WPA Outcomes for First-Year Composition	Where *The Allyn & Bacon Guide* Addresses These Outcomes
PROCESSES By the end first-year composition, students should • Be aware that it usually takes multiple drafts to create and complete a successful text • Develop flexible strategies for generating, revising, editing, and proofreading • Understand writing as an open process that permits writers to use later invention and rethinking to revise their work • Understand the collaborative and social aspects of writing processes • Learn to critique their own and others' works • Learn to balance the advantages of relying on others with the responsibility of doing their part • Use a variety of technologies to address a range of audiences	Part 3, "A Guide to Composing and Revising," Skills 1–20 Additionally, all Writing Project chapters in Part 2 have substantial process components, including questions for peer review. A variety of technologies is used to produce genres such as scientific posters, advocacy ads, PowerPoint presentations, and desktop-published material, as well as conventional print essays, in Part 2.
KNOWLEDGE OF CONVENTIONS By the end of first-year composition, students should • Learn common formats for different kinds of texts • Develop knowledge of genre conventions ranging from structure and paragraphing to tone and mechanics • Practice appropriate means of documenting their work • Control such surface features as syntax, grammar, punctuation, and spelling	Part 1, "A Rhetoric for Writers," Concepts 7, 11, and 12 Part 4, "A Rhetorical Guide to Research," Skills 28–33 Handbook (Regular Edition) Additionally, all Writing Project chapters in Part 2 explain the format, tone, and style appropriate for a wide range of genres.
COMPOSING IN ELECTRONIC ENVIRONMENTS By the end of first year composition, students should • Use electronic environments for drafting, reviewing, revising, editing, and sharing texts • Locate, evaluate, organize, and use research material collected from electronic sources, including scholarly library databases; other official databases (e.g., federal government databases); and informal electronic networks and internet sources • Understand and exploit the differences in the rhetorical strategies and in the affordances available for both print and electronic composing processes and texts	Chapter 25, "Assembling a Portfolio" Part 4, "A Rhetorical Guide to Research," Skills 22–26 Additionally, the Writing Project chapters in Part 2 make frequent reference to electronic formats and processes, including desktop-published material, posters, advocacy ads, and PowerPoint presentations.

THE ALLYN & BACON GUIDE TO WRITING

BRIEF EDITION

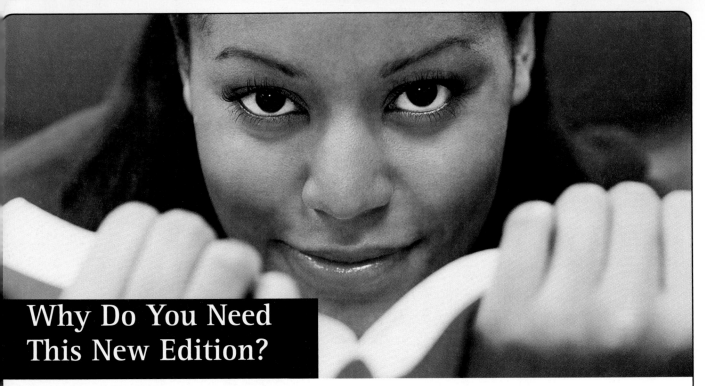

Why Do You Need This New Edition?

If you're wondering why you should buy this new edition of *The Allyn & Bacon Guide to Writing*, here are a few great reasons!

1. Chapters 1 through 4 have been streamlined and reorganized into 12 key concepts all writers need to know—whether writing for a composition course, other college courses, the workplace, or the civic arena.
2. Six new writing projects your instructor may assign include new assignments, instruction, and samples to guide you as you practice different types of writing useful in other college courses as well as in your career and civic life (Chapters 7, 8, 9, 10, 11, 16).
3. New annotated Framework charts present at a glance the typical structures of many kinds of writing projects to help you organize the papers you write (Part 2).
4. A newly organized presentation of 33 key skills involved in the writing and research processes will help you perform specific tasks, such as writing introductions and conclusions, searching online databases, and evaluating Web sources (Chapters 17–23).
5. New readings have been added on engaging and current topics, such as online social networking sites, job outsourcing, and gender stereotyping, that model the different writing projects your instructor may assign (Part 2).
6. New Strategies charts detail ways of accomplishing various writing tasks, such as creating a persuasive essay and outlining a speech, to help you break down large assignments into manageable, productive tasks.
7. New Source Samples show you where to find author, title, and publication information in online database articles, Web articles, and blogs that you will need in order to cite and document sources in researched papers (Chapter 23).
8. New model MLA- and APA-style research papers show you how to format a researched essay and cite sources in two academic styles you will use in other college courses (Chapters 10, 23).
9. New guides that correlate every chapter to the first-year composition learning outcomes recommended by the Council of Writing Program Administrators help you recognize the thinking, drafting, revising, and researching skills *The Allyn & Bacon Guide* will help you develop and practice (Parts 1, 2, 3, 4, 5, 6).
10. A new appendix, "A Guide to Avoiding Plagiarism," provides additional concrete suggestions for quoting, summarizing, and paraphrasing to give you the information you need to avoid unintentionally plagiarizing.
11. A dynamic e-book version of *The Allyn & Bacon Guide to Writing* provides access to comprehensive grammar, writing, and research resources on MyCompLab to give you extra practice with your writing skills.

THE ALLYN & BACON GUIDE TO WRITING

BRIEF EDITION

FIFTH EDITION

John D. Ramage
Arizona State University

John C. Bean
Seattle University

June Johnson
Seattle University

Longman
New York San Francisco Boston
London Toronto Sydney Tokyo Singapore Madrid
Mexico City Munich Paris Cape Town Hong Kong Montreal

Acquisitions Editor: Lauren A. Finn
Senior Development Editor: Marion B. Castellucci
Senior Marketing Manager: Sandra McGuire
Senior Supplements Editor: Donna Campion
Senior Media Producer: Stefanie Liebman
Production Manager: Donna DeBenedictis
Project Coordination, Text Design, and Electronic Page Makeup: Elm Street Publishing Services
Cover Design Manager: John Callahan
Cover Designer: Kay Petronio
Cover Image: Courtesy of Shutterstock
Art Studio: Elm Street Publishing Services
Photo Researcher: Rebecca Karamehmedovic
Senior Manufacturing Buyer: Alfred C. Dorsey
Printer and Binder: Worldcolor Taunton
Cover Printer: Phoenix Color Corporation

For permission to use copyrighted material, grateful acknowledgment is made to the copyright holders on pp. 699–703, which are hereby made part of this copyright page.

Library of Congress Cataloging-in-Publication Data
Ramage, John D.
The Allyn & Bacon guide to writing / John D. Ramage, John C. Bean, June Johnson.— [5th ed.; Complete ed.].
p. cm.
Includes index.
ISBN-13: 978-0-205-74175-5 (Complete edition)
ISBN-10: 0-205-74175-4 (Complete edition)
ISBN-13: 978-0-205-74176-2 (Brief edition)
ISBN-10: 0-205-74176-2 (Brief edition)
[etc.]
1. English language—Rhetoric—Handbooks, manuals, etc. 2. English language—Grammar—Handbooks, manuals, etc. 3. Report writing—Handbooks, manuals, etc. 4. College readers. I. Title: Allyn and Bacon guide to writing. II. Bean, John C. III. Johnson, June, 1953 IV. Title.

PE1408.R18 2009
808'.042—dc22

2007041532

This book includes 2009 MLA guidelines.

ISBN-13: 978-0-205-74175-5 (Complete Edition)
ISBN-10: 0-205-74175-4 (Complete Edition)
ISBN-13: 978-0-205-74176-2 (Brief Edition)
ISBN-10: 0-205-74176-2 (Brief Edition)
ISBN-13: 978-0-205-74177-9 (Concise Edition)
ISBN-10: 0-205-74177-0 (Concise Edition)

Longman
is an imprint of

4 5 6 7 8 9 10—WCT—12 11 10

Visit us at **www.ablongman.com**

BRIEF CONTENTS

Detailed Contents ix
Writing Projects xxvii
Thematic Contents xxix
Preface xxxvi

PART 1 A RHETORIC FOR WRITERS

1 Thinking Rhetorically about Good Writing 5
2 Thinking Rhetorically about Your Subject Matter 28
3 Thinking Rhetorically about How Messages Persuade 49
4 Thinking Rhetorically about Style and Document Design 66

PART 2 WRITING PROJECTS

WRITING TO LEARN
5 Seeing Rhetorically: The Writer as Observer 89
6 Reading Rhetorically: The Writer as Strong Reader 109

WRITING TO EXPLORE
7 Writing an Autobiographical Narrative 150
8 Writing an Exploratory Essay or Annotated Bibliography 175

WRITING TO INFORM
9 Writing an Informative Essay or Report 208

WRITING TO ANALYZE AND SYNTHESIZE
10 Analyzing Field Research Data 239
11 Analyzing Images 285
12 Analyzing a Short Story 320
13 Analyzing and Synthesizing Ideas 346

WRITING TO PERSUADE
14 Writing a Classical Argument 377
15 Making an Evaluation 423
16 Proposing a Solution 447

PART 3 A GUIDE TO COMPOSING AND REVISING

17 Writing as a Problem-Solving Process 489
18 Composing and Revising Closed-Form Prose 506
19 Composing and Revising Open-Form Prose 546

PART 4 A RHETORICAL GUIDE TO RESEARCH

20 Asking Questions, Finding Sources 573
21 Evaluating Sources 592
22 Incorporating Sources into Your Own Writing 611
23 Citing and Documenting Sources 626

PART 5 WRITING FOR ASSESSMENT

24 Essay Examinations: Writing Well Under Pressure 663
25 Assembling a Portfolio and Writing a Reflective Essay 677

Appendix: A Guide to Avoiding Plagiarism 693
Acknowledgments 701
Index 707

DETAILED CONTENTS

Writing Projects *xxvii*
Thematic Contents *xxix*
Preface *xxxvi*

PART 1 A RHETORIC FOR WRITERS

1 THINKING RHETORICALLY ABOUT GOOD WRITING 5

CONCEPT 1 Good Writing Can Vary from Closed to Open Forms. 6
David Rockwood, ***A Letter to the Editor*** 7
Thomas Merton, ***A Festival of Rain*** 8
Distinctions between Closed and Open Forms of Writing 9
Where to Place Your Writing along the Continuum 10
CONCEPT 2 Good Writers Pose Questions about Their Subject Matter. 12
Shared Problems Unite Writers and Readers 12
Posing Your Own Subject-Matter Questions 13
Brittany Tinker, ***Can the World Sustain an American Standard of Living?*** 14
CONCEPT 3 Good Writers Write for a Purpose to an Audience within a Genre. 19
How Writers Think about Purpose 19
How Writers Think about Audience 22
How Writers Think about Genre 24
Chapter Summary 26
BRIEF WRITING PROJECT 1 POSING A GOOD SUBJECT-MATTER PROBLEM 26
BRIEF WRITING PROJECT 2 UNDERSTANDING RHETORICAL CONTEXT 27

2 THINKING RHETORICALLY ABOUT YOUR SUBJECT MATTER 28

CONCEPT 4 Professors Value "Wallowing in Complexity." 29

Learning to Wallow in Complexity 29

Seeing Each Academic Discipline as a Field of Inquiry and Argument 30

CONCEPT 5 Good Writers Use Exploratory Strategies to Think Critically about Subject-Matter Questions. 32

Freewriting 32

Focused Freewriting 34

Idea Mapping 34

Dialectic Talk 35

Playing the Believing and Doubting Game 36

Believing and Doubting Paul Theroux's Negative View of Sports 37

CONCEPT 6 A Strong Thesis Statement Surprises Readers with Something New or Challenging. 41

Trying to Change Your Reader's View of Your Subject 41

Giving Your Thesis Tension through "Surprising Reversal" 42

CONCEPT 7 Thesis Statements in Closed-Form Prose Are Supported Hierarchically with Points and Particulars. 45

How Points Convert Information to Meaning 45

How Removing Particulars Creates a Summary 46

How to Use Points and Particulars When You Revise 47

Chapter Summary 48

BRIEF WRITING PROJECT PLAYING THE BELIEVING AND DOUBTING GAME **48**

3 THINKING RHETORICALLY ABOUT HOW MESSAGES PERSUADE 49

CONCEPT 8 Messages Persuade through Their Angle of Vision. 50

Recognizing the Angle of Vision in a Text 50

Analyzing Angle of Vision 54

CONCEPT 9 Messages Persuade through Appeals to *Logos, Ethos,* and *Pathos.* 55

CONCEPT 10 Nonverbal Messages Persuade through Visual Strategies That Can Be Analyzed Rhetorically. 57

Visual Rhetoric 57

The Rhetoric of Clothing and Other Consumer Items 60

Chapter Summary 63

BRIEF WRITING PROJECT ANALYZING ANGLE OF VISION IN TWO PASSAGES ABOUT NUCLEAR ENERGY 64

4 **THINKING RHETORICALLY ABOUT STYLE AND DOCUMENT DESIGN 66**

CONCEPT 11 Good Writers Make Purposeful Stylistic Choices. 67

Factors That Affect Style 67

Abstract Versus Concrete Words: Moving Up or Down the Scale of Abstraction 69

Wordy Versus Streamlined Sentences: Cutting Deadwood to Highlight Your Ideas 73

Coordination Versus Subordination: Using Sentence Structure to Control Emphasis 73

Inflated Voice Versus a Natural Speaking Voice: Creating a Persona 75

CONCEPT 12 Good Writers Make Purposeful Document Design Choices. 76

Using Type 77

Using Space and Laying Out Documents 78

Using Color 79

Using Graphics and Images 79

Examples of Different Document Designs 79

Chapter Summary 82

BRIEF WRITING PROJECT CONVERTING A PASSAGE FROM SCIENTIFIC TO POPULAR STYLE 83

PART 2 WRITING PROJECTS

WRITING TO LEARN

5 **SEEING RHETORICALLY: THE WRITER AS OBSERVER 89**

Exploring Rhetorical Observation 89

Understanding Observational Writing 93

Why "Seeing" Isn't a Simple Matter 93

How to Analyze a Text Rhetorically 96

WRITING PROJECT TWO CONTRASTING DESCRIPTIONS OF THE SAME PLACE AND A SELF-REFLECTION **98**

Exploring Rationales and Details for Your Two Descriptions 99

Generating Details 100

Shaping and Drafting Your Two Descriptions 101

Using *Show* Words Rather than *Tell* Words 102

Revising Your Two Descriptions 103
Generating and Exploring Ideas for Your Self-Reflection 104
Questions for Peer Review 104

READINGS

Clash on the Congo: Two Eyewitness Accounts 105
Tamlyn Rogers (student), ***Two Descriptions of the Same Classroom and a Self-Reflection*** **106**

6 READING RHETORICALLY: THE WRITER AS STRONG READER 109

Exploring Rhetorical Reading 109
Andrés Martin, ***On Teenagers and Tattoos*** 110
Understanding Rhetorical Reading 114
What Makes College-Level Reading Difficult? 114
Using the Reading Strategies of Experts 115
Reading with the Grain and Against the Grain 116
Understanding Summary Writing 117
Sean Barry (student), ***Summary of Martin's Article*** 118
Understanding Strong Response Writing 121
Strong Response as Rhetorical Critique 122
Strong Response as Ideas Critique 122
Strong Response as Reflection 125
Strong Response as a Blend 126
Sean Barry (student), ***Why Do Teenagers Get Tattoos? A Response to Andrés Martin*** 127
Writing a Summary/Strong Response of a Visual-Verbal Text 129
WRITING PROJECT A SUMMARY 131
Generating Ideas: Reading for Structure and Content 131
Drafting and Revising 133
Questions for Peer Review 134
WRITING PROJECT A SUMMARY/STRONG RESPONSE ESSAY 135
Exploring Ideas for Your Strong Response 135
Writing a Thesis for a Strong Response Essay 138
Shaping and Drafting 139
Revising 140
Questions for Peer Review 140

READINGS

Thomas L. Friedman, ***30 Little Turtles*** 142

Stephanie Malinowski (student), ***Questioning Thomas L. Friedman's Optimism in "30 Little Turtles"*** 143
David Horsey, ***Today's Economic Indicator (editorial cartoon)*** 146
Mike Lane, ***Labor Day Blues (editorial cartoon)*** 147
Froma Harrop, ***New Threat to Skilled U.S. Workers*** 148

WRITING TO EXPLORE

7 **WRITING AN AUTOBIOGRAPHICAL NARRATIVE 150**

Exploring Autobiographical Narrative 151
Understanding Autobiographical Writing 152
Autobiographical Tension: The Opposition of Contraries 152
How Literary Elements Work in Autobiographical Narratives 153
WRITING PROJECT AUTOBIOGRAPHICAL NARRATIVE 157
Generating and Exploring Ideas 157
Shaping and Drafting Your Narrative 158
Revising 159
Questions for Peer Review 159
WRITING PROJECT LITERACY NARRATIVE 160
What Is a Literacy Narrative? 160
Typical Features of a Literacy Narrative 161
Generating and Exploring Ideas 162
Shaping and Drafting Your Literacy Narrative 163
Revising 164
Questions for Peer Review 164
READINGS
Kris Saknussemm, ***Phantom Limb Pain*** 165
Patrick José (student), ***No Cats in America?*** 167
Anonymous (student), ***Masks*** 169
Jennifer Ching (student), ***Once Upon a Time*** 171

8 **WRITING AN EXPLORATORY ESSAY OR ANNOTATED BIBLIOGRAPHY 175**

Exploring Exploratory Writing 176
Understanding Exploratory Writing 177
WRITING PROJECT AN EXPLORATORY ESSAY 179

Generating and Exploring Ideas 180
Taking "Double-Entry" Research Notes 181
Shaping and Drafting 183
Revising 186
Questions for Peer Review 186
WRITING PROJECT AN ANNOTATED BIBLIOGRAPHY 187
What Is an Annotated Bibliography? 187
Features of Annotated Bibliography Entries 187
Examples of Annotation Entries 188
Writing a Critical Preface for Your Annotated Bibliography 189
Shaping, Drafting, and Revising 189
Questions for Peer Review 190
READINGS
James Gardiner (student), ***How Do Online Social Networks Affect Communication?*** 191
James Gardiner (student), ***What Is the Effect of Online Social Networks on Communication Skills? An Annotated Bibliography*** 196
Jane Tompkins, ***"Indians": Textualism, Morality, and the Problem of History*** 199

WRITING TO INFORM

9 WRITING AN INFORMATIVE ESSAY OR REPORT 208
Exploring Informative (and Surprising) Writing 209
EnchantedLearning.com, ***Tarantulas*** 209
Rod Crawford, ***Myths about "Dangerous" Spiders*** 210
Understanding Informative Writing 212
Need-to-Know Informative Prose 212
Informative Reports 214
Informative (and Surprising) Articles 215
WRITING PROJECT A SET OF INSTRUCTIONS 217
Generating and Exploring Ideas 218
Shaping and Drafting 218
Revising 219
Questions for Peer Review 219
WRITING PROJECT INFORMATIVE WORKPLACE REPORT 219
Generating and Exploring Ideas 220
Shaping and Drafting 220

Revising 221
Questions for Peer Review 221
WRITING PROJECT INFORMATIVE (AND SURPRISING) ARTICLE 221
Generating and Exploring Ideas 222
Shaping, Drafting, and Revising 223
Questions for Peer Review 225
READINGS
Kerry Norton, *Winery Yeast Preparation Instructions* 226
Pew Research Center, *Muslim Americans: Middle Class and Mostly Mainstream* 228
Kerri Ann Matsumoto (student), *How Much Does It Cost to Go Organic?* 231
Cheryl Carp (student), *Behind Stone Walls* 232
Shannon King (student), *How Clean and Green Are Hydrogen Fuel-Cell Cars?* 234
Eugene Robinson, *You Have the Right to Remain a Target of Racial Profiling* 236

WRITING TO ANALYZE AND SYNTHESIZE

10 **ANALYZING FIELD RESEARCH DATA 239**

Exploring the Analysis of Field Research Data 239
Understanding the Analysis of Field Research Data 240
The Structure of an Empirical Research Report 240
How Readers Typically Read a Research Report 242
Posing Your Research Question 243
Collecting Data through Observation, Interviews, or Questionnaires 245
Reporting Your Results in Text, Tables, and Graphs 252
Analyzing Your Results 256
Following Ethical Standards 259
WRITING PROJECT AN EMPIRICAL RESEARCH REPORT 260
Generating Ideas for Your Empirical Research Report 261
Designing Your Empirical Study and Drafting the Introduction and Method Sections 261
Doing the Research and Writing the Rest of the Report 262
Revising Your Report 262
Questions for Peer Review 262
Writing in Teams 264
WRITING PROJECT A SCIENTIFIC POSTER 265
What Is a Scientific Poster? 265
Content of a Poster 265
Features of an Effective Poster 265

Designing, Creating, and Revising Your Poster 266
Questions for Peer Review 268

READINGS

Gina Escamilla, Angie L. Cradock, and Ichiro Kawachi, ***Women and Smoking in Hollywood Movies: A Content Analysis*** 269

Lauren Campbell, Charlie Bourain, and Tyler Nishida (students), ***A Comparison of Gender Stereotypes in SpongeBob SquarePants and a 1930s Mickey Mouse Cartoon (APA-Style Research Paper)*** 275

Lauren Campbell, Charlie Bourain, and Tyler Nishida (students), ***SpongeBob SquarePants Has Fewer Gender Stereotypes than Mickey Mouse (scientific poster)*** 284

11 **ANALYZING IMAGES 285**

Exploring Image Analysis 286

Understanding Image Analysis 289
How Images Create a Rhetorical Effect 289
How to Analyze an Advertisement 295
How Advertisers Target Specific Audiences 296
Sample Analysis of an Advertisement 298
Cultural Perspectives on Advertisements 301

WRITING PROJECT ANALYSIS OF TWO VISUAL TEXTS 307
Exploring and Generating Ideas for Your Analysis 308
Shaping and Drafting Your Analysis 309
Revising 309
Questions for Peer Review 310

READINGS

Paul Messaris, from ***Visual Persuasion: The Role of Images in Advertising*** 311

Stephen Bean (student), ***How Cigarette Advertisers Address the Stigma Against Smoking: A Tale of Two Ads*** 316

12 **ANALYZING A SHORT STORY 320**

Exploring Literary Analysis 321
Evelyn Dahl Reed, ***The Medicine Man*** 321

Understanding Literary Analysis 322
The Truth of Literary Events 323
Writing (about) Literature 323

WRITING PROJECT AN ANALYSIS OF A SHORT STORY 326

Reading the Story and Using Reading Logs 327
Generating and Exploring Ideas 329
Shaping, Drafting, and Revising 331
Questions for Peer Review 332
READINGS
Alice Walker, ***Everyday Use (For Your Grandmama)*** 332
Sherman Alexie, ***The Lone Ranger and Tonto Fistfight in Heaven*** 339
Betsy Weiler (student), ***Who Do You Want to Be? Finding Heritage in Walker's "Everyday Use"*** 343

13 **ANALYZING AND SYNTHESIZING IDEAS 346**

Exploring the Analysis and Synthesis of Ideas 347
Nikki Swartz, ***Mobile Phone Tracking Scrutinized*** 347
Terry J. Allen, ***Reach Out and Track Someone*** 348
Understanding Analysis and Synthesis 350
Posing a Synthesis Question 350
Synthesis Writing as an Extension of Summary/Strong Response Writing 352
Student Example of a Synthesis Essay 352
Kate MacAulay (student), ***Technology's Peril and Potential*** 353
WRITING PROJECT A SYNTHESIS ESSAY 356
Ideas for Synthesis Questions and Readings 356
Using Learning Logs 357
Exploring Your Texts through Summary Writing 357
Exploring Your Texts' Rhetorical Strategies 359
Exploring Main Themes and Similarities and Differences in Your Texts' Ideas 360
Generating Ideas of Your Own 362
Taking Your Position in the Conversation: Your Synthesis 363
Shaping and Drafting 365
Writing a Thesis for a Synthesis Essay 366
Organizing a Synthesis Essay 367
Revising 368
Questions for Peer Review 368
READINGS
Dee, ***Comprehensive Immigration Reform: PROs and ANTIs*** 370
Byron Williams, ***Immigration Frenzy Points Out Need for Policy Debate*** 371
Victor Davis Hanson, ***The Global Immigration Problem*** 372

Mike Crapo, ***Immigration Policy Must Help Economy While Preserving Ideals*** 374
Trapper John, ***The Progressive Case Against the Immigration Bill*** 375

WRITING TO PERSUADE

14 WRITING A CLASSICAL ARGUMENT 377

Exploring Classical Argument 378
Understanding Classical Argument 379
Stages of Development: Your Growth as an Arguer 379
Creating an Argument Frame: A Claim with Reasons 380
Articulating Reasons 382
Articulating Unstated Assumptions 383
Using Evidence Effectively 385
Evaluating Evidence: The STAR Criteria 387
Addressing Objections and Counterarguments 389
Responding to Objections, Counterarguments, and Alternative Views 392
Appealing to *Ethos* and *Pathos* 393
A Brief Primer on Informal Fallacies 395
WRITING PROJECT A CLASSICAL ARGUMENT 397
Generating and Exploring Ideas 399
Shaping and Drafting 401
Revising 403
Questions for Peer Review 403

READINGS
Ross Taylor (student), ***Paintball: Promoter of Violence or Healthy Fun?*** 404
William Sweet, ***Why Uranium Is the New Green*** 407
Stan Eales, ***Welcome to Sellafield (editorial cartoon)*** 411
Los Angeles Times, **No to Nukes** 412
Leonard Pitts, Jr., ***Spare the Rod, Spoil the Parenting*** 415
A. J. Chavez (student), ***The Case for (Gay) Marriage*** 417

15 MAKING AN EVALUATION 423

Exploring Evaluative Writing 424
Understanding Evaluation Arguments 427
The Criteria-Match Process 427
The Role of Purpose and Context in Determining Criteria 429

Other Considerations in Establishing Criteria 429
Using a Planning Schema to Develop Evaluation Arguments 431
Conducting an Evaluation Argument: An Extended Example 432
WRITING PROJECT AN EVALUATION ARGUMENT 436
Generating and Exploring Ideas 437
Shaping and Drafting 438
Revising 439
Questions for Peer Review 439
READINGS
Jackie Wyngaard (student), ***EMP: Music History or Music Trivia?*** 440
Diane Helman and Phyllis Bookspan, **Sesame Street:** ***Brought to You by the Letters M-A-L-E*** 442
Teresa Filice (student), **Parents: The Anti-Drug:** ***A Useful Site*** 444

16 PROPOSING A SOLUTION 447

Exploring Proposal Writing 448
Understanding Proposal Writing 449
Special Demands of Proposal Arguments 450
Developing an Effective Justification Section 451
Proposals as Visual Arguments and PowerPoint Presentations 455
WRITING PROJECT A PROPOSAL ARGUMENT 455
Generating and Exploring Ideas 456
Shaping and Drafting 457
Revising 458
Questions for Peer Review 458
WRITING PROJECT ADVOCACY AD OR POSTER 459
Using Document Design Features 459
Exploring and Generating Ideas 459
Shaping and Drafting 460
Revising 461
Questions for Peer Review 461
WRITING PROJECT PROPOSAL SPEECH WITH VISUAL AIDS 461
Developing, Shaping, and Outlining Your Proposal Speech 462
Designing Your Visual Aids 463
Delivering Your Speech 467
Revising 468
Questions for Peer Review 468

READINGS
Jane Kester (student), ***A Proposal to Reduce High-Risk Drinking Through Student Awareness Workshops (oral presentation with visual aids)*** 469
Rebekah Taylor (student), ***A Proposal to Provide Cruelty-Free Products on Campus*** 472
Jennifer Allen, ***The Athlete on the Sidelines*** 477
Dylan Fujitani (student), ***"The Hardest of the Hardcore": Let's Outlaw Hired Guns in Contemporary American Warfare*** 479

PART 3 A GUIDE TO COMPOSING AND REVISING

17 WRITING AS A PROBLEM-SOLVING PROCESS 489

SKILL 1 Understand Why Expert Writers Use Multiple Drafts. 490
Why Expert Writers Revise So Extensively 492
An Expert's Writing Processes Are Recursive 493
SKILL 2 Revise Globally as Well as Locally. 493
SKILL 3 Develop Ten Expert Habits to Improve Your Writing Processes. 496
SKILL 4 Use Peer Reviews to Help You Think Like an Expert. 498
Become a Helpful Reader of Classmates' Drafts 498
Use a Generic Peer Review Guide 500
Participate in Peer Review Workshops 503
Respond to Peer Reviews 505
Chapter Summary 505

18 COMPOSING AND REVISING CLOSED-FORM PROSE 506

SKILL 5 Understand Reader Expectations. 507
Unity and Coherence 507
Old before New 509
Forecasting and Fulfillment 510
SKILL 6 Convert Loose Structures into Thesis/Support Structures. 511
And Then Writing, or Chronological Structure 511
All About Writing, or Encyclopedic Structure 512
Engfish Writing, or Structure without Surprise 514
SKILL 7 Plan and Visualize Your Structure. 514
Use Scratch Outlines Early in the Writing Process 515

Before Making a Detailed Outline, "Nutshell" Your Argument 515
Articulate a Working Thesis and Main Points 517
Sketch Your Structure Using an Outline, Tree Diagram, or Flowchart 517
Let the Structure Evolve 520

SKILL 8 Create Effective Titles. 521

SKILL 9 Create Effective Introductions. 522
What Not to Do: The "Funnel" Introduction 522
From Old to New: The General Principle of Closed-Form Introductions 522
Typical Elements of a Closed-Form Introduction 524
Forecast the Whole with a Thesis Statement, Purpose Statement, or Blueprint Statement 525

SKILL 10 Create Effective Topic Sentences for Paragraphs. 527
Place Topic Sentences at the Beginning of Paragraphs 527
Revise Paragraphs for Unity 528
Add Particulars to Support Points 529

SKILL 11 Guide Your Reader with Transitions and Other Signposts. 530
Use Common Transition Words to Signal Relationships 531
Write Major Transitions between Parts 533
Signal Transitions with Headings and Subheadings 533

SKILL 12 Bind Sentences Together by Placing Old Information before New Information. 533
The Old/New Contract in Sentences 533
How to Make Links to the "Old" 535
Avoid Ambiguous Use of "This" to Fulfill the Old/New Contract 537
How the Old/New Contract Modifies the Rule "Avoid Weak Repetition" 537
How the Old/New Contract Modifies the Rule "Prefer Active over Passive Voice" 538

SKILL 13 Learn Four Expert Moves for Organizing and Developing Ideas. 539
The *For Example* Move 539
The *Summary/However* Move 540
The *Division-into-Parallel Parts* Move 541
The *Comparison/Contrast* Move 542

SKILL 14 Write Effective Conclusions. 543

19 COMPOSING AND REVISING OPEN-FORM PROSE 546

SKILL 15 Make Your Narrative a Story, Not an *And Then* Chronology. 547
Patrick Klein (student), ***Berkeley Blues*** 547
Depiction of Events through Time 551
Connectedness 552

Tension or Conflict 552
Resolution, Recognition, or Retrospective Interpretation 553
SKILL 16 Write Low on the Ladder of Abstraction. 554
Concrete Words Evoke Images and Sensations 554
Use Revelatory Words and Memory-Soaked Words 556
SKILL 17 Disrupt Your Reader's Desire for Direction and Clarity. 557
Disrupt Predictions and Make Odd Juxtapositions 558
Leave Gaps 558
SKILL 18 Tap the Power of Figurative Language. 559
SKILL 19 Expand Your Repertoire of Styles. 561
SKILL 20 Use Open-Form Elements to Create "Voice" in Closed-Form Prose. 562
Introduce Some Humor 563
Use Techniques from Popular Magazines 564
READING
Annie Dillard, *Living Like Weasels* 566

PART 4 A RHETORICAL GUIDE TO RESEARCH

20 ASKING QUESTIONS, FINDING SOURCES 573

An Overview of Research Writing 573
SKILL 21 Argue Your Own Thesis in Response to a Research Question. 574
Formulating a Research Question 574
Establishing Your Role as a Researcher 575
A Case Study: James Gardiner's Research on Online Social Networks 577
SKILL 22 Understand Differences among Kinds of Sources. 578
Looking at Sources Rhetorically 578
SKILL 23 Use Purposeful Strategies for Searching Libraries, Databases, and Web Sites. 582
Checking Your Library's Home Page 583
Finding Books: Searching Your Library's Online Catalog 583
Finding Print Articles: Searching a Licensed Database 584
Illustration of a Database Search 586
Finding Cyberspace Sources: Searching the World Wide Web 588

21 EVALUATING SOURCES 592

SKILL 24 Read Sources Rhetorically and Take Purposeful Notes. 592

Read with Your Own Goals in Mind 592

Read Your Sources Rhetorically 593

Take Purposeful Notes 595

SKILL 25 Evaluate Sources for Reliability, Credibility, Angle of Vision, and Degree of Advocacy. 597

Reliability 597

Credibility 597

Angle of Vision and Political Stance 598

Degree of Advocacy 600

SKILL 26 Use Your Rhetorical Knowledge to Evaluate Web Sources. 600

The Web as a Unique Rhetorical Environment 600

Criteria for Evaluating a Web Source 601

Analyzing Your Own Purposes for Using a Web Source 604

22 INCORPORATING SOURCES INTO YOUR OWN WRITING 611

Roger D. McGrath, *The Myth of Violence in the Old West* 611

SKILL 27 Keep Your Focus on Your Own Argument. 613

Writer 1: An Analytical Paper on Causes of Violence in Contemporary Society 613

Writer 2: A Persuasive Paper Supporting Gun Control 614

Writer 3: An Informative Paper Showing Shifting Definitions of Crime 614

SKILL 28 Know When and How to Use Summary, Paraphrase, Quotation, and Attributive Tags. 615

Effective Use of Summary, Paraphrase, or Quotation 615

Creating Rhetorically Effective Attributive Tags 617

SKILL 29 Understand the Mechanics of Quoting. 620

Quoting a Complete Sentence Introduced by an Attributive Tag 621

Inserting Quoted Words and Phrases into Your Own Sentences 621

Using Brackets to Modify a Quotation 622

Using Ellipses to Indicate Omissions from a Quotation 622

Using Single and Double Quotation Marks for a Quotation within a Quotation 623

Using Block Indentation for Quotations More than Four Lines Long 624

SKILL 30 Understand and Avoid Plagiarism. 624

23 **CITING AND DOCUMENTING SOURCES 626**

SKILL 31 Understand How Parenthetical Citations Work. 626

Connect the Body of the Paper to the Bibliography with Citations 626

Citation Problems with Database and Web Sources 627

SKILL 32 Cite and Document Sources Using MLA Style. 628

Cite from an Indirect Source 629

Cite Page Numbers for Downloaded Material 629

Document Sources in a Works Cited List 629

MLA Citation Models 630

James Gardiner (student), ***Why* Facebook *Might Not Be Good for You (MLA-Style Research Paper)*** 642

SKILL 33 Cite and Document Sources Using APA Style. 652

APA Formatting for In-Text Citations 652

Cite from an Indirect Source 653

Document Sources in a References List 653

APA Citation Models 653

Student Example of an APA-Style Research Paper 659

PART 5 WRITING FOR ASSESSMENT

24 **ESSAY EXAMINATIONS: WRITING WELL UNDER PRESSURE 663**

How Essay Exams Differ from Other Essays 664

Preparing for an Exam: Learning Subject Matter 664

Identifying and Learning Main Ideas 665

Applying Your Knowledge 665

Making a Study Plan 666

Analyzing Exam Questions 666

Understanding the Use of Outside Quotations 667

Recognizing Organizational Cues 667

Interpreting Key Terms 668

Dealing with the Limits of the Test Situation 673

Producing an "A" Response 675

Chapter Summary 676

25 ASSEMBLING A PORTFOLIO AND WRITING A REFLECTIVE ESSAY 677

Understanding Portfolios 678
Collecting Work for Paper and Electronic Portfolios 678
Selecting Work for Your Portfolio 679

Understanding Reflective Writing 679
Why Is Reflective Writing Important? 681

Reflective Writing Assignments 682
Single Reflection Assignments 682
Guidelines for Writing a Single Reflection 683
Comprehensive Reflection Assignments 684
Guidelines for Writing a Comprehensive Reflection 684
Guidelines for Writing a Comprehensive Reflective Letter 686

READINGS
Jaime Finger (student), ***A Single Reflection on an Exploratory Essay*** 687
Bruce Urbanik (student), ***A Comprehensive Reflective Letter*** 688

Appendix: A Guide to Avoiding Plagiarism 693
Acknowledgments 701
Index 707

WRITING PROJECTS

BRIEF PROJECTS

CHAPTER 1 Write a brief essay posing a problematic, significant, and interesting question. 26

Write two messages with different audiences, purposes, and genres, and explain the differences in your rhetorical choices in each message. 27

CHAPTER 2 Use the "believing and doubting game to explore a controversial assertion. 48

CHAPTER 3 Analyze the different angles of vision in two passages about nuclear energy. 64

CHAPTER 4 Transform a brief scientific report into a mini-article for a popular audience. 83

MAJOR PROJECTS

CHAPTER 5 Write two contrasting descriptions of the same place, and then analyze them, indicating what you learned. 98

CHAPTER 6 Write a summary of a reading. 131

Write a summary and strong response essay. 135

CHAPTER 7 Write an autobiographical narrative shaped by contrary experiences or opposing tensions. 157

Write a literacy narrative. 160

CHAPTER 8 Write an exploratory narrative of your engagement with a problem and your attempts to resolve it. 179

Write an annotated bibliography for a research project. 187

CHAPTER 9 Write a set of instructions. 217

Write an informative workplace report. 219

Write an informative article using the "surprising-reversal strategy. 221

CHAPTER 10 Write an empirical research report based on a field research project using questionnaires, interviews, or observations. 260

Create a scientific poster to present the key elements of your field research project. 265

CHAPTER 11 Analyze two print advertisements, posters, photographs, or paintings. 307

CHAPTER 12 Pose an interpretive question about a short story and respond to it analytically. (Project also uses reading log entries.) 326

CHAPTER 13 Analyze the ideas of other writers on a question and synthesize these ideas to arrive at your own point of view. (Project also uses learning log entries.) 356

CHAPTER 14 Write a persuasive argument in the classical style. 397

CHAPTER 15 Develop criteria for an evaluation and test your chosen case against the criteria. 436

CHAPTER 16 Write a proposal to solve a local problem or address a public issue. 455

Create a public affairs advocacy advertisement or poster. 459

Prepare a proposal speech with visual aids. 461

THEMATIC CONTENTS

The Allyn & Bacon Guide to Writing contains 61 essays—35 by professional writers and 26 by students. In addition, the text has more than 60 visual texts (such as advertisements, news photographs, posters, and Web sites) that can lead to productive thematic discussions. These essays and visual texts can be clustered thematically in the following ways.

ENERGY SOURCES AND SUSTAINABILITY

Wind turbines photograph 3

David Rockwood, A Letter to the Editor 7

Brittany Tinker (student), Can the World Sustain an American Standard of Living? 14

Two passages about nuclear energy 64

Arctic National Wildlife Refuge photographs and verbal texts 91

SUV advertisements 39, 301

Shannon King (student), How Clean and Green Are Hydrogen Fuel-Cell Cars? 234

William Sweet, Why Uranium Is the New Green 407

Stan Eales, Welcome to Sellafield (editorial cartoon) 411

Los Angeles Times, No to Nukes 412

THE INTERNET, CELL PHONES, SOCIAL RELATIONS, AND SURVEILLANCE

James Gardiner (student), How Do Online Social Networks Affect Communication? 191

James Gardiner (student), What Is the Effect of Online Social Networks on Communication Skills? An Annotated Bibliography 196

Nikki Swartz, Mobile Phone Tracking Scrutinized 347

Terry J. Allen, Reach Out and Track Someone 348

Kate MacAulay (student), Technology's Peril and Potential 353

James Gardiner (student), Why *Facebook* Might Not Be Good for You 643

IMMIGRATION

Mike Lane, Labor Day Blues (editorial cartoon) 147

Froma Harrop, New Threat to Skilled U.S. Workers 148

Pew Research Center, Muslim Americans: Middle Class and Mostly Mainstream 228

Immigration photographs 287, 288

Dee, Comprehensive Immigration Reform: PROs and ANTIs (blog) 370

Byron Williams, Immigration Frenzy Points Out Need for Policy Debate (blog) 371

Victor Davis Hanson, The Global Immigration Problem (blog) 372

Mike Crapo, Immigration Policy Must Help Economy While Preserving Ideals (blog) 374

Trapper John, The Progressive Case Against the Immigration Bill (blog) 375

EMPLOYMENT AND OUTSOURCING

Thomas L. Friedman, 30 Little Turtles 142

Stephanie Malinowski (student), Questioning Thomas L. Friedman's Optimism in "30 Little Turtles" 143

David Horsey, Today's Economic Indicator (editorial cartoon) 146

Mike Lane, Labor Day Blues (editorial cartoon) 147

Froma Harrop, New Threat to Skilled U.S. Workers 148

Dee, Comprehensive Immigration Reform: PROs and ANTIs (blog) 370

Byron Williams, Immigration Frenzy Points Out Need for Policy Debate (blog) 371

Victor Davis Hanson, The Global Immigration Problem (blog) 372

Mike Crapo, Immigration Policy Must Help Economy While Preserving Ideals (blog) 374

Trapper John, The Progressive Case Against the Immigration Bill (blog) 375

American Indian College Fund public affairs advocacy advertisement 661

VIOLENCE, PUBLIC SAFETY, AND INDIVIDUAL RIGHTS

Ross Taylor (student), Paintball: Promoter of Violence or Healthy Fun? 404

Women Against Gun Control Web site 571

Million Mom March Web site factoids 606

Roger D. McGrath, The Myth of Violence in the Old West 611

OTHER PUBLIC POLICY ISSUES

Stem Cells (editorial cartoon) 51

Army recruitment advertisement 87

Pew Research Center, Muslim Americans: Middle Class and Mostly Mainstream 228

Kerri Ann Matsumoto (student), How Much Does It Cost to Go Organic? 231

Eugene Robinson, You Have the Right to Remain a Target of Racial Profiling 236

Leonard Pitts, Jr., Spare the Rod, Spoil the Parenting 415

A. J. Chavez (student), The Case for (Gay) Marriage 417

Images and graphs about binge drinking 424, 426, 466, 469–471

Teresa Filice (student), *Parents: The Anti-Drug*: A Useful Site 444

Common Sense for Drug Policy, White Kids Are Much More Likely to Be Using (and Selling) Drugs! (public affairs advocacy advertisement) 454

Rebekah Taylor (student), A Proposal to Provide Cruelty-Free Products on Campus 472

Jane Kester (student), A Proposal to Reduce High-Risk Drinking Through Student Awareness Workshops (oral presentation with visual aids) 469

Jennifer Allen, The Athlete on the Sidelines 477

Dylan Fujitani (student), "The Hardest of the Hardcore": Let's Outlaw Hired Guns in Contemporary American Warfare 479

James Gardiner (student), Why *Facebook* Might Not Be Good for You 643

American Indian College Fund public affairs advocacy advertisement 661

RACE AND CLASS

The visual rhetoric of clothing photographs 62, 63

Clash on the Congo: Two Eyewitness Accounts 105

Patrick José, No Cats in America? 167

Jane Tompkins, "Indians": Textualism, Morality, and the Problem of History 199

Pew Research Center, Muslim Americans: Middle Class and Mostly Mainstream 228

Eugene Robinson, You Have the Right to Remain a Target of Racial Profiling 236

Paul Messaris, from *Visual Persuasion: The Role of Images in Advertising* 311

Multiethnic images in advertisements 314, 315

Stephen Bean (student), How Cigarette Advertisers Address the Stigma Against Smoking: A Tale of Two Ads 316

Immigration photographs 287, 288

Evelyn Dahl Reed, The Medicine Man 321

Alice Walker, Everyday Use (For Your Grandmama) 332

Sherman Alexie, The Lone Ranger and Tonto Fistfight in Heaven 339

Betsy Weiler (student), Who Do You Want to Be? Finding Heritage in Walker's "Everyday Use" 343

Dee, Comprehensive Immigration Reform: PROs and ANTIs (blog) 370

Byron Williams, Immigration Frenzy Points Out Need for Policy Debate (blog) 371

Victor Davis Hanson, The Global Immigration Problem (blog) 372

Mike Crapo, Immigration Policy Must Help Economy While Preserving Ideals (blog) 374

Trapper John, The Progressive Case Against the Immigration Bill (blog) 375

Common Sense for Drug Policy, White Kids Are Much More Likely to Be Using (and Selling) Drugs! (public affairs advocacy advertisement) 454

Patrick Klein (student), Berkeley Blues 547

American Indian College Fund public affairs advocacy advertisement 661

NATIVE AMERICAN EXPERIENCE AND OPPORTUNITIES

Jane Tompkins, "Indians": Textualism, Morality, and the Problem of History 199

Evelyn Dahl Reed, The Medicine Man 321

Sherman Alexie, The Lone Ranger and Tonto Fistfight in Heaven 339

American Indian College Fund public affairs advocacy advertisement 661

GENDER

Anonymous (student), Believing and Doubting Paul Theroux's Negative View of Sports 37

The visual rhetoric of clothing, photographs 62, 63

Dale Kunkel, Kirstie M. Cope, and Erica Biely, from Sexual Messages on Television: Comparing Findings from Three Studies 80

Deborah A. Lott, from The New Flirting Game 81

Army recruitment advertisement 87

Anonymous (student), Masks 169

Jennifer Ching (student), Once Upon a Time 171

Gina Escamilla, Angie L. Cradock, and Ichiro Kawachi, Women and Smoking in Hollywood Movies: A Content Analysis 268

Lauren Campbell, Charlie Bourain, and Tyler Nishida (students), A Comparison of Gender Stereotypes in *SpongeBob SquarePants* and a 1930s Mickey Mouse Cartoon 274

Lauren Campbell, Charlie Bourain, and Tyler Nishida (students), *SpongeBob SquarePants* Has Fewer Gender Stereotypes than Mickey Mouse (scientific poster) 283

Images of women in advertisements 299, 302, 304, 305, 306

A. J. Chavez (student), The Case for (Gay) Marriage 417

Diane Helman and Phyllis Bookspan, *Sesame Street*: Brought to You by the Letters M-A-L-E 442

Jennifer Allen, The Athlete on the Sidelines 477

Women Against Gun Control Web site 571

Million Mom March Web site 606

IDENTITY AND VALUES

Thomas Merton, Festival of Rain 8

Stem Cells (editorial cartoon) 51

The visual rhetoric of clothing photographs 62, 63

Army recruitment advertisement 87

Andrés Martin, On Teenagers and Tattoos 110

Sean Barry (student), Why Do Teenagers Get Tattoos? A Response to Andrés Martin 127

Kris Saknussemm, Phantom Limb Pain 165

Patrick José (student), No Cats in America? 167

Anonymous (student), Masks 169

Jennifer Ching (student), Once Upon a Time 171

Kerri Ann Matsumoto (student), How Much Does It Cost to Go Organic? 231

Cheryl Carp (student), Behind Stone Walls 232

Evelyn Dahl Reed, The Medicine Man 321

Alice Walker, Everyday Use (For Your Grandmama) 332

Sherman Alexie, The Lone Ranger and Tonto Fistfight in Heaven 339

Betsy Weiler (student), Who Do You Want to Be? Finding Heritage in Walker's "Everyday Use" 343

Kate MacAulay (student), Technology's Peril and Potential 353

Images and graphs about binge drinking 424, 426, 466, 469–471

Teresa Filice (student), *Parents: The Anti-Drug*: A Useful Site 444

Rebekah Taylor (student), A Proposal to Provide Cruelty-Free Products on Campus 472

Jane Kester (student), A Proposal to Reduce High-Risk Drinking Through Student Awareness Workshops (oral presentation with visual aids) 469

Patrick Klein (student), Berkeley Blues 547

Annie Dillard, Living Like Weasels 566

James Gardiner (student), Why *Facebook* Might Not Be Good for You 643

American Indian College Fund, public affairs advocacy advertisement 661

POPULAR CULTURE, MEDIA, AND ADVERTISING

Anonymous (student), Believing and Doubting Paul Theroux's Negative View of Sports 37

Norman Rockwell, *Doc Melhorn and the Pearly Gates* (painting) and High-Technology Medicine photograph 58, 59

The visual rhetoric of clothing photographs 62, 63

Dale Kunkel, Kirstie M. Cope, and Erica Biely, from Sexual Messages on Television: Comparing Findings from Three Studies (facsimile of first page of scholarly article) 80

Deborah A. Lott, from The New Flirting Game (facsimile of first page of popular magazine article) 81

Army recruitment advertisements 87

Andrés Martin, On Teenagers and Tattoos 110

Sean Barry (student), Why Do Teenagers Get Tattoos? A Response to Andrés Martin 127

James Gardiner (student), How Do Online Social Networks Affect Communication? 191

Gina Escamilla, Angie L. Cradock, and Ichiro Kawachi, Women and Smoking in Hollywood Movies: A Content Analysis 268

Lauren Campbell, Charlie Bourain, and Tyler Nishida (students), A Comparison of Gender Stereotypes in *SpongeBob SquarePants* and a 1930s Mickey Mouse Cartoon 274

Lauren Campbell, Charlie Bourain, and Tyler Nishida (students), *SpongeBob SquarePants* Has Fewer Gender Stereotypes than Mickey Mouse (scientific poster) 283

Images of women in advertisements 299, 302, 304, 305, 306

Paul Messaris, from *Visual Persuasion: The Role of Images in Advertising* 311

Multiethnic advertisements 314, 315

Stephen Bean (student), How Cigarette Advertisers Address the Stigma Against Smoking: A Tale of Two Ads 316

Kate MacAulay (student), Technology's Peril and Potential 353

Ross Taylor (student), Paintball: Promoter of Violence or Healthy Fun? 404

Images and graphs about binge drinking 424, 426, 466, 469–471

Experience Music Project photograph 433

Jackie Wyngaard (student), EMP: Music History or Music Trivia? 440

Diane Helman and Phyllis Bookspan, *Sesame Street*: Brought to You by the Letters M-A-L-E 442

Jane Kester (student), A Proposal to Reduce High-Risk Drinking Through Student Awareness Workshops (oral presentation with visual aids) 469

Jennifer Allen, The Athlete on the Sidelines 477

PARENTS, CHILDREN, AND FAMILY

Dale Kunkel, Kirstie M. Cope, and Erica Biely, from Sexual Messages on Television: Comparing Findings from Three Studies 80

Army recruitment advertisement 87

Andrés Martin, On Teenagers and Tattoos 110

Sean Barry (student), Why Do Teenagers Get Tattoos? A Response to Andrés Martin 127

Patrick José (student), No Cats in America? 167

Jennifer Ching (student), Once Upon a Time 171

Alice Walker, Everyday Use (For Your Grandmama) 332

Betsy Weiler (student), Who Do You Want to Be? Finding Heritage in Walker's "Everyday Use" 343

Leonard Pitts, Jr., Spare the Rod, Spoil the Parenting 415

Diane Helman and Phyllis Bookspan, *Sesame Street*: Brought to You by the Letters M-A-L-E 442

Teresa Filice (student), *Parents: The Anti-Drug*: A Useful Site 444

NATURE AND ECOLOGY

Wind turbines photograph 3

David Rockwood, A Letter to the Editor 7

Thomas Merton, A Festival of Rain 8

Brittany Tinker (student), Can the World Sustain an American Standard of Living? 14

Arctic National Wildlife Refuge photographs and verbal texts 91

EnchantedLearning.com, Tarantulas 209

Rod Crawford, Myths about "Dangerous" Spiders 210

Kerry Norton, Winery Yeast Preparation Instructions 226

Kerri Ann Matsumoto (student), How Much Does It Cost to Go Organic? 231

Rebekah Taylor (student), A Proposal to Provide Cruelty-Free Products on Campus 472

Annie Dillard, Living Like Weasels 566

PREFACE

Through four editions, *The Allyn & Bacon Guide to Writing* has been praised for its groundbreaking integration of composition research and rhetorical perspective. In regular, brief, and concise editions, the text has been adopted at a wide range of two- and four-year institutions where instructors admire its appeal to students, its focus on problem posing, its distinctive emphasis on writing and reading as rhetorical acts, its engaging classroom activities, and its effective writing assignments. Reviewers have consistently praised the book's theoretical coherence and explanatory power, which help students produce interesting, idea-rich essays and help composition teachers create pedagogically effective, challenging, and intellectually stimulating courses.

What's New in the Fifth Edition?

In this fifth edition, we have retained the signature strengths of the fourth edition while making substantial improvements that expand the text's coverage of genres within a more streamlined, modular organization. Users will be pleased to discover how easy it is to navigate among key concepts and skills and to refer students exactly to desired teaching points. Reflecting our continuing research in composition theory and practice while incorporating pedagogical insights and suggestions from users of the fourth edition, the book is particularly effective at helping students achieve the outcome goals established by the Council of Writing Program Administrators.

Major Changes

- **The new organization and design make the text more convenient for instructors and more accessible for students**. We have improved the sequencing of instruction by grouping material into teachable units called "Concepts" in Chapters 1 through 4 and "Skills" in Chapters 17 through 23. These condensed, self-contained units, with clear, brief explanations and examples, will reduce students' reading time while improving their comprehension. Simultaneously, instructors will appreciate the new ease of making daily reading assignments and referring students quickly to key concepts and skills without having to search through chapters.
- **New genres in the Writing Projects chapters give instructors more options for assignments across a wide range of writing situations.** Recent scholarship in genre theory has demonstrated that understanding genre is as important to students' rhetorical development as understanding audience or aim. Besides providing more Writing Project options, the newly added genres

strengthen the book's commitment to writing across the curriculum, appeal to students from diverse majors, and increase students' awareness of rhetorical contexts. The new genres include the:

- **literacy narrative** (Chapter 7);
- **annotated bibliography** (Chapter 8);
- **set of instructions** and the **workplace informative report** (Chapter 9);
- **scientific poster** (Chapter 10);
- option of **analyzing paintings for the image analysis** (Chapter 11); and
- **proposal speech with visual aids** (Chapter 16).

Each of these genres is illustrated with new readings or examples by student or professional writers. These new options increase the flexibility of the text, allowing instructors to focus primarily on academic genres or to create a mix of academic, personal, workplace, and civic genres.

- **Every chapter in the text is correlated to the Council of Writing Program Administrators' Outcomes Statement for First-Year Composition** to help administrators with program-wide assessment, to help graduate assistants connect the work of the Council to classroom practice and see how to correlate any learning outcomes to a textbook, and to help undergraduates recognize the skills they are developing and practicing (part opening pages and inside front cover).
- **In Part 2, the Writing Project chapters follow a reordered, streamlined, and consolidated structure.** Chapters now present an Explore activity, general instruction on the type of writing covered in the chapter, the Writing Project instructions, and finally the readings. This reorganization allows instructors to assign instructional material without having to skip over the readings, which were formerly in the middle of the chapter. It also helps students, since instructional material immediately follows the assignment itself. Peer review guidelines have been shortened to focus on the features of specific Writing Projects with a cross-reference to the generic revising questions in Chapter 17.
- **The fifth edition is shorter than the fourth edition, we happily note, despite the addition of genres, readings, visuals, and instructional graphics.** In response to reviewer comments about the length and density of the fourth edition, we have condensed the narrative and presented some instruction in at-a-glance graphics.
    - New **Strategies boxes** throughout the text present to-the-point ways to accomplish specific writing and research tasks and serve as easy reference and review for students.
    - New **Framework charts** in the Writing Projects chapters show ways to approach the organization of various types of writing.
- **Seventeen new professional readings and ten new student readings have been added, many of which have been selected to form thematic units.** As can be seen in the "Thematic Contents" (pp. xxix–xxxv), the readings in

the fifth edition form a wide range of thematic groupings. New thematic units include "Employment and Outsourcing," "The Internet, Cell Phones, Social Relations, and Surveillance," "Immigration," "Native American Experience and Opportunities," and "Energy Sources and Sustainability." Other thematic groupings from the fourth edition—such as units related to popular culture, media, and advertising; nature and ecology; guns and violence; and identity and values—have been updated with new readings, including both visual and verbal texts and a wide range of scholarly and popular genres, as can be seen in the catalog of genres on the inside back cover.

Specific Changes

- **Part 1 (Chapters 1–4) on rhetoric has been reorganized to highlight twelve key takeaway concepts**, making it easy for students to understand the concept on first reading and to review it quickly. The essence of each concept is identified in its title:

  CHAPTER 1
  Concept 1: Good writing can vary from closed to open forms.
  Concept 2: Good writers pose questions about their subject matter.
  Concept 3: Good writers write for a purpose to an audience within a genre.

  CHAPTER 2
  Concept 4: Professors value "wallowing in complexity."
  Concept 5: Good writers use exploratory strategies to think critically about subject-matter questions.
  Concept 6: A strong thesis statement surprises readers with something new or challenging.
  Concept 7: Thesis statements in closed-form prose are supported hierarchically with points and particulars.

  CHAPTER 3
  Concept 8: Messages persuade through their angle of vision.
  Concept 9: Messages persuade through appeals to *logos, ethos*, and *pathos.*
  Concept 10: Nonverbal messages persuade through visual strategies that can be analyzed rhetorically.

  CHAPTER 4
  Concept 11: Good writers make purposeful stylistic choices.
  Concept 12: Good writers make purposeful document design choices.

  With these concepts, Chapters 1 through 4 now provide students with a briefer yet more inclusive and powerful overview of rhetoric that will ground their study of college-level writing, reading, and thinking.

- **Chapter 1 now explains three foundational concepts that expand students' thinking about "good writing."** The basics of audience, purpose, and genre are now introduced here rather than in Chapter 3 to provide students with a better conceptual framework for understanding the flexible concept of "good writing." The important realization that the "rules" for good writing vary from closed to open forms prepares students to appreciate how writers' choices about structure and style depend on the nature of the subject-matter problem they are posing and on their purpose, audience, and genre. This chapter offers two Brief Writing Projects, giving instructors more options for a short writing-to-learn assignment on the second or third day of the course.

- **Chapters 2, 3, and 4 reflect the new ordering and sequencing of basic rhetorical instruction** that will help students produce rich and thoughtful work in response to the Writing Projects assignments in Part 2. Prewriting strategies have been moved from Chapter 17 into Chapter 2 to emphasize how writers use exploratory strategies to wrestle with subject-matter problems. In Chapter 4, the concept of different styles is now illustrated using academic and popular articles on *South Park*. New sections have been added on pruning wordiness and on controlling emphasis through coordination or subordination as ways of improving style. Throughout, new "For Writing and Discussion" exercises give students practice with the rhetorical concepts.
- **Numerous local changes improve each of the Writing Projects chapters in Part 2.** The addition of new genres in many chapters has already been mentioned. Additional improvements include the following:
    - **Chapter 6 on rhetorical reading has been substantially revised to clarify the genres of strong response, to increase students' grasp of concepts, and to provide engaging new readings for analysis.** Through consolidation and pruning, we have made this chapter shorter, clearer, and easier to teach. We identify the genres of strong response as "rhetorical critique," "ideas critique," "reflection," and "blend," and provide new exercises to clarify concepts as well as **a new Writing Project focusing on summary writing**. New readings focus on the important domestic and global economic issue of outsourcing.
    - **Chapter 7 on autobiographical narrative has a new literacy narrative Writing Project.** It includes key points to guide all stages of writing a literacy narrative, with examples from student literacy narratives, as well as a full-length student literacy narrative in the Readings section.
    - **In Chapter 8, a new Framework chart shows ways to approach an exploratory essay, and a new exploratory essay by student writer James Gardiner (on online social networks)** illustrates key thinking and researching moves. Gardiner also provides a model for the new **annotated bibliography Writing Project**. The readings in this chapter now include Jane Tompkins's provocative exploratory article "'Indians': Textualism, Morality, and the Problem of History."
    - **Chapter 10 on field research includes a new student APA empirical research report** on gender stereotyping in a Mickey Mouse and a *SpongeBob SquarePants* cartoon. The same research study is also presented as a **scientific poster**, a new Writing Project.

- **Chapter 11 on visual rhetoric contains new material on analyzing paintings and news photos**, expanding the fourth edition's focus on advertising. It also has a striking new opening exercise on immigration photos and a new **Framework chart** for analyzing visual texts.
- **In Chapter 12, Sherman Alexie's "The Lone Ranger and Tonto Fistfight in Heaven,"** an intercultural short story with strong student appeal, replaces the David Updike story "Summer."
- **Chapter 13 on synthesis has a new set of readings on immigration, all taken from blogs.** The opening exploration exercise focuses on the provocative issue of mobile phone tracking. In addition, **a new Flow Diagram** helps students organize their approach to writing a synthesis essay.
- **Chapter 14 on classical argument has been made more teachable** by eliminating Toulmin terminology such as "warrant" and "backing" while retaining the basic Toulmin schema, which powerfully helps students identify and analyze the underlying assumptions in arguments as well as the way that evidence is used to support reasons. The chapter has **a new Framework chart** to help students organize their argument and new readings on the controversy over nuclear power plants.
- **Chapter 15 has a new opening exercise on evaluating visual images** that oppose binge drinking, replacing the fourth edition's exercise on the upside-down map. The Writing Project instruction includes **a new Framework chart** for approaching an evaluation argument. A student paper in this chapter now evaluates an advocacy Web site.
- **Chapter 16 now includes material on delivering a proposal speech using PowerPoint visual aids.** This new module addresses the challenges and controversies over using PowerPoint. The chapter also includes **a new Framework chart** for organizing a proposal argument.
- **In Part 3, "A Guide to Composing and Revising," the instructional material is now organized as twenty "Skills"** to help students improve their writing by mastering important strategies and techniques. Chapter 17 has been substantially revised so that its ideas are clearly identified as skills and are presented in modules to follow the pattern of Chapters 18 and 19 and to make these writing process points more available to students.

- **Part 4, "A Rhetorical Guide to Research," has been condensed and organized into thirteen skills, making it easier to locate key teaching concepts.** Throughout this section, student James Gardiner's research project on online social networks, first introduced in Chapter 8, illustrates these research moves.
- **In Chapter 21, blogs have been added to our analysis of media**, and a new "For Writing and Discussion" exercise on investigating statistical "factoids" in advocacy ads helps students analyze angle of vision in research sources.
- **In Chapter 23, four new Source Samples show students where in their online database, Web site, and blog research sources** they can find the information they need to cite and document in MLA and APA style.

- **New annotated MLA and APA student model research papers are shown in full in Chapters 23 and 10** so that students can format their own MLA- and APA-style papers more accurately.
- **Part 5, "Writing for Assessment," replaces the fourth edition's "Writing for Special Occasions."** The new title emphasizes this part's clear focus on writing for assessment: essay examinations and portfolio reflections.
- **Throughout the text, our focus on visual rhetoric has been expanded.** Striking visual images appear at the beginning of the major parts of the text with explanatory captions that provoke critical thinking. Examples of visual or visual-verbal texts also appear in numerous For Writing and Discussion exercises throughout the text to provoke interest in how images influence audiences' responses and how they contribute to social conversations and controversies. For example, in Chapter 11, a new gallery of photos related to immigration directs students' attention to the way that images influence public opinion and policy. Similarly, in Chapter 15, a collection of visuals related to the problem of alcohol abuse on college campuses asks students to think about how they might use these visuals to create a campaign against binge drinking.
- **A handy new appendix, A Guide to Avoiding Plagiarism,** provides students with a deeper understanding of what constitutes plagiarism in an academic setting and gives step by step explanations and examples so that students can learn how to use sources effectively and cite them properly.

Distinctive Approach of *The Allyn & Bacon Guide to Writing*

The improvements in the fifth edition enhance the enduring strengths of *The Allyn & Bacon Guide to Writing* that have made this text pedagogically effective for students and intellectually satisfying for instructors. What follows are the distinctive features of our approach to teaching composition:

- **Integration of rhetorical theory with composition research.** The authors of this text are scholars in rhetoric, writing across the curriculum, critical thinking, global cultural studies, and composition pedagogy. Together, they bring to *The Allyn & Bacon Guide to Writing* a distinctive pedagogical approach that integrates rhetorical theory with composition research by treating writing and reading as rhetorical acts and as processes of inquiry, problem posing, and critical thinking. The text helps students learn important skills that transfer across disciplines and professional fields.
- **Classroom-tested assignments that guide students through all phases of the reading and writing processes and make frequent use of collaboration and peer review.** The Writing Projects promote intellectual growth and stimulate the kind of critical thinking valued in college courses. Numerous "For Writing and Discussion" exercises make it easy to incorporate active

learning into a course, while deepening students' understanding of concepts. The text's focus on the subject-matter question that precedes the thesis helps students see academic disciplines as fields of inquiry rather than as data banks of right answers.

- **Coverage of a wide range of genres and aims including academic, civic, and professional genres as well as personal and narrative forms.** By placing nonfiction writing on a continuum from closed-form prose (thesis-based) to open-form prose (narrative-based), the text presents students with a wide range of genres and aims and clearly explains the rhetorical function and stylistic features of different genres. The text focuses on closed-form writing for entering most academic, civic, and professional conversations, and on open-form writing for narrating ideas and experiences that resist closed-form structures and for creating stylistic surprise and pleasure.
- **Instructional emphases meet the Council of Writing Program Administrators (WPA) guidelines** for outcome goals in first-year composition courses. The correlation of the WPA Outcomes Statement with the fifth edition of *The Allyn & Bacon Guide to Writing* appears on the front endpapers, the part opening pages, and in the *Instructor's Resource Manual*, which was revised by Susanmarie Harrington of Indiana University Purdue University Indianapolis. In addition to helping instructors plan their courses, these correlations help with program-wide internal and external assessments.
- **Great flexibility for instructors.** Because the chapters on rhetoric, on Writing Projects, and on composing and research strategies have been designed as self-contained modules, users praise the ease with which they can select chapters and order them to fit the goals of their own courses. The addition of new genres in the fifth edition, as well as its improved, modular organization, increase the text's flexibility and ease of use.
- **Use of reader-expectation theory to explain how closed-form prose achieves maximum clarity and how open-form prose achieves its distinctive pleasures.** The skills explained in Chapter 18 on composing and revising closed-form prose (such as the reader's need for understanding the problem before encountering the thesis, for forecasting and signposts, for points before particulars, and for old information before new information) are taught as self-contained Skill lessons that can be easily integrated into a variety of course structures. These explanations show students why certain principles of closed-form prose (such as unified and coherent paragraphs with topic sentences) derive from the psychology of cognition rather than from the rule-making penchant of English teachers. The skills explained in Chapter 19 on open-form prose show how writers create pleasurable surprise through purposeful disruptions and violations of the conventions of closed-form prose.
- **Emphasis on teaching students to read rhetorically.** An often-noted strength of *The Allyn & Bacon Guide to Writing* is its method for teaching students to read rhetorically so that they can summarize complex readings and speak back to them armed with their own powers of analysis and critical thinking. This skill is crucial for undergraduate research in any discipline. In

its focus on rhetorical reading, the text teaches students to understand the differences between print and cyberspace sources; to analyze the rhetorical occasion, genre, context, intended audience, and angle of vision of sources; to evaluate sources according to appropriate criteria; and to negotiate the World Wide Web with confidence.

- **Coverage of visual rhetoric and document design** focuses on Web sites, advertisements, posters, and other texts where words and images work together for rhetorical effect.
- **A sequenced skill-based approach to research** teaches students expert strategies for conducting academic research in a rhetorical environment.
- **A friendly, encouraging tone** that respects students and treats them as serious learners.
- **Accessible readings on current and enduring questions** that illustrate rhetorical principles, represent a balance between professional and student writers, and invite thematic grouping.

Structure of *The Allyn & Bacon Guide to Writing*

Part 1, "A Rhetoric for Writers," provides a conceptual framework for *The Allyn & Bacon Guide to Writing* by showing how inquiring writers pose problems, pursue them through dialectic thinking and research, and try to solve them within a rhetorical context shaped by the writer's purpose, audience, and genre. Part 1 teaches twelve important rhetorical concepts that enable students to situate verbal and visual texts in a rhetorical context and to think critically about how any text tries to persuade its audience. It also awakens students to the problem-based nature of academic writing, where professors expect students to "wallow in complexity" by examining all evidence that bears on a problem and considering alternative views and arguments.

Part 2, "Writing Projects," consists of twelve self-contained assignment chapters arranged according to the aims of writing: to learn, to explore, to inform, to analyze and synthesize, and to persuade. The heart of each chapter is one or more Writing Projects designed to teach students the features of a genre while promoting new ways of seeing and thinking. The exploratory exercises for each Writing Project help students develop their skills at posing problems, generating ideas, delaying closure, valuing alternative points of view, and thinking dialectically. "Questions for Peer Review" focus on the important features in the assignments and facilitate detailed, helpful peer reviews. "Questions for Peer Review" are tailored to each Writing Project in order to help students evaluate one another's work. Each chapter concludes with a section of high-interest readings with questions for discussion.

Part 3, "A Guide to Composing and Revising," comprises three self-contained chapters of nuts-and-bolts strategies for composing and revising along the continuum from closed to open forms. Each "skill" covered in these chapters is conceived as a mini-lesson that can be incorporated into a class period. Chapter 17 explains how experienced writers use invention strategies, prewriting, and multiple drafts to manage the complexities of writing and suggests ways that students can improve their own writing processes. It also includes instruction on how to conduct peer reviews. Chapter 18 presents ten self-contained lessons—derived from reader-expectation theory—on composing and revising closed-form prose. Chapter 19 offers parallel explanations of open-form prose.

Part 4, "A Rhetorical Guide to Research," continues the sequence of skills as mini-lessons provided in Part 3. Students learn how to pose research questions and conduct searches (Chapter 20), evaluate sources (Chapter 21), incorporate sources into their own writing (Chapter 22), and cite and document sources according to MLA or APA style (Chapter 23). Throughout, research skills are taught within a rhetorical context with special attention given to the distinctions between peer-reviewed scholarly sources and other sources, to the rhetoric of Web sites, and to a political understanding of popular media.

Part 5, "Writing for Assessment," focuses on essay exams and portfolios. Chapter 24, drawing on research on timed writing, shows students how to plan and draft an exam essay by applying the principles of rhetorical understanding discussed throughout the text. Chapter 25 teaches students how to think metacognitively about their own composing processes, produce self-reflective evaluations of their own work, and assemble portfolios.

Strategies for Using *The Allyn & Bacon Guide to Writing*

The text's organization makes it easy to design a new syllabus or adapt the text to your current syllabus. Although there are many ways to use *The Allyn & Bacon Guide to Writing,* the most typical course design has students reading and discussing selected concepts from Chapters 1–4 (Part 1) during the opening weeks. The brief, informal write-to-learn projects in these chapters can be used either for homework assignments or for in-class discussion. In the rest of the course, instructors typically assign Writing Projects chapters from the array of options available in Part 2. While students are engaged with the Writing Projects in these chapters, instructors can work in mini-lessons on the writing and research "skills" in Parts 3 and 4. Typically during class sessions, instructors move back and forth between classroom exercises related directly to the current Writing Project (invention exercises, group brainstorming, peer review workshops) and discussions focused on instructional matter from the rest of the text. (For more specific suggestions on how to select and sequence materials, see the sample syllabi in the *Instructor's Resource Manual.*)

Using the Writing Projects in Part 2

Because each of the twelve assignment chapters in Part 2 is self-contained, instructors can select and organize the Writing Projects in the way that best fits their course goals and their students' needs. Here is an overview of the Writing Projects:

- The project in Chapters 5 on "seeing rhetorically" asks students to write **two descriptions of the same scene** for different rhetorical purposes and then to write a reflection of what they learned from this activity. Many instructors have praised the transformative power of this assignment for teaching angle of vision in texts.

- Chapter 6, on **summary/strong response**, teaches students how to write summaries of texts and to incorporate these summaries into their own prose. It also teaches "strong response" by showing students how to analyze the rhetorical strategies of a text, to join its conversation of ideas, to write reflectively about the personal meaning of the text for the writer, or to blend these kinds of strong responses. By also explaining how to integrate summaries and quotations into one's own prose, this chapter grounds students in the skills needed for college-level research.
- In Chapter 7, the Writing Projects on **autobiographical narrative** and the subgenre **literacy narrative** provide the text's primary "open-form" assignments. Introducing students to strategies of plot, character, and dramatic tension, the autobiographical narrative project often produces surprisingly sophisticated narratives. Some teachers like to give this assignment early in the course—on the grounds that personal writing should precede more academic forms. Others like to give it last—on the grounds that open-form writing is more complex and subtle than closed-form prose. We have found that either choice can work well. Teachers often pair Chapter 7 with Chapter 19, on composing and revising open-form prose.
- Chapter 8 offers two Writing Project options: an **exploratory essay** and an **annotated bibliography**. The exploratory essay asks students to narrate their engagement with a problem and their attempts to resolve it. Teachers may want to pair this chapter with Part 4 on research writing, using the exploratory essay as the first stage of a major research project. The annotated bibliography, which can also be used in conjunction with a later research assignment, can be assigned prior to the major assignment to stimulate invention.
- Chapter 9, on informative writing, provides three options: **a set of instructions**, **a workplace informative report**, and **a magazine article** that brings surprising, new information to its readers. The "surprising-reversal" strategy used in the last option introduces students to a powerful rhetorical move that can be used to enliven almost any kind of informative, analytical, or persuasive prose.
- Chapter 10 is the first of four chapters with an analysis/synthesis aim. Its Writing Project is an **APA empirical research report** (introduction, methods, results, and discussion) based on students' investigation of an empirical research question using questionnaires, interviews, or observations. An optional assignment for this chapter is a poster of the kind frequently displayed at scientific conferences.
- Chapter 11 introduces students to visual rhetoric. Its Writing Project is the **analysis of two contrasting visual texts** (advertisements, paintings, or photographs). The chapter's discussion of advertising allows instructors to use this assignment as an introduction to popular culture.
- Chapter 12 focuses on **analyzing a short story**, introducing students to inquiry and analysis in literary studies.

- Chapter 13 teaches students how to **analyze and synthesize ideas** from two or more readings addressing the same problem, helping students develop the advanced critical reading and thinking skills essential for success in any field.
- The Writing Project for Chapter 14 is a **classical argument** in which the writer supports his or her own claim with reasons and evidence but also summarizes and responds to opposing views through rebuttal or concessions. The assignment also teaches students how to identify the underlying assumptions of an argument and, if the audience is not apt to accept the assumptions, to articulate and support them.
- Chapter 15 teaches specific strategies for **evaluation arguments**, particularly how to determine the criteria for an evaluation and how to argue whether the phenomenon being evaluated meets the criteria. The Writing Project asks students to write an evaluation argument addressed to a skeptical audience.
- Chapter 16 focuses on proposal arguments. It offers three optional Writing Projects: a written proposal, either a **practical proposal or a policy proposal**; an **advocacy advertisement or poster**; and **a proposal speech supported with PowerPoint visuals**.

Supplements for *The Allyn & Bacon Guide to Writing*

The Allyn & Bacon Guide to Writing is supported by helpful supplements for instructors and students.

- **The *Instructor's Resource Manual*, Fifth Edition**, has been revised by Susanmarie Harrington of Indiana University Purdue University Indianapolis. The *Instructor's Resource Manual* integrates emphases for meeting the Council of Writing Program Administrators' guidelines for outcome goals in first-year composition courses. It continues to offer detailed teaching suggestions to help both experienced and new instructors; practical teaching strategies for composition instructors in a question-and-answer format; suggested syllabi for courses of various lengths and emphases; chapter-by-chapter teaching suggestions; answers to Handbook exercises; suggestions for using the text with nonnative speakers; suggestions for using the text in an electronic classroom; transparency masters for class use; and annotated bibliographies.
- **MyCompLab** (www.MyCompLab.com). **MyCompLab** is a Web application that offers comprehensive and integrated resources for every writer. With MyCompLab, students can access a dynamic e-book version of *The Allyn & Bacon Guide to Writing*; learn from interactive tutorials and instruction; practice and develop their skills with grammar; writing, and research exercises; share their writing and collaborate with peers; and receive comments on their writing from instructors and tutors. Go to http://www.mycomplab.com to register for these premiere resources and much more.

- **Other Supplements.** Pearson English has a wide array of other supplementary items—some at no additional cost, some deeply discounted—that are available for packaging with this text. Please contact your local Pearson representative to find out more.

Acknowledgments

We wish to give special thanks to the following composition scholars and teachers, who reviewed the fourth-edition text or the manuscript for the fifth edition, helping us understand how they use *The Allyn & Bacon Guide to Writing* in the classroom and offering valuable suggestions for improving the text:

Jeanette Adkins, Tarrant County College Northeast
Robert J. Affeldt, University of Texas—Pan American
Kathleen Baca, Doña Ana Community College
Larry Beason, University of South Alabama
Danika M. Brown, University of Texas—Pan American
Laura Carroll, Abilene Christian University
Chandra Speight Cerutti, East Carolina University
Ron Christiansen, Salt Lake Community College
Jesse S. Cohn, Purdue University North Central
Joseph Rocky Colavito, Northwestern State University
Michael Creeden, Florida International University
Cynthia Debes, Kansas State University
Chitralekha Duttagupta, Arizona State University
Tamara Fish, University of Houston
John Charles Goshert, Utah Valley State College
Kimberly Harrison, Florida International University
Annis H. Hopkins, Southern Illinois University Edwardsville
Melissa Ianetta, University of Delaware
Peggy Jolly, University of Alabama at Birmingham
Bonnie Lenore Kyburz, Utah Valley State College
Alfred G. Litton, Texas Woman's University
Kim Brian Lovejoy, Indiana University Purdue University Indianapolis
Carol Luvert, Hawkeye Community College
Josie Mills, Arapahoe Community College
Robert Saba, Florida International University
Gloria A. Shearin, Savannah State University
Scott Weeden, Indiana University Purdue University Indianapolis

We also give special thanks to Virginia Norton, an avid reader of political blogs, who helped us navigate the "blogosphere," identifying significant blogs and bloggers from right to left across the political spectrum, and who helped us choose the blogs on immigration for the readings in Chapter 13. We thank Professor Jeff Philpott in the Department of Communication at Seattle University for his advice in our Chapter 16 unit on PowerPoint presentations, and John Caster, artist and art teacher, for his suggestions for paintings to analyze in Chapter 11. Finally, we thank Professor Charles Paine of the University of New Mexico, whose insightful critiques of the fourth edition first guided us to attempt the streamlined, modular organization of the fifth edition as well as to expand our coverage of genres.

Thanks also to various scholars who have written commissioned sections of *The Allyn & Bacon Guide to Writing* for previous editions and whose work remains in the fifth edition. Thanks to Tim McGee of Philadelphia University, whose work still influences our material on oral presentation. Thanks also to Alice Gillam of the University of Wisconsin–Milwaukee, who authored the chapter on self-reflective writing (Chapter 25) and to Virginia Chappell of Marquette University, who contributed significantly to Chapter 12 on analyzing a short story. Finally, we wish to thank again Christy Friend of the University of South Carolina, Columbia, who wrote the chapter on essay examinations for the first edition.

Our deepest thanks and appreciation go to our editor, Lauren Finn, whose comprehensive view of the field, keen insights, and excellent people and communication skills make her a pleasure to work with. We are also particularly grateful to our development editor, Marion Castellucci, who has worked with us through multiple revisions and has become an invaluable part of our team. Her insight, sense of humor, professional experience, and extensive editorial knowledge have once again kept us on track and made the intense work of this revision possible.

We would also like to thank three Seattle University students who provided special research assistance for this edition as well as their perspective on important issues: James Gardiner, Teresa Filice, and Lauren Campbell. Most of all, we are indebted to all our students, who have made the teaching of composition such a joy. We thank them for their insights and for their willingness to engage with problems, discuss ideas, and, as they compose and revise, share with us their frustrations and their triumphs. They have sustained our love of teaching and inspired us to write this book.

Finally, John Bean thanks his wife, Kit, also a professional composition teacher, whose dedication to her students as writers and individuals manifests the sustaining values of our unique profession. John also thanks his children, Matthew, Andrew, Stephen, and Sarah, who have grown to adulthood since he began writing textbooks. June Johnson thanks her husband, Kenneth Bube, for his loving support, his interest in teaching, and his expert understanding of the importance of writing in mathematics and the sciences. Finally, she thanks her daughter, Jane Ellen, who has offered encouragement and support in countless ways.

John D. Ramage
John C. Bean
June Johnson

THE ALLYN & BACON GUIDE TO WRITING

PART 1

A RHETORIC FOR WRITERS

As the search for clean, renewable energy to relieve the pressure on oil gains momentum, photographs of wind turbines are appearing more frequently in magazines and newspapers. However, because this source of energy is controversial, *how* these massive technological windmills are depicted varies widely. Do they blend into the landscape or mar it with their industrial presence? Photographers and writers, conscious of the rhetorical effect of photos, carefully plan the impression they want photos of wind power to convey. This low-angle shot of wind turbines, emphasizing their size and power and hinting at barren hills in the background, participates in this public controversy.

This photograph is part of a discussion in Chapter 3, pp. 58–59, on the way that visuals make appeals to *logos*, *ethos*, and *pathos*.

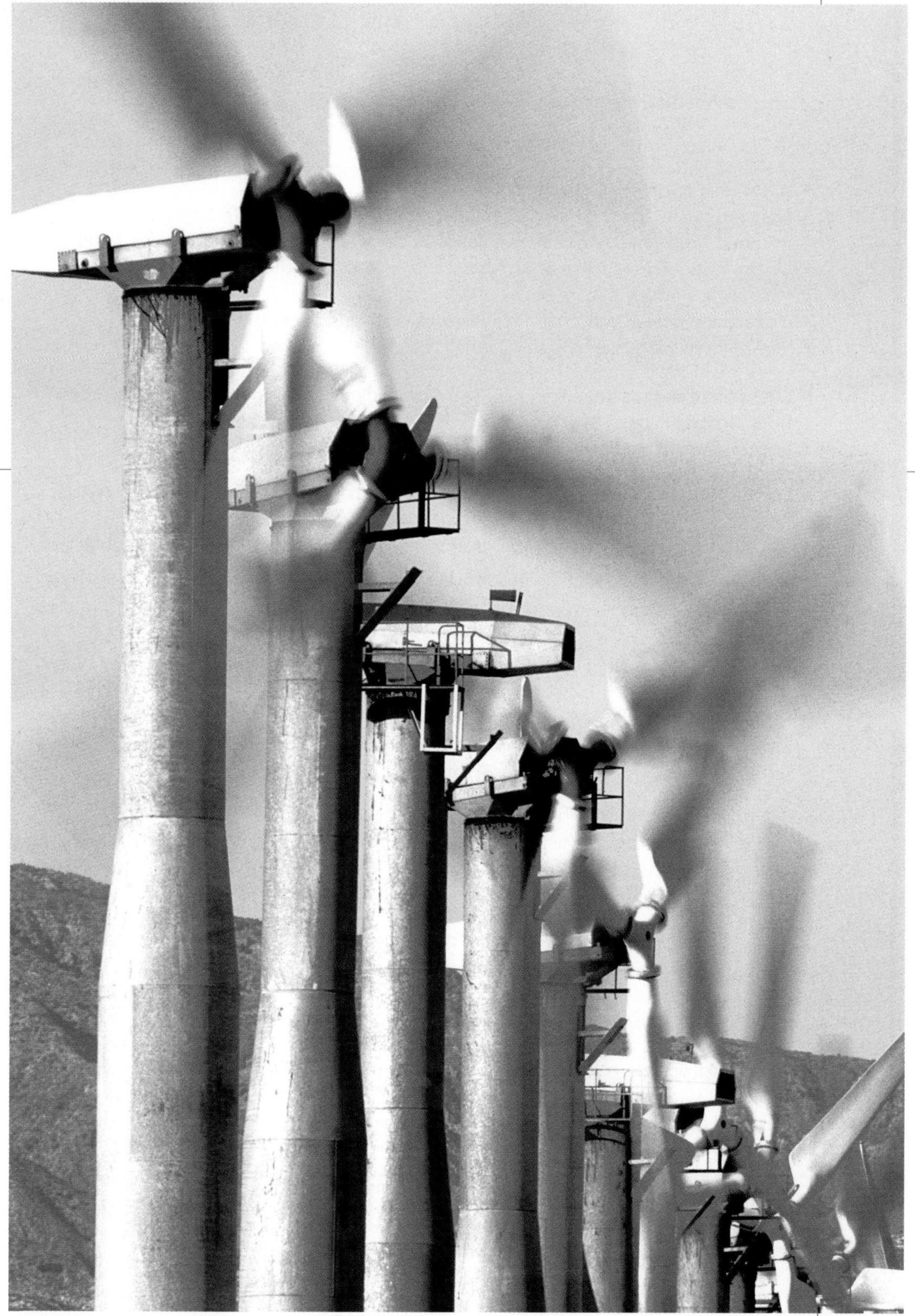

PART 1 A RHETORIC FOR WRITERS

Council of Writing Program Administrators Outcomes for First-Year Composition

CHAPTER 1 Thinking Rhetorically about Good Writing	
RHETORICAL KNOWLEDGE	• Focus on a purpose (Concept 3) • Respond to the needs of different audiences (Concepts 1 and 3) • Respond appropriately to different kinds of rhetorical situations (Concepts 1 and 3) • Use conventions of format and structure appropriate to the rhetorical situation (Concepts 1 and 3) • Understand how genres shape reading and writing (Concepts 1 and 3) • Write in several genres (Brief Writing Project 2)
CRITICAL THINKING, READING, AND WRITING	• Use writing and reading for inquiry, learning, thinking, and communicating (Concept 2; Brief Writing Project 1) • Integrate their own ideas with those of others (Concept 2)
KNOWLEDGE OF CONVENTIONS	• Learn common formats for different kinds of texts (Concepts 1 and 3; Brief Writing Projects) • Develop knowledge of genre conventions ranging from structure and paragraphing to tone and mechanics (Concepts 1 and 3; Brief Writing Projects)
CHAPTER 2 Thinking Rhetorically about Your Subject Matter	
CRITICAL THINKING, READING, AND WRITING	• Use writing and reading for inquiry, learning, thinking, and communicating (Concepts 4–6; Brief Writing Project) • Understand a writing assignment as a series of tasks, including finding, evaluating, analyzing, and synthesizing appropriate primary and secondary sources (Concepts 4–7) • Integrate their own ideas with those of others (Concepts 4 and 5)
CHAPTER 3 Thinking Rhetorically about How Messages Persuade	
CRITICAL THINKING, READING, AND WRITING	• Understand the relationships among language, knowledge, and power (Concepts 8 and 9; Brief Writing Project)
PROCESSES	• Use a variety of technologies to address a range of audiences (Concept 10)
CHAPTER 4 Thinking Rhetorically about Style and Document Design	
RHETORICAL KNOWLEDGE	• Adopt appropriate voice, tone, and level of formality (Concepts 11 and 12; Brief Writing Project) • Respond appropriately to different kinds of rhetorical situations (Concepts 11 and 12; Brief Writing Project) • Use conventions of format and structure appropriate to the rhetorical situation (Concepts 11 and 12; Brief Writing Project) • Understand how genres shape reading and writing (Concepts 11 and 12; Brief Writing Project)

THINKING RHETORICALLY ABOUT GOOD WRITING

CHAPTER 1

It seems to me, then, that the way to help people become better writers is not to tell them that they must first learn the rules of grammar, that they must develop a four-part outline, that they must consult the experts and collect all the useful information. These things may have their place. But none of them is as crucial as having a good, interesting question.

—Rodney Kilcup, Historian

hen new students enter our writing courses, we find that they are often concerned with rules:

- Can I use "I" in this paper?
- Is this paper supposed to have a thesis statement? Where should I put it?
- Do we need to have quotes?

However, instead of focusing on rules, we would like to begin by giving you a broader and deeper way to look at the writing you will do in your academic and professional life. One of our goals is to help you see writing as critical thinking. We'd like you to think of good writers as question askers and problem posers rather than as followers of rigidly prescribed rules. In particular, writers must work out their answers to two sorts of questions: questions about their *subject matter* (Will hydrogen fuel cell cars become a solution to the energy crisis? Does Hamlet change in the last act?) and questions about their *audience and purpose* (Who are my readers? How much do they already know or care about this question? What do I want them to see, know, or do?).

Before turning directly to the notion of writers as questioners and problem posers, we want to pause to consider another question: Why take a writing course? What benefits can you expect to get from studying writing at the college level?

First of all, the skills you learn in this course will be directly transferable to your other college courses, where you will have to write papers in a wide variety of styles. Lower-division (general education or core) courses often focus on general academic writing, while upper-division courses in your major introduce you to the specialized writing and thinking of your chosen field. What college professors value are the kinds of questioning, analyzing, and arguing skills that this course will help you develop. You will emerge from this course as a better reader and thinker and a clearer and more persuasive writer, able to meet the demands of different academic writing situations.

Effective writing skills are also essential for most professional careers. To measure the importance of writing to career success, researchers Andrea Lunsford and Lisa Ede surveyed randomly selected members of such professional organizations as the American Consulting Engineers Counsel, the American Institute of Chemists, the American Psychological Association, and the International City Management Association. They discovered that members of these organizations spend, on average, forty-four percent of their professional time writing, including (most commonly) letters, memos, short reports, instructional materials, and professional articles and essays.

Besides the pragmatic benefits of college and career success, learning to write well can bring you the personal pleasure of a richer mental life. As we show throughout this text, writing is closely allied to thinking and to the innate satisfaction you take in exercising your curiosity, creativity, and problem-solving ability. Writing connects you to others and helps you discover and express ideas that you would otherwise never think or say. Unlike speaking, writing gives you time to think deep and long about an idea. Because you can revise writing, it lets you pursue a problem in stages, with each draft reflecting a deeper, clearer, or more complex level of thought. Thus writing isn't just a way to express thought; it is a way to do the thinking itself. The act of writing stimulates, challenges, and stretches your mental powers and, when you do it well, is profoundly satisfying.

Having suggested some benefits of writing well, we now introduce you in this chapter to three important concepts about good writing:

Concept 1: Good writing can vary from closed to open forms of prose.

Concept 2: Good writers pose questions about their subject matter.

Concept 3: Good writers write for a purpose to an audience within a genre.

CONCEPT 1 Good writing can vary from closed to open forms.

In our experience, beginning college writers are often discomforted by the ambiguity of the rules governing writing. They often wish for some consistent rules: "Never use 'I' in a formal paper" or "Start every paragraph with a topic sentence." The problem is that different kinds of writing have different criteria for effectiveness, leaving the writer with rhetorical choices rather than with hard-and-fast formulas for success. You'll be able to appreciate this insight for yourself through the following exercise.

Read the following short pieces of nonfiction prose. The first is a letter to the editor written by a professional civil engineer in response to a newspaper editorial arguing for the development of wind-generated electricity. The second short piece is entitled "A Festival of Rain." It was written by the American poet and religious writer Thomas Merton, a Trappist monk. After reading the two samples carefully, proceed to the discussion questions that follow.

David Rockwood

A Letter to the Editor

1 Your editorial on November 16, "Get Bullish on Wind Power," is based on fantasy rather than fact. There are several basic reasons why wind-generated power can in no way serve as a reasonable major alternative to other electrical energy supply alternatives for the Pacific Northwest power system.

2 First and foremost, wind power is unreliable. Electric power generation is evaluated not only on the amount of energy provided, but also on its ability to meet system peak load requirements on an hourly, daily, and weekly basis. In other words, an effective power system would have to provide enough electricity to meet peak demands in a situation when the wind energy would be unavailable—either in no wind situations or in severe blizzard conditions, which would shut down the wind generators. Because wind power cannot be relied on at times of peak needs, it would have to be backed up by other power generation resources at great expense and duplication of facilities.

3 Secondly, there are major unsolved problems involved in the design of wind generation facilities, particularly for those located in rugged mountain areas. Ice storms, in particular, can cause sudden dynamic problems for the rotating blades and mechanisms which could well result in breakdown or failure of the generators. Furthermore, the design of the facilities to meet the stresses imposed by high winds in these remote mountain regions, in the order of 125 miles per hour, would indeed escalate the costs.

4 Thirdly, the environmental impact of constructing wind generation facilities amounting to 28 percent of the region's electrical supply system (as proposed in your editorial) would be tremendous. The Northwest Electrical Power system presently has a capacity of about 37,000 megawatts of hydro power and 10,300 megawatts of thermal, for a total of about 48,000 megawatts. Meeting 28 percent of this capacity by wind power generators would, most optimistically, require about 13,400 wind towers, each with about 1,000 kilowatt (one megawatt) generating capacity. These towers, some 100 to 200 feet high, would have to be located in the mountains of Oregon and Washington. These would encompass hundreds of square miles of pristine mountain area, which, together with interconnecting transmission facilities, control works, and roads, would indeed have major adverse environmental impacts on the region.

5 There are many other lesser problems of control and maintenance of such a system. Let it be said that, from my experience and knowledge as a professional engineer, the use of wind power as a major resource in the Pacific Northwest power system is strictly a pipe dream.

Thomas Merton
A Festival of Rain

1 Let me say this before rain becomes a utility that they can plan and distribute for money. By "they" I mean the people who cannot understand that rain is a festival, who do not appreciate its gratuity, who think that what has no price has no value, that what cannot be sold is not real, so that the only way to make something *actual* is to place it on the market. The time will come when they will sell you even your rain. At the moment it is still free, and I am in it. I celebrate its gratuity and its meaninglessness.

2 The rain I am in is not like the rain of cities. It fills the woods with an immense and confused sound. It covers the flat roof of the cabin and its porch with insistent and controlled rhythms. And I listen, because it reminds me again and again that the whole world runs by rhythms I have not yet learned to recognize, rhythms that are not those of the engineer.

3 I came up here from the monastery last night, sloshing through the corn fields, said Vespers, and put some oatmeal on the Coleman stove for supper. ... The night became very dark. The rain surrounded the whole cabin with its enormous virginal myth, a whole world of meaning, of secrecy, of silence, of rumor. Think of it: all that speech pouring down, selling nothing, judging nobody, drenching the thick mulch of dead leaves, soaking the trees, filling the gullies and crannies of the wood with water, washing out the places where men have stripped the hillside! What a thing it is to sit absolutely alone, in a forest, at night, cherished by this wonderful, unintelligible, perfectly innocent speech, the most comforting speech in the world, the talk that rain makes by itself all over the ridges, and the talk of the watercourses everywhere in the hollows!

4 Nobody started it, nobody is going to stop it. It will talk as long as it wants, this rain. As long as it talks I am going to listen.

5 But I am also going to sleep, because here in this wilderness I have learned how to sleep again. Here I am not alien. The trees I know, the night I know, the rain I know. I close my eyes and instantly sink into the whole rainy world of which I am a part, and the world goes on with me in it, for I am not alien to it.

FOR WRITING AND DISCUSSION

Comparing Rockwood's and Merton's Writing

Working in small groups or as a whole class, try to reach consensus on the following specific tasks:

1. What are the main differences between the two types of writing? If you are working in groups, help your recorder prepare a presentation describing the differences between Rockwood's writing and Merton's writing.
2. Create a metaphor, simile, or analogy that best sums up your feelings about the most important differences between Rockwood's and Merton's writing: "Rockwood's writing is like ..., but Merton's writing is like ... ."
3. Explain why your metaphors are apt. How do your metaphors help clarify or illuminate the differences between the two pieces of writing?

Now that you have done some thinking on your own about the differences between these two examples, turn to our brief analysis.

Distinctions between Closed and Open Forms of Writing

David Rockwood's letter and Thomas Merton's mini-essay are both examples of nonfiction prose. But as these examples illustrate, nonfiction prose can vary enormously in form and style. From the perspective of structure, we can place nonfiction prose along a continuum that goes from closed to open forms of writing (see Figure 1.1).

Of our two pieces of prose, Rockwood's letter illustrates tightly closed writing and falls at the far left end of the continuum because it has these elements:

- An explicit thesis in the introduction that informs readers of the point of the whole essay (i.e., wind-generated power isn't a reasonable alternative energy source in the Pacific Northwest)
- Unified and coherent paragraphs (i.e., "First and foremost, wind power is unreliable. ... Secondly, there are major unsolved problems. ... Thirdly, ...")
- Sustained development of that thesis without digressions

Once the thesis is stated, readers know the point of the essay and can predict its structure. (You might note that the five-paragraph essay sometimes taught in high school is a by-the-numbers way to teach closed-form prose.) Because its structure is transparent and predictable, the success of closed-form prose rests entirely on its ideas, which must "surprise" readers by asserting something new, challenging, doubtful, or controversial. It aims to change readers' view of the subject through the power of reason, logic, and evidence. Closed-form prose is what most college professors write in their scholarly research, what they most often expect from their students, and what is most common in professional and business contexts.

In contrast, Merton's "A Festival of Rain" falls toward the right end of the closed-to-open continuum because it exhibits these features:

- No reduction to a single, summarizable thesis (Merton clearly opposes the consumer culture that will try to "sell" you the rain, but what exactly does Merton mean by "festival" or by rain's "gratuity and its meaninglessness"?)
- The use of story or narrative as an organizing principle (i.e., the story of Merton's leaving the monastery to sleep in the rain-drenched cabin) through which a point emerges suggestively

Although open-form prose does not announce its thesis and support it with reasons and evidence, it does have a focus. As Merton's piece illustrates, the focus is more like a theme in fiction that readers might discuss and even dispute than like a thesis in argument.

Consider also the extent to which Merton violates the rules for closed-form prose. Instead of using transitions between paragraphs, Merton juxtaposes passages that tell the story of his camping trip ("I came up here from the monastery last night ...") with passages that make cryptic, interpretive comments about his experience ("The rain I am in is not like the rain of cities"). Unlike paragraphs in closed-form prose, which typically begin with topic sentences and are developed with supporting details, the paragraphs in Merton's piece have no clear hierarchical structure; paragraph 4, in fact, is only two lines long. These open-form elements

FIGURE 1.1
A Continuum of Essay Types: Closed to Open Forms

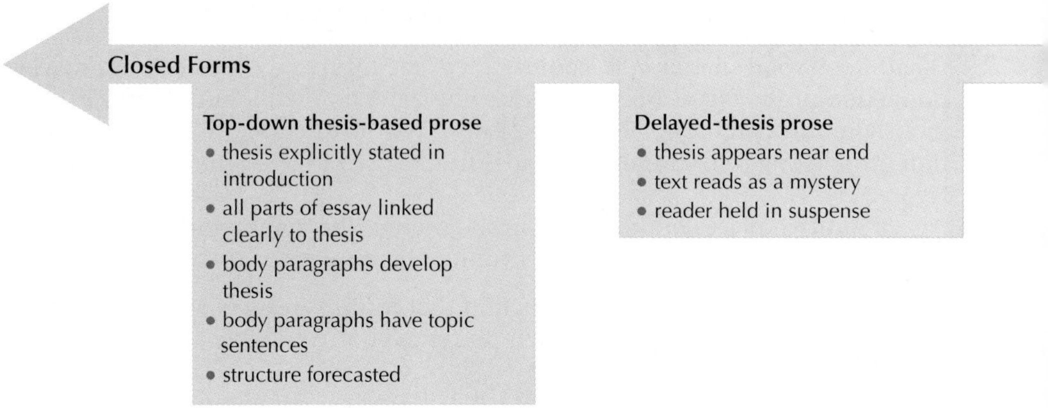

Closed Forms

Top-down thesis-based prose
- thesis explicitly stated in introduction
- all parts of essay linked clearly to thesis
- body paragraphs develop thesis
- body paragraphs have topic sentences
- structure forecasted

Delayed-thesis prose
- thesis appears near end
- text reads as a mystery
- reader held in suspense

often appear in personal essays, in blogs, in newspaper or magazine feature stories or character profiles, or in professional nonfiction.

As you can see from the continuum in Figure 1.1, essays can fall anywhere along the scale. Not all thesis-with-support writing has to be top down, stating its thesis explicitly in the introduction. In some cases writers choose to delay the thesis, creating a more exploratory, open-ended, "let's think through this together" feeling before finally stating the main point late in the essay. In some cases writers explore a problem without *ever* finding a satisfactory thesis, creating an essay that is thesis seeking rather than thesis supporting, an essay aimed at deepening the question, refusing to accept an easy answer. Such essays may replicate their author's process of exploring a problem and include digressions, speculations, conjectures, multiple perspectives, and occasional invitations to the reader to help solve the problem. When writers reach the far right-hand position on the continuum, they no longer state an explicit thesis. Instead, like novelists or short story writers, they embed their points in plot, imagery, dialogue, and so forth, leaving their readers to *infer* a theme from the text. This kind of writing is often called "literary nonfiction."

Where to Place Your Writing along the Continuum

Clearly, essays at opposite ends of this continuum operate in different ways and obey different rules. Because each position on the continuum has its appropriate uses, the writer's challenge is to determine which sort of writing is most appropriate in a given situation. Thus if you were writing a business proposal, a legal brief, or an academic paper for a scholarly audience, you would typically choose a closed-form structure, and your finished product would include elements such as the following:

- An explicit thesis in the introduction
- Forecasting of structure
- Cohesive and unified paragraphs with topic sentences

Open Forms

Thesis-seeking prose
- essay organized around a question rather than a thesis
- essay explores the problem or question, looking at it in many ways
- writer may or may not arrive at thesis

Theme-based narrative
- often organized chronologically or has storylike elements
- often used to heighten or deepen a problem, or show its human significance
- often has an implicit theme rather than a thesis
- often violates rules of closed-form prose by using literary techniques

- Clear transitions between sentences and between parts
- No digressions

But if you were writing an autobiographical narrative about, say, some turning point in your life, you would probably move toward the open end of the continuum and violate one or more of these conventions. Instead of a thesis-support structure, you might use the power of compelling stories, vivid characterization, dialogue, and evocative language to convey your ideas.

If we return now to the question about good writing posed at the beginning of this chapter, we can see that having a thesis statement, topic sentences, good transitions, and unified and coherent paragraphs are not qualities of "good prose" but simply of "closed-form prose." What makes a piece of closed-form prose "good," as we will see in the next section, is the extent to which it addresses a problem or question that matters to the reader and brings to the reader something new, surprising, or provocative. In contrast, we have seen that open-form prose can be "good" without having a thesis-driven hierarchical structure. Open-form prose conveys its pleasures and insights through narrative strategies rather than through thesis-with-support strategies.

FOR WRITING AND DISCUSSION

Thinking Personally about Closed and Open Forms

Do you and your classmates most enjoy writing prose at the closed or at the more open end of the continuum?

Individual task: Recall a favorite piece of writing that you have done in the past. Jot down a brief description of the kind of writing this was (a poem, a personal-experience essay, a piece of workplace writing, a research paper, a newspaper story, a persuasive argument). Where would you place this piece of writing on

(*continued*)

the closed-to-open continuum? Explore why you liked this piece of writing. Are you at your best in closed-form writing that calls for an explicit thesis statement and logical support? Or are you at your best in more open and personal forms?

Small-group or whole-class task: Share the results of the individual tasks. Is there a wide range of preferences in your class? If so, how do you account for this variance? If not, how do you account for the narrow range?

CONCEPT 2 Good writers pose questions about their subject matter.

In the previous section, we explained how the rules for good writing vary along a continuum from closed to open forms. In this section, we focus on the connection between writing and thinking. We show you how the spirit of inquiry drives the writing process. From your previous schooling, you are probably familiar with the term *thesis statement,* which is the main point a writer wants to make in an essay. However, you may not have thought much about the *question* that lies behind the thesis, which is the problem or issue that the writer is wrestling with. Behind every thesis statement is an explicit or implied thesis question, which is the problem or issue to which the thesis responds. An essay's thesis statement is actually the writer's answer to the writer's question, and it is this question that has motivated the writer's thinking. Experienced writers immerse themselves in subject-matter questions in pursuit of answers or solutions. They write to share their proposed solutions with readers who share their interests.

Shared Problems Unite Writers and Readers

Everywhere we turn, we see writers and readers forming communities based on questions or problems of mutual interest. Many college professors are engaged in research projects stimulated and driven by questions and problems. For example, at a recent workshop for new faculty members, we asked participants to write a brief description of the question or problem that motivated them to write a conference paper or article. Here is how a biochemistry professor responded:

> During periods of starvation, the human body makes physiological adaptations to preserve essential protein mass. Unfortunately, these adaptations don't work well during long-term starvation. After the body depletes its carbohydrate storage, it must shift to depleting protein in order to produce glucose. Eventually, this loss of functional protein leads to metabolic dysfunction and death. Interestingly, several animal species are capable of surviving for extensive periods without food and water while conserving protein and maintaining glucose levels. How do the bodies of these animals accomplish this feat? I wanted to investigate the metabolic functioning of these animals, which might lead to insights into the human situation.

As you progress through your college career, you will find yourself increasingly engaged with the kinds of questions that motivate your professors. All around college campuses you'll find clusters of professors and students asking questions about all manner of curious things from the reproductive cycles of worms and bugs to the structural properties of concrete, from the social significance of obscure poets to gender roles among the Kalahari Bushmen. A quick review of the magazine rack at any large supermarket reveals that similar communities have formed around everything from computers and cooking to hot rods and kayaks.

At the heart of all these communities of writers and readers is an interest in common questions and the hope for better or different answers. Writers write because they have something new or surprising or challenging to say in response to a question. Readers read because they share the writer's interest in the problem and want to deepen their understanding.

Posing Your Own Subject-Matter Questions

Where do good questions come from and how can you learn to pose them? At the outset, we should say that the kinds of questions we discuss in this chapter may lead you toward new and unfamiliar ways of thinking. Beginning college students typically value questions that have right answers. Students ask their professors questions because they are puzzled by confusing parts of a textbook, a lecture, or an assigned reading. They hope their professor will explain the confusing material clearly. Their purpose in asking these questions is to eliminate misunderstandings, not to open up controversy and debate. Although basic comprehension questions are important, they are not the kinds of inquiry questions that initiate strong college-level writing and thinking.

The kinds of questions that stimulate the writing most valued in college are open-ended questions that focus on unknowns rather than factual questions that have single right answers.* They invite multiple points of view or alternative hypotheses; they stimulate critical thinking and research. These are what historian Rodney Kilcup refers to when he says that writers should begin with a "good, interesting question" (see the epigraph to this chapter, p. 5). For Kilcup a good question sets the writer on the path of inquiry, critical thinking, analysis, and argument. The kinds of problems you will face vary from discipline to discipline, but they all require the thinker to make sense of complex data, to wrestle with alternative views, and eventually to stake out a claim and support it.

Our way of thinking about problems has been motivated by the South American educator Paulo Freire, who wanted his students (often poor, illiterate villagers) to become *problematizers* instead of memorizers. Freire opposed what he called "the banking method" of education, in which students deposited knowledge in their memory banks and then made withdrawals during exams. The banking method, Freire believed, left third world villagers passive and helpless to improve their situations in life. If students were taught to read and write using the banking method, they might learn the word *water* through drill-and-skill

*Cognitive psychologists call these "ill-structured" problems. An ill-structured problem has competing solutions, requiring the thinker to argue for the best solution in the absence of full and complete data or in the presence of stakeholders with different backgrounds, assumptions, beliefs, and values. In contrast, a "well-structured" problem eventually yields a correct answer. Math problems that can be solved by applying the right formulae and processes are well structured. That's why you can have the correct answers in the back of the book.

workbook sentences such as, "The water is in the well." With Freire's problematizing method, students might learn the word *water* by asking, "Why is the water dirty and who is responsible?" Freire believed that good questions have stakes and that answering the questions can make a difference in the world.

What constitutes a good subject-matter question? As a general principle, a question is a good one if it hooks your readers' interest and motivates their desire to read your solution. Generally, questions that lead to good college-level writing exhibit three main qualities:

- *A good question is problematic for your audience.* By "problematic," we mean that your intended readers should be initially motivated by the question and find it puzzling. Either they don't know the answer to the question or are considering answers different from your own. Your readers should be intrigued by the question, curious about how you will solve it.
- *A good question is significant.* In addition, a good question should have something at stake. Why does the problem matter? Who are its stakeholders? Why is the question worth pursuing? How will a community gain by considering the writer's solution? These are the "So what?" questions that a good college-level essay must address.
- *A good question is interesting to the writer.* Finally, you as writer need to be genuinely engaged with this question; it has to be a real question for you, a problem in which you feel invested. You can infuse your writing with vitality only when you, the writer, are truly curious about a question or passionately concerned about it.

One way to think about posing a problematic and significant question is to do a thought experiment. Imagine that you are assigned to write a one-page essay, the only goal of which is to pose a good question (not to answer the question or have a thesis). What follows is a student example of such an essay.

Brittany Tinker

Can the World Sustain an American Standard of Living?

Hooks reader's interest and provides background

Yesterday's class discussion about the growing demand for automobiles in China combined with all the problems of smog and air pollution in Beijing raised lots of dilemmas for me. Because the United States and other developed nations are already using up vast quantities of the world's oil, adding oil demands from China and other developing nations will cause the world to deplete its oil even sooner. Moreover, third world development adds even more to the air pollution and global warming caused by consumerism in the United States and other developed countries. So I wonder, what standard of living can the whole world sustain once third world countries expand their own economies?

States the question

Part of me hopes that the poor people in second and third world countries can one day enjoy the standard of living that I have had. The disparity between first world and second or third world countries hit me when I visited Nicaragua. Most Nicaraguans live in small, one-room homes made from corrugated tin and cinder blocks. The plumbing is underdeveloped and the electricity is inconstant. Most Nicaraguan families do not have enough food to provide adequate nutrition. But through economic development, I hope that these people can have the comforts that I and many other fortunate Americans have such as hot water, lots of nutritious food, numerous bedrooms, at least one car in the family, paved sidewalks or driveways, and a backyard, swimming pool, or hot tub.

Begins to show that the question is problematic by presenting one side of her dilemma

But another part of me sees that my own standard of living may be what's at fault; maybe this model for the good life won't work anymore. If second and third world countries attain the standard of living that I have been lucky enough to have, then air pollution, destruction of forests, global warming, and harm to wildlife, as well as the depletion of oil reserves, will pose even greater risks for the world than they already do. A lot of my classmates seem confident that scientists will discover alternative energy sources and solutions to pollution and global warming so that the whole world can live in comfort. But this pessimistic side of me doesn't share their confidence. Maybe the solution is for Americans to greatly reduce their own consumption and to begin reducing the environmental damage they have already created.

Shows the other side of her dilemma

So I am left wondering, Can the world sustain for everybody the standard of living I have enjoyed? This question is significant because there is so much at stake. If our model for the happy life is to have all the American luxuries, then the development of the third world might mean a much speedier destruction of the planet. If we hope to preserve the planet while eliminating the poverty and misery of third world people, then maybe Americans have to develop a new model for happiness. Is it possible for developing countries to find a new path to economic prosperity that shows the developed world a new model of preserving the environment?

Shows why question is significant

Note Brittany Tinker's strategy for getting her readers invested in her question. The end of her first paragraph states the question explicitly: "What standard of living can the whole world sustain once third world countries expand their own economies?" She then shows what makes this question problematic for her: On the one hand she wants third world countries to enjoy America's standard of living (paragraph 2—made vivid by concrete examples from her experience in Nicaragua). On the other hand, she isn't sure the world can produce enough resources and energy to sustain this standard of living (paragraph 3—made vivid by her listing of specific negative consequences to the environment and her skepticism about science's ability to rush to the rescue). Finally her fourth paragraph shows why the question is significant.

As the following charts show, there are a variety of strategies you can use for posing questions and showing how they are problematic and significant. We'll show you additional strategies for posing and exploring questions in Concepts 4 and 5 in Chapter 2.

STRATEGIES for Developing Questions and Showing Why They Are Problematic

Strategies for Developing a Question	Examples of Issues and Possible Questions	Strategies for Showing Readers How Question Is Problematic
A question arises when you:		
Are in disagreement with someone	Sam's argument in favor of nuclear power doesn't adequately address nuclear waste. **Question:** What can we do to dispose of nuclear waste safely?	Summarize the alternative viewpoint and show its weakness.
Are dissatisfied with currently proposed solutions	None of the proposed solutions to steroid use in baseball seems satisfactory. **Question:** What would be a good method to eliminate steroids from baseball?	Show weaknesses in current answers to the question.
Are equally swayed by alternative solutions or points of view	The arguments for and against building a fence between the United States and Mexico are both persuasive. **Question:** Will building a fence on the border between Mexico and the USA solve the problem of illegal immigration? Are there better solutions?	Summarize alternative solutions and viewpoints and show how they are equally attractive (or flawed).
Are dissatisfied with your earlier "easy" answer to a question	Part of me still strongly believes in wind power. But another part of me is persuaded by Rockwood's argument against wind power. **Question:** To what extent will wind power help meet our energy needs? Should taxes pay for research and development of wind power?	Show yourself divided: "Part of me thinks X, but another part of me thinks Y," or "I used to think X, but now I am leaning toward Y."
Are uncertain about the causes, consequences, purpose, or value of a phenomenon	My classmates disagree about whether hip-hop lyrics promote misogyny. **Question:** Are hip-hop lyrics damaging to gender relations?	Show disagreements about cause, consequence, purpose, or value.

Strategies for Developing a Question	Examples of Issues and Possible Questions	Strategies for Showing Readers How Question Is Problematic
Are puzzled by a phenomenon that doesn't match a theory	The "gay gene" theory for homosexual orientation doesn't seem to account for different sexual orientations in identical twins. **Question:** How can we explain different sexual orientations in identical twins?	Point out discrepancy between phenomenon and theory.
Are puzzled by a gap or inconsistency in evidence	The evidence linking childhood immunizations to autism is inconsistent. **Question:** To what extent are childhood immunizations a cause of autism? What other causes have scientific support?	Show how evidence is inconsistent, missing, or contradictory.
Are puzzled by some feature of a text, image, or other phenomenon	It's not clear to me why Merton calls the rain a "festival." **Question:** What does Merton mean by calling rain a "festival"?	Call reader's attention to the puzzling feature.

STRATEGIES for Showing That a Question Is Significant

Possible Strategies	Examples
Show how solving the problem will lead to practical, real-world benefits	If we could figure out how to increase a car's mileage substantially, we could cut down on fossil fuel use.
Show how solving a small knowledge problem will help us solve a larger problem	If we could better understand the role of the witches in *Macbeth*, we would better understand the social construction of gender in the Renaissance.

FOR WRITING AND DISCUSSION

Posing Your Own Problematic Question

Working in small groups or as a whole class, consider the short informative article below. Based on ideas sparked by discussion of this article, create five or more good questions connected to issues of energy and fuel consumption. Pose each question in a simple interrogative sentence that hooks a reader's interest. Then show how each question is both problematic and significant.

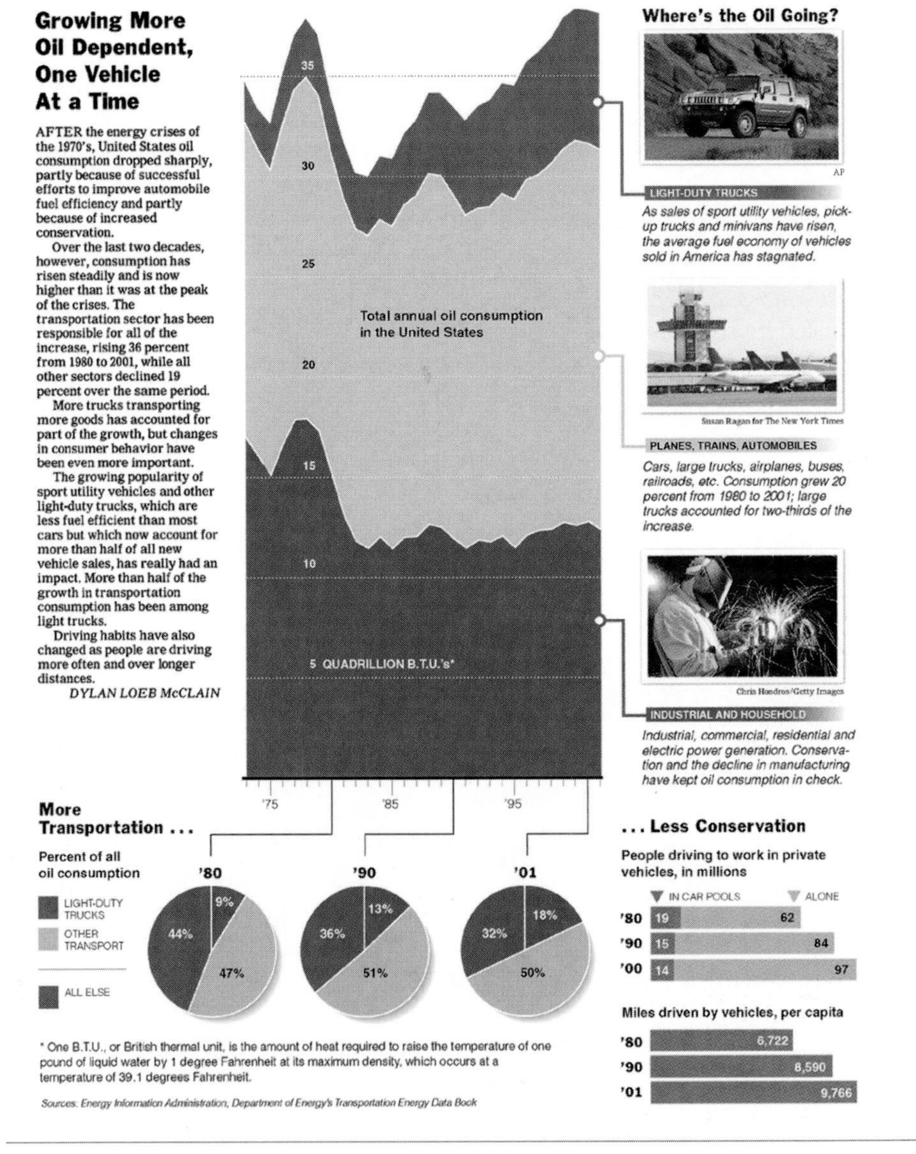

Growing More Oil Dependent, One Vehicle At a Time

AFTER the energy crises of the 1970's, United States oil consumption dropped sharply, partly because of successful efforts to improve automobile fuel efficiency and partly because of increased conservation.

Over the last two decades, however, consumption has risen steadily and is now higher than it was at the peak of the crises. The transportation sector has been responsible for all of the increase, rising 36 percent from 1980 to 2001, while all other sectors declined 19 percent over the same period.

More trucks transporting more goods has accounted for part of the growth, but changes in consumer behavior have been even more important.

The growing popularity of sport utility vehicles and other light-duty trucks, which are less fuel efficient than most cars but which now account for more than half of all new vehicle sales, has really had an impact. More than half of the growth in transportation consumption has been among light trucks.

Driving habits have also changed as people are driving more often and over longer distances.

DYLAN LOEB McCLAIN

Where's the Oil Going?

AP

LIGHT-DUTY TRUCKS

As sales of sport utility vehicles, pick-up trucks and minivans have risen, the average fuel economy of vehicles sold in America has stagnated.

Susan Ragan for The New York Times

PLANES, TRAINS, AUTOMOBILES

Cars, large trucks, airplanes, buses, railroads, etc. Consumption grew 20 percent from 1980 to 2001; large trucks accounted for two-thirds of the increase.

Chris Hondros/Getty Images

INDUSTRIAL AND HOUSEHOLD

Industrial, commercial, residential and electric power generation. Conservation and the decline in manufacturing have kept oil consumption in check.

More Transportation . . .

Percent of all oil consumption

	'80	'90	'01
LIGHT-DUTY TRUCKS	9%	13%	18%
OTHER TRANSPORT	47%	51%	50%
ALL ELSE	44%	36%	32%

. . . Less Conservation

People driving to work in private vehicles, in millions

	IN CAR POOLS	ALONE
'80	19	62
'90	15	84
'00	14	97

Miles driven by vehicles, per capita

'80	6,722
'90	8,590
'01	9,766

* One B.T.U., or British thermal unit, is the amount of heat required to raise the temperature of one pound of liquid water by 1 degree Fahrenheit at its maximum density, which occurs at a temperature of 39.1 degrees Fahrenheit.

Sources: Energy Information Administration, Department of Energy's Transportation Energy Data Book

CONCEPT 3 Good writers write for a purpose to an audience within a genre.

In the previous section we showed how good writers pose questions about their subject matter. In this final section we show how good writers also pose questions about their purpose, audience, and genre. (A *genre* is a recurring type of writing with established conventions such as a letter to the editor, a scholarly article, or a blog.) As good writers consider their subject matter, they also pose questions like these about their rhetorical situation:

- *About their purpose:* What am I trying to accomplish in this paper? What do I want my readers to know, believe, see, or do?
- *About their audience:* What are my readers' values and assumptions? What do they already know or believe about my subject? How much do they care about it?
- *About their genre:* What kind of document am I writing? What are its requirements for structure, style, and document design?

In the rest of this chapter, we will look more closely at these features of rhetorical context.

How Writers Think about Purpose

In this section, we want to help you think more productively about your purpose for writing, which can be examined from several different perspectives: your rhetorical aim, the motivating occasion that gets you going, and your desire to change your reader's view. All three perspectives will help you make your awareness of purpose work for you and increase your savvy as a writer. Let's look at each in turn.

Purpose as Rhetorical Aim

One powerful way to think about purpose is through the general concept of "rhetorical aim." In this text, we identify six different rhetorical aims of writing: to express, to explore, to inform, to analyze and synthesize, to persuade, and to reflect. Thinking of each piece of writing in terms of one or more of these rhetorical aims can help you understand typical ways that your essay can be structured and developed and can help you clarify your relationship with your audience. The writing projects in Part 2 of this text are based on these rhetorical aims. Table 1.1 gives you an overview of each of the six rhetorical aims and sketches out how the subject matter differs from aim to aim, how the writer's task and relationship to readers differ according to aim, and how a chosen aim affects the writing's genre and its position on the spectrum from open to closed forms.

Purpose as a Response to a Motivating Occasion

Another important way to think about purpose is to think about each piece of writing as a response to a particular motivating occasion. Almost all writing is

TABLE 1.1 Purpose as Rhetorical Aim

Rhetorical Aim	Focus of Writing	Relationship to Audience	Forms and Genres
Express or share (Chapter 7) May also include an artistic aim (Chapter 19)	Your own life, personal experiences, reflections	You share aspects of your life; you invite readers to walk in your shoes, to experience your insights	**Form:** Tends to have many open-form features **Sample genres:** journal, blog, personal Web site; personal essays or literacy narratives, often with artistic features
Explore or inquire (Chapter 8)	A significant subject-matter problem that puzzles writer	You take readers on your own intellectual journey by showing your inquiry process (raising questions, seeking evidence, considering alternative views)	**Form:** Follows open form in being narrative based; is thesis seeking rather than thesis supporting **Sample genres:** freewriting; research logs; articles and books focused on process of discovery
Inform or explain (Chapter 9)	Factual knowledge addressing a reader's need or curiosity	You provide knowledge that your readers need or want, or you arouse curiosity and provide new, surprising information. You expect readers to trust your authority	**Form:** Usually has a closed-form structure **Sample genres:** encyclopedia articles; instruction booklets; sales reports; technical reports; informative magazine articles; informative Web sites
Analyze, synthesize, or interpret (Chapters 10–13)	Complex subject matter that you can break down into parts and put together in new ways for greater understanding	Using critical thinking and possibly research, you challenge readers with a new way of understanding your subject. Skeptical readers expect you to support your thesis with good particulars	**Form:** Typically has a closed-form structure **Sample genres:** scholarly articles; experimental reports; many kinds of college research papers; public affairs magazine articles; many kinds of blogs
Persuade (Chapters 14–16)	Subject-matter questions that have multiple controversial answers	You try to convince readers, who may not share your values and beliefs, to accept your stance on an issue by providing good reasons and evidence and attending to alternative views	**Form:** Usually closed form, but may employ many open-form features for persuasive effect **Sample genres:** letters to the editor; op-ed pieces; advocacy pieces in public affairs magazines; advocacy Web sites; researched academic arguments

TABLE 1.1 *continued*

Rhetorical Aim	Focus of Writing	Relationship to Audience	Forms and Genres
Reflect (Chapter 25)	Subject matter closely connected to writer's interests and experience; often involves self-evaluation of an experience	Writing for yourself as well as for a reader, you seek to find personal meaning and value in an experience or course of study. You assume a sympathetic and interested reader	**Form:** Anywhere on the closed-to-open-form continuum **Sample genres:** memoirs, workplace self-evaluations; introductory letter for a portfolio; personal essays looking back on an experience

compelled by some sort of motivating occasion or exigency.* This exigency can be external (someone giving you a task and setting a deadline) or internal (your awareness of a problem stimulating your desire to bring about some change in people's views). Thus, when engineer David Rockwood read a newspaper editorial supporting wind-power projects, his own belief in the impracticality of wind power motivated him to write a letter to the editor in rebuttal (see p. 7). But he also knew that he had to write the letter within one or two days or else it stood no chance of being published. His exigency thus included both internal and external factors.

You might think that school is the only place where people are compelled to write. However, some element of external compulsion is present in nearly every writing situation, although this external compulsion is almost never the sole motivation for writing. Consider a middle manager requested by the company vice president to write a report explaining why his division's profits are down. The manager is motivated by several factors: He wants to provide a sound analysis of why profits have declined; he wants to propose possible solutions that will remedy the situation; he wants to avoid looking personally responsible for the dip in profits; he wants to impress the vice president in the hope that she will promote him to upper management; and so on.

College students' motivations for writing can be equally complex: In part, you write to meet a deadline; in part, you write to please the teacher and get a good grade. But ideally you also write because you have become engaged with an intellectual problem and want to say something significant about it. Our point here is that your purposes for writing are always more complex than the simple desire to meet an assignment deadline.

Purpose as a Desire to Change Your Reader's View

Perhaps the most useful way to think about purpose is to focus on the change you want to bring about in your audience's view of the subject. When you are given a

*An *exigency* is an urgent or pressing situation requiring immediate attention. Rhetoricians use the term to describe the event or occasion that causes a writer to begin writing.

See Chapter 2, Concept 6, for an explanation of surprise in thesis statements.

college writing assignment, this view of purpose engages you directly with the intellectual problem specified in the assignment. This view of purpose will be developed further in Concept 6 when we explain the importance of surprise as a measure of what is new or challenging in your essay. For most essays, you can write a one-sentence, nutshell statement about your purpose.

> My purpose is to give my readers a vivid picture of my difficult struggle with Graves' disease.
>
> My purpose is to explain how Thoreau's view of nature differs in important ways from that of contemporary environmentalists.
>
> My purpose is to persuade the general public that wind-generated electricity is not a practical energy alternative in the Pacific Northwest.

In closed-form academic articles, technical reports, and other business and professional pieces, writers often place explicit purpose statements in their introductions along with the thesis. In most other forms of writing, the writer uses a behind-the-scenes purpose statement to achieve focus and direction but seldom states the purpose explicitly. Writing an explicit purpose statement for a paper is a powerful way to nutshell the kind of change you want to bring about in your reader's view of the subject.

Chapter 18, Skill 9, shows you how purpose statements can be included in closed-form introductions.

How Writers Think about Audience

In our discussion of purpose, we have already had a lot to say about audience. What you know about your readers—their familiarity with your subject matter, their reasons for reading, their closeness to you, their values and beliefs—affects most of the choices you make as a writer.

In assessing your audience, you must first determine who that audience is—a single reader (for example, your boss), a select group (a scholarship committee; attendees at an undergraduate research conference), or a general audience. If you imagine a general audience, you will need to make some initial assumptions about their views and values. Doing so creates an "implied audience," giving you a stable rather than a moving target so that you can make decisions about your own essay. Once you have identified your audience, you can use the following strategies for analysis.

STRATEGIES for Analyzing Audience

Questions to Ask about Your Audience	Reasons for Asking the Question
How busy are my readers?	• Helps you decide on length, document design, and open versus closed features • In workplace writing, busy readers often require closed-form prose with headings that allow for skimming

Questions to Ask about Your Audience	Reasons for Asking the Question
What are my readers' motives for reading?	• If the reader has requested the document, you need only a short introduction • In most cases, your opening must hook your reader's interest
What is my relationship with my readers?	• Helps you decide on a formal or informal style • Helps you select tone—polite and serious or loose and slangy
What do my readers already know about my topic? Are my readers more or less expert than me, or do they have the same expertise?	• Helps you determine what will be old/familiar information for your audience versus new/unfamiliar information • Helps you decide how much background and context to include • Helps you decide to use or avoid in-group jargon and specialized knowledge
How interested are my readers in my topic? Do my readers already care about it?	• Helps you decide how to write the introduction • Helps you determine how to make the problem you address interesting and significant to your reader
What are my readers' attitudes toward my thesis? Do my readers share my beliefs and values?	• Helps you make numerous decisions about tone, structure, reference to alternative views, and use of evidence • Helps you decide on the voice and persona you want to project

To appreciate the importance of audience, consider how a change in audience can affect the content of a piece. Suppose you want voters to approve a bond issue to build a new baseball stadium. If most voters are baseball fans, you can appeal to their love of the game, the pleasure of a new facility, and so forth. But non-baseball fans won't be moved by these arguments. To reach them, you must tie the new stadium to their values. You can argue that it will bring new tax revenues, clean up a run-down area, revitalize local businesses, or stimulate tourism . Your purpose remains the same—to persuade taxpayers to fund the stadium—but the content of your argument changes if your audience changes.

In college, you often seem to be writing for an audience of one—your instructor. However, most instructors try to read as a representative of a broader audience. To help college writers imagine these readers, many instructors try to design writing assignments that provide a fuller sense of audience. They may ask you to write for the readers of a particular magazine or journal, or they may create case assignments with built-in audiences (for example, "You are an accountant in the firm of Numbers and Fudge; one day you receive a letter from ..."). If your instructor does not specify an audience, you can generally assume the audience to be what we like to call "the generic academic audience"—student peers who have approximately the same level of knowledge and expertise in the field as you do, who are engaged by the question you address, and who want to read your writing and be surprised in some way.

How Writers Think about Genre

The term *genre* refers to categories of writing that follow certain conventions of style, structure, approach to subject matter, and document design. Table 1.2 shows different kinds of genres.

The concept of genre creates strong reader expectations and places specific demands on writers. How you write any given letter, report, or article is influenced by the structure and style of hundreds of previous letters, reports, or articles written in the same genre. If you wanted to write for *Reader's Digest,* for example, you would have to use the conventions that appeal to its older, conservative readers: simple language, subjects with strong human interest, heavy reliance on anecdotal evidence in arguments, an upbeat and optimistic perspective, and an approach that reinforces the conservative *ethos* of individualism, self-discipline, and family. If you wanted to write for *Seventeen* or *Rolling Stone,* however, you would need to use quite different conventions.

To illustrate the relationship of a writer to a genre, we sometimes draw an analogy with clothing. Although most people have a variety of different types of clothing in their wardrobes, the genre of activity for which they are dressing (Saturday night movie date, job interview, wedding) severely constrains their choice and expression of individuality. A man dressing for a job interview might express his personality through choice of tie or quality and style of business suit; he probably wouldn't express it by wearing a Hawaiian shirt and sandals. Even when people deviate from a convention, they tend to do so in a conventional way. For example, teenagers who do not want to follow the genre of "teenager admired by adults" form their own genre of purple hair and pierced body parts.

TABLE 1.2 Examples of Genres

Personal Writing	Academic Writing	Popular Culture	Public Affairs, Civic Writing	Professional Writing	Literature
Letter Diary/journal Memoir Blog Text message E-mail MySpace page Personal essay Literacy narrative	Scholarly article Research paper Scientific report Abstract or summary Book review Essay exam Annotated bibliography Textual analysis	Articles for magazines such as *Seventeen, Ebony*, or *Vibe* Advertisements Hip-hop lyrics Fan Web sites Bumper stickers Reviews of books, films, plays, music	Letter to the editor Newspaper editorial Op-ed piece Advocacy Web site Political blog Magazine article on civic issue	Cover letter for a job application Résumé Business memo Legal brief Brochure Technical manual Instruction booklet Proposal Report Press release	Short story Novel Graphic novel Play Sonnet Epic poem Literary podcast

The concept of genre raises intriguing and sometimes unsettling questions about the relationship of the unique self to a social convention or tradition.

These same kinds of questions and constraints perplex writers. For example, academic writers usually follow the genre of the closed-form scholarly article. This highly functional form achieves maximum clarity for readers by orienting them quickly to the article's purpose, content, and structure. Readers expect this format, and writers have the greatest chance of being published if they meet these expectations. In some disciplines, however, scholars are beginning to publish more experimental, open-form articles. They may slowly alter the conventions of the scholarly article, just as fashion designers alter styles of dress.

FOR WRITING AND DISCUSSION

Thinking about Purpose, Audience, and Genre

1. This exercise, which is based on Table 1.1 on page 20, will help you appreciate how rhetorical aim connects to choices about subject matter as well as to audience and genre. As a class, choose one of the following topic areas or another provided by your instructor. Then imagine six different writing situations in which a hypothetical writer would compose an essay about the selected topic. Let each situation call for a different aim. How might a person write about the selected topic with an expressive aim? An exploratory aim? An informative aim? An analytic aim? A persuasive aim? A reflective aim? How would each essay surprise its readers?

automobiles	animals	hospices or nursing homes
homelessness	music	dating or marriage
advertising	energy crisis	sports injuries

Working on your own or in small groups, create six realistic scenarios, each of which calls for prose in a different category of aim. Then share your results as a whole class. Here are two examples based on the topic "hospices."

Expressive Aim — Working one summer as a volunteer in a hospice for dying cancer patients, you befriend a woman whose attitude toward death changes your life. You write an autobiographical essay about your experiences with this remarkable woman.

Analytic Aim — You are a hospice nurse working in a home care setting. You and your colleagues note that sometimes family members cannot adjust psychologically to the burden of living with a dying person. You decide to investigate this phenomenon. You interview "reluctant" family members in an attempt to understand the causes of their psychological discomfort so that you can provide better counseling services as a possible solution. You write a paper for a professional audience analyzing the results of your interviews.

(*continued*)

2. Working in small groups or as a whole class, develop a list of the conventions for one or more of the following genres:
   - Cell phone text messages as typically created by teenagers
   - A MySpace profile
   - The home page for a college or university Web site

Chapter Summary

- Good writing varies along a continuum from closed to open forms.
- Closed-form prose has an explicit thesis statement, topic sentences, unified and coherent paragraphs, and good transitions. Open-form prose uses narrative techniques such as storytelling, evocative language, surprising juxtapositions, and other features that violate the conventions of closed-form prose. Closed-form prose is "good" only if its ideas bring something new, provocative, or challenging to the reader.
- Good writers pose interesting, problematic, and significant questions about their subject matter.
- Writers analyze their purpose based on their rhetorical aim, their motivating occasion, or their desire to bring about change in the reader's view.
- Writers analyze their audiences to determine their readers' existing knowledge of (and interest in) the writer's subject matter and to assess their readers' values, beliefs, and assumptions.
- Writers attend to genre because different genres have defining conventions of structure and style to which writers must adhere.

BRIEF WRITING PROJECT 1

Posing a Good Subject-Matter Problem

This assignment asks you to write a brief problem-posing essay modeled after the thought exercise on pages 14–15 (see Brittany Tinker's essay as a possible model).

Write a one- to two-page (double-spaced) essay that poses a question about a problem that perplexes you on a subject matter of your choice or on one designated by your instructor. Besides explaining your question and providing needed background information, you should help readers see (1) why the question is problematic—that is, why it is a genuine problem with no easy right answers—and (2) why the question is significant or worth pursuing—that is, what benefit will come from solving it. Remember that your task here is to *pose* the question, not answer it.

This assignment may at first feel strange because students are often used to beginning school essays with a thesis statement. Your instinct is to *argue* something rather than to *ask* something. Trust us, however, when we suggest that this assignment is freeing. You do not need to have a thesis. All that this assignment asks for is a question that you find puzzling. Here are two examples of how our students have posed problematic and significant questions:

- *Are interspecies transplants ethical?* This student developed the problem with the case of a man who had a transplant of a baboon heart. On the one hand, she was ethically troubled by surgeons' "playing God" in doing such a transplant. On the other hand, she hoped that such transplants would save lives. She said the problem was significant because "it causes us to question the limits of medical research and to ask what it means to be human."
- *Should rap music be censored?* This student agreed that rap lyrics are often "vile, misogynistic, homophobic, and obscene." In part of herself she believed that this music should be kept away from children. But in another part of herself she believed in free speech and the possible social good of expressing politically incorrect thoughts. She thought this question was significant because it involves larger issues of individual freedom versus the public good.

Understanding Rhetorical Context

BRIEF WRITING PROJECT 2

The purpose of this brief write-to-learn assignment is to let you experience firsthand how rhetorical context influences a writer's choices. The whole assignment, which has three parts, should be no more than two pages (double-spaced) in length.

Part 1: Using popular e-mail style based on text messaging (abbreviations, no capitals, and so forth), compose a brief e-mail message to a friend explaining that you have to miss a social event because you are sick; then ask for a possible rescheduling. (Make up details as you need them.) Give the e-mail message a subject line appropriate for this informal style.

Part 2: Compose an e-mail message to your professor explaining that you cannot meet an assignment deadline because you are sick and asking for an extension. (Use the same sickness details from Part 1.) Create a subject line appropriate for this new context.

Part 3: Using Parts 1 and 2 as illustrative examples, explain to someone who has not read Chapter 1 of this text why a difference in your rhetorical context caused you to make different choices in these two e-mails. In your explanation use the terms "purpose," "audience," and "genre." Your goal is to teach your audience the meanings of these terms.

For additional writing, reading, and research resources, go to **www.MyCompLab.com** and choose **Ramage/Bean/Johnson's *The Allyn & Bacon Guide to Writing,* Fifth Edition.**

CHAPTER 2

THINKING RHETORICALLY ABOUT YOUR SUBJECT MATTER

"In management, people don't merely 'write papers,' they solve problems," said [business professor A. Kimbrough Sherman]. ... He explained that he wanted to construct situations where students would have to "wallow in complexity" and work their way out, as managers must.

—*A. Kimbrough Sherman, Management Professor, Quoted by Barbara E. Walvoord and Lucille P. McCarthy*

In the previous chapter we explained how the rules for good writing vary along a continuum from closed to open forms, how writers pose subject-matter questions, and how they think rhetorically about their purpose, audience, and genre. In this chapter we show how writers think rhetorically about their "subject matter"—that is, how they think about what is unknown, puzzling, or controversial in their subject matter and about how their view of the subject might be different from their audience's. Because this chapter concerns academic writing, we focus on closed-form prose—the kind of thesis-governed writing most often required in college courses and often required in civic and professional life. As we will show, thesis-governed writing requires a behind-the-scenes ability to think rigorously about a problem and then to make a claim* based on your own solution to the problem. This claim should bring something new, interesting, useful, or challenging to readers.

To prepare you for the kinds of writing you will do in college and beyond, this chapter introduces you to four new concepts with significant explanatory power.

Concept 4: Professors value "wallowing in complexity."

Concept 5: Good writers use exploratory strategies to think critically about subject-matter questions.

Concept 6: A strong thesis statement surprises readers with something new or challenging.

Concept 7: Thesis statements in closed-form prose are supported hierarchically with points and particulars.

*In this text we use the words *claim* and *thesis statement* interchangeably. As you move from course to course, instructors typically use one or the other of these terms. Other synonyms for *thesis statement* include *proposition, main point,* or *thesis sentence.*

These concepts transfer across most academic disciplines and, if you employ them effectively, will markedly increase your ability to write engaging and meaningful prose targeted to the audience of your choice.

CONCEPT 4 Professors value "wallowing in complexity."

As we explained in the previous chapter, good writers pose problematic questions about their subject matter. Here we emphasize the critical thinking that such problems entail. We don't mean to make this focus on problems sound scary. Indeed, humans pose and solve problems all the time and often take great pleasure in doing so. Psychologists who study critical and creative thinking see problem solving as a productive and positive activity. According to one psychologist, "Critical thinkers are actively engaged with life. ... They appreciate creativity, they are innovators, and they exude a sense that life is full of possibilities."* By explaining the kinds of problems that writers pose and struggle with and the benefits of dwelling with these problems and learning to explore them, we hope to increase your own engagement and pleasure in becoming a writer.

Learning to Wallow in Complexity

As students start to adapt to the demands of college, they often wonder about professors' expectations: What do professors want? Many beginning students imagine that professors want students to comprehend course concepts as taught in textbooks and lectures and to show their understanding on exams. Such comprehension is important, but it is only a starting point. As management professor A. Kimbrough Sherman explains in the epigraph to this chapter, college instructors expect students to wrestle with problems by applying the concepts, data, and thought processes they learn in a course to new situations. As Sherman puts it, students must learn to "wallow in complexity" and work their way out.

Wallowing in complexity is not what most first-year college students aspire to do. New college students tend to shut down their creative thinking processes too quickly and head straight for closure to a problem. Harvard psychologist William Perry, who has studied the intellectual development of college students, found that few of them become skilled wallowers in complexity until late in their college careers. According to Perry, most students come to college as "dualists," believing that all questions have right or wrong answers, that professors know the right answers, and that the student's job is to learn them. Of course, these beliefs are partially correct. First-year students who hope to become second-year students must indeed understand and memorize mounds of facts, data, definitions, and basic concepts.

As students progress to an intermediate stage of development beyond dualism, students become what Perry calls "multiplists." At this stage students believe that since the experts disagree on many questions, all answers are equally valid and profes-

*Academic writers regularly document their sources. Two standard methods for documenting sources in student papers and in many professional scholarly articles are the MLA and APA citation systems explained in Chapter 23. In this text we have cited our sources in an "Acknowledgments" section. To find our source for this quotation (or the quotations from Kilcup or Kimbrough in the epigraphs), see the Acknowledgments at the end of the text.

sors want students merely to have an opinion and to state it strongly. A multiplist believes that a low grade on an essay indicates simply that the teacher didn't like his or her opinion. Multiplists are often cynical about professors and grades; to them, college is a game of guessing what the teacher wants to hear. Students emerge into Perry's final stages—what we call "relativism" and "commitment in relativism"—when they are able to take a position in the face of complexity and to justify that decision through reasons and evidence while weighing and acknowledging contrary reasons and counterevidence. Professor Sherman articulates what is expected at Perry's last stages—wading into the messiness of complexity and working your way back out.

Thus true intellectual growth requires the kind of problematizing we discussed in Chapter 1. It requires students to *do* something with their new knowledge, to apply it to new situations, to conduct the kinds of inquiry, research, analysis, and argument pursued by experts in each discipline. The kinds of problems vary from discipline to discipline, but they all require the writer to use reasons and evidence to support a tentative solution. Because your instructors want you to learn how to do the same kind of thinking, they often phrase essay exam questions or writing assignments as open-ended problems. They are looking not for one right answer, but for well-supported arguments that acknowledge alternative views. A C paper and an A paper may have the same "answer" (identical thesis statements), but the C writer may have waded only ankle deep into the mud of complexity, whereas the A writer wallowed in it and worked a way out.

What skills are required for successful wallowing? Specialists in critical thinking have identified the following:

CRITICAL THINKING SKILLS NEEDED FOR "WALLOWING IN COMPLEXITY"

1. The ability to pose problematic questions
2. The ability to analyze a problem in all its dimensions—to define its key terms, determine its causes, understand its history, appreciate its human dimension and its connection to one's own personal experience, and appreciate what makes it problematic or complex
3. The ability (and determination) to find, gather, and interpret facts, data, and other information relevant to the problem (often involving library, Internet, or field research)
4. The ability to imagine alternative solutions to the problem, to see different ways in which the question might be answered and different perspectives for viewing it
5. The ability to analyze competing approaches and answers, to construct arguments for and against alternatives, and to choose the best solution in light of values, objectives, and other criteria that you determine and articulate
6. The ability to write an effective argument justifying your choice while acknowledging counterarguments

We discuss and develop these skills throughout this text.

Seeing Each Academic Discipline as a Field of Inquiry and Argument

In addition to these general thinking abilities, critical thinking requires what psychologists call "domain-specific" skills. Each academic discipline has its own characteristic ways of approaching knowledge and its own specialized habits of mind. The questions asked by psychologists differ from those asked by historians or anthropologists; the evidence and assumptions used to support arguments in literary analysis differ from those in philosophy or sociology. As illustrations, here are some examples of how different disciplines might pose different questions about hip-hop:

- *Psychology:* To what extent do hip-hop lyrics increase misogynistic or homophobic attitudes in male listeners?
- *History:* What was the role of urban housing projects in the early development of hip-hop?
- *Sociology:* How does the level of an individual's appreciation for rap music vary by ethnicity, class, age, geographic region, and gender?
- *Rhetoric/Composition:* What images of urban life do the lyrics of rap songs portray?
- *Marketing and Management:* How did the white media turn a black, urban phenomenon into corporate profits?
- *Women's Studies:* What influence does hip-hop music have on the self-image of African-American women?

As these questions suggest, when you study a new discipline, you must learn not only the knowledge that scholars in that discipline have acquired over the years, but also the processes they used to discover that knowledge. It is useful to think of each academic discipline as a network of conversations in which participants exchange information, respond to each other's questions, and express agreement and disagreement. As each discipline evolves and changes, its central questions evolve also, creating a fascinating, dynamic conversation that defines the discipline. Table 2.1 provides examples of questions that scholars have debated over the years as well as questions they are addressing today.

TABLE 2.1 Scholarly Questions in Different Disciplines

Field	Examples of Current Cutting-Edge Questions	Examples of Historical Controversies
Anatomy	What is the effect of a pregnant rat's alcohol ingestion on the development of fetal eye tissue?	In 1628, William Harvey produced a treatise arguing that the heart, through repeated contractions, caused blood to circulate through the body. His views were attacked by followers of the Greek physician Galen.
Literature	To what extent does the structure of a work of literature, for example Conrad's *Heart of Darkness*, reflect the class and gender bias of the author?	In the 1920s, a group of New Critics argued that the interpretation of a work of literature should be based on close examination of the work's imagery and form and that the intentions of the writer and the biases of the reader were not important. These views held sway in U.S. universities until the late 1960s, when they came increasingly under attack by deconstructionists and other postmoderns, who claimed that author intentions and reader's bias were important parts of the work's meaning.

(*continued*)

TABLE 2.1 *continued*

Field	Examples of Current Cutting-Edge Questions	Examples of Historical Controversies
Rhetoric/ Composition	How does hypertext structure and increased attention to visual images in Web-based writing affect the composing processes of writers?	Prior to the 1970s, college writing courses in the United States were typically organized around the rhetorical modes (description, narration, exemplification, comparison and contrast, and so forth). This approach was criticized by the expressivist school associated with the British composition researcher James Britton. Since the 1980s, composition scholars have proposed various alternative strategies for designing and sequencing assignments.
Psychology	What are the underlying causes of gender identification? To what extent are differences between male and female behavior explainable by nature (genetics, body chemistry) versus nurture (social learning)?	In the early 1900s under the influence of Sigmund Freud, psychoanalytic psychologists began explaining human behavior in terms of unconscious drives and mental processes that stemmed from repressed childhood experiences. Later, psychoanalysts were opposed by behaviorists, who rejected the notion of the unconscious and explained behavior as responses to environmental stimuli.

CONCEPT 5 Good writers use exploratory strategies to think critically about subject-matter questions.

One of the important discoveries of research in rhetoric and composition is the extent to which experienced writers use writing to generate and discover ideas. Not all writing, in other words, is initially intended as a final product for readers. The very act of writing—often without concern for audience, structure, or correctness—can stimulate the mind to produce ideas. Moreover, when you write down your thoughts, you'll have a record of your thinking that you can draw on later. In Chapter 17 we explain this phenomenon more fully, showing you how to take full advantage of the writing process for invention of ideas and revision for readers. In this section we describe five strategies of exploratory writing and talking: freewriting; focused freewriting; idea mapping; dialectic talk in person, in class discussions, or in electronic discussion boards; and playing the believing and doubting game.

Freewriting

Freewriting, also sometimes called *nonstop writing* or *silent, sustained writing,* asks you to record your thinking directly. To freewrite, put pen to paper (or sit at your computer screen, perhaps turning *off* the monitor so that you can't see what you are writing) and write rapidly, *nonstop*, for ten to fifteen minutes at a stretch. Don't worry about grammar, spelling, organization, transitions, or other features of edited writing. The object is to think of as many ideas as possible. Some freewriting looks like stream of consciousness. Some is more organized and focused, although it lacks the logical connections and development that would make it suitable for an audience of strangers.

Many freewriters find that their initial reservoir of ideas runs out in three to five minutes. If this happens, force yourself to keep your fingers moving. If you can't think of anything to say, write, "Relax" over and over (or "This is stupid" or "I'm stuck") until new ideas emerge.

What do you write about? The answer varies according to your situation. Often you will freewrite in response to a question or problem posed by your instructor. Sometimes you will pose your own questions and use freewriting to explore possible answers or simply generate ideas.

The following freewrite, by student writer James Gardiner, formed the starting point for his later exploration of issues connected to online social networks such as MySpace.com and Facebook.com. It was written in response to the prompt "What puzzles you about the new digital age?" We will return to James's story occasionally throughout this text. You can read his final paper in Chapter 23, pages 643–651, where he argues that online social networks can have unexpected detrimental effects on many users. You can also read his earlier exploratory paper (Chapter 8, pp. 191–196), which narrates the evolution of his thinking as he explored the popularity of MySpace and Facebook.

JAMES GARDINER'S INITIAL FREEWRITE

Hmm, what puzzles me about the new digital age? Let's see, let's see, OK I'm puzzled by what life used to be like before there was so much technology. I'm amazed by the growing role that technology has on the lives of people my age. It seems that my generation is spending an increasing amount of time surfing the net, talking on cell phones, listening to MP3 players, playing video games, and watching digital television. I wonder what type of effect these new technologies will have on our society as a whole and if the positive aspects that they bring into the lives of their users outweigh the negative aspects. Are kids happier now that they have all this technology? Hmm. What is the effect of text-messaging rather than talking directly to people? Also what about online social networks like Myspace and Facebook? A lot of my friends have a profile on these sites. I've never joined one of these networks or created a profile. What is my reason for avoiding them? Think. Think. OK, for one thing, I have seen how much time people can spend on these sites and I already feel that I spend enough time checking emails and voicemails. Here's another thing—I am a little hesitant to display personal information about myself on a website that can be viewed by anyone in the world. I feel I am a generally private person and there is something about posting personal details of my life in cyberspace that makes me a little uneasy. As these online social networks increase in popularity and membership, I am puzzled by how my generation will be affected by them. Although people use the sites to communicate with one another, they are usually (physically) alone at their computer. I wonder how this new type of online communication will affect other forms of interpersonal communication skills in the "real world." I also question whether young people should be encouraged to limit their time on these networks and what specifically they should use these sites for. [out of time]

Note how this freewrite rambles, moving associatively from one topic or question to the next. Freewrites often have this kind of loose, associative structure. The value of such freewrites is that they help writers discover areas of interest or rudimentary beginnings of ideas. When you read back over one of your freewrites, try to find places that seem worth pursuing. Freewriters call these places "hot spots," "centers of interest," "centers of gravity," or simply "nuggets" or "seeds." Because we believe this technique is of great value to writers, we suggest that you use it to generate ideas for class discussions and essays.

Focused Freewriting

Freewriting, as we have just described it, can be quick and associational, like brainstorming aloud on paper. Focused freewriting, in contrast, is less associational and aimed more at developing a line of thought. You wrestle with a specific problem or question, trying to think and write your way into its complexity and multiple points of view. Because the writing is still informal, with the emphasis on your ideas and not on making your writing grammatically or stylistically polished, you don't have to worry about spelling, punctuation, grammar, or organizational structure. Your purpose is to deepen and extend your thinking on the problem. Some instructors will create prompts or give you specific questions to ponder, and they may call this kind of exploratory writing "focused freewriting," "learning log responses," "writer's notebook entries," or "thinking pieces."

Examples of focused freewriting can be found in the learning log entries on pp. 357–364 in Chapter 13.

Idea Mapping

Another good technique for exploring ideas is *idea mapping,* a more visual method than freewriting. To make an idea map, draw a circle in the center of a page and write down your broad topic area (or a triggering question or your thesis) inside the circle. Then record your ideas on branches and subbranches that extend out from the center circle. As long as you pursue one train of thought, keep recording your ideas on subbranches off the main branch. But as soon as that chain of ideas runs dry, go back and start a new branch.

Often your thoughts will jump back and forth between one branch and another. This technique will help you see them as part of an emerging design rather than as strings of unrelated ideas. Additionally, idea mapping establishes at an early stage a sense of hierarchy in your ideas. If you enter an idea on a subbranch, you can see that you are more fully developing a previous idea. If you return to the hub and start a new branch, you can see that you are beginning a new train of thought.

An idea map usually records more ideas than a freewrite, but the ideas are not as fully developed. Writers who practice both techniques report that they can vary the kinds of ideas they generate depending on which technique they choose. Figure 2.1 shows a student's idea map made while he was exploring issues related to the grading system.

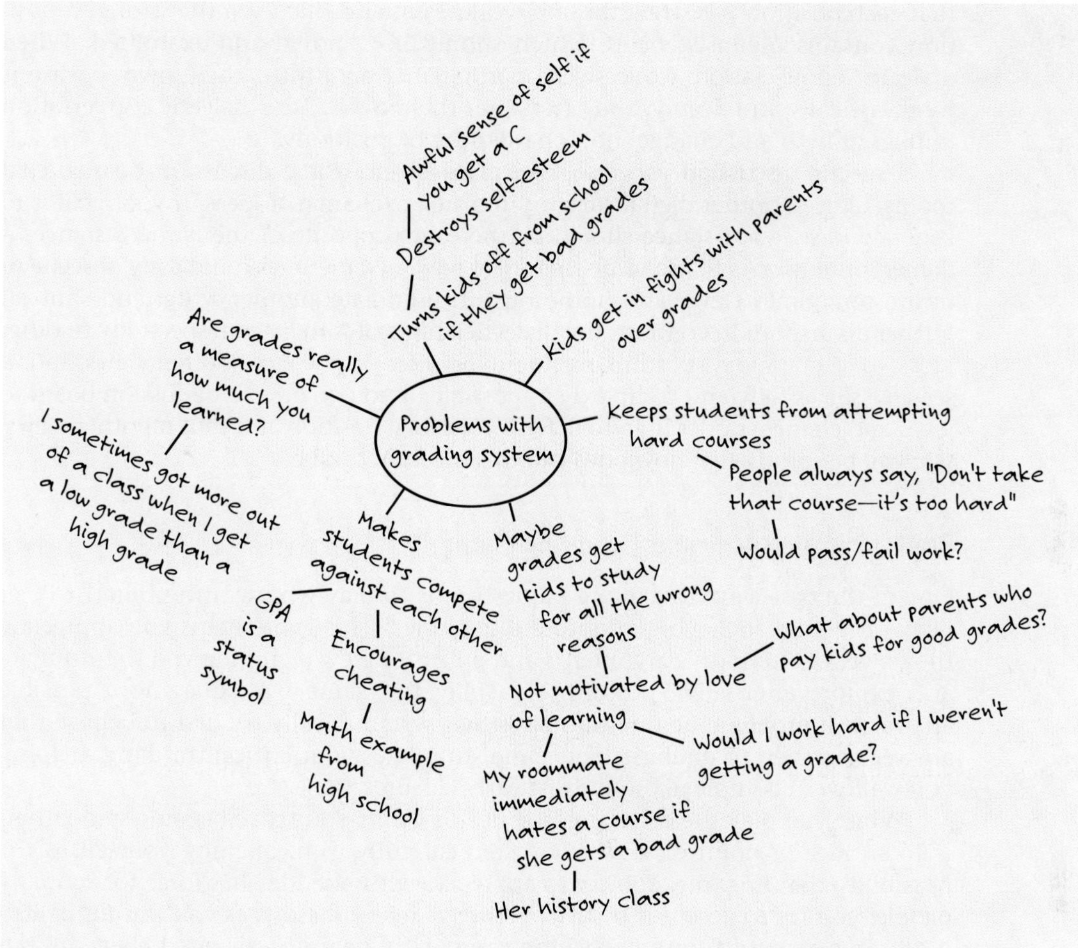

FIGURE 2.1 Idea Map on Problems with the Grading System

Dialectic Talk

Another effective way to explore the complexity of a topic is through face-to-face discussions with others, whether in class, over coffee in the student union, or late at night in bull sessions. Not all discussions are productive; some are too superficial and scattered, others too heated. Good ones are *dialectic*—participants with differing views on a topic try to understand each other and resolve their differences by examining contradictions in each person's position. The key to dialectic conversation is careful listening, which is made possible by an openness to each other's views. A dialectic discussion differs from a talk show shouting match or a pro/con debate in which proponents of opposing positions, their views set in stone, attempt to win the argument. In a dialectic discussion, participants assume that each position has strengths and weaknesses and that even the strongest position contains inconsistencies, which should be exposed and examined. When dialectic conversation works well, participants scrutinize their own positions more critically and deeply, and often alter their views. True dialectic conversation implies growth and change, not a hardening of positions.

Dialectic discussion can also take place in electronic discussion boards, chat rooms, blogs, or other digital sites for informal exchange of ideas. If your goal is to generate ideas, your stance should be the exact opposite of the flamer's stance. A flamer's intention is to use brute rhetorical power (sometimes mindlessly obscene or mean, sometimes clever and humorous) to humiliate another writer and shut off further discussion. In contrast, the dialectician's goal is to listen respectfully to other ideas, to test new ways of thinking, to modify ideas in the face of other views, and to see an issue as fully and complexly as possible. If you go on to a discussion board to learn and change, rather than to defend your own position and shut off other views, you will be surprised at how powerful this medium can be.

Playing the Believing and Doubting Game

One of the best ways to explore a question is to play what writing theorist Peter Elbow calls the "believing and doubting game." This game helps you appreciate the power of alternative arguments and points of view by urging you to formulate and explore alternative positions. To play the game, you imagine a possible answer to a problematic question and then systematically try first to believe that answer and then to doubt it. The game stimulates your critical thinking, helping you wallow in complexity and resist early closure.

When you play the believing side of this game, you try to become sympathetic to an idea or point of view. You listen carefully to it, opening yourself to the possibility that it is true. You try to appreciate why the idea has force for so many people; you try to accept it by discovering as many reasons as you can for believing it. It is easy to play the believing game with ideas you already believe in, but the game becomes more difficult, sometimes even frightening and dangerous, when you try believing ideas that seem untrue or disturbing.

The doubting game is the opposite of the believing game. It calls for you to be judgmental and critical, to find fault with an idea rather than to accept it. When you doubt a new idea, you try your best to falsify it, to find counterexamples that disprove it, to find flaws in its logic. Again, it is easy to play the doubting game with ideas you don't like, but it, too, can be threatening when you try to doubt ideas that are dear to your heart or central to your own worldview.

Here is how one student played the believing and doubting game with the following assertion from professional writer Paul Theroux that emphasizing sports is harmful to boys.

> Just as high school basketball teaches you how to be a poor loser, the manly attitude towards sports seems to be little more than a recipe for creating bad marriages, social misfits, moral degenerates, sadists, latent rapists and just plain louts. I regard high school sports as a drug far worse than marijuana.

Believing and Doubting Paul Theroux's Negative View of Sports

Believe

1 Although I am a woman I have a hard time believing this because I was a high school basketball player and believe high school sports are *very* important. But here goes. I will try to believe this statement even though I hate it. Let's see. It would seem that I wouldn't have much first-hand experience with how society turns boys into men. I do see though that Theroux is right about some major problems. Through my observations, I've seen many young boys go through humiliating experiences with sports that have left them scarred. For example, a 7-year-old boy, Matt, isn't very athletic and when kids in our neighborhood choose teams, they usually choose girls before they choose Matt. I wonder if he sees himself as a sissy and what this does to him? I have also experienced some first-hand adverse effects of society's methods of turning boys into men. In our family, my dad spent much of his time playing football, basketball, and baseball with my brother. I've loved sports since I was very young so I was eager to play. In order to play with them, I had to play like a boy. Being told you threw or played like a girl was the worst possible insult you could receive. The phrase, "be tough" was something I heard repeatedly while I was growing up. Whenever I got hurt, my dad would say, "Be tough." It didn't matter how badly I was hurt, I always heard the same message. Today, I think, I have a very, very difficult time opening up and letting people get to know me, because for so long I was taught to keep everything inside. Maybe sports does have some bad effects.

Doubt

2 I am glad I get to doubt this too because I have been really mad at all the sports bashing that has been going on in class. I think much of what Theroux says is just a crock. I know that the statement "sports builds character" is a cliché, but I really believe it. It seems to me that the people who lash out at sports clichés are those who never experienced these aspects of athletics and therefore don't understand them. No one can tell me that sports didn't contribute to some of my best and most meaningful friendships and growing experiences. I am convinced that I am a better person because through sports I have had to deal with failure, defeat, frustration, sacrificing individual desires for the benefit of the team, and so on. After my last high school basketball game when after many years of mind games, of hating my coach one minute and the next having deep respect for him, of big games lost on my mistakes, of hours spent alone in the gym, of wondering if the end justifies the means, my coach put his arm around me and told me he was proud. Everything, all the pain, frustration, anxiety, fear, and sacrifice of the past years seemed so worthwhile. You might try to tell me that this story is hackneyed and trite, but I won't listen because it is a part of me, and some thing you will never be able to damage or take away. I think athletes share a special bond. They know what it is like to go through the physical pain of practice time and again. They understand the wide variety of emotions felt (but rarely expressed). They also know what a big role the friendships of teammates and coaches play in an athlete's life.

We admire this writer a great deal—both for the passion with which she defends sports in her doubting section and for the courage of walking in a sports basher's shoes in the believing section. This exercise clearly engaged and stretched her thinking.

FOR WRITING AND DISCUSSION

Using Exploratory Writing to Generate Ideas

1. **Generating questions using freewriting and discussion**
   For this task, your goal is to generate several interesting questions, using the template *"What is puzzling, controversial, or unknown about X?"*
   Individual task: Freewrite for five minutes in response to the above template. For "X" plug in a broad subject-matter area such as "college athletics," "gender," "climate change," "popular music," "the Internet," "health care," "poverty," "my workplace," and so forth. Your instructor might specify the same topic area for the whole class or let you choose your own. Thus you might freewrite on "What is puzzling about poverty in America?" or "What is controversial about working at Bill's Big Boy Burgers?" or "What is unknown [to me] about sexual orientation?"
   Small-group or whole-class task: Working in small groups or as a whole class, share some of the questions you posed while freewriting. See if you can reach consensus on several questions that meet the criteria for problematic, significant, and interesting as explained in Concept 2.

2. **Generating questions using idea mapping and discussion**
   Repeat the process used in Exercise 1 using a different topic area for X. This time, instead of freewriting for five minutes, use the strategy of idea mapping. Which technique works better for you, freewriting or idea mapping? How are they similar or different in the way they stimulate thinking?

3. **Generating questions through close observation of texts, artifacts, or phenomena**
   Another powerful way to generate questions is through close observation of a piece of written text (what literary critics call "close reading"), a visual text, a graph or table, an artifact (a building, the dashboard of a car, a holiday table setting), or a phenomenon (crowd behavior at a football game, individual behavior in an elevator, the sniffing behavior of a dog on a walk). Working at first individually and then in small groups or as a whole class, generate questions based on finding aspects of a text, artifact, or phenomenon that you find puzzling. Identify a puzzling feature and try to generate several possible explanations for the feature, none of which seems conclusive or totally satisfactory. We offer three texts here—a Hummer ad, a poem, and a table about oil consumption (p. 40) as possible texts for you to consider. Your instructor might ask you to focus instead on an artifact or phenomenon that he or she will identify.

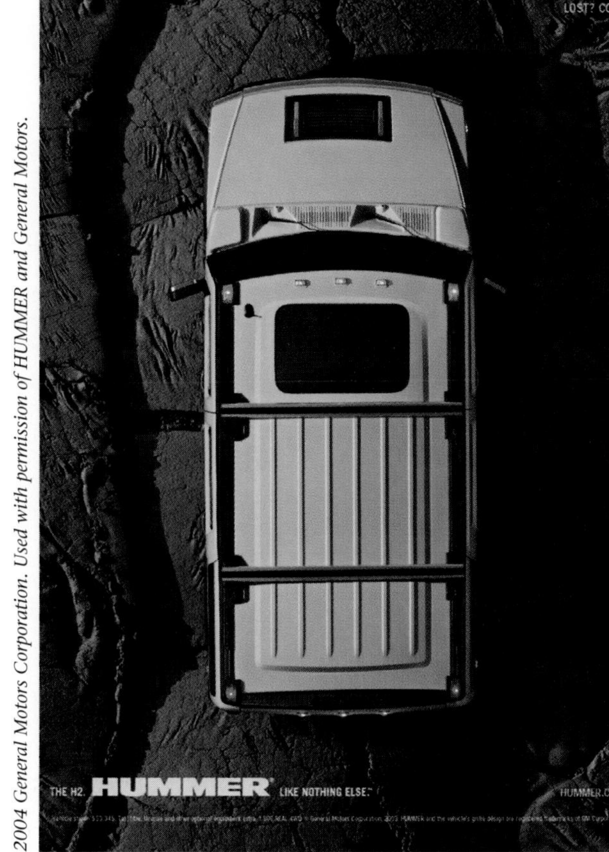

General Motors Ad for the Hummer

next to of course god america i

"next to of course god america i
love you land of the pilgrims' and so forth oh
say can you see by the dawn's early my
country 'tis of centuries come and go

and are no more what of it we should worry
in every language even deafanddumb
thy sons acclaim your glorious name by gorry
by jingo by gee by gosh by gum
why talk of beauty what could be more beautiful than these heroic happy dead
who rushed like lions to the roaring slaughter
they did not stop to think they died instead
then shall the voice of liberty be mute?"

He spoke. And drank rapidly a glass of water

—*e. e. cummings*

Energy Supply and Disposition by Type of Fuel: 1960 to 2003

[In quadrillion British thermal units (Btu) (42.80 represents 42,800,000,000,000,000 Btu). For Btu conversion factors, see source and text, this section]

Year	Production									Net imports total[6]	Consumption					
						Renewable energy[4]										
	Total[1]	Crude oil[2]	Natural gas	Coal	Nuclear power[3]	Total[1]	Hydro-electric power	Biofuel[5]	Solar energy		Total[1]	Petro-leum[7]	Natural gas[8]	Coal	Nuclear power	Renewable energy[4] total
1960	42.80	14.93	12.66	10.82	(Z)	2.93	1.61	1.32	(NA)	2.71	45.09	19.92	12.39	9.84	(Z)	2.93
1970	63.50	20.40	21.67	14.61	0.24	4.08	2.63	1.43	(NA)	5.71	67.84	29.52	21.79	12.26	0.24	4.08
1973	63.58	19.49	22.19	13.99	0.91	4.43	2.86	1.53	(NA)	12.58	75.71	34.84	22.51	12.97	0.91	4.43
1974	62.37	18.57	21.21	14.07	1.27	4.77	3.18	1.54	(NA)	12.10	73.99	33.45	21.73	12.66	1.27	4.77
1975	61.36	17.73	19.64	14.99	1.90	4.72	3.15	1.50	(NA)	11.71	72.00	32.73	19.95	12.66	1.90	4.72
1976	61.60	17.26	19.48	15.65	2.11	4.77	2.98	1.71	(NA)	14.59	76.01	35.17	20.35	13.58	2.11	4.77
1977	62.05	17.45	19.57	15.75	2.70	4.25	2.33	1.84	(NA)	17.90	78.00	37.12	19.93	13.92	2.70	4.25
1978	63.14	18.43	19.49	14.91	3.02	5.04	2.94	2.04	(NA)	17.19	79.99	37.97	20.00	13.77	3.02	5.04
1979	65.95	18.10	20.08	17.54	2.78	5.17	2.93	2.15	(NA)	16.60	80.90	37.12	20.67	15.04	2.78	5.17
1980	67.24	18.25	19.91	18.60	2.74	5.49	2.90	2.48	(NA)	12.10	78.29	34.20	20.39	15.42	2.74	5.49
1981	67.01	18.15	19.70	18.38	3.01	5.47	2.76	2.59	(NA)	9.41	76.34	31.93	19.93	15.91	3.01	5.47
1982	66.57	18.31	18.32	18.64	3.13	5.99	3.27	2.62	(NA)	7.25	73.25	30.23	18.51	15.32	3.13	5.99
1983	64.11	18.39	16.59	17.25	3.20	6.49	3.53	2.83	(NA)	8.06	73.10	30.05	17.36	15.89	3.20	6.49
1984	68.83	18.85	18.01	19.72	3.55	6.43	3.39	2.88	(Z)	8.68	76.74	31.05	18.51	17.07	3.55	6.43
1985	67.65	18.99	16.98	19.33	4.08	6.03	2.97	2.86	(Z)	7.58	76.47	30.92	17.83	17.48	4.08	6.03
1986	67.09	18.38	16.54	19.51	4.38	6.13	3.07	2.84	(Z)	10.13	76.78	32.20	16.71	17.26	4.38	6.13
1987	67.61	17.67	17.14	20.14	4.75	5.69	2.63	2.82	(Z)	11.59	79.23	32.87	17.74	18.01	4.75	5.69
1988	68.95	17.28	17.60	20.74	5.59	5.49	2.33	2.94	(Z)	12.93	82.84	34.22	18.55	18.85	5.59	5.49
1989[9]	69.36	16.12	17.85	21.35	5.60	6.29	2.84	3.06	0.06	14.11	84.96	34.21	19.71	19.07	5.60	6.29
1990	70.73	15.57	18.33	22.46	6.10	6.13	3.05	2.66	0.06	14.06	84.67	33.55	19.73	19.17	6.10	6.13
1991	70.36	15.70	18.23	21.59	6.42	6.16	3.02	2.70	0.06	13.19	84.60	32.85	20.15	18.99	6.42	6.16
1992	69.93	15.22	18.38	21.63	6.48	5.91	2.62	2.85	0.06	14.44	85.95	33.53	20.84	19.12	6.48	5.91
1993	68.26	14.49	18.58	20.25	6.41	6.16	2.89	2.80	0.07	17.01	87.58	33.84	21.35	19.84	6.41	6.16
1994	70.68	14.10	19.35	22.11	6.69	6.06	2.68	2.94	0.07	18.33	89.25	34.67	21.84	19.91	6.69	6.06
1995	71.16	13.89	19.08	22.03	7.08	6.67	3.21	3.07	0.07	17.75	91.22	34.55	22.78	20.09	7.08	6.67
1996	72.47	13.72	19.34	22.68	7.09	7.14	3.59	3.13	0.07	19.07	94.22	35.76	23.20	21.00	7.09	7.14
1997	72.39	13.66	19.39	23.21	6.60	7.08	3.64	3.01	0.07	20.70	94.73	36.27	23.33	21.45	6.60	7.08
1998	72.79	13.24	19.61	23.94	7.07	6.56	3.30	2.83	0.07	22.28	95.15	36.93	22.94	21.66	7.07	6.56
1999	71.65	12.45	19.34	23.19	7.61	6.60	3.27	2.89	0.07	23.54	96.77	37.96	23.01	21.62	7.61	6.60
2000	71.22	12.36	19.66	22.62	7.86	6.16	2.81	2.91	0.07	24.97	98.90	38.40	23.92	22.58	7.86	6.16
2001	71.79	12.28	20.20	23.53	8.03	5.29	2.20	2.64	0.07	26.39	96.38	38.33	22.91	21.95	8.03	5.29
2002	70.93	12.16	19.49	22.70	8.14	5.96	2.67	2.79	0.06	25.74	98.03	38.40	23.66	21.98	8.14	5.96
2003[10]	70.47	12.15	19.64	22.31	7.97	6.15	2.78	2.88	0.06	26.97	98.16	39.07	22.51	22.71	7.97	6.15

NA Not available. Z Less than 5 trillion. [1]Includes types of fuel not shown separately. [2]Includes lease condensate. [3]Data on the generation of electricity in the United States represent net generation, which is gross output of electricity (measured at the generator terminals) minus power plant use. Nuclear electricity generation data are gross outputs of electricity. [4]End-use consumption and electricity net generation. [5]Wood, waste, and alcohol (ethanol blended into motor gasoline). [6]Imports minus exports. [7]Petroleum products supplied, including natural gas plant liquids and crude oil burned as fuel. [8]Includes supplemental gaseous fuels. [9]There is a discontinuity in this time series between 1989 and 1990 due to the expanded coverage of nonelectric utility use of renewable energy beginning in 1990. [10]Preliminary.

Source: U.S. Energy Information Administration, Annual Energy Review 2003. *See also <http://www.eia.doe.gov/emeu/aer/overview.html> (released September 2004).*

CONCEPT 6 A strong thesis statement surprises readers with something new or challenging.

The strategies for exploring ideas that we offered in the previous section can prepare you to move from posing problems to proposing your own solutions. Your answer to your subject-matter question becomes your thesis statement. In this section we show that a good thesis surprises its readers either by bringing something new to the reader or by pushing against other possible ways to answer the writer's question.

Thus a strong thesis usually contains an element of uncertainty, risk, or challenge. A strong thesis implies a naysayer who could disagree with you. According to composition theorist Peter Elbow, a thesis has "got to stick its neck out, not just hedge or wander. [It is] something that can be quarreled with." Elbow's sticking-its-neck-out metaphor is a good one, but we prefer to say that a strong thesis *surprises* the reader with a new, unexpected, different, or challenging view of the writer's topic. By surprise, we intend to connote, first of all, freshness or newness for the reader. Many kinds of closed-form prose don't have a sharply contestable thesis of the sticking-its-neck-out kind highlighted by Elbow. A geology report, for example, may provide readers with desired information about rock strata in an exposed cliff, or a Web page for diabetics may explain how to coordinate meals and insulin injections during a plane trip across time zones. In these cases, the information is surprising because it brings something new and significant to intended readers.

In other kinds of closed-form prose, especially academic or civic prose addressing a problematic question or a disputed issue, surprise requires an argumentative, risky, or contestable thesis. In these cases also, surprise is not inherent in the material but in the intended readers' reception; it comes from the writer's providing an adequate or appropriate response to the readers' presumed question or problem.

In this section, we present two ways of creating a surprising thesis: (1) trying to change your reader's view of your subject; and (2) giving your thesis tension.

Trying to Change Your Reader's View of Your Subject

To change your reader's view of your subject, you must first imagine how the reader would view the subject *before* reading your essay. Then you can articulate how you aim to change that view. A useful exercise is to write out the "before" and "after" views of your imagined readers:

> Before reading my essay, my readers think this way about my topic:
>
> ______________________________
>
> After reading my essay, my readers will think this different way about my topic:
>
> ______________________________

You can change your reader's view of a subject in several ways.* First, you can enlarge it. Writing that enlarges a view is primarily informational; it provides new ideas and data to add to a reader's store of knowledge about the subject. For

*Our discussion of how writing changes a reader's view of the world is indebted to Richard Young, Alton Becker, and Kenneth Pike, *Rhetoric: Discovery and Change* (New York: Harcourt Brace & Company, 1971).

example, suppose you are interested in the problem of storing nuclear waste (a highly controversial issue in the United States) and decide to investigate how Japan stores radioactive waste from its nuclear power plants. You could report your findings on this problem in an informative research paper. (Before reading my paper, readers would be uncertain how Japan stores nuclear waste. After reading my paper, my readers would understand the Japanese methods, possibly helping us better understand our options in the United States.)

Second, you can clarify your reader's view of something that was previously fuzzy, tentative, or uncertain. Writing of this kind often explains, analyzes, or interprets. This is the kind of writing you do when analyzing a short story, a painting, an historical document, a set of economic data, or other puzzling phenomena or when speculating on the causes, consequences, purpose, or function of something. Suppose, for example, that you are analyzing the persuasive strategies used in various clothing ads. You are intrigued by a jeans ad that you "read" differently from your classmates. (Before reading my paper, my readers will think that this jeans ad reveals a liberated woman, but after reading my paper they will see that the ad fulfills traditional gender stereotypes.)

Another kind of change occurs when an essay actually restructures a reader's whole view of a subject. Such essays persuade readers to change their minds or make decisions. For example, engineer David Rockwood, in his letter to the editor that we reprinted in Chapter 1 (p. 7), wants to change readers' views about wind power. (Before reading my letter, readers will believe that wind-generated electricity can solve our energy crisis, but after reading my letter they will see that the hope of wind power is a pipe dream.)

Surprise, then, is the measure of change an essay brings about in a reader. Of course, to bring about such change requires more than just a surprising thesis; the essay itself must persuade the reader that the thesis is sound as well as novel. Later in this chapter (Concept 7), we talk about how writers support a thesis through a network of points and particulars.

Giving Your Thesis Tension through "Surprising Reversal"

Another element of a surprising thesis is tension. By *tension* we mean the reader's sensation of being pulled away from familiar ideas toward new, unfamiliar ones. A strategy for creating this tension—a strategy we call "surprising reversal"—is to contrast your surprising answer to a question with your targeted audience's common answer, creating tension between your own thesis and one or more alternative views. Its basic template is as follows: "*Many people believe X (common view), but I am going to show Y (new, surprising view).*" The concept of surprising reversal spurs the writer to go beyond the commonplace to change the reader's view of a topic.

One of the best ways to employ this strategy is to begin your thesis statement with an "although" clause that summarizes the reader's "before" view or the counterclaim that your essay opposes; the main clause states the surprising view or position that your essay will support. You may choose to omit the *although* clause from your actual essay, but formulating it first will help you achieve focus and surprise in your thesis. The examples that follow illustrate the kinds of tension we have been discussing and show why tension is a key requirement for a good thesis.

Question	What effect has the cell phone had on our culture?
Thesis without Tension	The invention of the cell phone has brought many advantages to our culture.
Thesis with Tension	Although the cell phone has brought many advantages to our culture, it may also have contributed to an increase in risky behavior among boaters and hikers.
Question	Do reservations serve a useful role in contemporary Native American culture?
Thesis without Tension	Reservations have good points and bad points.
Thesis with Tension	Although my friend Wilson Real Bird believes that reservations are necessary for Native Americans to preserve their heritage, the continuation of reservations actually degrades Native American culture.

In the first example, the thesis without tension (cell phones have brought advantages to our culture) is a truism with which everyone would agree and hence lacks surprise. The thesis with tension places this truism (the reader's "before" view) in an *although* clause and goes on to make a surprising or contestable assertion. The idea that the cell phone contributes to risky behavior among outdoor enthusiasts alters our initial complacent view of the cell phone and gives us new ideas to think about.

In the second example, the thesis without tension may not at first seem tensionless because the writer sets up an opposition between good and bad points. But *almost anything* has good and bad points, so the opposition is not meaningful, and the thesis offers no element of surprise. Substitute virtually any other social institution (marriage, the postal service, the military, prisons), and the statement that it has good and bad points would be equally true. The thesis with tension, in contrast, is risky. It commits the writer to argue that reservations have degraded Native American culture and to oppose the counterthesis that reservations are needed to *preserve* Native American culture. The reader now feels genuine tension between two opposing views.

Tension, then, is a component of surprise. The writer's goal is to surprise the reader in some way, thereby bringing about some kind of change in the reader's view. Here are some specific strategies you can use to surprise a reader.

STRATEGIES for Surprising a Reader

- Give the reader new information or clarify a confusing concept.
- Make problematic something that seems nonproblematic by showing paradoxes or contradictions within it, by juxtaposing two or more conflicting points of view about it, or by looking at it more deeply or complexly than expected.
- Identify an unexpected effect, implication, or significance of something.
- Show underlying differences between two concepts normally thought to be similar or underlying similarities between two concepts normally thought to be different.
- Show that a commonly accepted answer to a question isn't satisfactory or that a commonly rejected answer may be satisfactory.
- Oppose a commonly accepted viewpoint, support an unpopular viewpoint, or in some other way take an argumentative stance on an issue.
- Propose a new solution to a problem or an unexpected answer to a question.

FOR WRITING AND DISCUSSION

Developing Questions into Thesis Statements

It is difficult to create thesis statements on the spot because a writer's thesis grows out of an exploratory struggle with a problem. However, in response to a question one can often propose a possible claim and treat it hypothetically as a tentative thesis statement put on the table for testing. What follows are several problematic questions, along with some possible audiences that you might consider addressing. Working individually, spend ten minutes considering possible thesis statements that you might pose in response to one or more of these questions. (Remember that these are tentative thesis statement that you might abandon after doing research.) Be ready to explain why your tentative thesis brings something new, enlightening, challenging, or otherwise surprising to the specified readers. Then, working in small groups or as a whole class, share your possible thesis statements. Finally, choose one or two thesis statements that your small group or the whole class thinks are particularly effective and brainstorm the kinds of evidence that would be required to support the thesis.

1. To what extent should the public support genetically modified foods? (possible audiences: readers of health food magazines; general public concerned about food choices; investors in companies that produce genetically modified seeds)
2. Should the government mandate more fuel-efficient cars? If so, how? (possible audiences: SUV owners; conservative legislators generally in favor of free markets; investors in the automobile industry)
3. Any questions that your class might have developed through discussing Chapter 1–2.

Here is an example:

Problematic question: What can cities do to prevent traffic congestion?

One possible thesis: Although many people think that building light-rail systems won't get people out of their cars, new light-rail systems in many cities have attracted new riders and alleviated traffic problems.

Intended audience: Residents of cities concerned about traffic congestion but skeptical about light-rail

Kinds of evidence needed to support thesis: Examples of cities with successful light-rail systems; evidence that many riders switched from driving cars; evidence that light-rail alleviated traffic problems

CONCEPT 7 Thesis statements in closed-form prose are supported hierarchically with points and particulars.

Of course, a surprising thesis is only one aspect of an effective essay. An essay must also persuade the reader that the thesis is believable as well as surprising. Although tabloid newspapers have shocking headlines ("Cloning Produces Three-Headed Sheep"), skepticism quickly replaces surprise when you look inside and find the article's claims unsupported. A strong thesis, then, must both surprise the reader and be supported with convincing particulars.

In fact, the particulars are the flesh and muscle of writing and comprise most of the sentences. In closed-form prose, these particulars are connected clearly to points, and the points precede the particulars. In this section, we explain this principle more fully.

How Points Convert Information to Meaning

When particulars are clearly related to a point, the point gives meaning to the particulars, and the particulars give force and validity to the point. Particulars constitute the evidence, data, details, examples, and subarguments that develop a point and make it convincing. By themselves, particulars are simply information—mere data without meaning.

In the following example, you can see for yourself the difference between information and meaning. Here is a list of information:*

- In almost all species on earth, males are more aggressive than females.
- Male chimpanzees win dominance by brawling.
- To terrorize rival troops, they kill females and infants.
- The level of aggression among monkeys can be manipulated by adjusting their testosterone levels.
- Among humans, preliminary research suggests that male fetuses are more active in the uterus than female fetuses.
- Little boys play more aggressively than little girls despite parental efforts to teach gentleness to boys and aggression to girls.

*The data in this exercise are adapted from Deborah Blum, "The Gender Blur," *Utne Reader* Sept. 1998: 45–48.

To make meaning out of this list of information, the writer needs to state a point—the idea, generalization, or claim—that this information supports. Once the point is stated, a meaningful unit (point with particulars) springs into being:

Point

Particulars

> **Aggression in human males may be a function of biology rather than culture.** In almost all species on earth, males are more aggressive than females. Male chimpanzees win dominance by brawling; to terrorize rival troops, they kill females and infants. Researchers have shown that the level of aggression among monkeys can be manipulated by adjusting their testosterone levels. Among humans, preliminary research suggests that male fetuses are more active in the uterus than female fetuses. Also, little boys play more aggressively than little girls despite parental efforts to teach gentleness to boys and aggression to girls.

Once the writer states this point, readers familiar with the biology/culture debate about gender differences immediately feel its surprise and tension. This writer believes that biology determines gender identity more than does culture. The writer now uses the details as evidence to support a point.

To appreciate the reader's need for a logical connection between points and particulars, note how readers would get lost if, in the preceding example, the writer included a particular that seemed unrelated to the point ("Males also tend to be taller and heavier than women"—a factual statement, but what does it have to do with aggression?) or if, without explanation, the writer added a particular that seemed to contradict the point ("Fathers play more roughly with baby boys than with baby girls"—another fact, but one that points to culture rather than biology as a determiner of aggression).

Obviously, reasonable people seek some kind of coordination between points and particulars, some sort of weaving back and forth between them. Writing teachers use a number of nearly synonymous terms for expressing this paired relationship: *points/particulars, generalizations/specifics, claims/evidence, ideas/details, interpretations/data, meaning/support.*

How Removing Particulars Creates a Summary

What we have shown, then, is that skilled writers weave back and forth between generalizations and specifics. The generalizations form a network of higher-level and lower-level points that develop the thesis; the particulars (specifics) support each of the points and subpoints in turn. In closed-form prose, the network of points is easily discernible because points are clearly highlighted with transitions, and main points are placed prominently at the heads of paragraphs. (In open-form prose, generalizations are often left unstated, creating gaps where the reader must actively fill in meaning.)

Being able to write summaries and abstracts of articles is an important academic skill. See Chapter 6 on strategies for writing summaries and strong responses, pp. 117–130.

If you remove most of the particulars from a closed-form essay, leaving only the network of points, you will have written a summary or abstract of the essay. As an example, reread the civil engineer's letter to the editor arguing against the feasibility of wind-generated power (p. 7). The writer's argument can be summarized in a single sentence:

> Wind-generated power is not a reasonable alternative to other forms of power in the Pacific Northwest because wind power is unreliable, because there are major

unsolved problems involved in the design of wind-generation facilities, and because the environmental impact of building thousands of wind towers would be enormous.

What we have done in this summary is remove the particulars, leaving only the high-level points that form the skeleton of the argument. The writer's thesis remains surprising and contains tension, but without the particulars the reader has no idea whether to believe the generalizations or not. The presence of the particulars is thus essential to the success of the argument.

FOR WRITING AND DISCUSSION

Analyzing Supporting Particulars

Compare the civil engineer's original letter with the one-sentence summary just given and then note how the engineer uses specific details to support each point. How do these particulars differ from paragraph to paragraph? How are they chosen to support each point?

How to Use Points and Particulars When You Revise

The lesson to learn here is that in closed-form prose, writers regularly place a point sentence in front of detail sentences. When a writer begins with a point, readers interpret the ensuing particulars not as random data but rather as *evidence* in support of that point. The writer depends on the particulars to make the point credible and persuasive.

This insight may help you understand two of the most common kinds of marginal comments that readers (or teachers) place on writers' early drafts. If your draft has a string of sentences giving data or information unconnected to any stated point, your reader is apt to write in the margin, "What's your point here?" or "Why are you telling me this information?" or "How does this information relate to your thesis?" Conversely, if your draft tries to make a point that isn't developed with particulars, your reader is apt to write marginal comments such as "Evidence?" or "Development?" or "Could you give an example?" or "More details needed."

Don't be put off by these requests; they are a gift. It is common in first drafts for main points to be unstated, buried, or otherwise disconnected from their details and for supporting information to be scattered confusingly throughout the draft or missing entirely. Having to write point sentences obliges you to wrestle with your intended meaning: Just what am I trying to say here? How can I nutshell that in a point? Likewise, having to support your points with particulars causes you to wrestle with the content and shape of your argument: What particulars will make this point convincing? What further research do I need to do to find these particulars? In Part 3 of this text, which is devoted to advice about composing and revising, we show how the construction and location of point sentences are essential for reader clarity. Part 3 also explains various composing and revising strategies that will help you create effective networks of points and particulars.

Chapter Summary

- Academic writing is rooted in interesting and significant questions shared by the writer's audience. What typically initiates the writing process is the problematic question that invites the writer to "wallow in complexity."
- Experienced writers use exploratory techniques such as freewriting, idea mapping, dialectic talk, and the believing and doubting game to generate ideas.
- A writer's thesis should bring something new or challenging to the reader. A good thesis tries to change the reader's view of the subject and often creates tension by pushing against alternative views.
- A writer supports a thesis through a hierarchical network of points and particulars.

BRIEF WRITING PROJECT

Playing the Believing and Doubting Game

Part 1: Play the believing and doubting game with one of the assertions listed here (or with another assertion provided by your instructor) by freewriting your believing and doubting responses. Spend fifteen minutes believing and then fifteen minutes doubting the assertion for a total of thirty minutes. When you believe an assertion, you agree, support, illustrate, extend, and apply the idea. When you doubt an assertion, you question, challenge, rebut, and offer counterreasons and counterexamples to the assertion.

1. Grades are an effective means of motivating students to do their best work.
2. MySpace is a good way to make new friends.
3. In recent years, advertising has made enormous gains in portraying women as strong, independent, and intelligent.
4. To help fight terrorism and promote public safety, individuals should be willing to give up some of their rights.
5. The United States should reinstate the draft.
6. It should be against the law to talk on a cell phone while driving.
7. Fencing at the U.S.–Mexico border is not an effective immigration policy.
8. More college classes should be taught online.

Part 2: Write a reflective paragraph in which you assess the extent to which the believing and doubting game extended or stretched your thinking. Particularly, answer these questions:

- What was difficult about this writing activity?
- To what extent did it make you take an unfamiliar or uncomfortable stance?
- How can believing and doubting help you wallow in complexity?

For additional writing, reading, and research resources, go to **www.MyCompLab.com** and choose **Ramage/Bean/Johnson's *The Allyn & Bacon Guide to Writing,* Fifth Edition.**

THINKING RHETORICALLY ABOUT HOW MESSAGES PERSUADE

CHAPTER 3

A way of seeing is also a way of not seeing.

—*Kenneth Burke, Rhetorician*

Every time an Indian villager watches the community TV and sees an ad for soap or shampoo, what they notice are not the soap and shampoo but the lifestyle of the people using them, the kind of motorbikes they ride, their dress and their homes.

—*Nayan Chanda, Indian-Born Editor of Yaleglobal Online Magazine*

In Chapters 1 and 2 we have focused on writing as a rhetorical act: When writers think rhetorically, they write to an audience for a purpose within a genre. We have also shown how academic writers pose subject-matter questions that engage their audience's interests, and they propose solutions to those problems that bring something new, surprising, or challenging to their audiences.

In this chapter we expand your understanding of a writer's choices by showing how messages persuade. We'll use the word *message* in its broadest sense to include verbal texts and nonverbal texts such as photographs and paintings or consumer artifacts such as clothing. When you understand how messages achieve their effects, you will be better prepared to analyze and evaluate those messages and to make your own choices about whether to resist them or accede to them.

This chapter will introduce you to three more important rhetorical concepts:

Concept 8: Messages persuade through their angle of vision.

Concept 9: Messages persuade through appeals to l*ogos*, *ethos*, and *pathos*.

Concept 10: Nonverbal messages persuade through visual strategies that can be analyzed rhetorically.

CONCEPT 8 Messages persuade through their angle of vision.

One way that messages persuade is through their "angle of vision," which is formed by the way the writer selects or omits details, chooses words with intended connotations, uses sentence structure and overall organization to emphasize certain points and de-emphasize others, adopts one kind of tone and style rather than another, and so forth. An angle of vision—which might also be called a lens, a filter, a perspective, a bias, a point of view—is persuasive because it controls what the reader "sees." Unless readers are rhetorically savvy, they can lose awareness that they are seeing the writer's subject matter through a lens that both reveals and conceals.

A classic illustration of angle of vision is the following thought exercise:

THOUGHT EXERCISE ON ANGLE OF VISION

> Suppose you attended a fun party on Friday night. (You get to choose what constitutes "fun" for you.) Now imagine that two people ask what you did on Friday night. Person A is your best friend, who missed the party. Person B is your grandmother. How would your descriptions of Friday night differ?

Clearly there isn't just one way to describe this party. Your description will be influenced by your purpose and audience. You will have to decide:

- What image of myself should I project? (For your friend you might construct yourself as a party animal; for Grandma you might construct yourself as a demure, soda-sipping observer of the party action.)
- What details should I include or leave out? (Does Grandma really need to know that the neighbors called the police?)
- How much emphasis do I give the party? (Your friend might want a full description. Grandma might want assurance that you are having some fun.)
- What words should I choose? (The colorful slang you use with your friend might not be appropriate for Grandma.)

You'll note that our comments about your rhetorical choices reflect common assumptions about friends and grandmothers. You might actually have a party-loving grandma and a geeky best friend, in which case Grandma might want the party details while your friend prefers talking about gigabytes or modern poetry. No matter the case, your rhetorical decisions are shaped by your particular knowledge of your audience and context.

Recognizing the Angle of Vision in a Text

This thought exercise illustrates a key insight of rhetoric: There is always more than one way to tell the same story, and no single way of telling it constitutes the whole truth. By saying that a writer writes from an "angle of vision," we mean that the writer cannot take a godlike stance that allows a universal, all-seeing, completely true, and whole way of knowing. Rather, the writer looks at the subject from a certain location, or, to use another metaphor, the writer wears a lens that colors or filters the topic in a certain way. The angle of vision, lens, or filter determines what part of a topic gets "seen" and what remains "unseen," what gets included or excluded from the writer's essay, what gets emphasized or de-emphasized, and so forth. It even determines what words get chosen out of an array of options—for example, whether you say "terrorist" or "freedom fighter," "public servant" or "politician," "homeless person" or "wino."

A good illustration of angle of vision is the political cartoon on stem cell research shown in Figure 3.1, which appeared in national newspapers in early summer 2001 when President Bush was contemplating his stance on federal funding for stem cell research. As the cartoon shows, nobody sees stem cells from a universal position. Each stakeholder has an angle of vision that emphasizes some aspects of stem cell research and de-emphasizes or censors other aspects. In the chart on page 52, we try to suggest how each of these angles of vision produces a different "picture" of the field.

FIGURE 3.1 Political Cartoon Illustrating Angle of Vision

In this cartoon, President Bush is cast as an inquirer trying to negotiate multiple perspectives. The cartoon treats Bush satirically—as if he were concerned only with the political implications of his decision. But if we think of him as seeking an ethically responsible stance, then his dilemma stands for all of us as writers confronting a problematic question. In such cases, we all have to forge our own individual stance and be ethically responsible for our decision, while acknowledging other stances and recognizing the limitations of our own.

Where do our stances come from? The stance we take on questions is partly influenced by our life experiences and knowledge, by our class and gender, by our ethnicity and sexual orientation, by our personal beliefs and values, and by our ongoing intentions and desires. But our stance can also be influenced by our rational and empathic capacity to escape from our own limitations and see the world from different perspectives, to imagine the world more fully. We have the power to take stances that are broader and more imaginative than our original limited vision, but we also never escape our own roots and situations in life.

The U. R. Riddle exercise on page 53 will help you understand the concept of "angle of vision" more fully.

Angles of Vision on Stem Cell Research

Angle of Vision	Words or Phrases Used to Refer to Stem Cells	Particulars That Get "Seen" or Emphasized
Disease sufferer	"Cluster of cells" that may help repair damaged tissues or grow new ones	The diseases that may be cured by stem cell research; the suffering of those afflicted; scientists as heroes; shelves of frozen stem cells; cells as objects that would just be thrown out if not used for research; emphasis on cures
Priest	"Embryo" as potential human life formed by union of sperm and egg	Moral consequences of treating human life as means rather than ends; scientists as Dr. Frankensteins; single embryo as potential baby
Scientist	"Blastocysts," which are better suited for research than adult stem cells	Scientific questions that research would help solve; opportunities for grants and scholarly publication; emphasis on gradual progress rather than cures
Businessperson	"Biogenetic investment opportunity"	Potential wealth for company that develops new treatments for diseases or injuries
President Bush (at time of cartoon, Bush was uncertain of his stance)	Afraid to say "cluster of cells," "embryo," or "blastocyst" because each term has political consequences	Political consequences of each possible way to resolve the stem cell controversy; need to appease supporters from the Right without appearing callous to sufferers of diseases; need to woo Catholic vote

FOR WRITING AND DISCUSSION

U. R. Riddle Letter

Background: Suppose that you are a management professor who is regularly asked to write letters of recommendation for former students. One day you receive a letter from a local bank requesting a confidential evaluation of a former student, one Uriah Rudy Riddle (U.R. Riddle), who has applied for a job as a management trainee. The bank wants your assessment of Riddle's intelligence, aptitude, dependability, and ability to work with people. You haven't seen U.R. for several years, but you remember him well. Here are the facts and impressions you recall about Riddle:

- Very temperamental student, seemed moody, something of a loner
- Long hair and very sloppy dress—seemed like a misplaced street person; often twitchy and hyperactive
- Absolutely brilliant mind; took lots of liberal arts courses and applied them to business
- Wrote a term paper relating different management styles to modern theories of psychology—the best undergraduate paper you ever received. You gave it an A+ and remember learning a lot from it yourself.
- Had a strong command of language—the paper was very well written
- Good at mathematics; could easily handle all the statistical aspects of the course
- Frequently missed class and once told you that your class was boring
- Didn't show up for the midterm. When he returned to class later, he said only that he had been out of town. You let him make up the midterm, and he got an A.
- Didn't participate in a group project required for your course. He said the other students in his group were idiots.
- You thought at the time that Riddle didn't have a chance of making it in the business world because he had no talent for getting along with people.
- Other professors held similar views of Riddle—brilliant, but rather strange and hard to like; an odd duck.

You are in a dilemma because you want to give Riddle a chance (he's still young and may have had a personality transformation of some sort), but you also don't want to damage your own professional reputation by falsifying your true impressions.

Individual task: Working individually for ten minutes or so, compose a brief letter of recommendation assessing Riddle; use details from the list to support your assessment. Role-play that you have decided to take a gamble with Riddle and give him a chance at this career. Write as strong a recommendation as possible while remaining honest. (To make this exercise more complex, your instructor might ask half the class to role-play a negative angle of vision in which you want to warn the bank against hiring Riddle without hiding his strengths or good points.)

(continued)

Task for group or whole-class discussion: Working in small groups or as a whole class, share your letters. Pick out representative examples ranging from the most positive to the least positive and discuss how the letters achieve their different rhetorical effects. If your intent is to support Riddle, to what extent does honesty compel you to mention some or all of your negative memories? Is it possible to mention negative items without emphasizing them? How?

Analyzing Angle of Vision

Chapter 5, "Seeing Rhetorically," develops this connection between seeing and interpreting in more detail.

Just as there is more than one way to describe the party you went to on Friday night, there is more than one way to write a letter of recommendation for U. R. Riddle. The writer's angle of vision determines what is "seen" or "not seen" in a given piece of writing—what gets slanted in a positive or negative direction, what gets highlighted, what gets thrown into the shadows. As rhetorician Kenneth Burke claims in the first epigraph for the chapter, "A way of seeing is also a way of not seeing." Note how the writer controls what the reader "sees." As Riddle's professor, you might in your mind's eye see Riddle as long-haired and sloppy, but if you don't mention these details in your letter, they remain unseen to the reader. Note too that your own terms "long-haired and sloppy" interpret Riddle's appearance through the lens of your own characteristic way of seeing—a way that perhaps values business attire and clean-cut tidiness. Another observer might describe Riddle's appearance quite differently, thus seeing what you don't see.

In an effective piece of writing, the author's angle of vision often works so subtly that unsuspecting readers—unless they learn to think rhetorically—will be drawn into the writer's spell and believe that the writer's prose conveys the "whole picture" of its subject rather than a limited picture filtered through the screen of the writer's perspective. To understand more clearly how an angle of vision is constructed, you can analyze the language strategies at work. Some of these strategies—which writers employ consciously or unconsciously to achieve their intended effects—are described here.

STRATEGIES for Constructing an Angle of Vision

Strategies	Examples
State your meaning or intentions directly.	Your letter for U. R. Riddle might say, "Riddle would make an excellent bank manager" or "Riddle doesn't have the personality to be a bank manager."
Select details that support your intended effect and omit those that do not. Instead of outright omission of data, de-emphasize some details while highlighting others.	If you are supporting Riddle, include all the positive data about Riddle and omit or downplay the negative data (or vice versa if you are opposing his candidacy).

Strategies	Examples
Choose words that frame the subject in a desired way or that have desired connotations.	If you call Riddle "an independent thinker who doesn't follow the crowd," you frame him positively in a value system that favors individualism. If you call him "a loner who thinks egocentrically," you frame him negatively in a value system that favors consensus and social skills. Calling him "forthright" will elicit a different response than calling him "rude."
Use metaphors, similes, or analogies to create an intended effect.	To suggest that Riddle has outgrown his earlier alienation, you might call him a "social late bloomer." If you think he's out of place in a bank, you could say his independent spirit would feel "caged in" by the routine of a banker.
Vary sentence structure to emphasize or de-emphasize ideas and details. Emphasize material by placing it at the end of a long sentence, in a short sentence surrounded by long sentences, or in a main clause rather than a subordinate clause.	Consider the difference between "Although Riddle had problems relating to other students in my class, he is a brilliant thinker" and "Although Riddle is a brilliant thinker, he had problems relating to other students in my class."

CONCEPT 9 Messages persuade through appeals to *logos, ethos,* and *pathos.*

Another way to think about the persuasive power of texts is to imagine writers or speakers trying to sway their audiences toward a certain position on an issue. In order to win people's consideration of their ideas, writers or speakers can appeal to what the classical philosopher Aristotle called *logos*, *ethos*, and *pathos*. These appeals are particularly important in argument when one takes a directly persuasive aim. But all kinds of messages, including writing with an expressive, informative, or analytic aim, can be strengthened by using these appeals.

Developing the habit of examining how these appeals are functioning in texts and being able to employ these appeals in your own writing will enhance your ability to read and write rhetorically. Let's look briefly at each:

A fuller discussion of these classical appeals appears in Chapter 14, "Writing a Classical Argument."

- *Logos* is the appeal to reason. It refers to the quality of the message itself—to its internal consistency, to its clarity in asserting a thesis or point, and to the quality of reasons and evidence used to support the point.
- *Ethos* is the appeal to the character of the speaker/writer. It refers to the speaker/writer's trustworthiness and credibility. One can often increase the *ethos* of a message by being knowledgeable about the issue, by appearing thoughtful and fair, by listening well, and by being respectful of alternative points of view. A writer's accuracy and thoroughness in crediting sources and profes-

sionalism in caring about the format, grammar, and neat appearance of a document are part of the appeal to *ethos*.

- *Pathos* is the appeal to the sympathies, values, beliefs, and emotions of the audience. Appeals to *pathos* can be made in many ways. *Pathos* can often be enhanced through evocative visual images, frequently used in Web sites, posters, and magazine or newspaper articles. In written texts, the same effects can be created through vivid examples and details, through connotative language, and through empathy with the audience's beliefs and values.

To see how these three appeals are interrelated, you can visualize a triangle with points labeled *Message, Audience,* and *Writer* or *Speaker*. Rhetoricians study how effective communicators consider all three points of this *rhetorical triangle*. (See Figure 3.2.)

We encourage you to ask questions about the appeals to *logos, ethos,* and *pathos* every time you examine a text. For example, is the appeal to *logos* weakened by the writer's use of scanty and questionable evidence? Has the writer made a powerful appeal to *ethos* by documenting her sources and showing that she is an authority on the issue? Has the writer relied too heavily on appeals to *pathos* by using numerous heart-wringing examples? Later chapters in this textbook will help you use these appeals well in your own writing as well as analyze these appeals in others' messages.

FIGURE 3.2 Rhetorical Triangle

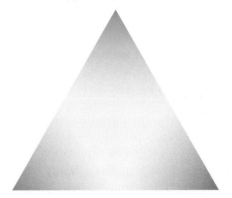

Message

Logos: *How can I make my ideas internally consistent and logical? How can I find the best reasons and support them with the best evidence?*

Audience

Pathos: *How can I make the readers open to my message? How can I best engage my readers' emotions and imaginations? How can I appeal to my readers' values and interests?*

Writer or Speaker

Ethos: *How can I present myself effectively? How can I enhance my credibility and trustworthiness?*

CONCEPT 10 Nonverbal messages persuade through visual strategies that can be analyzed rhetorically.

To us, one of the most pleasurable aspects of rhetorical thinking is analyzing the rhetorical power of visual images or identifying rhetorical factors in people's choices about clothing, watches, cars, tattoos, and other consumer items.

Visual Rhetoric

Just as you can think rhetorically about texts, you can think rhetorically about photographs, drawings, paintings, statues, buildings, and other visual images. In Chapter 11, we deal extensively with visual rhetoric, explaining how color, perspective, cropping, camera angle, foreground/background, and other visual elements work together to create a persuasive effect. In this chapter, we intend only to introduce you to the concept of visual rhetoric and to suggest its importance. Consider, for example, the persuasive power of famous photographs from the war in Iraq. Early in the war, several widely publicized images, particularly the film footage of the toppling of the statue of Saddam Hussein and the "Mission Accomplished" photograph of President Bush wearing a pilot's flight suit on the deck of the aircraft carrier *Abraham Lincoln*, served to consolidate public support of the war. Later, certain images began eating away at public support. For example, an unauthorized picture of flag-draped coffins filling the freight deck of a military transport plane focused attention on those killed in the war. Particularly devastating for supporters of the war were the images of American prison guards sexually humiliating Iraqi prisoners in the Abu Ghraib prison. Images like these stick in viewers' memories long after specific texts are forgotten.

What gives visual images this persuasive power? For one thing, visual texts, like verbal texts, persuade through their angle of vision, which controls what the viewer sees and doesn't see. (Note that "angle of vision" is itself a visual metaphor.) To appreciate the effect of angle of vision in paintings and photographs, consider the impact of visual images on our cultural discussions of health care. In the early and middle decades of the twentieth century, a powerful concept of the "family doctor" emerged. This "family doctor" was envisioned as a personable, caring individual—usually a fatherly or grandfatherly male—with a stethoscope around his neck and a little black bag for making house calls. This image was deeply embedded in the American psyche through a series of paintings by Norman Rockwell, several of which were reproduced on the cover of the influential *Saturday Evening Post* (see Figure 3.3).

These paintings are now part of our cultural nostalgia for a simpler era and help explain some of the cultural resistance in the United States to impersonal HMOs, where medical decisions seem made by insurance bureaucrats. Yet, we also want our doctors to be high-tech. In the last few decades, the image of doctors in the popular imagination, especially furthered by advertising, has shifted away from idealized Norman Rockwell scenes to images of highly specialized experts using the latest technological equipment. Figure 3.4 (p. 59) suggests the kinds of high-tech imagery

FIGURE 3.3 A Norman Rockwell Painting of a Family Doctor

"Doc Melhorn and the Pearly Gates" by Norman Rockwell, inside illustration from The Saturday Evening Post, December 24, 1938. Printed by permission of the Norman Rockwell Family Agency. Copyright © 1938 the Norman Rockwell Family Entities.

that now characterizes popular media portrayal of doctors. However, in many current articles about health care in the United States, the Norman Rockwell paintings of the family doctor are still invoked to represent an older ideal of what people are looking for in their doctors.

Visual images also appeal to *logos*, *ethos*, and *pathos*. Consider how visual images make implicit arguments (*logos*) while also appealing to our values and emotions (*pathos*) and causing us to respond favorably or unfavorably to the painter or photographer (*ethos*). Consider, for example, the wind farm photograph that is shown as a part opener on page 3.

In this striking image, the dominance of the whirling turbines conveys the implicit argument (*logos*) that wind farms can generate plentiful energy. The pho-

FIGURE 3.4 A Modern High-Tech Image of a Doctor

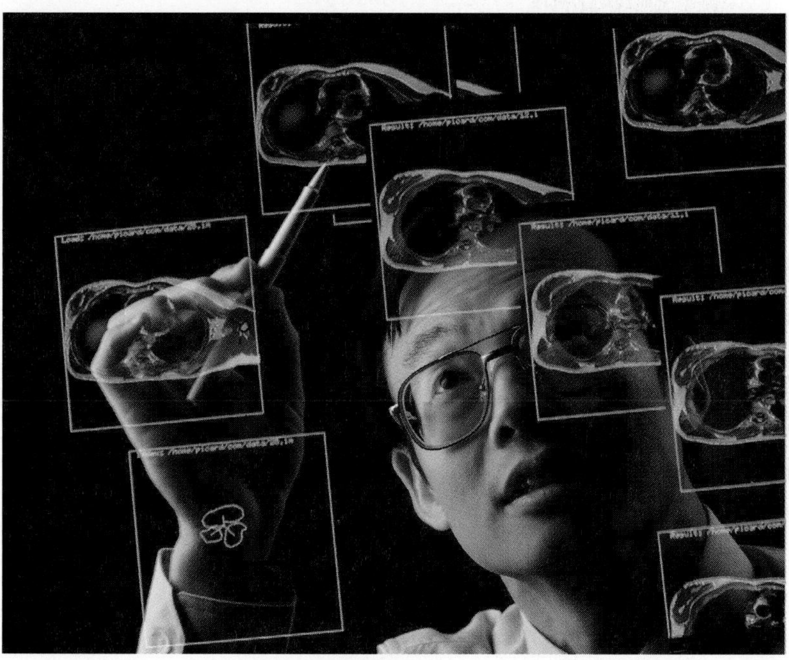

tograph's angle of vision, which emphasizes the size and power of these wind towers against a hint of a background of barren hills and blue sky, could be used to counter David Rockwood's disparagement of wind power in his letter to the editor in Chapter 1 and could instead help to build confidence in this technology. Whereas Rockwood emphasizes damage to "pristine wilderness" as an argument against wind power, this photograph suggests that wind towers can be located productively on arid land. The contrast between Rockwood's "pristine wilderness" and the photograph's barren hills also illustrates the use of *pathos* in argument. To enlist environmentalists' opposition to wind power, Rockwood evokes their love of wilderness. In contrast, the photograph minimizes environmental concerns (no beautiful landscape being destroyed, no birds flying into the turbines, no air pollution), evoking instead positive feelings about technology, analogous to photographs from another era of steam locomotives pulling freight across the plains or of gleaming rows of turbines in the powerhouses of dams. The *ethos* of the photograph is harder to analyze. The photographer is obviously a professional, who uses upward camera placement to emphasize the technological power of the wind turbines. Whether one is favorably impressed by this photograph or not depends on one's sense of how much the photograph seems "natural" as opposed to being framed for political effect.

FOR WRITING AND DISCUSSION

Analyzing Visual Messages

Working in small groups or as a whole class, explore your answers to the following questions:

1. What implicit arguments (*logos*) are made by the Norman Rockwell painting (Figure 3.3) and the photograph of the high-tech doctor (Figure 3.4)? Consider how each image makes a claim in response to the question "What are the traits of a good doctor?" Also, how does each image evoke a system of values and by doing so appeal to the viewers' emotions and beliefs (*pathos*)?
2. What specific details contribute to the persuasive impact of the painting or photograph? Why, for example, does Rockwell choose an upholstered chair for the doctor to sit on rather than, say, a hard-backed kitchen chair? Why is the little boy standing up rather than lying in bed looking sick? Why is the photograph framed so that we see the doctor's face looking through some sort of glass window covered with slide transparencies rather than, say, having the doctor look at slides attached to a white board or chart?
3. To what extent do the visual images help you form an impression of Norman Rockwell himself or of the photographer who took the high-tech photograph? How would you characterize your impression of the *ethos* of each visual?
4. Why is it in the interest of HMOs and insurance companies to portray high-tech images of doctors? How might the influence of the Norman Rockwell view of doctors serve the interests of alternative health care providers such as naturopathic physicians?

The Rhetoric of Clothing and Other Consumer Items

Not only do visual images have rhetorical power, but so do many of our consumer choices. To help you appreciate the rhetoric of consumer choice, we cite a view of rhetoric proposed by twentieth-century rhetorician Kenneth Burke, who claims that humans are "beings that by nature respond to symbols." Burke's point is that humans communicate by symbolic means and that symbols persuade in both direct and indirect ways. To understand what Burke means by humans as symbol-using beings, consider the difference in flirting behavior between peacocks and humans. When peacocks flirt, they spread their beautiful tails, do mating dances, and screech weirdly to attract females, but the whole process is governed by instinct. Peacocks don't have to choose among different symbolic actions such as buying an Armani tail versus buying a Wal-Mart tail or driving to the mating grounds in the right car. Unlike a peacock, a flirting human must make symbolic choices, all of which involve consequences. Consider how what you wear might contribute to the effectiveness of your flirting behavior (For males: Feedlot cap? Doo rag? Preppy sweater? Baggy, low-riding pants? For females: Skirt and tights? Low-cut jeans, halter top, and belly ring? Gothic make-up, black dress, and open-fingered black gloves?). Each of these choices sends signals about the groups you identify with. Your choice of language (for example, big words versus street slang) or conversation topics (football versus art films) gives further hints of your identity and values. All these choices carry symbolic significance about the identity you wish to project to the world. Rhetoricians study, among other things, how these symbols are constructed within a given culture and how they operate to persuade audiences toward certain beliefs or actions.

Given this brief background, consider the rhetorical thinking that goes into our choice of clothes. We choose our clothes not only to keep ourselves covered and warm but also to project our identification with certain social groups. For example, if you want to be identified as a skateboarder, a preppy socialite, a gang member, a pickup-driving NASCAR fan, or a junior partner in a corporate law firm, you know how to select clothes and accessories that convey that identification. The way you dress communicates where you fit (or how you want to be perceived as fitting) within a class and social structure. For the most part, clothing codes are arbitrary, based on a system of differences. For example, there is no universal "truth" saying that long, baggy basketball shorts are more attractive than short basketball shorts or that cargo pants are more beautiful than stirrup pants, even though one style may feel current and one out-of-date.

How do these symbolic codes get established? They can be set by fashion designers, by advertisers, or by trendy groups or individuals. The key to any new clothing code is to make it look different in some distinctive way from an earlier code or from a code of another group. Sometimes clothing codes develop to show rebellion against the values of parents or authority figures. At other times they develop to show new kinds of group identities.

Clothing codes are played on in conscious ways in fashion advertisements so that consumers become very aware of what identifications are signaled by different styles and brands. This aspect of consumer society is so ubiquitous that one of the marks of growing affluence in third world countries is people's attention to the rhetoric of consumer goods. Consider the second epigraph to this chapter, which indicates that villagers in India watching TV ads notice not only the soap or shampoo but also the brands of motorbikes and the lifestyles of the people in the ads. Buying a certain kind of consumer good projects a certain kind of status or group or class identity. Our point, from a rhetorical perspective, is that in making a consumer choice, many people are concerned not only with the quality of the item itself but also with the symbolic messages that the item sends to different audiences. Note that the same item can send quite different messages to different groups: A Rolex watch might enhance one's credibility at a corporate board meeting while undercutting it at a barbecue for union workers. Or consider the clothing choices of preteen girls who want to dress like female pop rock stars. They often do so to fit in with their friends, perhaps unaware of the whole array of cultural messages that these clothes convey to other social groups.

FOR WRITING AND DISCUSSION

Analyzing the Rhetoric of Clothing

Working in small groups or as a whole class, do a rhetorical analysis of the consumer items shown in Figures 3.5, 3.6, 3.7, and 3.8.

1. In each case, see if you can reach consensus on why persons might have chosen a particular way of dressing. How does the clothing style project a desire to identify with certain groups or to shock or reject certain groups? How do the clothing choices help establish and enhance the wearer's sense of identity?
2. When you and your friends make consumer purchases, to what extent are you swayed by the internal quality of the item (its materials and workmanship) versus the rhetorical messages it sends to an audience (its signals about social identity and standing)? (Note: Advertisers have long known that consumers, when queried, say: "I buy to please myself." However, advertisers' extensive psychological research suggests that consumers are intensely aware of audience: "I buy to maintain and project a certain way of being perceived by others.")
3. How does the rhetoric of clothing extend to other consumer items such as cars, vacations, recreational activities, home furnishings, music, and so forth?

FIGURE 3.5

FIGURE 3.6

FIGURE 3.7

FIGURE 3.8

Chapter Summary

In this chapter we have looked briefly at rhetorical theory in order to explain the persuasive power of both verbal and nonverbal texts.

- Any text necessarily looks at its subject from a perspective—an angle of vision—that emphasizes some details while minimizing others.

- You can analyze angle of vision by considering the writer's word choices and the selection and arrangement of evidence.
- The classical appeals of *logos, ethos,* and *pathos* are strategies for increasing the effectiveness of messages.
- Rhetorical thinking can be applied to images and to various kinds of consumer choices.

BRIEF WRITING PROJECT

Analyzing Angle of Vision in Two Passages about Nuclear Energy

Background and Readings

This brief writing project will give you practice at analyzing the angle of vision in different texts. This assignment focuses on two passages about nuclear power plants. Read the two passages; then we will describe your writing task.

The first passage is from the Bush administration's *National Energy Policy: Reliable, Affordable, and Environmentally Sound Energy for America's Future.* The document was written by an energy task force chaired by Vice President Dick Cheney. This passage is an overview paragraph on nuclear power from the opening chapter of the document; the last sentence of the passage is from a later section on recommendations for increasing energy supplies:

PASSAGE 1

> Nuclear power plants serve millions of American homes and businesses, have a dependable record for safety and efficiency, and discharge no greenhouse gases into the atmosphere. As noted earlier, these facilities currently generate 20 percent of all electricity in America, and more than 40 percent of electricity generated in 10 states in the Northeast, South, and Midwest. Other nations, such as Japan and France, generate a much higher percentage of their electricity from nuclear power. Yet the number of nuclear plants in America is actually projected to decline in coming years, as old plants close and none are built to replace them. … [Later the Cheney document makes the following recommendation:] Provide for the safe expansion of nuclear energy by establishing a national repository for nuclear waste, and by streamlining licensing of nuclear power plants.

The second passage is from an op-ed piece by columnist Marianne Means. It was entitled "Bush, Cheney Will Face Wall of Opposition If They Try to Resurrect Nuclear Power."

PASSAGE 2

> Washington—Vice President Dick Cheney, head of the presidential task force studying our energy needs, favors building new nuclear power plants—and he's oddly casual about it.
>
> The industry has been moribund in this country since the partial meltdown at Three Mile Island more than two decades ago set off fierce emotional resistance to an unreliable technology capable of accidentally spreading deadly radiation. No new

plants have been ordered since then. Only 20 percent of our electricity is generated by nuclear power.

But President Bush has instructed Cheney to look into the prospect of resurrecting and developing nuclear power as a major part of a broad new energy policy. Cheney argues that modern, improved reactors operate safely, economically and efficiently. "It's one of the safest industries around," he says unequivocally.

There remains, however, a little problem of how to dispose of the plants' radioactive waste. Cheney concedes that issue is still unsolved. "If we're going to go forward with nuclear power, we need to find a way to resolve it," he said Sunday in an NBC "Meet the Press" interview.

No state wants to be the repository of the more than 40,000 tons of high-level nuclear waste currently accumulating at 103 commercial reactor sites around the country. This spent fuel is so deadly it can remain a potential threat to public health and safety for thousands of years. A leak could silently contaminate many miles of groundwater that millions of people depend on.

Your task: Contrast the differences in angle of vision in these two passages by analyzing how they create their different rhetorical effects. Consider factors such as overt statements of meaning, selection/omission of details, connotations of words and figures of speech, and sentence emphasis. To help guide your analysis, reread the section "Analyzing Angle of Vision" on page 54. Your goal here is to explain to your readers how these two passages create different impressions of nuclear power.

For additional writing, reading, and research resources, go to **www.MyCompLab.com** and choose **Ramage/Bean/Johnson's *The Allyn & Bacon Guide to Writing,* Fifth Edition.**

CHAPTER 4

THINKING RHETORICALLY ABOUT STYLE AND DOCUMENT DESIGN

Style is everything, and nothing. It is not that, as is commonly supposed, you get your content and soup it up with style; style is absolutely embedded in the way you perceive.

—Martin Amis, Author

...[C]larity and excellence in thinking is very much like clarity and excellence in the display of data. When principles of design replicate principles of thought, the act of arranging information becomes an act of thought.

—Edward Tufte, Visual Design Researcher and Consultant

In Chapters 1, 2, and 3, we explained the importance of thinking rhetorically about your writing. In this chapter, we focus on the rhetorical effect of different choices in writing style and document design. We show how the arrangement and selection of your words and the format and layout of your document can increase or decrease the effectiveness of your prose.

Our two epigraphs for this chapter suggest the significance of these concerns. As explained by Amis and Tufte, one's choices about style and document design reflect one's thinking. The goal of effective style and document design is clear communication—emphasizing for the audience what the writer intends as important and meaningful. Style and document design are not decorative add-ons to jazz up dull content but rather means of guiding an audience to see what matters. In a famous article about the dangers of PowerPoint presentations, Edward Tufte argues that the gee-whiz features of this software can seduce users into concentrating on decorative effects rather than clear communication. He suggests that the *Challenger* spacecraft disaster might have been avoided had it not been for a jumbled PowerPoint slide that buried key data about the temperature sensitivity of O-rings. He shows how the buried data could have been highlighted to make its story vivid—thereby gaining the attention of NASA managers. For Tufte, design is part of the message itself. Tufte's work on the visual display of information can be extended to all aspects of document design and even to style: What matters is the communication of meaning, not the decorative effects.

To build on your understanding of rhetorical effectiveness, this chapter presents two concepts.

Concept 11: Good writers make purposeful stylistic choices.

Concept 12: Good writers make purposeful document design choices.

CONCEPT 11 Good writers make purposeful stylistic choices.

To grow as an effective writer, you need to become increasingly aware of your stylistic choices. By *style*, we mean an interactive combination of the words you choose and the way you arrange them in sentences. To use a phrase often cited by composition instructors, an effective style means "the right words in the right places." Writers can say essentially the same thing in a multitude of ways, each placing the material in a slightly different light, subtly altering meaning and slightly changing the effect on readers. Good writers know how to adjust their style in a piece of writing to fit their purpose, audience, and genre. In this section, we illustrate the stylistic options open to you and explain how you might go about making stylistic choices.

Factors That Affect Style

As we see in Figure 4.1, style is a complex composite of many factors, and for each of these, writers have many options. By *style*, rhetoricians mean the way these different factors work together in a piece of writing. Style refers to analyzable textual features on a page such as the abstractness or specificity of a writer's word choices and length and complexity of sentences. Style also includes *voice* or *persona*: that is, the reader's impression of the writer projected from the page. Through your stylistic choices, you create an image of yourself in your readers' minds. This image can be cold or warm, insider or outsider, humorous or serious, detached or passionate, scholarly or hip, antagonistic or friendly, and so forth. In addition, writers adopt an attitude toward their subject matter and their audience—called the *tone* of a piece of writing—that is conveyed by the writer's choice of words and sentence style.

What style you adopt depends on your purpose, audience, and genre. Consider, for example, the differences in style in two articles about the animated sitcom *South Park*. The first passage comes from an academic journal in which the author analyzes how race is portrayed in *South Park*. The second passage is from a popular magazine, where the author argues that despite *South Park*'s vulgarity, the sitcom has a redeeming social value.

FIGURE 4.1 Ingredients of Style

Ways of shaping sentences	Types of words	Voice or persona	Tone
Long/short Simple/complex Many modifiers/few modifiers Normal word order/frequent inversions or interruptions Mostly main clauses/many embedded phrases and subordinate clauses	Abstract/concrete Formal/colloquial Unusual/ordinary Specialized/general Metaphorical/literal Scientific/literary	Expert/layperson Scholar/student Outsider/insider Political liberal/conservative Neutral observer/active participant	Intimate/distant Personal/impersonal Angry/calm Browbeating/sharing Informative/entertaining Humorous/serious Ironic/literal Passionately involved/aloof

PASSAGE FROM SCHOLARLY JOURNAL

In these cartoons, multiplicity encodes a set of nonwhite identities to be appropriated and commodified by whiteness. In the cartoon world, obscene humor and satire mediate this commodification. The whiteness that appropriates typically does so by virtue of its mobile positioning between and through imagined boundaries contrarily shown as impassible to black characters or agents marked as black. Let me briefly turn to an appropriately confusing example of such a character in *South Park*'s scatological hero extraordinaire, Eric Cartman. ... Eric Cartman's yen for breaking into Black English and interactions with black identities also fashion him an appropriator. However, Cartman's voice and persona may be seen as only an avatar, one layer of textual identity for creator Trey Parker, who may be regarded in one sense as a "blackvoice" performer.

—Michael A. Chaney, "Representations of Race and Place in *Static Shock, King of the Hill,* and *South Park*"

PASSAGE FROM POPULAR MAGAZINE

Despite the theme song's chamber of commerce puffery, *South Park* is the closest television has ever come to depicting hell on earth. Its inhabitants are, almost without exception, stupid, ignorant or venal—usually all three. Its central characters are four eight-year-olds: Stan, the high-achiever, Kyle, the sensitive Jew, Kenny, whose grisly death each week prompts the tortured cry, "Oh my God! They've killed Kenny! Those bastards!" and Eric Cartman, who has become the Archie Bunker of the '90s, beloved by millions. My 12-year-old son informs me that many of his schoolmates have taken to speaking permanently in Cartman's bigoted and usually furiously inarticulate manner. A (mild) sample: any display of human sensitivity is usually met by him with the rejoinder: "Tree-hugging hippie crap!" This has led to predictable calls for *South Park*, which is usually programmed late in the evening, to be banned altogether.

—Kevin Michael Grace, "*South Park* Is a Snort of Defiance Against a World Gone to Hell"

FOR WRITING AND DISCUSSION

Analyzing Differences in Style

Working in small groups or as a whole class, analyze the differences in the styles of these two samples.

1. How would you describe differences in the length and complexity of sentences, in the level of vocabulary, and in the degree of formality?
2. How do the differences in styles create different voices, personas, and tones?
3. Based on clues from style and genre, who is the intended audience of each piece? What is the writer's purpose? How does each writer hope to surprise the intended audience with something new, challenging, or valuable?
4. How are the differences in content and style influenced by differences in purpose, audience, and genre?

In the sections that follow, we highlight some ways of thinking about style that will be particularly relevant to you in your college writing.

Abstract Versus Concrete Words: Moving Up or Down the Scale of Abstraction

Although there are many ways that word choices affect style, we will consider first a writer's choice between abstract and concrete words. In Chapter 2, we explained how writers use particulars—examples, details, numerical data, and other kinds of evidence—to support their points. We said that strong writing weaves back and forth between points and particulars; points give meaning to particulars and particulars flesh out and develop points, making them credible and convincing. However, the distinction between points and particulars is a matter of context. The same sentence might serve as a point in one context and as a particular in another. What matters is the relative position of words and sentences along a scale of abstraction. As an illustration of such a scale, consider Figure 4.2, in which words or concepts descend from abstract and general to concrete and specific.

Where you pitch a piece of writing on the scale of abstraction helps determine its style, with high-on-the-scale writing creating an abstract or theoretical effect and low-on-the-scale writing creating a more vivid and concrete effect. In descriptive and narrative prose, writers often use sensory details that are very low on the scale of abstraction. Note how shifting down the scale improves the vividness of the following passage.

FIGURE 4.2
Pitching Words or Concepts on the Scale of Abstraction

Abstract or general: High on the scale of abstraction	Clothes	Building	Global problems	Sam exhibited gendered play behavior
	• Footwear	• Residence	• Finding food for the world's growing population	• Sam exhibited male play behavior
	• Shoes	• Vacation home	• Producing farm food in developing countries	• Sam played with stereotypical boy toys
	• Sandals	• Mountain cabin	• Growing traditional crops versus growing commercial crops in developing countries	• Sam played with trucks and fire engines
	• Flip-flops	• A-frame cabin in the mountains	• Traditional farming versus planting genetically modified commercial crops in India	• Sam played aggressively with his Tonka trucks and fire engines
Specific or concrete: Low on the scale of abstraction	• Purple platform flip-flops with rhinestones	• Three-story A-frame mountain cabin with a large deck overlooking the alpine lake	• Growing the traditional crops of mandua and jhangora versus growing genetically modified soy beans in Northern India for sale on the global market	• Sam gleefully smashed his toy Tonka truck into the coffee table

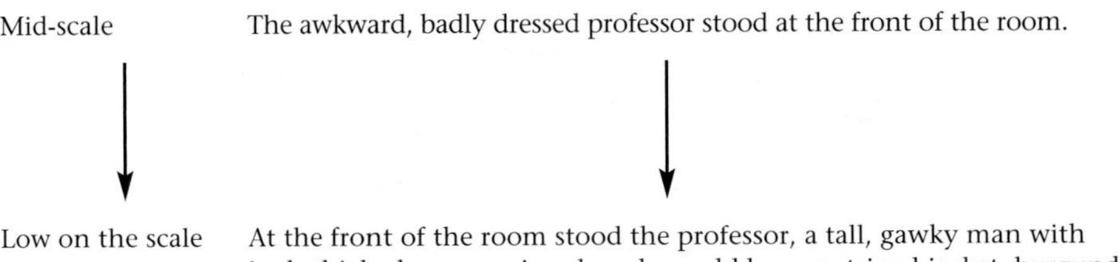

Mid-scale
The awkward, badly dressed professor stood at the front of the room.
Low on the scale
At the front of the room stood the professor, a tall, gawky man with inch-thick glasses, a wispy beard, an old brown-striped jacket, burgundy and gray plaid pants, and a green tie with blue koalas.

The details in the more specific passage help you experience the writer's world. They don't just tell you that the professor was dressed weirdly; they *show* you.

In closed-form prose such specific sensory language is less common, so writers need to make choices about the level of specificity that will be most effective based on their purpose, audience, and genre. Note the differences along the level of abstraction in the following passages:

PASSAGE 1: FAIRLY HIGH ON SCALE OF ABSTRACTION

Although lightning produces the most deaths and injuries of all weather-related accidents, the rate of danger varies considerably from state to state. Florida has twice as many deaths and injuries from lightning strikes as any other state. Hawaii and Alaska have the fewest.

Point sentence

Particulars high on scale of abstraction

—Passage from a general interest informative article on weather-related accidents

PASSAGE 2: LOWER ON SCALE OF ABSTRACTION

Florida has twice as many deaths and injuries from lightning strikes as any other state, with many of these casualties occurring on the open spaces of golf courses. Florida golfers should carefully note the signals of dangerous weather conditions such as darkening skies, a sudden drop in temperature, an increase in wind, flashes of light and claps of thunder, and the sensation of an electric charge on one's hair or body. In the event of an electric storm, golfers should run into a forest, get under a shelter, get into a car, or assume the safest body position. To avoid being the tallest object in an area, if caught in open areas, golfers should find a low spot, spread out, and crouch into a curled position with feet together to create minimal body contact with the ground.

Point sentence

Particulars at midlevel on scale

Particulars at lower level on scale

—Passage from a safety article aimed at Florida golfers

Both of these passages are effective for their audience and purpose. Besides sensory details, writers can use other kinds of particulars that are low on the scale of abstraction such as quotations or statistics. Civil engineer David Rockwood uses low-on-the-scale numerical data about the size and number of wind towers to convince readers that wind generation of electricity entails environmental damage.

See Rockwood's letter to the editor, p. 7.

Other kinds of closed-form writing, however, often remain high on the scale. Yet even the most theoretical kind of prose will move back and forth between several layers on the scale. Your rhetorical decisions about level of abstraction are important because too much high-on-the-scale writing can become dull for readers, while too much low-on-the-scale writing can seem overwhelming or pointless. Each of the assignment chapters in Part 2 of this text gives advice on finding the right kinds and levels of particulars to support each essay.

FOR WRITING AND DISCUSSION

Choosing Details for Different Levels on the Scale of Abstraction

The following exercise will help you appreciate how details can be chosen at different levels of abstraction to serve different purposes and audiences. Working in small groups or as a whole class, invent details at appropriate positions on the scale of abstraction for each of the following point sentences.

(*continued*)

1. The big game was a major disappointment. You are writing an e-mail message to a friend who is a fan (of baseball, football, basketball, another sport) and missed the game; use midlevel details to explain what was disappointing.
2. Although the game stank, there were some great moments. Switch to low-on-the-scale details to describe one of these "great moments."
3. Advertising in women's fashion magazines creates a distorted and unhealthy view of beauty. You are writing an analysis for a college course on popular culture; use high-to-midlevel details to give a one-paragraph overview of several ways these ads create an unhealthy view of beauty.
4. One recent ad, in particular, conveys an especially destructive message about beauty. Choose a particular ad and describe it with low-on-the-scale details.
5. In U.S. politics, there are several key differences between Republicans and Democrats. As part of a service-learning project, you are creating a page on "American Politics" for a Web site aimed at helping international students understand American culture. Imagine a two-columned bulleted list contrasting Republicans and Democrats and construct two or three of these bullets. Choose details at an appropriate level on the scale of abstraction.
6. One look at Pete's pickup, and you knew immediately he was an in-your-face Republican (Democrat). You are writing a feature story for your college newspaper about Pete, a person who has plastered his pickup with political signs, bumper stickers, and symbols. Choose details at an appropriate level on the scale of abstraction.

Wordy Versus Streamlined Sentences: Cutting Deadwood to Highlight Your Ideas

We began our discussion of style by explaining how style, when effective, emphasizes what the writer deems important. During the drafting stage, writers often produce verbose passages that clutter their intended meaning with unnecessary words and roundabout expressions. These long, wordy sentences are not grammatically wrong, but they are rhetorically weak. They ask readers to wade through lots of extra words and phrases to figure out the writer's points. As experienced writers revise, they prune deadwood, combine sentences, and use other strategies to make their prose as efficient and economical as possible. Their aim is to create streamlined sentences that keep the reader on track. In essence, writers learn to cut out extra phrases and words—deadwood—to create direct, lively sentences. In the following examples, consider how cutting words creates a leaner, more streamlined style:

Wordy/Verbose	**Streamlined**
As a result of the labor policies established by Bismarck, the working-class people in Germany were convinced that revolution was unnecessary for the attainment of their goals and purposes.	Bismarck's labor policies convinced the German working class that revolution was unnecessary.
In recent times a new interest has been apparent among many writers to make the language as it is used by specialists in the areas of government, law, and medicine more available to be understood and appreciated by readers who are not specialists in the afore-mentioned areas.	Recently writers have tried to make the language of government, law, and medicine more accessible to nonspecialist readers.

Coordination Versus Subordination: Using Sentence Structure to Control Emphasis

Experienced writers often vary the length and structure of their sentences to emphasize main ideas. For example, a writer can emphasize an idea by placing it in a main clause or by placing it in a short sentence surrounded by longer sentences. We illustrated this phenomenon in Concept 8 in our discussion of the U. R. Riddle exercise, where variations in sentence structure created different emphases on Riddle's good or bad points:

> Although Riddle is a brilliant thinker, he had problems relating to other students in my class. (Emphasizes Riddle's personal shortcomings.)
>
> Although Riddle had problems relating to other students in my class, he is a brilliant thinker. (Emphasizes Riddle's intelligence.)

Neither of these effects would have been possible had the writer simply strung together two simple sentences.

> Riddle is a brilliant thinker. Riddle also had problems relating to other students in my class.

In this version, both points about Riddle are equally emphasized, leaving the reader confused about the writer's intended meaning.

Our point is that effective use of subordination can help writers emphasize main ideas. Stringing together a long sequence of short sentences—or simply joining them with coordinate conjunctions like *and, or, so,* or *but*—creates a choppy effect that fails to distinguish between more important and less important ideas. Each sentence gets equal emphasis whether or not the ideas in each sentence are equally important. Often a writer can sharpen the focus of a passage by subordinating some of the ideas. Consider the differences in the following examples.

Excessive Coordination	**Focused through Subordination**
Hisako usually attends each lab meeting. However, she missed the last one. She took the train to Boston to meet her sister. Her sister was arriving from Tokyo.	Although Hisako usually attends each lab meeting, she missed the last one because she took the train to Boston to meet her sister, who was arriving from Tokyo.
I am a student at Sycamore College, and I live in Watkins Hall. I am enclosing a proposal that concerns a problem with dorm life. There is too much drinking, so nondrinking students don't have an alcohol-free place to go, and so the university should create an alcohol-free dorm, and they should strictly enforce this no-alcohol policy.	As a Sycamore College student living in Watkins Hall, I am enclosing a proposal to improve dorm life. Because there is too much drinking on campus, there is no place for nondrinking students to go. I propose that the university create an alcohol-free dorm and strictly enforce the no-alcohol policy.

In the excessively coordinated sentences, each sentence or main clause gets equal emphasis, leaving the reader uncertain about the writer's main point. In the first example above, is the focus on Hisako's missing the lab meeting, on her taking the train to Boston, or on her sister's arriving from Tokyo? In the second example what is more important—the fact that the writer is a student at Sycamore College, that the writer lives in Watkins Hall, or that the writer is proposing a solution to a campus problem? In each case, the revised passage is easier to process because less important material is subordinated, focusing the reader's attention on main ideas. (The revision of the first passage offers an explanation for Hisako's missed lab meeting. The revision of the second passage emphasizes the campus problem and the proposed solution.)

Inflated Voice Versus a Natural Speaking Voice: Creating a Persona

College students often wonder what style—and particularly, what voice—is appropriate for college papers. For most college assignments, we recommend that you approximate your natural speaking voice to give your writing a conversational academic style. By "natural," we mean a voice that strives to be plain and clear while retaining the engaging quality of a person who is enthusiastic about the subject.

Of course, as you become an expert in a discipline, you often need to move toward a more scholarly voice. For example, the prose in an academic journal article can be extremely dense in its use of technical terms and complex sentence structure, but expert readers in that field understand and expect this voice. Students sometimes try to imitate a dense academic style before they have achieved the disciplinary expertise to make the style sound natural. The result can seem pretentiously stilted and phony—what we call here an "inflated" style. Writing with clarity and directness within your natural range will usually create a more effective and powerful voice. Consider the difference in the following examples:

Inflated Style

As people advance in age, they experience time-dependent alterations in their ability to adapt to environmental change. However, much prior research on the aging process has failed to differentiate between detrimental changes that result from an organism's aging process itself and detrimental changes resulting from a disease process that is often associated with aging.

Natural Speaking Voice Style

As people get older, they are less able to adapt to changes in their environment. Research on aging, however, hasn't always distinguished between loss of function due to aging itself and loss due to diseases common among older people.

Although the "natural voice" style is appropriate for most college papers, especially those written for lower-division courses, many professors construct assignments asking you to adopt different voices and different styles. It is important to understand the professor's assignment and to adopt the style and voice appropriate for the assigned rhetorical situation.

FOR WRITING AND DISCUSSION

Revising Passages to Create a More Effective Style

Working individually or in small groups, try to improve the style of the following passages by cutting deadwood, by combining sentences to eliminate excessive coordination, or by achieving a more natural speaking voice.

1. It is unfortunate that the mayor acted in this manner. The mayor settled the issue. But before he settled the issue he made a mistake. He fostered a public debate that was very bitter. The debate pitted some of his subordinates against each other. These subordinates were in fact key subordinates. It also caused many other people to feel inflamed passions and fears as a result of the way the mayor handled the issue.
2. Text production with an informative aim attempts to replicate essential information about what happened in a world event. An epitome of informative text production is a news story. Text production with a persuasive aim attempts to instigate a transformation in the reader's behaviors or systems of belief. An epitome of persuasive production is an op-ed piece.
3. Then my view of rap began to change. I started to listen to the female rappers introduced to me by my friends. One time was during my sophomore year. We were sent home from school because of a bomb threat. We danced to *The Miseducation of Lauryn Hill* in my living room. I liked what Lauryn was saying. Women hip-hop artists have something different to offer in a male-dominated industry. It has been women artists who converted me into a hip-hop fan. Some female rappers merely follow in the footsteps of male rappers. They do this by rapping about money, sex, or

(*continued*)

violence. The truly great female rappers do something different. They provide female listeners a sense of self-empowerment and identity. They provide a woman's perspective on many topics. They often create a hopeful message. This message counters the negativity of male rap. Through their songs, good female rappers spread positive, unique messages. These messages benefit not only African-Americans, but females of any race.

CONCEPT 12 Good writers make purposeful document design choices.

Document design sends readers strong rhetorical messages and offers writers rhetorical opportunities and constraints. Document design refers to the visual features of a text. The "look" of a document is closely bound to the rhetorical context, to the way writers seek to communicate with particular audiences for particular purposes, and to the audience's expectations for that genre of writing. In this section, we explain the main components of document design.

As a writer in an academic setting, you will usually be producing manuscript (typed pages of text) rather than a publication-ready document, and you will mainly be considering these features of document design: margins, font style and size, location of page numbers, and line spacing. As an academic writer, you generally produce manuscripts following the style guidelines of the Modern Language Association (MLA), the American Psychological Association (APA), or some other scholarly organization. In business and professional settings, you employ different kinds of manuscript conventions for writing letters, memoranda, or reports.

Attention to document design and the appearance of your manuscripts is an important part of academic writing. For example, in an academic article, the overt function of documentation and a bibliography is to enable other scholars to track down your cited sources. But a covert function is to create an air of authority for you, the writer, to assure readers that you have done your professional work and are fully knowledgeable and informed. Your image is also reflected in your manuscript's form, appearance, and editorial correctness. Sloppy or inappropriately formatted manuscripts, grammatical errors, misspelled words, and other problems hurt your *ethos* and send a message that you are unprofessional.

In contrast to manuscript, today's writers are sometimes asked to use desktop publishing software to produce camera-ready or Web-ready documents that have a professional visual appeal (such as a pamphlet or brochure, a Web page, a poster, a marketing proposal that incorporates visuals and graphics, or some other piece with a "professionally published" look). Occasionally in your manuscript documents, you may want to display ideas or information visually—for example, with graphs, tables, or images.

See Chapter 10 for suggestions about when and how to use graphics and tables.

The main components of document design are use of type, use of space and layout, use of color, and use of graphics or images.

Using Type

Type comes in different typeface styles, or fonts, that are commonly grouped in three font families: serif fonts that have tiny extensions on the letters, which make them easier to read in long documents; sans serif fonts that lack these extensions on the letters and are good for labels, headings, and Web documents; and specialty fonts, often used for decorative effect, that include script fonts and special symbols. Common word processing programs usually give you a huge array of fonts. Some examples of different fonts are shown in the chart on page 78.

Fonts also come in different sizes, measured in points (one point = 1/72 of an inch). Much type in printed texts is set in ten or twelve points. In addition, fonts can be formatted in different ways: boldface, italics, underlining, or shading.

Font style and size contribute to the readability and overall impression of a text. Scholarly publications use few, plain, and regular font styles that don't draw attention to the type. Their use of fonts seeks to keep the readers' focus on the content of the document, to convey a serious tone, and to maximize the readers' convenience in grappling with the ideas of the text. (Teachers regularly expect a conservative font such as CG Times, Times New Roman, or Courier New for academic papers. Were you to submit an academic paper in a specialty or scripted font, you'd make a "notice me" statement, analogous to wearing a lime green jumpsuit to a college reception.) In academic papers, boldface can be used for headings and italics can be used for occasional emphasis, but otherwise design flourishes are seldom used.

Popular magazines, on the other hand, tend to use fonts playfully and artistically, using a variety of fonts and sizes to attract readers' attention initially and to make a document look pleasingly decorative on the page. Although the body text of articles is usually the same font throughout, the opening page often uses a variety of fonts and sizes, and font variations may occur throughout the text to highlight key ideas for readers who are reading casually or rapidly.

Examples of Font Styles

Font Style	Font Name	Example
Serif fonts	Times New Roman	Have a good day!
	Courier New	Have a good day!
Sans serif fonts	Arial	Have a good day!
	Century Gothic	Have a good day!
Specialty fonts	Monotype Corsiva	*Have a good day!*
	Symbol	Ηαϖε α γοοδ δαψ!

Using Space and Laying Out Documents

Layout refers to how the text is formatted on the page. Layout includes the following elements:

- The size of the page itself
- The proportion of text to white space
- The arrangement of text on the page (single or multiple columns, long or short paragraphs, spaces between paragraphs)
- The size of the margins
- The use of justification (alignment of text with the left margin or both margins)
- The placement of titles
- The use of headings and subheadings to signal main and subordinate ideas and main parts of the document
- The spacing before and after headings
- The use of numbered or bulleted lists
- The use of boxes to highlight ideas or break text into visual units

Academic and scholarly writing calls for simple, highly functional document layouts. Most scholarly journals use single or double columns of text that are justified at both margins to create a regular, even look. (In preparing an academic manuscript, however, justify only the left-hand margin, leaving the right margin ragged.) Layout—particularly the presentation of titles and headings and the formatting of notes and bibliographic data—is determined by the style of the individual journal, which treats all articles identically. The layout of scholarly documents strikes a balance between maximizing the amount of text that fits on a page and ensuring readability by using headings and providing adequate white space in the margins.

In contrast, popular magazines place text in multiple columns that are often varied and broken up by text in boxes or by text wrapped around photos or drawings. Readability is important, but so is visual appeal and entertainment: Readers must enjoy looking at the pages. Many popular magazines try to blur the distinction between content and advertising so that ads become part of the visual appeal. This is why, in fashion magazines, the table of contents is often buried a dozen or more pages into the magazine. The publisher wants to coax readers to look at the ads as they look for the contents. (In contrast, the table of contents for most academic journals is on the cover.)

Using Color

Colors convey powerful messages and appeals, even affecting moods. While manuscripts are printed entirely in black ink, published documents often use color to identify and set off main ideas or important information. Color-tinted boxes can indicate special features or allow magazines to print different but related articles on the same page.

Academic and scholarly articles and books use color minimally, if at all, relying instead on different font styles and sizes to make distinctions in content. Popular magazines, on the other hand, use colors playfully, artistically, decoratively, and strategically to enhance their appeal and, thus, their sales. Different colors of type may be used for different articles within one magazine or within articles themselves. Some articles may be printed on colored paper to give variety to the whole magazine.

The rhetorical use of visuals is introduced in Chapter 3, Concept 10. More detailed discussion of tables and graphs is found in Chapter 10, pp. 252–255, and of drawings and photographs throughout Chapter 11.

Using Graphics and Images

Graphics include visual displays of information such as tables, line graphs, bar graphs, pie charts, maps, cartoons, illustrations, and photos.

As with the use of type, space, and color, the use of graphics indicates the focus, seriousness, function, and complexity of the writing. In scientific articles and books, many of the important findings of the articles may be displayed in complex, technical graphs and tables. Sources of information for these graphics are usually prominently stated, with key variables clearly labeled. In the humanities and social sciences, content-rich photos and drawings also tend to be vital parts of an article, even the subject of the analysis.

Popular magazines typically use simple numeric visuals (for example, a colorful pie chart or a dramatic graph) combined with decorative use of images, especially photos. If photos appear, it is worthwhile to consider how they are used. For example, do photos aim to look realistic and spontaneous like documentary photos of disaster scenes, sports moments, or people at work, or are they highly constructed, aesthetic photos? (Note that many political photos are meant to look spontaneous but are actually highly scripted—for example, a photograph of the president mending a fence with a horse nearby.) Are they concept (thematic) photos meant to illustrate an idea in an article (for example, a picture of a woman surrounded by images of pills, doctors, expensive medical equipment, and wrangling employers and insurance agents, to illustrate an article on health care costs)? The use of photos and illustrations can provide important clues about a publication's angle of vision, philosophy, or political leaning. For example, the *Utne Reader* tends to use many colored drawings rather than photos to illustrate its articles. These funky drawings with muted colors suit the magazine's liberal, socially progressive, and activist angle of vision.

Understanding the political slant of magazines, newspapers, and Web sites is essential for researchers. See Chapter 21, Skills 25 and 26.

Examples of Different Document Designs

As examples of different document designs, consider the opening pages of a scholarly article on flirting from *The Journal of Sex Research* (Figure 4.3) and a more popular article on flirting from *Psychology Today* (Figure 4.4) Discussion questions about the opening pages are in the For Writing and Discussion exercise that follows.

FIGURE 4.3 Opening Page from Article in *The Journal of Sex Research*

Sexual Messages on Television: Comparing Findings From Three Studies

Dale Kunkel, Kirstie M. Cope, and Erica Biely
University of California Santa Barbara

Television portrayals may contribute to the sexual socialization of children and adolescents, and therefore it is important to examine the patterns of sexual content presented on television. This report presents a summary view across three related studies of sexual messages on television. The content examined ranges from programs most popular with adolescents to a comprehensive, composite week sample of shows aired across the full range of broadcast and cable channels. The results across the three studies identify a number of consistent patterns in television's treatment of sexual content. Talk about sex and sexual behaviors are both found frequently across the television landscape, although talk about sex is more common. Most sexual behaviors tend to be precursory in nature (such as physical flirting and kissing), although intercourse is depicted or strongly implied in roughly one of every eight shows on television. Perhaps most importantly, the studies find that TV rarely presents messages about the risks or responsibilities associated with sexual behavior.

Sexual socialization is influenced by a wide range of sources, including parents, peers, and the mass media (Hyde & DeLameter, 1997). In trying to understand the process by which young people acquire their sexual beliefs, attitudes, and behaviors, the study of media provides information about potential socializing messages that are an important part of everyday life for children and adolescents (Greenberg, Brown, & Buerkel-Rothfuss, 1993). The significance of media content in this realm stems from a number of unique aspects surrounding its role in the lives of youth, including its early accessibility and its almost universal reach across the population.

Electronic media, and television in particular, provide a window to many parts of the world, such as sexually-related behavior, that would otherwise be shielded from young audiences. Long before many parents begin to discuss sex with their children, answers to such questions as "When is it OK to have sex?" and "With whom does one have sexual relations?" are provided by messages delivered on television. These messages are hardly didactic, most often coming in the form of scripts and plots in fictional entertainment programs. Yet the fact that such programs do not intend to teach sexual socialization lessons hardly mitigates the potential influence of their portrayals.

While television is certainly not the only influence on sexual socialization, adolescents often report that they use portrayals in the media to learn sexual and romantic scripts and norms for sexual behavior (Brown, Childers, & Waszak, 1990). Indeed, four out of ten (40%) teens say they have gained ideas for how to talk to their boyfriend or girlfriend about sexual issues directly from media portrayals (Kaiser Family Foundation, 1998).

Just as it is well established that media exposure influences social behaviors such as aggression and social stereotyping, there is a growing body of evidence documenting the possible effects of sexual content on television (Huston, Wartella, & Donnerstein, 1998). For example, two studies have reported correlations between watching television programs high in sexual content and the early initiation of sexual intercourse by adolescents (Brown & Newcomer, 1991; Peterson, Moore, & Furstenberg, 1991), while another found heavy television viewing to be predictive of negative attitudes toward remaining a virgin (Courtright & Baran, 1980). An experiment by Bryant and Rockwell (1994) showed that teens who had just viewed television dramas laden with sexual content rated descriptions of casual sexual encounters less negatively than teens who had not viewed any sexual material.

Another important aspect of sexual socialization involves the development of knowledge about appropriate preventative behaviors to reduce the risk of infection from AIDS or other sexually-transmitted diseases. When teenagers begin to engage in sexual activity, they assume the risk of disease as well as the risk of unwanted pregnancy, and it appears that many lack adequate preparation to avoid such negative consequences.

Two Americans under the age of 20 become infected with HIV every hour (Office of National AIDS Policy, 1996). Almost one million teenagers become pregnant every year in the United States (Kirby, 1997). In the face of these sobering statistics, it is important to consider the extent to which media portrayals engage in or overlook concerns such as these, which are very serious issues in the lives of young people today.

In summary, media effects research clearly suggests that television portrayals contribute to sexual socialization.

The Family Hour Study was supported by the Henry J. Kaiser Family Foundation (Menlo Park, CA) and Children Now (Oakland, CA). The Teen Study was the Master's Thesis for Kirstie M. Cope. The V-Chip Study was supported by the Henry J. Kaiser Family Foundation. The authors wish to thank Carolyn Colvin, Ed Donnerstein, Wendy Jo Farinola, Ulla Foehr, Jim Potter, Vicky Rideout, and Emma Rollin, each of whom made significant contributions to one or more of the studies summarized here.

Address correspondence to Dr. Dale Kunkel, Department of Communication, University of California Santa Barbara, Santa Barbara, CA 93106: e-mail: kunkel@ahshaw.ucsb.edu.

The Journal of Sex Research Volume 36, Number 3, August 1999: pp. 230–236 230

FIGURE 4.4 Opening Page from Article in *Psychology Today*

THE NEW

Flirting Game

IT MAY BE AN AGES-OLD, BIOLOGICALLY-DRIVEN ACTIVITY, BUT TODAY IT'S ALSO PLAYED WITH ARTFUL SELF-AWARENESS AND EVEN CONSCIOUS CALCULATION.

By Deborah A. Lott

To hear the evolutionary determinists tell it, we human beings flirt to propagate our genes and to display our genetic worth. Men are constitutionally predisposed to flirt with the healthiest, most fertile women, recognizable by their biologically correct waist-hip ratios. Women favor the guys with dominant demeanors, throbbing muscles and the most resources to invest in them and their offspring.

Looked at up close, human psychology is more diverse and perverse than the evolutionary determinists would have it. We flirt as thinking individuals in a particular culture at a particular time. Yes, we may express a repertoire of hardwired non-verbal expressions and behaviors—staring eyes, flashing brows, opened palms—that resemble those of other animals, but unlike other animals, we also flirt with conscious calculation. We have been known to practice our techniques in front of the mirror. In other words, flirting among human beings is culturally modulated as well as biologically driven, as much art as instinct.

In our culture today, it's clear that we do not always choose as the object of our desire those people the evolutionists might deem the most biologically desirable. After all, many young women today find the pale, androgynous, scarcely muscled yet emotionally expressive Leonardo DiCaprio more appealing than the burly Tarzans (Arnold Schwartzenegger, Bruce Willis, etc.) of action movies. Woody Allen may look nerdy but he's had no trouble winning women—and that's not just because he has material resources, but because humor is also a precious cultural commodity. Though she has no breasts or hips to speak of, Ally McBeal still attracts because there's ample evidence of a quick and quirky mind.

In short, we flirt with the intent of assessing potential lifetime partners, we flirt to have easy, no-strings-attached sex, and we flirt when we are not looking for either. We flirt because, most simply, flirtation can be a liberating form of play, a game with suspense and ambiguities that brings joys of its own. As Philadelphia-based social psychologist Tim Perper says, "Some flirters appear to want to prolong the interaction because it's pleasurable and erotic in its own right, regardless of where it might lead."

Here are some of the ways the game is currently being played.

TAKING The Lead

When it comes to flirting today, women aren't waiting around for men to make the advances. They're taking the lead. Psychologist Monica Moore, Ph.D. of Webster University in St. Louis, Missouri, has spent more than 2000 hours observing women's flirting maneuvers in restaurants, singles bars and at parties. According to her findings, women give non-verbal cues that get a flirtation rolling fully two-thirds of the time. A man may think he's making the first move because he is the one to literally move from wherever he is to the woman's side, but usually he has been summoned.

By the standards set out by evolutionary psychologists, the women who attract the most

42 PHOTOGRAPHY BY FRANK VERONSKY

Psychology Today November/December 1998

FOR WRITING AND DISCUSSION

Analyzing Rhetorical Effect

Working individually or in small groups, analyze how content, style, genre, and document design are interrelated in these articles.

1. How does the document design of each article—its use of fonts, layout, color, and graphics—identify each piece as a scholarly article or an article in a popular magazine? From your own observation, what are typical differences in the document design features of an academic article and a popular magazine article?
2. What makes the style and document design of each article appropriate for its intended audience and purpose?
3. What is the function of the abstract (article summary) at the beginning of the academic journal article? What is the function of the large-font "leads" at the beginning of popular articles?
4. Consider the photograph in the *Psychology Today* article shown in Figure 4.4. Is it a realistic, candid "documentary" photo? Is it a scripted photo? Is it a concept photo aimed at illustrating the article's thesis or question? What aspects of the *Psychology Today* photo appeal to psychological themes and interests and make it appropriate for the content, audience, and genre of the article? Why do you think a magazine like *Psychology Today* would devote so much space to a photograph?
5. When you download an article from an electronic database (unless it is in pdf format), you often lose visual cues about the article's genre such as document design, visuals, and so forth. Even when an article is in pdf format, you lose cues about its original print context—the kind of magazine or journal the article appeared in, the magazine's layout and advertisements, and its targeted audience. How do these visual cues in the original print version of an article provide important contextual information for reading the article and using it in your own research? Why do experienced researchers prefer the original print version of articles rather than downloaded articles whenever possible?

Chapter Summary

This chapter has expanded your awareness of rhetorical choices by focusing your attention on style and document design.

- Four main factors contribute to a writer's style: word choice, sentence structure, voice or persona, and tone. Writers create different styles to fit different rhetorical contexts. We also examined the rhetorical effects of moving up and down the scale of abstraction, of cutting deadwood from verbose passages, of using coordination and subordination to emphasize main ideas, and of adopting a natural speaking voice style in your writing.

- Document design contributes to your *ethos* as a writer and to the rhetorical effectiveness of your writing. We have shown how type, space, layout, color, and graphics create different rhetorical effects suitable to your particular audience, purpose, and genre.

Converting a Passage from Scientific to Popular Style

BRIEF WRITING PROJECT

This assignment asks you to try your hand at translating a piece of writing from one rhetorical context to another. As background, you need to know that sometimes *Reader's Digest* includes a section called "News from the World of Medicine," which contains one or more mini-articles reporting on recent medical research. The writers of these pieces scan articles in medical journals, select items of potential interest to the general public, and translate them from a formal, scientific style into a popular style. Here is a typical example of a *Reader's Digest* mini-article:

COMPLETE ARTICLE FROM *READER'S DIGEST*

"For Teeth, Say Cheese," Penny Parker

Cheese could be one secret of a healthy, cavity-free smile, according to a recent study by a professor of dentistry at the University of Alberta in Edmonton, Canada.

In the study, John Hargreaves found that eating a piece of hard cheese the size of a sugar cube at the end of a meal can retard tooth decay. The calcium and phosphate present in the cheese mix with saliva and linger on the surface of the teeth for up to two hours, providing protection against acid attacks from sweet food or drink.

Now compare this style with the formal scientific style in the following excerpts, the introduction and conclusion of an article published in the *New England Journal of Medicine*.

EXCERPT FROM SCIENTIFIC ARTICLE IN A MEDICAL JOURNAL.

From "Aspirin as an Antiplatelet Drug," Carlo Patrono

Introduction: The past 10 years have witnessed major changes in our understanding of the pathophysiologic mechanisms underlying vascular occlusion and considerable progress in the clinical assessment of aspirin and other antiplatelet agents. The purpose of this review is to describe a rational basis for antithrombotic prophylaxis and treatment with aspirin. Basic information on the molecular mechanism of action of aspirin in inhibiting platelet function will be integrated with the appropriate clinical pharmacologic data and the results of randomized clinical trials. ...

Conclusions: Aspirin reduces the incidence of occlusive cardiovascular events in patients at variable risk for these events. Progress in our understanding of the molecular mechanism of the action of aspirin, clarification of the clinical pharmacology of its effects on platelets, and clinical testing of its efficacy at low doses have contributed to a downward trend in its recommended daily dose. The present recommendation of a single loading dose of 200–300 mg followed by a daily dose of 75–100 mg is based on findings that this dose is as clinically efficacious as higher doses and is safer than higher doses. The satisfactory safety profile of low-dose aspirin has led to ongoing trials of the efficacy of a combination of aspirin and low-intensity oral anti-coagulants in high-risk patients. Finally, the efficacy of a cheap drug such as aspirin in preventing one fifth to one third of all important cardiovascular events should not discourage the pharmaceutical industry from attempting to develop more effective antithrombotic drugs, since a sizeable proportion of these events continue to occur despite currently available therapy.

Assume that you are a writer of mini-articles for the medical news section of *Reader's Digest*. Translate the findings reported in the article on aspirin into a *Reader's Digest* mini-article.

Although the style of the medical article may seem daunting at first, a little work with a good dictionary will help you decipher the whole passage. We've reproduced excerpts from the article's introduction and all of the final section labeled "Conclusions." These two sections provide all the information you need for your mini-article.

For additional writing, reading, and research resources, go to **www.MyCompLab.com** and choose **Ramage/Bean/Johnson's *The Allyn & Bacon Guide to Writing,* Fifth Edition.**

PART

2

WRITING PROJECTS

This ad for the United States Army highlights qualities traditionally associated with patriotic military service to the country: respect, honor, and courage. Note that this poster does not depict soldiers in uniform on a battlefield or in the midst of a drill. Consider the way the images of the father and daughter and the words in this ad connect character-building, family relationships, the Army, and success. Think about how gender functions in this ad by focusing on the young woman's long hair, tasteful makeup, and earnest manner. This advertisement is part of a For Writing and Discussion exercise in Chapter 11.

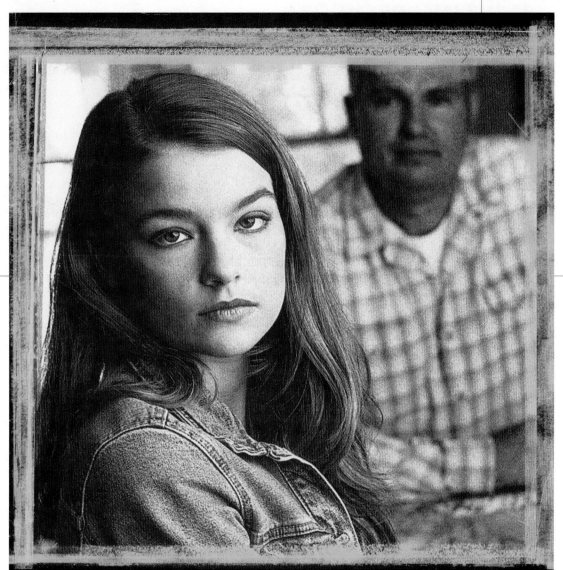

YOU TAUGHT HER ABOUT RESPECT, HONOR AND COURAGE. IS IT ANY SURPRISE THAT NOW SHE WANTS TO USE THEM?

She'll experience the most challenging training, use the latest technology and get the strongest support. Every drill and every mission will reinforce in her that character always leads to success. Encourage her to consider becoming a Soldier – AN ARMY OF ONE.®

AN ARMY OF ONE®

GOARMY.COM

PART 2 WRITING PROJECTS

Council of Writing Program Administrators Outcomes for First-Year Composition

RHETORICAL KNOWLEDGE	• Focus on a purpose: • To learn (Ch. 5, 6) • To explore (Ch. 7, 8) • To inform (Ch. 9) • To analyze/synthesize (Ch. 10–13) • To persuade (Ch. 14–16) • Respond to the needs of different audiences • Respond appropriately to different kinds of rhetorical situations • Use conventions of format and structure appropriate to the rhetorical situation • Adopt appropriate voice, tone, and level of formality • Understand how genres shape reading and writing (Readings and Thinking Critically activities) • Write in several genres: • Two Descriptions with a Reflection (Ch. 5) • Summary and Strong Response (Ch. 6) • Autobiographical Narrative, Literacy Narrative (Ch. 7) • Exploratory Essay, Annotated Bibliography (Ch. 8) • Set of Instructions, Informative Workplace Report, Informative and Surprising Article (Ch. 9) • Empirical Research Report, Scientific Poster (Ch. 10) • Analysis of Two Visual Texts (Ch. 11) • Analysis of a Short Story (Ch. 12) • Synthesis Essay (Ch. 13) • Classical Argument (Ch. 14) • Evaluation Argument (Ch. 15) • Proposal Argument, Advocacy Ad or Poster, Proposal Speech with Visual Aids (Ch. 16)
CRITICAL THINKING, READING, AND WRITING	• Use writing and reading for inquiry, learning, thinking, and communicating (Exploratory activities, For Writing and Discussion activities, Readings, and Thinking Critically activities) • Understand a writing assignment as a series of tasks, including finding, evaluating, analyzing, and synthesizing appropriate primary and secondary sources • Integrate their own ideas with those of others (Ch. 6, Summary/Strong Response; Ch. 8, Exploratory Essay; Ch. 13, Synthesis Essay; Ch. 14–16, Arguments)
PROCESSES	• Be aware that it usually takes multiple drafts to create a successful text • Develop flexible strategies for generating, revising, editing, and proofreading • Understand writing as an open process that permits writers to use later invention and re-thinking to revise their work • Understand the collaborative and social aspects of writing processes (Ch. 10, team writing; For Writing and Discussion activities, Questions for Peer Review) • Learn to critique their own and others' work (Questions for Peer Review) • Learn to balance the advantages of relying on others with the responsibility of doing their part (Ch. 10, team writing) • Use a variety of technologies to address a range of audiences (Ch. 10, Scientific Poster; Ch. 16, Advocacy Ad, Proposal Speech with Visual Aids)
KNOWLEDGE OF CONVENTIONS	• Develop knowledge of genre conventions ranging from structure and paragraphing to tone and mechanics • Practice appropriate means of documenting their work (Ch. 6, Summary/Strong Response; Ch. 8, Exploratory Essay, Annotated Bibliography; Ch. 10, Empirical Research Report; Ch. 13, Synthesis Essay; Ch. 14–16, Arguments)
COMPOSING IN ELECTRONIC ENVIRONMENTS	• Understand and exploit the differences in the rhetorical strategies and in the affordances available for both print and electronic composing processes and texts (Ch. 9, Desktop-published Article; Ch. 10, Scientific Poster; Ch. 16, Advocacy Ad, Proposal Speech with Visual Aids)

SEEING RHETORICALLY
The Writer as Observer

CHAPTER 5

In this chapter you will learn to write a description of a scene using sensory details to appeal to sight, sound, touch, smell, and even taste. You will also engage the important rhetorical concept "angle of vision" that we introduced in Chapter 3 (Concept 8). If you have written descriptions, you may have imagined that you were creating a true, accurate, and objective description of your scene. But consider what happens to a description assignment if we give it a rhetorical twist. Suppose we asked you to write *two* descriptions of the same scene from two different perspectives (caused, say, by different purposes or moods) and then to analyze how the two descriptions differ. We could then ask you to reflect on the extent to which any description of a scene is objective as opposed to being shaped by the author's selection of details, choice of words, and other factors. You would then be thinking rhetorically about how words create certain effects.

Our goal is to help you understand more fully the rhetorical concept of "angle of vision." The writing assignment for this chapter will ask you to create

- two contrasting (but equally factual) descriptions of the same scene and then to write a short self-reflection about what you learned about angle of vision from this rhetorical experiment.

This "writing-to-learn" assignment will teach you some principles of good descriptive writing while also showing you some of the subtle ways that language and perception are interconnected.

Exploring Rhetorical Observation

One of the intense national debates of the last decade has been whether the federal government should permit oil exploration in the Coastal Plain of the Arctic National Wildlife Refuge (ANWR). Arguments for and against drilling in the ANWR have regularly appeared in newspapers, magazines, blogs, and advocacy Web sites. Nearly every argument contains descriptions of the ANWR that operate rhetorically to advance the writer's position. In the following two exercises, we ask you to analyze the angle of vision of several verbal or visual texts.

Exercise One

The following passages—one from a pro-exploration advocacy group called Arctic Power and one from former President Jimmy Carter—show two different ways that the ANWR can be described. Read the two descriptions and then proceed to the questions that follow.

ARCTIC POWER'S DESCRIPTION OF THE ANWR

These facts [about ANWR] are not as pretty or as emotionally appealing [as the descriptions of ANWR by anti-exploration writers]. But they are important for anyone involved in the ANWR debate. On the coastal plain, the Arctic winter lasts for 9 months. It is dark continuously for 56 days in midwinter. Temperatures with the wind chill can reach –110 degrees F. It's not pristine. There are villages, roads, houses, schools, and military installations. It's not a unique Arctic ecosystem. The coastal plain is only a small fraction of the 88,000 square miles that make up the North Slope. The same tundra environment and wildlife can be found throughout the circumpolar Arctic regions. The 1002 Area [the legal term for the plot of coastal plain being contested] is flat. That's why they call it a plain. [...]

Some groups want to make the 1002 Area a wilderness. But a vote for wilderness is a vote against American jobs.

JIMMY CARTER'S DESCRIPTION OF THE ANWR

Rosalynn [Carter's wife] and I always look for opportunities to visit parks and wildlife areas in our travels. But nothing matches the spectacle of wildlife we found on the coastal plain of America's Arctic National Wildlife Refuge in Alaska. To the north lay the Arctic Ocean; to the south rolling foothills rose toward the glaciated peaks of the Brooks Range. At our feet was a mat of low tundra plant life, bursting with new growth, perched atop the permafrost.

As we watched, 80,000 caribou surged across the vast expanse around us. Called by instinct older than history, this Porcupine (River) caribou herd was in the midst of its annual migration. To witness this vast sea of caribou in an uncorrupted wilderness home, and the wolves, ptarmigan, grizzlies, polar bears, musk oxen and millions of migratory birds, was a profoundly humbling experience. We were reminded of our human dependence on the natural world.

Sadly, we were also forced to imagine what we might see if the caribou were replaced by smoke-belching oil rigs, highways and a pipeline that would destroy forever the plain's delicate and precious ecosystem.

Working as a whole class or in small groups, address the following questions:

1. How do the different descriptions create an angle of vision that serves the political interests of each party? (Hint: How does the Arctic Power description make the ANWR seem like a favorable place to drill for oil? How does Carter's description make it seem like an unfavorable place to drill for oil? What does each writer see and not see?)
2. Assuming that both the Arctic Power and the Carter descriptions are factually accurate, how do they achieve different rhetorical effects?
3. Why does Arctic Power refer to the ANWR as "the 1002 area" while Carter refers to it as "a precious ecosytem"? Why does Carter not mention "villages, roads, housing, schools, and military installations" (noted by Arctic Power)? Why does Arctic Power not mention "this vast sea of caribou" (noted by Carter)?
4. Why does Carter imagine "smoke-belching oil rigs, highways, and pipelines" replacing the caribou while Arctic Power imagines "American jobs"?

Exercise Two

What follows are three North Alaskan photographs. Observe the photographs and then discuss the questions that follow.

FIGURE 5.1 Polar Bear with Cubs

FIGURE 5.2 Caribou and Truck

FIGURE 5.3 ANWR Coastal Plain

1. Suppose that you are a publicity writer for an oil company. You need to create a pamphlet or Web page arguing that the ANWR should be opened for oil drilling. Which photograph or photographs would you choose for your document? Why?
2. Suppose that you are opposed to oil drilling. Which photograph or photographs make a visual claim against oil drilling?

Exercise Three

Figure 5.4 is a page from a pamphlet produced by Arctic Power, an advocacy group in favor of drilling for oil. The pamphlet's text is accompanied by a photograph labeled "Wildlife grow accustomed to oil operations at Prudhoe Bay." (We accessed this pamphlet through the organization's Web site.) Observe the photograph, read the text, and then address the questions that follow.

1. How does the text in this pamphlet create an angle of vision supportive of oil drilling? What details about the ANWR are included in this passage? What details are omitted?
2. Why did the pamphlet makers choose the photograph of bears on a pipeline? What is the visual claim of the photograph? For the pamphlet maker's purpose, how might this photograph be more rhetorically effective than any of the photographs shown in Figures 5.1, 5.2, and 5.3? (Hint: How does the photograph address concerns of environmentalists?)

FIGURE 5.4 Pamphlet Page from the Arctic Power Advocacy Group

Wildlife grow accustomed to oil operations at Prudhoe Bay.

ANWR has the nation's best potential for major additions to U.S. oil supplies

Most geologists think the Coastal Plain of the Artic National Wildlife Refuge has the best prospects for major additions to U.S. domestic oil supply. This is the part of ANWR set aside by Congress in 1980 for further study of its petroleum potential. There is a good chance that very large oil and gas fields, equal to the amount found at Prudhoe Bay further west, could be discovered in ANWR's coastal plain.

The Coastal Plain has very attractive geology and lies between areas of the Alaska North Slope and the Canadian Beaufort Sea where there have been major oil and gas discoveries. Oil and gas deposits have been discovered near ANWR's western border, and a recent oil discovery may result in the first pipeline built to the western boundary of the Coastal Plain.

Although the Coastal Plain was reserved for study of its oil potential, Congress must act to open it for oil and gas exploration. Alaskans and residents of the North Slope, including the Inupiat community of Kaktovik, within ANWR, widely support exploring the Coastal Plain.

Understanding Observational Writing

In this section, we elaborate on the concept of angle of vision, showing how previous knowledge, cultural background, interests, and values influence perceptions. We'll also show you some ways to analyze a passage rhetorically.

Why "Seeing" Isn't a Simple Matter

On the face of it, terms such as *observation, perception,* and *seeing* seem nonproblematic. Objects are objects, and the process of perceiving an object is immediate and automatic. However, perception is never a simple matter. Consider what we call "the expert-novice phenomenon": Experts on any given subject notice details about that subject that the novice overlooks. An experienced bird-watcher can distinguish dozens of kinds of swallows by subtle differences in size, markings, and behaviors, whereas a non-bird-watcher sees only a group of birds of similar size and shape. Similarly, people observing an unfamiliar game (for example, an American watching cricket or a Nigerian watching baseball) don't know what actions or events have meaning and, hence, don't know what to look for.

In addition to prior knowledge, cultural differences affect perception. An American watching two Japanese business executives greet each other might not know that they are participating in an elaborate cultural code of bowing, eye contact, speech patterns, and timing of movements that convey meanings about social status. An Ethiopian newly arrived in the United States and an American sitting in a doctor's office will see different things when the nurse points to one of them to come into the examination room: The American notices nothing remarkable about the scene; he or she may remember what the nurse was wearing or something about the wallpaper. The Ethiopian, on the other hand, is likely to remember the nurse's act of pointing, a gesture of rudeness used in Ethiopia only to beckon children or discipline dogs. Again, observers of the same scene see different things.

Your beliefs and values can also shape your perceptions, often creating blind spots. You might not notice data that conflict with your beliefs and values. Or you might perceive contradictory data at some level, but if they don't register in your mind as significant, you disregard them. Consider, for example, how advocates of gun control focus on a child's being accidentally killed because the child found a loaded firearm in Dad's sock drawer, while opponents of gun control focus on burglaries or rapes being averted because the home owner had a pistol by the bedside. The lesson here is that people note and remember whatever is consistent with their worldview much more readily than they note and remember inconsistencies. What you believe is what you see.

Another factor determining what you see is mood. When people are upbeat they tend to see things through "rose-colored glasses"—a cliché with a built-in reference to angle of vision. When you are in a good mood, you see the flowers in a meadow. When you are depressed, you see the discarded wrappers from someone's pack of gum.

More direct and overt is the influence of rhetorical purpose. Consider again the case of the Arctic National Wildlife Refuge mentioned earlier in this chapter. Jimmy Carter's view of the ANWR as a "spectacle of wildlife" is juxtaposed against Arctic Power's view of the ANWR as a "flat" plain where "the Arctic winter lasts for 9 months." Note how each way of seeing the ANWR serves the political purposes of the author. Opponents of oil exploration focus on the unspoiled beauty of the land, listing fondly the names of different kinds of animals that live there. What remains "unseen" in their descriptions are the native villages and military installations on the Coastal Plain and any references to economic issues, the U.S. need for domestic oil, or jobs. In contrast, supporters of oil exploration shift the focus from the caribou herds (their descriptions don't "see" the animals), to the bleak and frigid landscape and the native communities that would benefit from jobs.

This example suggests the ethical dimension of description. Rhetorical purpose entails responsibility. All observers must accept responsibility for what they see and for what they make others see because their descriptions can have real-world consequences—for example, no jobs for a group of people or potential harm to an animal species and an ecosystem. We should reiterate, however, that neither perspective on the ANWR is necessarily dishonest; each is true in a limited way. In any description, writers necessarily—whether consciously or unconsciously—include some details and exclude others. But the writer's intent is nevertheless to influence the reader's way of thinking about the described phenomenon, and ethical readers must be aware of what is happening. By noting what is *not there,* readers can identify a piece's angle of vision and analyze it. The reader can see the piece of writing not as the whole truth but as one person's perspective that can seem like the whole truth if one simply succumbs to the text's rhetorical power.

Finally, let's look at one more important factor that determines angle of vision—what we might call a writer's "guiding ideology" or "belief system." We touched on this point earlier when we showed how one's belief system can create blind spots. Let's examine this phenomenon in more depth by seeing how different beliefs about the role of women in primitive societies cause two anthropologists to describe a scene in different ways. What follows are excerpts from the works of two female anthropologists studying the role of women in the !Kung tribe* of the African Kalahari Desert (sometimes called the "Bushmen"). Anthropologists have long been interested in the !Kung because they still hunt and forage for food in the manner of their prehistoric ancestors.

Here is how anthropologist Lorna Marshal describes !Kung women's work:

MARSHAL'S DESCRIPTION

Women bring most of the daily food that sustains the life of the people, but the roots and berries that are the principal plant foods of the Nyae Nyae !Kung are apt to be tasteless, harsh and not very satisfying. People crave meat. Furthermore, there is only drudgery in digging roots, picking berries, and trudging back to the encampment with heavy loads and babies sagging in the pouches of the karosses: there is no splendid excitement and triumph in returning with vegetables.

—Lorna Marshal, *The !Kung of Nyae Nyae*

And here is how a second anthropologist describes women's work:

DRAPER'S DESCRIPTION

A common sight in the late afternoon is clusters of children standing on the edge of camp, scanning the bush with shaded eyes to see if the returning women are visible. When the slow-moving file of women is finally discerned in the distance, the

*The word *!Kung* is preceded by an exclamation point in scholarly work to indicate the unique clicking sound of the language.

children leap and exclaim. As the women draw closer, the children speculate as to which figure is whose mother and what the women are carrying in the karosses. [...]

!Kung women impress one as a self-contained people with a high sense of self-esteem. There are exceptions—women who seem forlorn and weary—but for the most part, !Kung women are vivacious and self-confident. Small groups of women forage in the kalahari at distances of eight to ten miles from home with no thought that they need the protection of the men or of the men's weapons should they encounter any of the several large predators that also inhabit the Kalahari.

—P. Draper, "!Kung Women: Contrasts in Sexual Egalitarianism in Foraging and Sedentary Contexts"

As you can see, these two anthropologists "read" the !Kung society in remarkably different ways. Marshal's thesis is that !Kung women are a subservient class relegated to the heavy, dull, and largely thankless task of gathering vegetables. In contrast, Draper believes that women's work is more interesting and requires more skill than other anthropologists have realized. Her thesis is that there is an egalitarian relationship between men and women in the !Kung society.

The source of data for both anthropologists is careful observation of !Kung women's daily lives. But the anthropologists are clearly not seeing the same thing. When the !Kung women return from the bush at the end of the day, Marshal sees their heavy loads and babies sagging in their pouches, whereas Draper sees the excited children awaiting the women's return.

So which view is correct? That's a little like asking whether the ANWR is an "unspoiled wilderness" or a "bleak and forbidding land." If you believe that women play an important role in !Kung society, you "see" the children eagerly awaiting the women's return at the end of the day, and you note the women's courage in foraging for vegetables "eight to ten miles from home." If you believe that women are basically drudges in this culture, then you "see" the heavy loads and babies sagging in the pouches of the karosses. The details of the scene, in other words, are filtered through the observer's interpretive screen.

How to Analyze a Text Rhetorically

Our discussion of two different views of the ANWR and two different views of the role of women in !Kung society shows how a seemingly objective description of a scene reflects a specific angle of vision that can be revealed through analysis. Rhetorically, a description subtly persuades the reader toward the author's angle of vision. This angle of vision isn't necessarily the author's "true self" speaking, for authors *create* an angle of vision through the rhetorical choices they make while composing. We hope you will discover this insight for yourself while doing the assignment for this chapter.

For a more complete explanation of these five strategies, see the discussion of how an angle of vision is constructed in Chapter 3, Concept 8.

In this section we describe five textual strategies writers often use (consciously or unconsciously) to create the persuasive effect of their texts. By analyzing a writer's use of these strategies, you can uncover the writer's angle of vision. Each strategy creates textual effects that you can discuss in your rhetorical analysis.

STRATEGIES

Writers Use to Create a Persuasive Effect	
Strategies	**Examples of How Writers Use the Strategies**
1. State your meaning or intended effect directly.	The first anthropologist, Marshal, says that "there is only drudgery in digging roots," casting her view in negative terms. The second anthropologist, Draper, says, "!Kung women impress one as a self-contained people with a high sense of self-esteem," announcing a more positive perspective.
2. Select details that convey your intended effect and omit those that don't.	Marshal selects details about the tastelessness of the vegetables and the heaviness of the women's loads, creating an impression that women's work is thankless and exhausting. Draper selects details about the excitement of the children awaiting their mothers' return and the fearlessness of the mothers as they forage "eight to ten miles from home," creating an impression of self-reliant women performing an essential task.
3. Choose words with connotations that convey your intended effect.	Marshal chooses words connoting listlessness and fatigue such as *drudgery, trudging, heavy,* and *sagging.* Draper chooses words connoting energy: The children *scan* the bush, *leap and exclaim,* and *speculate,* while the women *forage.*
4. Use figurative language (metaphors, similes, and analogies) that conveys your intended effect.	One writer opposing oil drilling in the ANWR says that oil companies are "salivating" for new oil-drilling opportunities. He equates oil companies with drooling dogs, giving readers an unpleasant vision of the oil companies' eagerness to get at the ANWR's oil reserves.
5. Use sentence structure to emphasize and de-emphasize your ideas.	Marshal uses sentence structure to create a negative impression of the !Kung women's plant-gathering role: Women bring most of the daily food that sustains the life of the people, but the roots and berries that are the principal plant foods of the Nyae Nyae !Kung are apt to be tasteless, harsh and not very satisfying. People crave meat. The short sentence following the long sentence receives the most emphasis, giving readers the impression that meat is more important than the women's vegetables.

FOR WRITING AND DISCUSSION

Analyzing Descriptions

What follows is a student example of two contrasting descriptions written for the assignment in this chapter. Working individually, analyze the descriptions rhetorically to explain how the writer has created contrasting impressions through overt statements of meaning, selection and omission of details, word choice, figurative language, and sentence structure. Spend approximately ten minutes freewriting your analysis. Then, working in small groups or as a whole class, share your analyses, trying to reach agreement on examples of how the writer has created different rhetorical effects by using the five strategies just described.

DESCRIPTION 1—POSITIVE EFFECT

Light rain gently drops into the puddles that have formed along the curb as I look out my apartment window at the corner of 14th and East John. Pedestrians layered in sweaters, raincoats, and scarves and guarded with shiny rubber boots and colorful umbrellas sip their steaming hot triple-tall lattes. Some share smiles and pleasant exchanges as they hurry down the street, hastening to work where it is warm and dry. Others, smelling the aroma of French roast espresso coming from the coffee bar next to the bus stop, listen for the familiar rumbling sound that will mean the 56 bus has arrived Radiant orange, yellow, and red leaves blanket the sidewalk in the areas next to the maple trees that line the road. Along the curb a mother holds the hand of her toddler, dressed like a miniature tugboat captain in yellow raincoat and pants, who splashes happily in a puddle.

DESCRIPTION 2—NEGATIVE EFFECT

A solemn grayness hangs in the air, as I peer out the window of my apartment at the corner of 14th and East John. A steady drizzle of rain leaves boot-drenching puddles for pedestrians to avoid. Bundled in rubber boots, sweaters, coats, and rain-soaked scarves, commuters clutch Styrofoam cups of coffee as a defense against the biting cold. They lift their heads every so often to take a small sip of caffeine, but look sleep-swollen nevertheless. Pedestrians hurry past each other, moving quickly to get away from the dismal weather, the dull grayness. Some nod a brief hello to a familiar face, but most clutch their overcoats and tread grimly on, looking to avoid puddles or spray from passing cars. Others stand at the bus stop, hunched over, waiting in the drab early morning for the smell of diesel that means the 56 bus has arrived. Along the curb an impatient mother jerks the hand of a toddler to keep him from stomping in an oil-streaked puddle.

WRITING PROJECT

Two Contrasting Descriptions of the Same Place and a Self-Reflection

Your writing project for this chapter is to write two descriptions and a reflection. The assignment has two parts:*

*For this assignment, we are indebted to two sources: (1) Richard Braddock, *A Little Casebook in the Rhetoric of Writing* (Englewood Cliffs, NJ: Prentice-Hall, 1971); and (2) Kenneth Dowst, "Kenneth Dowst's Assignment," *What Makes Writing Good?* Eds. William E. Coles, Jr., and James Vopat (Lexington, MA: D. C. Heath, 1985), pp. 52–57).

Part A: Find an indoor or outdoor place where you can sit and observe for fifteen or twenty minutes in preparation for writing a focused description of the scene that will enable your readers to see what you see. Here is the catch: You are to write *two* descriptions of the scene. Your first description must convey a favorable impression of the scene, making it appear pleasing or attractive. The second description must convey a negative, or unfavorable, impression, making the scene appear unpleasant or unattractive. Both descriptions must contain only factual details and must describe exactly the same scene from the same location at the same time. It's not fair, in other words, to describe the scene in sunny weather and then in the rain or otherwise to alter factual details. Each description should be one paragraph long (approximately 125–175 words).

Part B: Self-Reflection on What You Learned (300–400 words): Attach to your two descriptions a self-reflection about what you have learned from doing this assignment. This self-reflection should include your own rhetorical analysis of your two descriptions and explain some of the insights you have gained into the concepts of "angle of vision" and "seeing rhetorically."

Part A of the assignment asks you to describe the same scene in two different ways, giving your first description a positive tone and the second description a negative one. You can choose from any number of scenes: the lobby of a dormitory or apartment building, a view from a park bench or a window, a favorite (or disliked) room, a scene at your workplace, a busy street, a local eating or drinking spot, whatever. Part B of the assignment asks you to write a self-reflection in which you do a rhetorical analysis of your two descriptions and explore what you have learned from this exercise about seeing rhetorically. Because this assignment results in a thought exercise rather than in a self-contained essay requiring an introduction, transitions between parts, and so forth, you can label your sections simply "Descriptions" and "Self-Reflection." A student example of this assignment is found on pages 106–108. An additional example of two contrasting scenes is found on page 105.

Strategies for doing a rhetorical analysis are explained in Chapter 3, pp. 54–55, and in this chapter, p. 97.

Since the assignment for this chapter has two parts—Part A, calling for two contrasting descriptions, and Part B, calling for a self-reflection—we address each part separately.

Exploring Rationales and Details for Your Two Descriptions

To get into the spirit of this unusual assignment, you need to create a personal rationale for why you are writing two opposing descriptions. Our students have been successful imagining any one of the following three rationales:

Rationales for Writing Opposing Descriptions

Different Moods

One approach is to imagine observing your scene in different moods. How could I reflect a "happy" view of this scene? How could I reflect a "sad" view of this scene? Be sure, however, to focus entirely on a description of the scene, not on your mood itself. Let the mood determine your decisions about details and wording, but don't put yourself into the scene. The reader should infer the mood from the description.

Verbal Game

Here you see yourself as a word wizard trying consciously to create two different rhetorical effects for readers. In this scenario, you don't worry how you feel about the scene but how you want your reader to feel. Your focus is on crafting the language to influence your audience in different ways.

Different Rhetorical Purposes

In this scenario, you imagine your description in service of some desired action. You might want authorities to improve an ugly, poorly designed space (for example, a poorly designed library reading room). Or you might want to commend someone for a particularly functional space (for example, a well-designed computer lab). In this scenario, you begin with a strongly held personal view of your chosen scene—something you want to commend or condemn. One of your descriptions, therefore, represents *the way you really feel*. Your next task is to see this same scene from an opposing perspective. To get beyond your current assessment of the scene—to recognize aspects of it that are inconsistent with your beliefs—you need to "defamiliarize" it, to make it strange. Artists sometimes try to disrupt their ordinary ways of seeing by drawing something upside down or by imagining the scene from the perspective of a loathsome character—whatever it takes to wipe away "the film of habit" from the object.

The student who wrote the example on pages 106–108 worked from this last rationale. She disliked one of her classrooms, which she found unpleasant and detrimental to learning. In choosing this place, she discovered that she valued college classrooms that were well equipped, comfortable, quiet, modernized, reasonably roomy, and unaffected by outside weather conditions. It was easy for her to write the negative description of this room, which used details showing how the scene violated all her criteria. However, she had trouble writing the positive description until she imagined being inside the head of someone totally different from herself.

Generating Details

Once you have chosen your scene, you need to compose descriptions that are rich in sensory detail. Good description should be packed with sensory detail—sights, sounds, smells, textures, even on occasion tastes—all contributing to a dominant impression that gives the description focus.

One way to train yourself to notice sensory details is to create a two-column sensory chart. As you observe your scene for fifteen or twenty minutes note details that appeal to each of the senses and then try describing them, first positively (left column) and then negatively (right column). One student, observing a scene in a local tavern, made these notes in her sensory chart:

Positive Description	**Negative Description**
Taste	**Taste**
salted and buttered popcorn	salty, greasy popcorn
frosty pitchers of beer	half-drunk pitchers of stale, warm beer
big bowls of salted-in-the-shell peanuts on the tables	mess of peanut shells and discarded pretzel wrappers on tables and floor
Sound	**Sound**
hum of students laughing and chatting	din of high-pitched giggles and various obnoxious frat guys shouting at each other
the jukebox playing oldies but goodies from the early Beatles	jukebox blaring out-of-date music

[She continued with the other senses of odor, touch, and sight]

Shaping and Drafting Your Two Descriptions

Once you have decided on your rationale for the two descriptions, observed your scene, and made your sensory chart, compose your two descriptions. You will need to decide on an ordering principle for your descriptions. It generally makes sense to begin with an overview of the scene to orient your reader.

> From the park bench near 23rd and Maple, one can watch the people strolling by the duck pond.
>
> By eight o'clock on any Friday night, Pagliacci's Pizzeria on Broadway becomes one of the city's most unusual gathering places.

Then you need a plan for arranging details. There are no hard-and-fast rules here, but there are some typical practices. You can arrange details in the following ways:

- By spatially scanning from left to right or from far to near
- By using the written equivalent of a movie zoom shot: begin with a broad overview of the scene, then move to close-up descriptions of specific details

Compose your pleasant description, selecting and focusing on details that convey a positive impression. Then compose your unpleasant description. Each description should comprise one fully developed paragraph (125–175 words).

Using *Show* Words Rather than *Tell* Words

In describing your scenes, use *show* words rather than *tell* words. *Tell* words interpret a scene without describing it. They name an interior, mental state, thus telling the reader what emotional reaction to draw from the scene.

TELL WORDS

There was a *pleasant* tree in the backyard.
There was an *unpleasant* tree in the backyard.

In contrast, *show* words describe a scene through sensory details appealing to sight, sound, smell, touch, and even taste. The description itself evokes the desired effect without requiring the writer to state it overtly.

SHOW WORDS

A *spreading elm* tree *bathed* the backyard with *shade*. [evokes positive feelings]

An *out-of place elm, planted too close to the house, blocked our view of the mountains.* [evokes negative feelings]

The "scale of abstraction" is explained in Chapter 4, Concept 11, pp. 69–72.

Whereas *show* words are particulars that evoke the writer's meaning through sensory detail, *tell* words are abstractions that announce the writer's intention directly (Strategy 1 on p. 97). An occasional *tell* word can be useful, but *show* words operating at the bottom of the "scale of abstraction" are the flesh and muscle of descriptive prose.

Inexperienced writers often try to create contrasting impressions of a scene simply by switching *tell* words.

WEAK: OVERUSE OF *TELL* WORDS

The smiling merchants happily talked with customers trying to get them to buy their products. [positive purpose]

The annoying merchants kept hassling customers trying to convince them to buy their products. [negative purpose]

In this example, the negative words *annoying* and *hassling* and the positive words *smiling* and *happily* are *tell* words; they state the writer's contrasting intentions, but they don't describe the scene. Here is how the student writer revised these passages using *show* words.

STRONG: CONVERSION TO *SHOW* WORDS

One of the merchants, selling thick-wooled Peruvian sweaters, nodded approvingly as a woman tried on a richly textured blue cardigan in front of the mirror. [positive purpose]

One of the merchants, hawking those Peruvian sweaters that you find in every open-air market, tried to convince a middle-aged woman that the lumpy, oversized cardigan she was trying on looked stylish. [negative purpose]

Here are some more examples taken from students' drafts before and after revision:

Draft with *Tell* Words	**Revision with *Show* Words**
Children laugh and point animatedly at all the surroundings.	Across the way, a small boy taps his friend's shoulder and points at a circus clown.
The wonderful smell of food cooking on the barbecue fills my nose.	The tantalizing smell of grilled hamburgers and buttered corn on the cob wafts from the barbecue area of the park, where men in their cookout aprons wield forks and spatulas and drink Budweisers.
The paintings on the wall are confusing, dark, abstract, demented, and convey feelings of unhappiness and suffering.	The paintings on the wall, viewed through the smoke-filled room, seem confusing and abstract—the work of a demented artist on a bad trip. Splotches of black paint are splattered over a greenish-yellow background like bugs on vomit.

Revising Your Two Descriptions

The following checklist of revision questions will help you improve your first draft:

1. *How can I make my two descriptions more parallel—that is, more clearly about the same place at the same time*? The rules for the assignment ask you to use only factual details observable in the same scene at the same time. It violates the spirit of the assignment to have one scene at a winning basketball game and the other at a losing game. Your readers' sense of pleasure in comparing your two descriptions will be enhanced if many of the same details appear in both descriptions.
2. *Where can I replace* tell *words with* show *words*? Inexperienced writers tend to rely on *tell* words rather than give the reader sensory details and visual impressions. Find words that deliver prepackaged ideas to the reader (*pleasant, happy, depressing, annoying, pretty*, and so forth) and rewrite those sentences by actually describing what you see, hear, smell, touch, and taste. Pay particular attention to this advice if you are choosing "different moods" as your rationale for two descriptions.
3. *How can I make the angle of vision in each description clearer? How can I clarify my focus on a dominant impression*? Where could you use words with vividly appropriate connotations? Where could you substitute specific words for general ones by writing lower on the scale of abstraction? For example, consider synonyms for the generic word *shoe*. Most people wear shoes, but only certain people wear spiked heels or riding boots. Among words for kinds of sandals, *Birkenstocks* carries a different connotation from *Tevas* or *strappy espadrilles with faux-metallic finish*. Search your draft for places where you could substitute more colorful or precise words for generic words to convey your dominant impression more effectively.

Generating and Exploring Ideas for Your Self-Reflection

Writing self-reflections constitutes a powerful learning strategy. See Chapter 25 on the practice and value of self-reflective writing.

Part B of this Writing Project asks you to write a self-reflection about what you have learned. Your reflection should begin with a rhetorical analysis of your two descriptions in which you explain how you created your positive versus negative effects. Focus on how you used the strategies introduced in Chapter 3 (pp. 54–55) and summarized in the chart "Strategies Writers Use to Create a Persuasive Effect" on page 97. In the rest of your self-reflection, explore what you have learned from reading this chapter and doing this exercise. You are invited to consider questions like these:

- What rationale or scenario did you use for explaining to yourself why one might write opposing descriptions—different moods? verbal game? different rhetorical purposes? something else? Which description was easier for you to write and why?
- What new insights did you come away with? Specifically, what have you learned about the concept "angle of vision" and about ways writers can influence readers? What, if anything, was disturbing or challenging about the concepts developed in this chapter?
- Throughout this text we urge you to read rhetorically, that is, to be aware of how a text is constructed to influence readers. How has this chapter advanced your ability to read rhetorically?

Questions for Peer Review

In addition to the generic peer review questions explained in Chapter 17, Skill 4, ask your peer reviewers to address these questions:

1. The two descriptions
   a. How could the two descriptions be made more parallel or more detailed and vivid?
   b. Where might the writer replace *tell* words with *show* words? How could the writer include more sensory details appealing to more of the senses?
   c. If the writer has used only one or two of the strategies for creating contrast (direct statement of meaning, selection of details, word choice, figurative language, sentence structure), how might he or she use other strategies?
2. Self-reflection
   a. In the rhetorical analysis section, how many of the five strategies listed on page 97 does the writer include? How effectively does the writer use examples from his or her two descriptions to illustrate the chosen strategies? How might the rhetorical analysis section be improved?
   b. What does the writer say he or she has learned from doing this assignment? How could the writer's insights be expanded, explained more clearly, or developed more thoroughly?

The first reading for this chapter consists of two eyewitness accounts of an event that occurred on the Congo River in Africa in 1877.* The first account is by the famous British explorer Henry Morton Stanley, who led an exploration party of Europeans into the African interior. The second account is by the African tribal chief Mojimba, as told orally to a Belgian missionary, Fr. Frassle, who recorded the story. The conflicting accounts suggest the complexity of what happens when different cultures meet for the first time.

Clash on the Congo: Two Eyewitness Accounts

Henry Morton Stanley's Account

1 We see a sight that sends the blood tingling through every nerve and fibre of the body ... a flotilla of gigantic canoes bearing down upon us. A monster canoe leads the way ... forty men on a side, their bodies bending and swaying in unison as with a swelling barbarous chorus they drive her down towards us ... the warriors above the manned prow let fly their spears. ... But every sound is soon lost in the ripping crackling musketry. ... Our blood is up now. It is a murderous world, and we feel for the first time that we hate the filthy vulturous ghouls who inhabit it. ... We pursue them ... and continue the fight in the village streets with those who have landed, hunt them out into the woods, and there only sound the retreat, having returned the daring cannibals the compliment of a visit.

Mojimba's Account

2 When we heard that the man with the white flesh was journeying down the [Congo] we were open-mouthed with astonishment. ... He will be one of our brothers who were drowned in the river .... We will prepare a feast, I ordered, we will go to meet our brother and escort him into the village with rejoicing! We donned our ceremonial garb. We assembled the great canoes. ... We swept forward, my canoe leading, the others following, with songs of joy and with dancing, to meet the first white man our eyes had beheld, and to do him honor. But as we drew near his canoes there were loud reports, bang! bang! And fire-staves spat bits of iron at us. We were paralyzed with fright ... they were the work of evil spirits! "War! That is war!" I yelled. ... We fled into our village—they came after us. We fled into the forest and flung ourselves on the ground. When we returned that evening our eyes beheld fearful things: our brothers, dead, dying, bleeding, our village plundered and burned, and the water full of dead bodies. The robbers and murderers had disappeared.

THINKING CRITICALLY
about the *Two Accounts*

Our purpose in presenting these two accounts is to raise the central problem examined in this chapter: the rhetorical nature of observation—that is, how

*These readings are taken from Donald C. Holsinger, "A Classroom Laboratory for Writing History," *Social Studies Review* 31.1 (1991): 59–64. The role-playing exercise following the readings is also adapted from this article.

observation is shaped by values, beliefs, knowledge, and purpose and therefore represents an angle of vision or one perspective.

1. How do the two accounts differ?
2. What is common to both accounts? Focusing on common elements, try to establish as many facts as you can about the encounter.
3. How does each observer create a persuasive effect by using one or more of the five strategies described on page 97 (overt statement of meaning, selection/omission of details, connotations of words, figurative language, ordering and shaping of sentences)?
4. What differences in assumptions, values, and knowledge shape these two interpretations of events?
5. As a class, try the following role-playing exercise:

   Background: You are a newspaper reporter who has a global reputation for objectivity, accuracy, and lack of bias. You write for a newspaper that has gained a similar reputation and prides itself on printing only the truth. Your editor has just handed you two eyewitness accounts of an incident that has recently occurred in central Africa. You are to transform the two accounts into a brief front-page article (between sixty and ninety words) informing your readers what happened. You face an immediate deadline and have no time to seek additional information.

   Task: Each class member should write a sixty- to ninety-word newspaper account of the event, striving for objectivity and lack of bias. Then share your accounts.
6. As a class, play the believing and doubting game with this assertion: "It is possible to create an objective and unbiased account of the Congo phenomenon."

Our second reading is student writer Tamlyn Rogers' essay written for this assignment. We include the full text of her two descriptions, but print only excerpts from her self-reflection in order to avoid influencing your own rhetorical analyses or reflections on what you learned from this assignment.

Tamlyn Rogers

Two Descriptions of the Same Classroom and a Self-Reflection

Part A: The Two Descriptions

Description 1—positive effect: The high ceiling and plainness of this classroom on the second floor of the Administration Building make it seem airy, spacious, and functional. I sense that this classroom, which is neither dusty and old nor sterile and modern, has a well-used, comfortable feel like the jeans and favorite sweater you put on to go out for pizza with friends. Students around me, who are focused on the assignment, read the instructor's notes on the chalkboard, thumb through their texts, and jot down ideas in their notebooks spread out on the spacious two-person tables. In the back of the room, five students cluster around a table and talk softly and intently about the presentation they are getting ready to make to the class. Splashes of spring sunshine filtering through the blinds on the tall windows brighten the room with natural light, and a breeze pungent with the scent of newly mown grass wafts through the open ones, sweeps over the students writing at their desks, and passes out through the door to the hall. As I glance out the window, I see a view that contributes to the quiet harmony of the environment: bright pink and red rhododendron bushes and manicured beds of spring flowers ring the huge lawn where a few students are studying under the white-blossomed cherry trees.

Description 2—negative effect: The high ceiling of this classroom on the second floor of the Administration Building cannot relieve the cramped, uncomfortable feeling of this space, which is filled with too many two-person tables, some of them crammed together at awkward angles. A third of the chalkboard is blocked from my view by the bulky television, VCR, and overhead projector that are stacked on cumbersome carts and wreathed in electrical cords. Students around me, working on the assignment, scrape their chairs on the bare linoleum floor as they try to see the chalkboard where some of the instructor's notes are blotted out by the shafts of sunlight piercing through a few bent slats in the blinds. In the back of the room, five students cluster around a table, trying to talk softly about their presentation, but their voices bounce off the bare floors. Baked by the sun, the classroom is so warm that the instructor has allowed us to open the windows, but the wailing sirens of ambulances racing to the various hospitals surrounding the campus distract us. The breeze full of the smell of mown lawn brings warm air from outside into this stuffy room. Several students besides me gaze longingly out the window at the bright pink and red rhododendrons in the garden and at the students reading comfortably in the shade under the white-blossomed cherry trees.

Part B: Self-Reflection

In writing the two descriptions, I used most of the strategies for creating rhetorical effects discussed in the text. In deliberately changing my angle of vision from positive to negative, I realized how much the connotation of individual words can convey particular ideas to readers. For example, in the positive description to get across the idea of a comfortably studious environment, I used words such as "airy," "spacious," "focused," and "quiet harmony." But in my negative description, I wanted readers to feel the unpleasantness of this room so I used words like "cramped," "crammed," "blocked," and "bulky." I also created different effects by including or excluding certain details. For example, in the positive description, I mentioned the "splashes of sunshine" coming through the window, but in the negative description I mentioned the "wailing sirens of ambulances." [She continues with this rhetorical analysis, explaining and illustrating the other strategies she used.]

I learned several things from doing this assignment. First ... [She then explains what she learned from doing the assignment and also notes how she has begun to notice similar rhetorical strategies being used in some of her recent reading.]

THINKING CRITICALLY

about "Two Descriptions of the Same Classroom and a Self-Reflection"

1. In her self-reflection, Tamlyn Rogers explains how she uses two of the five strategies summarized on page 97: connotation of words and selection/omission of details. (We omitted the rest of her rhetorical analysis.) Which remaining strategies—direct statement of intention, figurative language, and use of sentence structure—do you think she might have profitably discussed in her rhetorical analysis?
2. What do you see as the strengths and weaknesses of Tamlyn's attempt to create two contrasting descriptions of the same scene?

For additional writing, reading, and research resources, go to **www.MyCompLab.com** and choose **Ramage/Bean/Johnson's *The Allyn & Bacon Guide to Writing,* Fifth Edition.**

READING RHETORICALLY

The Writer as Strong Reader

CHAPTER 6

Many new college students are surprised by the amount, range, and difficulty of reading they have to do in college. Every day they are challenged by reading assignments ranging from scholarly articles and textbooks on complex subject matter to primary sources such as Plato's dialogues or Darwin's *Voyage of the Beagle*.

The goal of this chapter is to help you become a more powerful reader of academic texts, prepared to take part in the conversations of the disciplines you study. To this end, we explain two kinds of thinking and writing essential to your college reading:

- Your ability to listen carefully to a text, to recognize its parts and their functions, and to summarize its ideas
- Your ability to formulate strong responses to texts by interacting with them, either by agreeing with, interrogating, or actively opposing them

To interact strongly with texts, you must learn how to read them both with and against the grain. When you read *with the grain* of a text, you see the world through its author's perspective, open yourself to the author's argument, apply the text's insights to new contexts, and connect its ideas to your own experiences and personal knowledge. When you read *against the grain* of a text, you resist it by questioning its points, raising doubts, analyzing the limits of its perspective, or even refuting its argument. We say that readers who respond strongly to texts in this manner read *rhetorically*; that is, they are aware of the effect a text is intended to have on them, and they critically consider that effect, entering into or challenging the text's intentions.

The two writing projects in this chapter introduce you to several of the most common genres of academic writing:

- the summary
- various kinds of strong response essays, which usually incorporate a summary of the text to which the writer is responding.

Exploring Rhetorical Reading

As an introduction to rhetorical reading, we ask you to imagine that you are investigating how attitudes toward tattoos have changed in American society in the last ten years. In your investigation, you are consulting both popular and scholarly sources, and you have come across a short article in the scholarly publication the *Journal of the American Academy of Child and Adolescent Psychiatry*. Before reading this article by Dr. Andrés Martin, "On Teenagers and Tattoos," which appeared in a 1997 edition of this journal, complete the following opinion survey. Respond to each statement using a 1–5 scale, with 1 meaning "strongly agree" and 5 meaning "strongly disagree."

1. For teenagers, getting a tattoo is like following any other fad such as wearing the currently popular kind of shoe or hairstyle.
2. Teenagers who get tattoos are expressing deep psychological needs.
3. Because tattoos are so common today among young adults, they can no longer serve as a meaningful form of rebellion or self-definition.
4. With the growth of the tattoo removal industry, people, especially teens, no longer regard tattoos as an irreversible marking of their skins.
5. An article from a 1997 psychiatry journal can provide useful insights into current trends in American teens' choices to get tattoos.

When you have finished rating your degree of agreement with these statements, read Martin's article, using whatever note-taking, underlining, or highlighting strategies you normally use when reading for a class. When you have finished reading, complete the exercises that follow.

Andrés Martin, M.D.

On Teenagers and Tattoos

The skeleton dimensions I shall now proceed to set down are copied verbatim from my right arm, where I had them tattooed: as in my wild wanderings at that period, there was no other secure way of preserving such valuable statistics.

Melville/*Moby-Dick CII*

1 Tattoos and piercings have become a part of our everyday landscape. They are ubiquitous, having entered the circles of glamour and the mainstream of fashion, and they have even become an increasingly common feature of our urban youth. Legislation in most states restricts professional tattooing to adults older than 18 years of age, so "high end" tattooing is rare in children and adolescents, but such tattos are occasionally seen in older teenagers. Piercings, by comparison, as well as self-made or "jailhouse" type tattoos, are not at all rare among adolescents or even among schoolage children. Like hairdo, makeup, or baggy jeans, tattoos and piercings can be subject to fad influence or peer pressure in an effort toward group affiliation. As with any other fashion statement, they can be construed as bodily aids in the inner struggle toward identity consolidation, serving as adjuncts to the defining and sculpting of the self by means of external manipulations. But unlike most other body decorations, tattoos and piercings are set apart by their irreversible and permanent nature, a quality at the core of their magnetic appeal to adolescents.

2 Adolescents and their parents are often at odds over the acquisition of bodily decorations. For the adolescent, piercings or tattoos may be seen as personal and beautifying statements, while parents may construe them as oppositional and enraging affronts to their authority. Distinguishing bodily adornment from self-mutilation may indeed prove challenging, particularly when a family is in disagreement over a teenager's motivations and a clinician is summoned as the final arbiter. At such times it may be most important to realize jointly that the skin can all too readily become but another battleground for the tensions of the age, arguments having less to do with tattoos and piercings than with core issues such as separation from the family matrix. Exploring the motivations and significance underlying tattoos (Grumet, 1983) and piercings can go a long way toward resolving such differences and can become a novel and additional way of getting to know teenagers. An interested and nonjudgmental appreciation of teenagers' surface presentations may become a way of making contact not only in their terms but on their turfs: quite literally on the territory of their skins.

3 The following three sections exemplify some of the complex psychological underpinnings of youth tattooing.

Identity and the Adolescent's Body

4 Tattoos and piercing can offer a concrete and readily available solution for many of the identity crises and conflicts normative to adolescent development. In using such decorations, and by marking out their bodily territories, adolescents can support their efforts at autonomy, privacy, and insulation. Seeking individuation, tattooed adolescents can become unambiguously demarcated from others and singled out as unique. The intense and often disturbing reactions that are mobilized in viewers can help to effectively keep them at bay, becoming tantamount to the proverbial "Keep Out" sign hanging from a teenager's door.

5 Alternatively, [when teenagers feel] prey to a rapidly evolving body over which they have no say, self-made and openly visible decorations may restore adolescents' sense of normalcy and control, a way of turning a passive experience into an active identity. By indelibly marking their bodies, adolescents can strive to reclaim their bearings within an environment experienced as alien, estranged, or suffocating or to lay claim over their evolving and increasingly unrecognizable bodies. In either case, the net outcome can be a resolution to unwelcome impositions: external, familial, or societal in one case; internal and hormonal in the other. In the words of a 16-year-old girl with several facial piercings, and who could have been referring to her body just as well as to the position within her family, "If I don't fit in, it is because *I* say so."

Incorporation and Ownership

6 Imagery of a religious, deathly, or skeletal nature, the likenesses of fierce animals or imagined creatures, and the simple inscription of names are some of the time-tested favorite contents for tattoos. In all instances, marks become not only memorials or recipients for clearly held persons or concepts; they strive for incorporation, with images and abstract symbols gaining substance on becoming a permanent part of the individual's skin. Thickly embedded in personally meaningful representations and object relations, tattoos can become not only the ongoing memento of a relationship,

but at times even the only evidence that there ever was such a bond. They can quite literally become the relationship itself. The turbulence and impulsivity of early attachments and infatuations may become grounded, effectively bridging oblivion through the visible reality of tattoos.

7 *Case Vignette.* A, a 13-year-old boy, proudly showed me his tattooed deltoid. The coarsely depicted roll of the dice marked the day and month of his birth. Rather disappointed, he then uncovered an immaculate back, going on to draw for me the great "piece" he envisioned for it. A menacing figure held a hand of cards: two aces, two eights, and a card with two sets of dates. A's father had belonged to "Dead Man's Hand," a motorcycle gang named after the set of cards (aces and eights) that the legendary Wild Bill Hickock had held in the 1890s when shot dead over a poker table in Deadwood, South Dakota. A had only the vaguest memory of and sketchiest information about his father, but he knew he had died in a motorcycle accident: the fifth card marked the dates of his birth and death.

8 The case vignette also serves to illustrate how tattoos are often the culmination of a long process of imagination, fantasy, and planning that can start at an early age. Limited markings, or relatively reversible ones such as piercings, can at a later time scaffold toward the more radical commitment of a permanent tattoo.

The Quest for Permanence

9 The popularity of the anchor as a tattoo motif may historically have had to do less with guild identification among sailors than with an intense longing for rootedness and stability. In a similar vein, the recent increase in the popularity and acceptance of tattoos may be understood as an antidote or counterpoint to our urban and nomadic lifestyles. Within an increasingly mobile society, in which relationships are so often transient—as attested by the frequencies of divorce, abandonment, foster placement, and repeated moves, for example—tattoos can be a readily available source of grounding. Tattoos, unlike many relationships, can promise permanence and stability. A sense of constancy can be derived from unchanging marks that can be carried along no matter what the physical, temporal, or geographical vicissitudes at hand. Tattoos stay, while all else may change.

10 *Case Vignette.* A proud father at 17, B had had the smiling face of his 3-month-old baby girl tattooed on his chest. As we talked at a tattoo convention, he proudly introduced her to me, explaining how he would "always know how beautiful she is today" when years from then he saw her semblance etched on himself.

11 The quest for permanence may at other times prove misleading and offer premature closure to unresolved conflicts. At a time of normative uncertainties, adolescents may maladaptively and all too readily commit to a tattoo and its indefinite presence. A wish to hold on to a current certainty may lead the adolescent to lay down in ink what is valued and cherished one day but may not necessarily be in the future. The frequency of self-made tattoos among hospitalized, incarcerated, or gang-affiliated youths suggests such motivations: a sense of stability may be a particularly dire need under temporary, turbulent, or volatile conditions. In addition, through their designs teenagers may assert a sense of bonding and allegiance to a group larger than themselves. Tattoos may attest to

powerful experiences, such as adolescence itself, lived and even survived together. As with *Moby Dick's* protagonist Ishmael, they may bear witness to the "valuable statistics" of one's "wild wandering(s)": those of adolescent exhilaration and excitement on the one hand; of growing pains, shared misfortune, or even incarceration on the other.

12 Adolescents' bodily decorations, at times radical and dramatic in their presentation, can be seen in terms of figuration rather than disfigurement, of the natural body being through them transformed into a personalized body (Brain, 1979). They can often be understood as self-constructive and adorning efforts, rather than prematurely subsumed as mutilatory and destructive acts. If we bear all of this in mind, we may not only arrive at a position to pass more reasoned clinical judgment, but become sensitized through our patients' skins to another level of their internal reality.

References

Brain, R. (1979). *The Decorated Body*. New York: Harper & Row.
Grumet, G. W. (1983). Psychodynamic implications of tattoos. *Am J Orthopsychiatry*, 53:482–492.

THINKING CRITICALLY
about "On Teenagers and Tattoos"

1. Summarize in one or two sentences Martin's main points.
2. Freewrite a response to this question: In what way has Martin's article caused me to reconsider my answers to the opinion survey?
3. Working in small groups or as a whole class, compare the note-taking strategies you used while reading this piece. (a) How many people wrote marginal notes? How many underlined or highlighted? (b) Compare the contents of these notes. Did people highlight the same passage or different passages? (c) Individually, look at your annotations and highlights and try to decide why you wrote or marked what you did. Share your reasons for making these annotations. The goal of this exercise is to make you more aware of your thinking processes as you read.
4. Working as a whole class or in small groups, share your responses to the questionnaire and to the postreading questions. To what extent did this article change people's thinking about the reasons teenagers choose to tattoo their bodies? What were the most insightful points in this article?
5. Assume that you are looking for substantial, detailed information about changes in American attitudes toward tattooing. What parts of this article are useful? How might a psychiatrist writing about tattoos today differ from Martin in 1997?

Understanding Rhetorical Reading

In this section we explain why college-level reading is often difficult for new students and offer suggestions for improving your reading process based on the reading strategies of experts. We then show you the importance of reading a text both with the grain and against the grain—skills you need to summarize a text and respond to it strongly.

What Makes College-Level Reading Difficult?

The difficulty of college-level reading stems in part from the complexity of the subject matter. Whatever the subject—from international monetary policies to the intricacies of photosynthesis—you have to wrestle with new and complex materials that might perplex anyone. But in addition to the daunting subject matter, several other factors contribute to the difficulty of college-level reading:

- *Vocabulary.* Many college-level readings—especially primary sources—contain unfamiliar technical language that may be specific to an academic discipline: for example, the terms *identity consolidation, normative, individuation,* and *object relations* in the Martin text or words like *existentialism* and *Neoplatonic* in a philosophy textbook. In academia, words often carry specialized meanings that evoke a whole history of conversation and debate that may be inaccessible, even through a specialized dictionary. You will not fully understand them until you are initiated into the disciplinary conversations that gave rise to them.
- *Unfamiliar rhetorical context.* As we explained in Part 1, writers write to an audience for a purpose arising from some motivating occasion. Knowing an author's purpose, occasion, and audience will often clarify confusing parts of a text. For example, you can understand the Martin article more easily if you know that its author, writing in a scientific journal, is offering advice to psychiatrists about how to counsel tattooed teens and their families. A text's internal clues can sometimes help you fill in the rhetorical context, but often you may need to do outside research.
- *Unfamiliar genre.* In your college reading, you will encounter a range of genres such as textbooks, trade books, scholarly articles, scientific reports, historical documents, newspaper articles, op-ed pieces, and so forth. Each of these makes different demands on readers and requires a different reading strategy.
- *Lack of background knowledge.* Writers necessarily make assumptions about what their readers already know. Your understanding of Martin, for example, would be more complete if you had a background in adolescent psychology and psychiatric therapy.

FOR WRITING AND DISCUSSION

Appreciating the Importance of Background Knowledge

The importance of background knowledge can be easily demonstrated any time you dip into past issues of a newsmagazine or try to read articles about an unfamiliar culture. Consider the following passage from a 1986 *Newsweek* article.

How much background knowledge do you need before you can fully comprehend this passage? What cultural knowledge about the United States would a student from Ethiopia or Indonesia need?

> Throughout the NATO countries last week, there were second thoughts about the prospect of a nuclear-free world. For 40 years nuclear weapons have been the backbone of the West's defense. For almost as long American presidents have ritually affirmed their desire to see the world rid of them. Then, suddenly, Ronald Reagan and Mikhail Gorbachev came close to actually doing it. Let's abolish all nuclear ballistic missiles in the next 10 years, Reagan said. Why not all nuclear weapons, countered Gorbachev. OK, the president responded, like a man agreeing to throw in the washer-dryer along with the house.
>
> What if the deal had gone through? On the one hand, Gorbachev would have returned to Moscow a hero. There is a belief in the United States that the Soviets need nuclear arms because nuclear weapons are what make them a superpower. But according to Marxist-Leninist doctrine, capitalism's nuclear capability (unforeseen by Marx and Lenin) is the only thing that can prevent the inevitable triumph of communism. Therefore, an end to nuclear arms would put the engine of history back on its track.
>
> On the other hand, Europeans fear, a nonnuclear United States would be tempted to retreat into neo-isolationism.
>
> —Robert B. Cullen, "Dangers of Disarming," *Newsweek*

Working in small groups or as a class, identify words and passages in this text that depend on background information or knowledge of culture for complete comprehension.

Using the Reading Strategies of Experts

In Chapter 17, we describe the differences between the writing processes of experts and those of beginning college writers. There are parallel differences between the reading processes of experienced and inexperienced readers, especially when they encounter complex materials. In this strategies chart we describe some expert reading strategies that you can begin applying to your reading of any kind of college-level material.

STRATEGIES for Reading Like an Expert

Strategies	What to Do	Comments
Reconstruct the rhetorical context.	Ask questions about purpose, audience, genre, and motivating occasion.	If you read an article that has been anthologized (as in the readings in this textbook), note any information you are given about the author, publication, and genre. Try to reconstruct the author's original motivation for writing.

(*continued*)

Strategies	What to Do	Comments
Take notes.	Make extensive marginal notes as you read.	Expert readers seldom use highlighters, which encourage passive, inefficient reading.
Get in the dictionary habit.	Look up words whose meaning you can't get from context.	If you don't want to interrupt your reading, check off words to look up when you are done.
Match your reading speed to your goals.	Speed up when skimming or scanning for information. Slow down for complete comprehension or detailed analysis.	Robert Sternberg, a cognitive psychologist, discovered that novice readers tend to read everything at about the same pace, no matter what their purpose. Experienced readers know when to slow down or speed up.
Read a complex text in a "multi-draft" way.	Read a text two or three times. The first time, read quickly, skimming ahead rapidly, looking at the opening sentences of paragraphs and at any passages that sum up the writer's argument or clarify the argument's structure. Pay particular attention to the conclusion, which often ties the whole argument together.	Rapid "first-draft reading" helps you see the text's main points and structure, thus providing background for a second reading. Often, experienced readers reread a text two or three times. They hold confusing passages in mental suspension, hoping that later parts of the essay will clarify earlier parts.

Reading With the Grain and Against the Grain

For an explanation of the believing and doubting game, see Chapter 2, Concept 5.

The reading and thinking strategies that we have just described enable skilled readers to interact strongly with texts. Your purpose in using these strategies is to read texts both with the grain and against the grain, a way of reading that is analogous to the believing and doubting game we introduced in Chapter 2. This concept is so important that we have chosen to highlight it separately here.

When you read with the grain of a text, you practice what psychologist Carl Rogers calls "empathic listening," in which you try to see the world through the author's eyes, role-playing as much as possible the author's intended readers by adopting their beliefs and values and acquiring their background knowledge. Reading with the grain is the main strategy you use when you summarize a text, but it comes into play also when you develop a strong response. When making with-the-grain points, you support the author's thesis with your own arguments and examples, or apply or extend the author's argument in new ways.

When you read against the grain of a text, you question and perhaps even rebut the author's ideas. You are a resistant reader who asks unanticipated questions, pushes back, and reads the text in ways unforeseen by the author. Reading against the grain is a key part of creating a strong response. When you make against-the-grain points, you challenge the author's reasoning, sources, examples, or choices of language. You present alternative lines of reasoning, deny the writer's values, or raise points or specific data that the writer has omitted. With the grain and against the grain thinking moves are shown in the following strategies chart.

STRATEGIES for Reading with and Against the Grain

Reading with the Grain	Reading Against the Grain
• Listen to the text, read with the author, and withhold judgments. • Extend and support the author's thesis with your own points and examples. • Apply the author's argument in new ways.	• Challenge, question, and resist the author's ideas. • Rebut the author's ideas with counterreasoning and counterexamples. • Point out what the author has left out or overlooked, and note what the author has *not* said.

Strong readers develop their ability to read in both ways—with the grain and against the grain. Throughout the rest of the chapter, we show you different ways to apply these strategies in your reading and writing.

Understanding Summary Writing

Summaries (often called abstracts) are condensed versions of texts that extract and present main ideas in a way that does justice to the author's intentions. A summary, as fairly and objectively as possible, states the main ideas of a longer text, such as an article or even a book. Not only will you frequently write summaries as a student, you will often encounter summaries as a stand-alone genre. Summaries at the beginning of articles, in prefaces to books, and on book jackets help readers determine if they want to read the article or book. Your professors send abstracts of proposed papers to conference committees in hopes of getting the paper accepted for presentation. Engineers or business executives place "executive summaries" at the beginning of proposals or major reports. In the "literature review" section of scientific papers, summaries of previous research are used to demonstrate gaps in knowledge that the present researchers will try to fill. Writing summaries is a particularly important part of research writing, where you often present condensed views of other writers' arguments, either in support of your own view or as alternative views you must analyze or respond to.

Summary writing fosters a close encounter between you and the text and demonstrates your understanding of it. In writing a summary, you must distinguish between main and subordinate points and provide even coverage of the entire article. Writing summaries challenges you to convey clearly the main ideas of a text—ideas that are often complex—in a limited number of words. Often, summaries are written to certain specifications, say, one-tenth of the original article, or 200 words, or 100 words. Although the words "summary" and "abstract" are often used interchangeably, the term "abstract" is usually used for a stand-alone summary at the head of a published article or for the summary you create of your own longer piece of writing. In this chapter, we focus on the summaries you create of someone else's texts.

If you are incorporating a summary of an article into your own writing, you will need to frame it so that readers can easily distinguish your own ideas from the ideas of the author you are summarizing. You do so by putting quotation marks around any passages that use the writer's original wording, by citing the article using the appropriate documentation style, and by using frequent attributive tags (sometimes called "signaling phrases") such as "Martin says," "according to Martin," or "Martin maintains." Typically, writers also introduce the summary with appropriate contextual information giving the author's name and perhaps also the title and genre (in research writing this information is repeated in the "Works Cited" or "References" list). The first sentence of the summary typically presents the main idea or thesis of the entire article. Here is a summary of the Martin article as it might be incorporated into one's own paper (the writer is using the MLA citation and documentation style).

Chapter 22 provides additional instruction on summarizing, paraphrasing, and quoting sources. It also explains how to work sources smoothly into your own writing and avoid plagiarism.

Identification of the article, journal, and author

Thesis of article

Attributive tag

Transition

Attributive tag

Transition and attributive tag

Transition and attributive tag

Inclusion of short quotation from article. MLA documentation style; number in parentheses indicates page number of original article where quotation is found

Attributive tag

Attributive tag

> In "On Teenagers and Tattoos," published in the *Journal of the American Academy of Child and Adolescent Psychiatry*, Dr. Andrés Martin advises fellow psychiatrists to think of teenage tattooing not as a fad or as a form of self-mutilation but as an opportunity for clinicians to understand teenagers better. Martin examines three different reasons that teenagers get tattoos. First, he argues that tattoos help teenagers establish unique identities by giving them a sense of control over their evolving bodies and over an environment perceived as adverse and domineering. Second, he believes that a tattooed image often symbolizes the teen's relationship to a significant concept or person, making the relationship more visible and real. Finally, says Martin, because teens are disturbed by modern society's mobility and fragmentation and because they have an "intense longing for rootedness and stability" (112), the irreversible nature of tattoos may give them a sense of permanence. Martin concludes that tattoos can be a meaningful record of survived teen experiences. He encourages

therapists to regard teen tattoos as "self-constructive and adorning efforts," rather than as "mutilatory and destructive acts" (113) and suggests that tattoos can help therapists understand "another level of [teenagers'] internal reality" (113). [195 words]

Another short quotation

Brackets indicate that the writer changed the material inside the brackets to fit the grammar and context of the writer's own sentence

Works Cited

Martin, Andrés. "On Teenagers and Tattoos." *Journal of the American Academy of Child and Adolescent Psychiatry* 36 (1997): 860–61. Rpt. in *The Allyn & Bacon Guide to Writing*. John D. Ramage, John C. Bean, and June Johnson. 5th ed. New York: Longman, 2009. 110–13. Print.

Martin article cited completely using MLA documentation form; in a formal paper, the "works cited" list begins on a new page.

Note in this example how the use of attributive tags, quotation marks, and citations makes it easy to tell that the writer is summarizing Martin's ideas rather than presenting his or her own ideas. Note too the writer's attempt to remain neutral and objective and not to impose his or her own opinions. To avoid interjecting your own opinions, you need to choose your verbs in attributive tags carefully. Consider the difference between "Smith argues" and "Smith rants." The second verb, by moving beyond neutrality, reveals the writer's judgment of the author's ideas.

In an academic setting, then, think of summaries as short, tightly written pieces that retain an author's main ideas while eliminating the supporting details. In the writing projects for this chapter, we'll explain the strategies you can use to write a good summary. The following chart lists the criteria for incorporating a summary effectively into your own prose.

Criteria for an Effective Summary Incorporated into Your Own Prose

- Represents the original article accurately and fairly.
- Is direct and concise, using words economically.
- Remains objective and neutral, not revealing the writer's own ideas on the subject, but, rather, only the original author's points.
- Gives the original article balanced and proportional coverage.
- Uses the writer's own words to express the original author's ideas.
- Distinguishes the summary writer's ideas from the original author's ideas by using attributive tags (such as "according to Martin" or "Martin argues that").
- Uses quotations sparingly, if at all, to present the original author's key terms or to convey the flavor of the original.
- Is a unified, coherent piece of writing in its own right.
- Cites and documents the text the writer is summarizing and any quotations used according to an appropriate documentation system.

FOR WRITING AND DISCUSSION

Determining What Is a Good Summary

This exercise asks you to work with the "Criteria for an Effective Summary Incorporated into Your Own Prose" on page 119 as you analyze the strengths and weaknesses of three summaries of the same article: "Protect Workers' Rights" by Bruce Raynor, published in the *Washington Post* on September 1, 2003. Imagine three student writers assigned to summarize this editorial in approximately 200 words. The first of the summaries below we have rated as excellent. Read the excellent summary first and then determine how successful the other summaries are.

SUMMARY 1 (AN EXCELLENT SUMMARY OF THE RAYNOR ARTICLE)

In Bruce Raynor's op-ed article "Protect Workers' Rights," originally published in the *Washington Post* on September 1, 2003, union official Raynor argues that workers everywhere are threatened by the current rules of globalization that allow corporations and governments to seek out the cheapest and least regulated labor around the world. Using the example of the Pillowtex Corporation that recently shut down its plant in Kannapolis, North Carolina, he shows how ending manufacturing that has played a long and major role in the economies of towns leaves workers without severance pay, medical insurance, money to pay taxes and mortgages, and other options for employment. According to Raynor, in the last three years, millions of jobs have been lost in all branches of American manufacturing. While policymakers advise these workers to seek education to retool for white-collar jobs, Raynor points out that fields such as telemarketing and the computer industry are also losing millions of jobs. Furthermore, outsourcing has caused a drop in wages in the United States. The same dynamic of jobs moving to countries with cheaper and less stringent safety and health regulation has recently caused Mexican and Bangladeshi workers to lose their jobs to Chinese workers. Raynor concludes with a call to protect the rights of workers everywhere by rewriting the "rules for the global economy" (A25). (214 words)

Work Cited

Raynor, Bruce. "Protect Workers' Rights." *Washington Post* 1 Sept. 2003: A25. Print.

SUMMARY 2

The closing of the Pillowtex Corporation's factories in the United States represents a loss of sixteen textile plants and about 6,500 jobs, according to Bruce Raynor, president of UNITE, a union of textile workers.

The workers left in Kannapolis, North Carolina, former home of one of the largest Pillowtex plants, are experiencing financial problems as they are unable to buy medical insurance, pay their taxes or mortgages or find other jobs.

Raynor argues that the case of the Pillowtex workers is representative of workers in other industries such as metals, papers, and electronics and that "this is the longest decline since the Great Depression" with about three million jobs gone in the last three years.

He then explains that white-collar jobs are not safe either because millions of jobs in telemarketing, claims adjusting, and even government are predicted to go overseas in the next five years. Furthermore, Raynor states that the possibility of outsourcing jobs leads to lowering of wages within the United States, as "outsourcing has forced down hourly wage rates by 10 percent to 40 percent for many U.S. computer consultants" (A25).

However, according to Raynor, the developing countries like Mexico and Bangladesh that have acquired manufacturing jobs are also threatened by countries like China who can offer employees who are willing to work for even lower wages and under worse conditions.

Raynor concludes that "a prosperous economy requires that workers be able to buy the products that they produce" (A25) and that workers everywhere need to be protected. (251 words)

Work Cited

Raynor, Bruce. "Protect Workers' Rights." *Washington Post* 1 Sept. 2003: A25. Print.

SUMMARY 3

In his article "Protect Workers' Rights," Bruce Raynor, president of UNITE, a textile workers' union, criticizes free trade and globalization for taking away workers' jobs. Using the Pillowtex Corporation's closing of its plant in Kannapolis, North Carolina, as his prime example, Raynor claims that outsourcing has destroyed the economy of this town and harmed workers across the United States. Raynor threatens that millions of white-collar jobs are also being lost and going to be lost in the next five years. Raynor complains that the whole national and global economy is falling apart and is going to get worse. He implies that the only solution is to keep jobs here in the United States. He maintains that workers around the world are also suffering when factories are moved from one developing country to another that has even more favorable conditions for the corporations. Raynor naively fails to factor in the role of consumers and the pressures on corporations into his defense of workers' rights. Clearly, Raynor loves unions and hates corporations; he probably fears that he is going to lose his own job soon. (183 words)

Understanding Strong Response Writing

We have said that the summary or abstract is an important academic genre and that summary writing is an essential academic skill. Equally important is strong response writing in which you identify and probe points in a text, sometimes by examining how a piece is written and often by inserting your own ideas into the text's conversation. "Strong response" is an umbrella term that incorporates a wide variety of ways that you can speak back to a text. In all cases, you are called on to do your own critical thinking by generating and asserting your own responses to the text.

In this section we will explain four different genres of strong response writing:

- Rhetorical critique
- Ideas critique
- Reflection
- Blended version of all three of these

Strong Response as Rhetorical Critique

A strong response as rhetorical critique analyzes a text's rhetorical strategies and evaluates how effectively the author achieves his or her intended goals. When writing a rhetorical critique, you discuss how a text is constructed, what rhetorical strategies it employs, and how effectively it appeals to *logos*, *ethos*, and *pathos*. In other words, you closely analyze the text itself, giving it the same close attention that an art critic gives a painting, a football coach gives a game film, or a biologist gives a cell formation. The close attention can be with the grain, noting the effectiveness of the text's rhetorical strategies, or against the grain, discussing what is ineffective or problematic about these strategies. Or an analysis might point out both the strengths and weaknesses of the text's rhetorical strategies.

> **Example:** Suppose that you are writing a rhetorical critique of an article appearing in a conservative business journal that advocates oil exploration in the Arctic National Wildlife Refuge (ANWR). You might analyze the article's rhetorical strategies (for example, How is it shaped to appeal to a conservative, business-oriented audience? How has the writer's angle of vision filtered the evidence for his or her argument? How does the writer make himself or herself seem credible to this audience?). You would also evaluate the argument (for example, What are the underlying assumptions and beliefs on which the argument is based? Is the logic sound? Is the evidence accurate and current?).

Rhetorical critiques are usually closed-form, thesis-driven essays. The essay has a thesis that captures the writer's overall assessment of the text and maps out the specific points that the writer will develop in the analysis. When writing a rhetorical critique, your goal is to find a few rhetorical points that you find particularly intriguing, important, or disturbing to discuss and probe. Typically, your analysis zeroes in on some key features that you, the writer, find noteworthy. In the following strategies chart, we suggest the kinds of questions you can ask about a text to construct a rhetorical critique.

QUESTION-ASKING STRATEGIES for Writing a Rhetorical Critique

Ask Questions about Any of the Following:	Examples
Audience and purpose: • Who is the intended audience? • What is the writer's purpose? • How well does the text suit its particular audience and purpose?	Examine how Andrés Martin writes to other psychiatrists (rather than to a general audience) with the purpose of convincing them that probing the motives behind a teenage patient's tattoos can help them understand the teenager at a deeper level. Examine how the text uses language and evidence to support this purpose.

Ask Questions about Any of the Following:	Examples
Influence of genre on the shape of the text: • How has the genre affected the author's style, structure, and use of evidence?	Examine how the scientific genre accounts for the clinical tone of the article, for some of its jargon, and for its use of case studies as evidence.
Author's style: • How do the author's language choices and sentence length and complexity contribute to the impact of the text?	Examine how Martin uses both psychological language and clear descriptive sentences with concrete details. Consider what the *Moby Dick* references contribute to this scientific journal article.
Appeal to *logos*, the logic of the argument: • How well has the author created a reasonable, logically structured argument?	Examine how well Martin uses logical points to support his claim and make his claim persuasive.
Use of evidence: • How reputable, relevant, current, sufficient, and representative is the evidence?	Examine how Martin uses a combination of his own analysis and evidence from case studies to develop each point. Question whether the 1997 publication date makes his evidence no longer current.
Appeal to *ethos* and the credibility of the author: • How well does the author persuade readers that he/she is knowledgeable, reliable, credible, and trustworthy?	Examine how Martin establishes himself as a credible authority to other psychiatrists. Examine the effects of genre and style in creating this *ethos*. Examine whether this *ethos* is effective for readers who are not psychiatrists.
Appeal to *pathos*: • How well does the writer appeal to readers' emotions, sympathies, and values?	Examine how Martin uses case studies to appeal to his readers' emotions—especially the 17-year-old father with the tattoo of his baby girl or the 13-year-old boy with tattooed dice and future plans for a "Dead Man's Hand" tattoo to commemorate his dead father.
Author's angle of vision: • How much does the author's angle of vision or interpretive filter dominate the text, influencing what is emphasized or omitted?	Examine how Martin's angle of vision restricts his examples to tattooed teenagers who come for psychiatric therapy. Had he interviewed a wider range of teenagers, he might have reached different conclusions.

For a rhetorical critique, you would probably not choose all of these questions but would select three or four to highlight. Your goal is to make insightful observations about how a text works rhetorically and to support your points with examples and short quotations from the text.

Strong Response as Ideas Critique

A second kind of strong response focuses on the ideas at stake in the text. Rather than treat the text as an artifact to analyze rhetorically (as in a rhetorical critique), you treat it as a voice in a conversation—one perspective on an issue or one solution to a problem or question. Your strong response examines how the ideas of the original author mesh or conflict with your own. Based on your own critical thinking, personal experiences, and research, to what extent do you agree or disagree with the writer's thesis? A with-the-grain reading of a text would support all or some of the text's ideas, while also supplying additional evidence or extending the argument, perhaps applying it in a new context. An against-the-grain reading would challenge the writer's ideas, point out flaws and holes in the writer's thinking, and provide counterexamples and rebuttals. You might agree with some ideas and disagree with others in the text. In any case, in an ideas critique you speak back to the text from your own experience, background, reading, and thoughtful wrestling with the writer's ideas.

> **Example:** In response to the article in the conservative business journal on drilling for oil in the ANWR, you would give your own views on oil exploration in the ANWR to support or challenge the writer's views, to raise new questions, and otherwise to add your voice to the ANWR conversation. You might supply additional reasons and evidence for drilling, or you might oppose drilling in the ANWR by providing counterreasoning and counterexamples.

When you write an ideas critique you are thus joining an important conversation about the actual subject matter of a text. Because much academic and professional writing focuses on finding the best solution to complex problems, this kind of strong response is very common. Usually this genre requires closed-form, thesis-governed prose. The following strategies chart suggests questions you can ask about a text to enter into its conversation of ideas.

QUESTION-ASKING STRATEGIES for Writing an Ideas Critique

Questions to Ask	Examples
Where do I agree with this author? (with the grain)	Consider how you might amplify or extend Dr. Andrés Martin's ideas. Build on his ideas by discussing examples of acquaintances who have marked significant moments in their lives (graduation, deaths of relatives, divorces) with tattoos.
What new insights has this text given me? (with the grain)	Explore Martin's idea that teens use tattoos to record relationships. Think of how people's choice of tattoos might have deeper meanings about friendships or connections with a group.

Questions to Ask	Examples
Where do I disagree with this author? (against the grain)	Challenge Martin's view of tattoos as having special significance by showing that tattoos have become a commonplace mainstream phenomenon among teens and adults alike.
What points has the author overlooked or omitted? (against the grain)	Recognize that Martin is writing at a time when tattoo removal was uncommon, so he speaks of tattoos as entirely permanent. Today the availability of laser removal of tattoos might change the way people think about them.
What new questions or problems has the text raised? (with or against the grain)	Explain how Martin's highly sympathetic attitude toward tattoos portrays body modification in a wholly positive and creative light, while glossing over health risks and long-term costs.
What are the limitations or consequences of this text? (with or against the grain)	Discuss how Martin's view of tattoos was progressive for its time, but doesn't explain why tattoos and piercing have become increasingly popular in recent years.

Because critiques of ideas appear in many contexts where writers search for the best solutions to problems, this kind of thinking is essential for academic research. In writing research papers, writers typically follow the template "This other writer has argued A, but I am going to argue B." Often the writer's own view (labeled "B") results from the writer's having wrestled with the views of others. Because this kind of dialectic thinking is so important to academic and professional life, we treat it further in Chapter 8 on exploratory writing, in Chapter 13 on analysis and synthesis, and in Chapter 14 on classical argument. Each of these chapters encourages you to articulate alternative views and respond to them.

Strong Response as Reflection

A third kind of strong response is often called a "reflection" or a "reflection paper." (An instructor might say, for example, "Read Andrés Martin's article on teenage tattooing and write a reflection about it.") Generally, a reflection assignment is an introspective genre; it invites you to connect the reading to your own personal experiences, beliefs, and values. In a reflection paper, the instructor is particularly interested in how the reading has affected you personally—what memories it has triggered, what personal experiences it relates to, what values and beliefs it has challenged, what dilemmas it poses, and so forth. A reflection paper is often more exploratory, open-ended, musing, and tentative than a rhetorical critique or an ideas critique, which are usually closed form and thesis governed.

Example: In response to the article in the conservative business journal on drilling for oil in the ANWR, you might explore how the reading creates a dilemma for you. You might reflect on your own wilderness experiences, musing about the importance of nature in your own life. But at the same time, you acknowledge that you are aware of the need for oil and of your own reluctance to give up owning a car. You build your reflective paper around a personal conflict in values.

Here are some strategies you can use to generate ideas for a reflective strong response:

QUESTION-ASKING STRATEGIES for Writing a Reflective Strong Response

Questions to Ask	Examples
What personal memories or experiences does this text trigger?	Explore how Andrés Martin's case studies of teenagers with tattoos trigger your own reflections about tattoos. If you have one, why did you get it? If you don't, why not?
What personal values or beliefs does this text reinforce or challenge?	Explore the extent to which you can relate to the tattooed teenagers in Martin's case studies. How are your values or beliefs similar to or different from theirs? Does Martin's analysis of their situations make sense to you?
What questions, dilemmas, or problems does this text raise for me?	Explore how Martin's text has raised problems for you. Perhaps you feel ambivalent about body piercing and tattoos and see them more as self-mutilation rather than meaningful art. You could explore the layers of your own thinking about tattoos.
What new insights, ideas, or thoughts of my own have been stimulated by this text?	Explore any possible new "aha" moments that might have struck you while reading Martin. For example, suppose the use of tattoos to "control" a situation struck you as similar to the way anorexics talk about starvation as control.

As you can tell from these questions, a reflective strong response highlights your own personal experiences and beliefs in conversation with the text. Whereas the focus of a rhetorical critique is on analyzing the way the text works rhetorically and the focus of an ideas critique is on taking a stance on the ideas at stake in the text, a reflective response focuses on the personal dimension of reading the text. Reflections call for a degree of self-disclosure or self-exploration that would be largely absent from the other kinds of strong responses.

Strong Response as a Blend

It should be evident that the boundaries among these genres overlap and that a strong response could easily blend features of each of the preceding genres. In trying to decide how to respond strongly to a text, you often don't have to confine yourself to a pure genre but can mix and match different kinds of responses. You can analyze and critique a text's rhetorical strategies, show how the text challenges your own personal values and beliefs, and also develop your own stance on the text's ideas. In writing a blended response, you can emphasize what is most important to you, while not limiting yourself to only one approach.

Before we turn to the writing projects for this chapter, we show you an example of a student summary/strong response that uses a blend of rhetorical critique and a critique of Martin's ideas. Note that the essay begins by identifying the question under discussion: Why do teenagers get tattoos? It then summarizes the article by Andrés Martin.* Immediately following the summary, the student writer states his thesis, followed by his strong response, which contains both rhetorical points and points about the causes of teenage tattooing.

Sean Barry (student)

Why Do Teenagers Get Tattoos? A Response to Andrés Martin

My sister has one. My brother has one. I have one. Just take a stroll downtown and you will see how commonplace it is for someone to be decorated with tattoos and hung with piercings. In fact, hundreds of teenagers, every day, allow themselves to be etched upon or poked into. What's the cause of this phenomenon? Why do so many teenagers get tattoos?

Introduces topic and sets context

Dr. Andrés Martin has answered this question from a psychiatrist's perspective in his article "On Teenagers and Tattoos," published in the *Journal of the American Academy of Child and Adolescent Psychiatry*. Martin advises fellow psychiatrists to think of teenage tattooing as a constructive opportunity for clinicians to understand teenagers better. Martin examines three different reasons that teenagers get tattoos. First, he argues that tattoos help teenagers establish unique identities by giving them a sense of control over their evolving bodies and over an environment perceived as adverse and domineering. Second, he believes that a tattooed image often symbolizes the teen's relationship to a significant concept or person, making the relationship more visible and real. Finally, says Martin, because teens are disturbed by modern society's mobility and fragmentation and because they have an "intense longing for rootedness and stability" (112), the irreversible nature of tattoos may give them a sense of permanence. Martin concludes that tattoos can be a meaningful record of survived teen experiences. Although Martin's analysis has relevance and some strengths, I think he overgeneralizes and over-romanticizes teenage tattooing, leading him to overlook other causes of teenage tattooing such as commercialization and teenagers' desire to identify with a peer group as well as achieve an individual identity.

Summary of Martin's article

Thesis statement

thesis: his opinion

(*continued*)

*In this essay the student writer uses a shortened version of his 195-word summary that was used as an illustration on pages 118–119.

With-the-grain point in support of Martin's ideas

Some of Martin's points seem relevant and realistic and match my own experiences. I agree that teenagers sometimes use tattoos to establish their own identities. When my brother, sister, and I all got our tattoos, we were partly asserting our own independence from our parents. Martin's point about the symbolic significance of a tattoo image also connects with my experiences. A Hawaiian guy in my dorm has a fish tattooed on his back, which he says represents his love of the ocean and the spiritual experience he has when he scuba dives.

Rhetorical point about Martin's audience, purpose, and genre that has both with-the-grain and against-the-grain elements

Martin, speaking as a psychiatrist to other psychiatrists, also provides psychological insights into the topic of teen tattooing even though this psychological perspective brings some limitations, too. In this scholarly article, Martin's purpose is to persuade fellow psychiatrists to think of adolescent tattooing in positive rather than judgmental terms. Rather than condemn teens for getting tattoos, he argues that discussion of the tattoos can provide useful insights into the needs and behavior of troubled teens (especially males). But this perspective is also a limitation because the teenagers he sees are mostly youths in psychiatric counseling, particularly teens struggling with the absence of or violent loss of a parent and those who have experience with gangs and prison-terms. This perspective leads him to overgeneralize. As a psychological study of a specific group of troubled teens, the article is informative. However, it does not apply as well to most teenagers who are getting tattoos today.

Against-the-grain rhetorical point: Barry analyzes use of quotations from Moby Dick

Besides overgeneralizing, Martin also seems to romanticize teenage tattooing. Why else would a supposedly scientific article begin and end with quotations from *Moby Dick*? Martin seems to imply a similarity between today's teenagers and the sailor hero Ishmael who wandered the seas looking for personal identity. In quoting *Moby Dick*, Martin seems to value tattooing as a suitable way for teenagers to record their experiences. Every tattoo, for Martin, has deep significance. Thus, Martin casts tattooed teens as romantic outcasts, loners, and adventurers like Ishmael.

Transition to writer's own analysis

Against-the-grain point: writer's alternative theory

In contrast to Martin, I believe that teens are influenced by the commercial nature of tattooing, which has become big business aimed at their age group. Every movie or television star or beauty queen who sports a tattoo sends the commercial message that tattoos are cool: "A tattoo will help you be successful, sexy, handsome, or attractive like us." Tattoo parlors are no longer dark dives in seedy, dangerous parts of cities, but appear in lively commercial districts; in fact, there are several down the street from the university. Teenagers now buy tattoos the way they buy other consumer items.

Against-the-grain point: writer's second theory

Furthermore, Martin doesn't explore teenagers' desire not only for individuality but also for peer group acceptance. Tattooing is the "in" thing to do. Tattooing used to be defiant and daring, but now it is popular and more acceptable among teens. I even know a group of sorority women who went together to get tattoos on their ankles. As tattooing has become more mainstreamed, rebels/trendsetters have turned to newer and more outrageous practices, such as branding and extreme piercings. Meanwhile, tattoos bring middle-of-the-road teens the best of both worlds: a way to show their individuality and simultaneously to be accepted by peers.

Conclusion and summary

In sum, Martin's research is important because it examines psychological responses to teen's inner conflicts. It offers partial explanations for teens' attraction to tattoos and promotes a positive, noncritical attitude toward tattooing. But I think the article is limited by its overgeneralizations based on the psychiatric focus, by its tendency to romanticize tattooing, by its lack of recognition of the commercialization of tattooing, and by its underemphasis on group belonging and peer pressure. Teen tattooing is more complex than even Martin makes it.

Work Cited

Martin, Andrés. "On Teenagers and Tattoos." *Journal of the American Academy of Child and Adolescent Psychiatry* 36 (1997): 860–61. Rpt. in *The Allyn & Bacon Guide to Writing*. John D. Ramage, John C. Bean, and June Johnson. 5th ed. New York: Longman, 2009. 110–13. Print.

Complete citation of article in MLA format

In the student example just shown, Sean Barry illustrates a blended strong response that intermixes rhetorical critique of the article with his own views on tattooing. He analyzes Martin's article rhetorically by pointing out some of the limitations of a psychiatric angle of vision and by showing the values implications of Martin's references to *Moby Dick*. He adds his own ideas to the conversation by supporting two of Martin's points using his own personal examples. But he also reads Martin against the grain by arguing that Martin, perhaps influenced by his romantic view of tattoos, fails to appreciate the impact on teenagers of the commercialization of tattooing and the importance of peer group acceptance. Clearly, Sean Barry illustrates what we mean by a strong reader.

For another example of a student's summary/strong response essay—in this case the strong response is primarily a rhetorical critique—see Stephanie Malinowski's "Questioning Thomas L. Friedman's Optimism in '30 Little Turtles'" in the Readings section of this chapter, pages 143–145. The Friedman article is found on pages 142–143.

Writing a Summary/Strong Response of a Visual-Verbal Text

In our increasingly visual world, many genres of texts—advocacy sites on the Web, public affairs advocacy ads, advertisements, posters for political and environmental campaigns, brochures, and leaflets—combine verbal and visual elements. As we discuss in Concept 10 in Chapter 3 and Concept 12 in Chapter 4, visual images such as photographs, drawings, and paintings can also be read rhetorically, and indeed many of these visuals do much of the rhetorical work of the document.

Visual-verbal texts are often rhetorically complex and very interesting to examine and critique. A strong response to a visual-verbal text might examine many of the same features we identified for verbal texts—for example, how well the text connects with the intended audience, carries out its purposes, and fulfills readers' expectations for its genre. In critiquing a visual-verbal text, you might consider analyzing any of the features listed on page 130. For our examples, we have used a booklet entitled *Compassionate Living* produced by the People for the Ethical Treatment of Animals (PETA), which you can find at this Web address: www.peta2.com/college/pdf/CompassionateLiving.pdf.

QUESTION-ASKING STRATEGIES for Analyzing a Visual-Verbal Text

Ask Questions about Any of the Following:	Examples
Use of type, layout, color, and image: • How effectively do these features contribute to the rhetorical effect of the document? • How effectively are these features used to influence the intended audience?	Examine how the booklet *Compassionate Living* created by the People for the Ethical Treatment of Animals (PETA) achieves a user-friendly appearance through its use of pleasant-colored boxes of text; photographs of animals, people, and products; a layout that divides each page into boxes and columns; and readable headings in different type sizes.
Relationship between image and verbal text: • Do the words comment on images, or do images illustrate words? • How much rhetorical work is performed by the visual images in the text?	In the *Compassionate Living* booklet, examine how text is used to present explanations, information, and slogans ("Real environmentalists don't eat meat") and attention-grabbing headings (for example, "Bulldozing the sea" and "Chicken hell") and how the photographs illustrate these ideas and provide visual variety.
Appeals to *logos, ethos,* and *pathos:* • How effectively do the images convey or support main points? • Does the whole document seem credible and ethical? • How do the images affect the emotions and sympathies of the audience?	Examine to what extent the *Compassionate Living* guide builds credibility with its information, explanations, and proposals for a lifestyle without animal products; discuss the effect of the disturbing photos and narrative anecdotes about cruelty and animal suffering. Consider the extent to which the argument for a vegan lifestyle is rationally and persuasively supported.
Author's angle of vision: • How much has the author's angle of vision or interpretive filter dominated the text, influencing what is emphasized and what is left out? • What is the rationale for including various images?	Examine the extent to which the *Compassionate Living* booklet, in promoting "a kinder lifestyle" and faulting humans' treatment of animals, focuses on a pro-vegan perspective and excludes other perspectives. What views about humans' relationship to animals is left out of this short guide?

WRITING PROJECT

A Summary

Write a summary of an article assigned by your instructor for an audience who has not read the article. Write the summary using attributive tags and providing an introductory context as if you were inserting it into your own longer paper (see the model on p. 127). The word count for your summary will be specified by your instructor. Try to follow all the criteria for a successful summary listed on page 119, and use MLA documentation style, including a Works Cited entry for the article that you are summarizing. (Note: Instead of an article, your instructor may ask you to summarize a longer text such as a book or a visual-verbal text such as a Web page or an advocacy brochure. We address these special cases at the end of this section.)

Generating Ideas: Reading for Structure and Content

Once you have been assigned an article to summarize, your first task is to read it carefully a number of times to get an accurate understanding of it. Remember that summarizing involves the essential act of reading with the grain as you figure out exactly what an article is saying. In writing a summary, you must focus on both a text's structure and its content. In the following steps, we recommend a process that will help you condense a text's ideas into an accurate summary. As you become a more experienced reader and writer, you'll follow these steps without thinking about them.

Step 1: The first time through, read the text fairly quickly for general meaning. If you get confused, keep going; later parts of the text might clarify earlier parts.

Step 2: Read the text carefully paragraph by paragraph. As you read, write gist statements in the margins for each paragraph. A *gist statement* is a brief indication of a paragraph's function in the text or a brief summary of a paragraph's content. Sometimes it is helpful to think of these two kinds of gist statements as "what it does" statements and "what it says" statements.* A "what it does" statement specifies the paragraph's function—for example, "summarizes an opposing view," "introduces another reason," "presents a supporting example," "provides statistical data in support of a point," and so on. A "what it says" statement captures the main idea of a paragraph by summarizing the paragraph's content. The "what it says" statement is the paragraph's main point, in contrast to its supporting ideas and examples. Sometimes an explicit topic sentence makes the main point easy to find, but often you have to extract the main point by shrinking an argument

*For our treatment of "what it does" and "what it says" statements, we are indebted to Kenneth A. Bruffee, *A Short Course in Writing*, 2nd ed. (Cambridge, MA: Winthrop, 1980).

down to its essence. In some cases, you may be uncertain about the main point. If so, select the point that you think a majority of readers would agree is the main one.

When you first practice detailed readings of a text, you might find it helpful to write complete *does* and *says* statements on a separate sheet of paper rather than in the margins until you develop the internal habit of appreciating both the function and content of parts of an essay. Here are *does* and *says* statements for selected paragraphs of Andrés Martin's essay on teenage tattooing:

Paragraph 1: *Does*: Introduces the subject and sets up the argument. *Says*: The current popularity of tattoos and piercings is partly explained as an aid toward finding an identity, but the core of their appeal is their irreversible permanence.

Paragraph 2: *Does*: Narrows the focus and presents the thesis. *Says*: To counsel families in disagreement over tattoos, psychiatrists should exhibit a nonjudgmental appreciation of teen tattoos and use them to understand teenagers better.

Paragraph 4: *Does*: Discusses the first complex motivation behind youth tattooing. *Says*: Teens use tattoos to handle identity crises and to establish their uniqueness from others.

Paragraph 5: *Does*: Elaborates on the first motivation, the identity issue. *Says*: Tattoos provide teens with a sense of control over their changing bodies and over an environment perceived as adverse and domineering.

Paragraph 11: *Does*: Complicates the view of teens' use of tattoos to find permanence and belonging. *Says*: Although tattoos may unrealistically promise the resolution to larger conflicts, they may at least record the triumphs and miseries of adolescent turbulence, including gang and prison experience.

Paragraph 12: *Does*: Sums up the perspective and advice of the article. *Says*: Psychiatrists should regard adolescent tattoos positively as adornment and self-expression and employ tattoos to help understand teens' identities and sense of reality.

You may occasionally have difficulty writing a *says* statement for a paragraph because you may have trouble deciding what the main idea is, especially if the paragraph doesn't begin with a closed-form topic sentence. One way to respond to this problem is to formulate the question that you think the paragraph answers. If you think of chunks of the text as answers to a logical progression of questions, you can often follow the main ideas more easily. Rather than writing *says* statements in the margins, therefore, some readers prefer writing *says* questions. *Says* questions for the Martin text may include the following: What is the most constructive approach clinicians can take to teen tattooing when these tattoos have become the focus of family conflict? What psychological needs and problems are teenagers acting out through their tattoos? Why does the permanence of tattoos appeal to young people?

No matter which method you use—*says* statements or *says* questions—writing gist statements in the margins is far more effective than underlining or highlighting in helping you recall the text's structure and argument.

Step 3: After you have analyzed the article paragraph by paragraph, try locating the article's main divisions or parts. In longer closed-form articles, writers often forecast the shape of their essays in their introductions or use their conclusions to sum up main points. For example, although Martin's article is short, it uses both a forecasting statement and subheads to direct readers through its main points. The article is divided into several main chunks as follows:

- Introductory paragraphs, which establish the problem to be addressed and narrow the focus to a clinical perspective (paragraphs 1–2)
- A one-sentence organizing and predicting statement (paragraph 3)
- A section explaining how tattoos may help adolescents establish a unique identity (paragraphs 4–5)
- A section explaining how tattoos help teens incorporate onto their bodies a symbolic ownership of something important to them (paragraphs 6–8)
- A section explaining how tattoos represent and satisfy teens' search for permanence (paragraphs 9–11)
- A conclusion that states the thesis explicitly and sums up Martin's advice to fellow psychiatrists (paragraph 12)

Instead of listing the sections of your article, you might prefer to make an outline or tree diagram of the article showing its main parts.

Outlines and tree diagrams are discussed in Chapter 18, Skill 7.

Drafting and Revising

Once you have determined the main points and grasped the structure of the article you are summarizing, combine and condense your *says* statements into clear sentences that capture the gist of the article. These shortened versions of your *says* statements will make up most of your summary, although you might mention the structure of the article to help organize the points. For example, you might say, "[Author's name] makes four main points in this article. ... The article concludes with a call to action. ... " Because representing an article in your own words in a greatly abbreviated form is a challenge, most writers revise their sentences to find the clearest, most concise way to express the article's ideas accurately. Choose and use your words carefully to stay within your word limit.

The procedures for summarizing articles can work for book-length texts and visual-verbal texts as well. For book-length texts, your *does* and *says* statements may cover chapters or parts of the book. Book introductions and conclusions as well as chapter titles and introductions may provide clues to the author's thesis and subthesis to help you identify the main ideas to include in a book summary. For verbal-visual texts such as a public affairs advocacy ad, product advertisement, Web page, or brochure, examine the parts to see what each contributes to the whole. In your summary, help your readers visualize the images, comprehend the parts, and understand the main points of the text's message. For example, here is a brief summary of the PETA booklet *Compassionate Living* that we discussed on page 130.

> The PETA guide *Compassionate Living* consists of twenty-four pages. The front of the booklet states the title and shows inviting pictures of animals. The guide sets up "What's Inside" under six main headings: "Compassionate eating," "Compassionate shopping," "Compassionate clothing," "Animal-friendly apparel," "Compassionate entertainment," and "Compassionate living." Then the booklet states claims and raises questions, provides support and answers, and uses boxed text as well as cute photos of animals and photos of cruelty to animals to illustrate its points. Its argument is that ... [here you would summarize the main ideas from the sections].

Plan to create several drafts of all summaries to refine your presentation and wording of ideas. Group work may be helpful in these steps.

FOR WRITING AND DISCUSSION

Finding Key Points in an Article

If the whole class or a group of students is summarizing the same article, brainstorm together and then reach consensus on the main ideas that you think a summary of that article should include to be accurate and complete. Then reread your own summary and check off each idea.

When you revise your summary, consult the criteria on page 119 in this chapter as well as the Questions for Peer Review that follow.

Questions for Peer Review

In addition to the generic peer review questions explained in Chapter 17, Skill 4, ask your peer reviewers to address these questions:

1. In what way do the opening sentences provide needed contextual information and then express the overall thesis of the text? What information could be added or more clearly stated?
2. How would you evaluate the writer's representation and coverage of the text's main ideas in terms of accuracy, balance, and proportion? What ideas have been omitted or overemphasized?
3. Has the writer treated the article fairly and neutrally? If judgments have crept in, where could the writer revise?
4. How could the summary use attributive tags more effectively to keep the focus on the original author's ideas?
5. Has the writer used quotations sparingly and cited them accurately? Has the writer translated points into his or her own words? Has the writer included a Works Cited?
6. Where might the writer's choice of words and phrasing of sentences be revised to improve the clarity, conciseness, and coherence of the summary?

A Summary/Strong Response Essay

WRITING PROJECT

In response to a text assigned by your instructor, write a "summary/strong response" essay that incorporates a 150–250 word summary of the article. In your strong response to that reading, speak back to its author from your own critical thinking, personal experience, values, and, perhaps, further reading or research. Unless your instructor assigns a specific kind of strong response (rhetorical critique, ideas critique, or reflection), write a blended response in which you are free to consider the author's rhetorical strategies, your own agreement or disagreement with the author's ideas, and your personal response to the text. Think of your response as your analysis of how the text tries to influence its readers rhetorically and how your wrestling with the text has expanded and deepened your thinking about its ideas. As you work with ideas from the text, remember to use attributive tags, quotation marks for any quoted passages, and MLA documentation to distinguish your own points about the text from the author's ideas and language.

Exploring Ideas for Your Strong Response

Earlier in the chapter we presented the kinds of strong responses you may be asked to write in college. We also provided examples of the questions you can ask to generate ideas for different kinds of strong response. Your goal now is to figure out what you want to say. Your first step, of course, is to read your assigned text with the grain, listening to the text so well that you can write a summary of its argument. Use the strategies described in the previous writing project to compose your summary of the assigned text.

After you have written your summary, which demonstrates your full understanding of the text, you are ready to write a strong response. Because your essay cannot discuss every feature of a text or every idea the text has evoked, you will want to focus on a small group of points that enable you to bring readers a new, enlarged, or deepened understanding of the text. You may decide to write a primarily with-the-grain response, praising, building on, or applying the text to a new context, or a primarily against-the-grain response, challenging, questioning, and refuting the text. Our students generally say it is easier to write a strong response that questions or disagrees with a text rather than agrees with it. However, both approaches have challenges. If your strong response primarily agrees with the text, you must be sure to extend it and apply the ideas rather than simply make your strong response one long summary of the article. If your strong response primarily disagrees with the text and criticizes it, you must be sure to be fair and accurate in your criticisms. Here we give you some specific rereading strategies that will stimulate ideas for your strong response, as well as an example of Sean Barry's marginal response notes to Martin's article (Figure 6.1).

See Chapter 1, Concept 3, for a discussion of audience analysis.

STRATEGIES

for Rereading to Stimulate Ideas for a Strong Response

Strategies	What to Do	Comments
Take notes.	Make copious marginal notes while rereading, recording both with-the-grain and against-the-grain responses.	Writing a strong response requires a deep engagement with texts. For example, in Figure 6.1, observe how Sean Barry's notes incorporate with-the-grain and against-the-grain responses and show him truly talking back to and interacting with Martin's text.
Identify "hot spots" in the text.	Mark all hot spots with marginal notes. After you've finished reading, find these hot spots and freewrite your responses to them in a reading journal.	By "hot spot" we mean a quotation or passage that you notice because you agree or disagree with it or because it triggers memories or other associations. Perhaps the hot spot strikes you as thought provoking. Perhaps it raises a problem or is confusing yet suggestive.
Ask questions.	Write several questions that the text caused you to think about. Then explore your responses to those questions through freewriting, which may trigger more questions.	Almost any text triggers questions as you read. A good way to begin formulating a strong response is to note these questions.
Articulate your difference from the intended audience.	Decide who the writer's intended audience is. If you differ significantly from this audience, use this difference to question the author's underlying assumptions, values, and beliefs.	Your gender, age, class, ethnicity, sexual orientation, political and religious beliefs, interests, values, and so forth, may cause you to feel estranged from the author's imagined audience. If the text seems written for straight people and you are gay, or for Christians and you are a Muslim or an atheist, or for environmentalists and you grew up in a small logging community, you may well resist the text. Sometimes your sense of exclusion from the intended audience makes it difficult to read a text at all.

Andrés Martin, M.D.

On Teenagers and Tattoos

Quotation from a novel?

A strange beginning for a scientific article

The skeleton dimensions I shall now proceed to set down are copied verbatim from my right arm, where I had them tattooed: as in my wild wanderings at that period, there was no other secure way of preserving such valuable statistics.

—Melville/ Moby Dick CII

What do 19th-century sailors have to do with 21st century teens?

1 Tattoos and piercings have become a part of our everyday landscape. They are ubiquitous, having entered the circles of glamour and the mainstream of fashion, and they have even become an increasingly common feature of our urban youth. Legislation in most states restricts professional tattooing to adults older than 18 years of age, so "high end" tattooing is rare in children and adolescents, but such tattoos are occasionally seen in older teenagers. Piercings, by comparison, as well as self-made or "jailhouse" type tattoos, are not at all rare among adolescents or even among schoolage children. Like hairdo, makeup, or baggy jeans, tattoos and piercings can be subject to fad influence or peer pressure in an effort toward group affiliation. As with any other fashion statement, they can be construed as bodily aids in the inner struggle toward identity consolidation, serving as adjuncts to the defining and sculpting of the self by means of external manipulations. But unlike most other body decorations, tattoos and piercings are set apart by their irreversible and permanent nature, a quality at the core of their magnetic appeal to adolescents.

Larger tattooing scene?

Idea here: the body as a concrete record of experience?

I like the phrase "the defining and sculpting of the self"—sounds creative, like art

This idea is surprising and interesting. It merits lots of discussion.

2 Adolescents and their parents are often at odds over the acquisition of bodily decorations. For the adolescent, piercings or tattoos may be seen as personal and beautifying statements, while parents may construe them as oppositional and enraging affronts to their authority. Distinguishing bodily adornment from self-mutilation may indeed prove challenging, particularly when a family is in disagreement over a teenager's motivations and a clinician is summoned as the final arbiter. At such times it may be most important to realize jointly that the skin can all too readily become but another battleground for the tensions of the age, arguments having less to do with tattoos and piercings than with core issues such as separation from the family matrix. Exploring the motivations and significance underlying tattoos (Grumet, 1983) and piercings can go a long way toward resolving such differences and can become a novel and additional way of getting to know teenagers. An interested and nonjudgmental appreciation of teenagers' surface presentations may become a way of making contact not only in their terms but on their turfs: quite literally on the territory of their skins.

These terms show the main opposing views on tattoos.

Which teenagers? All teenagers?

Is he speaking only to psychiatrists? Does this clinical perspective have other applications?

Good open-minded, practical approach to teen tattoos

3 The following three sections exemplify some of the complex psychological underpinnings of youth tattooing.

I like Martin's focus on complexity

FIGURE 6.1 Student's Marginal Notes on Martin's Text

FOR WRITING AND DISCUSSION

Practicing Strong Response Reading Strategies

What follows is a short passage by writer Annie Dillard in response to a question about how she chooses to spend her time. This passage often evokes heated responses from our students.

> I don't do housework. Life is too short. ... I let almost all my indoor plants die from neglect while I was writing the book. There are all kinds of ways to live. You can take your choice. You can keep a tidy house, and when St. Peter asks you what you did with your life, you can say, "I kept a tidy house, I made my own cheese balls."

Individual task: Read the passage and then briefly freewrite your reaction to it.

Group task: Working in groups or as a whole class, develop answers to the following questions:

1. What values does Dillard assume her audience holds?
2. What kinds of readers are apt to feel excluded from that audience?
3. If you are not part of the intended audience for this passage, what in the text evokes resistance?

Articulate Your Own Purpose for Reading

You may sometimes read a text against the grain if your purposes for reading differ from what the author imagined. Normally you read a text because you share the author's interest in a question and want to know the author's answer. In other words, you usually read to join the author's conversation. But suppose that you wish to review the writings of nineteenth-century scientists to figure out what they assumed about nature (or women, or God, or race, or capitalism). Or suppose that you examine a politician's metaphors to see what they reveal about his or her values, or analyze *National Geographic* for evidence of political bias. In these cases, you will be reading against the grain of the text. In a sense, you would be blindsiding the authors—while they are talking about topic X, you are observing them for topic Y. This method of resistant reading is very common in academia.

Writing a Thesis for a Strong Response Essay

A thesis for a strong response essay should map out for readers the points that you want to develop and discuss. These points should be risky and contestable; your thesis should surprise your readers with something new or challenging. Your thesis might focus entirely on with-the-grain points or entirely on against-the-grain points, but most likely it will include some of both. Avoid tensionless thesis statements such as "This article has both good and bad points."

See Chapter 2, Concept 6, for a discussion of surprising thesis statements.

Here are some thesis statements that students have written for strong responses in our classes. Note that each thesis includes at least one point about the rhetorical strategies of the text.

EXAMPLES OF SUMMARY/STRONG RESPONSE THESIS STATEMENTS

- In "The Beauty Myth," Naomi Wolf makes a very good case for her idea that the beauty myth prevents women from ever feeling that they are good enough; however, Wolf's argument is geared too much toward feminists to be persuasive for a general audience, and she neglects to acknowledge the strong social pressures that I and other men feel to live up to male standards of physical perfection.
- Although Naomi Wolf in "The Beauty Myth" uses rhetorical strategies persuasively to argue that the beauty industry oppresses women, I think that she overlooks women's individual resistance and responsibility.
- Although the images and figures of speech that Thoreau uses in his chapter "Where I Lived, and What I Lived For" from *Walden* wonderfully support his argument that nature has valuable spiritually renewing powers, I disagree with his antitechnology stance and with his extreme emphasis on isolation as a means to self-discovery.
- In "Where I Lived, and What I Lived For" from *Walden*, Thoreau's argument that society is missing spiritual reality through its preoccupation with details and its frantic pace is convincing, especially to twenty-first century audiences; however, Thoreau weakens his message by criticizing his readers and by completely dismissing technological advances.
- Although the booklet *Compassionate Living* by People for the Ethical Treatment of Animals (PETA) uses the design features of layout, color, and image powerfully, its extreme examples, its quick dismissal of alternative views, and its failure to document the sources of its information weaken its appeal to *ethos* and its overall persuasiveness.

FOR WRITING AND DISCUSSION

Examining Thesis Statements for Strong Response Critiques

Working individually or in groups, identify the points in each of the thesis statements in the preceding section and briefly state them. Think in terms of the ideas you are expecting the writers to develop in the body of the essay. As a follow-up to this exercise, you might share in your groups your own thesis statements for your strong response essays. How clearly does each thesis statement lay out points that the writer will probe? As a group, discuss what new, important perspectives each thesis statement promises to bring to readers and how each thesis suits a rhetorical critique, ideas critique, or some combination of these.

Shaping and Drafting

Most strong response essays call for a short contextualizing introduction to set up your analysis. In the essay on pages 127–129, student writer Sean Barry begins by noting the popularity of tattoos and then poses the question that Andrés Martin will address: What is the cause of teenagers' getting tattoos? Student writer Stephanie Malinowski (pp. 143–145) uses a similar strategy. She begins by tapping into her readers' experiences with outsourcing, and then poses the question that Thomas Friedman addresses in his op-ed piece: Should Americans support or question the practice of outsourcing?

Both student writers pose a question that gives direction and purpose to their critique, and both include a short summary of the article that gives readers a foundation for the critique before they present the points of the article they will address in their strong responses.

Each of the thesis statements in the preceding section as well as Sean's and Stephanie's thesis statements identifies and maps out two or more points that readers will expect to see developed and explained in the body of the essay. In a closed-form, thesis-driven strong response, readers will also expect the points to follow the order in which they are presented in the thesis. If your strong response is primarily a rhetorical critique, your evidence will come mainly from the text you are analyzing. If your strong response is primarily an ideas critique, your evidence is apt to come from personal knowledge of the issue or from further reading or research. If your strong response is primarily reflective, much of your evidence will be based on your own personal experiences and inner thoughts. A blended response, of course, can combine points from any of these perspectives.

Each point in your thesis calls for a lively discussion, combining general statements and specifics that will encourage readers to see this text your way. Just as you do in your summary, you must use attributive tags to distinguish between the author's ideas and your own points and responses. In addition, you must document all ideas gotten from other sources as well as place all borrowed language in quotation marks or block indentations according to MLA format and include a Works Cited in MLA format. Most strong response essays have short conclusions, just enough commentary to bring closure to the essay.

Revising

In a summary/strong response essay, you may want to work on the summary separately before you incorporate it into your whole essay. Use the peer review questions for summaries (p. 134) for that part of your essay. You will definitely want to get feedback from readers to make your strong response as clear, thorough, and compelling as possible.

Questions for Peer Review

In addition to the generic peer review questions explained in Chapter 17, Skill 4, ask your peer reviewers to address these questions:

1. How appealingly do the title and introduction of the essay set up the topic of critique, convey the writer's interest, and lay a foundation for the summary of the article and the writer's thesis?
2. How could the writer's thesis statement be clearer in presenting several focused points about the text's rhetorical strategies and ideas?
3. How could the body of the strong response follow the thesis more closely?
4. Where do you, the reader, need more clarification or support for the writer's points? How could the writer develop with-the-grain or against-the-grain points more appropriately?
5. Where could the writer work on the effectiveness of attributive tags, quotations, and documentation?

READINGS

The readings for this chapter touch on the larger questions: What jobs will be available and promising when you graduate from college? How is globalization affecting the U.S. economy and employment opportunities? Specifically, these readings address the issue of outsourcing or offshoring, the business practice of moving jobs from developed countries like the United States to poor, developing countries like Mexico, China, and India. Outsourcing offers companies a large qualified workforce willing to work for lower wages and often more lenient environmental and safety regulations for factories. About thirty years ago, companies began moving their manufacturing abroad; later call centers, which handle customer service, and back office jobs, such as data entry, insurance claims, and payroll, followed manufacturing. In the last ten years, highly skilled jobs in information technology (IT), computer programming, and product design have also moved abroad. Basically, any work that can be conducted via the Internet—that is, with services handled electronically—can be outsourced.

Outsourcing's seemingly limitless potential, along with other factors, have sparked fiery public debates. Its increasing popularity as a business practice has coincided with a decrease in the normal rate of job creation in the United States as well as an increase in the unemployment and poverty rates as tracked by the Bureau of Labor Statistics, causing people to argue about these questions:

- Which factor is more responsible for the loss of American jobs: advances in automation or outsourcing?
- Who is benefiting from outsourcing: American consumers and stockholders, American corporations, foreign workers, the American economy, or geopolitical relations?
- What is the best solution to global economic competition: protecting American workers by restricting outsourcing, continuing to allow companies to outsource freely to remain competitive, or compensating American workers for job loss due to outsourcing?

The readings that follow address these questions from different perspectives. You can use these readings in various ways. Your instructor may choose one of these pieces as the subject of your assignments for this chapter. You can also use the readings to build your knowledge base on these issues. Representing a few of the many voices in this public controversy, these articles and political cartoons help form a rhetorical context for each other. We think you will find them useful in illuminating the rhetorical strategies and angle of vision of the text that you are analyzing. Because your task is to summarize your assigned piece and respond strongly to it, we omit the questions for analysis for all but the student essay by Stephanie Malinowski.

Our first reading is an op-ed piece by prominent journalist Thomas L. Friedman, published in the *New York Times* on February 29, 2004. Friedman is known for his pro–free trade enthusiasm and his two books on globalization, *The Lexus and the Olive Tree* (1999) and *The World Is Flat: A Brief History of the Twenty-First Century* (2005).

Thomas L. Friedman

30 Little Turtles

1 Indians are so hospitable. I got an ovation the other day from a roomful of Indian 20-year-olds just for reading perfectly the following paragraph: "A bottle of bottled water held 30 little turtles. It didn't matter that each turtle had to rattle a metal ladle in order to get a little bit of noodles, a total turtle delicacy. The problem was that there were many turtle battles for less than oodles of noodles."

2 I was sitting in on an "accent neutralization" class at the Indian call center 24/7 Customer. The instructor was teaching the would-be Indian call center operators to suppress their native Indian accents and speak with a Canadian one—she teaches British and U.S. accents as well, but these youths will be serving the Canadian market. Since I'm originally from Minnesota, near Canada, and still speak like someone out of the movie "Fargo," I gave these young Indians an authentic rendition of "30 Little Turtles," which is designed to teach them the proper Canadian pronunciations. Hence the rousing applause.

3 Watching these incredibly enthusiastic young Indians preparing for their call center jobs—earnestly trying to soften their t's and roll their r's—is an uplifting experience, especially when you hear from their friends already working these jobs how they have transformed their lives. Most of them still live at home and turn over part of their salaries to their parents, so the whole family benefits. Many have credit cards and have become real consumers, including of U.S. goods, for the first time. All of them seem to have gained self-confidence and self-worth.

4 A lot of these Indian young men and women have college degrees, but would never get a local job that starts at $200 to $300 a month were it not for the call centers. Some do "outbound" calls, selling things from credit cards to phone services to Americans and Europeans. Others deal with "inbound" calls—everything from tracing lost luggage for U.S. airline passengers to solving computer problems for U.S. customers. The calls are transferred here by satellite or fiber optic cable.

5 I was most taken by a young Indian engineer doing tech support for a U.S. software giant, who spoke with pride about how cool it is to tell his friends that he just spent the day helping Americans navigate their software. A majority of these call center workers are young women, who not only have been liberated by earning a decent local wage (and therefore have more choice in whom they marry), but are using the job to get M.B.A.'s and other degrees on the side.

6 I gathered a group together, and here's what they sound like: M. Dinesh, who does tech support, says his day is made when some American calls in with a problem and is actually happy to hear an Indian voice: "They say you people are really good at what you do. I am glad I reached an Indian." Kiran Menon, when asked who his role model was, shot back: "Bill Gates—[I dream of] starting my own company and making it that big." I asked C. M. Meghna what she got most out of the work: "Self-confidence," she said, "a lot of self-confidence, when people come to you with a problem and you can solve it—and having a lot of independence." Because the call center teams work through India's night—which corresponds to America's day—"your biological clock goes haywire," she added. "Besides that, it's great."

7 There is nothing more positive than the self-confidence, dignity and optimism that comes from a society knowing it is producing wealth by tapping its own brains—men's and women's—as opposed to one just tapping its own oil, let alone one that is so lost it can find dignity only through suicide and "martyrdom."

8 Indeed, listening to these Indian young people, I had a déjà vu. Five months ago, I was in Ramallah, on the West Bank, talking to three young Palestinian men, also in their 20's, one of whom was studying engineering. Their hero was Yasir Arafat. They talked about having no hope, no jobs and no dignity, and they each nodded when one of them said they were all "suicide bombers in waiting."

9 What am I saying here? That it's more important for young Indians to have jobs than Americans? Never. But I am saying that there is more to outsourcing than just economics. There's also geopolitics. It is inevitable in a networked world that our economy is going to shed certain low-wage, low-prestige jobs. To the extent that they go to places like India or Pakistan—where they are viewed as high-wage, high-prestige jobs—we make not only a more prosperous world, but a safer world for our own 20-year-olds.

Our second reading is a summary/strong response essay by student writer Stephanie Malinowski in response to the Friedman article. It follows primarily a "rhetorical critique" strategy for the strong response.

Stephanie Malinowski

Questioning Thomas L. Friedman's Optimism in "30 Little Turtles"

1 You are struggling to fix a problem that arises when you are downloading new computer software on to your computer. You're about to give up on the whole thing when an idea hits you: call the software company itself to ask for assistance. Should you be surprised when the person who answers the phone to help you is based in India? Should Americans support or question outsourcing?

2 In "30 Little Turtles," an op-ed piece that appeared in the *New York Times* on February 29, 2004, journalist and foreign affairs columnist Thomas L. Friedman argues that outsourcing call center jobs from the Western world to India is transforming the lives of Indian workers and benefiting geopolitics. Friedman supports his argument by detailing his experience visiting a call center in India. He claims that the Indians working to serve Canadian and American markets are happy with how their work has improved their lives. Friedman points out that the working Indian women feel liberated now that they are making a decent wage and can afford such things as a college education. He describes Indian workers' view of their jobs, using words such as "self-confidence" and "independence." At the end of his article, Friedman states that he doesn't favor Indian employment over American employment but that outsourced jobs in countries like India or Pakistan create both prosperity and global security.

Although Friedman's article clearly conveys to its audience how some Indian workers are benefiting from outsourcing, his argument relies heavily on personal experience and generalizations. I also think his condescending attitude hurts his argument, and he concludes his article too abruptly, leaving readers with questions.

3 Friedman succeeds in portraying the positive side of outsourcing to his *New York Times* readers who may be questioning the rationale for outsourcing. Friedman interviews the recipients of American jobs to see outsourcing from their perspective. Reading Friedman's article is an enlightening experience for Americans trying to understand how outsourcing is benefiting workers in other countries. Friedman's opening is vivid and captures the readers' interest by detailing his experience inside an Indian call center. He quotes the Indian workers expressing the joys of working for American and Canadian people. These workers testify to the financial and personal gains these jobs have brought. One woman says that she feels good about her job and herself "when people come to you with a problem and you can solve it" (142). The article is so full of optimism that the reader can't help but empathize with the Indians and feel happy that outsourcing has transformed their lives. Through these emotional appeals, Friedman succeeds in making readers who may have big reservations about outsourcing think about the human dimension of outsourcing.

4 However, Friedman also makes large generalizations based on his few personal experiences, lessening the credibility of his article. The first sentence of the article reads, "Indians are so hospitable." So are *all* Indians "so hospitable"? Friedman seems to make this generalization about national character based on the fact that he was applauded by a room full of Indians after reading a tongue twister paragraph in a perfect Canadian accent. I can see why Friedman appreciates his warm reception, but "feel good" moments can hardly provide evidence for the soundness of global economic policies. Friedman generalizes further about what he sees and hears in the call center room. He talks about the Indian employees in these terms: "All of them seem to have gained self-confidence and self-worth" (142). From this single observation, Friedman makes the assumption that almost every Indian working an outsourcing job must be gaining, and that the overall experience has done wonders for their lives. However, other articles that I have read have mentioned that call center work is basically a deadend job and that $200 a month is not a big salary. Later in his conclusion, Friedman states that "we make not only a more prosperous world, but a safer world for our own 20-year-olds" (143). Can this conclusion be drawn from one visit to a call center where Indians expressed gratitude for their outsourcing work?

5 An even bigger problem with Friedman's article is the condescending way in which he describes the Indian workers. I think he portrays the culture as being incompetent before the American and Canadian outsourcing jobs came to improve their accents and their lives. One statement that conveys condescension is this remark: "Watching these incredibly enthusiastic young Indians preparing for their call center jobs—earnestly trying to soften their t's and roll their r's—is an uplifting experience ..." (142). This passage reminds me of the delight and pride of parents witnessing their children's growth milestones. Friedman is casting the accent neutralization of the Indian workers as overcoming a barrier in order to reach success. Friedman's conde-

scending tone is apparent again when he restates the words of one American caller to an Indian worker, "They say you people are really good at what you do. I am glad I reached an Indian" (142). I see Friedman's reason for including this quote; he wants the reader to know that Indian workers are being valued for their work. However, the words that the American uses, which Friedman deliberately chooses to include in his article, "you people," suggest that Indians are a whole other kind of people different from American workers in their skills. Friedman's condescension also appears when he says that these are "low-wage, low-prestige jobs" (143). This remark is full of problems because it puts down the Indians taking the jobs and the Americans who have lost them, and it misrepresents the outsourcing scene that now includes many highly skilled prestigious jobs.

6 I also think that Friedman weakens his article by concluding abruptly and introducing new ideas to readers that leave them with unanswered questions. Friedman asks the reader, "What am I saying here? That it's more important for young Indians to have jobs than Americans?" (143). This point seems like a relevant question to investigate, but its weakness is that Friedman never even mentions any place in his article the loss that American workers are experiencing. At the end of the article, readers are left with questions. For example, the last sentence reads, "we make not only a more prosperous world, but a safer world for our own 20-year-olds" (143). Although Friedman is implying that outsourcing improves our relationships with other countries and enhances our national safety, nowhere in the article does he substantiate this claim. He seems to have thrown this statement into the conclusion just to end the article on a happy note.

7 Giving a human face to outsourcing is a good idea; however, Friedman does not support his main argument well, and this article comes across as a simplistic, unexplored view of outsourcing. I and other readers are left needing to look for answers to serious questions about outsourcing elsewhere.

Work Cited

Friedman, Thomas L. "30 Little Turtles." *New York Times* 29 Feb. 2004. Rpt. in *The Allyn & Bacon Guide to Writing*. John D. Ramage, John C. Bean, and June Johnson. 5th ed. New York: Longman, 2009. 142–43. Print.

THINKING CRITICALLY

about "Questioning Thomas L. Friedman's Optimism in '30 Little Turtles'"

1. What rhetorical points has Stephanie Malinowski chosen to analyze in her strong response essay?
2. What examples and quotations from Friedman's article work particularly well as support for her points? Where might she have included more support?

3. Where does Stephanie use attributive tags effectively?
4. If you were to write a rhetorical critique of Friedman's article, what points would you select to analyze?
5. If you were to write an ideas critique, what would you choose to focus on? Where would you agree and disagree with Friedman?

Our third and fourth readings consist of two political cartoons that tell stories about employment and U.S. involvement in outsourcing. As you read these cartoons, identify the characters, the story line, the angle of vision, and the argument each presents.

David Horsey, two-time Pulitzer Prize winner for editorial cartoons, publishes regularly in the *Seattle Post-Intelligencer*. This cartoon was originally published in that newspaper on June 4, 2003.

David Horsey

Today's Economic Indicator

The second cartoon, by Mike Lane, appeared in the *Baltimore Sun* in 2003 and was posted on Cagle Cartoons on August 27, 2003. Lane, a prize-winning and well-known liberal editorial cartoonist, left the Baltimore newspaper in 2004 after thirty-two years.

Mike Lane

Labor Day Blues

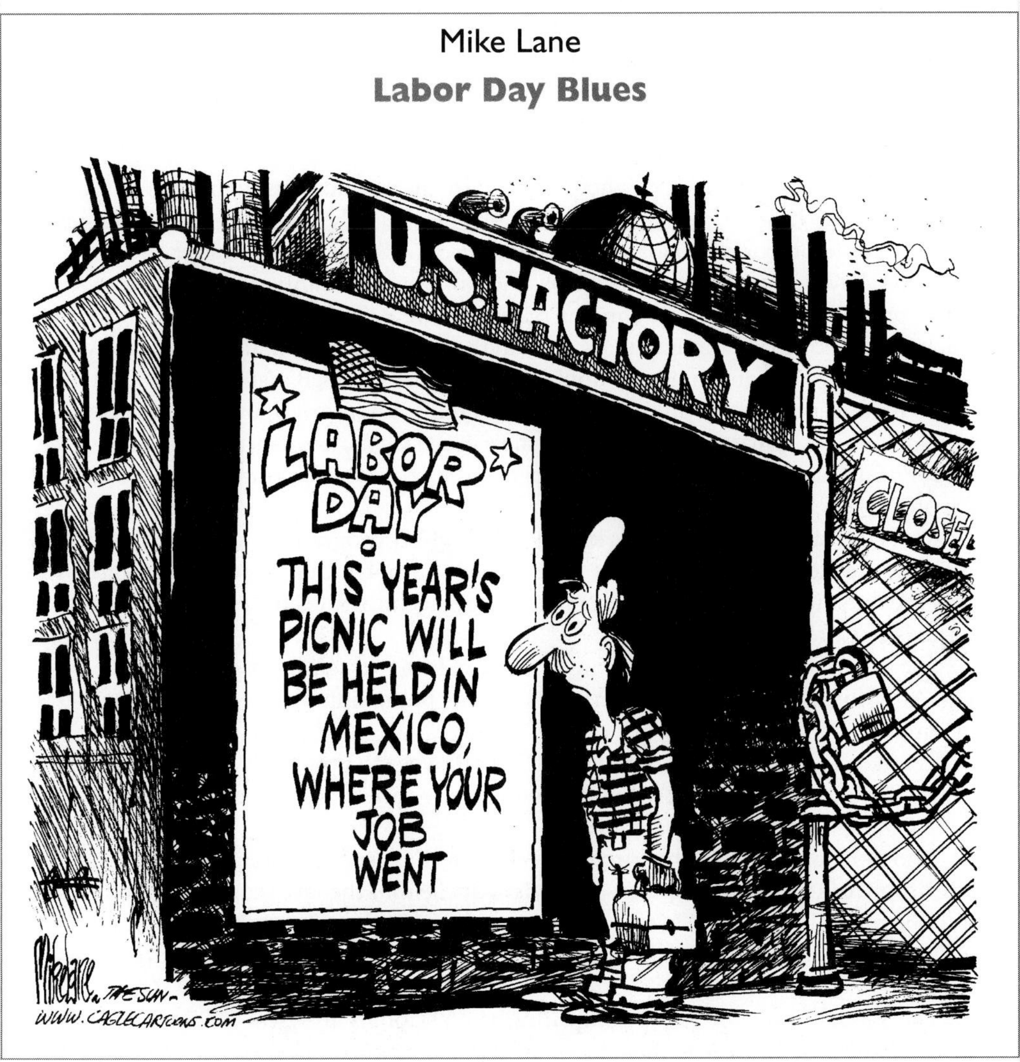

Our fifth reading is an op-ed piece by editorial writer and syndicated columnist Froma Harrop, who writes regularly for the *Providence Journal* and whose columns appear frequently in newspapers around the country. She is known for the articulate, forthright expression of her liberal views on current issues. This piece appeared in the *Seattle Times* on April 17, 2007.

Froma Harrop

New Threat to Skilled U.S. Workers

1 The master plan, it seems, is to move perhaps 40 million high-skill American jobs to other countries. U.S. workers have not been consulted.

2 Princeton economist Alan Blinder predicts that these choice jobs could be lost in a mere decade or two. We speak of computer programming, bookkeeping, graphic design and other careers once thought firmly planted in American soil. For perspective, 40 million is more than twice the total number of people now employed in manufacturing.

3 Blinder was taken aback when, sitting in at the business summit in Davos, Switzerland, he heard U.S. executives talk enthusiastically about all the professional jobs they could outsource to lower-wage countries. And he's a free trader.

4 What America can do to stop this is unclear, but it certainly doesn't have to *speed up* the process through a government program. We refer to the H-1B visa program, which allows educated foreigners to work in the United States, usually for three years. Many in Congress want to nearly double the number of H-1B visas, to 115,000 a year.

5 To the extent that the program helps talented foreign graduates of U.S. universities stay in this country while they await their green cards, it performs a useful service. But for many companies, the visa has become just a tool for transferring American jobs offshore.

6 Ron Hira has studied the dark side of the H-1B program. A professor of public policy at the Rochester Institute of Technology, he notes that the top applicants for visas are outsourcing companies, such as Wipro Technologies of India and Bermuda-based Accenture.

7 The companies bring recruits in from, say, India to learn about American business. After three years here, the workers go home better able to interact with their U.S. customers.

8 In other cases, companies ask their U.S. employees to train H-1B workers who then replace them at lower pay. "This is euphemistically called, 'knowledge transfer,'" Hira says. "I call it 'knowledge extraction.' "

9 Another rap against the program is that it's used to depress the wages of American workers. The program's defenders argue that the law requires companies to pay "the prevailing wage."

10 But "prevailing wage" is a legalism, Hira says. It does not translate into "market wage."

11 The median pay for H-1B computing professionals in fiscal 2005 was $50,000, which means half earn less than that. An American information-technology worker with a bachelor's degree makes more than $50,000 in an entry-level job.

12 Businesses bemoan the alleged shortage of Americans trained to do the work. But wait a second—the law of supply and demand states that a shortage of something causes its price to rise. Wages in information technology have been flat.

13 The companies fret that not enough young Americans are studying science and technology. Well, cutting the pay in those fields isn't much of an incentive, is it?

14 The threat that they will outsource if they can't bring in foreign temps is a hollow one. "There's nothing stopping those companies from working offshore anyway," Hira says. "They're not patriotic."

15 This vision for a competitive America seems to be a few rich U.S. executives commandeering armies of foreign workers. They don't have to train their domestic workforce. They don't have to raise pay to American standards.

16 A provision for revving up the H-1B program is contained in the immigration bill that last year passed the Senate. The co-sponsors, Democrat Ted Kennedy of Massachusetts and Republican John McCain of Arizona, have contended that their legislation requires employers to search for U.S. workers first. It does not.

17 Skilled U.S. workers had better start looking out for their interests. No one else is.

For additional writing, reading, and research resources, go to **www.MyCompLab.com** and choose **Ramage/Bean/Johnson's *The Allyn & Bacon Guide to Writing,* Fifth Edition.**

CHAPTER 7

WRITING AN AUTOBIOGRAPHICAL NARRATIVE

This chapter focuses on the rhetorical aim we have called "writing to express or share." This chapter's writing projects ask you to write an autobiographical narrative about something significant in your own life. But rather than state the significance up front in a thesis, you let it unfold in storylike fashion. This narrative structure places autobiographical writing at the open end of the closed-to-open-form continuum, making it more like a nonfiction "short story" than a traditional academic essay. Consequently, many instructors pair this chapter with Chapter 19, which discusses in more detail the features of open-form prose. The student essays in this chapter, as well as "Berkeley Blues" in Chapter 19 (pp. 547–549), were written for assignments like the ones in this chapter.

Autobiographical writing can help us explore, deepen, and complicate our perceptions of the world. Some of the most profound and influential science writing for general audiences—for example, the work of James Watson, Loren Eiseley, Jay Gould, Rachel Carson, and others—is narrative based, with the writer telling the story of intellectual discovery or narrating his or her wrestling with a problem. In addition to telling stories to convey the complexity and significance of phenomena, we use stories to reveal ourselves. In this regard, autobiographical writing, like certain forms of conversation, fills a very basic need in our daily lives—the need for intimacy or nontrivial human contact. One of the best measures we have of our closeness to other human beings is our willingness or reluctance to share with them our significant life stories, the ones that reveal our aspirations or humiliations.

We also use others' stories, particularly during adolescence, to monitor our own growth. Many of us once read (and still read) the stories of such people as Anne Frank, Maya Angelou, Helen Keller, Malcolm X, and Laura Ingalls Wilder in search of attitudes and behaviors to emulate. Reading their stories becomes a way of critiquing and understanding our own stories.

The writing projects for this chapter address two genres of narrative writing:

- An autobiographical narrative on any significant event or moment in your life that uses the narrative strategies of plot, character, and setting to develop tension, move the story forward, and give it significance
- A literacy narrative that uses the same narrative strategies but is centered on the writer's experience with language, reading, writing, school and teachers, or education

Both kinds of narratives draw on the sensibility that you bring to the ordinary as well as to the unique events of your life. Good autobiographical narrative does not depend on your having led an exciting life with highly dramatic moments. You need not have dated a movie star, won an X-Game skateboard competition, or survived an earthquake to share something lively or meaningful about your life. Likewise, an effective literacy narrative doesn't depend on your having learned to read when you were two or having won a national short story writing contest at age twelve. On the contrary, some of the most memorable autobiographical and literacy narratives relate ordinary experiences in a vivid manner that shares the writer's humiliations, aspirations, self-discoveries, and revelations. All of us have experienced a first day at a new school or job, a rival or sibling who seemed to best us at every turn, or a conflict with a parent, teacher, employer, lover, or friend. Everyone enjoys hearing good writers describe their unique methods of coping with and understanding these universal situations. It is precisely because readers have experienced these things that they can project themselves easily into the writer's world. This chapter shows you how to write an autobiographical story by finding a significant moment in your life and writing about it compellingly using literary techniques.

Exploring Autobiographical Narrative

One of the premises of this book is that good writing is rooted in the writer's perception of a problem. Problems are at the center not only of thesis-based writing but also of narrative writing. In effective narration, the problem usually takes the form of a *contrary,* two or more things in opposition—ideas, characters, expectations, forces, worldviews, or whatever. Three kinds of contraries that frequently form the plots of autobiographical narratives are the following:

1. *Old self versus new self.* The writer perceives changes in himself or herself as a result of some transforming or breakthrough moment or event.
2. *Old view of person X versus new view of person X.* The writer's perception of a person (favorite uncle, childhood hero, scary teacher) changes as a result of some revealing moment; the change in the narrator's perception of person X also indicates growth in the narrator's self-perception.
3. *Old values versus new values that threaten, challenge, or otherwise disrupt the old values.* The writer confronts an outsider (or a new, unfamiliar situation such as a class or a learning task) that challenges his or her worldview, or the writer undergoes a crisis that creates a conflict in values.

Prior to class discussion, freewrite for ten minutes about episodes in your own life that fit one or more of these typical plots. Then, working in small groups or as a whole class, share your discoveries. Your goal is to begin seeing that each person's life is a rich source of stories.

In considering experiences for a narrative, think of *significant* not as "unusual" or "exciting" but as "revealing" or "conveying an unexpected meaning or insight." Thought of in this way, a significant moment in a story might be a gesture, a remark, a smile, a way of walking or tying a shoe, the wearing of a certain piece of clothing, or the carrying of a certain object in a purse or pocket. Invent a short scene in which a gesture, smile, or brief action reverses one character's feelings about, or understanding of, another character.

1. You thought that Maria had led a sheltered life until ____________________.
2. You thought Mr. Watson was a scary old miser until ____________________.
3. Marco (Jillian) seemed the perfect date until ____________________.

In each case, think of specific details about one revealing moment that reverse your understanding. Here is an example of a scene:

> My dad seemed unforgivingly angry at me until he suddenly smiled, turned my baseball cap backward on my head, and held up his open palm for a high five. "Girl, if you don't change your ways, you're going to be as big a high school screw-up as your old man was."

Understanding Autobiographical Writing

Autobiographical writing may include descriptions of places and people and depictions of events that are more entertaining than enlightening. However, the spine of most autobiographical writing is a key moment or event, or a series of key moments or events, that shapes or reveals the author's emerging character or growth in understanding.

Autobiographical Tension: The Opposition of Contraries

Key events in autobiography are characterized by a clash of opposing values or points of view. These oppositions are typically embodied in conflicts between characters or in divided feelings within the narrator. The contraries in a story can often be summed up in statements such as these:

> My best friend from the eighth grade was suddenly an embarrassment in high school.
>
> My parents thought I was too young to drive to the movies when in fact I was ready to ride off with Iggy's Motorcycle Maniacs.
>
> The school I had dreamed of attending turned into a nightmarish prison.
>
> The subject I had hated most in middle school—science—became my passion in high school.
>
> The job that bored me and made all my muscles ache rescued me from a hopeless summer.

Consider the differences between "Berkeley Blues" (pp. 547–549) and "The Stolen Watch" (pp. 549–550).

An autobiographical piece without tension is like an academic piece without a problem or a surprising thesis. No writing is more tedious than a pointless "So what?" narrative that rambles on without tension. (You can read such a narrative in our discussion of the difference between a "story" and an "*and then* chronology" in Chapter 19. It is a good example of what *not* to do for this assignment.)

Like the risky thesis statement in closed-form writing, contrariety, or opposition, creates purpose and focus for open-form writing. It functions as an organizing principle, helping the writer determine what to include or omit. It also sets a direction for the writer. When a story is tightly wound and all the details contribute to the story line, the tension moves the plot forward as a mainspring moves the hands of a watch. The tension is typically resolved when the narrator experiences a moment of recognition or insight, vanquishes or is vanquished by a foe, or changes status.

How Literary Elements Work in Autobiographical Narratives

The basic elements of a literary narrative that work together to create a story are plot, character, setting, and theme.

The Importance of Plot

By *plot* we mean the basic action of the story, including the selection and sequencing of scenes and events. Often stories don't open with the earliest chronological moment; they may start *in medias res* ("in the middle of things") at a moment of crisis and then flash backward to fill in earlier details that explain the origins of the crisis. What you choose to include in your story and where you place it are concerns of plot. The amount of detail you choose to devote to each scene is also a function of plot. How a writer varies the amount of detail in each scene is referred to as a plot's *pacing*.

Plots typically unfold in the following stages: (a) an arresting opening scene; (b) the introduction of characters and the filling in of background; (c) the building of tension or conflict through oppositions embedded in a series of events or scenes; (d) the climax or pivotal moment when the tension or conflict comes to a head; and (e) reflection on the events of the plot and their meaning.

To help you recognize story-worthy events in your own life, consider the following list of pivotal moments that have figured in numerous autobiographical narratives:

Possible Focuses for Autobiographical Narratives

Moments of enlightenment or coming to knowledge: understanding a complex idea for the first time, recognizing what is meant by love or jealousy or justice, mastering a complex skill, seeing some truth about yourself or your family that you previously hadn't seen

Passages from one realm to the next: from innocence to experience, from outsider to insider or vice versa, from child to adult, from novice to expert, from what you once were to what you now are

Confrontation with the unknown: with people or situations that challenged or threatened your old identity and values

Moments of crisis or critical choice: moments that tested your mettle or your system of values.

Major choices: about the company you keep (friends, love interests, cliques, larger social groups) and the effects of those choices on your integrity and the persona you project to the world

Problems with people: problems maintaining relationships without compromising your own growth or denying your own needs

Problems accepting limitations and necessities: confronting the loss of dreams, the death of intimates, the failure to live up to ideals, or the difficulty of living with a chronic illness or disability

Contrasts between common wisdom and your own unique knowledge or experience: doing what people said couldn't be done, failing at something others said was easy, finding value in something rejected by society, finding bad consequences of something widely valued

The Importance of Character

Which characters from your life will you choose to include in your autobiography? The answer to that question depends on the nature of the tension that moves your story forward. Characters who contribute significantly to that tension or who represent some aspect of that tension with special clarity belong in your story. Whatever the source of tension in a story, a writer typically chooses characters who exemplify the narrator's fears and desires or who forward or frustrate the narrator's growth in a significant way.

Sometimes writers develop characters not through description and sensory detail but through dialogue. Particularly if a story involves conflict between people, dialogue is a powerful means of letting the reader experience that conflict directly. The following piece of dialogue, taken from African-American writer Richard Wright's classic autobiography *Black Boy,* demonstrates how a skilled writer can let dialogue tell the story, without resorting to analysis and abstraction. In the following scene, young Wright approaches a librarian in an attempt to get a book by Baltimore author and journalist H. L. Mencken from a whites-only public library. He has forged a note and borrowed a library card from a sympathetic white coworker and is pretending to borrow the book in his coworker's name.

> "What do you want, boy?"
>
> As though I did not possess the power of speech, I stepped forward and simply handed her the forged note, not parting my lips.
>
> "What books by Mencken does he want?" she asked.
>
> "I don't know ma'am," I said avoiding her eyes.
>
> "Who gave you this card?"
>
> "Mr. Falk," I said.
>
> "Where is he?"
>
> "He's at work, at the M— Optical Company," I said. "I've been in here for him before."
>
> "I remember," the woman said. "But he never wrote notes like this."
>
> Oh, God, she's suspicious. Perhaps she would not let me have the books? If she had turned her back at that moment, I would have ducked out the door and never gone back. Then I thought of a bold idea.
>
> "You can call him up, ma'am," I said, my heart pounding.
>
> "You're not using these books are you?" she asked pointedly.
>
> "Oh no ma'am. I can't read."
>
> "I don't know what he wants by Mencken," she said under her breath.
>
> I knew I had won; she was thinking of other things and the race question had gone out of her mind.
>
> —Richard Wright, *Black Boy*

It's one thing to hear *about* racial prejudice and discrimination; it's another thing to *hear* it directly through dialogue such as this. In just one hundred or so words of conversation, Wright communicates the anguish and humiliation of being a "black boy" in the United States in the 1920s.

Another way to develop a character is to present a sequence of moments or scenes that reveal a variety of behaviors and moods. Imagine taking ten photographs of your character to represent his or her complexity and variety and then arranging them in a collage.

The Importance of Setting

Elements of setting are selected as characters are selected, according to how much they help readers understand the conflict or tension that drives the story. When you write about yourself, what you notice in the external world often reflects your inner world. In some moods you are apt to notice the expansive lawn, beautiful flowers, and swimming ducks in the city park; in other moods you might note the litter of paper cups, the blight on the roses, and the scum on the duck pond. The setting typically relates thematically to the other elements of a story. In "Berkeley Blues" (pp. 547–549), for example, the author contrasts the swimming pools and sunsets of his hometown to the grit and darkness of inner-city Berkeley. The contrast in settings mirrors the contrast in the worldviews of the high school debaters and the homeless person who confronts them.

FOR WRITING AND DISCUSSION

Capturing a Setting

In writing an autobiographical narrative, one of the challenges is to use words to capture scenes so vividly that readers can see in their own minds what you are describing and can share in your experience vicariously. The four photos in Figures 7.1 through 7.4 depict four common scenes: a wooded stream, a high school football field, an elementary school classroom, and an amusement ride at a fair. For this exercise, choose one of these photos, and imagine a scene from your own life that might have taken place there.

Your goal in this exercise is to freewrite a vivid description of a setting, imagining that you are there. Describe the setting fully. What do you see? Hear? Smell? Once you have described the setting, imagine several characters entering this location and what conflict might play out. Try writing a short scene that portrays some tension. Then share your descriptions with your classmates, discussing how your settings might be used in an autobiographical narrative.

FIGURE 7.1 A Wooded Stream

FIGURE 7.2 A High School Football Field

(continued)

FIGURE 7.3 An Elementary School Classroom

FIGURE 7.4 Amusement Ride at a Fair

The Importance of Theme

The word *theme* is difficult to define. Themes, like thesis statements, organize the other elements of the essay. But a theme is seldom stated explicitly and is never proved with reasons and factual evidence. Readers ponder—even argue about—themes, and often different readers are affected very differently by the same theme. Some literary critics view theme as simply a different way of thinking about plot. To use a phrase from critic Northrop Frye, a plot is "what happened" in a story, whereas the theme is "what happens" over and over again in this story and others like it. To illustrate this distinction, we summarize student writer Patrick José's autobiographical narrative "No Cats in America?", one of the essays in the Readings section of this chapter, from a plot perspective and from a theme perspective:

José's essay is on pp. 167–168.

> **Plot Perspective** It's the story of a Filipino boy who emigrates with his family from the Philippines to the United States when he is in the eighth grade. On the first day of school, he is humiliated when classmates snicker at the lunch his mother packed for him. Feeling more and more alienated each day, he eventually proclaims, "I hate being Filipino!"
>
> **Theme Perspective** It's the story of how personal identity is threatened when people are suddenly removed from their own cultures and immersed into new ones that don't understand or respect difference. The story reveals the psychic damage of cultural dislocation.

As you can see, the thematic summary goes beyond the events of the story to point toward the larger significance of those events. Although you may choose not to state your theme directly for your readers, you need to understand that theme to organize your story. This understanding usually precedes and guides your decisions about what events and characters to include, what details and dialogue to use, and what elements of setting to describe. But sometimes you need to reverse the process and start out with events and characters that, for whatever reason, force themselves on you, and then figure out your theme after you've written for a while. In other words, theme may be something you discover as you write.

Autobiographical Narrative

WRITING PROJECT

Write a narrative essay about something significant in your life using the literary strategies of plot, character, and setting. Develop your story through the use of contraries, creating tension that moves the story forward and gives it significance. You can discuss the significance of your story explicitly, perhaps as a revelation, or you can imply it. (The readings at the end of this chapter illustrate different options.) Use specific details and develop contraries that create tension.

This assignment calls for a story. In Chapter 19, we argue that narrative qualifies as a story only when it depicts a series of connected events that create for the reader a sense of tension or conflict that is resolved through a new understanding or change in status. Your goal for this assignment is to write a story about your life that fulfills these criteria. The suggestions that follow will help you.

Generating and Exploring Ideas

Choosing a Plot

For some of you, identifying a plot—a significant moment or insight arising out of contrariety—will present little problem; perhaps you have already settled on an idea that you generated in one of the class discussion exercises earlier in this chapter. However, if you are still searching for a plot idea, you may find the following list helpful:

- A time when you took some sort of test that conferred new status on you (Red Cross lifesaving exam, driver's test, SAT, important school-or work-related test, entrance exam, team tryout). If you failed, what did you learn from it or how did it shape you? If you succeeded, did the new status turn out to be as important as you had expected it to be?
- A situation in which your normal assumptions about life were challenged (an encounter with a foreign culture, a time when a person you'd stereotyped surprised you).
- A time when you left your family for an extended period or forever (going to college, getting married, entering the military, leaving one parent for another after their divorce).
- A time that plunged you into a crisis (being the first person to discover a car crash, seeing a robbery in progress, being thrown in with people who were repugnant to you, facing an emergency).
- A situation in which you didn't fit or fulfill others' expectations of you, or a situation in which you were acknowledged as a leader or exceeded others' expectations of you (call to jury duty, assignment to a new committee, being placed in charge of an unfamiliar project).
- A time when you overcame your fears to do something for the first time (first date, first public presentation, first challenge in a new setting).

- A situation in which you learned how to get along amicably with another human being, or a failed relationship that taught you something about life (your first extended romantic relationship; your relationship with a difficult sibling, relative, teacher, or boss; getting a divorce).
- A time when a person who mattered to you (parent, spouse, romantic interest, authority figure) rejected you or let you down, or a time when you rejected or let down someone who cared for you.
- A time when you made a sacrifice on behalf of someone else, or when someone else made a sacrifice in your name (taking in a foster child, helping a homeless person, caring for a sick person).
- A time when you were irresponsible or violated a principle or law and thereby caused others pain (you shoplifted or drank when underage and were caught, you failed to look after someone entrusted to your care).
- A time when you were criticized unjustly or given a punishment you didn't deserve (you were accused of plagiarizing a paper that you'd written, you were blamed unjustly for a problem at work).
- A time when you were forced to accept defeat, death, or the loss of a dream or otherwise learned to live with reduced expectations.
- A time when you experienced great joy (having a baby, getting your dream job) or lived out a fantasy.

Shaping and Drafting Your Narrative

Once you've identified an event about which you'd like to write, you need to develop ways to show readers what makes that event particularly story-worthy. In thinking about the event, consider the following questions:

HOW TO START

- What are the major contraries or tensions in this story?
- What events and scenes portraying these contraries might you include in your narrative?
- What insights or meaning do you think your story suggests? How would you articulate for yourself the theme of your narrative?
- How might you begin your narrative?

HOW TO THINK ABOUT AND DEVELOP CHARACTERS AND SETTING

- What characters are important in this story?
- How will you portray them—through description, action, dialogue?
- What settings or scenes can you re-create for readers?
- What particulars or physical details will make the setting, characters, and conflicts vivid and memorable?

HOW TO THINK ABOUT AND DEVELOP THE PLOT OF YOUR NARRATIVE

- How might you arrange the scenes in your story?
- What would be the climax, the pivotal moment of decision or insight?

HOW TO CONCLUDE YOUR NARRATIVE

- What resolution can you bring to the tensions and conflicts in your story?

- How can you convey the significance of your story? What will make it something readers can relate to?
- How can the ending of your narrative leave readers thinking about larger human issues and concerns?

When stuck, writers often work their way into a narrative by describing in detail a vividly recalled scene, person, or object. You may not be able to include all the descriptive material, but in the act of writing exhaustively about this one element, the rest of the story may begin to unfold for you, and forgotten items and incidents may resurface. In the course of describing scenes and characters, you will probably also begin reflecting on the significance of what you are saying. Try freewriting answers to such questions as "Why is this important?" and "What am I trying to do here?" Then continue with your rough draft. Remember that it is the storyteller's job to put readers into the story by providing enough detail and context for the readers to see why the event is significant.

Revising

Testing your narrative out on other readers can give you valuable feedback about your effectiveness in grabbing and holding their interest and conveying an insight. Plan to write several drafts of your narrative.

Questions for Peer Review

In addition to the generic peer review questions explained in Chapter 17, skill it ask your peer reviewers to address these questions:

OPENING AND PLOT

1. How could the title and opening paragraphs more effectively hook readers' interest and prepare them for the story to follow?
2. How might the writer improve the tension, structure, or pacing of the scenes?
3. How could the writer improve the connections between scenes or use a different organization such as a collage of scenes or flashbacks to enhance the clarity or drama of the narrative?

CHARACTERIZATION

4. Where might the writer provide more information about characters or describe them more fully?
5. Where might the writer use dialogue more effectively to reveal character?

SETTING, THEME, AND LANGUAGE

6. How might the writer make the setting more vivid and connected to the action and significance of the story?
7. What insight or revelation do you get from this story? How could the narrative's thematic significance be made more memorable or powerful?
8. Where do you find examples of specific language? Where could the writer use more concrete language?

WRITING PROJECT

Literacy Narrative

Write an autobiographical narrative that focuses on your experiences with language, reading, writing, or education. You could explore positive or negative experiences in learning to read or write, breakthrough moments in your development as a literate person, or some educational experiences that have shaped your identity as a person or student. Incorporate the literary elements of plot, character, setting, theme, and descriptive language in the telling of your story. Think of your task as finding new significance for yourself in these experiences and sharing your discoveries with your readers in ways that hold their interest and bring them new understanding.

What Is a Literacy Narrative?

A literacy narrative is a particular kind of narrative that recounts a writer's personal experience with language, reading, writing, and thinking skills, or with education as a process and a social institution. Literacy narratives are a frequently encountered and important genre. The academic and public fascination with literacy narratives has grown out of—and contributed to—contemporary discussions about cultural diversity in the United States, the importance of education, and the connections among education, social status, and citizenship. A number of contemporary educators, leaders, and well-known writers have reflected on the ways that their access to education and their educational experiences have shaped them. Much attention has also been given to historical literacy narratives—to the ways that learning to read and write influenced leaders and writers in the past. For example, one of the most famous literacy narratives is by Frederick Douglass, the ex-slave and abolitionist leader who describes learning to read and write as the key to his liberation from slavery. Another well-known literacy narrative is by Zitkala-Sa (Gertrude Bonnin), a Native American woman who exposes the forceful assimilation tactics employed by the missionary schools to separate Native American children from their tribes in the late nineteenth and early twentieth centuries. Perhaps the most famous literacy narrative is by Helen Keller, who recounts the moments when an understanding of language broke through the isolation created by her blindness and deafness. More recently, literacy narratives by immigrants from many cultures have explored the role of education in thwarting or encouraging their integration into American society.

Writing a literacy narrative in college classes has become a popular way for students to explore their adjustment to the social and intellectual life of college communities, to make fruitful links between their earlier educational experiences with reading and writing and the demands of college, and to take ownership of their own education. Thinking about your own literacy experiences compels you to ponder your educational path and your own ideas of the purpose of education. In contemplating the way that ethnic, economic, gender, class, and regional considerations have shaped your own learning to read and write, you will experience the pleasure of self-discovery and cultural insight.

Typical Features of a Literacy Narrative

Literacy narratives resemble other autobiographical narratives in their open-form structure and their inclusion of some or all of these literary features: a plot built on some tensions and presented as well-sequenced scenes, vivid descriptions of settings, well-drawn characters, dialogue, and theme. Like other autobiographical narratives, literacy narratives rely on vivid, concrete language to make settings and dramatic moments come alive for readers. While literacy narratives share many elements with other autobiographical narratives, they differ in their attention to the following features:

DISTINCTIVE FEATURES OF LITERACY NARRATIVES

- A focus on a writer's experience with language, reading, writing, schooling, teachers, or some other important aspect of education.
- A focus on bringing an insight about the significance of learning, language, reading, or writing to readers through an implied theme (although this theme might be explicitly stated, most likely at the end of the narrative).
- A focus on engaging readers and connecting them to an understanding of the writer's educational/learning experience, prompting them to think about their own educational experiences and larger questions about the purpose and value of education.

FOR WRITING AND DISCUSSION

Analyzing Features of Literacy Narratives

Read the following passages that depict key moments in two students' literacy experiences, and answer the questions about them that direct your attention to specific features.

EXCERPT FROM MEGAN LACY'S LITERACY NARRATIVE

... I was placed in the remedial reading group. Our books had red plastic covers while the other kids had books with yellow covers that looked gold to me. When it was reading time, the rest of the red group and I congregated around a rectangular wood table where Mrs. Hinckley would direct each of us to read a passage from the story aloud. The first time this happened, my stomach dropped. Even the remedial kids were sounding out the words, but I had no idea what those symbols on the page meant.

When my turn came, I muttered meekly, "I can't. ..."

"Don't say 'can't' in my classroom!" Mrs. Hinckley snapped. Then, more gently, she said, "Just sound it out. ..."

I did as she recommended and could hardly believe what was happening. I was reading. I felt superhuman with such a power. After that moment, I read to my mom every night. ...

EXCERPT FROM JEFFREY CAIN'S LITERACY NARRATIVE

In the Walla Walla Public Library, I remember the tomato soup colored carpet, the bad oil paintings of pioneers fording the Columbia River, the musty smell,

(*continued*)

the oak card catalog with brass knobs, the position of the clock when I first read Jerzi Kosinski's *The Painted Bird.*

"Just read it," my sister-in-law said. "I know you don't read much fiction, but just read this one," she pleaded.

Reluctantly, at first, I turned the pages. But each word covertly seduced me; slowly the odyssey of the dark-skinned gypsy affected my spirit like an exotic opiate, until Lehki's painted bird lay pecked to death on the ground. The image haunted my conscience for days. During some of my more restless nights, I was chased like the characters by Nazis through the Black Forest.

Who was this Kosinski? Why did his book affect me this way? How and why did he write like this? Did all writers write like Kosinski?

The novel incited a series of questions that forced me to begin writing notes and summarizing my thoughts. I began a reading journal and my development as a writer shadowed my habits as a reader. ...

1. What learning experiences concerning reading or writing have Megan and Jeffrey chosen to focus on?
2. How do Megan and Jeffrey create tension and the sense of an unfolding plot in their literacy narratives?
3. What details of setting and what descriptive language do these student writers use to involve readers in their experiences?
4. Based on the excerpts you have read from these literacy narratives, how would you articulate the theme of each piece?
5. What educational memories of your own have these excerpted literacy narratives triggered?

Generating and Exploring Ideas

To discover ideas that you could fruitfully explore in your literacy narrative, try asking yourself the following questions:

QUESTIONS ABOUT YOUR EXPERIENCES WITH READING AND WRITING

- What problems or obstacles did you encounter in learning to read and write and how did you overcome them?
- What are your earliest memories of learning to read?
- What can you remember about learning to write or things you have written?
- What role have reading and writing played in your life so far?
- What important changes and their causes can you identify in your communication skills?

QUESTIONS ABOUT ADJUSTING TO COLLEGE OR EDUCATIONAL CHALLENGES

- What educational challenges have you experienced so far in adjusting to college? (Or earlier, in adjusting to middle school or high school?)
- What holes or weaknesses in your knowledge and education are you concerned about?
- If you are a first-generation college student, an international student, or a recent immigrant, how has this background influenced your attitudes toward college?

- How is cultural diversity or the size and power of the college or university affecting your views of education?

QUESTIONS ABOUT YOUR EXPERIENCES WITH LANGUAGE

- When has your command of spoken or written language served you well? Failed you?
- If you are bilingual, how has your knowledge of these two languages shaped your identity and your view of the world?
- What barriers or opportunities has language created for you?

QUESTIONS ABOUT INFLUENTIAL TEACHERS OR MENTORS

- What people have helped or hindered your learning to read or write?
- How has a teacher or someone else changed your view of yourself as a literate person or your view of education?

QUESTIONS ABOUT THE CONNECTIONS BETWEEN EDUCATION AND SOCIAL STATUS OR CITIZENSHIP

- What do you see as the important uses of reading and writing?
- What do you think is the importance of literacy for social and economic success?
- How has education affected your role as a citizen of the United States and the global community?

FOR WRITING AND DISCUSSION

Discovering Experiences with Literacy

Use one of the questions in the preceding lists to help you probe your own life for an experience with literacy. Freewrite for ten to fifteen minutes on this question. As you freewrite, think about what key moments in your life—presented as scenes—this question uncovers. What particularly interests you about these moments? How can you make this experience relevant to readers?

Shaping and Drafting Your Literacy Narrative

In addition to applying the contraries listed on page 151—old self versus new self, old view of X versus new view of X, and old values versus new threatening or challenging values—the following questions can help you shape and map out your narrative in terms of tensions, scenes, and unfolding story.

QUESTIONS FOR FINDING THE UNDERLYING PATTERN OF YOUR LITERACY EXPERIENCE

- Can you portray your literacy experience in terms of change and contrast (I used to be/Now I am)?
- What memorable, breakthrough, or transformative moments can you highlight in this experience?
- Can you depict your literacy experience as a journey or process?
- Can you portray your literacy experience in an action/significance or what happened/interpretation pattern?

While some literacy narratives will follow a clear chronological pattern or a tightly connected scene sequence, others may assume the pattern of a collage or a series of snapshots of key moments in your development. Your challenge is to find what pattern best fits the story you want to tell. Note how in her literacy narrative on pages 171–174 student writer Jennifer Ching has adopted an unfolding structure of scenes narrating her key memories about reading and writing.

Revising

In writing about experiences that are very close to you, it is particularly important to get responses from readers. Your readers can help you determine how effectively you are capturing and holding their attention and conveying the significance behind your experiences.

Questions for Peer Review

In addition to the generic peer review questions explained in Chapter 17, Skill 4, ask your peer reviewers to address these questions:

PLOT AND STRUCTURE

1. How can the writer make the title and opening of this narrative focus on literacy more clearly and create more interest for readers?
2. How might the writer improve the tension, structure, sequence, or pacing of the scenes?

SETTING AND CHARACTERIZATION

3. Where does the writer do a good job of putting readers in the scene? How might the writer select, shape, or describe setting more effectively to create a lively story and convey its significance?
4. How might the writer improve characterization (through description? dialogue?) to portray his/her literacy experience?

LANGUAGE AND THEME

5. Where does the writer's use of specific, concrete language enhance the story's interest? What changes in descriptive language would heighten the appeal and meaning of this narrative?
6. What insight, revelation, or new understanding about the importance of reading, writing, or education does this narrative offer you? How can the narrative's thematic significance be made more memorable or powerful?

Our first reading is by Kris Saknussemm, a poet and fiction writer. He is the author of the dystopian, futuristic novel *Zanesville* (2005), and his poems and short stories have appeared in literary magazines around the country, including *The Boston Review, New Letters, The Antioch Review,* and *ZYZZYVA*. This selection is taken from his autobiographical work in progress.

Kris Saknussemm

Phantom Limb Pain

1 When I was 13 my sole purpose was to shed my baby fat and become the star halfback on our football team. That meant beating out Miller King, the best athlete at my school. He was my neighbor and that mythic kid we all know—the one who's forever better than us—the person we want to be.

2 Football practice started in September and all summer long I worked out. I ordered a set of barbells that came with complimentary brochures with titles like "How to Develop a He-Man Voice." Every morning before sunrise I lumbered around our neighborhood wearing ankle weights loaded with sand. I taught myself how to do Marine push-ups and carried my football everywhere so I'd learn not to fumble. But that wasn't enough. I performed a ceremony. During a full moon, I burned my favorite NFL trading cards and an Aurora model of the great quarterback Johnny Unitas in the walnut orchard behind our house, where Miller and I'd gotten into a fight when we were seven and I'd burst into tears before he even hit me.

3 Two days after my ceremony, Miller snuck out on his older brother's Suzuki and was struck by a car. He lost his right arm, just below the elbow. I went to see him the day after football practice started—after he'd come back from the hospital. He looked pale and surprised, but he didn't cry. It was hard to look at the stump of limb where his arm had been, so I kept glancing around his room. We only lived about 200 feet away, and yet I'd never been inside his house before. It had never occurred to me that he would also have on his wall a poster of Raquel Welch from *One Million Years B.C.*

4 I went on to break all his records that year. Miller watched the home games from the bench, wearing his jersey with the sleeve pinned shut. We went 10–1 and I was named MVP, but I was haunted by crazy dreams in which I was somehow responsible for the accident—that I'd found the mangled limb when it could've been sewn back on—and kept it in an aquarium full of vodka under my bed.

5 One afternoon several months later, toward the end of basketball season, I was crossing the field to go home and I saw Miller stuck going over the Cyclone fence—which wasn't hard to climb if you had both arms. I guess he'd gotten tired of walking around and hoped no one was looking. Or maybe it was a matter of pride. I'm sure I was the last person in the world he wanted to see—to have to accept assistance from. But even that challenge he accepted. I helped ease him down the fence, one diamond-shaped hole at a time. When we were finally safe on the other side, he said to me, "You know, I didn't tell you this during the season, but you did all right. Thanks for filling in for me."

6 We walked home together, not saying much. But together. Back to our houses 200 feet apart. His words freed me from my bad dreams. I thought to myself, how many things I hadn't told him. How even without an arm he was more of a leader. Damaged but not diminished, he was still ahead of me. I was right to have admired him. I grew bigger and a little more real from that day on.

THINKING CRITICALLY
about "Phantom Limb Pain"

Perhaps the first thing the reader realizes about Saknussemm's narrative is that the climactic event—one boy helping another climb down a Cyclone fence—is a small action; however, it has a big psychological and emotional meaning for the narrator. The events leading to this moment have prepared us to understand the writer's revelation of his new relationship to his rival. Saknussemm's last paragraph comments on the preceding narrative, making connections and pulling out threads of meaning.

1. Saknussemm chooses to leave a lot unsaid, depending on his readers to fill in the gaps. Why do you suppose that he had never been inside Miller King's house before? Why does he feel "somehow responsible for the accident"? What details does Saknussemm use to sketch in Miller's admirable traits?

See Chapter 19, Skill 16, for a discussion of concrete language including revelatory words and memory-soaked words. See Chapter 5, pp. 102–103, for a discussion of *show* words and *tell* words.

2. What examples can you find in this narrative of revelatory words, memory-soaked words, and other concrete words low on the ladder of abstraction? Where does Saknussemm use words that *show* what is happening in the narrative instead of simply telling readers?

3. In closed-form prose, writers seldom use sentence fragments. In open-form prose, however, writers frequently use fragments for special effects. Note the two fragments in Saknussemm's final paragraph: "But together. Back to our houses 200 feet apart." Why does Saknussemm use these fragments? What is their rhetorical effect?

4. Part of Saknussemm's style in this narrative is to use understatement and minimalistic language while also using words that resonate with multiple meanings. For example, he lets readers imagine what Miller would look like trying to climb the Cyclone fence with one arm. However, some phrases and words are figurative and symbolic. What does Saknussemm mean by the phrases "grew bigger" and "a little more real" in his final sentence? How do the ideas of size and of reality versus illusion play a role in this narrative and relate to the theme?

For a different approach to narrative, consider student writer Patrick José's "No Cats in America?" Unlike Saknussemm's narrative, José's includes plentiful description. Note also how José creates tension through contrasts in his narrative:

between an ideal image of America and a factual image, between life in the Philippines and life in California.

Patrick José (student)

No Cats in America?

1 "There are no cats in America." I remember growing up watching *An American Tail* with my sisters and cousins. Ever since I first saw that movie, I had always wanted to move to America. That one song, "There Are No Cats in America," in which the Mousekewitz family is singing with other immigrating mice, had the most profound effect on me. These were Russian mice going to America to find a better life—a life without cats. At first, I thought America really had no cats. Later, I learned that they meant that America was without any problems at all. I was taught about the American Dream with its promise of happiness and equality. If you wanted a better life, then you better pack up all your belongings and move to America.

2 However, I loved living in the Philippines. My family used to throw the best parties in Angeles City. For a great party, you need some delicious food. Of course there would be lechon, adobo, pancit, sinigang, lumpia, and rice. We eat rice for breakfast, lunch, and dinner, and rice even makes some of the best desserts. (My mom's bibingka and puto are perfect!) And you mustn't forget the drinks. San Miguel and Coke are usually sufficient. But we also had homemade mango juice and coconut milk. And a party wouldn't be a party without entertainment, right? So in one room, we had the gambling room. It's usually outside the house. Everybody would be smoking and drinking while playing mahjong. And sometimes, others would play pepito or pusoy dos. Music and dancing is always a must. And when there are firecrackers, better watch out because the children would go crazy with them.

3 Then one day, a mixed feeling came over me. My dad told us that he had gotten a job ... in California. In the span of two months, we had moved to America, found a small apartment, and located a small private Catholic school for the kids. We did not know many people in California that first summer. We only had ourselves to depend on. We would go on car trips, go to the beach, cook, play games. In August, I thought we were living the American Dream.

4 But at the end of summer, school began. I was in the eighth grade. I had my book bag on one shoulder, stuffed with notebooks, folder paper, calculators, a ruler, a pencil box, and my lunch. I still can remember what I had for lunch on the first day of school—rice and tilapia and, in a small container, a mixture of vinegar, tomatoes, and bagoong. My mom placed everything in a big Tupperware box, knowing I eat a lot.

5 When I walked into the classroom, everyone became quiet and looked at me. I was the only Filipino in that room. Everyone was white. We began the day by introducing ourselves. When it got to my turn, I was really nervous. English was one of the courses that I took in the Philippines, and I thought I was pretty proficient at it. But when I first opened my mouth, everyone began to laugh. The teacher told everyone to

hush. I sat down, smiling faintly not understanding what was so funny. I knew English, and yet I was laughed at. But it had nothing to do with the language. It was my accent.

6 Some students tried to be nice, especially during lunch. But it didn't last long. I was so hungry for my lunch. I followed a group of students to the cafeteria and sat down at an empty table. Some girls joined me. I didn't really talk to them, but they asked if they could join me. As I opened my Tupperware, I saw their heads turn away. They didn't like the smell of fish and bagoong. The girls left and moved to another table of girls. From the corner of my eye I saw them looking and laughing at me. I tried to ignore it, concentrating on eating my lunch as I heard them laugh. In the Philippines, the only way to eat fish and rice is with your hands. But that was in the Philippines. My manners were primitive here in America. I was embarrassed at the smell, was embarrassed at the way I ate, was embarrassed to be me.

7 When I got home, I lied to my parents. I told them school was great and that I was excited to go back. But deep down, I wanted to go back to the Philippines. When lunch came the next day, I was hungry. In my hand was my lunch. Five feet away was the trash. I stood up, taking my lunch in my hands. Slowly, I walked my way towards the trashcan, opened the lid, and watched as my lunch filled the trashcan. Again, I told my parents I enjoyed school.

8 When my grades began to suffer, the teacher called my parents and scheduled an appointment. The next day, my parents came to the classroom, and when they started talking to the teacher I heard laughter in the background. It humiliated me to have my classmates hear my parents talk.

9 That night, my parents and I had a private discussion. They asked why I lied to them. I told them everything, including my humiliation. They told me not to worry about it, but I pleaded for us to return to the Philippines. My parents said no. "Living here will provide a better future for you and your sisters," they said. Then the unexpected came. I didn't know what I was thinking. I yelled to them with so much anger, "I hate being Filipino!" Silence filled the room. Teardrops rolled down my cheeks. My parents were shocked, and so was I.

10 I went to my room and cried. I didn't mean what I said. But I was tired of the humiliation. Lying on my bed, with my eyes closed, my mind began to wander. I found myself in the boat with the Mousekewitz family singing, "There are no cats in America." If only they knew how wrong they were.

THINKING CRITICALLY
about "No Cats in America?"

Patrick José lets the reader infer his essay's significance from the details of the narrative and from their connection to the framing story of the fictional mice and cats.

1. How do the settings help you understand José's theme at different points in the story?
2. What would you say is the story's climax or pivotal moment?

3. José's title, first paragraph, and last paragraph are about a children's movie that features the Mousekewitz's song proclaiming that there are no cats in America. How does the "no cats" image function as both part of the underlying tension of this narrative and as a symbolic vehicle for conveying the theme of José's essay? What is the insight that José has achieved at the end?
4. During a rough draft workshop, José asked his peer reviewers whether he should retain his description of parties in the Philippines, which he thought was perhaps unconnected to the rest of the story. His classmates urged him to keep those details. Do you agree with their advice? Why?
5. For Filipinos and Filipinas, the specific names of foods and party games would be rich examples of memory-soaked words. For other readers, however, these names are foreign and strange. Do you agree with José's decision to use these specific ethnic names? Why?

See Chapter 19, Skill 16, for a discussion of the power of memory-soaked words.

The next example was written in a first-year composition course by a student writer who wishes to remain anonymous.

Masks

1 Her soft, blond hair was in piggytails, as usual, with ringlets that bounced whenever she turned her head. As if they were springs, they could stretch, then shrink, then bounce, excited by the merest movement of her head. Never was there a hair that wasn't enclosed in those glossy balls which always matched her dress. I knew the only reason she turned her head was so they'd bounce. Because it was cute. Today, she wore a pink dress with frills and lace and impeccably white tights. Her feet, which swayed back and forth underneath her chair, were pampered with shiny, black shoes without a single scuff. She was very wise, sophisticated beyond her kindergarten years.

2 I gazed at her and then looked down at my clothes. My green and red plaid pants and my yellow shirt with tiny, blue stars showed the day's wear between breakfast, lunch, and recess. Showing through the toe of my tenny runners was my red sock.

3 At paint time, I closely followed behind her, making sure I painted at the easel next to hers. She painted a big, white house with a white picket fence and a family: Mom, Dad, and Daughter. I painted my mom, my brother, and myself. I, then, painted the sky, but blue streaks ran down our faces, then our bodies, ruining the picture.

4 The next day, I wore my hair in piggytails. I had done it all by myself, which was obvious due to my craftsmanship. She pointed and giggled at me when I walked by. I also wore a dress that day but I didn't have any pretty white tights. The boys all gathered underneath me when I went on the monkeybars to peak at my underwear to chant, "I see London, I see France, I see Tiffy's underpants."

5 When the day was done, she ran to the arms of her mother that enveloped her in a loving and nurturing hug. She showed her mother her painting, which had a big, red star on it.

6 "We'll have to put this up on the refrigerator with all of your others," her mother said. I had thrown my painting away. I looked once more at the two of them as they walked hand in hand towards their big, white house with a white picket fence. I trudged to my babysitter's house. I wouldn't see my mother until six o'clock. She had no time for me, for my paintings, for my piggytails. She was too busy working to have enough money to feed my brother and me.

7 Digging absently through books and folders, I secretly stole a glance at her, three lockers down. Today she wore her Calvins and sported a brand new pair of Nikes. As always, at the cutting edge of fashion. If I wanted Nikes, I could pay for them myself, or so said my mother. In the meantime, I had to suffer with my cheap, treadless Scats. As I searched for a pen, her giggle caught my attention. Three of her friends had flocked around her locker. I continued searching for a pen but to no avail. I thought of approaching and borrowing one but I was fearful that they would make fun of me.

8 "Jim and Brad called me last night and both of them asked me to go to the show. Which one should I pick?" She asked. My mom wouldn't let me go out on dates until I was a sophomore in high school. We were only in seventh grade and she was always going out with guys. Not that it mattered that I couldn't date, yet. Nobody had ever asked me out.

9 "My hair turned out so yucky today. Ick," she commented. She bent down to grab a book and light danced among the gentle waves of her flowing, blond mane. Her radiant brown eyes and adorable smile captivated all who saw her. Once captured, however, none was allowed past the mask she'd so artfully constructed to lure them to her. We were all so close to her, so far away. She was so elusive, like a beautiful perfume you smell but can't name, like the whisper that wakes you from a dream and turns out to belong to the dream.

10 As she walked into the library, I heard a voice whisper, "There she is. God, she's beautiful." She was wearing her brown and gold cheerleader outfit. Her pleated skirt bounced off her thighs as she strutted by. Her name, "Kathy," was written on her sweater next to her heart and by it hung a corsage. As she rounded the corner, she flicked her long, blond curls and pivoted, sending a ripple through the pleats of the skirt. She held her head up high, befitting one of her social standing: top of the high school food chain. She casually searched the length of the library for friends. When she reached the end of the room, she carefully reexamined every table, this time less casually. Her smile shaded into a pout. She furrowed her face, knitting her eyebrows together, and saddening her eyes. People stared at her until she panicked.

11 She was bolting toward the door when she spotted me. She paused and approached my table. Putting on her biggest smile, she said, "Oh hi! Can I sit by you?" Thrilled at the possibility of at last befriending her, I was only too happy to have her sit with me. As she sat down, she again scanned the expanse of the library.

12 "So, who does the varsity basketball team play tonight?" I asked.

13 "Great Falls Central," she replied. "Make sure you're there! ... How's the Algebra assignment today?!"

14 "Oh, it's okay. Not too tough," I said.

15 "John always does my assignments for me. I just hate Algebra. It's so hard."

16 We stood up in silence, suddenly painfully aware of our differences. She glanced in the reflection of the window behind us, checked her hair, then again scanned the room.

17 "There's Shelly! Well, I'll see you later," she said.

18 She rose from the table and fled to her more acceptable friend.

19 The next day, she walked down the hall surrounded by a platoon of friends. As we passed, I called out "Hi!" but she turned away as if she didn't know me, as if I didn't exist.

20 I, then, realized her cheerleader outfit, her golden locks, her smile were all a mask. Take them away and nothing but air would remain. Her friends and their adoration were her identity. Without them she was alone and vulnerable. I was the powerful one. I was independent.

THINKING CRITICALLY
about "Masks"

1. What are the main contrarieties, or oppositions, in this piece?
2. Where does the writer's description of the setting help to portray the characters?
3. This piece focuses on the narrator's movement toward a significant recognition. What is it she recognizes? If you were a peer reviewer for this writer, would you recommend eliminating the last paragraph, expanding it, or leaving it as it is? Why?
4. In Chapter 19, we quote writer John McPhee's advice to prefer specific words over abstract ones—brand names, for example, rather than generic names. This student writer follows this advice throughout her essay. Where does she use details and specific words with particular effectiveness?

The discussion of concrete language is in Chapter 19, Skill 16.

Our fourth reading is a literacy narrative by student writer Jennifer Ching, written for an assignment like the one in this chapter.

Jennifer Ching (student)

Once Upon a Time

1 When I was three years old, I learned that words were the cure to help my dad stop smoking.

2 "MOE Q. MCGLUTCH, YOU SMOKE TOO MUCH!" I would yell whenever he lit up a cigarette.

3 After dinner, when the halo-cloud of smoke enveloped the entire dining room ceiling, I asked my father to read me *Moe. Q. McGlutch,* a story about a donkey who smoked too much. Each page ended with someone in the donkey's family saying, "Moe Q. McGlutch, you smoke too much." I would loudly proclaim this line for my father.

4 "And so, Moe. Q.'s brother said to him ... " Pop read.

5 "MOE. Q. MCGLUTCH, YOU SMOKE TOO MUCH!" I yelled, bending closely to his ear.

6 Words are powerful, I learned. Pop quit smoking within a few weeks of my mother's discovery of that book in the library.

7 The San Francisco Merced Branch Library, an air-conditioned, musty smelling building, was a place where I began to love the sounds of words. I can still see my mother, squatting down and flipping through the crisp cellophane covers of slim volumes of children's books as my legs dangled from a wooden reading table and I tried to read. My eyes were always bigger than my muscles; if I wanted to check out books, my mom said, I would have to help carry some. She bought me a small green cloth backpack which I crammed with books. Hunched over and looking somewhat like a troll for my four years, I would toddle home, obediently trotting at my mother's side.

8 At night, I curled up on my parents' bed. Snuggled safely between them, I visited different people, places, and time periods all in one night. I baked bread in *The Midnight Kitchen,* sailed away on *The Maggie B.*, celebrated a birthday on *June Seventh,* and visited *Where the Wild Things Are.*

9 The appreciation my parents fostered for good literature and, consequently, an appreciation for words remained with me throughout my education. I remembered the stories they read when I entered first grade, where I began to create my own stories. Clutching a thick charcoal pencil, I wrote my first stories on wide-line control paper.

10 "My grandparents have a dog, Fitzherbert Martin Junior Wong," I wrote. "When he hears the wood cabinet open he runs to the kitchen because he thinks he will eat a treat. I feed him doggie doughnuts. They are purple, green, yellow, and red. I think he likes the red ones. I make him sit down before he eats. 'Woof,' he says. The end."

11 After I turned in my story, Mrs. Komm, my teacher, called me to her desk.

12 "Jennifer, look," she said, waving her red pen as my nose bumped the top of her desk. "You really don't need to make your periods as big as cannon balls. They need to be much smaller. No more cannon balls."

13 As big as *cannon balls*? That was all she was going to say about my story? I had received my first lesson in criticism about my writing.

14 In the fourth grade, when the class began to write short stories, I unintentionally started a game which my classmates called, "See Who Can Write More Than Jennifer."

15 "Yours are always sooooo long," my classmates said. "Why do you do all that work?"

"I need to make up for my math grade," I would tell them. That was not really
16 true. To me, writing those creative stories was not work; it was actually fun.

17 "How many pages is yours?" I would be asked the day the stories were due.

18 "Seven or eight pages," I would say.

19 "Wow," my classmates said, amazed.

20 One day, Paul Kim waved his hand in the air. "Can I read mine?," he asked our teacher.

21 Paul crossed quickly to the front of the room. He stood there, nervously shuffling his feet and, with sticky palms, jiggled the pennies in his pocket with his left hand. The other hand clutched what looked like an entire pack of wide-rule binder paper.

22 "Hee-hee," he giggled, as his eyes scoped the class. He grinned broadly and proclaimed "MINE'S 14 PAGES LONG!"

23 I rolled my eyes. The class rumor mill was right; Paul did try to use up the entire pack of binder paper.

24 Most of the class was asleep by page seven, the page where Paul met space aliens of some kind.

25 "Hee-hee," he giggled. "And then—hee-hee, hee-hee. The aliens—hee-hee, hee-hee—the aliens—hee-hee, hee-hee ... ha ha ha ha ha ha ha ... "

26 "Paul, why don't you just sit down?" my teacher said, kindly but with a note of irritation in her voice.

27 "Thank goodness," I thought, suddenly realizing that length did not necessarily make a story better. I elbowed the girl next to me, who was drooling on her desk. "Wake up. We're spared."

28 I did not encounter the concept of The Thesis Statement until my senior year of high school. "It's the main point you want to make in your paper," said my English teacher, Mrs. Sanderson.

29 It was so organized, so structured. I stared blankly at the screen. What did she mean, an argument? What is proof? I tried to make a point and strung a series of quotations together as proof.

30 "There," I thought, printing off the paper. "This must be an argument."

31 But it wasn't an argument. Neither were the ones following. Paper after paper was returned with the same comment: "good ideas, but the organization, structure, etc. need some more work ... You also need to be more explicit with your ideas."

32 I was discouraged with myself and my writing. I began to look at reading and writing as a chore, something I had to get through in order to do my homework. Even though I enjoyed the class, I dreaded writing the argumentative papers. I didn't really appreciate what was causing my problem until in our first-year college writing class we discussed the difference between open-form and closed-form writing. Yes. I knew immediately that I liked the story approach.

33 In retrospect, I think my dread at writing arguments arose from the way I was raised. In my family, I was not raised to pick one side and argue it out; I was always taught to consider all sides of an issue. If my cousins and I argued, for example, my grandfather would sit us all down and hear everyone's version of the argument. By the time everyone was done crying and telling their story, we had forgotten what initially started the disagreement.

34 Perhaps my not being "explicit" enough in my argumentative writing arose from the implicit understanding of certain things in my family. When I visited my relatives, I would always greet them in order of "importance": first my great-grandmother, then my grandfather, then my grandmother, etc. To do otherwise would insult the family. It was implicitly understood in my family that I would not talk about certain things, such as repeating the playground poems I heard in school. Once, when I was playing with one of my aunts, I chanted, "Stick a needle in my eye if I lie!" My grandparents stared at me, horrified that I would have said something so blatantly "violent." In my family, certain bold statements are better left unsaid.

35 Mrs. Sanderson began to show me that there was a kind of power in making bold assertions, and that argumentative writing was useful and powerful. It was very difficult for me, though, and I was a bit intimidated when she announced this was the only kind of writing that we would be doing in college.

36 Although I hope to become more comfortable with argumentative writing in this course, I do not think that it will become "second nature" to me as it is with some of my classmates who were in high school debate or who love to argue. I am much more comfortable writing about Moe. Q. McGlutch, my family, the Merced Branch Library, Fitzherbert Martin Junior Wong, and Mrs. Sanderson. They have shown me that words can be powerful in more than one way.

THINKING CRITICALLY
about "Once Upon a Time"

1. How does Jennifer Ching engage readers' interest in her literacy narrative? How does she use dialogue?
2. What conflicts and breakthrough moments does Jennifer depict? What personal and family/cultural obstacles does she overcome?
3. Where has she used language effectively?
4. How would you sum up what Jennifer has learned about herself, reading, writing, and language in recounting her experiences?
5. What insights about your own experiences with reading, writing, and school has this literacy narrative brought to you?

For additional writing, reading, and research resources, go to **www.MyCompLab.com** and choose **Ramage/Bean/Johnson's *The Allyn & Bacon Guide to Writing,* Fifth Edition.**

WRITING AN EXPLORATORY ESSAY OR ANNOTATED BIBLIOGRAPHY

CHAPTER 8

In Part 1, we explained how writers wrestle with subject-matter problems. Most academic writers testify that writing projects truly begin when they become engaged with a question or problem and commit themselves to an extensive period of exploration. During exploration, experienced writers may radically redefine the problem and then later alter or even reverse their initial thesis. As we have noted, however, inexperienced writers sometimes truncate this process, closing off the period of exploratory thinking. Asserting a thesis too soon can prevent writers from acknowledging an issue's complexity, whereas dwelling with a question invites writers to contemplate multiple perspectives, entertain new ideas, and let their thinking evolve.

This chapter introduces you to two genres of writing built on exploratory thinking:

- **The exploratory essay.** An exploratory essay narrates a writer's research process. When you write an exploratory essay, you pose a question or problem and dwell with it even if you can't solve it. You provide a chronological account of your thinking about your question as your research progresses. Your narration recounts your attempt to examine your question's complexity, to explore alternative solutions, and to arrive at a solution or answer. Because your exploration often requires library or Internet research, many instructors pair this project with Part 4 of this text, "A Rhetorical Guide to Research."
- **The annotated bibliography.** In an annotated bibliography, a writer summarizes and briefly critiques the research sources he or she used while exploring a problem. Although an annotated bibliography doesn't capture the internal flow of your discovery process, it encourages exploration and inquiry, provides a valuable "tracing" of your work, and creates a useful guide for others interested in your research problem.

Even though academic and professional readers tend to expect and need thesis-driven arguments and reports, exploratory essays are becoming more common in scholarly journals, and annotated bibliographies are a frequently encountered academic genre. Exploratory essays exist in embryo in the research or lab notebooks of scholars. Also, scholars occasionally take readers into the kitchen of academic discovery and write stand-alone essays about their discovery process. Jane

Tompkins's essay "'Indians': Textualism, Morality, and the Problem of History" in the Readings section of this chapter is an example of a scholar narrating her inquiry process.

For student writers, both the exploratory essay and the annotated bibliography generally serve as an intermediate stage in the research process. Student James Gardiner's exploratory paper and annotated bibliography in this chapter's Readings section are products of the exploratory phase of his research project about online social networking, which later resulted in a closed-form researched argument. You can compare his exploratory essay with the final thesis-driven argument, which appears in Chapter 23.

Exploring Exploratory Writing

Through our work in writing centers, we often encounter students disappointed with their grades on essay exams or papers. "I worked hard on this paper," they tell us, "but I still got a lousy grade. What am I doing wrong? What do college professors want?"

To help you answer this question, consider the following two essays written for a freshman placement examination in composition at the University of Pittsburgh, in response to the following assignment:

> Describe a time when you did something you felt to be creative. Then, on the basis of the incident you have described, go on to draw some general conclusions about "creativity."

How would you describe the differences in thinking exhibited by the two writers? Which essay do you think professors rated higher?

ESSAY A

I am very interested in music, and I try to be creative in my interpretation of music. While in high school, I was a member of a jazz ensemble. The members of the ensemble were given chances to improvise and be creative in various songs. I feel that this was a great experience for me, as well as the other members. I was proud to know that I could use my imagination and feelings to create music other than what was written.

Creativity to me means being free to express yourself in a way that is unique to you, not having to conform to certain rules and guidelines. Music is only one of the many areas in which people are given opportunities to show their creativity. Sculpting, carving, building, art, and acting are just a few more areas where people can show their creativity.

Through my music I conveyed feelings and thoughts which were important to me. Music was my means of showing creativity. In whatever form creativity takes, whether it be music, art, or science, it is an important aspect of our lives because it enables us to be individuals.

ESSAY B

Throughout my life, I have been interested and intrigued by music. My mother has often told me of the times, before I went to school, when I would "conduct" the orchestra on her records. I continued to listen to music and eventually started to play the guitar and the clarinet. Finally, at about the age of twelve, I started to sit down and to try to write songs. Even though my instrumental skills were far from my own high standards, I would spend much of my spare time during the day with a guitar around my neck, trying to produce a piece of music.

Each of these sessions, as I remember them, had a rather set format. I would sit in my bedroom, strumming different combinations of the five or six chords I could play, until I heard a series which sounded particularly good to me. After this, I set the music to a suitable rhythm (usually dependent on my mood at the time), and ran through the tune until I could play it fairly easily. Only after this section was complete did I go on to writing lyrics, which generally followed along the lines of the current popular songs on the radio.

At the time of the writing, I felt that my songs were, in themselves, an original creation of my own; that is, I, alone, made them. However, I now see that, in this sense of the word, I was not creative. The songs themselves seem to be an oversimplified form of the music I listened to at the time.

In a more fitting sense, however, I *was* being creative. Since I did not purposely copy my favorite songs, I was, effectively, originating my songs from my own "process of creativity." To achieve my goal, I needed what a composer would call "inspiration" for my piece. In this case the inspiration was the current hit on the radio. Perhaps, with my present point of view, I feel that I used too much "inspiration" in my songs, but, at the time, I did not.

Creativity, therefore, is a process which, in my case, involved a certain series of "small creations" if you like. As well, it is something the appreciation of which varies with one's point of view, that point of view being set by the person's experience, tastes, and his own personal view of creativity. The less experienced tend to allow for less originality, while the more experienced demand real originality to classify something a "creation." Either way, a term as abstract as this is perfectly correct, and open to interpretation.

Working as a whole class or in small groups, analyze the differences between Essay A and Essay B. What might cause college professors to rate one essay higher than the other? What would the writer of the weaker essay have to do to produce an essay more like the stronger?

Understanding Exploratory Writing

The essential move for exploratory thinking and writing is to keep a problem alive through consideration of multiple solutions or points of view. The thinker identifies a problem, considers a possible solution or point of view, explores its strengths and weaknesses, and then moves on to consider another possible solution or viewpoint. The thinker resists closure—that is, resists settling too soon on a thesis.

To show a mind at work examining multiple solutions, let's return to the two student essays you examined in the previous exploratory activity (p. 176). The fundamental difference between Essay A and Essay B is that the writer of Essay B treats the concept of "creativity" as a true problem. Note that the writer of Essay A is satisfied with his or her initial definition:

> Creativity to me means being free to express yourself in a way that is unique to you, not having to conform to certain rules and guidelines.

The writer of Essay B, however, is *not* satisfied with his or her first answer and uses the essay to think through the problem. This writer remembers an early creative experience—composing songs as a twelve-year-old:

> At the time of the writing, I felt that my songs were, in themselves, an original creation of my own; that is, I, alone, made them. However, I now see that, in this sense of the word, I was not creative. The songs themselves seem to be an oversimplified form of the music I listened to at the time.

This writer distinguishes between two points of view: "On the one hand, I used to think *x*, but now, in retrospect, I think *y*." This move forces the writer to go beyond the initial answer to think of alternatives.

The key to effective exploratory writing is to create a tension between alternative views. When you start out, you might not know where your thinking process will end up; at the outset you might not have formulated an opposing, countering, or alternative view. Using a statement such as "I used to think ..., but now I think" or "Part of me thinks this ..., but another part thinks that ..." forces you to find something additional to say; writing then becomes a process of inquiry and discovery.

The second writer's dissatisfaction with the initial answer initiates a dialectic process that plays one idea against another, creating a generative tension. In contrast, the writer of Essay A offers no alternative to his or her definition of creativity. This writer presents no specific illustrations of creative activity (such as the specific details in Essay B about strumming the guitar) but presents merely space-filling abstractions ("Sculpting, carving, building, art, and acting are just a few more areas where people can show their creativity"). The writer of Essay B scores a higher grade, not because the essay creates a brilliant (or even particularly clear) explanation of creativity; rather, the writer is rewarded for thinking about the problem dialectically.

We use the term *dialectic* to mean a thinking process often associated with the German philosopher Hegel, who said that each thesis ("My act was creative") gives rise to an antithesis ("My act was not creative") and that the clash of these opposing perspectives leads thinkers to develop a synthesis that incorporates some features of both theses ("My act was a series of 'small creations'"). You initiate dialectic thinking any time you play Elbow's believing and doubting game or use other strategies to place alternative possibilities side by side.

See Chapter 2, Concept 5, for an explanation of the believing and doubting game.

Essay B's writer uses a dialectic thinking strategy that we might characterize as follows:

1. Sees the assigned question as a genuine problem worth puzzling over.
2. Considers alternative views and plays them off against each other.
3. Looks at specific examples and illustrations.
4. Continues the thinking process in search of some sort of resolution or synthesis of the alternative views.
5. Incorporates the stages of this dialectic process into the essay.

These same dialectic thinking habits can be extended to research writing where the researcher's goal is to find alternative points of view on the research question, to read sources rhetorically, to consider all the relevant evidence, to search for a resolution or synthesis of alternative views, and to use one's own critical thinking to arrive at a thesis.

Keeping a Problem Open

FOR WRITING AND DISCUSSION

1. Working individually, read each of the following questions and write out the first plausible answer that comes to your mind.
   - Why on average are males more attracted to video games than females? Are these games harmful to males?
   - Have online social networks such as MySpace or Facebook improved or harmed the lives of participants? Why?
   - The most popular magazines sold on college campuses are women's fashion and lifestyle magazines such as *Glamour, Elle,* and *Cosmopolitan.* Why do women buy these magazines? Are these magazines harmful?
2. As a whole class, take a poll to determine the most common first-response answers for each of the questions. Then explore other possible answers and points of view. The goal of your class discussion is to postulate and explore answers that go against the grain of or beyond the common answers. Try to push deeply into each question so that it becomes more complex and interesting than it may at first seem.
3. How would you use library and Internet research to deepen your exploration of these questions? Specifically, what keywords might you use in a database search? What databases would you use?

See Chapters 20–22 for instructions on doing college-level academic research.

An Exploratory Essay

WRITING PROJECT

Choose a question, problem, or issue that genuinely perplexes you. At the beginning of your exploratory essay, explain why you are interested in this chosen problem, why the question is significant and worth exploring, and why you have been unable to reach a satisfactory answer. Then write a first-person, chronologically organized narrative account of your thinking process as you investigate your question through research, talking with others, and doing your own reflective thinking. Your research might involve reading articles or other sources assigned by your instructor, doing your own library or Internet research, or doing field research through interviews and observations. As you reflect on your research, you can also draw on your own memories and experiences. Your goal is to examine your question, problem, or issue from a variety of perspectives, assessing the strengths and weaknesses of different positions and points of view. By the end of your essay, you may or may not have reached a satisfactory solution to your problem. You will be rewarded for the quality of your exploration and thinking processes. In other words, your goal is not to answer your question but to report on the process of wrestling with it.

This assignment asks you to dwell on a problem—and not necessarily to solve that problem. Your problem may shift and evolve as your thinking progresses. What matters is that you are actively engaged with your problem and demonstrate why it is problematic.

Generating and Exploring Ideas

Your process of generating and exploring ideas is, in essence, the *subject matter* of your exploratory essay. This section will help you get started and keep going.

Posing Your Initial Problem

Your instructor may assign a specific problem to be investigated. If not, then your first step is to choose a question, problem, or issue that currently perplexes you. Perhaps a question is problematic for you because you haven't yet had a chance to study it (Should the United States turn to nuclear power for generating electricity? How can we keep children away from pornography on the Internet?). Maybe the available data seem conflicting or inconclusive (Should postmenopausal women take supplemental estrogen?). Or, possibly, the problem or issue draws you into an uncomfortable conflict of values (Should we legalize the sale of organs for transplant? Should the homeless mentally ill be placed involuntarily in state mental hospitals?).

The key to this assignment is to choose a question, problem, or issue *that truly perplexes you*. The more clearly readers sense your personal engagement with the problem, the more likely they are to be engaged by your writing. (Note: If your instructor pairs this assignment with a later one, be sure that your question is appropriate for the later assignment. Check with your instructor.)

Here are several exercises to help you think of ideas for this essay:

- Make a list of issues or problems that both interest and perplex you. Then choose two or three of your issues and freewrite about them for five minutes or so. Explore why you are interested in the problem and why it seems problematic to you. Use as your model James Gardiner's freewrite on page 33, which marked the origin of his exploratory paper for this chapter. Share your questions and your freewrites with friends and classmates because doing so often stimulates further thinking and discovery.
- If your exploratory essay is paired with a subsequent assignment, read the assignment to help you ask a question that fits the context of the final paper you will write.
- A particularly valuable kind of problem to explore for this assignment is a public controversy that might come to your attention through newspaper, television, or radio coverage; your reading of magazines or books; or personal experiences. Often such issues involve disagreements about facts and values that merit open-ended exploration. This assignment invites you to explore and clarify where you stand on such public issues as gay marriage, immigration, health care reform, ending the Iraq war, racial profiling, energy policies, and so forth. Make a list of currently debated public controversies that you

would like to explore. Use the following trigger question: "I don't know where I stand on the issue of ________." Share your list with classmates and friends.

Formulating a Starting Point

After you've chosen a problem or issue, you are ready to draft a first version of the introduction to your exploratory essay in which you identify the problem or issue you have chosen, show why you are interested in it and find it perplexing, and show its significance. You might start out with a sharp, clearly focused question (Should the United States build a fence between the United States and Mexico?). Often, however, formulating the question will turn out to be part of the *process* of writing the exploratory paper. Many writers don't start with a single, focused question but rather with a whole cluster of related questions swimming in their heads. This practice is fine as long as you have a direction in which to move after the initial starting point. Even if you do start with a focused question, it is apt to evolve as your thinking progresses.

In the introduction to an exploratory essay, a writer explains his or her research question or starting-point problem. For example, James Gardiner opens his essay by noting the popularity of online social networks such as MySpace and Facebook and mentioning the shocked look of his friends when he tells them he doesn't have a Facebook profile (see p. 191). He then introduces the questions he wants to investigate—why students are attracted to Facebook or MySpace, how students use the sites, and how their communication skills are being affected. Another student, Dylan Fujitani, opened his essay by explaining his shock when seeing a newspaper photograph of mutilated corpses hanging from a bridge in Falluja, Iraq. Later, he discovered that the bodies were not American soldiers but hired contractors. This experience gave rise to a number of issues he wanted to explore about mercenary soldiers under the general question, "Is the use of private contractors in military roles a good idea?"

Dylan Fujitani's final argument essay appears on pp. 479–483.

Taking "Double-Entry" Research Notes

After you have formulated your starting point, you need to proceed with your research. To develop the kind of academic research skills you will need for success in college, you should take purposeful notes as you read, following the strategies explained under Skill 24 (on taking effective notes) in Part 4, "A Rhetorical Guide to Research." Whereas novice researchers avoid taking notes and instead simply collect a file folder of photocopied or downloaded-and-printed articles, experienced researchers use note taking as a discipline to promote strong rhetorical reading. We recommend "double-entry" notes in which you have one section for summarizing key points, recording data, noting page numbers for useful quotations, and so forth, and another section for writing your own strong response to each source, explaining how it advanced your thinking, raised questions, or pulled you in one direction or another.

We also recommend that you keep your notes in a research journal or in separate computer files. What follows is James Gardiner's double-entry research notes for one of the articles he used in his exploratory essay. When you read his full essay in Chapter 23, you'll be able to see how he used this article at a crucial place in his research.

James's Double-Entry Research Log Entry for *Financial Times* Article

Date of entry so you can reconstruct chronological order → February 24

Bibliographic citation following assigned format, in this case MLA → Bowley, Graham. "The High Priestess of Internet Friendship." *Financial Times Weekend Magazine* 27 Oct. 2006. *LexisNexis Academic*. Web. 22 Feb. 2007.

Rhetorical notation about genre, purpose, audience → Newspaper feature article in journalistic style

Reading notes in column 1 on content of the source

Include full quotations if you won't keep a copy of the full source

Strong response notes in column 2 show reactions to the source

Reading Notes	Strong Response Notes
—Begins with Danah Boyd, an expert on OSNs. Talks about how she enjoyed Internet connections when she was growing up. Says the Internet "could change the way all of us order our world, interact with each other, get information and do business." (p. 1 of printout)	*—I want to find out more about Danah Boyd.* *—good quote*
—Two-page section on history of OSNs beginning with Friendster.	
—Returns to profile of Boyd. Boyd compares MySpace to an "electronic version of the local mall" (p. 2). She claims that these public spaces are no longer available so kids have gone virtual.	*—I don't think I agree with this; kids still hang out at malls.*
—Quote from blogger Cory Doctorow on OSN messages as "simple grooming exercises" (p. 3)—not serious talk—just saying "hi" online.	*—good quote; I should use it.*
—Paragraph on the "explosion of self-expression" on the sites—poems, songs, pictures, etc.—everyone trying to self-express creatively.	*—very interesting; I should try to use it.*
—Generational shift in attitudes toward privacy. Compares kids on OSNs trying to become celebrities like Paris Hilton (p. 3)—mentions Christine Dolce (AKA ForBiddeN) as example of someone who achieved celebrity status.	*—very important for my research question*
—Quotes Boyd: OSNs are about "identity production"—kids are trying to "write themselves into being." Quotes researcher Fred Stutzman about kids using OSN profiles like their bedroom walls—their private place where they can invite friends. They are "testing out identities." (p. 4)	*—I have another article by Stutzman; should read it soon. —great analogy*

Reading Notes	Strong Response Notes
—Has a section on online games; also has a section on how sociologists are doing interesting experiments seeing how news travels on OSNs.	*—I don't quite understand the experiments*
—Raises some questions about dangers—stalkers—especially dangers to minors. How legislators are trying to come up with laws to make it harder for stalkers to find victims.	*—good for challenging OSNs and constructing alternative views*
—Returns to Boyd, who says these dangers are "painfully overblown." Boyd really supports OSNs as places where kids can "negotiate this new world."	*—important points; good longer quote on p. 5*
— Last part focuses on commercial aspects of OSNs; they apparently aren't yet big moneymakers. Also if there is too much advertising, kids might not like the OSN as well.	*—points make sense; might use them*

Strong response summary:
Very useful article, not scholarly but fairly deep and well-researched. I can use it to give arguments in favor of Facebook, MySpace, or other OSNs. However, Danah Boyd doesn't support OSNs in the same way that many other supporters do. Most supporters talk about how OSNs help young people enlarge their list of friends and have a feeling of connection, etc. Boyd is much more edgy and sees the dangers out there and all the role playing and phoniness. Boyd seems to like that unstable atmosphere where the rules and norms aren't really clear. She thinks that the online world is really helping students learn to find their identities and discover who they are. I still have reservations, though. I like the parts of the article where Bowley talks about students wanting to become celebrities and competing with each other for the most friends because that seems like self-enhancement rather than making connections. Also Boyd doesn't seem worried about all the time young people spend at these sites. I need to do more research into the downside of OSNs.

Shaping and Drafting

Your exploratory essay records the history of your researching and thinking process (what you read or whom you talked to, how you responded, how your thinking evolved). Along the way you can make your narrative more colorful and grounded by including your strategies for tracking down sources, your conversations with friends, your late-night trips to a coffee shop, and so forth. What you will quickly discover about this exploratory assignment is that it forces you actually to do the research. Unless you conduct your research in a timely fashion, you won't have any research process to write about.

Exploratory essays can be composed in two ways—what we might call the "real-time strategy" and the "retrospective strategy."

STRATEGIES for Composing an Exploratory Essay

Strategies	Advantages
Real-time strategy. Compose the body of the essay during the actual process of researching and thinking.	Yields genuine immediacy—like a sequence of letters or e-mails sent home during a journey.
Retrospective strategy. Look back over your completed research notes and then compose the body of the essay.	Allows for more selection and shaping of details and yields a more artistically designed essay.

In either case, the goal when writing with an exploratory aim is to reproduce the research and thinking process, taking the readers on the same intellectual and emotional journey you have just traveled. The exploratory essay has the general organizational framework shown in Figure 8.1.

There are a number of keys to writing successful exploratory papers. As you draft, pay particular attention to the following:

- *Show how you chose sources purposively and reflectively rather than randomly.* As you make a transition from one source to the next, help your reader see your thought processes. Note the following examples of bridging passages that reveal the writer's purposeful selection of sources:

  > For the next stage of my research, I wanted to explore in more detail what students actually did while online in an OSN. I located my next source by searching through the Academic Search complete database (from James Gardiner's essay, para. 6, p. 193).

  > After reading Friedman's views of how globalization was changing lives in India and China, I realized that I needed to talk to some students from these countries, so I grabbed my backpack and headed to the International Student Center.

- *Give your draft both open-form and closed-form features.* Because your exploratory paper is a narrative, it follows an unfolding, open-form structure. Many of your paragraphs should open with chronological transitions such as "I *started* by reading," "*Early the next morning,* I headed for the library to ..." or "On the *next* day, I decided," or "*After* finishing ... I *next* looked at. ..." At the same time, your summaries of your sources and your strong responses to them should be framed within closed-form structures with topic sentences and logical transitions: "This article, in raising objections to genetic screening of embryos, began changing my views about new advances in reproductive technology. Whereas before I felt ..., now I feel. ..."
- *Show yourself wrestling with ideas.* Readers want to see how your research stimulates your own thinking. Throughout, your paper should show you responding strongly to your sources. Here is a good example from James's paper on online social networks.

FIGURE 8.1 Framework for an Exploratory Essay

Introduction (one or more paragraphs)	• Establishes that your question is complex, problematic, and significant • Shows why you are interested in it • Presents relevant background You can begin with your question or build up to it, using it to end your introductory section.
Body section 1 on first source	• Introduces your first source and shows why you started with it • Provides rhetorical context and information about the source • Summarizes the source's content and argument • Offers your strong response to this source, frequently including both with-the-grain and against-the-grain points • Talks about what this source contributes to your understanding of your question: What did you learn? What value does this source have for you? What is missing from this source that you want to consider? Where do you want to go from here?
Body section 2 on second source	• Repeats the process with a new source selected to advance the inquiry • Explains why you selected this source (to find an alternative view, pursue subquestions, find more data, and so forth) • Summarizes the source's argument • Provides a strong response • Shows how your cumulative reading of sources is shaping your thinking or leading to more questions
Body sections 3, 4, 5, etc., on additional sources	• Continues the process
Conclusion	• Wraps up your intellectual journey and explains where you are now in your thinking and how your understanding of your problem has changed • Presents your current answer to your question based on all that you have read and learned so far, or explains why you still can't answer your question, or explains what further research you might do
Works Cited or References list	• Includes a complete list of citations in MLA or APA format, depending on your assignment

After considering the views of Boyd and Stutzman, I felt I understood why they think that OSNs give young people the opportunity for self-definition and self-expression. However, I still had doubts about the beneficial effects of OSNs. They still seem to me to send superficial messages about a person's identity. I found myself wondering if it is detrimental to spend all that time in virtual space rather than actually being with one's friends. I felt I needed to start looking for articles that examine the dangers of OSNs.

Although you might feel that sentences that show your mind talking its way through your research will sound too informal, they actually work well in exploratory essays to create interest and capture your critical thinking.

Revising

Because an exploratory essay describes the writer's research and thinking in chronological order, most writers have little trouble with organization. When they revise, their major concern is to improve their essay's interest level by keeping it focused and lively. Often drafts need to be pruned to remove extraneous details and keep the pace moving. Frequently, introductions can be made sharper, clearer, and more engaging. Peer reviewers can give you valuable feedback about the pace and interest level of an exploratory piece. They can also help you achieve the right balance between summarizing sources and showing the evolution of your own thinking. As you revise, make sure you use attributive tags and follow proper stylistic conventions for quotations and citations.

Questions for Peer Review

In addition to the generic peer review questions explained in Chapter 17, Skill 4, ask your peer reviewers to address these questions:

POSING THE PROBLEM:

1. In the introduction, how has the writer tried to show that the problem is interesting, significant, and problematic? How could the writer engage you more fully with the initial problem?
2. How does the writer provide cues that his/her purpose is to explore a question rather than argue a thesis? How might the opening section of the draft be improved?

NARRATING THE EXPLORATION:

3. Is the body of the paper organized chronologically so that you can see the development of the writer's thinking? Where does the writer provide chronological transitions?
4. Part of an exploratory essay involves summarizing the argument of each new research source. Where in this draft is a summary of a source particularly clear and well developed? Where are summary passages either undeveloped or unclear or too long? How could these passages be improved?
5. Another part of an exploratory paper involves the writer's strong response to each source. Where in this draft is there evidence of the writer's own critical thinking and questioning? Where are the writer's ideas particularly strong and effective? Where are the writer's own ideas undeveloped, unclear, or weak?
6. Has the writer done enough research to explore the problem? How would you describe the range and variety of sources that the writer has consulted? Where does the writer acknowledge how the kinds of sources shape his or her perspective on the subject? What additional ideas or perspectives do you think the writer should consider?

An Annotated Bibliography

WRITING PROJECT

Create an annotated bibliography that lists the research sources you have used for your exploratory project. Because annotated bibliographies can vary in the number, length, and kinds of entries, follow guidelines provided by your instructor. Some instructors may also require a critical preface that explains your research question and provides details about how you selected the bibliographic sources.

What Is an Annotated Bibliography?

Bibliographies are alphabetized lists of sources on a given topic, providing readers with the names of authors, titles, and publication details for each source. Unlike a plain list of sources, an *annotated bibliography* also includes the writer's "annotation" or commentary on each source. These annotations can be either *summary-only* or *evaluative*.

- **A summary-only annotation** provides a capsule of the source's contents without any additional comments from the bibliography's author.
- **An evaluative annotation** adds the author's critique or assessment of the work, including comments about the source's rhetorical context, its particular strengths or weaknesses, and its usefulness or value.

Whichever type is used, the length of the annotation is a function of its audience and purpose. Brief annotations comprise only a few sentences (one standard approach—to be described later—uses three sentences) while longer annotations can be up to 150 words. Brief annotations are most common when the annotated bibliography has numerous entries; longer annotations, which allow for fuller summaries and more detailed analyses, are often more helpful for readers but can make an annotated bibliography too long if there are many sources.

Annotated bibliographies serve several important functions. First, writing an annotated bibliography engages researchers in exploratory thinking by requiring that they read sources rhetorically like experts, entering critically into scholarly conversations. Annotated bibliographies can also be valuable time-saving tools for new researchers in a field. By providing overview information about potential sources, they help new researchers determine whether a particular source might be useful for their own purposes. Think of source annotations as analogous to short movie reviews that help you select your next film. (What's this movie about? How good is it?) Additionally, annotated bibliographies can establish the writer's *ethos* by showing the depth, breadth, and competence of the writer's research. (A good annotated bibliography proves that you have read and thought about your sources.)

Features of Annotated Bibliography Entries

Each entry has two main parts, the bibliographic citation and the annotation. The *bibliographic citation* should follow the conventions of your assigned documentation

See Skills 32 and 33 in Chapter 23.

style such as the Modern Language Association (MLA) or the American Psychological Association (APA).

An *evaluative annotation* (the most common kind) typically includes three elements. In a three-sentence evaluative annotation, each element is covered in one sentence.

- **Rhetorical information**, including the source's rhetorical context, particularly its genre and (if not implied by the genre) its purpose and audience. Is this source a scholarly article? An op-ed piece? A blog? What is the author's purpose and who is the intended audience? Are there any political biases that need to be noted?
- **A summary of the source's content.** In some cases, a writer simply lists what is covered in the source. Whenever possible, however, summarize the source's actual argument. (Note: In a *summary-only* annotation, this summary is the only element included.)
- **The writer's evaluation of the source.** What are the source's particular strengths or weaknesses? How useful is the source for specific purposes? How might the writer use the source for his or her research project? (Or, if the annotated bibliography comes at the end of the project, how did the writer use the source?)

Examples of Annotation Entries

Here are examples of different kinds of annotations based on James Gardiner's research notes for one of his sources (see pp. 182–183):

SUMMARY-ONLY ANNOTATION

Bowley, Graham. "The High Priestess of Internet Friendship." *Financial Times Weekend Magazine* 27 Oct. 2006. *LexisNexis Academic*. Web. 22 Feb. 2007.

In this feature story, Bowley explains the development of OSNs from their origins in *Friendster* to their current popularity in *MySpace* and *Facebook*. He also traces further developments of OSNs and explains their difficulties in making profits through commercial advertising. Finally, Bowley uses interviews with researchers to show how young people use OSNs to maintain social relationships and to play with different identities through self-expression.

EVALUATIVE ANNOTATION

Bowley, Graham. "The High Priestess of Internet Friendship." *Financial Times Weekend Magazine* 27 Oct. 2006. *LexisNexis Academic*. Web. 22 Feb. 2007.

This article is a feature story in the "Arts and Weekend" section of the *Financial Times Weekend Magazine*. Bowley's information comes from interviews with researchers who study online social networks (OSNs). Bowley explains the development of OSNs from their origins in *Friendster* to their current popularity in *MySpace* and *Facebook*, traces further developments of OSNs, and explains their difficulties in making profits through commercial advertising. Bowley also shows how young people use OSNs to maintain social relationships and to play with different identities through self-expression. A particularly valuable section mentions the dangers of OSNs, such as sexual predators. However, Danah Boyd, a researcher whom Bowley quotes extensively, defends OSNs as a place where young people can explore their identities and "negotiate this new world." This article gives a mostly positive view of OSNs and goes beyond other articles by showing how OSNs provide a new space for "identity production."

THREE-SENTENCE EVALUATIVE ANNOTATION

Bowley, Graham. "The High Priestess of Internet Friendship." *Financial Times Weekend Magazine* 27 Oct. 2006. *LexisNexis Academic*. Web. 22 Feb. 2007.

This article is a journalistic feature story written for readers of a major business and finance newspaper. It gives the history of online social networks (OSN) including *Friendster*, *MySpace*, and *Facebook*, explains their difficulties in making money through commercial advertising, and shows how young people use OSNs to maintain social relationships and to play with different identities through self-expression. This is a valuable article that gives a mostly positive view of OSNs by showing how they provide a new space for "identity production" and self-expression.

Writing a Critical Preface for Your Annotated Bibliography

Scholars who publish annotated bibliographies typically introduce them with a critical preface that explains the scope and purpose of the bibliography. When you write a critical preface for your own annotated bibliography, you have a chance to highlight your critical thinking and show the purposeful way that you conducted your research. Typically the critical preface includes the following information:

- A contextual overview that shows the purpose of the annotated bibliography and suggests its value and significance for the reader
- The research question posed by the author
- The dates during which the bibliography was compiled
- An overview of the number of items in the bibliography and the kinds of material included

A student example of an annotated bibliography with a critical preface is found in the Readings section of this chapter (pp. 196–198).

Shaping, Drafting, and Revising

The key to producing a good annotated bibliography is to take good research notes as you read. Compare the various versions of the above annotations with James Gardiner's research notes (pp. 182–183). Before composing your annotated bibliography, make sure that you understand your instructor's preferences for the number of entries required and for the length and kinds of annotations. Arrange the bibliography in alphabetical order as you would in a "Works Cited" (MLA format) or "References" (APA format) list.

The specific skills needed for an annotated bibliography are taught in various places in this text. If you are having problems with aspects of an annotated bibliography, you can find further instruction as follows.

Problems with:	**Where to Find Help**
Formatting the citations.	Refer to Chapter 23, Skill 32 for MLA style, and Skill 33 for APA style.
Describing the rhetorical context and genre.	Review Chapter 21, Skill 24, and reread Chapter 1, Concept 3.
Writing a summary.	Read Chapter 6, pages 117–121, on summary writing; read also Chapter 22, Skill 28.
Writing an evaluation.	Use the strategies for strong response in Chapter 6, pages 121–126, and also Chapter 21, Skills 24–26.
Wordiness—the annotation is more than 150 words.	See Chapter 4, Concept 11, on wordy versus streamlined sentences.

Questions for Peer Review

The following questions are based on the assumption that your instructor requires evaluative annotations and a critical preface. Adjust the questions to fit a different assignment.

CRITICAL PREFACE

1. Where does the writer explain the following: The purpose and significance of the bibliography? The research question that motivated the research? The dates of the research? The kinds of sources included?
2. How could the critical preface be improved?

BIBLIOGRAPHIC CITATIONS

3. Does each citation follow MLA or APA conventions? Pay particular attention to the formatting of sources downloaded from a licensed database or from the Web.
4. Are the sources arranged alphabetically?

ANNOTATIONS

5. Where does each annotation include the following: Information about genre or rhetorical context? A capsule summary of the source's contents? An evaluative comment?
6. Identify any places where the annotations are confusing or unclear or where the writer could include more information.
7. How could one or more of the annotations be improved?

READINGS

Our first reading is an exploratory essay by student writer James Gardiner on online social networks. After completing the exploratory essay, James continued his research, writing an argument on potential negative consequences of OSNs. James's final argument is our sample MLA student research paper in Chapter 23 (pp. 643–651).

James Gardiner (student)

How Do Online Social Networks Affect Communication?

1 Walk into any computer lab located at any college campus across the country and you'll see dozens of students logged onto an online social network (OSN). In the last few years, the use of these networks has sky-rocketed among Internet users, especially young adults. As a college student, I am one of the few people I know who does not have a profile on either *MySpace* or *Facebook*, and I'm constantly met with shocked looks when I inform my fellow students of this. Today, OSNs have become a staple in the life of most American young people. Although I was conscious that OSNs were impacting the way young people communicate with each other, I was largely unaware of the specific ways that people used these OSNs or how their communication skills were being affected by this new technology. For this research project, I decided to pursue the question, How are online social networks influencing the way young people communicate with each other? This question deserves to be examined because the more people move toward these new modes of communication, the more influence these networks will have on society as a whole. I suspect that these new virtual communities are changing the way people communicate with one another to an incredible degree.

2 Before I could focus on the impact of OSNs on people's communication skills, I first needed to learn more about who used these networks and for what specific purposes they joined them. I started by reading a short news article, "The Web of Social Networking," from *U.S. News & World Report* (Green), to give me a basic understanding of this phenomenon. I learned that by far the two most popular OSNs are *MySpace* and *Facebook*. *MySpace* is a general networking site that allows anybody to access it. *Facebook* is geared more toward college students, and until recently a user needed a university e-mail address to join. According to Green, in 2005, *MySpace* was one of the 20 most popular sites on the Internet while *Facebook* was the top site for 18- to 24-year-olds. Moreover, Green points out that 60% of *Facebook* members logged in daily. This high number surprised me.

3 Needing more in-depth information about how young people use OSNs, I next turned to the *Pew Internet Project* website, based on a recommendation from my composition instructor. Pew is a non-partisan, non-profit research center that examines the social impact of the Internet. On the website, I found the results of the Parents and Teens 2006 survey in which researchers conducted telephone interviews of 935 teenagers and their parents living in the United States. The key findings include the following, which I quote from this report:

- 55% of online teens have created a personal profile on OSNs.
- 66% of teens who have created a profile say that their profile is not visible to all Internet users. They limit access to their profiles.
- 48% of teens visit social networking websites daily or more often; 26% visit once a day, 22% visit several times a day.
- Older girls ages 15–17 are more likely to have used social networking sites and created online profiles; 70% of older girls have used an online social network compared with 54% of older boys, and 70% of older girls have created an online profile, while only 57% of older boys have done so. (Lenhart and Madden 2)

The survey reveals how young people were using OSNs as tools to communicate with each other. It states that 91% of users logged on to keep in touch with their regularly seen friends, while 82% used the sites to stay in touch with distant friends. The survey also indicates that 49% use the sites to make new friends (Lenhart and Madden 2).

4 The Pew survey gave me a clearer picture of how and why young people are using OSNs. Although I wasn't surprised to learn that over half of all online teens were members of OSNs, I was caught off guard by the frequency that these teens logged on to these sites. I was also unaware that almost half of all social networking teens used these sites to meet new people. These discoveries helped me to better form my understanding of OSNs as I proceeded with my investigation focusing on their effects on communication skills.

5 I was now several days into my project. Because I am kind of a private person, I would be hesitant to put much personal information on a profile. Since all online social networks are comprised of profiles created by their members, I thought it would be a good idea to next examine how extensively these people disclosed personal information. By plugging "personal information" and "Online Social Networks" into *Google*, I located a study titled, "An Evaluation of Identity-Sharing Behavior in Social Network Communities" by Frederic Stutzman, a graduate student at the School of Information and Library Science at the University of North Carolina in Chapel Hill. In this scholarly piece from a conference, Stutzman recounts how his research attempted to uncover how much and what kind of identity information young people are disclosing in OSNs. Stutzman identified a random sample of UNC students and asked them to complete a survey about their use of these social networks and their feelings about disclosure of identity information. The results showed that 90% of UNC undergraduates have a *Facebook* profile. At the heart of Stutzman's article is a graph that shows the percentage of polled students who disclose certain personal information on their *Facebook* page. For example, 75% of users post a photograph, 65% post relationship information, 55% disclose political views, and 35% disclose sexual orientation (sec. 4.3). Stutzman concludes that as the Internet grew in popularity and the tools and places for self-expression became more widely available and easier to use, many people went from wanting to be anonymous online to revealing a lot of personal information.

6 I was taken aback by the percentage of students willing to put their photographs and other personal information online. What kinds of photographs did they actually put online? How did the whole profile contribute to the way they communicated? For the next stage of my research, I wanted to explore in more detail what students actually did while online in an OSN. I located my next source by searching through the *Academic Search Complete* database. I was fortunate to come upon a very helpful article. It was a

feature article in the international business newspaper *Financial Times*. Its author, Graham Bowley, bases much of his information on an interview with OSN researcher Danah Boyd. Through a *Google* search, I found Boyd's personal website, where I learned that she is a PhD candidate at the University of California-Berkeley and a Fellow at the University of Southern California Annenberg Center for Communications. Her research focuses on "how people negotiate a presentation of self to unknown audiences in mediated contexts" (Boyd). According to Bowley, Boyd is widely known online as "the high priestess of Internet friendship" for her writings and research on the subject. His interview with Boyd confirms findings that I found in the Pew survey that while some OSN users try to find new friends on the Internet, the majority were not using OSNs for that purpose. Instead, according to Bowley, "they were using it to reinforce existing relations with the group of friends they already had from their offline lives. For them, *MySpace* had become an electronic version of the local mall or park, the place they went to with their friends when they just wanted to hang out." Besides a "virtual hang out," OSNs offer young people a way to stay in touch with friends by allowing them to view their friends' profiles and leave short messages or comments. According to Cory Doctorow, another person interviewed by Bowley, this practice can be likened to "simple grooming exercises—in the same way that other primates groom each other to reinforce their relationships" (qtd. in Bowley).

7 Throughout the article, Bowley shows why Boyd supports OSNs. Boyd believes that "online social networks have become a vital space for young people to express themselves and build their personal identities" (Bowley). What I find interesting is that she particularly seems to like some of the edgy, unstable, dangerous aspects of OSNs that cause parents to be nervous about having their children online.

> Is there porn on MySpace? Of course. And bullying, sexual teasing and harassment are rampant among teenagers. It is how you learn to make meaning, cultural roles, norms. These kids need to explore their life among strangers. Teach them how to negotiate this new world. They need these public spaces now that other public spaces are closed to them. They need a place that is theirs. We should not always be chasing them and stopping them from growing up. (qtd. in Bowley)

Danah Boyd's observations have helped me understand how OSNs provide a place for self-expression as well as for communication with friends. She says that online sites give students practice at "identity production," where they can construct an identity through the kinds of items they post in their profile while also getting feedback and recognition from their friends. I got further understanding of this aspect of OSNs from another researcher interviewed by Bowley, Fred Stutzman (a person whose article on Internet identity-sharing I had already read). Stutzman calls students' OSN profiles an online version of their bedroom wall. Just as young people place posters on bedroom walls to express their special interests, they place items (pictures, music, and so forth) in their profiles to express themselves while also searching for an identity. "They are tuning into an audience," explains Stutzman. "One of the things students do at college is they test out identities. Maybe that is one new thing we are seeing now—more rapid changes of identity. Online you get feedback and you can change at a moment's notice" (qtd. in Bowley).

8 After considering the views of Boyd and Stutzman, I felt I understood why they think that OSNs give young people the opportunity for self-definition and self-expression. However, I still had doubts about the beneficial effects of OSNs. They still seem to me to send superficial messages about a person's identity. I found myself wondering if it is detrimental to spend all that time in virtual space rather than actually being with one's friends. I felt I needed to start looking for articles that examine the dangers of OSNs.

9 Although the next two sources I found didn't focus on the dangers of OSNs, they did provide interesting information on how students use *Facebook* to gain information about people they have met offline. The first article, another proceeding from an academic conference, reports data from two surveys of 1,440 first-year students at Michigan State University who had profiles on *Facebook*. Results show that "users are largely employing *Facebook* to learn more about people they meet offline, and are less likely to use the site to initiate new connections" (Lampe, Ellison, and Steinfield 167). The study reveals that *Facebook* users primarily use *Facebook* as a tool to investigate people they've already met offline. My second article, "Click Clique: *Facebook*'s Online College Community," written by Libby Copeland and published in the reputable newspaper the *Washington Post* in December of 2004, gives specific examples of this new social practice. One student explains how she would meet someone new at a friend's party that interested her and minutes later would be in her friend's room looking at his *Facebook* profile. Another student used the site to learn about the people in his classes: "If you meet someone in class and can't remember his name, you can look him up on the class lists kept on the *Facebook*. You can also research his interests, gathering information that you keep to yourself when you talk to him so he won't ever know you looked him up." Copeland also cites another student, who went as far as to call *Facebook* a "Stalker book."

10 After learning more about how users of OSNs practice self-disclosure, how they interact with friends online, and how they used the networks to find out information about people, I wanted to address something that had caught me off guard earlier in my research: the frequency with which OSN members are logged on to the community. Copeland mentions how much time students spent logged onto *Facebook*. She uses the term "Facebook Trance," which describes a person who loses track of all time and stares at the screen for hours. Copeland quotes one student who says "You stare into it [*Facebook* profiles] FOR-EV-ER." For the next stage of my research, I wanted to learn more about this "Facebook trance" and about the concept of Internet addiction.

11 I discovered that there is a lot of material on Internet addiction, so I started with an article appearing in the *Educational Psychology Review* in 2005 (Chou, Condron, and Belland). This is a long, scholarly article most of which doesn't talk directly about OSNs. Nevertheless, parts of the article are valuable. In contrast to most of my research so far, this article sheds light on the potential problems of OSNs—the other side of this double-edged communication sword. One section states that 13% of respondents (in one of the studies the authors reviewed) reported that Internet use had interfered with "their academic work, professional performance, or social lives." Among them, about 2% perceived the Internet as having an "overall negative effect on their daily lives" (369). Although OSNs can help to maintain and create new relationships, the authors claim that

"over-dependence on online relationships may result in significant problems with real-life interpersonal and occupational functioning" (381). Students may believe that they are "in touch" with people, when in actuality they are physically alone with their computers. Although online communication can be used to enhance relationships, this article warns that it can become a problem when it begins to replace offline interaction.

12 After learning some of the ways that online social networks affect their users' communication skills, I have concluded that these networks can improve the ability to communicate, but if overused can negatively affect these skills. Although OSNs are offering their users new tools to express themselves, stay in touch with friends, and meet new people, these networks can turn counterproductive when a person becomes addicted and thus isolated from offline interpersonal interactions.

13 As I continue with my research, I am not sure what thesis I will assert for my final project. I still want to do more research on the negative effects of OSNs. For example, I haven't found studies that explore the possible phoniness of *Facebook* relationships. I remember a passage from Copeland where one user labels *Facebook* interaction as "communication lean." According to this student, "It's all a little fake—the 'friends'; the profiles that can be tailored to what others find appealing; the 'groups' that exist only in cyberspace." I'm still thinking about that quotation. Do OSNs contribute to deeper, more meaningful relationships or do they promote a superficial phoniness? I hope to explore this issue further before writing my major paper.

Works Cited

Bowley, Graham. "The High Priestess of Internet Friendship." *Financial Times Weekend Magazine* 27 Oct. 2006. *LexisNexis Academic*. Web. 22 Feb. 2007.

Boyd, Danah. Home page. Web. 21 Feb. 2007.

Chou, Chien, Linda Condron, and John C. Belland. "A Review of the Research on Internet Addiction." *Educational Psychology Review* 17.4 (2005): 363–89. *Academic Search Complete*. Web. 22 Feb. 2007.

Copeland, Libby. "Click Clique: *Facebook*'s Online College Community." *Washingtonpost.com*. Washington Post, 28 Dec. 2004. Web. 24 Feb. 2007.

Green, Elizabeth Weiss. "The Web of Social Networking." *U.S. News & World Report* 14 Nov. 2005: 58. *Academic Search Complete*. Web. 15 Feb. 2007.

Lampe, Cliff, Nicole Ellison, and Charles Steinfield. "A Face(book) in the Crowd: Social Searching Versus Social Browsing." *Proceedings of the 2006 20th Anniversary Conference on Computer Supported Cooperative Work*. 2006: 167–70. *The ACM Digital Library*. Web. 24 Feb. 2007.

Lenhart, Amanda, and Mary Madden. "Social Networking Websites and Teens: An Overview." *Pew Internet & American Life Project*. Pew Research Center, 3 Jan. 2007. Web. 19 Feb. 2007.

Stutzman, Frederic. "An Evaluation of Identity-Sharing Behavior in Social Network Communities." *Proceedings of the 2006 iDMAa and IMS Code Conference*. Oxford, OH, 2006. Web. 20 Feb. 2007. <http://www.ibiblio.org/fred/pubs/stutzman_pub4.pdf>.

THINKING CRITICALLY

about "How Do Online Social Networks Affect Communication?"

1. Earlier in this chapter, we suggested ways to organize and strengthen an exploratory essay. Where do you see James including the following features: (a) A blend of open-form narrative moves with closed-form focusing sentences? (b) A purposeful selection of sources? (c) A consideration of the rhetorical context of his sources—that is, an awareness of the kinds of sources he is using and how the genre of the source influences its content? (d) Reflective/critical thinking that shows his strong response to his sources? Where might he develop these features further?
2. Trace the evolution of James's ideas in this paper. How does his thinking evolve? What subquestions does he pose? What issues connected to his main question does he pursue?
3. Read James's argument for limiting use of OSNs on pages 643–651. What new research did he do for his final argument? How do you see the exploratory paper contributing to James's argument in the final paper? How do differences in purpose (exploration versus persuasion) lead to different structures for the two papers?
4. What are the strengths and weaknesses of James's exploration of OSNs?

Our next reading is an excerpt from James's annotated bibliography based on the same research he did for his exploratory paper. We have used James's research for both examples so that you can compare an exploratory paper with an annotated bibliography. His original annotated bibliography contained six entries. We have printed three of these, along with his critical preface. Additionally, the annotated bibliography entry for Graham Bowley is shown on page 188.

James Gardiner (student)

What Is the Effect of Online Social Networks on Communication Skills?

An Annotated Bibliography

Critical Preface

1 Today, online social networks (OSNs) such as *MySpace* and *Facebook* have become staples in the lives of most American young people. Although I was conscious that OSNs were impacting the way young people communicate with each other, I was largely unaware of the specific ways that the people used these OSNs or how their communication skills were being affected by this new technology. For this research project, I set out to discover how online social networks influence the way young peo-

ple communicate with each other. I posed several specific questions that I hoped my research could help me answer: (1) Why are OSNs so popular? (2) How do young people use OSNs? (3) How do OSNs affect communication skills? And (4) To what extent might OSNs be harmful or detrimental? These questions deserve to be examined because as more people move toward these new modes of communication, these networks will increasingly influence society as a whole.

2 I conducted this research during a one-week period in late February 2007. The bibliography contains different kinds of sources: two articles from popular magazines or newspapers; three articles from scholarly journals; and one survey report from a major Internet site devoted to research on people's use of the Internet. These sources gave me preliminary answers to all my initial research questions. They show why young people are attracted to OSNs and why and how they use them. Particularly valuable for my research are the articles by Bowley and by Lampe, Ellison, and Steinfield showing the positive potential of OSNs and the article by Chou, Condron, and Belland showing the possible negative potential if persons become addicted to OSNs.

Annotated Bibliography

Chou, Chien, Linda Condron, and John C. Belland. "A Review of the Research on Internet Addiction." *Educational Psychology Review* 17.4 (2005): 363–89. *Academic Search Complete*. Web. 22 Feb. 2007.

This lengthy academic article written for scholars reviews research on Internet addiction. It has four sections: (1) explanations of how Internet addiction is defined and assessed; (2) problems created by Internet addiction and variables such as gender or psychosocial traits associated with addiction; (3) explanations for why the Internet creates addictions; and (4) ways to treat Internet addiction. For my project, section 2 on problems was most valuable. In one study 13% of respondents reported that Internet use interfered with their personal lives or academic performance. Although Internet addiction didn't seem as harmful as other addictions, the authors observed that too much dependence on online relationships can interfere with real relationships. The tables in this article show the key findings from dozens of research studies.

Lampe, Cliff, Nicole Ellison, and Charles Steinfield. "A Face(book) in the Crowd: Social Searching Versus Social Browsing." *Proceedings of the 2006 20th Anniversary Conference on Computer Supported Cooperative Work*. 2006: 167–70. *The ACM Digital Library*. Web. 24 Feb. 2007.

This scholarly research report is based on questionnaires about *Facebook* usage received from 1,440 first-year students at Michigan State University in fall 2006. The researchers investigated whether students used *Facebook* primarily to meet new people ("social browsers") or to maintain or develop friendships with persons whom they had already met ("social searchers.") The findings contradicted the popular view that *Facebook* users are social browsers. Rather, the majority of respondents used the network to keep in touch with existing friends or to find out additional information about classmates or other recent acquaintances. This article has useful data about perceived audiences for profiles (peers rather than professors or administrators) and about primary reasons for using *Facebook*. The article provided insights into why *Facebook* is popular.

Lenhart, Amanda, and Mary Madden. "Social Networking Websites and Teens: An Overview." *Pew Internet & American Life Project*. Pew Research Center, 3 Jan. 2007. Web. 19 Feb. 2007.

This source is an online memo from researchers working for the Pew Internet and American Life Project, a non-profit research organization. It reports the results of a telephone survey of a random national sample of 935 youths aged 12 to 17 in fall 2006. The document has numerous tables showing demographic data about teens' use of OSNs, the most popular sites, the frequency of use, and the reasons teens give for using the sites. Because of the scientific method of polling, this article provides reliable data for understanding how teens currently use OSNs.

THINKING CRITICALLY

about "What Is the Effect of Online Social Networks on Communication Skills? An Annotated Bibliography"

1. Explain how James includes the three common elements of an evaluative annotation (genre/rhetorical context, summary of content, evaluation) in each of his annotations.
2. Compare James's annotated bibliography with his exploratory essay (pp. 191–196), noting differences between the way each source is described in the bibliography versus the essay. What insights do you get from the exploratory essay that are missing from the bibliography? What information about the sources comes through more clearly in the bibliography than in the essay?
3. How might James use information and points in this annotated bibliography in his researched argument?

The third example of exploratory writing is an excerpt from a scholarly article by literary critic Jane Tompkins. First published in the scholarly journal *Critical Inquiry*, Tompkins's article focuses on the problem of how different historians portray Native Americans. This problem was a surprise for Tompkins, who began her research in pursuit of another topic. Note how deftly Tompkins uses an open-form structure to recount both personal and scholarly revelations. Although it is too long to print in full here, the entire article follows the narrative shape of Tompkins's thinking process, beginning with the discovery and evolution of a "problem of my own."

Jane Tompkins
"Indians":
Textualism, Morality, and the Problem of History

This passage introduces the problem by relating a childhood memory about Indians.

1 When I was growing up in New York City, my parents used to take me to an event in Inwood Park at which Indians—real American Indians dressed in feathers and blankets—could be seen and touched by children like me. This event was always a

disappointment. It was more fun to imagine that you *were* an Indian in one of the caves in Inwood Park than to shake the hand of an old man in a headdress who was not overwhelmed at the opportunity of meeting you. After staring at the Indians for a while, we would take a walk in the woods where the caves were, and once I asked my mother if the remains of a fire I had seen in one of them might have been left by the original inhabitants. After that, wandering up some stone steps cut into the side of the hill, I imagined I was a princess in a rude castle. My Indians, like my princesses, were creatures totally of the imagination, and I did not care to have any real exemplars interfering with what I already knew.

2 I already knew about Indians from having read about them in school. Over and over we were told the story of how Peter Minuit had bought Manhattan Island from the Indians for twenty-four dollars' worth of glass beads. And it was a story we didn't mind hearing because it gave us the rare pleasure of having someone to feel superior to, since the poor Indians had not known (as we eight-year-olds did) how valuable a piece of property Manhattan Island would become. Generally, much was made of the Indian presence in Manhattan; a poem in one of our readers began: "Where we walk to school today / Indian children used to play," and we were encouraged to write poetry on this topic ourselves. So I had a fairly rich relationship with Indians before I ever met the unprepossessing people in Inwood Park. I felt that I had a lot in common with them. They, too, liked animals (they were often named after animals); they, too, made mistakes—they liked the brightly colored trinkets of little value that the white men were always offering them; they were handsome, warlike, and brave and had led an exciting, romantic life in the forest long ago, a life such as I dreamed of leading myself. I felt lucky to be living in one of the places where they had definitely been. Never mind where they were or what they were doing now.

3 My story stands for the relationship most non-Indians have to the people who first populated this continent, a relationship characterized by narcissistic fantasies of freedom and adventure, of a life lived closer to nature and to spirit than the life we lead now. As Vine Deloria, Jr., has pointed out, the American Indian Movement in the early seventies couldn't get people to pay attention to what was happening to Indians who were alive in the present, so powerful was this country's infatuation with people who wore loincloths, lived in tepees, and roamed the plains and forests long ago. The present essay, like these fantasies, doesn't have much to do with actual Indians, though its subject matter is the histories of European-Indian relations in seventeenth-century New England. In a sense, my encounter with Indians as an adult doing "research" replicates the childhood one, for while I started out to learn about Indians, I ended up preoccupied with a problem of my own.

This section explains the focus of this paper and then makes a transition to the academic problem it will explore.

4 This essay enacts a particular instance of the challenge poststructuralism poses to the study of history. In simpler language, it concerns the difference that point of view makes when people are giving accounts of events, whether at first or second hand. The problem is that if all accounts of events are determined through and through by the observer's frame of reference, then one will never know, in any given case, what really happened.

Poststructuralism is a critical theory that, among other things, denies that truth can be directly understood and stated clearly.

This section provides an overview of Tompkins's exploration of the problem.

Here Tompkins shows why her problem is problematic.

Here she shows why her problem is significant.

5 I encountered this problem in concrete terms while preparing to teach a course in colonial American literature. I'd set out to learn what I could about the Puritans' relations with American Indians. All I wanted was a general idea of what had happened between the English settlers and the natives in seventeenth-century New England; poststructuralism and its dilemmas were the furthest thing from my mind. I began, more or less automatically, with Perry Miller, who hardly mentions the Indians at all, then proceeded to the work of historians who had dealt exclusively with the European-Indian encounter. At first, it was a question of deciding which of these authors to believe, for it quickly became apparent that there was no unanimity on the subject. As I read on, however, I discovered that the problem was more complicated than deciding whose version of events was correct. Some of the conflicting accounts were not simply contradictory, they were completely incommensurable, in that their assumptions about what counted as a valid approach to the subject, and what the subject itself was, diverged in fundamental ways. Faced with an array of mutually irreconcilable points of view, points of view which determined what was being discussed as well as the terms of the discussion, I decided to turn to primary sources for clarification, only to discover that the primary sources reproduced the problem all over again. I found myself, in other words, in an epistemological quandary, not only unable to decide among conflicting versions of events but also unable to believe that any such decision could, in principle, be made. It was a moral quandary as well. Knowledge of what really happened when the Europeans and the Indians first met seemed particularly important, since the result of that encounter was virtual genocide. This was the kind of past "mistake" which, presumably, we studied history in order to avoid repeating. If studying history couldn't put us in touch with actual events and their causes, then what was to prevent such atrocities from happening again?

This paragraph states the purpose of the essay and forecasts its exploratory shape.

6 For a while, I remained at this impasse. But through analyzing the process by which I had reached it, I eventually arrived at an understanding which seemed to offer a way out. This essay records the concrete experience of meeting and solving the difficulty I have just described (as an abstract problem, I thought I had solved it long ago). My purpose is not to throw new light on antifoundationalist epistemology—the solution I reached is not a new one—but to dramatize and expose the troubles antifoundationalism gets you into when you meet it, so to speak, in the road.

Antifoundationalism rejects the notion that truth can be verified using laws, events, or texts.

Here Tompkins describes the start of her intellectual journey.

7 My research began with Perry Miller. Early in the preface to *Errand into the Wilderness*, while explaining how he came to write his history of the New England mind, Miller writes a sentence that stopped me dead. He says that what fascinated him as a young man about his country's history was "the massive narrative of the movement of European culture into the vacant wilderness of America." "Vacant?" Miller, writing in 1956, doesn't pause over the word "vacant," but to people who read his preface thirty years later, the word is shocking. In what circumstances could someone proposing to write a history of colonial New England *not* take account of the Indian presence there?

8 The rest of Miller's preface supplies an answer to this question, if one takes the trouble to piece together its details. Miller explains that as a young man, jealous of

older compatriots who had had the luck to fight in World War I, he had gone to Africa in search of adventure. "The adventures that Africa afforded," he writes, "were tawdry enough, but it became the setting for a sudden epiphany" (p. vii). "It was given to me," he writes, "disconsolate on the edge of a jungle of central Africa, to have thrust upon me the mission of expounding what I took to be the innermost propulsion of the United States, while supervising, in that barbaric tropic, the unloading of drums of case oil flowing out of the inexhaustible wilderness of America" (p. viii). Miller's picture of himself on the banks of the Congo furnishes a key to the kind of history he will write and to his mental image of a vacant wilderness; it explains why it was just there, under precisely these conditions, that he should have had his epiphany.

9 The fuel drums stand, in Miller's mind, for the popular misconception of what this country is about. They are "tangible symbols of [America's] appalling power," a power that everyone but Miller takes for the ultimate reality (p. ix). To Miller, "the mind of man is the basic factor in human history," and he will plead, all unaccommodated as he is among the fuel drums, for the intellect—the intellect for which his fellow historians, with their chapters on "stoves or bathtubs, or tax laws," "the Wilmot Proviso" and "the chain store," "have so little respect" (p. viii, ix). His preface seethes with a hatred of the merely physical and mechanical, and this hatred, which is really a form of moral outrage, explains not only the contempt with which he mentions the stoves and bathtubs but also the nature of his experience in Africa and its relationship to the "massive narrative" he will write.

In this section, Tompkins presents a series of particulars to illustrate the point that Miller had a biased and limited perspective that prevented him from truly "seeing" the Indians.

10 Miller's experiences in Africa are "tawdry," his tropic is barbaric because the jungle he stands on the edge of means nothing to him, no more, indeed something less, than the case oil. It is the nothingness of Africa that precipitates his vision. It is the barbarity of the "dark continent," the obvious (but superficial) parallelism between the jungle at Matadi and America's "vacant wilderness" that releases in Miller the desire to define and vindicate his country's cultural identity. To the young Miller, colonial Africa and colonial America are—but for the history he will bring to light—mirror images of one another. And what he fails to see in the one landscape is the same thing he overlooks in the other: the human beings who people it. As Miller stood with his back to the jungle, thinking about the role of mind in human history, his failure to see that the land into which European culture had moved was not vacant but already occupied by a varied and numerous population, is of a piece with his failure, in his portrait of himself at Matadi, to notice *who* was carrying the fuel drums he was supervising the unloading of.

11 The point is crucial because it suggests that what is invisible to the historian in his own historical moment remains invisible when he turns his gaze to the past. It isn't that Miller didn't "see" the black men, in a literal sense, any more than it's the case that when he looked back he didn't "see" the Indians, in the sense of not realizing they were there. Rather, it's that neither the Indians nor the blacks *counted* for him, in a fundamental way. The way in which Indians can be seen but not counted is illustrated by an entry in Governor John Winthrop's journal, three hundred years before, when he recorded that there had been a great storm with high winds "yet through God's great

mercy it did no hurt, but only killed one Indian with the fall of a tree." The juxtaposition suggests that Miller shared with Winthrop a certain colonial point of view, a point of view from which Indians, though present, do not finally matter.

Here Tompkins describes the next step in her journey. Vaughan's book is explicitly about Puritans and Indians, so she expects it to answer questions that Miller didn't address.

12 A book entitled *New England Frontier: Puritans and Indians, 1620–1675*, written by Alden Vaughan and published in 1965, promised to rectify Miller's omission. In the outpouring of work on the European-Indian encounter that began in the early sixties, this book is the first major landmark, and to a neophyte it seems definitive. Vaughan acknowledges the absence of Indian sources and emphasizes his use of materials which catch the Puritans "off guard." His announced conclusion that "the New England Puritans followed a remarkably humane, considerate, and just policy in their dealings with the Indians" seems supported by the scope, documentation, and methodicalness of his project (*NEF*, p. vii). The author's fair-mindedness and equanimity seem everywhere apparent, so that when he asserts "the history of interracial relations from the arrival of the Pilgrims to the outbreak of King Philip's War is a credit to the integrity of both peoples," one is positively reassured (*NEF*, p. viii).

Tompkins begins showing the reader why Vaughan is also not a reliable source of truth about Indians.

13 But these impressions do not survive an admission that comes late in the book, when, in the course of explaining why works like Helen Hunt Jackson's *Century of Dishonor* had spread misconceptions about Puritan treatment of the Indians, Vaughan finally lays his own cards on the table.

> The root of the misunderstanding [about Puritans and Indians]... lie[s] in a failure to recognize the nature of the two societies that met in seventeenth century New England. One was unified, visionary, disciplined, and dynamic. The other was divided, self-satisfied, undisciplined, and static. It would be unreasonable to expect that such societies could live side by side indefinitely with no penetration of the more fragmented and passive by the more consolidated and active. What resulted, then, was not—as many have held—a clash of dissimilar ways of life, but rather the expansion of one into the areas in which the other was lacking. [*NEF*, p. 323]

In these transitional paragraphs, Tompkins shows how the reader plays an active role in shaping the meaning of a written text. The perspective of scholars who were deeply affected by the tumultuous cultural changes of the 1960s exposed Vaughan's racial biases. Finally, Tompkins leaves the scholars of the past behind, preparing us for "an entirely different picture of the European-Indian encounter."

14 From our present vantage point, these remarks seem culturally biased to an incredible degree, not to mention inaccurate: was Puritan society unified? If so, how does one account for its internal dissensions and obsessive need to cast out deviants? Is "unity" necessarily a positive culture trait? From what standpoint can one say that American Indians were neither disciplined nor visionary, when both these characteristics loom so large in the ethnographies? Is it an accident that ways of describing cultural strength and weakness coincide with gender stereotypes—active/passive, and so on? Why is one culture said to "penetrate" the other? Why is the "other" described in terms of "lack"?

15 Vaughan's fundamental categories of apprehension and judgment will not withstand even the most cursory inspection. For what looked like even-handedness when he was writing *New England Frontier* does not look that way anymore. In his introduction to *New Directions in American Intellectual History*, John Higham writes that by the end of the sixties

> the entire conceptual foundation on which [this sort of work] rested [had] crumbled away. ... Simultaneously, in sociology, anthropology, and history, two working assumptions ... came under withering attack: first, the assumption that societies tend to be integrated, and second, that a shared culture maintains that

> integration. ... By the late 1960s all claims issued in the name of an "American mind" were subject to drastic skepticism.

"Clearly," Higham continues, "the sociocultural upheaval of the sixties created the occasion" for this reaction. Vaughan's book, it seemed, could only have been written before the events of the sixties had sensitized scholars to questions of race and ethnicity. It came as no surprise, therefore, that ten years later there appeared a study of European-Indian relations which reflected the new awareness of social issues the sixties had engendered. And it offered an entirely different picture of the European-Indian encounter.

16 Francis Jennings's *The Invasion of America* (1975) rips wide open the idea that the Puritans were humane and considerate in their dealings with the Indians. In Jennings's account, even more massively documented than Vaughan's, the early settlers lied to the Indians, stole from them, murdered them, scalped them, captured them, tortured them, raped them, sold them into slavery, confiscated their land, destroyed their crops, burned their homes, scattered their possessions, gave them alcohol, undermined their systems of belief, and infected them with diseases that wiped out ninety percent of their numbers within the first hundred years after contact.

Here begins the third stage of Tompkins's journey. Now she is exploring the work of a post-1960s scholar with a radically different perspective on Puritans and Indians.

17 Jennings mounts an all-out attack on the essential decency of the Puritan leadership and their apologists in the twentieth century. The Pequot War, which previous historians had described as an attempt on the part of Massachusetts Bay to protect itself from the fiercest of the New England tribes, becomes, in Jennings's painstakingly researched account, a deliberate war of extermination, waged by whites against Indians. It starts with trumped-up charges, is carried on through a series of increasingly bloody reprisals, and ends in the massacre of scores of Indian men, women, and children, all so that Massachusetts Bay could gain political and economic control of the southern Connecticut Valley. When one reads this and then turns over the page and sees a reproduction of the Bay Colony seal, which depicts an Indian from whose mouth issue the words "Come over and help us," the effect is shattering.

18 But even so powerful an argument as Jennings's did not remain unshaken by subsequent work. Reading on, I discovered that if the events of the sixties had revolutionized the study of European-Indian relations, the events of the seventies produced yet another transformation. The American Indian Movement, and in particular the founding of the Native American Rights Fund in 1971 to finance Indian litigation, and a court decision in 1975 which gave the tribes the right to seek redress for past injustices in federal court, created a climate within which historians began to focus on the Indians themselves. "Almost simultaneously," writes James Axtell, "frontier and colonial historians began to discover the necessity of considering the American natives as real determinants of history and the utility of ethnohistory as a way of ensuring parity of focus and impartiality of judgment." In Miller, Indians had been simply beneath notice; in Vaughan, they belonged to an inferior culture; and in Jennings, they were the more or less innocent prey of power-hungry whites. But in the most original and provocative of the ethnohistories, Calvin Martin's *Keepers of the Game*, Indians became complicated, purposeful human beings, whose lives were spiritually motivated to a high degree. Their relationship to the animals they hunted, to the natural environ-

Tompkins begins showing how Jennings's view is also limited by his own perspective.

Before she moves to the fourth stage of her journey, Tompkins helps readers get their bearings by briefly reviewing the path she has taken.

ment, and to the whites with whom they traded became intelligible within a system of beliefs that formed the basis for an entirely new perspective on the European-Indian encounter.

Tompkins begins the fourth stage of her journey by summarizing the work of Calvin Martin, a modern scholar motivated by the desire to explore a problem: Why did the Indians willingly participate in the fur trade, a self-destructive pursuit?

19 Within the broader question of why European contact had such a devastating effect on the Indians, Martin's specific aim is to determine why Indians participated in the fur trade which ultimately led them to the brink of annihilation. The standard answer to this question had always been that once the Indian was introduced to European guns, copper kettles, woolen blankets, and the like, he literally couldn't keep his hands off them. In order to acquire these coveted items, he decimated the animal populations on which his survival depended. In short, the Indian's motivation in participating in the fur trade was assumed to be the same as the white European's—a desire to accumulate material goods. In direct opposition to this thesis, Martin argues that the reason why Indians ruthlessly exploited their own resources had nothing to do with supply and demand, but stemmed rather from a breakdown of the cosmic worldview that tied them to the game they killed in a spiritual relationship of parity and mutual obligation.

20 The hunt, according to Martin, was conceived not primarily as a physical activity but as a spiritual quest, in which the spirit of the hunter must overmaster the spirit of the game animal before the kill can take place. The animal, in effect, *allows* itself to be found and killed, once the hunter has mastered its spirit. The hunter prepared himself through rituals of fasting, sweating, or dreaming which revealed the identity of his prey and where he can find it. The physical act of killing is the least important element in the process. Once the animal is killed, eaten, and its parts used for clothing or implements, its remains must be disposed of in ritually prescribed fashion, or the game boss, the "keeper" of that species, will not permit more animals to be killed. The relationship between Indians and animals, then, is contractual; each side must hold up its end of the bargain, or no further transactions can occur.

21 What happened, according to Martin, was that as a result of diseases introduced into the animal population by Europeans, the game suddenly disappeared, began to act in inexplicable ways, or sickened and died in plain view, and communicated their diseases to the Indians. The Indians, consequently, believed that their compact with the animals had been broken and that the keepers of the game, the tutelary spirits of each animal species whom they had been so careful to propitiate, had betrayed them. And when missionization, wars with the Europeans, and displacement from their tribal lands had further weakened Indian society and its belief structure, the Indians, no longer restrained by religious sanctions, in effect, turned on the animals in a holy war of revenge.

Tompkins speculates that Indians' perceptions of events differed so radically from those of European settlers' that "conflict was inevitable."

22 Whether or not Martin's specific claim about the "holy war" was correct, his analysis made it clear to me that, given the Indians' understanding of economic, religious, and physical processes, an Indian account of what transpired when the European settlers arrived here would look nothing like our own. Their (potential, unwritten) history of the conflict could bear only a marginal resemblance to Eurocentric views. I began to think that the key to understanding European-Indian relations was to see them as an encounter between wholly disparate cultures, and that

therefore either defending or attacking the colonists was beside the point since, given the cultural disparity between the two groups, conflict was inevitable and in large part a product of mutual misunderstanding.

23 But three years after Martin's book appeared, Shepard Krech III edited a collection of seven essays called *Indians, Animals, and the Fur Trade*, attacking Martin's entire project. Here the authors argued that we don't need an ideological or religious explanation for the fur trade. As Charles Hudson writes,

Now Tompkins begins stage five of her journey, summarizing a collection of essays that run counter to Martin's way of thinking.

> The Southeastern Indians slaughtered deer (and were prompted to enslave and kill each other) because of their position on the outer fringes of an expanding modern world-system. ... In the modern world-system there is a core region which establishes *economic* relations with its colonial periphery. ... If the Indians could not produce commodities, they were on the road to cultural extinction. ... To maximize his chances for survival, an eighteenth-century Southeastern Indian had to ... live in the interior, out of range of European cattle, forestry, and agriculture. ... He had to produce a commodity which was valuable enough to earn him some protection from English slavers.

24 Though we are talking here about Southeastern Indians, rather than the subarctic and Northeastern tribes Martin studied, what really accounts for these divergent explanations of why Indians slaughtered the game are the assumptions that underlie them. Martin believes that the Indians acted on the basis of perceptions made available to them by their own cosmology; that is, he explains their behavior as the Indians themselves would have explained it (insofar as he can), using a logic and a set of values that are not Eurocentric but derived from within Amerindian culture. Hudson, on the other hand, insists that the Indians' own beliefs are irrelevant to an explanation of how they acted, which can only be understood, as far as he is concerned, in the terms of a Western materialist economic and political analysis. Martin and Hudson, in short, don't agree on what counts as an explanation, and this disagreement sheds light on the preceding accounts as well. From this standpoint, we can see that Vaughan, who thought that the Puritans were superior to the Indians, and Jennings, who thought the reverse, are both, like Hudson, using Eurocentric criteria of description and evaluation. While all three critics (Vaughan, Jennings, and Hudson) acknowledge that Indians and Europeans behave differently from one another, the behavior differs, as it were, within the order of the same: all three assume, though only Hudson makes the assumption explicit, that an understanding of relations between the Europeans and the Indians must be elaborated in European terms. In Martin's analysis, however, what we have are not only two different sets of behavior but two incommensurable ways of describing and assigning meaning to events. This difference at the level of explanation calls into question the possibility of obtaining any theory-independent account of interaction between Indians and Europeans.

Tompkins again helps readers get their bearings by summarizing her understanding of what she has learned up to this point in her journey.

Then she reiterates the basic poststructuralist dilemma posed earlier: How can you get at the truth about an event when every account is biased?

25 At this point, dismayed and confused by the wildly divergent views of colonial history the twentieth-century historians had provided, I decided to look at some primary materials. I thought, perhaps, if I looked at some firsthand accounts and at some scholars looking at those accounts, it would be possible to decide which experts were right and which were wrong by comparing their views with the evidence. Captivity

Tompkins describes a new strategy for determining which perspectives are valid.

narratives seemed a good place to begin, since it was logical to suppose that the records left by whites who had been captured by Indians would furnish the sort of first-hand information I wanted. …

In the essay's final section, Tompkins works out her solution to the problem she has examined. Here the ellipses indicate a long section we have omitted in which she analyzes a variety of historical documents.

26 After a while it began to seem to me that there was something wrong with the way I had formulated the problem. …

27 My problem presupposed that I couldn't judge because I didn't know what the facts were. All I had, or could have, was a series of different perspectives, and so nothing that would count as an authoritative source on which moral judgments could be based. But, as I have just shown, I did judge, and that is because, as I now think, I did have some facts. I seemed to accept as facts that ninety percent of the native American population of New England died after the first hundred years of contact, that tribes in eastern Canada and the northeastern United States had a compact with the game they killed, that Comanches had subjected a captive girl to casual cruelty, that King Philip smoked a pipe, and so on. It was only where different versions of the same event came into conflict that I doubted the text was a record of something real. And even then, there was no question about certain major catastrophes. I believed that four hundred Pequots were killed near Saybrook, that Winthrop was the Governor of the Massachusetts Bay Colony when it happened, and so on. My sense that certain events, such as the Pequot War, did occur in no way reflected the indecisiveness that overtook me when I tried to choose among the various historical versions. In fact, the need I felt to make up my mind was impelled by the conviction that certain things *had* happened that shouldn't have happened. Hence it was never the case that "what happened" was completely unknowable or unavailable. It's rather that in the process of reading so many different approaches to the same phenomenon I became aware of the difference in the attitudes that informed these approaches. This awareness of the interests motivating each version cast suspicion over everything, in retrospect, and I ended by claiming that there was nothing I could know. This, I now see, was never really the case. But how did it happen?

Tompkins acknowledges and demonstrates how her own method of reading all these documents reflects her own historical perspective.

28 Someone else, confronted with the same materials, could have decided that one of these historical accounts was correct. Still another person might have decided that more evidence was needed in order to decide among them. Why did I conclude that none of the accounts was accurate because they were all produced from some particular angle of vision? Presumably there was something in my background that enabled me to see the problem in this way. …

29 What this means for the problem I've been addressing is that I must piece together the story of European-Indian relations as best I can, believing this version up to a point, that version not at all, another almost entirely, according to what seems reasonable and plausible, given everything else that I know. And this, as I've shown, is what I was already doing in the back of my mind without realizing it, because there was nothing else I *could* do. If the accounts don't fit together neatly, that is not a reason for rejecting them all in favor of a metadiscourse about epistemology; on the contrary, one encounters contradictory facts and divergent points of view in practically every phase of life, from deciding whom to marry to choosing the right brand of cat food, and one decides as best one can given the evidence available. It is only the nature of the academic situation which makes it appear that one can linger on the threshold of decision

in the name of an epistemological principle. What has really happened in such a case is that the subject of debate has changed from the question of what happened in a particular instance to the question of how knowledge is arrived at. The absence of pressure to decide what happened creates the possibility for this change of venue.

30 The change of venue, however, is itself an action taken. In diverting attention from the original problem and placing it where Miller did, on "the mind of man," it once again ignores what happened and still is happening to American Indians. The moral problem that confronts me now is not that I can never have any facts to go on, but that the work I do is not directed toward solving the kinds of problems that studying the history of European-Indian relations has awakened me to.

THINKING CRITICALLY
about "'Indians'"

1. Tompkins's essay is about her struggle to find out "what had happened between the English settlers and the natives in seventeenth-century New England." Explain in your own words why Tompkins's study of various historians didn't lead to a direct answer to her question.
2. Tompkins's journey begins with her shocked revelation that historian Perry Miller (one of the great U.S. historians writing in the 1950s) didn't "see" the Indians. He talks instead about the movement of European culture into the "vacant wilderness" of America. To try to understand Miller, Tompkins reads his discussion of his experience in Africa. Tompkins concludes: "[W]hat is invisible to the historian in his own historical moment remains invisible when he turns his gaze to the past." What does Tompkins mean? How does Miller's preface support her claim?
3. Trace the competing theses of each of the historians that Tompkins reads. How does Tompkins show that each thesis is "determined through and through by the observer's frame of reference"?
4. One fact on which historians agree is that Native Americans participated in the fur trade by exchanging furs for guns, copper kettles, and woolen blankets. Historians disagree, however, on why Native Americans sold furs to the white traders. What is the traditional explanation? How does Calvin Martin's explanation (in *Keepers of the Game*) differ from the traditional view? How does Charles Hudson attack Martin?
5. In the final section of her essay, Tompkins explains her own solution to the dilemma she has explored. In your own words, how does she resolve her dilemma? Do you find her resolution satisfactory? How does her resolution give rise to the "moral problem" she poses in her last sentence?

CHAPTER 9 WRITING AN INFORMATIVE ESSAY OR REPORT

As a reader, you regularly encounter writing with an informative aim, ranging from the instruction booklet for an MP3 player to a newspaper feature story on the African AIDS crisis. Informative documents include encyclopedias, cook-books, news articles, instruction booklets, voters' pamphlets, and various kinds of reports, as well as informative Web sites and magazine articles. In some informative prose, visual representations of information such as diagrams, photographs, maps, tables, and graphs can be as important as the prose itself.

A useful way to begin thinking about informative writing is to classify it according to the reader's motivation for reading. From this perspective, we can place informative prose in three categories.

In the first category, readers are motivated by an immediate need for information such as the need to set the clock on a new microwave, study for a driver's test, or, in a more complex instance, make a major repair on an aircraft engine using the technical documentation supplied by the manufacturer. In these need-to-know instances, what readers want from informative prose is precision, accuracy, and clarity.

In the second category, readers are motivated by their own curiosity about a subject. For example, readers might turn to encyclopedias for information on the rings of Saturn or to newspapers or Internet news services for the latest information on the war against terror. In the work world, managers scan industry magazines looking for information about competitors, new products, or new markets.

Informative writing in these two categories does not necessarily contain a contestable thesis. Documents are organized effectively, of course, but they often follow a chronological step-by-step organization (as in a recipe) or an "all-about" topic-by-topic organization (as in an encyclopedia article on, say, Pakistan divided into "Geography," "Climate," "Population," "History," and so forth). The writer provides factual information about a subject without necessarily shaping the information specifically to support a thesis.

In contrast, the third category of informative writing *is* thesis-based and is therefore aligned with other kinds of thesis-based prose. The thesis brings new or surprising information to readers who may not be initially motivated by a need-to-know occasion or by their own curiosity. In fact, readers might not be initially interested in the writer's topic at all, so the writer's first task is to hook readers' interest—often by having an effective opening that arouses curiosity, hints that readers' current knowledge about a topic might have holes or gaps, and motivates their desire to learn something new, surprising, or different. Such pieces are commonly encountered in newspaper feature stories or in magazine articles where the reader is enticed by an intriguing title or in academic pieces where a researcher may have new information or a new point of view. An excellent strategy for creating this motivation to read is the technique of "surprising reversal," which we explain later in this chapter.

The writing projects in this chapter are based on three typical genres with an informative aim:

- A set of instructions
- A workplace informative report
- An informative (and surprising) magazine article or academic article

Exploring Informative (and Surprising) Writing

Let's say that you have just watched an old James Bond movie featuring a tarantula in Bond's bathroom. Curious about tarantulas, you do a quick Web search and retrieve the following short informative pieces. Read each one, and then proceed to the questions that follow.

Our first mini-article comes from the Web site EnchantedLearning.com, a commercial site aimed at providing interesting, fact-filled learning lessons for children.

EnchantedLearning.com

Tarantulas

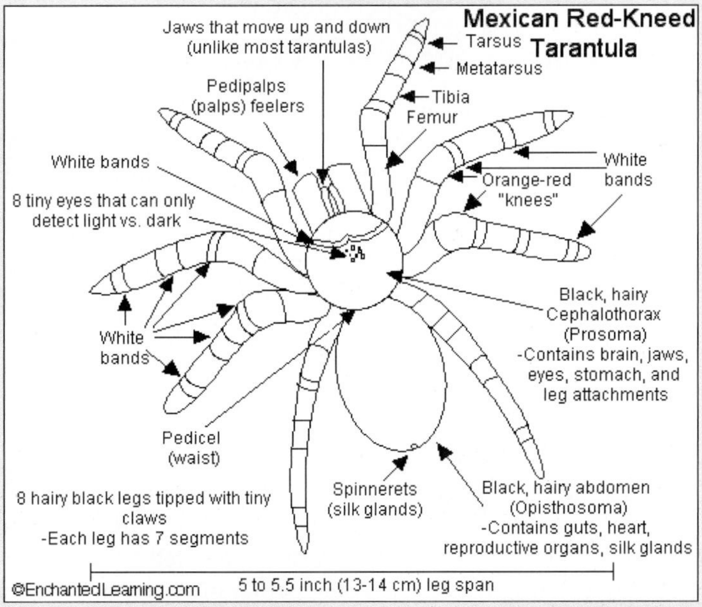

1 Tarantulas are large hairy spiders that live in warm areas around the world, including South America, southern North America, southern Europe, Africa, southern

Asia, and Australia. The greatest concentration of tarantulas is in South America. There are about 300 species of tarantulas. The biggest tarantula is *Pseudotherathosa apophysis*, which has a leg span of about 13 inches (33 cm). These arachnids have a very long life span; some species can live over 30 years.

2 **Habitat:** Some tarantulas live in underground burrows; some live on the ground, and others live in trees. They live in rain forests, deserts, and other habitats.

3 **Diet:** Tarantulas are carnivores (meat-eaters). They eat insects (like grasshoppers and beetles), other arachnids, small reptiles (like lizards and snakes), amphibians (like frogs), and some even eat small birds. Tarantulas kill their prey using venomous fangs; they also inject a chemical into the prey that dissolves the flesh. Tarantulas can crush their prey using powerful mouthparts. No person has ever died of a tarantula bite.

4 **Anatomy:** Tarantulas have a hairy two-part body and very strong jaws (with venomous fangs). They have eight hairy legs; each leg has 2 tiny claws at the end and a cushioning pad behind the claws. The hairs on the body and legs are sensitive to touch, temperature, and smell. Tarantulas have a hard exoskeleton and not an internal skeleton.

The second mini-article comes from the Web site of the University of Washington's Burke Museum. The author of this piece is the curator of arachnids at the Burke Museum.

Rod Crawford

Myths about "Dangerous" Spiders

1 **Myth: Tarantulas are dangerous or deadly to humans.**

2 **Fact:** Outside of southern Europe (where the name is used for a wolf spider, famous in medieval superstition as the alleged cause of "tarantella" dancing), the word tarantula is most often used for the very large, furry spiders of the family Theraphosidae.

3 Hollywood is squarely to blame for these spiders' toxic-to-humans reputation. Tarantulas are large, photogenic and easily handled, and therefore have been very widely used in horror and action-adventure movies. When some "venomous" creature is needed to menace James Bond or Indiana Jones, to invade a small town in enormous numbers, or to grow to gigantic size and prowl the Arizona desert for human prey, the special-effects team calls out the tarantulas!

4 In reality, the venom of these largest-of-all-spiders generally has **very low toxicity to humans**. I myself was once bitten by a Texan species and hardly even felt it. None of the North American species or those commonly kept as pets are considered to pose even a mild bite hazard. There are some reports that a few tropical species may have venom more toxic to vertebrates, but human bite cases haven't been reported, so we can't know for sure.

5 The only health hazard posed by keeping pet tarantulas comes from the irritating chemicals on the hairs of the abdomen, which can cause skin rashes or inflammation of eyes and nasal passages. To prevent such problems, simply keep tarantulas away from your face and wash your hands after handling one.

European tarantula
Lycosa tarentula
Southern Europe; body length 2–3 cm
(photo courtesy of Manuel J. Cabrero)
Click image to enlarge

Pink toe tarantula
Avicularia avicularia
Brazil to Trinidad; body length 6–7 cm
(photo courtesy of Ron Taylor)
Click image to enlarge

Both the *European wolf spiders (**left**)* originally called tarantulas, and the *theraphosid spiders (**right**),* often kept as pets and called tarantulas now, have been reputed dangerous to humans. They aren't.

6 Compared to common pets such as dogs, tarantulas are not dangerous at all. (For more information see the American Tarantula Society.)

THINKING CRITICALLY
about "Tarantulas" and "Myths about 'Dangerous' Spiders"

1. Why do you think the reading from EnchantedLearning.com uses a diagram of a tarantula while the Burke Museum Web site uses photographs? How is each choice connected to the piece's targeted audience and purpose?
2. How would you describe the difference in organizational strategies for each of the readings? To us, one of these has an "all-about" topic-by-topic structure while the other has a thesis-based structure. Which is which? How is this difference connected to the targeted audience and purpose? How does the difference affect the way details are selected and arranged?
3. One might suppose that informational writing would be unaffected by the writer's angle of vision—that facts would simply be facts and that informational pieces on the same topic would contain the same basic information. Yet these two short pieces give somewhat different impressions of the tarantula. For example, how do these readings differ in the way they portray the bite of the tarantula? How else do they differ in overall effect?

Understanding Informative Writing

In informative writing, the writer is assumed to have more expertise than the reader on a given subject. The writer's aim is to enlarge the reader's view of the subject by bringing the reader new information. The writer's information can come from a variety of sources:

- From field research such as observations, interviews, questionnaires, and so forth
- From library or Internet research
- From the writer's preexisting expertise in a subject
- From the writer's own personal experiences

We turn now to a closer look at three typical genres with an informative aim.

Need-to-Know Informative Prose

As anyone who has tried to write instructions or explain a process knows, the obstacles to clarity are numerous. An ambiguous term, a mislabeled diagram, a missing step, or the inclusion of digressive, nonessential information can leave your readers baffled. Technical writers and engineers use the wonderful term "COIK" (Clear Only If Known) for passages that make perfect sense to insiders but leave outsiders scratching their heads in confusion. Here is an example of a COIK passage in an instruction booklet for setting up a DVD player. This passage occurs in the early "Preparation" stage where the new DVD owner is still trying to figure out where to plug in cables.

COIK PASSAGE FROM DVD INSTRUCTION BOOKLET

About the Scanning Mode

> Depending on the material source format, DVD VIDEO discs can be classified into two types: film source and video source (note that some DVD Video discs contain both film source and video source). Film sources are recorded as 24-frame-per-second information, while (NTSC) video sources are recorded as 30-frame-per-second (60-field-per-second interlaced) information. When the unit plays back a film source material, uninterlaced progressive output signals are created using the original information. When a video source material is played back, the unit interleaves lines between the interlaced lines on each to create the interpolated picture and outputs as the progressive signal.

"Huh?" says the bewildered new owner, still trying to figure out where to plug in the red and white wires. There are two main problems with this passage: (1) It is written to tech-heads rather than to general readers, and (2) the information is not needed for hooking up a DVD unit to a TV.

Instruction booklets created by product manufacturers are often so notoriously confusing that a whole industry has arisen around producing clear, fun-to-read instructions or explanations. Examples include the *For Dummies* series (*Excel for Dummies*) or the *Idiot's Guide* series (*The Complete Idiot's Guide to Success as a Real Estate Agent*). Many people find that humor eases the frustration of complex directions or explanations and can often create a soothing effect opposite of

COIK. (COIK makes you feel like an inadequate outsider; humor welcomes you into the family of the confused.)

For an example of clear, easy-to-follow instructions, consider Figure 9.1, which explains how to roast peppers.

FIGURE 9.1 Roasting Peppers

ROASTING PEPPERS
1. Slice $\frac{1}{4}$ inch from the top and bottom of the pepper. Then gently remove the stem from the top lobe.
2. Pull the core out of the pepper.
3. Make a slit down one side of the pepper, then lay it flat, skin side down. Use a sharp knife to remove all the ribs and seeds.
4. Arrange the strips of peppers and the top and bottom lobes on a baking sheet, skin-side up. Flatten the strips with the palm of your hand.
5. Adjust the oven rack to its top position. If the rack is more than $3\frac{1}{2}$ inches from the heating element, set a jelly-roll pan, bottom up, on the rack under the baking sheet.
6. Roast until the skin of the peppers is charred and puffed up like a balloon but the flesh is still firm. You may steam the peppers at this point or not, as you wish. Start peeling where the skin has charred the most.

FOR WRITING AND DISCUSSION

Giving Instructions

1. How did you read the instructions for roasting peppers (Figure 9.1)? Did you focus primarily on the text or the drawings? Do you agree that these instructions are clear?
2. Try the following exercise in giving instructions:
   a. Ask someone in the class who knows how to make a good paper airplane to explain that process verbally to your course instructor. (If the explainer needs to make the airplane in order to visualize each step, make sure that the instructor can't see what the explainer is doing.) Your instructor will try to follow the verbal directions exactly. Note how often the instructor makes a wrong move, requiring a revision of the instructions.
   b. Now have the expert actually demonstrate the process.
   c. Divide into small groups and try to create instructions for making a paper airplane using both verbal text and diagrams, which you must design and draw.

Informative Reports

Although the term *report* can have numerous meanings, we will define "report" as any document that presents the results of a fact-finding or data-gathering investigation. Sometimes report writers limit themselves to presenting the newly discovered information, while at other times they go further by analyzing or interpreting the information in an effort to understand causes, consequences, functions, or purposes. Reports of various kinds are among the most common genres that you will read and write as workplace professionals. Often managers have to prepare periodic reports to supervisors on sales, operations, expenses, or team productivity. Equally important are solicited reports, usually assigned by supervisors to individuals or task forces, requesting individuals to investigate a problem, gather crucial information, and report the results. Depending on the size of the task, turn-around time may be as little as a few days to as long as several months. The writer's goal is to gather the requested information, organize it effectively, and present it as concisely and crisply as possible.

In the workplace, informative reports can be of intense interest to planners or decision makers. The text of the report should be concise, with a tightly closed-form structure often broken into sections marked by headings. Individual points might be bulleted. Numeric data are usually displayed in graphs or tables. Long reports usually include a cover page and a table of contents and often begin with an "executive summary" that condenses the main findings into a paragraph. Shorter reports are usually written in a memorandum format. In many cases, writers prepare both a hard copy of the report and a PowerPoint version for oral presentation.

Workplace reports, whether periodic or solicited, are generally written to audiences already interested in the information and expecting the report. Introductions are therefore quite different from those where the writer must arouse readers' interest or curiosity. Instead of a title, short reports usually have an informative "subject line" that identifies the report's topic and purpose. The introduction typically creates a brief context for the report, states its purpose, and maps its structure. Here is an example of an introduction:

PROTOTYPE INTRODUCTION FOR A SOLICITED REPORT

To: Ms. Polly Carpenter, Business Manager
From: Ralph Hiner
Subject: Projected costs for the new seed catalog

As you requested, I have researched the projected costs for the new seed catalog. This memo provides background on the marketing plan, itemizes projected expenses, and presents an overall figure for budget planning.

For an example of a short informative report, see "Muslim Americans: Middle Class and Mostly Mainstream" on pages 228–229.

The following exercise will give you a taste of workplace report writing. Suppose that you are a marketing researcher for a company that designs and produces new video games. One day you receive the following memo from your manager:

To: Ima Newbie
From: Big Boss
Subject: Information about gender differences in video game playing

The marketing team wants to investigate differences in the amount of time male and female college students spend playing video games and in the kinds of video games that each gender enjoys. I want you to conduct appropriate research at local colleges using questionnaires, interviews, and focus groups. Specifically, the marketing team wants to know approximately how many minutes per week an average college male versus a college female spends playing video games. Also investigate whether there is any difference in the kinds of games they enjoy. We need your report by the end of the month.

FOR WRITING AND DISCUSSION

Producing a Workplace Report

1. Assume that your classroom is a "focus group" for Ima Newbie's investigation. As a class, create an informal questionnaire to gather the information that Ima will need for her report.
2. Give the questionnaire to the class and tabulate results.
3. Working individually or in small groups, prepare a memo to Big Boss reporting your results.

For guidance on developing a questionnaire, see Chapter 10, p. 249.

Informative (and Surprising) Magazine or Academic Articles

Another commonly encountered genre is the informative article found in magazines or academic journals. Depending on the magazine or journal, informative articles can range from the frivolous (celebrity news) to the serious (declining sea turtle populations). In this section we focus on a specific kind of article—a thesis-based informative article aimed at general audiences. Because readers are assumed to be browsing through the pages of a magazine, the writer's rhetorical challenge is to arouse the reader's curiosity and then to keep the reader reading by providing interesting new information. The writer's first task is to hook the reader on a question and then to provide a surprising thesis that gives shape and purpose to the information. A good way to focus and sharpen the thesis, as we will show, is to use the "surprising-reversal" strategy.

Let's begin by revisiting the difference between an encyclopedic (or "all-about") informative piece and a thesis-based piece. To appreciate this distinction, consider again the difference between the EnchantedLearning.com Web site on tarantulas (pp. 209–210) and the Burke Museum piece "Myths about 'Dangerous' Spiders" (pp. 210–211). The EnchantedLearning.com piece is a short "all-about" report organized under the topic headings "Habitat," "Diet," and "Anatomy." The writer of the Web site may simply have adapted an encyclopedia article on tarantulas into a format for children. In contrast, the Burke Museum piece by Rod

Crawford is thesis-based. Crawford wishes to refute the myth that "[t]arantulas are dangerous or deadly to humans." He does so by providing information on the low toxicity of tarantula venom to humans and the relative painlessness of bites. All of Crawford's data focus on the danger potential of tarantulas. There are no data about habitat, diet, or other aspects of tarantula life—material that would be included if this were an all-about report. Because the piece also includes data about misconceptions of tarantulas, it follows the basic pattern of surprising reversal: "Many people believe that tarantulas are toxic to humans, but I will show that tarantulas are not dangerous at all."

Surprising reversal, as we explained in Chapter 2, is our term for a strategy in which the writer's thesis pushes sharply against a counterthesis. This structure automatically creates a thesis with tension focused on a question or problem. Because of its power to hook and sustain readers, examples of surprising-reversal essays can be found in almost any publication—from scholarly journals to easy-reading magazines. Here, for example, is an abstract of an article from the table of contents of the *Atlantic Monthy*.

"REEFER MADNESS" BY ERIC SCHLOSSER

> Marijuana has been pushed so far out of the public imagination by other drugs, and its use is so casually taken for granted in some quarters of society, that one might assume it had been effectively decriminalized. In truth, the government has never been tougher on marijuana offenders than it is today. In an era when violent criminals frequently walk free or receive modest jail terms, tens of thousands of people are serving long sentences for breaking marijuana laws.

This article asserts a surprising, new position that counters a commonly held view.

Commonly Held, Narrow, or Inaccurate View	Surprising View
Because marijuana laws are no longer enforced, marijuana use has effectively become decriminalized	The government has never been tougher on marijuana offenders than it is today.

A similar pattern is often found in scholarly academic writing, which typically has the following underlying shape:

> Whereas other scholars say X, Y, or Z, my research reveals Q.

Because the purpose of academic research is to advance knowledge, an academic article almost always shows the writer's new view against a background of prevailing views (what other scholars have said). This kind of tension is what often makes thesis-based writing memorable and provocative.

The writer's surprising information can come from personal experience, field research, or library/Internet research. If a college writer bases an informative piece on research sources and documents them according to academic conventions, the magazine genre doubles as an effective college research paper by combining academic citations with a tone and style suitable for general readers. Shannon King's article on hydrogen cars (p. 231) is an example of a student research paper written in magazine article style.

When using the surprising-reversal strategy, keep in mind that *surprise* is a relative term based on the relationship between you and your intended audience. You don't have to surprise everyone in the world, just those who hold a mistaken or narrow view of your topic. The key is to imagine an audience less informed about your topic than you are. Suppose, as an illustration, that you have just completed an introductory economics course. You are less informed about economics than your professor, but more informed about economics than persons who have never had an econ class. You might therefore bring surprising information to the less informed audience:

> The average airplane traveler thinks that the widely varying ticket pricing for the same flight is chaotic and silly, but I can show how this pricing scheme makes perfect sense economically. [written to the "average airplane traveler," who hasn't taken an economics course]

This paper would be surprising to your intended audience, but not to the economics professor. From a different perspective, however, you could also write about economics to your professor because you might know more than your professor about, say, how students struggle with some concepts:

> Many economics professors assume that students can easily learn the concept of "elasticity of demand," but I can show why this concept was particularly confusing for me and my classmates. [written to economics professors who aren't aware of student difficulties with particular concepts]

Additionally, your surprising view doesn't necessarily have to be diametrically opposed to the common view. Perhaps you think the common view is *incomplete* or *insufficient* rather than *dead wrong*. Instead of saying, "View X is wrong, where as my view, Y, is correct," you can say, "View X is correct and good as far as it goes, but my view, Y, adds a new perspective." In other words, you can also create surprise by going a step beyond the common view to show readers something new.

A Set of Instructions

WRITING PROJECT

Write instructions for a process that poses difficulty for your target audience. Imagine readers who need to know the information that you are providing. Using words and, where appropriate, drawings or other images, give instructions that your readers can easily follow.

Many processes that seem easy to an experienced person can be hard to explain to new learners. A real-world opportunity for writing instructions can often be found in service-learning projects. For example, a homeless shelter might need to post procedures that volunteers should follow in preparing and serving meals or to publish an informative brochure explaining how to apply for housing assistance and other services. Other real-world opportunities can be focused on a campus need (for example, instructions for first-year students on how to set up a digital portfolio or how to use a new registration system) or by a specific classroom need (instructions for fellow classmates on how to import figures from a spreadsheet into a word processing program or how to use a certain library database). Your instructor might also make this a short, low-stakes assignment by asking you, say, to write instructions—suitable for placing in a hotel room—on how to set the alarm on the bedstand clock or to write instructions for elderly Mr. Jones, who just bought his first computer, on how to use a Web search engine.

Your instructor may also give you a free choice of topics. If you choose your own topic, be sure to get your instructor's approval in terms of scope and difficulty level. (It is much easier to explain how to boil water or to change the oil in a car than it is to explain how to make a pie chart using a spreadsheet program.)

For an example of instructional writing, see Kerry Norton's instructions for yeast preparation at a winery (pp. 226–227).

Generating and Exploring Ideas

If you have free choice of topics, you need to select a process that you understand well but that can be troublesome for new learners. To help you think of ideas for your paper, try the following brainstorming strategies:

- *Think of areas in which you have special skills or expertise.* Make a list of your hobbies (stamp collecting, gardening, video games, cooking, car mechanics, fantasy sports); your special skills (playing a musical instrument, surfing the Web, playing a certain position in soccer or another sport, fly-fishing, cleaning house, laying bricks); past experiences that give you "insider" knowledge (running a campaign, serving in an office or club, planning a trip, organizing an event); or any other areas where you think you might be able to teach a skill or process to a new learner (programming an MP3 player, using library databases, creating a digital slide show, recuperating from a broken leg).
- *In any specific area in which you have experience or expertise, brainstorm difficulties that new learners have.* Choose several possibilities from your list of special expertise and role-play being a new learner in this area. Make an idea map identifying difficulties or problems that a newcomer encounters.

Shaping and Drafting

As much as possible, break the process into stages that you can highlight with headings. Within each stage, explain the process clearly and, where appropriate, draw diagrams or figures. If your instructions start becoming too long, detailed, and involved, you may need to narrow your subject. For example, instead of explaining how to walk with crutches with your leg in a cast, you might focus only on going down stairs on crutches, on taking a shower, or on strengthening your arms and shoulders. Eliminate extraneous details or other digressions so that your reader can concentrate on each important step, one stage at a time. Readers also appreciate, where appropriate, being told *why* they are supposed to do something as well as *what* they are supposed to do. Notice in Kerry Norton's instructions for preparing the yeast for winemaking (pp. 226–227) how often he explains the rationale behind each step.

Revising

Unlike most pieces of writing, instructions actually produce observable behaviors in readers. You can give your instructions to a new learner and actually observe whether the instructions work. We therefore recommend that you road test your early drafts on readers, asking them, if feasible, to actually follow the instructions. You can then revise those sections where the new learners get thrown off track. It is also helpful to ask your readers—while you watch them—to think out loud as they go through each step. When they verbalize their thinking, you can assess not only if they understand what they are supposed to do but also if they understand the purpose or rationale for each step.

Questions for Peer Review

In addition to the generic peer review questions explained in Chapter 17, Skill 4, ask your peer reviewers to address these questions:

1. How well can you follow these instructions? What places might lead to confusion?
2. Where does the writer explain the purpose and rationale of key steps or stages? Are there places where you need more explanation of *why* as well as *what*?
3. If the instructions include diagrams or drawings, how effective are they? If not, would the instructions be clearer if some visuals were added? How so?

Informative Workplace Report

WRITING PROJECT

Write a short workplace report based on data you have gathered from observations, interviews, questionnaires, or library/Internet research. Your report should respond to one of the following scenarios or to a scenario provided by your instructor:

- Your boss runs a chain of health food stores that sell high-nutrition smoothies. Because sales have been flat, she wants to create an advertising campaign to attract more customers to her smoothie bars. She has heard that the boutique coffee drinks sold at coffee shops such as Starbucks or Tullys are actually high in calories and fat. She has asked you to research the nutritional information on coffee drinks. She would also like you to compare the fat/calorie content of various coffee drinks to that of cheeseburgers, fries, and milkshakes sold at fast-food restaurants. She's hoping that the information you provide will help her launch a campaign to lure customers from coffee shops to her smoothie bars.
- You are doing a service-learning project for a health maintenance organization. Your manager plans to produce a series of public service advertisements devoted to health issues. One advertisement will focus on the dangers of hearing loss. The manager asks you to research the dangers of

hearing loss posed to young people who wear ear-buds plugged into MP3 players. "Has there been any research on this subject?" he asks. "If so, what does it say?"

- The manager for this same health maintenance organization (previous scenario) also plans a public service advertisement on sleep and alertness. He asks you to investigate the sleep habits of a random selection of college students. How much sleep does the average student get during the week? What percentage of students sleep less than seven hours per night? To what extent do students catch up on sleep during the weekends? Do students report feeling sleepy in class? Is there any difference by gender?

This assignment asks you to report the results of your own research gathered either through library/Internet research or through observation, interviews, or questionnaires. Write your report in the form of a memorandum to your supervisor, providing the requested information in a closed-form, crisply presented style.

Generating and Exploring Ideas

Your initial goal is to use effective research strategies to find the information requested by your supervisor. If your report draws on library/Internet research, consult Part 4 of this textbook on doing research. Skills 22–26 explain strategies for finding and evaluating research sources; Skills 27–30 explain how to summarize sources for your own purposes and to incorporate them into your own writing using paraphrase and brief quotations. If your report draws on field research, consult Chapter 10 on analyzing data. Particularly helpful will be pages 247–251 on using questionnaires and interviews and pages 252–255 on reporting your results in words and graphics.

Shaping and Drafting

Although there is no one correct way to organize a workplace informative report, such reports typically have the following sections:

- A subject line that identifies the subject of the report
- An overview passage that references the supervisor's initial request, states the purpose of the report, and maps out the structure. (See the prototype introduction on p. 214.)
- A section explaining the writer's research process—e.g., the steps the writer went through to gather the information
- A major section providing the requested information. Typically, numeric data are displayed in graphs or tables and referenced in the writer's text. How to incorporate graphs and tables into your own prose is explained in Chapter 10, pages 252–255.

Revising

As you revise, make sure that your graphics (if you used them) and your words tell the same story and reinforce each other. The principle of "independent redundancy" explained in Chapter 10 (pp. 254–255) isn't as stringently followed in workplace reports as it is in scientific papers, but your text should still make explicit reference to your graphics while also explaining the same thing in words as the graphics show visually. As you edit, try to achieve a clear, concise style that allows your supervisor to read quickly; show your respect for the busy business environment that places many simultaneous demands on managers. When you have a near-final draft, exchange it with a classmate for a peer review.

Questions for Peer Review

In addition to the generic peer review questions explained in Chapter 17, Skill 4, ask your peer reviewers to address these questions:

1. Does the document have a professional appearance (memo format, pleasing use of white space, appropriate use of headings)?
2. Do the subject line and opening overview passage effectively explain the report's occasion, purpose, and structure?
3. Does the writer explain how the research was conducted?
4. Does the report clearly address the supervisor's initial questions? How might the presentation of the information be improved?
5. If the report uses graphics, are the graphics referenced in the text? Are they clear with appropriate titles and labels? How might they be improved?

Informative (and Surprising) Article

WRITING PROJECT

Using field research, library/Internet research, or your own personal experience, write an informative magazine or academic article in a tone and style suitable for general readers. Your rhetorical task is to arouse your readers' curiosity by posing an interesting question and then responding to it with information that is new to the targeted audience. In many cases, you can sharpen your thesis by using the surprising-reversal strategy: You imagine readers who hold a mistaken or overly narrow view of your topic; your purpose is to give them a new, surprising view.

Depending on the wishes of your instructor, this assignment can draw primarily on field research (see Kerri Ann Matsumoto's "How Much Does It Cost to Go Organic?" p. 231), library/Internet research (see Shannon King's "How Clean and Green Are Hydrogen Fuel-Cell Cars?" pp. 234–236), or personal experience (see Cheryl Carp's essay "Behind Stone Walls," pp. 232–233). In each of these cases, the article enlarges the targeted audience's view of a subject in a surprising way. Matsumoto "desktop-published" her essay in two-column format to look like a magazine article. King and Carp both write in a relaxed style suitable for magazine publication. King's article also serves as an example of a short academic research article.

For this assignment, try to avoid issues calling for persuasive rather than informative writing. With persuasive prose, you imagine a resistant reader who may argue back. With informative prose, you imagine a more trusting reader, one willing to learn from your experience or research. Although you hope to enlarge your reader's view of a topic, you aren't necessarily saying that your audience's original view is wrong, nor are you initiating a debate. For example, suppose a writer wanted to develop the following claim: "Many of my friends think that having an alcoholic mother would be the worst thing that could happen to you, but I will show that my mother's disease forced our family closer together." In this case the writer isn't arguing that alcoholic mothers are good or that everyone should have an alcoholic mother. Rather, the writer is simply offering readers a new, unexpected, and expanded view of what it might be like to have an alcoholic mother.

Generating and Exploring Ideas

If you do field research or library/Internet research for your article, start by posing a research question. As you begin doing initial research on your topic area, you will soon know more about your topic than most members of the general public. Ask yourself, "What has surprised me about my research so far? What have I learned that I didn't know before?" Your answers to these questions can suggest possible approaches to your paper. Kerri Ann Matsumoto, for example, wondered how expensive it would be to switch to organic vegetables. Shannon King began her research believing that fuel-cell technology produced totally pollution-free energy. She didn't realize that one needs to burn fossil fuels in order to produce the hydrogen. This initial surprise shaped her paper. She decided that if this information surprised her, it should surprise others also.

What follows are two exercises you can try to generate ideas for your paper.

Individual Task to Generate Ideas

Here is a template that can help you generate ideas by asking you to think specifically about differences in knowledge levels between you and various audiences.

> I know more about X [topic area] than [specific person or persons].

For example, you might say, "I know more about [computer games/gospel music/the energy crisis] than [my roommate/my high school friends/my parents]." This exercise helps you discover subjects about which you already have expertise compared to other audiences. Likewise, you can identify a subject that interests you, do a couple of hours of research on it, and then ask: "Based on just this little amount of research, I know more about X than my roommate." Thinking in this way, you might be able to create an intriguing question that you could answer through your research.

Small-Group Task to Generate Ideas

Form small groups. Assign a group recorder to make a two-column list, with the left column titled "Mistaken or Narrow View of X" and the right column titled "Groupmate's Surprising View." Using the surprising-reversal strategy, brainstorm ideas for article topics until every group member has generated at least one entry for the right-hand column. Here is a sample list entry:

Mistaken or Narrow View of X	Groupmate's Surprising View
Football offensive lineman is a no-brain, repetitive job requiring size, strength, and only enough brains and athletic ability to push people out of the way.	Jeff can show that being an offensive lineman is an interesting job that requires mental smarts as well as size, strength, and athletic ability.

To help stimulate ideas, you might consider topic areas such as the following:

- *People:* computer programmers, homeless people, cheerleaders, skateboarders, gang members, priests or rabbis, feminists, house-spouses, mentally ill or developmentally disabled persons.
- *Activities:* washing dishes, climbing mountains, wrestling, modeling, gardening, living with a chronic disease or disability, owning a certain breed of dog, riding a subway at night, entering a dangerous part of a city.
- *Places:* particular neighborhoods, particular buildings or parts of buildings, local attractions, junkyards, places of entertainment, summer camps.
- *Other similar categories:* groups, animals and plants, and so forth; the list is endless.

Next, go around the room, sharing with the entire class the topics you have generated. Remember that you are not yet committed to writing about any of these topics.

Here are some examples from recent students:

> A common misconception about Native Americans is that they lived in simple harmony with the earth, but my research reveals that they often "controlled" nature by setting fire to forests to make farming easier or to improve hunting.
>
> To the average person, pawnshops are disreputable places, but my experience shows that pawnshops can be honest, wholesome businesses that perform a valuable social service.
>
> Most of my straight friends think of the film *Frankenstein* as a monster movie about science gone amuck, but to the gay community it holds a special and quite different meaning.

Shaping, Drafting, and Revising

An informative article based on field research often has a structure similar to that of a scientific paper except that its style is more informal and less detailed. You will note that Kerri Ann Matsumoto's essay on the cost of organic food poses a research question (How much extra does it cost to buy organic food over non-organic food?); explains her process (did comparison pricing for a chicken stir-fry for a family of four at an organic and a non-organic store); presents her findings in both words and graphics (organic foods cost more); and suggests the significance of her research (the advantages of organic foods versus the advantages of spending the extra money in other ways). The structure of the popular version is thus quite similar to the scientific version: problem, method, findings, significance.

Both Carp's article on prisoners and King's article on hydrogen cars have a surprising-reversal shape:

- An introduction that engages the reader's interest in a question and provides needed context and background.
- A section that explains the common or popular answer to the writer's question.
- A section that gives the writer's surprising answer developed with information derived from personal experience in Carp's case or from library/Internet research in King's case.

To create the "surprising-reversal" feel, consider delaying your thesis until after you have explained your audience's common, expected answer to your opening question. This delay in presenting the thesis creates a more open-form feel that readers often find engaging.

As a way of helping you generate ideas, we offer the following five questions. Questions 1, 2, and 4 are planning questions that will help you create broad point sentences to form your essay's skeletal framework. These questions call for one-sentence generalizations. Questions 3 and 5 are freewriting prompts to help you generate supporting details. For these two questions, freewrite rapidly, either on paper or at your computer. Following each question, we speculate about what Carp or King might have written if they had used the same questions to help them get started on their essays.

1. *What question does your essay address?* (Carp might have asked, "What is it like to visit inmates in a maximum-security prison?" King might have asked, "Will hydrogen fuel-cell automobiles solve our nation's energy and pollution crises?")
2. *What is the common, expected, or popular answer to this question held by your imagined audience?* (Carp might have said, "Visiting these prisoners will be scary because prisoners are sex-starved, dangerous people." King might have said, "Most people believe that hydrogen fuel-cell cars will solve our country's pollution and energy crises."
3. *What examples and details support your audience's view?* Expand on these views by developing them with supporting examples and details. (Carp might have brainstormed details about concealed razor blades, drugs, prison violence, her friends' fear, and so on. King might have noted her research examples praising fuel-cell technology such as the Bush/Cheney National Energy Report or California Governor Arnold Schwarzenegger's desire to build hydrogen fuel stations across the state.)
4. *What is your own surprising view?* (Carp might have answered, "Visiting the prison is uplifting because prisoners can be kind, creative, and generous." King might have said, "Although hydrogen fuel-cell cars are pollution free, getting the hydrogen in the first place requires burning fossil fuels.")
5. *What examples and details support this view? Why do you hold this view? Why should a reader believe you?* Writing rapidly, spell out the evidence that sup-

ports your point. (Carp would have done a freewrite on all the experiences she had that changed her views about prisoners. Later she would have selected the most powerful ones and refined them for her readers. King would have done a freewrite about her research discoveries that hydrogen has to be recovered from carbon-based fossils or from electrolysis of water—all of which means continued use of pollution-causing fossil fuels.)

After you finish exploring your responses to these five trigger questions, you will be well on your way to composing a first draft of your article. Now finish writing your draft fairly rapidly without worrying about perfection.

Once you have your first draft on paper, the goal is to make it work better, first for yourself and then for your readers. If you discovered ideas as you wrote, you may need to do some major restructuring. Check to see that the question you are addressing is clear. If you are using the surprising-reversal strategy, make sure that you distinguish between your audience's common view and your own surprising view. Apply the strategies for global revision explained in Chapter 17.

Questions for Peer Review

In addition to the generic peer review questions explained in Chapter 17, Skill 4, ask your peer reviewers to address these questions:

1. What is the question the paper addresses? How effective is the paper at hooking the reader's interest in the question?
2. If the paper uses the surprising-reversal strategy, where does the writer explain the common or popular view of the topic? Do you agree that this is the common view? How does the writer develop or support this view? What additional supporting examples, illustrations, or details might make the common view more vivid or compelling?
3. What is the writer's surprising view? Were you surprised? What details does the writer use to develop the surprising view? What additional supporting examples, illustrations, or details might help make the surprising view more vivid and compelling?
4. If the paper uses field research, where does the writer do each of the following: (a) explain the problem or question to be addressed; (b) explain the process for gathering information; (c) report the findings; and (d) suggest the significance of the findings?
5. Is the draft clear and easy to follow? Is the draft interesting? How might the writer improve the style, clarity, or interest level of the draft?
6. If the draft includes graphics, are they effective? Do the words and the visuals tell the same story? Are the visuals properly titled and labeled? How might the use of visuals be improved?
7. If the instructor asks writers to "desktop-publish" their papers to look like articles, is the document design effective? Are the graphics readable? How might the visual design of the paper be improved?

READINGS

The readings for this chapter comprise various types of informative prose ranging from need-to-know instructions to informative magazine articles using surprising reversal. Our first reading, written by a winemaker for a major winery, explains the process for yeast preparation—a crucial first step in the winemaking process. In an e-mail to us, the winemaker explained some of the kinds of writing he does on the job: "I do a lot of writing for our employees in the form of procedures. [These procedures are] an attempt to instruct in a non-ambiguous manner (we are currently rewriting all of these with help from the cellar crew, who are pointing out the ambiguous portions)." Imagine that you have just been hired by this company and told to prepare the yeast. Could you follow these instructions?

Kerry Norton

Winery Yeast Preparation Instructions

Attention! The dried yeast that we use to ferment grapes and grape juice is alive! If you follow these instructions, the yeast will grow and successfully ferment the grapes into wine. If you do not follow these instructions, the yeast may die and the wine could be ruined. Every yeast manufacturer's instructions are a little different, but they are all similar to the following procedure.

Always follow these instructions exactly.

Before you start, warm the tank to the inoculation temperature listed in the work order.

1. Weigh out the proper amount and type of yeast in a **DRY** container. Mix the proper amount of water in a pail or bucket (or buckets). Close the box of yeast up tightly after you are done with it!!! We use 10 Liters of water for each Kilogram of yeast. The water **must** be close to **104 degrees F. (40 degrees C.)**. The easiest way to do this is to start with hot water, then add cold water until you have a lot of water at 104 degrees F., then dump out the excess.
2. Stir in the weighed yeast very gently. Do not stir any harder than necessary to get the yeast wet. You don't have to dissolve it—just get it wet and stirred in.
3. Wait **10–20 minutes**, no more and no less. Then stir the starter gently and add enough juice or must from the tank to increase the volume of the starter about 1/2. It should be foaming gently by this time.
4. Wait 10 minutes, then add more juice or grapes to double the volume of the starter.
5. Wait another 10 minutes, then add the starter to the tank.
6. Make sure that the cooling jacket is set to the proper fermentation temperature and that the valves are set to cool and not heat the tank.

What happens if...

I weigh out the wrong kind of yeast? Yeast add flavor to the wine, and the yeast you accidentally picked out may make the wine taste different than it should. If you haven't added water yet, put the yeast back into the container it came from or in a plastic bag, label it clearly, and seal the container tightly. If you have already added water, ask your supervisor what to do.

I forget to close up the box of yeast? The yeast are alive and OK as long as they stay dry. If the yeast gets damp, it loses strength and will not ferment well. Make sure you keep it dry until you are ready to use it!

I don't get the water temperature right? Too hot, and you kill or stun the yeast. Too cold, and the yeast will not grow fast enough. Get the temperature as close to 104 degrees as you can.

I use the electric stirrer when I dissolve the yeast? The yeast cells are very fragile when you first add water, and the electric stirrer kills some of them. Stir by hand and save the electric stirrer until the yeast is rehydrated.

I forget to add juice after 10–20 minutes? The yeast is hungry and it needs to eat! As soon as it is rehydrated, it needs some juice or grapes so it can start fermenting. If you leave it more than 30 minutes after adding the water, throw away the starter and start over. If less than 30 minutes, add the juice and see if the starter starts to foam. If it isn't doing anything, it is probably no good and you need to throw it away and start over.

I use too small a bucket and it foams over? Then you are losing your yeast onto the floor. Put it into a bigger bucket.

I skip the steps where I add the juice to the starter? This is done to let the yeast adjust itself from its rehydration temperature of 104 degrees F. down to the temperature of the juice or grapes. If the temperature difference is too much, it stresses the yeast and then it won't ferment well. It is important to do these steps, so don't shortcut them.

Remember, it is the yeast that ferment sugar into alcohol, add their own flavors, and make the wine taste good. If we make them comfortable, they will be happy and will do their job well.

THINKING CRITICALLY
about "Winery Yeast Preparation Instructions"

1. How has Kerry Norton attempted to avoid COIK in these instructions? Give some specific examples of ways he has adapted these instructions for workers, many of whom may have only a high school education or less.

2. Norton informed us that the material after the heading "What happens if …" was created after conversations with the cellar crew. Norton asked them all the kinds of things that might go wrong in making the yeast and then created this section. Do you find this section effective? Why or why not?

3. With respect to the three classical appeals of *logos*, *ethos*, and *pathos* (see pp. 55–56), how has Norton tried to make these instructions as effective as possible? *Logos*: Do the instructions seem knowledgeable and complete? *Ethos*: What kind of persona does Norton construct here? What image of the "boss" is conveyed in these instructions? *Pathos*: Where do these instructions show awareness for the concerns and point of view of the audience?

Our second reading, "Muslim Americans: Middle Class and Mostly Mainstream," illustrates an informative report. Based on field and research data compiled by the Pew Research Center for the People and the Press, this reading is the widely disseminated summary of the Center's longer, more detailed report. The complete report can be read on the Pew Research Center's Web site at http://people-press.org. This report summary has many features of a workplace document except that it is addressed to a general audience rather than a specific workplace audience.

The Pew Research Center for the People and the Press

Muslim Americans: Middle Class and Mostly Mainstream

1 The first-ever, nationwide, random sample survey of Muslim Americans finds them to be largely assimilated, happy with their lives, and moderate with respect to many of the issues that have divided Muslims and Westerners around the world.

2 The Pew Research Center conducted more than 55,000 interviews to obtain a national sample of 1,050 Muslims living in the United States. Interviews were conducted in English, Arabic, Farsi and Urdu. The resulting study, which draws on Pew's survey research among Muslims around the world, finds that Muslim Americans are a highly diverse population, one largely composed of immigrants. Nonetheless, they are decidedly American in their outlook, values and attitudes. This belief is reflected in Muslim American income and education levels, which generally mirror those of the public.

3 Key findings include:

- Overall, Muslim Americans have a generally positive view of the larger society. Most say their communities are excellent or good places to live.
- A large majority of Muslim Americans believe that hard work pays off in this society. Fully 71% agree that most people who want to get ahead in the U.S. can make it if they are willing to work hard.
- The survey shows that although many Muslims are relative newcomers to the U.S., they are highly assimilated into American society. On balance, they believe that Muslims coming to the U.S. should try and adopt American customs, rather than trying to remain distinct from the larger society.

Muslim Americans: Who Are They?

	Total
Proportion who are...	%
Foreign-born Muslims	**65**
Arab region	24
Pakistan	8
Other South Asia	10
Iran	8
Europe	5
Other Africa	4
Other	6
Native-born Muslims	**35**
African American	20
Other	15
	100
Foreign-born Muslims	**65**
Year immigrated:	
2000–2007	18
1990–1999	21
1980–1989	15
Before 1980	11
Native-born Muslims	**35**
Percent who are...	
Converts to Islam	21
Born Muslim	14

And by nearly two-to-one (63%–32%) Muslim Americans do not see a conflict between being a devout Muslim and living in a modern society.

- Roughly two-thirds (65%) of adult Muslims in the U.S. were born elsewhere. A relatively large proportion of Muslim immigrants are from Arab countries, but many also come from Pakistan and other South Asian countries. Among native-born Muslims, roughly half are African American (20% of U.S. Muslims overall), many of whom are converts to Islam.
- Based on data from this survey, along with available Census Bureau data on immigrants' nativity and nationality, the Pew Research Center estimates the total population of Muslims in the United States at 2.35 million.
- Muslim Americans reject Islamic extremism by larger margins than do Muslim minorities in Western European countries. However, there is somewhat more acceptance of Islamic extremism in some segments of the U.S. Muslim public than others. Fewer native-born African American Muslims than others completely condemn al Qaeda. In addition, younger Muslims in the U.S. are much more likely than older Muslim Americans to say that suicide bombing in the defense of Islam can be at least sometimes justified. Nonetheless, absolute levels of support for Islamic extremism among Muslim Americans are quite low, especially when compared with Muslims around the world.
- A majority of Muslim Americans (53%) say it has become more difficult to be a Muslim in the U.S. since the Sept. 11 terrorist attacks. Most also believe that the government "singles out" Muslims for increased surveillance and monitoring.
- Relatively few Muslim Americans believe the U.S.-led war on terror is a sincere effort to reduce terrorism, and many doubt that Arabs were responsible for the 9/11 attacks. Just 40% of Muslim Americans say groups of Arabs carried out those attacks.

U.S. Muslims More Mainstream

Percent low-income compared with general public

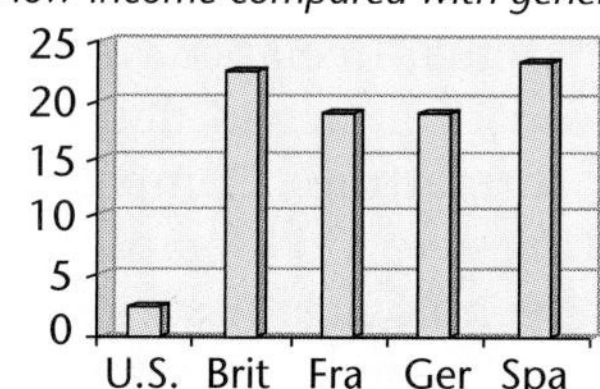

Life is better for women here than in Muslim countries

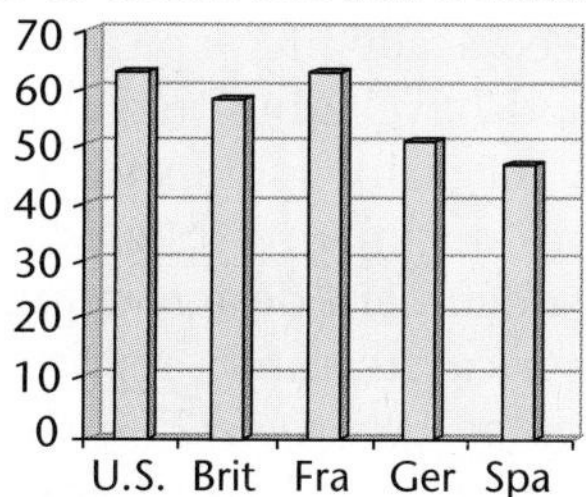

Think of self as Muslim first, not American/British/French/German/Spanish

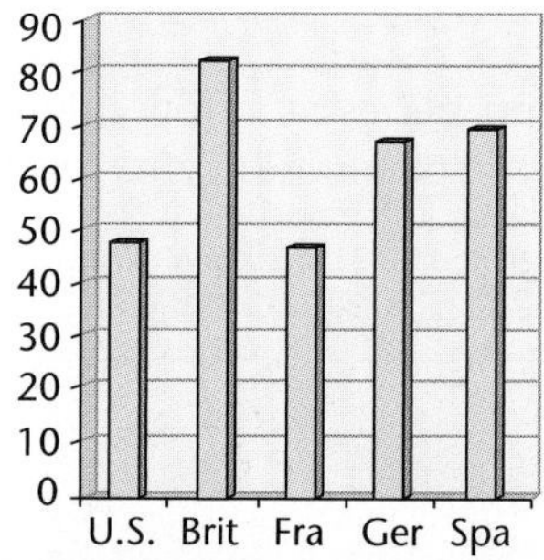

Very concerned about Islamic extremism in the world these days

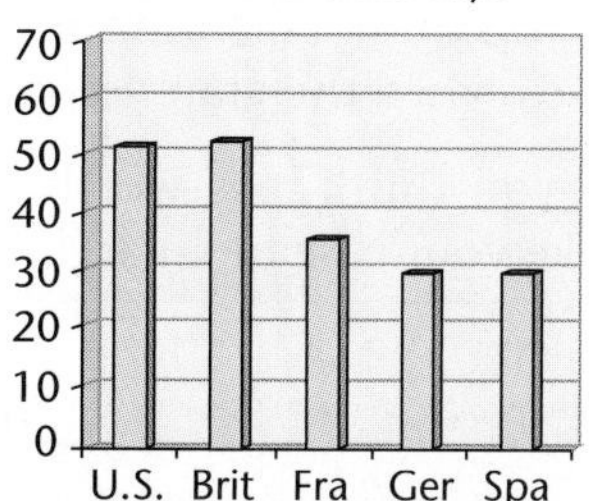

THINKING CRITICALLY
about "Muslim Americans: Middle Class and Mostly Mainstream"

1. Note how this document includes the typical features, with some modifications, of a typical workplace report (see bulleted list on p. 220). Where does the document include the following:
   a. An overview sentence that orients readers to the purpose and content of the document?
   b. An explanation of the writer's research process?
   c. Presentation of the writer's findings using both verbal text and graphics?
2. Typically, informative writing is valuable to the extent that it brings something needed, new, or surprising to the audience and therefore enlarges their view of the topic. What did you find new, surprising, or otherwise worthwhile in this informative report?

Our third reading, by student writer Kerri Ann Matsumoto (p. 231), is formatted to look like a popular magazine article (see p. 231).

THINKING CRITICALLY
about "How Much Does It Cost to Go Organic?"

1. In our teaching, we have discovered that students appreciate the concept of genre more fully if they occasionally "desktop-publish" a manuscript to look like a magazine article, a poster, or a brochure rather than a standard double-spaced academic paper. If Kerri Ann had been an actual freelance writer, she would have submitted this article double-spaced with attached figures, and the magazine publisher would have done the formatting. Compare Kerri Ann's document design for "How Much Does It Cost to Go Organic?" with the document design required by the American Psychological Association for empirical research reports—the student essay on gender in cartoons in Chapter 10, pages 274–281. How does document design itself signal differences in genre? To what extent has Kerri Ann made this article *sound* like a popular magazine article as well as look like one?
2. Do you think Kerri Ann used graphics effectively in her essay? How might she have revised the graphics or the wording to make the paper more effective?
3. Do you think it is worth the extra money to go organic? How would you make your case in an argument paper with a persuasive aim?

HOW MUCH DOES IT COST TO GO ORGANIC?

Kerri Ann Matsumoto

Organic foods, grown without pesticides, weed killers, or hormone additives, are gaining popularity from small privately owned organic food stores to large corporate markets. With the cost of living rising, how much can a family of four afford to pay for organically grown food before it becomes too expensive?

To find out more information about the cost of organic foods, I went to the Rainbow Market, which is a privately owned organic food store, and to a nearby Safeway. I decided to see what it would cost to create a stir-fry for a family of four. I estimated that the cost of organic vegetables for the stir-fry would cost $3.97. Non-organic vegetables for the same stir-fry, purchased at Safeway, would cost $2.37. If we imagined our family eating the same stir fry every night for a year, it would cost $1,499 for organic and $865 for non-organic for a difference of $584.

After pricing vegetables, I wanted to find out how much it would cost to add to the stir-fry free-range chicken fed only organic feeds, as opposed to non-organic factory farmed chicken. For good quality chicken breasts, the organic chicken was $6.99 per pound and the non-organic was $3.58 per pound. Projected out over a year, the organic chicken would cost $5,103 compared to $2,613 for non-organic chicken.

Comparative Cost of Ingredients in an Organic Versus Non-Organic Stir-Fry

	Vegetables per day	Chicken per day	Total per day	Total per year
Organic	$3.97	$13.98	$17.95	$6552
Non-Organic	$2.37	$7.16	$9.53	$3478

If we add the cost of chicken and vegetables together (see the table and the graph), we can compute how much more it would cost to feed our family of four organic versus non-organic chicken stir-fry for a year.

My research shows that over the course of one year it will cost $6,552 per year to feed our family organic stir-fry and $3,478 for non-organic for a difference of $3,074. If a family chose to eat not only organic dinner, but also all organic meals, the cost of food would sharply increase.

Before going to the Rainbow Market I knew that the price of organic foods was slightly higher than non-organic. However, I did not expect the difference to be so great. Of course, if you did comparison shopping at other stores, you might be able to find cheaper organic chicken and vegetables. But my introductory research suggests that going organic isn't cheap.

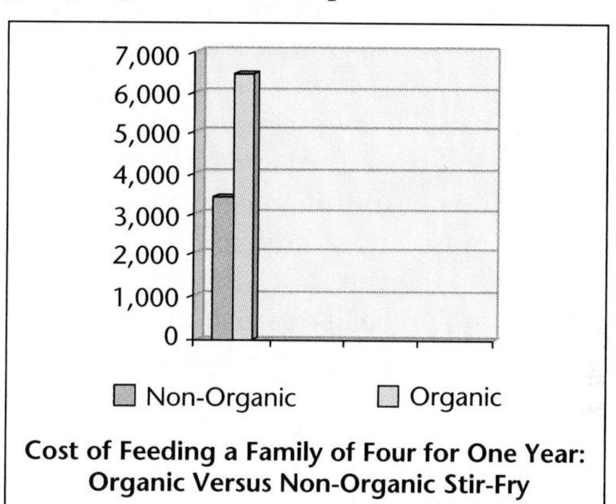

Cost of Feeding a Family of Four for One Year: Organic Versus Non-Organic Stir-Fry

Is it worth it? Many people today have strong concerns for the safety of the foods that they feed to their family. If you consider that organic vegetables have no pesticides and that the organic chicken has no growth hormone additives, the extra cost may be worth it. Also if you are concerned about cruelty to animals, free-range chickens have a better life than caged chickens. But many families might want to spend the $3,074 difference in other ways. If you put that money toward a college fund, within ten years you could save over $30,000. So how much are you willing to pay for organic foods?

Our next reading is by student writer Cheryl Carp, whose experience with volunteer outreach in a maximum-security prison enabled her to enlarge her readers' views of prisoners with life sentences. This paper, which uses the surprising-reversal strategy, illustrates how personal experiences can be used for an informative aim.

Cheryl Carp (student)

Behind Stone Walls

1 For about eight hours out of every month I am behind the stone walls of the Monroe State Penitentiary. No, that's not the sentencing procedure of some lenient judge; I am part of a group of inmates and outsiders who identify themselves as Concerned Lifers. Concerned Lifers is an organization operating both inside and outside of prison walls. Inside Monroe there are close to thirty men who take part in the organization and its activities, all of whom have been given life sentences. Concerned Lifers outside the prison visit the prisoners, take part in the organization's meetings, and then split into various small groups for personal conversation. I became involved in this exciting group as a personal sponsor (able to visit the prison alone for special activities) after attending my first meeting inside Monroe State Penitentiary. That first drive to Monroe seemed to take forever. Looking out the window of that twelve-seater van filled with apprehensive first-time volunteers, I kept my eyes on the evening sky and tried to imagine what it would be like to be shut up in prison for life, never to see this beautiful scenery again. I was not scared, but I was nervous and could feel my pulse rate steadily rise as I began to see the green and white road signs to the prison. As the van slowly climbed the hill to the guard tower at the top, I wondered what it would be like to visit this maximum security prison.

2 Many people believe that visiting a prison would be frightening. Most people typically picture dangerous men lurking in every corner. The guards are yelling and the men are fighting; the men are covered with tattoos, probably carrying concealed razor blades and scowling menacingly. People think that prisons are a haven for rampant homosexuality and illegal drugs. Common belief is that the inmates are like locked animals, reaching out between the iron bars of their cages. These men are seen as sex-starved, eagerly waiting for a female body to enter their domain. The atmosphere is one of suspense, with sub-human men ready at any moment to break free and run. People I've spoken to express a fear of danger to themselves and almost a threat to their lives. They wonder how I have the nerve to do it.

3 But visiting a prison to me is an uplifting experience, far from frightening. Since that initial visit, I have returned many times to organize and participate in a clown group. The clown group is made up of about twenty of the inmates in the Concerned Lifers group and myself. The prisoners meet and rehearse once a week, and I join them every other week to critique their progress, give them pointers, and do various exercises to improve their ability.

4 The only frightening part of a visit is getting through all the guards and their red tape. Last week I drove up the hill to the guard tower, identified myself and my affiliation, and was told to "park to the left" by a disembodied voice coming from a loud-

speaker. After going through many metal security doors, being checked by a metal detector that even picks up the nails in your shoes, and being escorted by numerous guards, I finally got to be with the people I had come to see.

5 The most enjoyable, exciting, and friendly time I spend at the prison is the time I spend with the boys. These people are no longer "the prisoners" or "the inmates," but are now individuals. Visiting the prison is not a frightening experience because the men inside become people, people full of emotions, creativity, and kindness. These qualities are evident in the activities and projects these men become involved in or initiate themselves. For example, one young lifer named Ken became interested in Japanese paper folding—origami. In order to pursue his interest in origami, he requested a book on the subject from the prison librarian and proceeded to teach himself. A few weeks later, I saw origami creations everywhere—flowers, dragons, and birds—all made by the guys and all done carefully and beautifully. Ken had taught his fellow inmates. Another great thing that this group has undertaken is the sponsorship of four children through an orphan relief program. The men make almost nothing at their various jobs within the prison, but what they do make they are more than willing to share, some thing many of us never seem to "get around to."

6 It is true that the men value the presence of a female, but not for sexual reasons. The men inside Monroe are hungry for outside companionship and understanding. They're hungry for a woman's viewpoint and conversation. They have treated me as a friend, valued my conversation, and never made sexual advances. The men behind the walls are reaching through their bars not menacingly, but pleadingly—begging the outside world to take a good look at them. The men need to be looked at as people and as fellow humans in this world. Most of them are aching for a second chance at life and relationships. This is not a place for outsiders to fear, but a place to which outsiders can bring light, hope, and understanding.

7 My point is not to condone the crimes that these men may have committed in the past, but to look to the present and the future by seeing these men not as "inmates," but as individual people trying to succeed in the kind of life they now have to live.

THINKING CRITICALLY
about "Behind Stone Walls"

1. What is the audience that Cheryl Carp imagines?
2. For this audience, what is the common view of prisoners that Cheryl Carp attempts to reverse?
3. What is her own surprising view?
4. What are the strengths and weaknesses of Cheryl's essay?

The next reading, by student writer Shannon King, is a short academic research paper using the surprising-reversal strategy. Shannon's paper uses research information to enlarge her readers' understanding of hydrogen fuel-cell vehicles by showing that hydrogen fuel is not as pollution-free as the general public believes.

Shannon King (Student)

How Clean and Green Are Hydrogen Fuel-Cell Cars?

1 The United States is embroiled in a controversy over energy and pollution. We are rapidly using up the earth's total supply of fossil fuels, and many experts think that children being born today will experience the end of affordable oil. One energy expert, Paul Roberts, believes that serious oil shortages will start occurring by 2015 when the world's demand for oil will outstrip the world's capacity for further oil production. An equally serious problem is that the burning of fossil fuels spews carbon dioxide into the atmosphere, which increases the rate of global warming.

2 One hopeful way of addressing these problems is to develop hydrogen fuel cell cars. According to Karim Nice, the author of the fuel cell pages on the *HowStuffWorks* Web site, a fuel cell is "an electrochemical energy conversion device that converts hydrogen and oxygen into water, producing electricity and heat in the process." A hydrogen-fueled car is therefore an electric car, powered by an electric motor. The car's electricity is generated by a stack of fuel cells that act like a battery. In the hydrogen fuel cell, the chemicals that produce the electricity are hydrogen from the car's pressurized fuel tank, oxygen from the air, and special catalysts inside the fuel cell. The fuel cell releases no pollutants or greenhouse gases. The only waste product is pure water.

3 To what extent will these pollution-free fuel cells be our energy salvation? Are they really clean and green?

4 Many people think so. The development of hydrogen fuel cells has caused much excitement. I know people who say we don't need to worry about running out of oil because cars of the future will run on water. One recent *New York Times* advertisement produced by General Motors has as its headline, "Who's driving the hydrogen economy?" The text of the ad begins by saying "The hydrogen economy isn't a pipe dream. ... The hydrogen economy is the endgame of a multifaceted strategy General Motors set in motion years ago, with steps that are real, progressive, and well-underway" (General Motors). The Web site for the Hydrogen Fuel Cell Institute includes a picture of a crystal clear blue sky landscape with a large letter headline proclaiming "At long last, a technology too long overlooked promises to transform society. "At the bottom of the picture are the words, "Offering clean & abundant power, hydrogen-based fuel cells could soon end our reliance on oil and minimize emissions of pollution and global-warming gases." According to CNN News, the Bush administration has proposed devoting 1.7 billion dollars of federal funds to developing hydrogen fuel cells (CNN). The biggest nationally known proponent of hydrogen fuel cells is California Governor Arnold Schwarzenegger, who signed an Executive Order that California's "21 interstate freeways shall be designated as the 'California Hydrogen Highway Network.'" (California). In this executive order, Schwarzenegger envisions

> a network of hydrogen fueling stations along these roadways and in the urban centers that they connect, so that by 2010, every Californian will have access to hydrogen fuel, with a significant and increasing percentage produced from clean, renewable sources. (2)

Schwarzenegger's optimism about the hydrogen highway sums up the common view that hydrogen is a clean alternative energy source that is abundant throughout nature. All we have to do is bottle it up, compress it, and transport it to a network of new "gas stations" where the gas being pumped is hydrogen.

5 But what I discovered in my research is that hydrogen is not as green as most people think. Although hydrogen fuel cells appear to be an environmentally friendly alternative to fossil fuels, the processes for producing hydrogen actually require the use of fossil fuels. The problem is that pure hydrogen doesn't occur naturally on earth. It has to be separated out from chemical compounds containing hydrogen, and that process requires other forms of energy. What I discovered is that there are only two major ways to produce hydrogen. The first is to produce it from fossil fuels by unlocking the hydrogen that is bonded to the carbon in coal, oil, or natural gas. The second is to produce it from water through electrolysis, but the power required for electrolysis would also come mainly from burning fossil fuels. These problems make hydrogen fuel cell cars look less clean and green than they first appear.

6 One approach to creating hydrogen from fossil fuels is to use natural gas. According to Matthew L. Wald, writing in a *New York Times* article, natural gas is converted to hydrogen in a process called "steam reforming." Natural gas (made of hydrogen and carbon atoms) is mixed with steam (which contains hydrogen and oxygen atoms) to cause a chemical reaction that produces pure hydrogen. But it also produces carbon dioxide, which contributes to global warming. According to Wald, if fuel cell cars used hydrogen from steam reforming, they would emit 145 grams of global warming gases per mile compared to 374 grams an ordinary gas-powered car would emit. The good news is that using hydrogen power would cut carbon emissions by more than half. The bad news is that these cars would still contribute to global warming and consume natural gas. Moreover, Wald suggests that the natural gas supply is limited and that natural gas has many better, more efficient uses than converting it to hydrogen.

7 Another method for producing hydrogen would come from coal, which is the cheapest and most abundant source of energy. However, the current method of generating electricity by burning coal is the leading source of carbon dioxide emission. At Ohio University, engineers state we still have enough coal to last us two hundred and fifty years and that we should find some better uses for coal. The engineers have received a 4 million dollar federal grant to investigate the production of hydrogen from coal. They plan on mixing coal with steam, air, and oxygen under high temperatures and pressure to produce hydrogen and carbon monoxide ("Ohio University"). But this too would generate greenhouse gases and is a long way off from producing results.

8 The next likely source of hydrogen is to produce it directly from water using an electrolyzer. Wald explains that the electrolyzer uses an electrical current to break down water molecules into hydrogen and oxygen atoms. Creating hydrogen through electrolysis sounds like a good idea because its only waste product is oxygen. But the hazardous environmental impact is not in the electrolysis reaction, but in the need to generate electricity to run the electrolyzer. Wald claims that if the electricity to run the electrolyzer came from a typical coal-fired electrical plant, the carbon dioxide emissions for a fuel cell car would be 17 percent worse than for today's gasoline powered cars. One solution would be to run the electrolyzer with wind-generated or nuclear-

powered electricity. But wind power would be able to produce only a small fraction of what would be needed, and nuclear power brings with it a whole new set of problems including disposal of nuclear waste.

9 Although there seem to be various methods of producing hydrogen, the current sources being considered do not fulfill the claim that hydrogen fuel cell technology will end the use of fossil fuels or eliminate greenhouse gases. The problem is not with the fuel cells themselves but with the processes needed to produce hydrogen fuel. I am not arguing that research and development should be abandoned, and I hope some day that the hydrogen economy will take off. But what I have discovered in my research is that hydrogen power is not as clean and green as I thought.

Works Cited

California. Executive Dept. "Executive Order S-7-04." 20 Apr. 2004. Web. 24 May 2004. <http://www.its.ucdavis.edu/hydrogenhighway/Executive-Order.pdf>.

CNN. "The Issues/George Bush." *CNN.com*. Cable News Network, 2004. Web. 23 May 2004. <http://www.cnn.com/ELECTION/2004/special/president/issues/index.bush.html>.

General Motors. Advertisement. *New York Times* 28 July 2004: A19. Print.

Hydrogen Fuel Cell Institute. Wilder Foundation, 2001. Web. 27 May 2004.

Nice, Karim, and Jonathan Strickland. "How Fuel Cells Work." *HowStuffWorks.com*. HowStuffWorks, 18 Sept. 2000. Web. 27 May 2004.

"Ohio University Aims to Use Coal to Power Fuel Cells." *Fuel Cell Today*. N.p., 24 Nov. 2003. Web. 3 June 2004.

Roberts, Paul. "Running Out of Oil—and Time." *Los Angeles Times*. Common Dreams News Center, 6 Mar. 2004. Web. 23 Mar. 2004.

Wald, Matthew L. "Will Hydrogen Clear the Air? Maybe Not, Some Say." *New York Times* 12 Nov. 2003: C1. Print.

THINKING CRITICALLY

about "How Clean and Green Are Hydrogen Fuel-Cell Cars?"

1. Explain Shannon King's use of the surprising-reversal strategy. What question does she pose? What is the common answer? What is her surprising answer? How effectively does she use research data to support her surprising answer?

2. The line between information and persuasion is often blurred. Some might argue that Shannon's essay has a persuasive aim that argues against hydrogen fuel-cell cars rather than an informative aim that simply presents surprising information about hydrogen production. To what extent do you agree with our classification of Shannon's aim as primarily informative rather than persuasive? Can it be both?

Our final essay, by syndicated columnist Eugene Robinson, illustrates how an informative article for the general public can be based on data from a major research study—in this case a statistical report by the federal Bureau of Justice. At first glance, the study seems to indicate that no racial profiling occurs at the rate at which white, African-American, and Hispanic drivers are pulled over by police. But in this op-ed piece Robinson pushes deeper into the statistics and presents information showing that "driving while black" is "unsafe at any speed."

Eugene Robinson

You Have the Right to Remain a Target of Racial Profiling

1 Washington—This just in: Driving while black is still unsafe at any speed, even zero miles per hour. The same goes for driving while brown.

2 The federal Bureau of Justice Statistics released a report Sunday showing that white, African-American and Hispanic drivers are equally likely to be pulled over by police for an alleged traffic offense. In 2005, the year covered by the study, black drivers were actually less likely—by a tiny margin—to be stopped by police than drivers belonging to the other groups. You might be tempted to conclude that the constitutional imperative of equal protection had finally been extended to America's streets and highways.

3 But you would be wrong. The study reports that African-American and Hispanic drivers who are stopped by police are more than twice as likely as whites to be subjected to a search. Specifically, police searched only 3.6 percent of white drivers pulled over in a traffic stop, while they searched 9.5 percent of African-Americans who obeyed the flashing lights and 8.8 percent of Hispanics.

4 The report says the "apparent disparities" between racial groups "do not constitute proof that police treat people differently along demographic lines," since there could be "countless other factors and circumstances" that go into the decision of whom to spread-eagle on the hood.

5 All right, those figures alone might not constitute "proof" of bias that would convince a jury beyond a reasonable doubt. They are pretty compelling, though, especially when you also consider that black and Hispanic drivers are much more likely to experience "police use of force" than whites.

6 And besides, the following paragraph in the report pretty effectively demolishes that "move along, folks, nothing to see here" disclaimer about bias:

7 "Police actions taken during a traffic stop were not uniform across racial and ethnic categories. Black drivers (4.5 percent) were twice as likely as white drivers (2.1 percent) to be arrested during a traffic stop, while Hispanic drivers (65 percent) were more likely than white (56.2 percent) or black (55.8 percent) drivers to receive a ticket.

8 "In addition, whites (9.7 percent) were more likely than Hispanics (5.9 percent) to receive a written warning, while whites (18.6 percent) were more likely than blacks (13.7 percent) to be verbally warned by police."

9 African Americans have been putting up with the "driving while black" thing for so long that we've become somewhat cynical. For example, nearly three-quarters of whites and Hispanics who were pulled over for allegedly running a red light or a stop sign were willing to concede that they had been caught dead to rights, while nearly half of African Americans in that situation believed they had committed no infraction. About 90 percent of white drivers detained for some sort of vehicle defect, such as a busted taillight, thought the stop was legitimate, as opposed to 67 percent of black drivers.

10 Think that's just paranoia? Then try to reconcile the counterintuitive fact that while blacks are much more likely than whites to be arrested in a traffic stop, they are also more likely to be released with no enforcement action, not even a warning. This looks to me like powerful evidence that racial profiling is alive and well. It suggests there was no good reason to stop those people.

11 "About one in 10 searches during a traffic stop uncovered evidence of a possible crime," the report says. What could be wrong with that? Isn't that what police should be doing—enforcing the nation's laws, capturing criminals, making law-abiding Americans that much safer?

12 Of course that's what we pay our police officers to do, but not selectively. Whites, too, drive around with drugs, illegal weapons, open containers of alcohol or other contraband in their cars. The numbers in the report suggest that if white drivers stopped by police were searched at the same rate as blacks or Hispanics, police would uncover evidence of tens of thousands of additional crimes each year, doubtless putting thousands of dangerous people behind bars.

13 But, of course, we don't want a society in which everybody is being patted down by police officers all the time. We don't want a society in which people have to stand by the side of the road, fuming, while police arbitrarily rummage through the stuff in their cars—shopping bags, children's toys, McDonald's wrappers—on the off chance of finding something illegal.

14 If you're black or brown, though, may I see your license and registration, please?

THINKING CRITICALLY

about "You Have the Right to Remain a Target of Racial Profiling"

1. Nationally syndicated African-American columnist Eugene Robinson highlights statistical data to support his thesis about subtle but pervasive racial discrimination. In doing so, he gives his report a "surprising-reversal structure." What is the common view, seemingly supported by the report, that Robinson believes is mistaken? What is his surprising view? How does he use report data to support his surprising view?

2. What pieces of information from the report do you find most compelling in supporting Robinson's thesis?

3. Analyze this piece from the perspectives of *logos*, *ethos*, and *pathos*.

ANALYZING FIELD RESEARCH DATA

CHAPTER 10

Field research—which uses strategies such as questionnaires, interviews, or direct observation—is one of the most powerful methods that scholars use to investigate our world. If you plan to major in the social or physical sciences or in professional fields such as business, nursing, or education, this chapter will introduce you to two common genres of scientific writing:

- The empirical research report
- The scientific poster

If your major is in the humanities, this chapter will familiarize you with ways that scientists gather and interpret research data as they investigate empirical questions. (By "empirical," we mean investigations based on direct observation of events or phenomena or on systematically gathered statistical data.) The writing projects for this chapter ask you to pose an empirical research question about a phenomenon that interests you and then to collect relevant data through observation, through interviews, or through a questionnaire that you design. You will present your findings in a scientific style—either a research report or a poster or both.

Our own classroom experience suggests that you will find the research and writing called for in this chapter intellectually engaging and enjoyable. You will discover that there are hundreds of empirical questions that you can ask and investigate on a small scale yourself. You will actually produce new knowledge that is interesting to you and others.

Exploring the Analysis of Field Research Data

The following task, which anticipates some of the research issues discussed later in this chapter, will help you begin thinking about the analysis of field research data.

Suppose you want to find out whether there is any difference in the exercise habits of male versus female college students. (Rather than exercise habits, you might choose to investigate gender differences for other activities such as playing video games, reading magazines, watching television, surfing the Internet, or doing homework.) You might hypothesize that there are no gender differences in the percentage of male versus female students who exercise regularly or in the amount of time spent exercising by men versus women. However, you might speculate that the kinds of exercise vary by gender. For example, you might hypothesize that male students spend more time than females on muscle-building activities such as weight training or on pickup team sports such as basketball or touch football. Conversely, you might hypothesize that female students select exercises aimed at weight loss, muscle toning, and psychological well-being. Your study will help you confirm or disconfirm your initial hypothesis.

1. Working in small groups, create your own hypothesis in answer to the research question, "Are there gender differences in the exercise habits of male versus female college students?" Then create a short questionnaire (or set of interview questions) that will give you the data needed to confirm or disconfirm your hypothesis. At a minimum, your group's questionnaire will have to provide data on two variables: the respondent's gender and the amount of time each week the respondent typically spends on physical exercise. You might also wish to determine the kinds of exercise preferred by the respondents and their motivations for exercising, but try to develop an uncluttered questionnaire that yields answers that you can count and tabulate.
2. Choose one or more of the questionnaires you created in small groups and field-test them on the class. Ask class members—on a volunteer basis—to try responding to the questions. Your goal here is to discover whether the questions might be unclear or ambiguous.
3. As a class, discuss problems that arose in creating the questionnaire and then in responding to the questions. Were any questions unclear? Did they yield answers that could be counted and tabulated? How would you revise your questionnaire based on difficulties you encountered?
4. Suppose on two successive days you gave one of your class's questionnaires to all students entering your college library and tabulated the results. To what extent would the results be generalizable to the whole student body? Generalizable to college students overall? Generalizable to the public at large?
5. Discuss the ethics of this study. Might some students feel embarrassed or even harmed by this study if their answers were made public? Is it any one's business how much a person exercises? How might safeguards be built into the study to minimize the chances of any person's being made to feel uncomfortable?

Understanding the Analysis of Field Research Data

The Structure of an Empirical Research Report

A framework chart for a typical research report is shown in Figure 10.1. Formatting conventions call for section headings so that readers can quickly find the sections labeled "Introduction," "Method," "Results," and "Discussion." What is noteworthy about this structure is that the main sections of a research report follow the logic of the scientific method, as the following explanation suggests.

Introduction (Stage 1: Posing the question) Scientists begin by posing a research question and formulating their own hypothetical answer based on their initial theories, assumptions, hunches, and reasoning. The "Introduction" section of the research report corresponds to this stage: It describes the research question, explains its

FIGURE 10.1 Framework for an Empirical Research Report*

(Title Page)	• For format of an APA title page and body of research report, see pages 274–281 • Gives title of paper and author's name; short version of title appears before the page number in the upper right-hand corner of this and all subsequent pages
ABSTRACT	• Provides a 120-word or less summary of paper (research question, methods, major findings, significance of study)
INTRODUCTION	• Explains the problem to be investigated • Shows importance and significance of the problem • *Reviews previous studies examining the same problem (called a "literature review") and points to conflicts in these studies or to unknowns meriting further investigation*† • Poses the determinate research question(s) to be investigated • Presents the researcher's hypothesis
METHOD	• Describes how the study was done (enables future researchers to replicate the study exactly) • Often has subheadings such as "Participants," "Materials," and "Procedure" • Often provides operative definitions of key concepts in the problem/hypothesis
RESULTS	• Presents the researcher's findings or results • Often displays findings in figures, charts, or graphs as well as describes them in words • Usually does not present raw data or behind-the-scenes mathematics; data focus on composite results • *Presents statistical analysis of data to show confidence levels and other advanced statistical implications or meanings*†
DISCUSSION	• Presents the researcher's analysis of the results • Interprets and evaluates the collected data in terms of the original research question and hypothesis • Speculates on causes and consequences of the findings • Shows applications and practical or theoretical significance of the study • Usually includes a section pointing out limitations and possible flaws in the study and suggests directions for future research
REFERENCES	• Bibliographic listing of cited sources • For format of APA references, see Chapter 23, Skill 33, and page 281.
APPENDICES	• Provides place to include questionnaires or other materials used in study

*Based on guidelines in *Publication Manual of the American Psychological Association,* 5th ed., Washington, DC.: APA, 2001, pp. 10–30.

†Italicized sections are not required for the writing project in this chapter.

significance, and reviews previous scientific research addressing the same or a similar question. (Note: The writing projects for this chapter do not ask you to do a literature review.) Typically, the introduction ends with the scientist's hypothesis predicting what the observed data will show.

Method (Stage 2: Collection data) Scientists develop a method for collecting the data needed to confirm or disconfirm the hypothesis. The materials and methods used to conduct the research, along with operational definitions of any key terms, are described in detail in the "Method" section of the report. The Method section is like a recipe that allows future researchers to replicate the research process exactly. It also allows peer reviewers to look for possible flaws or holes in the research design.

Results (Stage 3: Determining results) Scientists examine the collected data carefully. The findings are reported in the "Results" section, usually displayed in tables or graphs as well as described verbally. To help determine the extent to which researchers can have confidence in the gathered data, expert researchers perform a variety of statistical tests that show, among other things, whether the results might be attributable simply to chance. (The writing projects for this chapter do not require statistical tests.)

Discussion (Stage 4: Analyzing results) Finally, scientists interpret and analyze their findings, drawing conclusions about what the findings mean and how the research advances knowledge. This stage of the scientific process corresponds to the "Discussion" section of the research report. Typically, the Discussion section also points to limitations and flaws in the research design and suggests directions for future research.

Other Sections

In addition to the four main sections, research reports often include an abstract of 120 words or less that summarizes the research problem, research design, results, and major implications of the study. The abstract allows readers at a glance to get a basic understanding of the research. At the end of the report, a "References" section lists bibliographic details about any cited sources. Finally, scientists can add in the "Appendices" section, copies of questionnaires used, interview questions asked, or special calculations that might interest readers.

How Readers Typically Read a Research Report

What is unusual about research reports is that readers typically don't read them in a linear fashion. The advantage of a well-marked structure is that readers can skim a report first and then, if they're interested, read it carefully in an order that meets their needs. Readers will typically skim the Introduction to understand the problem under investigation and then skip directly to the Discussion section, where the researcher's findings are analyzed in depth. Readers with special interest in the question being investigated may then go back to read the Introduction, Method section, and Results section in detail to evaluate the soundness of the research design and the accuracy and reliability of the data. Some readers may follow a different order. For example, researchers primarily interested in developing new research designs might read the Method section first to learn how the research was conducted. Our point is that the conventional format of a research report allows readers to tailor their reading practices to their own interests.

We will now go back through the sections of a research report, offering you suggestions for doing the kinds of thinking needed at each stage of the research process.

Posing Your Research Question

When you pose your research question for this writing project, you need to appreciate the difference between the broad, open-ended questions we have emphasized throughout this text and the very narrow questions that scientists use when doing empirical studies. Scientists, of course, pose big, open-ended questions all the time: What is the origin of the universe? What is the role of nature versus nurture in human gender behavior? What would it be like to ride upon a beam of light (a question Einstein asked in formulating his theory of relativity)? But when they conduct actual research, scientists transform these big, speculative, indeterminate questions into narrow determinate questions. By "determinate," we mean questions that can be answered either with yes or no or with a single fact, number, or range of numbers. The kinds of determinate questions that scientists typically ask can be placed in five categories in ascending order of complexity (see Table 10.1).*

As you study Table 10.1, you will see that it moves from descriptive questions aimed at identifying, measuring, and describing a phenomenon (categories 1, 2, and 3) to explanatory questions aimed at discovering the causes or consequences of a phenomenon (category 5). A question in the first category simply asks whether a phenomenon exists. Within the second category, researchers are interested in measuring some aspect of that existence—the phenomenon's size, temperature, frequency, and so forth. Categories 3 through 5 focus increasingly on causality. Category 3 determines how the phenomenon differs from other, related phenomenon, where the identification of differences would stimulate speculative thinking about causes. Category 4 focuses on the discovery of how two or more phenomena are correlated—that is, how they vary together. For example, recent research has suggested that women who work night shifts and sleep during the day develop breast cancer at higher rates than women who sleep at night. However, the existence of a correlation doesn't explain what causes the correlation. Within category 5, researchers try to create experiments or develop other research methods that will establish actual cause and effect.

*Table 10.1 is based on an unpublished paper by psychologist Robert Morasky, "Model of Empirical Research Question." Morasky's model was used for the section on "Asking Empirical Research Questions for Science" in John C. Bean and John D. Ramage, *Form and Surprise in Composition: Writing and Thinking Across the Curriculum* (New York: Macmillan, 1986), pp. 183–189.

TABLE 10.1 Asking Determinate Research Questions

Question Type	Explanation	Natural Science Example	Social Science Example	Question That You Might Ask for This Chapter's Writing Project
1. *Existence Questions:* "Does X exist in domain Y?"	Often researchers simply want to determine if a given phenomenon occurs or exists within a given domain	Do fragments of fungi exist in Precambrian sediments?	Do racial stereotypes exist in current world history textbooks?	Do advertisements for computers appear in women's fashion magazines?
2. *Measurement Questions:* "How large/small/fast/much/many/bright is X?"	Here researchers want to measure the extent to which something occurs (percentages) or the degree or size of a phenomenon	How hot is the surface of Venus?	What percentage of homeless persons suffer from mental illness?	What percentage of children's birthday cards currently displayed at local stores contain gender stereotyping?
3. *Comparison Questions:* "Is X greater/less than Y or different from Y?"	Researchers frequently want to study how two events, groups, or phenomena differ according to greater or less amounts of some measure	Is radiation from Io greater in volcanic areas than in nonvolcanic areas?	Is the incidence of anorexia greater among middle-class women than among working-class women?	Do humanities majors report fewer study hours per week than nonhumanities majors?
4. *Correlation Questions:* "If X varies, does Y vary?"	This is a more complex kind of comparison question in which researchers determine whether differences in X are accompanied by corresponding differences in Y	Does the aggression level of male rats vary with testosterone levels in their blood?	Do students' evaluations of their teachers vary with the grades they expect to receive for the course?	Does students' satisfaction with university food services vary with their family size?
5. *Experimental Questions:* "Does a variation in X cause a variation in Y?"*	Here researchers move beyond correlations to try to determine the direct causes of a certain phenomenon	If male rats are forced into stress situations to compete for food, will the level of testosterone in their blood increase?	Will preschool children taken shopping after watching TV commercials for high-sugar cereals ask for such cereals at a higher rate than children in a control group who did not see the commercials?	Will persons shown a Monsanto ad promoting biotech corn reveal a more favorable attitude toward genetically modified foods than a control group not shown the ad?

** Direct experiments can be difficult to design and conduct in some of the social sciences. Also, experimental questions often raise ethical issues whenever experiments place human subjects in psychological stress, cause physical pain and suffering to laboratory animals, or otherwise bring harm to individuals.* *See pages 259–260 for further discussion of ethical issues in research.*

FOR WRITING AND DISCUSSION

Generating Research Questions

This exercise encourages you to brainstorm ideas for your own research question. The goal here is not to settle on a research question but to get a feeling for the range of options you might choose for your own investigation.

Background: The following list shows how students might use the five categories in Table 10.1 to frame questions about the exercise habits of college students.

CATEGORIES OF RESEARCH QUESTIONS APPLIED TO STUDY OF EXERCISE HABITS

1. *Existence Questions ("Does X exist in domain Y?"):* Does "yoga" appear as an exercise choice among the respondents to this questionnaire?
2. *Measurement Questions ("How large/small/fast/much/many/bright is X?"):* On average, how many hours per week do female (and male) college students devote to physical exercise? Or, what percentage of females (and males) report five or more hours per week of physical exercise?
3. *Comparison Questions ("Is X greater/less than Y or different from Y?"):* Do a higher percentage of male college students than female college students report five or more hours per week of physical exercise?
4. *Correlation Questions ("If X varies, does Y vary?"):* Do students who report studying more than thirty hours per week exercise more than students who report studying fewer than thirty hours per week?
5. *Experimental Questions ("Does a variation in X cause a variation in Y?"):* Will an experimental group of students asked to keep an exercise log exercise more regularly than a control group of students who do not keep such a log?

Individual task: Spend ten minutes thinking of possible ideas for your own research project. Try using the five categories of questions to stimulate your thinking, but don't worry whether a question exactly fits one category or the other. Remember to ask determinate questions that can be answered by yes/no or by a single number, percentage, or range of numbers.

Group task: Working in small groups or as a whole class, share your initial ideas, using your classmates' proposed research questions to stimulate more of your own thinking. Your goal is to generate a wide range of possible research questions you might like to investigate.

Collecting Data through Observation, Interviews, or Questionnaires

Once you have formulated your research question, you need to develop a plan for collecting the needed data. In this section, we give you suggestions for conducting your research through direct observation, interviews, or questionnaires.

Using Observation to Gather Information

The key to successful observation of human behavior or other natural phenomena is having a clear sense of your purpose combined with advance preparation. We offer the following practical strategies for carrying out observational research:

STRATEGIES for Using Observation to Collect Data

Strategies	What to Do	Comments
Determine the purpose and scope of your observation.	Think ahead about the subject of your observation and the details, behaviors, or processes involved. Make a list.	Some phenomena can be observed only once; others can be observed regularly. If you plan on a series of observations, the first one can provide an overview or baseline, while subsequent observations can enable you to explore your subject in more detail or note changes over time.
Make arrangements ahead of time.	In making requests, state clearly who you are and what the purpose of your observation is. Be cordial in your requests and in your thanks after your observations.	If you need to ask permission or get clearance for your observation, be sure to do so long before you plan to start the observation.
Take clear, usable notes while observing.	Bring note-taking materials—either a laptop or plenty of paper, a clipboard or binder with a hard surface for writing, and good writing utensils. Document your notes with exact indications of location, time, and names and titles of people (if relevant).	Make sure that your notes are easy to read and well labeled with helpful headings.
Go through your notes soon afterward.	Fill in gaps and elaborate where necessary. You might then write a first draft while your observations are still fresh in your mind.	Don't let too much time go by, or you will not be able to reconstruct details or recapture thoughts you had while observing.

Here are two examples of how students have used direct observation to conduct research:

- A student wanting to know how often people violated a "Do Not Walk on the Grass" sign on her campus observed a lawn for one week during mornings between classes and counted persons who took a shortcut across the grass rather than followed the sidewalks. She also recorded the gender of shortcut-takers to see if there were any gender differences in this behavior.

- A student research team hypothesized that episodes of the cartoon *SpongeBob SquarePants* would contain fewer gender stereotypes than episodes of a 1930s Mickey Mouse cartoon. The researchers watched the cartoons in one-minute segments and for each segment recorded the presence of behaviors that they categorized as stereotypical or nonstereotypical male behavior and stereotypical or nonstereotypical female behavior. (You can read their research report and their poster in the Readings section of this chapter.)

Conducting Interviews

Interviews can be an effective way to gather field research information. They can range from formal interviews lasting thirty or more minutes to quick, informal interviews, in which the researcher hopes only for brief answers to a few key questions. The researcher might even conduct an interview over the telephone, without a face-to-face meeting. As an example of informal interviews, consider the hypothetical case of a researcher investigating why customers at a local grocery store choose to buy or not buy organic vegetables. This researcher might ask persons buying vegetables if they would be willing to be briefly interviewed. (The researcher would need to be very polite, keep the interviews brief, and get the store manager's permission in advance.)

In other kinds of field research studies, you might rely on longer, formal interviews with persons whose background or knowledge is relevant to your research question. Although asking a busy professional for an interview can be intimidating, many experts are generous with their time when they encounter a student who is interested in their field. To make interviews as useful as possible, we suggest several strategies.

STRATEGIES
for Conducting an Interview

Strategies	What to Do	Comments
	Before the Interview	
Consider your purpose.	Determine what you hope to learn from the interview. Think about your research question and the aim of the paper you are planning to write.	This thinking will help you focus the interview.
Learn about your subject.	Research important subjects related to your research question and the person you will be interviewing. Although you needn't become an expert, you should be conversant about your subject.	Ideally, interviews should give you knowledge or perspectives unavailable in books or articles.

(continued)

Strategies	What to Do	Comments
	Before the Interview (*continued*)	
Formulate your questions.	Develop a range of questions, including short-answer questions like the following: How long have you been working in this field? What are the typical qualifications for this job? Create open-ended questions, which should be the heart of your interview. For example: What changes have you seen in this field? What solutions have you found to be the most successful in dealing with ... ? What do you see as the causes of ... ? Questions framed in this way will elicit the information you need but still allow the interviewee to answer freely.	Be as thorough with your questions as possible. Most likely you will have only one chance to interview this person. Avoid yes-or-no questions that can stall conversation with a one-word answer. Avoid leading questions. The more you lead the interviewee to the answers you want, the less valid your research becomes.
Gather your supplies.	If you plan to record the interview, be sure to get your interviewee's permission, and spend time familiarizing yourself with recording equipment. Bring a laptop or pad of paper to take notes.	Using a recorder allows you to focus your attention on the substance of the interview. Most likely, you will want to take notes even if you are recording.
	During the Interview	
Manage your time.	Arrive on time. Also agree to a time limit for the interview and stick to it. (If necessary, you can request a second interview, or your interviewee may be willing to stay longer.)	You will show a lack of professionalism if you are not particularly careful to respect the interviewee's time.
Be courteous.	Thank the interviewee for his or her time. During the interview, listen attentively. Don't interrupt.	Your attitude during the interview can help set up a cordial and comfortable relationship between you and the person you are interviewing.
Take notes.	Take down all the main ideas and be accurate with quoted material. Don't hesitate to ask if you are unsure about a fact or statement or if you need to double-check what the person intended to say.	If you are recording the interview, you can double-check quotations later.
Be flexible.	Ask your questions in a logical order, but also be sensitive to the flow of the conversation. If the interviewee rambles away from the question, don't jump in too fast.	You may learn something valuable from the seeming digression. You may even want to ask unanticipated questions if you have delved into new ideas.

Strategies	What to Do	Comments
	After the Interview	
Go through your notes soon afterward.	No matter how vivid the words are in your mind, take time *very* soon after the interview to go over your notes, filling in any gaps, or to transcribe your tape.	What may seem unforgettable at the moment is all too easy to forget later. Do not trust your memory alone.

Using Questionnaires

In constructing a questionnaire, your goal is to elicit responses that are directly related to your research question and that will give you the data you need to answer the question. The construction of a questionnaire—both its wording and its arrangement on the page—is crucial to its success. As you design your questionnaire, imagine respondents with only limited patience and time. Keep your questionnaire clear, easy to complete, and as short as possible, taking care to avoid ambiguous sentences. Proofread it carefully, and pilot it on a few volunteer respondents so that you can eliminate confusing spots. Some specific examples of types of questions often found on questionnaires are shown in Figure 10.2.

When you have designed the questions you will ask, write an introductory comment that explains the questionnaire's purpose. If possible, encourage responses by explaining why the knowledge gained from the questionnaire will be beneficial to others. Make your completed questionnaire as professionally attractive and easy to read and fill out as possible. As an example, Figure 10.3 shows a questionnaire, introduced with an explanatory comment, prepared by a student investigating the parking problems of commuter students on her campus.

When you distribute your questionnaire, try to obtain a random sample. For example, if you assessed student satisfaction with a campus cafeteria by passing out questionnaires to those eating in the cafeteria at noon on a particular day, you might not achieve a random sampling of potential cafeteria users. You would miss those who avoid the cafeteria because they hate it; also, the distribution of noon users of the cafeteria might be different from the distribution of breakfast or dinner users. Another problem with sampling is that people who feel strongly about an issue are more likely to complete a questionnaire than those who don't feel strongly. The student who prepared the parking questionnaire for example, is likely to get a particularly high rate of response from those most angry about parking issues, and thus her sample might not be representative of all commuter students.

In some situations, random sampling may be unfeasible. For the assignment for this chapter, check with your instructor whether a "convenience sample" would be acceptable (for example, you would pass out questionnaires to persons in your dorm or in your class as a matter of convenience, even though these persons would not represent a random sample of the larger population).

FIGURE 10.2 Types of Questions Used in Questionnaires

1. Fixed-choice question

Compared to other campuses with which you are familiar, this campus's use of alcohol is (mark one):

—— greater than other campuses'
—— less than other campuses'
—— about the same as other campuses'

2. Open-ended question

How would you say alcohol use on this campus compares to other campuses?

Comment: Fixed-choice questions are easier to tabulate and report statistically; open-ended questions can yield a wider variety of insights but are impractical for large numbers of respondents.

3. Question with operationally defined rather than undefined term

Undefined term: Think back over the last two weeks. How many times did you engage in binge drinking?
Operationally defined term: Think back over the last two weeks. How many times have you had four or more drinks in a row?

Comment: An "operational definition" states empirically measurable criteria for a term. In the first version of the question, the term "binge drinking" might mean different things to different persons. Moreover, respondents are apt to deny being binge drinkers given that it is an unflattering categorization. In the revised question, the term "binge drinking" is replaced with an observable and measurable behavior; respondents are more apt to give an honest response.

4. Category question

What is your current class standing?

—— freshman
—— sophomore
—— junior
—— senior
—— other (please specify)

Comment: In category questions, it is often helpful to have an "Other" category for respondents who do not fit neatly into any of the other categories.

5. Scaled-answer question

This campus has a serious drinking problem (circle one):

strongly agree	agree	neither agree nor disagree	disagree	strongly disagree
5	4	3	2	1

How much drinking goes on in your dormitory on Friday or Saturday nights?

a lot	some	not much	none

Comment: Although scaled-answer questions are easy to tabulate and are widely used, the data can be skewed by the subjective definitions of each respondent (one person's "a lot" may be another person's "not much").

FIGURE 10.3 Example of a Questionnaire

Dear Commuter Student:
I am conducting a study aimed at improving the parking situation for commuter students. Please take a few moments to complete the following questionnaire, which will provide valuable information that may lead to specific proposals for easing the parking problems of commuters. If we commuter students work together with the university administration, we may be able to find equitable solutions to the serious parking issues we face. Please return the questionnaires to the box I have placed at the south entrance to the Student Union Building.

1. When do you typically arrive on campus?
   Before 8 A.M. ______
   Between 8 A.M. and 9 A.M. ______
   Between 9 A.M. and noon ______
   During noon hour ________
   Between 1 P.M. and 5 P.M. _____
   Between 5 P.M. and 7 P.M. _____
   After 7 P.M. _____
2. How frequently do you have problems finding a place to park?
   Nearly every day ____
   About half the time ____
   Occasionally ____
   Almost never ____
3. When the first lot you try is full, how long does it typically take you to find a place to park (for those who buy a commuter parking permit)?
   Less than 10 minutes ___
   10–15 minutes ___
   More than 15 minutes ___
4. For those who use street parking only, how long does it take you to find a place to park?
   Less than 10 minutes ___
   10–15 minutes ___
   More than 15 minutes ___
5. Do you currently carpool?
   Yes ____
   No ____
6. The university is considering a proposal to raise parking fees for single-driver cars and lower them for car pools. If you don't currently carpool, how difficult would it be to find a car-pool partner?
   Impossible ___
   Very difficult ___
   Somewhat difficult ___
   Fairly easy ___
7. If finding a car-pool partner would be difficult, why?
   Few fellow students live in my neighborhood ___
   Few fellow students match my commuting hours ___
   Other ___
8. What suggestions do you have for improving the parking situation for commuter students?

FOR WRITING AND DISCUSSION

Developing a Research Plan

Write a possible research question that you might investigate for your project. Working individually, consider ways that you might use one of the research methods just discussed—observation, interviews, or questionnaires—to answer your question. Begin designing your research plan, including procedures for observations or formulation of questions for your questionnaire or interviews. Then, working in small groups or as a whole class, share your brainstorming. Your goal is to develop the beginnings of a research plan. Help each other talk through the stages of a possible investigation.

Reporting Your Results in Text, Tables, and Graphs

Once you have completed your research and tabulated your findings, you are ready to write the "Results" section of your paper, which reports your findings in words often supplemented with tables and graphs.* Do not report raw data. Rather, create composite results by tabulating totals or calculating averages and report these results in words and in appropriate graphics. Try to report your data in such a way that readers can quickly see whether the data support or do not support your hypothesis. In reporting results, your aim is to create a scientific *ethos* that is objective and unbiased. Your purpose is to help readers understand your findings concisely and clearly. In this section we will first explain the kinds of graphics you might choose for your report. Then we'll explain some of the skills needed to make sure that your words and graphics tell the same story in a clear, easy-to-follow manner.

For a discussion of *ethos,* see Chapter 3, Concept 9.

Tables

Halfway between a picture and a list, a table presents data in columns (vertical groupings) and rows (horizontal groupings), thereby allowing readers to see relationships relatively quickly. Table 10.2 displays data of a student researcher who

TABLE 10.2 Number, Percentage, and Purchase Choices of Impulse Buyers

		Impulse Buyers		Number of Shoppers Who Purchased Each Item (Some shoppers bought more than one item.)				
	Total Shoppers	Number	Percent	Magazine	Tabloid	Candy/gum/cigarettes	Toy	Other
Day 1	75	22	29	18	10	10	5	7
Day 2	107	38	36	26	12	20	9	11
Day 3	90	29	30	21	12	17	8	10
Total	272	89	33	65	34	47	22	28

*In professional reports, the "Results" section also includes a statistical analysis of the data to determine confidence levels and statistical significance. For your assignment for this chapter, you do not need to do a statistical analysis, which requires a course in statistics.

was investigating the number of people who bought "impulse items" in the checkout line at a local grocery store. She wanted to see how often people added to their carts items such as magazines, tabloids, candy, novelty toys, or convenience goods like mini-flashlights or nail files.

Line Graphs

A line graph can tell a story more dramatically than a table because it makes the relationship between two variables immediately visible. It achieves this effect by converting numerical data into a series of points on a grid and connecting them to create flat, rising, or falling lines. Figure 10.4 shows a line graph created by a student interested in interviewing international students about their experiences in the humanities college at his university. As background, he obtained registration data from his university's Web site and created this graph, which shows enrollment patterns for international students from 1998 to 2008 within the humanities college. By convention, the horizontal axis contains the predictable, known variable, such as time or some other sequence, arranged in a predictable order. The vertical axis contains the unpredictable variable that forms the graph's story.

Pie Charts

Pie charts, as their name suggests, depict different percentages of a total (the pie) in the form of slices. Pie charts tell the story of how the whole is divided into different-sized parts. Pie charts can tell a particularly dramatic story if one piece of the pie is larger or smaller than one would expect. Two pie charts placed side by side can often tell the story of how two different cases divide up the pie differently. Figure 10.5 was created by a team of students investigating why customers chose a Starbucks coffee shop close to their campus as opposed to a locally owned coffee shop several blocks away. They used side-by-side pie charts to show the importance of "atmosphere" at the locally owned shop, Café Vita, versus "convenience" for customers at Starbucks.

FIGURE 10.4 International Student Enrollment in Humanities College, 1998–2008

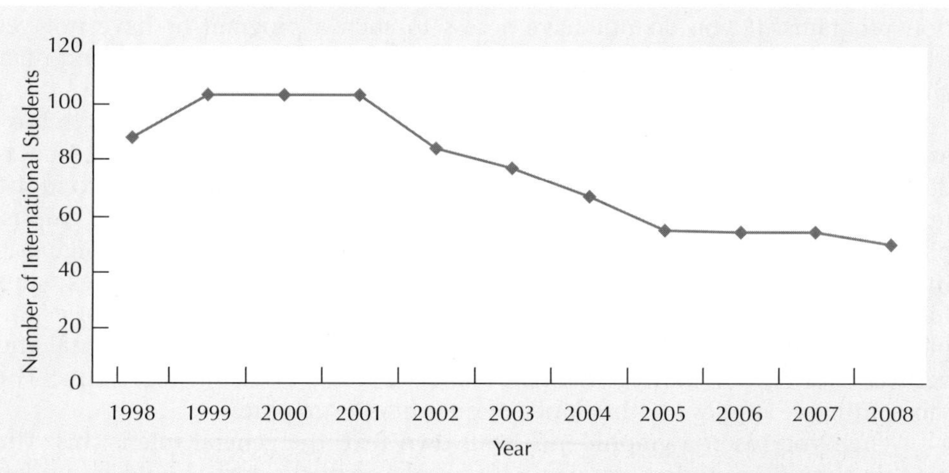

FIGURE 10.5 Factors That Are Important to Customers When Choosing Starbucks or Café Vita

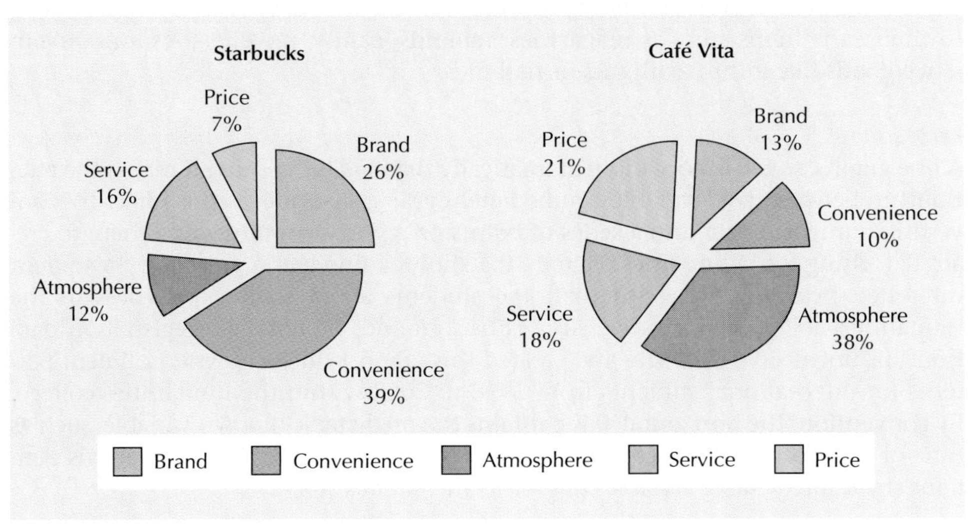

Bar Graphs

Bar graphs use columns of varying lengths to contrast two or more quantities. They quickly allow readers to make comparisons between different groups across a variable such as time. The key to clarity is the wording of the title (which tells the reader what the bar graph is supposed to show), the labels on the horizontal and vertical axes, and the legend, which tells readers what each column represents. The legends often make use of color, shadings, or different patterns of hash marks. The bar graph in Figure 10.6 was created by a student investigating students' responses to the question, "If you were to achieve the 'good life,' what would be your ideal car?" (The phrase "N=35" in the title indicates the number of respondents was thirty-five.)

Incorporating Graphics into Your Research Report

Quantitative graphics can now be made quickly using spreadsheet or presentation programs. If you do not have access to such a program or have not yet learned how to use them, you can also make your graphics with pencil and ruler and tape or scan them into your document.

In newspapers and popular magazines, writers often include graphics in boxes or sidebars without specifically referring to them in the text. However, in academic papers, graphics are always labeled, numbered, titled, and referred to in the text. By convention, tables are listed as "Tables," while line graphs, bar graphs, pie charts, or any other kinds of drawings or photographs are labeled as "Figures." In addition to numbering and labeling, each graphic needs a title that explains fully what information is being displayed. In the title for a bar graph, for example, some part of the title has to correspond to the labels on the horizontal and vertical axes and to the legends that show what each column represents. The same principle applies to other kinds of quantitative graphics.

When you insert a graphic into your own text, the general rule is this: The graphic should be understandable without the text; the text should be understandable without the graphic; and the text and graphic should tell the same story. Refer explicitly to each of your graphics and explain to your readers what you want them to see in the graphic—a referencing convention called "independent redundancy." You can easily understand this principle if you imagine giving a PowerPoint presentation. When a graphic comes on the screen, you would tell the audience in words what the graphic signifies, and you would probably also point to appropriate places on the graphic. The same principle applies in writing as shown in Figure 10.6, which illustrates how the author who produced the bar graph on "dream car preferences" inserted that graphic into his own text.

FIGURE 10.6 Example of a Student Text with Referenced Graphic

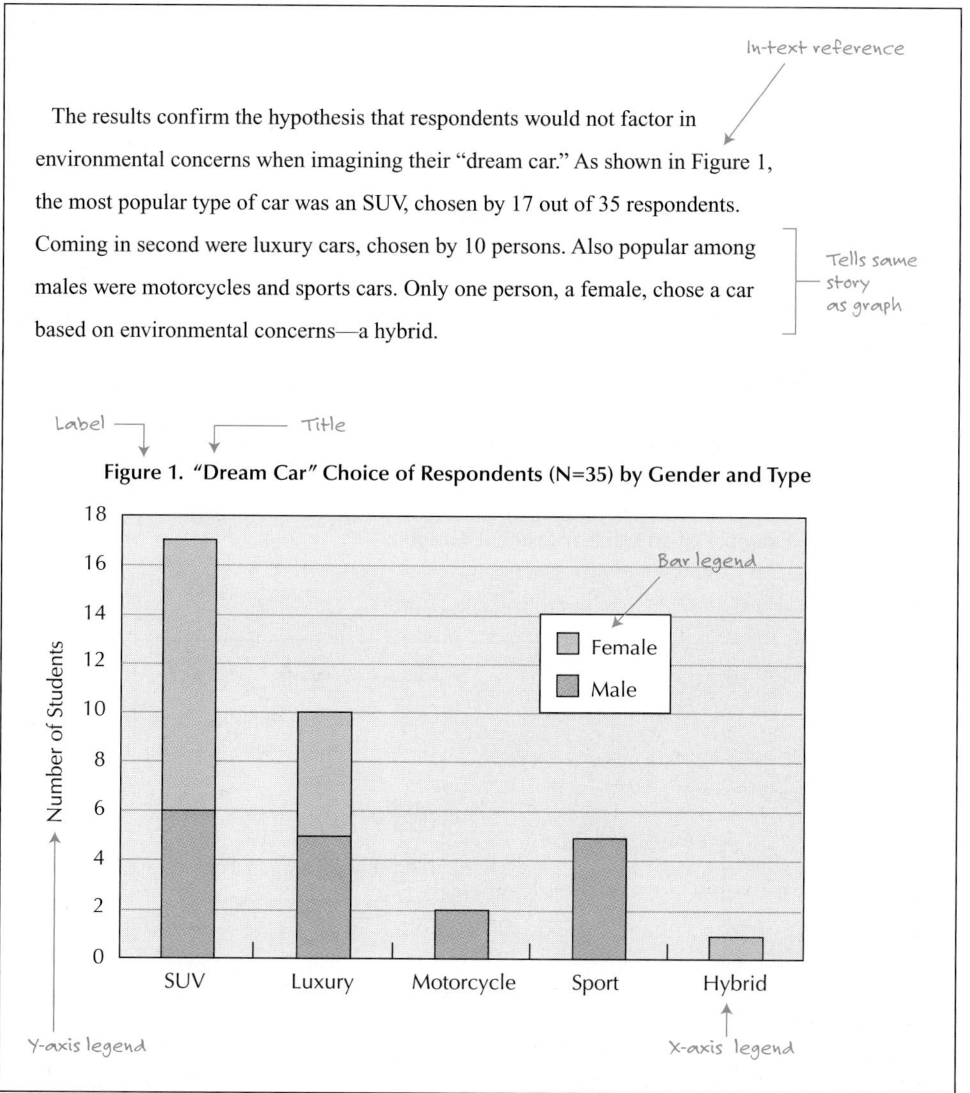

The results confirm the hypothesis that respondents would not factor in environmental concerns when imagining their "dream car." As shown in Figure 1, the most popular type of car was an SUV, chosen by 17 out of 35 respondents. Coming in second were luxury cars, chosen by 10 persons. Also popular among males were motorcycles and sports cars. Only one person, a female, chose a car based on environmental concerns—a hybrid.

FOR WRITING AND DISCUSSION

Revising a Poor Graph

Background: A frequent problem with graphics designed by inexperienced writers is unclear purpose (What is this graphic supposed to show? What is its story?). Often this confusion comes from a missing or incomplete title, from missing or misleading labels for the *x*- and *y*-axes, or from inclusion of extraneous information.

Your task: Working in small groups or as a whole class, explain what is confusing about the graphic in Figure 10.7. The writer's purpose is to explain respondents' answers to the question, "Which fast-food restaurant produces the best chicken nuggets?" What do you think the *x*- (horizontal) axis and *y*- (vertical) axis are supposed to represent? How could you rewrite the title and the axis labels in order to make the graphic easier to comprehend at a glance? Assuming that the vertical axis represents number of respondents, try telling this story using a pie chart (based on percentages) rather than a bar graph.

Analyzing Your Results

The "Discussion" section of a research report is devoted to the writer's analysis of the results. This section most resembles a thesis-governed essay addressing an open-ended problem. Think of your Discussion section as answering the following question: Now that I have reported my results, what do these results mean? (What do I learn from the results? How do they confirm or disconfirm my initial assumptions and theories? How are these results important or significant?)

The Discussion section should open with a thesis statement that indicates whether your findings support or do not support your original hypothesis and that summarizes or forecasts the other main points of your analysis. Here is an

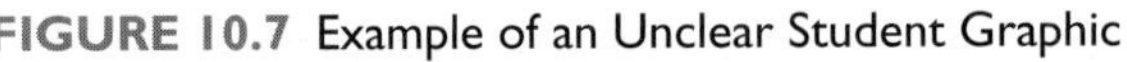

FIGURE 10.7 Example of an Unclear Student Graphic

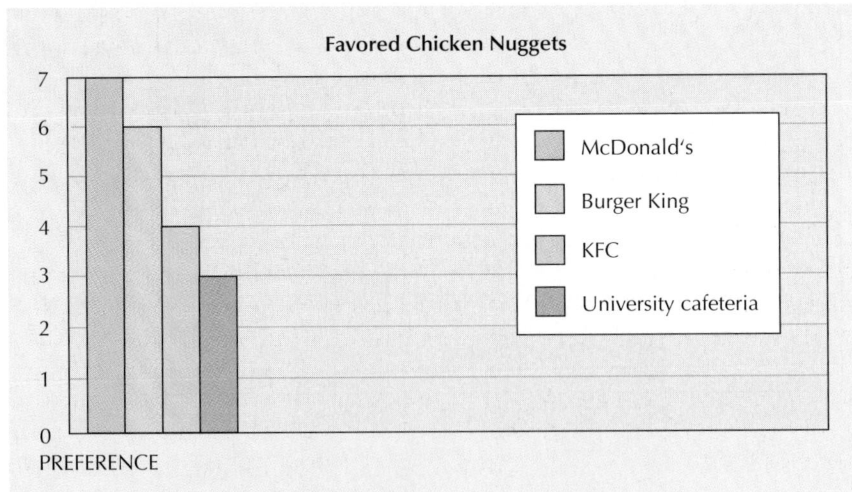

example of how a thesis statement from a professional research report entitled "Marital Disruption and Depression in a Community Sample" is connected to the research problem in the Introduction:

DESCRIPTION OF PROBLEM FROM "INTRODUCTION"

> *Explanation of problem*: "Researchers have long known that recently divorced persons tend to show high degrees of depression, but the direction of causation is unknown: Does divorce cause depression or does depression cause divorce?"
>
> *Research question*: "Does marital disruption contribute to higher levels of depression in recently divorced persons?"
>
> *Hypothesis*: "Marital disruption contributes to higher levels of depression in recently divorced persons."

Early in the Discussion section, the authors create an explicit thesis statement that directly responds to the hypothesis:

THESIS STATEMENT FROM THE "DISCUSSION" SECTION

> "According to the results, marital disruption does in fact cause a significant increase in depression compared to pre-divorce levels within a period of three years after the divorce."

Although there are no formulas for the Discussion section of a research report, most reports contain the following four conventional features:

- Identification of significant patterns and speculation about causes
- Implications and significance of the results
- Limitations of the study
- Suggestions for further research

Let's look at each in turn.

Identification of Significant Patterns and Speculation about Causes

The first part of a Discussion section often points out patterns that the researcher considers significant. The most important patterns are those that bear directly on the researcher's hypothesis. For example, in studying exercise habits of college students, you might find that, contrary to your hypothesis, women exercise more than men. Depending on other findings derived from your questionnaire, you might note additional patterns—for example, that persons claiming to be on a diet exercise more than those who don't or that persons who are regular runners tend to spend more time studying than do persons who play lots of pickup team sports.

The discovery of significant patterns leads naturally to speculation about causes. Understanding how a certain event or condition leads to other events or conditions contributes to our knowledge of the world and often may have practical consequences for improving the world or our situation in it. Because of scientists' interest in the underlying causes of a phenomenon, researchers typically use the Discussion section of a report to speculate about the causes of significant patterns. Often a researcher suggests several different, alternative explanations of the data, each explanation opening up avenues for further research. As you contemplate questions raised by your research, consider the following ways that data may suggest causality:

- *Causality induced from a recurring pattern*: If you regularly start to sneeze after petting a cat but not after petting a dog, you can induce, as an initial hypothesis, that you are allergic in some way to cats even though you can't directly explain the mechanism. You were able to make this induction only after you recognized a pattern. In the social sciences, descriptive studies help reveal such patterns. For example, psychologists attempting to understand the causes of anorexia have discovered that many (but not all) anorexics come from perfectionist, highly work-oriented homes that emphasize duty and responsibility. This frequently recurring element is thus a suspected causal factor leading to anorexia.
- *Causality hypothesized from correlations*: *Correlation* is a statistical term indicating the probability that two events or phenomena will occur together. For example, various studies have shown a correlation between creativity and left-handedness. (The percentage of left-handed people within a sample of highly creative people is considerably higher than the percentage of left-handed people in the general population.) But does being left-handed cause a person to be more creative? Or does some other factor cause both left-handedness and creativity? The presence of this puzzling correlation leads scientists to speculate about its causes and to design further research that might pin down an answer.
- *Causality demonstrated through experimental control of variables*: In some cases, scientists try to resolve causal questions through direct experiment. By controlling variables and testing them one at a time, scientists can sometimes isolate causal factors quite precisely. For example, through experimentation, scientists now know that a particular bacterium causes typhoid fever and that particular antibiotics will kill that bacterium. Controlled experiments in psychology have demonstrated that prolonged deprivation of sunlight can cause depression in certain individuals (a condition known as *seasonal affective disorder*).

We have mentioned these approaches to causal analysis to stimulate your thinking about possible patterns you might see in your data or about interesting or puzzling correlations. These in turn might lead you to speculate why your findings turned out as they did or suggest implications for further study.

FOR WRITING AND DISCUSSION

Analyzing Results

Working in small groups or as a whole class, speculate on possible explanations for each of the following phenomena:

1. White female teenagers are seven times more likely to smoke than African-American female teenagers (a finding based on several professional studies).
2. When asked about the "car of their dreams," ninety-one percent of students polled listed an SUV, luxury car, or high-performance sports car. Only three percent specifically mentioned a fuel-conserving vehicle such as a hybrid.

Implications and Significance of the Results

Another typical portion in the Discussion section focuses on the implications and significance of your research—the "So what?" question. What is important about this research? How does it advance our knowledge? What, if any, are its practical applications? For example, the discovery that white female teenagers smoke at a higher rate than African-American female teenagers could lead to speculation on ways to reduce teenage smoking among white females or offer clues into the psyches of white versus African-American women. (One theory proposed in the scientific literature is that white women are more obsessed with weight and body image than African-American women and see smoking as a way to suppress appetite). Or, to take our other example, the study showing that only five percent of students mentioned a fuel-conserving car as their "dream car" could lead to speculation on how consumer preferences might be changed to promote the goal of environmental preservation.

Limitations of the Study

Another common feature of the Discussion section is the researcher's skeptical analysis of his or her own research methods and data. It may seem counterintuitive that authors would explicitly point out problems with their own research, but this honesty is part of the scientific *ethos* aimed at advancing knowledge. By nature, scientists are skeptical and cautious. Typically, authors go out of their way to mention possible flaws and other limitations of their studies and to caution other scholars against overgeneralizing from their research. They might refer to problems in sample size or duration of the study, flaws in the research design that might contaminate results, possible differences between an experimental group and a control group, or lack of statistical confidence in the data.

Your own research for this assignment will probably exhibit a number of problems that would limit other researchers' confidence in your findings. To increase your own *ethos* as a scientific writer, you should make these objections yourself as part of the Discussion section.

Suggestions for Further Research

At the conclusion of their Discussion sections, researchers often suggest avenues for future research. Typically they show how their own research raises new questions that could be profitably explored. You might try this approach at the conclusion of your own Discussion section by mentioning one or more questions that you think would be the logical next steps for researchers interested in your area of study.

Following Ethical Standards

When research involves human subjects, researchers must be scrupulous in adhering to ethical standards. In the past, there have been horrible cases of unethical research using human subjects. Among the most notorious are Nazi medical experiments on Jews in concentration camps during World War II or the Tuskegee syphilis study in which four hundred low-income African-American males with syphilis were denied treatment—even though a cure for syphilis had been discovered—because the researchers wanted to continue studying the progress of the untreated disease. Likewise, certain psychological experiments, once highly regarded in the middle of the twentieth century, are now considered by many to have been unethical. For example, the famous Milgram experiments on obedience to authority revealed the extent to which research subjects would administer what they thought were painful electric shocks to another human being when told to do so by an authority figure. This experiment depended on deception: The research subjects were unsuspecting participants in a faked laboratory scenario designed by the researchers (the authority figure and the screaming human being receiving the shock were really actors).

As a response to problems like these, in 1979 the National Institutes of Health (a federal agency) established ethical guidelines for biomedical research, instigating widespread efforts among all scientific organizations to develop ethical standards for any kind of research using human subjects. Today, almost all colleges and universities have Institutional Review Boards that provide oversight for such research. In the case of your own research, for example, consider how certain items on a questionnaire might cause stress to a potential respondent or be considered an invasion of his or her privacy. It's one thing to ask persons if they prefer a Mac to a PC; it is quite another to ask them if they have ever cheated on an exam or gotten drunk at a party. As a general rule, the kind of first-time research that you do for this writing project will not require oversight from your university's Institutional Review Board, but you should nevertheless adhere to the following guidelines:

- *Obtain informed consent.* Explain to potential respondents the purpose of your research, your methods for collecting data, and the way your data will be used. In the case of interviews, reach agreement on whether the respondent will be named or anonymous. Obtain direct permission for recording the session.
- *Explain that participation in your study is voluntary.* Do not apply any kind of personal or social pressure that would make it difficult for a respondent to say no.
- *In the case of questionnaires, explain that no respondent will be individually identified and that results will be reported as statistical aggregates.* If possible, ensure that all responses are anonymous to you (don't try to identify handwriting or otherwise match responses to an identified individual). If such anonymity is impossible (for example, you might be conducting an oral survey), then assure the respondent that you will keep all answers confidential.
- *If any of your respondents are minors, check with your instructor because human-subject regulations are particularly strict in such instances.* Parents or guardians generally have to give consent for interviews with their children.

WRITING PROJECT

An Empirical Research Report

The assignment for this project is a modified version of a standard empirical research report. We have omitted advanced features that would be required of upper-division science majors, such as a statistical analysis of the data or a review of previous research.

Write a scientific report in APA style that presents and analyzes your research findings in response to an empirical question about a phenomenon, behavior, or event. Your research can be based on direct observations, interviews, or questionnaires. Your report should have a title page and abstract, followed by the four main sections of a research report: Introduction, Method, Results, and Discussion. Also include a "References" page if you cite any sources.

An example of a student empirical research report written for this writing project is found on pages 274–281. In the Introduction section of this report, the student researchers present a brief review of the literature based on readings in gender identity that the instructor had used in class for this unit. In most cases, you will not be expected to have a similar section in your report.

Generating Ideas for Your Empirical Research Report

In addition to the ideas presented earlier in this chapter, here are some suggestions for possible research projects:

- Using a questionnaire to gather evidence, investigate students' usage patterns or levels of satisfaction with some aspect of student services on your campus (for example, computer labs, security escorting service, student newspaper, recreational facilities in the student union, study skills workshops).
- Using direct observation, investigate the degree of gender stereotyping in randomly selected children's birthday cards from a local card store or supermarket. Or investigate adherence to road rules at a chosen intersection, testing variables such as car type, weather conditions, time of day, amount of traffic, and so forth.
- Using interviews or a questionnaire, investigate the way students spend their time during a typical week (for example, studying, watching television, playing video games, logging into Facebook or MySpace, playing recreational sports, working, and so forth). You might also try to determine whether there are differences in these patterns depending upon factors such as gender, major, GPA, ethnicity, career aspirations, job status, part time/full time, or commuter/residential.

Designing Your Empirical Study and Drafting the Introduction and Method Sections

To design your study, you'll need to begin with a determinate research question that can be answered with yes/no or with a number, range of numbers, or percentage. Review pages 243–244 on asking a determinate research question.

We recommend that you write a draft of your Introduction and your Method section *before* you do the actual research. Drafting these sections first not only gets them out of the way but helps you think through your whole research process. Drafting your Introduction helps you understand your purpose more clearly and serves to clarify your research question and hypothesis. Drafting the Method section helps you plan exactly the steps you will take to do the research. If your research uses a questionnaire, make sure that it is carefully designed and revised before you start distributing it. Many research projects are ruined when the researcher discovers that the questionnaire had ambiguous questions or didn't ask the right questions. Before proceeding with the research itself, we recommend that you get preliminary feedback from peers or your instructor on the clarity of your research question and the design of your methods.

Doing the Research and Writing the Rest of the Report

Your next step is to do the research, record your raw numbers, and do the calculations needed for creating composite numbers that answer your research question. What follows is brief advice on drafting the rest of the report.

- *Writing the Results section:* This section simply presents your results both in words and in graphics. Reread pages 254–255 for advice on how to reference graphs and tables.
- *Writing the Discussion section:* Novice science writers often have trouble determining what goes in the Results section versus the Discussion section. The Results section answers the question, "What are my findings?" In contrast, the "Discussion" section addresses the question, "What do my findings mean?" It is the place where you bring your own critical thinking to bear on your results, creating your own thesis and argument. Reread page 242 to understand the typical features of a Discussion section.
- *Writing the Abstract:* When you have finished your draft, write a summary (no more than 120 words) of your report. In a few sentences indicate the broad problem you are investigating and the narrower purpose of your research; state your research question and your hypothesis. Then briefly describe your methods. In the last half of the abstract, describe your results and the extent to which they support your hypothesis. Conclude by suggesting the significance and implications of your research.

Revising Your Report

Because a scientific report follows a conventional structure, you should check your draft against the framework chart on page 241 (Figure 10.1). Make sure you have placed the right type of material in the appropriate section. Inside each section, revise for effective transitions, conciseness, and clarity. Getting feedback from peers can be very helpful.

Questions for Peer Review

In addition to the generic peer review questions explained in Chapter 17, Skill 4, ask your peer reviewers to address these questions:

TITLE AND ABSTRACT

1. Can you suggest improvements to the title to better focus the paper and pique reader interest?
2. Where does the abstract describe the research question and hypothesis? Where does it briefly summarize the methods? Where does it briefly state the results? Where does it discuss the significance of the results?
3. Can you suggest improvements for the abstract?

INTRODUCTION

4. Where does the writer present the research question(s) and hypothesis(es)? Can you suggest ways to improve the focus of the research question(s) and hypothesis(es)?
5. Where does the writer suggest the importance or significance of the research question? What overall suggestions might you make to improve the introduction?

METHOD

6. Will the writer's method provide the data necessary to answer the research question? How would you suggest the writer improve the overall research design to provide clearer or more focused findings?
7. If you had to replicate the writer's research, where might you have problems?

RESULTS

8. Are the writer's results clearly stated in both words and graphics?
9. Where does the writer demonstrate "independent redundancy" by referencing graphics and explaining in words what a graphic is supposed to show? Where does the writer need to explain a graphic's point in more detail?
10. Are the graphics well designed so that you can interpret them without reference to the text? What suggestions might you have for improving the titles, labels, legends, and overall design of graphics?

DISCUSSION

11. Where is the thesis statement that shows whether the research supports the hypothesis? Can you suggest ways to improve the thesis?
12. Where does the writer: (a) Identify significant patterns in the data and speculate about possible causes? (b) Show the significance and importance of the study? (c) Describe the limitations of the study? (d) Suggest ideas for future research or next steps?
13. What can you suggest to improve the writer's discussion of possible causes, significance, limitations, or future research? What additional ideas or insights can you offer?

Writing in Teams

Because professional field research is often done in teams, resulting in jointly authored articles, your instructor may ask you to work in teams to plan and carry out your research projects. In such cases, instructors sometimes ask team members to write their own individual reports and sometimes require jointly authored reports. If you are assigned to write in teams, consider our advice for team-writing as shown in the following strategies chart.

STRATEGIES for Team-Writing of Documents

Strategies	What the Team Does	What an Individual Does
Do as a group what teams do best. Do as individuals what individuals do best.	• Brainstorm ideas. • Set goals; plan and organize. • Develop research questions and methods. • Divide up the work. • Tabulate and analyze results. • Give feedback on ideas.	• Write drafts of each section. • Revise drafts of each section. • Edit for uniform voice and style. • Format the paper in APA style.
Talk through your document before you write it.	• Plan what will go into each section by taking notes on a large sheet of paper.	• Understand the contents of each section and feel qualified to write any section as assigned.
Draft individually; revise as a team.	• Assign the drafting of each section. • Review drafts for accuracy, completeness, clarity, development, and style. • Assign the revision of each section. • Repeat the team-review process for the revised draft.	• Volunteer to draft the section with which you are most comfortable. • Make copies of your drafted section for team members to review. • Revise the section you are assigned.
Prepare the final document.	• Assign one person to do the final editing so that it seems written in one voice. • Assign one person to edit for APA formatting and style.	• Edit and prepare the final draft. • Check APA formatting and style.

A Scientific Poster

WRITING PROJECT

Publish the results of your empirical research project as a scientific poster suitable for display at an undergraduate research conference. Your poster should combine visual and verbal elements to hook participants' interest in your project, show your research question and results, and provide a frame for further personal discussion of your research.

A professional example of a poster is shown in Figure 10.8, and a student example is found in the Readings section, page 284.

What Is a Scientific Poster?

A poster is a common means of disseminating research at a scientific conference.* Unlike a fifteen-minute talk to a sitting audience (which is the other means of presentation at a conference), a poster presentation occurs in a large room where dozens of researchers display their work on posters taped to walls or placed upright on tables. As researchers stand next to their displays, conference participants wander around the room, perusing posters and stopping to talk to researchers whose work particularly interests them. The advantage of a poster is that conference participants can talk in depth about the research, using the poster as a reference point.

Content of a Poster

The content of a scientific poster, like an abstract, follows the same structure as the research report. In fact, a poster is sometimes called an "illustrated abstract." The opening section indicates the large research problem being addressed and the specific objective of your research (your question and hypothesis). Another section briefly explains your methods. The main section—which is the payoff of your research—highlights your key results and their significance. Designing an effective graphic to display your results—and making it readable from four feet away—is crucial.

Features of an Effective Poster

The function of a poster is to highlight the results of your research while simultaneously attracting an audience by its visual interest and its rhetorically effective choices about what is included. Scientists often design their posters using publishing software (Microsoft PowerPoint can be used for making posters) and then print them on a poster-sized sheet using a plotting printer. A typical poster size is thirty-six by fifty-four inches, the largest sheet that most plotting printers can handle. If you don't

*Our discussion of posters is indebted to two excellent Web sites: Hess, G. R., K. Tosney, and L. Liegel. 2006. Creating Effective Poster Presentations. http://www.ncsu.edu/project/posters, visited July 25, 2007 and Purrington, C. B. 2006. Advice on designing scientific posters. http://www.swarthmore.edu/NatSci/cpurrin1/posteradvice.htm. Accessed July 25, 2007.

FIGURE 10.8 An Award-Winning Poster by Practicing Scientists

Southern Flounder Exhibit Temperature-Dependent Sex Determination

J. Adam Luckenbach*, John Godwin and Russell Borski
Department of Zoology, Box 7617, North Carolina State University, Raleigh, NC 27695

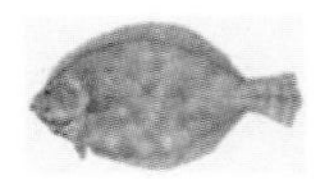

Introduction

Southern flounder (*Paralichthys lethostigma*) support valuable fisheries and show great promise for aquaculture. Female flounder are known to grow faster and reach larger adult sizes than males. Therefore, information on sex determination that might increase the ratio of female flounder is important for aquaculture.

Objective

This study was conducted to determine whether southern flounder exhibit temperature-dependent sex determination (TSD), and if growth is affected by rearing temperature.

Methods

- Southern flounder broodstock were strip spawned to collect eggs and sperm for *in vitro* fertilization.
- Hatched larvae were weaned from a natural diet (rotifers/*Artemia*) to high protein pelleted feed and fed until satiation at least twice daily.
- Upon reaching a mean total length of 40 mm, the juvenile flounder were stocked at equal densities into one of three temperatures 18, 23, or 28°C for 245 days.
- Gonads were preserved and later sectioned at 2-6 microns.
- Sex-distinguishing markers were used to distinguish males (spermatogenesis) from females (oogenesis).

Histological Analysis

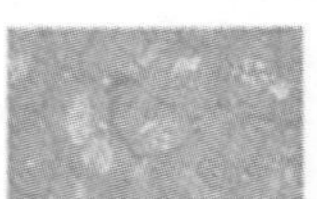

Male Differentiation

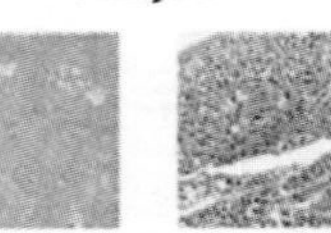

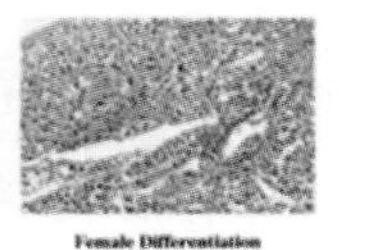

Female Differentiation

Temperature Affects Sex Determination

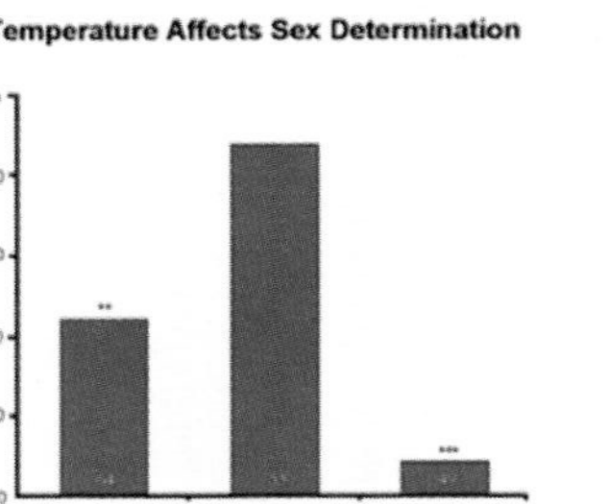

(**P < 0.01 and ***P < 0.001 represent significant deviations from a 1:1 male:female sex ratio)

Rearing Temperature Affects Growth

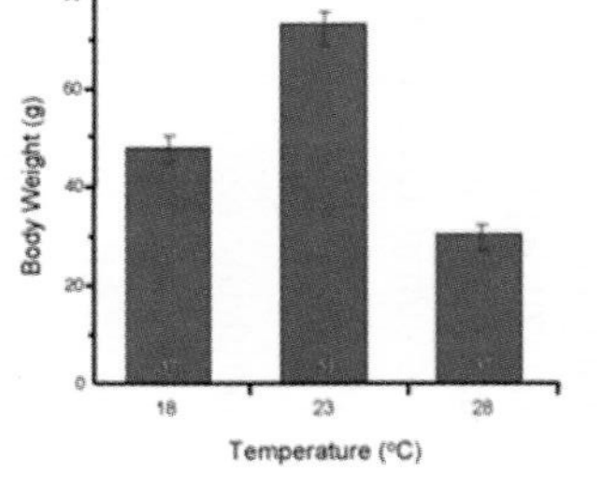

Growth Does Not Differ by Sex

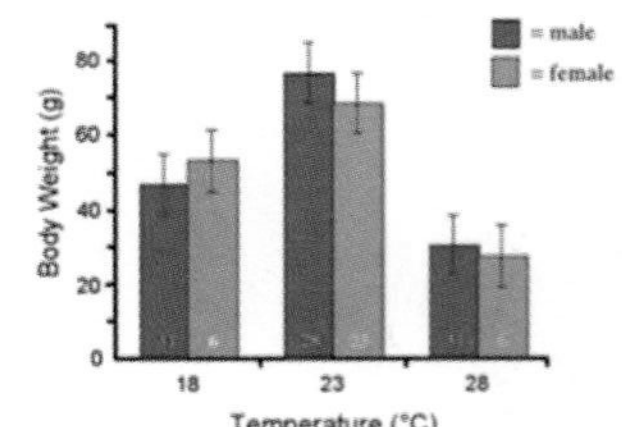

Results

- Sex was discernible in most fish greater than 120 mm long.
- High (28°C) temperature produced 4% females.
- Low (18°C) temperature produced 22% females.
- Mid-range (23°C) temperature produced 44% females.
- Fish raised at high or low temperatures showed reduced growth compared to those at the mid-range temperature.
- Up to 245 days, no differences in growth existed between sexes.

Conclusions

- These findings indicate that sex determination in southern flounder is temperature-sensitive and temperature has a profound effect on growth.
- A mid-range rearing temperature (23°C) appears to maximize the number of females and promote better growth in young southern flounder.
- Although adult females are known to grow larger than males, no difference in growth between sexes occurred in age-0 (< 1 year) southern flounder.

Acknowledgements

The authors acknowledge the Saltonstall-Kennedy Program of the National Marine Fisheries Service and the University of North Carolina Sea Grant College Program for funding this research. Special thanks to Lea Ware and Beth Shimps for help with the work.

have access to these professional tools, you can print sections of your poster using regular paper, arrange the sheets on poster board, and tape them in place.

An effective poster has the following features:

- Is readable from four feet away (text fonts should be at least 24 points; heading fonts should be 36 points)
- Uses phrases rather than sentences with text elements limited to fifty words or fewer
- Uses lots of white space with content arranged in columns
- Where appropriate, uses headings to tell your story
- Uses effective visual elements to supplement text, to create a balanced appearance, and to tell your story visually
- Has an easy-to-follow structure; readers know where to start and what sequence to follow

The most common poster mistake is using small fonts to cram in more text. An effective poster takes a "sound-bite" approach; it entices viewers into discussion with the research team rather than tries to substitute for the whole paper. Figure 10.8 shows an award-winning poster by practicing research scientists.

Designing, Creating, and Revising Your Poster

Begin by blocking sections of your poster for your Title, Introduction, Method, Results, and Discussion. Determine what graphics or drawings will make your poster visually attractive and meaningful. Then begin creating sound-bite headings and text, limiting text blocks to fifty words or fewer. Create several different mock-ups of your poster, in order to find a version that best conveys your research while remaining visually interesting and readable from four feet away. Note that researchers often change the title of the original research report for their posters, as well as captions for figures, in order to highlight key meanings (again following the sound-bite principle):

	Original Research Report	**Poster**
Title	A Comparison of Gender Stereotypes in *SpongeBob SquarePants* and a 1930s Mickey Mouse Cartoon	*SpongeBob SquarePants* Has Fewer Gender Stereotypes than Mickey Mouse
Figure caption	Figure 1: Stereotypical Behaviors by Gender in *SpongeBob SquarePants* and Mickey Mouse	More Non-Stereotypical Behavior for Males and Females in *SpongeBob SquarePants*

Also, a poster often recasts the writer's research question and hypothesis as an "objective":

OBJECTIVE STATEMENT FOR POSTER

To determine whether *SpongeBob SquarePants* has fewer gender stereotypes than a 1930s Mickey Mouse cartoon.

Once you have created a poster that satisfies your goals, you are ready for a peer review.

Questions for Peer Review

Ask your peer reviewers to address these questions:

1. Is the poster visually attractive with balanced placement of visual and verbal elements and with plenty of white space? Where are possible problem areas that make the poster cluttered, unattractive, or too text-oriented?
2. Are all elements of the poster, including the legends and axis labels on graphics, readable from four feet away? If not, how can the problem be resolved?
3. What features of the poster make it easy to navigate? Can you tell where to start reading and where to go next from beginning to end?
4. How do the headings and other visual elements highlight the key points of the research? Is the objective of the research (usually a recasting of the writer's question and hypothesis) clearly highlighted? Where might readers need more highlighting of the results and significance of the research?
5. Are there any places where the poster is confusing? What clarification do readers need?

READINGS

The following readings show a professional and a student example of a research report followed by a student example of a poster. The first reading, by authors from the Department of Health and Social Behavior in the Harvard School of Public Health, was published in the peer-reviewed scholarly journal *The American Journal of Public Health* in March 2000. You should find this article generally accessible even though the specific meaning of terms such as "odds ratios" or "confidence levels" may be unclear. As with most scientific articles, you can skim those portions of "Results" that focus on statistical analyses, moving on to those parts of the article that you can understand.

Gina Escamilla, B.A., Angie L. Cradock, M.S., and Ichiro Kawachi, M.D., Ph.D.

Women and Smoking in Hollywood Movies:

A Content Analysis

1 According to the Centers for Disease Control and Prevention, over one third (34.7%) of female high school students in a national survey reported smoking at least 1 cigarette in the previous month, up 10% since 1993 and 32% since 1991.[1] Cigarette smoking is initiated primarily in adolescence. Among adult regular smokers, 71% reported having formed the habit before the age of 18 years.[2]

2 Television and popular films have contributed to the allure of smoking. A recent study found that young adults smoked in about 75% of music videos.[3] Although tobacco industry documents suggest that manufacturers have not engaged in deliberate product placement in Hollywood movies since the late 1980s,[4] recent evidence indicates that smoking continues to be depicted at very high levels. Moreover, the gap between the prevalence of tobacco use in movies and in actual life has steadily widened through the 1990s.[5] A recent analysis of G-rated children's animated films found that more than two thirds featured tobacco or alcohol use in story plots, with no clear reference made to the adverse health consequences associated with these substances.[6]

3 Popular film actresses are likely to be role models for young women and adolescent girls. The way that movie stars portray cigarette smoking on the screen may influence young girls' attitudes toward the habit. In this study, we analyzed the portrayal of smoking by 10 leading Hollywood actresses.

Methods

Selection of Actresses

4 We selected 10 leading Hollywood actresses by surveying the 1997 issues of 5 popular magazines that had the highest readership among women aged 18 to 24 years, according to *Simmons Study of Media and Markets*.[7] Magazine titles from the "Special Interest" and "Women's Magazines" categories were selected if the editorial descriptions taken from *Bacon's Magazine Directory*[8] included 1 or more of the following key words or phrases: entertainment, contemporary or current, Hollywood, celebrity, film or movie, personality profiles, women in their 20s, or young women. All issues for the period January 1997 through December 1997 were obtained for the

magazines *Cosmopolitan, Glamour, Vogue, Vanity Fair*, and *Rolling Stone*. Each issue was analyzed for the appearance of female film stars. Advertisements were excluded, and the search was limited to women whose careers are primarily in film. The number of magazine appearances was tallied for each actress, and the 10 actresses with the greatest number of appearances were selected.

Selection of Films

5 A list of films starring each selected actress was generated from the Web site www.tvguide.com. This Web site, maintained by TV Guide Entertainment Network, provides information on the cast, credits, and reviews for some 35,000 movies. Five titles released between 1993 and 1997 were randomly selected for each of the 10 actresses. We excluded period dramas as well as movies in which the actresses did not play a lead or major supporting role. The title, year of release, rating (R, NC-17, PG, PG-13, G), and genre of each film were recorded.

Content Analysis

6 We followed the analytic approach described by Hazan et al.[9] Each film was divided into 5-minute intervals. The occurrence of smoking episodes in each interval was recorded on a coding sheet. We recorded both actual and implied smoking behavior (e.g., holding or smoking a lit or unlit tobacco product); the presence of cigarettes or other smoking paraphernalia (e.g., cigars, matches, and ashtrays); and environmental messages, including "no smoking" signs, tobacco advertising, and tobacco merchandise. Additionally, we recorded smoker characteristics (e.g., gender; whether lead, supporting, or other character); location (i.e., outdoors or in a bar, restaurant, home, or car); the social context of the event (i.e., smoking alone or with others and whether consideration was shown to nonsmokers). We also noted verbal and nonverbal tobacco messages (i.e., positive or negative consequences of smoking behavior and discussion about tobacco products, including positive, negative, or mixed reference to tobacco use). To establish interrater reliability, 5 films (10% of total sample) were randomly selected and independently rated by graduate student coders (G. Escamilla and A. L. Cradock). The coders had 99% agreement on all of the parameters examined regarding the depiction of smoking.

7 After viewing each film, the coders also completed a qualitative assessment of smoking themes and behaviors, addressing contextual issues such as the emotional valence attached to the smoking behavior and the significance of smoking for the character portrayed. All statistical analyses were performed with Stata.[10]

Results

8 The 50 films, representing approximately 96 hours of footage, were broken down into 1116 5-minute intervals (excluding introductions and credits). Of these, 317 (28.4%) of the intervals depicted smoking behavior (Table 1). Cigarettes were the most common tobacco product shown (23.9%). Over half of the smoking episodes (58.7%) occurred in the presence of others who were not smoking.

9 As Table 2 indicates, smoking was significantly more likely to be depicted in R-rated or unrated films than in PG/PG-13-rated films ($P < .001$). Although the percentage of lead actors or supporting actors shown smoking was similar for men and women (38% and 42%, respectively), sex differences were apparent according to the

TABLE 1 Depiction of Smoking Behavior and Paraphernalia, Smoking Context, and Location of Smoking Behaviors in 50 Hollywood Movies

	No. of 5-Min Intervals	Total 5-Min Movie Intervals, % (n = 1116)	Intervals Containing Smoking Behavior, % (n = 317)
Smoking behavior and paraphernalia			
Smoking (actual or implied) behavior	317	28.4	—
Cigarettes	267	23.9	—
Cigarette packs	64	5.7	—
Matches/lighter	108	9.7	—
Cigars, pipes, or smokeless tobacco	71	6.4	—
Ashtray	105	9.4	—
Social context of smoking behavior[a]			
Alone	46	—	14.5
With others (nonsmokers)	186	—	58.7
With others, including smokers and nonsmokers	71	—	22.4
Consideration shown to nonsmokers	5	—	1.6
Location of smoking behavior[b]			
Bar/lounge	25	—	7.9
Home/apartment	84	—	26.5
Restaurant	28	—	8.8
Car	40	—	12.6
Outside	103	—	32.5
Other location	69	—	21.8

[a]*A total of 4.4% of intervals depicted incidental smoking of characters other than the lead/supporting actors.*
[b]*Percentages total more than 100 as smoking may have occurred in more than one context in the same interval.*

TABLE 2 Odds Ratios (ORs) and 95% Confidence Intervals (95% CIs) for the Occurrence of Smoking Behavior in R-Rated/Unrated Movies

	OR[a]	95% CI
Overall smoking behavior	1.62	1.20–2.14
Smoking by male lead or supporting actor	2.48	1.55–3.97
Smoking by female lead or supporting actor	1.23	0.88–1.86

[a]*Referent is PG/PG-13 movies.*

film's rating. Males in lead or supporting roles were 2.5 times more likely to be shown smoking in R-rated/unrated movies than in PG/PG-13-rated films (P <.001). By contrast, the portrayal of smoking by a female lead or supporting character was not significantly different according to the movie's rating; that is, female actresses were *equally likely* to light up in movies aimed at juvenile audiences as in those aimed at mature audiences.

10 Smoking was also more likely to be depicted in the movies starring younger actresses. The mean age of the 10 actresses was 29.3 years (range = 21–40 years). When we categorized actresses according to quartiles by age, movies starring actresses in the youngest quartile featured 3.6 times as many intervals depicting smoking as did movies starring actresses in the oldest age group (95% confidence interval [95% CI] = 2.4, 5.4).

11 Negative messages regarding tobacco product use (e.g., depictions of the consequences of the use of tobacco products, such as coughing or grimacing at the smell of smoke) were more common than positive messages (30 vs 23) among the 50 films viewed. However, only 9 of 22 messages in PG/PG-13 films depicted smoking in a negative light, compared with 21 of 31 messages in R-rated/unrated films; that is, movies aimed at young audiences were *less* likely (odds ratio = 0.33; 95% CI = 0.11, 1.01) to carry negative messages associated with tobacco use than were movies made for mature audiences.

12 In a qualitative analysis of the social context of smoking, sex differences were detected in the themes associated with tobacco use. Women were likely to be portrayed using tobacco products to control their emotions, to manifest power and sex appeal, to enhance their body image or self-image, to control weight, or to give themselves a sense of comfort and companionship. Men were more likely to be depicted using tobacco products to reinforce their masculine identity; to portray a character with power, prestige, or significant authority; to show male bonding; or to signify their status as a "protector" (the last 3 themes were associated with cigar smoking).

Discussion

13 The results of this study raise concerns about exposure to smoking in popular movies. According to social learning theory, by paying attention to the behaviors of a person who possesses the qualities, skills, and capacities one hopes to achieve, a young observer learns to model these behaviors.[11] Among third- through sixth-grade students who had smoked, having role models who smoked was more common, and having beliefs about the adverse consequences of smoking was less common than among their peers who never smoked.[12]

14 The prevalence of smoking by both female (42%) and male (38%) lead or supporting actors was substantially higher than the national smoking prevalence for females (24.3%) and males (29.2%) aged 18 to 44.[13] This discrepancy is significant, given that adolescents who overestimate smoking prevalence among young people and adults are more likely to become smokers themselves.[2] In the films viewed, over half of the smoking episodes occurred in the presence of others who were not smoking, and in fewer than 2% of the intervals was consideration shown to nonsmokers (e.g., smoker leaves the room or asks permission to smoke). The depiction of smoking in Hollywood would thus appear to reinforce smoking as an acceptable and normative behavior in society. While most young people older than 18 years are able to acknowledge that on-screen smoking is part of a movie role, this may be more difficult for younger females aged 12 to 17 years, among whom smoking initiation is taking place.

15 Our qualitative analysis of smoking identified several themes related to smoking. One of the most prominent themes was using smoking to control emotion, which was specific to female characters and occurred during times of stress or difficulty, when the character was trying to regain or establish control, to repress or deny emotion, or to exit a negative or threatening situation.

16 Important limitations of this study should be noted. First, the sampling of magazine titles was limited to those with the highest readership among women aged 18 to 24 years. On the other hand, given the content and focus of the magazines, it is highly likely that they are widely read by adolescent girls. Surveying the issues of only 5 magazines may have biased our sample of actresses. However, a recent study on the influence of movie stars on adolescent smoking identified 6 of the 10 actresses in our sample as being the "most favorite" among girls. [14] Given that African American and Latina women have become targets for tobacco advertisements, it would also be informative to survey movies starring actresses of different racial/ethnic backgrounds. Future studies need to be extended to popular male actors as well. Finally, replication of our findings through the use of raters who are unaware of the hypotheses would be desirable, since the smoking-related themes emerging from our qualitative analyses may have been biased.

17 Our findings, in conjunction with those of others,[14] suggest the need for the development of policies—such as the adoption of a voluntary code of ethics by the entertainment industry—to eliminate the depiction of smoking in ways that appeal to adolescent audiences.

References

1. Centers for Disease Control and Prevention. Tobacco use among high school students—United States, 1997. *MMWR Morb Mortal Wkly Rep*. 1998; 47:229–233.
2. *Preventing Tobacco Use Among Young People: A Report of the Surgeon General*. Atlanta, Ga: National Center for Chronic Disease Prevention and Health Promotion, Office on Smoking and Health; 1994.
3. DuRant, RH, Rome ES, Rich M, Allred E, Emans SJ, Woods ER. Tobacco and alcohol use behaviors portrayed in music videos: a content analysis. *Am J Public Health*, 1997;87:1131–1135.
4. http://www.philipmorries.com/getallimg.asp.DOC_ID=2025863645/3659. Accessed July 1998.
5. Stockwell TF, Glantz SA. Tobacco use is increasing in popular films. *Tob Control*. 1997; 6:282–284.
6. Goldstein AO, Sobel RA, Newman GR. Tobacco and alcohol use in G-rated children's animated films. *JAMA*, 1999; 281:1131–1136.
7. Simmons Market Research Bureau. *Simmons Study of Media and Markets, M1*. New York, NY: Simmons Market Research Bureau; 1994; 0162–0163.
8. *Bacon's Magazine Directory: Directory of Magazines and Newsletters*. Chicago, III: Bacon's Information Inc; 1988.
9. Hazan AR, Lipton HL, Glantz S. Popular films do not reflect current tobacco use. *Am J Public Health*. 1994; 84:998–1000.
10. *Stata Statistical Software: Release 5.0*. College Station, Tex: Stata Corporation; 1997.

11. Greaves L. *Mixed Messages: Women, Tobacco and the Media*. Ottawa, Ontario: Health Canada; 1996.
12. Greenlund KJ, Johnson CC, Webber LS, Berenson GS. Cigarette smoking attitudes and first use among third- through sixth-grade students: the Bogalusa Heart Study. *Am J Public Health*. 1997; 87: 1345–1348.
13. Centers for Disease Control and Prevention. Cigarette smoking among adults—United States, 1995. *MMWR Morb Mortal Wkly Rep*. 1997; 46: 1217–1220.
14. Distefan JM, Gilpin EA, Sargent JD, Pierce JP. Do movie stars encourage adolescents to start smoking? Evidence from California. *Prev Med*. 1999; 28: 1–11.

THINKING CRITICALLY

about "Women and Smoking in Hollywood Movies: A Content Analysis"

1. The introduction to this article doesn't state its research question directly, even though a question is clearly implied. In your own words, what is the question these researchers are asking? Why is this question significant?
2. How did the researchers determine which actresses they were going to study? How did they select the films for each actress? How did they analyze smoking behavior within the films selected for study?
3. What were their findings?
4. In the Discussion section, where do the researchers (a) analyze causes and effects connected to their findings, (b) suggest the significance of their study, (c) point out limitations of their study, and (d) suggest areas for further research?

Our second reading, which was written for this chapter's writing project, was jointly authored by a team of three students. We have reproduced it in manuscript format to illustrate the form and documentation style of the APA (American Psychological Association) system for research papers. For further explanation of APA style, see Chapter 23, Skill 33.

Running head: GENDER STEREOTYPES 1

Include shortened title and page number on each page. On p. 1, include "Running head."

A Comparison of Gender Stereotypes in *SpongeBob SquarePants* and a 1930s Mickey Mouse Cartoon

Lauren Campbell, Charlie Bourain, and Tyler Nishida

November 10, 2006

Center title and authors.

APA Style

Brief abstract summarizes paper and appears on a separate page.

Abstract

Researchers in gender identity have continually argued whether gender differences are biological or social. Because television is a prime place for teaching children gender differences through socialization, we studied the extent of gender stereotyping in two1930s Mickey Mouse cartoons and two recent *SpongeBob SquarePants* cartoons. We analyzed the cartoons in one-minute increments and recorded the number of gender stereotypical and gender-non-stereotypical actions in each increment. Our results confirmed our hypothesis that *SpongeBob SquarePants* would have fewer gender stereotypes than Mickey Mouse. This study is significant because it shows that in at least one contemporary cartoon males and females have a range of acceptable behaviors that go beyond traditional gender stereotypes.

GENDER STEREOTYPES 3

A Comparison of Gender Stereotypes in *SpongeBob SquarePants* and a 1930s Mickey Mouse Cartoon

Repeat title before body of paper

Researchers in gender identity have long argued over the role of biology versus culture in causing gendered behavior. Pinker (2005) has argued that biology plays a more significant role in gender identity. In contrast, Barres (2006) has argued that culture plays the more significant role in gender identity. Proponents of socialization over biology have shown that cultural influences begin at a very young age. For example, Clearfield and Nelson (2006) show that mothers are more verbal and nurturing towards girls but are more focused on promoting independence and use more commands with boys.

Also of interest are the effects of media and popular culture on children and adults. A large part of a child's life is spent watching cartoons; therefore we believe it is important to find how much of a role gender stereotypes play in the media. In response to this question, we have examined data about gender stereotypes from two different kinds of children's cartoons. The first is a recent, somewhat controversial cartoon called *SpongeBob SquarePants*. The other is a popular 1930s Mickey Mouse cartoon.

Double-space all text.

The purpose of our study is to see if there is a difference in the extent of gender stereotypes between *SpongeBob SquarePants* and the earlier Mickey Mouse cartoon. We asked the following research question: To what extent has *SpongeBob SquarePants* rejected or reinforced gender stereotypes compared to the Mickey Mouse cartoon? Our hypothesis is that *SpongeBob SquarePants* will show fewer gender stereotypes than the older Mickey Mouse cartoon. We believe this because SpongeBob SquarePants has been attacked by some conservative religious groups as a gay character (Kirkpatrick, 2005). We hypothesize that this characterization comes from the cartoon's male characters' not exhibiting stereotypical male behaviors. In contrast, we believe that the older Mickey

Use italics for titles.

Center section headings in bold.

Reference tables in text.

Mouse cartoon will show Mickey exhibiting stereotypical male behavior and Minnie stereotypical female behavior.

Methods

To analyze the cartoons, we developed four specific categories for coding the data: Stereotypical Female Action, Stereotypical Male Action, Non-Stereotypical Female Action, and Non-Stereotypical Male Action. For each category we developed certain criteria that can be viewed in Table 1.

We watched two episodes of each cartoon (obtained from the Internet) in one-minute intervals. After each minute, we stopped the cartoon and waited for each team member to record his or her analysis. We all watched the same episodes at the same time, but recorded our data separately and later compiled the data after the last episode had been watched.

Table 1

Coding Criteria for Gender Stereotypes

Category	Criteria for Making Category Decision
Stereotypical Female Action	Female character behaves in a timid, submissive, or passive way; breaks into tears; shows caring, nurturing, empathic, or motherly behavior; dresses in stereotypical way (frilly clothes, dresses, feminine accessories)
Stereotypical Male Action	Male character behaves in an aggressive, fearless, or competitive way; is cocky or taunting; shows physical strength; dresses in stereotypical male way
Non-Stereotypical Female Action	Female character exhibits stereotypical male behavior
Non-Stereotypical Male Action	Male character exhibits stereotypical female behavior

Here is a representative example of how we applied our coding scheme: In one one-minute segment from *SpongeBob SquarePants*, SpongeBob and his friend Patrick decide to lift weights. While lifting weights, SpongeBob infuriates a body building fish who is much bigger and stronger than SpongeBob. SpongeBob runs away in fear while his friend Sandy (the female squirrel) stands up to the mean body building fish. She then makes sure SpongeBob is okay before she returns to lifting weights. We coded this example as containing a stereotypical male action (body building fish), a non-stereotypical male action (SpongeBob showing fear), a stereotypical female action (Sandy expressing concern for others), and non-stereotypical female actions (Sandy challenging the fish and also lifting weights).

Results

Our results (see Figure 1) show that the Mickey Mouse cartoon had a higher percentage of stereotypical male and female actions than did *SpongeBob SquarePants*, which had an almost equal amount of non-stereotypical and stereotypical gendered actions.

Reference figures in text.

As shown in Figure 1, female actions in *SpongeBob SquarePants* were 59% gender stereotypical and 40% gender non-stereotypical while in Mickey Mouse female actions were 84% gender stereotypical and only 16% gender non-stereotypical. Similarly, male actions in *SpongeBob SquarePants* were 48% gender stereotypical and 52% gender non-stereotypical, while in Mickey Mouse male actions were 87% gender stereotypical and 12% gender non-stereotypical.

Discussion

Our hypothesis that *SpongeBob SquarePants* will have fewer gender stereotypes than the Mickey Mouse cartoon was confirmed. The data show that overall *SpongeBob SquarePants* is the more gender-neutral cartoon, showing balance between non-stereotypical and stereotypical actions, while Mickey Mouse showed strong gender stereotypes.

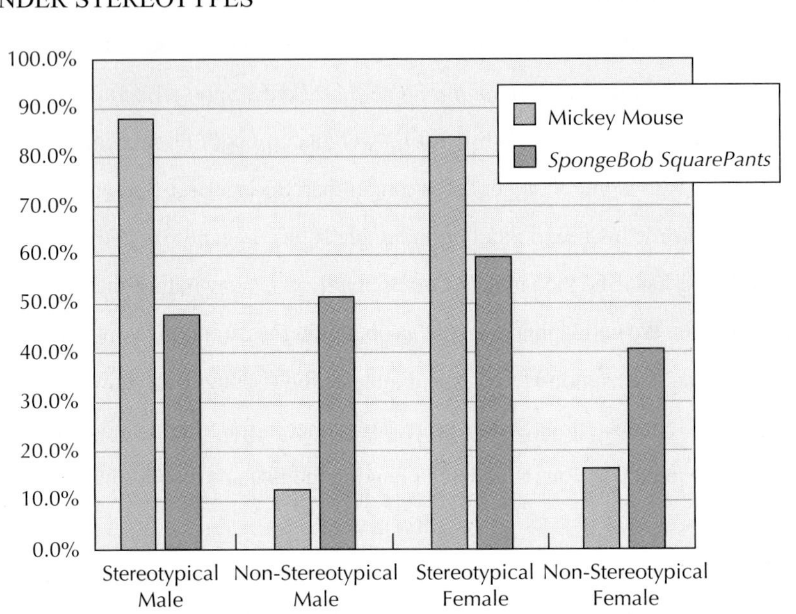

Figure 1. Stereotypical Behaviors by Gender in *SpongeBob SquarePants* and Mickey Mouse.

The study we have done is important because it shows that *SpongeBob SquarePants* does not reveal gender stereotyping in the stereotypical ways exhibited in the Mickey Mouse cartoon. In *SpongeBob SquarePants*, almost every gender stereotypical action (like SpongeBob acting tough or macho) was followed by a gender non-stereotypical action (like SpongeBob crying). This was not the case for Mickey Mouse, where there were many more gender stereotypical actions (for instance, Mickey Mouse rescuing Minnie Mouse) than gender non-stereotypical actions (for instance, Mickey Mouse quivering in fear).

The trends found in the *SpongeBob SquarePants* and Mickey Mouse cartoons suggest to us that these cartoons reveal ways that society's view of gender is evolving. In *SpongeBob SquarePants*, the greater variation and complexity of behavior may reflect such cultural and social changes as women and mothers in the workforce, stay-at-home dads raising the kids, shared household responsibilities, women in the military, and nontraditional families. These recent social and cultural changes have complicated our culture's views of gender, and we speculate that it is these less rigid gender restrictions that we glimpse in *SpongeBob SquarePants*. However, there is still a cultural war going on over gender roles in the media. Our class's discussion of advertising showed that the media in the 21st century still promote gender stereotypes, and the continuation of these stereotypes could explain why *SpongeBob SquarePants* has been controversial and has come under attack from cultural conservatives.

A potential limitation of our study could be that we didn't observe enough episodes of the two cartoons to get a representative sample. Another limitation was our difficulty in deciding how to code continuous actions that lasted more than one minute. For example, in a one-minute segment, *SpongeBob SquarePants* characters would exhibit many different actions, while actions in Mickey Mouse would last longer. For example, there might be a chase scene in which Mickey exhibited the same male action for several minutes or a scene where Minnie cried for several minutes. Should we count the chase scene or the crying scene as one action or as several because it continued across one-minute increments? We decided to count the same continuous action as several actions. Making another choice might have changed our data.

For future studies, researchers could ask questions like the following: Do other modern cartoons follow the trend of *SpongeBob SquarePants*? New research could compare *SpongeBob SquarePants* with other recent cartoons like *The Justice League* or *Jimmy Neutron* to see if they follow *SpongeBob SquarePants*' gender-neutral tendencies. If we believe that gender stereotyping is harmful, furthering the research on gender stereotypes in the media could help identify how to promote a more gender-neutral society in the future.

APA Style

GENDER STEREOTYPES 8

Center heading.

References

Use initials for first names.

Place date after author's name.

Italicize publication names.

Use initial cap for article titles.

Check that everything cited in report is in References list (except personal communications).

Barres, B. A. (2006, July 13). Does gender matter? *Nature, 442*, 133–136.

Clearfield, M., & Nelson, N. (2006, January). Sex differences in mothers' speech and play behavior with 6-, 9-, and 14-month-old infants. *Sex Roles, 54*(1/2), 127–137.

Kirkpatrick, D. (2005, January 20). Conservatives pick soft target: A cartoon sponge. *The New York Times*. Retrieved from http://www.nytimes.com

Pinker, S. (2005, February 7). The science of difference. Sex ed. *The New Republic Online*. Retrieved from http://www.tnr.com

THINKING CRITICALLY
about "A Comparison of Gender Stereotypes in *SpongeBob SquarePants* and a 1930s Mickey Mouse Cartoon"

1. Explain how this paper follows the genre conventions for a scientific report.
2. To what extent do you think the authors' research design was effective? Are you persuaded that *SpongeBob SquarePants* has moved away from gender stereotypes?
3. This research project was part of a class unit on issues in gender identity that included the readings by Pinker, Barres, and Clearfield and Nelson referred to in the introduction. What does this brief "review of the literature" add to the paper? How much more extensive is the review of the literature in the previous reading by Escamilla, Cradock, and Kawachi?
4. The authors located the reference to Kirkpatrick on their own. How does the use of this source contribute to the paper?
5. How might the authors expand their speculations about causes of new approaches to gender in cartoons and their ideas about the significance of the study? How has this study inspired you to think about gender and cartoons?

Our final reading is the poster created by the authors of the *SpongeBob SquarePants* paper for presentation at a poster session (see page 284).

THINKING CRITICALLY
about "*SpongeBob SquarePants* Has Fewer Gender Stereotypes than Mickey Mouse"

1. To what extent does this poster present the same scientific content as the complete research report? If you attended a conference, would you rather listen to a fifteen-minute talk by the authors or view their poster and ask them questions? Why?
2. How does this poster employ the "sound-bite" principle by using minimal text connected to visual elements?
3. In what ways do you think this poster is effective? What questions would you want to ask the creators of this poster?

SpongeBob SquarePants Has Fewer Gender Stereotypes than Mickey Mouse

Lauren Campbell, Charlie Bourain, and Tyler Nishida

Introduction

Television cartoons may influence children's learning of gender stereotypes. Knowing how a contemporary cartoon portrays gender stereotypes would help us understand messages children receive.

Objective

We wanted to see if there is a difference in gender stereotypes between *SpongeBob SquarePants* and a 1930s Mickey Mouse cartoon.

Method

We analyzed cartoons in one-minute increments.

We coded behavior in four categories:

- *Stereotypical female* [timid, passive, tearful; caring, motherly; wearing frilly clothes, accessories]
- *Stereotypical male* [aggressive, fearless, competitive; cocky; showing physical strength; wearing typical male clothing]
- *Non-stereotypical female* [female exhibiting stereotypical male action]
- *Non-stereotypical male* [male exhibiting stereotypical female action]

Results

More Non-Stereotypical Behavior for Males and Females in SpongeBob

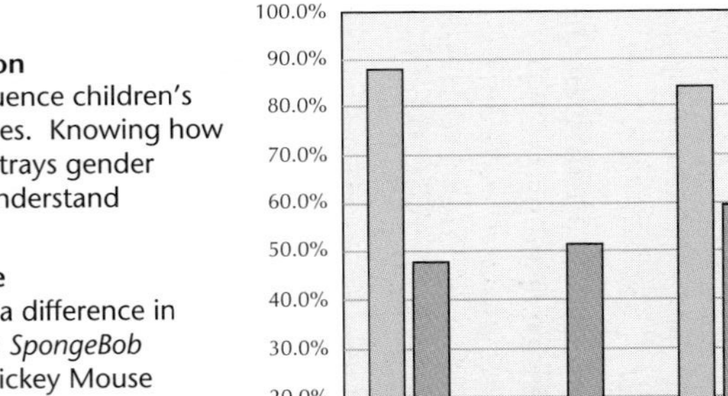

- *SpongeBob SquarePants* has almost equal ratio of stereotypical and non-stereotypical behaviors for both males and females (49%/51% for males; 59%/41% females)
- Mickey Mouse has mostly stereotypical behaviors (88%/12% for males; 84%/16% for females)

Discussion

SpongeBob SquarePants showed males and females engaged in wider range of behavior with fewer gender stereotypes than Mickey Mouse.

- *SpongeBob SquarePants* intermixed gender stereotypical action (SpongeBob acting tough, Sandy being nurturing) and non-stereotypical behavior (SpongeBob crying, Sandy rescuing SpongeBob)
- Mickey Mouse had mostly gender stereotypical actions (Mickey rescuing Minnie, who is in tears).

These differences may match changes in culture since 1930s (women's movement, working women, stay-at-home dads) and may explain why *SpongeBob SquarePants* has been attacked by cultural conservatives.

ANALYZING IMAGES

CHAPTER 11

This chapter asks you to analyze images in order to understand their persuasive power—a skill often called "visual literacy." By *visual literacy,* we mean your awareness of the importance of visual communication and your ability to interpret or make meaning out of images and graphics (photos, paintings, illustrations, icons, charts, graphs, and other visual displays of data). In this chapter, we seek to enhance your visual literacy by focusing on the way that images influence our conceptual and emotional understanding of a phenomenon and the way that they validate, reveal, and construct the world.

This chapter is the second of four assignment chapters on writing to analyze and synthesize. As you may recall from Chapter 1, Concept 3, when you write to analyze and synthesize, you apply your own critical thinking to a puzzling object or to puzzling data and offer your own new ideas to a conversation. Your goal is to raise interesting questions about the object or data being analyzed—questions that perhaps your reader hasn't thought to ask—and then to provide tentative answers to those questions, supported by points and particulars derived from your own close examination of the object or data.

See Table 1.1, pp 20–21, for an explanation of the aims of writing.

The word *analysis* derives from a Greek word meaning "to dissolve, loosen, undo." Metaphorically, analysis means to divide or dissolve the whole into its constituent parts, to examine these parts carefully, to look at the relationships among them, and then to use this understanding of the parts to better understand the whole—how it functions, what it means. Synonyms for writing to analyze might be *writing to interpret, clarify,* or *explain.*

In this chapter, we introduce you to a common academic genre: a comparative analysis of two visual texts (such as two advertisements, two photos, two posters, two paintings, or any other visual texts). In this kind of analysis, you need to think of images rhetorically in terms of how and why they were created and for whom. In turn, your close examination of images and their rhetorical contexts can be useful in your own career and civic life. For instance, your understanding of the relationship between words and images in advertising can be readily transferred to other rhetorical settings such as designing a brochure or Web site or writing any kind of document that incorporates images and depends on document design.

We begin by thinking about the cultural importance of images. Consider how British cultural critic John Berger, in his book *About Looking,* sketches the pervasive use of photographs shortly after the invention of the camera.

> The camera was invented by Fox Talbot in 1839. Within a mere 30 years of its invention as a gadget for an elite, photography was being used for police filing, war

reporting, military reconnaissance, pornography, encyclopedic documentation, family albums, postcards, anthropological records (often, as with the Indians in the United States, accompanied by genocide), sentimental moralizing, inquisitive probing (the wrongly named "candid camera"), aesthetic effects, news reporting and formal portraiture. The speed with which the possible uses of photography were seized upon is surely an indication of photography's profound, central applicability to industrial capitalism.

One of photography's purposes—as Berger hints—is to create images that "have designs on" us, that urge us to believe ideas, buy things, go places, or otherwise alter our views or behaviors. Information brochures use carefully selected photographs to enhance a product's image (consider how the photographs on your college's Web site or view book have been selected). News photographs editorialize their content (during the Vietnam War a newspaper photograph of a naked Vietnamese child running screaming toward the photographer while a napalm bomb explodes behind her turned many Americans against the war; and recently, the images of forlorn, emaciated children in Africa have accompanied newspaper stories about programs to fight HIV/AIDS). And advertisements urge us not only to buy a certain product but to be a certain kind of person with certain values.

Visual literacy was introduced in Chapter 3, Concept 10, with images of doctors (pp. 58–59) and in Chapter 5 with images of the Arctic National Wildlife Refuge (pp. 91–93).

The images we examine in this chapter represent those that you are likely to encounter as a citizen and a student: news photos, advertisements, and paintings by well-known artists. Studying ways to analyze these images will enhance your visual literacy and make you a more perceptive cultural critic. The chapter's main focus—on visual rhetoric used in product advertisements—relates to Berger's assertion that photographs have a "profound, central applicability to industrial capitalism" and will help you understand how ads both convey and help construct our cultural values; our self-image; our ideas about gender, race, and class; and our sense of what is normal or ideal. Such understanding will sharpen your powers of observation and analysis, equipping you to respond independently to the rhetorical persuasiveness of all images and to counter manipulation, prejudice, and injustice.

Exploring Image Analysis

To introduce you to the concept of image analysis, we provide two related exercises to stimulate your thinking and discussion. The exercises ask you to interact with a gallery of photographs on the issue of immigration reform. Many of these photographs first appeared accompanying news stories.

Immigration reform is one of the most complex issues facing the United States today. Although it concerns immigrants from any spot on the globe, the problem is particularly acute with respect to immigrants from Mexico and Central America. What kinds of immigration reforms would lead to a just and effective U.S. policy? This issue is complicated by the history of the United States and Mexico, by geography (the 1,900-mile border between the two countries), and by economic policies such as the North American Free Trade Agreement

(NAFTA). Immigrants are drawn to the United States by the availability of employment not found in their own countries. U.S. citizens benefit from the inexpensive labor, which in turn influences the low prices of services and goods. Besides having a sizable Mexican-American citizenry, the United States has within its borders an estimated 11.1 million illegal immigrants. All these factors give rise to a number of controversial questions: Should the United States increase border security and focus on building impassable barriers? Should it deport illegal immigrants or explore easier routes to making them citizens? Should it crack down on employers of illegal immigrants or should it implement a guest worker program to legitimize immigrant labor?

Because immigration policy reform involves complicated political, economic, and cultural issues with many stakeholders and large stakes, public debate about these issues is particularly susceptible to manipulation by the rhetorical appeal of images. The following exercise asks you to examine a gallery of photos, Figures 11.1 through 11.8, related to the United States–Mexico immigration problem.

FIGURE 11.1 Wall between Tijuana, Mexico, and the United States

FIGURE 11.2 Immigrants Crossing the Border Illegally

FIGURE 11.3 Protestors Marching for Compassionate Treatment of Immigrants

FIGURE 11.4 Immigrants Saying Their Citizenship Pledge

FIGURE 11.5 Immigrant Farmworkers

FIGURE 11.6 U.S. Democratic Representative Loretta Sanchez from Los Angeles

FIGURE 11.7 Mexican Restaurant in the Southwest

FIGURE 11.8 Taco Bell

Working individually or in groups, consider the rhetorical effect of these photos from news and photo sites, first by recording your responses to these photos and then by speculating how you might use these images to increase the persuasiveness of different positions on immigration reform.

Task 1: Analyzing the Photos

1. What objects, people, or places stand out in each photo? Does the photo look candid or staged, taken close-up or from a distance? How does the angle of

the photo (taken from below or above the subject) and the use of color contribute to the effect?
2. What is the dominant impression conveyed by each photo?
3. For each pair of photos, examine how their similarities and differences convey different rhetorical impressions of immigrants, of Latino culture, or of the role of immigrants or ethnic diversity in U.S. culture.

Task 2: Using the Photos Rhetorically

Now imagine how you might use these photos to enhance the persuasiveness of particular claims. Choose one or two photos to support or attack each claim below and explain what the photo could contribute to the argument. How might the photo be used to make emotional appeals to viewers? How might it shape viewers' impressions and thoughts about the issue? Within your own argument, how would you label the photograph?

a. The United States should seal off its border with Mexico by building a wall and increasing border patrols.
b. The United States should allow guest workers to enter the United States and work here for up to six years before having to return to Mexico.
c. The United States should offer amnesty and citizenship to immigrants who are currently in the United States illegally.
d. The United States benefits from the cultural importance and influence of its Latino/Latina citizens.

Understanding Image Analysis

In preparation for analyzing all kinds of visual texts intended to have specific rhetorical effects, let's look at some strategies to help you examine key features.

How Images Create a Rhetorical Effect

An image can be said to have a rhetorical effect whenever it moves us emotionally or intellectually. We might identify with the image or be repelled by it; the image might evoke our sympathies, trigger our fears, or call forth a web of interconnected ideas, memories, and associations. An image's rhetorical effect derives from both its angle of vision or perspective and from the composition of the image itself. In photographs, the angle of vision is a function of camera placement and techniques (special lighting, lenses, or filters); in paintings, it is a function of the artist's position and compositional techniques (kinds of paint or ink, brushstrokes, and so forth). We will look first at angle of vision and then at the way the image is composed.

Angle of Vision and Techniques

To analyze an image, begin by considering the angle of vision or perspective of the artist or photographer—the placement of the painter's easel or the photographer's camera—and the special techniques employed.*

*Our ideas in this section are indebted to Paul Messaris, *Visual Persuasion: The Role of Images in Advertising* (Thousand Oaks, CA: Sage, 1997).

STRATEGIES

for Analyzing an Image's Angle of Vision and Techniques

What to Examine	Rhetorical Effects To Consider
Examine distance from the subject: Is the photograph or painting a close-up, medium perspective, or distant perspective?	• Close-ups tend to increase the intensity of the image and suggest the importance of the subject. • Long shots tend to blend the subject into the environment.
Note the orientation of the image with respect to the artist/camera: Is the artist/camera positioned in front of or behind the subject? Is the artist/camera positioned below the subject, looking up (a low-angle perspective), or above the subject, looking down (a high-angle perspective)?	• Front-view perspectives tend to emphasize the persons in the image. • Rear-view perspectives often emphasize the scene or setting. • In photography, a low-angle camera tends to grant superiority, status, and power to the subject. • A high-angle camera can comically reduce the subject to childlike status. • A level angle tends to imply equality.
Look at where the eyes gaze: Which persons in the image, if any, gaze directly at the camera or artist or look away?	• Looking directly at the camera/artist implies power. • Looking away can imply deference or shyness.
Consider point of view: Does the photographer/artist strive for an "objective effect," with the camera/artist outside the scene and observing it? Or does the photographer/artist create a "subjective effect," as if he/she is in the scene?	• Many photographs or paintings have a standard objective view. • In photography, subjective shots are fairly common: The camera appears to be the eyes of someone inside the scene, involving the viewer as an actor in the scene and creating intensity.
Evaluate the artistic presentation: Has the photographer/artist used highly artistic techniques for special effects? In photography, these effects include film or digital techniques, filters for special effects, or the distorting or merging of images. In painting, they involve choices of ink/paint and kinds of application techniques.	• Making parts of the image crisp and in focus and others slightly blurred can affect viewers' impressions. • Using filters can alter the mood and dominant impression. • Distorting or merging images can create fanciful effects (a city blending into a desert or a woman blending into a tree), or create visual parodies (a Greek statue wearing jeans).

If you are analyzing a photograph, be aware of various ways that a photographic image can be manipulated or falsified: staging images (scenes that appear to be real but are really staged); altering images (for example, airbrushing, reshaping body parts, or constructing a composite image such as putting the head of one person on the body of another); selecting images or parts of images (such as cropping photographs so that only parts of the body or only parts of a scene are shown); and mislabeling (putting a caption on a photograph that misrepresents what it actually is).

FOR WRITING AND DISCUSSION

Examining Angle of Vision and Camera Techniques in Three Photographs

Look at three photographic images of bears: Figure 5.1 (Chapter 5, p. 91), Figure 5.4 (Chapter 5, p. 93), and the Nikon camera advertisement, Figure 11.9 (p. 293). Then, working in small groups or as a whole class, analyze the camera techniques of each photograph, and explain how these techniques are rhetorically effective for the purpose of the message to which each is attached.

Compositional Features

In addition to analyzing the artist's/photographer's angle of vision and techniques, you need to analyze the compositional features of the image. What is included in the image and what is excluded? How are details of the image arranged? (Note: When photographs are used in product advertisements, every detail down to the props in the photograph or the placement of a model's hands are consciously chosen.)

See Chapter 4, Concept 12, for a discussion of document design.

STRATEGIES for Analyzing the Compositional Features of Images

What to Examine	Examples of Questions to Ask
Examine the settings, furnishings, and all other included details: If an indoor setting, list all furnishings and other details such as paintings on walls, furniture styles, objects on tables, the kind and color of rugs, and the arrangement of rooms; or if scene is outdoors, list the kinds of details included.	• Is the room formal or informal; neat, lived-in, or messy? • If the setting is outdoors, what are the features of the landscape: urban or rural, mountain or meadow? • If there are birds or animals, why a crow rather than a robin?

(continued)

What to Examine	Examples of Questions to Ask
Consider the social meaning of objects: Note how objects signal differences in values, social class, or lifestyle. Note the symbolic significance of objects.	• What is the emotional effect of the objects in a den: for example, duck decoys and fishing rods versus computers and high-tech printers? • What is the social significance of the choice of dog breed: for example, a groomed poodle versus an English sheepdog or mutt? • What could a single rose, a bouquet of daisies, or a potted fuchsia symbolize?
Consider the characters, roles, and actions: Create the story behind the image. In a product advertisement determine if the models are instrumental (acting out real-life roles) or decorative (staged just to be attractive visually).	• Who are these people and what are they doing? • In product advertisements, are female models used instrumentally (depicted as mechanics working on cars or as a consumer buying a car) or are they used decoratively (bikini-clad and lounging on the hood of the latest truck)?
Observe how models are dressed, posed, and accessorized: Note facial expressions, eye contact, and gestures.	• What are the models' hairstyles and what cultural and social significance do they have? • How well are they dressed? • How are they posed?
Observe the relationships among actors and among actors and objects: Look at how position signals importance and dominance.	• Who is looking at whom? • Who is above or below whom? • Who or what is in the foreground or background?
Consider what social roles are being played out and what values appealed to: Note how body position, style of dress, and use of objects or props might indicate class, status, or power.	• Are the gender roles traditional or nontraditional? • Are the relationships romantic, erotic, friendly, formal, uncertain? • What are the power relationships among characters?
Analyze the rhetorical context of the image: If a photograph, note whether the image accompanies a news story, a poster, a Web site, or an advertisement. Consider the relationship between the image and the words. Consider the document design. If a painting, note how it functions in its setting (in a museum, a coffee shop, the wall of someone's living room).	• How does the image function within the context? • How does it contribute to the rhetorical effect of the whole to which it is a part? • If an ad, how do layout, color, and type style function? • What is the style of language (for example, connotations, double entendres, puns)? • What kind of product information is included or excluded from the ad?

FIGURE 11.9 Nikon Ad

The camera for those who look at this picture and think, "Gosh, how'd they open up the shadows without blowing out the highlights?"
When staring into the mouth of a 10 ft. grizzly bear, you tend to think about life. Limbs. And how handy legs are. Not the fill-flash ratio needed to expose teeth about to rip your leg off.
Nikon created the N90 specifically for complicated situations like this. When you have no time to think. A brown bear on brown earth, about to mangle a brown shoe. So instead of overexposing this picture like other cameras might, the N90™ works for you, properly analyzing the situation and delivering an accurate exposure.
Here's how it does it. The 3D Matrix Meter divides the scene into eight segments. It measures the brightness in each one of the segments and then compares them for contrast. D-type lenses incorporate the subject's distance which allows the N90 to calculate the proper ambient light exposure.
The SB-25 Speedlight fires a rapid series of imperceptible pre-flashes to determine the bear's reflectance. And then provides the precise amount of fill-flash needed to lighten the bear's dark brown fur, without overexposing his slightly yellow teeth.
The N90 can give you near-perfect exposures when other cameras would be fooled. Or, for that matter, eaten.
Professionals trust the N90. So you can too. Because it works just as well on children eating ice cream as it does on bears eating people.

The N90 System

Nikon
We take the world's greatest pictures.

See the Nikon N90 at authorized dealers where you see this symbol. Nikon Data Link System available Winter '93. For more on our MasterCard, call 1-800-NIKON-35.

Photograph by Galen Rowell/Mountain Light. Courtesy of Nikon.

FOR WRITING AND DISCUSSION

Analyzing Compositional Features in Two Paintings

Background: The following exercise asks you to apply the analysis strategies presented in the previous section to the examination of two paintings that could become your subject for this chapter's writing project. Examine the painting *Rhetoricians at a Window* by Dutch painter Jan Steen, which appears on page 487, and *Nighthawks,* a painting by American artist Edward Hopper, shown in Figure 11.10. Although a class in art history would give you a more sophisticated art vocabulary and an historical background to contextualize and

(*continued*)

discuss these paintings, the strategies we have just presented for analyzing the angle of vision and compositional features of images will help you generate plenty of ideas. As you observe the two paintings, you may find the following background information useful:

BACKGROUND FOR JAN STEEN'S *RHETORICIANS AT A WINDOW*

- ***About Steen:*** Jan Havickszoon Steen (1626–1679) was a Dutch painter during the Baroque period (roughly the end of the sixteenth to the beginning of the eighteenth centuries); he was a contemporary of the painter Rembrandt and was a popular painter during his lifetime.
- ***About his art:*** Although he also painted landscapes, he is known as a genre painter—that is, a painter of scenes from everyday life: tavern life, family scenes, holidays. As the owner of a tavern, Steen probably observed human behavior closely, as indicated by his paintings' insightful views of human nature.
- ***About this painting:*** *Rhetoricians at a Window* is oil on canvas and was painted between 1662 and 1666. The term *rhetorician* commonly described classical scholars and speechmakers.

BACKGROUND FOR EDWARD HOPPER'S *NIGHTHAWKS*

- ***About Hopper:*** Edward Hopper (1882–1967) was an American illustrator and painter who studied under Robert Henri, one of the artists of the Ashcan School, whose paintings are characterized by their harsh depictions of urban life. Hopper also admired the realism of Ernest Hemingway's writing.
- ***About his art:*** Hopper is known as a realistic painter of American scenes and is remembered for his portrayals of America during the Depression and of the effects of big, modern cities on their inhabitants.

FIGURE 11.10 *Nighthawks* by Edward Hopper

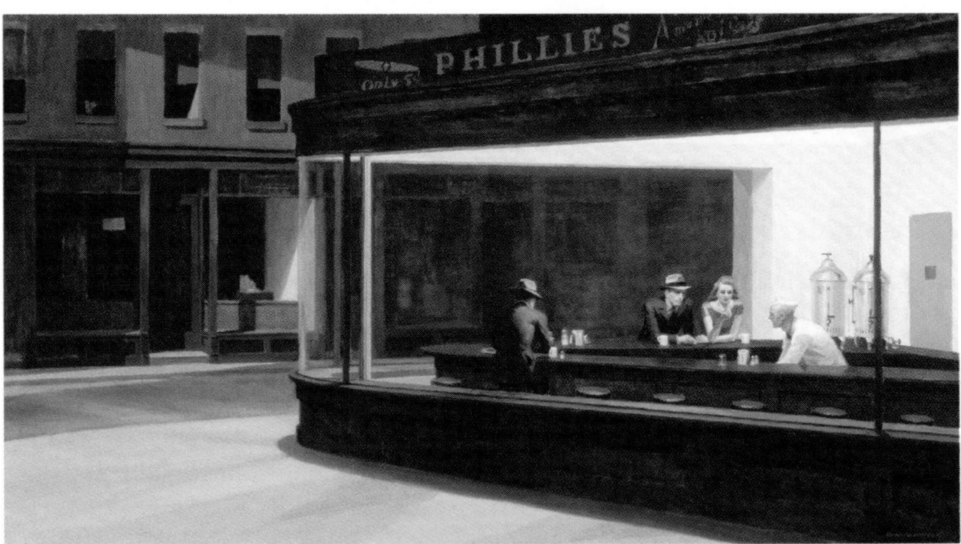

- ***About this painting:*** *Nighthawks* (1942), an oil painting on canvas, depicts a restaurant in Greenwich Village in New York City.

Your task: Working individually or in small groups, analyze both of these paintings:

- Begin by applying the strategies for analyzing an image's angle of vision and techniques (p. 290).
- Then apply the strategies for analyzing the compositional features of images (pp. 291–292).
- After you have analyzed the visual features of the paintings, consider why the artists titled them as they did. Why the title *Rhetoricians at a Window*? Why the title *Nighthawks*?
- Finally, what are the thematic differences between these two paintings? What view or feeling about life or about the artist's world is conveyed in each painting? What way of seeing or thinking are these paintings persuading you to adopt?

How to Analyze an Advertisement

Now that you have a general understanding of how to analyze the persuasive strategies of visual images, we turn to a specific application—modern advertising. The goal of advertisers is to put viewers in the mood to buy a certain product. The strategies they employ—both in their painstakingly precise and intentional creation of every detail in a photograph and in the way they make the photograph interact with the words of the ad—are fascinating to study. We begin with a brief explanation of the context within which advertisers work.

Understanding an Advertiser's Goals and Strategies

Although some advertisements are primarily informational—explaining why the company believes its product is superior—most advertisements involve parity products such as soft drinks, deodorants, breakfast cereals, toothpaste, and jeans. (*Parity* products are products that are roughly equal in quality to their competitors and so can't be promoted through any rational or scientific proof of superiority.)

Advertisements for parity products usually use psychological and motivational strategies to associate a product with a target audience's (often subconscious) dreams, hopes, fears, desires, and wishes, suggesting that the product will magically dispel these fears and anxieties or magically deliver on values, desires, and dreams. Using sophisticated research techniques, advertisers study how people's fears, dreams, and values differ according to their ethnicity, gender, educational level, socioeconomic class, age, and so forth; this research allows advertisers to tailor their appeals precisely to the target audience.

Furthermore, advertisers often focus on long-range advertising campaigns rather than on just a single ad. Their goal is not simply to sell a product but to build brand loyalty or a relationship with consumers that will be long lasting. (Think of how the brand Marlboro has a different image from the brand Winston, or how the GAP has tried to improve its corporate image through its RED campaign that appeals to consumers' concern about global social justice.) Advertisers try to convert a brand name from a label on a can or on the inside of a sweater to a field of qualities, values, and imagery that lives inside the heads of its targeted consumers. An ad campaign, therefore, uses subtle repetition of themes through a variety of individual ads aimed at building up a psychological link between the product and the consumer. Advertisers don't just want you to buy Nikes rather than Reeboks, but also to see yourself as a Nike kind of person who attributes part of your identity to Nike. Some ad campaigns have been brilliant at turning whole segments of a population into loyal devotees of a brand. Among the most famous campaigns are the long-lived Marlboro cowboy ads, the independent female theme of Virginia Slims ads, the milk mustaches on celebrities in the "Got Milk?" ads, and the sophisticated and artsy poster ads for Absolut vodka.

How Advertisers Target Specific Audiences

When advertisers produce an ad, they create images and copy intended to appeal to the values, hopes, and desires of a specific audience. How do they know the psychological attributes of a specific audience? Much of the market research on which advertisers rely is based on an influential demographic tool developed by SRI Research called the "VALS" (Values And Lifestyle System).* This system divides consumers into three basic categories with further subdivisions:

1. ***Needs-driven consumers.*** Poor, with little disposable income, these consumers generally spend their money only on basic necessities.
   - *Survivors:* Live on fixed incomes or have no disposable income. Advertising seldom targets this group.
   - *Sustainers:* Have very little disposable income, but often spend what they have impulsively on low-end, mass-market items.
2. ***Outer-directed consumers.*** These consumers want to identify with certain in-groups, to "keep up with the Joneses," or to surpass them.
   - *Belongers:* Believe in traditional family values and are conforming, nonexperimental, nostalgic, and sentimental. They are typically blue-collar or lower middle class, and they buy products associated with Mom, apple pie, and the American flag.
   - *Emulators:* Are ambitious and status conscious. They have a tremendous desire to associate with currently popular in-groups. They are typically young, have at least moderate disposable income, are urban and upwardly mobile, and buy conspicuous items that are considered "in."
   - *Achievers:* Have reached the top in a competitive environment. They buy to show off their status and wealth and to reward themselves for their hard climb up the ladder. They have high incomes and buy top-of-the-line luxury items that say "success." They regard themselves as leaders and persons of stature.

*Our discussion of VALS is adapted from Harold W. Berkman and Christopher Gibson, *Advertising,* 2nd ed. (New York: Random House, 1987), pp. 134–137.

3. ***Inner-directed consumers.*** These consumers are individualistic and buy items to suit their own tastes rather than to symbolize their status.
   - *I-am-me types:* Are young, independent, and often from affluent backgrounds. They typically buy expensive items associated with their individual interests (such as mountain bikes, stereo equipment, or high-end camping gear), but may spend very little on clothes, cars, or furniture.
   - *Experiential types:* Are process-oriented and often reject the values of corporate America in favor of alternative lifestyles. They buy organic foods, make their own bread, do crafts and music, value holistic medicine, and send their children to alternative kindergartens.
   - *Socially conscious types:* Believe in simple living and are concerned about the environment and the poor. They emphasize the social responsibility of corporations, take on community service, and actively promote their favorite causes. They have middle to high incomes and are usually very well educated.

No one fits exactly into any one category, and most people exhibit traits of several categories, but advertisers are interested in statistical averages, not individuals. When a company markets an item, it enlists advertising specialists to help target the item to a particular market segment. Budweiser is aimed at belongers, while upscale microbeers are aimed at emulators or achievers. To understand more precisely the fears and values of a target group, researchers can analyze subgroups within each of these VALS segments by focusing specifically on women, men, children, teenagers, young adults, or retirees or on specified ethnic or regional minorities. Researchers also determine what kinds of families and relationships are valued in each of the VALS segments, who in a family initiates demand for a product, and who in a family makes the actual purchasing decisions. Thus, ads aimed at belongers depict traditional families; ads aimed at I-am-me types may depict more ambiguous sexual or family relationships. Advertisements aimed at women can be particularly complex because of women's conflicting social roles in our society. When advertisers target the broader category of gender, they sometimes sweep away VALS distinctions and try to evoke more deeply embedded emotional and psychological responses.

FOR WRITING AND DISCUSSION

Designing Ads

You own a successful futon factory that has marketed its product primarily to experiential types. Your advertisements have associated futons with holistic health, spiritualism (transcendental meditation, yoga), and organic wholesomeness (all-natural materials, gentle people working in the factory, incense and sitar music in your retail stores, and so forth). You have recently expanded your factory and now produce twice as many futons as you did six months ago. Unfortunately, demand hasn't increased correspondingly. Your market research suggests that if you are going to increase demand for futons, you have to reach other VALS segments.

(*continued*)

Working in small groups, develop ideas for a magazine or TV advertisement that might sell futons to one or more of the other target segments in the VALS system. Your instructor can assign a different target segment to each group, or each group can decide for itself which target segment constitutes the likeliest new market for futons.

Groups should then share their ideas with the whole class.

Sample Analysis of an Advertisement

With an understanding of possible photographic effects and the compositional features of ads, you now have all the background knowledge needed to begin doing your own analysis of ads. To illustrate how an analysis of an ad can reveal the ad's persuasive strategies, we show you our analysis of an ad for Coors Light (Figure 11.11) that ran in a variety of women's magazines. First, consider the contrast between the typical beer ads that are aimed at men (showing women in bikinis, fulfilling adolescent male sexual fantasies, or men on fishing trips or in sports bars, representing male comradeship and bonding) and this Coors Light ad with its "Sam and Me" theme.

Rather than associating beer drinking with a wild party, this ad associates beer drinking with the warm friendship of a man and a woman, with just a hint of potential romance. The ad shows a man and a woman, probably in their early- to mid-twenties, in relaxed conversation; they are sitting casually on a tabletop, with their legs resting on chair seats. The woman is wearing casual pants, a summery cotton top, and informal shoes. Her braided, shoulder-length hair has a healthy, mussed appearance, and a braid comes across the front of her shoulder. She is turned away from the man, leans on her knees, and holds a bottle of Coors Light. Her sparkling eyes are looking up, and she smiles happily, as if reliving a pleasant memory. The man is wearing slacks, a cotton shirt with the sleeves rolled up, and scuffed tennis shoes with white socks. He also has a reminiscing smile on his face, and he leans on the woman's shoulder. The words "Coors Light. Just between friends." appear immediately below the picture next to a Coors Light can.

This ad appeals to women's desire for close friendships and relationships. Everything about the picture signifies long-established closeness and intimacy—old friends rather than lovers. The way the man leans on the woman shows her strength and independence. Additionally, the way they pose, with the woman slightly forward and sitting up more than the man, results in their taking up equal space in the picture. In many ads featuring male-female couples, the man appears larger and taller than the woman; this picture signifies mutuality and equality.

The words of the ad help interpret the relationship. Sam and the woman have been friends since the first grade, and they are reminiscing about old times. The relationship is thoroughly mutual. Sometimes he brings the Coors Light and sometimes she brings it; sometimes she does the listening and sometimes he

FIGURE 11.11 Beer Ad Aimed at Women

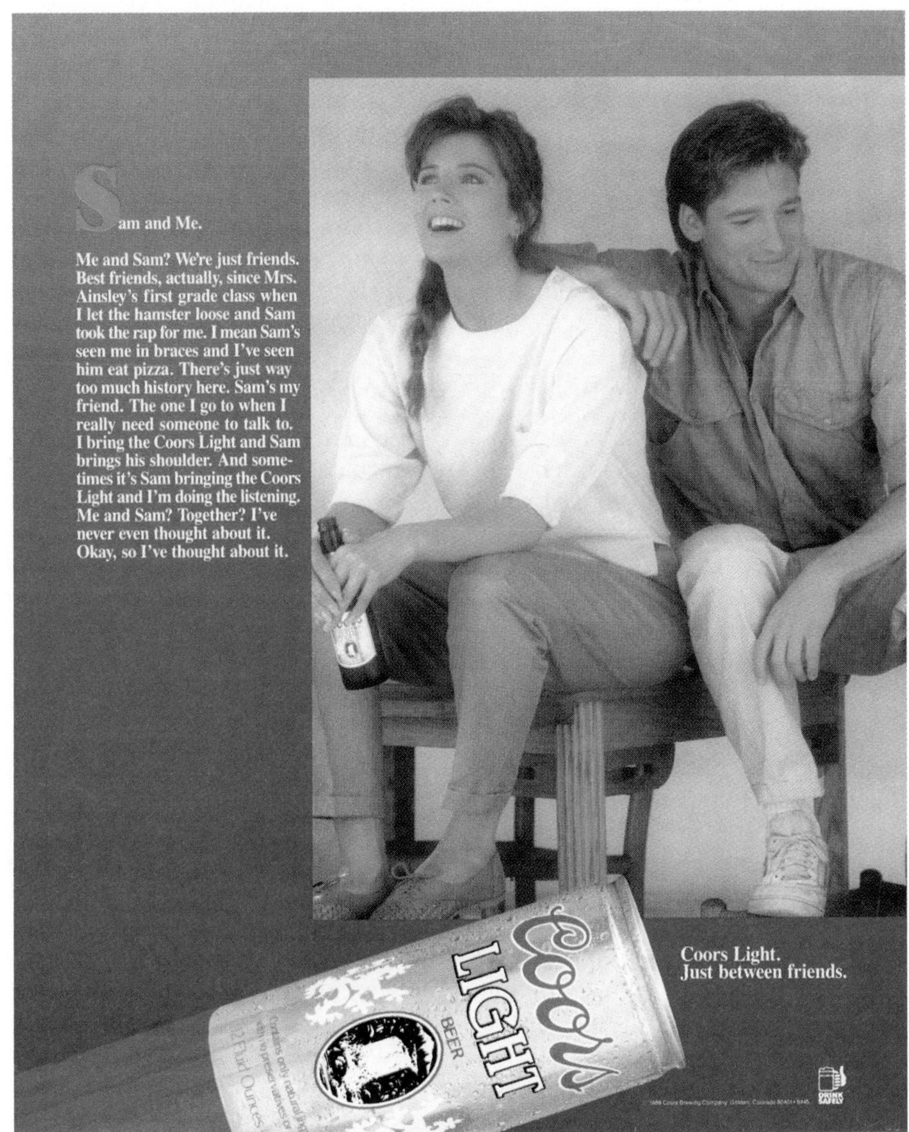

Coors Brewing Company.

does; sometimes she leans on his shoulder and sometimes he leans on hers. Sometimes the ad says, "Sam and me"; sometimes it says, "me and Sam." Even the "bad grammar" of "Sam and me" (rather than "Sam and I") suggests the lazy, relaxed absence of pretense or formality.

These two are reliable, old buddies. But the last three lines of the copy give just a hint of potential romance: "Me and Sam? Together? I've never even thought about it. Okay, so I've thought about it." Whereas beer ads targeting men portray women as sex objects, this ad appeals to many women's desire for relationships and for romance that is rooted in friendship rather than sex.

And why the name "Sam"? Students in our classes have hypothesized that Sam is a "buddy" kind of name rather than a romantic-hero name. Yet it is more modern and more interesting than other buddy names such as "Bob" or "Bill" or "Dave." "A 'Sam,'" said one of our students, "is more mysterious than a 'Bill'." Whatever associations the name strikes in you, be assured that the admakers spent hours debating possible names until they hit on this one.

For an additional ad analysis, see the sample student essay (pp. 316–318).

FOR WRITING AND DISCUSSION

Analyzing Two SUV Ads

This exercise asks you to analyze two advertisements for sport-utility vehicles: a Jeep Grand Cherokee ad, which appeared in the March 2004 edition of *Brio*, an upscale, elegant, glamorous Japanese magazine (Figure 11.12), and an ad for the Hummer, which appeared in magazines like *Sports Illustrated* (see the Hummer ad in Chapter 2, p. 39). Note: In the full magazine-size version of the Jeep Cherokee ad, two shadowy figures are visible—the driver and the woman looking down on the Jeep from the lighted window high up in the building.

Working individually or in groups, address the following tasks:

1. Analyze the angle of vision of each ad as well as the use of any special camera techniques. Use the strategies chart on page 290.
2. Analyze the compositional features of each ad using the strategies chart on pages 291–292.
3. Pose questions raised by your analyses of each ad. For example, why does the Jeep Cherokee ad have the strange waterfall effect on the right side of the picture? Why did the Hummer ad designer choose this particular angle of vision?
4. Analyze the rhetorical appeals made by each ad. Who is the target audience for each ad? To what values does each ad appeal? How do the angle of vision, camera techniques, and compositional features of each ad work together to create appeals to those values? What roles do persons and vehicle play in each story? (Note: In the Japanese ad, the words in the upper left corner of the ad can be translated as, "Always have adventure in your heart. Jeep Grand Cherokee.")
5. Sport-utility vehicles are at the center of the public controversies over global warming, pollution of the environment, and the growing shortage of fossil fuel. Critics of SUVs commonly point out three ironies: (a) these vehicles, which are designed to take people out into nature, are contributing disproportionately to the destruction of nature; (b) these all-terrain vehicles are often used in urban driving that does not call for the size, power, or features of SUVs; and (c) these vehicles are gas-guzzlers in a time of rising gasoline prices, fuel shortages, and overdependence on imported oil. How do these ads work to deflect these criticisms and "hide" these ironies?

FIGURE 11.12 Jeep Grand Cherokee Ad

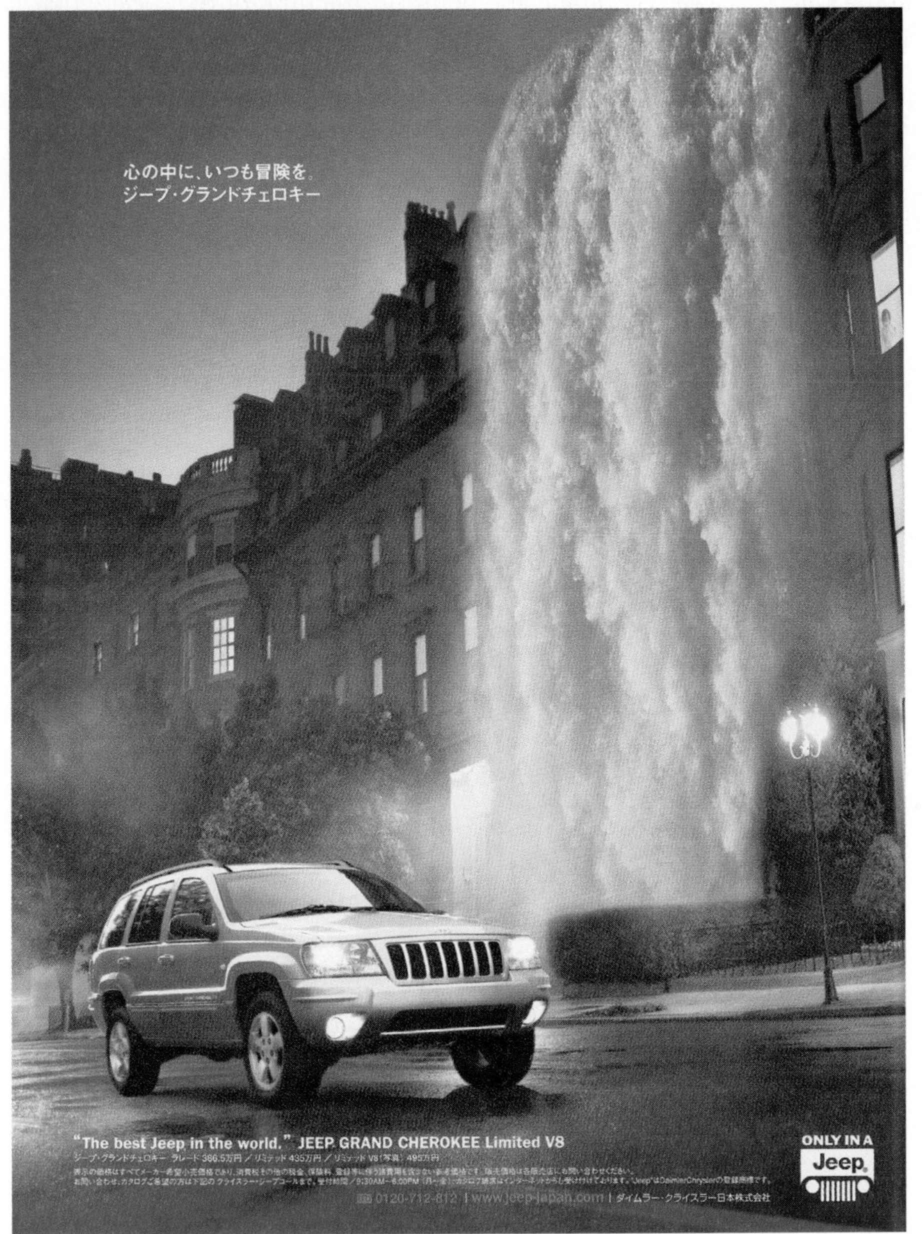

Courtesy Daimler Chrysler

Cultural Perspectives on Advertisements

There isn't space here to examine in depth the numerous cultural issues raised by advertisements, but we can introduce you to a few of them and provide some thought-provoking tasks for exploratory writing and talking. The key issue we want you to think about in this section is how advertisements not only reflect the cultural values and the economic and political structures of the society that produces them but also actively construct and reproduce that society.

For example, look at the 1924 advertisement for the Hoover vacuum cleaner shown in Figure 11.13. This ad appealed to a middle class that was becoming more dependent on household inventions as the use of domestic help became less common. In this ad, a well-dressed wife with carefully styled hair embraces her well-dressed husband as he returns from a day of work in the business world. Notice that the image and the words reinforce the idea of distinct gender roles

FIGURE 11.13
Hoover Ad

you darling!

"Give her a Hoover and you give her the Best"
The HOOVER
It BEATS ... as it Sweeps as it Cleans
ANOTHER year has slipped by since you last thought of giving her a Hoover.
But she has thought of it many times.
As cleaning days come and go she struggles resolutely with the only "tools" she has in her "workshop," your home.
And they are woefully inadequate, wasteful of time and strength.
As she wields her broom foot by foot across the dusty, dirty rugs her arms rebel and her back seems near to breaking.
Yet she tries to greet you with a smile when you come home at night.
In your heart you pay her tribute. "She's a brave little woman," you say.
But why put her courage to such an unfair test?
Why ask her to bear her burdens patiently when they can so easily be lifted?
The Hoover will save her strength.
The Hoover will speed her work.
The Hoover will safeguard her pride in a clean home.
You cannot afford to deny her these things for the small monthly payments which The Hoover costs.
Don't disappoint her again this Christmas!
Show her that you really do care, and throughout her lifetime your thoughtfulness will be ever in her mind.

while promoting pride in a comfortable, clean, and aesthetically pleasing home. The ad sells more than Hoover vacuum cleaners; it sells a vision of middle-class domestic harmony in which the wife's "natural" role is housecleaning.

In its depiction of gender roles, the Hoover ad now strikes us as very old-fashioned. However, cultural critics often argue that contemporary advertisements continue to depict women in culturally subordinate ways. In 1979, the influential sociologist and semiotician* Erving Goffman published a book called *Gender Advertising,* arguing that the way in which women are pictured in advertisements removes them from serious power. In many cases, Goffman's point seems self-evident. Women in advertisements are often depicted in frivolous, childlike, exhibitionistic, sexual, or silly poses that would be considered undignified for a man, such as the "Of Sound Body" Zenith ad (Figure 11.14). Women in advertisements are often fun to look at or enthralling to "gaze" at, but are seldom portrayed in positions of power. What distinguishes Goffman's work is his analysis of apparently positive portrayals of women in advertisements. He points out tiny details that differentiate the treatment of men from that of women. For example, when men hold umbrellas in an ad, it is usually raining, but women often hold umbrellas for decoration; men grip objects tightly, but women often caress objects or cup them in a gathering in or nurturing way. Female models dance and jump and wiggle in front of the camera (like children playing), whereas male models generally stand or sit in a dignified manner. Even when trying to portray a powerful and independent woman, ads reveal cultural signs that the woman is subordinate.

A decade later, another cultural critic, researcher Jean Kilbourne, made a more explicit argument against the way advertisements negatively construct women. In her films *Still Killing Us Softly* (1987) and *Slim Hopes: Advertising and the Obsession with Thinness* (1995), Kilbourne argues that our culture's fear of powerful women is embodied in advertisements that entrap women in futile pursuit of an impossible, flawless standard of beauty. Advertisements help construct the social values that pressure women (particularly middle-class white women) to stay thin, frail, and little-girlish and thus become perfect objects. In *Slim Hopes,* she claims that basically only one body type is preferred (the waif look or the waif-made-voluptuous-with-reconstructed-breasts look). Further, the dismemberment of women in ads—the focus on individual body parts—both objectifies women and intensifies women's anxious concentration on trying to perfect each part of their bodies. Kilbourne asserts that ads distort women's attitudes toward food through harmful and contradictory messages that encourage binging while equating moral goodness with thinness and control over eating. Ads convert women into lifelong consumers of beauty and diet products while undermining their self-esteem.

To what extent do the criticisms of Goffman or Kilbourne still apply to the most current advertisements? To what extent has advertising made gains in portraying women as strong, independent, intelligent, and equal with men in their potential for professional status? The picture painted by Goffman and Kilbourne is complicated by some new ads—for example, the new genre of physical fitness

*A *semiotician* is a person who studies the meanings of signs in a culture. A *sign* is any human-produced artifact or gesture that conveys meaning. It can be anything from a word to a facial expression to the arrangement of silverware at a dinner table.

ads that emphasize women's physical strength and capabilities as well as their sexuality and femininity. Ads for athletic products feature models with beautiful faces and skin and strong, trim, and shapely bodies. These ads strike different balances between female athleticism and sexuality, perhaps creating a more powerful view of women. (See the Nike "Hot Chick" ad, Figure 11.15.) It is also more common today to find ads picturing women in the military and in business roles

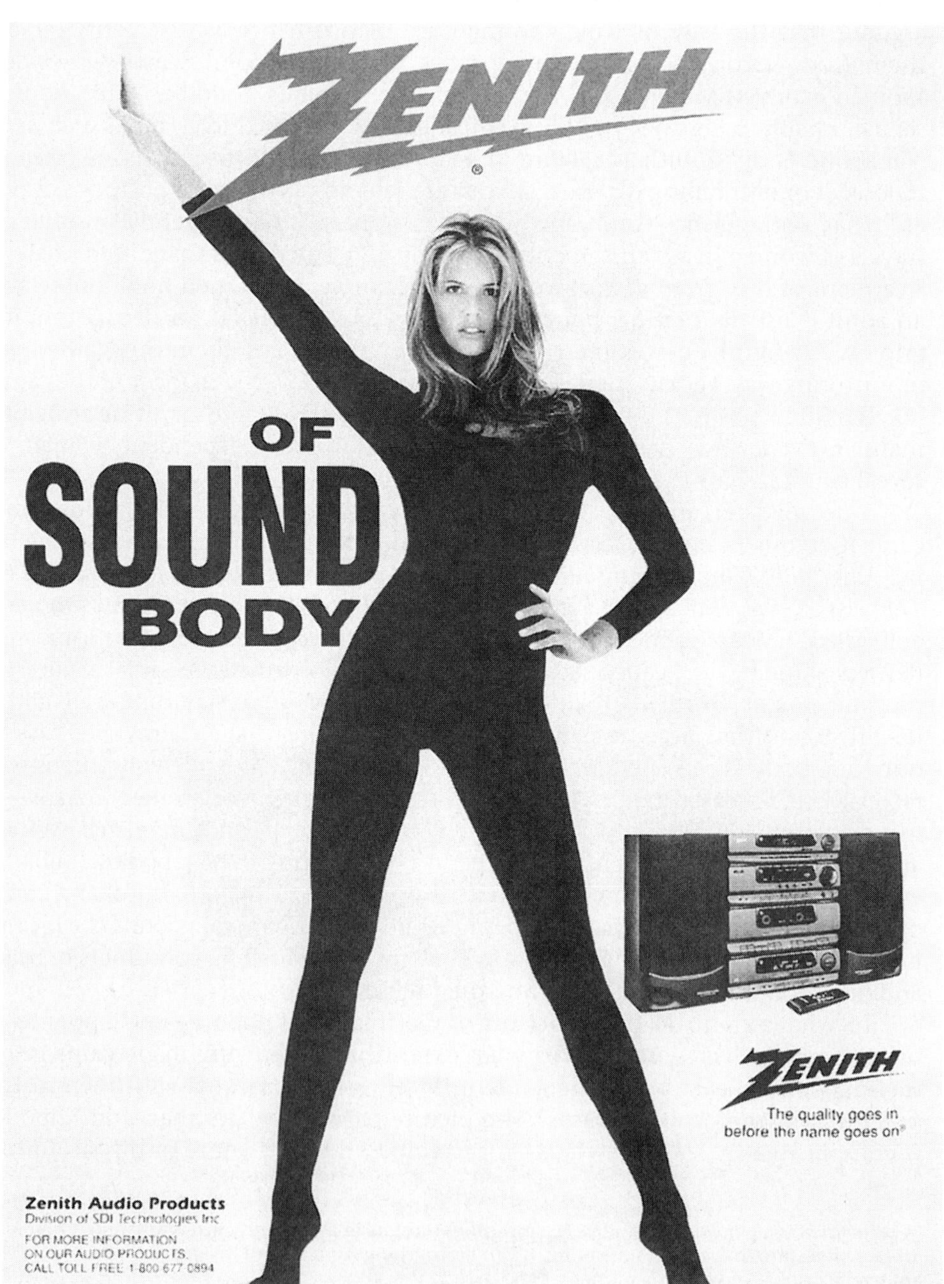

FIGURE 11.14
Zenith Audio Products Ad

FIGURE 11.15 Nike "Hot Chick" Ad

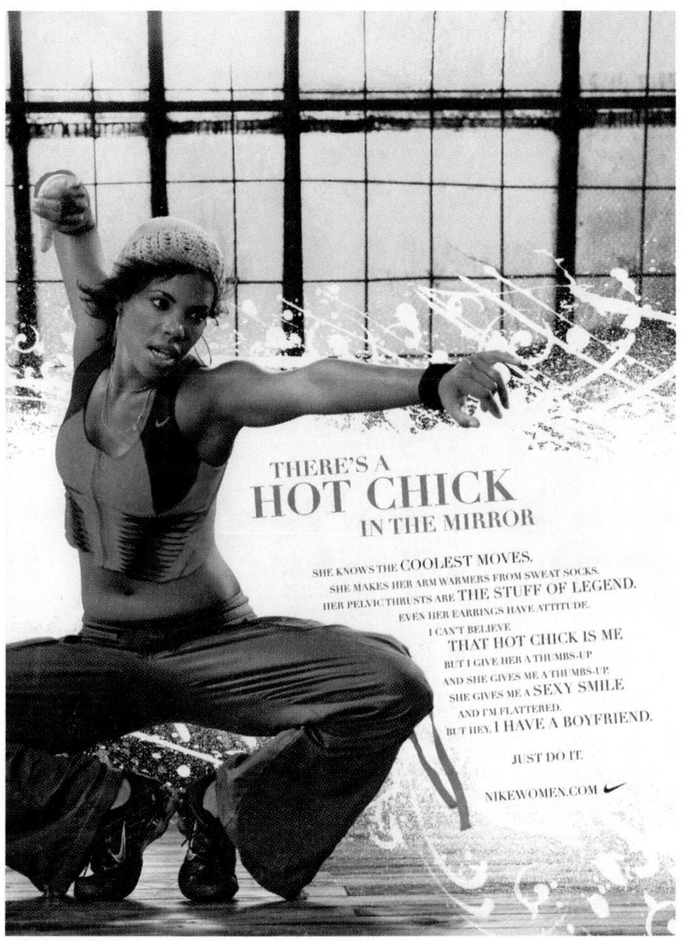

although these ads may send complex messages. For example, how would you describe the women in the U.S. Army ad on page 87 and in the "Simply Palm" ad in Figure 11.16?

FOR WRITING AND DISCUSSION

Examining Ads for Construction of Gender

To test for yourself the extent to which Goffman's and Kilbourne's claims about ads still apply, we invite you to explore this issue in the following sequence of activities, which combine class discussion with invitations for exploratory writing.

1. Examine the four ads discussed in the previous section: the Hoover ad (Figure 11.13); the "Of Sound Body" Zenith ad (Figure 11.14); the Nike "Hot Chick" ad (Figure 11.15); and the "Simply Palm" ad (Figure 11.16); as well as the U.S. Army ad (page 87). To what extent does each of these ads construct women

(*continued*)

FIGURE 11.16 "Simply Palm"

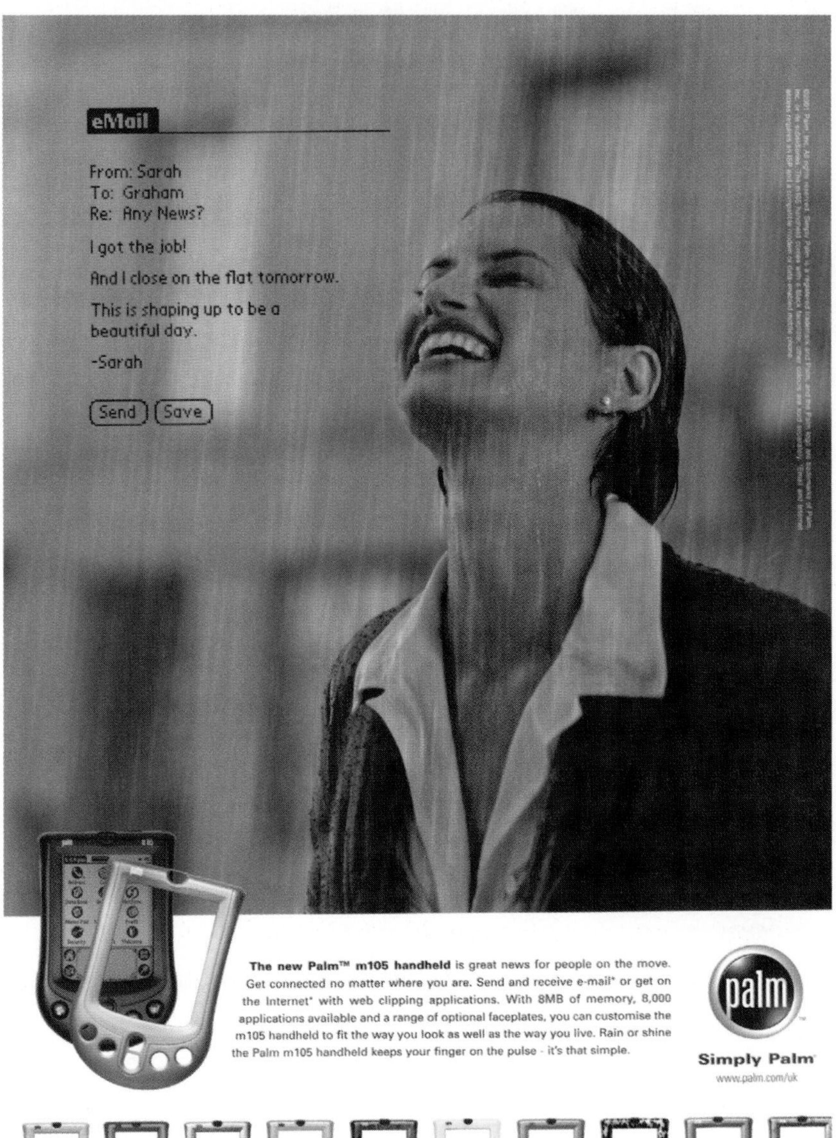

as lacking in power in the economic, political, and professional structures of our culture? Which ads, if any, treat women as powerful? Using these ads as your evidence, draw some conclusions about how the social roles for women have changed in the last eighty years. Freewrite your responses to the way women are constructed in these ads as preparation for class discussion.

2. Consider again the "Simply Palm" ad (Figure 11.16). To what extent would you call the woman in this ad an empowered professional? How might Goffman or Kilbourne argue that this ad subtly subordinates women? Try

playing the "What if they changed ... ?" game with this ad. What would be different if this ad featured a man rather than a woman to advertise the new Palm? How would the image change? How would the verbal text change?

3. Bring to class advertisements for women's clothing, perfumes, or accessories from recent issues of fashion and beauty magazines such as *Glamour, Elle, InStyle,* and *Vogue*. Study the ways that female models are typically posed in these ads. Then have male students assume the postures of the female models. How many of the postures, which look natural for women, seem ludicrous when adopted by men? To what extent are these postures really natural for women? To what extent do these postures illustrate Goffman's point that advertisements don't take women seriously?
4. Bring to class some examples of recent advertisements that you think portray women in a particularly positive and empowered way—ads that you think neither Goffman nor Kilbourne could deconstruct to show the subordination of women in our culture. Share your examples with the class and see whether your classmates agree with your assessment of these ads.
5. An excellent way to learn how to analyze advertisements is to create your own ad. For this exercise we invite you to create a laundry-soap ad aimed at men. According to an article in *American Demographics,* "Commercials almost never show men doing the laundry, but nearly one-fifth of men do at least seven loads a week. Men don't do as much laundry as women, but the washday gap may be closing. ... Yet virtually all laundry-detergent advertising is aimed at women."

   Working in small groups, create an idea for a laundry-detergent ad to be placed in a men's magazine such as *Men's Health, Sports Illustrated, Field and Stream,* or *Esquire*. Draw a rough sketch of your ad that includes the picture, the placement of words, and a rough idea of the content of the words. Pay particular attention to the visual features of your ad—the models' ages, ethnicity, social status or class, and dress; the setting, such as a self-service laundry or a home laundry; and other features. When you have designed a possible approach, explain why you think your ad would be successful.

Analysis of Two Visual Texts

WRITING PROJECT

Choose two print advertisements, posters, photographs, or paintings to analyze in a closed-form essay. Your two visual texts should have some common denominator: for example, they could be ads for the same product but for different consumer groups; they could be photographs of the same person or place taken or manipulated for different purposes; or they could be paintings with similar subject matter from different historical periods. Describe your two visual texts in detail so that your readers can easily visualize them without actually seeing them. For this closed-form analysis, choose several key points of contrast as the focus. Show how the details of the visual image—angle of vision, camera or paint techniques, compositional features—contribute to the image's rhetorical effect. If you are analyzing advertisements, also analyze how the visual images and the verbal text interact. In addition to analyzing the rhetorical appeals made by each ad, poster, photograph, or painting, you may also wish to evaluate or criticize your visual texts by commenting on the images of the culture they convey.

Exploring and Generating Ideas for Your Analysis

For the subject of your analysis, your instructor may allow you to choose your own visual images or may provide them for you. If you choose your own visual texts, be sure to follow your instructor's guidelines. In choosing your visual texts, look for some important commonality that will enable you to concentrate on similarities and differences in your analysis.

If you are writing about two ads, it is a good idea to find two ads that promote the same general product (for example, cars, perfume, watches, shampoo) to different target audiences or that make appeals to noticeably different value systems. Look for ads that are complex enough to invite detailed analysis. In comparing ads targeted at different demographic groups, you will want to think carefully about the audience-specific rhetorical appeals. For example, ad designers may vary their appeals to reach female versus male audiences or upper-middle-class versus lower-middle-class socioeconomic groups. Or the ads might vary in their appeals to reach African-American, Hispanic, or Asian markets. The student essay "How Cigarette Advertisers Address the Stigma Against Smoking" (pp. 316–318), written for this assignment, shows how choosing two ads for the same kind of product enables the writer to speculate about audience-specific appeals.

As a variation on this assignment, your instructor might ask you to analyze two photographs of a politician from magazines with different political biases; two news photographs from articles addressing the same story from different angles of vision; the images on the home pages of two Web sites presenting different perspectives on heated topics such as global warming, medical research using animals, or government spending on public transportation; or two advocacy ads for corporations or political causes that represent opposing views. Although these images, articles, and Web sites are not selling you a product per se, they are "selling" you a viewpoint on an issue, and thus you can apply the strategies in this chapter for analyzing camera techniques and use of details, props, and the posing of human figures to these other kinds of visual texts.

No matter what type of visual texts you are using, we suggest that you generate ideas and material for your analysis by using the question-asking strategies presented earlier in this chapter:

- Strategies for analyzing an image's angle of vision and techniques (p. 290)
- Strategies for analyzing the compositional features of images (pp. 291–292)

To help you generate more ideas, freewrite your responses to the following additional questions:

- How would this visual text have a different effect if some key features were changed? (For example, what if this character were holding a martini glass instead of a wine glass? What if the dog in the picture were a poodle rather than a black Lab? What if this model were a person of color rather than white?)
- Overall, to what fears, values, hopes, or dreams is this text appealing?

Shaping and Drafting Your Analysis

Your closed-form essay should be fairly easy to organize at the big-picture level, but each part will require its own organic organization depending on the main points of your analysis. At the big-picture level, you can generally follow a structure like the one shown in Figure 11.17.

If you get stuck, we recommend that you write your rough draft rapidly, without worrying about gracefulness or correctness, merely trying to capture your initial ideas. Many people like to begin with the description of the two visual texts and then write the analysis before writing the introduction and conclusion. After you have written your draft, put it aside for a while before you begin revising.

Revising

Most experienced writers make global changes in their drafts when they revise, especially when they are doing analytical writing. The act of writing a rough draft

FIGURE 11.17 Framework for an Analysis of Two Visuals

Introduction	• Hooks readers' interest; • Gives background on the two visual texts you are analyzing; • Sets up the similarities; • Poses the question your paper will address; • Ends with initial mapping in the form of a purpose or thesis statement.
General description of your two visual texts (ads, photographs, paintings)	• Describes each visual text in turn.
Analysis of the two visual texts	• Analyzes and contrasts each text in turn, using the ideas you generated from your observations, question asking, and close examination.
Conclusion	• Returns to the big picture for a sense of closure; • Makes final comments about the significance of your analysis;

generally leads to the discovery of more ideas. You may also realize that some of your original ideas aren't clearly developed or that the draft feels scattered or disorganized.

We recommend that you ask your classmates for a peer review of your draft early in the revising process to help you enhance the clarity and depth of your analysis.

Questions for Peer Review

In addition to the generic peer review questions explained in Chapter 17, Skill 4, ask your peer reviewers to address these questions:

1. How well do the title, introduction, and thesis set up an academic analysis?
2. Where does the writer capture your interest and provide necessary background information? How might the writer more clearly pose the question to be addressed and map out the analysis?
3. Where could the writer describe the visual texts more clearly so that readers can "see" them?
4. How has the writer established the complexity of the texts and their commonalities and differences?
5. How well has the writer used the questions about angle of vision, artistic techniques, and compositional features presented in this chapter to achieve a detailed and insightful analysis of the texts? Where could the writer add more specific details about settings, props, furniture, posing of characters, facial expressions, manners of dress, and so forth?
6. In what ways could the writer improve this analysis by clarifying, deepening, expanding, or reorganizing the analysis? How has the writer helped you understand something new about these two texts?

Our first reading is an excerpt from Paul Messaris's book *Visual Persuasion: The Role of Images in Advertising*. Messaris, a communications professor at the University of Pennsylvania, intended this book for an academic audience (hence his frequent parenthetical references to other scholars). His purpose is to analyze the distinctive features of visual communication and to examine the role of visual images in political campaigns and commercial advertising. In the following excerpt, Messaris explains his position on the ethical responsibility of advertisers. The particular question at issue is whether advertisers are being unethical when they display certain groups of people—in this passage, adolescents and African-Americans—in ways that are stereotypical, unrealistic, or potentially harmful to individuals or society.

Paul Messaris

From Visual Persuasion:

The Role of Images in Advertising

1 As we have seen, the iconicity* of images makes it possible for ads to elicit our attention and emotions by simulating various significant features of our real-world visual experiences. By virtue of their iconicity, visual ads are able to erect before our eyes a mirror world, with whose inhabitants we are invited to identify or to imagine that we are interacting. These acts of identification and imaginary interaction have real-world consequences. Some of the most revealing analyses of advertising have described the ways in which viewers use the characters they see in ads as reference points for their own evolving identities (Barthel, 1988; Ewen, 1988; Ewen & Ewen, 1982). For example, Carol Moog (1990) recalls how, as a young girl, she studied the posture of a woman in a refrigerator commercial to learn how to carry herself as an adult (p. 13). Together with fictional movies and TV programs, ads are a major source of images that young people can use to previsualize their places in the world of sexual and status relationships. It can be argued that advertisers have an ethical responsibility to take these circumstances into account in fashioning the images that they place before the public.

2 What might constitute a violation of this ethical responsibility? Critics of advertising images often focus on the discrepancy between the vision of life offered in ads and the needs or abilities of real people. Drawing on her practice as a psychotherapist, Moog (1990) cites the story of a young lawyer who expressed dissatisfaction with her life because she had not lived up to her potential as a member of "the Pepsi generation"—that is, "beautiful, sexy, happy, young people ... a generation that didn't slog through law school, work twelve-hour days, or break up with fiancés" (p. 15). Moog presents this vignette as a reminder of the fact that "advertisers are not in the business of making people feel better about themselves, they're in the *selling* business" (p. 16). As this statement implies, commercial advertising often does create a vision of a fantasy world that may become a source of dissatisfaction in people's real lives, and this is especially true of ads that use sex or status as part of their appeal. Some people may

**Iconicity* is an academic term (related to *icon*, meaning "image") referring to the power of images to influence a viewer. When you desire, for example, to meet a stranger in a Parisian café or to ride a horse through the pounding surf because you saw characters do these things in an ad, you experience the *iconic power* of the image.

find this practice objectionable in and of itself, although in my view it would be rather fatuous, as well as somewhat puritanical, to suggest that advertisers should stop purveying the images of "beautiful, sexy, happy young people" that led to Moog's client's distress. However, there is a related trend in advertising that does seem to me to raise especially troublesome ethical issues.

3 In recent years, ads aimed at young people have increasingly sought to appeal to an adolescent sense of frustration and resentment at the constricting demands of adult society. There may be a lingering element of this type of sentiment in the dissatisfaction expressed by Moog's client, but the kind of advertising to which I am referring is quite different from the old, Pepsi-generation style of happy, carefree images. Instead, these more recent ads, for products such as athletic shoes, off-road vehicles, or video games, often make a point of displaying abrasive, belligerent behavior and physical recklessness (cf. Lull, 1995, pp. 73–81). A defender of such ads might argue that they are simply being honest. Adolescents often have good reason to chafe at the standards imposed on them by older people and to recoil from the vision of the future that many of them face. The aggression and recklessness depicted in some of these ads are no doubt authentic expressions of how many young people feel. To put a happy face on those feelings could be considered hypocritical. Nevertheless, with due respect for such views, I would argue that the type of resentment exploited in these ads is unproductive at best, counterproductive at worst. Dissatisfaction that leads to impulsiveness and disregard for other people gains nothing from being expressed openly. In that sense, I would say that the ethics of this genre of advertising are certainly questionable.

4 This is not to say, however, that advertising aimed at young people should necessarily revert to the untroubled imagery of earlier times. It should be possible to portray and address youth honestly without pandering to the irresponsible tendencies that are sometimes associated with adolescence. For instance, despite the criticism that has recently been directed at the advertising of Calvin Klein, it seems to me that there are many Calvin Klein ads that manage to strike this balance quite effectively. In particular, the print ads for cK one fragrance have generated record-breaking sales while presenting a view of youthful sexuality that is remarkably unglamorized (compared to most other ads) and, furthermore, notably inclusive both racially and in terms of sexual orientation. This inclusiveness deserves special mention. The cK one ads are among the few examples of mass-produced imagery in which the mingling of people from different backgrounds appears relatively natural, rather than an artificial (albeit well-meaning) concoction of the media.

5 But, again, this comment should not be interpreted as a blanket endorsement of unvarnished naturalism in all of advertising. In a recent discussion of the portrayal of blacks and whites in the mass media, DeMott (1995) has argued that movies and ads present a phony picture of harmony between the races that serves to obscure the unpleasant truth about race relations in the United States. I do not find this argument persuasive. For one thing, information about racial friction is abundantly available elsewhere in the media. More importantly, though, I think it is a mistake to assume that people always look at advertising images expecting to see the way things really are in society. Almost by definition, the portrayals of the good life presented in ads carry with them the implicit

understanding that they are idealizations, not documentary reports (cf. Schudson, 1984). What people look for in such ads is a vision of the way things ought to be. Furthermore, when an ad is produced by a large corporation, people are likely to see this vision as an indicator of socially approved values—even though it also may be understood tacitly that those values do not correspond very closely to current social reality. From this perspective, the kinds of advertisements that DeMott criticizes—depictions of people from different racial and ethnic backgrounds living together in harmony and prosperity—are actually highly desirable. For example, an American Express Gold Card ad (attacked by DeMott) shows elegantly dressed blacks and whites occupying adjacent box seats in an opulent-looking theater or concert hall, while an ad for Chubb Insurance portrays two suburban families, one black, one white, posing together in a setting of obvious wealth. Such ads should be praised, not subjected to carping objections. In my view, they are models of the responsible use of advertising's iconic powers.

THINKING CRITICALLY
about "Visual Persuasion"

1. Messaris seeks to establish a middle position between two extreme views of advertisers' responsibility to viewers and consumers. How would you describe his view and the extremes he is reacting against?
2. Can you find examples of adolescent-directed ads portraying, in Messaris's words, "abrasive, belligerent behavior and physical recklessness"? What points can you raise in support of or against his censure of this type of ad?
3. Over the last two decades, the number of magazine ads featuring persons of color has increased substantially. Sometimes ads show multiracial groups. At other times, especially in middlebrow magazines such as *Parents' Magazine, Working Mother, Good Housekeeping,* and *Sports Illustrated,* ads now feature models from minority groups, where formerly the models would have been white. Observe closely the ads in Figures 11.18 through 11.21. To what extent do these ads present an equitable, harmonious multiracial and multicultural society? Do any of them contain racial or ethnic stereotypes? What vision of social reality, race, and class are these ads constructing?
4. Messaris refers to the argument of Benjamin DeMott that buddy movies featuring pals from different races or "happy harmony" ads showing blacks and whites together create a false sense that America no longer has a race problem. How do you think Messaris and DeMott would analyze the ads in Figures 11.18 through 11.21? Do you think the Dockers ad illustrates DeMott's idea of a "happy harmony" ad? How would you describe the difference in the image of the black males in the MetLife ad (Figure 11.18) and the Reeboks ad (Figure 11.20)? How do their clothes, positions, expressions, and attitudes differ and create different effects? What other features of the composition of the ads contribute to their impressions?

FIGURE 11.18 MetLife Ad

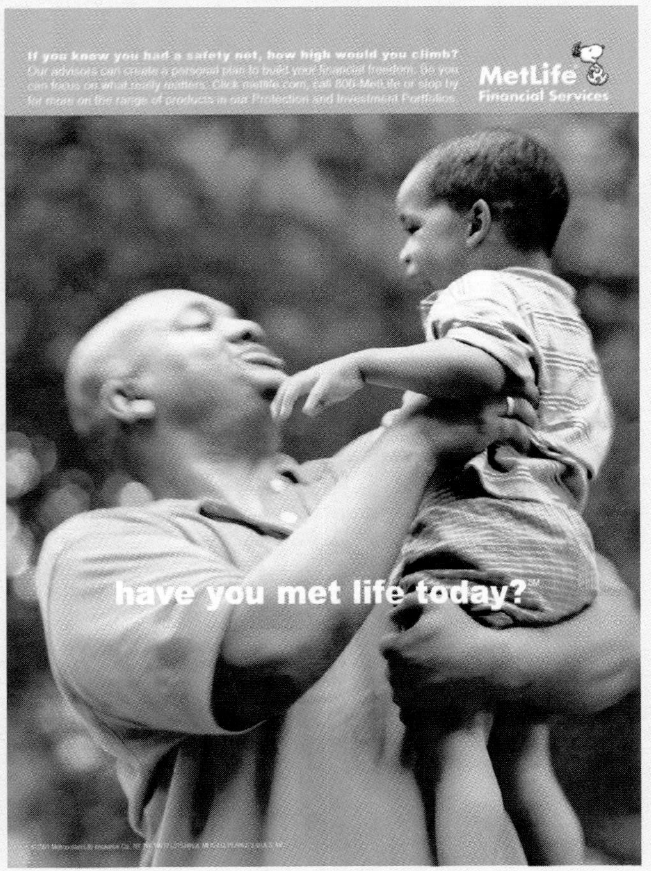

Courtesy of MetLife. PEANUTS (copyright) United Feature Syndicate, Inc.

FIGURE 11.19 PINE-SOL® Household Cleaner Ad

FIGURE 11.20 Reebok by Jay-Z Ad

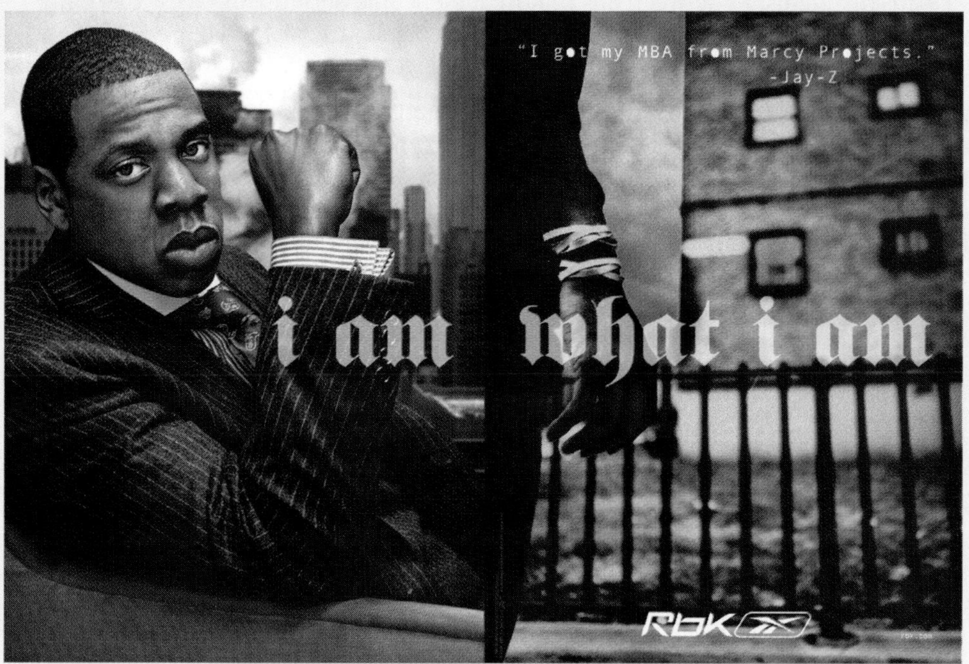

FIGURE 11.21 Dockers Ad

5. Messaris distinguishes between ads that include people of different races "naturally" and those that appear "artificial" and "concocted." Do the ads in Figures 11.18 and 11.20 seem to you to be natural or artificially concocted? Why or why not?

6. These ads also raise questions about the intersection of race and gender. We have asked how Messaris and DeMott might analyze these ads. Now ask how Goffman and Kilbourne might analyze them. Imagine the PINE-SOL Household Cleaner ad (Figure 11.19) using a white model rather than a black model (same pose, clothing, and body type with only the skin color changed). Would the ad work? Why or why not? Also consider the Dockers ad (Figure 11.21). This ad features a group of youthful to older adults, at least six women and two men, walking, talking, and laughing. Why did the ad designers choose this ratio of women to men, instead of an even number of men and women, or more men than women? Would the effect of the ad be different if more people were turning back towards a black woman or man, instead of apparently talking to the two white women on the left side of the ad? Why does the clothing on these models range from hot-weather to cold-weather clothes? What impression of this group do you think the ad designers were trying to achieve? How is that impression dependent upon the arrangement and posing of the models by gender and race?

The final reading is a student essay written in response to the assignment in this chapter. It contrasts the strategies of two different cigarette ads to make smoking appear socially desirable despite public sentiment to the contrary.

Stephen Bean (student)

How Cigarette Advertisers Address the Stigma Against Smoking:

A Tale of Two Ads

1 Any smoker can tell you there's a social stigma attached to smoking in this country. With smokers being pushed out of restaurants, airports, and many office buildings, how could anyone not feel like a pariah lighting up? While never associated with the churchgoing crowd, smoking is increasingly viewed as lower class or as a symbol of rebellion. Smoking has significantly decreased among adults while increasing among teenagers and young adults in recent years—a testament to its growing status as an affront to middle- and upper-class values. Cigarette advertisers are sharply tuned into this cultural attitude. They must decide whether to overcome the working-class/rebellious image of smoking in their advertisements or use it to their advantage. The answer to this question lies in what type of people they want an ad to target—the young? the rich? the poor?—and in what values, insecurities, and desires they think this group shares. Two contrasting answers to these questions are apparent in recent magazine ads for Benson & Hedges cigarettes and for Richland cigarettes.

2 The ad for Benson & Hedges consists of a main picture and a small insert picture below the main one. The main picture shows five women (perhaps thirty years old) sitting around, talking, and laughing in the living room of a comfortable and urbane home or upscale apartment. The room is filled with natural light and is tastefully decorated with antique lamps and Persian rugs. The women have opened a bottle of wine, and a couple of glasses have been poured. They are dressed casually but fashionably, ranging from slightly hip to slightly conservative. One woman wears a loose, black, sleeveless dress; another wears grungesque boots with a sweater and skirt. One of the women, apparently the hostess, sits on a sofa a bit apart from the others, smiles with pleasure at the conversation and laughter of her friends, and knits. Two of the women are smoking, and three aren't. No smoke is visible coming from the cigarettes. Underneath the main picture is a small insert photograph of the hostess—the one knitting in the main picture—in a different pose. She is now leaning back in pleasure, apparently after the party, and this time she is smoking a cigarette. Underneath the photos reads the slogan "For people who like to smoke."

3 The ad for Richland cigarettes shows a couple in their late twenties sitting in a diner or perhaps a tavern off the freeway. The remains of their lunch—empty burger and fries baskets, a couple of beer bottles—lie on the table. They seem to be talking leisurely, sharing an after-meal smoke. The man is wearing black jeans and a black T-shirt. The woman is wearing a pinkish skirt and tank top. Leaning back with her legs apart she sits in a position that signals sexuality. The slogan reads, "It's all right here." And at the bottom of the ad, "Classic taste. Right price." Outside the window of the diner you can see a freeway sign slightly blurred as if from heated air currents.

4 Whom do these different advertisements target? What about them might people find appealing? Clearly the Benson & Hedges ad is aimed at women, especially upper-middle-class women who wish to appear successful. As the media have noted lately, the social stigma against smoking is strongest among middle- and upper-class adults. My sense of the B&H ad is that it is targeting younger, college-educated women who feel social pressure to quit smoking. To them the ad is saying, "Smoking makes you no less sophisticated; it only shows that you have a fun side too. Be comfortable doing whatever makes you happy."

5 What choices did the advertisers make in constructing this scene to create this message? The living room—with its antique lamps and vases, its Persian rugs and hardcover books, and its wall hanging thrown over what appears to be an old trunk—creates a sense of comfortable, tasteful, upscale living. But figuring out the people in the room is more difficult. Who are these women? What is their story? What brought them together this afternoon? Where did their money come from? Are these professional women with high-paying jobs, or are they the wives of young bankers, attorneys, and stockbrokers? One woman has a strong business look—short hair feathered back, black sleeveless dress—but why is she dressed this way on what is apparently a Saturday afternoon? In contrast, another woman has a more hip, almost grunge look—slightly spiky hair that's long in the back, a loose sweater, a black skirt, and heavy black boots. Only one woman wears a wedding ring. It seems everything about these women resists easy definition or categorization. The most striking image in the ad is the hostess knitting. She looks remarkably domestic, almost motherly, with her

knees drawn close, leaning over her knitting and smiling to herself as others laugh out loud. Her presence gives the scene a feeling of safety and old-fashioned values amidst the images of independence. Interestingly, we get a much different image of the hostess in the insert picture placed just above the B&H logo. This picture shows the hostess leaning back pleasurably on the couch and smoking. The image is undeniably sexual. Her arms are back; she's deeply relaxed; the two top buttons of her blouse are open; her hair is slightly mussed; she smokes languidly, taking full pleasure in the cigarette, basking in the party's afterglow.

6 The opposing images in the advertisement (knitting/smoking, conservative/hip, wife/career, safe/independent, domestic/sexual) mean that these women can't easily be defined—as smokers or as anything else. For an ad promoting smoking, the cigarettes themselves take a back seat. In the main picture the cigarettes are hardly noticeable; the two women holding cigarettes do so inconspicuously and there is no visible smoke. The ad doesn't say so much that it is good to smoke, but that it is okay to smoke. Smoking will not make you less sophisticated. If anything, it only shows that you have an element of youth and fun. The slogan, "For people who like to smoke," targets nonsmokers as much as it does smokers—not so much to take up smoking but to be more tolerant of those who choose to smoke. The emphasis is on choice, independence, and acceptance of others' choices. The ad attacks the social stigma against smoking; it eases the conscience of "people who like to smoke."

7 While the B&H ad hopes to remove the stigma attached to smoking, the Richland ad feasts on it. Richland cigarettes aren't for those cultivating the upper-class look. The ad goes for a rebellious, gritty image, for beer drinkers, not wine sippers. While the story of the women in the B&H ad is difficult to figure out, the Richland ad gives us a classic image: a couple on the road who have stopped at a diner or tavern. Here the story is simpler: a man and woman being cool. They are going down the freeway to the big city. I picture a heavy American cruising car parked out front. Everything about the ad has a gritty, blue-collar feel. They sit at a booth with a Formica tabletop; the walls are bare, green-painted wood. The man is dressed in black with a combed-back, James Dean haircut. The woman wears a pink skirt with a tank top; her shoulder-length hair hasn't been fussed over, and she wears a touch of makeup. Empty baskets and bottles cluttering the table indicate they had a classic American meal—hamburgers, fries, and a beer—eaten for pleasure without politically correct worries about calories, polyunsaturated fats, cruelty to animals, or cancer. While the sexual imagery in the B&H ad is subtle, in the Richland ad it is blatant. The man is leaning forward with his elbows on the table; the woman is leaning back with her legs spread and her skirt pushed up slightly. Her eyes are closed. They smoke leisurely, and the woman holds the cigarette a couple of inches from her expecting lips. The slogan, "It's all right here," is centered beneath the woman's skirt. Smoking, like sex, is about pure pleasure—something to be done slowly. Far from avoiding working-class associations with smoking, this ad aims to reinforce them. The cigarettes are clearly visible, and, unlike the cigarettes in the B&H ad, show rings of rising smoke. This ad promotes living for the moment. The more rebellious, the better.

8 So we see, then, two different ways that cigarette companies address the stigma against smoking. The B&H ad tries to eliminate it by targeting middle-class, college-educated women. It appeals to upscale values, associating cigarette smoking with

choice, and showing that "people who like to smoke" can also knit (evoking warm, safe images of domestic life) or lean back in postparty pleasure (evoking a somewhat wilder, more sexual image). In contrast, the Richland ad exploits the stigma. It associates smoking with on-the-road freedom, rebellion, sexuality, and enjoyment of the moment. The smoke visibly rising from the cigarettes in the Richland ad and noticeably absent from the Benson & Hedges ad tells the difference.

THINKING CRITICALLY

about "How Cigarette Advertisers Address the Stigma Against Smoking"

1. Stephen Bean argues that the Benson & Hedges and the Richland ads use very different appeals to encourage their target audiences to smoke. What are the appeals he cites? Do you agree with Stephen's analysis?
2. Collect a variety of cigarette ads from current magazines, and analyze their various appeals. How do the ads vary according to their intended audiences? Consider ads targeted at men versus women or at audiences from different VALS segments.
3. What do you see as the strengths and weaknesses of Stephen's essay?

For additional writing, reading, and research resources, go to **www.MyCompLab.com** and choose **Ramage/Bean/Johnson's *The Allyn & Bacon Guide to Writing,* Fifth Edition.**

CHAPTER 12

ANALYZING A SHORT STORY

You've no doubt had more than one experience analyzing literature. For some students, such analysis is fun. It gives you a welcome break from densely packed textbook pages while stimulating your imagination. For others, the very word *literary* might trigger memories of mystifying class discussions and teachers' seemingly arbitrary decrees about the "hidden meaning" of something. Our goal in this chapter is to demonstrate that analyzing literature need not be either mystifying or arbitrary. In fact, analyzing literature is quite similar to analyzing just about any type of text or event: asking questions that you think will intrigue your reader as well as yourself and studying the text to find what answers it provides. What's different about literary analysis is that it opens up imaginative possibilities that can entertain and delight readers as well as inform them.

This chapter introduces you to a common genre encountered in English and literature courses:

- The literary analysis or critical interpretive essay, which poses an interpretive question about a literary text and offers an answer to the question supported by evidence from the text and the writer's critical thinking.

To begin understanding literary analysis, try to think of literature not so much as a collection of great books to be read, but rather as a way of reading. Or, put another way, you can choose to read anything literally or literarily. When you read something *literally*, you attempt to reduce its meaning to one clear set of statements and disregard other possible ways of reading the text. When you read something *literarily*, you read it playfully and openly, trying to see in it a wide range of possible meanings.

To help you understand the distinction we're drawing, consider the following analogy: A literal reading of an imaginative text is like a packaged bus tour of an unfamiliar city. Picture a bus filled with out-of-town conventioneers going from one landmark to the next, but missing the details of the city's lived life. The first step in moving beyond a literal to a literary understanding of a text, or a city, is to get off the bus. Stop being a tourist and become instead a traveler. Open yourself up to the otherness of a text the way travelers on foot open up to the sights and sounds of a new place to understand the diverse ways that humans create their lives. Reading literarily, experience the text on its own terms; that is, read it carefully, noticing and examining your reactions to what you have read. Travelers aren't driven by a desire to have been somewhere so they can tell others that they were there. Instead, they are driven by curiosity, a sense of wonder, a knack for recognizing resemblances in a world of apparent differences, and a capacity for being enthralled by the differences they do find.

To be a traveler rather than a tourist, you need to be an active participant in the process of constructing meaning from a text. Whereas tourists tend to write brief "We're here!" notes on postcards to friends, travelers are more likely to keep journals to help them remember and understand their experiences. They reflect on what they see and on relationships between what they see, do, and feel one day to what they've seen, done, or felt in the past or to what others have reported seeing, doing, and feeling in the same place.

In this way, travelers interpret what they experience. An interpretation focuses on an ambiguous aspect of a text or experience and says, "Here's what I think is most probable." Unlike a traditional argument, which obligates the writer to refute other points of view, an interpretation may simply point out alternative explanations of the ambiguity and then focus on the writer's own interpretation and the evidence that supports it.

Exploring Literary Analysis

As we have noted, any sort of text can be read either literally or literarily. However, texts do tend to invite one kind of reading over another. The following Navajo legend contains several signals that invite us to read literarily rather than literally. As you read this piece, note where those signals occur.

Retold by Evelyn Dahl Reed

The Medicine Man

1 There is a telling that, in the beginning, when the animals first came up from the darkness to live above the ground, Coyote was sent ahead by Thought Woman to carry a buckskin pouch far to the south.

2 "You must be very careful not to open the pouch," she told him, "or you will be punished."

3 For many days, Coyote ran southward with the pouch on his back. But the world was new, and there was nothing to eat along the way, so he grew very hungry. He wondered if there might be food in the pouch. At last, he took it from his back and untied the thongs. He looked inside and saw nothing but stars. Of course, as soon as he opened the pouch the stars all flew up into the sky, and there they are to this day.

4 "Now look what you've done," said Thought Woman. "For now you shall always get into trouble everywhere you go."

5 And because Coyote disobeyed, he was also made to suffer with the toothache. When the other animals were asleep, he could only sit and howl at the stars. Thus, he has been crying ever since the beginning of the world.

6 Sometimes he would ask the other animals to cure him, but they would only catch the toothache from him, and they, too, would cry.

7 One day he met Mouse, who lived in a little mound under the chaparral bush. "Friend Mouse," begged Coyote, "can you cure me of this toothache?"

8 Now it happened that while digging underground, as is his habit, Mouse had come upon a sweet-smelling root and had put it with the other herbs in the pouch he always carried. He was said to be very wise in the use of herbs.

9 "I don't know," said Mouse, "but I have just found a new root, and it may be that it will help you." He rubbed the root on Coyote's swollen cheek, and in a little while the toothache was gone.

10 This is how it happened that coyotes never hunt or kill field mice.

THINKING CRITICALLY
about "The Medicine Man"

1. List the signals in the text that led you to read this story literarily as opposed to literally. Summarize the most important differences between how you read this story and how you read the introduction to this chapter.

2. Devise questions about the legend that you think might produce different responses among your classmates. For example: Why is the woman named Thought Woman? Why is Thought Woman a female and not a male?

3. Explain why you think these questions will evoke different responses.

Understanding Literary Analysis

The Truth of Literary Events

As an introduction to literary analysis, let's discuss "The Medicine Man" and consider several questions that it, and other texts of its sort, pose to the reader. First, in what sense is the story true? What advantages are there to expressing a view of truth in a literary, rather than in a literal, way? Why might someone choose to tell such a story rather than approach the world scientifically? What other stories does "The Medicine Man" remind you of? How is it different from those stories? How are the characters in the story like and unlike characters you've known in real life?

"The Medicine Man" is immediately recognizable as literary; it's difficult, if not impossible, to read it literally. Animals can't talk, and galaxies can't be carted about in a buckskin pouch. We either make a leap of faith and license the author to play fast and loose with our conventional understanding of reality, or we put the story down, dismayed that anyone could think we'd be gullible enough to buy this twaddle.

The events of the story are presented to us as if they actually happened. We know better, but we go along with the ruse in order to enjoy the story. We know that when we read these sorts of texts, we can't demand a one-to-one correspondence between the words we read and the things, persons, and events to which they supposedly refer. We must read instead with what the poet Coleridge called "a Willing Suspension of Disbelief."

Suspending disbelief does not mean erasing it. While we're reading literarily, we are to some degree consciously suppressing skepticism and nagging doubts, leftovers of our literal-minded selves. Both ways of looking at the story—literal and literary—are open to us, and we consciously choose one over the other. While we're reading "The Medicine Man," we never really forget that coyotes can't talk. But if coyotes could talk, we can imagine them talking as this coyote talks.

The both/and principle allows us to become engrossed in the events in a fictional story, while at the same time standing back from the story to analyze how it works.

Writing (about) Literature

We put "about" in parentheses in this heading because in a sense, to write about literature is to write literature. When you read literarily you are an active cocreator of the text just as a musician is a cocreator of a concerto. This reading as performance is quite different from the more passive process of literal reading. Whereas the literal reader expects to find unambiguous, universally shared meaning in the text, the literary reader anticipates having to create meaning, which then must be justified to other readers and modified by them. For the literal reader, meaning is a commodity that is extracted intact from the text much as gold nuggets are sluiced from a stream. For the literary reader, meaning is more like a quilt constructed from bits and pieces of the text by many people who consult and argue and admire each other's skill and change each other's minds about which pieces to include and where to put them.

To participate in the reading process actively, to "write" your version of a text, you need to know the kinds of questions you might ask of it. To help you, we briefly summarize five critical elements of a literary text and the kinds of questions each element suggests.

For additional discussion of these elements and of open-form writing in general, refer to Chapter 7 and Chapter 19.

Asking Questions about Plot

Plot refers to the sequence of critical events in the story. The key term here is *critical*. A plot summary does not include everything that happens in a story; it focuses on the elements that most directly move the action of the story forward. One method of analyzing the plot is to begin by identifying what you see as the most critical single event or moment in a story. What is the most pivotal point, the one that prior events lead up to and that subsequent events derive from? Different readers are apt to pick different moments, indicating differences in the way they read the story. Your task is to identify your own choice and to be prepared to defend it. Remember, you are *performing* the story, not trying to figure out some unambiguous right meaning. As long as you have a rationale for your decision, you are acting as a literary critic.

Asking Questions about Setting

Although a setting is sometimes little more than a backdrop, like a black curtain behind a speaker on a stage, it can also serve to amplify or help explain the events and motivations of a story. Sometimes the setting acts as a symbol or serves the same function in a story that theme music serves in a movie, underscoring the text's primary themes and moods. A story could be set at the edge of a dark forest, on an ascent up a mountain, or in an inner city, with action moving back and forth between remote vacant lots and a warm kitchen. Sometimes setting plays an active role in the text, functioning almost as a character. A setting could thwart the protagonist's efforts to bring about change or to survive; for example, the collapse of a bridge could prevent a character from crossing a river. Does setting play a role in the story you are analyzing? If so, how would you characterize that role? Could you picture the events of the text taking place in a significantly different setting? Why or why not?

Asking Questions about Characters

Characters are the people who make the decisions that forward the plot and whose fortunes change as a result of the plot. You can understand characters in a text only in relationship to each other and to the direction of change in the text. The major character, sometimes called the *protagonist,* is typically the one most responsible for forwarding the plot. In action stories, these characters are pretty static: Dirty Harry or Batman may undergo occasional physical changes and disguises, but their characters tend not to grow or deepen. In other kinds of stories, the major character may change significantly in terms of fortune, insight, or understanding. Which characters change in the story you are examining? How do they change? Which characters do not change? Why do the characters change or not change?

To examine the characters' relationships with each other, you might start with the protagonist and consider the other characters according to how they help or hinder the protagonist. Characters may contribute to the plot by overt action or inaction, by recognizing or failing to recognize something of significance, by adapting to the situation of the story or by being inflexible. They can guide or misguide the protagonist, be a friend or foe, share or threaten the protagonist's values or beliefs, and so forth. What tensions, contrasts, and differing points of view do you see among the characters?

Asking Questions about Point of View

Perhaps the toughest element to perceive in a fictional work is point of view. It does not exist out there on the page as do character and plot. Point of view is the filter through which the reader views the action of a story. In some cases the impact of point of view on your perception of a character or event is obvious; in other cases it is not. The point of view can trick you into seeing an event in a particular way that you will have to revise when you realize that the narrator's perspective was limited, biased, or ironic. Often the narrator's values and perceptions are different from those of the author; you should never assume that the narrator of the story and the author are the same.

The two primary elements of point of view are time and person. Most stories are told in the past tense, a significant number in the present tense, and a few in the future tense. An almost equal number of stories are told in the first person (in which case the narrator is usually an actor in the story, although not always the main character) as in the third person (in which case the narrator tells the story from a position outside the tale). All choices of tense and person affect the reader's perception of a story. For example, a story told in the first-person present tense ("We ride back from the hunt at dusk") has an immediacy that a story told in the third-person past ("They rode back from the hunt at dusk") does not have. You learn about a first-person narrator both from what the narrator does or says in the plot and from how the narrator tells the story—what he or she includes or omits, the sentence structure, tone, or figures of speech that he or she adopts, and so forth. A third-person narrator may be objective (the narrator sees only the external actions of characters) or omniscient (the narrator can enter the minds and feelings of various characters). Sometimes a third-person narrator is omniscient with respect to one character but objective toward others.

Narrators can provide a full and complete sense of a given character (by entering that character's mind as an omniscient narrator) or a partial view only (by observing the character from the outside). Some stories feature multiple points of view through multiple narrators. For example, one character may discover a journal written by another character or may listen to a story told by another character.

The surest path to understanding point of view is to start with your feelings and attitudes toward characters and events and then to examine the extent to which point of view contributes to those attitudes. Do you trust the narrator? Do you like the narrator? Has the narrator loaded the dice, causing you to see characters or events in strongly slanted ways? Is the narrator scrupulously objective or ironic to the point that you're not quite sure what to make of his or her observations?

To ask questions about point of view, begin by asking whether the narrative is first or third person. Then ask whether the narrator's perspective is omniscient or limited. Does the narrator reveal bias or irony? Do you feel that there is more to the story than the narrator is telling you? What does the narrator leave out? How are the narrator's perceptions different from your own?

Asking Questions about Theme

If a plot is what happens in a story, then theme is the significance of what happens. Your response to the question, "So what?" after reading a story represents your notion of the story's theme. Sometimes, a theme is obvious—the main characters might discuss it, or the author might even state it outright. Often, however, a theme is veiled, and you have to infer it from the words and deeds of the characters.

One way to discover theme is simply to reflect on your immediate responses to characters or on passages that affected you particularly strongly. Consider questions such as these: How did this story change your view of something or the way you feel about something? Is this story trying to reveal something about racism? About endurance in a time of trial? About growth from one phase of life to another? About appearance versus reality? About conflicts between the individual and family? About exterior loss and interior gain? About rebellion from society? About what's really valuable versus what appears to be valuable? About establishing values in a confusing world?

You can often gain valuable insights into a story's theme by examining the connections among the various literary elements we have been discussing. These points of intersection may also help you generate significant interpretive questions.

WRITING PROJECT

An Analysis of a Short Story

Your writing project for this chapter has two parts—a formal essay analyzing a short story and a series of reading log entries that will prepare you to write your essay. Your entries in your reading log will give you an opportunity to explore your own understanding of the story, pose questions about it, and then compare your ways of reading and responding to it with your classmates' experiences of it. This process of writing about and discussing the story will help you find places in the text where readers' understandings differ, where ambiguities lead to uncertainties about some aspect of the story. These places will prompt *interpretive questions*—that is, questions for which the text contains evidence that supports more than one good thesis regarding, for example, events, motives, or meaning. Such questions are the perfect starting points for an interpretive paper like the one called for in the following assignment.

For help choosing or framing such questions, review Chapter 1, Concept 2, about posing interesting, problematic, and significant questions.

> Pose an interpretive question about a short story and respond to it analytically, showing your readers where and how the text of the story supports your interpretation. In the introduction to your essay, pose an interesting, problematic, and significant question about the story, one that can be answered several different ways according to the evidence in the text. Look for a question that might lead to differences in opinion among your classmates and that offers readers new insights into the story. Your task in this assignment is not to discover the right way to interpret the text, but to explain *your* way of reading some aspect of it.

Using a closed-form structure, present your thesis about the story and your supporting arguments. Before you give your thesis, make clear just what question you are putting to the text and why. It is this question that will engage your readers' interest and make them look forward to your analysis. Then, in the body of your paper, explain your own responses to this question, contrasting your answer with other possible interpretations that have been proposed by your classmates or that you yourself have considered. Without disputing the alternative interpretations, concentrate on showing your readers how you arrived at *your* interpretation and why you think that that interpretation is valuable. Use details from the story for support.

Reading the Story and Using Reading Logs

To help you settle on a good question for your paper and to develop and share ideas, we have prepared a series of reading log questions for you to use in exploring the story. Your reading log will help you the most if you write in response to each freewriting task.

The reading log entries will help you pose a good question about your assigned short story. Good literary questions call attention to problematic details of the text, stimulate conversation, and provoke readers to return to the text to reread and rethink. You know you have a good question if your classmates disagree about the answer and contribute their own differing views to the conversation. Sharing your reading log entries with classmates will help you generate and sustain a productive discussion about the short story.

Reading the First Time

We ask you now to read the short story your instructor has designated for this assignment. Task 1 asks you to stop several times along the way as you read. Tasks 2 and 3 should be written immediately after you finish reading.

Reading Log Task 1: As you read your assigned story, stop at several points and predict what you think will happen in the rest of the story. Make your first stop fairly early in the story, choose a second stopping place in the middle, and stop a third time near the end. In each case, predict what is going to happen next and note what in the text causes you to make your prediction. Freewrite for three or four minutes each time you stop.

Reading Log Task 2: As soon as you finish your reading, write down your immediate responses to the text—how it made you feel or think, what emotions it triggered, what issues it raised. Freewrite for five minutes.

Reading Log Task 3: Write down (a) what most interested you about the story and (b) the most important question you're left with after reading the text. Freewrite for a couple of minutes after several minutes of reflecting.

FOR WRITING AND DISCUSSION

Impressions and Questions

As a whole class or in small groups, share your responses to the reading log tasks. Because you need to begin your formal essay for this assignment with a problematic question, pay particular attention to your classmates' responses to (b) in Task 3—the most important question raised by the story. Perhaps you have a tentative answer that you would like to propose to someone else's question.

Analyzing the Plot

Reading Log Task 4: What is the single most important moment or event in your assigned story? Why do you see this moment as important or crucial? Freewrite for about ten minutes.

FOR WRITING AND DISCUSSION

Plot

As a whole class or in small groups, share your responses to Task 4. Which events did you choose and what are your arguments for selecting them? Take notes about how your classmates' interpretations differ.

Analyzing the Setting and Characters

Reading Log Task 5: What is worth noting about your assigned story's setting? What is the setting? How does it change? Consider multiple aspects of time, location, atmosphere, and so forth, to discern the role that setting plays in the unfolding events. Freewrite for ten minutes on your ideas about the importance of setting in the story.

Reading Log Task 6: Who do you think is the most important character in the story? How does this character change or grow as the story progresses? How do the other characters promote or inhibit change in the main character? How do they help you see and understand the changes? Freewrite for ten to fifteen minutes.

FOR WRITING AND DISCUSSION

Setting and Characters

Share your reading log entries for Tasks 5 and 6 and note differences in the interpretations of various members of the class. Remember that you are not seeking the one right answer to these questions. You are trying to determine how *you* read this story.

Analyzing Point of View

Reading Log Task 7: What is the story's point of view? What is the narrator's role in the unfolding of events? How do the narrator's perceptions filter your understanding of the story? Do you consider the narrator's perceptions reliable, or does the text suggest alternative understandings? Is the narrator's way of seeing part of what the story is about? Freewrite for ten minutes on ideas you generate by contemplating the story's point of view.

FOR WRITING AND DISCUSSION

Point of View

Share your reading log entry for Task 7 with your class and note differences in interpretations.

Revisiting the Story

Reading Log Task 8: Reread your response to Task 2, your first attempt to articulate ideas related to the story's theme. Then complete one of the following statements: (a) After further reflection on my assigned story, I think the author is trying to say something to readers about ________________. (b) Here is what this story makes me think about and see: ________________. Freewrite for ten minutes.

Reading Log Task 9: Look again at the place in the story that you identified in Task 4 as its most important moment or event. (a) What role do the elements of *character* that you identified in Task 6 play in this crucial passage? (b) Do elements of the story's *setting* contribute to your understanding of the importance of this passage? How do these details add to its impact? (c) How does *point of view* contribute to a reader's sense of the importance of the events and/or description in this passage? (d) Does your analysis of the interconnections of these literary elements give you new ideas or raise new questions for you about the story's *theme*? Freewrite for ten minutes.

FOR WRITING AND DISCUSSION

Theme and Critical Elements

Share your responses to Reading Log Tasks 8 and 9 with your class and note differences in the ways members of the class read this story.

The reading log entries you've completed in conjunction with your assigned story should help you considerably when you plan your essay. Begin that planning by writing out the question you will pose and explore in your paper. As we have seen, a good question, one that is problematic and significant, is one that promotes engaged conversation and differing points of view. To help you decide on a question, the reading log tasks in this section ask you to freewrite in response to several different "starter questions." After you decide on a question, you will need to explore ways to answer it, using textual details for support.

Generating and Exploring Ideas

To help you settle on a good problematic question for the introduction of your formal essay, we list several starter questions that focus on *turning points*—major changes in a story's character, plot, language, and point of view. You may want to begin with one of these questions and then refine it to make it more specific to the story.

After reviewing these questions, complete the two reading log tasks that follow.

Turning-Point Starter Questions about a Short Story

1. Changes in character
   a. How do circumstances change for each character? What sets each change of circumstance in motion?
   b. How does each character's understanding or knowledge change?
   c. How does your attitude toward each character change?
   d. How does each character's relationship to other characters change?

2. Changes in language
   a. How does the dialogue change? Do characters talk to each other differently at any point?
   b. How does the tone of the language change? Does it become lighter or darker at given points?
   c. How do the metaphors and similes change? Is there a pattern to that change?
3. Changes in point of view
   a. How does the narrator's attitude toward the characters and events change? Does the narrator move closer or farther away from characters and events at any point?
   b. How trustworthy or credible is the narrator? If the narrator is not credible, at what point do you first suspect him or her of unreliability?
4. Changes in setting
   a. How does the time or place depicted in the text change? How are other changes in the text related to these changes?

Reading Log Task 10: Using the turning-point starter questions to stimulate your thinking, pose five or six specific turning-point questions about your assigned story.

Reading Log Task 11: Choose one of your turning-point questions and explore your own answer to it.

Looking at turning points is not the only way to pose questions about a text. A second list of starter questions focuses on other considerations, such as theme, values, and character. Review the questions and then complete the two reading log tasks that follow.

Additional Starter Questions

1. How does the story's title contribute to your understanding of the story?
2. What does each of the major characters seek and want? What are each character's values?
3. Which character's beliefs and values are closest to your own? How so?
4. What are the main conflicts in the story? What or who blocks the characters from reaching their goals (remember, sometimes what blocks them may be inside them), and how much control do they have over achieving their ends?
5. How successful are the characters in achieving their goals and how do they respond to the outcome?
6. Among all the characters, who seems to best understand what happens and why?

Reading Log Task 12: Use these additional starter questions to pose two or three specific questions about your assigned story.

Reading Log Task 13: Choose one of your questions and explore your responses to it.

Choosing Your Problematic Question and Exploring Your Answer

You're now ready to choose the question that will initiate your essay and to explore your answer. For the final reading log tasks, freewrite rapidly to spill your ideas onto the paper and avoid writer's block. Before you begin, read over what you have written so far in your reading log to help you get the juices flowing.

Reading Log Task 14: Write out the question that you want to ask in your essay about your assigned short story. What makes this an interesting and significant question? Why don't you and your classmates immediately agree on the answer?

Reading Log Task 15: Freewriting as rapidly as you can, explore your answer to the question you asked in Task 14. Use textual details and your own critical thinking to create an argument supporting your answer.

Shaping, Drafting, and Revising

Reading Log Tasks 14 and 15 give you a head start on a rough draft. The best way to organize your literary analysis is to follow the problem-thesis pattern of closed-form prose:

First, begin with an introduction that poses your question about the text and shows readers why it is an interesting, problematic, and significant question. To show why your question is problematic, you may want to refer briefly to differing interpretations your classmates have suggested or you have considered. At the end of your introduction, be sure to include a thesis statement—a one-sentence summary answer to your question. Early in the introduction you may need to supply background about the story so that readers can understand your question.

Second, write the main body of your essay, in which you develop and support your thesis using textual details and argument. There is no formula for organizing the body. The major sections depend on your argument and the steps needed to make your case. If you haven't already summarized alternative interpretations in the introduction, you may choose to do so in the body. The key here is to create tension for your thesis and to demonstrate the significance of your interpretation.

Conclude by returning to your essay's big picture and suggesting why your answer to your opening question is significant. What larger implications does your analysis have for the story? What kind of changed view of the story do you want to bring about in your readers' minds? Why is this view important? You may choose to write about different value systems or different ways of reading that distinguish *your* analysis of the story from that of some of your classmates.

After you have produced a good rough draft, let it sit for a while. Then try it out on readers, who can follow the Questions for Peer Review. Based on your readers' advice, begin revising your draft, making it as clear as possible for your readers. Remember to start with the big issues and major changes and then work your way down to the smaller issues and minor changes.

Questions for Peer Review

In addition to the generic peer review questions provided in Chapter 17, Skill 4, ask your peer reviewers to address these questions:

INTRODUCTION:

1. Does the title arouse interest and forecast the problem to be addressed? How might the author improve the title?
2. How does the introduction capture your interest, explain the question to be addressed, and suggest why it is both problematic and significant?
3. Does the introduction conclude with the writer's thesis? Is the thesis surprising? How might the author improve the introduction?

ANALYSIS AND INTERPRETATION:

4. How has the writer shown that his or her thesis is in conflict with alternative interpretations or views?
5. How is the essay organized? Does the writer helpfully forecast the whole, place points before particulars, use transitions, and follow the old/new contract as explained in Chapter 18? How might the author improve or clarify the organization?
6. Where does the author quote from the story (or use paraphrase or other specific references to the text)? How are each of the author's points grounded in the text? What passages not cited might better support the argument? What recommendations do you have for improving the author's use of supporting details?
7. Where do you disagree with the author's analysis? What aspects of the story are left unexplained? What doesn't fit?

Here are two short stories to test your analytical skills. In addition, we include a student essay written for this chapter's writing project.

The first reading is "Everyday Use (For Your Grandmama)" by African-American writer Alice Walker. It was written in 1973.

Alice Walker

Everyday Use (For Your Grandmama)

1 I will wait for her in the yard that Maggie and I made so clean and wavy yesterday afternoon. A yard like this is more comfortable than most people know. It is not just a yard. It is like an extended living room. When the hard clay is swept clean as a floor and the fine sand around the edges lined with tiny, irregular grooves, anyone can come and sit and look up into the elm tree and wait for the breezes that never come inside the house.

2 Maggie will be nervous until after her sister goes: she will stand hopelessly in corners, homely and ashamed of the burn scars down her arms and legs, eying her sister with a mixture of envy and awe. She thinks her sister has held life always in the palm of one hand, that "no" is a word the world never learned to say to her.

3 You've no doubt seen those TV shows where the child who has "made it" is confronted, as a surprise, by her own mother and father, tottering in weakly from backstage. (A pleasant surprise, of course: What would they do if parent and child came on the show only to curse out and insult each other?) On TV mother and child embrace and smile into each other's faces. Sometimes the mother and father weep; the child wraps them in her arms and leans across the table to tell how she would not have made it without their help. I have seen these programs.

4 Sometimes I dream a dream in which Dee and I are suddenly brought together on a TV program of this sort. Out of a dark and soft-seated limousine I am ushered into a bright room filled with many people. There I meet a smiling, gray, sporty man like Johnny Carson who shakes my hand and tells me what a fine girl I have. Then we are on the stage and Dee is embracing me with tears in her eyes. She pins on my dress a large orchid, even though she has told me once that she thinks orchids are tacky flowers.

5 In real life I am a large, big-boned woman with rough, man-working hands. In the winter I wear flannel nightgowns to bed and overalls during the day. I can kill and clean a hog as mercilessly as a man. My fat keeps me hot in zero weather. I can work outside all day, breaking once to get water for washing; I can eat pork liver cooked over the open fire minutes after it comes steaming from the hog. One winter I knocked a bull calf straight in the brain between the eyes with a sledge hammer and had the meat hung up to chill before nightfall. But of course all this does not show on television. I am the way my daughter would want me to be: a hundred pounds lighter, my skin like an uncooked barley pancake. My hair glistens in the hot bright lights. Johnny Carson has much to do to keep up with my quick and witty tongue.

6 But that is a mistake. I know even before I wake up. Who ever knew a Johnson with a quick tongue? Who can even imagine me looking a strange white man in the eye? It seems to me I have talked to them always with one foot raised in flight, with my head turned in whichever way is farthest from them. Dee, though. She would always look anyone in the eye. Hesitation was no part of her nature.

7 "How do I look, Mama?" Maggie says, showing just enough of her thin body enveloped in pink skirt and red blouse for me to know she's there, almost hidden by the door.

8 "Come out into the yard," I say.

9 Have you ever seen a lame animal, perhaps a dog run over by some careless person rich enough to own a car, sidle up to someone who is ignorant enough to be kind to him? That is the way my Maggie walks. She has been like this, chin on chest, eyes on ground, feet in shuffle, ever since the fire that burned the other house to the ground.

10 Dee is lighter than Maggie, with nicer hair and a fuller figure. She's a woman now, though sometimes I forget. How long ago was it that the other house burned? Ten, twelve years? Sometimes I can still hear the flames and feel Maggie's arms sticking to me, her hair smoking and her dress falling off her in little black papery flakes. Her eyes seemed stretched open, blazed open by the flames reflected in them. And Dee. I see her standing off under the sweet gum tree she used to dig gum out of; a look of concentration on her face as she watched the last dingy gray board of the house fall in toward the red-hot brick chimney. Why don't you do a dance around the ashes? I'd wanted to ask her. She had hated the house that much.

11 I used to think she hated Maggie, too. But that was before we raised the money, the church and me, to send her to Augusta to school. She used to read to us without pity; forcing words, lies, other folks' habits, whole lives upon us two, sitting trapped and ignorant underneath her voice. She washed us in a river of make-believe, burned us with a lot of knowledge we didn't necessarily need to know. Pressed us to her with the serious way she read, to shove us away at just the moment, like dimwits, we seemed about to understand.

12 Dee wanted nice things. A yellow organdy dress to wear to her graduation from high school; black pumps to match a green suit she'd made from an old suit somebody gave me. She was determined to stare down any disaster in her efforts. Her eyelids would not flicker for minutes at a time. Often I fought off the temptation to shake her. At sixteen she had a style of her own: and she knew what style was.

13 I never had an education myself. After second grade the school was closed down. Don't ask me why: in 1927 colored asked fewer questions than they do now. Sometimes Maggie reads to me. She stumbles along good-naturedly but can't see well. She knows she is not bright. Like good looks and money, quickness passed her by. She will marry John Thomas (who has mossy teeth in an earnest face) and then I'll be free to sit here and I guess just sing church songs to myself. Although I never was a good singer. Never could carry a tune. I was always better at a man's job. I used to love to milk till I was hooked in the side in '49. Cows are soothing and slow and don't bother you, unless you try to milk them the wrong way.

14 I have deliberately turned my back on the house. It is three rooms, just like the one that burned, except the roof is tin; they don't make shingle roofs any more. There are no real windows, just some holes cut in the sides, like the portholes in a ship, but not round and not square, with rawhide holding the shutters up on the outside. This house is in a pasture, too, like the other one. No doubt when Dee sees it she will want to tear it down. She wrote me once that no matter where we "choose" to live, she will manage to come

see us. But she will never bring her friends. Maggie and I thought about this and Maggie asked me, "Mama, when did Dee ever *have* any friends?"

15 She had a few. Furtive boys in pink shirts hanging about on washday after school. Nervous girls who never laughed. Impressed with her they worshipped the well-turned phrase, the cute shape, the scalding humor that erupted like bubbles in lye. She read to them.

16 When she was courting Jimmy T she didn't have much time to pay to us, but turned all her faultfinding power on him. He *flew* to marry a cheap city girl from a family of ignorant flashy people. She hardly had time to recompose herself.

17 When she comes I will meet—but there they are!

18 Maggie attempts to make a dash for the house, in her shuffling way, but I stay her with my hand. "Come back here," I say. And she stops and tries to dig a well in the sand with her toe.

19 It is hard to see them clearly through the strong sun. But even the first glimpse of leg out of the car tells me it is Dee. Her feet were always neat-looking, as if God himself had shaped them with a certain style. From the other side of the car comes a short, stocky man. Hair is all over his head a foot long and hanging from his chin like a kinky mule tail. I hear Maggie suck in her breath. "Uhnnnh," is what it sounds like. Like when you see the wriggling end of a snake just in front of your foot on the road. "Uhnnnh."

20 Dee next. A dress down to the ground, in this hot weather. A dress so loud it hurts my eyes. There are yellows and oranges enough to throw back the light of the sun. I feel my whole face warming from the heat waves it throws out. Earrings gold, too, and hanging down to her shoulders. Bracelets dangling and making noises when she moves her arm up to shake the folds of the dress out of her armpits. The dress is loose and flows, and as she walks closer, I like it. I hear Maggie go "Uhnnnh" again. It is her sister's hair. It stands straight up like the wool on a sheep. It is black as night and around the edges are two long ponytails that rope about like small lizards disappearing behind her ears.

21 "Wa-su-zo-Tean-o!" she says, coming in on that gliding way the dress makes her move. The short stocky fellow with the hair to his navel is all grinning and he follows up with "Asalamalakim, my mother and sister!" He moves to hug Maggie but she falls back, right up against the back of my chair. I feel her trembling there and when I look up I see the perspiration falling off her chin.

22 "Don't get up," says Dee. Since I am stout it takes something of a push. You can see me trying to move a second or two before I make it. She turns, showing white heels through her sandals, and goes back to the car. Out she peeks next with a Polaroid. She stoops down quickly and lines up picture after picture of me sitting there in front of the house with Maggie cowering behind me. She never takes a shot without making sure the house is included. When a cow comes nibbling around the edge of the yard she snaps it and me and Maggie *and* the house. Then she puts the Polaroid in the back seat of the car, and comes up and kisses me on the forehead.

23 Meanwhile Asalamalakim is going through the motions with Maggie's hand. Maggie's hand is as limp as a fish, and probably cold, despite the sweat, and she keeps trying to pull it back. It looks like Asalamalakim wants to shake hands but wants to do

it fancy. Or maybe he don't know how people shake hands. Anyhow, he soon gives up on Maggie.

24 "Well," I say. "Dee."

25 "No, Mama," she says. "Not 'Dee,' Wangero Leewanika Kemanjo!"

26 "What happened to 'Dee'?" I wanted to know.

27 "She's dead," Wangero said. "I couldn't bear it any longer, being named after the people who oppress me."

28 "You know as well as me you was named after your aunt Dicie," I said. Dicie is my sister. She named Dee. We called her "Big Dee" after Dee was born.

29 "But who was she named after?" asked Wangero.

30 "I guess after Grandma Dee," I said.

31 "And who was she named after?" asked Wangero.

32 "Her mother," I said, and saw Wangero was getting tired. "That's about as far back as I can trace it," I said. Though, in fact, I probably could have carried it back beyond the Civil War through the branches.

33 "Well," said Asalamalakim, "there you are."

34 "Uhnnnh," I heard Maggie say.

35 "There I was not," I said, "before 'Dicie' cropped up in our family, so why should I try to trace it that far back?"

36 He just stood there grinning, looking down on me like somebody inspecting a Model A car. Every once in a while he and Wangero sent eye signals over my head.

37 "How do you pronounce this name?" I asked.

38 "You don't have to call me by it if you don't want to," said Wangero.

39 "Why shouldn't I?" I asked. "If that's what you want us to call you, we'll call you."

40 "I know it might sound awkward at first," said Wangero.

41 "I'll get used to it," I said. "Ream it out again."

42 Well, soon we got the name out of the way. Asalamalakim had a name twice as long and three times as hard. After I tripped over it two or three times he told me to just call him Hakim-a-barber. I wanted to ask him was he a barber, but I didn't really think he was, so I didn't ask.

43 "You must belong to those beef-cattle peoples down the road," I said. They said "Asalamalakim" when they met you, too, but they didn't shake hands. Always too busy: feeding the cattle, fixing the fences, putting up salt-lick shelters, throwing down hay. When the white folks poisoned some of the herd the men stayed up all night with rifles in their hands. I walked a mile and a half just to see the sight.

44 Hakim-a-barber said, "I accept some of their doctrines, but farming and raising cattle is not my style." (They didn't tell me, and I didn't ask, whether Wangero (Dee) had really gone and married him.)

45 We sat down to eat and right away he said he didn't eat collards and pork was unclean. Wangero, though, went on through the chitlins and corn bread, the greens and everything else. She talked a blue streak over the sweet potatoes. Everything delighted her. Even the fact that we still used the benches her daddy made for the table when we couldn't afford to buy chairs.

46 "Oh, Mama!" she cried. Then turned to Hakim-a-barber. "I never knew how lovely these benches are. You can feel the rump prints," she said, running her hands

underneath her and along the bench. Then she gave a sigh and her hand closed over Grandma Dee's butter dish. "That's it!" she said. "I knew there was something I wanted to ask you if I could have." She jumped up from the table and went over in the corner where the churn stood, the milk in it clabber by now. She looked at the churn and looked at it.

47 "This churn top is what I need," she said happily. "Didn't Uncle Buddy whittle it out of a tree you all used to have?"

48 "Yes," I said.

49 "Uh huh," she said happily. "And I want the dasher, too."

50 "Uncle Buddy whittle that, too?" asked the barber.

51 Dee (Wangero) looked up at me.

52 "Aunt Dee's first husband whittled the dash," said Maggie so low you almost couldn't hear her. "His name was Henry, but they called him Stash."

53 "Maggie's brain is like an elephant's," Wangero said, laughing. "I can use the churn top as a centerpiece for the alcove table," she said, sliding a plate over the churn, "and I'll think of something artistic to do with the dasher."

54 When she finished wrapping the dasher the handle stuck out. I took it for a moment in my hands. You didn't even have to look close to see where hands pushing the dasher up and down to make butter had left a kind of sink in the wood. In fact, there were a lot of small sinks; you could see where thumbs and fingers had sunk into the wood. It was beautiful light yellow wood, from a tree that grew in the yard where Big Dee and Stash had lived.

55 After dinner Dee (Wangero) went to the trunk at the foot of my bed and started rifling through it. Maggie hung back in the kitchen over the dishpan. Out came Wangero with two quilts. They had been pieced by Grandma Dee and then Big Dee and me had hung them on the quilt frames on the front porch and quilted them. One was in the Lone Star pattern. The other was Walk Around the Mountain. In both of them were scraps of dresses Grandma Dee had worn fifty and more years ago. Bits and pieces of Grandma Jarrell's Paisley shirts. And one teeny faded blue piece, about the size of a penny matchbox, that was from Great Grandpa Ezra's uniform that he wore in the Civil War.

56 "Mama," Wangero said sweet as a bird. "Can I have these old quilts?"

57 I heard something fall in the kitchen, and a minute later the kitchen door slammed.

58 "Why don't you take one or two of the others?" I asked. "These old things was just done by me and Big Dee from some tops your grandma pieced before she died."

59 "No," said Wangero. "I don't want those. They are stitched around the borders by machine."

60 "That'll make them last better," I said.

61 "That's not the point," said Wangero. "These are all pieces of dresses Grandma used to wear. She did all this stitching by hand. Imagine!" She held the quilts securely in her arms, stroking them.

62 "Some of the pieces, like those lavender ones, come from old clothes her mother handed down to her," I said, moving up to touch the quilts. Dee (Wangero) moved back just enough so that I couldn't reach the quilts. They already belonged to her.

63 "Imagine!" she breathed again, clutching them closely to her bosom.

64 "The truth is," I said, "I promised to give them quilts to Maggie, for when she marries John Thomas."

65 She gasped like a bee had stung her.

66 "Maggie can't appreciate these quilts!" she said. "She'd probably be backward enough to put them to everyday use."

67 "I reckon she would," I said. "God knows I been saving 'em for long enough with nobody using 'em. I hope she will!" I didn't want to bring up how I had offered Dee (Wangero) a quilt when she went away to college. Then she had told me they were old-fashioned, out of style.

68 "But they're *priceless!*" she was saying now, furiously; for she has a temper. "Maggie would put them on the bed and in five years they'd be in rags. Less than that!"

69 "She can always make some more," I said. "Maggie knows how to quilt."

70 Dee (Wangero) looked at me with hatred. "You just will not understand. The point is these quilts, *these* quilts!"

71 "Well," I said, stumped. "What would *you* do with them?"

72 "Hang them," she said. As if that was the only thing you *could* do with quilts.

73 Maggie by now was standing in the door. I could almost hear the sound her feet made as they scraped over each other.

74 "She can have them, Mama," she said, like somebody used to never winning anything, or having anything reserved for her. "I can 'member Grandma Dee without the quilts."

75 I looked at her hard. She had filled her bottom lip with checkerberry snuff and it gave her face a kind of dopey, hangdog look. It was Grandma Dee and Big Dee who taught her how to quilt herself. She stood there with her hands hidden in the folds of her skirt. She looked at her sister with something like fear but she wasn't mad at her. This was Maggie's portion. This was the way she knew God to work.

76 When I looked at her like that something hit me in the top of my head and ran down to the soles of my feet. Just like when I'm in church and the spirit of God touches me and I get happy and shout. I did something I never had done before: hugged Maggie to me, then dragged her on into the room, snatched the quilts out of Miss Wangero's hands and dumped them into Maggie's lap. Maggie just sat there on my bed with her mouth open.

77 "Take one or two of the others," I said to Dee.

78 But she turned without a word and went out to Hakim-a-barber.

79 "You just don't understand," she said, as Maggie and I came out to the car.

80 "What don't I understand?" I wanted to know.

81 "Your heritage," she said. And then she turned to Maggie, kissed her, and said, "You ought to try to make something of yourself, too, Maggie. It's really a new day for us. But from the way you and Mama still live you'd never know it."

82 She put on some sunglasses that hid everything above the tip of her nose and her chin.

83 Maggie smiled; maybe at the sunglasses. But a real smile, not scared. After we watched the car dust settle I asked Maggie to me bring me a dip of snuff. And then the two of us sat there just enjoying, until it was time to go in the house and go to bed.

The second reading is the title short story from Sherman Alexie's 1993 collection *The Lone Ranger and Tonto Fistfight in Heaven*. Alexie, who draws on his Native American background for much of his fiction, has written stories, novels, poems, and screenplays. The 1998 film *Smoke Signals* was based on one of his stories.

Sherman Alexie

The Lone Ranger and Tonto Fistfight in Heaven

1 Too hot to sleep so I walked down to the Third Avenue 7-11 for a Creamsicle and the company of a graveyard-shift cashier. I know that game. I worked graveyard for a Seattle 7-11 and got robbed once too often. The last time the bastard locked me in the cooler. He even took my money and basketball shoes.

2 The graveyard-shift worker in the Third Avenue 7-11 looked like they all do. Acne scars and a bad haircut, work pants that showed off his white socks, and those cheap black shoes that have no support. My arches still ache from my year at the Seattle 7-11.

3 "Hello," he asked when I walked into his store. "How you doing?"

4 I gave him a half-wave as I headed back to the freezer. He looked me over so he could describe me to the police later. I knew the look. One of my old girlfriends said I started to look at her that way, too. She left me not long after that. No, I left her and don't blame her for anything. That's how it happened. When one person starts to look at another like a criminal, then the love is over. It's logical.

• • •

5 "I don't trust you," she said to me. "You get too angry."

6 She was white and I lived with her in Seattle. Some nights we fought so bad that I would just get in my car and drive all night, only stop to fill up on gas. In fact, I worked the graveyard shift to spend as much time away from her as possible. But I learned all about Seattle that way, driving its back ways and dirty alleys.

7 Sometimes, though, I would forget where I was and get lost. I'd drive for hours, searching for something familiar. Seems like I'd spent my whole life that way, looking for anything I recognized. Once, I ended up in a nice residential neighborhood and somebody must have been worried because the police showed up and pulled me over.

8 "What are you doing out here?" the police officer asked me as he looked over my license and registration.

9 "I'm lost."

10 "Well, where are you supposed to be?" he asked me, and I knew there were plenty of places I wanted to be, but none where I was supposed to be.

11 "I got in a fight with my girlfriend," I said. "I was just driving around, blowing off steam, you know?"

12 "Well, you should be more careful where you drive," the officer said. "You're making people nervous. You don't fit the profile of the neighborhood."

13 I wanted to tell him that I didn't really fit the profile of the country but I knew it would just get me into trouble.

• • •

14 "Can I help you?" the 7-11 clerk asked me loudly, searching for some response that would reassure him that I wasn't an armed robber. He knew this dark skin and long, black hair of mine was dangerous. I had potential.

15 "Just getting a Creamsicle," I said after a long interval. It was a sick twist to pull on the guy, but it was late and I was bored. I grabbed my Creamsicle and walked back to the counter slowly, scanned the aisles for effect. I wanted to whistle low and menacingly but I never learned to whistle.

16 "Pretty hot out tonight?" he asked, that old rhetorical weather bullshit question designed to put us both at ease.

17 "Hot enough to make you go crazy," I said and smiled. He swallowed hard like a white man does in those situations. I looked him over. Same old green, red, and white 7–11 jacket and thick glasses. But he wasn't ugly, just misplaced and marked by loneliness. If he wasn't working there that night, he'd be at home alone, flipping through channels and wishing he could afford HBO or Showtime.

18 "Will this be all?" he asked me, in that company effort to make me do some impulse shopping. Like adding a clause onto a treaty. *We'll take Washington and Oregon and you get six pine trees and a brand-new Chrysler Cordoba.* I knew how to make and break promises.

19 "No," I said and paused. "Give me a Cherry Slushie, too."

20 "What size?" he asked, relieved.

21 "Large," I said, and he turned his back to me to make the drink. He realized his mistake but it was too late. He stiffened, ready for the gunshot or the blow behind the ear. When it didn't come, he turned back to me.

22 "I'm sorry," he said. "What size did you say?"

23 "Small," I said and changed the story.

24 "But I thought you said large."

25 "If you knew I wanted a large, then why did you ask me again?" I asked him and laughed. He looked at me, couldn't decide if I was giving him serious shit or just goofing. There was something about him I liked, even if it was three in the morning and he was white.

26 "Hey," I said. "Forget the Slushie. What I want to know is if you know all the words to the theme from 'The Brady Bunch'?"

27 He looked at me, confused at first, then laughed.

28 "Shit," he said. "I was hoping you weren't crazy. You were scaring me."

29 "Well, I'm going to get crazy if you don't know the words."

30 He laughed loudly then, told me to take the Creamsicle for free. He was the graveyard-shift manager and those little demonstrations of power tickled him. All seventy-five cents of it. I knew how much everything cost.

31 "Thanks," I said to him and walked out the door. I took my time walking home, let the heat of the night melt the Creamsicle all over my hand. At three in the morning I could act just as young as I wanted to act. There was no one around to ask me to grow up.

• • •

32 In Seattle, I broke lamps. She and I would argue and I'd break a lamp, just pick it up and throw it down. At first she'd buy replacement lamps, expensive and beautiful. But

after a while she'd buy lamps from Goodwill or garage sales. Then she just gave up the idea entirely and we'd argue in the dark.

33 "You're just like your brother," she'd yell. "Drunk all the time and stupid."

34 "My brother don't drink that much."

35 She and I never tried to hurt each other physically. I did love her, after all, and she loved me. But those arguments were just as damaging as a fist. Words can be like that, you know? Whenever I get into arguments now, I remember her and I also remember Muhammad Ali. He knew the power of his fists but, more importantly, he knew the power of his words, too. Even though he only had an IQ of 80 or so, Ali was a genius. And she was a genius, too. She knew exactly what to say to cause me the most pain.

36 But don't get me wrong. I walked through that relationship with an executioner's hood. Or more appropriately, with war paint and sharp arrows. She was a kindergarten teacher and I continually insulted her for that.

37 "Hey, schoolmarm," I asked. "Did your kids teach you anything new today?"

38 And I always had crazy dreams. I always have had them, but it seemed they became nightmares more often in Seattle.

39 In one dream, she was a missionary's wife and I was a minor war chief. We fell in love and tried to keep it secret. But the missionary caught us fucking in the barn and shot me. As I lay dying, my tribe learned of the shooting and attacked the whites all across the reservation. I died and my soul drifted above the reservation.

40 Disembodied, I could see everything that was happening. Whites killing Indians and Indians killing whites. At first it was small, just my tribe and the few whites who lived there. But my dream grew, intensified. Other tribes arrived on horseback to continue the slaughter of whites, and the United States Cavalry rode into battle.

41 The most vivid image of that dream stays with me. Three mounted soldiers played polo with a dead Indian woman's head. When I first dreamed it, I thought it was just a product of my anger and imagination. But since then, I've read similar accounts of that kind of evil in the old West. Even more terrifying, though, is the fact that those kinds of brutal things are happening today in places like El Salvador.

42 All I know for sure, though, is that I woke from that dream in terror, packed up all my possessions, and left Seattle in the middle of the night.

43 "I love you," she said as I left her. "And don't ever come back."

44 I drove through the night, over the Cascades, down into the plains of central Washington, and back home to the Spokane Indian Reservation.

• • •

45 When I finished the Creamsicle that the 7–11 clerk gave me, I held the wooden stick up into the air and shouted out very loudly. A couple lights flashed on in windows and a police car cruised by me a few minutes later. I waved to the men in blue and they waved back accidentally. When I got home it was still too hot to sleep so I picked up a week-old newspaper from the floor and read.

46 There was another civil war, another terrorist bomb exploded, and one more plane crashed and all aboard were presumed dead. The crime rate was rising in every city with populations larger than 100,000, and a farmer in Iowa shot his banker after foreclosure on his 1,000 acres.

47 A kid from Spokane won the local spelling bee by spelling the word *rhinoceros*.

• • •

48 When I got back to the reservation, my family wasn't surprised to see me. They'd been expecting me back since the day I left for Seattle. There's an old Indian poet who said that Indians can reside in the city, but they can never live there. That's as close to truth as any of us can get.

49 Mostly I watched television. For weeks I flipped through channels, searched for answers in the game shows and soap operas. My mother would circle the want ads in red and hand the paper to me.

50 "What are you going to do with the rest of your life?" she asked.

51 "Don't know," I said, and normally, for almost any other Indian in the country, that would have been a perfectly fine answer. But I was special, a former college student, a smart kid. I was one of those Indians who was supposed to make it, to rise above the rest of the reservation like a fucking eagle or something. I was the new kind of warrior.

52 For a few months I didn't even look at the want ads my mother circled, just left the newspaper where she had set it down. After a while, though, I got tired of television and started to play basketball again. I'd been a good player in high school, nearly great, and almost played at the college I attended for a couple years. But I'd been too out of shape from drinking and sadness to ever be good again. Still, I liked the way the ball felt in my hands and the way my feet felt inside my shoes.

53 At first I just shot baskets by myself. It was selfish, and I also wanted to learn the game again before I played against anybody else. Since I had been good before and embarrassed fellow tribal members, I knew they would want to take revenge on me. Forget about the cowboys versus Indians business. The most intense competition on any reservation is Indians versus Indians.

54 But on the night I was ready to play for real, there was this white guy at the gym, playing with all the Indians.

55 "Who is that?" I asked Jimmy Seyler.

56 "He's the new BIA chief's kid."

57 "Can he play?"

58 "Oh, yeah."

59 And he could play. He played Indian ball, fast and loose, better than all the Indians there.

60 "How long's he been playing here?" I asked.

61 "Long enough."

62 I stretched my muscles, and everybody watched me. All these Indians watched one of their old and dusty heroes. Even though I had played most of my ball at the white high school I went to, I was still all Indian, you know? I was Indian when it counted, and this BIA kid needed to be beaten by an Indian, any Indian.

63 I jumped into the game and played well for a little while. It felt good. I hit a few shots, grabbed a rebound or two, played enough defense to keep the other team honest. Then that white kid took over the game. He was too good. Later, he'd play college ball back East and would nearly make the Knicks team a couple years on. But we didn't know any of that would happen. We just knew he was better that day and every other day.

64 The next morning I woke up tired and hungry, so I grabbed the want ads, found a job I wanted, and drove to Spokane to get it. I've been working at the high school

exchange program ever since, typing and answering phones. Sometimes I wonder if the people on the other end of the line know that I'm Indian and if their voices would change if they did know.

65 One day I picked up the phone and it was her, calling from Seattle.

66 "I got your number from your mom," she said. "I'm glad you're working."

67 "Yeah, nothing like a regular paycheck."

68 "Are you drinking?"

69 "No, I've been on the wagon for almost a year."

70 "Good."

71 The connection was good. I could hear her breathing in the spaces between our words. How do you talk to the real person whose ghost has haunted you? How do you tell the difference between the two?

72 "Listen," I said. "I'm sorry for everything."

73 "Me, too."

74 "What's going to happen to us?" I asked her and wished I had the answer for myself.

75 "I don't know," she said. "I want to change the world."

• • •

76 These days, living alone in Spokane, I wish I lived closer to the river, to the falls where ghosts of salmon jump. I wish I could sleep. I put down my paper or book and turn off all the lights, lie quietly in the dark. It may take hours, even years, for me to sleep again. There's nothing surprising or disappointing in that.

77 I know how all my dreams end anyway.

The following student essay on Walker's "Everyday Use (For Your Grandmama)" was written in response to this chapter's assignment. What questions and comments would you have for its writer if you were in a peer review session?

Betsy Weiler (student)

Who Do You Want to Be?

Finding Heritage in Walker's "Everyday Use"

> "You just don't understand."
> "What don't I understand?"
> "Your heritage" (338).*

1 Whose heritage is Dee talking about? Is it her family's heritage or her ethnic heritage?

2 This exchange takes place near the end of Alice Walker's short story, "Everyday Use," when Dee is saying goodbye to her mother and her sister Maggie after a brief visit and an argument about some quilts. That visit was almost like a treasure hunt for Dee. It seems that Dee, who now has the name Wangero Leewanika Kemanjo, came to visit

*Numbers in parentheses indicate page numbers on which the quotation is found (in this case, page numbers in this text). This parenthetical citation system follows the MLA format. See Chapter 23.

because she wants to try to identify herself with the past. She wants to take parts of a butter churn and some family quilts back home with her, but Mama says "no" about the quilts because she promised them to Maggie. Dee thinks that Maggie can't "appreciate" the quilts and is "backward enough to put them to everyday use" (338). This confrontation over the quilts suggests that Dee may have learned a lot in college about her ethnic background as an African American, but she does not understand or appreciate her own family's heritage.

3 At first, a reader might think that Dee/Wangero has come home to express her appreciation for her family's heritage. While Mama is waiting for her, she expects that Dee will want to tear down the family house because it is just like the one that burned down when she was a child there. Dee hated that house. But when Dee arrives, before she even tells her mother her new name, she begins taking "picture after picture" of her mother and Maggie, "making sure the house is included" in every one (335). It seems that Dee is proud to include the house in her heritage—but is it her ethnic heritage or her family heritage? What will she do with the pictures? Are they something to remember her family with or are they something "artistic" that she will use to display her ethnic heritage?

4 When Dee explains her new name to her mother, she seems to have forgotten part of her family heritage. Wangero says that "Dee" is "dead" because "I couldn't bear it any longer, being named after the people who oppress me" (336). After her mother explains that she is actually named after Aunt Dee and Grandma Dee, Wangero Leewanika Kemanjo may gain some appreciation of the family tradition because she says that Mama doesn't have to call her the new name "if you don't want to." But Mama shows her own respect for her own daughter by saying "I'll get used to it."

5 When the treasure hunt part of the visit begins after the dinner, Dee's concern for ethnic heritage becomes clear. Dee wants items from the past that she identifies with her ethnic heritage. She jumps up from the table and declares that she needs the churn top. She asks, "Didn't Uncle Buddy whittle it [the churn] out of a tree you all used to have?" (337). She is talking about the churn top in terms of family heritage, but when she says that she intends to use it as a centerpiece on an alcove table, the reader understands that for Dee the churn is more significant for the ethnic heritage it represents. Many blacks could not afford to buy butter, so they had to make it themselves. (In fact, her mother is still using that churn to make butter.) She also wants the dasher from the churn. For Maggie and Mama, it is a tool in the present that represents family history. Maggie explains that Aunt Dee's first husband, Stash, whittled it; when Mama (the narrator) looks it over she notices the "small sinks" in the wood from the hands of people who had used it (including her own, no doubt). There is a strong contrast between their attitude toward the heirloom and Dee/Wangero's. She laughs at Maggie's story (family heritage), saying Maggie has a "brain ... like an elephant's" and announces that she herself will "think of something artistic to do with the dasher" (337). For all of them, the dasher represents the hard work blacks have had to struggle through, but for Mama and Maggie, it is a tool made by a family member to help with that work today. For Wangero it is an ethnic heritage object to display.

6 The final two items that Dee wants are the hand-stitched quilts that she digs out of Mama's trunk. They represent family heritage because they contain pieces of her ancestors' clothing, including a tiny piece from the blue uniform of a great-grandfather who

fought in the Civil War. That family heritage is very strong for Mama, who was planning to give the quilts to Maggie as a wedding present. She remembers, but doesn't say anything, that Dee/Wangero had refused to take a quilt with her to college because they were old fashioned. Dee loses her temper over the idea of Maggie using the quilts on a bed because "in five years they'd be in rags" (338). Mama says that then Maggie would make new ones. But Dee wants "*these* quilts," the ones with pieces of her own family's clothing. This may appear to be an appreciation of family heritage, but since Dee/Wangero wants to hang the quilts on the wall, not use them for a practical purpose, it seems that she wants to display a heritage that she doesn't want to live anymore.

7 Maggie is willing to give up the quilts, saying she can remember Grandma Dee without them, but Mama grabs the quilts back from Dee. The conflict here is not only about remembering but also about how to remember. Although Dee wants to preserve the original quilts with their antique pieces, she keeps separating herself from the family heritage that created them.

8 As Dee gets into the car to leave, she puts on a pair of sunglasses that hide "everything above the tip of her nose and her chin" (338). If, as the saying goes, the eyes are the windows to the soul, then Dee is hiding her soul. By wearing the sunglasses, Dee is hiding who she truly is and just wants to be identified with the color of her skin, her ethnic heritage. She tells Maggie that "[i]t's really a new day for us" although "from the way you ... live, you'd never know it" (338).

9 Mama and Maggie may live in a very old-fashioned setting, using old-fashioned tools every day, but Dee/Wangero's attitude about her family and its heirlooms shows that actually she is the person who does not understand her heritage.

THINKING CRITICALLY

about "Who Do You Want to Be? Finding Heritage in Walker's 'Everyday Use'"

1. The assignment for this chapter asks for an essay built around a problematic and significant interpretive question. Do you think that Betsy Weiler adequately addresses the assignment? Has she been successful in articulating a problematic question and indicating its importance for our understanding of the story?
2. Does Weiler's thesis statement respond adequately to the question? Does she supply enough details to support her analysis? Would the paper be better with more analysis of literary elements? What should she add or cut ?
3. What alternative answers to Weiler's interpretive question occur to you besides the ones she brings up? What evidence do you find in the text to support your analysis and interpretation?
4. What recommendations would you have for improving this essay?

For additional writing, reading, and research resources, go to **www.MyCompLab.com** and choose **Ramage/Bean/Johnson's *The Allyn & Bacon Guide to Writing,* Fifth Edition.**

CHAPTER 13 ANALYZING AND SYNTHESIZING IDEAS

In many of your college courses, you'll be asked to explore connections and contradictions among groups of texts. Distilling main points from more than one text, seeing connections among texts, commenting on meaningful relationships, and showing how the texts have influenced your own thinking on a question are all part of the thinking and writing involved in synthesis.

Synthesis, which is a way of seeing and coming to terms with complexities, is a counterpart to *analysis*. When you analyze something, you break it down into its parts to see the relationships among them. When you synthesize, you take one more step, putting parts together in some new fashion. The cognitive researcher Benjamin Bloom schematized "synthesis" as the fifth of six levels of thinking processes, ranked in order of complexity and challenge: knowledge, comprehension, application, analysis, *synthesis,* and evaluation. Bloom defined synthesis in these terms: "putting together of constituent elements or parts to form a whole requiring original creative thinking."* Synthesis drives those light-bulb moments when you exclaim, "Ah! Now I see how these ideas are related!"

A second useful and related way to think of synthesis is as a dialectical thinking process. Throughout this text, we have explained that college writing involves posing a significant question that often forces you to encounter clashing or contradictory ideas. Such conflicts intrigued the German philosopher Hegel, who posited that thinking proceeds dialectically when a thesis clashes against an antithesis, leading the thinker to formulate a synthesis encompassing dimensions of both the original thesis and the antithesis. When you write to synthesize ideas, your thinking exemplifies this dialectical process.

This Hegelian view is also discussed in Chapter 8, p. 181.

This chapter introduces you to an important academic genre:

- The synthesis essay, which moves beyond analysis to show how a writer interacts with a group of texts, explores their alternative perspectives on an issue, and presents a new, enlarged perspective of his or her own.

Synthesis is an especially important component of research writing, where you use synthesis to carve out your own thinking space on a research question while sifting through the writings of others. Synthesis, then, is the skill of wrestling with ideas from different texts or sources, trying to forge a new whole out of potentially confusing parts. It is the principal way you enter into a conversation on a social, civic, or scholarly issue.

*Benjamin Bloom, *Taxonomy of Educational Objectives: Handbook I: Cognitive Domain* (New York: David McKay, 1956).

Exploring the Analysis and Synthesis of Ideas

To introduce you to some of the essential thinking moves involved in analyzing and synthesizing, we offer this exercise that asks you to read two articles on the question, "What effect are cell phones having on our lives as American citizens?" The first reading, "Mobile Phone Tracking Scrutinized" by Nikki Swartz, was published in the *Information Management Journal* for March/April 2006. This journal bills itself as "the leading source of information on topics and issues central to the management of records and information worldwide" (www.arma.org). The second reading, "Reach Out and Track Someone" by Terry J. Allen, appeared in the May 2006 edition of *In These Times,* a publication "dedicated to informing and analyzing popular movements for social, environmental and economic justice" (www.inthesetimes.com/about/). Read these pieces carefully and then do the exercises that follow.

Nikki Swartz

Mobile Phone Tracking Scrutinized

1 Nearly 200 million Americans have cell phones, but many of them are not aware that wireless technology companies, as well as the U.S. government, track their movements through signals emitted by their handsets.

2 Cellular providers, including Verizon Wireless and Cingular Wireless, know, within about 300 yards, the location of their subscribers whenever a phone is turned on. Even if the phone is not in use, it still communicates with cell tower sites, and the wireless provider keeps track of the phone's position as it travels. These companies are marketing services that turn handsets into even more precise global positioning devices for driving or allowing parents to track the whereabouts of their children.

3 In recent years, law enforcement officials have used cellular technology as a tool for easily and secretly monitoring the movements of suspects. But this kind of surveillance, which investigators have been able to conduct with easily obtained court orders, has now come under tougher legal scrutiny.

4 *The New York Times* reports that, in the last four months of 2005, three federal judges denied prosecutors the right to get cell phone tracking information from wireless companies without first showing "probable cause" that a crime has been or is being committed—the same standard applied to requests for search warrants.

5 The rulings, issued by magistrate judges in New York, Texas, and Maryland, underscore the growing debate over privacy rights and government surveillance in the digital age. Wireless providers keep cell phone location records for varying lengths of time, from several months to years, and have said that they turn over cell location information when presented with a court order to do so.

6 Prosecutors argue that having such data is crucial to finding suspects, corroborating their whereabouts with witness accounts, or helping build a case for a wiretap on the phone. The government has routinely used records of cell phone calls and caller locations to show where a suspect was at a particular time, with access to those records obtainable under a lower legal standard.

7 But it is unclear how often prosecutors have asked courts for the right to obtain cell-tracking data as a suspect is moving. And the government is not required to report publicly when it makes such requests.

8 Prosecutors, while acknowledging that they must get a court order before obtaining real-time cell-site data, argue that a 1994 amendment to the 1986 Stored Communications Act—a standard that calls for the government to show "specific and articulable facts" that demonstrate that the records sought are "relevant and material to an ongoing investigation"—is actually lower than the probable-cause hurdle. In the cell-tracking cases, some legal experts say that the Stored Communications Act refers only to records of where a person has been—historical location data—but does not address live tracking.

9 Prosecutors in the recent cases also unsuccessfully argued that the expanded police powers under the USA PATRIOT Act could be read as allowing cell phone tracking.

10 The magistrate judges, however, ruled that surveillance by cell phone because it acts like an electronic tracking device that can follow people into homes and other personal spaces must meet the same high legal standard required to obtain a search warrant to enter private places.

11 "The distinction between cell site data and information gathered by a tracking device has practically vanished," wrote Stephen W. Smith, a magistrate in Federal District Court in the Southern District of Texas, in his ruling. He added that when a phone is monitored, the process is usually "unknown to the phone users, who may not even be on the phone."

12 In a digital era, the stream of data that carries a telephone conversation or an e-mail message contains a great deal of information, including when and where the communications originated. And that makes it harder for courts to determine whether a certain digital surveillance method invokes Fourth Amendment protections against unreasonable searches.

Terry J. Allen

Reach Out and Track Someone

1 If you are one of the more than 200 million Americans with a cell phone nestled in your pocket, authorities may be able to find you any time day or night—even if you never make or receive a call.

2 You know the Verizon ad where a lockstep crowd personifies the network that accompanies its customer everywhere? Well, within that seemingly friendly horde, a hightech Big Brother is lurking.

3 Most people know that when they make a mobile call—during a 911 emergency, for example—authorities can access phone company technology to pin down their location, sometimes to within a few feet.

4 A lesser-known fact: Cell phone companies can locate you any time you are in range of a tower and your phone is on. Cell phones are designed to work either with

global positioning satellites or through "pings" that allow towers to triangulate and pinpoint signals. Any time your phone "sees" a tower, it pings it.

5 That is what happened last month when a New York City murder highlighted the existence of the built-in capability of phones to locate people even when they aren't making calls.

6 The case of Imette St. Guillen captivated the New York City media as only the murder of a young, attractive, middle-class, white female can. One piece of evidence leading to the arrest of Darryl Littlejohn, the bouncer at the club where St. Guillen was last seen, was what police called "cell phone records." In fact, it was not an actual call that placed Littlejohn at the crime scene. Instead, according to the *New York Daily News,* police traced Littlejohn's route the day of the murder by tracking the "pings" of his cell phone, which were "stored" in a tower and "later retrieved from T-Mobile by cops."

7 Telecom companies and government are not eager to advertise that tracking capability. Nor will companies admit whether they are archiving the breadcrumb trail of pings from a cell phone so that they—or authorities—can trace back, after the fact, where the customer had been at a particular time. "Of course, there is that capability," says Bruce Schneier, chief technical officer with Counterpane Internet Security. "Verizon and the other companies have access to that information and the odds are zero that they wouldn't sell it if it is legal and profitable. This is capitalism after all."

8 But legality can be so tricky to pin down, especially when national security and corporate profits are involved. Communications companies and government have been repeatedly caught collaborating in highly questionable practices. Warrantless wiretapping, now sparking cries for Bush's impeachment, was implemented by the NSA accessing the "gateway" switches that route calls around the globe. Most of these switches are controlled by AT&T, MCI and Sprint.

9 Recently, the Electronic Frontier Foundation (EFF) said it had internal AT&T documents and a sworn statement by retired AT&T technician Mark Klein showing that the company's use of a "dragnet surveillance" was "diverting Internet traffic into the hands of the NSA wholesale."

10 It is likely that authorities are also accessing cell phone call records and conducting real-time tracing of hapless Palestinians who donated to clinics and liberal activists who dared march for peace. And if the administration's record is a guide, it is interpreting privacy protection laws relating to cell phones in ways that bend and perhaps batter the Constitution.

11 "I think there's a substantial worry that location information about cell phone users is being released without a court order," EFF Staff attorney Kevin Bankston told CNN.

12 Echoing the Bush administration's rationale for warrantless wiretapping, the Justice Department argues that time lost justifying a search warrant can mean dangerous delays. Several judges around the country have disagreed. Citing officials' failure to show probable cause, they have denied government requests for cell phone tracking. According to EFF, a New York magistrate revealed that "the Justice Department had routinely been using a baseless legal argument to get secret authorizations from a number of courts, probably for many years."

13 "Justice Department officials countered that courts around the country have granted many such orders in the past without requiring probable cause," the Oct. 28 *Washington Post* reported.

14 Real-time tracking technology also opens disturbing entrepreneurial opportunities. Anyone who provides their kids, spouse or employees with a software-readied cell phone can secretly monitor them on the web. Wherify.com "locates loved ones within feet/meters in about a minute," and allows subscribers to "view location on both street and aerial mapping, to include date/time stamp, lat/long and block address" and "set breadcrumb schedule for periodic locates." Another Internet business promises to sell you the calling records for any phone number you provide. (Note to readers: If you have Karl Rove's number, I'll cough up the $100 fee to get a look.)

15 But as far as invasiveness goes, the ability of the government to secretly track and find you anywhere, anytime, ranks right up with a pelvic exam in Times Square.

INDIVIDUAL TASKS

1. How would you describe each writer's perspective or angle of vision on cell phones? In one or two sentences, summarize each writer's main points in these passages.
2. List ideas that these pieces have in common.
3. List any contradictions or differences you see in these pieces.
4. Freewrite your own response to these readings for five minutes, exploring what questions they raise for you or personal experiences that they might remind you of.

GROUP OR WHOLE-CLASS TASKS

5. Working in small groups or as a whole class, try to reach consensus answers to questions 1, 2, and 3.
6. Share your individual responses to question 4. What are the major questions and issues raised by your group or the whole class? What different views of cell phones in particular and technology in general emerged?

Understanding Analysis and Synthesis

Posing a Synthesis Question

As we have shown throughout this text, most academic and professional writing begins with the posing of a problem. Writing a synthesis essay follows the same principle. The need to synthesize ideas usually begins when you pose a problematic question that sends you off on an intellectual journey through a group of texts. The synthesis or focusing question directs you to look for ways that a group of texts are connected and ways that they differ in their approaches to a particular problem or issue. A synthesis question helps you zero in on a problem that these texts address or that you are trying to solve through exploring these texts. Your goal is to achieve your own informed view on that question, a view that reflects your intellectual wrestling with the ideas in your sources and in some way integrates ideas from these sources with your own independent thinking.

Although synthesis writing appears in college courses across the curriculum, how these assignments are set up varies widely. Sometimes instructors will specify the texts and the questions that you are to explore whereas at other times you will be asked to choose your texts and articulate your own synthesis questions. The following examples show typical synthesis assignments that you might encounter in different disciplines, with both the texts and synthesis questions provided in each case.

Environmental Politics Course

Texts to Be Analyzed	Synthesis Questions
Garrett Hardin's essay on overpopulation, "The Tragedy of the Commons," from *Science* (1968)	Are there any common assumptions about the world's environment in these readings?
Kenneth E. Boulding's essay "Economics of the Coming Spaceship Earth" (1966)	What problems and solutions appear in these readings?
A chapter from Ron Bailey's *The True State of the Planet* (1995)	What direction would you take in proposing a solution?
A chapter from Al Gore's *An Inconvenient Truth* (2006)	

American Literature Survey Course

Texts to Be Analyzed	Synthesis Questions
Selections from the *Lowell Offering,* a publication produced in Lowell, Massachusetts, in the 1840s, featuring the writings of young female factory workers	What common questions about changes in women's social roles in the 1800s emerge in these texts?
Historian Gerda Lerner's essay "The Lady and the Mill Girl: Changes in the Status of Women in the Age of Jackson 1800–1840" (1969)	Which text gives you the clearest understanding of the problems with women's changing roles and why?
Herman Melville's short story "The Paradise of Bachelors and the Tartarus of Maids" (1835)	

Film Criticism Course

Films to Be Analyzed	Synthesis Questions
Drums along the Mohawk (1939) *Fort Apache* (1948) *Dances with Wolves* (1990) *Smoke Signals* (1998)	What similarities and differences do you see in these films' representations of Native Americans? How do you explain these differences?

Synthesis Writing as an Extension of Summary/Strong Response Writing

In Chapter 6, we introduced you to writing summaries of texts and responding strongly to them through critique of their rhetorical strategies and ideas. It is helpful to think of synthesis writing as an extension of those skills. In writing a synthesis essay, you use both with-the-grain and against-the-grain thinking. You listen carefully to texts as you summarize them to determine their main points. You also conduct—at least informally in your exploratory stages—a critique of both the rhetorical features and the ideas of these texts. This analysis builds the platform from which you create a synthesis of ideas—that is, from which you begin your own independent thinking based on the synthesis question that ties your texts together.

A synthesis essay differs from a summary/strong response essay in that a synthesis extends the process to more texts with the aim of bringing them into conversation with each other. A synthesis essay shows how you have taken apart, made sense of, assessed, and recombined the ideas of these texts. A synthesis essay most likely incorporates the following features:

To review summary/strong response writing, see Chapter 6.

TYPICAL FEATURES OF A SYNTHESIS ESSAY

- A statement of the synthesis question that shows your interest in the texts and presents this question as problematic and significant
- Short summaries of these texts to give your readers a sense of the readings you are working with
- A thesis that indicates how you have analyzed and synthesized the readings to arrive at a new perspective
- Your analysis of key points in these texts, determined in part by the synthesis question
- Your new view that combines ideas gathered from readings with your own independent ideas

Student Example of a Synthesis Essay

Before we move to the writing project for this chapter—and to the idea-generating strategies of student writers who are analyzing and synthesizing texts—we show you a student example of a synthesis essay. This example, by student writer Kate MacAulay, was written for the writing project for this chapter and addressed the assigned question, "What effect is technology having on humanity and the quality of life in the twenty-first century?" The texts she was asked to analyze and synthesize are these two:

- George Ritzer, "The Irrationality of Rationality: Traffic Jams on Those 'Happy Trails.'" This is a chapter from Ritzer's widely discussed book *The McDonaldization of Society*. New Century Edition (Thousand Oaks, CA: Pine Forge Press, 2000).
- Sherry Turkle, "Who Am We?" published in the magazine *Wired* 4.1 (January 1996): 148–52, 194–99.

We have not reprinted these two lengthy texts; however, later in this chapter, we include Kate MacAulay's informal and analytical writing as well as that of another student writer in order to show you helpful steps in writing synthesis essays.

Kate MacAulay (student)

Technology's Peril and Potential

Recently in English class, we have been focusing on the question, What effect is technology having on humanity and the quality of life in the twenty-first century? We have had heated discussions about the use of cell phones, palm pilots, beepers, e-mail, chat rooms, and the Web. As part of my investigation of this question, I read two texts: a chapter from George Ritzer's book *The McDonaldization of Society*, entitled "The Irrationality of Rationality: Traffic Jams on Those 'Happy Trails,'" and an article published in the magazine *Wired* entitled "Who Am We?", by Sherry Turkle. In his chapter, Ritzer, a sociology professor, explains how technology has rationalized businesses and many facets of society following the McDonald's model. He argues that modern technology is causing loss of quality products, time, and relationships. In the McDonaldized system, where everything is designed logically for economy and convenience, things have become more artificial, and our relationships have become more superficial. In her article "Who Am We?", Sherry Turkle, a psychology professor at MIT, shows how computers and the Internet are transforming our views of ourselves and the way we interact socially. Focusing on computers' capacities for simulation and promoting interaction, Turkle has explored MUDs (multiuser domains), which allow people to create virtual identities. MUDs, Turkle believes, contribute to the formation of postmodern multiple selves and raise new questions about personal identity and morality. Although both Turkle and Ritzer identify problems in technology's influence and in society's responses to it, Turkle sees more potential and gain where Ritzer sees mostly peril and loss. Both articles made me question how we define our values and morality in this postmodern, technologically advanced world and persuaded me of the need for caution in embracing technology.

Introduces focusing questions and context

Introduces the texts to be analyzed

Brief summary of Ritzer's text

Brief summary of Turkle's text

Thesis statement with analytical points and synthesis points

Although Ritzer and Turkle both see technology as having some negative effects on human relations and the quality of life, they disagree about exactly where the most interesting and serious problems lie. Ritzer believes that the problems caused by technology are not problems within the individual, but problems imposed on the individual by McDonaldized systems. For example, Ritzer claims that fast-food restaurants encourage us to eat unhealthy food quickly and also contribute to "the disintegration

Analytical point: compares and contrasts Ritzer's and Turkle's ideas

Analyzes and elaborates on Ritzer's ideas

of the family" (141) by taking away family time. He also believes that rationalized systems create illusions of fun, reality, and friendliness. He talks about the "scripted interactions" (138) that employees are supposed to have with customers, where they are told exactly what to say to every customer, making interactions less real. Further, rationalized systems are dehumanizing in the kinds of jobs they create that "don't offer much in the way of satisfaction or stability" (137), benefiting only stockholders, owners, and employers.

Analyzes, contrasts, and elaborates on Turkle's ideas

In contrast, Turkle responds to technology's threat by focusing inward on technology's effect on the self and on relationships. While she is clearly intrigued by such Internet capabilities as multiuser domains, she acknowledges that this potential for multiple simultaneous identities threatens the wholeness of individuals, possibly damaging our emotional and psychological selves. Her concern is that people become addicted to these games because in the virtual world it is easy to create better "selves," to be what you wish you were. Turkle shows that people can lose themselves between the real world and the virtual world and be "imprisoned by the screens" (199). Although the virtual world is exciting and fun, she notes that "[o]ur experiences there are serious play" (199). She also examines cases of virtual characters who get into relationships with other characters, including cyber-sex relationships. She ponders the issue of cyber-sex immorality and adultery.

Analytical point: compares and contrasts Ritzer's and Turkle's ideas

Analyzes and elaborates on Ritzer's ideas

Presents writer's independent thinking

Despite Turkle and Ritzer's agreement that technology can damage us as a society, they disagree on their overall outlook and on our power to respond positively to technology's influence. I find Ritzer's views almost entirely negative. He believes that we are irreversibly damaged by technological advances because we are completely caught up in the McDonaldized system, with few parts of society left unchanged. Almost all of the family-owned neighborhood restaurants or mom-and-pop grocery stores have been taken over by franchises like Red Robin or Safeway. The costs of these rationalized systems, he says, are "inefficiency, illusions of various types, disenchantment, dehumanization, and homogenization" (124). In this chapter of his book, Ritzer doesn't mention any ways that our lives could be improved by these systems; he gives only examples of the way we are misled and damaged by them.

Analyzes, contrasts, and elaborates on Turkle's ideas

Presents writer's independent thinking

Turkle's approach strikes me as much more positive and balanced than Ritzer's. Optimistically, she explains that MUDs can give people self-knowledge that they can apply to real life: "[t]he anonymity of MUDs gives people the chance to express multiple and often unexplored aspects of the self, to play with their identity and to try out new ones" (152). Turkle sees an opportunity for us to grow as individuals and to learn to use technology in a positive way: "If we can cultivate awareness of what stands behind our screen personae, we are more likely to succeed in using virtual experience for personal transformation" (199). I think Turkle's views are more complex than Ritzer's. She believes that we have to take responsibility for our own habits and psychological responses to technology. She encourages us to be aware of how we interact with technology and believes that we can grow as individuals using this technology.

After reading these articles, I have realized how the continuing advancement of technology raises new moral questions. In a McDonaldized system, where everything is designed for convenience, there seem to be many places for morals to be left out of the picture. For example, is it okay for us to exchange real human interaction for convenience and saving time? Is there something wrong with our ethics when interesting and fulfilling jobs are eliminated by machines or replaced by dead-end, low-paying Mcjobs? Turkle too shows us how virtual worlds pose new moral questions for us. In MUDs, people can form virtual relationships, even cyber-sex relationships. The people behind the characters are real people, even if they are acting as someone else. If a married person has a cyber-sex relationship on a MUD, is he or she cheating? If a person commits a virtual assault or other crime that has no real-world, physical effects, should he or she feel guilty or sinful for the intention? Ritzer and Turkle have made me see how important these questions are.

Transition to writer's synthesis. Synthesis point discusses writer's own view

Elaborates on the connections the writer is making

Reading the articles made me strongly believe that we must use this technology in moderation in order to preserve individual qualities and our relationships. From our class discussions, I remember what Scott said about the way that the Internet connects people. He said that people like his uncle, who was severely injured on the job, use the Internet as a way of "getting out" to meet people and socialize. He pointed out how the Microsoft Gaming Zone has brought his uncle into an ongoing backgammon tournament through which he has made friends. Meanwhile his aunt has gotten a lot of pleasure out of playing and problem solving in the world of MUDs.

Synthesis point discusses writer's own view

But my own experience has left me concerned about the danger we face as emotional, social beings in the face of technology. The other night at a family gathering, one of my cousins, after discussing car buying with some of the relatives, got the urge to research new car prices. He left the room, logged onto the Internet, and spent the rest of the evening looking at cars and prices. We saw him only once the whole evening when he came out to get a slice of pie. My cousin's withdrawal from the conversation made me think about Ritzer's and Turkle's concerns that technology decreases real interactions among people.

Synthesis point discusses writer's own view

Ritzer and Turkle offer us a warning that technology can be damaging if we don't recognize and overcome its dangers. I would encourage us not to let ourselves become dominated by technology, not to let it take our full attention just because it is there, and not to overlook the complex moral questions that technology poses. The convenience that technology offers—our e-mail, cell phones, and debit cards—should help us save time that can be spent in nurturing our relationships with other people. The real challenge is to find ways to become even better people because of technology.

Transition and final connections

Conclusion

Works Cited

Ritzer, George. *The McDonaldization of Society*. Thousand Oaks: Pine Forge, 2000. Print.
Turkle, Sherry. "Who Am We?" *Wired* Jan. 1996: 148+. Print.

Complete citation of articles in MLA format

WRITING PROJECT

A Synthesis Essay

Write a synthesis essay that meets the following criteria:

- Addresses a synthesis question that your instructor provides or that you formulate for yourself
- Summarizes and analyzes the views of at least two writers on this question
- Shows how you have wrestled with different perspectives on the question and have synthesized these ideas to arrive at your own new view of the question.

Ideas for Synthesis Questions and Readings

The writing project for this chapter draws on the kinds of texts you will typically be asked to synthesize in your college courses. This text provides a number of options from which your instructor can choose. Some instructors may assign both the readings and the synthesis questions. Others may assign the readings but invite students to pose their own questions. Still others may leave both the questions and the readings up to the students. The following list of questions and readings found in this text gives you options for subject matter and focus for synthesis essays.

Reading Options for This Assignment

Synthesis Questions	Possible Readings
How have cell phones affected the lives of American citizens?	• Nikki Swartz, "Mobile Phone Tracking Scrutinized," pp. 347–348 • Terry J. Allen, "Reach Out and Track Someone," pp. 348–349
What are the biggest obstacles in managing the problem of undocumented immigrants? What should the United States do to make progress in solving this problem?	Two or more of the excerpts from blogs collected in the Readings section of this chapter, pp. 369–376
What should be our attitude toward outsourcing of American jobs? What is the most reasonable approach to solving problems caused by outsourcing?	• Thomas L. Friedman, "30 Little Turtles," pp. 142–143 • David Horsey, "Today's Economic Indicator," (editorial cartoon) p. 146 • Mike Lane, "Labor Day Blues," (editorial cartoon), p. 147 • Froma Harrop, "New Threat to Skilled U.S. Workers," pp. 148–149

Synthesis Questions	Possible Readings
Should the United States increase its production of electricity by building more nuclear power plants or by pursuing some other form of energy?	• David Rockwood, "A Letter to the Editor," p. 7 • William Sweet, "Why Uranium Is the New Green," pp. 407–410 • Stan Eales, "Welcome to Sellafield," (editorial cartoon) p. 411 • Editorial from the *Los Angeles Times,* "No to Nukes," pp. 412–414
What does it mean to be a Native American? How are we to understand the concept of "otherness"?	• Jane Tompkins, "'Indians': Textualism, Morality, and the Problem of History," pp. 199–207 • Sherman Alexie, "The Lone Ranger and Tonto Fistfight in Heaven," pp. 339–345 • American Indian College Fund Advocacy Ad, p. 661

Using Learning Logs

In our view, a productive way to generate ideas for your synthesis essay is to break your process into a series of incremental thinking steps that take you gradually from summaries of your chosen texts to an analysis of them and finally to a synthesis of their ideas with your own. The five learning log tasks in the sections that follow will guide you through this process. On several occasions you will have an opportunity to share your learning log explorations with classmates and to use these logs to generate further discussion of ideas. Your instructor will specify whether completion of these learning log tasks will be a requirement for this assignment. In our view, the learning log tasks work best if you keep your writing informal and exploratory with an emphasis on idea generation rather than on corrections and polish.

Exploring Your Texts through Summary Writing

Learning Log Task 1: Write a 200–250-word summary of each of the main texts you will use in your final paper.

As a starting point for grappling with a writer's ideas, writing careful summaries prompts you to read texts with the grain, adopting each text's perspective and walking in each author's shoes. When you summarize a text, you try to achieve an accurate, thorough understanding of it by stating its main ideas in a tightly distilled format.

Instructions on how to write a summary are found on pp. 131–134.

What follows are student Kara Watterson's summary of the book chapter by Ritzer and student Kate MacAulay's summary of Turkle's article—the two readings they will use in their synthesis essays. Notice how they use attributive tags to show that they are representing Ritzer's and Turkle's ideas as objectively as they can and that these ideas belong to Ritzer or Turkle, not to them.

Instructions on how to use attributive tags are found in Chapter 22, Skill 28.

KARA'S SUMMARY OF RITZER'S CHAPTER

In "The Irrationality of Rationality," the seventh chapter in *The McDonaldization of Society*, sociologist George Ritzer identifies a major sociological and economic problem: in an effort to find the most efficient way to run a business (what Ritzer calls "rationalizing"), more and more companies are following the franchise model pioneered by McDonald's. Although McDonaldization is efficient and economical for the companies, Ritzer argues it can be irrational, inconvenient, inefficient, and costly for consumers who often stand in long lines at fast-food restaurants and supermarkets. Ritzer also claims that McDonaldized systems cause people to forfeit real fun for manufactured fun and illusion. He cites the example of fake international villages at amusement parks and the fake friendliness of the "scripted interactions" (138) that employees are supposed to have with customers. Ritzer explains that our McDonaldized society has begun focusing more on quantity than quality. He believes that McDonaldized systems are dehumanizing: jobs "don't offer much in the way of satisfaction or stability" (137) and families hardly ever eat together any more, a situation that is contributing to the "disintegration of the family" (141). Ritzer also argues that by franchising everywhere, we are losing cultural distinctions. Whether you are in Japan or the United States, products are beginning to look the same. Finally, Ritzer shows that when companies become rationalized, they limit the possibility of connection between human beings. Citing examples from fast-food restaurants to hospitals, he states that there are many serious drawbacks to "our fast-paced and impersonal society" (140).

KATE'S SUMMARY OF TURKLE'S ARTICLE

In her *Wired* article "Who Am We?" psychologist and MIT professor Sherry Turkle explores how computers and the Internet are transforming our views of ourselves and the way we interact socially. Turkle believes that the Internet is moving us toward a "decentered" (149) sense of the self. She says that computers used to be thought of as "calculating machines" (149), but they are increasingly now seen as intelligent objects capable of interaction and simulation. She uses children's interactive computer games to illustrate how some people now think of computers as having personalities and psyches, which make them "fitting partners for dialog and relationship" (150). In the second half of her article, she argues that virtual life raises new moral issues. She uses the example of MUDs (multiuser domains), which allow people to create multiple and often simultaneous virtual identities by playing different characters. She presents examples of the relationships of cyber characters—often cyber-sex—that raise the question of whether cybersex is an act of real-life infidelity or adultery. Turkle concludes that it is easy for people to lose themselves between the real world and these virtual worlds. Because we have the ability to create better "selves" in the virtual world, it is possible to become addicted to virtual life and be "imprisoned by the screens" (199). According to Turkle, we are moving toward a "postmodernist culture of simulation" (149), and she cautions that it is more important than ever that we are very self-aware.

Summarizing Your Texts

FOR WRITING AND DISCUSSION

Working in small groups or as a whole class, share your summaries of your two chosen or assigned readings. What important main ideas does your group agree must be included in a summary of each text? What points are secondary and can be left out?

Exploring Your Texts' Rhetorical Strategies

Learning Log Task 2: Analyze the rhetorical strategies used in each of your texts (for example, the way your texts handle purpose; audience; genre; angle of vision; appeals to *logos, ethos,* and *pathos,* and use of evidence).

Explanations of these terms and concepts are found in Concepts 3, 7, and 8.

In order to analyze a text and synthesize its ideas, you need to consider the text rhetorically. To whom is the author writing and why? Do you see how the genre of each text influences some of the author's choices about language and structure? What angle of vision shapes each text and accounts for what is included and excluded? Do you share the values of the author or of his or her intended audience?

Here is Kara's learning log entry exploring the rhetorical contexts of the Ritzer and Turkle texts:

Instructions on how to write a rhetorical critique of a text are found in Chapter 6 on pp. 135–140.

KARA'S RESPONSE TO LEARNING LOG TASK 2

Although both George Ritzer and Sherry Turkle are scholars, their texts are not really written for scholarly audiences. Both would fall in the category of nonfiction books (articles) written for general audiences and both are written to raise audience awareness of sociological/cultural problems—in this case, the way that technological advances and the fast-food model of business are affecting the quality of life and the way that the Internet is affecting our sense of ourselves and our relationships.

Both Ritzer and Turkle have chosen to write in accessible language so that their ideas can easily be understood by a general audience, and both use many examples to build credibility. Still, because I had no previous personal background with multiuser domains, I found it challenging to imagine some of Turkle's descriptions of the virtual world of MUDs, but I did have previous experience with all of Ritzer's examples so I never felt in over my head while reading his chapters.

From Ritzer's angle of vision, McDonaldization has had a damaging and irreversible effect on the quality of contemporary life, and he is trying to prompt people to slow down this destructive process. His approach is quite one-sided, though. He does admit that "we undoubtedly have gained much from the rationalization of society in general" (132), but he does not develop this idea any further. He refuses to make any further concessions to the rationalization he is fighting. Instead of acknowledging contradicting ideas, Ritzer hammers his point strongly with example after example. By the end of the chapter, the reader is left with a glazed-over feeling, not really taking in the information.

Kara defines "rationalization" in the opening sentences of her summary of Ritzer, p. 358.

Turkle's angle of vision seems to include curiosity and exploration as well as concern about the way computers are transforming society. She seems to analyze more than argue. She is trying to get across her notion that the Internet lets people adopt many different characters and have multiple selves, for example when they play in MUDs and simulation games. So maybe, in claiming that computers are no longer calculating machines, Turkle, like Ritzer, is only presenting one limited view of her subject, the view that interests her as a psychologist who has written many books and articles on computers, and our changing sense of identity and community.

FOR WRITING AND DISCUSSION

Examining the Rhetorical Strategies of Your Texts

Working in small groups or as a whole class, share what each of you discovered in Learning Log Task 2. Try to reach consensus on the most important rhetorical features of each of the texts you are using for your synthesis essay.

Exploring Main Themes and Similarities and Differences in Your Texts' Ideas

Learning Log Task 3: Identify main issues or themes in your assigned or chosen texts. Then explore the similarities and differences in their ideas.

This learning log task asks you to identify main issues, ideas, or themes that surface in your texts as preparation for looking for similarities and differences among your texts. This process of thinking—comparison and contrast—will help you clarify your understanding of each reading and promote analysis of the underlying values, assumptions, and ideas of each author. Here are some questions that can guide your learning log writing at this stage of your thinking:

QUESTIONS TO HELP YOU GRAPPLE WITH SIMILARITIES AND DIFFERENCES IN YOUR TEXTS

- What main ideas or themes related to your synthesis question do you see in each text?
- What similarities and differences do you see in the way the authors choose to frame the issues they are writing about? How do their theses (either implied or stated) differ?
- What are the main similarities and differences in their angles of vision?
- What commonalities and intersections related to your synthesis question do you see in their ideas? What contradictions and clashes do you see in their ideas?
- What similarities and differences do you see in the authors' underlying values and assumptions?
- What overlap, if any, is there in these authors' examples and uses of terms?
- On the subject of your synthesis question, how would Author A respond to Author B?

Here are excerpts from Kara's and Kate's learning logs, showing their exploratory analyses of Ritzer's and Turkle's texts. Note how they each begin to organize comparisons by points, to make analytical connections among them, and to push themselves to think out exactly where these authors agree and differ.

EXCERPT FROM KARA'S RESPONSE TO LEARNING LOG TASK 3

Both Ritzer and Turkle make strong comments about health problems that may be caused by the particular type of technology they are dealing with. For Ritzer, the dangers that arise from McDonaldization can most easily be seen in fast-food restaurants and their fatty, unhealthy foods: "such meals are the last things many Americans need, suffering as they do from obesity, high cholesterol levels, high blood pressure, and perhaps diabetes" (133). He also considers the high level of stress created by our high-speed society that can cause heart attacks, panic attacks, maybe nervous breakdowns. Turkle, too, is concerned about the effects of technology on people's health, but her focus is people's psyches and minds. One person in her research study who creates different identities on the Internet thinks that "MUDding has ultimately made him feel worse about himself" (196). For Turkle, the Internet can be dangerous for what it can do to a person's psyche.

Both authors agree that technological advances are causing a loss of real human connection. McDonaldization fosters fake contact; employees are given guidelines about how to interact with customers and are programmed with what to say and what not to say: "rule Number 17 for Burger King workers is 'Smiles at all times'" (Ritzer 130). Quick sales, not real customer relations, are the main concern. For Turkle too, this loss of human contact is a dilemma. MUDs are not places where you truly get to know a person; they are places where people are acting out characters. These are not real friends that can aid you when you are feeling ill or down. Also, people are spending vast quantities of time logging on, spending time with a computer screen instead of family and friends. ...

EXCERPT FROM KATE'S RESPONSE TO LEARNING LOG TASK 3

... Last, I think that Turkle and Ritzer have very different attitudes about what they observe and claim is happening to society. Turkle seems to be a little more optimistic than Ritzer. While she sees the changes that advanced technology is causing in society, she seems to think that we, as human beings, have the ability to adjust to the changes facing us and to change ourselves in order to preserve our humanity. In contrast to that view, Ritzer seems to take the position that we are on a downward spiral and McDonaldized systems are destroying us and society as a whole. Ritzer and Turkle would have a really great discussion about all the negative effects that technology and rationality are having on individuals and society, but they would probably largely disagree on society's ability to bounce back and fix itself.

Generating Points about Themes, Shared Ideas, and Differences

FOR WRITING AND DISCUSSION

Working as a whole class or in small groups, share your analyses of similarities and differences in your chosen or assigned texts. Pay close attention to these two overarching questions: How are the texts similar and different? How do each author's assumptions, beliefs, purposes, and values account for these similarities and differences?

Generating Ideas of Your Own

Learning Log Task 4: In light of what you have read and thought about so far, explore your own views on the original synthesis question that has guided your probing of the texts.

One of your biggest challenges in writing a synthesis essay is to move beyond analysis to synthesis. A successful synthesis essay incorporates ideas from your texts and yet represents your own independent thinking, showing evidence of the dialectic process. You need to think about how the differing perspectives of Texts A and B have led you to new realizations that will let you enter the conversation of these texts. As you begin to formulate your synthesis views, you will also need to reassert your personal/intellectual investment in the conversation of the texts. You will need to take ownership of the ideas and to emerge with a clearer sense of your own views. You may also want to consider which text—in your mind—makes the most significant contribution to the question you are exploring. You may want to evaluate the texts to determine which has influenced your thinking the most and why. The following questions should help you use Learning Log Task 4 to generate ideas of your own.

QUESTIONS TO HELP YOU DEVELOP YOUR OWN VIEWS

- What do I agree with and disagree with in the texts I have analyzed?
- How have these texts changed my perception and understanding of an issue, question, or problem? (You might want to use these prompts: "I used to think _________, but now I think _________." "Although these texts have persuaded me that _________, I still have doubts about _________.")
- What do I see or think now that I didn't see or think before I read these texts?
- Related to my synthesis question, what new, significant questions do these texts raise for me?
- What do I now see as the main controversies?
- What is my current view on the focusing question that connects my texts and that all my texts explore?
- How would I position myself in the conversation of the texts?
- If I find one author's perspective more valid, accurate, interesting, or useful than another's, why is that?

To illustrate this learning log task, we show you excerpts from the explorations of both Kara and Kate.

EXCERPT FROM KARA'S RESPONSE TO LEARNING LOG TASK 4

When I was in Puerto Rico one spring break, I remember how excited my friend and I were to go to a burger place for dinner one night. It was so nice to have American food after days of eating fajitas and enchiladas. At the time, I did not think about how this American restaurant got to Puerto Rico; I was just glad it was there. However, after reading "The Irrationality of Rationality" by George Ritzer, I began to take a closer look at this experience. Both this article and "Who Am We?" have caused me to take a closer look at our society. ... What is it that causes people to surf the Internet for hours on end, to chat with people they have never met? What is this doing to our culture? Are we losing the distinctions evident when you travel from one region to the next, from one country to another? ...

EXCERPT FROM KATE'S RESPONSE TO LEARNING LOG TASK 4

Reading the articles by Ritzer and Turkle made me much more aware of a social problem that I didn't really pay attention to before. I didn't realize how much modern technology is changing our human relationships. For example, the other night I was at a family gathering, and some of my cousins began discussing the idea of purchasing a new car. After talking for a short while about how much it would cost and how to get the best deal, one of my cousins had that modern craving for wanting to know the answer immediately. He logged on to the Internet and spent the remainder of the evening looking at cars and prices, and had limited interaction with the family. It made me think about the articles and how things were becoming more immediate and less personal, and how interactions between machines and humans are decreasing the interactions between people. Why speak with another person who might not know the answer to a question or the solution to a problem when you can just log on to the Internet and find the right answer immediately? It makes me wonder what the Internet does not offer. ...

Taking Your Position in the Conversation: Your Synthesis

Learning Log Task 5: Reread your first four learning logs and consider how your own views on the synthesis question have evolved and emerged. Think about the risky, surprising, or new views that you can bring to your readers. In light of your reading and thinking, explore what you want to say in your own voice to show the connections you have made and the new insights you now have.

After you have discovered what you think about the texts you have analyzed—what ideas you accept and reject, what new questions you have formulated, how your ideas have been modified and transformed through your reading experience—you need to find a way to pull your ideas together. Your synthesis view should be the fruit of your intellectual work, a perspective that you have come to after reading the ideas of other writers, pondering them reflectively and keenly. Here are some questions that can help you articulate the points that you want to develop in your essay:

QUESTIONS TO HELP YOU FORMULATE AND DEVELOP YOUR SYNTHESIS VIEWS

- What discoveries have I made after much thought?
- What are the most important insights I have gotten from these readings?
- What is my intellectual or personal investment with the synthesis question at this point?

- Where can I step out on my own, even take a risk, in my thinking about the ideas discussed in these texts?
- What new perspective do I want to share with my readers?

What follows is an excerpt from Kara's learning log. Note how she is beginning to find her stance on the synthesis question of whether technology enriches or dehumanizes our lives.

EXCERPT FROM KARA'S RESPONSE TO LEARNING LOG TASK 5

What is technology doing to our relationships with one another? Both Ritzer and Turkle seem to be urging us away from dependency on technology, and these authors have made me aware of my complacence in accepting technology, but still I see value in technology that these writers don't discuss. ...

I find myself questioning these writers' views. Ritzer seems to believe that families go to McDonald's rather than eat family meals together. He doesn't consider that it is when people are on the road or out already that these restaurants are visited, not when they are sitting at home deciding what is for dinner. Turkle also speaks of the loss of connection that can arise from people constantly at their computers. She raises some very important questions about what technology is doing to our relationships and self-image, but I think she focuses too much on MUDs. How many people actually are doing this MUDding? Also, there are some valid things that come out of relationships on the Internet. I know of several examples of people who have met their future spouses through chat rooms and Online Social Networks. When I left for college, I was not sure whom I would stay in touch with, but because of the Internet, I am able to stay connected to people I would have drifted away from otherwise.

Also, while we note the dangers of technology, I think we need to remember the benefits as well. I agree that cell phones are overused, but how often have cell phones saved people in emergencies or aided people stranded on the road with car problems? I hope to be a doctor. I have great appreciation for the way that cameras can see inside a patient as surgeons are operating and thus reduce the risk of many surgeries. ...

FOR WRITING AND DISCUSSION

Generating Your Synthesis Points

Prior to the start of this task, work individually to write two or three main points that you want to make in the synthesis portion of your final essay. Working in small groups or as a whole class, share your short list of main points. Briefly explain to your group or to the whole class why these points interest you. Take notes on group ideas.

At this point, you might want to reread Kate MacAulay's synthesis essay (pp. 353–355) to see how it grew out of exploratory writing in her learning logs. Particularly note how she selected, organized, and developed points that emerged from her exploratory thinking.

Shaping and Drafting

Your main project in shaping and drafting your synthesis essay is to move from the kernels of good ideas that you generated in your learning logs to a focused, fully developed, and logically organized discussion of these ideas. Focusing and organizing your ideas for a synthesis essay are both challenging writing tasks. We offer some suggestions for developing the analysis and synthesis sections of your essay and then for formulating a thesis that will direct and hold together your essay.

For the analysis part of your essay, identify the points in Learning Log Tasks 2 and 3 that strike you as the most interesting, lively, profound, or significant. The following strategies will help you focus and develop these ideas.

STRATEGIES

for Shaping the Analytical Section of Your Essay

What to Consider in Planning the Analysis Section of Your Essay	Questions and Decisions
• Your analysis section lays the foundation for your synthesis. • The analysis section usually forms about one-half to two-thirds of your essay. • This section discusses several ways that your texts relate to your synthesis question.	• How many analytical points do you want to develop? • What are these points?
• Your analysis section should show that you have wallowed in the complexity of your texts. • It may include points about the rhetorical features of your texts (as in a rhetorical critique), and it may include points about the ideas (as in an ideas critique). • It should map out and explain a number of important similarities and differences in your texts.	Consider developing answers to these questions: • How do your texts frame the problem? How do they present different angles of vision? Where do they intersect in their perspectives and approaches? How do they argue and support their views with evidence? • How rhetorically effective are these texts? • What do the authors do to make their readers think?

For the synthesis part of your essay, use the following strategies to develop points that emerged for you from Learning Log Tasks 4 and 5.

STRATEGIES

for Shaping the Synthesis Section of Your Essay

What to Consider in Planning the Synthesis Section of Your Essay	Questions and Decisions
• Your essay should build to your synthesis section. • Typically your synthesis ideas form at least one-third of your essay.	• How can you best show where the texts and their authors promote your own independent thinking? • What synthesis points do you want to explore and discuss?
• The synthesis section of your essay should show your informed, independent thinking. • It should show how you have worked your way to a new understanding.	• What new insights have you developed through studying these texts? • What new perspectives have you gained through the contrast and/or clash of different ideas? • How much or how little have these texts changed your views and why?

Writing a Thesis for a Synthesis Essay

For a full explanation of thesis statements, purpose statements, and mapping statements, see Chapter 18, Skill 9.

See Chapter 2, Concept 6 for a discussion of how to avoid unsurprising, noncontestable thesis statements.

In a synthesis essay, your thesis statement is particularly important and challenging to write. It sets up your readers' expectations, promising an illuminating view of the texts you have worked with. It should reflect earnest intellectual work, promise insights achieved through serious reflection, be your own original connection of ideas, and contain some element of risk and newness. Avoid bland, noncontestable thesis statements such as "These articles have both good and bad points."

You will probably want to work back and forth between formulating your thesis statement and drafting the analysis and synthesis sections of your essay. We recommend that you map out a rough thesis, draft your essay, and then revise and sharpen your thesis. For a synthesis essay, it is sometimes difficult to write a one-sentence, high-level thesis statement that encompasses both your analysis and your synthesis points. In such cases, you can write two lower-level, more specific thesis statements—one for your analysis section and one for your synthesis section—and simply join them together. What is important is that your thesis forecasts your main analysis and synthesis points and creates a map for your reader. The following examples illustrate these different options.

LOW-LEVEL, TWO-SENTENCE THESIS

Lower-level thesis for analysis

Lower-level thesis for synthesis

Whereas Ritzer focuses on the way high-tech society makes us homogeneous and superficial, Turkle focuses on how the Internet unsettles traditional views of the self. Although I agree with Ritzer's argument that McDonaldization is dehumanizing, I think that role-playing in MUDs is actually a healthy way to oppose McDonaldization and expresses human desire to be creative, to develop the self, and to make human connections.

HIGH-LEVEL, ONE-SENTENCE THESIS

Ritzer's attack on technological society and Turkle's more optimistic belief that it offers opportunity for growth and discovery have together forced me to consider the superficiality and vulnerability of human relationships in our high-tech society.

Writer chooses high-level, one-sentence thesis rather than two lower-level theses

Organizing a Synthesis Essay

The biggest organizational decision you have to make in writing a synthesis essay is how much to summarize your texts and how to incorporate these summaries into your essay. Your decision should be guided by your audience's familiarity with the texts you are discussing and the complexity of the points you are making. Two ways of organizing a synthesis essay are shown in Figure 13.1.

FIGURE 13.1 Two Frameworks for a Synthesis Essay

Framework 1

Introduction and summary of both texts (several paragraphs)	• Presents the synthesis question and hooks readers • Summarizes the texts (unless your instructor posits that readers have already read the texts, in which case you can omit the summaries or reduce them to one or two sentences each) • Presents your thesis, which maps out your main analytical and synthesis points (Your thesis might come at the end of the paragraphs with your summaries or in a mini-paragraph of its own.)
Analytical section	• Includes paragraphs discussing and developing your analytical points
Synthesis section	• Includes paragraphs discussing and developing your synthesis points
Concluding paragraph	• Reiterates the values and limitations of the texts you have analyzed. • Pulls together your new insights • Leaves readers thinking about your views

Framework 2

Introduction	• Presents the synthesis question and hooks readers • Presents your thesis, which maps out your main analytical and synthesis points
Summary/analysis of first text	• Summarizes the first text • Analyzes the first text
Summary/analysis of second text	• Summarizes the second text • Analyzes the second text
Synthesis section	• Develops several main synthesis points
Concluding paragraph	• Reiterates values and limitations of the texts you have analyzed. • Pulls together your new insights • Leaves readers thinking about your views

Revising

As you revise your synthesis essay, make sure that you have set up the synthesis question effectively. Then work on clarifying and developing your analytical points while striving for an engaging style. Also consider how to make your synthesis views more clearly reflect your own wrestling with the texts' ideas. Think about finding the most interesting ways to show how these texts have enlarged and deepened your own views.

Questions for Peer Review

In addition to the generic peer review questions explained in Chapter 17, Skill 4, ask your peer reviewers to address these questions:

INTRODUCTION, SUMMARIES OF THE TEXT, AND THESIS

1. What works well about the writer's presentation of the synthesis question that connects the texts under examination? How could the writer better show this question's significance and problematic nature?
2. Where could the writer's summaries of the texts be expanded, condensed, or clarified? Where would the summaries be better located in the essay to help readers?
3. How could the thesis be made more focused, risky, and clear in setting up the writer's analytical and synthesis points?

ANALYTICAL SECTION OF THE ESSAY

4. How could the analytical points more clearly compare and contrast the authors' values, assumptions, angles of vision, or rhetorical strategies in addressing the synthesis question?
5. What further textual evidence could the writer add to develop these analytical points and make them more interesting or comprehensive?

SYNTHESIS SECTION OF THE ESSAY

6. How could the writer's synthesis points more clearly demonstrate the writer's thoughtful interaction with these texts?
7. What examples or other specifics could the writer include to develop these synthesis points more effectively?
8. How could the writer conclude this essay more effectively to leave readers with a new perspective on the texts and on the underlying question?

READINGS

The readings in this chapter immerse you in a network of issues about illegal immigration and immigration reform. (Also connected to this issue is the exercise on news photographs in Chapter 11, pp. 287–288.) These issues cut across political parties and continue to perplex citizens, policymakers, and immigrants. Experts estimate that eleven to twelve million people have illegally crossed the border between the United States and Mexico and are currently living and working in the United States. What caused these persons to risk the dangers of border crossing in order to work in the United States? What questions about human rights and domestic security does this problem raise? What forces are interfering with effective policy discussions and decision making to solve these problems?

For this chapter's readings, we present five blogs on these issues. ("Blog" is an abbreviation for "Web log.") Blogging has become a popular arena for political discourse worldwide as well as for discourse on any subject ranging from hobbies to sports to conspiracy theories. The blogosphere constitutes a new and rapidly evolving rhetorical context open to anyone who desires to create a blogsite or respond to postings on someone else's site. Persons often blog under online pseudonyms. Because a blogger tends to attract persons with similar interests and views, a blogsite serves as a "virtual café" for like-minded people to exchange views. Consequently, blogs often have an uncomfortable "insider feel" for persons trying to enter a blog conversation for the first time. They are also often characterized by informal, colloquial, and occasionally obscene language that wouldn't be encountered in print media. Some widely known and highly influential sites—such as the Daily Kos on the left or MichelleMalkin or Little Green Footballs on the right—are major players in United States political debate. Many people now think that skilled and knowledgeable bloggers play a more important "free press" investigative role in our democracy than do major newspapers dominated by corporate interests.

To avoid influencing your own analysis of these readings, we omit the discussion questions that typically follow in other chapters. However, as you read each blog, consider the particular blogsite that is hosting this piece (mentioned in the headnote) and also think about these general questions: How does the writer frame the issue? What is the writer's main argument? What types of evidence are included? What is distinctive about the way the writer expresses his or her ideas?

Our first blog is by a Mexican-American woman who identifies herself only as "Dee." According to her blogsite, Dee is a United States citizen with a Hispanic ethnicity. She holds a mid-level management position in a large corporation. Upset by the divisive discourse over immigration, Dee started her own blogsite called "Immigration Talk with a Mexican American: Truth, Honesty, and the American Way." In the blog reprinted below (posted on August 7, 2007), she sums up her placement of blogosphere views of immigration in two categories: the PROs (those who support comprehensive immigration reform) and the ANTIs (those who oppose it). She places herself firmly among the PROs. In this brief blog, her reference to the 12M stands for the estimated twelve million undocumented workers currently in the United States. Her use of abbreviations suggests the insider audience characteristic of blog discourse.

Dee

Comprehensive Immigration Reform: PROs and ANTIs

http://immigrationmexicanamerican.blogspot.com/2007/08/comprehensive-immigration-reform-pros.html

1 Our country is divided on how to resolve our Immigration issues in our country. Comprehensive Immigration Reform (CIR) is needed. Who is for CIR? PROs. Who is against CIR? ANTIs. What are their perspectives?

2 Pro Profile: There are many, many PRO groups. Each group has a different motivation and they rarely rally together. The largest group is Hispanic Americans. The ethnicities vary and include: Mexican, Central and South American, Cuban, Puerto Rican and more. The majority of PROs who post on the internet are from this group. Other Minority groups include Asian, Southern European, Middle Eastern, African. I only see their posts when I search the international sites. Other PRO groups who also rarely post include: Churches and Humanitarian groups, Businesses that prosper from sales to the 12M (e.g. Banks, Insurance Companies, Retail, etc.), Businesses experiencing Labor Shortages that hire the 12M (e.g. Farming, IT, Construction, Contractors, Retail, etc), Politicians with reasons to support the 12M (e.g. enhance Globalization, running for office, etc). And, of course, the illegal immigrants themselves. The majority of PROs who do post tend to have the following views: They advocate secure borders, sanctioning employers and comprehensive immigration reform (because the current program is broken). The biggest difference between the ANTIs and the PROs is, the PROs advocate a path to citizenship for the 12M, particularly since most of the 12M have worked and contributed to this country for + 5–20 years.

3 ANTI Profile: American. The majority are Anglos. (Anglos = white, Northern European ethnicity). Viewpoint: The majority advocate Deportation (mass or self) of the illegal immigrants in this country. Anything short of Deportation is termed Amnesty by the ANTIs. Many call for a 2000 mile southern border fence. They advocate for restrictive Official English laws even though English is already the National Language. They advocate for changing the 14th amendment and birthright citizenship, hoping to end, what they term "Anchor Babies." There are a few legal immigrants and minorities within their groups, but not many. There are a few politicians that support them, not many. There are hundreds of ANTI websites across the internet. There are hundreds of ANTI radio shows across the country. ANTIs tend to be very angry. They try their darndest to get African Americans to join forces with them citing their uncorroborated claim the 12M drag down the minimum wage. The ANTIs tend to forget the deep alliances between the two ethnic groups which were forged over the previous four decades when they marched together for civil rights. Some of the Worst Terms the ANTIs use: 3rd World Country, Mexifornia, return to American Values.

Our next reading is a blog by Byron Williams, an African-American syndicated columnist. According to his online biography, the Reverend Byron Williams is "a writer, theologian, and activist [who] fuses theology with public policy to bring a fresh social justice perspective to the public arena." He serves as pastor of the Resurrection Community Church in Oakland, California. This blog was posted on The Huffington Post on May 9, 2006.

Byron Williams

Immigration Frenzy Points Out Need for Policy Debate

http://www.huffingtonpost.com/byron-williams/immigration-frenzy-points_b_20717.html

1 As a child I recall Thanksgiving with mixed emotions. I enjoyed the big family feast with relatives I had not seen since the previous Thanksgiving, but I dreaded the days after. It was turkey ad nauseam. By the sixth day my father would make what he called "Turkey a la King," which was turkey remnants along with whatever else he could find to put in the pot.

2 As emotions flare on both sides of the immigration debate it has morphed into "Immigration a la King." But unlike my father's mysterious concoction, the ingredients are well known. It consists of one part legitimate public policy, one part ethnocentrism, and one part political pandering.

3 There is no doubting we need a legitimate public policy conversation around illegal immigration. The porous nature of America's borders coupled with the post 9/11 climate does warrant national concern.

4 If, however, we remove the legitimate public policy aspect, what's left? What's left is ugly, reactionary fear-based hatred symbolizing America at its worst.

5 With 9/11 approaching its 5th anniversary, why are we just getting around to dealing with immigration? Like a wounded, cornered animal, the Republican-led Congress and the president conveniently fan the flames of one of America's greatest tragedies, resurfacing fear, in order to gain short-term political points.

6 It is hard to embrace the concept that at this late date the administration and Congress are worried about Al Qaeda members coming across the border in man made tunnels or in the back of trucks when you consider the 9/11 attackers entered the country legally.

7 They have successfully created a climate where vigilantes known as the Minutemen—who do a disservice to the brave individuals who fought during the Revolutionary War by embracing the name—are viewed as patriotic by taking the law into their own hands allegedly protecting America's borders.

8 How many poor white southerners willingly accepted a death sentence by fighting for the Confederacy to protect a "southern way of life" in which they did not participate? They were seductively lured, in part, by the notion that all hell would break loose if emancipated African slaves were elevated to their same impoverished status.

9 The ethnocentrism and political pandering has sadly infected parts of the African American community. If one removes the veil of objecting to the comparisons between the civil rights movement and Hispanic immigration demonstrations, which a num-

ber of African Americans hide behind, they would discover the same fear that plagues the dominant culture.

10 This does not dismiss the obvious concerns about the plight of low-skilled African Americans who find themselves competing with immigrants for certain entry-level employment. But again, this is part of the much needed public policy debate that is submerged under the current political frenzy.

11 Freely throwing around words such "illegal" and "Al Qaeda" opens the door to dehumanization. And once an individual has been dehumanized that individual can be taken advantage of.

12 Even those who compassionately advocate for a guest worker program, forget that the last such program that existed on a large scale in this country was struck down by Abraham Lincoln on September 22, 1863.

13 There are legitimate concerns on both sides of this issue. But history has shown us there is something wrong when marginalized groups are systematically pitted against each other.

14 For all of the cries to protect the borders and the loss of job opportunities for low-skilled Americans, I doubt there would be 11 million undocumented individuals in the country if no one was hiring. There can be no legitimate immigration debate that does not hold the business community equally accountable for hiring undocumented individuals while paying less than a living wage.

15 Each individual must come to his or her decision as to how they feel about immigration. But the only way to have an authentic policy is to have an authentic policy debate—one that does not include the unnecessary ingredients that ultimately lead to dehumanization.

Our third reading by Victor Davis Hanson is a posting to Roundup: Historians' Take, a spot for "historians writing about the news," on the History News Network site. Victor Davis Hanson, a former professor of classics and now a Senior Fellow at the Hoover Institution, is known as a military historian, a political essayist, and a regular conservative columnist for the *National Review* and Tribune Media Services. He has published numerous books and his writing has appeared frequently in such well-known newspapers and journals as the *New York Times,* the *Wall Street Journal,* and the *American Spectator*. He also blogs regularly at Pajamas Media. This posting appeared on Wednesday, June 6, 2007.

Victor Davis Hanson

The Global Immigration Problem

http://hnn.us/roundup/entries/39776.html

1 Thousands of aliens crossing our 2,000-mile border from an impoverished Mexico reflect a much larger global one-way traffic problem.

2 In Germany, Turkish workers—both legal and illegal—are desperate to find either permanent residence or citizenship.

3 "Londonstan" is slang for a new London of thousands of unassimilated Pakistani nationals.

4 In France, there were riots in 2005 because many children of North African immigrants are unemployed—and unhappy.

5 Albanians flock to Greece to do farm work, and then are regularly deported for doing so illegally.

6 The list could go on.

7 So why do millions of these border-crossers head to Europe, the United States or elsewhere in the West?

8 Easy. Stable democracies and free markets ensure economic growth, rising standards of living and, thus, lots of jobs, while these countries' birth rates and native populations fall.

9 Employers may console themselves that they pay better than what the immigrants earned back at home. This might be true, but the wages are never enough to allow such newcomers to achieve parity with their hosts.

10 Naturally, immigrants soon get angry. And rather than showing thanks for a ticket out of the slums of Mexico City or Tunis, blatant hypocrisy can follow: the once thankful, but now exhausted, alien may wave the flag of the country he would never return to while shunning the culture of the host county he would never leave.

11 In the second generation—as we see from riots in France or gangs in Los Angeles—things can get even worse.

12 The moment illegal immigrants arrive, a sort of race begins: can these newcomers become legal, speak the host language and get educated before they age, get hurt or lose their job? If so, then they assimilate and their children are held up as models of diversity. If not, the end of the story can be welfare or jail.

13 Hypocrisy abounds on all sides. Free-marketers claim they must have cheap workers to stay competitive. Yet they also count on public subsidies to take care of their former employees when old, sick or in trouble.

14 Governments in countries such as Mexico and Morocco usually care far more about their emigrants once they are long gone. Then these poor are no longer volatile proof of their own failures, but victims of some wealthy foreign government's indifference. And these pawns usually send cash home.

15 The lower middle classes complain most about massive immigration, but then they have to compete with aliens for jobs, often live among them and don't use their services. The wealthier, who hire immigrants for low wages and see them only at work, often think mass immigration, even if illegal, is wonderful.

16 The lasting solution is not the status quo—or even walls, fines, deportation, amnesty or guest-worker programs. Instead, failed societies in Latin America, Africa and much of the Middle East must encourage family planning and get smarter about using their plentiful natural wealth to keep more of their own people home.

17 The remedy for the richer West?

18 It is past time to remember that paying our own poorer laborers more, doing some occasional physical work and obeying the laws—the immigration ones especially—are not icky or a bummer. Rather, this is the more ethical and, in the long run, cheaper approach.

19 There is a final irony. The more Western elites ignore their own laws, allow unassimilated ethnic ghettos and profit from an exploitive labor market, the more their own nations will begin to resemble the very places immigrants fled from.

Our final two pieces focus on disagreements over the "temporary guest worker" program that was part of an immigration reform bill considered (and ultimately rejected) by Congress in 2007. One provision of the bill would have allowed currently illegal immigrants to stay in the United States legally for up to six years as guest workers. In this excerpt from a posting on The Hill Blog, Republican Senator Mike Crapo from Idaho explains why he supported the guest worker provision of the bill, although he eventually voted against the bill for other reasons.

Senator Mike Crapo

Excerpt from "Immigration Policy Must Help Economy While Preserving Ideals"

http://blog.thehill.com/2007/07/07/immigration-policy-must-help-economy-while-preserving-ideals-sen-mike-crapo/

A robust economy hinges on having a temporary guest worker program to fill jobs that are not filled by American citizens. U.S.-based businesses need economic incentives to keep operations stateside. If they have a dependable labor pool at all skill levels, incentives to move operations overseas are greatly decreased. We appreciate consumer goods and agriculture products "Made in America." We can keep things that way by approaching immigration rationally and sensibly. Whatever the skill level, any temporary guest worker system must be enforceable and reliable for the worker and employer. Once Americans have been given "first right" to jobs, employers such as the agriculture industry must have access to a system that's cost-effective, not bureaucratic, and doesn't carry the risk of prosecution while employers are trying to comply with the law. Congress understands the urgency of reaching a workable solution and is moving in the right direction.

Our last piece is an excerpt from "The Progressive Case Against the Immigration Bill," which appeared in the liberal blog The Daily Kos on June 25, 2007. It gives a different view of the temporary guest worker program than that expressed by Senator Mike Crapo. The author of this piece is "Trapper John," the online identity for Jake McIntyre, who is a contributing editor for The Daily Kos.

Trapper John

Excerpt from "The Progressive Case Against the Immigration Bill"

http://www.dailykos.com/story/2007/6/25/73229/6647

1 This immigration bill is an historically bad bill, one that will undermine wage markets and which will permanently cripple skills training in vital sectors of the economy. ... [T]he fatal flaw in this bill isn't "amnesty"—it's the euphemistically termed "temporary worker program."

2 The temporary worker program has nothing to do with immigration policy. To the contrary—it is a guaranteed cheap labor program grafted on to an immigration bill. When most people think of "immigration" to the US, they think of people coming to America to build a new life for themselves and their families, just as their ancestors did. But the temporary worker program has nothing to do with building American families and American dreams. Under the program, *400,000–600,000 guest workers would enter the country every year* on two-year visas. Although the visas can be renewed twice, recipients would be denied any path to permanent residency or citizenship. In fact, the guest workers would be precluded from even applying for permanent residency while here on temporary visas.

3 In short, the "temporary workers" will be just that—"temporary," and "workers." Not "immigrants." And they can never be "Americans." Instead, we will have created a permanent caste of non-citizens with no hope of ever becoming citizens. A class of over half-a-million workers without a voice in the political process, here at the sole sufferance of their employers. And those employers won't have to pay their new indentured servants any more than the minimum wage. See, unlike the existing H-2B visa—the visa that governs most "unskilled" temporary workers in the US today—the proposed temporary worker program contains no requirements that employers pay their temporary help the federally determined "prevailing wage" for their occupation and the geographic area. Today, if a contractor can't find a qualified electrician to work on a project in Chicago, the contractor can apply for an H-2B visa. But the contractor is required to pay any foreign electrician entering the US on the H-2B no less than $53.57 per hour, including benefits. That's the prevailing wage for an electrician in Chicago, according to the Department of Labor. And by requiring H-2B sponsors to pay their foreign help the prevailing wage, the H-2B program limits the ability of employers to use guest workers as a tool to undermine wage markets. The proposed temporary worker plan changes all that.

4 Under the proposed plan, there is no wage floor. If the Chicago contractor can't find an electrician in the US to work on his project for $20 per hour, he can import a temporary worker who will. The result will be a swift collapse of wage markets in many industries populated by skilled non-professional workers, like construction. And all of a sudden, we'll be hearing that the work of an electrician is one of those "jobs Americans won't do," like fruit picking. The truth, of course, is that there is no

job that an American won't do for the right price. But by creating a steady flow of temporary workers with no ability to stay in the country for more than a couple years, and no practical ability to fight for better wages, the number of jobs that "Americans won't do" will grow dramatically. And they include a host of the jobs that sustain and nourish the middle class. The construction trades. Cosmetology. Culinary arts. These are jobs that take years to master, and consequently pay quite well, because not just anybody can do them. But by busting open the labor markets for these jobs, and opening them with no restrictions to folks from countries with much lower costs of living, we will strangle the middle class lives of the millions of Americans who have proudly earned their paychecks with their skills. ...

5 There's no question that we need immigration reform in this country. We need to find a way to bring the millions of immigrants laboring in the shadows into the light, and into our American family. And to the extent that we have bona fide labor shortages in this country, we need to address them through an expansion of legal immigration. But the price of immigration reform cannot be a temporary worker program that exploits foreign workers, limits real immigration, and guts wages for American workers.

For additional writing, reading, and research resources, go to **www.MyCompLab.com** and choose **Ramage/Bean/Johnson's *The Allyn & Bacon Guide to Writing,* Fifth Edition.**

WRITING A CLASSICAL ARGUMENT

CHAPTER 14

The writing project for this chapter introduces you to a classical way of arguing in which you take a stand on an issue, offer reasons and evidence in support of your position, and summarize and respond to alternative views. Your goal is to persuade your audience, who can be initially perceived as either opposed to your position or undecided about it, to adopt your position or at least to regard it more openly or favorably.

The need for argument arises whenever members of a community disagree on an issue. Classical rhetoricians believed that the art of arguing was essential for good citizenship. If disputes can be resolved through exchange of perspectives, negotiation of differences, and flexible seeking of the best solutions to a problem, then nations won't have to resort to war or individuals to fisticuffs.

The study of argumentation involves two components: truth seeking and persuasion:

- By *truth seeking,* we mean a diligent, open-minded, and responsible search for the best course of action or solution to a problem, taking into account all the available information and alternative points of view.
- By *persuasion,* we mean the art of making a claim* on an issue and justifying it convincingly so that the audience's initial resistance to your position is overcome and they are moved toward your position.

These two components of argument seem paradoxically at odds: Truth seeking asks us to relax our certainties and be willing to change our views; persuasion asks us to be certain, to be committed to our claims, and to get others to change their views. We can overcome this paradox if we dispel two common but misleading views of argument. The most common view is that argument is a fight as in "I just got into a horrible argument with my roommate." This view of argument as a fist-waving, shouting match in which you ridicule anyone who disagrees with you (popularized by radio and television talk shows and the Internet) entirely disregards argument as truth seeking, but it also misrepresents argument as persuasion because it polarizes people, rather than promoting understanding, new ways of seeing, and change.

Another common but misleading view is that argument is a pro/con debate modeled after high school or college debate matches or presidential debates. Although debating can be an excellent way to develop critical thinking skills, it

*By long-standing tradition, the thesis statement of an argument is often called its "claim."

misrepresents argument as a two-sided contest with winners and losers. Because controversial issues involve many different points of view, not just two, reducing an issue to pro/con positions distorts the complexity of the disagreement. Instead of thinking of *both* sides of an issue, we need to think of *all* sides. Equally troublesome, the debate image invites us to ask, "Who won the debate?" rather than "What is the best solution to the question that divides us?" The best solution might be a compromise between the two debaters or an undiscovered third position. The debate image tends to privilege the confident extremes in a controversy rather than the complex and muddled middle.

From our perspective, the best image for understanding argument is neither "fight" nor "debate" but the deliberations of a committee representing a wide spectrum of community voices charged with finding the best solution to a problem. From this perspective, argument is both a *process* and a *product.* As a process, argument is an act of inquiry characterized by fact-finding, information gathering, and consideration of alternative points of view. As a product, it is someone's contribution to the conversation at any one moment—a turn taking in a conversation, a formal speech, or a written position paper such as the one you will write for this chapter. The goal of argument as process is truth seeking; the goal of argument as product is persuasion. When members of a diverse committee are willing to argue persuasively for their respective points of view but are simultaneously willing to listen to other points of view and to change or modify their positions in light of new information or better arguments, then both components of argument are fully in play.

We cannot overemphasize the importance of both truth seeking and persuasion to your professional and civic life. Truth seeking makes you an informed and judicious employee and a citizen who delays decisions until a full range of evidence and alternative views are aired and examined. Persuasion gives you the power to influence the world around you, whether through letters to the editor or blogs on political issues or through convincing position papers for professional life. Whenever an organization needs to make a major decision, those who can think flexibly and write persuasively can wield great influence.

Exploring Classical Argument

An effective way to appreciate argument as both truth seeking and persuasion is to address an issue that is new to you and then watch how your own views evolve. Your initial position will probably reflect what social scientists sometimes call your personal *ideology*—that is, a network of basic values, beliefs, and assumptions that tend to guide your view of the world. However, if you adopt a truth-seeking attitude, your initial position may evolve as the conversation progresses. In fact, the conversation may even cause changes in some of your basic beliefs, since ideologies aren't set in stone and since many of us have unresolved allegiance to competing ideologies that may be logically inconsistent (for example, a belief in freedom of speech combined with a belief that hate speech should be banned). In this exercise we ask you to keep track of how your views change and to note what causes the change.

The case we present for discussion involves ethical treatment of animals.

> **Situation:** A bunch of starlings build nests in the attic of a family's house, gaining access to the attic through a torn vent screen. Soon the eggs hatch, and every morning at sunrise the family is awakened by the sound of birds squawking and wings beating against rafters as the starlings fly in and out of the house to feed the hatchlings. After losing considerable early morning sleep, the family repairs the screen. Unable to get in and out, the parent birds are unable to feed their young. The birds die within a day. Is this cruelty to animals?

1. Freewrite your initial response to this question. Was the family's act an instance of cruelty to animals (that is, was their act ethically justifiable or not)?
2. Working in small groups or as a whole class, share your freewrites and then try to reach a group consensus on the issue. During this conversation (argument as process), listen carefully to your classmates' views and note places where your own initial views begin to evolve.
3. So far we have framed this issue as an after-the-fact yes/no question: Is the family guilty of cruelty to animals? But we can also frame it as an open-ended, before-the-fact question: "What should the family have done about the starlings in the attic?" Suppose you are a family member discussing the starlings at dinner, prior to the decision to fix the vent screen. Make a list of your family's other options and try to reach class consensus on the two or three best alternative solutions.
4. At the end of the discussion, do another freewrite exploring how your ideas evolved during the discussion. What insights did you get about the twin components of argument, truth seeking and persuasion?

Understanding Classical Argument

Having introduced you to argument as both process and product, we now turn to the details of effective argumentation. To help orient you, we begin by describing the typical stages that mark students' growth as arguers.

Stages of Development: Your Growth as an Arguer

We have found that when we teach argument in our classes, students typically proceed through identifiable stages as their argumentative skills increase. While these stages may or may not describe your own development, they suggest the skills you should strive to acquire.

- ***Stage 1: Argument as personal opinion.*** At the beginning of instruction in argument, students typically express strong personal opinions but have trouble justifying their opinions with reasons and evidence and often create short, undeveloped arguments that are circular, lacking in evidence, and insulting to those who disagree. The following freewrite, written by a student first confronting the starling case, illustrates this stage:

> The family shouldn't have killed the starlings because that is really wrong! I mean that act was disgusting. It makes me sick to think how so many people are

> just willing to kill something for no reason at all. How are these parents going to teach their children values if they just go out and kill little birds for no good reason?!! This whole family is what's wrong with America!

This writer's opinion is passionate and heartfelt, but it provides neither reasons nor evidence why someone else should hold the same opinion.

- ***Stage 2: Argument structured as claim supported by one or more reasons.*** This stage represents a quantum leap in argumentative skill because the writer can now produce a rational plan containing point sentences (the reasons) and particulars (the evidence). The writer who produced the previous freewrite later developed a structure like this:

  The family's act constituted cruelty to animals

  - because the starlings were doing minimal harm.
  - because other options were available.
  - because the way they killed the birds caused needless suffering.

- ***Stage 3: Increased attention to truth seeking.*** In stage 3 students become increasingly engaged with the complexity of the issue as they listen to their classmates' views, conduct research, and evaluate alternative perspectives and stances. They are often willing to change their positions when they see the power of other arguments.
- ***Stage 4: Ability to articulate the unstated assumptions underlying their arguments.*** As we show later in this chapter, each reason in a writer's argument is based on an assumption, value, or belief (often unstated) that the audience must accept if the argument is to be persuasive. Often the writer needs to state these assumptions explicitly and support them. At this stage students identify and analyze their own assumptions and those of their intended audiences. Students gain increased skill at accommodating alternative views through refutation or concession.
- ***Stage 5: Ability to link an argument to the values and beliefs of the intended audience.*** In this stage students are increasingly able to link their arguments to their audience's values and beliefs and to adapt structure and tone to the resistance level of their audience. Students also appreciate how delayed-thesis arguments or other psychological strategies can be more effective than closed-form arguments when addressing hostile audiences.

The rest of this chapter helps you progress through these stages. Although you can read the remainder in one sitting, we recommend that you break your reading into sections, going over the material slowly and applying it to your own ideas in progress. Let the chapter's concepts and explanations sink in gradually, and return to them periodically for review. This section on "Understanding Classical Argument" comprises a compact but comprehensive course in argumentation.

Creating an Argument Frame: A Claim with Reasons

Somewhere in the writing process, whether early or late, you need to create a frame for your argument. This frame includes a clear question that focuses the argument, your claim, and one or more supporting reasons. Often your reasons, stated as *because* clauses, can be attached to your claim to provide a working thesis statement.

Finding an Arguable Issue

At the heart of any argument is an issue, which we can define as a question that invites more than one reasonable answer and thus leads to perplexity or disagreement. This requirement excludes disagreements based on personal tastes, where no shared criteria can be developed ("Baseball is more fun than soccer"). It also excludes purely private questions because issues arise out of disagreements in communities.

Issue questions are often framed as yes/no choices, especially when they appear on ballots or in courtrooms: Should gay marriage be legalized? Should the federal government place a substantial tax on gasoline to elevate its price? Is this defendant guilty of armed robbery? Just as frequently, they can be framed openly, inviting many different possible answers: What should our city do about skateboarders in downtown pedestrian areas? How can we best solve the energy crisis?

It is important to remember that framing an issue as a yes/no question does not mean that all points of view fall neatly into pro/con categories. Although citizens may be forced to vote yes or no on a proposed ballot initiative, they can support or oppose the initiative for a variety of reasons. Some may vote happily for the initiative, others vote for it only by holding their noses, and still others oppose it vehemently but for entirely different reasons. To argue effectively, you need to appreciate the wide range of perspectives from which people approach the yes/no choice.

How you frame your question necessarily affects the scope and shape of your argument itself. In our exploratory exercise we framed the starling question in two ways: (1) Was the family guilty of cruelty to animals? and (2) What should the family do about the starlings? Framed in the first way, your argument would have to develop criteria for "cruelty to animals" and then argue whether the family's actions met those criteria. Framed in the second way, you could argue for your own solution to the problem, ranging from doing nothing (waiting for the birds to grow up and leave, then fixing the screen) to climbing into the attic and drowning the birds so that their deaths are quick and painless. Or you could word the question in a broader, more philosophical way: When are humans justified in killing animals? Or you could focus on a subissue: When can an animal be labeled a "pest"?

FOR WRITING AND DISCUSSION

Identifying Arguable Issues

1. Working individually, make a list of several communities that you belong to and then identify one or more questions currently being contested within those communities. (If you have trouble, check your local campus and city newspapers or an organizational newsletter; you'll quickly discover a wealth of contested issues.) Then share your list with classmates.
2. Pick two or three issues of particular interest to you, and try framing them in different ways: as broad or narrow questions, as open-ended or yes/no questions. Place several examples on the chalkboard for class discussion.

Stating a Claim

Your claim is the position you want to take on the issue. It is your brief, one-sentence answer to your issue question:

> The family was not ethically justified in killing the starlings.
> The city should build skateboarding areas with ramps in all city parks.
> The federal government should substantially increase its taxes on gasoline.

You will appreciate argument as truth seeking if you find that your claim evolves as you think more deeply about your issue and listen to alternative views. Be willing to rephrase your claim to soften it or refocus it or even to reverse it as you progress through the writing process.

Articulating Reasons

Your claim, which is the position you take on an issue, needs to be supported by reasons and evidence. A *reason* (sometimes called a "premise") is a subclaim that supports your main claim. In speaking or writing, a reason is usually linked to the claim with such connecting words as *because, therefore, so, consequently,* and *thus.* In planning your argument, a powerful strategy for developing reasons is to harness the grammatical power of the conjunction *because;* think of your reasons as *because* clauses attached to your claim. Formulating your reasons in this way allows you to create a thesis statement that breaks your argument into smaller parts, each part devoted to one of the reasons.

For advice on how much of your supporting argument you should summarize in your thesis statement, see Chapter 18, Skill 9.

Suppose, for example, that you are examining the issue "Should the government legalize hard drugs such as heroin and cocaine?" Here are several different points of view on this issue, each expressed as a claim with *because* clauses:

ONE VIEW

Cocaine and heroin should be legalized

- because legalizing drugs will keep the government out of people's private lives.
- because keeping these drugs illegal has the same negative effects on our society that alcohol prohibition did in the 1920s.

ANOTHER VIEW

Cocaine and heroin should be legalized

- because taking drug sales out of the hands of drug dealers would reduce street violence.
- because decriminalization would cut down on prison overcrowding and free police to concentrate on dangerous crime rather than on finding drug dealers.
- because elimination of underworld profits would change the economic structure of the underclass and promote shifts to socially productive jobs and careers.

STILL ANOTHER VIEW

The government should not legalize heroin and cocaine

- because doing so will lead to an increase in drug users and addicts.
- because doing so will send the message that it is okay to use hard drugs.

Although the yes/no framing of this question seems to reduce the issue to a two-position debate, many different value systems are at work here. The first pro-legalization argument, libertarian in perspective, values maximum individual freedom. The second argument—although it too supports legalization—takes a community perspective valuing the social benefits of eliminating the black market drug-dealing culture. In the same way, individuals could oppose legalization for a variety of reasons.

FOR WRITING AND DISCUSSION

Generating *Because* Clauses

Working in small groups or as a whole class, generate a list of reasons for and against one or more of the following yes/no claims. State your reasons as *because* clauses. Think of as many *because* clauses as possible by imagining a wide variety of perspectives on the issue.

1. The school year for grades 1 through 12 should be lengthened to eleven months.
2. The federal government should place a substantial tax on gasoline.
3. The United States should adopt a single-payer, government-financed health system like that of Canada.
4. Playing violent video games is a harmful influence on teenage boys. [or] Women's fashion and style magazines (such as *Glamour* or *Seventeen*) are harmful influences on teenage girls.
5. The war on terror requires occasional use of "enhanced interrogation techniques" on some detainees.

Articulating Unstated Assumptions

So far, we have focused on the frame of an argument as a claim supported with one or more reasons. Shortly, we will proceed to the flesh and muscle of an argument, which is the evidence you use to support your reasons. But before turning to evidence, we need to look at another crucial part of an argument's frame: its *unstated assumptions*.

What Do We Mean by an Unstated Assumption?

Every time you link a claim with a reason, you make a silent assumption that may need to be articulated and examined. Consider this argument:

> The family was justified in killing the starlings because starlings are pests.

To support this argument, the writer would first need to provide evidence that starlings are pests (examples of the damage they do and so forth). But the persuasiveness of the argument rests on the unstated assumption that it is okay to kill pests. If an audience doesn't agree with that assumption, then the argument flounders unless the writer articulates the assumption and defends it. The complete frame of the argument must therefore include the unstated assumption.

Claim: The family was justified in killing the starlings.

Reason: Because starlings are pests.

Unstated assumption: It is ethically justifiable to kill pests.

It is important to examine the unstated assumption that connects any reason to its claim *because you must determine whether your audience will accept that assumption. If not, you need to make it explicit and support it.* Think of the unstated assumption as a general principle, rule, belief, or value that connects the reason to the claim. It answers your reader's question, "Why, if I accept your reason, should I accept your claim?"*

Here are a few more examples:

Claim with reason: Women should be allowed to join combat units because the image of women as combat soldiers would help society overcome gender stereotyping.

Unstated assumption: It is good to overcome gender stereotyping.

Claim with reason: The government should not legalize heroin and cocaine because doing so will lead to an increase in drug users.

Unstated assumption: It is bad to increase the number of drug users.

Claim with reason: The family was guilty of cruelty to animals in the starling case because less drastic means of solving the problem were available.

Unstated assumption: A person should choose the least drastic means to solve a problem.

FOR WRITING AND DISCUSSION

Identifying Unstated Assumptions

Identify the unstated assumptions in each of the following claims with reasons.

1. Cocaine and heroin should be legalized because legalizing drugs will keep the government out of people's private lives.
2. The government should raise gasoline taxes because the higher price would substantially reduce gasoline consumption.
3. The government should not raise gasoline taxes because the higher price would place undo hardship on low-income people.

*Our explanation of argument structure is influenced by the work of philosopher Stephen Toulmin, who viewed argument as a dynamic courtroom drama where opposing attorneys exchange arguments and cross-examinations before a judge and jury. Although we use Toulmin's strategies for analyzing an argument structure, we have chosen not to use his specialized terms, which include *warrant* (the underlying assumption connecting a reason to a claim), *grounds* (the evidence that supports the claim), *backing* (the evidence and subarguments that support the warrant), *conditions of rebuttal* (all the ways that skeptics could attack an argument or all the conditions under which the argument wouldn't hold), and finally *qualifier* (an indication of the strength of the claim). However, your instructor may prefer to use these terms and in that case may provide you with more explanation and examples.

4. The government should not raise gasoline taxes because other means of reducing gasoline consumption would be more effective.
5. The government is justified in detaining suspected terrorists indefinitely without charging them with a crime because doing so may prevent another terrorist attack.

Using Evidence Effectively

Inside your arguments, each of your reasons (as well as any unstated assumptions that you decide to state explicitly and defend) needs to be supported either by subarguments or by evidence. By "evidence" we mean facts, examples, summaries of research articles, statistics, testimony, or other relevant data that will persuade your readers to accept your reasons. Some reasons can be supported with personal-experience data, but many require more formal evidence—the kind you gather from library or field research. The kinds of evidence most often used in argument are the following:

Factual Data

Factual data can provide persuasive support for your arguments. (Of course, writers always select their facts through an angle of vision, so the use of facts doesn't preclude skeptics from bringing in counterfacts.) Here is how evolutionary biologist Olivia Judson used factual data to support her point that malaria-carrying mosquitoes cause unacceptable harm to human lives and wealth.

> Each year, malaria kills at least one million people and causes more than 300 million cases of acute illness. For children worldwide, it's one of the leading causes of death. The economic burden is significant too: malaria costs Africa more than $12 billion in lost growth each year. In the United States, hundreds of millions of dollars are spent every year on mosquito control.

Examples

An example from personal experience can often be used to support a reason. Here is how one student writer, arguing that her church building needs to be remodeled, used a personal example to support a reason.

> Finally, Sacred Heart Church must be renovated immediately because the terrazzo floor that covers the entire church is very dangerous. Four Sundays ago, during 11:00 Mass, nine Eucharistic Ministers went up to the altar to prepare for distributing communion. As they carefully walked to their assigned post on the recently buffed terrazzo floor, a loud crash of crystal echoed through the church. A woman moving to her post slipped on the recently buffed floor, fell to the ground, hit her head on the marble, and was knocked unconscious. People rushed to her aid, thinking she was dead. Fortunately she was alive, only badly hurt. This woman was my mother.

Besides specific examples like this, writers sometimes invent hypothetical examples, or *scenarios,* to illustrate an issue or hypothesize about the consequences of an event. (Of course, you must tell your reader that the example or scenario is hypothetical.)

Summaries of Research

Another common way to support an argument is to summarize research articles. Here is how a student writer, investigating whether menopausal women should use hormone replacement therapy to combat menopausal symptoms, used one of several research articles in her paper. The student began by summarizing research studies showing possible dangers of hormone replacement therapy. She then made the following argument:

> Another reason not to use hormone replacement therapy is that other means are available to ease menopausal symptoms such as hot flashes, irritability, mood changes, and sleep disturbance. One possible alternative treatment is acupuncture. One study (Cohen, Rousseau, and Carey) revealed that a randomly selected group of menopausal women receiving specially designed acupuncture treatment showed substantial decreases in menopausal symptoms as compared to a control group. What was particularly persuasive about this study was that both the experimental group and the control group received acupuncture, but the needle insertion sites for the experimental group were specifically targeted to relieve menopausal symptoms whereas the control group received acupuncture at sites used to promote general well-being. The researchers concluded that "acupuncture may be recommended as a safe and effective therapy for reducing menopausal hot flushes as well as contributing to the reduction in sleep disruptions" (299).*

Statistics

Another common form of evidence is statistics. Here is how one writer uses statistics to argue that the federal government should raise fuel-efficiency standards placed on auto manufacturers:

> There is very little need for most Americans to drive huge SUVs. One recent survey found that 87 percent of four-wheel-drive SUV owners had never taken their SUVs off-road (Yacobucci). ... By raising fuel-efficiency standards, the government would force vehicle manufacturers to find a way to create more earth-friendly vehicles that would lower vehicle emissions and pollution. An article entitled "Update: What You Should Know Before Purchasing a New Vehicle" states that for every gallon of gasoline used by a vehicle, 20 to 28 pounds of carbon dioxide are released into the environment. This article further states that carbon dioxide emissions from automobiles are responsible for 20 percent of all carbon dioxide released into the atmosphere from human causes.

Testimony

Writers can also use expert testimony to bolster a case. The following passage from a student essay arguing in favor of therapeutic cloning uses testimony from

*The examples in this section use the MLA (Modern Language Association) style for documenting sources. See Chapter 23 for full explanations of how to use both the MLA and APA (American Psychological Association) systems for citing and documenting sources.

a prominent physician and medical researcher. Part of the paragraph quotes this expert directly; another part paraphrases the expert's argument.

> As Dr. Gerald Fischbach, Executive Vice President for Health and Biomedical Sciences and Dean of Medicine at Columbia University, said in front of a United States Senate subcommittee: "New embryonic stem cell procedures could be vital in solving the persistent problem of a lack of genetically matched, qualified donors of organs and tissues that we face today." Along with organ regeneration, therapeutic cloning could potentially cure many diseases that currently have no cure. Fischbach goes on to say that this type of cloning could lead to the discovery of cures for diseases such as ALS, Parkinson's disease, Alzheimer's disease, diabetes, heart disease, cancer, and possibly others.

Subarguments

Sometimes writers support reasons not directly through data but through sequences of subarguments. Sometimes these subarguments develop a persuasive analogy, hypothesize about consequences, or simply advance the argument through a chain of connected points. In the following passage, taken from a philosophic article justifying torture under certain conditions, the author uses a subargument to support one of his main points—that a terrorist holding victims hostage has no "rights":

> There is an important difference between terrorists and their victims that should mute talk of the terrorist's "rights." The terrorist's victims are at risk unintentionally, not having asked to be endangered. But the terrorist knowingly initiated his actions. Unlike his victims, he volunteered for the risks of his deed. By threatening to kill for profit or idealism, he renounces civilized standards, and he can have no complaint if civilization tries to thwart him by whatever means necessary.

Rather than using direct empirical evidence, the author supports his point with a subargument showing how terrorists differ from victims and thus relinquish their claim to rights.

Evaluating Evidence: The STAR Criteria

To make your arguments as persuasive as possible, apply to your evidence what rhetorician Richard Fulkerson calls the STAR criteria:* (**S**ufficiency, **T**ypicality, **A**ccuracy, and **R**elevance), as shown in the chart on page 388.

It is often difficult to create arguments in which all your evidence fully meets the STAR criteria. Sometimes you need to proceed on evidence that might not be typical, verifiable, or as up-to-date as you would like. In such cases, you can often

*Richard Fulkerson, *Teaching the Argument in Writing,* Urbana: National Council of Teachers of English, 1996, pp. 44–53. In this section we are indebted to Fulkerson's discussion.

The STAR Criteria for Evaluating Evidence

STAR Criteria	Implied Question	Comments
Sufficiency	Is there enough evidence?	If you don't provide enough evidence, skeptical audiences can dismiss your claim as a "hasty generalization." To argue that marijuana is not a harmful drug, you would probably need more evidence than the results of one study or the testimony of a healthy pot smoker.
Typicality	Are the chosen data representative and typical?	If you choose extreme or rare-case examples, rather than typical and representative ones, your audience might accuse you of cherry-picking your data. Testimony from persons whose back pain was cured by yoga may not support the general claim that yoga is good for back pain.
Accuracy	Are the data accurate and up-to-date?	Providing recent, accurate data is essential for your own *ethos* as a writer. Data from 1998 on homelessness or inaccurately gathered data may be ineffective for a current policy argument.
Relevance	Are the data relevant to the claim?	Even though your evidence is accurate, up-to-date, and representative, if it's not pertinent to the claim, it will be ineffective. For example, evidence that nuclear waste is dangerous is not relevant to the issue of whether it can be stored securely in Yucca Mountain.

increase the effectiveness of your argument by qualifying your claim. Consider the difference between these two claims:

- **Strong claim:** Watching violent TV cartoons increases aggressive play behavior in boys.
- **Qualified claim:** Watching violent TV cartoons can increase aggressive play behavior in some boys.

To be made persuasive, the strong claim requires substantial evidence meeting the STAR criteria. In contrast, the qualified claim requires less rigorous evidence, perhaps only an example or two combined with the results of one study.

See Chapter 21, Skill 25, for advice on evaluating sources for reliability and bias. See Chapter 21, Skill 26, for help on evaluating Web sites.

As you gather evidence, consider also its source and the extent to which your audience will trust that source. While all data must be interpreted and hence are never completely impartial, careful readers are aware of how easily data can be skewed. Newspapers, magazines, blogs, and journals often have political biases and different levels of respectability. Generally, evidence from peer-reviewed scholarly journals is more highly regarded than evidence from secondhand sources. Particularly problematic is information gathered from Internet Web sites, which can vary wildly in reliability and degree of bias.

Addressing Objections and Counterarguments

Having looked at the frame of an argument (claim, reasons, and underlying assumptions) and at the kinds of evidence used to flesh out the frame, let's turn now to the important concern of anticipating and responding to objections and counterarguments. In this section, we show you an extended example of a student's anticipating and responding to a reader's objection. We then describe a planning schema that can help you anticipate objections and show you how to respond to counterarguments, either through refutation or concession. Finally, we show how your active imagining of alternative views can lead you to qualify your claim.

Anticipating Objections: An Extended Example

In our earlier discussions of the starling case, we saw how readers might object to the argument "The family was justified in killing the starlings because starlings are pests." What rankles these readers is the unstated assumption that it is okay to kill pests. Imagine an objecting reader saying something like this:

> It is *not* okay to get annoyed with a living creature, label it a "pest," and then kill it. This whole use of the term *pest* suggests that humans have the right to dominate nature. We need to have more reverence for nature. The ease with which the family solved their problem by killing living things sets a bad example for children. The family could have waited until fall and then fixed the screen.

Imagining such an objection might lead a writer to modify his or her claim. But if the writer remains committed to that claim, then he or she must develop a response. In the following example in which a student writer argues that it is okay to kill the starlings, note (1) how the writer uses evidence to show that starlings are pests; (2) how he summarizes a possible objection to his underlying assumption that killing pests is morally justified; and (3) how he supports his assumption with further arguments.

STUDENT ARGUMENT DEFENDING REASON AND UNDERLYING ASSUMPTION

The family was justified in killing the starlings because starlings are pests. *[Claim with reason]* Starlings are nonindigenous birds that drive out native species and multiply rapidly. When I searched "starlings pests" on Google, I discovered thousands of Web sites dealing with starlings as pests. Starlings are hated by farmers and gardeners because huge flocks of them devour newly planted seeds in spring as well as fruits and berries at harvest. A flock of starlings can devastate a cherry orchard in a few days. As invasive nesters, starlings can also damage attics by tearing up insulation and defecating on stored items. *[Evidence that starlings are pests]* Many of the Web site articles focused on ways to kill off starling populations. In killing the starlings, the family was protecting its own property and reducing the population of these pests.

Many readers might object to my argument, saying that humans should have a reverence for nature and not quickly try to kill off any creature they label a pest. Further, these readers might say that even if starlings are pests, the family could have waited until fall to repair the attic or found some other means of protecting their property without having to kill the baby starlings. *[Summary of a possible objection]* I too would have waited until fall if the birds in the attic had been swallows or some other native species without

Response to the objection

> starlings' destructiveness and propensity for unchecked population growth. But starlings should be compared to rats or mice. We set traps for rodents because we know the damage they cause when they nest in walls and attics. We don't get sentimental trying to save the orphaned rat babies. In the same way, we are justified in eliminating starlings as soon as they begin infesting our houses.

In the preceding example, we see how the writer uses evidence to support his reason and then, anticipating readers' objection to his underlying assumption, summarizes that objection and provides a response to it. One might not be convinced by the argument, but the writer has done a good job of trying to support both his reason (starlings are pests) and his underlying assumption (it is morally justifiable to kill pests).

Using a Planning Schema to Anticipate Objections

The arguing strategy used by the previous writer was triggered by his anticipation of objections. Note that a skeptical audience can attack an argument by attacking either a writer's reasons or a writer's underlying assumptions. This knowledge allows us to create a planning schema that can help writers develop a persuasive argument. This schema encourages writers to articulate their argument frame (reason and underlying assumption that links the reason back to the claim) and then to imagine what kinds of evidence could be used to support both the reason and the underlying assumption. Equally important, the schema encourages writers to anticipate counterarguments by imagining how skeptical readers might object to the writer's reason or underlying assumption or both. To create the schema, simply make a chart headed by your claim with reason and then make slots for your underlying assumption, for evidence/arguments in support of the reason, for evidence/arguments in support of the underlying assumption, and for ways that skeptics could object to the reason or the underlying assumption. Here is how another student writer used this schema to plan an argument on the starling case:

CLAIM WITH REASON

The family showed cruelty to animals because the way they killed the birds caused needless suffering.

UNDERLYING ASSUMPTION

If it is not necessary to kill an animal, then don't; if it is necessary, then the killing should be done in the least painful way possible.

EVIDENCE TO SUPPORT REASON

I've got to show how the birds suffered and also how the suffering was needless. The way of killing the birds caused the birds to suffer. The hatchlings starved to death, as did the parent birds if they were trapped inside the attic. Starvation is very slow and agonizing. The suffering was also needless since other means were available such as calling an exterminator who would remove the birds and either relocate them or kill them painlessly. If no other alternative was available, someone should have crawled into the attic and found a painless way to kill the birds.

EVIDENCE/ARGUMENTS TO SUPPORT UNDERLYING ASSUMPTION

I've got to convince readers it is wrong to make an animal suffer if you don't have to. Humans have a natural antipathy to needless suffering—our feeling of unease if we imagine cattle or chickens caused to suffer for our food rather than being cleanly and quickly killed. If a horse is incurably wounded, we put it to sleep rather then let it suffer. We are morally obligated to cause the least pain possible.

WAYS SKEPTICS MIGHT OBJECT

How could a reader object to my reason? A reader could say that killing the starlings did not cause suffering. Perhaps hatchling starlings don't feel pain of starvation and die very quickly. Perhaps a reader could object to my claim that other means were available: There is no other way to kill the starlings—impossibility of catching a bunch of adult starlings flying around an attic. Poison may cause just as much suffering. Cost of exterminator is prohibitive.

How could a reader object to my underlying assumption? Perhaps the reader would say that my rule to cause the least pain possible does not apply to animal pests. In class, someone said that worrying about the baby starlings was sentimental. Laws of nature condemn millions of animals each year to death by starvation or by being eaten alive by other animals. Humans occasionally have to take their place within this tooth-and-claw natural system.

How many of the ideas from this schema would the writer use in her actual paper? That is a judgment call based on the writer's analysis of the audience. In every case, the writer should support the reason with evidence because supporting a claim with reasons and evidence is the minimal requirement of argument. But it is not necessary to state the underlying assumption explicitly or provide backing for it unless the writer anticipates readers who will doubt it.

The same rule of thumb applies to the need for summarizing and responding to objections and counterarguments: Let your analysis of audience be your guide. If we imagined the preceding argument aimed at readers who thought it was sentimental to worry about the suffering of animal pests, the writer should make her assumption explicit and back it up. Her task would be to convince readers that humans have ethical responsibilities that exclude them from tooth-and-claw morality.

FOR WRITING AND DISCUSSION

Creating Argument Schemas

Working individually or in small groups, create a planning schema for the following arguments. For each claim with reason: (a) imagine the kinds of evidence needed to support the reason; (b) identify the underlying assumption; (c) imagine a strategy for supporting the assumption; and (d) anticipate possible objections to the reason and to the assumption.

1. ***Claim with reason:*** We should buy a hybrid car rather than an SUV with a HEMI engine because doing so will help the world save gasoline. (Imagine this argument aimed at your significant other, who has his or her heart set on a huge HEMI-powered SUV.)

(*continued*)

2. ***Claim with reason:*** Gay marriage should be legalized because doing so will promote faithful, monogamous relationships among lesbians and gay men. (Aim this argument at supporters of traditional marriage.)
3. ***Claim with reason:*** The war in Iraq was justified because it rid the world of a hideous and brutal dictator. (Aim this argument at a critic of the war.)

Responding to Objections, Counterarguments, and Alternative Views

We have seen how a writer needs to anticipate alternative views that give rise to objections and counterarguments. Surprisingly, one of the best ways to approach counterarguments is to summarize them fairly. Make your imagined reader's best case against your argument. By resisting the temptation to distort a counterargument, you demonstrate a willingness to consider the issue from all sides. Moreover, summarizing a counterargument reduces your reader's tendency to say, "Yes, but have you thought of ... ?" After you have summarized an objection or counterargument fairly and charitably, you must then decide how to respond to it. Your two main choices are to rebut it or concede to it.

Rebutting Opposing Views

When rebutting or refuting an argument, you can question the argument's reasons and supporting evidence or the underlying assumptions or both. In the following student example, the writer summarizes her classmates' objections to abstract art and then analyzes shortcomings in their reasons and grounds.

> Some of my classmates object to abstract art because it apparently takes no technical drawing talent. They feel that historically artists turned to abstract art because they lacked the technical drafting skills exhibited by Remington, Russell, and Rockwell. Therefore these abstract artists created an art form that anyone was capable of and that was less time consuming, and then they paraded it as artistic progress. But I object to the notion that these artists turned to abstraction because they could not do representative drawing. Many abstract artists, such as Picasso, were excellent draftsmen, and their early pieces show very realistic drawing skill. As his work matured, Picasso became more abstract in order to increase the expressive quality of his work. *Guernica* was meant as a protest against the bombing of that city by the Germans. To express the terror and suffering of the victims more vividly, he distorted the figures and presented them in a black and white journalistic manner. If he had used representational images and color—which he had the skill to do—much of the emotional content would have been lost and the piece probably would not have caused the demand for justice that it did.

Conceding to Counterarguments

In some cases, an alternative view can be very strong. If so, don't hide that view from your readers; summarize it and concede to it.

Making concessions to opposing views is not necessarily a sign of weakness; in many cases, a concession simply acknowledges that the issue is complex and that your position is tentative. In turn, a concession can enhance a reader's respect for you and invite the reader to follow your example and weigh the strengths of your own argument charitably. Writers typically concede to opposing views with transitional expressions such as the following:

admittedly	I must admit that	I agree that	granted
even though	I concede that	while it is true that	

After conceding to an opposing view, you should shift to a different field of values where your position is strong and then argue for those new values. For example, adversaries of drug legalization argue plausibly that legalizing drugs would increase the number of users and addicts. If you support legalization, here is how you might deal with this point without fatally damaging your own argument:

> Opponents of legalization claim—and rightly so—that legalization will lead to an increase in drug users and addicts. I wish this weren't so, but it is. Nevertheless, the other benefits of legalizing drugs—eliminating the black market, reducing street crime, and freeing up thousands of police from fighting the war on drugs—more than outweigh the social costs of increased drug use and addiction, especially if tax revenues from drug sales are plowed back into drug education and rehabilitation programs.

The writer concedes that legalization will increase addiction (one reason for opposing legalization) and that drug addiction is bad (the underlying assumption for that reason). But then the writer redeems the case for legalization by shifting the argument to another field of values (the benefits of eliminating the black market, reducing crime, and so forth).

Qualifying Your Claim

The need to summarize and respond to alternative views lets the writer see an issue's complexity and appreciate that no one position has a total monopoly on the truth. Consequently, writers often need to qualify their claims—that is, limit the scope or force of a claim to make it less sweeping and therefore less vulnerable. Consider the difference between the sentences "After-school jobs are bad for teenagers" and "After-school jobs are often bad for teenagers." The first claim can be refuted by one counterexample of a teenager who benefited from an after-school job. Because the second claim admits exceptions, it is much harder to refute. Unless your argument is airtight, you will want to limit your claim with qualifiers such as the following:

perhaps	maybe
in many cases	generally
tentatively	sometimes
often	usually
probably	likely
may *or* might (*rather than* is)	

You can also qualify a claim with an opening *unless* clause ("*Unless* your apartment is well soundproofed, you should not buy such a powerful stereo system").

Appealing to *Ethos* and *Pathos*

When the classical rhetoricians examined ways that orators could persuade listeners, they focused on three kinds of proofs: *logos,* the appeal to reason; *ethos,* the appeal to the speaker's character; and *pathos,* the appeal to the emotions and the sympathetic imagination. We introduced you to these appeals in Chapter 3, Concept 9, because they are important rhetorical considerations in any kind of writing. Understanding how arguments persuade through *logos, ethos,* and *pathos* is particularly helpful when your aim is persuasion. So far in this chapter we have focused on *logos.* In this section we examine *ethos* and *pathos.*

Appeal to Ethos

A powerful way to increase the persuasiveness of an argument is to gain your readers' trust. You appeal to *ethos* whenever you present yourself as credible and trustworthy. For most readers to accept your argument, they must perceive you as knowledgeable, trustworthy, and fair. We suggest three ways to enhance your argument's *ethos:*

1. Demonstrate that you know your subject well. If you have personal experience with the subject, cite that experience. Reflect thoughtfully on your subject, citing research as well as personal experience, and accurately and carefully summarize a range of viewpoints.
2. Be fair to alternative points of view. Scorning an opposing view may occasionally win you favor with an audience predisposed toward your position, but it will offend others and hinder critical analysis. As a general rule, treating opposing views respectfully is the best strategy.
3. Build bridges toward your audience by grounding your argument in shared values and assumptions. Doing so will demonstrate your concern for your audience and enhance your trustworthiness. Moreover, rooting your argument in the audience's values and assumptions has a strong emotional appeal, as we explain in the next section.

Appeals to Pathos

Besides appealing to *logos* and *ethos,* you might also appeal to what the Greeks called *pathos*. Sometimes *pathos* is interpreted narrowly as an appeal to the emotions and is therefore undervalued on the grounds that arguments should be rational rather than emotional. Although appeals to *pathos* can sometimes be irrational and irrelevant ("You can't give me a C! I need a B to get into medical school, and if I don't it'll break my ill grandmother's heart"), they can also arouse audience interest and deepen understanding of an argument's human dimensions. Here are some ways to use *pathos* in your arguments:

Use Vivid Language and Examples. One way to create *pathos* is to use vivid language and powerful examples. If you are arguing in favor of homeless shelters, for example, you can humanize your appeal by describing one homeless person:

> He is huddled over the sewer grate, his feet wrapped in newspapers. He blows on his hands, then tucks them under his armpits and lies down on the sidewalk with his shoulders over the grate, his bed for the night.

But if you are arguing for tougher laws against panhandling, you might let your reader see the issue through the eyes of downtown shoppers intimidated by "ratty, urine-soaked derelicts drinking fortified wine from a shared sack."

Find Audience-Based Reasons. The best way to think of *pathos* is not as an appeal to emotions but rather as an appeal to the audience's values and beliefs. For example, in engineer David Rockwood's argument against wind-generated power, Rockwood's final reason is that constructing wind-generation facilities will damage the environment. To environmentalists, this reason has emotional as well as rational power because its underlying assumption ("Preserving the environment is good") appeals to their values. It is an example of an audience-based reason, which we can define simply as any reason whose underlying assumption the audience already accepts and endorses. Such reasons, because they hook into the beliefs and values of the audience, appeal to *pathos*.

Rockwood's argument appears in Chapter 1, p. 7.

When you plan your argument, seek audience-based reasons whenever possible. Suppose, for example, that you are advocating the legalization of heroin and cocaine. If you know that your audience is concerned about their own safety in the streets, then you can argue that legalization of drugs will cut down on crime:

> We should legalize drugs because doing so will make our streets safer: It will cut down radically on street criminals seeking drug money, and it will free up narcotics police to focus on other kinds of crime.

If your audience is concerned about improving the quality of life for youths in inner cities, you might argue that legalization of drugs will lead to better lives for people in poor neighborhoods.

> We should legalize drugs because doing so will eliminate the lure of drug trafficking that tempts so many inner-city youth away from honest jobs and into crime.

Or if your audience is concerned about high taxes and government debt, you might say:

> We should legalize drugs because doing so will help us balance federal and state budgets: It will decrease police and prison costs by decriminalizing narcotics; and it will eliminate the black market in drugs, allowing us to collect taxes on drug sales.

In each case, you move people toward your position by connecting your argument to their beliefs and values.

A Brief Primer on Informal Fallacies

We'll conclude our explanation of classical argument with a brief overview of the most common informal fallacies. Informal fallacies are instances of murky reasoning that can cloud an argument and lead to unsound conclusions. Because they can crop up unintentionally in anyone's writing, and because advertisers and hucksters often use them intentionally to deceive, it is a good idea to learn to recognize the more common fallacies.

Post Hoc, Ergo Propter Hoc *("After This, Therefore Because of This")*

This fallacy involves mistaking sequence for cause. Just because one event happens before another event doesn't mean the first event caused the second. The connection may be coincidental, or some unknown third event may have caused both of these events.

Example When the New York police department changed its policing tactics in the early 1990s, the crime rate plummeted. But did the new police tactics cause the decline in crime? (Many experts attributed the decline to other causes.) Persons lauding the police tactics ("Crime declined because the NYPD adopted new tactics") were accused of the *post hoc* fallacy.

Hasty Generalization

Closely related to the *post hoc* fallacy is the hasty generalization, which refers to claims based on insufficient or unrepresentative data. Generally, persuasive evidence should meet the STAR criteria that we explained on page 388. Because the amount of evidence needed in a given case can vary with the audience's degree of skepticism, it is difficult to draw an exact line between hasty and justified generalizations.

Example The news frequently carries stories about vicious pit bulls. Therefore all pit bills must be vicious. [or] This experimental drug has been demonstrated safe in numerous clinical trials [based on tests using adult subjects]. Therefore this drug is safe for children.

False Analogy

Arguers often use analogies to support a claim. (We shouldn't go to war in Iraq because doing so will lead us into a Vietnam-like quagmire.) However, analogical arguments are tricky because there are usually significant differences between the two things being compared as well as similarities. (Supporters of the war in Iraq argued that the situation in Iraq in 2002 was very different from that in Vietnam in 1964.) Although it is hard to draw an exact line between a false analogy and an acceptable one, charges of false analogy are frequent when skeptical opponents try to refute arguments based on analogies.

Example Gun control will work in the United States because it works in England. [or] It's a mistake to force little Johnnie to take piano lessons because you can't turn a reluctant child into a musician any more than you can turn a tulip into a rose.

Either/Or Reasoning

This fallacy occurs when a complex, multisided issue is reduced to two positions without acknowledging the possibility of other alternatives.

Example Either you are pro-choice on abortion or you are against the advancement of women in our culture.

Ad Hominem *("Against the Person")*

When people can't find fault with an argument, they sometimes attack the arguer, substituting irrelevant assertions about that person's character for an analysis of the argument itself.

Example We should discount Senator Jones's argument against nuclear power because she has huge holdings in oil stock.

Appeals to False Authority and Bandwagon Appeals

These fallacies offer as support the fact that a famous person or "many people" already support it. Unless the supporters are themselves authorities in the field, their support is irrelevant.

Example Buy Freeble oil because Joe Quarterback always uses it in his fleet of cars. [or] How can abortion be wrong if millions of people support a woman's right to choose?

Non Sequitur *("It Does Not Follow")*

This fallacy occurs when there is no evident connection between a claim and its reason. Sometimes a *non sequitur* can be repaired by filling in gaps in the reasoning; at other times, the reasoning is simply fallacious.

Example I don't deserve a B for this course because I am a straight-A student.

Circular Reasoning

This fallacy occurs when you state your claim and then, usually after rewording it, you state it again as your reason.

Example Marijuana is injurious to your health because it harms your body.

Red Herring

This fallacy refers to the practice of raising an unrelated or irrelevant point deliberately to throw an audience off track. Politicians often employ this fallacy when they field questions from the public or press.

Example You raise a good question about my support of companies' outsourcing jobs to find cheaper labor. Let me tell you about my admiration for the productivity of the American worker.

Slippery Slope

The slippery slope fallacy is based on the fear that one step in a direction we don't like inevitably leads to the next step with no stopping place.

Example If we allow embryonic stem cells to be used for medical research, we will open the door for full-scale reproductive cloning.

A Classical Argument

WRITING PROJECT

Write a position paper that takes a stand on a controversial issue. Your introduction should present your issue, provide background, and state the claim you intend to support. In constructing your claim, strive to develop audience-based reasons. The body of your argument should summarize and respond to opposing views as well as present reasons and evidence in support of your own position. You will need to choose whether to summarize and refute opposing views before or after you have made your own case. Try to end your essay with your strongest arguments. Try also to include appeals to *pathos* and to create a positive, credible *ethos*.

We call this assignment a "classical" argument because it is patterned after the persuasive speeches of ancient Greek and Roman orators. In the terms of ancient rhetoricians, the main parts of a persuasive speech are the *exordium,* in which the speaker gets the audience's attention; the *narratio,* which provides needed background; the *propositio,* the speaker's thesis (claim); the *partitio,* a forecast of the main parts of the speech, equivalent to a blueprint statement; the *confirmatio,* the speaker's arguments in favor of the proposition; the *confutatio,* the refutation of opposing views; and the *peroratio,* the conclusion that sums up the argument, calls for action, and leaves a strong, lasting impression. Figure 14.1 is a framework chart showing the generic structure of a classical argument.

We cite these tongue-twisting Latin terms only to assure you that in writing a classical argument, you are joining a time-honored tradition that links you to Roman senators on the capitol steps. From their discourse arose the ideal of a democratic society based on superior arguments rather than on superior weaponry. Although there are many other ways to persuade audiences, the classical approach is a particularly effective introduction to persuasive writing.

FIGURE 14.1 Framework for a classical argument

• *Exordium* • *Narratio* • *Propositio* • *Partitio*	INTRODUCTION	• Attention-grabber (often a memorable scene) • Explanation of issue and needed background • Writer's thesis (claim) • Forecasting passage
• *Confirmatio*	PRESENTATION OF WRITER'S POSITION	• Main body of essay • Presents and supports each reason in turn • Each reason is tied to a value or belief held by the audience
• *Confutatio*	SUMMARY OF OPPOSING VIEWS	• Summary of views differing from writer's (should be fair and complete)
	RESPONSE TO OPPOSING VIEWS	• Refutes or concedes to opposing views • Shows weaknesses in opposing views • May concede to some strengths
• *Peroratio*	CONCLUSION	• Brings essay to closure • Often sums up argument • Leaves strong, lasting impression • Often calls for action or relates topic to a larger context of issues

Generating and Exploring Ideas

The tasks that follow are intended to help you generate ideas for your argument. Our goal is to help you build up a storehouse of possible issues, explore several of these possibilities, and then choose one for deeper exploration before you write your initial draft.

Finding an Issue

If you are having trouble finding an arguable issue for this writing project, consider the following strategies:

STRATEGIES for Finding an Arguable Issue

Strategies	Explanations
Make an inventory of various communities to which you belong.	Communities can include family, neighborhood, workplace, online networks, classroom, dormitory, religious or social group, campus, hometown, state, region, nation, the world, and so forth. Note the varied communities represented in the student argument examples in this text: Ross Taylor and the paintball community (pp. 404–406); A. J. Chavez and the gay community on a national issue (pp. 417–421); James Gardiner and online social network communities (pp. 191–198).
Brainstorm contested issues in these communities.	Ask questions like these: • What do members disagree about? • What causes these disagreements? • What values are in conflict? • What decisions must be made? • What problems must be solved? • How is this community in conflict with other communities?
Choose several issues for further exploration.	Through freewriting or idea mapping, explore your response to these questions: • What is my position on the issue and why? • What are alternative points of view? • Why do people disagree? Do they disagree about the facts of the case or about underlying values? What is at stake? • To argue my position, what further research will I need to do?

(continued)

Strategies	Explanations
Conduct and respond to initial research.	If your issue requires research, do a quick bibliographic survey and enough reading to get a good sense of the kinds of arguments that surround your issue and the alternative views that people have taken. Note: Check with your instructor on how much research is needed. In the Readings section, Ross Taylor's essay is based largely on personal experience. A. J. Chavez uses library/Internet research.
Brainstorm claims and reasons on various sides of the issue.	• State your own claim and possible *because* clause reasons in support of your claim. • Do the same thing for one or more opposing or alternative claims.

Conduct an In-Depth Exploration Prior to Drafting

The following set of tasks is designed to help you explore your issue in depth. Most students take one or two hours to complete these tasks; the time will pay off, however, because most of the ideas that you need for your rough draft will be on paper.

See the discussion of issue questions on p. 381.

1. Write out the issue your argument will address. Try phrasing your issue in several different ways, perhaps as a yes/no question and as an open-ended question. Try making the question broader, then narrower. Finally, frame the question in the way that most appeals to you.
2. Now write out your tentative answer to the question. This will be your beginning thesis statement or claim. Put a box around this answer. Next, write out one or more different answers to your question. These will be alternative claims that a neutral audience might consider.
3. Why is this a controversial issue? Is there insufficient evidence to resolve the issue, or is the evidence ambiguous or contradictory? Are definitions in dispute? Do the parties disagree about basic values, assumptions, or beliefs?
4. What personal interest do you have in this issue? How does the issue affect you? Why do you care about it? (Knowing why you care about it might help you get your audience to care about it.)
5. What reasons and evidence support your position on this issue? Freewrite everything that comes to mind that might help you support your case. This freewrite will eventually provide the bulk of your argument. For now, freewrite rapidly without worrying whether your argument makes sense. Just get ideas on paper.
6. Imagine all the counterarguments your audience might make. Summarize the main arguments against your position and then freewrite your response to each of the counterarguments. What are the flaws in the alternative points of view?
7. What kinds of appeals to *ethos* and *pathos* might you use to support your argument? How can you increase your audience's perception of your credibil-

ity and trustworthiness? How can you tie your argument to your audience's beliefs and values?

8. Why is this an important issue? What are the broader implications and consequences? What other issues does it relate to? Thinking of possible answers to these questions may prove useful when you write your introduction or conclusion.

Shaping and Drafting

Once you have explored your ideas, create a plan. Here is a suggested procedure:

Begin your planning by analyzing your intended audience. You could imagine an audience deeply resistant to your views or a more neutral, undecided audience acting like a jury. In some cases, your audience might be a single person, as when you petition your department chair to waive a requirement in your major. At other times, your audience might be the general readership of a newspaper, church bulletin, or magazine. When the audience is a general readership, you need to imagine from the start the kinds of readers you particularly want to sway. Here are some questions you can ask:

- ***How much does your audience know or care about your issue?*** Will you need to provide background? Will you need to convince them that your issue is important? Do you need to hook their interest? Your answers to these questions will particularly influence your introduction and conclusion.
- ***What is your audience's current attitude toward your issue?*** Are they deeply opposed to your position? If so, why? Are they neutral and undecided? If so, what other views will they be listening to?
- ***How do your audience's values, assumptions, and beliefs differ from your own?*** What aspects of your position will be threatening to your audience? Why? How does your position on the issue challenge your imagined reader's worldview or identity? What objections will your audience raise toward your argument? Your answers to these questions will help determine the content of your argument and alert you to the extra research you may have to do to respond to audience objections.
- ***What values, beliefs, or assumptions about the world do you and your audience share?*** Despite your differences with your audience, where can you find common links? How might you use these links to build bridges to your audience?

Your next step is to plan an audience-based argument by seeking audience-based reasons or reasons whose underlying assumptions you can defend. Here is a process you can use:

1. Create a skeleton, tree diagram, outline, or flowchart for your argument by stating your reasons as one or more *because* clauses attached to your claim. Each *because* clause will become the head of a main section or *line of reasoning* in your argument.
2. Use the planning schema on pages 390–391 to plan each line of reasoning. If your audience accepts your underlying assumption, you can concentrate on

supporting your reason with evidence. However, if your audience is apt to reject the underlying assumption for one of your lines of reasoning, then you'll need to state it directly and argue for it. Try to anticipate audience objections by exploring ways that an audience might question either your reasons or your underlying assumptions.

3. Using the skeleton you created, finish developing an outline or tree diagram for your argument. Although the organization of each part of your argument will grow organically from its content, the main parts of your classical argument should match the framework chart shown on page 398 (Figure 14.1).

This classical model can be modified in numerous ways. A question that often arises is where to summarize and respond to objections and counterarguments. Writers generally have three choices: One option is to handle opposing positions before you present your own argument. The rationale for this approach is that skeptical audiences may be more inclined to listen attentively to your argument if they have been assured that you understand their point of view. A second option is to place this material after you have presented your argument. This approach is effective for neutral audiences who don't start off with strong opposing views. A final option is to intersperse opposing views throughout your argument at appropriate moments. Any of these possibilities, or a combination of all of them, can be effective.

Another question often asked is, "What is the best way to order one's reasons?" A general rule of thumb when ordering your own argument is to put your strongest reason last and your second-strongest reason first. The idea here is to start and end with your most powerful arguments. If you imagine a quite skeptical audience, build bridges to your audience by summarizing alternative views early in the paper and concede to those that are especially strong. If your audience is neutral or undecided, you can summarize and respond to possible objections after you have presented your own case.

Revising

As you revise your argument, you need to attend both to the clarity of your writing (all the principles of closed-form prose described in Chapter 18) and also to the persuasiveness of your argument. As always, peer reviews are valuable, and especially so in argumentation if you ask your peer reviewers to role-play an opposing audience.

Questions for Peer Review

In addition to the generic peer review questions explained in Chapter 17, Skill 4, ask your peer reviewers to address these questions:

INTRODUCTION

1. How could the title be improved so that it announces the issue, reveals the writer's claim, or otherwise focuses your expectations and piques interest?

2. What strategies does the writer use to introduce the issue, engage your interest, and convince you that the issue is significant and problematic? What would add clarity and appeal?
3. How could the introduction more effectively forecast the argument and present the writer's claim? What would make the statement of the claim more focused, clear, or risky?

ARGUING FOR THE CLAIM

4. Consider the overall structure: What strategies does the writer use to make the structure of the paper clear and easy to follow? How could the structure of the argument be improved?
5. Consider the support for the reasons: Where could the writer provide better evidence or support for each line of reasoning? Look for the kinds of evidence for each line of reasoning by noting the writer's use of facts, examples, statistics, testimony, or other evidence. Where could the writer supply more evidence or use existing evidence more effectively?
6. Consider the support for the underlying assumptions: For each line of reasoning, determine the assumptions that the audience needs to grant for the argument to be effective. Are there places where these assumptions need to be stated directly and supported with arguments? How could support for the assumptions be improved?
7. Consider the writer's summary of and response to alternative viewpoints: Where does the writer treat alternative views? Are there additional alternative views that the writer should consider? What strategies does the writer use to respond to alternative views? How could the writer's treatment of alternative views be improved?

CONCLUSION

8. How might the conclusion more effectively bring completeness or closure to the argument?

READINGS

Our first reading, by student writer Ross Taylor, aims to increase appreciation of paintball as a healthy sport. An avid paintballer, Ross was frustrated by how many of his friends and acquaintances didn't appreciate paintball and had numerous misconceptions about it. The following argument is aimed at those who don't understand the sport or those who condemn it for being dangerous and violent.

Ross Taylor (student)

Paintball:

Promoter of Violence or Healthy Fun?

1 Glancing out from behind some cover, I see an enemy soldier on the move. I level my gun and start pinching off rounds. Hearing the incoming fire, he turns and starts to fire, but it is far too late. His entire body flinches when I land two torso shots, and he falls when I hit his leg. I duck back satisfied with another good kill on my record. I pop up this time again to scan for more enemy forces. Out of the corner of my eye I see some movement and turn to see two soldiers peeking out from behind a sewer pipe. I move to take cover again, but it's futile. I feel the hits come one by one hitting me three times in the chest and once on the right bicep before I fall behind the cover. I'm hit. It's all over—for me at least. The paintball battle rages on as I carefully leave the field to nurse my welts, which are already showing. Luckily, I watch my three remaining teammates trample the two enemy soldiers who shot me to win the game. This is paintball in all its splendor and glory.

2 Paintball is one of the most misunderstood and generally looked down upon recreational activities. People see it as rewarding violence and lacking the true characteristics of a healthy team sport like ultimate Frisbee, soccer, or pickup basketball. Largely the accusations directed at paintball are false because it is a positive recreational activity. Paintball is a fun, athletic, mentally challenging recreational activity that builds teamwork and releases tension.

3 Paintball was invented in the early 1980s as a casual activity for survival enthusiasts, but it has grown into a several hundred million dollar industry. It is, quite simply, an expanded version of tag. Players use a range of CO_2 powered guns that fire small biodegradable marbles of paint at approximately 250–300 feet per second. The result of a hit is a small splatter of oily paint and a nice dark bruise. Paintball is now played nationwide in indoor and outdoor arenas. Quite often variants are played such as "Capture the Flag" or "Assassination." In "Capture the Flag" the point is to retrieve the heavily guarded flag from the other team and return it to your base. The game of "Assassination" pits one team of "assassins" against the "secret service." The secret service men guard an unarmed player dubbed the "president." Their goal is get from point A to point B without the president's getting tagged. Contrary to popular belief, the games are highly officiated and organized. There is always a referee present. Barrel plugs are required until just before a game begins and must be reinserted as soon as the game ends. No hostages may be taken. A player catching another off guard at close range must first give the player the opportunity to surrender. Most importantly there is no physical contact between players. Punching, pushing, or butt-ending with the

gun is strictly prohibited. The result is an intense game that is relatively safe for all involved.

4 The activity of paintball is athletically challenging. There are numerous sprint and dives to avoid being hit. At the end of a game, typically lasting around 20 minutes, all the players are winded, sweaty, and ultimately exhilarated. The beginning of the game includes a mad dash for cover by both teams with heavy amounts of fire being exchanged. During the game, players execute numerous strategic moves to gain a tactical advantage, often including quick jumps, dives, rolls, and runs. While undercover, players crawl across broad stretches of playing field often still feeling their bruises from previous games. These physical feats culminate in an invigorating and physically challenging activity good for building muscles and coordination.

5 In addition to the athletic challenge, paintball provides strong mental challenge, mainly the need for constant strategizing. There are many strategic positioning methods. For example, the classic pincer move involves your team's outflanking an opponent from each side to eliminate his or her mobility and shelter. In the more sophisticated ladder technique, teammates take turns covering each other as the others move onward from cover to cover. Throughout the game, players' minds are constantly reeling as they calculate their positions and cover, their teammates' positions and cover, and their opponents' positions and strength. Finally, there is the strong competitive pull of the individual. It never fails to amaze me how much thought goes into one game.

6 Teamwork is also involved. Paintball takes a lot of cooperation. You need special hand signals to communicate with your teammates, and you have to coordinate, under rapidly changing situations, who is going to flank left or right, who is going to charge, and who is going to stay back to guard the flag station. The importance of teamwork in paintball explains why more and more businesses are taking their employees for a day of action with the intent of creating a closer knit and smooth-functioning workplace. The value of teamwork is highlighted on the Web site of a British Columbia facility, Action and Adventure Paintball, Ltd, which says that in paintball,

> as in any team sport, the team that communicates best usually wins. It's about thinking, not shooting. This is why Fortune 500 companies around the world take their employees to play paintball together.

An advantage of paintball for building company team spirit is that paintball teams, unlike teams in many other recreational sports, can blend very skilled and totally unskilled players. Women like paintball as much as men, and the game is open to people of any size, body type, and strength level. Since a game usually takes no more than seven to ten minutes, teams can run a series of different games with different players to have lots of different match-ups. Also families like to play paintball together.

7 People who object to paintball criticize its danger and violence. The game's supposed danger gets mentioned a lot. The public seems to have received the impression that paintball guns are simply eye-removing hardware. It is true that paintball can lead to eye injuries. An article by medical writer Cheryl Guttman in a trade magazine for ophthalmologists warns that eye injuries from paintball are on the rise. But the fact

is that Guttman's article says that only 102 cases of eye injuries from paintballs were reported from 1985 to 2000 and that 85 percent of those injured were not wearing the required safety goggles. This is not to say that accidents don't happen. I personally had a friend lose an eye after inadvertently shooting himself in the eye from a very close range. The fact of the matter is that he made a mistake by looking down the barrel of a loaded gun and the trigger malfunctioned. Had he been more careful or worn the proper equipment, he most likely would have been fine. During my first organized paintball experience I was hit in the goggles by a very powerful gun and felt no pain. The only discomfort came from having to clean all the paint off my goggles after the game. When played properly, paintball is an incredibly safe sport.

8 The most powerful argument against paintball is that it is inherently violent and thus unhealthy. Critics claim paintball is simply an accepted form of promoting violence against other people. I have anti-war friends who think that paintball glorifies war. Many new parents today try to keep their kids from playing cops and robbers and won't buy them toy guns. These people see paintball as an upgraded and more violent version of the same antisocial games they don't want their children to play. Some people also point to the connections between paintball and violent video games where participants get their fun from "killing" other people. They link paintball to all the other violent activities that they think lead to such things as gangs or school shootings. But there is no connection between school shootings and paintball. As seen in Michael Moore's *Bowling for Columbine*, the killers involved there went bowling before the massacre; they didn't practice their aim by playing paintball.

9 What I am trying to say is that, yes, paintball is violent to a degree. After all, its whole point is to "kill" each other with guns. But I object to paintball's being considered a promotion of violence. Rather, I feel that it is a healthy release of tension. From my own personal experience, when playing the game, the players aren't focused on hurting the other players; they are focused on winning the game. At the end of the day, players are not full of violent urges, but just the opposite. They want to celebrate together as a team, just as do softball or soccer teams after a game. Therefore I don't think paintball is an unhealthy activity for adults. (The only reason I wouldn't include children is because I believe the pain is too intense for them. I have seen some younger players cry after being shot.) Paintball is simply a game, a sport, that produces intense exhilaration and fun. Admittedly, paintball guns can be used in irresponsible manners. Recently there have been some drive-by paintballings, suggesting that paintball players are irresponsible and violent. However, the percentage of people who do this sort of prank is very small and those are the bad apples of the group. There will always be those who misuse equipment. For example, baseball bats have been used in atrocious beatings, but that doesn't make baseball a violent sport. So despite the bad apples, paintball is still a worthwhile activity when properly practiced.

10 Athletic and mentally challenging, team-building and fun—the game of paintball seems perfectly legitimate to me. It is admittedly violent, but it is not the evil activity that critics portray. Injuries can occur, but usually only when the proper safety equipment is not being used and proper precautions are ignored. As a great recreational activity, paintball deserves the same respect as other sports. It is a great way to get physical exercise, make friends, and have fun.

THINKING CRITICALLY

about "Paintball: Promoter of Violence or Healthy Fun?"

1. Before reading this essay, what was your own view of paintball? To what extent did this argument create for you a more positive view of paintball? What aspects of the argument did you find particularly effective or ineffective?
2. How effective are Ross's appeals to *ethos* in this argument? Does he create a persona that you find trustworthy and compelling? How does he do so or fail to do so?
3. How effective are Ross's appeals to *pathos?* How does he appeal to his readers' values, interests, and emotions in trying to make paintball seem like an exhilarating team sport? To what extent does he show empathy with readers when he summarizes objections to paintball?
4. How effective are Ross's appeals to *logos?* How effective are Ross's reasons and evidence in support of his claim? How effective are Ross's responses to opposing views?
5. What are the main strengths and weaknesses of Ross's argument?

Our next three readings focus on the issue of nuclear power—specifically, whether the United States should increase its production of electricity by building more nuclear power plants. The first of these readings, by electrical engineer and science writer William Sweet, appeared in the "Better Planet" section of the science magazine *Discover* in August 2007. Under the title "Why Uranium Is the New Green," it presents arguments in favor of greatly expanding our nuclear-generating capacity. William Sweet, a graduate of the University of Chicago and Princeton University, is the author of *Kicking the Carbon Habit: Global Warming and the Case for Nuclear and Renewable Energy* (Columbia University Press, 2006).

William Sweet

Why Uranium Is the New Green

1 ExxonMobil has thrown in the towel, terminating its campaign to convince the public that global warming is a hoax concocted by some pointy-headed intellectuals. All three major Democratic candidates for president, and some of the top Republican contenders as well, have promised serious action. Leading members of Congress have introduced a half dozen bills that would impose some kind of carbon regulation, and even the president now concedes that climate change is important.

2 Using coal to make electricity accounts for about a third of America's carbon emissions. As a result, tackling emissions from coal-fired power plants represents our best opportunity to make sharp reductions in greenhouse gases.

3 Fortunately, we already have the technology to do that. Unfortunately, right now the United States is addicted to coal, a cheap, abundant power source. Burning coal

produces more than half the country's electricity, despite its immense human and environmental costs. Particulates and other air pollutants from coal-fired power plants cause somewhere between 20,000 and 30,000 premature deaths in the United States *each year.* Fifty tons of mercury—one-third of all domestic mercury emissions—are pumped into the atmosphere annually from coal plants. In addition, the extraction of coal, from West Virginia to Wyoming, devastates the physical environment, and its processing and combustion produce gigantic volumes of waste.

4 For the last decade, coal-burning utilities have been fighting a rearguard action, resisting costly antipollution measures required by environmental legislation. At the same time, they have been holding out the prospect of "clean coal"—in which carbon is captured and stored as coal is burned. But clean-coal technologies have yet to be demonstrated on a large scale commercially, and by the admission of even the president's own climate-technology task force, clean coal doesn't have any prospect of making a big dent in the climate problem in the next 15 to 20 years.

5 By comparison, nuclear and wind power are proven technologies whose environmental risks and costs are thoroughly understood and which can make an immediate difference for the better.

6 The first thing to be appreciated about reactors in the United States is that they are essentially immune to the type of accident that occurred at Chernobyl in April 1986. Put simply, because of fundamental design differences, U.S. reactors cannot experience a sudden and drastic power surge, as happened at Chernobyl's Unit Number 4, causing it to explode and catch fire. In addition, the reliability of U.S. nuclear plants has been constantly improving. In 1980, American nuclear power plants were generating electricity only 56 percent of the time because they frequently needed special maintenance or repair. By 2004, reactor performance had improved to the point of generating electricity over 90 percent of the time.

7 Our regulatory regime, which was enormously strengthened in the wake of the 1979 Three Mile Island accident (during which no one was hurt, by the way), is indisputably much better than the Soviet system, which bred endemic incompetence. Management of U.S. nuclear power plants has improved dramatically since Three Mile Island, and security has been tightened significantly since 9/11 (though more remains to be done). By comparison with other tempting terrorist targets like petrochemical complexes, reactors are well fortified.

8 What about the problem of storing radioactive waste? It is overrated from an engineering standpoint and pales in comparison with the challenges associated with the permanent sequestration of immense quantities of carbon, as required by clean-coal systems. Though the wastes from nuclear power plants are highly toxic, their physical quantity is surprisingly small—barely more than 2,000 tons a year in the United States. The amount of carbon dioxide emitted by our coal plants? Nearly 2 *billion* tons.

9 Let us say it plainly: Today coal-fired power plants routinely kill tens of thousands of people in the United States each year by way of lung cancer, bronchitis, and other ailments; the U.S. nuclear economy kills virtually no one in a normal year.

10 Perhaps the most serious concern about increasing our reliance on nuclear power is whether it might lead to an international proliferation of atomic bombs. Contrary to

a stubborn myth, however, countries do not decide to build nuclear weapons because they happen to get nuclear reactors first; they acquire nuclear reactors because they want to build nuclear weapons. This was true of France and China in the 1950s, of Israel and India in the '60s and '70s, and it's true of Korea and Iran today. Does anybody honestly think that whether Tehran or Pyongyang produces atomic bombs depends on how many reactors the United States decides to build in the next 10 to 20 years?

11 Ultimately, the replacement of old, highly polluting coal-fired power plants by nuclear reactors is essentially no different from deciding, after putting sentimental considerations aside, to replace your inexpensive and reliable—but obsolete—1983 Olds Omega with a 2007 Toyota Camry or BMW 3 Series sedan.

12 All that said, it's important to be clear about nuclear energy's limits. It's likely that the construction of at least one new nuclear power plant will be initiated by the end of this year, ending a two-decade drought in new nuclear plant construction. But by its own estimates, the U.S. nuclear industry can handle only about two new nuclear reactor projects annually at its present-day capacity.

13 Obviously, given these limits, a lot of new wind generation, conservation, and improvements in energy use will also be needed. Wind is especially important because, despite the hopes of many, solar power just isn't going to cut it on a large scale in the foreseeable future. Right now, on a dollar per megawatt basis, solar installations are six or seven times as expensive as wind.

14 Wind turbines already generate electricity almost as inexpensively as fossil fuels. Thanks to a two cents per kiolwatt-hour production incentive from the U.S. government, they are being built at a rate that will increase the amount of wind-generated electricity by nearly three gigawatts a year. Taking into account that wind turbines produce electricity only about a third of the time, that's roughly the equivalent of building one standard one-gigawatt nuclear power plant a year.

15 Currently, nuclear and wind energy (as well as clean coal) are between 25 and 75 percent more expensive than old-fashioned coal at current prices (not including all the hidden health and environmental costs of coal), so it will take a stiff charge on coal to induce rapid replacement of obsolete plants. A tax or equivalent trading scheme that increases the cost of coal-generated electricity by, say, 50 percent would stimulate conservation and adoption of more efficient technologies throughout the economy and prompt replacement of coal by some combination of wind, nuclear, and natural gas. Proceeds from the tax or auctioned credits could (and should) be used to compensate regions and individuals most adversely affected by the higher costs, like the poor.

16 For the last six years, the U.S. government, with well-orchestrated support from industry, has told the American people that we can't afford to attack global warming aggressively. That's nonsense. We're the world's richest country, and we use energy about twice as extravagantly as Europe and Japan. It's no surprise that we account for a quarter of the globe's greenhouse-gas emissions.

17 What the United States needs to do is get in step with the Kyoto Protocol, both to establish its bona fides with the other advanced industrial countries and to give countries like India and China an incentive to accept mandatory carbon limits. That implies cutting U.S. carbon emissions by 25 percent as soon as possible.

18 The United States could do that by simply making the dirtiest and most inefficient coal plants prohibitively expensive by means of the carbon tax or trading systems mentioned above.

19 All we need to move decisively on carbon reduction is a different kind of political leadership at the very top. Surprisingly, it's the muscle-bound action-movie star who runs California who has best captured the spirit of what's needed. Last September, the day Arnold Schwarzenegger signed a bill committing his state to a program of sharp greenhouse-gas reductions, he told an ABC interviewer that climate change kind of "creeps up on you. And then all of a sudden it is too late to do something about it. We don't want to go there."

THINKING CRITICALLY
about "Why Uranium Is the New Green"

1. This article includes most of the features typically associated with classical argument—a claim with supporting reasons, a summary of alternative or opposing views, and responses to those views.
   a. What are the chief reasons that Sweet supports nuclear-generated electricity?
   b. What arguments against nuclear-generated electricity does Sweet mention or summarize?
   c. Where and how does he respond to those alternative views or opposing arguments?
2. From the perspective of *logos,* what reasons and evidence in favor of nuclear-generated power do you find most effective in Sweet's argument? Are there weaknesses in his argument? Where and how?
3. In what ways, and with what effectiveness, does Sweet appeal to *pathos* and *ethos*?
4. One of the chief arguments against nuclear power is the problem of storing nuclear waste. How would you analyze rhetorically Sweet's method of responding to that objection? How effective is his response?

Making a case against nuclear power, our next reading is a cartoon by Stan Eales, one of the most prominent cartoonists working in Europe today. Eales was born in 1962 and has a degree in graphic design from Auckland, New Zealand. Sellafield is a famous nuclear power site in England with a long, controversial history. It was the home of the world's first commercial nuclear power plant and is currently a storage site for radioactive waste as well as a major research facility on nuclear power. Sellafield has been the subject of numerous documentaries and protest rallies, including a famous 1992 Greenpeace rally that featured bands such as U2, Public Enemy, and Kraftwerk.

Stan Eales

Welcome to Sellafield

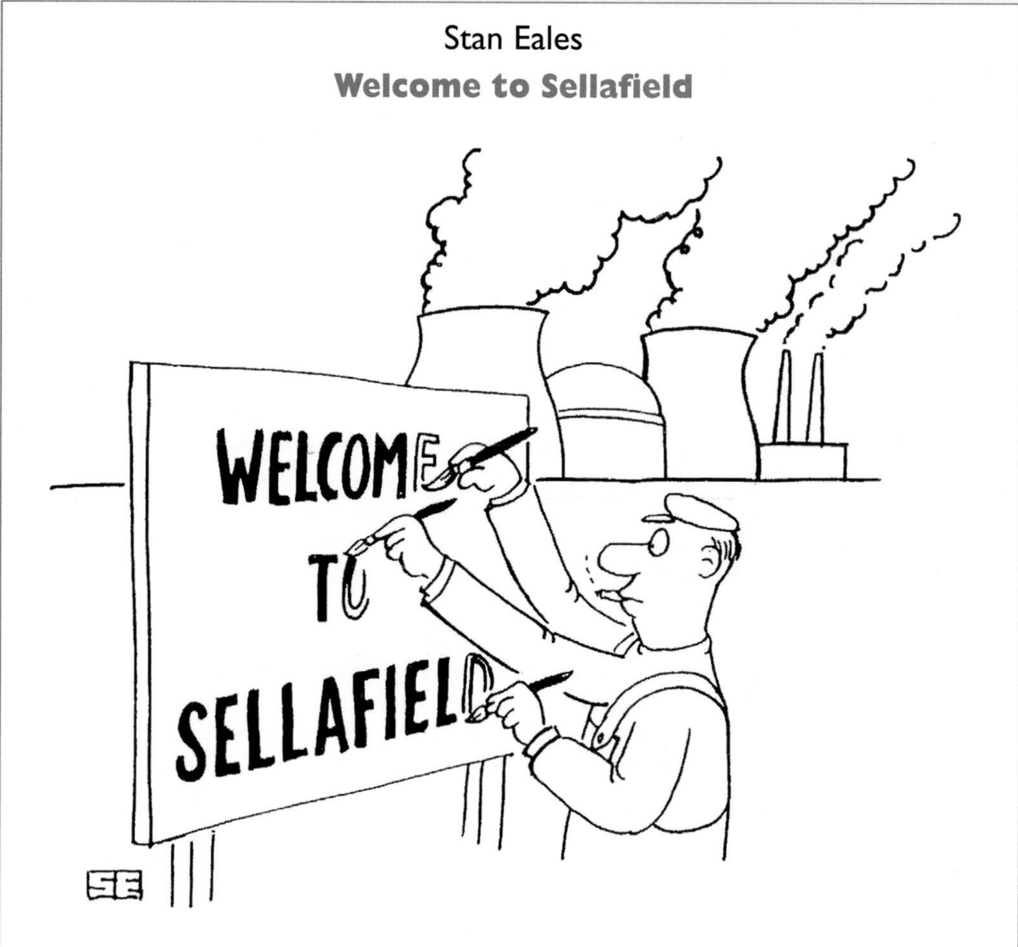

THINKING CRITICALLY
about "Welcome to Sellafield"

1. Translate Eales's cartoon into a verbal argument by finishing this sentence: "Nuclear energy is bad because ________________."
2. Cartoons get their power from their ability to encapsulate a complex argument in a striking visual image. In your own words, explain how this cartoon uses *logos, pathos,* and *ethos* to create its persuasive effect.
3. How would William Sweet (previous reading) respond to this cartoon?

Our last nuclear power reading is an editorial appearing in the *Los Angeles Times* on July 23, 2007. It responds to a growing public reassessment of nuclear power as a possible solution to global warming. Its immediate context is the July 2007 earthquake in Japan that damaged a nuclear power plant, causing leakage of a small amount of contaminated water.

Editorial from the *Los Angeles Times*

No to Nukes

1 Japan sees nuclear power as a solution to global warming, but it's paying a price. Last week, a magnitude 6.8 earthquake caused dozens of problems at the world's biggest nuclear plant, leading to releases of radioactive elements into the air and ocean and an indefinite shutdown. Government and company officials initially downplayed the incident and stuck to the official line that the country's nuclear plants are earthquake-proof, but they gave way in the face of overwhelming evidence to the contrary. Japan has a sordid history of serious nuclear accidents or spills followed by cover-ups.

2 It isn't alone. The U.S. government allows nuclear plants to operate under a level of secrecy usually reserved for the national security apparatus. Last year, for example, about nine gallons of highly enriched uranium spilled at a processing plant in Tennessee, forming a puddle a few feet from an elevator shaft. Had it dripped into the shaft, it might have formed a critical mass sufficient for a chain reaction, releasing enough radiation to kill or burn workers nearby. A report on the accident from the Nuclear Regulatory Commission was hidden from the public, and only came to light because one of the commissioners wrote a memo on it that became part of the public record.

3 The dream that nuclear power would turn atomic fission into a force for good rather than destruction unraveled with the Three Mile Island disaster in 1979 and the Chernobyl meltdown in 1986. No U.S. utility has ordered a new nuclear plant since 1978 (that order was later canceled), and until recently it seemed none ever would. But rising natural gas prices and worries about global warming have put the nuclear industry back on track. Many respected academics and environmentalists argue that nuclear power must be part of any solution to climate change because nuclear power plants don't release greenhouse gases.

4 They make a weak case. The enormous cost of building nuclear plants, the reluctance of investors to fund them, community opposition and an endless controversy over what to do with the waste ensure that ramping up the nuclear infrastructure will be a slow process—far too slow to make a difference on global warming. That's just as well, because nuclear power is extremely risky. What's more, there are cleaner, cheaper, faster alternatives that come with none of the risks.

Glowing Pains

5 Modern nuclear plants are much safer than the Soviet-era monstrosity at Chernobyl. But accidents can and frequently do happen. The Union of Concerned Scientists cites 51 cases at 41 U.S. nuclear plants in which reactors have been shut down for more than a year as evidence of serious and widespread safety problems.

6 Nuclear plants are also considered attractive terrorist targets, though that risk too has been reduced. Provisions in the 2005 energy bill required threat assessments at nuclear plants and background checks on workers. What hasn't improved much is the risk of spills or even meltdowns in the event of natural disasters such as earthquakes,

making it mystifying why anyone would consider building reactors in seismically unstable places like Japan (or California, which has two, one at San Onofre and the other in Morro Bay).

7 Weapons proliferation is an even more serious concern. The uranium used in nuclear reactors isn't concentrated enough for anything but a dirty bomb, but the same labs that enrich uranium for nuclear fuel can be used to create weapons-grade uranium. Thus any country, such as Iran, that pursues uranium enrichment for nuclear power might also be building a bomb factory. It would be more than a little hypocritical for the U.S. to expand its own nuclear power capacity while forbidding countries it doesn't like from doing the same.

8 The risks increase when spent fuel is recycled. Five countries reprocess their spent nuclear fuel, and the Bush administration is pushing strongly to do the same in the U.S. Reprocessing involves separating plutonium from other materials to create new fuel. Plutonium is an excellent bomb material, and it's much easier to steal than enriched uranium. Spent fuel is so radioactive that it would burn a prospective thief to death, while plutonium could be carried out of a processing center in one's pocket. In Japan, 200 kilograms of plutonium from a waste recycling plant have gone missing; in Britain, 30 kilograms can't be accounted for. These have been officially dismissed as clerical errors, but the nuclear industry has never been noted for its truthfulness or transparency. The bomb dropped on Nagasaki contained six kilograms.

9 Technology might be able to solve the recycling problem, but the question of what to do with the waste defies answers. Even the recycling process leaves behind highly radioactive waste that has to be disposed of. This isn't a temporary issue: Nuclear waste remains hazardous for tens of thousands of years. The only way to get rid of it is to put it in containers and bury it deep underground—and pray that geological shifts or excavations by future generations that have forgotten where it's buried don't unleash it on the surface.

10 No country in the world has yet built a permanent underground waste repository, though Finland has come the closest. In the U.S., Congress has been struggling for decades to build a dump at Yucca Mountain in Nevada but has been unable to overcome fierce local opposition. One can hardly blame the Nevadans. Not many people would want 70,000 metric tons of nuclear waste buried in their neighborhood or transported through it on the way to the dump.

11 The result is that nuclear waste is stored on-site at the power plants, increasing the risk of leaks and the danger to plant workers. Eventually, we'll run out of space for it.

Goin' Fission?

12 Given the drawbacks, it's surprising that anybody would seriously consider a nuclear renaissance. But interest is surging; the NRC expects applications for up to 28 new reactors in the next two years. Even California, which has a 31-year-old ban on construction of nuclear plants, is looking into it. Last month, the state Energy Commission held a hearing on nuclear power, and a group of Fresno businessmen plans a ballot measure to assess voter interest in rescinding the state's ban.

13 Behind all this is a perception that nuclear power is needed to help fight climate change. But there's little chance that nuclear plants could be built quickly enough to make much difference. The existing 104 nuclear plants in the U.S., which supply

roughly 20% of the nation's electricity, are old and nearing the end of their useful lives. Just to replace them would require building a new reactor every four or five months for the next 40 years. To significantly increase the nation's nuclear capacity would require far more.

14 The average nuclear plant is estimated to cost about $4 billion. Because of the risks involved, there is scarce interest among investors in putting up the needed capital. Nor have tax incentives and subsidies been enough to lure them. In part, that's because the regulatory process for new plants is glacially slow. The newest nuclear plant in the U.S. opened in 1996, after having been ordered in 1970—a 26-year gap. Though a carbon tax or carbon trading might someday make the economics of nuclear power more attractive, and the NRC has taken steps to speed its assessments, community opposition remains high, and it could still take more than a decade to get a plant built.

15 Meanwhile, a 2006 study by the Institute for Energy and Environmental Research found that for nuclear power to play a meaningful role in cutting greenhouse gas emissions, the world would need to build a new plant every one to two weeks until mid-century. Even if that were feasible, it would overwhelm the handful of companies that make specialized parts for nuclear plants, sending costs through the roof.

16 The accelerating threat of global warming requires innovation and may demand risk-taking, but there are better options than nuclear power. A combination of energy-efficiency measures, renewable power like wind and solar, and decentralized power generators are already producing more energy worldwide than nuclear power plants. Their use is expanding more quickly, and the decentralized approach they represent is more attractive on several levels. One fast-growing technology allows commercial buildings or complexes, such as schools, hospitals, hotels or offices, to generate their own electricity and hot water with micro-turbines fueled by natural gas or even bio-fuel, much more efficiently than utilities can do it and with far lower emissions.

17 The potential for wind power alone is nearly limitless and, according to a May report by research firm Standard & Poor's, it's cheaper to produce than nuclear power. Further, the amount of electricity that could be generated simply by making existing non-nuclear power plants more efficient is staggering. On average, coal plants operate at 30% efficiency worldwide, but newer plants operate at 46%. If the world average could be raised to 42%, it would save the same amount of carbon as building 800 nuclear plants.

18 Nevertheless, the U.S. government spends more on nuclear power than it does on renewables and efficiency. Taxpayer subsidies to the nuclear industry amounted to $9 billion in 2006, according to Doug Koplow, a researcher based in Cambridge, Mass., whose Earth Track consultancy monitors energy spending. Renewable power sources, including hydropower but not ethanol, got $6 billion, and $2 billion went toward conservation.

19 That's out of whack. Some countries—notably France, which gets nearly 80% of its power from nuclear plants and has never had a major accident—have made nuclear energy work, but at a high cost. The state-owned French power monopoly is severely indebted, and although France recycles its waste, it is no closer than the U.S. to approving a permanent repository. Tax dollars are better spent on windmills than on cooling towers.

THINKING CRITICALLY
about "No to Nukes"

1. This article, like William Sweet's, includes the typical elements associated with classical argument.
   a. What are the editorial writer's chief arguments against nuclear power?
   b. What arguments in favor of nuclear power does this editorial mention or summarize?
   c. How and where does the editorial writer respond to these alternative views?
2. From the perspective of *logos,* what reasons and evidence opposing nuclear-generated power do you find most effective in this editorial? Are there weaknesses in the editorial's arguments? Where and how?
3. In what ways, and with what effectiveness, does the editorial appeal to *pathos* and *ethos*?
4. Both Sweet and the editorial writer have high hopes for wind energy. In fact, the editorial writer concludes by saying, "Tax dollars are better spent on windmills than on cooling towers." How would David Rockwood (see Rockwood's letter to the editor in Chapter 1, p. 7) respond to both writers?
5. Where do you place yourself on the spectrum from "strong support of nuclear power" to "strong opposition to nuclear power"? What new research evidence would be required to persuade you to move in one direction or the other along this spectrum?

Our next reading changes pace, moving from the global issue of nuclear energy to the family issue of how we should discipline our children. "Spare the Rod, Spoil the Parenting" is an op-ed piece by *Miami Herald* columnist Leonard Pitts, Jr. In this editorial, Pitts jumps into the ongoing controversy over corporal punishment, children's rights, childrearing practices, and spanking. Leonard Pitts, one of the nation's foremost African-American opinion writers, won the Pulitzer Prize for commentary in 2004. He is the author of *Becoming Dad: Black Men and the Journey to Fatherhood.*

Leonard Pitts, Jr.

Spare the Rod, Spoil the Parenting

1 I hate to tell you this, but your kid is spoiled. Mine aren't much better.

2 That, in essence, is the finding of a recent Time/CNN poll. Most of us think most of our kids are overindulged, materialistic brats.

3 If you're waiting for me to argue the point, you're in the wrong column.

4 No, I only bring it up as context to talk about a controversial study released late last month. It deals with corporal punishment—spanking—and it has outraged those who oppose the practice while rearming those who support it.

5 It seems that Dr. Diana Baumrind, a psychologist at the University of California at Berkeley, followed 164 middle-class families from the time their children were in preschool until they reached their 20s. She found that most used some form of corporal punishment. She further found that, contrary to what we've been told for years, giving a child a mild spanking (defined as open-handed swats on the backside, arm or legs) does not leave the child scarred for life.

6 Baumrind, by the way, opposes spanking. Still, it's to her credit as an academic that her research draws a distinction other opponents refuse to. That is, a distinction between the minor punishments practiced by most parents who spank and the harsher variants practiced by a tiny minority (shaking and blows to the head or face, for example).

7 Yes, children whose parents treat them that severely are, indeed, more likely to be maladjusted by the time they reach adolescence. And, yes, the parents themselves are teetering dangerously close to child abuse.

8 But does the same hold true in cases where corporal punishment means little more than swatting a misbehaving backside?

9 For years, the official consensus from the nation's child-rearing experts was that it did. Maybe that's about to change. We can only hope.

10 For my money, there was always something spurious about the orthodoxy that assured us all corporal punishment, regardless of severity, was defacto abuse. Nevertheless, we bought into it, with the result being that parents who admitted to spanking were treated as primitive dolts and heaped with scorn. They were encouraged to negotiate with misbehaving children in order to nurture their self-esteem.

11 But the orthodoxy was wrong on several fronts.

12 In the first place, it's plainly ridiculous—and offensive—to equate a child who has been swatted on the butt with one who has been stomped, scalded or punched. In the second, the argument that reasonable corporal punishment leads inevitably to mental instability always seemed insupportable and has just been proven so by Baumrind's study. And in the third, have you ever tried to "negotiate" with a screaming 5-year-old? It may do wonders for the child's self-esteem, but, I promise, it's going to kill yours. Your sanity, too.

13 Don't get me wrong, contrary to what its proponents sometimes claim, corporal punishment is not a panacea for misbehavior. Rearing a child requires not just discipline, but also humor, love and some luck.

14 Yet the very fact that spanking must be exonerated by a university study suggests how far afield we've wandered from what used to be the central tenet of family life: parents in charge. Ultimately, it probably doesn't matter whether that tenet is enforced by spanking or other corrective measures, so long as it is enforced.

15 I've seen too many children behave with too grand a sense of entitlement to believe that it is. Heard too many teachers tell horror stories of dealing with kids from households where parents are not sovereign, adult authority not respected. As a culture, we seem to have forgotten that the family is not a democracy, but a benign dictatorship.

16 Small wonder our kids are brats.

17 So the pertinent question isn't: To spank or not to spank? Rather, it's: Who's in charge here? Who is teaching whom? Who is guiding whom?

18 The answer used to be obvious. It's obvious no more. And is it so difficult to see where that road leads? To understand that it is possible to be poisoned by self-esteem, and that a spoiled child becomes a self-centered adult ill-equipped to deal with the vagaries and reversals of life?

19 Some folks think it's abuse when you swat a child's backside. But maybe, sometimes, it's abuse when you don't.

THINKING CRITICALLY
about "Spare the Rod, Spoil the Parenting"

1. In the introductory paragraphs of this op-ed piece, Leonard Pitts, Jr., mentions the rhetorical situation that has called forth his argument. What contemporary research is prompting Pitts's column?
2. Pitts's argument takes a stand on the issue question, "Is spanking a good childrearing practice?" What claim does he make in this argument? What reasons and evidence does he offer to support this claim?
3. Where does Pitts acknowledge and respond to opposing views?
4. To understand the intensity of the social controversy on this issue, we suggest that you search the keywords "spanking" and "corporal punishment" using an online database and the Web. What different positions do you find represented in articles and by advocacy Web sites such as the site for the Center for Effective Discipline? How would these sources challenge Pitts's position and evidence?

The last reading is by student writer A. J. Chavez, who wrote this paper for the classical argument assignment in this chapter. In proposing the legalization of gay marriage, A. J. Chavez draws on personal knowledge and experience, some Internet research, and information from an anthropology course he was taking simultaneously with first-year composition.

A. J. Chavez (student)
The Case for (Gay) Marriage

1 "What if it was a gay world? And you were straight?" a recent TV spot asks (the ad can be viewed at commercialcloset.org—see "What If" in Works Cited). The camera pans across a hospital waiting room, filled with gay and lesbian couples. There, a middle-aged man sits, waiting. "Your partner's in a coma. She's not responding," a young male doctor says to him. "Unfortunately, since the state doesn't recognize your marriage, I can't grant you spousal visitation. If she were to wake, or a family member gave consent—I wish

there was more I could do. I'm sorry." After that, the camera quickly zooms out from the man's heartbroken face. The scene blurs, and a female voiceover reads the fact that appears on the screen: "hospital visitation: just one of over 1000 rights granted to a legally married couple." Next, the scene fades into a black screen with a blue rectangle that has a yellow equal sign on it. The female voiceover continues, "Support equality for all Americans. Millionformarriage.org." This spot, sponsored by the Human Rights Campaign, the largest queer political organization in the United States, shows a scenario that undoubtedly happens every day in America, just with the tables turned. According to a report from the United States General Accounting Office, released after the passage of the federal Defense of Marriage Act of 1996, there are at least 1,049 federal laws in the U.S. code that relate to rights specific to marriage (2). Some are obvious, like Social Security or Veterans' Administration benefits upon the death of a spouse for the surviving spouse and children. Others are not so obvious, but equally important, such as the federally guaranteed right of an employee to take time off from work to care for an ill spouse or the so-called "spousal privilege" of not having to testify against a husband or wife in court. Currently, marriage rights are denied to a small, but still significant group in America—gays and lesbians, a group of which I am a part. We are denied the same rights enjoyed by straight people, simply because we are attracted to and love members of our own sex and have chosen to live open, honest lives, instead of closeted ones.

2 In opposition to the current Congressional proposal to amend the Constitution by defining marriage as a union between a man and a woman, I am proposing the nationwide legalization of same-sex marriage. First of all, gay marriage is the easiest way to ensure equality for all. Civil unions can only go part of the way. Secondly, the government must define marriage through a secular framework that respects the spirit of laws already in place, not a religious one that would violate separation between church and state. Third, the costs to taxpayers for legalizing gay marriage would be negligible. Some studies even suggest it would save taxpayer money. Finally, anthropological evidence exists for the existence of what we would refer to today as "gay marriage" across a long time span and wide range of cultures, demonstrating that it is not abnormal or perverted.

3 There are many arguments against gay marriage. Some are definitional, such as "Marriage is between a man and a woman." Other claims against gay marriage stem from concern for the well-being of children raised by gay or lesbian couples from previous straight marriages, adoption, or reproductive assistance. Still others arise out of respect for the Hebrew and Christian scriptures, the moral code from which most of Western civilization has lived by for thousands of years—certain passages in them prohibit homosexual relations. Another objection is that marriage is reserved for procreation, and that gay marriage, obviously, cannot serve this end. Additionally, there is the argument that legal options already exist for gay couples that offer some of the benefits of marriage, such as power of attorney or living will. Some politicians claim that marriage is something that should be left to the states to decide how to define and deal with individually. Furthermore, there is the argument that the legalization of gay marriage will open the doors to the legalization of more radical unions, such as adult-child unions or polygamy. Last, some members of America's queer community oppose gay marriage because they see it as just an attempt to copy and live a hetero lifestyle.

4 My first reason for legalizing gay marriage is that it is the easiest and most effective way to ensure equal rights for all in this country. Currently, sexual minorities receive no explicit protection from federal anti-discrimination acts, such as Title VII from the Civil Rights Act of 1964, which only prohibits discrimination in employment based on "race, color, religion, sex, or national origin." Employers are not required to offer the same benefits to the significant others of gay employees as they do to straight employees. With gay marriage, they would be obliged under laws that protect the rights of married couples to do so. Civil unions relegate gays and lesbians to second-class status. Civil unions or domestic partnerships are offered only by a few states, but can be disregarded by neighboring anti-gay states because of the federal Defense of Marriage Act. Civil unions can guarantee protections only at the state level, and at that, only the state they were issued in. Gay marriage, with its protections, would help prevent discrimination toward sexual minorities from prejudiced individuals. Here, it becomes clear that marriage laws should not just be left to the states, as some politicians who would rather not take a stand on the issue suggest, because if they are, patchwork laws will continue to develop across the nation. Some states will prohibit same-sex marriages and civil unions, while others will provide civil unions, and, perhaps in the future, gay marriage. A clear, federal standard for the inclusion of gay marriage will also prevent possible loopholes in marriage or civil union laws for inappropriate unions between adults and children or among more than two partners.

5 Second, for public policy, marriage, like all other things, needs to be defined through a non-religious, secular framework. The separation of church and state has always been an important tenet in American government. Allowing religious dogma to define marriage violates this tenet, setting up a dangerous precedent for further unification of church and state. If gay marriage were legalized, religions would still be allowed to distinguish what they do and do not see as "marriage." The Human Rights Campaign Web site provides the example of the Catholic church, which does not bless second marriages after divorce. Yet people can still file for divorce and then remarry if they see fit. In this case, the state recognizes a legal marriage that is not officially sanctioned by the church ("I Believe God Meant"). Also, while certain passages of the Bible prohibit sexual relationships between members of the same sex, others condone slavery and polygamy—both practices that would not be approved in American society today. Clearly, appeals to the Bible cannot be used to determine public policy. We would not only violate the important principle of separation between church and state, but by strict Biblical interpretation of morality, we could theoretically have a polygamous, slave-owning society.

6 Another compelling reason for legalizing same-sex marriage is the money that could actually be *saved* in state budgets every year. The FAQ section on marriage on the Human Rights Campaign Web site explains how government savings could add up through increased reliance between gay and lesbian couples on each other, reducing reliance on government assistance programs such as Temporary Assistance to Needy Families (welfare), Supplemental Security Income (disability), food stamps and Medicaid. The Web site cites two economic studies by professors at UCLA and the University of Massachusetts, Amherst, who examined possible savings to state governments in California and New Jersey if domestic benefits were extended to same-sex

couples. According to these studies, the savings were projected to be $10.6 million in California and $61 million in New Jersey ("Won't This Cost"). Additionally, the legalization of gay marriage would provide medical insurance benefits for thousands of currently uninsured children. While gay and lesbian couples obviously cannot conceive children on their own, plenty raise children from previous, heterosexual marriages, adopt children. or use reproductive assistance such as surrogate mothers or assisted insemination to bear their own children. The fact that many gay and lesbian partners are raising children shows the fallacy in claiming that gays should not be allowed to marry because they can't procreate. If we used the logic of procreation in determining whether to grant marriage rights, we would have to ban marriage between elderly couples, between sterile straight couples, and between those who plan to use birth control to prevent pregnancy. Of course, we would never ban such marriages because we recognize the value of having a life partner. Extending marriage benefits to gay partners brings the same benefits to them, with the additional benefit to the states of reducing reliance on state assistance programs and bringing medical insurance to many children.

7 My final reason for the legalization of gay marriage is that same-sex unions have existed across all cultures and time. This is important to recognize, because Judeo-Christian societies like ours tend to discount the legitimacy or even existence of such unions, and of so-called "sexual minorities." Such disregard can be explained by the histories of Judaism and Christianity, says Ted Fortier, Ph.D., a cultural anthropologist at Seattle University. In early Jewish societies, largely due to problems with underpopulation, he notes, any sexual activity without procreative power was considered taboo. Also, in Christian medieval Europe, disease and famine required that the people have all the labor possible to produce food. Again, all nonprocreative sex was labeled taboo. For anthropological purposes, Fortier defines marriage as "a union between a woman and another person." This definition, however, can be quite broad, he says. The "woman" can actually be a man playing a feminine role. He explains that in our culture, we look at gender as a biological concept, instead of a socially determined one. He gives examples of different cultures that distinguish certain men who take on womanly roles as being a third gender, such as that of Tahiti, where every village has a man that takes on the role of a woman, or the Native American *berdache* role, another womanly role played by a man. These men raise children just like the other adults. For the most part, Fortier claims, throughout all societies and cultures marriage has always been about securing resources and property—known as "alliance theory" in anthropology. Looking at our own society with this concept in mind, we see that marriage is utilized in the same way—as a stabilizing combination of tangible and intangible resources that leads to benefits to society, often including the raising of children. Law professor Mark Strasser, in an essay entitled "State Interests in Recognizing Same-Sex Marriage," mentions that "there is no evidence that children will not thrive when raised by same-sex parents and, indeed, some evidence that children may be better off in certain ways when they are raised by same-sex parents than when they are raised by different-sex parents" (37). Strasser refers to the increased tolerance and appreciation of differences that children of gays and lesbians typically have and the innumerable studies over the years that show these children grow up

just as well-adjusted and are no more likely to be homosexual than children living with straight parents. The government, therefore, should recognize and extend marriage protections to same-sex couples as well. While there are some gay/lesbian/bisexual/transgender people who think gay marriage is just a futile attempt to copy mainstream, straight society, and that the government should not bother legalizing it, entering into any union is based on the mutual choice of two individuals. GLBT persons who find the institution of marriage unsavory would still not be forced by the government to marry if gay marriage were legalized.

8 The case for gay marriage is a strong one indeed, similar to earlier struggles for interracial marriage, which was legalized only relatively recently in American history. Gay marriage will result in an unprecedented addition of formal protections to America's last marginalized minority—the queer community. Studies suggest that it will save individual states millions of dollars in revenue on an annual basis. Gay marriage is not sick or a perversion—it exists across all cultures and times in one form or another and was stigmatized in Judeo-Christian traditions for the practical purpose of achieving as high of a population as possible. It is impossible to turn on a television set or open a newspaper now without seeing a reference to gay marriage. Legalizing gay marriage affirms both the "liberal" ideal of equality and the "conservative" value of community stability and individual rights. It also affirms the dignity of all of mankind.

Works Cited

Fortier, Ted. Personal interview, 26 Feb. 2004.

Human Rights Campaign. Advertisement. *The Commercial Closet.* Commercial Closet Association, 2004. Web. 2 Mar. 2004.

"I Believe God Meant Marriage for Men and Women." *Human Rights Campaign.* Human Rights Campaign, 20 Feb. 2004. Web. 15 Mar. 2004.

Strasser, Mark. "State Interests in Recognizing Same-Sex Marriage." *Marriage and Same Sex Unions: A Debate.* Ed. Lynn D. Wardle et al. Westport: Praeger, 2003. Print.

United States. General Accounting Office. *Categories of Laws Involving Marital Status.* Letter of transmittal. By Barry R. Bedrick. 31 Jan. 1997. Web. 16 Mar. 2004. <http://www.gao.gov/archive/1997/og97016.pdf>.

"Won't This Cost Taxpayers Too Much Money?" *Human Rights Campaign.* Human Rights Campaign, 2004. Web. 15 Mar. 2004.

THINKING CRITICALLY
about "The Case for (Gay) Marriage"

1. In classical arguments there is often an overlap between the reasons used to support one's own claim and the reasons used to rebut opposing views. In such cases the distinction between support and rebuttal can become blurred (not a problem so long as the argument remains clear). In this essay, where

does A. J. Chavez summarize the arguments opposing the legalization of gay marriage? How many of these arguments does he respond to as the argument proceeds? Where does he add supporting reasons in favor of gay marriage that aren't initially framed as rebuttals?

2. How effectively does A. J. create appeals to *ethos* in this argument? How would you characterize his persona based on tone, reasonableness, and empathy for opposing views?
3. On the gay marriage issue, opponents of gay marriage can range from conservative audiences with strong religious arguments against same-sex marriage to very liberal gay audiences who believe that gays shouldn't imitate heterosexual relationships. How well does A. J. use appeals to *pathos* to connect with his imagined readers at both ends of this spectrum? How does he appeal to the values, beliefs, and emotions of his audiences? Point out specific passages where you think he is successful or unsuccessful.
4. How would you assess the appeals to *logos* in this argument? Are A. J.'s uses of reasons and evidence persuasive?
5. What do you see as the major strengths and weaknesses of this argument?

For additional writing, reading, and research resources, go to **www.MyCompLab.com** and choose **Ramage/Bean/Johnson's *The Allyn & Bacon Guide to Writing,* Fifth Edition.**

MAKING AN EVALUATION

CHAPTER 15

People make evaluations all the time. What is the best laptop computer for my purposes? Which elective course should I take next term? In professional life the stakes for evaluations are often high: How should I evaluate this employee's job performance? Which plan of action will be best for our company?

Evaluation arguments usually involve a two-step critical thinking process: (1) establishing and rank-ordering the criteria for the evaluation and (2) matching the individual case to the criteria. Thus, when you choose an elective course for next term, you'll first have to establish your criteria. What do you value most—high interest level? High (or low) level of work and challenge? Convenient time slot? Relevance to your major? Reputation of the teacher? You'll then need to match each of your possible courses to these criteria.

This chapter instructs you in a systematic procedure for making an evaluation. Research suggests that most college assignments require some form of evaluative thinking. According to one study by Barbara Walvoord and Lucille McCarthy, college assignments often take the form of "good/better/best" questions:

Is X good (or bad)?	How good is the current system of health care in the United States?
Which is better—X or Y?	Which is the better health care system—the current U.S. system or the Canadian system?
Among available options, which is best?	Among the three congressional bills aimed at improving the U.S. health care system, which is best?

The writing project for this chapter asks you to make an evaluation argument in which you imagine a skeptical audience that has some degree of initial resistance to your evaluation. (You can imagine the critical disagreements raised by the questions about U.S. health care in the previous example.) This kind of evaluation has a persuasive rather than a purely informational aim and thus differs from, say, a movie or restaurant review that simply notes the good points and bad points of the thing being evaluated.

An evaluation argument is a frequently encountered subcategory of classical argument. If you wrote a classical argument for Chapter 14, you may have already addressed an evaluation issue. For example, the starling case used in Chapter 14 involves evaluation issues: Of the various options for dealing with the starling problem, was the family's solution a good one? This chapter simply looks at this specific kind of argument in more depth. (The next chapter looks in depth at proposal arguments, another common subcategory of classical argument.) Because evaluation arguments help communities make choices about actions, beliefs, or values, they are among the most important kinds of arguments to understand.

Exploring Evaluative Writing

To introduce you to evaluative thinking, we ask you to explore a provocative evaluative question:

> **Situation:** You are a member of a student group planning a workshop on the dangers of binge drinking. Universities around the country are trying to address this problem, which has been shown to have dangerous short-range and long-range consequences. The goals of your workshop are (1) to raise awareness of the consequences of binge drinking and other forms of alcohol abuse; (2) to work toward changing the "culture of drinking" that exists on college campuses across the country; and (3) to promote responsible, safe, and legal behavior regarding alcohol. Your particular committee is in charge of creating a poster for displaying around campus to promote student interest in the workshop. Your committee is choosing among four possible visuals (shown in Figures 15.1–15.4) to use in this poster. You want to choose the "best" visual for your poster in order to reach a range of students from your particular college or university. You'll need to consider not only the design and subject matter of each visual but also its suitability for reaching students on your particular campus, given its size, location, culture, and mission.

In Chapter 16, we present a proposal argument on reducing binge drinking.

FIGURE 15.1 Graph Correlating Alcohol Consumption and Academic Performance

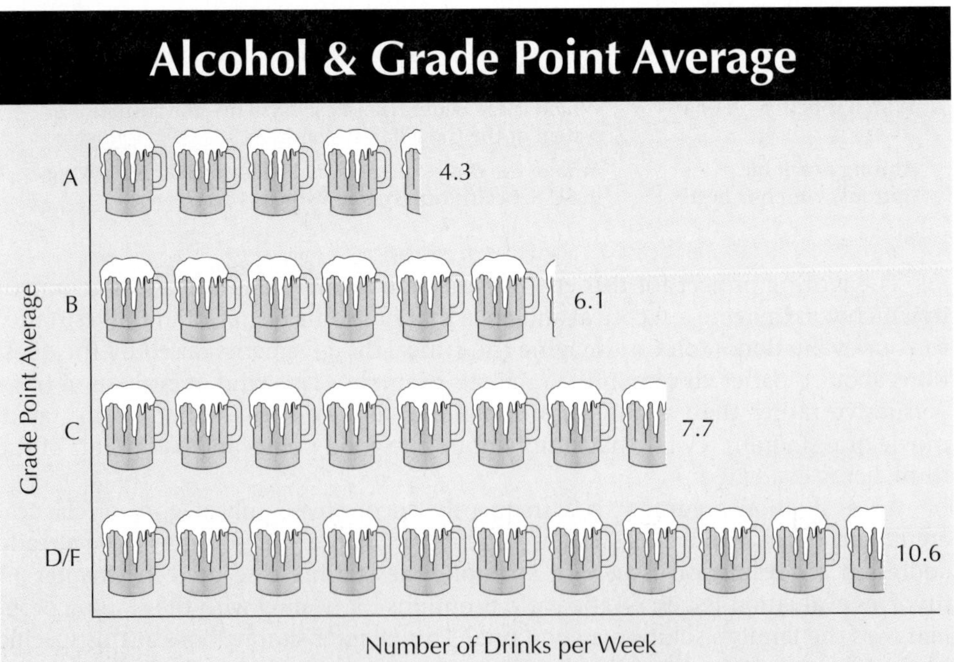

FIGURE 15.2 Nineteenth-Century Prohibition Cartoon

1. After studying Figures 15.1–15.4, freewrite your initial responses to them. What is striking or memorable about each? What is confusing? What message does each convey? How well do the dominant impression and message of each visual fit with the purpose of your workshop on binge drinking and with your academic institution?
2. Working in small groups or as a whole class, create the best argument that you can for selecting one of these visuals for your poster. Frame each argument as a

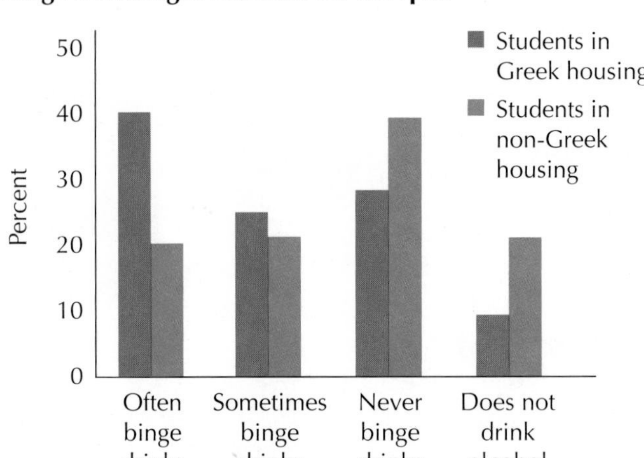

FIGURE 15.3 Graphic Showing Percentage of Students Reporting Substance Abuse by Housing Type

FIGURE 15.4 A Social Norms Campaign Poster

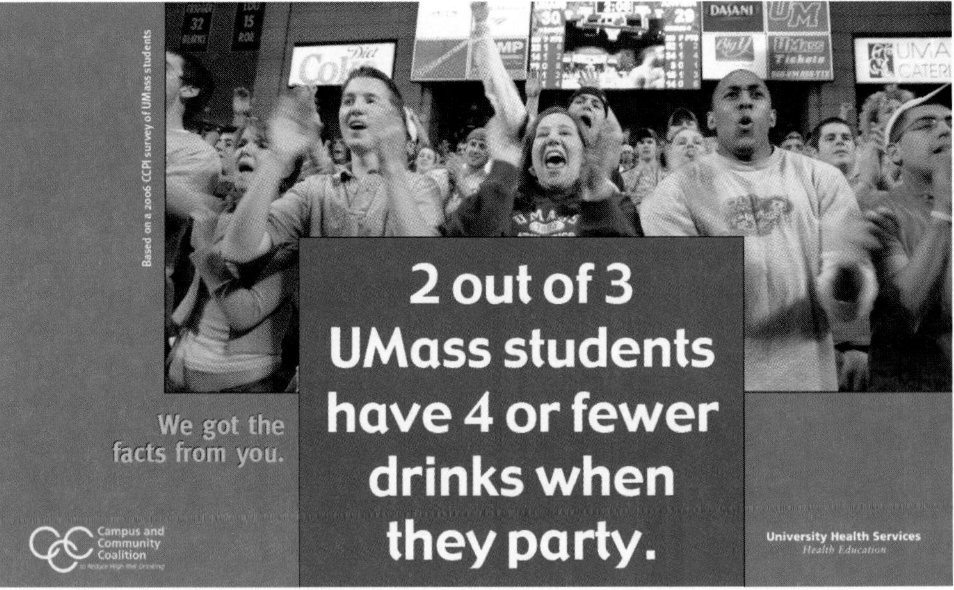

claim with reasons, stating each reason as a *because* clause (for example, "The graph using the beer glasses is best because ... , because ... ," etc.).

3. When the class reaches consensus about the best visual, write the frame of the justifying argument on the chalkboard as a claim with *because* clauses. If you wish, you can also write a dissenting argument on the board or list reasons for rejecting certain visuals as well as supporting others. Then articulate the unstated assumption behind each *because* clause. As we will show in the next section, these unstated assumptions are the criteria for your evaluation argument.

Understanding Evaluation Arguments

The Criteria-Match Process

Evaluation arguments involve what we call a *criteria-match* process. The first step in this process is to establish criteria; the second step is to show how well your subject matches these criteria. Here are several examples:

- Which students should be awarded the prestigious presidential scholarship?
  Criteria task: What are the criteria for the presidential scholarship?
  Match task: Which of the candidates best meets the criteria?
- Is hospitalization an effective treatment program for eating disorders?
  Criteria task: What are the criteria for an effective treatment for eating disorders?
  Match task: Does hospitalization meet these criteria?
- Is Michael Moore's *Sicko* a great documentary film?
  Criteria task: What are the criteria for a great documentary film?
  Match task: Does *Sicko* meet these criteria?
- Which is the best visual for the poster advertising this school's workshop on the dangers of binge drinking?
  Criteria task: What are the criteria for the best visual in this context?
  Match task: Which visual best meets the criteria?

In each of these cases, it is possible to articulate criteria while anticipating that different stakeholders might argue for different criteria or consider certain criteria more important than others and thus might weight the criteria differently. For example, on the poster issue, one group of designers might argue this way:

ARGUMENT FOR CHOOSING A VISUAL WITH NUMERIC GRAPHS

One of the two numeric graphs is the best visual for our poster ...
- because a graph succinctly highlights the problem of binge drinking.
- because it takes a factual approach.
- because it stimulates intelligent questions.

The unstated assumptions behind these reasons are the criteria for this argument. In other words, the argument states that a good visual should meet these criteria:

1. It should highlight the problem of binge drinking;
2. It should take a factual approach (as opposed to an imaginative or emotional approach); and
3. It should stimulate intelligent questions.

Based on these criteria, Figure 15.1 or 15.3 would be the best choice. (The argument would then need to be refined further to choose the better of these two options.)

But other poster designers might present a different argument:

ARGUMENT FOR CHOOSING A VISUAL WITH IMAGES

One of the two visuals with images is the best visual for our poster ...
- because these images are eye-catching and dramatic.
- because they have emotional and imaginative appeal.
- because they have a personal, immediate impact.

The unstated assumptions behind this argument set up a different set of criteria. For these poster designers, a good visual is:

1. eye-catching;
2. emotionally appealing; and
3. personal and immediate.

Based on these criteria, the social norms campaign poster with the photo of the college students cheering or the nineteenth-century Prohibition cartoon would be more effective. (Again, a further argument would be needed to narrow the choice to one.)

The preceding argument focuses on disagreements over the criteria. Evaluation arguments can also focus on disagreements over the match. For example, consider a family deciding what used car to buy. They might agree on the criteria—let's say, (1) low cost, (2) safety, and (3) reliability. But they might disagree whether a specific car meets the criteria. In terms of cost, Car A may be initially cheaper than Car B but may get lower gas mileage and have a higher frequency-of-repair record. In this match argument, the family would be arguing over whether Car A or Car B best meets the low-cost criterion.

FOR WRITING AND DISCUSSION

Establishing and Applying Criteria

Whenever you evaluate something, you first need to establish criteria—that is, for any given class of items, you have to determine the qualities, traits, behaviors, or features that constitute excellence for members of that class. Then you need to match those criteria to a single member of that class—the thing you are evaluating. The following simple exercise will give you practice in thinking in this systematic, two-stage way:

1. Working individually, make a list of criteria that are important to you in choosing a career. These criteria are apt to differ from person to person. Some people might place "high income" at the top of their list, while others might put "prestige," "leadership opportunities," "adventure," "being outdoors," or "time for family and leisure" at the top. Then rank your criteria from highest to lowest priority.
2. Share your criteria lists in small groups or as a whole class. Then write on the chalkboard two or three representative lists of criteria.
3. Finally, write several different careers on the board and match them to the lists of criteria. Which possible careers come out on top for you? Which ones come out on top based on the criteria lists placed on the board? Possible careers to consider include these: grade school/high school teacher, lawyer, auto mechanic, airplane pilot, bus driver, military officer, hedge fund manager, engineer, computer technician, insurance salesperson, accountant, small business owner, plumber, commercial artist, homemaker, nurse/physician/dentist, chiropractor/optometrist, social worker, police officer.
4. When disagreements arise, try to identify whether they are disagreements about criteria or disagreements about the facts of a given career.

The Role of Purpose and Context in Determining Criteria

Ordinarily, criteria are based on the purpose of the class to which the thing being evaluated belongs. For example, if you asked a professor to write a recommendation for you, he or she would need to know what you were applying for—A scholarship? Internship in a law office? Peace Corps volunteer? Summer job in a national park? The qualities of a successful law office intern differ substantially from those of a successful Peace Corps worker in Uganda. The recommendation isn't about you in the abstract but about you fulfilling the purposes of the class "law office intern" or "Peace Corps volunteer." Similarly, if you were evaluating a car, you would need to ask, "a car for what purpose?"—Reliable family transportation? Social status (if so, what social group?)? Environmental friendliness?

Decisions about purpose are often affected by context. For example, a union member, in buying a car, might specify an American-made car while a subscriber to *Mother Jones* magazine might specify high gas mileage and low pollution. To see how context influences criteria, consider a recent review of Seattle's soup kitchens appearing in a newspaper produced by homeless people. In most contexts, restaurant reviews focus on the quality of food. But in this review the highest criterion was the sense of dignity and love extended to homeless people by the staff.

FOR WRITING AND DISCUSSION

Working with Purpose and Criteria

1. Working in small groups or as a whole class, decide how you would evaluate a local eatery as a place to study. How would you evaluate it as a place to take a date, a place to hang out with friends, or a place to buy a nutritious meal?
2. As a whole class or in small groups, discuss how this individual exercise helped you realize how criteria for excellence vary when you place the same item into different classes with different purposes.

Other Considerations in Establishing Criteria

Establishing the criteria for evaluation arguments can entail other considerations besides purpose and context. We examine these considerations in this section.

The Problem of Apples and Oranges

To create meaningful evaluations, you need to avoid the problem of mixing apples and oranges. Try to place the thing you are evaluating into the smallest applicable class. That way, apples compete only with other apples, not with other members of the next-larger class, "fruit," where they have to go head-to-head against bananas, peaches, and oranges. You would therefore evaluate Kobe Bryant against other basketball players rather than against golfers and race car drivers. And if you were to evaluate a less talented basketball player, you might do so within the subclass of "point guard" or "power forward" or "off-the-bench scorer" rather than the general class "basketball player."

The Problem of Standards: What's Commonplace Versus What's Ideal

When we determine criteria, we often encounter the problem of what's commonplace versus what's ideal. Do we praise something because it is better than average, or do we condemn it because it is less than ideal? Do we hold it to absolute standards or to common practice? Do we censure someone for paying a housekeeper under the table to avoid taxes (failure to live up to an ideal), or do we overlook this behavior because it is so common? Is it better for high schools to pass out free contraceptives because teenagers are having sex anyway (what's *commonplace*), or is it better not to pass them out in order to support abstinence (what's *ideal*)?

There is no easy way to decide which standard to use. The problem with the "ideal" is that nothing may ever measure up. The problem with the "commonplace" is that we may lower our standards and slip into a morally dangerous relativism. In deciding which standard to follow, we need to recognize the limitations of each, to make the best choice we can, and to use the same standard for all items being evaluated.

The Problems of Necessary, Sufficient, and Accidental Criteria

In identifying criteria, we often recognize that some are more important than others. Suppose you said, "I will be happy with any job as long as it puts food on my table and gives me time for my family." In this case the criteria "adequate income" and "time for family," taken together, are *sufficient,* meaning that once these criteria are met, the thing being rated meets your standard for excellence. Suppose you said instead, "I am hard to please in my choice of a career, which must meet many criteria. But I definitely will reject any career that doesn't put enough food on my table or allow me time for my family." In this case the criteria of "adequate income" and "time for family" are *necessary* but not *sufficient,* meaning that these two criteria have to be met for a career to meet your standards, but that other criteria must be met also.

Besides necessary and sufficient criteria, there are also *accidental* criteria, which are added bonuses but not essential. For example, you might say something like, "Although it's not essential, having a career that would allow me to be outside a lot would be nice." In this case "being outside" is an *accidental* criteria (nice but not required).

The Problem of Seductive Empirical Measures

Empirical data can help you evaluate all sorts of things. If you are buying an automobile, you can be helped a great deal by knowing the numbers for its horsepower and acceleration, for its fuel economy and frequency-of-repair record, and for its potential resale value. But sometimes the need to make defensible evaluative decisions leads people to empirical measures that disastrously oversimplify complex matters. Every year, for example, new crops of potential professional athletes are scrutinized minutely for their records in the forty-yard dash, the bench press, the vertical jump, and so forth. Every year, some of the people who max out on these empirical measures flop ingloriously in actual competition because they lack qualities that are difficult if not impossible to measure empirically, whereas other athletes, with more modest scores, achieve great success thanks to these same invisible qualities.

Quantifiable measures can be helpful, of course. But they are so concrete and they make comparisons so easy that they can seduce you into believing that you can make complex judgments by comparing numbers. It's all too easy to fall into the trap of basing college admissions on SAT scores, scholarships on grade point averages, or the success of a government policy on tax dollars saved.

The Problem of Cost

A final problem in establishing criteria is cost. A given X may be far superior to any other Xs in its class, but it may also cost far more. Before you move from evaluating an X to acting on your evaluation (by buying, hiring, or doing X), you must consider cost, whether it is expressed as dollars, time, or lost opportunity. There's little question, for example, that a Lexus is superior to a Nissan Sentra according to most automotive criteria. But are the differences sufficient to justify the additional thirty thousand or so dollars that the Lexus costs?

Using a Planning Schema to Develop Evaluation Arguments

In Chapter 14, we showed you how to use a planning schema to develop ideas for an argument (pp. 390–391). The schema encourages writers to articulate their argument frame (each reason and the underlying assumption that links the reason back to the claim) and then to imagine what kinds of evidence could be used to support both the reason and the underlying assumption. Equally important, the schema encourages writers to anticipate counterarguments by imagining how skeptical readers might object to the writers' reasons or underlying assumptions or both.

Let's say that you are the student member of a committee to select a professor for an outstanding teaching award. Several members of the committee want to give the award to Professor M. Mouse, a popular sociology professor at your institution. You are opposed. One of your lines of reasoning is that Professor Mouse's courses aren't rigorous. Here is how you could develop this line of reasoning using the planning schema explained in Chapter 14.

CLAIM WITH REASON

Professor Mouse does not deserve the teaching award because his courses aren't rigorous.

EVIDENCE TO SUPPORT THE REASON

I need to provide evidence that his courses aren't rigorous. From the dean's office records, I have discovered that eighty percent of his students get As or high Bs; a review of his syllabi shows that he requires little outside reading and only one short paper; he has a reputation in my dorm of being fun and easy.

UNDERLYING ASSUMPTION (CRITERION)

Having rigorous academic standards is a necessary criterion for the university teaching award.

EVIDENCE/ARGUMENTS TO SUPPORT THE ASSUMPTION

I need to show why I think rigorous academic standards are necessary. Quality of teaching should be measured by the amount that students learn. Good teaching is more than a popularity contest. Good teachers draw high-level performance from their students and motivate them to put time and energy into learning. High standards lead to the development of skills that are demanded in society.

WAYS SKEPTICS MIGHT OBJECT

How could someone attack my reason and evidence? Might a person say that Mouse has high standards? Could someone show that students really earned the high grades? Are the students I talked to not representative? Could someone say that Mouse's workload and grading patterns meet or exceed the commonplace behavior of faculty in his department?

How could someone attack my underlying assumption? Could someone argue that rigorous academic standards aren't as important as other criteria—that this is an accidental not a necessary criterion? Could a person say that Mouse's goal—to inspire interest in sociology—is best achieved by not loading students down with too many papers and too much reading, which can appear to be busywork? (I'll need to refute this argument.) Could someone say that the purpose of giving the university teaching award is public relations and it is therefore important to recognize widely popular teachers who will be excellent speakers at banquets and other public forums?

Conducting an Evaluation Argument: An Extended Example

Now that we have explored some potential difficulties in establishing and defending criteria for an evaluation, let's consider in more detail the process of making an evaluation argument.

The student examples in this section focus on the evaluation of a rock and roll museum in Seattle, Washington, called Experience Music Project (EMP). Designed by world-famous architect Frank Gehry (who is known for his creation of the Guggenheim Museum in Bilbao, Spain, the Aerospace Hall in Los Angeles, and other famous buildings around the world), EMP was sponsored by Microsoft cofounder Paul Allen as a tribute to rock singer Jimi Hendrix and to rock music itself. In Figure 15.5, you can see this innovative structure, which has sparked much controversy (is it a wonder or an eyesore?). Sharing some characteristics with the Rock and Roll Hall of Fame and Museum in Cleveland, Ohio, EMP features some permanent exhibits—the Hendrix Gallery, the Guitar Gallery (tracing the development of guitars from the 1500s to the electric guitars of today), Milestones (including displays from rhythm and blues to hip-hop and current rap artists), and Northwest Passage (focusing on popular music in Seattle, from jazz and rhythm and blues to heavy metal, punk, grunge, and the contemporary music scene). EMP also includes Sound Lab (where visitors can play instruments using interactive technology), On Stage (where visitors can pretend to be rock stars playing before a cheering crowd), Artist's Journey (a ride involving motion platform technology), three restaurants, and a store. (To see for yourself what EMP is and how it looks on the inside, you can

FIGURE 15.5 Experience Music Project, Seattle, Washington

go to its Web site at www.emplive.com. A Web search on Frank Gehry will show you photos of his prizewinning architecture.)

Let's now turn to the specific steps of making an evaluation argument.

Step 1: Determining the Class to Which X Belongs and the Purposes of that Class

When you conduct an evaluation argument, you must first assign your person/object/phenomenon (the X you are evaluating) to a category or class and then determine the purposes of that class. Often people disagree about an evaluation because they disagree about the arguer's choice of category for X. EMP, as students soon discovered, could be placed in several different categories, leading to different criteria for evaluation. Here are typical classes proposed by students:

- A tourist attraction (for an audience of visitors to Seattle)
- A museum of rock history (for people interested in the development of rock as an art form)
- A rock and roll shrine (for rock fans who want to revere their favorite artists and feel part of the rock scene for a day)

Clearly these classes have different purposes. The purpose of a tourist attraction is to offer a unique, fun place to spend the day during a visit to Seattle. The purpose of a rock museum is to teach about the history of its subject in an informative, interesting, and accessible way. The purpose of a rock and roll shrine is to honor famous rock stars, bring visitors into their lives and work, and let them experience the music scene.

Step 2: Determining and Weighting Criteria

The criteria for your evaluation are directly connected to the purposes of the class to which X belongs. The following lists show typical criteria chosen by different students for each of the classes listed in Step 1:

A good *tourist attraction* should
- be entertaining and enjoyable.
- be affordable and worth the price, not simply out to gouge tourists' wallets.
- be unique—something tourists wouldn't find in another city.

A good *museum of rock history* should
- have a clear, well-organized layout that is easy to navigate.
- display objects of clear aesthetic or historical significance.
- teach the public by providing clear, meaningful information about rock music.
- arouse interest in rock as an art form and encourage the public's appreciation and involvement.

A good *rock and roll shrine* should
- take fans up close and personal into the lives of major artists.
- encourage fans to appreciate the complexity of rock and the skills of artists.
- help fans experience the rock scene and fantasize about being rock stars themselves.

In addition to identifying criteria, you should arrange them in order of importance so that you build to your most important criterion. In each of the preceding examples, students placed their most important criterion last.

Step 3: Determining the Extent to Which X Meets Your Criteria for the Class

A third step in constructing an evaluation argument is to make your match argument: To what extent does X meet or not meet the criteria you have formulated? The following examples show how three students framed the match part of their evaluation arguments on EMP. Note how each student matches EMP to the specific criteria he or she has selected.

Experience Music Project is a tourist trap rather than an attraction because
- the headphones and heavy computerized MEGs (Museum Exhibit Guides) keep everyone isolated, making companionship difficult.
- the arrangement of exhibits is chaotic, leading to frustration and repetition of the same experiences.
- it doesn't give any substance, just endless music trivia.
- it's too expensive and commercial, leaving the tourist feeling ripped-off.

Experience Music Project is a good museum of rock and roll history because
- it covers a range of popular music styles from jazz and blues to reggae, punk, grunge, and hip-hop.
- it provides interesting information on musicians, musical styles, and key moments in popular music history.
- it makes people excited about popular music and its history through the museum's interactive exhibits and technologically advanced museum guide devices.

For rock fans, Experience Music Project is a good rock and roll shrine because

- it gives illuminating insights into the lives and artistry of many rock musicians.
- it gives an in-depth look at some of the greats like Jimi Hendrix and helps fans really appreciate the talent of these musicians.
- the "onstage" room lets fans fulfill a fantasy by pretending they are rock stars.

Step 4: Determining What Alternative Views You Must Respond to in Your Evaluation Argument

Finally, in constructing your evaluation argument you need to determine whether your intended audience is likely to object to (1) the class in which you have placed your object; (2) the criteria you have developed for assessing your object; or (3) the degree to which your object matches the criteria you have chosen. You have numerous options for accommodating your audience's doubts or objections. For example, if your proposed class is controversial, you might choose to justify it in your introduction. If your criteria might be controversial, you could address objections before you start the match part of your argument. If you think your match argument will raise doubts, you could intersperse alternative views throughout or treat them separately near the end of your argument. Any of these methods can work.

In the Readings section of this chapter, we include a student writer's complete evaluation argument on the Experience Music Project.

FOR WRITING AND DISCUSSION

Responding to Objections

Consider how student writer Katie Tiehen confronts and responds to alternative views. After reading this typical passage from her argument, answer the questions that follow:

> ... Some may challenge my contention that EMP is an ineffective museum of rock history by arguing that a day spent at EMP is entertaining and fun. I'll be the first to admit that EMP is fun. From a rock and roll fan's perspective, EMP is nonstop entertainment, a musical paradise. I felt like a five-year-old on Christmas morning when I saw Eric Clapton's guitar, Jimi Hendrix's personal journals, and walls plastered in punk memorabilia. These items, coupled with video documentaries and hands-on activities, provided hours of enjoyment. Because of the fun factor, it's easy for people to jump of EMP's defense. However, it is not the entertainment value of EMP that I am questioning. There's no doubt that it is a fun and amusing place to visit. The problem arises when one tries to classify EMP as an historical museum, which should provide visitors with access to objects of lasting historical significance. Some entertainment is fine, but not to the point that it clouds the true purpose of the museum as it does in EMP's case. After two visits, I still couldn't tell you where rock and roll originated, but I could tell you that the line to play the drums in Sound Lab is really long. Entertainment is the main purpose of EMP and it shouldn't be.

(continued)

1. What objections to her argument does Katie anticipate (doubts about her proposed class for EMP, her criteria, or her match argument)?
2. How does Katie respond to alternative views—by conceding points and shifting back to her own perspective or by refuting alternative views with counterreasons and counterexamples?

WRITING PROJECT An Evaluation Argument

Write an argument in which you use evaluative thinking to persuade your audience to see the value (or lack of value) of the person, place, thing, event, or phenomenon that you are evaluating. The introduction to your argument should hook your audience's interest in your evaluation question. The body of your argument should establish criteria for evaluating your chosen subject, and then show how your subject meets or does not meet the criteria. Depending on the degree of controversy surrounding your subject, follow the procedure for other arguments by summarizing alternative views and responding to them through either concession or refutation.

For this assignment you need to pose an evaluative question that is important to your audience and invites multiple views. This question can arise from any of the various communities to which you belong: family, school, work, social or religious communities, or the civic communities of town, city, region, or nation. For example: What telephone plan (automobile, method of paying for your college education, day care facility) is best for your family? How effective is your school's intramural sports program, service-learning program, writing center, online registration system? How effective is your employer's incentive program (office layout, customer relations office, dress code)? Is establishing a national ID system or profiling airline passengers a good way to combat terrorism? Which movie deserves an Academy Award? Is art therapy a valuable contribution to clinical psychological practice?

In some cases, you may choose to evaluate a controversial person, event, thing, or phenomenon—something that engenders lively disagreement within a particular community. (For example: Is "Nimbletoes" Nelson a good quarterback?) When your subject is controversial, you need to consider alternative evaluations and show why yours is better.

In other cases, you may choose to evaluate something that is not directly controversial. Your purpose might be to help a specific audience determine how to spend their time or money. For example, is taking an art gallery walk a good way for students to spend a Saturday afternoon in your city? You might consider writing your evaluation for a specific forum. For example, you might write a review for a parents magazine evaluating whether the *Harry Potter* movies are good family films. Or you might write an editorial for your school newspaper explaining why tutoring with the local children's literacy project is a good experience for education majors.

Generating and Exploring Ideas

For your evaluation essay, you will try either to change your readers' assessment of a controversial person, event, thing, or phenomenon or help your readers decide whether an event or thing is worth their time or money.

If you have not already chosen an evaluation issue, try thinking about evaluative questions within the various communities to which you belong:

Local civic community: evaluative questions about transportation, land use, historical monuments, current leaders, political bills or petitions, housing, parking policies, effectiveness of police

National civic community: evaluative questions about public education, environmental concerns, economic policies, responses to terrorism, Supreme Court decisions, foreign policies, political leaders

Your university community: evaluative questions about academic or sports programs, campus life programs, first-year or transfer student orientation, clubs, dorm life, campus facilities, financial-aid programs, campus security, parking, cultural programs

Your scholarly community or disciplinary community in your major: evaluative questions about internships, study abroad programs, general studies programs, course requirements, first-year studies, major curriculum, advising, course sequences, teaching methods, homework requirements, academic standards, recent books or articles, new theories in a field, library resources, laboratory facilities, Web site sources of primary documents or numerical data in a field

Culture and entertainment issues within your social or family communities: evaluative questions about restaurants, movies, plays, museums, TV shows, musicians, video games, entertainment Web sites, concerts, books, paintings, sports figures, buildings

Consumer issues within your social or family communities: evaluative questions about computer systems, CDs, cars, clothing brands, stores, products, e-commerce

Work communities: Evaluative questions about supervisors or subordinates, office efficiency, customer relations, advertising and marketing, production or sales, record keeping and finance, personnel policies

Another good strategy for finding a topic is to think about a recent review or critique with which you disagree—a movie or restaurant review, a sportswriter's assessment of a team or player, an op-ed column or blog assessing a government official or proposed legislation. How would you evaluate this controversial subject differently?

Once you have chosen a possible controversial topic, use the following strategies to help you explore and develop ideas for your evaluation argument.

STRATEGIES

for Developing an Evaluative Claim

Strategies	Questions to Ask and Steps to Follow
Place the X you will evaluate in the smallest and most meaningful category for your intended audience.	For the audience you have in mind, what is the smallest, most relevant class in which to place your X? For example, Is Super Eye 2000 a good digital camera *for novices on a low-cost budget* (not simply, is it a good digital camera)?
Determine the criteria you will use to make your evaluation meaningful and helpful to your audience.	What are the purposes of the class in which you have placed your subject? Use freewriting or idea mapping to explore the qualities a member of that class needs to have to achieve those purposes.
Think about the objections to your criteria your audience might raise.	How will you justify your criteria? What reasoning and evidence will you use?
Think about how you will weight or rank your criteria.	Which of your criteria is most important and why?
Evaluate your subject by matching it to each of your criteria.	Why does your subject match or not match each of the criteria? Freewrite to find examples and counterexamples.

Shaping and Drafting

In drafting your evaluation argument, you have two key developmental and organizational questions to consider: (1) Will you have to defend your choice of criteria as well as complete the match part of your argument? (2) Where should you locate and respond to alternative views? Your answers to these questions will depend on your specific evaluation claim and on your audience. In the readings at the end of this chapter, you will notice that student writers Jackie Wyngaard (pp. 440–441) and Teresa Filice (pp. 444–446) chose different approaches to handling alternative views. We recommend that you consider trying different organizations for your evaluation argument. The framework chart shown in Figure 15.6 is a good place to start.

FIGURE 15.6 Framework for an Evaluation Argument

Introduction	• Presents your issue • Shows why evaluating X is problematic or controversial • Presents your evaluation claim and your criteria
Argument	• States criterion 1 and defends it if necessary • Shows that X meets/does not meet criterion 1 • States criterion 2 and defends it if necessary • Shows that X meets/does not meet criterion 2 • Continues with additional criteria and match arguments
Treatment of alternative or opposing views	• Summarizes objections to your criteria or your match • Responds to these objections
Conclusion	• Sums up your evaluation

Revising

As you revise, think of ways that you can make your evaluation clearer and more useful for your audience. Consider ways to sharpen your criteria and build up the match part of your argument to make your evaluation more persuasive.

Questions for Peer Review

In addition to the generic peer review questions explained in Chapter 17, Skill 4, ask your peer reviewers to address these questions:

INTRODUCTION

1. How well do the title and introduction capture your interest, provide needed background, and identify the controversy or importance of the subject?
2. How well has the writer established the evaluative question, the claim, and the criteria? How could these be improved?

THE CRITERIA-MATCH ARGUMENT

3. How fitting and persuasive is the writer's choice of criteria for evaluating this subject? How could the writer support or defend his/her criteria and the weighting of those criteria more clearly or persuasively?
4. How does the writer support and develop the match part of the argument? What evidence helps readers see that the X being evaluated meets or fails to meet each criterion? How could the writer improve the match argument?
5. Where does the writer summarize and address alternative views? How could this treatment of alternative views be improved?

READINGS

The first reading is a student essay by Jackie Wyngaard evaluating the Experience Music Project in Seattle, Washington.

Jackie Wyngaard (student)

EMP:

Music History or Music Trivia?

1 Along with other college students new to Seattle, I wanted to see what cultural opportunities the area offers. I especially wanted to see billionaire Paul Allen's controversial Experience Music Project (known as EMP), a huge, bizarre, shiny, multicolored structure that is supposed to resemble a smashed guitar. Brochures say that EMP celebrates the creativity of American popular music, but it has prompted heated discussions among architects, Seattle residents, museumgoers, and music lovers, who have questioned its commercialism and the real value of its exhibits. My sister recommended this museum to me because she knows I am a big music lover and a rock and roll fan. Also, as an active choir member since the sixth grade, I have always been intrigued by the history of music. I went to EMP expecting to learn more about music history from exhibits that showed a range of popular musical styles, that traced historical connections and influences, and that enjoyably conveyed useful information. However, as a museum of rock history, EMP is a disappointing failure.

2 EMP claims that it covers the history of rock and roll from its roots to the styles of today, but it fails at this task because it isolates musicians and styles without explaining historical progressions or cultural influences. For instance, the museum doesn't show how Elvis Presley's musical style was influenced by his predecessors like Chuck Berry and Muddy Waters. It doesn't show how early folk and blues influenced Bob Dylan's music. It doesn't show how early jazz paved the way for rock and roll. How are these isolated and separate EMP exhibits connected? How did rock and roll progress from the '50s "Let's Go to the Hop" beats to the laid-back guitar riffs of the '60s and '70s? How did '70s music become the heavy metal, head-banger rock of the '80s and '90s? How did these styles lead to rap? The exhibits show the existence of these different styles, but they don't help viewers understand the historical developments or historical context. While it is interesting to see a peace patch once owned by Janis Joplin, this exhibit does not explain either the social and political events of the time or Joplin's political views.

3 Another fault of EMP is that it omits many influential groups and musicians, particularly women. For example, there is no display about the Beatles, the Rolling Stones, Led Zeppelin, or the Doors. The exhibits also exclude many major female artists who made substantial contributions to popular music. I found nothing about Joan Baez, Ella Fitzgerald, Aretha Franklin, Carly Simon, or Joni Mitchell. I was also surprised that there were few women mentioned in the Northwest Passage exhibit. Weren't more women involved in the Seattle music scene? As a woman interested in music, I felt left out by EMP's overall neglect of women musicians.

4 Perhaps most frustrating about EMP is the way exhibits are explained through the awkward, difficult-to-use handheld computer called a Museum Exhibit Guide (MEG).

The explanations are hard to access and then disappointing in their content. I wanted to hear a landmark song that an artist wrote or an interesting analysis of the artist's musical style. Instead, I listened to "how Elvis made the leather jacket famous" and other random trivia. The MEG also offers too many choices for each exhibit, like a Web page with a dozen links. But after all the time and effort, you learn nothing that increases your understanding or stimulates your thinking about music history. The MEGs themselves are very heavy, clunky, and inconvenient. If you don't point this gadget exactly at the activator, nothing happens. It took me a good ten minutes to figure out how to get the device to play information for me, and many of my classmates had to keep going back to the booth to get new batteries or other repairs. The museum would be much more effective if visitors had the option of just reading about the displays from plaques on the walls.

5 I know that many people will disagree with my assessment of EMP. They'll point to the fun of the interactive exhibits and the interesting collection of album covers, crushed velvet costumes, concert clips, famous guitars, and old jukeboxes. But a good museum has to be more than a display of artifacts and an array of hands-on activities. Pretending you're a rock star by performing on stage with instruments doesn't tell you how a certain style of music came about. Displaying trivial information about Elvis's leather jacket or Janis Joplin's feather boa doesn't help you appreciate the importance of their music. Devoting half an exhibit to punk rock without any analysis of that style doesn't teach you anything. In short, the museum displays frivolous trivia tidbits without educational substance.

6 Music lovers hoping for an educational experience about the rock and roll era of musical history will be disappointed by EMP. And this is without the additional insult of having to shell out $19.95 to get in the door. Speaking for serious music lovers and students of music history, I have to say that EMP is a failure.

THINKING CRITICALLY
about "EMP: Music History or Music Trivia?"

1. What strategies particularly appropriate for evaluation arguments does Jackie Wyngaard use in her introduction?
2. How has Jackie chosen to classify Experience Music Project? What criteria does she choose?
3. In the match part of her argument, what evidence does Jackie use to support her assessment of Experience Music Project?
4. What alternative views does she acknowledge and where in her argument does she choose to treat them? Does she anticipate objections to her criteria or to the match part of her argument? What other objections might people raise to her argument?
5. What do you find persuasive about her arguments? How might this evaluation argument be improved?

The second reading aims at changing its readers' assessment of the children's television program *Sesame Street.* It posits just one criterion—a good children's program should not be sexist—and then focuses exclusively on demonstrating that *Sesame Street* is sexist. Its authors are both attorneys and mothers of young children.

Diane Helman and Phyllis Bookspan

Sesame Street:

Brought to You by the Letters M-A-L-E

1 A recent report released by the American Association of University Women, "How Schools Shortchange Women," finds that teachers, textbooks, and tests are, whether intentionally or unintentionally, giving preferential treatment to elementary-school boys. As a result, girls who enter school with equal or better academic potential than their male counterparts lose confidence and do not perform as well.

2 An earlier study about law students, published in the *Journal of Legal Education,* found a similar disparity. "Gender Bias in the Classroom" found that male law students are called upon in class more frequently than females, speak for longer periods of time, and are given more positive feedback by law professors.

3 The article raised some disturbing questions about whether women and men receive truly equal education in American law schools.

4 Unfortunately, this insidious gender bias appears long before our children enter school and pervades even the television show *Sesame Street.* Yes, *Sesame Street* is sexist! But, just as in the story of the emperor and his new clothes, many of us do not notice the obvious.

5 The puppet stars of the show, Bert and Ernie, and all the other major *Sesame Street* animal characters—Big Bird, Cookie Monster, Grover, Oscar the Grouch, Kermit the Frog, and Mr. Snuffleupagus—are male. Among the secondary characters, including Elmo, Herry Monster, Count VonCount, Telly Monster, Prairie Dawn, and Betty Lou, only a very few are girls.

6 The female Muppets always play children, while the males play adult parts in various scenes. In a recently aired skit "Squeal of Fortune," this disparity is evident when the host of the show introduces the two contestants. Of Count VonCount of Transylvania the host asks, "What do you do for a living?" to which the count responds authoritatively, "I count!" Of Prairie Dawn, he inquires, "And how do you spend your day?" Sure, it would be silly to ask a schoolgirl what she does for a living. But none of the female Muppets on *Sesame Street* are even old enough to earn a living.

7 Further, almost all the baby puppet characters on *Sesame Street* are girls. For example, Snuffie's sibling is Baby Alice; in books, Grover's baby cousin is a girl, and when Herry Monster's mother brings home the new baby—it's a girl. Since babies are totally dependent and fairly passive, the older (male) relatives take care of them and provide leadership.

8 Also, the female Muppets almost never interact with each other. In sharp contrast, consequential and caring friendships have been fully developed between male

Muppets: Ernie and Bert; Big Bird and Snuffie; even Oscar the Grouch and his (male) worm, Squirmy.

9 Any parent of toddlers or preschoolers can testify that the "girls" on *Sesame Street* are not very popular. Children ask their parents for Bert and Ernie dolls, not Baby Alice. Is this just because the girls are not marketed via books, tapes, placemats and toy dolls the same way the boys are? Or is it that the *Sesame Street* writers simply have not developed the girls into the same types of lovable, adorable personalities that belong to the main characters?

10 Interestingly and peculiarly, the minor "girls" look more human than most of the well-loved animal roles. They are not physically cuddly, colorful or bizarre, as are the more important male characters. Prairie Dawn has ordinary blonde hair and brown eyes—nothing even remotely similar to Big Bird's soft yellow feathers or Cookie Monster's wild, bright blue, mane.

11 Yes, we believe that *Sesame Street* is one of the best shows on television for small children. Our children—boys and girls—are regular viewers. In addition to its educational value, lack of violence and emphasis on cooperation, the adult characters on the show are admirably balanced in terms of avoiding sexual stereotypes.

12 But even the best of the bunch has room for improvement. Just as elementary through professional school educators must learn to be more sensitive to subtle and unintentional gender bias, so too should the folks at Children's Television Network. We can stop sexism from seeping into our children's first "formal" educational experience.

13 The message was brought to you by the letter F: fairness for females.

THINKING CRITICALLY
about "Sesame Street"

1. This essay spends no time on the criteria part of the argument ("Sexism is bad") and all its time on the match argument ("*Sesame Street* exhibits sexism"). Why do the authors feel no need to defend the criterion?
2. Do the authors convince you that *Sesame Street* is sexist?
3. If you agree with the argument that *Sesame Street* is sexist, should that criterion be sufficient for undermining the popular assessment of *Sesame Street* as a model educational program for children?

The final reading, an essay by student writer Teresa Filice, uses the criteria for evaluating Web sites found in Chapter 21, Skill 26—authority, objectivity or clear disclosure of advocacy, coverage, accuracy, and currency—to evaluate the site Parents: the Anti-Drug (www.theantidrug.com). Although an evaluation of material on the Internet could focus on the home page or even on one link of a Web site, Teresa has chosen to examine whether this advocacy site as a whole accomplishes its purposes effectively.

Teresa Filice

Parents: The Anti-Drug: A Useful Site

1 The United States' War on Drugs seems to make little progress, and the drug use of American teenagers remains a rampant problem; however, positive, forward-thinking groups have risen to the occasion and sought to meet the challenge, as anyone who listens to radio ads or reads popular news magazines will testify. While the Reagan-sponsored "Just say no" mantra toward drugs still prevails in some households, some anti-drug organizations are promoting open and honest communication between parents and their teens. These groups offer information and fresh perspectives on helping parents talk to their children about illegal substances. In my exploration of how the Web has been enlisted in this campaign against teen drug use, I chose to analyze the site of *Parents: The Anti-Drug* to determine if it is a good advocacy Web site. My evaluation employed the following well-accepted criteria: the breadth of coverage, the accuracy and currency of the information provided, and the site's openness about its mission, goals, and supporters. Despite some strong misgivings in the disclosure area of the Web site, I concluded that it is still a worthwhile advocacy site on the topic of teens and drug prevention, specifically in regards to the current, extensive information it provides on teens and drug use.

2 Initially, I had difficulty discovering what organizations and special interest groups were sponsoring this site, so the site failed to meet the criterion of clear disclosure of advocacy or objectivity. After clicking on the "About Us" link (which was fairly difficult to find), I found out that the site jumps to another Web site for the *Media Campaign*, sponsored by the Office of National Drug Control Policy (http://www.mediacampaign.org). The Office of National Drug Control Policy is a government sponsored organization, and the Media Campaign site contains links to the White House Web site. Though *Parents: The Anti-Drug* and the *Media Campaign* Web sites are not outrightly politically biased, further scrutiny reveals glimpses of the current conservative political administration in both sites. There is an entire section of *Parents: The Anti-Drug* dedicated to faith leaders and faith-based activities to keep teens away from illegal substances.

3 In addition, I noticed that this advocacy organization's site speaks about and to parents and teens in a traditional, middle-class family setting and therefore limits its coverage and usefulness. Most of the advice the site offers is based on the fact that teens will have parents with enough time (which often means money as well) to spend with them. While most parents may want to spend quality time with their children, many American parents literally cannot afford time for their children. The site also constantly refers to life in the suburbs and suburban values. One of the boys in the Prescription video states, "I couldn't be a drug addict ... I'm from the suburbs." In addition, some of the advice given to parents seems simplistic and unrealistic. For example, the site offers somewhat unrealistic suggestions for "summer activities" for parents to keep their children out of dangerous situations where drugs might be present: "Encourage them to write a song, and then let them record it; build, and maintain a birdfeeder; encourage them to paint a mural; and make homemade ice cream together" (http://www.theantidrug.com/SchoolsOut/activity_checklist.asp?action=form).

This site seems to be imagining a specific, limited audience with somewhat old-fashioned values.

4 Despite these flaws and this one area of narrowness, *Parents: The Anti-Drug* has a wide range of information and appears committed to transmitting important factual material to viewers. The site provides an extensive breadth of coverage and accurate information on teen behavior, recreational drugs, and motivating factors for teen drug use. The home page of the site is divided into three panels: "Learn," "Evaluate," and "Take Action," each of which offers numerous links such as "Signs & Symptoms," "Hear Real Stories and Advice," and "Find Help Locally." The "Drug Information" page (http://www.theantidrug.com/drug_info/), which is easily accessible from the home page, offers comprehensive information on a wide variety of drugs, including more recent offenders such as prescription drugs and Ecstasy. In each subsequent section, the site presents basic drug information, the health risks, and the signs that a person might be using that drug. Additionally, each link for the various drugs offers further links with specifics about that drug. The site also has specific "Feature Articles" on topics such as "Keep Your Teen Athlete Drug-Free" and "Teens, Drugs, and Violence." The section on "Teens, Drugs, and Violence" contains documented scientific and social development statistics on the rates of teen drug use and violence. It also has links to other advocacy sites that target gang activity and bullying at school. The "Studies and Research" section (http://www.theantidrug.com/news/studies-and-research.aspx) lists several articles from well-respected medical journals such as the *Journal of Preventative Medicine* and the *American Journal of Public Health*, as well as presenting the authors' credentials. I concluded that the entire site provides well-documented sources for the statistics it uses.

5 *Parents: The Anti-Drug* also shows its worth by meeting the important criterion of currency. The site is surprisingly current and exemplifies a fairly progressive attitude toward and direct approach to drug prevention. *Parents: The Anti-Drug* favors discussion and open communication with teens, as opposed to criticizing their beliefs. The "Teens Today" section cheekily reminds parents that "teens today are less likely to drink, smoke, commit a crime, or get pregnant or drop out of school, compared to their parents' generation" (http://www.theantidrug.com/advice/inside-teens-today.asp). The "Kids Eye View" section provides a voice for the teens themselves, offers a glimpse as to why certain teenagers choose to engage in this activity, and includes video diaries. The site also uses videos to give it a sense of immediacy. For example, on the "Prescription Drug Abuse" video, a teenage girl with brown curly hair comes into focus on the screen. Her name is Sara and she is nineteen years old. She recalls for the camera her path toward prescription drug addiction that began in her own home. She says, "I could find them [prescriptions] in my kitchen cupboard ... My parents wouldn't notice it, without the smell of marijuana" (http://www.theantidrug.com/drug_info/prescription_video.asp). Most parents never want to see their children share this young woman's struggles with addiction, rehab, and the subsequent consequences of both. With material like these videos, this site shows its relevance and awareness of the urgency of the problem and offers helpful advice.

6 Although the site *Parents: The Anti-Drug* has some weaknesses, its strengths compensate well for these deficiencies. I spent many hours poring over the *Parents: The*

Anti-Drug Web site. It bothered me greatly that the site emphasized middle-class values and did not fully disclose its government sponsorship. However, after taking some time away from viewing the Web site, I decided to imagine what a visit to this site would mean to parents desperate to communicate with their child. This Web site provides numerous valuable recommendations and, most importantly, provides credible and ample information on a subject that many parents need to understand. Though the site may appear unrealistic in places to older teens, I think it does effectively reach its target group and does qualify as a good advocacy Web site.

Work Cited

Parents: The Anti-Drug. The National Youth Anti-Drug Media Campaign, n.d. Web. 20 May 2007.

THINKING CRITICALLY

about "*Parents: The Anti-Drug*: A Useful Site"

1. In her evaluation argument, Teresa Filice evaluates the advocacy site Parents: The Anti-Drug for its usefulness for parents. How might her evaluation criteria vary if she were evaluating this site for a different audience—for example, teens or the medical profession?
2. What opposing views does Teresa Filice acknowledge in her argument? How does she respond to them?
3. Where do examples work well to support the match part of her argument?
4. From your own use of advocacy Web sites, what evaluation criteria would you add to the typical ones listed here in the headnote, applied in this argument, and presented in more detail in Chapter 21, Skill 26?

PROPOSING A SOLUTION

CHAPTER 16

Proposal arguments call an audience to action. They make a claim that some action should or ought to be taken. Sometimes referred to informally as *should arguments,* proposals are among the most common kinds of arguments that you will write or read.

Some proposals aim to solve local, practical matters. For example, Rebekah Taylor's proposal in this chapter (pp. 472–476) advocates that campus stores carry products that are not tested on animals. Practical proposals generally target a specific audience (usually the person with the power to act on the proposal) and are typically introduced with a "letter of transmittal," in which the writer briefly summarizes the proposal, explains its purpose, and courteously invites the reader to consider it. In business and industry, effective practical proposals are crucial for financial success. For example, many kinds of businesses—construction and engineering firms, ad agencies, university research teams, nonprofit agencies, and others—generate most of their new revenue from effective, competitive proposals.

Another kind of proposal, often called a policy proposal, is aimed at more general audiences instead of specific decision makers. These proposals typically address issues of public policy with the aim of swaying public support toward the writer's proposed solution. Policy proposals might address the problems of prison overcrowding, out-of-control health care costs, national security and terrorism, and so forth. Typically, policy proposals require researched sources. Student writer Dylan Fujitani's proposal that the United States military not use civilian contractors in combat roles in Iraq illustrates a researched policy proposal (see pp. 479–483).

The power of proposal arguments can often be enhanced through visual images, which can appeal to both *logos* and *pathos.* In fact, proposal arguments sometimes take the form of striking visual-verbal texts such as posters or advocacy advertisements calling an audience to action. Because these arguments must be brief, catchy, clear, and lively, they often employ document design—fonts, layout, graphics, images, and color—to maximum advantage.

Additionally, proposal arguments are frequently delivered as speeches when, for example, a manager proposes a course of action to a board of directors or a citizen speaks for or against a proposal at an open-mike public hearing. In formal settings, a speaker's proposal can be enhanced visually by means of presentation software such as PowerPoint.* In fact, a PowerPoint presentation—when it is done well—can harness the forces of both verbal and visual argument. PowerPoint slides used by student writer Jane Kester in her proposal speech advocating campus workshops against high-risk drinking are shown in the Readings section of this chapter.

The writing projects for this chapter cover the range of genres just described:

- A written proposal—either a practical proposal or a researched policy proposal
- An advocacy advertisement or a poster calling for action
- A proposal speech with visual aids created through PowerPoint or other means.

No matter what genre you choose, when you make a proposal argument you must first determine whether the problem you are addressing is already known to your audience. If so, then written or spoken proposals can follow the shape of classical argument described in Chapter 14, in which you introduce the issue, present the claim, provide supporting reasons for the claim, summarize and respond to alternative views, and provide a conclusion. If you wrote an argument for Chapter 14, you may have chosen a proposal issue. A. J. Chavez's essay in that chapter, in which he argues that gay marriages should be legalized, is a proposal argument (see pp. 417–421).

In many cases, however, the problem you wish to address is not known to your audience (or the audience doesn't take the problem seriously). In effect, you must create the issue you wish to address by calling the readers' attention to the problem and then proposing and justifying a course of action. The rest of this chapter focuses on strategies for the second type of proposal, in which part of the arguer's task is to convince the audience that a problem exists, that it is serious, and that some action should be taken to resolve it.

Exploring Proposal Writing

The following activity introduces you to the thinking processes involved in writing a proposal argument.

1. In small groups, identify and list several major problems facing students in your college or university.
2. Decide among yourselves which problems are most important and rank them in order of importance.
3. Choose your group's number-one problem and explore answers to the following questions. Group recorders should be prepared to present answers to the class as a whole.
   a. Why is the problem a problem?
   b. For whom is the problem a problem?
   c. How will these people suffer if the problem is not solved? Give specific examples.

*PowerPoint, which is a registered trademark of Microsoft, has become the common name for all kinds of computer-created and -projected slides. However, other companies also make presentation software. We use the term "PowerPoint presentation" because its use has become ubiquitous in business and industry. We intend the term to include any kind of oral presentation supported by visual aids developed on presentation software. Most businesses and professions now expect new management-level hires to be adept at using presentation software in oral presentations.

d. Who has the power to solve the problem?
e. Why hasn't the problem been solved up to this point?
f. How can the problem be solved? Create a proposal for a solution.
g. What are the probable benefits of acting on your proposal?
h. What costs are associated with your proposal?
i. Who will bear these costs?
j. Why should this proposal be enacted?
k. What makes this proposal better than alternative proposals?

4. As a group, draft an outline for a proposal argument in which you do the following:
   a. Describe the problem and its significance.
   b. Propose your solution to the problem.
   c. Justify your proposal by showing how the benefits of adopting it outweigh the costs.
5. Recorders for each group should write the group's outline on the board and be prepared to present the group's argument orally to the class.

Understanding Proposal Writing

All proposals have one feature in common—they offer a solution to a problem. For every proposal, there is always an alternative course of action, including doing nothing. Your task as a proposal writer is threefold: You must demonstrate that a significant problem exists; propose a solution to the problem; and justify the solution, showing that benefits outweigh costs and that the proposed solution will fix the problem better than alternative solutions would. Accordingly, a proposal argument typically has three main parts:

1. *Description of the problem.* The description often begins with background. Where does the problem show up? Who is affected by the problem? How long has the problem been around? Is it getting worse? You may add an anecdote or some kind of startling information or statistics to give the problem presence. Typically, this section also analyzes the problem. What are its elements? What are its causes? Why hasn't it been solved before? Why are obvious solutions not adequate or workable? Finally, the description shows the problem's significance. What are the negative consequences of not solving the problem?
2. *Proposal for a solution.* This section describes your solution and shows how it would work. If you don't yet have a solution, you may choose to generate a planning proposal calling for a committee or task force to study the problem and propose solutions at a later date. The purpose of a planning proposal is to call attention to a serious problem. In most cases, however, this section should propose a detailed solution, showing step-by-step how it would solve the problem and at what cost.
3. *Justification.* Here you persuade your audience that your proposal should be enacted. Typically you show that the benefits of your proposal outweigh the costs. You also need to show why your proposed solution is better than alternative solutions. Point out why other possible approaches would not solve

the problem, would provide fewer benefits, or would cost significantly more than your proposed solution.

In the following sections, we look at some of the distinctive demands of proposal writing. We then show you a powerful strategy for developing the justification section of a proposal.

Special Demands of Proposal Arguments

To get the reader to take action—the ultimate purpose of a proposal—requires you to overcome some difficult challenges. Here we examine the special demands that proposal arguments make on writers and offer suggestions for meeting them.

Creating Presence

To convince readers that a problem really exists, you must give it *presence;* that is, you must help readers *see* and *feel* the problem. Writers often use anecdotes or examples of people suffering from the problem or cite startling facts or statistics to dramatize the problem. For example, a student proposing streamlined checkout procedures in the hotel where she worked gave presence to her problem by describing a family that missed its flight home because of a slow checkout line. Her description of this family's frustration—including angry complaints overheard by people waiting to check in—convinced her boss that the problem was worth solving. To persuade your readers to act on your proposal, you need to involved them both mentally *and* emotionally in your argument.

Appealing to the Interest and Values of Decision Makers

Proposal writers sometimes appeal directly to readers' idealism, urging them to do the right thing. But writers also need to show how doing the right thing converges with their readers' own best interests. Show decision makers how acting on your proposal will benefit *them* directly. The author of the hotel checkout proposal argued that her solution would enhance customer satisfaction, an idea that she knew her boss would find more compelling than the notion of making life easier for desk clerks.

Overcoming Inherent Conservatism

People are inherently resistant to change. One of the most famous proposals of all time, the Declaration of Independence, is notable for the way in which it anticipates its audience's resistance to change: "Prudence, indeed, will dictate that governments long established should not be changed for light and transient causes; and accordingly, all experience hath shown, that mankind are more disposed to suffer, while evils are sufferable, than to right themselves by abolishing the forms to which they are accustomed."

To restate this passage as folk wisdom, "Better the devil you know than the one you don't know." Most people expect the status quo to have its problems, flaws, and frustrations. They live with and adapt to familiar imperfections. Unless they can be persuaded that change will make things markedly better, they will "suffer, while evils are sufferable" rather than risk creating new, possibly insufferable evils.

The challenge of proving that something needs to be changed is compounded by the fact that the status quo often appears to be working. If its shortcomings were readily apparent, people would probably already have fixed them. It is much harder to stir an audience to action when the problem you depict entails lost potential (things could be better), rather than palpable evil (look at all the suffering).

Predicting Consequences

People also resist change because they fear unforeseen bad consequences and doubt predictions of good consequences. Everyone has experienced the disappointment of failed proposals: Your favorite sports team makes a major trade—and then does worse; a company you invested in went through a major reorganization—and promptly went into the red; voters elect a new leader who promises major reforms—and nothing happens. Although most people do not become true cynics, they are understandably cautious about accepting the rosy scenarios contained in most proposals.

The more uncertain your proposal's consequences, the more clearly you must show *how* the proposal will bring about those consequences. To persuade your audience that your predictions are realistic, identify the links in the chain and show how each one leads to the next. Whenever possible, cite similar proposals that yielded the sorts of results you are predicting.

Evaluating Consequences

Compounding the problem of predicting consequences is the difficulty of figuring out whether those consequences are good or bad and for whom. For example, any alternative to the current health care system will contain changes that simultaneously advantage one segment of your audience (say, patients) and disadvantage another (say, doctors, insurance companies, or taxpayers). Indeed, if any health care proposal benefited all segments of your audience, it would probably have been adopted long ago.

It can also be difficult to identify the appropriate standard of measurement to use in calculating a proposal's costs and benefits. Often you must try to balance benefits measured in apples against costs measured in oranges. For instance, suppose that a health care proposal will reduce the cost of insurance by limiting coverage. How would you balance the dollars saved on your insurance bill against the suffering of persons denied a potentially lifesaving medical procedure? Some cost-benefit analyses try to reduce all consequences to one scale of measure—usually money. This scale may work well in some circumstances, but it can lead to grotesquely inappropriate conclusions in others.

With these challenges in mind, we now set forth some strategies for making proposals as effective as possible.

Developing an Effective Justification Section

The distinctions between proposals and other kinds of arguments dictate a special variety of support for proposals. Experienced proposal writers often use a *three-strategy approach* to help them develop their justification sections. They brainstorm justifying reasons by focusing sequentially on principles, consequences, and precedents or analogies, as explained in the following strategies chart.

STRATEGIES for Developing a Justification Section

Strategies	What to Do	Templates and Comments	Examples
Argument from principle	Argue that an action should (should not) be taken because it is right (wrong) according to some value, assumption, principle, or belief you share with your audience.	We should (should not) do (this action) because (this action) is ______________. Fill in the blank with a belief or value that the audience holds: *good, honest, fair,* and so on.	"We should create publicly financed jobs for poor people because doing so is both charitable and just."
Argument from consequence	Argue that an action should (should not) be taken because doing so will lead to consequences that you and your audience think are good (bad).	We should (should not) do (this action) because (this action) will lead to these good (bad) consequences: ________, ________, and ________. Use consequences that your audience will agree are good or bad, as needed.	"We should create publicly financed jobs for poor people because doing so will provide them with money for food and housing, promote a work ethic, and produce needed goods and services."
Argument from precedent or analogy	Argue that an action should (should not) be taken because doing so is similar to what was done in another case, which turned out well (badly).	We should (should not) do (this action) because doing (this action) is like ________, which turned out to be good (bad). Use precedents or analogies that are similar to your proposed action and that will have good (bad) associations for your audience.	*Precedent:* "We should create publicly financed jobs for poor people because doing so will alleviate poverty just as a similar program has helped the poor in Upper Magnesia." *Analogy:* " ... because doing so is like teaching the poor how to fish rather than giving them fish."

Each of these argumentation strategies was clearly evident in a public debate in Seattle, Washington, over a proposal to raise county sales taxes to build a new baseball stadium. Those favoring the stadium put forth arguments such as these:

> We should build the new stadium because preserving our national pastime for our children is important (*argument from principle*), because building the stadium will create new jobs and revitalize the adjacent Pioneer Square district (*argument from consequence*), and because building the stadium will have the same beneficial effects on the city that building Camden Yards had in Baltimore (*argument from precedent*).

Those opposing the stadium created arguments using the same strategies:

> We should not build the stadium because it is wrong to subsidize rich owners and players with tax dollars (*argument from principle*), because building a stadium diverts tax money from more important concerns such as low-income housing (*argument from consequence*), and because Toronto's experience with Skydome shows that once the novelty of a new stadium wears off, attendance declines dramatically (*argument from precedent*).

FOR WRITING AND DISCUSSION

Using Different Strategies to Develop Support

Working individually or in small groups, use the strategies of principle, consequence, and precedent/analogy to create *because* clauses that support (or oppose) the following proposals. Try to have at least one *because* clause from each of the strategies, but generate as many reasons as possible.

Example:

Claim	Spanking children should be made illegal.
Principle	Because it is wrong to cause bodily pain to children.
Consequence	Because it teaches children that it is okay to hit someone out of anger; because it causes children to obey rules out of fear rather than respect; because it can lead children to be abusive parents.
Precedent/analogy	Because spanking a child is like throwing dishes or banging your fists against a wall—it relieves your anger but turns the child into an object.

1. The school year for grades K–12 should/should not be extended to eleven months.
2. "Enhanced interrogation techniques" (such as sleep deprivation, stressful positions, or water boarding) should/should not be used on suspected terrorists.
3. An impenetrable fence should/should not be built between the United States and Mexico.
4. Marijuana should/should not be legalized.
5. The federal government should/should not enact a substantially increased tax on gasoline.

FIGURE 16.1 A One-Page Advocacy Advertisement from a Magazine

WHITE KIDS ARE MUCH MORE LIKELY TO BE USING (AND SELLING) DRUGS!

CAN YOU FIND ANYTHING WRONG WITH THESE PICTURES??

According to the federal Centers for Disease Control, he's 4 times more likely than his African-American classmate to be a regular cocaine user.

White high-school students who are current users of cocaine: 4.1%[1]

Chance of a white person ever trying an illicit drug in their lifetime: 42%[2]

Percent of felony drug defendants in state courts who are white: 37%[3]

Percent of white drug felons given probation or nonincarceration sentence by state courts: 32%[4]

Percent of white drug felons sentenced to prison by state courts each year: 27%[5]

According to the Justice Department, if he's arrested on drug charges, he's 1-1/2 times more likely than his white classmate to be sent to prison.

African-American high-school students who are current users of cocaine: 1.1%[1]

Chance of an African-American person ever trying an illicit drug in their lifetime: 37.7%[2]

Percent of felony drug defendants in state courts who are black: 61%[3]

Percent of black drug felons given probation or nonincarceration sentence by state courts: 25%[4]

Percent of black drug felons sentenced to prison by state courts each year: 43%[5]

BLACK KIDS ARE MORE LIKELY TO GO TO PRISON!

Note:

According to the US Justice Department and the Office of National Drug Control Policy, drug users typically buy their drugs from sellers of their own racial or ethnic background. Research of Ethnicity & Race of Drug Sellers and Users: US Dept. of Justice National Institute of Justice & the Office of National Drug Control Policy, "Crack, Powder Cocaine, and Heroin: Drug Purchase and Use Patterns in Six U.S. Cities, " December 1997, p.1, 16, and p. 15, Table 16.

Sources:

[1] Data on drug use by high-school students: Youth Risk Behavior Survey 1999, Centers for Disease Control, reported in Morbidity and Mortality Weekly Report, Vol. 49, No. SS-5, p. 66, Table 24.

[2] Data on lifetime prevalence of drug use: US Dept. of HHS Substance Abuse and Mental Health Services Administration, "Summary of Findings from the 1999 National Household Survey on Drug Abuse," August 2000, p. G-13, Table G-13.

[3] Demogaphic data on felony drug defendants in state courts: US Dept. of Justice Bureau of Justice Statistics. "Felony Defendants in Large Urban Counties, 1996," October 1999, p.4, Table 3

[4] Demographic data on felony drug defendants in state courts: US Dept. of Justice Bureau of Justice Statistics, "State Court Sentencing of Convicted Felons, 1996," February 2000, p. 13, Table 2.5

[5] Demographic data on felony drug defendants in state courts: US Dept. of Justice Bureau of Justice Statistics, "State Court Sentencing of Convicted Felons, 1996," February 2000, p. 13, Table 2.5

Kevin B. Zeese, President, Common Sense for Drug Policy
3220 "N" Street, NW, #141, Washington, D.C. 20007 * 703-354-9050 * fax 703-354-5695 * info@csdp.org
For more information, visit www.csdp.org and www.drugwarfacts.org

Proposals as Visual Arguments and PowerPoint Presentations

Proposal arguments are often enhanced by photographs, drawings, graphs, or other images. Frequently we encounter proposal arguments as condensed, attention-grabbing verbal-visual texts such as posters or flyers, paid advertisements in newspapers or magazines, brochures, or Web pages in advocacy Web sites. Their creators know the arguments must work fast to capture our attention, give presence to a problem, advocate a solution, and enlist our support. These advocacy ads frequently use photographs, images, or icons that are arresting or in some way memorable and that appeal to a reader's emotions and imagination.

As an example of a one-page advocacy ad, consider Figure 16.1, which is sponsored by the organization Common Sense for Drug Policy. Note how the advocacy advertisement makes its view of the problem real and urgent to readers by using disturbing black-and-white drawings, varied type sizes and fonts, and powerful lists of evidence. It also gains credibility through its documentation of sources, presented at the bottom of the page.

For a somewhat different approach to a visual proposal argument, consider the part opener image shown on page 661. This advocacy ad, sponsored by the American Indian College Fund, uses striking portrait and landscape photography and simple but powerful claims to make appeals for financial support for tribal colleges. Note how this ad employs familiar images of the West (the grassy plain and towering rock formation) yet resists stereotypes in the contemporary figure of the young Navajo woman.

Since proposal arguments are often delivered orally rather than visually as ads, speakers frequently create visual aids with presentation software like PowerPoint. Although effectively designed slides can enhance the impact of a speech, PowerPoint presentations are controversial among communication experts. Used poorly, PowerPoint can detract from an argument rather than enhance it. A Web search reveals wonderfully satirical diatribes against PowerPoint—including Lincoln's Gettysburg address imagined as a PowerPoint presentation, complete with Lincoln's mumbling, grumbling, off-the-cuff remarks as he tries to connect his laptop to the projector. Despite all the ways that PowerPoint can go wrong, using it to produce effective visual aids can enhance an argument's appeals to *logos, pathos,* and *ethos*. In the last writing project for this chapter, we offer advice on powerful ways to use PowerPoint in support of a proposal speech.

A Proposal Argument

WRITING PROJECT

Call your audience's attention to a problem, propose a solution to that problem, and present a justification for your solution. You have two choices (or your instructor may limit you to just one): (a) create a practical proposal, with a letter of transmittal, proposing a nuts-and-bolts solution to a local problem; or (b) write a more general policy proposal, addressing a public issue, in the form of a feature editorial for a particular (state, local, or college) newspaper. If you choose (b), your instructor might ask you to do substantial research and model your proposal after a magazine or journal article.

Generating and Exploring Ideas

If you have trouble thinking of a proposal topic, try making an idea map of local problems you would like to see solved. Consider some of the following starting points:

Finding a Proposal Issue

Problems at your university: dorm, parking, registration system, grading system, campus appearance, clubs, curriculum, intramural program

Problems in your city or town: dangerous intersections, ugly areas, inadequate lighting, a poorly designed store, a shopping center that needs a specific improvement

Problems at your place of work: office design, flow of customer traffic, merchandise display, company policies, customer relations

Problems related to other aspects of your life: hobbies, recreational time, life as a consumer, and so forth

Another approach is to freewrite your response to these trigger statements:

I would really like to solve the problem of ___________.
I believe that X should ___________. (Substitute for X words such as *my instructor, the president, the school administration, Congress, my boss,* and so forth.)

Note that the problem you pose for this paper can be personal, but shouldn't be private; that is, others should be able to benefit from a solution to your personal problem. For example, your inability to find child care for your daughter is a private problem. But if you focus your proposal on how zoning laws discourage development of in-home day care—and propose a change in those zoning laws to permit more in-home day care centers—then your proposal will benefit others.

Using Stock Issues to Explore Your Problem

Once you have decided on a proposal issue, explore it by freewriting your responses to the following questions. These questions are often called *stock issues,* since they represent generic, or stock, questions that apply to almost any kind of proposal.

1. Is there a problem here that has to be solved?
2. Will the proposed solution really solve this problem?
3. Can the problem be solved in a simpler way without disturbing the status quo?
4. Is the proposed solution practical enough that it really stands a chance of being implemented?
5. What will be the positive and negative consequences of the proposal?

You might also try freewriting your responses to the questions in the exploratory exercise on pages 448–449. Although these questions cover much the same territory as the stock issues, their different presentation might stimulate additional thought.

Finally, try thinking of justifications for your solution by using the three-strategy approach described on page 452.

Avoiding Presupposing Your Solution in Your Problem Statement

A common mistake of inexperienced proposal writers is to write problem statements that presuppose their solutions. As a restaurant server, suppose you notice that customers want coffee refills faster than servers can provide them. To solve this problem, you propose placing carafes of hot coffee at each table. When describing your problem, don't presuppose your solution: "The problem is that we don't have carafes of hot coffee at the tables." Rather, describe the problematic situation itself: annoyed customers clamoring for coffee and harassed servers trying to bring around refills. Only by giving presence to the original problem can you interest readers in your proposed solution, which readers will compare to other possible approaches (including doing nothing).

Here is another example:

> Weak: The problem is that the Student Union doesn't stay open late enough at night.
>
> Better: The problem is that students who study late at night don't have an attractive, convenient place to socialize or study; off-campus coffee houses are too far to walk to at night; dorm lounges aren't attractive or conducive to study; late-nighters make noise in the dorms instead of going to a convenient place.

Shaping and Drafting

In Figure 16.2, we show a typical organizational plan for a proposal argument that you might use if you get stuck while composing the first draft of your essay.

Introduction	• Presents and describes a problem that needs solving, giving it presence • Gives background including previous attempts to solve the problem • Argues that the problem is solvable (optional)
Presentation of the proposed solution	• States the solution succinctly • Explains the specifics of the solution
Summary and rebuttal of opposing views	*Policy proposal:* • Presents opposing view(s) • Rebuts opposing view(s) *Practical proposal:* • Presents alternative solution(s) • Explains why alternative solution(s) are inferior
Justification	• Persuades readers that the proposal should be implemented • Presents and develops Reasons 1, 2, and so forth • Reasons to support the proposed solution may be arguments from principle, consequence, and precedent or analogy
Conclusion	• Asks readers to act (sometimes incorporated into the last sentences of the final supporting reason)

FIGURE 16.2 Framework of a Proposal Argument

Revising

After you have completed your first draft and begun to clarify your argument for yourself, you are ready to start making your argument clear and persuasive for your readers. Use the strategies for clear closed-form prose outlined in Chapter 18. At this stage, feedback from peer readers can be very helpful.

Questions for Peer Review

In addition to the generic peer review questions explained in Chapter 17, Skill 4, ask your peer reviewers to address these questions:

INTRODUCTION AND STATEMENT OF PROBLEM:

1. How could the title more effectively focus the paper and pique your interest? How could the title be improved?
2. How does the writer convince you that a problem exists and that it is significant (worth solving) and solvable? How does the writer give the problem presence? How could the writer improve the presentation of the problem?

PROPOSED SOLUTION:

3. How could the writer's thesis more clearly propose a solution to the problem? Could the thesis be made more precise?
4. Could the writer give you more details about the solution so that you can understand it and see how it works? How could the writer make the solution clearer?

JUSTIFICATION:

5. In the justification section, how could the writer provide stronger reasons for acting on the proposal? Where could the reasons be better supported with more details and evidence? How could the reasons appeal more to the values and beliefs of the audience?
6. Can you help the writer think of additional justifying arguments (arguments from principle, from consequences, from precedent or analogy)? How could the writer improve support for the proposal?
7. Where does the writer anticipate and address opposing views or alternative solutions? How does the writer convince you that the proposed solution is superior to alternative solutions?
8. Has the writer persuaded you that the benefits of this proposal will outweigh the costs? Who will pay the costs and who will get the benefits? What do you think the gut reaction of a typical decision maker would be to the writer's proposal?
9. Can you think of other, unforeseen costs that the writer should acknowledge and address? What unforeseen benefits could the writer mention?
10. How might the writer improve the structure and clarity of the argument? Where might the writer better apply the principles of clarity from Chapter 18?

Advocacy Ad or Poster

WRITING PROJECT

Create a one-page advocacy ad or poster that presents a controversial public problem and calls for action and support. Consider how you will use all the features of visual arguments—type sizes and fonts, layout, color, and images and graphics—to grab the attention of your audience, construct a compelling sketch of the problem, and inform your audience what course of action you want them to take. In this advocacy piece, you need to capture your proposal argument in a highly condensed form, while making it visually clear and memorable. Your instructor might ask you instead to create a longer brochure-length handout or a Web page.

Using Document Design Features

To interpret and drive home the problem presented in photos or drawings, advocacy ads employ different type sizes and fonts. Large-type text in these documents frequently takes the form of slogans or condensed thesis statements written in an arresting style. Here are some examples of large boldfaced copy from advocacy literature that the authors of this text have encountered recently:

- "Abstinence: It works every time. ... " (from a newspaper advocacy ad sponsored by Focus on the Family, asking readers to donate money to promote abstinence education)
- "Educating, Organizing, Fighting to end the barbarism, racism, unfairness, and shame of judicial homicide in our lifetime" (from an advocacy ad in the *Progressive* asking readers to donate money to Death Penalty Focus to end capital punishment)
- "Expectant Mothers Deserve Compassionate Health Care—Not Prison!" (an advocacy advertisement from Common Sense for Drug Policy; this one appeared in the *National Review*)

To outline and justify their solutions, creators of advocacy ads often put main supporting reasons in bulleted lists and sometimes enclose carefully selected facts and quotations in boxed sidebars. To add an authoritative *ethos,* the ads often include footnotes and bibliographies in fine print.

Another prominent feature of these condensed, highly visual arguments is their direct call for a course of action: Go to an advocacy Web site to find out more information on how to support a cause; cut out a postcard-like form to send to a decision maker; vote for or against the proposition or the candidate; write a letter to a political representative; or donate money to a cause.

Exploring and Generating Ideas

The first stage of your invention process should be the same as that for a longer proposal argument. Choose a controversial public issue that needs immediate attention or a neglected issue about which you want to arouse public passion. As with a longer proposal argument, consider your audience in order to identify the values and beliefs on which you will base your appeal.

Shaping and Drafting

When you construct your argument, the limited space available puts high demands on you, the writer, to be efficient in your choice of words and in your use of document design. Your goal is to have a memorable impact on your readers in order to promote the action you advocate. When creating a condensed advocacy ad, we suggest that you consider the following question-asking strategies to help you design your ad:

STRATEGIES for Choosing Design Features for an Advocacy Ad

Features and Strategies to Consider	Questions to Ask
Medium: Choose the most appropriate medium for your rhetorical purpose.	Will your advocacy argument be a poster, a flyer, a one-page advertisement in a newspaper or magazine, a brochure, or a Web page?
Giving Presence to the Problem: Choose the most effective visual features to create appeals to *pathos.*	What would be the best means to establish the urgency and importance of the problem: graphic elements, cartoon images, photos?
Presenting the Core of the Proposal: Decide on how you will condense your argument and convey it clearly.	What type size, font, and layout will be the most powerful in presenting your claim and justifying your reasons for your intended audience? How much verbal text do you want to use?
Accentuating Key Phrases: Decide what key phrases could highlight the parts or the main points of this argument.	What memorable phrases or slogans could you use to convey your argument? How condensed or detailed should your argument be?
Clarifying the Call for Action: Decide what you are asking your audience to do.	How can document design clarify the course of action and the direct demand on the audience that this argument is proposing?
Using Color for Impact: Decide whether you will use color. Note: For some media, color might be cost-prohibitive.	If color is an option, how could you use color to enhance the overall impact of your advocacy argument? How could you use black-and-white images effectively?

Revising

Because visual elements are subject to personal and varied interpretation even more so than verbal text, you will want to try out your advocacy ad on a group of readers who can role-play your intended audience. Ask your readers to focus on the messages that your advocacy piece sends, the emotional impact of the piece, and the credibility and professionalism it conveys.

Questions for Peer Review

In addition to the generic peer review questions explained in Chapter 17, Skill 4, ask your peer reviewers to address these questions:

1. How clear is the argument of this advocacy ad? Where could the presentation of the problem, the claim, and the reasons be clearer?
2. What design features (type, layout, images and graphics, and color) work particularly well in this advocacy ad? Where could the designer make improvements?
3. To what course of action is the ad calling the audience? How could this appeal to take action be clearer and more powerful?
4. How could the designer enhance his/her credibility and authority? How could the designer make this advocacy argument more compelling and memorable in this medium?

Proposal Speech with Visual Aids

WRITING PROJECT

Deliver a proposal argument as a prepared but extemporaneous speech of approximately five to eight minutes supported with visual aids created on presentation software such as PowerPoint or through other means. Your speech should present a problem, propose a solution, justify the solution with reasons and evidence, and defend it against objections or alternative solutions. As you deliver your speech, use appropriate visual aids to give presence to the problem, highlight points, provide memorable data or evidence, or otherwise enhance appeals to *logos, ethos,* and *pathos.* Although the following explanations focus on PowerPoint (or equivalent presentation software), low-tech means of using visual aids (for example, overhead transparencies or flip charts) can also be effective. Follow the guidelines provided by your instructor.

As you contemplate this project, consider its three different components: creating the speech itself, designing the visuals, and delivering the speech. As you create your proposal argument, think *aurally* by imagining your audience listening to a speech rather than reading a written text and think *visually* by considering how visual aids can increase the clarity and persuasive power of your argument.

Developing, Shaping, and Outlining Your Proposal Speech

This project asks you to deliver your proposal speech extemporaneously. To speak extemporaneously means to spend ample time preparing the speech, but not to read it from a script or to recite it from memory. Instead, the speaker talks directly to the audience with the aid of an outline or note cards.

Long before the delivery of the speech, the speaker should have engaged in the same sort of composing process that precedes a finished essay, including giving attention to both subject-matter and rhetorical problems. Effective speakers typically spend an hour of preparation time per minute of speaking time. Much of this work focuses on creating a well-developed sentence outline for the speech. Finding the balance between a speech that is too impromptu and one that is too "scripted," and therefore begs for an audience of readers, is a main consideration in creating a speech.

One way to accommodate the needs of listeners is to make your speech even more closed form than are closed-form essays. To help an audience grasp an argument aurally, speakers need to forecast their points and provide aural signals. The most common formula for a speech is sometimes called the "tell 'em rule." It says: Tell 'em what you are about to say, say it, and then tell 'em what you just said. This redundancy greatly enhances an audience's ability to follow a spoken argument without a text. This "tell 'em rule" serves audience-based needs for unity and coherence, for receiving old information before new information, and for forecasting and fulfillment. Another important way to help your audience follow your speech is to use attributive tags to indicate who and when you are quoting: "According to Pat Miller, a clinical psychologist at Children's Hospital, ... " These attributive tags signal a quotation and also indicate why the quoted material is important.

In developing the content for your speech, follow the suggestions for idea generation and development covered in the first writing project for this chapter, pages 456–457. Also try the following strategies:

STRATEGIES for Creating Effective Speech Outlines

Strategies	Rationales and Explanations of How They Work
Plan the structure and content of your speech with the needs of your audience in mind.	How can you make the problem come alive for your audience and make your solution understandable and persuasive? What background information or defined terms does your audience need? What kinds of evidence will you need to show the seriousness of the problem and to support your reasons for enacting the proposal? What objections will your listeners be apt to raise? How can you motivate action?

Strategies	Rationales and Explanations of How They Work
Create a complete-sentence outline of your argument; use parallel structures, coordination, and subordination to clarify relationships among ideas.	See Chapter 18, Skill 7, for advice about different kinds of outlines, particularly the advantage of complete-sentence outlines, which state meanings rather than topics. Since you won't be writing out the complete argument in prose, this outline will be the written frame for your speech.
Build into your outline places for explicit signposting to help the audience follow your speech.	Indicate where you are in your speech: "My second reason is that. . . ." "As I stated earlier. . . ."
Early on, practice saying your speech in a normally paced speaking voice to determine its length.	Often speeches can cover much less ground than a written argument. By timing the speech when it is still in its rough draft stage, you will know whether you must cut or add material.

Designing Your Visual Aids

If you use presentation software such as PowerPoint to design your visual aids, focus on making your argument clear and persuasive rather than on demonstrating your technical wizardry.* A common mistake with PowerPoint presentations—in addition to producing boring or jumbled slides—is to make too many slides, to overdesign them, or to become enamored with special effects rather than with the ideas in the speech. Typically, PowerPoint slides fall into three categories as shown in Table 16.1: text-based, symbol-based, and image-based slides.

Slide Titles: Topic Phrases Versus Complete-Sentence Assertions

Many communication researchers object to Microsoft's default PowerPoint template that encourages short topic phrases for the title of a slide. The "title" box uses a large (for example, Arial 44-point bold) font that limits the number of words at the top of the slide. Dissatisfied with this approach, many researchers argue that complete sentences are more effective than topic phrases for conveying meanings, and they recommend writing complete-sentence assertions at the top of the slide. To do so, however, one has to override the PowerPoint default to use a smaller font. Professor Michael Alley recommends using an Arial 28-point bold font for slide headlines. This font is large enough to be seen throughout the room, but small enough to allow a two-line complete sentence for the headline.

*Our discussion of visual aids designed on PowerPoint is indebted to advice from our rhetorician colleague, Professor Jeffrey Philpott in the Department of Communication at Seattle University. We are also indebted to the work of Professor Michael Alley of Virginia Technical University. Alley's Web site at http://writing.eng.vt.edu/slides.html provides an overview of rhetorical objections to PowerPoint and shows the value of an assertion-evidence design for slides rather than a topic-subtopic design.

TABLE 16.1 Typical Kinds of PowerPoint Slides

Type of Slide	Illustration	Comment
Text-based	Key Ideas	• Indicates structure • Emphasizes main points • Can show all points at once (forecasts structure) or can be projected one bullet at a time (emphasizes development of argument-in-progress)
Symbols	Cause Effect	• Can make relationships vivid and memorable
Photographs, drawings, graphs, maps, or other images	Windpower: Pros and Cons	• Can illustrate an idea, create *pathos*, present graphic evidence, or serve other functions

Here are some examples of the differences between a topic phrase and a complete-sentence assertion:

For more on the value of complete-sentence outlines, see Chapter 18, Skill 7.

Topic Phrase Versus Complete-Sentence Assertion for Slide Title

Topic Phrase Slide Title	Assertion Slide Title
Problems with Metal Detectors in Schools	Schools should not use metal detectors as a way of reducing violence.
Consequences of High-Risk Drinking	Workshops will help students confront the consequences of high-risk drinking.

We recommend the assertion approach wherever possible. Student writer Jane Kester uses this approach for most of her slides in her argument against high-risk drinking (see pp. 469–471 in the Readings section).

Given this background, we offer the following strategies for creating your visual aids.

STRATEGIES

for Creating Effective Visual Aids

Strategies	Rationales and Explanations of How They Work
Make sure each visual aid (slide) is graphically interesting, relevant, functional, and directly connected to the points of your speech.	Visual aids (slides) should be visual and integral to your presentation. Create your speech first and then create visuals.
Use meaningful features as visual aids; don't use cutesy bells and whistles.	PowerPoint has special effects like exploding figures, words circling into position, and little buses wheeling across the screen. Using these special effects can distract the audience from the content of your speech; it creates the ethos of a technical whiz rather than a serious presenter of a proposal.
Use slides as a way to visually enhance meaning or impact. Do not use them as index cards of talking points.	If you convert your outline into slides, you simply replicate rather than enhance the speech. Use images (rather than words) wherever possible. Think visually.
Make slides simple, neat, and big enough for everyone to see.	PowerPoint wisely limits the number of words in a line. Include no more than eight to ten lines of text per slide. Don't create slides that need to be read as text.
Where appropriate, follow an assertion-evidence design, rather than a topic-subtopic design. Titles (headlines) should be complete sentences that state a point.	The assertion-evidence design promotes audience understanding by emphasizing meanings. (See examples on p. 464.) Note: You'll need to change the PowerPoint title font to 28-point Arial bold.
Use different font sizes and spacing to indicate hierarchy.	The headline font should be the largest font on the slide. Subordinate points should be in smaller font size.
Limit the number of visual aids you use.	Communication experts advise speakers to use no more than one visual aid per minute of presentation. In many parts of the speech, the screen can be blank.

Examples of Effective Slides

One criterion for effective slides is to use functional rather than decorative images. To see this criterion at work, consider Figure 16.3, the opening slide of student writer Jane Kester's PowerPoint presentation proposing a solution to the

FIGURE 16.3 PowerPoint Slide Showing Functional Use of Visuals

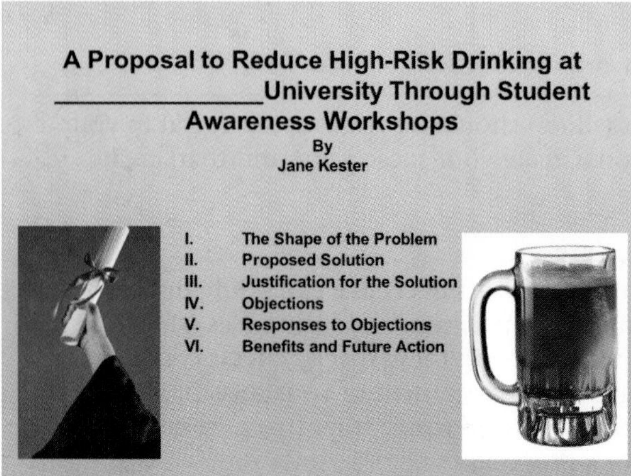

FIGURE 16.4 PowerPoint Slide Showing Parallelism, Coordination, and Subordination

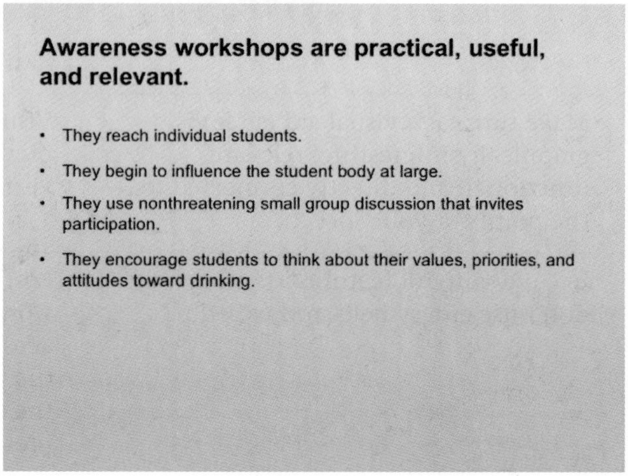

Awareness workshops are practical, useful, and relevant.

- They reach individual students.
- They begin to influence the student body at large.
- They use nonthreatening small group discussion that invites participation.
- They encourage students to think about their values, priorities, and attitudes toward drinking.

problem of binge drinking. In this opening slide, the outline of the proposal argument prepares the audience for the presentation to follow. The visuals—the image of the diploma raised high in celebration at graduation and the mug of beer—also set up the audience's expectations by illustrating the key tension that the proposal explores: How can students use their college experience successfully for intellectual and personal growth? How can they avoid becoming derailed or injured by excessive drinking? By conveying the tensions between the long-term goal of the diploma and the short-term pleasure of the beer, these images are functional rather than merely decorative. They contribute both to the *logos* of the argument and to its *pathos*. Moreover, the professional look of the slide helps establish the *ethos* of the speaker.

Another feature of good visuals is effective use of coordination, subordination, and parallel structure. Another of Jane Kester's slides, shown in Figure 16.4, illustrates these features. This slide uses the complete-sentence assertion-evidence structure we recommended earlier. The headline is a full sentence set in a larger type size than the bulleted subpoints. Note that each bulleted subpoint maintains parallel grammatical structure.

Delivering Your Speech

Adapting your argument to be delivered orally as a speech requires some special considerations. First, it is important that you allow plenty of time to practice delivering your speech. You can practice before a mirror, with a recorder, or in front of friends until you are confident about the length of your speech and your ability to deliver it with minimal prompting from your notes. In addition, you should think about these important strategies for successful speechmaking:

STRATEGIES

for Successfully Delivering Speeches

Strategies	What to Do
Control your volume and pace.	• Speak loudly enough to be heard and add emphasis by speaking louder or softer. • Speed up to get through details quickly and slow down for points you want to stress.
Use posture and gestures to your advantage.	• Stand straight and tall to help your breathing and projection. • Use natural gestures or a few carefully planned ones. • Avoid distracting or nervous gestures.
Maintain eye contact with your audience and look at every member of your audience.	• Know your speech well enough that you can look at your audience, not read your note cards. • Make steady and even eye contact with your audience.
Show enthusiasm and passion for the issue of your speech.	• Make your audience care about your issue through your own enthusiasm. • Show your audience that your issue is important by the energy you put into your delivery. • Also, use your enthusiasm to help you control nervousness.
Use note cards, PowerPoint slides, visual aids, and handouts effectively.	• Control the flow of ideas and information that comes through your slides and visual aids. • Keep your audience listening to you rather than reading handouts or the projector screen.
Overcome nervousness by controlling your hands, your breathing, and the volume of your voice.	• Take deep breaths and speak slightly louder than usual to help your body relax. • Use a podium if one is available.

Revising

After practicing your speech on your own or in front of an informal audience, think about ways you can improve the clarity of your message, your use of visual aids, and your delivery. After you make these improvements, practice the final outline of your speech a number of times to develop familiarity and confidence.

Questions for Peer Review

In addition to the generic peer review questions explained in Chapter 17, Skill 4, many of which will pertain to your outlined speech, ask your informal audience/reviewers to address these questions:

CONTENT OF THE SPEECH:

1. How well does this speech follow the problem-solution-justification-opposing views-rebuttal structure? How could the speaker improve the clarity of these parts of the speech?
2. How has the speaker tailored the speech to the audience? What could make the speech more lively and easier to follow?
3. Does this speech fit the time limit specified by the assignment? If not, what changes could develop or condense the speech?

USE OF VISUAL AIDS:

4. How functional, simple, clear, and illustrative are the visual aids? Which visual aids enhance the impact of the speech? If any are unclear or distracting, what could improve them?
5. How well do the visual aids support the message of the speech? Where could the speaker more effectively employ the strategies for using PowerPoint or other visual aids?

DELIVERY:

6. Where could the speaker improve his/her volume, enunciation, eye contact, posture, and gestures?
7. How well does the speaker maintain control of his/her material, visual aids, and manner? What suggestions do you have for the speaker to improve his or her enthusiasm and composure?

READINGS

Our first reading is a selection of slides from Jane Kester's PowerPoint speech proposing student workshops on her campus to reduce high-risk drinking. Jane's assignment was to research a proposal argument on a university or local issue and prepare her argument as a ten-minute speech using PowerPoint to enhance the impact of the proposal. The opening slide shown in Figure 16.3 on page 466, the additional slide shown in Figure 16.4 on page 466, and the slides shown here will provide you with enough of the frame of her speech so that you can comment on her proposal argument and her use of visual aids.

Jane Kester (student)

A Proposal to Reduce High-Risk Drinking Through Student Awareness Workshops

1

High-risk drinking is a major problem nationwide.

For students between 18-24 years of age, drinking yearly causes:

- 1,700 **DEATHS,** including car crashes (Hingson, 2005)
- 400,000 instances of **UNSAFE SEX** (2002)
- 97,000 cases of **SEXUAL ABUSE, SEXUAL ASSAULT, OR DATE RAPE**

2

High-risk drinking is a major problem on our campus.

2006 SURVEY of Freshmen, Sophomores, and Juniors showed that during last year:

20% had used false IDs to obtain alcohol.

39% admitted to underage drinking.

44% went off campus to drink more than once.

30% said they had been drunk at least once.

27% said they had received a Student Code of Conduct violation for drinking.

17% missed at least one class from drinking.

3

Proposal: The campus should establish student awareness workshops to reduce high-risk drinking.

These workshops will be effective because:

- They will engage students in confronting the consequences of high-risk drinking for both drinkers and nondrinkers.
- They will help change the "culture of drinking."
- Similar workshops have proven successful at other institutions in providing a foundation for tackling this complex problem.

4

Description of Student Awareness Workshops

- Workshops will be held during the first week of every term.
- Workshops will be voluntary but highly recommended and promoted in the residence halls.
- Workshops will involve small-group discussion.
- Workshops will be led by trained staff, graduate students, and undergraduate peer advisors.
- Attendees will receive movie passes.

5

Workshops will help students confront the consequences of high-risk drinking for student drinkers.

Consequences to academic performance

- Missing classes
- Getting behind on course work
- Doing poor work or failing tests

Correlation between drinking and grades

- A students average 3.1 drinks per week
- B students average 4.4 drinks per week
- C students average 5.6 drinks per week
- D and F students average 9.5 drinks per week

(http://www.bacchusnetwork.org/alcohol-academics.asp)

6

Workshops will help students confront the dangerous consequences to nondrinkers.

According to the 1999 Harvard survey, nondrinkers reported:

- property damage
- interrupted study and sleep
- unwanted sexual advances
- physical violence
- sexual assaults (www.alcoholpolicymd.com)

7

Workshops will expose the misconceptions promoted by the culture of drinking.

Misconception #1:
Beer is less intoxicating than other types of alcoholic beverage.

Reality:
One 12-ounce can of beer, one 4 ounce glass of wine, or one normal mixed drink or cocktail are all equally intoxicating.

8

Benefits and Future Action

- Workshops help students realize it is okay not to drink and the university will help students with alcohol abuse problems.
- Workshops can lead to:
  - individual commitment to safe, responsible choices
  - more funding for alcohol-free entertainment (dances, movies, sports, and games)
- Workshops send the message that extreme drinking
  - is not a "rite of passage"
  - is not a main part of the college experience

THINKING CRITICALLY

about "A Proposal to Reduce High-Risk Drinking Through Student Awareness Workshops"

1. Consider the way that Jane Kester draws attention to her key ideas with visual aids using images. What is effective about her use of images? Which of Jane's slides best exhibit the key principles for slides explained in this chapter? Which slides could be improved?
2. What images might Jane have used to illustrate the following ideas in her proposal?
   a. the reality that only time, not a cold shower, fresh air, or caffeine, can help a person sober up
   b. the life-changing and life-threatening consequences of drinking: damage to health, car accidents, and possible death from alcohol poisoning
3. What kinds of evidence might Jane have used to support her third reason that "workshops have proven successful at other institutions in providing a foundation for tackling this complex problem"? How might she have designed a visual aid for this part of her argument?
4. What objections to her argument do you think she anticipated? How might she have addressed these objections?
5. Do you think her concluding slide is effective? How might she have strengthened the concluding portion of her speech?

Our second reading, by student writer Rebekah Taylor, is a practical proposal entitled "A Proposal to Provide Cruelty-Free Products on Campus." Because practical proposals are aimed at a specific audience, they are often accompanied by a letter of transmittal that introduces the writer, sets the context, and summarizes the proposal. We reproduce here Rebekah's transmittal letter followed by her proposal. We also show you the appearance of her title page. Because of potential legal problems, we have had to omit the names of specific colleges as well as the specific brand names and companies.

____________ Hall, Room 356
May 15, 2001

Mr. Charles Ramos
Director of Residence Life
____________ University
Street
City, State, Zip

Dear Mr. Ramos:

1 Enclosed is my proposal that the campus store add cruelty-free products to its inventory. Currently, there are no toiletry or household products sold on campus that

are not tested on animals, forcing students like myself, who are concerned about animal welfare, to go off-campus.

2 My proposal would provide concerned students with needed products that are clearly designated as "cruelty free."

3 I believe that if these new products were offered on campus, they would be popular with students, would bring attention to the issue of animal testing, and would be in strong accordance with our university's mission statement.

4 Thank you for taking the time to read and consider this proposal.

Sincerely,
Rebekah Taylor

Following the letter of transmittal is the proposal's cover or title page.

A PROPOSAL TO PROVIDE CRUELTY-FREE PRODUCTS ON CAMPUS

Submitted to Mr. Charles Ramos
Director of Residence Life

Rebekah Taylor
__________ University Student

If this were the actual proposal, the first page would begin on a new page following the cover page.

Problem

1 The __________ University campus store does not offer toiletry or household products that are not tested on animals. Students who desire to purchase cruelty-free products on campus cannot do so.

2 A quick look inside the campus store reveals nearly every kind of product a student might desire or need. Shampoo, deodorant, soap, detergent, toothpaste, and eyedrops crowd shelves. Most of these products, manufactured by respected companies such as* __________ and others, have well-known names: __________, __________, __________, __________. Unfortunately, these companies all test their products on animals.

3 Those who understand that cruelty to animals runs rampant in these companies try their hardest not to buy from them. These conscientious shoppers support companies such as __________ and __________ that have made staunch commitments to quality product testing without the use of animals. To buy these cruelty-free products, conscientious students now have to go off-campus—a situation that is problematic in two ways:

*In the proposal argument that Rebekah Taylor actually submitted, she named specific companies and specific brand names. For textbook publication, these names had to be deleted.

- *First, students without cars have to walk or take the bus, potentially jeopardizing their safety.* Many students attending this university do not own cars, and the nearest store that carries cruelty-free products is about five blocks away from campus. Although this walk is safe during the day, at night it can be dangerous, especially for women, but when students desperately need toiletry products, they'll often go to the store after dark to get them.
- *Second, many students cannot afford to spend money off-campus.* Many students are not employed and don't have any real money to speak of. Frequently students find themselves flat broke, except for the money on their campus cards. They need to be able to use their cards on campus to buy personal and household products.

So conscientious students face a dilemma because they have no on-campus options for buying cruelty-free products. Often students must go against their principles by buying products made by companies that they strongly do not want to support.

4 In the past I have asked campus store personnel to stock cruelty-free items, but I was told that none of their purveyors offer this service and that the expense would be too great. However, I believe the benefits of solving this problem would outweigh the costs. The following proposal explains an approach the university can take.

Proposal

5 The campus store should offer students basic toiletry and household products that are not tested on animals. These products should be clearly distinguished on the shelves with a placard reading, "NOT TESTED ON ANIMALS."

6 If enacted, this proposal would provide students with cruelty-free options for such products as toothpaste, deodorant, shampoo, soap, shaving products, laundry detergent, dish soap, and all-purpose cleaner. One cruelty-free brand of each of these products would be sufficient. This proposal would not prevent students from buying the products they normally do because it would add new products to the store inventories; it would not replace any existing products.

7 To enact this proposal, the campus store can select among numerous producers of cruelty-free brands. _________ could provide toothpaste and floss, shampoos, deodorants, and soap. _________ offers excellent shaving products that are cruelty free. A conscientious company called "_________" could provide laundry detergent, dish soap, and cleaning sprays.

8 Perhaps one of the university's many purveyors could be persuaded to carry brands like these. If that is the case, providing cruelty-free products would only require adding new inventory from an already existing source. This situation would be ideal because the products could be easily delivered to campus along with other goods that the store already provides. If the university's purveyors will not offer such brands, they might still be easily acquired from a new purveyor, or from a local warehouse store. Based on phone calls I have made, I know of several warehouse stores in our area that offer natural and cruelty-free products in bulk. These companies might provide delivery services just as the university's current purveyors do.

9 If a new purveyor could not be found, and if the warehouse stores in the area could not deliver, concerned students might volunteer to personally obtain cruelty-free products from neighborhood stores and transport them to the school.

10 An important part of my proposal is that designated areas on campus store shelves would be provided for cruelty-free products. These areas would be clearly identified with a sign so that compassionate students would know which products are cruelty free. This aspect of the proposal is very important because it would draw the attention of students to the issue of animal testing and encourage them to consider seriously which products they want to buy. The hope is not only to offer cruelty-free products on campus, but to create a dialogue on the issue of animal testing.

Justification

11 There are four important reasons why __________ University should act on this proposal.

Success at Other Universities

12 First, other colleges and universities have enacted similar proposals to help combat animal testing and have had great success with the new products. I have researched two such places—__________ College and __________ College—and have discovered that cruelty-free products are very popular with students.

13 For example, the campus stores at __________ College in Iowa underwent a massive product change about five years ago in response to student protests against the __________ products sold on campus. These students knew that __________ is one of the corporate world's most ardent supporters of animal testing. The cruelty-free products that replaced __________ sold exceedingly well. Similarly, at __________ College in Colorado students raised an outcry when one of these cruelty-free products was almost pulled from the shelves. Our university should look to success stories such as these when considering whether or not to offer cruelty-free products on campus.

In Line with University Mission

14 Second, offering cruelty-free products on campus would be an action in line with our university's efforts to be a progressively minded, service- and value-oriented school. In many ways, __________ University has shown itself to be a leader in social change. This university has proved eager to become involved in struggles against all kinds of injustice. The most recent examples are the mission to Iraq to help people impoverished by U.N. sanctions and the addition of environmentally friendly, shade-grown coffee in the university coffee shops. These actions challenged current social practices and demonstrated clearly that many of our students are willing to fight for human rights and for the global ecosystem and endangered species. These actions are consistent with __________ University's official mission "to look critically at the society in which we live and at its institutions" (Mission Statement). It is time now to look critically at corporations that contribute to the suffering of animals by subjecting them to cruel, unnecessary experiments. At the very least, __________ University should allow its students the right to choose not to support such corporations.

Student Convenience and Safety

15 Third, offering cruelty-free products would allow students to purchase needed items on campus and to use the money on their University One Cards to do so. Simply put, if cruelty-free products were offered on campus, students would be safer and less inconvenienced because they would not have to worry about off-campus transportation or security. In addition, the ability to purchase such products with the One Card would allow numerous students who otherwise could not have afforded to do so to buy what they need.

Promise of Economic Success

16 Finally, many students at this university would choose cruelty-free products over other brands if they were available on campus. In a short survey I conducted winter quarter, many students said they would support a proposal to introduce cruelty-free products to the stores on campus. This survey of fifty randomly selected students revealed that over half (56%) are more than "somewhat concerned" about animal testing. The survey also showed that almost three-quarters (72%) would buy cruelty-free products instead of products tested on animals if they were offered on campus. Additionally, compassionate students who have gone off-campus to buy cruelty-free products would start spending their money at the campus store.

Conclusion

17 Past social actions by the students, faculty, and administration of __________ University reveal a long-held belief that real progress means real change. In hope of bettering the school and society, this university has always been willing to challenge the status quo. It is time to challenge the status quo again. To continue the university's efforts to fight injustice in the world, to take conscientious action on the issue of animal testing as other respected colleges have, and to honor the wishes of many students, the university's campus store should offer cruelty-free products. Taking this action would help our university remain faithful to its mission.

THINKING CRITICALLY

about "A Proposal to Provide Cruelty-Free Products on Campus"

1. What strategies does Rebekah Taylor use to convince the Director of Residence Life that a problem exists?
2. What strategies (including arguments from principle, consequence, and precedent) does Rebekah employ to persuade university administrators that her proposal is workable and that the benefits outweigh the costs?
3. How does Rebekah tie her proposal to the values and beliefs of her audience—the Director of Residence Life in particular and university administrators in general?
4. If you were Mr. Charles Ramos, the Director of Residence Life to whom this proposal is addressed, how effective would you find this proposal? What are its chief strengths and weaknesses?

Our third reading, an op-ed piece from the *New York Times* (February 20, 2004), proposes that competitive cheerleading be recognized as a varsity sport. It was written by Jennifer Allen, the daughter of former Washington Redskins football coach George Allen. She has also written a memoir about growing up female in a football family, *Fifth Quarter: The Scrimmage of a Football Coach's Daughter.*

Jennifer Allen

The Athlete on the Sidelines

1 It's midseason in cheer nation. This winter, thousands of girls will travel on college all-star teams to take part in competitions across the country. Practicing more than 20 hours a week, they will refine a routine of back flips, handsprings, round-offs and splits—all perfectly synchronized and timed to an Olympic second. Their goal: first place. Their game: competitive cheerleading, one of the fastest-growing sports for women in America.

2 Last year, the University of Maryland became the first Division I N.C.A.A. institution to recognize competitive cheerleading as a varsity sport. That means team members are accorded the same benefits as other campus athletes—a coaching and medical staff; locker rooms; help with academics; help dealing with the press. By the 2005–06 academic year, Maryland will provide 12 full scholarships to competitive cheerleaders. The question is this: What took so long?

3 (Time out for a definition. Competitive cheerleading overlaps with but is not identical to the spirit squads you see, say, on the sidelines of a Saturday afternoon college football game. The teams we're talking about do cheer at school games, but they also compete against other schools in cheerleading competitions where they perform high-risk routines under high-pressure circumstances.)

4 For too many years, cheerleading has been the subject of derision. *Sports Illustrated* has lampooned it. Many Americans fail to distinguish it from the sideline shows the Dallas Cowboys cheerleaders put on. Back when I was a cheerleader in high school in the late 70s, we were called a sideshow. In those days, we performed at every sporting event—football, basketball and baseball. We practiced three days a week; purchased our own uniforms (skirts, sweaters, trunks, socks, saddle shoes) and were responsible for our own steady supply of bandages. Ace bandages. There were plenty of injuries, mostly to ligaments. After a big game, my knee would swell. My dad would offer a diagnosis—water on the knee—bandage it up, and then prescribe 50 reps on the knee machine. But cheerleaders weren't allowed in the school weight room.

5 Today, more than 200,000 high-school and college students attend cheerleading camps each year; at least 15 percent of them participate in competitions. The Universal Cheerleading Association feeds its competitions to ESPN for lively weekend fare. When these events were televised last year, they drew an average audience of 334,000 homes.

6 For all its popularity, though, the sport is governed—or not governed—by a patchwork of entities. Schools may treat cheerleaders as athletes—but they don't have to. Some offer little more than a uniform and a game-day parking pass; others offer

scholarships; none offer the full range of support and benefit that Maryland does for competitive cheerleading. What's more, cheerleading is not even recognized by the N.C.A.A. as a sport.

7 Given the nature of competitive cheerleading, this seems like a risky proposition. Think about it: in what other sport is an athlete tossed more than 30 feet in the air—smiling—before spiraling down into the arms of a trusted teammate? Lifts and tosses and catches are the mainstay of competitive cheerleading. "Fliers" do not wear hip pads or kneepads or helmets. There is little to protect a cheerleader from awkward or poor landings on the gym floor.

8 Not surprisingly, cheerleading is the No. 1 cause of serious sports injuries to women, according to the National Center for Catastrophic Sport Injury Research, ahead of gymnastics and track. From 1980 to 2001, emergency room visits for cheerleading injuries rose fivefold.

9 Pushing colleges to recognize competitive cheerleading as a sport will surely help to cut down on injuries. Right now, the American Association of Cheering Coaches and Advisers publishes a manual and administers a safety certification program, but only a fraction of coaches have been certified. Many cheerleaders try dangerous stunts without proper training, coaching and supervision.

10 Of course, convincing other schools to make competitive cheerleading an official sport won't be easy. According to Deborah Yow, Maryland's athletic director, it took more than a year to make sure that the university's cheerleading squad would meet all the guidelines set forth by the Department of Education's Office of Civil Rights. While the department does not define what is or is not a "sport," it does determine whether a university's given activity—such as cheerleading—can be considered a sport in order to comply with Title IX.

11 Is Maryland's action entirely altruistic? Probably not. It doubtless relieves some Title IX pressure. But what's wrong with that? And would it be so wrong to ask the N.C.A.A. to sponsor and govern the sport? After all, when the big collegiate cheerleading competitions begin next month, hundreds of thousands of people will tune in, acknowledging the importance of cheerleading. More N.C.A.A. colleges would be wise to follow suit.

THINKING CRITICALLY
about "The Athlete on the Sidelines"

1. As in most proposal arguments, Allen's first task is to convince readers that a problem exists. She has to persuade readers to take competitive cheerleading seriously and to show them why it is problematic for competitive cheerleaders not to be granted varsity sport status. What are her strategies for convincing us that a problem exists? How effective is she?

2. How does Allen justify her claim that cheerleading should be recognized as a sport? According to her argument, what are the benefits that will come from making cheerleading a varsity sport? What costs does she acknowledge? What additional costs might you point to if you were skeptical of her claim?

3. Overall, how persuasive is her argument? In your response to this question, focus on the strengths and weaknesses of her appeals to *logos*, *ethos*, and *pathos*.
4. If you are persuaded by her argument and if you are attending an institution where competitive cheerleading could exist, how might you persuade the administration on your campus to make cheerleading a varsity sport? (Who are the decision makers for this issue? What arguments would most motivate them? What are the constraints that must be overcome?)

Our last reading, by student writer Dylan Fujitani, is a researched policy argument that addresses the problem of civilian contractors taking military roles in Iraq.

Dylan Fujitani (student)

"The Hardest of the Hardcore":

Let's Outlaw Hired Guns in Contemporary American Warfare

1 On March 31, 2004, America was shocked by the news that four civilians had been brutally killed, mutilated, and hung up on a bridge in Falluja, Iraq. This horrific event publicized the little-known role of civilian "contractors" in the Iraq war. The public's unawareness that some of these contractors are armed to the teeth is hardly surprising, however, because the language used to refer to non-military personnel in Iraq is often so vague that one can scarcely tell whether a reference to a contractor means a truck driver working for Halliburton or a South African mercenary with a history of killing blacks under the apartheid government working for a private security company. These personnel are often referred to using such broad and mundane terms as "security consultants" or simply "civilian contractors." But in reality, the jobs involved and the kinds of people doing them vary so greatly that these catchall labels are inaccurate. Persons referred to as "civilian contractors" are often well-armed ex-military personnel who took an early retirement to double their pay by working for one of many private security firms hired by the Pentagon. With their obvious training and heavy weaponry, these contractors bear a striking resemblance to soldiers, but one enormous difference sets them apart from the regular troops of the U.S. military: They are actually civilians who can be hired without even the symbolic approval of Congress. Without the need for approval, contractors give the Pentagon the flexibility of outsourcing certain military jobs to private security companies. Despite being paid much more than regular troops, contractors may actually cost less when military benefits and retirement are taken into account.

2 Soldiers for hire have historically been called mercenaries. A case could be made that this term is inapplicable in Iraq because contractors in Iraq are being hired to *support* the military's operations, not to fight the war itself. It is true that many of these civilians are support personnel who should not be called mercenaries—for example, highly specialized technicians or drivers of supply trucks—even though these persons may carry a weapon in case of an attack. But some of these personnel replace soldiers in combat roles historically filled by the military. According to Joshua Hammer of the

New Republic, these jobs include guarding the Baghdad airport, protecting oil fields, escorting convoys, training local police, and serving as prison interrogators (18). The use of these mercenaries circumvents public and congressional scrutiny of some aspects of war. Their non-military status gives virtual legal immunity to heavily armed individuals who often have questionable backgrounds, who profit from violent conflict, and who ultimately have responsibility to no one but their employers. In light of these dangerous developments, the use of mercenary soldiers must be halted or brought under intense congressional scrutiny.

3 Using mercenaries in war is problematic for six major reasons. First, the deployment of mercenaries disguises the true cost of war to the American public. According to *New York Times* reporter David Barstow, there are roughly 20,000 mercenaries on the ground in Iraq supporting U.S. military operations, and these numbers are not included in reports of the number of American soldiers in Iraq. These 20,000 private contractors make up the second largest contingent in Iraq, surpassing even the British deployment ("Privatizing Warfare"), yet they have received relatively little media attention even as their numbers continue to increase. The use of contractors enables the Pentagon to get by with a smaller number of actual troops through outsourcing to private military companies. Only the deployments of actual troops are reported, so the Pentagon appears to have done more with less. According to a Baghdad-based security consultant, "If you're going to keep the number of troops down, this is the way to do it. ... The expense is the same or more. But politically it's much less expensive" (qtd. in Daragahi). The use of mercenaries in Iraq blurs the high cost of war in the public eye, both in terms of dollars and in terms of human lives. Contractors have suffered casualties, yet the public scarcely hears of their death toll unless they are mutilated and publicly exhibited. Furthermore, with the service of a civilian mercenary in Iraq costing as much as $1,500 dollars a day ("Privatizing Warfare"), contractor use is consuming an enormous portion of the funding allocated for reconstruction. *New York Times* reporter David Barstow asserts that "security costs could claim up to 25 percent of the $18 billion budgeted for reconstruction," diverting capital from important reconstruction projects like school and road construction. Thus, the use of mercenaries in Iraq makes it more difficult for the American public to determine the true cost of war.

4 The second major problem with use of mercenaries is that as a group they have no national loyalties and ultimately answer to their employers, not the armed forces. According to the Brookings Institution's P. W. Singer, "during the Persian Gulf War, a 'very small number' of private contractors working at an air base in Saudi Arabia fled from fear that chemical weapons might be used" (qtd. in Bredemeier). In using mercenaries, the Pentagon is outsourcing what the *New York Times* calls its "core responsibilities" ("Privatizing Warfare"), and despite the importance of these tasks, the jobs are being assigned to people who can basically leave whenever they want to. As P. W. Singer has pointed out, a soldier faces a court-martial for refusing to face battle, whereas a contractor merely loses his job (Bredemeier). In addition, the mercenaries and regular military personnel sometimes have poor working relationships. Since contractors are not required to abide by normal military procedures, mercenaries can pretty much operate any way they want, sometimes to the armed forces' disliking.

Writing in the *New Republic*, Joshua Hammer explains the attitudes of the Marines who had been with the four contractors killed in Falluja the day before their deaths. Quoting a Marine officer, Hammer writes, "We would have told them not to do it [take an unauthorized shortcut through Baghdad]." According to Hammer, the officer "angrily called the contractors 'cowboys' and said they had failed to inform anyone on the base of their plans, a direct violation of military policy" (19). Relying on such a large number of poorly supervised and unaccountable mercenaries to fill crucial roles leaves the United States dangerously vulnerable to the future uncertainties of war.

5 Another problem with the use of mercenaries is their civilian status, creating legal ambiguity and making discipline extremely difficult if not impossible. Phillip Carter, a former U.S. Army officer, writing for the e-magazine *Slate*, commented that the involvement of private contractors in the Abu Ghraib prison abuse scandal brought the issue of discipline to the forefront ("How to Discipline"). According to Carter, mercenaries don't fit the Geneva convention definition of "non-combatants" (since they are armed), or of "lawful combatants" (since they don't wear uniforms or fit within a military chain of command). Rather, "they fall into an international legal gray zone" ("Hired Guns"). This problem is highlighted in an editorial from the *Economist*, which pointed out that the "great sanction on wrongdoing—the law—does not really operate. Regular soldiers are subject to courts-martial or international law. But it is not clear what law applies to private security firms" ("Dangerous Work"). Borzou Daragahi, in a piece for the *Post-gazette.com*, wrote that contractors are not subject to the Uniform Code of Military Justice and that there are military personnel who are very uncomfortable with their seemingly untouchable status. Contractors' fuzzy legal status with regard to military justice and international law is highly problematic.

6 Some have argued against these claims of virtual immunity, saying that in reality a lot can be done to discipline law-breaking private contractors. Carter says that possible disciplinary measures include termination of contracts, prohibition from bidding for future contracts, criminal prosecution, and civil suits ("How to Discipline"). All of these penalties, however, are at "the discretion of the agency that issued the original contract," or in this case, presumably the Pentagon. Although Carter effectively makes the point that contractors are not entirely immune from discipline, many of these forms of punishment ultimately amount to nothing more than loss of the job. Carter admits that government contractors are "shielded" from civil suits by a legal doctrine called the "government contractor" defense. Under the current circumstances in Iraq where offensive and defensive roles are becoming increasingly muddied, the only form of punishment contractors are concerned with is financial. This virtual legal immunity is striking considering the strict rules that govern the actions of military personnel. The threat of mere financial punishment cannot be expected to deter mercenaries from possible abusive and criminal behavior. Their legal status must be clarified as soon as possible in both domestic and international law.

7 The fourth major problem with mercenaries is that private military companies frequently hire employees with questionable backgrounds. Inadequate governmental oversight has allowed private companies to hire known war criminals who have been or continue to be paid with American taxpayer dollars. According to journalist Louis Nevaer, writing for the *National Catholic Reporter*, roughly 1,500 South African mer-

cenaries are now in Iraq, many of them former Apartheid-era mercenaries, some of whom have even confessed to killing blacks. Nevaer states that there are "terrorists ... and war criminals on the payrolls of companies contracted by the Pentagon." He gives the example of a former South African police officer who was "a member of the Vlakplass death squad that terrorized blacks under apartheid." Not only are the personal histories of the mercenaries questionable, but their motivations are also dubious. Joshua Hammer in his *New Republic* article "Cowboy Up" describes what he observed of these private contractors in Baghdad:

> [M]ost of the contractors are the hardest of the hard core—veterans of such elite outfits as the U.S. Special Forces; the Rhodesian Selous Scouts, the former special forces of the Rhodesian white regime; and Executive Outcomes, the now-disbanded South African mercenary army that fought in Sierra Leone and Angola. These men thrive on the danger of working in war zones. (19)

Given the current uncertainly about the legal status of private contractors, and given the fact that actual American military personnel could be targeted in retaliation for the behavior of mercenaries, Congress must quickly act to regulate hiring practices of private military companies to screen against the hiring of terrorists, war criminals, or anyone who would potentially misrepresent the United States.

8 The fifth problem with the use of mercenaries is that the growth of the private security industry entices many of America's most experienced soldiers to leave the military for higher paying contractor jobs. Eric Schmitt and Tom Shanker, writing in the *New York Times*, explain the lure of contractors' salaries:

> Senior enlisted members of the Army Green Berets or Navy Seals with 20 years or more experience now earn about $50,000 in base pay, and can retire with a $23,000 pension. But private security companies ... are offering salaries of $100,000 to nearly $200,000 a year to the most experienced of them.

The military is losing some of its finest soldiers to the private sector where their expertise goes to the highest bidder. The use of mercenaries must be swiftly restrained and eventually halted lest the military be gradually stripped of its edge and become further reliant upon the expertise of private military companies.

9 Finally, the sixth major problem regarding the use of mercenaries is that the rapid increase in their numbers is creating large international interest groups who will *want war* in the long run. For mercenaries, war means fortune and excitement, and peace means a boring period of unemployment. The creation of such groups who thrive off violent conflict is dangerous on a very fundamental level. In the interests of peace, mercenaries and any other war profiteers must not be encouraged through governmental employment. The business of war has proven lucrative, and the free market must not be allowed to encourage way any more than it already does.

10 The expanded use of mercenaries in American warfare has given rise to numerous problems that must be addressed immediately. Among the obvious, their use hides the true cost of war from the American people; contractors' backgrounds and loyalties are questionable; and they have been given a great reason to hope for war in the world. These problems must be addressed swiftly and immediately, particularly by Congress. Mercenaries are used because they are cheaper, both economically and

politically, but they also serve the critical purpose of circumventing the scrutiny of Congress and the people of the United States. Action must be taken now to disable this circumvention of democracy and to protect legitimate uses of war from market forces, lawlessness, and the abuse of power.

Works Cited

Barstow, David. "Security Companies: Shadow Soldiers in Iraq." *New York Times* 19 Apr. 2004: A1+. *Lexis-Nexis*. Web. 19 May 2004.

Bredemeier, Kenneth. "Thousands of Private Contractors Support U.S. Forces in Persian Gulf." *Washington Post.* Washington Post, 3 Mar. 2003: E01. Web. 19 May 2004.

Carter, Phillip. "Hired Guns: What to Do about Military Contractors Run Amok." *Slate* 9 Apr. 2004. Web. 12 June 2004.

---."How to Discipline Private Contractors." *Slate* 4 May 2004. Web. 19 May 2004.

"Dangerous Work." *Economist* 10 Apr. 2004: 22–23. *Academic Search Premier*. Web. 23 May 2004.

Daragahi, Borzou. "In Iraq, Private Contractors Lighten Load on U.S. Troops." *Post-gazette.com*. PG Publishing, 28 Sept. 2003. Web. 19 May 2004.

Hammer, Joshua. "Cowboy Up." *New Republic* 24 May 2004: 18–19. *Academic Search Premier*. Web. 23 May 2004.

Nevaer, Louis. "Many Hired Guns in Iraq Have War Crimes Pasts." *National Catholic Reporter* 14 May 2004: 10. Print.

"Privatizing Warfare." Editorial. *New York Times* 21 Apr. 2004: A22. *Lexis-Nexis*. Web. 19 May 2004.

Schmitt, Eric, and Tom Shanker. "Big Pay Luring Military's Elite to Private Jobs." *New York Times* 30 Mar. 2004: A1+. *Lexis-Nexis*. Web. 19 May 2004.

THINKING CRITICALLY

about "'The Hardest of the Hardcore': Let's Outlaw Hired Guns in Contemporary American Warfare"

1. Many people are unaware that a problem might exist with civilian contractors in Iraq. Dylan's major rhetorical task, therefore, is to persuade readers that a problem exists. To what extent do you think he convinces readers that the use of civilian contractors to fulfill military roles constitutes a problem? Point to passages that you think are or are not persuasive in building his case.

2. The structure of Dylan's paper is almost entirely devoted to showing that a problem exists. However, his proposed solution is vague: either to eliminate the use of contractors in military roles entirely or to demand more congressional oversight. Dylan's strategy is typical for "planning proposals" (see p. 449) where the writer points out a problem but is unable to propose a clear

plan for solving it. Does this strategy work for you? Do you think Dylan needs to propose a more specific solution, or is it enough that he simply identifies a problem?

3. Overall, how would you evaluate the *logos* of this argument? How effective is Dylan's use of reasons and evidence to convince you that the continued use of civilian contractors in military roles is a problem that requires some action?

4. How effective are Dylan's appeals to *ethos* and *pathos*? To what extent does Dylan project a credible and trustworthy persona? To what extent does he connect his argument to the values and beliefs of his audience, appealing to readers' emotions and sympathies as well as to their minds?

For additional writing, reading, and research resources, go to **www.MyCompLab.com** and choose **Ramage/Bean/Johnson's *The Allyn & Bacon Guide to Writing,* Fifth Edition.**

PART 3

A GUIDE TO COMPOSING AND REVISING

This painting by Dutch artist Jan Havickszoon Steen is entitled *Rhetoricians at a Window*. Steen, a contemporary of Rembrandt, painted during the mid-1600s. During this period, the term "rhetorician" (a translation of the Dutch *rederijker*) referred to amateur poets, dramatists, and orators whose performances provided popular entertainment. What view of the intellectual life is provided by this painting? Consider how the positioning of these figures, with the town orator-poets leaning out of the window and with the painter seeing this scene from outside and below the room, contributes to the dominant impression of the painting.

This image is part of a discussion of two contrasting paintings in Chapter 11, pages 293–294, that focuses on how the angle of vision and compositional features of paintings contribute to thematic effect.

The Philadelphia Museum of Art/Art Resources, NY

PART 3 A GUIDE TO COMPOSING AND REVISING

Council of Writing Program Administrators Outcomes for First-Year Composition

CHAPTER 17 Writing as a Problem-Solving Process

PROCESSES	• Be aware that it usually takes multiple drafts to create and complete a successful text (Skill 1) • Develop flexible strategies for generating, revising, editing, and proofreading (Skills 2 and 3) • Understand writing as an open process that permits writers to use later invention and re-thinking to revise their work (Skills 2 and 3) • Understand the collaborative and social aspects of writing processes (Skill 4) • Learn to critique their own and others' works (Skill 4) • Learn to balance the advantages of relying on others with the responsibility of doing their part (Skill 3)

CHAPTER 18 Composing and Revising Closed-Form Prose

CHAPTER 19 Composing and Revising Open-Form Prose

RHETORICAL KNOWLEDGE	• Respond to the needs of different audiences (Skills 5 and 6) • Respond appropriately to different kinds of rhetorical situations (Skills 6 and 15) • Use conventions of format and structure appropriate to the rhetorical situation (Skills 5–9 and 12–17) • Understand how genres shape reading and writing (Skills 6, 8, 15, and 17)
KNOWLEDGE OF CONVENTIONS	• Learn common formats for different kinds of texts (Skills 8, 9, and 14) • Develop knowledge of genre conventions ranging from structure and paragraphing to tone and mechanics (Skills 10–12, 16, 18–20).

WRITING AS A PROBLEM-SOLVING PROCESS

CHAPTER 17

I rewrite as I write. It is hard to tell what is a first draft because it is not determined by time. In one draft, I might cross out three pages, write two, cross out a fourth, rewrite it, and call it a draft. I am constantly writing and rewriting. I can only conceptualize so much in my first draft—only so much information can be held in my head at one time; my rewriting efforts are a reflection of how much information I can encompass at one time. There are levels and agenda which I have to attend to in each draft.*

—*Description of Revision by an Experienced Writer*

I read what I have written and I cross out a word and put another word in; a more decent word or a better word. Then if there is somewhere to use a sentence that I have crossed out, I will put it there.*

—*Description of Revision by an Inexperienced Writer*

Blot out, correct, insert, refine,
Enlarge, diminish, interline;
Be mindful, when invention fails,
To scratch your head, and bite your nails.

—*Jonathan Swift*

In Part 1 of this text, we explained twelve rhetorical concepts aimed at helping you think about your subject matter from the perspective of purpose, audience, and genre. In Part 3, we turn to the nuts and bolts of actually composing and revising your essays. Part 3 has three self-contained chapters that can be read in whatever order best fits your instructor's course plan. The present chapter focuses on writing as a problem-solving process, while Chapters 18 and 19 teach strategies for composing and revising closed-form and open-form prose.

*From Nancy Sommers, "Revision Strategies of Student Writers and Experienced Adult Writers," *College Composition and Communication* 31 (October 1980): 291–300.

In this chapter, we explain how experienced writers use multiple drafts to manage the complexities of writing and suggest ways that you can improve your own writing processes. The four skills explained in this chapter will help you appreciate how and why expert writers revise, understand global as well as local revision, develop expert habits for composing and revising, and use peer reviews to help you think like an expert. As you practice applying these skills to your college writing projects, you will become more confident in your growing ability as a writer.

SKILL 1 Understand why expert writers use multiple drafts.

We begin this chapter with a close look at how expert writers compose and why they need multiple drafts. A writer's goal in composing and revising is to discover good ideas and make them clear to readers. But as composition theorist Peter Elbow has asserted, "meaning is not what you start out with" but "what you end up with." Thus composing is a discovery process. In the early stages of writing, experienced writers typically discover what they are trying to say, often deepening and complicating their ideas rather than clarifying them. Only in the last drafts will such writers be in sufficient control of their ideas to shape them elegantly for readers.

It's important not to overgeneralize, however, because no two writers compose exactly the same way; moreover, the same writer may use different processes for different kinds of prose. Some writers outline their ideas before they write; others need to write extensively before they can outline. Some write their first drafts very slowly, devoting extensive thought and planning to each emerging paragraph; others write first drafts rapidly, to be sure to get all their ideas on paper, and then rework the material part by part. Some prefer to work independently, without discussing or sharing their ideas; others seek out classmates or colleagues to help them hash out ideas and rehearse their arguments before writing them down. Some seek out the stillness of a library or private room; others do their best writing in noisy cafeterias or coffee shops.

The actual mechanics of composing differ from writer to writer as well. Some writers create first drafts directly at a keyboard, whereas others require the reassuring heft of a pen or pencil. Among writers who begin by planning the structure of their work, some make traditional outlines (perhaps using the outline feature of their word processors), whereas others prefer tree diagrams or flowcharts. Some of those who use word processors revise directly at the computer, whereas others print out a hard copy, revise with pen, and then type the changes into the computer.

Tree diagrams and flowcharts are explained in Chapter 18, Skill 7.

Also, writers often vary their composing processes from project to project. A writer might complete one project with a single draft and a quick editing job, but produce a half dozen or more drafts for another project.

What most distinguishes expert from novice writers is their willingness to keep revising their work until they feel it is ready to go public. They typically work much harder at drafting and revising than do novice writers, taking more runs at their subject. Expert writers also make more substantial alterations in their drafts during revision—what we call "global" rather than "local" revision. This difference between expert and novice writers might seem counterintuitive. One might think that novices would need to revise more than experts. But decades of research on the writing process of experts reveals how extensively experts revise. Compare the first two quotations that open this chapter—one from an experienced and one from an inexperienced writer. The experienced writer crosses out pages and starts over while the inexperienced writer crosses out a word or two. The experienced writer feels cognitive overload while drafting, having to attend to many different "levels and agendas" at once. In contrast, the inexperienced writer seems to think only of replacing words or perhaps moving a sentence. Figure 17.1 shows the first page of a first draft of a magazine article written by an experienced freelance writer.

FIGURE 17.1 Draft Page of Experienced Writer

Minoan/Assyrian/Etruscan too—check dates of gold bees, procession fibulae, etc!— contemp.? earlier? Story of Jewelry

In Ancient Greece, ~~the craft of jewelry making~~ [as in other parts of the Classical world, goldsmithing] was raised to a high art. [Work it—wooden] Classical goldsmiths worked the metal in its unrefined state, as it was extracted from the earth. Usually, the natural alloy was roughly equivalent to 22 karat gold. [later?] Using pine resin as an organic glue, mouth blow-pipes, and brick furnaces, ~~they~~ [goldsmiths] bonded surfaces without the use of solder, creating jewels of fabulous delicacy and seeming fragility. Yet many of these bonds ~~were strong enough to~~ [have] endure[d] more than two millennia, withstanding the ravages of entombment, grave robbers, dozens of wearers, and finally, ~~curatorial~~ [misguided] conservation [attempts]. [All later] Today, as museum-goers marvel at the [delicately] repoussed and richly granulated surfaces of a rosette earring or a ram's head necklace finial, they may wonder whether these were the creations of earthly beings or of angels. In fact, historical evidence seems to indicate that most of the Greek ~~goldsmiths used children to do the intricate work, perhaps at great expense to the children's health and especially their eyesight.~~

[live children, not angels, were the agency of the intricate work, —children indentured at the tender age of nine or ten, and ~~condem~~ often rendered sightless before they reached maturity.]

more transition

Check accent-sp?

here or later?

have to explain-size of granules, control required, etc. Have to have pix!

verify

cringe ~~to bathe their young faces in flames~~

Was this system— or slavery?

pressed into service

Lead?

Backing into corner? Want disc. of technology as well as social evils-maybe frame?? Beauty/achievements framed by sadness of human cost??

Why Expert Writers Revise So Extensively

To help you understand this puzzling difference between beginning and experienced writers, let's consider *why* expert writers revise. If they are such good writers, why don't they get it right the first time? To use the language from Part 1, expert writers need multiple drafts to help them pose, pursue, and solve problems—both subject-matter problems and related rhetorical problems about purpose, audience, and genre. Faced with many choices, experienced writers use multiple drafts to break a complex task into manageable subtasks. Let's look more closely at some of the functions that revising can perform for writers.

- **Multiple drafts help writers overcome the limits of short-term memory.** Cognitive psychologists have shown that working memory—often called short-term memory—has remarkably little storage space. People use short-term memory to hold the data on which they are actively focusing at any given moment when solving a problem, reading a text, writing a draft, or performing other cognitive tasks. (Note how the experienced writer quoted in our epigraph says, "I can only conceptualize so much in my first draft—only so much information can be held in my head at one time. ... ") Writing a draft captures these ideas from short-term memory and stores them on paper. When you reread these stored ideas, you can note problem areas, think of new ideas, see material that doesn't fit, recall additional information, and so forth. You can then begin working on a new draft, focusing on one problem at a time.
- **Multiple drafts help accommodate shifts and changes in the writer's ideas.** Early in the writing process, expert writers often are unsure of what they want to say or where their ideas are leading; they find that their ideas shift and evolve as their drafts progress. Often, writing a draft leads the writer to reformulate the initial problem, to revise the thesis statement, or otherwise to discover new ideas that need to be accommodated. An expert writer's finished product often is radically different from the first draft—not simply in form and style but also in actual content.
- **Multiple drafts help writers clarify audience and purpose.** While thinking about their subject matter, experienced writers also ask questions about audience and purpose: Who are my readers? What do they already know and believe about my subject? How am I trying to change their views? What image of myself do I want to project? In the process of drafting and revising, the answers to these questions may evolve so that each new draft reflects a deeper or clearer understanding of audience and purpose.
- **Multiple drafts help writers create structure and coherence for readers.** Whereas the ideas in early drafts often follow the order in which writers conceived them, later drafts are often restructured—sometimes radically—to meet readers' needs. A typical kind of restructuring occurs when writers discover that their conclusions are clearer than their introductions. Having discovered and clarified their ideas while drafting, writers must shift their conclusion back to the introduction and rewrite the essay to follow the newly discovered order. Writing teachers sometimes call this transformation a

movement from writer-based to reader-based prose.* The composing and revising skills taught in Chapter 18 will help you learn how to revise your drafts from a reader's perspective.

- **Multiple drafts let writers save correctness for late in the writing process.** Late in the revision process, experienced writers turn their energy toward finding usage errors, punctuating effectively, checking their spelling, and revising sentences until they are concise, clear, graceful, and pleasing to the ear.

An Expert's Writing Processes Are Recursive

Given this background on why expert writers revise, we can now see that for expert writers, the writing process is recursive rather than linear. Writers continually cycle back to earlier stages as their thinking evolves. Sometimes writers develop a thesis statement early in the writing process. But just as frequently they formulate a thesis during an "aha!" moment of discovery later in the process, perhaps after several drafts. ("So *this* is my point! Here is my argument in a nutshell!") Even very late in the process, while checking usage and punctuation, experienced writers are apt to think of new ideas, thus triggering more revision. Furthermore, a writer might be "early in the process" for one part of a draft and "late in the process" for another. Frequently, a writer can also reconceptualize the argument late in the process and seemingly "start over"—but the time has not been wasted since the whole process has led to the writer's new ideas.

SKILL 2 Revise globally as well as locally.

To think like an expert writer, you need to appreciate the difference between "global" and "local" revision. You revise *locally* whenever you make changes to a text that affect only the one or two sentences that you are currently working on. In contrast, you revise *globally* when a change in one part of your draft drives changes in other parts of the draft. Global revision focuses on the big-picture concerns of ideas, structure, purpose, audience, and genre. Consider this analogy: When you revise globally you think of your essay as an ecosystem where alterations in one component (the introduction of a new predator, the loss of a food source, climate change) can alter the whole system. By analogy, what you say in the introduction of your essay shapes what you do in the middle of the essay. Revisions you make in the middle of the essay might lead you to rewrite the whole introduction or to change the tone or point of view throughout the essay. The parts, in other words, all connect to an integrated whole. Moreover, every large ecosystem contains many smaller subsystems. Not only can you revise a whole paper globally, but you can also revise sections or paragraphs globally.

Because they blend into each other, there is no hard-and-fast line that distinguishes global from local revision. Our point is simply that expert writers often

*The terms "writer-based" and "reader-based" prose come from Linda Flower, "Writer-Based Prose: A Cognitive Basis for Problems in Writing." College English, 1979, 41.1, 19–37.

make substantial changes to their first drafts. Moreover, this passion for revision is one of the distinguishing characteristics of expert as opposed to novice writers. What follows are some on-the-page strategies that you can adopt to practice the global revision strategies of experts:*

ON-THE-PAGE STRATEGIES

for Doing Global and Local Revision

Strategies to Use on the Page	Reasons
Throw out the whole draft and start again.	• Original draft helped writer discover ideas and see the whole territory. • New draft needs to be substantially refocused and restructured.
Cross out large chunks and rewrite from scratch.	• Original passage was unfocused; ideas have changed. • New sense of purpose or point meant that the whole passage needed reshaping. • Original passage was too confused or jumbled for mere editing.
Cut and paste; move parts around; (then write new transitions, mapping statements, and topic sentences).	• Parts didn't follow in logical order. • Parts occurred in the order writer thought of them rather than the order needed by readers. • Conclusion was clearer than introduction; part of conclusion had to be moved to introduction. • Revised thesis statement required different order for parts.
Add /revise topic sentences of paragraphs; insert transitions.	• Reader needs signposts to see how parts connect to previous parts and to whole. • Revision of topic sentences often requires global revision of paragraph.
Make insertions; add new material.	• Supporting particulars needed to be added: examples, facts, illustrations, statistics, other evidence (usually added to bodies of paragraphs). • New section was needed or more explanation was needed for a point. • Gaps in argument needed to be filled in.

*We have chosen to say "on the page" rather than "on the screen" because global revision is often facilitated by a writer's working off double-spaced hard copy rather than a computer screen. See pages 496–497 for our advice on using hard copy for revision.

Strategies to Use on the Page	Reasons
Delete material.	• Material is no longer needed or is irrelevant. • Deleted material may have been good but went off on a tangent.
Recast sentences (cross out and rewrite portions; combine sentences; rephrase sentences; start sentences with a different grammatical structure).	• Passage violated old/new contract (see pp. 533–538). • Passage was wordy/choppy or lacked rhythm or voice. • Grammar was tangled, diction odd, or meaning confused. • Passage lost focus of topic sentence of paragraph.
Edit sentences to correct mistakes.	• Writer found comma splices, fragments, dangling modifiers, nonparallel constructions, or other problems of grammar and usage. • Writer found spelling errors, typos, repeated or omitted words.

FOR WRITING AND DISCUSSION

Revising a Paragraph Globally

Choose an important paragraph in the body of a draft you are currently working on. Then write your answers to these questions about that paragraph.

1. Why is this an important paragraph?
2. What is its main point?
3. Where is that main point stated?

Now—as an exercise only—write the main point at the top of a blank sheet of paper, put away your original draft, and, without looking at the original, write a new paragraph with the sole purpose of developing the point you wrote at the top of the page.

When you are finished, compare your new paragraph to the original. What have you learned that might help you revise your original?

Here are some typical responses of writers who have tried this exercise:

> I recognized that my original paragraph was unfocused. I couldn't find a main point.
>
> I recognized that my original paragraph was underdeveloped. I had a main point but not enough particulars supporting it.
>
> I began to see that my draft was scattered and that I had too many short paragraphs.
>
> I recognized that I was making a couple of different points in my original paragraph and that I needed to break it into separate paragraphs.
>
> I recognized that I hadn't stated my main point (or that I had buried it in the middle of the paragraph).

(*continued*)

I recognized that there was a big difference in style between my two versions and that I had to choose which version I liked best. (It's not always the "new" version!)

SKILL 3 Develop ten expert habits to improve your writing processes.

Now that you understand why experts revise more extensively than novices and what they do on the page, we describe in Skill 3 the habitual ways of thinking and acting that experts use when they write. Our hope is that this description will help you develop these same habits for yourself. Because one of the best ways to improve your writing process is to do what the experts do, we offer you the following ten habits of experienced writers, expressed as advice:

1. ***Use exploratory writing and talking to discover and clarify ideas.*** Don't let your first draft be the first time you put your ideas into written words. Use exploratory writing such as freewriting, focused freewriting, and idea mapping (see Chapter 2, Concept 5) to generate ideas and deepen your thinking. Also seek out opportunities to talk about your ideas with classmates or friends in order to clarify your own thinking and appreciate alternative points of view. Whenever possible, talk through your draft with a friend; rehearse your argument in conversation as practice for putting it in writing.
2. ***Think rhetorically from the start.*** From the very start of a writing project, experts think about the effect they want their writing to have on readers. Develop this same habit. As you compose and revise, particularly concentrate on formulating the question or problem that your thesis will address and look for ways to engage readers' interest in that question. In seeking a thesis, look for ways to change your readers' view of your subject. ("Before reading my paper, my readers will think X about my topic. But after reading my paper, my readers will think Y.") Learning to think habitually about purpose and audience will serve you well in any writing context ranging from first-year composition through advanced papers in your major to your business or professional life.
3. ***Schedule your time.*** Plan for exploration, drafting, revision, and editing. Don't begin your paper the night before it is due. Give ideas time to ruminate in your mind. Recognize that your ideas will shift, branch out, even turn around as you write. Allow some time off between writing the first draft and beginning revision. Experienced writers build in time for revision.
4. ***Discover what methods of drafting work best for you.*** Some people compose rough drafts directly on the computer; others write longhand. Some make outlines first; others plunge directly into drafting and make outlines later. Some revise extensively on the computer as they are drafting; others plough ahead until they have a complete draft before they start revising. Some people sit at their desk for hours at a time; others need to get up and walk around every couple of minutes. Some people need a quiet room; others work best in a coffee shop. Discover the methods that work best for you.

5. ***For early drafts, reduce your expectations.*** Many novice writers get writer's block by trying to make drafts perfect as they go along. In contrast, expert writers expect the first draft to be an unreadable mess (often they call the first draft a "zero draft" or a "garbage draft" because they don't expect it to be good). They use the first draft merely to get their ideas flowing and to get some words on paper, knowing they will revise later. In short, don't aim for perfection in your first draft. If you get blocked, keep writing. Just get some ideas on paper.
6. ***Revise on double- or triple-spaced hard copy.*** Although many experienced writers revise on the screen without going through paper drafts, there are powerful advantages in printing occasional paper drafts. Research suggests that writers are apt to make more global changes in a draft if they work from hard copy. Because they can see the whole draft at once without having to scroll through a file, they can see more easily how the parts connect to the whole. They can look back at page two while revising page six. We suggest that you occasionally print out a double-or triple-spaced hard copy of your draft and then mark it up aggressively. Cross out text to be changed and write new text in the blank spaces between the lines. Make inserts. Draw arrows. (See again Figure 17.1, which shows how a professional writer marks up a draft.) When your draft gets too messy, keyboard your changes into your computer and begin another round of revision.
7. ***As you revise, think increasingly about the needs of your readers.*** Experts use first drafts to help them clarify their ideas for themselves but not necessarily for readers. In many respects, writers of first drafts are talking to themselves. Through global revision, however, writers gradually convert "writer-based prose" to "reader-based prose." Writers begin to employ consciously the skills of reader-expectation theory that we explain in detail in Chapter 18.
8. ***Exchange drafts with others.*** Get other people's reactions to your work in exchange for your reactions to theirs. Experienced writers regularly seek critiques of their drafts from trusted readers. Later in this chapter we explain procedures for peer review of drafts.
9. ***Save correctness for last.*** To revise productively, concentrate first on the big questions: Do I have good ideas in this draft? Am I responding appropriately to the assignment? Are my ideas adequately organized and developed? Save questions about exact wording, grammar, mechanics, and documentation style for later. These concerns are important, but they cannot be efficiently attended to until after higher-order concerns are met. Your first goal is to create a thoughtful, richly developed draft.
10. ***To meet deadlines and bring the process to a close, learn how to* satisfice.** Our description of the writing process may seem formidable. Technically, it seems, you could go on revising forever. How can you ever know when to stop? There is no ready answer to that question, which is more a psychological than a technical problem. Expert writers have generally learned how to *satisfice,* a term coined by influential social scientist Herbert Simon from two root words, *suffice* and *satisfy*. It means to do the best job you can under the circumstances considering your time constraints, the pressures of other demands on you, and the difficulty of the task. Expert writers begin the writing process early and get as far as they can before their deadline looms. Then they let the deadline give them the

energy for intensive revision. From lawyers preparing briefs for court to engineers developing design proposals, writers have used deadlines to help them put aside doubts and anxieties and to conclude their work, as every writer must. "Okay, it's not perfect, but it's the best I can do for now."

FOR WRITING AND DISCUSSION

Analyzing Your Own Writing Process

When you write, do you follow a process resembling the one we just described? Have you ever

- had a writing project grow out of your engagement with a problem or question?
- explored ideas by talking with others or by doing exploratory writing?
- made major changes to a draft because you changed your mind or otherwise discovered new ideas?
- revised a draft from a reader's perspective by consciously trying to imagine and respond to a reader's questions, confusions, and other reactions?
- road tested a draft by trying it out on readers and then revising it as a result of what they told you?

Working in groups or as a whole class, share stories about previous writing experiences that match or do not match the description of experienced writers' processes. To the extent that your present process differs, what strategies of experienced writers might you like to try?

SKILL 4 Use peer reviews to help you think like an expert.

One of the best ways to become a better reviser is to see your draft from a *reader*'s rather than a *writer*'s perspective. As a writer, you know what you mean; you are already inside your own head. But you need to see what your draft looks like to readers—that is, to people who are not inside your head.

A good way to learn this skill is to practice reading your classmates' drafts and have them read yours. In this section we offer advice on how to respond candidly to your classmates' drafts and how to participate in peer reviews.

Become a Helpful Reader of Classmates' Drafts

When you respond to a writer's draft, learn to make *readerly* rather than *writerly* comments. For example, instead of saying, "Your draft is disorganized," say, "I got lost when … ." Instead of saying, "This paragraph needs a topic sentence," say, "I had trouble seeing the point of this paragraph." In other words, describe your mental experience in trying to understand the draft rather than use technical terms to point out problem areas or to identify errors.

When you help a writer with a draft, your goal is both to point out where the draft needs more work and to brainstorm with the writer possible ways to improve the draft. Begin by reading the draft all the way through at a normal reading speed. As you read, make mental notes to help focus your feedback. We recommend that you also mark passages that you find confusing. Write "G!" for "Good" next to parts that you like. Write "?" next to places where you want to ask questions.

After you have read the draft, use the following strategies for making helpful responses, either in writing or in direct conversation with the writer.

STRATEGIES

for Responding Helpfully to a Classmate's Draft

Kinds of Problems Noted	Helpful Responses
If the ideas in the draft seem thin or undeveloped, or if the draft is too short	• Help the writer brainstorm for more ideas. • Help the writer add more examples, better details, more supporting data or arguments.
If you get confused or lost in some parts of the draft	• Show the writer where you got confused or miscued in reading the draft ("I started getting lost here because I couldn't see why you were giving me this information" or "I thought you were going to say X, but then you said Y"). • Have the writer talk through ideas to clear up confusing spots.

If you get confused or lost at the "big-picture" level	• Help the writer sharpen the thesis: suggest that the writer view the thesis as the answer to a controversial or problematic question; ask the writer to articulate the question that the thesis answers.
	• Help the writer create an outline, tree diagram, or flowchart (see Chapter 18, Skill 7).
	• Help the writer clarify the focus by asking him or her to complete these statements about purpose:
	  • The purpose of this paper is ________.
	  • The purpose of this section (paragraph) is ________.
	  • Before reading my paper, my reader will think X. But after reading my paper, my reader will think Y.

If you can understand the sentences but can't see the point	• Help the writer articulate the meaning by asking "So what?" questions, making the writer bring the point to the surface. ("I can understand what you are saying here but I don't quite understand why you are saying it. What do these details have to do with the topic sentence of the paragraph? Or what does this paragraph have to do with your thesis?") • Help the writer create transitions, new topic sentences, or other means of making points clear.
If you disagree with the ideas or think the writer has avoided alternative points of view	• Play devil's advocate to help the writer deepen and complicate ideas. • Show the writer specific places where you had queries or doubts.

Use a Generic Peer Review Guide

When participating in peer reviews, writers and reviewers often appreciate a list of guiding questions or checkpoints. What follows is a list of generic questions that can be used for peer-reviewing many different kinds of drafts. In each assignment chapter for Part 2 of this text, we have created additional peer review questions tailored specifically to that chapter's rhetorical aim and genres. For any given peer review session, your instructor may specify which generic or assignment-specific questions you are to use for the peer review.

Generic Peer Review Guide

For the writer

Prepare two or three questions you would like your peer reviewer to address while responding to your draft. The questions can focus on some aspect of your draft that you are uncertain about, on one or more sections where you particularly seek help or advice, on some feature that you particularly like about your draft, or on some part you especially wrestled with. Write out your questions and give them to your peer reviewer along with your draft.

For the reviewer

Basic overview: Read the draft at a normal reading speed from beginning to end. As you read do the following:

- Mark a "?" next to any passages that you find confusing, that somehow slow down your reading, or that raise questions in your mind.
- Mark a "G" next to any passages where you think the writing is particularly good, strong, or interesting.

Going into more depth: Prior to discussion with the writer, complete the following tasks:

- Identify at least one specific place in the draft where you got confused. Make notes for why you got confused, using readerly rather than writerly comments.
- Identify one place in the draft where you think the ideas are thin or need more development. Make discussion notes.
- Identify one place where you might write "So what?" after the passage. These are places where you don't understand the significance or importance of the writer's points. These are also places where you can't see how certain sentences connect to a topic sentence or how certain paragraphs or sections connect to the thesis statement.
- Identify at least one place where you could play devil's advocate or otherwise object to the writer's ideas. Make notes on the objections or alternative views that you will raise with the writer.

Evaluating the writer's argument: Look at the draft's effectiveness from the perspective of the classical rhetorical appeals:

- *Logos:* How effectively does the writer use reasons and evidence to support his or her claim? How effectively does the writer use details, particulars, examples, and other means as evidence to support points? How logical are the points and how clearly are they connected?

- *Ethos:* What kind of image does the writer project? How effective is the tone? How trustworthy, reliable, knowledgeable, and fair does this writer seem?
- *Pathos:* How effectively does the writer engage the audience's interest? How effectively does the writer tie into the audience's beliefs and values? To what extent does the writer make the reader care about the topic?

Noting problems of grammar and editing: Mark the draft wherever you notice problems in grammar, spelling, punctuation, documentation form, or other issues of mechanics.

Summing up: Create a consolidated summary of your review:

- Sum up the strengths of the draft.
- Identify two or three main weaknesses or problem areas.
- Make two or three suggestions for revision.

FOR WRITING AND DISCUSSION

Practicing a Peer Review

Background: In the following exercise, we invite you to practice a peer review by responding to a student's draft ("Should the University Carpet the Dorm Rooms?" below) or to another draft provided by your instructor. The "Carpets" assignment asked students to take a stand on a local campus issue. Imagine that you have exchanged drafts with this student and that your task is to help this student improve the draft through both global and local revision.

Individual task: Read the draft carefully following the instructions in the "Generic Peer Review Guide". Write out your responses to the bulleted items under "Going into more depth," "Evaluating the writer's argument," and "Summing up."

Small group or whole class: Share your responses. Then turn to the following additional tasks:

1. With the instructor serving as a guide, practice explaining to the writer where or how you got confused while reading the draft. Readers often have difficulty explaining their reading experience to a writer. Let several class members role-play being the reader. Practice using language such as "I like the way this draft started because … ." "I got confused when … ." "I had to back up and reread when … ." "I saw your point here, but then I got lost again because … ." Writing theorist Peter Elbow calls such language a "movie of your mind."
2. Have several class members role-play being devil's advocates by arguing against the writer's thesis. Where are the ideas thin or weak?

(*continued*)

Should the University Carpet the Dorm Rooms?

Tricia, a university student, came home exhausted from her work-study job. She took a blueberry pie from the refrigerator to satisfy her hunger and a tall glass of milk to quench her thirst. While trying to get comfortable on her bed, she tipped her snack over onto the floor. She cleaned the mess, but the blueberry and milk stains on her brand-new carpet could not be removed.

Tricia didn't realize how hard it was to clean up stains on a carpet. Luckily this was her own carpet.

A lot of students don't want carpets. Students constantly change rooms. The next person may not want carpet.

Some students say that since they pay to live on campus, the rooms should reflect a comfortable home atmosphere. Carpets will make the dorm more comfortable. The carpet will act as insulation and as a soundproofing system.

Paint stains cannot be removed from carpets. If the university carpets the rooms, the students will lose the privilege they have of painting their rooms any color. This would limit students' self-expression.

The carpets would be an institutional brown or gray. This would be ugly. With tile floors, the students can choose and purchase their own carpets to match their taste. You can't be an individual if you can't decorate your room to fit your personality.

According to Rachel Jones, Assistant Director of Housing Services, the cost will be $300 per room for the carpet and installation. Also the university will have to buy more vacuum cleaners. But will vacuum cleaners be all that is necessary to keep the carpets clean? We'll need shampoo machines too.

What about those stains that won't come off even with a shampoo machine? That's where the student will have to pay damage deposit costs.

There will be many stains on the carpet due to shaving cream fights, food fights, beverage parties, and smoking, all of which can damage the carpets.

Students don't take care of the dorms now. They don't follow the rules of maintaining their rooms. They drill holes into the walls, break mirrors, beds, and closet doors, and leave their food trays all over the floor.

If the university buys carpets our room rates will skyrocket. In conclusion, it is a bad idea for the university to buy carpets.

Participate in Peer Review Workshops

If you are willing to respond candidly to a classmate's draft—in a readerly rather than a writerly way—you will be a valuable participant in peer review workshops. In a typical workshop, classmates work in group of two to six to respond to each other's rough drafts and offer suggestions for revisions. These workshops are most helpful when group members have developed sufficient levels of professionalism and trust to exchange candid responses. A frequent problem in peer review workshops is that classmates try so hard to avoid hurting each other's feelings that they provide vague, meaningless feedback. Saying, "Your paper's great. I really liked it. Maybe you could make it flow a little better" is much less helpful than saying, "Your issue about environmental pollution in the Antarctic is well defined in the first paragraph, but I got lost in the second paragraph when you began discussing penguin coloration."

Responsibilities of Peer Reviewers and Writers

Learning to respond conscientiously and carefully to others' work may be the single most important thing you can do to improve your own writing. When you review a classmate's draft, you are not acting as a teacher, but simply as a fresh reader. You can help the writer appreciate what it's like to encounter his or her text for the first time. Your primary responsibility is to articulate your understanding of what the writer's words say to you and to identify places where you get confused, where you need more details, where you have doubts or queries, and so on.

When you play the role of writer during a workshop session, your responsibilities parallel those of your peer reviewers. You need to provide a legible rough draft, preferably typed and double-spaced, that doesn't baffle the reader with hard-to-follow corrections and confusing pagination. Your instructor may ask you to bring copies of your draft for all group members. During the workshop, your primary responsibility is to *listen,* taking in how others respond to your draft without becoming defensive. Many instructors also ask writers to formulate two or three specific questions about their drafts—questions they particularly want their reviewers to address. These questions might focus on something writers particularly like about their drafts or on specific problem areas or concerns.

Initial Exchange of Drafts

Once you exchange drafts with a classmate, you can either read the drafts silently or follow along on the hard copy as each writer reads his or her draft aloud. If time permits, we value reading drafts aloud. Reading expressively, with appropriate emphasis, helps writers distance themselves from their work and hear it anew. When you read your work silently to yourself, it's all too easy to patch up bits of broken prose in your head or to slide through confusing passages. But if you stumble over a passage while reading aloud, you can place a check mark in the margin to indicate where further attention is needed. Another benefit to reading aloud is perhaps more symbolic than pragmatic: Reading your work to others means that you are claiming responsibility for it, displaying your intention to reach a range of readers other than the teacher. And knowing that you will have to read your work aloud will encourage you to have that work in the best possible shape before bringing it to class.

After you've read each other's drafts, the next stage of your peer review may take one of several forms, depending on your instructor's preference. We describe here two basic strategies: response-centered workshops, and advice-centered workshops. Additional strategies often build on these approaches.

Response-Centered Workshops

This process-oriented, non-intrusive approach places maximum responsibility on the writer for making decisions about what to change in a draft. After the writer reads the draft aloud, group members follow this procedure:

1. All participants take several minutes to make notes on their copies of the manuscript. We recommend using the system described in the Generic Peer Review Guide.
2. Group members take turns describing to the writer their responses to the piece—where they agreed or disagreed with the writer's ideas, where they got confused, where they wanted more development, and so forth. Group members do not give advice; they simply describe their own personal response to the draft as written.
3. The writer takes notes during each response but does not enter into a discussion. The writer listens without trying to defend the piece or explain what he or she intended.

No one gives the writer explicit advice. Group members simply describe their reactions to the piece and leave it to the writer to make appropriate changes.

Advice-Centered Workshops

In this more product-oriented and directive approach, peer reviewers typically work in pairs. Each writer exchanges drafts with a partner, reviews the draft carefully, and then writes specific advice on how to improve the draft. This method works best when peer reviewers use specific questions selected by the instructor from the Generic Peer Review Guide or from genre-specific questions for each assignment in Part 2.

A variation on this approach, which allows peer reviewers to collaborate in pairs when analyzing a draft, uses the following process:

1. The instructor divides the class into initial groups of four.
2. Each group then divides into pairs; each pair exchanges drafts with the other pair.
3. The members of each pair collaborate to compose jointly written reviews of the two drafts they have received.
4. The drafts and the collaboratively written reviews are then returned to the original writers. If time remains, the two pairs meet to discuss their reviews.

When two students collaborate to review a draft, they often produce more useful and insightful reviews than when working individually. In sharing observations and negotiating their responses, they can write their reviews with more confidence and reduce the chances of idiosyncratic advice.

However, because each pair has received two drafts and has to write two peer reviews, this approach takes more class time. Instructors can speed up this process by setting up the groups of four in advance and asking pairs to exchange and read drafts prior to the class meeting. Class time can then be focused on collaborative writing of the reviews.

Respond to Peer Reviews

After you and your classmates have gone over each other's papers and walked each other through the responses, everyone should identify two or three things about his or her draft that particularly need work. Before you leave the session, you should have some notion about how you want to revise your paper.

You may get mixed or contradictory responses from different reviewers. One reviewer may praise a passage that another finds confusing or illogical. Conflicting advice is a frustrating fact of life for all writers, whether students or professionals. Such disagreements reveal how readers cocreate a text with a writer: Each brings to the text a different background, set of values, and way of reading.

It is important to remember that you are in charge of your own writing. If several readers offer the same critique of a passage, then no matter how much you love that passage, you probably need to follow their advice. But when readers disagree, you have to make your own best judgment about whom to heed.

Once you have received advice from others, reread your draft again slowly and then develop a revision plan, allowing yourself time to make sweeping, global changes if needed. You also need to remember that you can never make your draft perfect. Plan when you will bring the process to a close so that you can turn in a finished product on time and get on with your other classes and your life.

Chapter Summary

This chapter has focused on the writing processes of experts, showing how experienced writers use multiple drafts to solve subject-matter and rhetorical problems. We have also offered advice on how to improve your own writing processes. Particularly, beginning college writers need to understand the kinds of changes writers typically make in drafts, to role-play a reader's perspective when they revise, and to practice the revision strategies of experts. Because peer reviewing is a powerful strategy for learning how to revise, we showed you how to make "readerly" rather than "writerly" comments on a rough draft and how to participate productively in peer review workshops.

For additional writing, reading, and research resources, go to **www.MyCompLab.com** and choose **Ramage/Bean/Johnson's *The Allyn & Bacon Guide to Writing,* Fifth Edition.**

CHAPTER 18

COMPOSING AND REVISING CLOSED-FORM PROSE

[Form is] an arousing and fulfillment of desires. A work has form insofar as one part of it leads a reader to anticipate another part, to be gratified by the sequence.

—*Kenneth Burke, Rhetorician*

I think the writer ought to help the reader as much as he can without damaging what he wants to say; and I don't think it ever hurts the writer to sort of stand back now and then and look at his stuff as if he were reading it instead of writing it.

—*James Jones, Writer*

Chapter 17 explained four skills for composing and revising based on the writing practices of experts. In this chapter we present ten more skills that focus specifically on closed-form prose. This chapter is not intended to be read in one sitting, lest you suffer from information overload. To help you learn the material efficiently, we present each skill as a self-contained lesson that can be read comfortably in half an hour or less and discussed in class as part of a day's session. You will benefit most from these lessons if you focus on one lesson at a time and then return to the lessons periodically as you progress through the term. Each lesson's advice will become increasingly meaningful and relevant as you gain experience as a writer.

The first lesson (Skill 5)—on learning to understand reader expectations—is intended as a theoretical overview to the rest of the chapter. The remaining nine lessons can then be assigned and read in any order your instructor desires. You will learn how to convert loose structures into thesis/support structures (Skill 6); how to plan and visualize your structure (Skill 7); how to write effective titles (Skill 8) and introductions (Skill 9); how to use topic sentences, transitions, and the old/new contract to guide your readers through the twists and turns of your prose (Skills 10–12); how to perform several common writer's "moves" for developing your ideas (Skill 13); and how to write good conclusions (Skill 14). Together these lessons will teach you strategies for making your closed-form prose reader-friendly, well structured, clear, and persuasive.

SKILL 5 Understand reader expectations.

In this opening lesson, we show you how to think like a reader. Imagine for a moment that your readers have only so much *reader energy*, which they can use either to follow and respond to your ideas (the result you want) or to puzzle over what you are trying to say (the result you don't want).* Skilled readers make predictions about where a text is heading based on clues provided by the writer. When readers get lost, the writer has often failed to give clues about where the text is going or has failed to do what the reader predicted. "Whoa, you lost me on the turn," a reader might say. "How does this passage relate to what you just said?" To write effective closed-form prose, you need to help readers see how each part of your text is related to what came before. (Sometimes with open-form prose, surprise or puzzlement may be the very effect you want to create. But with closed-form prose, this kind of puzzlement is fatal.)

In this lesson we explain what readers of closed-form prose need in order to predict where a text is heading. Specifically we show you that readers need three things in a closed-form text:

- They need unity and coherence.
- They need old information before new information.
- They need forecasting and fulfillment.

Let's look at each in turn.

Unity and Coherence

Together the terms *unity* and *coherence* are defining characteristics of closed-form prose, as shown in Figure 18.1. *Unity* refers to the relationship between each part of an essay and the larger whole. *Coherence* refers to the relationship between adjacent sentences, paragraphs, and parts. The following thought exercise will explore your own expectations for unity and coherence:

THOUGHT EXERCISE 1

Read the following two passages and try to explain why each fails to satisfy your expectations as a reader:

A. Recent research has given us much deeper—and more surprising—insights into the father's role in childrearing. My family is typical of the east side in that we never had much money. Their tongues became black and hung out of their mouths. The back-to-basics movement got a lot of press, fueled as it was by fears of growing illiteracy and cultural demise.

*For the useful term *reader energy,* we are indebted to George Gopen and Judith Swan, "The Science of Scientific Writing," *American Scientist* 78 (1990): 550–559. In addition, much of our discussion of writing in this chapter is indebted to the work of Joseph Williams, George Gopen, and Gregory Colomb. See especially Gregory G. Colomb and Joseph M. Williams, "Perceiving Structure in Professional Prose: A Multiply Determined Experience," in Lee Odell and Dixie Goswamie (eds.), *Writing in Nonacademic Settings* (New York: The Guilford Press, 1985), pp. 87–128.

FIGURE 18.1 Unity and Coherence in Closed-Form Prose

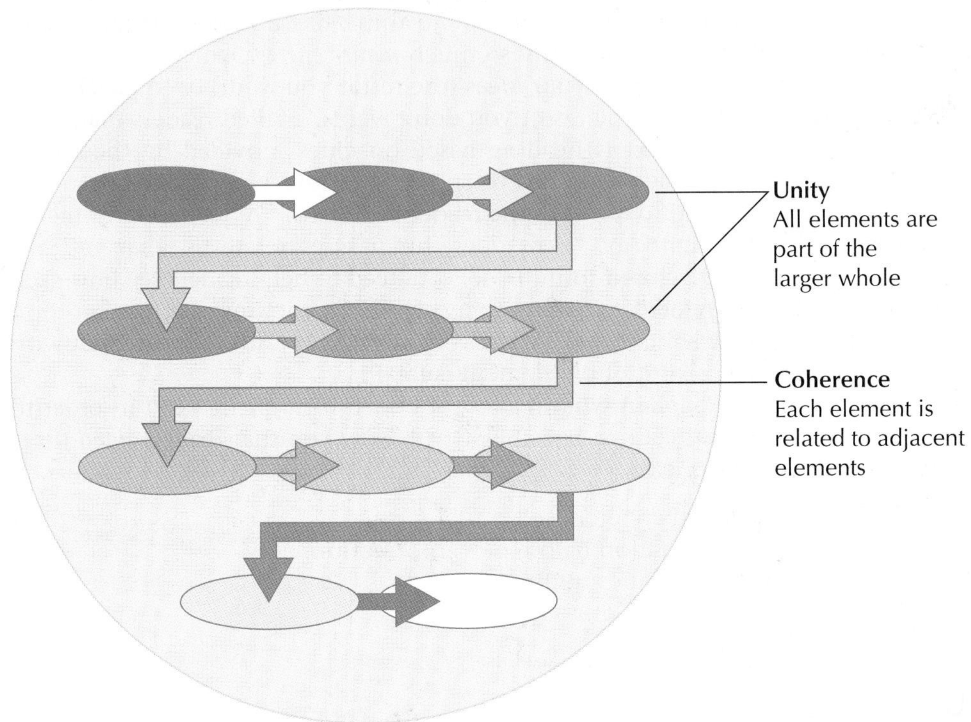
Unity
All elements are part of the larger whole
Coherence
Each element is related to adjacent elements

B. Recent research has given us much deeper—and more surprising—insights into the father's role in childrearing. Childrearing is a complex process that is frequently investigated by psychologists. Psychologists have also investigated sleep patterns and dreams. When we are dreaming, psychologists have shown, we are often reviewing recent events in our lives.

If you are like most readers, Passage A comically frustrates your expectations because it is a string of random sentences. Because the sentences don't relate either to each other or to a larger point, Passage A is neither unified nor coherent.

Passage B frustrates expectations in a subtler way. If you aren't paying attention, Passage B may seem to make sense because each sentence is linked to the one before it. But the individual sentences don't develop a larger whole: The topics switch from a father's role in childrearing to psychology to sleep patterns to the function of dreams. This passage has coherence without unity.

To fulfill a reader's expectations, then, a closed-form passage must be both unified and coherent:

C. (*Unified and coherent*) Recent research has given us much deeper—and more surprising—insights into the father's role in childrearing. It shows that in almost all of their interactions with children, fathers do things a little differently from mothers. What fathers do—their special parenting style—is not only highly complementary to what mothers do but is by all indications important in its own right. [The passage continues by showing the special ways that fathers contribute to childrearing.]

This passage makes a unified point—that fathers have an important role in childrearing. Because all the parts relate to that whole (unity) and because the connections from sentence to sentence are clear (coherence), the passage satisfies our expectations: It makes sense.

Because achieving unity and coherence is a major goal in revising closed-form prose, we'll refer frequently to these concepts in later lessons.

Old before New

One dominant way that readers process information and register ideas is by moving from already known (old) information to new information. In a nutshell, this concept means that new material is meaningful to a reader only if it is linked to old material that is already meaningful. To illustrate this concept, consider the arrangement of names and numbers in a telephone directory. Because we read from left to right, we want people's names in the left column and the telephone numbers in the right column. A person's name is the old, familiar information we already know and the number is the new, unknown information that we seek. If the numbers were in the left column and the names in the right, we would have to read backward.

You can see the same old-before-new principle at work in the following thought exercise:

THOUGHT EXERCISE 2

You are a passenger on an airplane flight into Chicago and need to transfer to Flight 16 to Memphis. As you descend into Chicago, the flight attendant announces transfer gates. Which of the following formats is easier for you to process? Why?

Option A		**Option B**	
To Atlanta on Flight 29	Gate C12	Gate C12	Flight 29 to Atlanta
To Dallas on Flight 35	Gate C25	Gate C25	Flight 35 to Dallas
To Memphis on Flight 16	Gate B20	Gate B20	Flight 16 to Memphis

If you are like most readers, you prefer Option A, which puts old information before new. In this case, the old/known information is our destination (cities arranged alphabetically) and perhaps our flight number (To Memphis on Flight 16). The new/unknown information is Gate B20. Option B causes us to expend more energy than does Option A because it forces us to hold the number of each gate in memory until we hear its corresponding city and flight number. Whereas Option A allows us to relax until we hear the word "Memphis," Option B forces us to concentrate intensely on each gate number until we find the meaningful one.

The principle of old before new has great explanatory power for writers. At the level of the whole essay, this principle helps writers establish the main structural frame and ordering principle of their argument. An argument's frame derives from the writer's purpose to change some aspect of the reader's view of the topic. The reader's original view of the topic—what we might call the common, expected, or ordinary view—constitutes old/known/familiar material. The writer's surprising view constitutes the new/unknown/unfamiliar material. The writer's hope is to move readers from their original view to the writer's new and different view. By understanding what constitutes old/familiar information to readers, the writer can determine how much background to provide, how to anticipate readers' objections, and how to structure material by moving from the old to the new. We treat these matters in more depth in Skills 8 and 9, on writing effective titles and introductions.

At the sentence level, the principle of old before new also helps writers create coherence between adjacent parts and sentences. Most sentences in an essay should contain both an old element and a new element. To create coherence, the writer begins with the old material, which links back to something earlier, and then puts the new material at the end of the sentence. (See the discussion of the old/new contract in Skill 12.)

Forecasting and Fulfillment

Finally, readers of closed-form prose expect writers to forecast what is coming and then to fulfill those forecasts. To appreciate what we mean by forecasting and fulfillment, try one more thought exercise:

THOUGHT EXERCISE 3

Although the following paragraph describes a simple procedure in easy-to-follow sentences, most readers still scratch their heads in bewilderment. Why? What makes the passage difficult to understand?

> The procedure is actually quite simple. First, you arrange things into different groups. Of course, one pile may be sufficient depending on how much there is to do. If you have to go somewhere else due to lack of facilities, that is the next step; otherwise, you are pretty well set. Next you operate the machines according to the instructions. After the procedure is completed, one arranges the materials into different groups again. Then they can be put in their appropriate places. Eventually, they will be used once more and the whole cycle will have to be repeated. However, that is part of life.

Most readers report being puzzled about the paragraph's topic. Because the opening sentence doesn't provide enough context to tell them what to expect, the paragraph makes no forecast that can be fulfilled. Now try rereading the paragraph, but this time substitute the following opening sentence:

> The procedure for washing clothes is actually quite simple.

With the addition of "for washing clothes," the sentence provides a context that allows you to predict and understand what's coming. In the language of cognitive psychologists, this new opening sentence provides a schema for interpretation. A *schema* is the reader's mental picture of a structure for upcoming material. The new opening sentence allows you as reader to say mentally, "This paragraph will describe a procedure for washing clothes and argue that it is simple." When the schema proves accurate, you experience the pleasure of prediction and fulfillment. In the language of rhetorician Kenneth Burke, the reader's experience of form is "an arousing and fulfillment of desires."

What readers expect from a closed-form text, then, is an ability to predict what is coming as well as regular fulfillment of those predictions. Writers forecast what is coming in a variety of ways: by writing effective titles and introductions, by putting points at the beginning of paragraphs, by creating effective transitions and mapping statements, and by using effective headings and subheadings if appropriate for the genre. To meet their readers' needs for predictions and fulfillment, closed-form writers start and end with the big picture. They tell readers where they are going before they start the journey, they refer to this big picture at key transition points, and they refocus on the big picture in their conclusion.

SKILL 6 Convert loose structures into thesis/support structures.

In Skill 5 we described readers' expectations for unity and coherence, old information before new, and forecasting and fulfillment. In academic contexts, readers also expect closed-form prose to have a thesis/support structure. As we explained in Chapter 2, most closed-form academic writing—especially writing with the aim of analysis or persuasion—is governed by a contestable or risky thesis statement. Because developing and supporting a thesis is complex work requiring much critical thought, writers sometimes retreat into loose structures that are easier to compose than a thesis-based argument with points and particulars.

In this lesson we help you better understand thesis-based writing by contrasting it with prose that looks like thesis-based writing but isn't. We show you three common ways in which inexperienced writers give the appearance of writing thesis-based prose while actually retreating from the rigors of making and developing an argument. Avoiding the pitfalls of these loose structures can go a long way toward improving your performance on most college writing assignments.

And Then Writing, or Chronological Structure

Chronological structure, often called "narrative," is the most common organizing principle of open-form prose. It may also be used selectively in closed-form prose to support a point. But sometimes the writer begins recounting the details of a story until chronological order takes over, driving out the thesis-based structure of points and particulars.

To a large degree, chronological order is the default mode we fall into when we aren't sure how to organize material. For example, if you were asked to analyze a fictional character, you might slip into a plot summary instead. In much the same way, you might substitute historical chronology ("First A happened, then B happened ...") for historical analysis ("B happened because A happened ..."); or you might give a chronological recounting of your research ("First I discovered A, then I discovered B ...") instead of organizing your material into an argument ("I question A's account of this phenomenon on the grounds of my recent discovery of B ...").

The tendency toward loose chronological structure is revealed in the following example from a student's essay on Shakespeare's *The Tempest*. This excerpt is from the introduction of the student's first draft:

PLOT SUMMARY—*AND THEN* WRITING

Prospero cares deeply for his daughter. In the middle of the play Prospero acts like a gruff father and makes Ferdinand carry logs in order to test his love for Miranda and Miranda's love for him. In the end, though, Prospero is a loving father who rejoices in his daughter's marriage to a good man.

Here the student seems simply to retell the play's plot without any apparent thesis. (The body of her rough draft primarily retold the same story in more detail.) However, during an office conference, the instructor discovered that the student regarded her sentence about Prospero's being a loving father as her thesis. In fact, the student had gotten in an argument with a classmate over whether Prospero was a good person or an evil one. The instructor helped her convert her draft into a thesis/support structure:

REVISED INTRODUCTION—THESIS/SUPPORT STRUCTURE

Many persons believe that Prospero is an evil person in the play. They claim that Prospero exhibits a harsh, destructive control over Miranda and also, like Faust, seeks superhuman knowledge through his magic. However, I contend that Prospero is a kind and loving father.

This revised version implies a problem (What kind of father is Prospero?), presents a view that the writer wishes to change (Prospero is harsh and hateful), and asserts a contestable thesis (Prospero is a loving father). The body of her paper can now be converted from plot summary to an argument with reasons and evidence supporting her claim that Prospero is loving.

This student's revision from an *and then* to a thesis/support structure is typical of many writers' experience. Because recounting events chronologically is a natural way to organize, many writers—even very experienced ones—lapse into long stretches of *and then* writing in their rough drafts. However, experienced writers have learned to recognize these *and then* sections in their drafts and to rework this material into a closed-form, thesis-based structure.

All About Writing, or Encyclopedic Structure

Whereas *and then* writing turns essays into stories by organizing details chronologically, *all about* writing turns essays into encyclopedia articles by piling up details in heaps. When *all about* writing organizes these heaps into categories, it can appear to be well organized: "Having told you everything I learned about educational opportunities in Cleveland, I will now tell you everything I learned about the Rock and Roll Hall of Fame." But the categories do not function as points and particulars in support of a thesis. Rather, like the shelving system in a library, they are simply ways of arranging information for convenient retrieval, not a means of building a hierarchical structure.

To illustrate the differences between *all about* writing and thesis-based writing, consider the case of two students choosing to write term papers on the subject of female police officers. One student is asked simply to write "all about" the topic; the other is asked to pose and investigate some problem related to female police officers and to support a thesis addressing that problem. In all likelihood, the first student would produce an initial outline with headings such as the following:

I. History of women in police roles
   A. Female police or soldiers in ancient times
   B. 19th century (Calamity Jane)
   C. 1900s–1960
   D. 1960–present
II. How female police officers are selected and trained
III. A typical day in the life of a female police officer
IV. Achievements and acts of heroism of female police officers
V. What the future holds for female police officers

Such a paper is a data dump that places into categories all the information the writer has uncovered. It is riskless, and, except for occasional new information, surpriseless. In contrast, when a student focuses on a significant question—one that grows out of the writer's own interests and demands engagement—the writing can be quite compelling.

Consider the case of a student, Lynnea, who wrote a research paper entitled "Women Police Officers: Should Size and Strength Be Criteria for Patrol Duty?" Her essay begins with a group of male police officers complaining about being assigned to patrol duty with a new female officer, Connie Jones (not her real name), who is four feet ten inches tall and weighs ninety pounds. Here is the rest of the introduction to Lynnea's essay.

> Connie Jones has just completed police academy training and has been assigned to patrol duty in ____________. Because she is so small, she has to have a booster seat in her patrol car and has been given a special gun, since she can barely manage to pull the trigger of a standard police-issue .38 revolver. Although she passed the physical requirements at the academy, which involved speed and endurance running, situps, and monkey bar tests, most of the officers in her department doubt her ability to perform competently as a patrol officer. But nevertheless she is on patrol because men and women receive equal assignments in most of today's police forces. But is this a good policy? Can a person who is significantly smaller and weaker than her peers make an effective patrol officer?

Lynnea examined all the evidence she could find—through library and field research (interviewing police officers)—and arrived at the following thesis: "Because concern for public safety overrides all other concerns, police departments should set stringent size and strength requirements for patrol officers, even if these criteria exclude many women." This thesis has plenty of tension because it sets limits on equal rights for women. Because Lynnea considers herself a feminist, it caused her considerable distress to advocate setting these limits and placing public safety ahead of gender equity. The resulting essay was engaging precisely because of the tension it creates and the controversy it engenders.

Engfish Writing, or Structure without Surprise

Unlike the chronological story and the *all about* paper, the *engfish* essay has a thesis.* But the thesis is a riskless truism supported with predictable reasons—often structured as the three body paragraphs in a traditional five-paragraph theme. It is fill-in-the-blank writing: "The food service is bad for three reasons. First, it is bad because the food is not tasty. Blah, blah, blah about tasteless food. Second, it is bad because it is too expensive. Blah, blah, blah about the expense." And so on. The writer is on autopilot and is not contributing to a real conversation about a real question. In some situations, writers use *engfish* intentionally: bureaucrats and politicians may want to avoid saying something risky; students may want to avoid writing about complex matters that they fear they do not fully understand. In the end, using *engfish* is bad not because what you say is *wrong*, but because what you say couldn't *possibly be* wrong. To avoid *engfish*, stay focused on the need to surprise your reader.

FOR WRITING AND DISCUSSION

Developing a Thesis/Support Structure

As a class, choose a topic from popular culture such as TV talk shows, tattooing, eating disorders, rock lyrics, or something similar.

1. Working as a whole class or in small groups, give examples of how you might write about this topic in an *and then* way, an *all about* way, and an *engfish* way.
2. Then develop one or more questions about the topic that could lead to thesis/support writing. What contestable theses can your class create?

SKILL 7 Plan and visualize your structure.

As we explained in Skill 6, closed-form writing supports a contestable thesis through a hierarchical network of points and particulars. One way to visualize this structure is to outline its skeleton, an exercise that makes visually clear that not all points are on equal levels. The highest-level point is an essay's thesis statement, which is usually supported by several main points that are in turn supported by subpoints and sub-subpoints, all of which are supported by their own particulars. In this lesson we show you how to create such a hierarchical structure for your own papers and how to visualize this structure through an outline, tree diagram, or flowchart.

At the outset, we want to emphasize two important points. First, structural diagrams are not rigid molds, but flexible planning devices that evolve as your thinking

*The term *engfish* was coined by the textbook writer Ken Macrorie to describe a fishy kind of canned prose that bright but bored students mechanically produce to please their teachers. See Ken Macrorie, *Telling Writing* (Rochelle Park, NJ: Hayden Press, 1970).

shifts and changes. The structure of your final draft may be substantially different from your initial scratch outline. In fact, we want to show you how your outlines or diagrams can help you generate more ideas and reshape your structure.

Second, outlines or diagrams organize *meanings*, not topics. Note that in all our examples of outlines, diagrams, and flowcharts, we write *complete sentences* rather than phrases in the high-level slots. We do so because sentences can make a point, which conveys meaning, unlike a phrase, which identifies a topic but doesn't make an assertion about it. Any point—whether a thesis, a main point, or a subpoint—is a contestable assertion that requires its own particulars for support. By using complete sentences rather than phrases in an outline, the writer is forced to articulate the point of each section of the emerging argument.

With this background, we now proceed to a sequence of steps you can take to plan and visualize a structure.

Use Scratch Outlines Early in the Writing Process

Many writers can't make a detailed outline of their arguments until they have written exploratory drafts. At these early stages, writers often make brief scratch outlines that list the main ideas they want to develop initially or they make a list of points that emerged from a freewrite or a very early draft. Here is student writer James Gardiner's initial scratch outline for his argument that online social networks can have harmful consequences:

We first introduced James's research problem in Chapter 2, pp. 33–34. James's final paper is shown in Chapter 23, pp. 643–651.

Despite their benefits, online social networks have some possible harms.

- Introduction
  - Attention-grabber
  - Show growing popularity of OSNs
  - Give my thesis
- Show the potential harm of OSNs.
  - They can lead to lower grades
  - They might promote superficial relationships (no nonverbal communication)
  - They can promote narcissism (I've got to explain this and show the research of Twenge about OSNs as narcissistic competition for the coolest profiles)
  - They can lead to future embarrassment (posting too much personal information—explain how athletic departments are forbidding athletes to have profiles on OSNs
- Give some advice on how to avoid harm.

Before Making a Detailed Outline, "Nutshell" Your Argument

As you explore your topic and begin drafting, your ideas will gradually become clearer and more structured. You can accelerate this process through a series of short exercises that will help you "nutshell" your argument.

The six exercises cause you to look at your argument from different perspectives, helping you clarify the question you are addressing, articulate the kind of change you want to make in your audience's view of your topic, and directly state your purpose, thesis, and tentative title. The authors of this text often use this exercise in one-on-one writing conferences to help students create an initial focus from a swirl of ideas. We recommend that you write out your responses to each exercise as a preliminary step in helping you visualize your structure.

Exercises for Nutshelling Your Argument

Exercise 1 What puzzle or problem initiated your thinking about X?

Exercise 2 *(Paradigm: Many people think X, but I am going to argue Y.)*

Before reading my paper, my readers will think this about my topic:

______________________________.

But after reading my paper, my readers will think this new way about my topic:

______________________________.

Exercise 3 The purpose of my paper is ______________.

Exercise 4 My paper addresses the following question: ______________.

Exercise 5 My one-sentence summary answer to the above question is this:

______________________________.

Exercise 6 A tentative title for my paper is this: ______________

______________________________.

Here are James Gardiner's responses to these questions:

Exercise 1: I was initially puzzled why so many students used online social networks. I didn't have a profile on Facebook or MySpace and wondered what the advantages and disadvantages of OSNs might be.

Exercise 2: Before reading my paper, my readers will believe that OSNs have few detrimental consequences. After reading my paper, my readers will appreciate the potential dangers of OSNs.

Exercise 3: The purpose of this paper is to point out potential negative consequences of OSNs.

Exercise 4: What should students watch out for when using OSNs? What are the possible negative consequences of OSNs?

Exercise 5: Overuse of OSNs can contribute to a decline in grades, to a superficial view of relationships, to an increase in narcissism, and to possible future embarrassment.

Exercise 6: Some Dangers of Online Social Networks

Articulate a Working Thesis and Main Points

Once you have nutshelled your argument, you are ready to visualize a structure containing several sections, parts, or chunks, each of which is headed by a main point and supported with particulars. Try answering these questions:

1. My working thesis statement is:
2. The main sections or chunks needed in my paper are:

Here are James Gardiner's answers to these questions:

1. Despite the benefits of online social networks such as MySpace or Facebook, these networks can have negative consequences such as a decline in grades, a superficial view of relationships, an increase in narcissism, and possible future embarrassment.
2. I'll need (a) an introduction that shows the increased use of OSNs and suggests their benefits and (b) a main body that shows the negative consequences. The main body will have four chunks: (1) a decline in grades; (2) superficial view of relationships; (3) increase in narcissism; and (4) possible future embarrassment.

Sketch Your Structure Using an Outline, Tree Diagram, or Flowchart

At this point you can make an initial structural sketch of your argument and use the sketch to plan out the subpoints and particulars necessary to support the main points. We offer you three different ways to visualize your argument: outlines, tree diagrams, and flowcharts. Use whichever strategy best fits your way of thinking and perceiving.

Outlines

The most common way of visualizing structure is the traditional outline, which uses letters and numerals to indicate levels of points, subpoints, and particulars. If you prefer outlines, we recommend that you use the outlining feature of your word processing program, which allows you to move and insert material and change heading levels with great flexibility.

Figure 18.2 shows James Gardiner's detailed outline for his argument. Note that, except in the introduction, James uses complete sentences rather than phrases for each level.

The importance of complete sentences is explained at the beginning of this skill, p. 515.

Tree Diagrams

A tree diagram displays a hierarchical structure visually, using horizontal and vertical space instead of letters and numbers. Figure 18.3 shows James's argument as a tree diagram. His thesis is at the top of the tree. His main reasons, written as point sentences, appear as branches beneath his claim. Supporting evidence and arguments are displayed as subbranches beneath each reason.

FIGURE 18.2
James Gardiner's Outline

Thesis: Despite the benefits of online social networks like MySpace or Facebook, these networks can have negative consequences such as a decline in grades, a superficial view of relationships, an increase in narcissism, and possible future embarrassment.

I Introduction
  A Attenion-grabber about walking into any computer lab
  B Media evidence shows a large increase in the popularity of OSNs among young people.
  C The term "Facebook Trance" indicates possible harms of OSNs.
  D Thesis paragraph

II Admittedly, OSNs have positive benefits.
  A They provide a way to stay in close contact with friends and family.
  B Researcher Danah Boyd says that OSNs give young people a place to experiment with identities and voices.
  C They provide a way to get quick additional information about someone you've met in class or at a party.

III Despite these benefits, OSNs have potential negative consequences.
  A They can have a negative effect on grades.
    1 Researcher Tamyra Pierce found that high school students with MySpace accounts were more likely to report a decline in grades than those without accounts.
    2 Her data show heavy use of OSNs among as many as 59 percent of students, taking time away from school, work, and sleep.
    3 Other writers apply the high school study to college.
  B OSNs have a tendency to promote superficial relationships.
    1 A study by Chou, Condron, and Belland shows that for some users, online relationships can result in problems with real-life interpersonal relationships.
    2 Another researcher, Matsuba, found that online relationships might hinder some people from developing an adult identity.
    3 A possible contributing factor to the superficiality of online relationships might be the absence of nonverbal communication.
  C OSNs might also contribute to a rise in narcissism.
    1 Researcher Jean Twenge says that today's students are more narcissistic than those of previous generations.
    2 She claims that OSNs are an outlet for self-loving tendencies.
      (a) Creation of online profiles spark a desire for self-expression more than relationship with others.
      (b) Young people compete to have the coolest sites and the most "friends."
      (c) OSNs are about self-promotion rather than connections and friendships.
  D OSNs might lead to future embarrassment.
    1 Many young people imagine an audience of only immediate friends rather than teachers, parents, or future employers.
    2 They often place too much private information on their sites.
      (a) Ludwig gives the example of a college student posting an overly revealing photograph of herself in a Catwoman costume.
      (b) She claims that material posted on sites is often "racy, embarrassing, or squeamishly intimate."
    3 Many college coaches forbid their athletes from creating profiles on OSNs.
      (a) Xiong cites specific examples from the University of Minnesota at Duluth.
      (b) Xiong cites examples of athletes embarrassing the team by posting photographs of drinking parties.

IV Although these dangers are real there are ways to minimize them.
  A I suggest that young people minimize their time online and avoid finding online substitutes for real friendships.
  B My advice is that today's students use OSNs as advanced e-mail-type communication rather than a place to loiter.

FIGURE 18.3 James's Tree Diagram

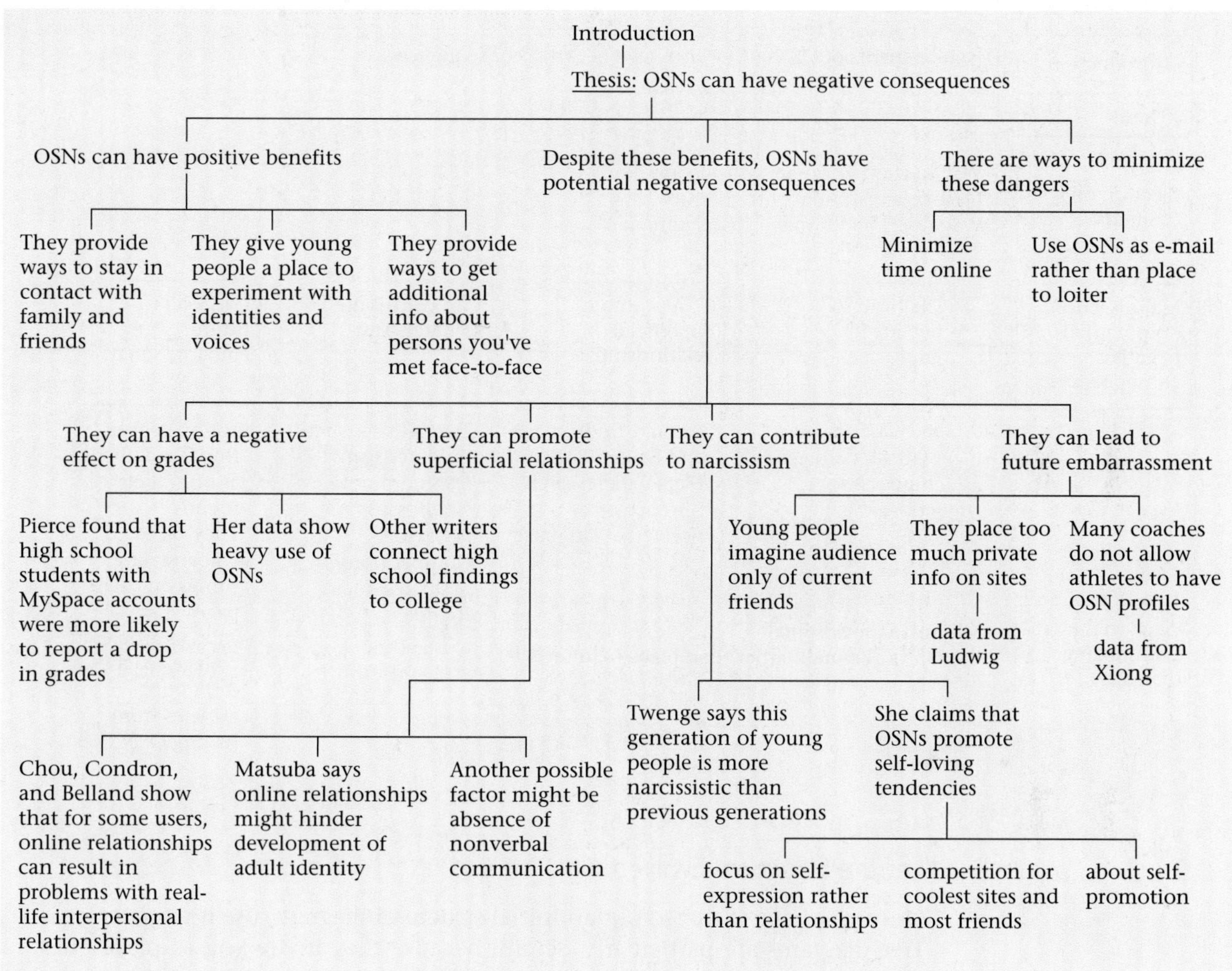

Unlike outlines, tree diagrams allow us to *see* the hierarchical relationship of points and particulars. When you develop a point with subpoints or particulars, you move down the tree. When you switch to a new point, you move across the tree to make a new branch. Our own teaching experience suggests that for many writers, this visual/spatial technique, which engages more areas of the brain than the more purely verbal outline, produces fuller, more detailed, and more logical arguments than does a traditional outline.

Flowcharts

Many writers prefer an informal, hand-sketched flowchart as an alternative to an outline or tree diagram. The flowchart presents the sequence of sections as separate boxes, inside which (or next to which) the writer notes the material needed to fill each box. A flowchart of James's essay is shown in Figure 18.4.

FIGURE 18.4 James's Flowchart

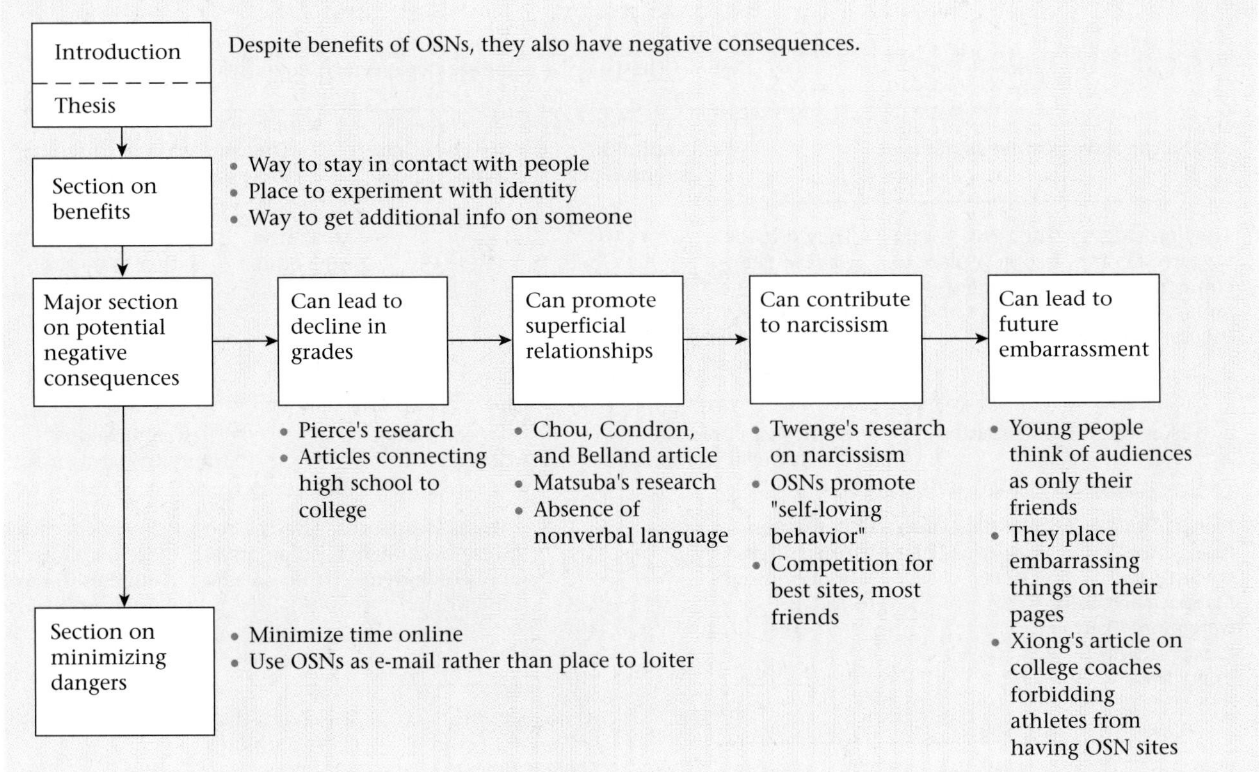

Let the Structure Evolve

Once you have sketched out an initial structural diagram, use it to generate ideas. Tree diagrams are particularly helpful because they invite you to place question marks on branches to "hold open" spots for new points or supporting particulars. If you have only two main points, for example, you could draw a third main branch and place a question mark under it to encourage you to think of another supporting idea. Likewise, if a branch has few supporting particulars, add question marks beneath it. The trick is to think of your structural diagrams as evolving sketches rather than rigid blueprints. As your ideas grow and change, revise your structural diagram, adding or removing points, consolidating and refocusing sections, moving parts around, or filling in details.

FOR WRITING AND DISCUSSION

Making Outlines, Tree Diagrams, or Flowcharts

Working individually, make a traditional outline, tree diagram, and flowchart of David Rockwood's argument against wind-generated electricity on page 7 or of another reading designated by your instructor. Use complete sentences at the top levels. Then convene in small groups to make a group outline, tree diagram, and flowchart of the assigned reading, combining and revising from your individual versions. Finally, make a list of the advantages and disadvantages of each method of representing structure. Which methods work best for different members of the class?

SKILL 8 Create effective titles.

Good titles follow the principle of old before new information that we introduced in Skill 5. A good title needs to have something old (a word or phrase that hooks into a reader's existing interests) and something new (a word or phrase that forecasts the writer's thesis or purpose). Here is an example of an academic title.

> "Style as Politics: A Feminist Approach to the Teaching of Writing" [This title attracts scholars interested either in style or in feminist issues in writing (old); it promises to analyze the political implications of style (new).]

As this example shows, your title should provide a brief but detailed overview of what your paper is about. Academic titles are typically longer and more detailed than are titles in popular magazines. They usually follow one of four conventions:

1. Some titles simply state the question that the essay addresses:

   "Will Patriarchal Management Survive Beyond the Decade?"

2. Some titles state, often in abbreviated form, the essay's thesis:

   "The Writer's Audience Is Always a Fiction"

3. Very often the title is the last part of the essay's purpose statement:

   "The Relationship between Client Expectation of Improvement and Psychotherapy Outcome"

4. Many titles consist of two parts separated by a colon. To the left of the colon the writer presents key words from the essay's issue or problem or a "mystery phrase" that arouses interest; to the right the author places the essay's question, thesis, or summary of purpose:

   "Money and Growth: An Alternative Approach"
   "Deep Play: Notes on a Balinese Cockfight"
   "Fine Cloth, Cut Carefully: Cooperative Learning in British Columbia"

Although such titles might seem overly formal to you, they indicate how much a closed-form writer wishes to preview an article's big picture. Although their titles may be more informal, popular magazines often use these same strategies. Here are some titles from *Redbook* and the business magazine *Forbes*:

> "Is the Coffee Bar Trend About to Peak?" (question)
> "A Man *Can* Take Maternity Leave—And Love It" (abbreviated thesis)
> "Why the Department of Education Shouldn't Take Over the Student Loan Program" (last part of purpose statement)
> "Feed Your Face: Why Your Complexion Needs Vitamins" (two parts linked by colon)

Composing a title for your essay can help you find your focus when you get bogged down in the middle of a draft. Thinking about your title forces you to *nutshell* your ideas by seeing your project's big picture. It causes you to reconsider your purpose and to think about what's old and what's new for your audience.

SKILL 9 Create effective introductions.

Because effective titles and introductions give readers a big-picture overview of a paper's argument, writers often can't compose them until they have finished one or more exploratory drafts. But as soon as you know your essay's big picture, you'll find that writing titles and introductions follows some general principles that are easy to learn.

What Not to Do: The "Funnel Introduction"

Some students have been taught an opening strategy, sometimes called the "funnel," that encourages students to start with broad generalizations and then narrow down to their topics. This strategy often leads to vapid generalizations in the opening sentences, as the following example shows:

> Since time immemorial people have pondered the question of freedom. What it means to be free was asked by the great philosophers of ancient Greece and Rome, and the question has echoed through the ages up until the present day. One modern psychologist who asked this question was B. F. Skinner, who wanted to study whether humans had free will or were programmed by their environment to act the way they did. ...

Here the writer eventually gets to his subject, B. F. Skinner. But the opening sentences are snoozers. A better approach, as we will show, is to hook immediately into your readers' interests.

From Old to New: The General Principle of Closed-Form Introductions

We introduced the principle of old before new in Skill 5. See pp. 507–511.

Whereas the broad-to-narrow strategy is mechanical, the strategy we show you in this lesson, based on the principle of old information before new information, is dynamic and powerful. Old information is something your readers already know and find interesting before they start reading your essay. New information is the surprise of your argument, the unfamiliar material that you add to your readers' understanding.

Because the writer's thesis statement forecasts the new information the paper will present, a thesis statement for a closed-form essay typically comes *at the end of the introduction*. What precedes the thesis is typically the old, familiar information that the reader needs in order to understand the conversation that the thesis joins. In most closed-form prose, particularly in academic prose, this old information is the problem or question that the thesis addresses. A typical closed-form introduction has the following shape:

PROBLEM
[old information]
↓
THESIS
[new information]

The length and complexity of your introduction is a function of how much your reader already knows and cares about the question or problem your paper addresses. The function of an introduction is to capture the reader's interest in the first few sentences, to identify and explain the question or problem that the essay addresses, to provide any needed background information, and to present the thesis. You can leave out any of the first three elements if the reader is already hooked on your topic and already knows the question you are addressing. For example, in an essay exam you can usually start with your thesis statement because you can assume the instructor already knows the question and finds it interesting.

To illustrate how an effective closed-form introduction takes the reader from the question to the thesis, consider how the following student writer revised his introduction to a paper on Napster.com:

ORIGINAL INTRODUCTION (CONFUSING)

> Napster is all about sharing, not stealing, as record companies and some musicians would like us to think. Napster is an online program that was released in October of '99. Napster lets users easily search for and trade mp3s—compressed, high-quality music files that can be produced from a CD. Napster is the leading file sharing community; it allows users to locate and share music. It also provides instant messaging, chat rooms, an outlet for fans to identify new artists, and a forum to communicate their interests.

Thesis statement

Background on Napster

Most readers find this introduction confusing. The writer begins with his thesis statement before the reader is introduced to the question that the thesis addresses. He seems to assume that his reader is already a part of the Napster conversation, and yet in the next sentences, he gives background on Napster. If the reader needs background on Napster, then the reader also needs background on the Napster controversy. In rethinking his assumptions about old-versus-new information for his audience, this writer decided he wants to reach general newspaper readers who may have heard about a lawsuit against Napster and are interested in the issue but aren't sure of what Napster is or how it works. Here is his revised introduction:

REVISED INTRODUCTION (CLEARER)

> Several months ago the rock band Metallica filed a lawsuit against Napster.com, an online program that lets users easily search for and trade mp3s—compressed, high-quality music files that can be produced from a CD. Napster.com has been wildly popular among music lovers because it creates a virtual community where users can locate and share music. It also provides instant messaging, chat rooms, an outlet for fans to identify new artists, and a forum to communicate their interests. But big-name bands like Metallica, alarmed at what they see as lost revenues, claim that Napster.com is stealing their royalties. However, Napster is all about sharing, not stealing, as some musicians would like us to think.

Triggers readers' memory of lawsuit

Background on Napster

Clarification of problem (Implied question: Should Napster be shut down?)

Thesis

This revised introduction fills in the old information the reader needs in order to recall and understand the problem; then it presents the thesis.

Typical Elements of a Closed-Form Introduction

Now that you understand the general principle of closed-form introductions, let's look more closely at its four typical features or elements:

An Opening Attention-Grabber. The first few sentences in an introduction have to capture your reader's interest. If you aren't sure your reader is already interested in your problem, you can begin with an attention-grabber (what journalists call the "hook" or "lead"), which is typically a dramatic vignette, a startling fact or statistic, an arresting quotation, an interesting scene, or something else that taps into your reader's interests. Attention-grabbers are uncommon in academic prose (where you assume your reader will be initially engaged by the problem itself) but frequently used in popular prose. The student writer of the Napster paper initially toyed with the following attention-grabber to begin his essay:

> How many times have you liked one or two songs on a CD but thought the rest of it was garbage? How many times have you burned your own customized CDs by finding your favorite music on Napster.com? Well, that opportunity is about to be lost if Metallica wins its lawsuit against Napster.

He decided not to use this attention-grabber, however, because he wanted to reach audiences who weren't already users of Napster. He decided that these general readers were already interested in the lawsuit and didn't need the extra zing of an attention-grabber.

The first brief writing project in Chapter 1 teaches you how to show that a question is problematic and significant. See p. 27.

Explanation of the Question to Be Investigated. If you assume that your reader already knows about the problem and cares about it, then you need merely to summarize it. This problem or question is the starting point of your argument. Closed-form writers often state the question directly in a single sentence ending with a question mark, but sometimes they imply it, letting the reader formulate it from context. If you aren't sure whether your audience fully understands the question or fully cares about it, then you need to explain it in more detail, showing why it is both problematic and significant.

Background Information. In order to understand the conversation you are joining, readers sometimes need background information—perhaps a definition of key terms, a summary of events leading up to the problem you're presenting, factual details needed for basic understanding of the problem, and so forth. In scientific papers, this background often includes a review of the preexisting literature on the problem. In the Napster introduction, the writer devotes several sentences to background on Napster.com.

A Preview of the Whole. The final element of a closed-form introduction sketches the big picture of your essay by giving readers a sense of the whole. This preview is initially new information for your readers (this is why it comes at the end of the introduction). Once stated, however, it becomes old information that readers will use to locate their position in their journey through your argument. By predicting what's coming, this preview initiates the pleasurable process of forecasting/fulfillment that we discussed in Skill 5. Writers typically forecast the whole by stating their thesis,

See this chapter's opening epigraph from rhetorician Kenneth Burke, p. 506.

but they can also use a purpose statement or a blueprint statement to accomplish the same end. These strategies are the subject of the next section.

Forecast the Whole with a Thesis Statement, Purpose Statement, or Blueprint Statement

The most succinct way to forecast the whole is to state your thesis directly. Student writers often ask how detailed their thesis statements should be and whether it is permissible, sometimes, to delay revealing the thesis until the conclusion—an open-form move that gives papers a more exploratory, mystery-novel feel. It is useful, then, to outline briefly some of your choices as a writer. To illustrate a writer's options for forecasting the whole, we use James Gardiner's research paper on online social networks that we discussed in Skill 7.

To see the choices James Gardiner actually made, see his complete essay on pp. 643–651.

STRATEGIES for Forecasting the Whole

Options	Strategies	Examples
Short thesis	State claim without summarizing your supporting argument or forecasting your structure.	Online social networks can have negative consequences.
Detailed thesis	Summarize whole argument; may begin with an *although* clause that summarizes the view you are trying to change.	Despite the benefits of online social networks like MySpace or Facebook, these networks can have negative consequences such as a decline in grades, a superficial view of relationships, an increase in narcissism, and possible future embarrassment.
Purpose statement	State your purpose or intention without summarizing the argument. A purpose statement typically begins with a phrase such as "My purpose is to ..." or "In the following paragraphs I wish to ..."	My purpose in this essay is to show the potential negative consequences of online social networks.
Blueprint or mapping statement	Describe the structure of your essay by announcing the number of main parts and describing the function or purpose of each one.	After discussing briefly the positive benefits of online social networks, I will describe four potential negative consequences. Finally I will suggest ways to avoid these consequences by using OSNs wisely.

In addition you have at least two other options:

- *Multisentence summary.* In long articles, academic writers often use all three kinds of statements—a purpose statement, a thesis statement, and a blueprint statement. While this sort of extensive forecasting is common in academic and business writing, it occurs less frequently in informal or popular essays. James decided that his paper wasn't complex enough to justify an extensive multisentence overview.
- *Thesis question.* When writers wish to delay their thesis until the middle or the end of their essays, letting their arguments slowly unfold and keeping their stance a mystery, they often end the introduction with a question. This open-form strategy invites readers to join the writer in a mutual search for the answer.

  > Although online social networks like MySpace and Facebook are widely popular and seem to have no negative consequences, something about them makes me wary and uncomfortable. I am wondering whether use of online social networks might be harmful in some way. Are there any dangers associated with OSNs? [This approach would have required a different tone and structure from the paper James actually wrote.]

Which of these options should a writer choose? There are no firm rules to help you answer this question. How much you forecast in the introduction and where you reveal your thesis is a function of your purpose, audience, and genre. The more you forecast, the clearer your argument is and the easier it is to read quickly. You minimize the demands on readers' time by giving them the gist of your argument in the introduction, making it easier to skim your essay if they don't have time for a thorough reading. The less you forecast, the more demands you make on readers' time: You invite them, in effect, to accompany you through the twists and turns of your own thinking process, and you risk losing them if they become confused, lost, or bored. For these reasons, academic writing is generally closed form and aims at maximum clarity. In many rhetorical contexts, however, more open forms are appropriate.

Chapter 1, Concept 1, gives more advice on when to choose closed or open forms.

If you choose a closed-form structure, we can offer some advice on how much to forecast. Readers sometimes feel insulted by too much forecasting, so include only what is needed for clarity. For short papers, readers usually don't need to have the complete supporting argument forecast in the introduction. In longer papers, however, or in especially complex ones, readers appreciate having the whole argument forecast at the outset. Academic writing in particular tends to favor explicit and often detailed forecasting.

FOR WRITING AND DISCUSSION

Revising a Title and Introduction

Individual task: Choose an essay you are currently working on or have recently completed and examine your title and introduction based on the advice in Skills 8 and 9. Ask yourself these questions:

- What audience am I imagining? What do I assume are my readers' initial interests that will lead them to read my essay (the old information I must hook into)? What is new in my essay?

- Do I have an attention-grabber? Why or why not?
- Where do I state or imply the question or problem that my essay addresses?
- Do I explain why the question is problematic and significant? Why or why not?
- For my audience to understand the problem, do I provide too much background information, not enough, or just the right amount?
- What strategies do I use to forecast the whole?

Based on your analysis of your present title and introduction, revise as appropriate.

Group task: Working with a partner or in small groups, share the changes you made in your title or introduction and explain why you made the changes.

SKILL 10 Create effective topic sentences for paragraphs.

In our lesson on outlining (Skill 7) we suggested that you write complete sentences rather than phrases for the high-level slots of the outline in order to articulate the *meaning* or *point* of each section of your argument. In this lesson we show you how to place these points where readers expect them: near the beginning of the sections or paragraphs they govern.

When you place points before particulars, you follow the same principle illustrated in Skill 5 with the flight attendant announcing the name of the city before the departure gate (the city is the old information, the departure gate the new information). When you first state the point, it is the new information that the next paragraph or section will develop. Once you have stated it, it becomes old information that helps readers understand the meaning of the particulars that follow. If you withhold the point until later, the reader has to keep all the particulars in short-term memory until you finally reveal the point that the particulars are supposed to support or develop.

Place Topic Sentences at the Beginning of Paragraphs

Readers of closed-form prose need to have point sentences (usually called "topic sentences") at the beginnings of paragraphs. However, writers of rough drafts often don't fulfill this need because, as we explained in Chapter 17, drafting is an exploratory process in which writers are often still searching for their points as they compose. Consequently, in their rough drafts writers often omit topic sentences entirely or place them at the ends of paragraphs, or they write topic sentences that misrepresent what the paragraphs actually say. During revision, then, you should check your body paragraphs carefully to be sure you have placed accurate topic sentences near the beginning.

What follow are examples of the kinds of revisions writers typically make. We have annotated the examples to explain the changes the writer has made to make the paragraphs unified and clear to readers. The first example is from a later draft of the essay on the dorm room carpets from Chapter 17 (pp. 502–503).

Revision–Topic Sentence First

Topic sentence placed first

Another reason for the university not to buy carpets is the cost. ^According to Rachel Jones, Assistant Director of Housing Services, the initial purchase and installation of carpeting would cost $300 per room. Considering the number of rooms in the three residence halls, carpeting amounts to a substantial investment. Additionally, once the carpets are installed, the university would need to maintain them through the purchase of more vacuum cleaners and shampoo machines. This money would be better spent on other dorm improvements that would benefit more residents, such as expanded kitchen facilities and improved recreational space. ~~Thus carpets would be too expensive.~~

In the original draft, the writer states the point at the end of the paragraph. In his revision he states the point in an opening topic sentence that links back to the thesis statement, which promises "several reasons" that the university should not buy carpets for the dorms. The words "Another reason" thus link the topic sentence to the argument's big picture.

Revise Paragraphs for Unity

In addition to placing topic sentences at the heads of paragraphs, writers often need to revise topic sentences to better match what the paragraph actually says, or revise the paragraph to better match the topic sentence. Paragraphs have unity when all their sentences develop the point stated in the topic sentence. Paragraphs in rough drafts are often not unified because they reflect the writer's shifting, evolving, thinking-while-writing process. Consider the following paragraph from an early draft of an argument against euthanasia by student writer Dao Do. Her peer reviewer labeled it "confusing." What makes it confusing?

We look at more examples from Dao's essay later in this chapter.

Early Draft–Confusing

First, euthanasia is wrong because no one has the right to take the life of another person. Some people say that euthanasia or suicide will end suffering and pain. But what proofs do they have for such a claim? Death is still mysterious to us; therefore, we do not know whether death will end suffering and pain or not. What seems to be the real claim is that death to those with illnesses will end <u>our</u> pain. Such pain involves worrying over them, paying their medical bills, and giving up so much of our time. Their deaths end our pain rather than theirs. And for that reason, euthanasia is a selfish act, for the outcome of euthanasia benefits us, the nonsufferers, more. Once the sufferers pass away, we can go back to our normal lives.

The paragraph opens with an apparent topic sentence: "Euthanasia is wrong because no one has the right to take the life of another person." But the rest of the paragraph doesn't focus on that point. Instead, it focuses on how euthanasia benefits the survivors more than the sick person. Dao had two choices: to revise the paragraph to fit the topic sentence or to revise the topic sentence to fit the paragraph. Here is her revision, which includes a different topic sentence and an additional sentence midparagraph to keep particulars focused on the opening point. Dao unifies this paragraph by keeping all its parts focused on her main point: "Euthanasia ... benefits the survivors more than the sick person."

Revision for Unity

First, euthanasia is wrong because it benefits the survivors more than the sick person. ~~First, euthanasia is wrong because no one has the right to take the life of another person.~~ Some people say that euthanasia or suicide will end *the sick person's* suffering and pain. But what proofs do they have for such a claim? Death is still mysterious to us; therefore, we do not know whether death will end suffering and pain or not. *Moreover, modern pain killers can relieve most of the pain a sick person has to endure.* What seems to be the real claim is that death to those with illnesses will end our pain. Such pain involves worrying over them, paying their medical bills, and giving up so much of our time. Their deaths end our pain rather than theirs. And for that reason, euthanasia is a selfish act, for the outcome of euthanasia benefits us, the nonsufferers, more. Once the sufferers pass away, we can go back to our normal lives.

Revised topic sentence better forecasts focus of paragraph

Keeps focus on "sick person"

Concludes subpoint about sick person

Supports subpoint about how euthanasia benefits survivors

A paragraph may lack unity for a variety of reasons. It may shift to a new direction in the middle, or one or two sentences may simply be irrelevant to the point. The key is to make sure that all the sentences in the paragraph fulfill the reader's expectations based on the topic sentence.

Add Particulars to Support Points

Just as writers of rough drafts often omit point sentences from paragraphs, they also sometimes leave out the particulars needed to support a point. In such cases, the writer needs to add particulars such as facts, statistics, quotations, research summaries, examples, or further subpoints. Consider how adding additional particulars to the following draft paragraph strengthens student writer Tiffany Linder's argument opposing the logging of old-growth forests.

DRAFT PARAGRAPH: PARTICULARS MISSING

One reason that it is not necessary to log old-growth forests is that the timber industry can supply the world's lumber needs without doing so. For example, we have plenty of new-growth forest from which timber can be taken (Sagoff 89). We could also reduce the amount of trees used for paper products by using other materials besides wood for paper pulp. In light of the fact that we have plenty of trees and ways of reducing our wood demands, there is no need to harvest old-growth forests.

REVISED PARAGRAPH: PARTICULARS ADDED

Added particulars support subpoint that we have plenty of new-growth forest

Added particulars support second subpoint that wood alternatives are available

One reason that it is not necessary to log old-growth forests is that the timber industry can supply the world's lumber needs without doing so. For example, we have plenty of new-growth forest from which timber can be taken as a result of major reforestation efforts all over the United States (Sagoff 89). In the Northwest, for instance, Oregon law requires every acre of timber harvested to be replanted. According to Robert Sedjo, a forestry expert, the world's demand for industrial wood could be met by a widely implemented tree farming system (Sagoff 90). We could also reduce the amount of trees used for paper products by using a promising new innovation called Kenaf, a fast-growing annual herb which is fifteen feet tall and is native to Africa. It has been used for making rope for many years, but recently it was found to work just as well for paper pulp. In light of the fact that we have plenty of trees and ways of reducing our wood demands, there is no need to harvest old-growth forests.

FOR WRITING AND DISCUSSION

Revising Paragraphs for Points-First Structure

Individual task: Bring to class a draft-in-progress for a closed-form essay. Pick out several paragraphs in the body of your essay and analyze them for "points-first" structure. For each paragraph, ask the following questions:

- Does my paragraph have a topic sentence near the beginning?
- If so, does my topic sentence accurately forecast what the paragraph says?
- Does my topic sentence link to my thesis statement or to a higher-order point that my paragraph develops?
- Does my paragraph have enough particulars to develop and support my topic sentence?

Group task: Then exchange your draft with a partner and do a similar analysis of your partner's selected paragraphs. Discuss your analyses of each other's paragraphs and then help each other plan appropriate revision strategies. If time permits, revise your paragraphs and show your results to your partner. [Note: Sometimes you can revise simply by adding a topic sentence to a paragraph, rewording a topic sentence, or making other kinds of local revisions. At other times, you may need to cross out whole paragraphs and start over, rewriting from scratch after you rethink your ideas.]

SKILL 11 Guide your reader with transitions and other signposts.

As we have explained earlier, when readers read closed-form prose, they expect each new sentence, paragraph, and section to link clearly to what they have already read. They need a well-marked trail with signposts signaling the twists and turns along the way. They also need resting spots at major junctions where they can review where they've been and survey what's coming. In this lesson, we show you how transition words as well as summary and forecasting passages can keep your readers securely on the trail.

Use Common Transition Words to Signal Relationships

Transitions are like signposts that signal where the road is turning and limit the possible directions that an unfolding argument might take. Consider how the use of "therefore" and "nevertheless" limits the range of possibilities in the following examples:

> While on vacation, Suzie caught the chicken pox. Therefore, ____________.
> While on vacation, Suzie caught the chicken pox. Nevertheless, ____________.

"Therefore" signals to the reader that what follows is a consequence. Most readers will imagine a sentence similar to this one:

> Therefore, she spent her vacation lying in bed itchy, feverish, and miserable.

In contrast, "nevertheless" signals an unexpected or denied consequence, so the reader might anticipate a sentence such as this:

> Nevertheless, she enjoyed her two weeks off, thanks to a couple of bottles of calamine lotion, some good books, and a big easy chair overlooking the ocean.

Here is a list of the most common transition words and phrases and what they signal to the reader:*

Words or Phrases	**What They Signal**
first, second, third, next, finally, earlier, later, meanwhile, afterward	*sequence*—First we went to dinner; then we went to the movies.
that is, in other words, to put it another way, — (dash), : (colon)	*restatement*—He's so hypocritical that you can't trust a word he says. To put it another way, he's a complete phony.
rather, instead	*replacement*—We shouldn't use the money to buy opera tickets; rather, we should use it for a nice gift.
for example, for instance, a case in point	*example*—Mr. Carlyle is very generous. For example, he gave the janitors a special holiday gift.
because, since, for	*reason*—Taxes on cigarettes are unfair because they place a higher tax burden on the working class.
therefore, hence, so, consequently, thus, then, as a result, accordingly, as a consequence	*consequences*—I failed to turn in the essay; therefore I flunked the course.
still, nevertheless	*denied consequence*—The teacher always seemed grumpy in class; nevertheless, I really enjoyed the course.

(*continued*)

*Although all the words on the list serve as transitions or connectives, grammatically they are not all equivalent, nor are they all punctuated the same way.

Words or Phrases	What They Signal
although, even though, granted that (*with* still)	*concession*—Even though the teacher was always grumpy, I still enjoyed the course.
in comparison, likewise, similarly	*similarity*—Teaching engineering takes a lot of patience. Likewise, so does teaching accounting.
however, in contrast, conversely, on the other hand, but	*contrast*—I disliked my old backpack immensely; however, I really like this new one.
in addition, also, too, moreover, furthermore	*addition*—Today's cars are much safer than those of ten years ago. In addition, they get better gas mileage.
in brief, in sum, in conclusion, finally, to sum up, to conclude	*conclusion or summary*—In sum, the plan presented by Mary is the best choice.

FOR WRITING AND DISCUSSION

Using Transitions

This exercise is designed to show you how transition words govern relationships between ideas. Working in groups or on your own, finish each of the following statements using ideas of your own invention. Make sure what you add fits the logic of the transition word.

1. Writing is difficult; therefore __________.
2. Writing is difficult; however, __________.
3. Writing is difficult because __________.
4. Writing is difficult. For example, __________.
5. Writing is difficult. To put it another way, __________.
6. Writing is difficult. Likewise, __________.
7. Although writing is difficult, __________.
8. __________ In sum, writing is difficult.

In the following paragraph, various kinds of linking devices have been omitted. Fill in the blanks with words or phrases that would make the paragraph coherent. Clues are provided in brackets.

Writing an essay is a difficult process for most people. __________ [contrast] the process can be made easier if you learn to practice three simple techniques. __________ [sequence] learn the technique of nonstop writing. When you are first trying to think of ideas for an essay, put your pen to your paper and write nonstop for ten or fifteen minutes without letting your pen leave the paper. Stay loose and free. Let your pen follow the waves of thought. Don't worry about grammar or spelling. __________ [concession] this technique won't work for everyone, it helps many people get a good cache of ideas to draw on. A __________ [sequence] technique is to write your rough draft rapidly without worrying about being perfect. Too many writers try to get their drafts right the first time. __________ [contrast] by learning to live with imperfection, you will save yourself headaches and a wastepaper basket full of crumpled paper. Think of your first rough draft as a path hacked out of the jungle—as part of an exploration, not as a completed highway. As a __________ [sequence] technique, try printing out a triple-spaced copy to allow space for revision. Many beginning writers don't leave enough space to revise. ___________ [consequence] these writers never get in the habit of crossing out chunks of their rough draft and writing revisions in the blank spaces. After you have revised your rough draft until it is too messy to work from anymore, you can ___________ [sequence] enter your changes into your word processor and print out a fresh draft, again setting your text on triple-space. The resulting blank space invites you to revise.

Write Major Transitions between Parts

In long closed-form pieces, writers often put *resting places* between major parts—transitional passages that allow readers to shift their attention momentarily away from the matter at hand to get a sense of where they've been and where they're going. Often such passages sum up the preceding major section, refer back to the essay's thesis statement or opening blueprint plan, and then preview the next major section. Here are three typical examples:

> So far I have looked at a number of techniques that can help people identify debilitating assumptions that block their self-growth. In the next section, I examine ways to question and overcome these assumptions.
>
> Now that the difficulty of the problem is fully apparent, our next step is to examine some of the solutions that have been proposed.
>
> These, then, are the major theories explaining why Hamlet delays. But let's see what happens to Hamlet if we ask the question in a slightly different way. In this next section, we shift our critical focus, looking not at Hamlet's actions, but at his language.

Signal Transitions with Headings and Subheadings

In many genres, particularly scientific and technical reports, government documents, business proposals, textbooks, and long articles in magazines or scholarly journals, writers conventionally break up long stretches of text with headings and subheadings. Headings are often set in different type sizes and fonts and mark transition points between major parts and subparts of the argument.

SKILL 12 Bind sentences together by placing old information before new information.

The previous skill focused on marking the reader's trail with transitions. This skill will enable you to build a smooth trail without potholes or washed-out bridges.

The Old/New Contract in Sentences

A powerful way to prevent gaps is to follow the old/new contract—a writing strategy derived from the principle of old before new that we explained and illustrated in Skill 5. Simply put, the old/new contract asks writers to begin sentences with something old—something that links to what has gone before—and then to end sentences with new information.

To understand the old/new contract more fully, try the following thought exercise. We'll show you two passages, both of which explain the old/new contract. One of them, however, follows the principle it describes; the other violates it.

THOUGHT EXERCISE

Which of these passages follows the old/new contract?

VERSION 1

The old/new contract is another principle for writing clear closed-form prose. Beginning your sentences with something old—something that links to what has gone before—and then ending your sentences with new information that advances the argument is what the old/new contract asks writers to do. An effect called *coherence,* which is closely related to *unity,* is created by following this principle. Whereas the clear relationship between the topic sentence and the body of the paragraph and between the parts and the whole is what *unity* refers to, the clear relationship between one sentence and the next is what *coherence* relates to.

VERSION 2

Another principle for writing clear closed-form prose is the old/new contract. The old/new contract asks writers to begin sentences with something old—something that links to what has gone before—and then to end sentences with new information that advances the argument. Following this principle creates an effect called *coherence,* which is closely related to unity. Whereas *unity* refers to the clear relationship between the body of a paragraph and its topic sentence and between the parts and the whole, *coherence* refers to the clear relationship between one sentence and the next, between part and part.

If you are like most readers, you have to concentrate much harder to understand Version 1 than Version 2 because it violates the old-before-new way that our minds normally process information. When a writer doesn't begin a sentence with old material, readers have to hold the new material in suspension until they have figured out how it connects to what has gone before. They can stay on the trail, but they have to keep jumping over the potholes between sentences.

To follow the old/new contract, place old information near the beginning of sentences in what we call the *topic position* and place new information that advances the argument in the predicate or *stress position* at the end of the sentence. We associate topics with the beginnings of sentences simply because in the standard English sentence, the topic (or subject) comes before the predicate—hence the notion of a "contract" by which we agree not to fool or frustrate our readers by breaking with the "normal" order of things. The contract says that the old, backward-linking material comes at the beginning of the sentence and that the new, argument-advancing material comes at the end.

FOR WRITING AND DISCUSSION

Practicing the Old/New Contract

Here are two more passages, one of which obeys the old/new contract while the other violates it. Working in small groups or as a whole class, reach consensus on which of these passages follows the old/new contract. Explain your reasoning by showing how the beginning of each sentence links to something old.

PASSAGE A

Play is an often-overlooked dimension of fathering. From the time a child is born until its adolescence, fathers emphasize caretaking less than play. Egalitarian feminists may be troubled by this, and spending more time in caretaking may be wise for fathers. There seems to be unusual significance in the father's style of play. Physical excitement and stimulation are likely to be part of it. With older children more physical games and teamwork that require the competitive testing of physical and mental skills are also what it involves. Resemblance to an apprenticeship or teaching relationship is also a characteristic of fathers' play: Come on, let me show you how.

PASSAGE B

An often-overlooked dimension of fathering is play. From their children's birth through adolescence, fathers tend to emphasize play more than caretaking. This emphasis may be troubling to egalitarian feminists, and it would indeed be wise for most fathers to spend more time in caretaking. Yet the fathers' style of play seems to have unusual significance. It is likely to be both physically stimulating and exciting. With older children it involves more physical games and teamwork that require the competitive testing of physical and mental skills. It frequently resembles an apprenticeship or teaching relationship: Come on, let me show you how.

How to Make Links to the "Old"

To understand how to link to "old information," you need to understand more fully what we mean by "old" or "familiar." In the context of sentence-level coherence, we mean everything in the text that the reader has read so far. Any upcoming sentence is new information, but once the reader has read it, it becomes old information. For example, when a reader is halfway through a text, everything previously read—the title, the introduction, half the body—is old information to which you can link to meet your readers' expectations for unity and coherence.

In making these backward links, writers have three targets:

1. They can link to a key word or concept in the immediately preceding sentence (creating coherence).
2. They can link to a key word or concept in a preceding point sentence (creating unity).
3. They can link to a preceding forecasting statement about structure (helping readers map their location in the text).

Writers have a number of textual strategies for making these links. In Figure 18.5 our annotations show how a professional writer links to old information within the first five or six words of each sentence. What follows is a compendium of these strategies:

- ***Repeat a key word.*** The most common way to open with something old is to repeat a key word from the preceding sentence or an earlier point sentence. In our example, note the number of sentences that open with "father," "father's," or "fathering." Note also the frequent repetitions of "play."
- ***Use a pronoun to substitute for a key word.*** In our example, the second sentence opens with the pronouns "It," referring to "research," and "their," refer-

FIGURE 18.5 How a Professional Writer Follows the Old/New Contract

Recent research has given us much deeper—and more surprising—insights into the father's role in childrearing. It shows that in ~~almost all of~~ their interactions with children, fathers do things a little differently from mothers. What fathers do—their special parenting style—is not only highly complementary to what mothers do but is by all indications important in its own right.

For example, an often-overlooked dimension of fathering is play. ~~From~~ their children's birth through adolescence, fathers tend to emphasize play more than caretaking. This may be troubling to egalitarian feminists, and it would indeed be wise for most fathers to spend more time in caretaking.

Yet ~~the~~ fathers' style of play seems to have unusual significance. It ~~is likely to~~ be both physically stimulating and exciting. With older children it ~~involves more physical games~~ and teamwork that require the competitive testing ~~of physical~~ and mental skills. It ~~frequently~~ resembles an apprenticeship or teaching relationship: Come on, let me show you how.

David Popenoe, "Where's Papa?" from *Life Without Father: Compelling New Evidence that Fatherhood and Marriage Are Indispensable for the Good of Children and Society.*

Refers to "research" in previous sentence

Refers to "fathers" in previous sentence

Rephrases idea of "childrearing"

Repeats "fathers" from previous sentence

Transition tells us new paragraph will be an example of previous concept

Rephrases concept in previous paragraph

Refers to "fathers"

New information that becomes topic of this paragraph

Pronoun sums up previous concept

Repeats words "father" and "play" from the topic sentence of the preceding paragraph

"It" refers to fathers' style of play

ring to "fathers." The last three sentences open with the pronoun "It," referring to "father's style of play."

- ***Summarize, rephrase, or restate earlier concepts.*** Writers can link to a preceding sentence by using a word or phrase that summarizes or restates a key concept. In the second sentence, "interactions with children" restates the concept of childrearing. Similarly, the phrase "an often-overlooked dimension" refers to a concept implied in the preceding paragraph—that recent research reveal something significant and not widely known about a father's role in childrearing. An "often-overlooked dimension" sums up this idea. Finally, note that the pronoun "This" in the second paragraph sums up the main concept of the previous two sentences. (But see our warning on p. 537 about the overuse of "this" as a pronoun.)
- ***Use a transition word.*** Writers can also use transition words such as *first* ... , *second* ... , *third* ... , or *therefore* or *however* to cue the reader about the logical relationship between an upcoming sentence and the preceding ones. Note how the second paragraph opens with "For example," indicating that the upcoming paragraph will illustrate the concept identified in the preceding paragraph.

These strategies give you a powerful way to check and revise your prose. Comb your drafts for gaps between sentences where you have violated the old/new contract. If the opening of a new sentence doesn't refer back to an earlier word, phrase, or concept, your readers could derail, so use what you have learned to repair the tracks.

Applying the Old/New Contract to Your Own Draft

FOR WRITING AND DISCUSSION

Individual task: Bring to class a draft-in-progress for a closed-form essay. On a selected page, examine the opening of each sentence. Place a vertical slash in front of any sentence that doesn't contain near the beginning some backward-looking element that links to old, familiar material. Then revise these sentences to follow the old/new contract.

Group task: Working with a partner, share the changes you each made on your drafts. Then on each other's pages, work together to identify the kinds of links made at the beginning of each sentence. (For example, does the opening of a sentence repeat a key word, use a pronoun to substitute for a key word, rephrase or restate an earlier concept, or use a transition word?)

As we discussed in Skill 5, the principle of old before new has great explanatory power in helping writers understand their choices when they compose. In this last section, we give you some further insights into the old/new contract.

Avoid Ambiguous Use of "This" to Fulfill the Old/New Contract

Some writers try to fulfill the old/new contract by frequent use of the pronoun *this* to sum up a preceding concept. Occasionally such usage is effective, as in our example passage on fathers' style of play when the writer says: "*This* may be troubling to egalitarian feminists." But frequent use of *this* as a pronoun creates lazy and often ambiguous prose. Consider how our example passage might read if many of the explicit links were replaced by *this*:

LAZY USE OF *THIS* AS PRONOUN

> Recent research has given us much deeper—and more surprising—insights into **this.** It shows that in doing **this**, fathers do things a little differently from mothers. **This** is not only highly complementary to what mothers do but is by all indications important in its own right.
>
> For example, an often-overlooked dimension of **this** is play.

Perhaps this passage helps you see why we refer to *this* (used by itself as a pronoun) as "the lazy person's all-purpose noun-slot filler."*

How the Old/New Contract Modifies the Rule "Avoid Weak Repetition"

Many students have been warned against repetition of the same word (or *weak repetition*, as your teacher may have called it). Consequently, you may not be aware that repetition of key words is a vital aspect of unity and coherence. The repeated words

*It's acceptable to use *this* as an adjective, as in "this usage"; we refer here only to *this* used by itself as a pronoun.

create what linguists call "lexical strings" that keep a passage focused on a particular point. Note in our passage about the importance of fathers' style of play the frequent repetitions of the words *father* and *play*. What if the writer had worried about repeating *father* too much and reached for his thesaurus?

UNNECESSARY ATTEMPT TO AVOID REPETITION

Recent research has given us much deeper—and more surprising—insights into the **male parent's** role in childrearing. It shows that in almost all of their interactions with children, **patriarchs** do things a little differently from mothers. What **sires** do. ...

For example, an often-overlooked dimension of **male gender parenting** is. ...

You get the picture. Keep your reader on familiar ground through repetition of key words.

How the Old/New Contract Modifies the Rule "Prefer Active over Passive Voice"

Another rule that you may have learned is to use the active voice rather than the passive voice. In the active voice the doer of the action is in the subject slot of the sentence, and the receiver is in the direct object slot, as in the following examples:

The dog caught the Frisbee.
The women wrote letters of complaint to the boss.
The landlord raised the rent.

In the passive voice the receiver of the action becomes the subject and the doer of the action either becomes the object of the preposition *by* or disappears from the sentence:

The Frisbee was caught by the dog.
Letters of complaint were written (by the women) to the boss.
The rent was raised (by the landlord).

Other things being equal, the active voice is indeed preferable to the passive because it is more direct and forceful. But in some cases, other things *aren't* equal, and the passive voice is preferable. *What the old/new contract asks you to consider is whether the doer or the receiver represents the old information in a sentence.* Consider the difference between the following passages:

Second Sentence, Active Voice	My great-grandfather was a skilled cabinetmaker. He made this dining room table near the turn of the century.
Second Sentence, Passive Voice	I am pleased that you stopped to admire our dining room table. It was made by my great-grandfather near the turn of the century.

In the first passage, the opening sentence is about *my great-grandfather*. To begin the second sentence with old information ("He," referring to "great-grandfather"), the writer uses the active voice. The opening sentence of the second passage is about the *dining room table*. To begin the second sentence with old information ("It," referring to "table"), the writer must use the passive voice, since the table is the receiver of the action. In both cases, the sentences are structured to begin with old information.

SKILL 13 Learn four expert moves for organizing and developing ideas.

Writers of closed-form prose often employ a conventional set of moves to organize parts of an essay. In using the term *moves*, we are making an analogy with the "set moves" or "set plays" in such sports as basketball, volleyball, and soccer. For example, a common set move in basketball is the "pick," in which an offensive player without the ball stands motionless in order to block the path of a defensive player who is guarding the dribbler. Similarly, certain organizational patterns in writing occur frequently enough to act as set plays for writers. These patterns set up expectations in the reader's mind about the shape of an upcoming stretch of prose, anything from a few sentences to a paragraph to a large block of paragraphs. As you will see, these moves also stimulate the invention of ideas. Next, we describe four of the most powerful set plays.*

The *For Example* Move

Perhaps the most common set play occurs when a writer makes an assertion and then illustrates it with one or more examples, often signaling the move explicitly with transitions such as *for example, for instance,* or *a case in point is* ... . Here is how student writer Dao Do used the *for example* move to support her third reason for opposing euthanasia:

FOR EXAMPLE MOVE

My third objection to euthanasia is that it fails to see the value in suffering. Suffering is a part of life. We see the value of suffering only if we look deeply within our suffering. For example, I never thought my crippled uncle from Vietnam was a blessing to my grandmother until I talked to her. My mother's little brother was born prematurely. As a result of oxygen and nutrition deficiency, he was born crippled. His tiny arms and legs were twisted around his body, preventing him from any normal movements such as walking, picking up things, and lying down. He could only sit. Therefore, his world was very limited, for it consisted of his own room and the garden viewed through his window. Because of his disabilities, my grandmother had to wash him, feed him, and watch him constantly. It was hard, but she managed to care for him for forty-three years. He passed away after the death of my grandfather in 1982. Bringing this situation out of Vietnam and into Western society shows the difference between Vietnamese and Western views. In the West, my uncle might have been euthanized as a baby. Supporters of euthanasia would have said he wouldn't have any quality of life and that he would have been a great burden. But he was not a burden on my grandmother. She enjoyed taking care of him, and he was always her company after her other children got married and moved away. Neither one of them saw his defect as meaningless suffering because it brought them closer together.

Topic sentence

Transition signalling the move

Extended example supporting point

This passage uses a single, extended example to support a point. You could also use several shorter examples or other kinds of illustrating evidence such as

*You might find it helpful to follow the set plays we used to write this section. This last sentence is the opening move of a play we call "division into parallel parts." It sets up the expectation that we will develop four set plays in order. Watch for the way we chunk them and signal transitions between them.

facts or statistics. In all cases the *for example* move creates a pattern of expectation and fulfillment. This pattern drives the invention of ideas in one of two ways: It urges the writer either to find examples to develop a generalization or to formulate a generalization that shows the point of an example.

FOR WRITING AND DISCUSSION

Practicing the *For Example* Move

Working individually or in groups, develop a plan for supporting one or more of the following generalizations using the *for example* move:

1. Another objection to state sales taxes is that they are so annoying.
2. Although assertiveness training has definite benefits, it can sometimes get you into real trouble.
3. Sometimes effective leaders are indecisive.

The *Summary/However* Move

This move occurs whenever a writer sums up another person's viewpoint in order to qualify or contradict it or to introduce an opposing view. Typically, writers use transition words such as *but, however, in contrast,* or *on the other hand* between the parts of this move. This move is particularly common in academic writing, which often contrasts the writer's new view with prevailing views. Here is how Dao uses a *summary/however* move in the introduction of her essay opposing euthanasia:

SUMMARY/HOWEVER MOVE

Issue over which there is disagreement

Summary of opposing viewpoint

Transition to writer's viewpoint

Statement of writer's view

Should euthanasia be legalized? My classmate Martha and her family think it should be. Martha's aunt was blind from diabetes. For three years she was constantly in and out of the hospital, but then her kidneys shut down and she became a victim of life support. After three months of suffering, she finally gave up. Martha believes this three-month period was unnecessary, for her aunt didn't have to go through all of that suffering. If euthanasia were legalized, her family would have put her to sleep the minute her condition worsened. Then, she wouldn't have had to feel pain, and she would have died in peace and with dignity. However, despite Martha's strong argument for legalizing euthanasia, I find it wrong.

The first sentence of this introduction poses the question that the essay addresses. The main body of the paragraph summarizes Martha's opposing view on euthanasia, and the final sentence, introduced by the transition "However," presents Dao's thesis.

FOR WRITING AND DISCUSSION

Practicing the *Summary/However* Move

For this exercise, assume that you favor development of wind-generated electricity. Use the *summary/however* move to acknowledge the view of civil engineer David Rockwood, whose letter opposing wind-generated electricity you read in Chapter 1 (p. 7). Assume that you are writing the opening paragraph of your own essay. Follow the pattern of Dao's introduction: (a) begin with a one-sentence issue or question; (b) summarize Rockwood's view in approximately one hundred words; and (c) state your own view, using *however* or *in contrast* as a transition. Write out your paragraph on your own, or work in groups to write a consensus paragraph. Then share and critique your paragraphs.

The *Division-into-Parallel-Parts* Move

Among the most frequently encountered and powerful of the set plays is the *division-into-parallel-parts* move. To initiate the move, a writer begins with an umbrella sentence that forecasts the structure and creates a framework. (For example, "Freud's theory differs from Jung's in three essential ways" or "The decline of the U.S. space program can be attributed to several factors.") Typical overview sentences either specify the number of parts that follow by using phrases such as "two ways," "three differences," or "five kinds," or they leave the number unspecified, using words such as *several, a few*, or *many*. Alternatively, the writer may ask a rhetorical question that implies the framework: "What are some main differences, then, between Freud's theory and Jung's? One difference is. ..."

To signal transitions from one part to the next, writers use two kinds of signposts in tandem. The first is a series of transition words or bullets to introduce each of the parallel parts. Here are typical series of transition words:

First ... Second ... Third ... Finally ...
First ... Another ... Still another ... Finally ...
One ... In addition ... Furthermore ... Also ...

The second kind of signpost, usually used in conjunction with transitions, is an echolike repetition of the same grammatical structure to begin each parallel part.

> I learned several things from this course. First, *I learned that* [development]. Second, *I learned that* [development]. Finally, *I learned that* [development].

The *division-into-parallel-parts* move can be used within a single paragraph, or it can control larger stretches of text in which a dozen or more paragraphs may work together to complete a parallel series of parts. (For example, you are currently in the third part of a parallel series introduced by the mapping sentence on p. 539: "Next, we describe four of the most powerful set plays.") Here is an example of a student paragraph organized by the *division-into-parallel-parts* move.

DIVISION-INTO-PARALLEL-PARTS MOVE

In this paper I will argue that political solutions to homelessness must take into account four categories of homeless people. A first category is persons who are out of work and seek new jobs. Persons in this category may have been recently laid off, unable to meet their rental payments, and forced temporarily to live out of a car or van. They might quickly leave the ranks of the homeless if they can find new jobs. A second category includes the physically disabled or mentally ill. Providing housing addresses only part of their problems since they also need medical care and medication. For many, finding or keeping a job might be impossible. A third category is the street alcoholic or drug addict. These persons need addiction treatment as well as clothing and shelter and will not become productive citizens until they become sober or drug free. The final category includes those who, like the old railroad "hobo," choose homelessness as a way of life.

Mapping statement forecasts "move"
Transition to first parallel part
Transition to second parallel part
Transition to third parallel part
Final transition completes "move"

Instead of transition words, writers can also use bullets followed by indented text:

USE OF BULLETS TO SIGNAL PARALLEL PARTS

The Wolf Recovery Program is rigidly opposed by a vociferous group of ranchers who pose three main objections to increasing wolf populations:

- They perceive wolves as a threat to livestock. [development]
- They fear the wolves will attack humans. [development]
- They believe ranchers will not be compensated by the government for their loss of profits. [development]

FOR WRITING AND DISCUSSION

Practicing the *Division-into-Parallel-Parts* Move

Working individually or in small groups, use the *division-into-parallel-parts* move to create, organize, and develop ideas to support one or more of the following point sentences.

1. To study for an exam effectively, a student should follow these [specify a number] steps.
2. Why do U.S. schoolchildren lag so far behind European and Asian children on standardized tests of mathematics and science? One possible cause is … [continue].
3. Constant dieting is unhealthy for several reasons.

The *Comparison/Contrast* Move

A common variation on the *division-into-parallel-parts* move is the *comparison/contrast* move. To compare or contrast two items, you must first decide on the points of comparison (or contrast). If you are contrasting the political views of two presidential candidates, you might choose to focus on four points of comparison: differences in their foreign policy, differences in economic policy, differences in social policy, and differences in judicial philosophy. You then have two choices for organizing the parts: the *side-by-side pattern,* in which you discuss all of candidate A's views and then all of candidate B's views; or the *back-and-forth pattern,* in which you discuss foreign policy, contrasting A's views with B's views, then move on to economic policy, then social policy, and then judicial philosophy. Figure 18.6 shows how these two patterns would appear on a tree diagram.

There are no cut-and-dried rules that dictate when to use the *side-by-side pattern* or the *back-and-forth pattern*. However, for lengthy comparisons, the *back-and-forth pattern* is often more effective because the reader doesn't have to store great amounts of information in memory. The *side-by-side pattern* requires readers to remember all the material about A when they get to B, and it is sometimes difficult to keep all the points of comparison clearly in mind.

FIGURE 18.6 Two Ways to Structure a Comparison or Contrast

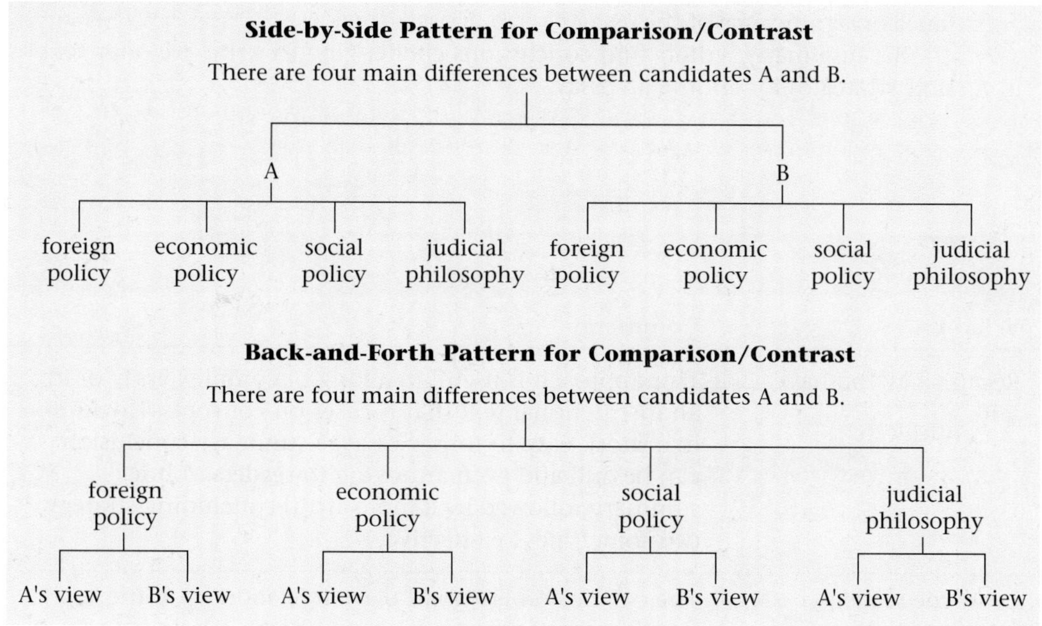

FOR WRITING AND DISCUSSION

Practicing the *Comparison/Contrast* Move

Working individually or in groups, create tree diagrams for stretches of text based on one or more of the following point sentences, all of which call for the *comparison/contrast* move. Make at least one diagram follow the *back-and-forth pattern* and at least one diagram follow the *side-by-side pattern.*

1. To understand U.S. politics, an outsider needs to appreciate some basic differences between Republicans and Democrats.
2. Although they are obviously different on the surface, there are many similarities between the Boy Scouts and a street gang.
3. There are several important differences between closed-form and open-form writing.

SKILL 14 Write effective conclusions.

Conclusions can best be understood as complements to introductions. In both the introduction and the conclusion, writers are concerned with the essay as a whole more than with any given part. In a conclusion, the writer attempts to bring a sense of completeness and closure to the profusion of points and particulars laid out in the body of the essay. The writer is particularly concerned with helping the reader move from the parts back to the big picture and to understand the importance or significance of the essay.

Because many writers find conclusions challenging to write, we offer six possible strategies for ending an essay.

STRATEGIES for Concluding an Essay

Strategies	What to Do	Comments
***Simple summary* conclusion**	Recap what you have said.	This approach is useful in a long or complex essay or in an instructional text that focuses on concepts. However, in a short, easy-to-follow essay, a summary conclusion can be dull and even annoying to readers. A brief summary followed by a more artful concluding strategy can sometimes be effective.
***Larger significance* conclusion**	Draw the reader's attention to the importance or the applications of your argument.	The conclusion is a good place to elaborate on the significance of your problem by showing how your proposed solution to a question leads to understanding a larger, more significant question or brings practical benefits to individuals or society. If you posed a question about values or about the interpretation of a confusing text or phenomenon, you might show how your argument could be applied to related questions, texts, or phenomena.
***Proposal* conclusion**	Call for action.	Often used in analyses and arguments, a *proposal* conclusion states the action that needs to be taken and briefly explains its advantages over alternative actions or describes its beneficial consequences. If your paper analyzes the negative consequences of shifting from a graduated to a flat-rate income tax, your conclusion may recommend an action such as modifying or opposing the flat tax.
	Call for future study.	A *call-for-future-study* conclusion indicates what else needs to be known or resolved before a proposal can be offered. Such conclusions are especially common in scientific writing.

Strategies	What to Do	Comments
***Scenic* or *anecdotal* conclusion**	Use a scene or brief story to illustrate the theme without stating it explicitly.	Often used in popular writing, a scene or anecdote can help the reader experience the emotional significance of the topic. For example, a paper favoring public housing for the homeless may end by describing an itinerant homeless person collecting bottles in a park.
***Hook and return* conclusion**	Return to something mentioned at the beginning of the essay.	If the essay begins with a vivid illustration of a problem, the conclusion can return to the same scene or story but with some variation to indicate the significance of the essay.
***Delayed-thesis* conclusion**	State the thesis for the first time at the end of the essay.	This strategy is effective when you are writing about complex or divisive issues and you don't want to take a stand until you have presented all sides. The introduction of the essay merely states the problem, giving the essay an exploratory feel.

FOR WRITING AND DISCUSSION

Writing Conclusions

Choose a paper you have just written and write an alternative conclusion using one of the strategies discussed in this lesson. Then share your original and revised conclusions in groups. Have group members discuss which one they consider most effective and why.

For additional writing, reading, and research resources, go to **www.MyCompLab.com** and choose **Ramage/Bean/Johnson's *The Allyn & Bacon Guide to Writing,* Fifth Edition.**

CHAPTER 19

COMPOSING AND REVISING OPEN-FORM PROSE

Good writing is supposed to evoke sensation in the reader—not the fact that it's raining, but the feel of being rained upon.

—*E. L. Doctorow, Novelist*

Much of this book focuses on closed-form prose where "good writing" means having a surprising thesis supported with effective points and particulars arranged hierarchically into unified and coherent paragraphs. But there are many kinds of good writing, and we probably all share the desire at times to write in ways other than tightly argued, thesis-governed, closed-form prose. In our epigraph, novelist E. L. Doctorow suggests another way to think of "good writing": Writing that evokes sensations, that triggers in the reader's imagination the very feel of the rain.

Chapter 7 on autobiographical narrative discusses plot, characterization, setting, and theme.

In this chapter, we shift our attention from closed- to open-form writing. Open-form prose differs from closed-form prose in its basic features, in the challenges and options it presents writers, in the demands it places on its readers, and in the mental and emotional pleasures it creates. Open-form writing, of the kind we discuss here, is often called *literary nonfiction* because it uses literary techniques and strategies such as story, plot, characterization, setting, and theme.

For essays that blend open and closed elements, see Cheryl Carp's "Behind Stone Walls" (pp. 232–233), and Jennifer Ching's "Once Upon a Time" (pp. 171–174).

Of course, it should be remembered that writing exists on a continuum from closed to open forms and that many features of open-form prose can appear in primarily closed-form texts. In fact, many of the example essays in this book combine elements of both open and closed styles. At the extremes of the continuum, closed- and open-form writing are markedly different, but the styles can be blended in pleasing combinations.

As we have discussed throughout this text, writing at the closed end of the spectrum seeks to be efficient and reader-friendly. By forecasting what's coming, placing points first, using clear transitions, and putting old information before new, closed-form writers place maximum emphasis on delivering clear ideas that readers can grasp quickly. In contrast, open-form writers, by violating or simply stretching those same conventions, set up a different kind of relationship with readers. They often provide more pleasure in reading, but just as often demand more patience and tolerance of ambiguity. They are likely to take readers backstage to share the process of their thinking. They often cast themselves in the role of narrators or characters reporting their quest for understanding and all the coincidences, disappointments, puzzling advice, and confusion they experienced along the way. In this process of sharing, they make readers codiscoverers of ideas and insights.

Open-form prose is also characterized by its emphasis on an aesthetic use of language—that is, language used to please and entertain. Without the benefit of a thesis or points appearing first to convey meaning, open-form prose depends on the very specificity of words, the ability of words to create mental pictures, to appeal to readers' senses and emotions, and to conjure up memories.

Our goal in this chapter is to give you some practical lessons on how to write effective open-form prose. But we need to acknowledge at the outset that, whereas closed-form prose is governed by a few widely accepted conventions, one of the main features of open-form prose is its freedom to play with conventions in a bewildering variety of ways. Consequently, our discussion of open-form writing seeks more to introduce you to guiding principles rather than to treat open-form writing exhaustively.

SKILL 15 Make your narrative a story, not an *and then* chronology.

We have said that open-form prose is narrative based and uses the strategies of a story. In this first lesson we want you to think more deeply about the concept of a story—particularly how a story differs from an *and then* chronology. Both a story and an *and then* chronology depict events happening in time. But there are important differences between them. At the start of this lesson, we'd like you to try your own hand at articulating the differences between a story and an *and then* chronology. Read the following example of a student's autobiographical narrative and then respond to the questions that follow.

And then writing is also discussed in Chapter 18, Skill 6.

Patrick Klein (student)

Berkeley Blues

1 It was a cold night. That is nothing new in San Francisco, but something made this night particularly frigid. It was early February and the whole city, including the Berkeley section where we were staying, was still held tight in the firm grip of winter. It had also rained that afternoon and the air, having been cleared by the storm, was cold and sharp. It hurt the back of your throat when you inhaled and turned into mist when you exhaled. As the six of us hurriedly walked in a huddled mass, the water that was lying in puddles on the dimly lit sidewalk jumped out of our way as we slammed our dress shoes down into its dregs. We silently decided on our destination and slipped into the grungy, closet-like pizza joint. We took the only seats the place had and as we pulled them into a circle, we all breathed a sigh of relief.

2 This was our first night at Berkeley. We were there for a debate tournament to be held the next day at the university. On this night, however, we were six high school

sophomores in search of food. So, dressed in our suits and ties (we were required to wear them) and heavy coats, we ventured out of the university and entered the city of Berkeley.

3 Berkeley is an interesting place. Many might have romantic notions of a bunch of shaggy intellectuals discussing French existentialism while sipping cappuccino, but while this might have been the case a few decades ago, the reality is that Berkeley is a ghetto. The place is filled with grungy closet shops while newspapers cover the sidewalks and the people lying on them. The university is divided from this ghetto by a two-lane street.

4 As the six of us crossed the two-lane street that fateful night, my thoughts drifted to my own neighborhood, which up until that moment had been the extent of my world.

5 McCormick Ranch, Arizona, is a sheltered place. To a certain extent it's mostly white, with little crime and few domestic problems. Everybody has a pool, at least two cars, and a beautiful desert sunset every night. I had everything I ever wanted. It seemed very gentle and dreamlike compared to the harsh slum we found ourselves in.

6 When we made it into the pizza place and moved the chairs into a protective circle around a square table, anxiety about our "hostile" environment was quickly swept away with hot, greasy pizza. We ate until we were content and were trying to decide how to divide the few remaining pieces among ourselves when it happened.

7 The pizza place was separated from the rest of humanity by a large window. Our table was directly in front of that window and two feet from the door. People had been passing the window and probably remarking on the six well-dressed kids inside, but we paid them no mind and they all walked by without incident. Still, our hearts were seized with terror every time a human being would pass that window, and we hoped with all that we could muster that every one of them would continue on. We were almost right.

8 On this night, when six young yuppie kids from an upper middle-class world decided to risk it and go eat pizza in a ghetto, he walked by. He didn't look any different from others we'd seen that night. Black. Dirty. Tired. Cold. His clothes consisted of a grimy, newspaper-stained jacket, a T-shirt with who-knows-how-old dirt on it, flimsy pants with holes at the knees, and tattered excuses for shoes. He was not quite up to par with our Gucci loafers and Armani jackets.

9 He shuffled past the window and glanced in. We didn't notice. He stopped. We noticed. Twelve eyes glanced up as casually as they could and six hearts stopped beating for a second. Yep, still there. All eyes went back to the floor, except for two. Those eyes belonged to Chad, and in some act of defiance, his eyes met the poor man's eyes and glared.

10 The man opened the door. "We're all going to die," I thought. "All my hopes and dreams are going to end here, in a stupid pizza place, at the hands of a crazy black bum."

11 He took something out of his pocket.

12 It was shiny.

13 I couldn't look.

14 A knife.

15 No. It was a flask. He took a swig from it, and, still propping the door open with his sagging frame, spoke the most jolting, burning words I've ever heard.

16 "I love you," he said. "All of you." He glanced at Chad, "Even you." He stepped back and said, "I know what you think of me, but I still love you." I will probably never forget those words or how he said them with a steady, steely voice.

17 Then he left. That was it. Gone. It took about five minutes for anyone to talk. When the talking started, we exchanged jokes and responded with empty, devastating laughter.

18 We soon left the shop. It had grown colder outside and we quickly returned to our climate-controlled hotel room. We had just eaten a filling meal and paid for it with our own money. We were all about fifteen. The man we had encountered was probably in his fifties. He had no roof, no money, or food. It seemed strange that I owned more than an adult, but in truth, he had more than I. He was able to love us when we ostracized him and thought stereotypically about him.

19 I remember later trying to rationalize my sickening behavior by thinking that there is nothing wrong with being and acting afraid in a strange environment. I tried to use my age as an excuse. Nothing worked. I was guilty of fearing a fellow human being because of his color and my preset notions of bums.

20 To this day I still think about what difference, if any, it would have made if we had given him our leftover pizza. It might have eased my conscience. It was a very cold night and we had made it colder.

FOR WRITING AND DISCUSSION

And Then Chronology Versus Story

Individual task: Now that you have read "Berkeley Blues," read the following autobiographical narrative entitled "The Stolen Watch," which was submitted by a student as a draft for an assignment on narrative writing.

The Stolen Watch

Last fall and winter I was living in Spokane with my brother, who during this time had a platonic girlfriend come over from Seattle and stay for a weekend. Her name was Karen, and we became interested in each other and I went over to see her at the first of the year. She then invited me to, supposedly, the biggest party of the year, called the Aristocrats' Ball. I said sure and made my way back to Seattle in February. It started out bad on Friday, the day my brother and I left Spokane. We left town an hour late, but what's new. Then my brother had to stop along the way and pick up some parts; we stayed there for an hour trying to find this guy. It all started out bad because we arrived in Seattle and I forgot to call Karen. We were staying at her brother's house and after we brought all our things in, we decided to go to a few bars. Later that night we ran into Karen in one of the bars, and needless to say she

(*continued*)

was not happy with me. When I got up the next morning I knew I should have stayed in Spokane, because I felt bad vibes. Karen made it over about an hour before the party. By the time we reached the party, which drove me crazy, she wound up with another guy, so her friends and I decided to go to a few bars. The next morning when I was packing, I could not find my watch and decided that someone had to have taken it. We decided that it had to have been the goon that Karen had wound up with the night before, because she was at her brother's house with him before she went home. So how was I going to get my watch back?

We decided the direct and honest approach to the problem would work out the best. We got in contact and confronted him. This turned out to be quite a chore. It turned out that he was visiting some of his family during that weekend and lived in Little Harbor, California. It turned out that Karen knew his half brother and got some information on him, which was not pretty. He had just been released by the army and was trained in a special forces unit, in the field of Martial Arts. He was a trained killer! This information did not help matters at all, but the next bit of information was just as bad if not worse. Believe it or not, he was up on charges of attempted murder and breaking and entering. In a way, it turned out lucky for me, because he was in enough trouble with the police and did not need any more. Karen got in contact with him and threatened him that I would bring him up on charges if he did not return the watch. His mother decided that he was in enough trouble and sent me the watch. I was astounded, it was still working and looked fine. The moral of the story is don't drive 400 miles to see a girl you hardly know, and whatever you do, don't leave your valuables out in the open.

Group task: Share your responses to the following questions:

1. How does your experience of reading "Berkeley Blues" differ from your experience of reading "The Stolen Watch"? Try to articulate the different ways you reacted to the two pieces while in the process of reading them.
2. Based on the differences between these two pieces, how would you define a "story"? Begin by brainstorming all the ways that the two pieces differ. Then try to identify the essential differences that make one a "story" and the other and *and then* chronology.

Now that you have tried to define a story for yourselves, we would like to explain our own four criteria for a story: depiction of events through time, connectedness, tension, and resolution. If we combine these criteria into a sentence, it would read like this: A story depicts events that are connected causally or thematically to create a sense of tension that is resolved through action, insight, or understanding. These four criteria occurring together turn a chronology into a story.

Depiction of Events through Time

The essence of storytelling is the depiction of events through time. Whereas thesis-based writing descends from problem to thesis to supporting reasons and evidence, stories unfold linearly, temporally, from event to event. You may start in the middle of the action and then jump backward and forward, but you always encounter some sequence of events happening in time. This temporal focus creates a sense of "onceness." Things that happen at a point in time happen only once, as the classic fairy-tale opening "Once upon a time" suggests. When you compose and revise a narrative, you want to try to capture the "onceness" of that experience. As the essayist E. B. White once advised a young writer, "Don't write about Man but about a man."

Consider how Val Plumwood, a professor of women's studies and author of the book *Feminism and the Mastery of Nature,* depicts the events leading up to a disturbing encounter with a crocodile. (Later in the story, the reader sees how this encounter shapes her understanding of humans' place in the food chain and the need for a respectful, rather than a dominating, attitude toward other animals.)

> In the early wet season, Kakadu's paper-bark wetlands are especially stunning, as the water lilies weave white, pink, and blue patterns of dreamlike beauty over the shining thunderclouds reflected in their still waters. Yesterday, the water lilies and the wonderful bird life had enticed me into a joyous afternoon's idyll as I ventured onto the East Alligator Lagoon for the first time in a canoe lent by the park service. "You can play about on the backwaters," the ranger had said, "but don't go onto the main river channel. The current's too swift, and if you get into trouble, there are the crocodiles. Lots of them along the river!" I followed his advice and glutted myself on the magical beauty and bird life of the lily lagoons, untroubled by crocodiles.
>
> Today, I wanted to repeat the experience despite the drizzle beginning to fall as I neared the canoe launch site. I set off on a day trip in search of an Aboriginal rock art site across the lagoon and up a side channel. The drizzle turned to a warm rain within a few hours, and the magic was lost. The birds were invisible, the water lilies were sparser, and the lagoon seemed even a little menacing. I noticed now how low the 14-foot canoe sat in the water, just a few inches of fiberglass between me and the great saurian, close relatives of the ancient dinosaurs. ...
>
> After hours of searching the maze of shallow channels in the swamp, I had not found the clear channel leading to the rock art site, as shown on the ranger's sketch map. When I pulled my canoe over in driving rain to a rock outcrop for a hasty, sodden lunch, I experienced the unfamiliar sensation of being watched. Having never been one for timidity, in philosophy or in life, I decided, rather than return defeated to my sticky trailer, to explore a clear, deep channel closer to the river I had traveled the previous day.
>
> The rain and wind grew more severe, and several times I pulled over to tip water from the canoe. The channel soon developed steep mud banks and snags. Farther on, the channel opened up and was eventually blocked by a large sandy bar. I pushed the canoe toward the bank, looking around carefully before getting out of the shallow and pulling the canoe up. I would be safe from crocodiles in the canoe—I had been

> told—but swimming and standing or wading at the water's edge were dangerous. Edges are one of the crocodile's favorite food-capturing places. I saw nothing, but the feeling of unease that had been with me all day intensified.

In this example of literary nonfiction, Plumwood persuades readers to appreciate the beauties of the exotic Australian rain forest as well as its dangers. Note how her method includes the depicting of events that happen once in time—her wondrous first day of exploration, the ranger's warning to stay away from the main river, her second day's unsuccessful search by canoe for a site of Aboriginal rock art, and then her emerging discovery that in the increasing intensity of the rainstorm, she had reached the junction with the main river. Plumwood's powerful narrative becomes the basis for a profound concluding reflection on what she calls humans' "ecological identity."

Connectedness

The events of a story must also be connected, not merely spatially or sequentially, but causally or thematically. When discussing "The Stolen Watch" in the previous exercise, you might have asked yourselves, "What does all that stuff about forgetting to call Karen and stopping for parts, etc., have to do with the stolen watch? Is this story about the watch or about confronting a potential killer?" If so, you instinctively understood the concept of connectedness. Stories are more than just chronicles of events. Novelist E. M. Forster offered the simplest definition of a story when he rejected "The king dies and then the queen died," but accepted "The king died and then the queen died ... of grief." The words "of grief" connect the two events to each other in a causal relationship, converting a series of events into a patterned, meaningfully related sequence of events. Now examine this passage to see the connections the writer establishes between the scenes.

THEMATIC AND CAUSAL CONNECTEDNESS

> I have been so totally erased from nature lately, like a blackboard before school starts, that yesterday when I was in the Japanese section of San Francisco, Japantown, I saw the sidewalk littered with chocolate wrappers.
>
> There were hundreds of them. Who in the hell has been eating all these chocolates? I thought. A convention of Japanese chocolate eaters must have passed this way.
>
> Then I noticed some plum trees on the street. Then I noticed that it was autumn. Then I noticed that the leaves were falling as they will and as they must every year. Where had I gone wrong?
>
> —Richard Brautigan, "Leaves"

Brautigan's narrative becomes a story only when you realize that the "chocolate wrappers" are really plum leaves; the two images are connected by the writer's changed perception, which illuminates the thematic question raised at the beginning and end: Why has he become "so totally erased from nature"? As you write, connect the elements of your narrative causally and thematically.

Tension or Conflict

The third criterion for a story—tension or conflict—creates the anticipation and potential significance that keep the reader reading. In whodunit stories, the tension follows from attempts to identify the murderer or to prevent the murderer from doing in yet another victim. In many comic works, the tension is generated by confusion or misunderstanding that drives a wedge between people who would normally be close. Tension always involves contraries, such as those between one belief and another, between opposing values, between the individual and the environment or the social order, between where I am now and where I want to be or used to be. In the following passage, see how the contraries create dramatic tension that engages readers.

DRAMATIC TENSIONS

Straddling the top of the world, one foot in China and the other in Nepal, I cleared the ice from my oxygen mask, hunched a shoulder against the wind, and stared absently down at the vastness of Tibet. I understood on some dim, detached level that the sweep of earth beneath my feet was a spectacular sight. I'd been fantasizing about this moment, and the release of emotion that would accompany it, for many months. But now that I was finally here, actually standing on the summit of Mount Everest, I just couldn't summon the energy to care.

It was early in the afternoon of May 10, 1996. I hadn't slept in fifty-seven hours. The only food I'd been able to force down over the preceding three days was a bowl of ramen soup and a handful of peanut M&M's. Weeks of violent coughing had left me with two separated ribs that made ordinary breathing an excruciating trial. At 29,028 feet up in the troposphere, so little oxygen was reaching my brain that my mental capacity was that of a slow child. Under the circumstances, I was incapable of feeling much of anything except cold and tired.

—Jon Krakauer, *Into Thin Air*

Notice how this passage presents several contraries or conflicts: the opposition between the narrator's expectation of what it would be like to stand on the top of Mount Everest and the actuality once he's there; and the opposition between the physical strength and stamina of the climber and the extreme danger of climbing this mountain. The reader wonders how Krakauer reached the summit with no sleep, almost no food, and a violent and agonizing cough; more important, the reader wonders why he kept on climbing. We can ask this important query of any narrative: What conflicts and tensions are prompting readers' ongoing questions and holding their interest?

Resolution, Recognition, or Retrospective Interpretation

The final criterion for a story is the resolution or retrospective interpretation of events. The resolution may be stated explicitly or implied. Fables typically sum up the story's significance with an explicit moral at the end. In contrast, the interpretation of events in poetry is almost always implicit. Note how the following haiku collapses events and resolution.

RESOLUTION

A strange old man
stops me,
Looking out of my deep mirror.

—Hitomaro, *One Hundred Poems from the Japanese*

In this tiny story, two things happen simultaneously. The narrator is stopped by a "strange old man" and the narrator looks into a mirror. The narrator's *recognition* is that he is that same old man. This recognition—"That's me in the mirror; when I wasn't looking, I grew old!"—in turn ties the singular event of the story back to more universal concerns and the reader's world.

The typical direction of a story, from singular event(s) to general conclusion, reverses the usual points-first direction of closed-form essays. Stories force readers to read inductively, gathering information and looking for a pattern that's confirmed or unconfirmed by the story's resolution. This resolution is the point *toward* which readers read. It often drives home the significance of the narrative. Typically, a reader's satisfaction or dissatisfaction with a story hinges on how well the resolution manages to explain or justify the events that precede it. Writers need to ask: How does my resolution grow out of my narrative and fit with the resolution the reader has been forming?

FOR WRITING AND DISCUSSION

Identifying Criteria for "Story"

1. Working as a whole class or in small groups, return to Patrick Klein's essay "Berkeley Blues" and explain how it qualifies as a story rather than an *and then* chronology. How does it meet all four of the criteria: depiction of events through time, connectedness, tension, and resolution?
2. Consider again "The Stolen Watch." It seems to meet the criterion of "depiction of events through time," but it is weak in connectedness, tension, and resolution. How could the writer revise the chronology to make it a story? Brainstorm several different ways that this potentially exciting early draft could be rewritten.
3. If you are working on your own open-form narrative, exchange drafts with a classmate. Discuss each others' drafts in light of this lesson's focus on story. To what extent do your drafts exhibit the features of a story rather than of an *and then* chronology? Working together, develop revision plans that might increase the story elements in your narratives.

SKILL 16 Write low on the scale of abstraction.

In Chapter 4 we introduced the concept of "scale of abstraction," in which words can be arranged from the very abstract (living creatures, clothing) down to the very specific (our dog Charley, a Rhodesian Ridgeback with floppy ears; my hippie Birkenstocks with the saltwater stains; see Chapter 4, Concept 11). In this lesson we show why and how open-form writers stay low on the scale of abstraction through their use of concrete words, revelatory words, and memory-soaked words.

Concrete Words Evoke Images and Sensations

To appreciate the impact of specific, concrete language, look again at the opening sentence of Val Plumwood's narrative about her encounter with crocodiles (p. 551):

> In the early wet season, Kakadu's paper-bark wetlands are especially stunning, as the water lilies weave white, pink, and blue patterns of dreamlike beauty over the shining thunderclouds reflected in their still waters.

Here is how that same passage might sound if rewritten a level higher on the scale of abstraction:

> In the early wet season the Kakadu landscape is especially stunning as the water plants weave their colorful patterns of dreamlike beauty over the clouds reflected in the water's surface.

For further discussion of specific, sensory words, see Chapter 5, pp. 102–103, on *show* words versus *tell* words.

This is still quite a nice sentence. But something is lost when you say "landscape" rather than "paper-bark wetlands," "clouds" rather than "thunderclouds," or "colorful" rather than "white, pink, and blue." The lower you write on the scale of abstraction, the more you tap into your readers' storehouse of particular memories and images.

The power of concrete words has been analyzed by writer John McPhee in a widely quoted and cited interview. When asked why he wrote the sentence "Old white oaks are rare because they had a tendency to become bowsprits, barrel staves, and queen-post trusses" instead of a more generic sentence such as, "Old white oaks are rare because they were used as lumber," he responded in a way that reveals his love of the particular:

> There isn't much life in [the alternative version of the sentence]. If you can find a specific, firm, and correct image, it's always going to be better than a generality, and hence I tend, for example, to put in trade names and company names and, in an instance like this, the names of wood products instead of a general term like "lumber." You'd say "Sony" instead of "tape recorder" if the context made it clear you meant to say tape recorder. It's not because you're on the take from Sony, it's because the image, at least to this writer or reader, strikes a clearer note.

Some readers might complain that the particulars "bowsprits, barrel staves, and queen-post trusses" don't help readers' understanding, as do particulars in closed-form prose, but instead give most readers a moment's pause. Today most barrel staves and bowsprits are made of metal, not oak, and few contemporary readers encounter them on a regular basis no matter what they're made of. Furthermore, few readers at any time could readily identify "queen-post trusses," a technical term from the building trade. Instead of smoothly completing the reader's understanding of a point, McPhee's particulars tend to arrest and even sidetrack, sending the reader in pursuit of a dictionary.

But if McPhee's examples momentarily puzzle, it's the sort of puzzlement that can lead to greater understanding. Precisely because they are exotic terms, these words arouse the reader's curiosity and imagination. "Exotic language is of value," says McPhee. "A queen-post truss is great just because of the sound of the words and what they call to mind. The 'queen,' the 'truss'—the ramifications in everything."

For McPhee, the fact that these words trip up the reader is a point in their favor. If McPhee had said that old white oaks are rare these days because they became parts of "ships, barrels, and roofs," no one would blink or notice. If you were to visualize the items, you'd probably call up some ready-made pictures that leave little trace in your mind. You also wouldn't hear the sounds of the words. (In this regard, notice McPhee's emphasis on images sounding "a clearer note.")

Your forward progress toward the point would be unimpeded, but what would be lost? A new glimpse into a lost time when oak trees were used to make exotic items that today exist mostly in old books and memories.

Another quality also recommends words that readers trip over, words such as *bowsprit, barrel stave,* and *queen-post truss:* their power to persuade the reader to believe in the world being described. Tripping over things, whether they're made of steel or words, forces the reader to acknowledge their independence, the reality of a world outside the reader's own head. For this reason, writers of formula fiction—thrillers, westerns, romances, and the like—will load their texts with lots of little details and bits of technical information from the time and place they describe. Because their stories are otherwise implausible (e.g., the description of the Evil Empire's doomsday machine), they need all the help they can get from their details (the size of the toggle bolts used to keep the machine in place while it's blasting out intergalactic death rays) to convince readers that the story is real.

Use Revelatory Words and Memory-Soaked Words

As we have seen, concrete language, low on the scale of abstraction, can evoke imaginative experiences for readers. Two particularly powerful kinds of concrete language are revelatory words and memory-soaked words. By *revelatory* words we mean specific details that reveal the social status, lifestyle, beliefs, and values of people. According to writer Tom Wolfe, carefully chosen details can reveal a person's *status life*—"the entire pattern of behavior and possessions through which people express their position in the world or what they think it is or hope it to be." Wolfe favors writing that records "everyday gestures, habits, manners, customs, styles of furniture, clothing, decoration, styles of traveling, eating, keeping house, modes of behaving toward children, servants, superiors, inferiors, peers, plus the various looks, glances, poses, styles of walking and other symbolic details that might exist within a scene." Thus subtle differences in a person's status life might be revealed in details about fast food (a Big Mac versus a Subway turkey wrap), body piercing (pierced ears versus pierced tongue), a watch (a Timex versus a TAG Heuer) or music (Kenny Chesney versus Busta Rhymes). In "Berkeley Blues," Patrick Klein and his classmates are economically revealed as upper-middle-class people by their attire—"Armani jackets" and "Gucci loafers."

Another way to create powerful concrete language is through *memory-soaked* words. Such words trigger a whole complex of ideas, emotions, and sensations in readers who share memories from a particular era. People who grew up in the 1950s, for example, might have deep associations with 45-rpm records, the Ed Sullivan show, or the words "duck tail" or "tail fins." For Vietnam veterans, Nancy Sinatra's "These Boots Were Made for Walking" or the whirr of helicopter blades might evoke strong memories. Persons growing up in the 1970s or 1980s might remember "Cookie Monster," "Pez guns," or 8-track tapes. In recent years, our students have come up with these memory-soaked words from their own childhoods: American Girl dolls, Power Rangers, Ghostbuster action figures, Super Nintendo, and Uno (card game).

FOR WRITING AND DISCUSSION

Working Low on the Scale of Abstraction

1. Working in small groups or as a whole class, try your own hand at using revelatory words to reveal status life. Create a list of specific details that you might associate with each of the following: middle school girls at a slumber party; friends at a tailgate party before a football game; the kitchen of an upscale urban apartment of a two-profession couple who subscribe to *Gourmet* magazine; the kitchen of a middle-class, middle America family with three kids and a collection of *Good Housekeeping* magazines; the kitchen of an apartment shared by college students. (If you are describing kitchens, for example, consider the different *status life* signaled by ketchup versus stone ground mustard or by an iceberg lettuce salad with ranch dressing versus an almond mandarin salad.)
2. Also try your hand at finding memory-soaked words. Make a list of specific words and names associated with your childhood that you now rarely hear or see. Share your list with others in your group and identify the items that have the strongest associations.
3. If you are working on your own open-form narrative, exchange drafts with a classmate and, working together, find specific examples where each of you has successfully used concrete, revelatory, or memory-soaked words. Then find passages that could be profitably revised by moving down a level on the scale of abstraction or by adding concrete details that follow the advice in this lesson.

SKILL 17 Disrupt your reader's desire for direction and clarity.

The epigraph to Chapter 18 by the philosopher Kenneth Burke speaks about form as "an arousing and fulfillment of desires." In closed-form prose, we can easily see this process at work: The writer previews what he or she is going to say, arousing the reader's desire to see the general outline fleshed out with specifics, and then fulfills that desire speedily through a presentation of pertinent points and particulars.

In more open-form prose, the fulfillment of desire follows a less straightforward path. Writers offer fewer overviews and clues, leaving readers less sure of where they're headed; or writers mention an idea and then put it aside for a while as they pursue some other point whose relevance may seem tenuous. Rather than establish the direction or point of their prose, writers suspend that direction, waiting until later in the prose to show how the ideas are meaningfully related. In other words, the period of arousal is longer and more drawn out; the fulfillment of desire is delayed until the end, when the reader finally sees how the pieces fit together.

Open-form prose gives you the opportunity to overlay your narrative core with other patterns of ideas—to move associatively from idea to idea, to weave a complex pattern of meaning in which the complete picture emerges later. Often the way you achieve these surprising twists and turns of structure and meaning is by playing with the conventions of closed-form prose. For example, in the autobiographical narrative "Berkeley Blues," Patrick Klein breaks the cardinal closed-form rule that pronouns should refer only to previously stated antecedents; he introduces the stranger only as *he* and gradually reveals that person's identity. This violation creates an aura of mystery and suspense. Here in this lesson we describe some of your open-form options for surprising your readers and delaying their fulfillment of desires.

Disrupt Predictions and Make Odd Juxtapositions

Open-form writers frequently violate the principle of forecasting and mapping that we stressed in Chapter 18. Consider the following introduction to an essay:

PASSAGE WITH DISRUPTED PREDICTIONS AND ODD JUXTAPOSITIONS

Whose bones? What feathers?

Birds? What birds?

What do birds have to do with how the brain works? Where is this writer going?

> I suppose their little bones have years ago been lost among the stones and winds of those high glacial pastures. I suppose their feathers blew eventually into the piles of tumbleweed beneath the straggling cattle fences and rotted there in the mountain snows, along with dead steers and all the other things that drift to an end in the corners of the wire. I do not quite know why I should be thinking of birds over the *New York Times* at breakfast, particularly the birds of my youth half a continent away. It is and funny thing what the brain will do with memories and how it will treasure them and finally bring them into odd juxtapositions with other things, as though it wanted to make a design, or get some meaning out of them, whether you want it or not, or even see it.
>
> —Loren Eisley, "The Bird and the Machine"

Note the sequence of ideas from bones to birds to breakfast over *The New York Times* to comments about the workings of the brain. In fact, in this essay it takes Eisley six full paragraphs in which he discusses mechanical inventions to return to the birds with the line: "... or those birds, I'll never forget those birds. ..."

Throughout these paragraphs, what drives the reader forward is curiosity to discover the connections between the parts and to understand the meaning of the essay's title "The Bird and the Machine." Actually, Eisley's comment about the brain's "odd juxtapositions" of memories with "other things, as though it wanted to make a design, or get some meaning out of them" could be a description of this open-form technique we've called "disrupting predictions and making odd juxtapositions." Open-form writers can choose when "odd juxtapositions" are an appropriate strategy for inviting the reader to accompany the discovering, reflecting writer on a journey toward meaning.

Leave Gaps

An important convention of closed-form prose is the old/new contract, which specifies that the opening of every sentence should link in some way to what has gone before. Open-form prose often violates this convention, leaving *gaps* in the text, forcing the reader to puzzle over the connection between one part and the next.

The following passage clearly violates the old/new contract. This example recounts the writer's thoughts after startling a weasel in the woods and exchanging glances with it.

PASSAGE WITH INTENTIONAL GAPS

> What goes on in [a weasel's brain] the rest of the time? What does a weasel think about? He won't say. His journal is tracks in clay, a spray of feathers, mouse blood and bone: uncollected, unconnected, loose-leaf, and blown.
>
> I would like to learn, or remember, how to live. I come to Hollins Pond not so much to learn how to live as, frankly, to forget about it.
>
> —Annie Dillard, "Living Like Weasels"

Gap caused by unexplained or unpredicted shift from weasel to philosophic musing

Dillard suddenly switches, without transition, from musing about the mental life of a weasel to asserting that she would like to learn how to live. What is the connection between her encounter with the weasel and her own search for how to live? Dillard's open-form techniques leave these gaps for readers to ponder and fill in, inviting us to participate in the process of arriving at meaning. Just as open-form writers can deliberately avoid predicting or mapping statements, they also have the liberty to leave gaps in a text when it suits their purpose.

FOR WRITING AND DISCUSSION

Disrupting Reader Expectations

If you are currently working on an open-form narrative, exchange drafts with a classmate. Discuss in what way the strategies explained in this lesson might be appropriate for your purposes. Where might you currently "explain too much" and benefit by juxtaposing scenes without explanatory filler? Where might you use other strategies from this lesson?

SKILL 18 Tap the power of figurative language.

Open-form writers often use figurative language in situations in which closed-form writers would use literal language. In this brief lesson, we show you some of the power of figurative language.

When journalist Nicholas Tomalin describes a captured Vietnamese prisoner as young and slight, the reader understands him in a literal way, but when, a moment later, he compares the prisoner to "a tiny, fine-boned wild animal," the reader understands him in a different way; the reader understands not only what the subject looks like—his general physical attributes—but how that particular boy appears in that moment to those around him—fierce, frightened, trapped.

Metaphors abound when literal words fail. When writers encounter eccentric people or are overwhelmed by the strangeness of their experiences, they use *figurative language*—imaginative comparisons—to explain their situation and their reactions to it. Figurative language—similes, metaphors, and personifications—enables the writer to describe an unfamiliar thing in terms of different, more familiar things. The surprise of yoking two very unlike things evokes from the reader a perception, insight, or emotional experience that could not otherwise be communicated. The originality and vividness of the imaginative comparison frequently resonates with meaning for readers and sticks in their minds long afterward.

In the following passage, Isak Dinesen describes an experience that most of us have not had—seeing iguanas in the jungle and shooting one. After reading this passage, however, we have a striking picture in our minds of what she saw and a strong understanding of what she felt and realized.

PASSAGE USING FIGURATIVE LANGUAGE

In the Reserve I have sometimes come upon the Iguana, the big lizards, as they were sunning themselves upon a flat stone in a riverbed. They are not pretty in shape, but nothing can be imagined more beautiful than their coloring. They shine like a heap of precious stones or like a pane cut out of an old church window. When, as you approach, they swish away, there is a flash of azure, green and purple over the stones, the color seems to be standing behind them in the air, like a comet's luminous tail.

Similes heaped up

Simile

Once I shot an Iguana. I thought that I should be able to make some pretty things from his skin. A strange thing happened then, that I have never afterwards forgotten. As I went up to him, where he was lying dead upon his stone, and actually while I was walking a few steps, he faded and grew pale, all color died out of him as in one long sigh, and by the time that I touched him he was gray and dull like a lump of concrete. It was the live impetuous blood pulsating within the animal, which had radiated out all that glow and splendor. Now that the flame was put out, and the soul had flown, the Iguana was as dead as a sandbag.

Metaphor of dying applied to color

Simile

Metaphor

Simile

—Isak Dinesen, "The Iguana"

The figurative language in this passage enables readers to share Dinesen's experience. It also compacts a large amount of information into sharp, memorable images.

FOR WRITING AND DISCUSSION

Using Figurative Language

1. Figurative language can fall flat when it takes the form of clichés ("I stood transfixed like a bump on a log") or mixed metaphors ("Exposed like a caterpillar on a leaf, he wolfed down his lunch before taking flight"). But when used effectively, figurative language adds powerfully compressed and meaningful images to a passage. Working individually or in small groups, find examples of figurative language in one or more of the example essays in this chapter or in Chapter 7 (pp. 165–174). See if you can reach consensus on what makes a particular instance of figurative language effective or ineffective. As an initial example, consider this passage from the student essay "Masks" (pp. 169–171): "She was so elusive, like a beautiful perfume you smell but can't name, like the whisper that wakes you from a dream and turns out to belong to the dream."
2. If you are currently working on an open-form narrative, exchange drafts with a classmate. See if you can find instances of figurative language in your current drafts and analyze their effectiveness. Perhaps you can also discover places where figurative language could be profitably added to the text.

SKILL 19 Expand your repertoire of styles.

In Chapter 4, we introduced you to the concept of style, which is a combination of sentence structure, word choice, and rhythm that allows writers to vary their emphasis and tone in a variety of ways. In this lesson, we show you how to expand your repertoire of styles through a classic method of teaching in which you try to imitate other writers' styles. This rhetorical practice—called "creative imitation"—has a long history beginning with the rhetoricians of classical Greece and Rome. When you do creative imitation, you examine a passage from an expert stylist and try to emulate it. You substitute your own subject matter, but you try to imitate the exact grammatical structures, lengths and rhythms of the sentences, and the tones of the original passage. The long-range effect of creative imitation is to expand your stylistic choices; the more immediate effect is to increase your skill at analyzing a writer's style. Most practitioners find that creative imitation encourages surprising insights into their own subject matter (when seen through the lens of the original writer's style) as well as a new understanding of how a particular piece of writing creates its special effects.

See Chapter 4, Concept 11, for a discussion of style.

You begin a creative imitation by asking questions such as these: What is distinctive about the sentences in this passage of writing? How do choices about sentence length and complexity, kinds of words, figures of speech, and so forth create a writer's voice? After close examination of the passage, you then think of your own subject matter that could be appropriately adapted to this writer's style.

To help you understand creative imitation, we provide the following example. In this passage, the writer, Victoria Register-Freeman, is exploring how relations between young men and women today threaten to undo some of the twentieth century's progress toward gender equality. In the section of her article that precedes this passage, Register-Freeman explains how she, as a single mother, taught her boys to cook, sew, do laundry, and "carry their weight domestically." But then, as she explains in this passage, teenage girls undid her attempts at creating gender equality:

REGISTER-FREEMAN PASSAGE

> Then came puberty and hunkhood. Over the last few years, the boys' domestic skills have atrophied because handmaidens have appeared en masse. The damsels have driven by, beeped, phoned and faxed. Some appeared so frequently outside the front door they began to remind me of the suction-footed Garfields spread-eagled on car windows. While the girls varied according to height, hair color and basic body type, they shared one characteristic. They were ever eager to help the guys out.
>
> —Victoria Register-Freeman, "My Turn: Hunks and Handmaidens"

Register-Freeman's voice projects the image of a concerned mother and feminist social critic. Her tone includes a range of attitudes: serious, personal, factual, ironic, frustrated. Note how this passage begins and ends with short, clipped sentences. The second sentence states a problem that the next three sentences develop with various kinds of details. The third sentence includes a series of colorful verbs; the fourth uses a metaphor (the ever-present girls compared to Garfields on car windows). The fifth sentence builds to the point in the sixth sentence, which is delivered bluntly and simply.

Here is one writer's attempt at a creative imitation:

CREATIVE IMITATION OF REGISTER-FREEMAN

Then came prosperity and popularity. Over the last ten years, Seattle's special charms have faded because expansion has occurred too rapidly. Traffic has multiplied, thickened, amplified, and slowed. Traffic jams appeared so often on the freeways and arterials they began to remind me of ants swarming over spilled syrup. While the congestion varied according to time, seasons, and weather conditions, it had one dominant effect. It increasingly threatened to spoil the city's beauty.

FOR WRITING AND DISCUSSION

Practicing Style through Creative Imitation

1. Do your own creative imitation of the passage from Register-Freeman.
2. Choose one or both of the following passages for creative imitation. Begin by jotting down all the specific observations you can make about the stylistic features of the passage. Then choose a topic that matches the topic of the original in its degree of lightness or seriousness and its depth. Explore your topic by presenting it using the sentence structures and kinds of words used in the original. Try to imitate the original phrase by phrase and sentence by sentence. You may find it helpful to use a dictionary and thesaurus.

    a. Africa is mystic; it is wild; it is a sweltering inferno; it is a photographer's paradise, a hunter's Valhalla, as escapist's Utopia. It is what you will, and it withstands all interpretations. It is the last vestige of a dead world or the cradle of a shiny new one. To a lot of people, as to myself, it is just "home." It is all of these things but one thing—it is never dull.

    —Beryl Markham, "Flying Elsewhere," *West with the Night*

    b. The disease was bubonic plague, present in two forms: one that infected the bloodstream, causing the buboes and internal bleeding, and was spread by contact; and a second, more virulent pneumonic type that infected the lungs and was spread by respiratory infection. The presence of both at once caused the high mortality and speed of contagion. So lethal was the disease that cases were known of persons going to bed well and dying before they woke, of doctors catching the illness at bedside and dying before the patient.

    —Barbara Tuchman, "This Is the End of the World," *A Distant Mirror*

SKILL 20 Use open-form elements to create "voice" in closed-form prose.

So far we have been talking about features of open-form prose in its purer forms. Sometimes, however, writers wish simply to loosen basically closed-form prose by combining it with some features of open-form prose. If, for example, an academic wanted to share new developments in a field with a popular audience, he or she would be well-advised to leaven his or her prose with some elements of open-form writing. In this final lesson, we offer several pieces of advice for loosening up closed-form prose.

Introducing Some Humor

Humor is rare in tightly closed prose because humor is nonfunctional—it doesn't *have* to be there for a writer to make a point—and closed-form prose values efficiency, getting what you have to say said in the most economical fashion.

Humor is closely related to one of the mainsprings of open-form style, surprise. Humor typically depends on sudden twists and abrupt changes in direction. In physical comedy, pratfalls are funny in direct proportion to the audience's inability to see them coming. In verbal humor, the less clearly the audience sees the punch line coming, the more it makes the audience laugh.

Humor is particularly valuable in that it can make imposing subjects more manageable for readers. Just as humor can deflate pretensions and bring down the high and the mighty in an instant, it can make difficult and foreign subjects less anxiety producing. Formal, abstract language can put readers off, estranging them from the subject; humor has the power to "de-strange" a subject, to allow the audience to look at it long enough to understand it. Many popular books on science and many of the best instructional books on car repair, cooking, money management, and others of life's drearier necessities use a humorous style to help their phobic readers get on with life.

To appreciate the effect of humor, consider the following passages from two different instructional books on how to operate the database program Paradox. The first passage, from *Windows in 21 Days,* uses a clear, humor-free, closed-form style.

> In this book, you learn by following detailed step-by-step exercises based on real-world problems in database application design. Every exercise leads you further into the power of "Paradox for Windows" as you develop the components of an automated application. This section does the following: explains the assumptions and conventions used in this book; lists the hardware and software requirements and setup needed to run Paradox for Windows and use this book efficiently; and offers some suggestions for strategies to get the most from this book. The step-by-step exercises make it easy.

Now note the different effect produced by the following passage from one of the hugely popular *For Dummies* books:

> Welcome to *Paradox for Windows for Dummies,* a book that's not afraid to ask the tough questions like "When's lunch?" and "Who finished the cookie dough ice cream?" If you're more interested in food (or Australian Wombats, for that matter) than you are in Paradox for Windows, this book is for you. If you're more interested in Paradox for Windows, please get some professional help before going out into society again.
>
> My goal is to help you get things done despite the fact that you're using Paradox. Whether you're at home, in your office, or at home in your office (or even if you just *feel* like you live at work) *Paradox for Windows for Dummies* is your all-in-one guidebook through the treacherous, frustrating, and appallingly technical world of the relational database.

FOR WRITING AND DISCUSSION

Thinking about Humor

1. Which of these two instructional books would you prefer to read?
2. The second passage says that the world of relational databases is "treacherous, frustrating, and appallingly technical," whereas the first stresses that

(*continued*)

the "step-by-step exercises [in the book] make it easy." Why do you suppose the humorous passage stresses the difficulty of databases whereas the humorless passage stresses the ease of a step-by-step approach? Is it good strategy for the humorous writer to stress the difficulty of Paradox?

3. Under what rhetorical circumstances are humorous instructions better than strictly serious instructions? When is a strictly serious approach better?

Use Techniques from Popular Magazines

Writers who publish regularly for popular audiences develop a vigorous, easy-reading style that differs from the style of much academic writing. The effect of this difference is illustrated by the results of a famous research study conducted by Michael Graves and Wayne Slater at the University of Michigan. For this study, teams of writers revised passages from a high school history textbook.* One team consisted of linguists and technical writers trained in producing closed-form texts using the strategies discussed in Chapter 18 (forecasting structure, putting points first, following the old/new contract, using transitions). A second team consisted of two *Time-Life* book editors.

Whereas the linguists aimed at making the passages clearer, the *Time-Life* writers were more concerned with making them livelier. The result? One hundred eleventh-grade students found the *Time-Life* editors' version both more comprehensible and more memorable. Lack of clarity wasn't the problem with the original textbook; unbearable dryness was the problem. According to the researchers, the *Time-Life* editors did not limit themselves

> to making the passages lucid, well-organized, coherent, and easy to read. Their revisions went beyond such matters and were intended to make the texts interesting, exciting, vivid, rich in human drama, and filled with colorful language.

To see how they achieved this effect, let's look at their revision. Here is a passage about the Vietnam War taken from the original history text:

ORIGINAL HISTORY TEXT

> The most serious threat to world peace developed in Southeast Asia. Communist guerrillas threatened the independence of the countries carved out of French Indo-China by the Geneva conference of 1954. In South Vietnam, Communist guerrillas (the Viet Cong) were aided by forces from Communist North Vietnam in a struggle to overthrow the American-supported government. ...
>
> Shortly after the election of 1964, Communist gains prompted President Johnson to alter his policy concerning Vietnam. American military forces in Vietnam were increased from about 20,000 men in 1964 to more than 500,000 by 1968. Even so, North Vietnamese troops and supplies continued to pour into South Vietnam.

Here is the *Time-Life* editors' revision:

HISTORY PRESENTED IN POPULAR MAGAZINE STYLE

> In the early 1960s the greatest threat to world peace was just a small splotch of color on Kennedy's map, one of the fledgling nations sculpted out of French Indo-China by the Geneva peacemakers of 1954. It was a country so tiny and remote that most Americans had never uttered its name: South Vietnam. ...

*The study involved three teams, but for purposes of simplification we limit our discussion to two.

Aided by Communist North Vietnam, the Viet Cong guerrillas were eroding the ground beneath South Vietnam's American-backed government. Village by village, road by road, these jungle-wise rebels were waging a war of ambush and mining: They darted out of tunnels to head off patrols, buried exploding booby traps beneath the mud floors of huts, and hid razor-sharp bamboo sticks in holes. ...

No sooner had Johnson won the election than Communist gains prompted Johnson to go back on his campaign promise. The number of American soldiers in Vietnam skyrocketed from 20,000 in 1964 to more than 500,000 by 1968. But in spite of GI patrols, leech-infested jungles, swarms of buzzing insects, and flash floods that made men cling to trees to escape being washed away—North Vietnamese troops streamed southward without letup along the Ho Chi Minh Trail.

What can this revision teach you about invigorating closed-form prose? What specifically are the editors doing here?

First, notice how far the level of abstraction drops in the revision. The original is barren of sensory words; the revision is alive with them ("South Vietnam" becomes a "small splotch of color on Kennedy's map"; "a struggle to overthrow the American-supported government" becomes "[They] buried exploding booby traps beneath the mud floors of huts, and hid razor-sharp bamboo sticks in holes").

Second, notice how much more dramatic the revision is. Actual scenes, including a vision of men clinging to trees to escape being washed away by flash floods, replace a chronological account of the war's general progress. According to the editors, such scenes, or "nuggets"—vivid events that encapsulate complex processes or principles—are the lifeblood of *Time-Life* prose.

Finally, notice how the revision tends to delay critical information for dramatic effect, moving information you would normally expect to find early on into a later position. In the first paragraph, the *Time-Life* writers talk about "the greatest threat to world peace" in the early 1960s for five lines before revealing the identity of that threat—South Vietnam.

FOR WRITING AND DISCUSSION

Enlivening Closed-Form Prose with Open-Form Elements

Here is a passage from a student argument opposing women's serving on submarines. Working individually or in small groups, enliven this passage by using some of the techniques of the *Time-Life* writers.

Not only would it be very expensive to refit submarines for women personnel, but having women on submarines would hurt the morale of the sailors. In order for a crew to work effectively, they must have good morale or their discontent begins to show through in their performance. This is especially crucial on submarines, where if any problem occurs, it affects the safety of the whole ship. Women would hurt morale by creating sexual tension. Sexual tension can take many forms. One form is couples' working and living in a close space with all of the crew. When a problem occurs within the relationship, it could affect the morale of those directly involved and in the workplace. This would create an environment that is not conducive to good productivity. Tension would also occur if one of the women became pregnant or if there were complaints of sexual harassment. It would be easier to deal with these problems on a surface ship, but in the small confines of a submarine these problems would cause more trouble.

READING

To conclude this chapter we present a famous short example of open-form prose—Annie Dillard's "Living Like Weasels." The exercises that follow the reading will help you review the lessons in this chapter.

Annie Dillard

Living Like Weasels

1 A weasel is wild. Who knows what he thinks? He sleeps in his underground den, his tail draped over his nose. Sometimes he lives in his den for two days without leaving. Outside, he stalks rabbits, mice, muskrats, and birds, killing more bodies than he can eat warm, and often dragging the carcasses home. Obedient to instinct, he bites his prey at the neck, either splitting the jugular vein at the throat or crunching the brain at the base of the skull, and he does not let go. One naturalist refused to kill a weasel who was socketed into his hand deeply as a rattlesnake. The man could in no way pry the tiny weasel off, and he had to walk half a mile to water, the weasel dangling from his palm, and soak him off like a stubborn label.

2 And once, says Ernest Thompson Seton—once, a man shot an eagle out of the sky. He examined the eagle and found the dry skull of a weasel fixed by the jaws to his throat. The supposition is that the eagle had pounced on the weasel and the weasel swiveled and bit as instinct taught him, tooth to neck, and nearly won. I would like to have seen that eagle from the air a few weeks or months before he was shot: was the whole weasel still attached to his feathered throat, a fur pendant? Or did the eagle eat what he could reach, gutting the living weasel with his talons before his breast, bending his beak, cleaning the beautiful airborne bones?

3 I have been reading about weasels because I saw one last week. I startled a weasel who startled me, and we exchanged a long glance.

4 Twenty minutes from my house, through the woods by the quarry and across the highway, is Hollins Pond, a remarkable piece of shallowness, where I like to go at sunset and sit on a tree trunk. Hollins Pond is also called Murray's Pond; it covers two acres of bottomland near Tinker Creek with six inches of water and six thousand lily pads. In winter, brown-and-white steers stand in the middle of it, merely dampening their hooves; from the distant shore they look like miracle itself, complete with miracle's nonchalance. Now, in summer, the steers are gone. The water lilies have blossomed and spread to a green horizontal plane that is terra firma to plodding blackbirds, and tremulous celling to black leeches, crayfish, and carp.

5 This is, mind you, suburbia. It is a five-minute walk in three directions to rows of houses, though none is visible here. There's a 55 mph highway at one end of the pond, and a nesting pair of wood ducks at the other. Under every bush is a muskrat hole or a beer can. The far end is an alternating series of fields and woods, fields and woods, threaded everywhere with motorcycle tracks—in whose bare clay wild turtles lay eggs.

6 So. I had crossed the highway, stepped over two low barbed-wire fences, and traced the motorcycle path in all gratitude through the wild rose and poison ivy of the pond's shoreline up into high grassy fields. Then I cut down through the woods to the mossy fallen tree where I sit. This tree is excellent. It makes a dry, upholstered bench at

the upper, marshy end of the pond, a plush jetty raised from the thorny shore between a shallow blue body of water and a deep blue body of sky.

7 The sun had just set. I was relaxed on the tree trunk, ensconced in the lap of lichen, watching the lily pads at my feet tremble and part dreamily over the thrusting path of a carp. A yellow bird appeared to my right and flew behind me. It caught my eye. I swiveled around—and the next instant, inexplicably, I was looking down at a weasel, who was looking up at me.

8 Weasel! I'd never seen one wild before. He was ten inches long, thin as a curve, a muscled ribbon, brown as fruitwood, soft-furred, alert. His face was fierce, small and pointed as a lizarad's; he would have made a good arrowhead. There was just a dot of chin, maybe two brown hairs' worth, and then the pure white fur began that spread down his underside. He had two black eyes I didn't see, any more than you see a window.

9 The weasel was stunned into stillness as he was emerging from beneath an enormous shaggy wild rose bush four feet away. I was stunned into stillness twisted backward on the tree trunk. Our eyes locked, and someone threw away the key.

10 Our look was as if two lovers, or deadly enemies, met unexpectedly on an overgrown path when each had been thinking of something else: a clearing blow to the gut. It was also a bright blow to the brain, or a sudden beating of brains, with all the charge and intimate grate of rubbed balloons. It emptied our lungs. It felled the forest, moved the fields, and drained the pond; the world dismantled and tumbled into that black hole of eyes. If you and I looked at each other that way, our skulls would split and drop to our shoulders. But we don't. We keep our skulls. So.

11 He disappeared. This was only last week, and already I don't remember what shattered the enchantment. I think I blinked, I think I retrieved my brain from the weasel's brain, and tried to memorize what I was seeing, and the weasel felt the yank of separation, the careening splashdown into real life and the urgent current of instinct. He vanished under the wild rose. I waited motionless, my mind suddenly full of data and my spirit with pleadings, but he didn't return.

12 Please do not tell me about "approach-avoidance conflicts." I tell you I've been in that weasel's brain for sixty seconds, and he was in mine. Brains are private places, muttering through unique and secret tapes—but the weasel and I both plugged into another tape simultaneously, for a sweet and shocking time. Can I help it if it was a blank?

13 What goes on in his brain the rest of the time? What does a weasel think about? He won't say. His journal is tracks in clay, a spray of feathers, mouse blood and bone: uncollected, unconnected, loose-leaf, and blown.

14 I would like to learn, or remember, how to live. I come to Hollins Pond not so much to learn how to live as, frankly, to forget about it. That is, I don't think I can learn from a wild animal how to live in particular—shall I suck warm blood, hold my tail high, walk with my footprints precisely over the prints of my hands?—but I might learn something of mindlessness, something of the purity of living in the physical senses and the dignity of living without bias or motive. The weasel lives in necessity and we live in choice, hating necessity and dying at the last ignobly in its talons. I would like to live as I should, as the weasel lives as he should. And I suspect that for

me the way is like the weasel's: open to time and death painlessly, noticing everything, remembering nothing, choosing the given with a fierce and pointed will.

15 I missed my chance. I should have gone for the throat. I should have lunged for that streak of white under the weasel's chin and held on, held on through mud and into the wild rose, held on for a dearer life. We could live under the wild rose wild as weasels, mute and uncomprehending. I could very calmly go wild. I could live two days in the den, curled, leaning on mouse fur, sniffing bird bones, blinking, licking, breathing musk, my hair tangled in the roots of grasses. Down is a good place to go, where the mind is single. Down is out, out of your ever-loving mind and back to your careless senses. I remember muteness as a prolonged and giddy fast, where every moment is a feast of utterance received. Time and events are merely poured, unremarked, and ingested directly, like blood pulsed into my gut through a jugular vein. Could two live that way? Could two live under the wild rose, and explore by the pond, so that the smooth mind of each is as everywhere present to the other, and as received and as unchallenged, as falling snow?

16 We could, you know. We can live any way we want. People take vows of poverty, chastity, and obedience—even of silence—by choice. The thing is to stalk your calling in a certain skilled and supple way, to locate the most tender and live spot and plug into that pulse. This is yielding, not fighting. A weasel doesn't "attack" anything; a weasel lives as he's meant to, yielding at every moment to the perfect freedom of single necessity.

17 I think it would be well, and proper, and obedient, and pure, to grasp your one necessity and not let it go, to dangle from it limp wherever it takes you. Then even death, where you're going no matter how you live, cannot you part. Seize it and let it seize you up aloft even, till your eyes burn out and drop; let your musky flesh fall off in shreds, and let your very bones unhinge and scatter, loosened over fields, over fields and woods, lightly, thoughtless, from any height at all, from as high as eagles.

THINKING CRITICALLY
about "Living Like Weasels"

Working in small groups or as a whole class, use the questions that follow to guide your close examination of Dillard's structural and stylistic choices.

1. How does Dillard's essay meet the criteria for a story—events depicted in time, connectedness, tension, and resolution? What final resolution or interpretation does Dillard offer?

2. Find ten examples of Dillard's use of specific words and concrete language. Try rewording some of these examples at a higher level of abstraction and then compare Dillard's "low on the scale" version with your "higher on the scale" version.

3. Choose three consecutive paragraphs in this essay and examine how Dillard employs gaps between sentences to stimulate readers to think actively about the questions she is raising. Try tracking her ideas from sentence to sentence

in these paragraphs. Where does she disrupt readers' expectations by violating conventions of closed-form prose?

4. Find ten examples of figurative language and explain how these are particularly effective in holding the reader's interest and portraying the intensity or meaning of her experience.

5. Suppose that you were going to do a stylistic imitation of one of Dillard's paragraphs. Choose a paragraph that you think is particularly interesting stylistically and explain why you have chosen it.

6. Imagine the entry on "weasels" in an encyclopedia. How could you use some of Dillard's strategies to make a typical closed-form encyclopedia article more lively?

For additional writing, reading, and research resources, go to **www.MyCompLab.com** and choose **Ramage/Bean/Johnson's *The Allyn & Bacon Guide to Writing,* Fifth Edition.**

PART 4

A RHETORICAL GUIDE TO RESEARCH

This screen capture shows the home page of Women Against Gun Control (www.wagc.com), a grassroots organization dedicated to supporting women's right to defend themselves. This organization participates in pro-gun political activism, legislative research, media awareness, distribution of print resources, and gun-related education. The Web site itself uses color, images, other design features, and bold text to stake out its position in the complex controversy over women's role in the hotly contested, larger issue of gun control. This Web site home page is featured in a class discussion exercise in Chapter 21.

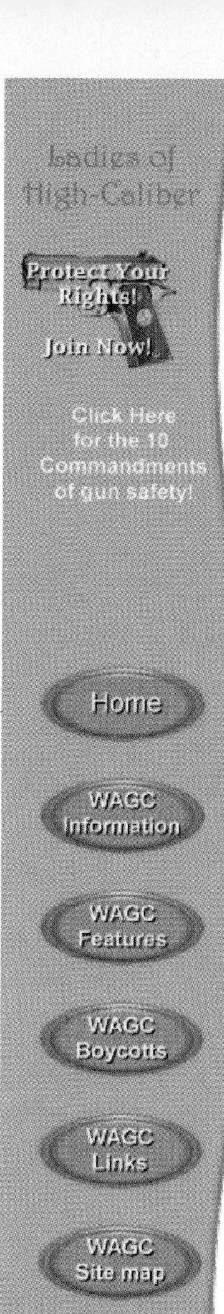

"The Second Amendment IS the Equal

Click here to sign and read our new forum board!

WAGC sends amicus brief to the U.S. Supreme Court!

Click Here (Opens New Window)

Click here to read a press release regarding this hearing.

Click here for a special message from WAGC President, Janalee Tobias

Contact Us

Postal Address

- WAGC

  PO Box 95357
  South Jordan, UT
  84095

Telephone

- 801-328-9660

E-Mail

- info@wagc.com
- State and Local Chapters
- webmaster

It's a Fact:

RECENT RESEARCH INDICATES THAT GUNS ARE USED DEFENSIVELY 2.5 MILLION TIMES PER YEAR.

It's not surprising then, that more women than ever want to keep their rights to own and carry a gun.
The reason is simple: Women **are** concerned about becoming victims of crime. Guns give women a fighting chance against crime.

Join Women Against Gun Control.
Take the Women Against Gun Control Pledge and you qualify for a membership in Women Against Gun Control, a grass roots volunteer organization dedicated to preserving our gun rights.

Join thousands of women (and men) in sending a powerful message throughout the world.

"Guns **SAVE** Lives. We do **NOT** support gun control. Gun Control does **NOT** control crime!"

2nd Amendment
A well regulated Militia being necessary to the security of a free State, the right of the people to keep and bear Arms shall not be infringed.

"The Second Amendment IS Homeland Security."

Special Article
Have gun, will not fear it anymore

Rosie O' Donnel

Hillary Clinton

Janet Reno

Diane Feinstein

Want Americans to believe all women support gun control...

If women are disarmed, a rapist will never hear...

"STOP OR I'LL SHOOT!"

Looking for Pro-Second Amendment and Pro-Freedom Books? Check Out These Book Reviews and Help Support This Site!

Support WAGC Efforts with the Utah GIRAFFE Society!

Get your pin in honor of WAGC!

PART 4 A RHETORICAL GUIDE TO RESEARCH

Council of Writing Program Administrators Outcomes for First-Year Composition

CHAPTER 20 Asking Questions, Finding Sources

RHETORICAL KNOWLEDGE	• Focus on a purpose (Skill 21)
CRITICAL THINKING, READING, AND WRITING	• Use writing and reading for inquiry, learning, thinking, and communicating (Skill 21) • Understand a writing assignment as a series of tasks, including finding, evaluating, analyzing, and synthesizing appropriate primary and secondary sources (Skills 21–23)
COMPOSING IN ELECTRONIC ENVIRONMENTS	• Locate, evaluate, organize, and use research material collected from electronic sources, including scholarly library databases; other official databases; and informal electronic networks and Internet sources (Skills 22, 23) • Understand and exploit the differences in the rhetorical strategies and in the affordances available for both print and electronic composing processes and texts (Skill 22)

CHAPTER 21 Evaluating Sources

RHETORICAL KNOWLEDGE	• Understand how genres shape reading and writing (Skill 24)
CRITICAL THINKING, READING, AND WRITING	• Use writing and reading for inquiry, learning, thinking, and communicating (Skills 24–26) • Understand a writing assignment as a series of tasks, including finding, evaluating, analyzing, and synthesizing appropriate primary and secondary sources (Skills 24–26)) • Understand the relationships among language, knowledge, and power (Skills 25 and 26)
KNOWLEDGE OF CONVENTIONS	• Develop knowledge of genre conventions ranging from structure and paragraphing to tone and mechanics (Skill 24)
COMPOSING IN ELECTRONIC ENVIRONMENTS	• Locate, evaluate, organize, and use research material collected from electronic sources, including scholarly library databases; other official databases; and informal electronic networks and Internet sources (Skills 24–26)

CHAPTER 22 Incorporating Sources into Your Own Writing

CRITICAL THINKING, READING, AND WRITING	• Integrate their own ideas with those of others (Skills 27–30)

CHAPTER 23 Citing and Documenting Sources

KNOWLEDGE OF CONVENTIONS	• Learn common formats for different kinds of texts (Skills 32–33) • Practice appropriate means of documenting their work (Skills 31–33)
COMPOSING IN ELECTRONIC ENVIRONMENTS	• Locate, evaluate, organize, and use research material collected from electronic sources, including scholarly library databases; other official databases; and informal electronic networks and Internet sources (Skills 32, 33)

ASKING QUESTIONS, FINDING SOURCES

CHAPTER 20

Our goal in Part 4 is to explain the skills you'll need for successful college-level research papers. We'll show you how to apply your growing knowledge of rhetoric and composition to research tasks by explaining how to find and evaluate research sources and to integrate them into your own arguments. After presenting a brief overview to research writing, this chapter will focus on three skills:

- Skill 21: Argue Your Own Thesis in Response to a Research Question
- Skill 22: Understand Differences among Kinds of Sources
- Skill 23: Use Purposeful Strategies for Searching Libraries, Databases, and Web Sites

The remaining chapters in Part 4 will show you how to evaluate sources (Chapter 21), how to incorporate sources into your own writing (Chapter 22), and how to cite and document your sources (Chapter 23).

An Overview of Research Writing

Although the research paper is a common writing assignment in college, students are often baffled by their professor's expectations. Many students think of research writing as finding information on a topic or as finding quotations to support a thesis rather than as wrestling with a question or problem. One of our colleagues calls these sorts of papers "data dumps": The student backs a truckload of data up to the professor's desk, unloads it, and says, "Here's what I found out about sweatshops, Professor Jones. Enjoy!" Another colleague calls papers full of long quotations "choo-choo train papers": big boxcars of quotations coupled together with little patches of a student's own writing.

But a research paper shouldn't be a data dump or a train of boxcar quotations. Instead, it should follow the same principles of writing discussed throughout this text. A research paper should pose an interesting and significant problem and respond to it with a contestable thesis. Research sources should be used purposefully. At first, you use research sources to help you explore a problem and synthesize ideas. Then, inside your own argument, you also use research sources purposefully to supply background, supporting evidence, alternative points of view, or other kinds of details. Moreover, your research data should come from credible sources that are documented in a formal, academic style.

Much of the writing you encounter in popular magazines has the characteristics of a research paper—a thesis and support—but not the documentation that college professors expect. That documentation makes all the difference because new knowledge is inevitably built on the work of others. In academic culture, authors who hope to gain credibility for new findings and ideas must explain the roots of their work as well as show how they reached their conclusions. By documenting their sources according to appropriate conventions, research writers establish a credible *ethos* and provide a valuable resource for others who wish to locate the same sources.

Many of the writing projects in this text invite your use of research sources. In fact, your instructor may pair the material in Part 4 with specific writing projects from Part 2. As you study this material, keep in mind your twofold purpose in doing research:

1. To develop an answer to your research question by finding relevant information and data and by synthesizing this information, blending it with your own thinking
2. To position yourself in a conversation with other voices that have addressed the same question

SKILL 21 Argue your own thesis in response to a research question.

Formulating a Research Question

Question asking is introduced in Chapter 1, Concept 2.

The best way to avoid writing a data dump or a jumble of quotations is to begin with a good research question. A good question keeps you in charge of your writing. It reminds you that your task is to answer this question for yourself, in your own voice, through your own critical thinking, applied to your own research sources. Skilled researchers don't seek the "perfect source" that answers their question. Rather, they know that they must create an answer themselves out of a welter of data and conflicting points of view, synthesizing ideas and forging their own informed view.

To stay in charge of your writing, you need to focus your research on a question rather than on a topic. Suppose a friend sees you doing research in the library and asks what your research paper is about. Consider differences in the following answers:

> **Topic Focus**: I am doing a paper on eating disorders.
>
> **Question Focus**: I'm trying to sort out what the experts say is the best way to treat severe anorexia nervosa. Is inpatient or outpatient treatment more effective?
>
> **Topic Focus**: I am doing my paper on gender-specific toys for children.
>
> **Question Focus**: I am puzzled about some of the effects of gender-specific toys. Do boys' toys, such as video games, toy weapons, and construction sets, develop intellectual and physical skills more than girls' toys do?

As these scenarios suggest, a topic focus invites you to collect information without a clear purpose—a sure road toward data dumping. In contrast, a question focus requires you to be a critical thinker who must assess and weigh data and understand multiple points of view. A topic focus encourages passive collection of information. A question focus encourages active construction of meaning.

How do you arrive at a research question? Ideally, good research questions arise from your own intellectual curiosity—a desire to resolve something that truly puzzles you. Often questions emerge from conflicting points of view in class discussions or from controversies or unknowns you encounter while reading. In most cases your initial research question will evolve as you do your research. You may make it broader or narrower, or refocus it on a newly discovered aspect of your original problem. You can test the initial feasibility of your research question by considering the following prompts:

- Are you personally interested in this question?
- Is the question both problematic and significant?
- Is the question limited enough for the intended length of your paper?
- Is there a reasonable possibility of finding information on this question based on the time and resources you have available?
- Is the question appropriate for your level of expertise?

Establishing Your Role as a Researcher

After you have formulated your research question, you need to consider the possible roles you might play as a researcher. Your role is connected to the aim or purpose of your paper—to explore, to inform, to analyze, or to persuade. To appreciate your options, consider the following strategies based on typical roles researchers can play:

STRATEGIES for Establishing Your Role as a Researcher

Aims and Roles	What to Do	Examples of Research Questions
Informative aim—reporter of information that fills a knowledge gap	Find, synthesize, and report data related to an information question.	• What is the United States doing to protect nuclear sites from terrorism? • How are math skills taught in local elementary schools?
Informative aim (primarily)—reporter of the current best thinking on a problem	Research the current thinking of experts on some important problem and report what the experts think.	• What are the views of experts on the causes of homosexuality? • What do researchers consider the possible dangers of online social networks?

(*continued*)

Aims and Roles	What to Do	Examples of Research Questions
Informative and analytical aims—conductor of original field research in response to an empirical question	Pose a problem that requires field or laboratory research, conduct the research, and present results in a scientific report. Often, include a "review of the literature" section.	• To what extent do pictures of party drinking appear on Facebook profiles at our campus? • Does topsoil downwind from a copper refinery show dangerous levels of heavy metals?
Informative, analytical, or persuasive aim—reviewer of a controversy	Investigate and report differing arguments on various sides of a controversy. (If you simply report alternative arguments, the aim is informative. If you evaluate these arguments, the paper takes on an analytical or persuasive aim.)	• What are the arguments for and against granting amnesty and eventual U.S. citizenship to illegal immigrants? • What are the differing arguments concerning a single-payer Canadian-style health care system in the United States?
Persuasive aim—advocate for a position in a controversy	Assert a position using research data for background, for support, or for alternative views.	• Should the United States grant amnesty and eventual citizenship to illegal immigrants? (Writer argues yes or no.) • What is the best means of providing universal health care for U.S. citizens? (Writer argues for a specific approach.)
Analytical or persuasive aim—critical thinker who proposes an answer to an interpretive or theoretical question; positioning oneself within a critical conversation	Do your own original analysis of a text, phenomenon, or data source, but also relate your views to what others have said about the same or similar questions. Do research to find relevant primary sources or to re-create the scholarly conversation. (This is perhaps the most common role taken by scholars in the humanities.)	• How does Hobbes's view of the effective prince differ from Machiavelli's? • What view of the religious dimension of life does Shakespeare seem to hold in *Hamlet*? • What was Edward Hopper's intention in calling his painting of a New York diner "Nighthawks"?

FOR WRITING AND DISCUSSION

Using Research Roles to Generate Research Questions

Working individually or in small groups, develop research questions on a general topic such as music, health, sports, use of fossil fuels, a literary work, or some other topic specified by your instructor. Develop questions that would be appropriate for each of the following roles:

1. Reporter of information to fill a knowledge gap
2. Reporter of the current best thinking of experts on a problem
3. Original field or laboratory researcher
4. Reviewer of a controversy
5. Advocate in a controversy
6. Critical thinker about an interpretive or theoretical question in conversation with other thinkers
7. Miscellaneous (good questions that don't fit neatly into any of these other roles)

A Case Study: James Gardiner's Research on Online Social Networks

To illustrate how a student writer poses a research question and argues his own thesis, let's return to James Gardiner's investigation of online social networks (OSNs) such as MySpace and Facebook. We first introduced James's research in Chapter 2, where we reprinted his initial musings about OSNs in the form of a five-minute freewrite (pp. 33–34). James's original problem was his uncertainty about why OSNs are so popular and why he himself had chosen not to have a Facebook profile. In his original freewrite, he said, "I am a little hesitant to display personal information about myself on a website that can be viewed by anyone in the world." He also was afraid that joining an OSN would take up too much time.

Later in the course he decided to investigate OSNs for a major research project. His research process is narrated in his exploratory essay in Chapter 8, pages 191–196. His initial research question was, "How are online social networks influencing the way young people communicate with each other?" As he began reading articles about OSNs, he noted that many articles were highly favorable: Researchers who studied OSNs regarded them as new ways for teenagers to maintain relationships with friends, to explore their own self-images, and to practice constructing online identities. However, James remained somewhat skeptical of OSNs and, late in his initial research, he encountered the term "Facebook trance" and located an article on Internet addictions. He became more and more interested in exploring the negative aspects of OSNs. At the conclusion of his exploratory essay, James sums up the direction he would like to move in further research:

> As I continue with my research, I am not sure what thesis I will assert for my final project. I still want to do more research on the negative effects of OSNs. For example, I haven't found studies that explore the possible phoniness of Facebook relationships. I remember a passage from Copeland where one user labels Facebook interaction as "communication lean." According to this student, "It's all a little fake—the 'friends'; the profiles that can be tailored to what others find appealing; the 'groups' that exist only in cyberspace." I'm still thinking about that quotation. Do OSNs contribute to deeper, more meaningful relationships or do they promote a superficial phoniness? I hope to explore this issue further before writing my major paper.

James's exploratory research gave him a solid background on OSNs, enabling him to bring his own critical thinking to bear on his research sources. In order to convert his exploratory narrative into a closed-form research paper, he eventually created a thesis statement focused on potential dangers of OSNs. You can read his final paper in Chapter 23, pages 643–651.

FOR WRITING AND DISCUSSION

Following James Gardiner's Research Process

Working individually, read James's exploratory paper (pp. 191–196) and his final research paper (pp. 643–651). Then, working in small groups or as a whole class, try to reach consensus answers to the following questions:

1. Trace the steps in James's thinking from the time he first becomes interested in OSNs until he finally settles on their possible negative effects. What were the key moments that shaped his thinking? How did his thinking evolve?
2. We have used James's story as an example of a student in charge of his own writing. Where do you see James doing active critical thinking? Where do you see instances of what we have called "rhetorical reading"—that is, places where James asks questions about an author's purpose, angle of vision, and selection of evidence? How is his final paper different from a data dump or a choo-choo train paper?

SKILL 22 Understand differences among kinds of sources.

To be an effective researcher, you need to understand the differences among the many kinds of books, articles, and Web sites you are apt to encounter—for example, the differences between scholarly books and trade books, between peer-reviewed journals and popular magazines, and between print sources and cyberspace-only sources. Before we describe strategies for finding sources (covered in the section devoted to Skill 23), we want to explain these differences, which are important for the following reasons:

- Different kinds of sources are found through different kinds of searches.
- For any particular research question, some kinds of sources are more useful than others.
- Knowing the differences among kinds of sources speeds your learning of search strategies, making you a more efficient and sophisticated researcher.
- Knowing what kind of source something is helps you read it rhetorically.

Looking at Sources Rhetorically

The best way to understand different kinds of sources is to view them rhetorically. Table 20.1, "A Rhetorical Overview of Print Sources," shows how print sources (books, scholarly journals, magazines, newspapers) can be categorized according to genre, publisher, author, and angle of vision. The last column in Table 20.1 identifies contextual clues that will help you recognize what category a print source belongs to. Later, when we discuss strategies for understanding the rheto-

TABLE 20.1 A Rhetorical Overview of Print Sources

Genre and Publisher	Author and Angle of Vision	How to Recognize Them
	Books	
SCHOLARLY BOOKS • University/academic presses • Nonprofit • Selected through peer review	**Author:** Professors, researchers **Angle of vision:** Scholarly advancement of knowledge	• University press on title page • Specialized academic style • Documentation and bibliography
TRADE BOOKS (NONFICTION) • Commercial publishers (for example, Penguin Putnam) • Selected for profit potential	**Author:** Journalists, freelancers, scholars aiming at popular audience **Angle of vision:** Varies from informative to persuasive; often well researched and respected, but sometimes shoddy and aimed for quick sale	• Covers designed for marketing appeal • Popular style • Usually documented in an informal rather than an academic style
REFERENCE BOOKS—MANY IN ELECTRONIC FORMAT • Publishers specializing in reference material • For-profit through library sales	**Author:** Commissioned scholars **Angle of vision:** Balanced, factual overview	• Titles containing words such as *encyclopedia, dictionary,* or *guide* • Found in reference section of library or online through library Web site
	Periodicals	
SCHOLARLY JOURNALS • University/academic presses • Nonprofit • Articles chosen through peer review • Examples: *Journal of Abnormal Psychology, Review of Metaphysics*	**Author:** Professors, researchers, independent scholars **Angle of vision:** Scholarly advancement of knowledge; presentation of research findings; development of new theories and applications	• Not sold on magazine racks • No commercial advertising • Specialized academic style • Documentation and bibliography • Cover often has table of contents • Often can be found in online databases
PUBLIC AFFAIRS MAGAZINES • Commercial, "for-profit" presses • Manuscripts reviewed by editors • Examples: *Harper's, Commonweal, National Review*	**Author:** Staff writers, freelancers, scholars for general audiences **Angle of vision:** Aims to deepen public understanding of issues; magazines often have political bias of left, center, or right	• Long, well-researched articles • Ads aimed at upscale professionals • Often has reviews of books, theater, film, and the arts • Often can be found in online databases or on the Web
TRADE MAGAZINES • Commercial, "for-profit" presses • Focused on a profession or trade • Examples: *Advertising Age, Automotive Rebuilder, Farm Journal*	**Author:** Staff writers, industry specialists **Angle of vision:** Informative articles for practitioners; advocacy for the profession or trade	• Title indicating trade or profession • Articles on practical job concerns • Ads geared toward a particular trade or profession

(continued)

TABLE 20.1 Continued

Genre and Publisher	Author and Angle of Vision	How to Recognize Them
	Periodicals (*continued*)	
NEWSMAGAZINES AND NEWSPAPERS • Newspaper chains and publishers • Examples: *Time, Newsweek, Washington Post, Los Angeles Times*	**Author:** Staff writers and journalists; occasional freelance pieces **Angle of vision:** News reports aimed at balance and objectivity; editorial pages reflect perspective of editors; op-ed pieces reflect different perspectives	• Readily familiar by name, distinctive cover style • Widely available on newsstands, by subscription, and on the Web • Ads aimed at broad, general audience
POPULAR NICHE MAGAZINES • Large conglomerates or small presses with clear target audience • Focused on special interests of target audience • Examples: *Seventeen, People, TV Guide, Car and Driver, Golf Digest*	**Author:** Staff or freelance writers **Angle of vision:** Varies—in some cases content and point of view are dictated by advertisers or the politics of the publisher	• Glossy paper, extensive ads, lots of visuals • Popular; often distinctive style • Short, undocumented articles • Credentials of writer often not mentioned

ric of Web sites (Chapter 21, Skill 26), we provide a similar "Rhetorical Overview of Web Sites" in Table 21.3 (pp. 602–604). We suggest that you take a few moments now to peruse the information in these tables so that you can begin to appreciate the distinctions we are making among types of research sources.

Books Versus Periodicals Versus Web Sites

The simple physical differences among these three types of sources are obvious—books are substantial physical objects that libraries store on shelves. Magazines and scholarly journals—categorized together as periodicals—are similarly printed on paper and kept on library shelves, typically in bound volumes that combine a year's worth of issues. (*Periodical* indicates that a publication appears at regular intervals—that is, periodically, usually more often than once a year.) What's important to know as a researcher is that the contents of print publications are stable—in great contrast to materials published on Web sites, which might change hourly. If you work from print sources, you can be sure that others will be able to track down your sources for their own projects. Furthermore, print publications generally go through an editorial review process that helps ensure accuracy and reputability. In contrast, Web-only documents from individuals or small organizations may be unedited and thus unreliable. The stability and reputability of print sources is good, but the editing, fact-checking, shipping, and storage that make them possible all cost money. Furthermore, in a world of rapidly changing circumstances and ideas, periodicals and reference books are increasingly being published in electronic formats, sometimes in conjunction with paper issues, sometimes in electronic form only.

These changes mean that when evaluating and citing sources, researchers must now pay attention to matters not even imagined just a decade ago. It used to be as obvious as the paper in front of you what kind of source you were using. Now, for students and faculty alike, the evidence of time well spent on research is an armload of downloaded printouts or photocopies. Does each of your sources have markers that show its origin? Was it photocopied from a print resource? Printed from a reference CD? Downloaded from a database? Printed from the Web (and if so, who wrote it when and why?). All these matters will impact the credibility of your sources as well as the citation formats you use to document these sources.

Details about licensed databases and how they differ from the Web are covered later in this chapter, pp. 584–589.

If you download and print material from an unfamiliar periodical, whether from a database or directly from the Web, be aware that you may lose important contextual clues about the author's purpose and angle of vision—clues that would be immediately apparent in the original journal or magazine through the table of contents, statement of editorial policy, or advertisements targeting specific audiences. (The increasing availability of *.pdf* or *portable document format* files, which reproduce the appearance of the original print page, makes understanding publication contexts much easier. When .pdf format is available, take advantage of it.) The more savvy you become at recognizing distinctions among different kinds of sources—especially electronic ones—the more you can read sources rhetorically and document them accurately.

Scholarly Books Versus Trade Books

Note in Table 20.1 the distinction between scholarly books, which are peer-reviewed and published by nonprofit academic presses, and trade books, which are published by for-profit presses with the intention of making money. By "peer review," which is a highly prized concept in academia, we mean the selection process by which scholarly manuscripts get chosen for publication. When manuscripts are submitted to an academic publisher, the editor sends them for independent review to experienced scholars who judge the rigor and accuracy of the research and the significance and value of the argument. The process is highly competitive and weeds out much shoddy or trivial work.

In contrast, trade books are not peer-reviewed by independent scholars. Instead, they are selected for publication by editors whose business is to make a profit. Fortunately, it can be profitable for popular presses to publish superbly researched and argued intellectual material because college-educated people, as lifelong learners, create a demand for intellectually satisfying trade books written for the general reader rather than for the highly specialized reader. These can be excellent sources for undergraduate research, but you need to separate the trash from the treasure. Trade books are aimed at many different audiences and market segments and can include sloppy, unreliable, and heavily biased material.

Scholarly Journals Versus Magazines

Like scholarly books, scholarly journals are academic, peer-reviewed publications. Although they may look like magazines, they almost never appear on newsstands; they are nonprofit publications subsidized by universities for disseminating high-level research and scholarship.

In contrast, magazines are intended to make a profit through sales and advertising revenues. Fortunately for researchers, a demand exists for intellectually satisfying magazines, just as for sophisticated trade books. Many for-profit magazines publish highly respectable, useful material for undergraduate or professional researchers, but many magazines publish shoddy material. As Table 20.1 shows, magazines fall into various categories aimed at different audiences.

Print Sources Versus Cyberspace Sources

Another crucial distinction exists between print sources and cyberspace sources. Much of what you can retrieve from a computer was originally published in print. What you download is simply an electronic copy of a print source, either from a library-leased database or from someone's Web site. (The next section shows you how to tell the difference.) In such cases, you often need to consider the article's original print origins for appropriate cues about its rhetorical context and purpose. But much cyberspace material, having never appeared in print, may never have undergone either peer review or editorial review. To distinguish between these two kinds of cyberspace sources, we call one kind a "print/cyberspace source." (something that has appeared in print and is made available on the Web or through library-leased databases) and the other a "cyberspace-only source." When you use a cyberspace-only source, you've got to take special care in figuring out who wrote it, why, and for what audience. Also, you need to document cyberspace-only material differently from print material retrieved electronically.

FOR WRITING AND DISCUSSION

Identifying Types of Sources

Your instructor will bring to class a variety of sources—different kinds of books, scholarly journals, magazines, and downloaded material. Working individually or in small groups, try to decide which category in Table 20.1 each piece belongs to. Be prepared to justify your decisions on the basis of the cues you used to make your decision.

SKILL 23 Use purposeful strategies for searching libraries, databases, and Web sites.

In the previous section, we explained differences among the kinds of sources you may encounter in a research project. In this section, we explain how to find these sources by using your campus library's online catalog (for locating books and other library resources, including paper copies of periodicals), library-leased electronic databases (for finding articles in journals and magazines), and Web search engines for finding material on the World Wide Web.

Checking Your Library's Home Page

We begin by focusing on the specialized resources provided by your campus library. Your starting place and best initial research tool will be your campus library's home page. This portal will lead you to two important resources: (1) the library's online catalog and (2) direct links to the periodicals and reference databases leased by the library. Here you will find indexes to a wide range of articles in journals and magazines and direct access to frequently used reference materials, including statistical abstracts, biographies, dictionaries, and encyclopedias. Furthermore, many academic library sites post lists of good research starting points, organized by discipline, including Web sites librarians have screened.

In addition to checking your library's home page, make a personal visit to your library to learn its features and especially to note the location of a researcher's best friend and resource: the reference desk. Make use of reference librarians—they are there to help you.

Finding Books: Searching Your Library's Online Catalog

Your library's holdings are listed in its online catalog. Most of the entries are for books, but an academic library also has a wealth of other resources such as periodical collections, government records and reports, newspapers, video and audio recordings, maps, encyclopedias, and hundreds of specialized reference works that your reference librarian can help you use.

Indexed by subject, tittle, and author, the online catalog gives you titles of books and other library-owned resources relevant to your research area. Note that the catalog lists the titles of journals and magazines in the library's periodical collection (for example, *Journal of Abnormal Psychology, Atlantic Monthly*), but does *not* list the titles of individual articles within these periodicals. As we explain later in this section, you can search the contents of periodicals by using a licensed database. Methods of accessing and using online catalogs vary from institution to institution, so you'll need to learn the specifics of your library's catalog through direct experience.

Subject Searches Versus Keyword Searches

At the start of a research project, before researchers know the names of specific authors or book titles, they typically search by subject or by keywords. Your own research process will be speedier if you understand the difference between these kinds of searches.

- *Subject searches.* Subject searches use predetermined categories published in the reference work *Library of Congress Subject Headings*. This work informs you that, for example, material on "street people" would be classified under the heading "homeless persons." If the words you use for a subject search don't yield results, seek help from a librarian, who can show you how to use the subject heading guide to find the best word or phrase.
- *Keyword searches.* Keyword searches are not based on predetermined subject categories. Rather, the computer locates the keywords you provide in titles, abstracts, introductions, and sometimes bodies of text. Keyword searches in online catalogs are usually limited to finding words and phrases in titles. We explain more about keyword searches in the upcoming section on using licensed databases, whose search engines look for keywords in bodies of text as well as in titles.

Learning Your Library's Shelving System

With a little experience you will find yourself efficiently jotting down call numbers and locating what you need within your library's shelving system. Most college and university libraries use the Library of Congress classification system, but some may have an older section organized by the Dewey Decimal System, which is often used in public libraries. When you are looking for a periodical, you will need to consult the "location" notes on a catalog entry so that you can determine where your library shelves its scholarly journals and magazines.

Finding Print Articles: Searching a Licensed Database

For many research projects, useful sources are print articles from your library's periodical collection, including scholarly journals, public affairs magazines, newspapers or newsmagazines, and niche magazines related to your research area. Some of these articles are available through the free-access portions of the World Wide Web, but many of them are not. Rather, they may be located physically in your library's periodical collection (or in that of another library and available through interlibrary loan) or located electronically in vast databases leased by your library.

What Is a Licensed Database?

Electronic databases of periodical sources are produced by for-profit companies that index articles in thousands of periodicals and construct engines that can search the database by author, title, subject, keyword, date, genre, and other characteristics. In most cases the database contains an abstract of each article, and in many cases it contains the complete text of the article that you can download and print. These databases are referred to by several different generic names: "licensed databases" (our preferred term), "periodicals databases," or "subscription services." Because access to these databases is restricted to fee-paying cus-

FIGURE 20.1 Licensed Database Versus Free-Access Portions of Internet

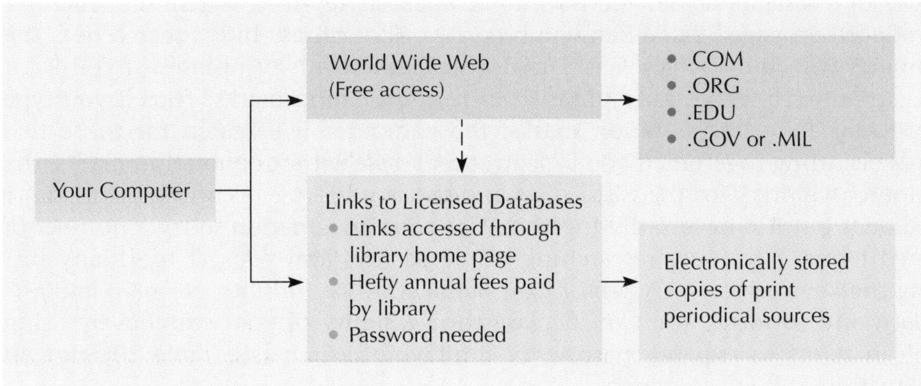

tomers, they can't be searched through Web engines like Google. Most university libraries allow students to access these databases from a remote computer by using a password. You can therefore use the Internet to connect your computer to licensed databases as well as to the World Wide Web (see Figure 20.1).

Although the methods of accessing licensed databases vary from institution to institution, we can offer some widely applicable guidelines. Most likely your library has online one or more of the following databases:

- *EBSCOhost*: Includes citations and abstracts from journals in most disciplines as well as many full-text articles from thousands of journals.
- *ProQuest:* Gives access to full text of articles from magazines and journals in many subject areas; may include full-text articles from newspapers.
- *FirstSearch Databases:* Incorporates multiple specialized databases in many subject areas, including WorldCat, which contains records of books, periodicals, and multimedia formats from libraries worldwide.
- *Lexis-Nexis Academic Universe:* Is primarily a full-text database covering current events, business, and financial news; includes company profiles and legal, medical, and reference information.
- *JSTOR:* Offers full text of scholarly journal articles across many disciplines; you can limit searches to specific disciplines.

Given the variability of these and many other resources, we once again refer you to your campus library's Web site and the librarians at the reference desk (who often answer questions by e-mail). There you will find the best advice about where to look for what. Then, when you decide to use a specific source for your research project, be sure to include in your notes the names of both the database and the database company because, as we explain in Chapter 23, you will need to include that information when you cite your sources.

MLA and APA formats for citing information and texts retrieved from licensed electronic databases are presented in Chapter 23, Skill 32 (MLA) and Skill 33 (APA).

More on Keyword Searching

To use an online database, you need to be adept at keyword searching, which we introduced on page 584. When you type a word or phrase into a search box, the computer will find sources that contain the same words or phrases. If you want the computer to search for a phrase, put it in quotation marks. Thus if you type "*street people*" using quotation marks, the computer will search for those two words occurring together. If you type in *street people* without quotation marks, the computer will look for the word *street* and the word *people* occurring in the same document but not necessarily together. Use your imagination to try a number of related terms. If you are researching gendered toys and you get too many hits using the keyword *toys,* try *gender toys, Barbie, G.I. Joe, girl toys, boy toys, toys psychology,* and so forth. You can increase the flexibility of your searches by using Boolean terms to expand, narrow, or limit your search (see Table 20.2 for an explanation of Boolean searches).

Illustration of a Database Search

As an illustration of a database search, we'll use student writer James Gardiner's research on online social networks. Figure 20.2 shows the results from James's search using the keywords *online relationships* and *loneliness* on the database

TABLE 20.2 Boolean Search Commands

Command and Function	Research Example	What to Type	Search Result
X OR Y (Expands your search)	You are researching Barbie dolls and decide to include G.I. Joe figures.	"Barbie doll" OR "G.I. Joe"	Articles that contain either phrase
X AND Y (Narrows your search)	You are researching the psychological effects of Barbie dolls and are getting too many hits under *Barbie dolls.*	"Barbie dolls" AND psychology	Articles that include both the phrase "Barbie dolls" and the word *psychology*
X NOT Y (Limits your search)	You are researching girls' toys and are tired of reading about Barbie dolls. You want to look at other popular girls' toys.	"girl toys" NOT Barbie	Articles that include the phrase "girl toys" but exclude *Barbie*

FIGURE 20.2 Sample Results List from a Search Using EBSCOhost

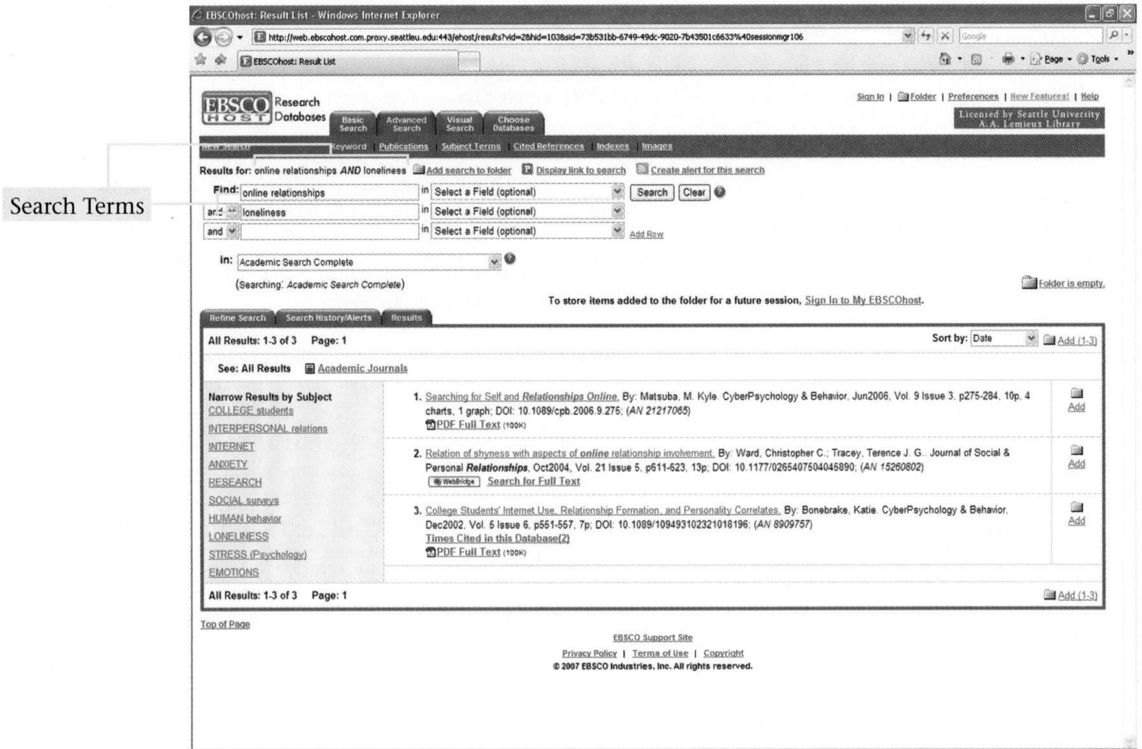

EBSCOhost. As the figure shows, EBSCOhost returned three articles from scholarly journals that deal in some way with online relationships and loneliness. The first article, "Searching for Self and Relationships Online," comes from an academic journal (*CyberPsychology & Behavior*) and a full text of the article is available online in .pdf format. To get more information, James clicked on the name of the article. The resulting screen, which is shown in Figure 23.1 (p. 634), gives an abstract of the article as well as complete data about when and where the article was published in print. (We placed this screen in Chapter 23 on documentation, rather than here, to show how it provides the information you'll need for your Works Cited list.) Based on the abstract, James downloaded the .pdf file and eventually used this article in his final research paper. (See the entry under "Matsuba" in his Works Cited list on p. 651.)

A particularly valuable feature of databases is the way that you can limit or expand your searches in a variety of useful ways. Here are some strategies for focusing, narrowing, or expanding your list of sources:

STRATEGIES for Narrowing or Expanding Your Searches on Licensed Databases

What You Want	What to Do
Only scholarly articles in peer-reviewed journals	Check the box for "peer-reviewed" articles in the database search box (different databases have different procedures—ask a librarian).
Only short articles (or only long articles)	Specify length of articles you want in the advanced search feature.
Only magazine articles or only newspaper articles	Specify in the advanced search feature.
Articles within a certain range of dates	Specify the dates in the advanced search feature.
Only articles for which "full text" is available	Check the box for "full text" in the database search box.
Only articles from periodicals carried by your library	Check method used by database. (Most databases accessed through your library will indicate whether your library carries the magazine or journal.)
All articles	Don't check any of the limiting boxes.
To narrow (or expand) the focus of the search	• Experiment with different keywords. • Use Boolean techniques: *online relationships* AND *friendship*; *online relationships* OR *MySpace* (see Table 20.2). • Try different databases. • Ask your reference librarian for help.

After you've identified articles you'd like to read, locate physically all those available in your library's periodical collection. (This way you won't lose important contextual cues for reading them rhetorically.) For those unavailable in your library, print them from the database (if full text is provided), or order them through interlibrary loan.

Finding Cyberspace Sources: Searching the World Wide Web

Another valuable resource is the World Wide Web. To understand the logic of Web search engines, you need to know that the Internet is divided into restricted

FIGURE 20.3 First Few Hits from Google

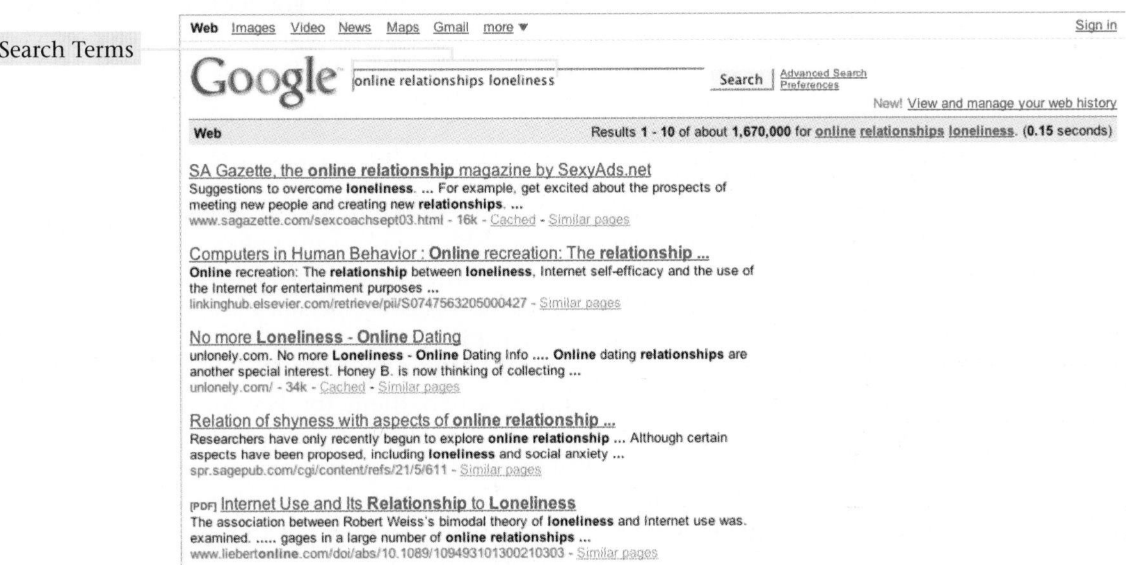

sections open only to those with special access rights and a "free-access" section. Web engines such as Google search only the free-access portion of the Internet. When you type keywords into a Web search engine, it searches for matches in material made available on the Web by all the users of the world's network of computers—government agencies, corporations, advocacy groups, information services, individuals with their own Web sites, and many others.

The following example will quickly show you the difference between a licensed database search and a Web search. When we entered the keywords *online relationships* and *loneliness* into EBSCOhost, we received three hits from scholarly journals (see Figure 20.2). In contrast, when we typed *online relationships loneliness* into Google, we received "about 1,670,000" hits. The first screen for this search is shown in Figure 20.3. (Typical Web search engines don't use the Boolean operators AND, OR, or NOT, although some have advanced search options that allow you to narrow or expand a search.)

FOR WRITING AND DISCUSSION

Comparing a Licensed Database Search and a Web Search

Working in small groups or as a whole class, see if you can reach consensus on the following questions:

1. How does a licensed database search differ from a Web search? In your own words, explain what is being searched in each case.
2. There is no way that James or any other researcher could scroll through more than a million hits. However, just the first five hits on Google (see

(continued)

Figure 20.3) offer interesting possibilities for James's research. Which of these sites might be worth exploring and why? As you look at each hit, pay attention to the URL, as well as to the description, to see if you can predict the kind of organization that sponsors the site. (Skill 26 in Chapter 21 explains in detail how to analyze Web sites.)

Using Web Search Engines

Although the hits you receive from a Web search frequently include useless, shoddy, trivial, or irrelevant material, the Web's resources for researchers are breathtaking. At your fingertips you have access to government documents and statistics, legislative and corporate white papers, court cases, persuasive appeals of advocacy groups, consumer information—the list is almost endless.

The World Wide Web can be searched by a variety of engines that collect and categorize individual Web files and search them for keywords. Most of these engines will find not only text files but also graphic, audio, and video files. Different engines search the Web in different ways, so it is important that you try a variety of search engines when you look for information. For example, a service offered by Google is "Google Scholar," with which you can limit a Web search to academic or scholarly sources. (But you will still need to turn to your library's collection or licensed databases for a full text of the source.) On campus, reference librarians and disciplinary experts can give you good advice about what has worked well in the past for particular kinds of searches. On the Web, an additional resource is NoodleTools.com, which offers lots of good advice for choosing the best search engine.

Determining Where You Are on the Web

As you browse the Web looking for resources, clicking from link to link, try to figure out what site you are actually in at any given moment. This information is crucial, both for properly documenting a Web source and for reading the source rhetorically.

To know where you are on the Web, begin by identifying the home page, which is the material to the left of the first single slash in the URL (universal resource locator). The generic structure of a typical URL looks like this: http://www.servername.domain/directory/subdirectory/filename.filetype

Here is a specific example, the URL for the NINDS (National Institute of Neurological Disorders and Stroke) Cerebral Aneurysm Information Page:

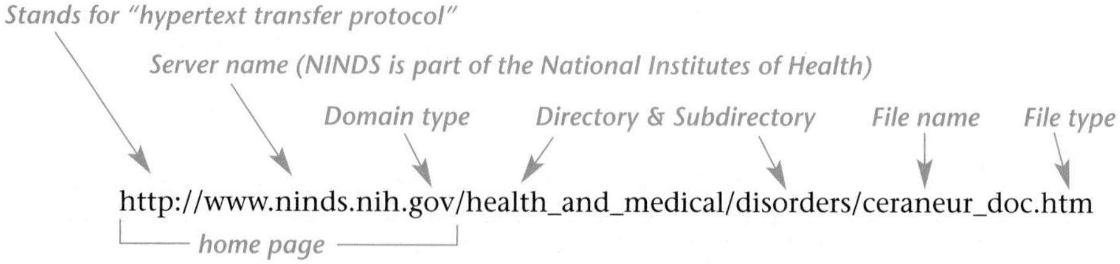

Stands for "hypertext transfer protocol"
Server name (NINDS is part of the National Institutes of Health)
Domain type
Directory & Subdirectory
File name
File type

http://www.ninds.nih.gov/health_and_medical/disorders/ceraneur_doc.htm

home page

In some URLs, the domain name is followed by an abbreviation signaling that the Web site is located in a country other than the United States, as in this URL for the home page of the National Institute for Research Advancement in Japan:

Country abbreviation

http://www.nira.go.jp

When you click on a link in one site, you may be sent to a totally different site. To determine the home page of this new site, simply note the root URL immediately following the "www."* To view the home page directly, delete the codes to the right of the initial home page URL in your computer's location window and hit Enter. You will then be linked directly to the site's home page, where you may be able to find an "About" link through which you can gather information about the purpose and sponsors of the page. As we discuss in later chapters, being able to examine a site's home page helps you read the site rhetorically and document it properly.

This chapter has shown you how to locate sources. In the next chapter, we'll discuss the crucial skills of evaluating sources and determining how you might use them in your own argument.

For additional writing, reading, and research resources, go to **www.MyCompLab.com** and choose **Ramage/Bean/Johnson's *The Allyn & Bacon Guide to Writing,* Fifth Edition.**

*Not all URLs begin with "www" after the first set of double slashes. Our description doesn't include variations of the most typical URL types. You can generally find the home page of a site by eliminating all codes to the right of the first slash mark after the domain or country name.

CHAPTER 21

EVALUATING SOURCES

In Chapter 20, we explained the importance of posing a good research question, of understanding the different kinds of sources, and of using purposeful strategies for searching libraries, databases, and Web sites. In this chapter we explain three additional skills that will help you become a successful undergraduate researcher:

- Skill 24: Read sources rhetorically and take purposeful notes.
- Skill 25: Evaluate sources for reliability, credibility, angle of vision, and degree of advocacy.
- Skill 26: Use your rhetorical knowledge to evaluate Web sources.

SKILL 24 Read sources rhetorically and take purposeful notes.

Once you've located a stack of books and magazine or journal articles, it's easy to feel overwhelmed. How do you begin reading all this material? There is no one right answer to this question. At times you need to read slowly with analytical closeness. At other times you can skim a source, looking only for its gist or for a needed piece of information. In this section, we offer some advice on how to read your sources with rhetorical savvy and take notes that will help you write your final paper.

Read with Your Own Goals in Mind

How you read a source depends to a certain extent on where you are in the research process. Early in the process, when you are in the thesis-seeking, exploratory stage, your goal is to achieve a basic understanding of your research area. You need to become aware of different points of view, learn what is unknown or controversial about your research question, see what values or assumptions are in conflict, and build up your store of background knowledge. As we saw in the case of James Gardiner, one's initial research question often evolves as one's knowledge increases and interests shift.

Given these goals, at the early stages of research you should select "overview" kinds of sources to get you into the conversation. In some cases, even an encyclopedia or specialized reference work can be a good start for getting general background.

As you get deeper into your research, your questions become more focused, and the sources you seek out become more specialized. Once you formulate a thesis and plan a structure for your paper, you can determine more clearly the sources you need. For example, after James Gardiner decided to focus on the negative aspects of online social networks, he began following up leads on Internet addiction, on OSNs as sites for narcissistic display, and on the possible superficiality of online relationships. At the same time he remained open-minded about the psychological and social benefits of OSNs.

Read Your Sources Rhetorically

To read your sources rhetorically, you should keep two basic questions in mind:

1. What was the source author's purpose in writing this piece?
2. What might be my purpose in using this piece?

Let's begin with the first question. The following chart sums up the strategies you can use to read your sources rhetorically, along with research tips for answering some of the questions you've posed.

STRATEGIES for Reading Your Sources Rhetorically

Questions to Ask	What to Do	Results
• Who is this author? • What are his or her credentials and affiliations?	• Look for the author's credentials at the end of the article or in the contributors' page. • Google the author's name. • In a database results list, click on the author's name for a list of other articles he/she has written.	• Helps you assess author's *ethos* and credibility. • Helps you establish author's angle of vision.
• What is this source's genre? • Who is the intended audience?	• If the source is downloaded, identify the original publication information. • If the source comes from a periodical, look at the print copy for clues about the audience (titles of other articles, ads, document design). • Use Table 20.1 for further clues about audience and genre. • If a Web-only source, see Skill 26.	• Helps you further determine the author's angle of vision as well as the source's reliability and credibility. • Helps explain rhetorical features of the source.

(*continued*)

Questions to Ask	What to Do	Results
• What is this author's purpose? • How is this author trying to change his/her audience's view of the topic?	• Determine whether the piece is primarily expressive, informational, analytical, or persuasive. • If the source comes from the Web, who is the site's sponsor? Read the "About us" material on the site's home page. • If it is a print source, determine the reputation and bias of the journal, magazine, or press (see Table 21.1, p. 599).	• Helps you evaluate the source for angle of vision and degree of advocacy. • Helps you decide how you might use the source in your own argument.
• What is this author's angle of vision or bias? • What facts, data, and other evidence does this author cite and what are the sources for the data? • What are this author's underlying values, assumptions, and beliefs? • What is omitted or censored from this text?	• Apply the rhetorical reading strategies explained in Chapter 6. • Evaluate the source for reliability, credibility, angle of vision, and degree of advocacy as explained in Skill 25. • If a Web source, evaluate it using strategies explained in Skill 26.	• Helps you bring your own critical thinking to bear on your sources. • Keeps your paper intellectually honest and interesting.

This chart reinforces a point we've made throughout this text: All writing is produced from an angle of vision that privileges some ways of seeing and filters out other ways. You should guard against reading your sources as if they present hard, undisputed facts or universal truths. For example, if one of your sources says that "Saint-John's-wort [an herb] has been shown to be an effective treatment for depression," some of your readers might accept that statement as fact; but many wouldn't. Skeptical readers would want to know who the author is, where his views have been published, and what he uses for evidence. Let's say the author is someone named Samuel Jones. Skeptical readers would ask whether

Jones is relying on published research, and if so, whether the studies have been peer-reviewed in reputable, scholarly journals and whether the research has been replicated by other scientists. They would also want to know whether Jones has financial connections to companies that produce herbal remedies and supplements. Rather than settling the question about Saint-John's-wort as a treatment for depression, a quotation from Jones might open up a heated controversy about medical research.

Reading rhetorically is thus a way of thinking critically about your sources. It influences the way you take notes, evaluate sources, and shape your argument.

Take Purposeful Notes

Taking good research notes serves two functions: First, it encourages you to read actively in order to summarize your sources' arguments and record usable information. Second, taking notes encourages you to do exploratory thinking—to write down ideas as they occur to you, to analyze sources as you read them, and to join your sources in conversation.

There are many ways to take notes, but we can offer several techniques that work especially well for other writers. First of all, you can try using a dialectic or double-entry journal. Divide a page in half; enter your informational notes on one side and your exploratory writing on the other. Another system is to record notes on index cards or in a computer file and then write out your exploratory thinking in a separate research journal. Still another method is to record informational notes on your computer in a regular font and then to use a boldfaced font for exploratory writing. Your objective here is to create a visual way to distinguish your informational notes from your exploratory thinking.

An example of double-entry notes can be found in Chapter 8, pp. 182–183.

A common practice of beginning researchers—one that experienced researchers almost never use—is *not* taking notes as they read and *not* doing any exploratory writing. We've seen students photocopy a dozen or more articles, but then write nothing as they read (sometimes they highlight passages with a marker), planning to rely later on memory to navigate through the sources. This practice reduces your ability to synthesize your sources and create your argument. When you begin drafting your paper, you'll have no notes to refer to, no record of your thinking-in-progress. Your only recourse is to revisit all your sources, thumbing through them one at a time—a practice that leads to passive cutting and pasting.

To take effective notes, make them purposeful—that is, imagine how you might use a given source in your research paper. Begin your notes on each source by recording all the bibliographic information that you will need for your "Works Cited" or "References" list (see Skill 32 or 33 depending on whether you are using MLA or APA citation form). Then take notes purposefully, moving back and forth between informational notes from the source and exploratory notes that record your own critical thinking in response to the source. The following chart shows the different functions that research sources might play in your argument and highlights appropriate note-taking strategies for each function.

STRATEGIES for Taking Notes According to Purpose

Function that Source Might Play in Your Argument	Strategies for Informational Notes	Strategies for Exploratory Notes
Provides background about your problem or issue	• Summarize the information. • Record specific facts and figures useful for background.	• Speculate on how much background your readers will need.
Gives an alternative view that you will mention briefly	• Summarize the source's argument in a couple of sentences; note its bias and perspective. • Identify brief quotations that sum up the source's perspective.	• Jot down ideas on how and why different sources disagree. • Begin making an idea map of alternative views.
Provides an alternative or opposing view that you might summarize fully and respond to	• Summarize the article fully and fairly (see Chapter 6 on summary writing). • Note the kinds of evidence used.	• Speculate about why you disagree with the source and whether you can refute the argument, concede to it, or compromise with it. • Explore what research you'll need to support your own argument.
Provides information or testimony that you might use as evidence	• Record the data or information. • If using authorities for testimony, quote short passages. • Note the credentials of the writer or person quoted.	• Record new ideas as they occur to you. • Continue to think purposefully about additional research you'll need.
Mentions information or testimony that counters your position or raises doubts about your argument	• Note counterevidence. • Note authorities who disagree with you.	• Speculate how you might respond to counterevidence.
Provides a theory or method that influences your approach to the issue	• Note credentials of the author. • Note passages that sparked ideas.	• Freewrite about how the source influences your method or approach.

When students work with downloaded or photocopied sources, they often ask whether they need to copy quotations into their notes. Generally, it is not necessary to transcribe quotations from sources that you will keep in your files. However, you should record in your notes the substance of the quotation and the page number so that you can quickly find it. If you won't have the source available when you write your paper, then you will need to copy quotations meticulously—exactly word for word—marking the quoted passage prominently with quotation marks. If you record information without directly quoting it, be sure that you restate it completely in your own words to avoid later problems with plagiarism.

For an explanation of how to avoid plagiarizing, see Chapter 22, Skill 30.

SKILL 25 Evaluate sources for reliability, credibility, angle of vision, and degree of advocacy.

When you read sources for your research project, you need to evaluate them as you go along. As you read each potential source, ask yourself questions about the author's reliability, credibility, angle of vision, and degree of advocacy.

Reliability

"Reliability" refers to the accuracy of factual data in a source as determined by external validation. If you check a writer's "facts" against other sources, do you find that the facts are correct? Does the writer distort facts, take them out of context, or otherwise use them unreasonably? In some controversies, key data are highly disputed—for example, the number of homeless people in the United States, the frequency of date rape, or the risk factors for many diseases. A reliable writer acknowledges these controversies and doesn't treat disputed data as fact. Furthermore, if you check out the sources used by a reliable writer, they'll reveal accurate and careful research—respected primary sources rather than hearsay or secondhand reports. Journalists of reputable newspapers (not tabloids) pride themselves on meticulously checking out their facts, as do editors of serious popular magazines. Editing is often minimal for Web sources, however, and they can be notoriously unreliable. As you gain knowledge of your research question, you'll develop a good ear for writers who play fast and loose with data.

Credibility

"Credibility" is similar to "reliability" but is based on internal rather than external factors. It refers to the reader's trust in the writer's honesty, goodwill, and trustworthiness and is apparent in the writer's tone, reasonableness, fairness in summarizing opposing views, and respect for different perspectives. Audiences differ in how much credibility they will grant to certain authors. Nevertheless, a writer can achieve a reputation for credibility, even among bitter political opponents, by applying to issues a sense of moral courage, integrity, and consistency of principle.

"Credibility" is synonymous with the classical term *ethos*. See pp. 55–56 and 393–394.

Angle of Vision and Political Stance

The concept of "angle of vision" was first introduced in Chapter 3, Concept 8. See also Chapter 5, which is devoted to a fuller analysis of angle of vision, and Chapter 6, which shows how an analysis of angle of vision helps you read a text with and against the grain.

How to analyze a writer's underlying assumptions is discussed in Chapter 6; the role of assumptions in argument is discussed in Chapter 14.

By "angle of vision," we mean the way that a piece of writing gets shaped by the underlying values, assumptions, and beliefs of its author, resulting in a text that reflects a certain perspective, worldview, or belief system. A text's angle of vision becomes apparent through both internal and external factors. Internally, factors such as the author's word choices (especially notice the connotations of words), selection and omission of details, figurative language, and grammatical emphasis combine with overt statements to reveal angle of vision. Of paramount importance are the assumptions that the writer assumes his or her readers will share. Externally, the politics and reputation of the author, along with the genre, market niche, and political reputation of the publication in which the material appears, will also provide useful clues about a writer's angle of vision and about the audience to whom she or he hopes to appeal and persuade.

To get at these external factors when you are evaluating a source, it is important to consider the writer's credentials, including any biographical information, which is often presented at the end of articles. Is the writer affiliated with an advocacy group or known for a certain ideology? (If you want more information about an author, try typing the author's name into a Web search engine. You will probably discover useful facts about her or his reputation and other publications.) Also note publishing data. If the source is an article, did it appear in a peer-reviewed scholarly journal or in a for-profit magazine or newspaper? What is the publication's reputation and editorial slant?

Your awareness of angle of vision is especially important if you are doing research on contemporary cultural or political issues. In Table 21.1, we have categorized some well-known political commentators, publications, policy research institutes (commonly known as *think tanks*), and blogs across the political spectrum from left/liberal to right/conservative.

Although the terms *liberal* and *conservative* or *left* and *right* often have fuzzy meanings, they provide a convenient shorthand for signaling a person's overall political stance or for pigeonholing opponents. (The "left" and "right" labels originated as references to the seating arrangements for radicals, who sat on the left, and nobility, who sat on the right, in the French National Assembly at the time of the French Revolution.) In the contemporary United States, "left–right" identities provide insight into views about the proper role of government in relation to the economy and social values. Liberals, tending to sympathize with labor and environmentalists, are typically comfortable with government regulation of economic matters while conservatives, who tend to sympathize with business interests, typically assert faith in free markets and favor a limited regulatory role for government. Some conservatives identify themselves as economic conservatives but social liberals; others side with workers' interests on many issues but are conservative on social issues. Social conservatives espouse traditional family values and advocate laws that would maintain these values (for example, a Constitutional amendment limiting marriage to a bond between a man and a woman). Liberals, on the other hand, tend to espouse individual choice regarding marital partnerships, abortion rights, and a wide range of other issues.

TABLE 21.1 Angles of Vision in U.S. Media and Think Tanks: A Sampling Across the Political Spectrum[1]

Commentators

Left	Left Center	Center	Right Center	Right
Barbara Ehrenreich	E. J. Dionne	Amitai Etzioni	David Brooks	Pat Buchanan
Al Franken	Ellen Goodman	Thomas Friedman	Midge Decter	Tucker Carlson
Bob Herbert	Nicholas Kristof	Kathleen Hall Jamieson	William Kristol	Linda Chavez
Michael Moore	William Raspberry	Kevin Phillips	William Safire	Ann Coulter
Bill Moyers	Mark Shields	Leonard Pitts	Andrew Sullivan	Rush Limbaugh
Salim Muwakkil	Fareed Zakaria	William Saletan	George Will	Bill O'Reilly
Daniel Schorr		Bob Woodward		Kathleen Parker

Newspapers and Magazines[2]

Left/Liberal	Center	Right/Conservative
The American Prospect	*Atlantic Monthly*	*American Spectator*
Harper's	*Business Week*	*Fortune*
Los Angeles Times	*Christian Science Monitor*	*National Review*
Mother Jones	*Commentary*	*Reader's Digest*
The Nation	*Commonweal*	*Reason*
New York Times	*Foreign Affairs*	*Wall Street Journal*
Salon	*New Republic*	*Washington Times*
Sojourners	*Slate*	*Weekly Standard*
	Washington Post	

Blogs

Liberal/Left	Moderate/Independent	Right/Conservative
americablog.com	newmoderate.blogspot.com	andrewsullivan.theatlantic.com
atrios.blogspot.com	politics-central.blogspot.com	conservativeblogger.com
crooksandliars.com	rantingbaldhippie.com	instapundit.com
dailykos.com	stevesilver.net	littlegreenfootballs.com
digbysblog.blogspot.com	themoderatevoice.com	michellemalkin.com
firedoglake.com	watchingwashington.blogspot.com	polipundit.com
huffingtonpost.com		powerlineblog.com
mediamatters.com		redstate.com
salon.com/opinion/greenwald/		
talkingpointsmemo.com		

Think Tanks

Left/Liberal	Center	Right/Conservative
Center for Defense Information	The Brookings Institution	American Enterprise Institute
Center for Media and Democracy (sponsors Disinfopedia.org)	Carnegie Endowment for International Peace	Cato Institute (Libertarian)
Institute for Policy Studies	Council on Foreign Relations	Center for Strategic and International Studies
Open Society Institute (Soros Foundation)	Jamestown Foundation	Heritage Foundation (sponsors Townhall.com)
Urban Institute	National Bureau of Economic Research	Project for the New American Century
	Progressive Policy Institute	

[1]*For further information about the political leanings of publications or think tanks, ask your librarian about* Gale Directory of Publications and Broadcast Media *or* NIRA World Directory of Think Tanks.

[2]*Newspapers are categorized according to positions they take on their editorial page; any reputable newspaper strives for objectivity in news reporting and includes a variety of views on its op-ed pages. Magazines do not claim and are not expected to present similar breadth and objectivity.*

Some issues will inevitably confound the distinction between liberals and conservatives. For example, in debates over immigration laws, liberals and conservatives have both found themselves agreeing with former opponents and clashing with former allies. Advocates for relatively open borders include liberals interested in protecting civil rights and conservatives interested in increasing the pool of low-cost labor. Meanwhile, their opposition includes liberals concerned about protecting organized labor and conservatives who oppose increased government spending for bilingual education and health care.

Finally, many persons regard themselves as "centrists." In Table 21.1 the column labeled "Center" includes commentators who seek out common ground between the left and the right and who often believe that the best civic decisions are compromises between opposing views. Likewise, centrist publications and institutes often approach issues from multiple points of view, looking for the most workable solutions.

Degree of Advocacy

By "degree of advocacy" we mean the extent to which an author unabashedly takes a persuasive stance on a contested position as opposed to adopting a more neutral, objective, or exploratory stance. For example, publications affiliated with advocacy organizations (the Sierra Club, the National Rifle Association) will have a clear editorial bias. When a writer has an ax to grind, you need to weigh carefully the writer's selection of evidence, interpretation of data, and fairness to opposing views. Although no one can be completely neutral, it is always useful to seek out authors who offer a balanced assessment of the evidence. Evidence from a more detached and neutral writer may be more trusted by your readers than the arguments of a committed advocate. For example, if you want to persuade corporate executives on the dangers of global warming, evidence from scholarly journals may be more persuasive than evidence from an environmentalist Web site or from a freelance writer for a leftist popular magazine such as *Mother Jones*.

Skill 26 Use your rhetorical knowledge to evaluate Web sources.

In the previous section we focused on reading sources rhetorically by asking questions about a source's reliability, credibility, angle of vision, and degree of advocacy. In this section we focus on evaluating sources from the World Wide Web.

The Web as a Unique Rhetorical Environment

The amount of resources available on the World Wide Web is mind-boggling. In addition to familiar entertainment and commercial sites, the Web can provide access to highly specialized data banks, historical archives, government documents, blogosphere commentary, scholarly portals useful for academic researchers, and much more. The Web is also a great vehicle for democracy, giving voice to the otherwise voiceless. Anyone with a cause and a rudimentary knowledge of Web design can create a site. Before the invention of the Web, people with a message had to stand on street corners passing out flyers or put money into creating newsletters or advocacy advertisements. The Web, in contrast, is cheap. The result is a rhetorical medium that differs in significant ways from print.

Consider, for example, the difference in the way writers attract readers. Magazines displayed on racks attract readers through interest-grabbing covers and teaser headlines inviting readers to look inside. Web sites, however, can't begin attracting readers until the readers have found them through links from another site or through a "hit" from a Web search. Research suggests that Web surfers stay connected to a site for no more than thirty seconds unless something immediately attracts their interest; moreover, they seldom scroll down to see the bottom of a page. The design of a home page—the arrangement and size of the print, the use of images and colors, the locations and labels of navigational buttons—must hook readers immediately and send a clear message about the purpose and contents of the site. If the home page is a confused jumble or simply a long, printed text, the average surfer will take one look and move on.

The biggest difference between the Web and print is the Web's hypertext structure. Users click from link to link rather than read linearly down the page. Users often "read" a Web page as a configuration of images and strategically arranged text that is interspersed with bullets, boxes, and hot links. Long stretches of linear text are usually found only deep within a site, usually through links to .pdf files or other archived or posted documents.

Criteria for Evaluating a Web Source

When you evaluate a Web source, we suggest that you ask five different kinds of questions about the site in which the source appeared, as shown in Table 21.2. These questions, developed by scholars and librarians as points to consider when you are evaluating Web sites, will help you determine the usefulness of a site or source for your own purposes.

As a researcher, the first question you should ask about a potentially useful Web source should be, Who placed this piece on the Web and why? You can begin answering this question by analyzing the site's home page, where you will often find navigational buttons linking to "Mission," "About Us," or other identifying information about the site's sponsors. You can also get hints about the site's purpose by asking, What kind of Web site is it? Different kinds of Web sites have different purposes, often revealed by the domain identifier following the server name (for example, .com, .net, .org, .edu, .gov, or .mil). Table 21.3, "A Rhetorical Overview of Web Sites," describes key rhetorical elements of different types of sites. Knowing who sponsors a site and analyzing the sponsor's purpose for creating the site will prepare you to read the site rhetorically.

See Chapter 15, pp. 444–446, for Teresa Filice's essay evaluating the advocacy site "Parents: The Anti-Drug."

TABLE 21.2 Criteria for Evaluating Web Sites

Criteria	Questions to Ask
1. Authority	• Is the document author or site sponsor clearly identified? • Does the site identify the occupation, position, education, experience, or other credentials of the author? • Does the home page or a clear link from the home page reveal the author's or sponsor's motivation for establishing the site? • Does the site provide contact information for the author or sponsor such as an e-mail or organization address?
2. Objectivity or Clear Disclosure of Advocacy	• Is the site's purpose clear (for example, to inform, entertain, or persuade)? • Is the site explicit about declaring its point of view? • Does the site indicate whether the author is affiliated with a specific organization, institution, or association? • Does the site indicate whether it is directed toward a specific audience?
3. Coverage	• Are the topics covered by the site clear? • Does the site exhibit a suitable depth and comprehensiveness for its purpose? • Is sufficient evidence provided to support the ideas and opinions presented?
4. Accuracy	• Are the sources of information stated? • Do the facts appear to be accurate? • Can you verify this information by comparing this source with other sources in the field?
5. Currency	• Are dates included in the Web site? • Do the dates apply to the material itself, to its placement on the Web, or to the time the site was last revised and updated? • Is the information current, or at least still relevant, for the site's purpose? For your purpose?

TABLE 21.3 A Rhetorical Overview of Web Sites

Type of Site	Author/Sponsor and Angle of Vision	Characteristics
.COM OR .BIZ (A COMMERCIAL SITE CREATED BY A BUSINESS OR CORPORATION)		
• Either of these suffixes signals a for-profit operation; this group includes major periodicals and publishers of reference materials • Purpose is to enhance image, attract customers, market products and services, provide customer service • Creators are paid by salary or fees and often motivated by desire to design innovative sites • Also in the business category: specialized suffixes .aero (for sites related to air travel), .pro (for professionals—doctors, lawyers, accountants)	**Author:** Difficult to identify individual writers; sponsoring company often considered the author **Angle of vision:** Purpose is to promote the point of view of the corporation or business; links are to sites that promote same values	• Links are often to other products and services provided by company • Photographs and other visuals used to enhance corporate image

TABLE 21.3 continued

Type of Site	Author/Sponsor and Angle of Vision	Characteristics
.ORG (A NONPROFIT ORGANIZATION OR ADVOCACY GROUP)		
• Note: Sites with the ".museum" suffix have similar purposes and feel. • Sometimes purpose is to provide accurate, balanced information (for example, the American Red Cross site) • May function as a major information portal, such as NPR.org, PBS.org, a think tank, or a museum (for example, the Heritage Foundation, the Art Institute of Chicago, or the Museum of Modern Art) • Frequently, purpose is to advocate for or explain the organization (for example, the Ford Foundation or local charity sites); thus, advocacy for fund-raising or political views is likely (for example, Persons for the Ethical Treatment of Animals [PETA] site or blog portals [Cursor.org])	**Author:** Often hard to identify individual writers; sponsoring organization often considered the author; some sites produced by amateurs with passionate views; others produced by well-paid professionals **Angle of vision:** Purpose is to promote views of sponsoring organization and influence public opinion and policy; many encourage donations through the site	• Advocacy sites sometimes don't announce purpose on home page • You may enter a node of an advocacy site through a link from another site and not realize the political slant • Facts/data selected and filtered by site's angle of vision • Often uses visuals for emotional appeal
.EDU (AN EDUCATIONAL SITE ASSOCIATED WITH A COLLEGE OR UNIVERSITY)		
• Wide range of purposes • Home page aimed at attracting prospective students and donors • Inside the site are numerous subsites devoted to research, pedagogy, libraries, student employment, and so forth	**Author:** Professors, staff, students **Angle of vision:** Varies enormously from personal sites of professors and students to organizational sites of research centers and libraries; can vary from scholarly and objective to strong advocacy on issues	• Often an .edu site has numerous "subsites" sponsored by the university library, art programs, research units • Links to .pdf documents may make it difficult to determine where you are in the site—e.g., professor's course site, student site, administrative site
.GOV OR .MIL (SPONSORED BY A GOVERNMENT AGENCY OR MILITARY UNIT)		
• Provides enormous range of basic data about government policy, bills in Congress, economic forecasts, and so forth • Aims to create good public relations for agency or military unit	**Author:** Development teams employed by the agency; sponsoring agency is usually considered the author **Angle of vision:** Varies—informational sites publish data and government documents with an objective point of view; agency sites also promote agency's agenda—e.g., Dept. of Energy, Dept. of Labor	• Typical sites (for example, www.energy.gov, the site of the U.S. Dept. of Energy) are extremely layered and complex and provide hundreds of links to other sites • Valuable for research • Sites often promote values/assumptions of sponsoring agency
PERSONAL WEB SITE (.NAME OR .NET)		
• An individual contracts with a server to publish the site; many personal Web sites have .edu affiliation • Promotes hobbies, politics; provides links according to personal preferences	**Author:** Anyone can create a personal Web site **Angle of vision:** Varies from person to person	• Credentials/bias of author often hard to determine • Irresponsible sites might have links to excellent sites; tracing links is complicated • Probably not designed for fast download

(continued)

TABLE 21.3 continued

Type of Site	Author/Sponsor and Angle of Vision	Characteristics
.INFO (INFORMATION PROVIDER—UNRESTRICTED, SO BECOMING A CATCHALL)		
• Libraries and library information materials • Regulations, hours, procedures, resources from local governments (e.g., www.lowermanhattan.info) • Publicity brochures for local organizations (e.g., Celtic Heritage Society, hobby groups) • Consumer alerts • Lodging, restaurants, bike rental, hiking trails, or other travel advice from tourist bureaus • Privately authored materials	**Author:** Varies widely from small public and private offices with an information mandate to individuals or groups with an ax to grind **Angle of vision:** Varies from genuinely helpful (Where can bicycles be loaded onto the ferry?) to business motives (Where can you find books or movies about bicycles?) to thinly disguised advocacy (e.g., "Debunking the Myths about Gun Control")	• Makes some information easier to find through advanced searches that specify the domain type • If author is identified, credentials difficult to determine • Information will be filtered through author(s) and sponsor(s) • Quality of editing and fact-checking will vary

Analyzing Your Own Purposes for Using a Web Source

Besides analyzing a sponsor's purpose for establishing a Web site, you also need to analyze your own purpose for using the site. To illustrate strategies for evaluating a Web site, we'll use as examples two hypothetical student researchers who are interested in the civic controversy over gun control. In both cases, the students are particularly interested in women's concerns about gun control.

Our first student researcher asked the question, "How are women represented and involved in the public controversy over gun control?" She did an initial Google search using "women gun control" as keywords and found dozens of pro-gun and anti-gun sites sponsored by women or by women's organizations. The home page of one such site, sponsored by the organization Women Against Gun Control, is shown on the opening page of Part 4 (p. 571). Fascinated by the Annie Oakley–like image (gun-toting cowgirl) on this home page, our researcher decided to focus her project on the ways that women depict themselves on pro-gun and anti-gun sites and on the kinds of arguments they make. These Web sites thus became primary sources for this student's project.

Our second researcher was more directly interested in determining her own stance in the gun control debate. She was trying to decide, from a woman's perspective, whether to advocate for gun control laws or to oppose gun control—whether even to join the National Rifle Association (NRA) and perhaps buy a gun and learn to shoot. As a researcher, her dilemma was how much she could use data about guns, crime, firearm accidents, and violence against women obtained from these sites. The sites for her were mostly secondary rather than primary sources.*

Let's look at each student's research process in turn.

*The terms *primary* and *secondary* sources are relative terms often used by researchers to differentiate between original data (primary sources) and data filtered through another researcher's perspective (secondary sources). Thus the Women Against Gun Control site (see p. 571) is a primary source for someone doing a rhetorical analysis of gun Web sites, but it is a secondary source for statistical data about gun violence.

Researcher 1: Using Women and Guns Web Sites for Rhetorical Analysis

Our first student quickly found herself immersed in a vigorous national conversation on gun control by women's groups and by traditionally male-dominated groups seeking support or membership from women. Her research goal was to analyze these sites rhetorically to understand the ways that women frame their interests and represent themselves. She discovered that the angle of vision of each kind of site—whether pro-gun or anti-gun—led to the filtering of evidence in distinctive ways. For example, women's groups advocating gun control emphasized accidental deaths from guns (particularly of children), suicides from easy access to guns, domestic violence turned deadly, guns in schools, and gun-related crime (particularly juvenile crime). In contrast, women's groups opposing gun control emphasized armed resistance to assaults and rapes, inadequate police responses to crime, the right of individuals to protect themselves and their families, and the Second Amendment right to keep and bear arms. (Women's anti-gun control sites often framed the gun control issue as pro-self-defense versus anti-self-defense.) She also noted that most of these sites made powerful use of visual elements—icons, colors (bright pink in particular), and well-known symbols—to enhance their emotional appeals. For instance, anti-gun control sites often had patriotic themes with images of waving American flags, stern-eyed eagles, and colonial patriots with muskets. Pro-gun control sites often had pictures of young children, with an emphasis on innocence, childhood fun, and family.

Researcher 1 noted that many of these sites tailored their appeals directly to women. The most well-known of the pro-gun control sites is the Million Mom March Organization, which describes itself (on the "About us" link) as "the nation's largest, non-partisan, grassroots organization leading the fight to prevent gun violence. ... " Its mission statement ends with these words; "With one loud voice, we will continue to cry out that we love our children more than the gun lobby loves its guns." In Figure 21.1, we have reproduced some images, text boxes for anecdotes, and "fact statements" from this site's home page.

For Researcher 1, it is evident that both this site and the Women Against Gun Control site, as well as other pro-gun or anti-gun sites, are useful and relevant for her purpose of analyzing rhetorically how women are portrayed in the Second Amendment debate.

FOR WRITING AND DISCUSSION

Analyzing the Rhetorical Elements of Two Home Pages

Working in small groups or as a whole class, try to reach consensus answers to the following questions about how Web sites seek to draw in readers. Go to www.wagc.com and www.millionmommarch.org or use the illustrations on pages 571 and 606.

1. How are the images of women in the Women Against Gun Control site different from those on the Million Mom March page? How do pieces of text (such as "Ladies of High-Caliber" on the Women Against Gun Control site or one of the "facts" on the Million Mom March site) contribute to the visual-verbal effects of the home pages?

(continued)

FIGURE 21.1 Images, Anecdotes, and Fact Statements from the Million Mom March Home Page (www.millionmommarch.org)

What started as one of the largest marches on Washington is now a national network of 75 Million Mom March Chapters that work locally in the fight against gun violence and the devastation it causes.

contact your local chapter

why i march

I march for my son, Chad, who was an innocent victim of gun violence.

- *Rita*

Read Rita's story.
Read stories from other moms.

Other anecdotes cycle through this box

fact file

15,000 kids were killed by firearms in the last five years

Other "facts" that cycle into "Fact File" every five seconds

- One child or a teen is killed by firearms every 3 hours
- A person is killed by a gun every 17 minutes in America
- More than 176 Americans go to an ER with a firearm injury every day
- 34 percent of America's children live in a home with at least one firearm
- On average, more than a thousand kids commit suicide with a firearm every year

2. In the Women Against Gun Control (WAGC) page, what seems to be the Web designer's intention in the use of color, curved background lines, and images?
3. How does the home page for each site use *logos, ethos,* and *pathos* to sway readers toward its point of view?

Researcher 2: Using Women and Guns Web Sites for Data on Guns and Gun Violence
Researcher 2 intends to create her own research-based argument on whether women should support or oppose gun control. Her dilemma is this: To what extent can she use "facts" appearing on these sites (such as the statement on the Women Against Gun Control site that "guns are used defensively 2.5 million times per year")?

She frequently encountered equivalent kinds of pithy statistical statements. In her initial Web search, she found an article entitled "Women Are the Real Victims of Handgun Control" by Kelly Ann Connolly, who is identified as the director of the Nevada State Rifle and Pistol Association. The site, www.armedandsafe.com, includes a biographical note indicating that Connolly is a public school teacher with a master's degree and that her husband is a former California Deputy Sheriff and police officer.

Connolly argues that a woman can walk confidently down any street in America if she is carrying a concealed weapon and is skilled in using it. She offers as support anecdotes of women who fought off rapists and cites numerous statistics, attributing the sources to "Bureau of Justice Statistics (1999)." Here are some examples from her article:

- 3 out of 4 American women will be a victim of violent crime at least once in their lifetime.
- 2 million women are raped each year, one every 15 seconds.
- Rapists know they have only a 1 in 605 chance of being caught, charged, convicted, and sentenced to serving time.

The purpose of these statistics is to increase women's anxiety about the prevalence of rape and other violent crimes and to reduce women's confidence in the police or justice system to protect them. The implied solution is to buy a pistol and learn how to use it.

How should our second researcher proceed in evaluating such an article for her own research purposes? Her first step is to evaluate the site itself. She found the home page by deleting extensions from the URL and looking directly at the home page (www.armedandsafe.com), which turned out to be the commercial site of a husband-and-wife team who run a firing range and give lessons in the use of rifles, pistols, and machine guns. The site obviously advocated Second Amendment rights and promoted gun ownership as a means of domestic and personal security. The images on the home page, showing a fierce eagle emerging from a collage of the American flag, the burning World Trade Center towers, and an aircraft carrier, were meant to reflect the patriotic sentiments that tend to dominate pro-gun Web sites. Researcher 2 could easily evaluate this site against the five criteria:

1. **Authority:** She could clearly tell that this was the commercial site of a firing range, run by its owners, a teacher and a former law enforcement official.

2. **Advocacy:** The site clearly advocated Second Amendment rights and gun ownership.
3. **Coverage:** The site did not cover gun-control issues in a complex way. Every aspect of the site was filtered to support its pro-gun vision.
4. **Accuracy:** At this point she was unable to check the accuracy of the site's data against other sources, but she assumed that all data would be rhetorically filtered and selected to promote the site's angle of vision.
5. **Currency:** Both anecdotal and statistical data were dated, taken primarily from the 1990s.

Based on this analysis, how might Researcher 2 use Connolly's article from this site? Our view is that the article could be very useful as one perspective on the gun-control controversy. It is a fairly representative example of the argument that guns can increase a woman's sense of confidence and well-being, and it clearly shows the kinds of rhetorical strategies such articles use—statistics on rape, descriptions of guns as equalizers in empowering women, and so forth. A summary of this article's argument could therefore be effective for presenting the pro-gun point of view.

As a source of factual data, however, the article is unusable. It would be irresponsible for her to claim that "3 out of 4 American women will be a victim of violent crime at least once in their lifetime" and to cite Connolly's article as an authoritative source. (Similarly, she would be irresponsible to claim that "a person is killed by a gun every 17 minutes in America" and give the Million Mom March site as a source.) Researcher 2 should instead look at primary data on crime statistics and guns compiled by trustworthy sources such as the Department of Justice, the FBI, state police departments, or peer-reviewed research by scholars (government statistics are all easily available from the Web). One purpose of reading sources rhetorically is to appreciate how much advocates for a given position will filter data. Trying to find the original data and to interpret it for yourself are two of the challenges of responsible research.

FOR WRITING AND DISCUSSION

Unpacking Factoids in Advocacy Web Sites

Consider the following two "factoids" from the sites we have just discussed:

Factoid 1: "3 out of 4 American women will be a victim of violent crime at least once in their lifetime." [from the Connolly article "Women Are the Real Victims of Handgun Control"]

Factoid 2: "A person is killed by a gun every 17 minutes in America." [from the Million Mom March home page]

Working individually or in small groups, try to reach consensus on the following questions. (When doing your own back-of-the-envelope calculations, consider the population of the United States to be 300 million people, with half of those being women.)

1. Based on the two primary sources shown here below, try to determine
   a. how these factoids were computed.
   b. how accurate they seem to be.

***SOURCE 1:* DATA ON VIOLENT CRIME RATES BY GENDER OF VICTIM, 1973–2003**

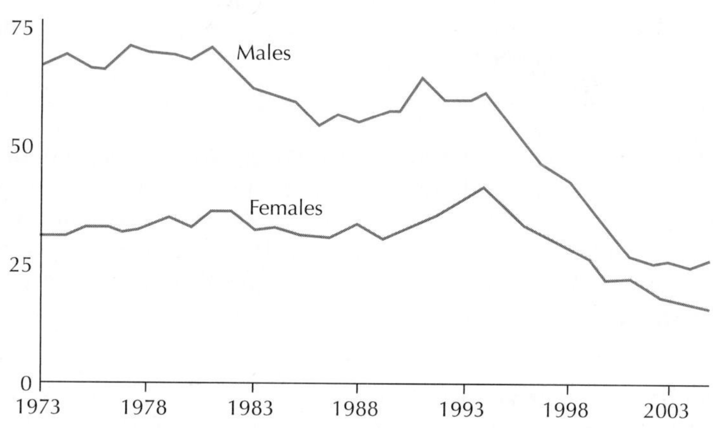

Adjusted victimization rate per 1,000 persons age 12 and over. The violent crimes included are rape, robbery, aggravated and simple assault, and homicide.

Source: Bureau of Justice Statistics, Department of Justice (http://ojp.usdoj.gov/bjs/glance/vsx2.htm).

***SOURCE 2:* DATA ON DEATH BY FIREARMS**

Firearm—In 2003, 30,136 persons died from firearm injuries in the United States (…), accounting for 18.4 percent of all injury deaths in 2003. Firearm suicide and homicide, the two major component causes, accounted for 56.1 and 39.6 percent, respectively, of all firearm injury deaths in 2003. In 2003, the age-adjusted death rate for firearm injuries was 10.3 deaths per 100,000 U.S. standard population. Males had an age-adjusted rate that was 6.8 times that for females, the black population had a rate that was 2.1 times that of the white population, and the non-Hispanic population had a rate that was 1.3 times that of the Hispanic population (…). The decrease between 2002 and 2003 in the age-adjusted death rate for firearm injuries was not statistically significant (…).

Source: Centers for Disease Control and Prevention. "Deaths: Final Data for 2003." *National Vital Statistics Reports* 54.13 (2006). 2 Sept. 2007 <http://www.cdc.gov/nchs/data/nvsr/nvsr54/nvsr54_13.pdf>.

2. Why do the factoids on each site have a different rhetorical impact than the original data displayed in statistical graphs and tables would? How do the factoids spin raw data in favor of a certain angle of vision?
3. Why do we say that Researcher 2 would be irresponsible if she used either the Connolly article or the Million Mom March Web site as a source of data on gun issues?
4. Note in the graph on violent crime (Source 1 above) how sharply crime rates fell from 1993 to 2003. Scholars have debated extensively the causes of this decline. How does this graph suggest the importance of "currency" when evaluating evidence?

In this chapter we have focused on evaluating sources, particularly on reading sources rhetorically and taking purposeful notes; on evaluating sources for reliability, credibility, angle of vision, and degree of advocacy; and on using your rhetorical knowledge to evaluate Web sources. In the next chapters, we turn to the skills you will need to incorporate your sources into your own prose and to cite and document them according to academic conventions.

For additional writing, reading, and research resources, go to **www.MyCompLab.com** and choose **Ramage/Bean/Johnson's *The Allyn & Bacon Guide to Writing,* Fifth Edition.**

INCORPORATING SOURCES INTO YOUR OWN WRITING

CHAPTER 22

So far, we have covered strategies for finding research sources (Chapter 20) and for evaluating them (Chapter 21). In this chapter, we focus on the skills you will need to incorporate sources into your own writing. Specifically, we'll focus on the following skills:

- Skill 27: Keep your focus on your own argument.
- Skill 28: Know when and how to use summary, paraphrase, quotation, and attributive tags.
- Skill 29: Understand the mechanics of quoting.
- Skill 30: Understand and avoid plagiarism.

Many of the examples in this chapter will be based on the following short article about violence in the Old West. This chapter will be most useful to you if you read the article first.

Roger D. McGrath

The Myth of Violence in the Old West

1 It is commonly assumed that violence is part of our frontier heritage. But the historical record shows that frontier violence was very different from violence today. Robbery and burglary, two of our most common crimes, were of no great significance in the frontier towns of the Old West, and rape was seemingly nonexistent.

2 Bodie, one of the principal towns on the trans-Sierra frontier, illustrates the point. Nestled high in the mountains of eastern California, Bodie, which boomed in the late 1870s and early 1880s, ranked among the most notorious frontier towns of the Old West. It was, as one prospector put it, the last of the old-time mining camps.

3 Like the trans-Sierra frontier in general, Bodie was indisputably violent and lawless, yet most people were not affected. Fistfights and gunfights among willing combatants—gamblers, miners, and the like—were regular events, and stagecoach holdups were not unusual. But the old, the young, the weak, and the female—so often the victims of crime today—were generally not harmed.

4 Robbery was more often aimed at stagecoaches than at individuals. Highwaymen usually took only the express box and left the passengers alone. There were eleven stagecoach robberies in Bodie between 1878 and 1882, and in only two instances were passengers robbed. (In one instance, the highwaymen later apologized for their conduct.)

5 There were only ten robberies and three attempted robberies of individuals in Bodie during its boom years, and in nearly every case the circumstances were the same: the victim had spent the evening in a gambling den, saloon, or brothel; he had revealed that he had on his person a significant sum of money; and he was staggering home drunk when the attack occurred.

6 Bodie's total of twenty-one robberies—eleven of stages and ten of individuals—over a five-year period converts to a rate of eighty-four robberies per 100,000 inhabitants per year. On this scale—the same scale used by the FBI to index crime—New York City's robbery rate in 1980 was 1,140, Miami's was 995, and Los Angeles's was 628. The rate for the United States as a whole was 243. Thus Bodie's robbery rate was significantly below the national average in 1980.

7 Perhaps the greatest deterrent to crime in Bodie was the fact that so many people were armed. Armed guards prevented bank robberies and holdups of stagecoaches carrying shipments of bullion, and armed homeowners and merchants discouraged burglary. Between 1878 and 1882, there were only thirty-two burglaries—seventeen of homes and fifteen of businesses—in Bodie. At least a half-dozen burglaries were thwarted by the presence of armed citizens. The newspapers regularly advocated shooting burglars on sight, and several burglars were, in fact, shot at.

8 Using the FBI scale, Bodie's burglary rate for those five years was 128. Miami's rate in 1980 was 3,282, New York's was 2,661, and Los Angeles's was 2,602. The rate of the United States as a whole was 1,668, thirteen times that of Bodie.

9 Bodie's law enforcement institutions were certainly not responsible for these low rates. Rarely were robbers or burglars arrested, and even less often were they convicted. Moreover, many law enforcement officers operated on both sides of the law.

10 It was the armed citizens themselves who were the most potent—though not the only—deterrent to larcenous crime. Another was the threat of vigilantism. Highwaymen, for example, understood that while they could take the express box from a stagecoach without arousing the citizens, they risked inciting the entire populace to action if they robbed the passengers.

11 There is considerable evidence that women in Bodie were rarely the victims of crime. Between 1878 and 1882 only one woman, a prostitute, was robbed, and there were no reported cases of rape. (There is no evidence that rapes occurred but were not reported.)

12 Finally, juvenile crime, which accounts for a significant portion of the violent crime in the United States today, was limited in Bodie to pranks and malicious mischief.

13 If robbery, burglary, crimes against women, and juvenile crime were relatively rare on the trans-Sierra frontier, homicide was not: thirty-one Bodieites were shot, stabbed, or beaten to death during the boom years, for a homicide rate of 116. No U.S. city today comes close to this rate. In 1980, Miami led the nation with a homicide rate of 32.7; Las Vegas was a distant second at 23.4. A half-dozen cities had rates of zero. The rate for the United States as a whole in that year was a mere 10.2.

14 Several factors contributed to Bodie's high homicide rate. A majority of the town's residents were young, adventurous, single males who adhered to a code of conduct

that frequently required them to fight even if, or perhaps especially if, it could mean death. Courage was admired above all else. Alcohol also played a major role in fostering the settlement of disputes by violence.

15 If the men's code of conduct and their consumption of alcohol made fighting inevitable, their sidearms often made it fatal. While the carrying of guns probably reduced the incidence of robbery and burglary, it undoubtedly increased the number of homicides.

16 For the most part, the citizens of Bodie were not troubled by the great number of killings; nor were they troubled that only one man was ever convicted of murder. They accepted the killings and the lack of convictions because most of those killed had been willing combatants.

17 Thus the violence and lawlessness of the trans-Sierra frontier bear little relation to the violence and lawlessness that pervade American society today. If Bodie is at all representative of frontier towns, there is little justification for blaming contemporary American violence on our frontier heritage.

SKILL 27 Keep your focus on your own argument.

To do effective college-level research, you need to present your own argument, using research sources for your own purposes. In Skill 24 in the previous chapter, we explained how you should remain aware of your research goals when you take notes and evaluate sources. The strategies chart on page 593–594 shows some of the typical functions that research sources can serve in your own paper. How you incorporate a research source into your own argument—whether, for example, you summarize it fully or simply draw a few pieces of factual information from it—depends on your own purpose.

It follows, then, that there is no one right way of using a source. As an illustration, your use of Roger D. McGrath's article "The Myth of Violence in the Old West" would depend on your own research question, thesis, and purpose. In what follows we illustrate how three hypothetical writers, addressing three different research questions, use McGrath's article in different ways. In each case, the writer's goal is not to reproduce McGrath's article but to use the article in support of her own argument.

Writer 1: An Analytical Paper on Causes of Violence in Contemporary Society

The first hypothetical writer is analyzing the causes of violence in contemporary U.S. society. She wants to reject one possible cause—that contemporary violence grows out of our violent past. To make this point in her argument, she summarizes McGrath's article.

> Many people believe that violence is part of our Wild West heritage. But Roger McGrath, in his article "The Myth of Violence in the Old West," shows that frontier violence was very different from contemporary violence. He explains that in a typical frontier town, violence involved gunslingers who were "willing combatants," whereas today's typical victims—"the old, the young, the weak, and the female"—were unaffected by crime (611). Because the presence of an armed populace deterred robbery and burglary, theft was much less common in the Old West than today. On the other hand, McGrath explains, killings were fueled by guns, alcohol, and a code of conduct that invited fighting, so murders were much more frequent than in any U.S. city today (612). Thus, according to McGrath, there is little resemblance between violence on the frontier and violence in today's cities, so we cannot blame current violence on our tumultuous frontier past.

In this passage the author summarizes McGrath's argument in order to refute the violent frontier theory about the causes of contemporary violence. Presumably, this author will proceed to other causes of violence and will not return again to McGrath.

Writer 2: A Persuasive Paper Supporting Gun Control

In our next case, the hypothetical writer uses McGrath's article to argue in favor of gun control. The writer wants to refute the popular anti–gun-control argument that law-abiding citizens need to be armed to protect themselves against criminals.

> Opponents of gun control often argue that guns benefit society by providing protection against intruders. But such protection is deadly, as Roger McGrath shows in his study of violence in the frontier town of Bodie, California. Although guns reduced theft, as seen in the low rate of theft in the well-armed town of Bodie, the presence of guns also led to a homicide rate far above that of the most violent city in the U.S. today. The homicide rate in the frontier town of Bodie, California, for example, was 116 per 100,000, compared to the current national average of 10.2 per 100,000 (612). True, Bodie citizens reduced the theft rate by being heavily armed, but at a cost of a homicide rate more than ten times the current national average. To protect our consumer goods at the cost of so much human life is counter to the values of most Americans.

McGrath's article contains data (low rate of crimes against property, high homicide rate) that could be used on either side of the gun-control debate. This writer acknowledges the evidence from Bodie showing that gun possession reduces theft and then works that potentially damaging information into an argument for gun control. How might you use the McGrath article to oppose gun control?

Writer 3: An Informative Paper Showing Shifting Definitions of Crime

Looking at another facet of McGrath's article, the last hypothetical writer summarizes part of McGrath's article to support her thesis that a community's definition of crime is constantly shifting.

> Our notion of criminal activity shifts over time. For example, only a short time ago on the American frontier, murder was often ignored by law enforcement. Roger McGrath, in his discussion of violence in the frontier town of Bodie, California, during the 1870s and 1880s, showed that the townspeople accepted homicides as long as both the murderer and the victim were "willing combatants" who freely participated in gunfights (613). These young males who were the "willing combatants" in Bodie share many characteristics with modern gang members in that they were encouraged to fight by a "code of conduct." According to McGrath, "A majority of the town's residents were young, adventurous, single males who adhered to a code of conduct that frequently required them to fight even if ... it could mean death" (612–613). Today's gang members also follow a code of conduct that requires violence—often in the form of vengeance. Although joining a gang certainly makes youths "willing combatants," that status doesn't prevent prosecution in court. Today's "willing combatants" are criminals, but yesterday's "willing combatants" were not.

This writer uses McGrath's article to make a point completely different from McGrath's. But by extending and applying information from McGrath's article to a new context, the writer gathers fuel for her own argument about shifting definitions of the word *criminal*.

FOR WRITING AND DISCUSSION

Using Sources for a Purpose

Each of the hypothetical writers uses McGrath's article for a different purpose. Working individually or in groups, answer the following questions. Be ready to elaborate on and defend your answers.

1. What are the differences in the ways the writers use the original article? How are these differences related to differences in each writer's purpose?
2. What differences would you expect to find in the research notes each writer took on the McGrath article?
3. What makes each writer's paragraph different from a purposeless listing of random information?

SKILL 28 Know when and how to use summary, paraphrase, quotation, and attributive tags.

As a research writer, you need to incorporate sources gracefully into your own prose so that your paper's focus stays on your own argument. The choices you have available are summarizing a source's argument, paraphrasing a relevant portion of a source, or quoting the source directly. In all cases, you signal your use of the source through an attributive tag, a parenthetical citation, or both.

Effective Use of Summary, Paraphrase, or Quotation

The following chart gives you an overview of summaries, paraphrases, and quotations as ways of incorporating sources into your own prose.

STRATEGIES for Incorporating Sources into Your Own Prose

Strategies	What to Do	When to Use These Strategies
Summarize the source.	Condense a source writer's argument by keeping main ideas and omitting details (see Chapter 6, pp. 131–133).	• When the source writer's whole argument is important • When the source writer presents an alternative or opposing view • When the source writer's argument can be used in support of your own
Paraphrase the source.	Reproduce an idea from a source writer but translate the idea entirely into your own words; a paraphrase should be approximately the same length as the original.	• When you want to incorporate factual information from a source or to use one specific idea from a source • When you want to incorporate source data in your own voice • When you do not want to interrupt the flow of your argument
Quote short passages from the source using quotation marks.	Work brief quotations from the source smoothly into the grammar of your own sentences (see Skill 29 on the mechanics of quoting).	• When you need testimony from an authority (state the authority's credentials in an attributive tag) • In summaries, when you want to reproduce a source's voice, particularly if the language is striking or memorable • In lieu of paraphrase when the source language is memorable
Quote long passages from the source using the block method. (Note: This is used very rarely in scholarly writing.)	Results in a page with noticeably lengthy block quotations (see Skill 29).	• When you intend to analyze or critique the quotation—the quotation is followed by your detailed analysis of its ideas or rhetorical features • When the flavor and language of testimonial evidence is important

With practice, you'll be able to use all these strategies smoothly and effectively. Detailed instructions on how to write a summary of an article and incorporate it into your own prose with attributive tags are provided in Chapter 6, "Reading

Rhetorically." Summaries can be as short as a single sentence or as long as a paragraph. Writer 1's summary of the McGrath article is a good example of a graceful summary used in support of the writer's own thesis.

Unlike a summary, which is a condensation of a source's whole argument, a paraphrase translates a short passage from a source's words into the writer's own words. When you paraphrase, be careful to avoid reproducing the original writer's grammatical structure and syntax. If you mirror the original sentence structure while replacing some words with synonyms, you are plagiarizing rather than paraphrasing. Here is an acceptable paraphrase of a short passage from the McGrath article:

Skill 30 explains plagiarism in more detail.

ORIGINAL

There is considerable evidence that women in Bodie were rarely the victims of crime. Between 1878 and 1882 only one woman, a prostitute, was robbed, and there were no reported cases of rape. (There is no evidence that rapes occurred but were not reported.)

PARAPHRASE

According to McGrath, women in Bodie seldom suffered at the hands of criminals. Between 1878 and 1882, the only female robbery victim in Bodie was a prostitute. Also rape seemed nonexistent, with no reported cases and no evidence that unreported cases occurred (612).

Note that to avoid plagiarism, the writer has changed the sentence structure substantially. However, the writer still acknowledges the original source with the phrase "According to McGrath" and provides the page number.

These features of citation and documentation are covered in Chapter 23.

Creating Rhetorically Effective Attributive Tags

As we have shown in this section, whenever you use sources in your writing, you need to distinguish your source's words and ideas from your own. The most precise way of doing so is to use strategically placed attributive tags—short phrases like "according to McGrath," "McGrath says," "in McGrath's view," and so on. As we show in a moment, attributive tags can have a powerful rhetorical effect by letting you create the angle of vision from which you want your readers to view a source.

Using Attributive Tags to Separate Your Ideas from Your Source's

The previous examples of citing, summarizing, paraphrasing, and quoting use attributive tags to signal which ideas are the writer's and which are taken from another source. Here, for example, are excerpts from Writer 1's summary of McGrath, in which we have highlighted the attributive tags with boldfaced font. (The complete summary appears on p. 614.)

USE OF ATTRIBUTIVE TAGS

Many people believe that violence is part of our Wild West heritage. But **Roger McGrath, in his article "The Myth of Violence in the Old West,"** shows that frontier violence was very different from contemporary violence. **He explains** that. ... On the other hand, **McGrath explains**, killings were fueled. ... Thus, **according to McGrath**, there is little resemblance between violence on the frontier and violence in today's cities. ...

Using Parenthetical Citations without Attributive Tags and the Resulting Ambiguities

You can also indicate borrowed material by inserting the source author's name and appropriate page number in a parenthetical citation at the end of the borrowed material:

(McGrath 612)

However, this approach—which is common in some academic writing, particularly in the social sciences—can introduce two kinds of ambiguity. First, it does not clearly mark where the borrowed material begins or how far it extends. Second, it tends to imply that the borrowed material is a "fact" as opposed to an author's argument filtered through that author's angle of vision. Note these ambiguities in the following passage, where parenthetical citations are used without attributive tags:

AMBIGUOUS ATTRIBUTION

There are many arguments in favor of preserving old-growth forests. First, it is simply unnecessary to log these forests to supply the world's lumber. We have plenty of new-growth forest from which lumber can be taken (Sagoff 89–90). Recently there have been major reforestation efforts all over the United States, and it is common practice now for loggers to replant every tree that is harvested. These new-growth forests, combined with extensive planting of tree farms, provide more than enough wood for the world's needs. Tree farms alone can supply the world's demand for industrial lumber (Sedjo 90).

When confronted with this passage, skeptical readers might ask, "Who are Sagoff and Sedjo? I've never heard of them." It is also difficult to tell how much of the passage is the writer's own argument and how much is borrowed from Sagoff and Sedjo. Is this whole passage a paraphrase? Finally, the writer tends to treat Sagoff's and Sedjo's assertions as uncontested facts rather than as professional opinions. Compare the preceding version with this one, in which attributive tags are added:

CLEAR ATTRIBUTION

There are many arguments in favor of preserving old-growth forests. First, it is simply unnecessary to log these forests to supply the world's lumber. **According to environmentalist Carl Sagoff**, we have plenty of new-growth forest from which lumber can be taken (89–90). Recently there have been major reforestation efforts all over the United States, and it is common practice now for loggers to replant every tree that is harvested. These new-growth forests, combined with extensive planting of tree farms, provide more than enough wood for the world's needs. **According to forestry expert Robert Sedjo**, tree farms alone can supply the world's demand for industrial lumber (90).

We can now see that most of the paragraph is the writer's own argument, into which she has inserted the expert testimony of Sagoff and Sedjo, whose views are treated not as indisputable facts but as the opinions of authorities in this field.

Using Attributive Tags to Create Context and Shape Reader Response

When you introduce a source for the first time, you can use the attributive tag not only to introduce the source but also to shape your readers' attitudes toward the source. In the previous example, the writer wants readers to respect Sagoff and Sedjo, so she identifies Sagoff as an "environmentalist" and Sedjo as a "forestry expert." If the writer favored logging old-growth forests and supported the logging industry's desire to create more jobs, she might have used different tags: "Carl Sagoff, an outspoken advocate for spotted owls over people," or "Robert Sedjo, a forester with limited knowledge of world lumber markets."

When you compose an initial tag, you can add to it any combination of the following kinds of information, depending on your purpose, your audience's values, and your sense of what the audience already knows or doesn't know about the source:

STRATEGIES for Modifying Attributive Tags to Shape Reader Response

Add to Attributive Tags	Examples
Author's credentials or relevant specialty (enhances credibility)	Civil engineer David Rockwood, a noted authority on stream flow in rivers
Author's lack of credentials (decreases credibility)	City Council member Dilbert Weasel, a local politician with no expertise in international affairs
Author's political or social views	Left-wing columnist Alexander Cockburn [has negative feeling]; Alexander Cockburn, a longtime champion of labor [has positive feeling]
Title of source if it provides context	In her book *Fasting Girls: The History of Anorexia Nervosa,* Joan Jacobs Brumberg shows that [establishes credentials for comments on eating disorders]
Publisher of source if it adds prestige or otherwise shapes audience response	Dr. Carl Patrona, in an article published in the prestigious *New England Journal of Medicine*
Historical or cultural information about a source that provides context or background	In his 1960s book popularizing the hippie movement, Charles Reich claims that
Indication of source's purpose or angle of vision	Feminist author Naomi Wolfe, writing a blistering attack on the beauty industry, argues that

Our point here is that you can use attributive tags rhetorically to help your readers understand the significance and context of a source when you first introduce it and to guide your readers' attitudes toward the source.

FOR WRITING AND DISCUSSION

Evaluating the Use of a Passage

What follow are four different ways that a writer can use the same passage from a source to support a point about the greenhouse effect. Working in groups or as a whole class, rank the four methods from "most effective" to "least effective." Assume that you are writing a researched argument addressed to your college classmates.

1. ***Quotation without attributive tag***
   The greenhouse effect will have a devastating effect on the earth's environment: "Potential impacts include increased mortality and illness due to heat stress and worsened air pollution, as in the 1995 Chicago heat wave that killed hundreds of people. ... Infants, children and other vulnerable populations—especially in already-stressed regions of the world—would likely suffer disproportionately from these impacts" (Hall 19).
2. ***Quotation with attributive tag***
   The greenhouse effect will have a devastating effect on the earth's environment. David C. Hall, president of Physicians for Social Responsibility, claims the following: "Potential impacts include increased mortality and illness due to heat stress and worsened air pollution, as in the 1995 Chicago heat wave that killed hundreds of people. ... Infants, children and other vulnerable populations—especially in already-stressed regions of the world—would likely suffer disproportionately from these impacts" (19).
3. ***Paraphrase without attributive tag***
   The greenhouse effect will have a devastating effect on the earth's environment. One of the most frightening effects is the threat of diseases stemming from increased air pollution and heat stress. Infants and children would be most at risk (Hall 19).
4. ***Paraphrase with attributive tag***
   The greenhouse effect will have a devastating effect on the earth's environment. One of the most frightening effects, according to David C. Hall, president of Physicians for Social Responsibility, is the threat of diseases stemming from increased air pollution and heat stress. Infants and children would be most at risk (19).

SKILL 29 Understand the mechanics of quoting.

In Skill 28, we explained your options for incorporating a source into your own paper—summary, paraphrase, and quotation. When you choose to quote, you confront the mechanics of quoting—that is, the nuts and bolts of where to put the quotation marks, where to insert commas or colons, how to make changes in the quotation to fit the grammar of your own sentence, and how to leave something out. In this section, we cover the following instances concerning the mechanics of quoting:

- Quoting a complete sentence introduced by an attributive tag
- Inserting quoted words and phrases into your own sentences

- Using brackets to modify a quotation to fit the grammar of your own sentence or to provide context
- Using ellipses to indicate omissions from a quotation
- Using single and double quotation marks to indicate a quotation within a quotation
- Using block indentation for quotations more than four lines long

These explanations will cover the big picture about the mechanics of quoting. Additional explanations covering variations and specific cases can be found in any good handbook.

Quoting a Complete Sentence Introduced by an Attributive Tag

In some cases, you will want to quote a complete sentence from your source. Typically, you will include an attributive tag that tells the reader who is being quoted. At the end of the quotation, you usually indicate its page number in parentheses (see Skills 32 and 33 about parenthetical citation of a source in MLA and APA styles).

Original Passage	Quotation of a Complete Sentence	Explanation
It was the armed citizens themselves who were the most potent—though not the only—deterrent to larcenous crime.	According to McGrath, "It was the armed citizens themselves who were the most potent—though not the only—deterrent to larcenous crime" (612).	• Because the quotation is a complete sentence, it starts with a capital letter and is separated from the introductory phrase by a comma. • The page number in parentheses is inserted *after* the quotation mark but *before* the closing period.

Inserting Quoted Words and Phrases into Your Own Sentences

Often you don't want to quote a complete sentence but instead to work brief words and phrases from your source into your own grammatical structure. In these cases, you need to make sure that the grammatical structure of the quotation fits smoothly into the grammar of your own sentence.

Original Passage	Quoted Phrase Inserted into Writer's Own Sentence	Explanation
But the old, the young, the weak, and the female—so often the victims of crime today—were generally not harmed.	McGrath contrasts frontier violence to crime today, pointing out that today's typical crime victims are "the old, the young, the weak, and the female" and showing that these groups were not molested in Bodie (611).	• Because the quoted material is not a complete sentence, it is worked into the grammar of the writer's own sentence. • No comma introduces the quotation; commas should be used only to fit the grammar of the writer's own sentence. • The number in parentheses is the page number where the quotation is found in the original source.

Using Brackets to Modify a Quotation

Occasionally the grammar of a desired quotation doesn't match the grammatical structure of your own sentence, or the meaning of a quoted word is not clear because the passage has been removed from its original context. In these cases, use brackets to modify the quotation's grammar or to add a clarifying explanation. Place your changes or additions in brackets to indicate that the bracketed material is not part of the original wording. You should also use brackets to show a change in capitalization.

Original Passage	Quotation Modified with Brackets	Reason for Change/Explanation
The newspapers regularly advocated shooting burglars on sight, and several burglars were, in fact, shot at.	In Bodie, an armed citizenry successfully eliminated burglaries, aided by newspapers "regularly advocat[ing] shooting burglars on sight" (McGrath 612).	• The change inside the brackets modifies the quotation to fit the grammar of the writer's sentence. • The parenthetical citation identifies the source being quoted.
Highwaymen, for example, understood that while they could take the express box from a stagecoach without arousing the citizens, they risked inciting the entire populace to action if they robbed the passengers.	Public sentiment influenced what laws were likely to be broken. According to McGrath, "[W]hile they [highwaymen] could take the express box from a stagecoach without arousing the citizens, they risked inciting the entire populace to action if they robbed the passengers" (612).	• The writer converts a dependent clause into a complete sentence introduced with an attributive tag; the brackets are used to change a small letter to a capital letter. • The word *highwaymen* is inserted in brackets to supply missing context.

Using Ellipses to Indicate Omissions from a Quotation

Another way that writers modify quotations is to omit words from the quoted passage. To indicate an omission, use three spaced periods called an *ellipsis*. Placement of the ellipsis depends on where the omitted material occurs. In the middle of a sentence, each of the periods should be preceded and followed by a space. When your ellipsis comes at the boundary between sentences, use an additional period to mark the end of the first sentence. When a parenthetical page number must follow the ellipsis, insert it before the final (fourth) period in the sequence.

Original Passage	Omitted Material Marked by Ellipsis	Explanation
Finally, juvenile crime, which accounts for a significant portion of the violent crime in the United States today, was limited in Bodie to pranks and malicious mischief.	According to McGrath, "juvenile crime ... was limited in Bodie to pranks and malicious mischief" (612).	• Three spaced periods mark the place where material was omitted.

Original Passage	Omitted Material Marked by Ellipsis	Explanation
Bodie's law enforcement institutions were certainly not responsible for these low rates. Rarely were robbers or burglars arrested, and even less often were they convicted. Moreover, many law enforcement officers operated on both sides of the law.	"Bodie's law enforcement institutions were certainly not responsible for these low rates. Rarely were robbers or burglars arrested. … Moreover, many law enforcement officers operated on both sides of the law" (612).	• Omitted material comes at the end of the second sentence. A fourth period indicates the sentence boundary.
Bodie's law enforcement institutions were certainly not responsible for these low rates. Rarely were robbers or burglars arrested, and even less often were they convicted. Moreover, many law enforcement officers operated on both sides of the law.	"Bodie's law enforcement institutions were certainly not responsible for these low rates. Rarely were robbers or burglars arrested …" (612).	• Omitted material comes at the end of the second sentence. A parenthetical citation precedes the fourth period.

Using Single and Double Quotation Marks for a Quotation within a Quotation

Occasionally a passage that you wish to quote will already contain quotation marks. If you insert the passage within your own quotation marks, change the original double marks (") into single marks (') to indicate the quotation within the quotation. The same procedure works whether the quotation marks are used for quoted words or for a title. Make sure that your attributive tag signals who is being quoted. Because the McGrath article contains no internal quotation marks, we will use a different example to illustrate quotations within quotations.

Original Passage	Use of Single Quotation Marks to Indicate a Quotation within a Quotation	Explanation
And finally, we tend to stereotype because it helps us make sense out of a highly confusing world, a world which William James once described as "one great, blooming, buzzing confusion." [Passage from an article by Robert Heilbroner, who here quotes William James]	Robert Heilbroner explains why people tend to create stereotypes: "And finally, we tend to stereotype because it helps us make sense out of a highly confusing world, a world which William James once described as 'one great, blooming, buzzing confusion.' "	• Single quotation marks are placed around the William James quotation; double quotation marks are placed around the quotation from Heilbroner. • The writer's attributive tag notes Heilbroner; Heilbroner's own attributive tag notes James.

Using Block Indentation for Quotations More Than Four Lines Long

If your quoted passage uses more than four lines in your own paper, use the block indentation method rather than quotation marks. Block quotations are generally introduced with an attributive tag followed by a colon. The indented block of text, rather than quotation marks, signals that the material is a direct quotation. As we explained earlier, block quotations occur rarely in scholarly writing and are used primarily in cases where the writer intends to analyze the text being quoted. If you overuse block quotations, your paper becomes a collage of other people's voices.

Original Passage	**Block Quotation**	**Explanation**
Fistfights and gunfights among willing combatants—gamblers, miners, and the like—were regular events, and stagecoach holdups were not unusual. But the old, the young, the weak, and the female—so often the victims of crime today—were generally not harmed.	McGrath describes the people most affected by violence in the frontier town of Bodie: Fistfights and gunfights among willing combatants—gamblers, miners, and the like—were regular events, and stagecoach holdups were not unusual. But the old, the young, the weak, and the female—so often the victims of crime today—were generally not harmed. (611)	• The quotation is introduced with an attributive tag followed by a colon. • The block quotation is indented one inch. • There are *no quotation marks*. The block indentation itself signals a quotation. • The number in parentheses indicates the page number where the quotation is found in the original source. Note that in block quotations, the parentheses come after the closing period.

SKILL 30 Understand and avoid plagiarism.

Before we proceed in the next chapter to the nuts and bolts of documenting sources, we'd like you to understand the ethical issue of plagiarism. As you know from writing your own papers, developing ideas and putting them into words is hard work. *Plagiarism* occurs whenever you take someone else's work and pass it off as your own. Plagiarism has two forms: borrowing another person's ideas without giving credit through proper citation and borrowing another writer's language without giving credit through quotation marks or block indentation.

The second kind of plagiarism is far more common than the first, perhaps because inexperienced writers don't appreciate how much they need to change the wording of a source to make the writing their own. It is not enough just to change the order of phrases in a sentence or to replace a few words with synonyms. In the following example, compare the satisfactory paraphrase of a passage from McGrath's piece with a plagiarized version.

Original There is considerable evidence that women in Bodie were rarely the victims of crime. Between 1878 and 1882 only one woman, a prostitute, was robbed, and there were no reported cases of rape. (There is no evidence that rapes occurred but were not reported.)

Acceptable Paraphrase According to McGrath, women in Bodie rarely suffered at the hands of criminals (612). Between 1878 and 1882, the only female robbery victim in Bodie was a prostitute. Also rape seemed nonexistent, with no reported cases and no evidence that unreported cases occurred.

Plagiarism According to McGrath, there is much evidence that women in Bodie were seldom crime victims (612). Between 1878 and 1882 only one woman, a prostitute, was robbed, and there were no reported rapes. There is no evidence that unreported cases of rape occurred (612).

FOR WRITING AND DISCUSSION

Understanding Plagiarism

The writer of the plagiarized passage perhaps assumed that the accurate citation of McGrath is all that is needed to avoid plagiarism. Yet this writer is guilty of plagiarism. Why? How has the writer attempted to change the wording of the original? Why aren't these changes enough?

The best way to avoid plagiarism is to be especially careful at the note-taking stage. If you copy from your source, copy exactly, word for word, and put quotation marks around the copied material or otherwise indicate that it is not your own wording. If you paraphrase or summarize material, be sure that you don't borrow any of the original wording. Also be sure to change the grammatical structure of the original. Lazy note taking, in which you follow the arrangement and grammatical structure of the original passage and merely substitute occasional synonyms, leads directly to plagiarism.

Also remember that you cannot borrow another writer's ideas without citing them. If you summarize or paraphrase another writer's thinking about a subject, you should indicate in your notes that the ideas are not your own and be sure to record all the information you need for a citation. If you do exploratory reflection to accompany your notes, then the distinction between other writers' ideas and your own should be easy to recognize when it's time to incorporate the source material into your paper.

For additional writing, reading, and research resources, go to **www.MyCompLab.com** and choose **Ramage/Bean/Johnson's *The Allyn & Bacon Guide to Writing,* Fifth Edition.**

CHAPTER 23

CITING AND DOCUMENTING SOURCES

In the previous chapter we explained how to incorporate sources into your writing; in this chapter we focus on the nuts and bolts of documenting those sources in a way appropriate to your purpose, audience, and genre. Accurate documentation not only helps other researchers locate your sources but also contributes substantially to your own *ethos* as a writer. Specifically, this chapter helps you understand the general logic of parenthetical citation systems; the Modern Language Association (MLA) and American Psychological Association (APA) methods for in-text citations; the MLA and APA methods for documenting sources in a "Works Cited" or "References" list, respectively; and the MLA and APA styles for formatting academic papers.* As you use one or both of these methods in papers for various classes, your growing familiarity with the type of information expected in citations will make it easier to follow the formatting details in the models we provide as well as in other systems your professors may expect you to use.

An example of a research paper written in MLA style is James Gardiner's paper on pp. 643–651. An example of a research paper written in APA style is Campbell et al. on pp. 274–281.

SKILL 31 Understand how parenthetical citations work.

The most common forms of documentation today use what are called parenthetical citations. Both the MLA system, used primarily in the humanities, and the APA system, used primarily in the social sciences, follow a system of parenthetical citations.

Connect the Body of the Paper to the Bibliography with Citations

In both the MLA and APA systems, the writer places a complete bibliography at the end of the paper. In the MLA system this bibliography is called "Works Cited." In the APA system it is called "References." The bibliography is arranged alphabetically by author or by title (if an author is not named). The key to the systems' logic is this:

- Every source in the bibliography must be mentioned in the body of the paper.
- Conversely, every source mentioned in the body of the paper must be listed in the bibliography.

*Our discussion of MLA style is based on the *MLA Handbook for Writers of Research Papers,* 7th ed. (2009). Our discussion of APA style is based on the *Publication Manual of the American Psychological Association,* 5th ed. (Washington, D.C.: American Psychological Association, 2001) and the *APA Style Guide to Electronic References* (2007).

- There must be a one-to-one correspondence between the first word in each bibliographic entry (usually, but not always, an author's last name)* and the name used to identify the source in the body of the paper.

Suppose a reader sees this phrase in your paper: "According to Debra Goldstein. . . ." The reader should be able to turn to your bibliography and find an alphabetized entry beginning with "Goldstein, Debra." Similarly, suppose that in looking over your bibliography, your reader sees an article by "Guillen, Manuel." This means that the name "Guillen" has to appear in your paper in one of two ways:

- As an attributive tag: "Economics professor Manuel Guillen argues that. . . ."
- As a parenthetical citation, probably following a quotation: ". . . changes in fiscal policy" (Guillen 49).

Because this one-to-one correspondence is so important, let's illustrate it with some complete examples using the MLA formatting style:

If the body of your paper has this:	Then the Works Cited list must have this:
According to linguist Deborah Tannen, political debate in America leaves out the complex middle ground where most solutions must be developed. [**author cited in an attributive tag**]	Tannen, Deborah. *The Argument Culture: Moving from Debate to Dialogue.* New York: Random, 1998. Print.
In the 1980s, cigarette advertising revealed a noticeable pattern of racial stereotyping (Pollay, Lee, and Carter-Whitney). [**authors cited in parentheses**]	Pollay, Richard W., Jung S. Lee, and David Carter-Whitney. "Separate, but Not Equal: Racial Segmentation in Cigarette Advertising." *Journal of Advertising* 21.1 (1992): 45–57. Print.
In its award-winning Web site, the National Men's Resource Center offers advice to parents on how to talk with children about alcohol and drugs ("Talking"). [**shortened title used to identify source in Works Cited list**]	"Talking with Kids about Alcohol and Drugs." *Menstuff.* National Men's Resource Center, 1 Mar. 2007. Web. 26 June 2007.

Citation Problems with Database and Web Sources

Citation systems work well with print sources like books and journals because these sources can be retrieved in the same paper format from library to library all over the world. Both the MLA and APA systems have a basic format for citing

*Sometimes a source won't have a named author. In such cases your parenthetical citation should identify the source by title, shortened for efficiency, and your bibliographic entry should begin with those title words (for example, "Guidelines for Online Security" could be shortened in the parenthetical citation to "Guidelines" as long as no other source begins with that title). To cite a source from a Web site identified by a corporation or group's name (for example, "Centers for Disease Control"), you have the choice of beginning the entry with the title of the document you are citing or with the corporate author, whichever you think will make more sense in your text and will help readers find the source in the bibliography more easily.

books and articles. In general, you simply find a bibliographic model that matches your source and plug the information into the correct slots.

The case is more difficult when you download an article from a licensed database or the Web. First of all, scholarly organizations usually expect researchers to find the original print version rather than use the downloaded version. But for college students, it is often difficult to locate the original print source if their libraries don't have it. There are three main problems with relying on downloaded articles: (1) you can't be sure the electronic article is a completely accurate version of the print article; (2) the downloaded version often doesn't reproduce the images that appear in the print version and that may be important; (3) the downloaded version usually doesn't reproduce the page numbering of the original source, so there is no clear way to cite pages.* Because downloaded versions are unstable, you must include in your bibliographic entry all the publication information about the original print version of the article *plus* information about the electronic source.

When citing Web sources, you will encounter the most difficulty where material is updated frequently and sometimes disappears completely. You can't be sure that material available today from the Web will still be available tomorrow, not to mention twenty or more years from now. It is often hard to determine publication dates and authorship of material. Also, as with licensed database sources, page numbers are often impossible to specify for Web sites. Sometimes the only certain thing you'll know about a Web site is the URL in your browser's address bar and the date you accessed the site. At the very minimum, you have to include this information in the citation.

SKILL 32 Cite and document sources using MLA style.

To cite sources in your text using the MLA system, place the author's last name and the page number(s) in parentheses immediately after the material being cited. If an attributive tag already identifies the author, give only the page reference in parentheses. Once you have cited the author and it is clear that the same author's material is being used, you need cite only the page numbers in parentheses. The following examples show parenthetical documentation with and without an attributive tag. Note that the citation precedes the period. If you are citing a quotation, the parenthetical citation follows the quotation mark but precedes the final period.

> The Spanish tried to reduce the status of Filipina women who had been able to do business, get divorced, and sometimes become village chiefs (Karnow 41).

*Databases are increasingly offering some sources in .pdf format, which reproduces the original look of the article. In these cases, images are usually reproduced, and the original page formatting is maintained.

> According to Karnow, the Spanish tried to reduce the status of Filipina women who had been able to do business, get divorced, and sometimes become village chiefs (41).
>
> "And, to this day," Karnow continues, "women play a decisive role in Filipino families" (41).

A reader who wishes to look up the source will find the bibliographic information in the Works Cited section by looking for the entry under "Karnow." If more than one work by Karnow was used in the paper, the writer would include in the in-text citation an abbreviated title of the book or article following Karnow's name.

> (Karnow, *In Our Image* 41)

Cite from an Indirect Source

Occasionally you may wish to use a quotation that you have seen cited in one of your sources. You read Jones, who has a nice quotation from Smith, and you want to use Smith's quotation. What do you do? Whenever possible, find the quotation in its original source and cite that source. But if the original source is not available, cite the source indirectly by using the term "qtd. in" and list only the indirect source in your Works Cited list. In the following example, the writer wishes to quote a Buddhist monk, Thich Nhat Hanh, who has written a book entitled *Living Buddha, Living Christ*. However, the writer is unable to locate the actual book and instead has to quote from a review of the book by newspaper critic Lee Moriwaki. Here is how the writer would make the in-text citation:

> A Buddhist monk, Thich Nhat Hanh, stresses the importance of inner peace: "If we can learn ways to touch the peace, joy, and happiness that are already there, we will become healthy and strong, and a resource for others" (qtd. in Moriwaki C4).

The Works Cited list will have an entry for "Moriwaki" but not for "Thich Nhat Hanh."

Cite Page Numbers for Downloaded Material

When the materials you are citing are available in .pdf format, you can provide accurate page numbers for parenthetical citations. If you are working with text or HTML files, however, do not use the page numbers on a printout because they will not be consistent from printer to printer. If the item has numbered paragraphs, cite them with the abbreviation *par.* or *pars.*—for example, "(Jones, pars. 22–24)." In the absence of reliable page numbers for the original material, MLA says to omit page references from the parenthetical citation.

Document Sources in a Works Cited List

In the MLA system, you place a complete bibliography, titled "Works Cited," at the end of the paper. The list includes all the sources that you mention in your paper. However, it does not include works you read but did not use. Entries in the Works Cited list are arranged alphabetically by author, or by title if there is no author. Each entry includes the medium of publication, such as "Print" or "Web." You can see a complete Works Cited list on pages 650–651.

Here is a typical example of a work, in this case a book, cited in MLA form.

Karnow, Stanley. *In Our Image: America's Empire in the Philippines*. New York: Random, 1989. Print.

Two or More Listings for One Author

When two or more works by one author are cited, the works are listed alphabetically by title. For the second and all additional entries, type three hyphens and a period in place of the author's name.

Dombrowski, Daniel A. *Babies and Beasts: The Argument from Marginal Cases*. Urbana: U of Illinois P, 1997. Print.

---.*The Philosophy of Vegetarianism*. Amherst: U of Massachusetts P, 1984. Print.

The remaining pages in this section show examples of MLA formats for different kinds of sources, provide explanations and illustrations as needed, and give examples of the most frequently encountered variations and source types.

To see what citations look like when typed in a manuscript, see James Gardiner's Works Cited list on pp. 650–651.

MLA Citation Models

Books

General Format for Books

Author. *Title*. City of publication: Publisher, year of publication. Print.

One author

Pollan, Michael. *The Omnivore's Dilemma: A Natural History of Four Meals*. New York: Penguin, 2006. Print.

Two or more authors

Dombrowski, Daniel A., and Robert J. Deltete. *A Brief, Liberal, Catholic Defense of Abortion*. Urbana: U of Illinois P, 2000. Print.

Belenky, Mary, et al. *Women's Ways of Knowing: The Development of Self, Voice, and Mind*. New York: Basic, 1986. Print.

If there are four or more authors, you have the choice of listing all the authors in the order in which they appear on the title page or using "et al." (meaning "and others") to replace all but the first author. Your Works Cited entry and the parenthetical citation should match.

Second, later, or revised edition

Montagu, Ashley. *Touching: The Human Significance of the Skin*. 3rd ed. New York: Perennial, 1986. Print.

In place of "3rd ed.," you can include abbreviations for other kinds of editions: "Rev. ed." (for "Revised edition") or "Abr. ed." (for "Abridged edition").

Republished book (for example, a paperback published after the original hardback edition or a modern edition of an older work)

Hill, Christopher. *The World Turned Upside Down: Radical Ideas During the English Revolution*. 1972. London: Penguin, 1991. Print.

Wollstonecraft, Mary. *The Vindication of the Rights of Woman, with Strictures on Political and Moral Subjects*. 1792. Rutland: Tuttle, 1995. Print.

The date immediately following the title is the original publication date of the work.

Multivolume work

Churchill, Winston S. *A History of the English-Speaking Peoples*. 4 vols. New York: Dodd, 1956–58. Print.

Churchill, Winston S. *The Great Democracies*. New York: Dodd, 1957. Print. Vol. 4 of *A History of the English-Speaking Peoples*. 4 vols. 1956–58.

Use the first method when you cite the whole work; use the second method when you cite one individually titled volume of the work.

Article in familiar reference work

"Mau Mau." *The New Encyclopaedia Britannica*. 15th ed. 2002. Print.

Article in less familiar reference work

Ling, Trevor O. "Buddhism in Burma." *Dictionary of Comparative Religion*. Ed. S. G. F. Brandon. New York: Scribner's, 1970. Print.

Translation

De Beauvoir, Simone. *The Second Sex*. 1949. Trans. H. M. Parshley. New York: Bantam, 1961. Print.

Corporate author (a commission, committee, or other group)

American Red Cross. *Standard First Aid*. St. Louis: Mosby Lifeline, 1993. Print.

No author listed

The New Yorker Cartoon Album: 1975–1985. New York: Penguin, 1987. Print.

Edited Anthologies

An edited anthology looks like a regular book but has an editor rather than an author, and the contents are separate articles written by individual scholars. Anthologies might also be collections of short stories, poems, artwork, cartoons, or other kinds of documents. When you refer to the whole book, you cite the editor. When you refer to an individual work within the anthology, you cite the author of that work.

Citing the editor

O'Connell, David F., and Charles N. Alexander, eds. *Self Recovery: Treating Addictions Using Transcendental Meditation and Maharishi Ayur-Veda*. New York: Haworth, 1994. Print.

Citing an individual article

Royer, Ann. "The Role of the Transcendental Meditation Technique in Promoting Smoking Cessation: A Longitudinal Study." *Self Recovery: Treating Addictions Using Transcendental Meditation and Maharishi Ayur-Veda*. Ed. David F. O'Connell and Charles N. Alexander. New York: Haworth, 1994. 221–39. Print.

When you cite an individual article, give the inclusive page numbers for the article at the end of the citation, before the medium of publication.

Articles in Scholarly Journals Accessed in Print

The differences between a scholarly journal and a magazine are explained on page 582.

General Format for Scholarly Journals

Author. "Article Title." *Journal Title* volume number.issue number (year): page numbers. Print.

Note that all scholarly journal entries include both volume number and issue number, regardless of how the journal is paginated. For scholarly journal articles retrieved from an online database, see page 634.

One Author

Herrera-Sobek, Maria. "Border Aesthetics: The Politics of Mexican Immigration in Film and Art." *Western Humanities Review* 60.2 (2006): 60–71. Print.

Two or Three Authors

Pollay, Richard W., Jung S. Lee, and David Carter-Whitney. "Separate, but Not Equal: Racial Segmentation in Cigarette Advertising." *Journal of Advertising* 21.1 (1992): 45–57. Print.

Four or More Authors

Either list all the authors in the order in which they appear, or use "et al." (meaning "and others") to replace all but the first author.

Buck, Gayle A., et al. "Examining the Cognitive Processes Used by Adolescent Girls and Women Scientists in Identifying Science Role Models: A Feminist Approach." *Science Education* 92.4 (2008): 688–707. Print.

Articles in Magazines and Newspapers Accessed in Print

Magazine and newspaper articles are easy to cite. If no author is identified, begin the entry with the title or headline. Distinguish between news stories and editorials by putting the word "Editorial" after the title. If a magazine comes out weekly or biweekly, include the complete date ("27 Sept. 2007"). If it comes out monthly, then state the month only ("Sept. 2007").

General Format for Magazines and Newspapers

Author. "Article Title." *Magazine Title* [day] Month year: page numbers. Print.

Note: If the article continues in another part of the magazine or newspaper, add "+" to the number of the first page to indicate the nonsequential pages.

Magazine article with named author

Snyder, Rachel L. "A Daughter of Cambodia Remembers: Loung Ung's Journey." *Ms.* Aug.-Sept. 2001: 62–67. Print.

Magazine article without named author

"Daddy, Daddy." *New Republic* 30 July 2001: 2–13. Print.

Review of book, film, or performance

Schwarz, Benjamin. "A Bit of Bunting: A New History of the British Empire Elevates Expediency to Principle." Rev. of *Ornamentalism: How the British Saw Their Empire,* by David Cannadine. *Atlantic Monthly* Nov. 2001: 126–35. Print.

Kaufman, Stanley. "Polishing a Gem." Rev. of *The Blue Angel,* dir. Josef von Sternberg. *New Republic* 30 July 2001: 28–29. Print.

Lahr, John. "Nobody's Darling: Fascism and the Drama of Human Connection in *Ashes to Ashes*." Rev. of *Ashes to Ashes,* by Harold Pinter. The Roundabout Theater Co. Gramercy Theater, New York. *New Yorker* 22 Feb. 1999: 182–83. Print.

Follow this general model: Name of reviewer. "Title of Review." Rev. of *book, film, or play,* by Author/Playwright [for films, use name of director preceded by "dir."; for plays, add production data as in last example]. *Periodical Title* [day] Month year: inclusive pages. Print. Include company and theater information only for live performances.

Newspaper article

Henriques, Diana B. "Hero's Fall Teaches Wall Street a Lesson." *Seattle Times* 27 Sept. 1998: A1+. Print.

Page numbers in newspapers are typically indicated by a section letter or number as well as a page number. Include these designations exactly as they appear in the source. The "+" indicates that the article continues on one or more pages later in the newspaper.

Newspaper editorial

"Dr. Frankenstein on the Hill." Editorial. *New York Times* 18 May 2002: A22. Print.

Letter to the editor of a magazine or newspaper

Tomsovic, Kevin. Letter. *New Yorker* 13 July 1998: 7. Print.

Articles or Books from an Online Database

General Format for Material from Licensed Databases

Author. "Title." *Periodical Name* Print publication data including date and volume/issue numbers: pagination. *Database*. Web. Date of access.

Journal article retrieved from licensed database

Matsuba, M. Kyle. "Searching for Self and Relationships Online." *CyberPsychology & Behavior* 9.3 (2006): 275–84. *Academic Search Complete*. Web. 14 April 2007.

To see where each element in this citation was found, see Figure 23.1, which shows the online database screen from which the Matsuba article was accessed. For articles

FIGURE 23.1 Article Downloaded from an Online Licensed Database, with Elements Identified for an MLA-Style Citation

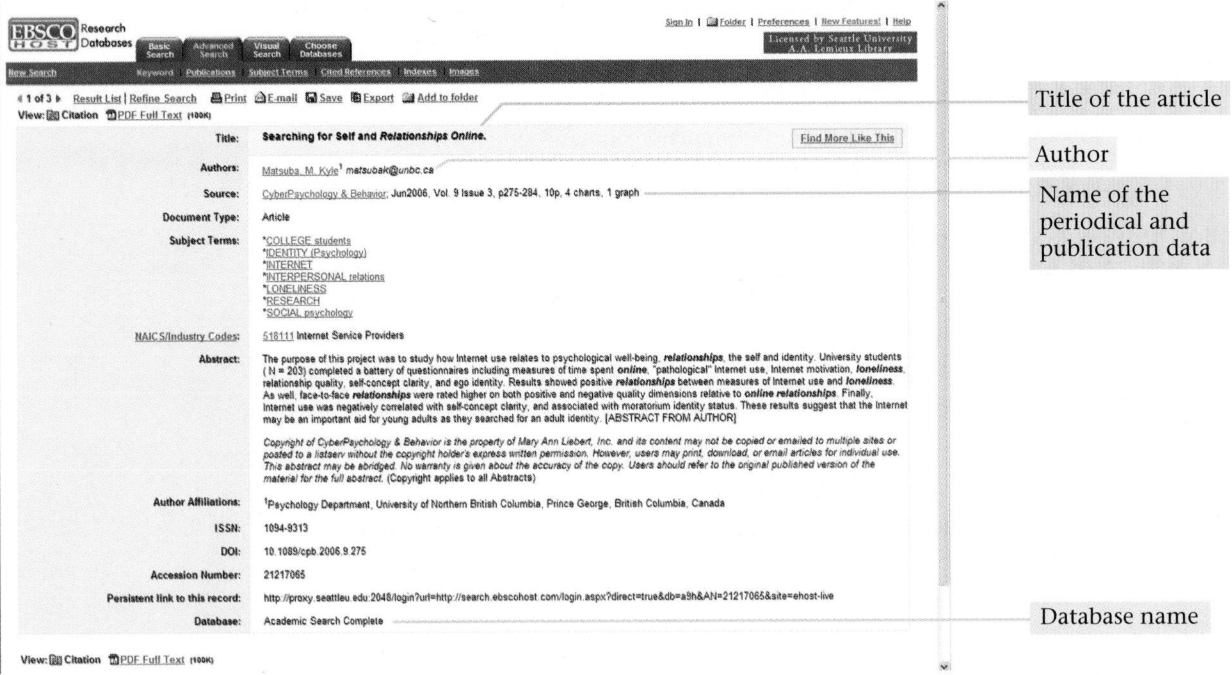

Matsuba, M. Kyle. "Searching for Self and Relationships Online." *CyberPsychology & Behavior* 9.3 (2006): 275–84. *Academic Search Complete*. Web. 14 Apr. 2007.

in databases, follow the formats for print magazines or scholarly journals, as relevant. When the database text provides only the starting page number of a multipage article, insert a plus sign after the number, before the period.

Broadcast transcript retrieved from licensed database

Conan, Neal. "Arab Media." *Talk of the Nation*. With Shibley Telhami. 4 May 2004. Transcript. *LexisNexis*. Web. 31 July 2004.

The label "Transcript" after the broadcast date indicates a text (not audio) version.

Reference material retrieved from licensed database

"Cicada." *Encyclopaedia Britannica Online*. 2004. *Encyclopaedia Britannica*. Web. 31 July 2004. <http://search.eb.com.libus.csd.mu.edu:80/eb/article?eu=84788>.

This example uses the MLA citation provided at the end of the Britannica article. The URL is unique to the database license for the academic library through which we accessed it; that is why it is included.

"Toni Morrison." *American Decades 1990–1999*. Ed. Tandy McConnell. Detroit: Gale Group, 2001. *Biography Resource Center*. Web. 14 Sept. 2003.

Papers and monographs from an information service

Information services such as ERIC (Educational Resources Information Center) or NTIS (National Technical Information Service) provide material to your library on microfiche or online, with indexes on CD-ROM or online. Much of the material from these services has not been published in major journals or magazines. Frequently they are typescripts of conference papers or other scholarly work disseminated on microfiche. Cite microfiche copies as you would cite print materials, using "Microform" as the medium of publication and then an accession number at the end.

Coll, Richard K., Sara Tofield, Brent Vyle, and Rachel Bolstad. "Free-Choice Learning at a Metropolitan Zoo." Annual Meeting of the National Association for Research in Science Teaching. Philadelphia. 23–26 Mar. 2003. Microform. ERIC ED 477832.

For online versions, follow the format for periodical articles from a licensed database, adding the database name after the accession number. Use "Web" as the medium of publication.

Coll, Richard K., Sara Tofield, Brent Vyle, and Rachel Bolstad. "Free-Choice Learning at a Metropolitan Zoo." Annual Meeting of the National Association for Research in Science Teaching. Philadelphia. 23–26 Mar. 2003. ERIC ED 477832. *Ovid*. Web. 26 July 2004.

E-book

Hanley, Wayne. *The Genesis of Napoleonic Propaganda, 1796–1799*. Columbia UP, 2002. *Gutenberg-e*. Web. 31 July 2004.

Machiavelli, Niccolo. *Prince*. 1513. *Bibliomania*. Web. 31 July 2004.

Information about the original print version, including a translator if relevant and available, should be provided.

Other Internet Sources

General Format for Web Sources

Author of the page or document, if available. "Title of page or document." *Title of the overall site, usually taken from the home page*. Sponsor of the site, date of publication online or last update of the site, if available. Web. Date you accessed the site. <URL of the specific document if it would be hard to locate without it>.

Barrett, John. "*MySpace* Is a Natural Monopoly." *ECommerce Times*. ECT News Network. 17 Jan. 2007. Web. 6 June 2007. < http://www.ecommercetimes.com/story/55185 .html>.

To see where each element of the Barrett citation comes from, see the Web article in Figure 23.2.

General Principles for Web Sources

As with print sources, the fundamental rule is to give your readers enough details to find the source you used. Since Web sites are frequently updated, altered, or dropped, it is important to provide the date that you accessed the material. In light of this variability, MLA advises that you print or download your Web and Internet sources. Here are a few additional useful principles for using the formats we provide:

- Always include the date on which you retrieved the material.
- Use "Web" as the medium of publication.
- Include a URL only if the item would be hard to locate without it.
- Provide the title of the overall Web site. This is usually found at the top of the site's home page. Also identify the name of the organization sponsoring the site (often available through an "About us" link) if it is different from the Web site title. For example, the Web site shown on page 637 is titled *ECommerce Times*, and the name of the sponsoring organization is ECT News Network; a citation for this site would include both names (the title italicized, the sponsor not italicized).
- If you wish to cite an entire Web site rather than a specific page or document, you need to provide only the title of the Web site, the sponsoring organization, the date of the latest update, the medium of publication (Web), and the date you accessed the Web site.

FIGURE 23.2 An Article Published on the Web, with Elements Identified for an MLA-Style Citation

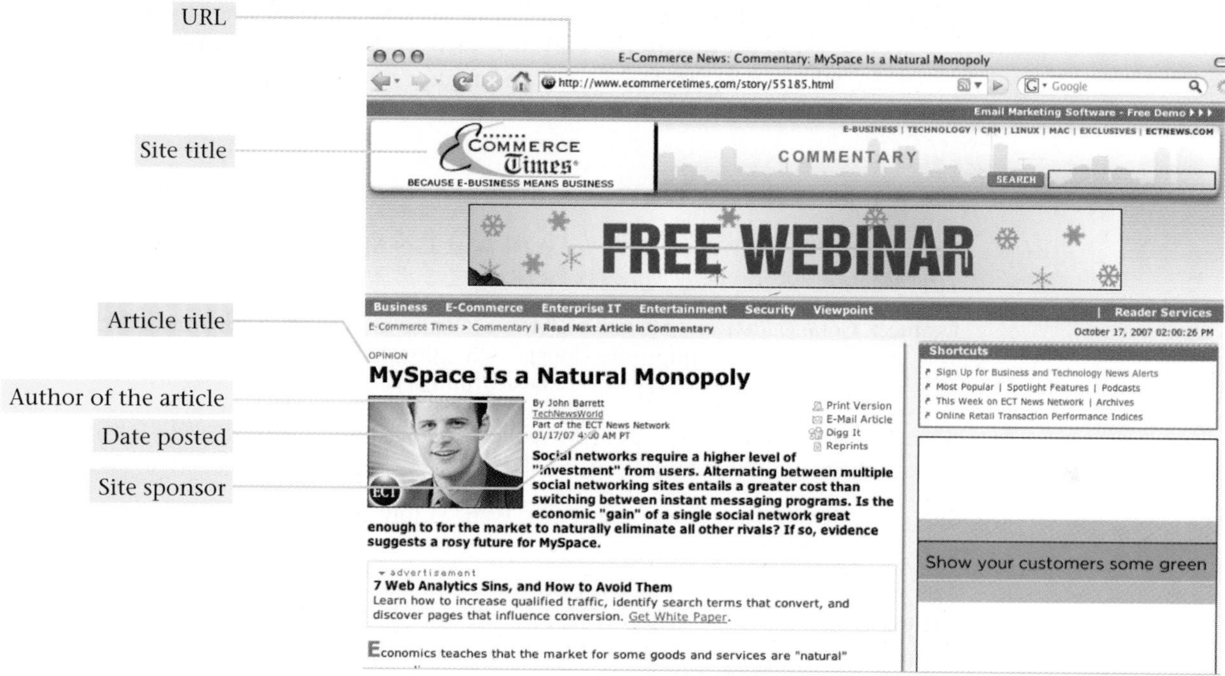

Barrett, John. "*MySpace* Is a Natural Monopoly." *ECommerce Times*. ECT News Network, 17 Jan. 2007. Web. 6 June 2007. <http://www.ecommercetimes.com/story/55185.html>.

- When you wish to cite a specific section or document within a Web site, you need to provide the section or document's title and, if available, its author. (As with print sources, if an author is not named, the citation should start with the title of the section or document.)
- When you are citing a specific document or section, include the date on which it was written, published, or posted to the site. If these facts are unavailable, use "n.d." for "no date."
- When citing a specific document, include its length in pages or paragraphs if these are indicated in the document itself. For example, .pdf documents show page numbers from paper publication, and some other documents indicate pagination from a print source. However, in most cases, you will not be able to provide the number of pages or paragraphs because they won't be specified. Do not include data about number of pages based on printouts because different computers and printers will process pages in different ways.
- Some sites provide model citations for use in a research paper. They may not be in MLA style, so be sure to convert them to MLA format.

- If you cannot locate the site sponsor, use "N.p." for "no publisher."
- If you do decide to include a URL in your citation, place it in angle brackets (<>) at the end of the entry after your access date, followed by a period. For accuracy, cut and paste the URL from the Web document into your citiation. If the URL is long and you need to break it over two lines, put the line break after a slash. Do not hyphenate a URL.

Entire Web site

BlogPulse. Intelliseek, n.d. Web. 24 July 2004.

Padgett, John B., ed. *William Faulkner on the Web*. U of Mississippi, 26 Mar. 2007. Web. 25 June 2007.

Agatucci, Cora. *Culture and Literature of Africa*. Course home page. Humanities Dept., Central Oregon Community College, Jan. 2007–May 2007. Web. 31 July 2007. <http://web.cocc.edu/cagatucci/classes/hum211/>.

African Studies Program. Home page. School of Advanced International Study, Johns Hopkins U., n.d. Web. 31 July 2007.

Sharpe, William F. Home page. May 2004. Web. 31 July 2004. <http://www.stanford.edu/~wfsharpe/>.

These examples show typical variations in the way to cite an entire Web site. The easiest case is the first, where you provide the site's title, its sponsoring organization, "Web," and your date of access. The second citation leads with the name of the site's editor and gives the date the site was last updated. The next two examples add the term "Home page" (not underlined) to signal the site's relation to a university course or program, and the final example refers to a personal home page that doesn't have a separate title.

Documents within a Web site

Marks, John. "Overview: Letter from the President." *Search for Common Ground*. Search for Common Ground, n.d. Web. 25 June 2007.

Gourlay, Alexander S. "Glossary." *The William Blake Archive*. Lib. of Cong., 2005. Web. 21 Jan. 2009.

"Ouch! Body Piercing." *Menstuff*. National Men's Resource Center, 1 Feb. 2001. Web. 17 July 2004. <http://www.menstuff.org/issues/byissue/fathersgeneral.html#bodypiercing>.

Bailey, Ronald. "The Impact of Science on Public Policy. Testimony before House Subcommittee on Energy and Mineral Resources. 108th Congress." *Reason Public Policy Institute*. Reason Public Policy Institute, 4 Feb. 2004. Web. 18 Sept. 2004.

Article from a newspaper or newswire site

Bounds, Amy. "Thinking Like Scientists." *Daily Camera* [Boulder]. Scripps Interactive Newspaper Group, 26 June 2007. Web. 26 June 2007.

"Great Lakes: Rwanda Backed Dissident Troops in DRC-UN Panel." *IRIN*. UN Office for the Coordination of Humanitarian Affairs, 21 July 2004. Web. 31 July 2004.

Broadcast transcript from a Web site

Woodruff, Judy, Richard Garnett, and Walter Dellinger. "Experts Analyze Supreme Court Free Speech Rulings." Transcript: background and discussion. *Online NewsHour*. PBS, 25 June 2007. Web. 26 June 2007.

Article from a scholarly e-journal

Welch, John R., and Ramon Riley. "Reclaiming Land and Spirit in the Western Apache Homeland." *American Indian Quarterly* 25.4 (2001): 5–14. Web. 19 Dec. 2001.

Blog posting

Wright, Jeremy. "*MySpace* Is the New Blogosphere." *Ensight.org*. N. pub., 21 Feb. 2006. Web. 6 June 2007. <http://www.ensight.org/archives/2006/02/21/myspace-is-the-new-blogosphere/>.

Follow the format for citing a Web site, using "N. pub." for "no publisher" if you cannot find the site sponsor. After the posting date, add "Web" and your access date. Include the URL if you think readers will have difficulty finding the posting. You can see where each element of the Wright blog citation comes from in Figure 23.3.

E-mail

Daffinrud, Sue. "Scoring Guide for Class Participation." Message to the author. 12 Dec. 2001. E-mail.

Use the subject line as the title of the e-mail. Use "E-mail" as the medium of publication.

FIGURE 23.3 A Blog Posting from the Web, with Elements Identified for an MLA-Style Citation

Wright, Jeremy. "*MySpace* Is the New Blogosphere." *Ensight.org*. N. pub., 21 Feb. 2006. Web. 6 June 2007. <http://www.ensight.org/archives/2006/02/21/myspace-is-the-new-blogosphere/>.

Miscellaneous Sources

Television or radio program

"Lie Like a Rug." *NYPD Blue*. Dir. Steven Bochco and David Milch. ABC. KOMO, Seattle, 6 Nov. 2001. Television.

For a program with episodes, begin with the episode name in quotation marks followed by the program name, italicized. If the program is part of a series (such as *Masterpiece Theatre*), add the series name, italicized, after the program title.

Film or video recording

Shakespeare in Love. Dir. John Madden. Perf. Joseph Fiennes and Gwyneth Paltrow. Screenplay by Marc Norman and Tom Stoppard. Universal Miramax, 1998. Film.

A minimal citation begins with the name of the film, italicized, and includes the name of the film company or the distributor and distribution date. Most citations also include the name of the director and may include the names of major performers and writers.

Shakespeare in Love. Dir. John Madden. Perf. Joseph Fiennes and Gwyneth Paltrow. Screenplay by Marc Norman and Tom Stoppard. Universal Miramax, 1998. Videocassette.

Cite the original film data. Then cite the recording medium (Videocassette, Laser disc, or DVD) last.

Podcast

Grammar Girl. "Ellipses." *Grammar Girl's Quick and Dirty Tips for Better Writing*. QD Now, 31 May 2007. Web. 6 June 2007.

Sound recording

Dylan, Bob. "Rainy Day Woman." *Bob Dylan MTV Unplugged*. Columbia, 1995. LP.

Begin the entry with what your paper emphasizes—for example, the artist's, composer's, or conductor's name—and adjust the elements accordingly. List the medium—CD, LP, Audiocassette—last.

Cartoon or advertisement

Trudeau, Garry. "Doonesbury." Comic strip. *Seattle Times* 19 Nov. 2001: B4. Print.

Banana Republic. Advertisement. *Details* Oct. 2001: 37. Print.

Interview

Castellucci, Marion. Personal interview. 7 Oct. 2007.

Lecture, speech, or conference presentation

Sharples, Mike. "Authors of the Future." Conference of European Teachers of Academic Writing. U of Groningen. Groningen, Neth. 20 June 2001. Lecture.

Government publications

Government publications are often difficult to cite because there are so many varieties. In general, follow these guidelines:

- Usually cite as author the government agency that produced the document. Begin with the highest level and then branch down to the specific agency:

  United States. Dept. of Justice. FBI.

  Idaho. Dept. of Motor Vehicles.

- Follow this with the title of the document, italicized.
- If a specific person is clearly identified as the author, you may begin the citation with that person's name, or you may list the author (preceded by the word "By") after the title of the document.

- Follow standard procedures for citing publication information for print sources or Web sources.

  United States. Dept. of Justice. FBI. *The School Shooter: A Threat Assessment Perspective*. By Mary Ellen O'Toole. 2000. Web. 16 Aug. 2001.

The in-text citation would be: (United States). If you have more than one U.S. government document, continue to narrow down the in-text citation: (United States. Dept. of Justice. FBI. *School Shooter*). Had this document been published in print rather than online, you would list the standard publishing information found on the title page. Typically the press would be the GPO (Government Printing Office).

James Gardiner (student), "Why *Facebook* Might Not Be Good for You" (MLA-Style Research Paper)

As an illustration of a student research paper written in MLA style, we present James Gardiner's paper on online social networks. James's process in producing this paper has been discussed in various places throughout the text.

Gardiner 1

Include your last name and page number on each page.

James Gardiner

Professor Johnson

Writing Seminar: Inquiry and Argument

15 May 2007

Why *Facebook* Might Not Be Good For You:

Some Dangers of Online Social Networks

Center title.

Walk into any computer lab located at any college campus across the country and you'll see dozens of students logged onto an online social network (OSN). In the last few years, the use of these networks has skyrocketed among Internet users, especially young adults. These new virtual communities are significantly influencing the way young people communicate and interact with one another. A report titled "E-Expectations: The Class of 2007" went so far as to label upcoming college freshmen "the Social-Networking Generation" (qtd. in Joly).

Indent paragraphs 5 spaces or 1/2inch.

Double-space all text.

In late 2006, the Pew Internet Project, a nonpartisan, nonprofit research group that examines the social impact of the Internet, reported that 55 percent of online teens have created a personal profile on OSNs and that 48 percent of teens visit social networking Web sites daily, with 22 percent visiting several times a day (Lenhart and Madden 2). The two most popular OSNs are *MySpace* and *Facebook*. *MySpace* is a general networking site that allows anyone to join, develop a profile, and display personal information. In less than four years of existence, *MySpace* has exploded to become the third most visited Web site on the Internet behind only *Google* and *Yahoo* ("Top Sites") with more than 100 million members (Joly). *Facebook* is geared more toward college students (until recently it required that a person attend a university to join the network) and is the number one site accessed by 18- to 24-year-olds. According to research studies cited in an article in the *Toronto Star*, 90 percent of all undergraduates log on to *Facebook* and 60 percent log on daily (George-Cosh W1). *Facebook*

Use 1-inch margins.

Italicize book and periodical titles and Web site names.

has also experienced unprecedented growth in its relatively short existence and now ranks as the seventh most visited site on the Internet ("Top Sites") and has a member base of more than 19 million (Joly).

With the use of OSNs increasing among young people, the term "Facebook trance" has emerged to describe a person who loses track of all time and stares at the screen for hours (Copeland). While "Facebook trance" might describe only an occasional and therefore harmless phenomenon, it gives rise to important questions: What are the possible negative consequences of OSNs? What should youthful users be watchful for and guard against? The purpose of this paper is to identify the possible harms of OSNs. I will suggest that overuse of OSNs can be a contributing factor to a decline in grades as well as to other problems such as a superficial view of relationships, an increase in narcissism, and possible future embarrassment.

I don't mean to deny that OSNs have positive consequences for young people. For one thing, they provide a "virtual hangout" that acts as a convenient and cost-effective way to stay in close contact with friends and family. According to the Pew survey, 91 percent of users use OSNs to keep in touch with their regularly seen friends, while 82 percent use the sites to stay in touch with distant friends (Lenhart and Madden). OSNs let young people regularly view their friends' profiles, leave short messages or comments, and share personal information. OSN researcher Danah Boyd also claims that these sites give young people a platform on which to experiment with identities, voice their opinions, and practice how they present themselves through personal data, pictures, and music placed in their profiles (Bowley). OSNs also assist them in learning more about people they've met offline. Used as an investigative tool, OSNs offer quick ways to get additional background information on someone. For example, a student could use an OSN to decide whom to partner with for a class project, to learn more about a new roommate, or to find

Gardiner 3

out more about someone he or she just met at a party, all by browsing classmates' profiles.

Despite these benefits, OSNs have a downside. One potential harm is that OSNs could have a negative effect on grades. One study shows a direct connection between the amount of time spent on the networks and declining grades in school. A college newspaper article entitled "Research Links *MySpace* Use to Drop in Grades" reports a survey of high school students conducted by Fresno State University professor Tamyra Pierce. Pierce found that students with *MySpace* accounts were significantly more likely than students without *MySpace* accounts to report a decline in grades since the previous year. According to Pierce, "We can't know for sure that *MySpace* caused the lower grades, but when compared to other after-school activities (work, sports, video games, etc.), only *MySpace* showed significance" (qtd. in "Research Links"). Pierce's research also revealed that 42 percent of polled students said they often had *MySpace* open while doing homework, and 34 percent stated that they would delay homework to spend time on social networking sites. Pierce adds that 59 percent of students reported spending "between 30 minutes and six hours daily on *MySpace*." Such heavy usage significantly takes time away from school work, extracurricular activities, and sleep. Although this specific study focused on high school students, it would be safe to assume that the results would be generally similar for college students. In fact, the results of the Fresno State study were reported in other college newspapers (Scrabis; Jimenez); the writers for these college newspapers usually included anecdotes from their own campuses about college students obsessed with OSNs. One Penn State student said of *MySpace*, "I keep getting rid of it and then getting it back again because I'm addicted. It's like cocaine" (qtd. in Scrabis).

Use quotation marks for article titles.

Use "qtd. in" for an author quoted in another source.

Another potential problem with OSNs is their tendency to promote superficial or unsatisfying relationships. According to Chou, Condron, and Belland, for some users "over-dependence on online relationships may result in significant problems with real-life interpersonal and occupational functioning" (381). When logged on to the network, students may believe that they are "in touch" with people, when actually they are physically alone with their computers. In a controversial 1998 article cited by Matsuba, Kraut and his colleagues suggested that extensive Internet use "was associated with declines in participants' communication with family members in the household, declines in the size of their social circle, and increases in their depression and loneliness" (qtd. in Matsuba 275). Matsuba conducted an extensive study to test Kraut's conclusions. Matsuba found that persons who scored high on measures of loneliness spent more time on the Internet than persons who scored low on the loneliness measures. In another facet of his study, Matsuba found that for persons who established online friendships, these friendships did not seem "as rich and diverse in quality compared to face-to-face friendships" (283). Matsuba concludes that while online communication can be used to enhance relationships, it can become a problem when it begins to replace offline interaction. He found that face-to-face friendships scored higher for both positive and negative aspects of relationships than did online friendships. He then speculates, "While it is possible that the internet is helping [lonely] people in their search, the possibility remains that the internet is hindering them in facing life in the 'real' world and thus preventing them from developing an adult identity" (283).

Matsuba's finding that face-to-face friendships are more "rich and diverse in quality" than online friendships has led me to speculate that a possible problem with OSNs is the complete lack of nonverbal communication exchanged between users. According to communications professor Julia T. Woods, "Scholars estimate that nonverbal behaviors account for 65 percent to 93 percent of the total meaning of communication" (132). Since the people interacting on OSNs are unable to view each other, they are unable to gauge the other's subtle body language, facial expressions, and voice tones that are such

Gardiner 5

vital ingredients of effective communication. Part of achieving the "adult identity" called for by Matsuba is learning to communicate nonverbally as well as verbally in an environment requiring real contact.

For me, a particularly interesting yet subtle danger of OSNs is their contribution to a rise in narcissism. In an article with the subtitle "Study Says Many Students Are Narcissists," journalist E. Hoover reports on the unpublished research of Jean M. Twenge, a psychology professor at San Diego State University, who says that new technology such as OSNs have "stoked the self-loving tendencies of modern students" (qtd. in Hoover A41). Twenge's recent research shows that college kids today are more narcissistic than college kids were in the 1980s; she labels the current generation of youth as "the most narcissistic in recent history" (Hoover). According to Hoover, Twenge defines narcissism as "excessive vanity and a sense of entitlement." Narcissists, Hoover reports, "tend to lack empathy for others, behave aggressively when insulted, and ignore the needs of those around them."

According to Twenge, narcissism finds expression on OSNs in the way that young people on *MySpace* and *Facebook* compete with each other to be heard. In another article reporting Twenge's research, Melissa Ludwig states that OSNs have "gone beyond touching base with friends to an arena where people vie for the most digital friends, the best videos, the coolest sites, and the biggest audience" (A15). She then quotes Twenge: "Now it all becomes a competition, seeking attention and seeking status rather than a true connection between people, or a meaningful connection." The work of Twenge and others suggests that the popularity of OSNs is partly the result of young people's finding an online way to express their narcissistic tendencies. The sites may contribute to self-expression more than to connection and friendship.

A final danger of OSNs is that persons will place on their sites material that they will later regret. Young people tend to think that their audiences are only their

Gardiner 6

like-minded friends and classmates. They often don't imagine their professors, their potential employers, or even their parents reading their sites. One journalist describes a *MySpace* profile in which a college student has posted photos of herself in "a skin-tight black leather Catwoman costume, two triangles of vinyl struggling to cover her silicone-enhanced breasts" (Ludwig A15). Ludwig continues:

Indent longer quotations 10 spaces or 1 inch.

Use ellipsis to show omitted words.

Use brackets when inserting explanatory words in quotation.

Cite page number after period.

> Much of the stuff floating around in cyberspace is tame, mundane even. But there also is plenty that's racy, embarrassing or squeamishly intimate. Bad or good, Generation Next is living out loud and doing it online, before a global audience, in a medium where digital archives may linger for a long, long time. . . . [Generation Nexters] still are too young to fully grasp the permanence of their online actions, and the possible consequences down the road. (A15)

One indication of this danger has already surfaced in the case of some sports teams. The University of Minnesota Duluth recently barred all athletes from creating profiles on *MySpace*, *Facebook*, and similar sites, a policy that, according to journalist Chao Xiong, aims to shield students and the school from bad press that might occur from the posting of inappropriate material. Xiong reports that athletic departments across the country are considering similar bans. One coach at the UM-Duluth campus said, "It was amazing to me how revealing people are with their lives on the Internet" (qtd. in Xiong 1A). (This coach had established her own *Facebook* profile in order to police the activities of her team members.) Xiong reports that across the country athletes have embarrassed their programs by posting pictures of themselves drinking blindfolded at parties or making disparaging comments about coaches or teammates. It is unclear whether coaches have the legal right to forbid their team members to place profiles on OSNs (some students are claiming violation of free speech rights). However, the fact that athletic programs are concerned about the impact of these

Gardiner 7

social networks shows the potential negative consequence of posting embarrassing material on OSNs.

Although I don't support the banning of *Facebook* or *MySpace* profiles for athletes or other students, I do think that young people should be aware of some of the problems associated with them. Two of the problems I have noted here—decline in grades and narcissistic competition for the coolest sites—could be avoided by students' simply limiting their time online. Knowing that OSNs can promote a superficial view of friendships might encourage people to use OSNs to stay in touch face-to-face with friends rather than try to find online substitutes for real friendships. Finally, young people should be aware that the materials they post on their profiles might one day come back to haunt them. To gain the maximum benefits of online social networks and avoid the pitfalls associated with them, my advice to today's students would be to use them as an advanced e-mail-type communication tool rather than as a place to loiter and waste valuable hours that they will never get back.

MLA Style

Start Works Cited list on a new page.

Center heading.

List sources alphabetically.

Use day-month-year format for dates.

Italicize database names.

Italicize periodical titles.

Use quotation marks for article titles.

Gardiner 8

Works Cited

Bowley, Graham. "The High Priestess of Internet Friendship." *Financial Times Weekend Magazine* 27 Oct. 2006. *LexisNexis Academic*. Web. 22 Feb. 2007.

Chou, Chien, Linda Condron, and John C. Belland. "A Review of the Research on Internet Addiction." *Educational Psychology Review* 17.4 (2005): 363-89. *Academic Search Complete*. Web. 22 Feb. 2007.

Copeland, Libby. "Click Clique: *Facebook*'s Online College Community." *Washingtonpost.com*. Washington Post, 28 Dec. 2004. Web. 24 Feb. 2007.

George-Cosh, David. "Social Net: Thousands of Local Students Build Friendships on *Facebook*." *TheStar.com*. Toronto Star, 20 Jan. 2007. Web. 15 Apr. 2007.

Hoover, E. "Here's You Looking at You, Kid: Study Says Many Students Are Narcissists." *Chronicle of Higher Education* 53.29 (9 Mar. 2007): A41. *Academic Search Complete*. Web. 14 Apr. 2007.

Jimenez, Eddie. "*MySpace* Adds to Overload for Teens." *Fresno Bee* 9 Mar. 2007. *Newspaper Source*. Web. 14 Apr. 2007.

Joly, Karine. "*Facebook*, *MySpace*, and Co." *University Business*. Professional Media Group, Apr. 2007. Web. 5 May 2007.

Lenhart, Amanda, and Mary Madden. "Social Networking Websites and Teens: An Overview." *Pew Internet & American Life Project*. Pew Research Center, 3 Jan. 2007. Web. 19 Feb. 2007.

Ludwig, Melissa. "LOOK@ME: Generation Next Is Living Out Loud and Online." *MySanAntonio.com*. San Antonio Express News, 15 Mar. 2007. Web. 15 Apr. 2007.

Matsuba, M. Kyle. "Searching for Self and Relationships Online." *CyberPsychology & Behavior* 9.3 (2006): 275-84. *Academic Search Complete*. Web. 14 Apr. 2007.

Gardiner 9

"Research Links *MySpace* Use to Drop in Grades." *FresnoStateNews.com*. California State U, 9 Mar. 2007. Web. 2 May 2007.

Scrabis, J. "*MySpace* Usage May Lower Grades in Both High School, College Students." *Daily Collegian.* Pennsylvania State U, 23 Mar. 2007. Web. 15 Apr. 2007.

"Top Sites for United States." *alexia.com*. N.p., n.d. Web. 2 May 2007. <http://www.alexia.com/site/ds/ top_sites?cc=US&ts_mode=country&lang=none>.

Woods, Julia T. *Interpersonal Communication: Everyday Encounters*. 5th ed. New York: Wadsworth, 2007. Print.

Xiong, Chao. "Not Their Space." *Minneapolis Star Tribune* 16 Apr. 2007. *LexisNexis*. Web. 2 May 2007.

Put URLs in angle brackets.

Italicize book titles.

Check that everything cited in paper is in Works Cited list.

SKILL 33 Cite and document sources using APA style.

In many respects, the APA style and the MLA style are similar and the basic logic is the same. In the APA system, the list where readers can find full bibliographic information is titled "References"; as in MLA format, it includes only the sources cited in the body of the paper. Pay careful attention to punctuation and format details in the models we present in this section. The distinguishing features of APA citation style are highlighted in the following list:

For an example of a student paper in APA style, see the report by Campbell et al. on pp. 274–281.

- APA style emphasizes the dates of books and articles and de-emphasizes the names of authors. Therefore the date of publication appears in parenthetical citations and is the second item mentioned in each entry in the References list.
- Only published or retrievable documents are included in the References list. Personal correspondence, e-mail messages, interviews, and lectures or speeches are referenced only through in-text citations.
- APA style uses fewer abbreviations and spells out the complete names of university presses. It uses an ampersand (&) instead of the word *and* for items in a series in both the References list and in-text citations.
- APA style capitalizes only the first word of titles and subtitles of books and articles. It doesn't place titles of articles in quotation marks.
- APA style uses only an initial for authors' or editors' first names in citations.
- APA style calls for every page of a periodical article to be listed in a reference, even when the pages are not continuous.
- Information about electronic sources such as Web documents and online database articles appears at the end of a citation. If an article or other document has been assigned a Digital Object Identifier (DOI), include the DOI at the end.
- If the Web document or article has no DOI, then cite the publication's home page URL. (If you found the article through a database like EBSCO's Academic Search Premier, do not cite the database or its URL since readers may find the article by searching elsewhere.) If you need to break a URL at the end of a line, do not use a hyphen. Instead, break it *before* a punctuation mark or *after* http://.
- For electronic sources, retrieval dates are necessary only if the material is likely to be changed or updated. Thus no retrival dates are needed for journal articles or books.
- For electronic documents without page numbers, APA suggests citing material by heading labels if they are available, and permits the writer to count paragraphs within a section. A parenthetical citation might then read: (Elrod, 2005, Introduction section, para. 7).

APA Formatting for In-Text Citations

When you make an in-text citation in APA style, you place inside the parentheses the author's last name and the year of the source as well as the page number if a particular passage or table is cited. The elements in the citation are separated by commas, and a "p." or "pp." precedes the page number(s). If a source has more than one author, use an ampersand (&) to join their names. When the author is mentioned in an attributive tag, include only the date (and page if applicable) in the parenthetical citation. The following examples show parenthetical documentation with and without attributive tags according to APA style:

> The Spanish tried to reduce the status of Filipina women who had been able to do business, get divorced, and sometimes become village chiefs (Karnow, 1989, p. 41).
>
> According to Karnow (1989), the Spanish tried to reduce the status of Filipina women who had been able to do business, get divorced, and sometimes become village chiefs (p. 41).

Cite from an Indirect Source

Ideally, if you want to use a quotation or data cited by one of your sources, you should track down the original source. When this isn't possible, APA style calls for using the phrase "as cited in" within the parenthetical reference. Only the indirect source would appear in the list of references. Here is an example:

> Morrison's data from the 1980s provides multiple examples of the phenomenon (as cited in Stephanbach, 2004, p. 828).

Document Sources in a References List

The APA References list at the end of a paper presents entries alphabetically in a hanging indentation format like that of MLA style. A typical entry would look like this:

Smith, R. (1995). *Body image in Western cultures, 1750–present.* London, England: Bonanza Press.

Two or More Listings for One Author

If you cite more than one item for an author, repeat the author's name each time and arrange the items in chronological order, beginning with the earliest. In cases where two works by an author appeared in the same year, arrange them in the list alphabetically by title, and then add a lowercase "a" or "b" (etc.) after the date so that you can distinguish between them in the in-text citations. As illustration, the following parenthetical citations refer to the hypothetical book and article cited in the sample entries that follow them:

> (Smith, 1999a)
> (Smith, 1999b)

Smith, R. (1999a). *Body image in non-Western cultures, 1750–present.* London, England: Bonanza Press.

Smith, R. (1999b). Eating disorders reconsidered. *Journal of Appetite Studies, 45*, 295–300.

APA Citation Models

Books

One author

Brumberg, J. J. (1997). *The body project: An intimate history of American girls.* New York, NY: Vintage.

Two or more authors

Dombrowski, D. A., & Deltete, R. J. (2000). *A brief, liberal, Catholic defense of abortion.* Urbana: University of Illinois Press.

Belenky, M., Clinchy, B. M., Goldberger, N. R., & Tarule, J. M. (1986). *Women's ways of knowing: The development of self, voice, and mind.* New York, NY: Basic Books.

APA style uses "et al." only for books and journal articles with more than seven authors.

Second, later, or revised edition

Montagu, A. (1986). *Touching: The human significance of the skin* (3rd ed.). New York, NY: Perennial Press.

The number of the edition goes in parentheses. One could also say "Rev. ed." for "Revised edition."

Republished book (for example, a paperback published after the original hardback edition or a modern edition of an older work)

Hill, C. (1991). *The world turned upside down: Radical ideas during the English revolution.* London, England: Penguin. (Original work published 1972)

The in-text citation should read: (Hill, 1972/1991).

Wollstonecraft, M. (1995). *The vindication of the rights of woman, with strictures on political and moral subjects.* Rutland, VT: Tuttle. (Original work published 1792)

The in-text citation should read: (Wollstonecraft, 1792/1995).

Multivolume work

Churchill, W. S. (1956–1958). *A history of the English-speaking peoples* (Vols. 1–4). New York, NY: Dodd, Mead.

Citation for all the volumes together. The in-text citation should read: (Churchill, 1956–1958).

Churchill, W. S. (1957). *A history of the English-speaking peoples: Vol. 4. The great democracies.* New York, NY: Dodd, Mead.

Citation for a specific volume. The in-text citation should read: (Churchill, 1957).

Article in reference work

Ling, T. O. (1970). Buddhism in Burma. In S. G. F. Brandon (Ed.), *Dictionary of comparative religion.* New York, NY: Scribner's.

Translation

De Beauvoir, S. (1961). *The second sex* (H. M. Parshley, Trans.). New York, NY: Bantam Books. (Original work published 1949)

The in-text citation should read: (De Beauvoir, 1949/1961).

Corporate author (a commission, committee, or other group)

American Red Cross. (1993). *Standard first aid.* St. Louis, MO: Mosby Lifeline.

Anonymous author

The New Yorker cartoon album: 1975–1985. (1987). New York, NY: Penguin Books.

The in-text citation may be a shortened version of the title such as: (*New Yorker*, 1987).

Edited Anthologies

Citing the editor

O'Connell, D. F., & Alexander, C. N. (Eds.). (1994). *Self recovery: Treating addictions using transcendental meditation and Maharishi Ayur-Veda*. New York, NY: Haworth Press.

Citing an individual article

Royer, A. (1994). The role of the transcendental meditation technique in promoting smoking cessation: A longitudinal study. In D. F. O'Connell & C. N. Alexander (Eds.), *Self recovery: Treating addictions using transcendental meditation and Maharishi Ayur-Veda* (pp. 221–239). New York, NY: Haworth Press.

The pattern is as follows: Author of article. (Year of publication). Title of article. In Name of editor (Ed.), *Title of anthology* (pp. inclusive page numbers of article). Place of publication: Name of press.

Articles in Scholarly Journals Accessed in Print

Scholarly journal that numbers pages continuously

Barton, E. L. (1993). Evidentials, argumentation, and epistemological stance. *College English, 55*, 745–769.

The pattern is as follows: Author. (Year of publication). Article title. *Name of Journal, volume number*, inclusive page numbers. Note that the volume number is italicized along with the title of the journal.

Scholarly journal that restarts page numbering with each issue

Pollay, R. W., Lee, J. S., & Carter-Whitney, D. (1992). Separate, but not equal: Racial segmentation in cigarette advertising. *Journal of Advertising, 21*(1), 45–57.

The citation includes the issue number in parentheses as well as the volume number. Note that the issue number and the parentheses are *not* italicized.

Articles in Magazines and Newspapers Accessed in Print

Magazine article with named author

Snyder, R. L. (2001, August/September). A daughter of Cambodia remembers: Loung Ung's journey. *Ms., 12*, 62–67.

Hall, S. S. (2001, March 11). Prescription for profit. *New York Times Magazine*, 40–45, 59, 91–92, 100.

The pattern is as follows: Author. (Year, Month [Day]). Title of article. *Name of Magazine, volume number [if stated in magazine]*, inclusive pages. If page numbers are discontinuous, identify every page, separating numbers with a comma.

Magazine article without named author

Daddy, daddy. (2001, July 30). *New Republic, 225*, 12–13.

Review of book or film

Schwarz, B. (2001, November). A bit of bunting: A new history of the British empire elevates expediency to principle [Review of the book *Ornamentalism: How the British saw their empire*]. *Atlantic Monthly, 288*, 126–135.

Kaufman, S. (2001, July 30). Polishing a gem [Review of the motion picture *The blue angel*]. *New Republic, 225*, 28–29.

Newspaper article

Henriques, D. B. (1998, September 27). Hero's fall teaches Wall Street a lesson. *Seattle Times*, pp. A1, A24.

Newspaper editorial

Dr. Frankenstein on the hill [Editorial]. (2002, May 18). *The New York Times*, p. A22.

Letter to the editor of a magazine or newspaper

Tomsovic, K. (1998, July 13). Culture clash [Letter to the editor]. *The New Yorker*, p. 7.

Print Articles or Books Downloaded from a Database

Print article downloaded from licensed database (with DOI)

Berke, J. H., & Schneider, S. (2007). Nothingness and narcissism. *Mental Health, Religion & Culture, 10*(4), 335–351. doi: 10.1080/13694670600722452

Print article downloaded from licensed database (no DOI)

Scharrer, E., Daniel, K. D., Lin, K.-M., & Liu, Z. (2006). Working hard or hardly working? Gender, humor, and the performance of domestic chores in television commercials. *Mass Communication and Society, 9*(2), 215–238. Retrieved from http://tandf.co.uk/journals/HMCS

The article as it appears in the database is shown in Figure 23.4. Note that the database name and URL are not cited, since readers may find the article elsewhere. Instead, the periodical's home page URL is provided in the "Retrieved from" statement.

Papers and monographs from an information service

Information services such as ERIC (Educational Resources Information Center) or NTIS (National Technical Information Service) provide material to your library on microfiche or online, offering indexes on CD-ROM or online. Much of the material from these services has not been published in major journals or magazines. Frequently they are typescripts of conference papers or other scholarly work disseminated on microfiche.

Coll, R. K., Tofield, S., Vyle, B., & Bolstad, R. (2003, March). *Free-choice learning at a metropolitan zoo*. Paper presented at the annual meeting of the National Association for Research in Science Teaching, Philadelphia, PA. (ERIC Document Reproduction Service No. ED477832)

If you retrieve the document online, add a retrieval statement indicating the date retrieved and the URL.

FIGURE 23.4 A Print Article Downloaded from an Online Licensed Database, with Elements Identified for an APA-Style Citation

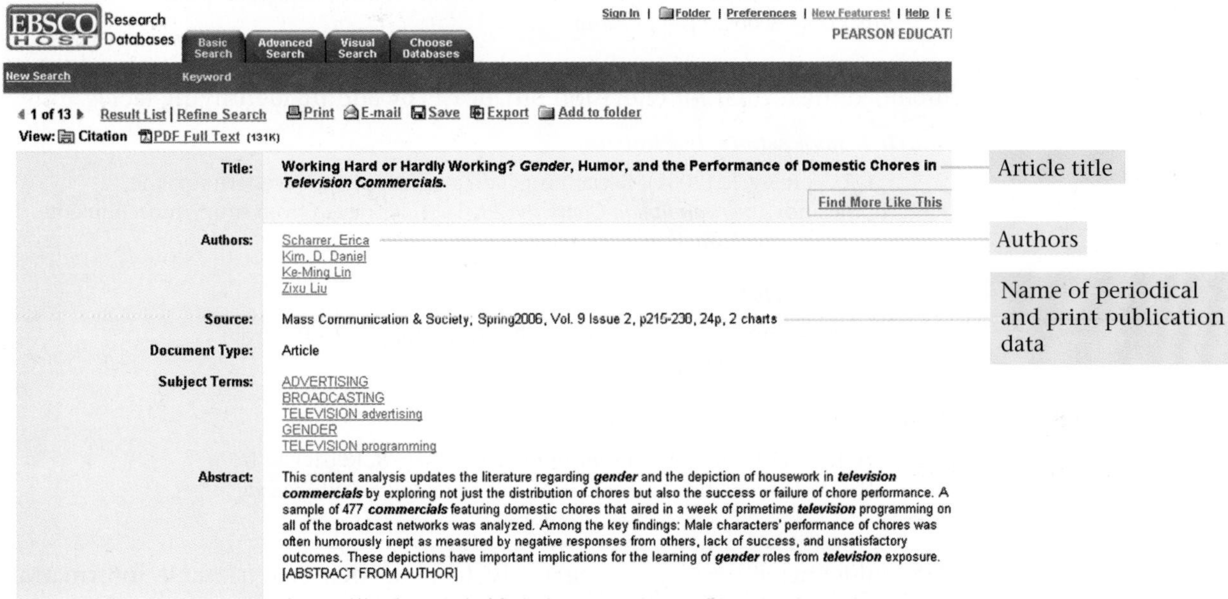

Scharrer, E., Daniel, K. D., Lin, K.-M., & Liu, Z. (2006). Working hard or hardly working? Gender, humor, and the performance of domestic chores in television commercials. *Mass Communication and Society, 9*(2), 215–238. Retrieved from http://www.tandf.co.uk/journals/HMCS

Web and Internet Sources

Documents within a Web site

Provide corporate authors when a document does not list an individual author. Use "n.d." if no publication date is provided.

Marks, J. (n.d.). *Overview: Letter from the president.* Retrieved June 25, 2007, from the Search for Common Ground Web site: http://www.sfcg.org/sfcg/sfcg_overview.html

United States Institute of Peace. (2000). *Advances in understanding international peacemaking.* Retrieved May 25, 2007, from http://www.usip.org/pubs/summaries /adv_intl.html

Article from a newspaper site

Bounds, A. (2007, June 26). Thinking like scientists. *Daily Camera* [Boulder]. Retrieved from http://www.dailycamera.com

Broadcast transcript from a Web site

Michels, S. (Correspondent), & Warner, M. (Anchor). (2004, July 28). The politics of 9/11 [Television transcript]. *News hour with Jim Lehrer.* Retrieved from http://www.pbs.org/newshour

Because the APA *Manual* doesn't have a model for broadcast transcripts, we modified the format for television broadcasts by adding identifying labels.

Article from a scholarly e-journal

Welch, J. R., & Riley, R. (2001). Reclaiming land and spirit in the western Apache homeland. *American Indian Quarterly, 25,* 5–14. Retrieved from http://muse.jhu.edu /journals/american_indian_quarterly

Reference material

Cicada. (2004). *Encyclopaedia Britannica.* Retrieved July 31, 2007, from http://www.britannica.com

E-book

Hoffman, F. W. (1981). *The literature of rock: 1954–1978.* Retrieved from http://www.netlibrary.com/ebook_info.asl?product_id=24355

E-mail, interviews, and personal correspondence

APA guidelines limit the References list to published or retrievable information. Cite personal correspondence in the body of your text, but not in the References list: "Daffinrud (personal communication, December 12, 2001) claims that. . . ."

Blog

CalEnergyGuy. (2004, July 27). Energy crisis impacts on the economy: Changes since 2001. [Web log post.] Retrieved from http://calenergy.blogspot.com

Miscellaneous Sources

Television program

Bochco, S., & Milch, D. (Directors). (2001, November 6). Lie like a rug [Television series episode]. In *NYPD blue.* New York, NY: American Broadcasting Company.

Podcast

Funke, E. (Host). (2007, June 26). [Audio podcast]. *ArtScene.* National Public Radio. Retrieved from http://www.npr.org

Film

Madden, J. (Director). (1998). *Shakespeare in love* [Motion picture]. United States: Universal Miramax.

Sound recording

Dwarf Music. (1966). Rainy day woman [Recorded by B. Dylan]. On *Bob Dylan MTV unplugged* [CD]. New York, NY: Columbia. (1995)

Follow this format: Writer of song or copyright holder. (Date of copyright). Title of song [Recorded by artist if different from writer]. On *Title of album* [Medium such as CD, record, or cassette]. Location: Record Label. (Date of album if different from date of song)

Unpublished paper presented at a meeting

Sharples, M. (2001, June 20). *Authors of the future*. Paper presented at the Conference of European Teachers of Academic Writing, Groningen, the Netherlands.

Government publications

O'Toole, M. (2000). *The school shooter: A threat assessment perspective*. Washington, DC: U.S. Federal Bureau of Investigation. Retrieved from http://www.fbi.gov/publications/school/school2.pdf

Student Example of an APA-Style Research Paper

An example of a paper in APA style is shown on pages 274–281.

PART 5

WRITING FOR ASSESSMENT

This advocacy ad, part of the ongoing campaign "If I Stay on the Rez" to raise money for tribal colleges, is sponsored by the American Indian College Fund. At the Web site www.collegefund.org, you can see the other campaign ads. Each ad spotlights a contemporary Native American man or woman against a striking landscape, briefly identifies the reservation and the tribal college, states a few persuasive facts and statistics about the success of these colleges, and provides contact information. Consider how these ads achieve the campaign's purpose "to shatter people's misconceptions about Indian people" (www.collegefund.org).

We refer to this ad in Chapter 16, page 455, in the discussion of proposals as visual arguments.

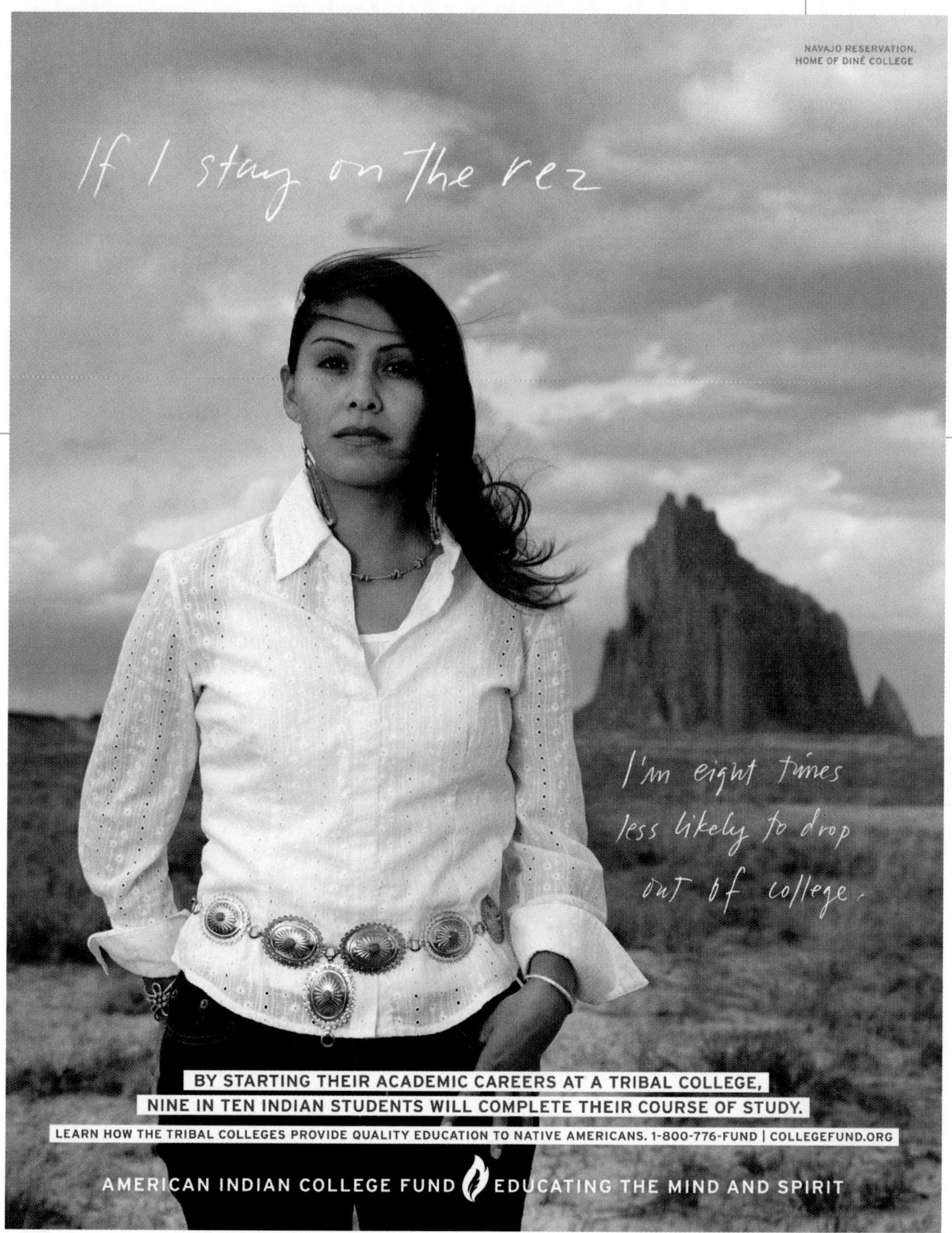
NAVAJO RESERVATION,
HOME OF DINÉ COLLEGE
If I stay on the rez
I'm eight times
less likely to drop
out of college.
BY STARTING THEIR ACADEMIC CAREERS AT A TRIBAL COLLEGE,
NINE IN TEN INDIAN STUDENTS WILL COMPLETE THEIR COURSE OF STUDY.
LEARN HOW THE TRIBAL COLLEGES PROVIDE QUALITY EDUCATION TO NATIVE AMERICANS. 1-800-776-FUND | COLLEGEFUND.ORG
AMERICAN INDIAN COLLEGE FUND
EDUCATING THE MIND AND SPIRIT

PART 5 WRITING FOR ASSESSMENT

Council of Writing Program Administrators Outcomes for First-Year Composition

CHAPTER 24 Essay Examinations: Writing Well under Pressure

RHETORICAL KNOWLEDGE	• Focus on a purpose • Respond appropriately to different kinds of rhetorical situations • Adopt appropriate voice, tone, and level of formality
CRITICAL THINKING, READING, AND WRITING	• Use writing and reading for inquiry, learning, thinking, and communicating

CHAPTER 25 Assembling a Portfolio and Writing a Reflective Essay

RHETORICAL KNOWLEDGE	• Focus on a purpose • Respond appropriately to different kinds of rhetorical situations
CRITICAL THINKING, READING, AND WRITING	• Understand the relationships among language, knowledge, and power
PROCESSES	• Learn to critique your own and others' work • Use a variety of technologies to address a range of audiences
COMPOSING IN ELECTRONIC ENVIRONMENTS	• Use electronic environments for drafting, reviewing, revising, editing, and sharing texts

CHAPTER 24

ESSAY EXAMINATIONS

Writing Well Under Pressure

I'm pretty good at writing research essays, but when I have to write under pressure, I freeze. Last time I took an essay test, I wrote two pages before I realized that I'd left out an important piece of my argument. By the time I had scratched out, made additions, and drawn arrows all over the page, my paper was such a mess that I couldn't decipher it. Needless to say, the instructor couldn't either.

—*Student A*

For me, the worst thing about exams is trying to figure out what the professor wants. The final in my European literature course was a perfect example: There was only one question. It started with a difficult-to-follow quotation from an author we hadn't studied, which we were supposed to apply to a whole slew of questions about novels we had read during the semester. The question went on for half a page (single-spaced!) and had at least five or six subsections. By the time I finished reading it, I didn't have a clue about where to start or how to cover so much ground in a single essay.

—*Student B*

As these students' comments indicate, taking essay exams, with the extra demands that exams place on writers, can be stressful and frustrating. When instructors give essay exams, they want to see how well students can restate, apply, and assess course material. Just as important, they want to see whether students can discuss in their own words what they have studied—whether they can participate in that discipline's discourse community. These twin demands make essay exams doubly challenging. Furthermore, not only must students master course material, but they must also write about it quickly and confidently.

Although you will rarely take exams after you leave college (unless you plan to attend graduate school), writing essay tests can help you develop skills relevant to many real-world situations. For example, in such fields as journalism, advertising, marketing, publishing, engineering, and teaching, you will need to compose documents on tight deadlines.

Even when you accept that it's important to learn how to write essay exams, you may wonder how you can possibly prepare for the kinds of exams you will face in all your college courses. These diverse courses will require that you adapt your exam essays to the course, instructor, and test question at hand. However, we can give you some useful guidelines and strategies that you can apply. This chapter shows you how to plan and write an essay exam and how to adapt to the unique requirements of in-class essay writing.

How Essay Exams Differ from Other Essays

Essay exams do share similarities with other assignments. Most of the instructions in this book apply to exam writing. For instance, you have learned how to respond to rhetorical context—audience, purpose, and genre—as you write an essay. Your audience for an essay exam is your instructor, so you need to ask yourself what your instructor values and wants. Does your instructor stress analysis of material or application of roles? Does your instructor encourage individual interpretations? Just as analyzing an audience helps you focus an out-of-class essay, so too can analyzing your instructor's expectations help you focus an exam response.

You also know the importance of knowing what you're talking about. Even the most brilliant writers will stumble on a test if they haven't bothered to attend class regularly, take notes, participate in class discussions, and keep up with the reading. Familiarity with the material lays the groundwork for a successful exam performance, just as thorough research and exploratory writing grounds a good paper.

However, not all the writing strategies you use for papers will serve you well in a test situation. Writing researcher Randall Popken, after reviewing more than two hundred sample exams in various disciplines, identified three skills unique to essay exam writing:

1. The ability to store, access, and translate appropriate knowledge into an organized essay
2. The ability to analyze quickly the specific requirements of an exam question and formulate a response to those requirements
3. The ability to deal with time pressure, test anxiety, and other logistical constraints of the exam situation

We examine each of these skills in the next section.

Preparing for an Exam: Learning Subject Matter

In an essay exam, you're on your own. You won't know beforehand which of the many pages of material you have studied in a class you'll be asked to synthesize and comment on. Although you may have studied hard and learned a great deal, you will have to display your knowledge in rapid, on-the-spot writing. Preparing for an exam involves finding efficient ways to organize, recall, and apply your knowledge so that you can easily construct an intelligent discussion on paper.

Identifying and Learning Main Ideas

No instructor will expect you to remember every single piece of information covered in class. Most instructors are happy if you can remember main ideas and theories, key terminology, and a few supporting examples. The best strategy when you study for an essay exam is to figure out what is most important and learn it first.

How do you determine the main ideas and key concepts? Sometimes they're obvious. Many professors outline their lectures on the board or distribute review sheets before each exam. If your professor does not provide explicit instructions, listen for a thesis statement, main points, and transitions in each lecture to determine the key ideas and relationships among them. For example,

> The *most important critics* of the welfare state are ...
>
> *Four developments* contributed to the reemergence of the English after the Norman invasion ...
>
> Hegel's dialectic was *most influenced by* Kant ...

Look for similar signals in your textbook and pay special attention to chapter summaries, subheadings, and highlighted terms. If the course involves a lot of discussion or if your professor prefers informal remarks to highly structured lectures, you may have to work harder to identify major points. But streamlining and organizing your knowledge in this way will keep you from feeling overwhelmed when you sit down to study.

Chapter 18, Skill 13, explains some of the main organizing moves writers use in the bodies of essays to clarify and develop their points.

Most instructors expect you to master more than the information they cover in class. Essay exams in humanities, social science, and fine arts courses often ask for an individual interpretation, argument, or critique. To prepare for such questions, practice talking back to course readings by developing your own positions on the viewpoints they express. If the professor has lectured on factors involved in mainstreaming schoolchildren with physical disabilities, look at your notes and try to define your own position on mainstreaming. If the textbook identifies salient features of Caravaggio's art, decide how you think his paintings compare to and differ from his contemporaries' work. Questioning texts and lectures in this way will help you personalize the material, expand your understanding, and take ownership of your education. Remember, though, that professors won't be impressed by purely subjective opinions; as you explore your views, search for evidence and arguments, not just from your own experience but the course as well, that you can use to support your ideas in the exam.

For specific strategies to help you understand and respond to reading material, review Chapter 6 and Chapter 13.

Applying Your Knowledge

In business, science, social science, and education courses, professors may ask you to apply a theory or method to a new situation. For example, they might ask you to show how "first in, last out" accounting might work in bookkeeping for a machine parts factory or how you might use psychodynamic concepts to analyze a hypothetical case study.

If you suspect that such a question might appear, use some study time to practice this kind of thinking. Brainstorm two or three current situations to which you could apply the theories or concepts you've been learning. Check local newspapers or browse the Web for ideas. Then freewrite for a few minutes on how you might organize an essay that puts the theory to work. For instance, if you've studied federal affirmative action law in a public administration course, you might ask the following questions: How has the recent decision by the U.S. Supreme Court in regard to the University of Michigan's affirmative action policies affected the use of race as a factor in college admissions? How might it apply to a local college trying to attract a diverse student body? You won't be able to predict exactly what will appear on the exam, but you can become skilled at transferring ideas into new settings.

Making a Study Plan

Once you've identified crucial subject matter, you need to develop a study plan. If you're a novice at studying for a major exam, try following some tried-and-true approaches.

- Review your instructor's previous exams. Don't be afraid to ask your instructor for general guidelines about the type, length, and format of questions he or she normally includes on tests.
- Generate your own practice questions and compose responses.
- Organize group study sessions with two to four classmates. Meet regularly to discuss readings, exchange practice questions, test each other informally, and critique each other's essays.

Avoid study techniques that are almost universally ineffective: Don't waste time trying to reread all the material or memorize passages word for word (unless the exam will require you to produce specific formulas or quotations). Don't set an unreasonable schedule. You can seldom learn the material adequately in one or two nights, and the anxiety produced by cramming can hurt your performance even more. Most important, don't stay up all night studying. Doing so can be worse than not studying at all, since sleep deprivation impairs your ability to recall and process information.

No matter how you decide to study, remember that the point of developing exam-preparation strategies isn't simply to do well on a single test, but to become comfortable with learning difficult, complex material and to acquire a level of intellectual confidence that will help you grow as a writer.

Analyzing Exam Questions

Whereas paper assignments typically ask you to address broad problems that can be solved in numerous possible ways, essay exams usually require much more narrowly focused responses. Essay exams feature well-defined problems with a very narrow range of right answers. They require you to recall a particular body of information and present it in a highly specific way. However, what your instructors are asking you to recall and how they want it presented will not always be clear to you. Exam questions often require interpretation.

Although the language of essay exams varies considerably across disciplines, professors typically draw on a set of conventional moves when they write exam prompts. Consider the following question from an undergraduate course in the history of the English language:

> Walt Whitman once wrote that English was not "an abstract construction of dictionary makers" but a language that had "its basis broad and low, close to the ground." Whitman reminds us that English is a richly expressive language because it comes from a variety of cultural sources. One of these is African-American culture. Write an essay discussing the major ways in which African-American culture and dialect have influenced the English language in the United States. Identify and illustrate at least three important influences: What were the historical circumstances? What important events and people were involved? What were the specific linguistic contributions?

This question presents an intimidating array of instructions, but it becomes manageable if you recognize some standard organizational features.

Understanding the Use of Outside Quotations

First, like many exam questions, this sample opens with a quotation from an author or work not covered in the course. Many students panic when they encounter such questions. "Whitman?! We didn't even study Whitman. What am I supposed to do now?" Don't worry. The primary function of such quotations is to encapsulate a general issue that the instructor wants you to address in your response. When you encounter an unfamiliar quotation, look carefully at the rest of the question for clues about what role the quotation should play in your essay. The point of the Whitman quotation is restated in the very next sentence—English is shaped by numerous cultural influences—and the function of the quotation is simply to reinforce that point. Because the rest of the question tells you specifically what kinds of cultural influences your response should address (African-American culture, three major linguistic contributions), you don't need to consider this quotation when you write your essay.

Sometimes professors will ask you to take a position on an unfamiliar quotation and support your argument with material covered in the course. Suppose that the question was, "What is your position on Whitman's view? Do you believe that English is enriched or corrupted by multicultural influences?" In this case the quotation is presented as the basis for a thesis statement, which you would then explain and support. A successful response might begin, "Whitman believes that multicultural influences make our language better, but this view is hopelessly naive for the following reasons ..." or "Whitman correctly argues that the contributions of different cultures enrich our language. Take these three examples. ..."

Recognizing Organizational Cues

The question itself can show you the best way to organize your response. Questions tend to begin with general themes that often suggest a thesis statement. Subsequent divisions tell you how to organize the essay into sections and in what order to introduce supporting points. For example, a successful response that follows the organization of our sample might be arranged as follows:

- A thesis stating that several contributions from African-American language and culture have enriched English
- Three supporting paragraphs, each discussing a different area of influence by
  1. summarizing historical circumstances
  2. noting important people and events
  3. providing one or two examples of linguistic contributions

Interpreting Key Terms

As do all exam questions, this one asks you to write about a specific body of information in a specific way. When you encounter a lengthy question such as this, first pick out the *noun phrases* that direct you to specific areas of knowledge: "African-American culture," "major influences on the English language in the United States," "historical circumstances," "important events and people," "linguistic contributions." Pay careful attention to words that modify these noun phrases. Does the question tell you how many influences to discuss? What kinds of examples to cite? Does the instructor include conjunctions, such as *or*, to give you a choice of topics, or does he or she use words such as *and* or *as well as* that require you to address all areas mentioned? Words such as *who, what, where*, and *why* also point to particular kinds of information.

After you've determined the specific areas you need to address, look for *directive verbs* that tell you what to do: *discuss, identify*, or *illustrate*, for example. These verbs define the horizons of your response. The strategies chart below defines some key directives that frequently appear in essay exams and provides sample questions for each. Meanings vary somewhat according to the course, the context of the question, and the professor's expectations, but you'll feel more confident if you have basic working definitions.

STRATEGIES for Responding to Common Essay-Question Verbs

Verbs	How to Respond	Example Questions
Analyze	Break an argument, concept, or approach into parts and examine the relations among them; discuss causes and effects; evaluate; or explain your interpretation. Look at the rest of the question to determine which strategies to pursue.	*Analyze* the various technical, acoustic, and aesthetic factors that might lead a musician to choose analog over digital recording for a live performance. Be sure to include the strengths and weaknesses of both methods in your discussion.

Verbs	How to Respond	Example Questions
Apply	Take a concept, formula, theory, or approach and adapt it to another situation.	Imagine that you've been hired to reengineer the operations of a major U.S. automaker. How might you *apply* the principles of Total Quality Management in your recommendations?
Argue	Take a position for or against an issue and give reasons and evidence to support that position.	*Argue* whether or not cloning should be pursued as a method of human reproduction. Be sure to account for the relationship between cloning and mitosis in your discussion.
Compare/ Contrast	Note the similarities (compare) or differences (contrast) between two or more objects or ideas.	*Compare* and *contrast* the leadership styles of Franklin Delano Roosevelt, John F. Kennedy, and Ronald Reagan, focusing on their uses of popular media and political rhetoric.
Construct	Assemble a model, diagram, or other organized presentation of your knowledge about a subject.	*Construct* a model of the writing process that illustrates the major stages writers go through when developing an idea into a finished text.
Critique	Analyze and evaluate an argument or idea, explaining both strengths and weaknesses.	Dinesh D'Souza's "Illiberal Education" sparked widespread controversy when it was published in 1991. Write an essay *critiquing* D'Souza's arguments against affirmative action, identifying both the strengths and weaknesses of his position. Use examples from the text, class discussion, and other class readings to illustrate your points.
Define	Provide a clear, concise, authoritative meaning for an object or idea. The response may include describing the object or idea, distinguishing it clearly from other objects or ideas, or providing one or more supporting examples.	How was "equality" *defined* by the Supreme Court in *Plessy v. Ferguson* (1896)? How did that definition influence subsequent educational policy in the United States?

(*continued*)

Verbs	How to Respond	Example Questions
Discuss	Comprehensively present and analyze important concepts, supported by examples or evidence. Cover several key points or examine the topic from several perspectives. Check the question for guidelines about what to include.	*Discuss* the controversy that surrounded Stanley Milgram's studies of authority and state your own position on the relevance and validity of the experiments.
Enumerate (or List)	List steps, components, or events pertaining to a larger phenomenon, perhaps briefly explaining and commenting on each item.	A two-year-old child falls from a swing on the playground and lies unconscious. As the head preschool teacher, *enumerate* the steps you would take from the time of the accident until the ambulance arrives.
Evaluate	Make a judgment about the worth of an object or idea, examining strengths and weaknesses.	*Evaluate* William Whyte's "Street Corner Society" as an ethnographic study. What are its methodological strengths and weaknesses? Do you believe the weaknesses make Whyte's research obsolete?
Explain	Clarify and state reasons to show how some object or idea relates to a more general topic.	*Explain* the relationship of centripetal force to mass and velocity and give an example to illustrate this relationship.
Identify	Describe some object or idea and explain its significance to a larger topic.	*Identify* the major phonetic characteristics of each of the following language groups of Africa, and provide illustrative examples: Koisan, Niger-Kordofanian, and Nilo-Saharan.
Illustrate	Give one or more examples, cases, or other concrete instances to clarify a general concept.	Define "monopoly," "public utility," and "competition," and give specific *illustrations* of each.
Prove	Produce reasons and evidence to establish that a position is logical, supportable, or factual.	Use your knowledge about the findings of the National Assessment of Educational Progress to *prove* that public schools either are or are not doing an adequate job of educating children to become productive U.S. citizens.

Verbs	How to Respond	Example Questions
Review	Briefly survey or summarize something.	*Review* the major differences between Socrates' conception of ethics and the ethical theories of his contemporaries in the fifth century B.C.E.
Summarize	Lay out the main points of a theory, argument, or event in a concise and organized manner.	*Summarize* Mill's definition of justice and explain how it differs from Kant's. Which definition comes closest to your own, and why?
Trace	Explain chronologically a series of events or the development of an idea.	Write an essay that *traces* the pathway of a nerve impulse through the nervous system, being sure to explain neuron structure, action potential, and the production and reception of neurotransmitters.

Our thanks to Michael C. Flanigan, who suggested some of the terms for this table, in "Processes of Essay Exams," manuscript. University of Oklahoma, 1991.

In some questions, directives are implied rather than stated directly. If a question asks, "Discuss the effects of Ronald Reagan's tax policies on the U.S. economy during the 1980s," you'll need to summarize what those policies were before you can assess their effects. Before you can take a position on an issue, you have to define what the controversy is about. In general, when you answer any question, you should include sufficient background information about the topic to convince your instructor that you're making an informed argument, whether or not the question specifically asks for background information.

FOR WRITING AND DISCUSSION

Analyze Essay Questions

This exercise will hone your ability to analyze essay questions. The following student essay, which received an A, was a response to one of the four closely related questions that follow it. The essay may address issues raised in two or more questions, but it is an A response to only one. Your task is to figure out which question the essay answers best.

Decide on your answer independently; then compare answers in small groups. Try to come to a consensus, referring to the strategies chart on pages

(*continued*)

668–671 to help resolve disagreements. As you discuss your responses, note any successful strategies that you may be able to adapt to your own writing.

FROM A BRITISH LITERATURE COURSE

Gulliver's Travels and *Frankenstein* portray characters whose adventures bring them face to face with the innate weaknesses and limitations of humankind. Victor Frankenstein and Lemuel Gulliver find out during their travels that humans are limited in reasoning capacity and easily corruptible, traits that cause even their best-intentioned projects to go awry. These characters reflect the critical view that Swift and Shelley take of human nature. Both believe that humans have a "dark side" that leads to disastrous effects.

In *Gulliver's Travels*, Gulliver's sea voyages expose him to the best and worst aspects of human civilization. Through Gulliver's eyes, readers come to share Swift's perception that no matter how good people's original intentions, their innate selfishness corrupts everything they attempt. All the societies Gulliver visits give evidence of this. For example, Lilliput has a system of laws once grounded on justice and morality, but that slowly were perverted by greedy politicians into petty applications. Even the most advanced society, Brobdingnag, has to maintain a militia even though the country is currently peaceful—since they acknowledge that because humans are basically warlike, peace can't last forever. By showing examples of varied cultures with common faults, Swift demonstrates what he believes to be innate human weaknesses. He seems to believe that no matter how much progress we make, human societies will eventually fall back into the same old traps.

Victor Frankenstein also experiences human limitations, this time in his own personality, as he pushes to gain knowledge beyond what any human has ever possessed. When he first begins his experiments to manufacture life in the laboratory, his goals are noble—to expand scientific knowledge and to help people. As he continues, he becomes more concerned with the power that his discovery will bring him. He desires to be a "god to a new race of men." Later, when the creature he creates wreaks havoc, Frankenstein's pride and selfishness keep him from confessing and preventing further deaths. Like the societies Gulliver observed, Frankenstein is a clear example of how human frailties corrupt potentially good projects.

Even though Swift and Shelley wrote during two different historical periods, they share a critical view of human nature. However, several unambiguously good characters in *Frankenstein*—including the old man and his daughter—suggest that Shelley feels more optimism that people are capable of overcoming their weaknesses, while Swift seems adamant that humans will eternally backslide into greed and violence. Basically, however, both works demonstrate vividly to readers the ever present flaws that prevent people and their societies from ever attaining perfection.

Which of the following questions does this essay address most successfully?

1. Contrast Swift's and Shelley's views of human nature, illustrating your points with specific examples from *Gulliver's Travels* and *Frankenstein*.
2. Analyze the use Swift and Shelley make of scientific knowledge to show the limits of human progress in *Gulliver's Travels* and *Frankenstein*, citing specific illustrations from each work.

3. Discuss the characters of Lemuel Gulliver in *Gulliver's Travels* and Victor Frankenstein in *Frankenstein:* What purpose does each serve in the text? How does each author use the character to illustrate important traits or concepts?
4. Many of the writers we've studied this semester explored the limitations of human potential in their work. Write an essay showing how any two of the following works deal with this idea: William Blake's *Songs of Innocence and Experience,* Jonathan Swift's *Gulliver's Travels,* Mary Shelley's *Frankenstein,* Percy Shelley's "Prometheus Unbound." Does each writer suggest a pessimistic or optimistic view of human nature? Be sure to support your argument with specific illustrations from each text.

Dealing with the Limits of the Test Situation

Suppose that you've organized the course material, studied faithfully, analyzed the exam questions, and know generally how you'll respond. You still need one more skill to succeed: the ability to thrive within the limits of a test situation. Here are some suggestions for handling the pressure.

Minimize Test Anxiety

Many students feel anxious if a test question looks unfamiliar or difficult. Others freeze up if they lose their train of thought midway through an essay. Still others panic when time begins to run out. But you can learn to anticipate potential disasters and brainstorm ways to handle them. If you tend to panic when a test question looks impossible on first reading, make a deal with yourself to close your eyes and count to ten and then read it again and try to block off the parts that you don't have to consider. If you usually run out of time, set a time limit when writing some practice questions so that you can get used to performing under pressure. Finally, make sure that you're in top form to take the exam: organize your supplies—including extra exam booklets and scratch paper, pens, and any testing aids your instructor allows—the night before; get plenty of sleep; eat breakfast; arrive at class a few minutes early; give yourself a pep talk. These measures will increase your confidence and head off debilitating nerves.

Manage Your Time

Lack of time when writing an essay exam is perhaps the hardest constraint for most people to deal with. Most writers produce their best work only after writing several drafts. You won't be able to compose a perfectly polished essay in an exam—there simply isn't time—so you will need to streamline your writing process through planning. After you have analyzed the exam question carefully, take a few minutes to jot down a quick outline or a list of key concepts you want to discuss. Exploratory writing techniques, such as tree diagrams and freewriting, can help you generate and arrange ideas. Prewriting gives you a sense of direction and helps you remember where the essay is going as you write.

For example, one undergraduate student jotted down this five-minute scratch outline in response to the following exam question in a Texas government course:

> What are the relative advantages and disadvantages of the district method versus the at-large method in municipal elections? Analyze the strengths and weaknesses of each and then either argue in favor of one method over the other or propose a different plan that avoids the limitations of both.

Thesis
District method
Advantages—history of discrimination and underrepresentation of minorities (examples)
    —race consciousness important for overcoming injustice
Disadvantages—encourages racial divisions
    —not necessary because much racism has been overcome; minorities may now be freely elected (ex. Sen. Barrientos, Ann Richards) BUT
At-large
Advantages—all citizens can work together for common good, not just concerned with narrow group interests
Disadvantages—majority rule may ignore important minority needs (ex. East Austin)
THESIS—B/c minorities have been and are still underrepresented in local government, the district method of local elections, while flawed, offers the best chance for these communities' voices to be heard.

Once you have a plan, you need to determine how much time to give to each answer. Many students' grades suffer because they blow all their time on the first question and then race through the rest of the exam. To determine how much time to allot each response, you need to solve a quick ratio problem. Divide the points assigned to a given question by the points for the whole exam; the result equals the percentage of time you should spend on that question. When you write your answer, follow the example of journalists and load critical information into your lead. Write a first paragraph that summarizes your whole answer (the student response in the For Writing and Discussion exercise on pp. 672–673 does this beautifully). Add examples and details to the extent that you have time, moving from more important to less important. If you can't finish a response in time, stop, but don't panic. You may have time to return to it later. If not, write a brief note directing the professor to your original notes or outline; let your professor know that you intended to write more but ran out of time. Many instructors will award partial credit for outlined responses.

Focus on the Important Things

You can save time by focusing only on elements important to your grade. Instructors don't expect dramatic, polished introductions and conclusions or artistically constructed sentences in an exam. They would rather you provide a clear thesis statement and explain your main points fully. Most instructors also value organization, although some grade almost entirely on content.

Instructors differ in how they treat errors in grammar, spelling, and punctuation. Some believe it's unfair to expect students to edit their work thoroughly in a short time and don't penalize such errors unless they interfere with the argument (as do garbled or fragmented sentences, for example). Other instructors deduct points for grammatical errors on the grounds that correct usage is always important. If your instructor is a stickler for these details, you may want to save the last five or ten minutes of the exam period for proofreading.

Even if you know a lot about a question, avoid writing more than it asks—unless, perhaps, you know absolutely nothing about one question and want to demonstrate extreme depth of understanding about the others to compensate. Extraneous material may make it difficult for your instructor to find the core of your argument.

Producing an "A" Response

No matter how committed you are to studying, planning, analyzing exam questions, and managing time constraints, your worries about essay tests probably come down to a single, inevitable question: What does an "A" response look like? Research suggests that most professors want closed-form, thesis-based prose that develops key ideas fully, drawing on supporting facts and examples. Although your essay's shape will be influenced by your individual writing style and the particular rhetorical context, the following summary of the points covered in this chapter can serve as a template for a successful essay:

- **Clear thesis statement**. Show your professor that you understand the big picture that the question addresses by including a thesis statement early on. Many professors recommend that you state your thesis clearly, though not necessarily stylishly, in the very first sentence.
- **Coherent organization**. Although a few instructors will read your essay only to see whether you've included important facts and concepts, most expect a logical presentation. Each paragraph should develop and illustrate one main point. Use transition words and phrases to connect each paragraph clearly to the thesis of the essay: "Another factor that led to the economic decline of the South was ..."; "In contrast to Hegel, Mill believed. ..." Show your instructor that you know where the essay's going, that you're developing your thesis.
- **Support and evidence**. When the question calls for supporting facts and examples, be specific. Don't assert or generalize unless you present names, dates, studies, examples, diagrams, or quotations from your reading as support.
- **Independent analysis and argument**. Your response should not be a pedestrian rehash of the textbook. When the question allows, present your own insights, criticisms, or proposals, making sure to support these statements with course material and relate them clearly to your thesis.
- **Conclusion**. Even if you're running short of time, write a sentence or two to tie together main points and restate your thesis. Your conclusion, even if brief, serves an important rhetorical function. It confirms that you've dealt adequately with the question and proved your point.

Clearly we can't teach you everything you need to know about exam writing in one chapter. Becoming comfortable with any genre of writing requires patience and experience. Practicing the suggestions in this chapter for preparing for essay exams, comprehending exam questions, and organizing your answers will help you build your mastery of this kind of writing.

FOR WRITING AND DISCUSSION

Take a Practice Exam

To gain some practical experience, your instructor may ask you to write an essay exam on one of the following topics. Use the preparation and prewriting strategies you've practiced in this chapter and any other strategies you find useful to prepare for the exam. Review the strategies for writing a successful response presented on pages 668–671 and, if possible, organize and conduct group study sessions with your classmates.

1. Imagine that you've been appointed to a campus committee charged with developing minimum requirements for writing assignments in undergraduate courses. Specifically, the committee is trying to decide whether to require professors to assign a final essay exam or a major research paper in core-curriculum courses. Write an essay in which you argue in favor of mandatory essay exams or mandatory research papers, using examples from your own experience and material from Chapters 1 through 4 and this chapter to support your position. You may want to consider some or all of the following questions in your discussion: Which kind of writing helps students learn the most? Which kind of writing most accurately gauges how well students know course material? Which kind of writing develops skills students are most likely to need in the future?
2. Explain the differences between closed-form and open-form prose as presented in Chapter 1 and Chapters 18 and 19. Illustrate your answer with examples taken from Ross Taylor's "Paintball" (pp. 404–406) and Annie Dillard's "Living Like Weasels" (pp. 566–568). Why does Taylor choose to write near the closed end of the closed-to-open continuum, whereas Dillard chooses to write near the open end?
3. Write an essay on a topic of your instructor's choice.

Chapter Summary

This chapter has discussed strategies for writing effective essay examinations under time pressure:

- Preparing for an exam involves identifying and learning main ideas, applying your knowledge, and following a study plan.
- Being able to analyze exam questions before writing is a key skill. You need to understand how quotations are used, recognize cues that will guide the organization of your essay, and interpret the key terms that indicate how you should approach answering the question.
- Overcoming anxiety and managing time are also important for success.
- An "A" response has a clear thesis statement, coherent organization, specific support and evidence, independent analysis and argument, and an effective conclusion.

For additional writing, reading, and research resources, go to **www.MyCompLab.com** and choose **Ramage/Bean/Johnson's *The Allyn & Bacon Guide to Writing,* Fifth Edition.**

ASSEMBLING A PORTFOLIO AND WRITING A REFLECTIVE ESSAY

CHAPTER 25

Reflection becomes a habit of mind, one that transforms.

—*Kathleen Blake Yancey, Writing and Composition Theorist*

Being an adult student, returning after a twelve-year layoff, working full-time and taking a twelve-credit load, I found that I really had to make time to reinvent my writing. These were times of incredible discovery and frustration. Odd as it seems, frustration breeds discovery.

—*William Jensen, Student*

Assembling a portfolio of your writing for a composition course, in which you select and present the work that best shows your progress or the work that represents your best writing for the term, engages you deeply in reflective self-evaluation. Sometimes this work includes rough drafts and informal writing such as freewrites and journal entries as well as polished, final drafts; at other times, it includes just the polished, final products. Almost always, however, writers have some or complete say in what goes into their final portfolio. Just as architects select their best designs or photographers select their best photographs to put into a portfolio to show a potential employer, so, too, do student writers assemble their best writing to demonstrate to the instructor or portfolio readers what they have learned and accomplished during the term.

Typically, writing portfolios also include a reflective letter or essay in which you discuss your portfolio choices and the learning they represent. The role of the accompanying reflective letter or essay is to offer the author's perspective on the writing in the portfolio, to give a behind-the-scenes account of the thinking and writing that went into the work, and to assess the writer's struggles and achievements during the term. This type of reflective writing, called a *comprehensive reflection*, demonstrates what you have learned from your writing over the course of the term, in order to transfer that learning to future writing situations. When you write a comprehensive reflection, you offer your perspective on a series of completed writing projects for presentation to an outside audience, either your instructor or a portfolio reader.

Another type of reflective essay focuses on a particular piece of writing. The aim of this type of reflective writing, called a *single reflection*, is to learn about a particular piece of writing in order to understand and often to revise it in the present or near future. When you write a single reflection, you formulate your ideas primarily for yourself and perhaps for a friendly, nonjudgmental audience.

In this chapter, we offer guidelines and suggestions for assembling a portfolio and writing both types of reflective essays.

Understanding Portfolios

Portfolios offer many advantages to writers. You may have more time to revise before presenting your work for evaluation since many instructors who assign portfolios do not assign grades to individual drafts. Through your comprehensive reflection, you can assess and comment on your writing and learning before someone else passes judgment. Further, the portfolio process helps you develop insights about your thinking and writing processes, insights that you can transfer to new writing situations. Finally, this experience can prepare you for work-related tasks because portfolios are increasingly required in job applications as well as in assessments for job promotions or merit-based increases.

Specific guidelines for preparing a writing portfolio vary from course to course, so you will need to check with each individual instructor for directions about what to include and how to organize your portfolio. You may be given a lot of leeway in what to include in your portfolio, or you may be required to submit a specific number or type of work. You may be asked to include only polished final works, or you may be asked to include process work, multiple drafts, journal entries, peer responses, research notes, and so on. However, no matter what the specific requirements are, the following general suggestions can help you manage the portfolio process.

Collecting Work for Paper and Electronic Portfolios

Crucial to your success in assembling a portfolio is careful organization and collection of your work throughout the term. This way, you will avoid the headache and wasted time caused by trying to hunt down lost or misplaced work.

If you are in a non-computer-based course, we recommend that you purchase an accordion-type file folder to keep and organize all of your work for the course. You can use the dividers to separate your work for individual writing projects. Include everything that contributed to your work on a particular writing project: the original assignment sheet, process work, multiple drafts, peer response sheets, teacher comments, reflective writing about the project, research notes, photocopied research articles, and so on. In addition to careful organization and storage of your work, you need to date and label all work so that you can reconstruct your work on a particular project and identify which draft is second or third, which peer response goes with which draft, and so on.

If you are in a computer-based course where most of the work is submitted electronically, then your portfolio will take electronic form. In this case, you will need to develop an electronic storage system. Specifically, you will need to establish separate electronic folders and files for all work related to specific writing projects and to save and back up all of that work. You may also have hard copy you need to save—say, of in-class handwritten peer responses. If this is the case, you will need to scan this material and save it electronically or develop two storage systems.

Besides the practical need to keep track of all your work in order to review and select the writing that you will include in your portfolio, the process of saving and organizing your work will cause you to attend to writing processes throughout the term, one of the key goals of portfolio teaching.

Selecting Work for Your Portfolio

Even if you are given explicit instructions about the number and type of writing to include in your portfolio, you will still have important choices to make about which completed pieces to include or which pieces to revise for inclusion. We suggest three general guidelines to consider as you review your writing and select work for your portfolio presentation.

- ***Variety:*** One purpose of portfolio assessment is to give a fuller picture of a writer's abilities. Therefore, it is important that you choose work that demonstrates your versatility—your ability to make effective rhetorical choices according to purpose, audience, and genre. What combination of writing samples best illustrates your ability to write effectively for different rhetorical situations and in different genres and media?
- ***Course goals:*** A second consideration is course goals. The goals are likely to be stated in the course syllabus and may include such things as "ability to demonstrate critical thinking in writing"; "ability to use multiple strategies for generating ideas, drafting, revising, and editing"; and "ability to demonstrate control over surface features such as syntax, grammar, punctuation, and spelling." Which pieces of writing most clearly demonstrate the abilities given as your course's goals, or which pieces can be revised to offer such a demonstration?
- ***Personal investment:*** Finally, be sure to consider which pieces of writing best reflect your personal investment and interest. If you are going to be revising the selected pieces multiple times during the last few weeks of class, you will want to make sure you choose work that holds your interest and has ideas you care about. Which pieces are you proudest of? Which were the most challenging or satisfying to write? Which present ideas you'd like to explore further?

Understanding Reflective Writing

Broadly defined, reflective writing is writing that describes, explains, interprets, and evaluates any past performance, action, belief, feeling, or experience. To *reflect* is to turn or look back, to reconsider something thought or done in the past from the perspective of the present.

Whether or not you record your thinking on paper, you think reflectively all the time. Suppose you ask your boss for a raise and get turned down. An hour later, as you cool your anger over coffee and a doughnut, you think of a particular point you could have made more effectively. On a larger scale, this kind of informal reflective thinking can be made more formal, systematic, and purposeful. Consider, for example, a football team that systematically reviews game videos to evaluate their own and their opponents' strategies and patterns of play. The camera's eye offers players and coaches new perspectives on their performance; it enables them to isolate, analyze, and evaluate specific moves that were unconsciously performed in the heat of the game.

Similar ways of thinking can be applied to any past performance. Writing reflectively encourages you to train your own camera's eye, metaphorically speaking, on the past. Reflective writing is now required in many jobs, and employees are asked to write an annual self-reflective review of their job performance. The following example comes from the performance review of a student who worked for a health maintenance organization. In this excerpt, she describes how she plans to make herself more productive in her job and then considers how this improvement will help the company's efficiency in general:

EXCERPT FROM A SELF-EVALUATION OF JOB PERFORMANCE

> To improve my claims processing knowledge, I signed up to take a CPT4 coding class. This will allow me to answer coding questions quickly without having to contact our Cost Containment Department. The Cost Containment Department will have more time to work on their projects if our department does not have to continually call to get answers to simple coding questions.

Similarly, a writer can look back reflectively on a writing performance. The following example is from an e-mail message sent by student writer Susan Meyers to her writing instructor concerning his comments on a draft of a paper she had written about the causes of anorexia. On the draft, the instructor had puzzled over a confusing sentence and suggested a revised version. Here is her e-mail response:

EXCERPT FROM A STUDENT REFLECTION ON A DRAFT

> I think that your suggested revision changes what I intended. I'd like that sentence to read: "Perhaps anorexics don't pursue desirability but are rather avoiding it." I am arguing not that anorexics want to be "undesirable" (as your sentence suggests) but rather that they want to avoid the whole issue; they want to be neutral. Sexuality and desire can be tremendously scary if you're in a position that places the value of your body over the value of your self/personage; one can feel that, by entering the sexual world of mature adults, one will lose hold of one's essential self. This is the idea I'm trying to express. Perhaps I should try to draft it some more. ... At any rate, thank you for pointing out the inadequacies of the topic sentence of this paragraph. I struggled with it, and I think your impulse is right: it needs to encompass more of a transition.

The synthesizing strategies in Chapter 13 for responding to multiple readings and arriving at your own enlarged views can also be applied to your own pieces of writing.

As these examples suggest, reflection involves viewing your writing from different perspectives, looking back on the past from the present, achieving a critical distance. Just as light waves are thrown or bent back from the surface of a mirror, so, too, reflective writing throws our experience, action, or performance back to us, allowing us to see it differently.

This process resembles the kind of dialectical thinking introduced in Chapter 8 on exploratory writing, where we explained how juxtaposing one thesis against its opposite can lead to a synthesis that incorporates some aspects of each of the opposing views. Similarly, the process of reexamining one's writing from a new perspective yields new insights and an enriched, more complicated understanding of a particular action, question, problem, or choice.

FOR WRITING AND DISCUSSION

Reflecting on a Past Experience

Working individually, think of a past experience that you can evaluate reflectively. This experience could be your performance in a job; participation in a sport, play, music recital, or other activity; development of a skill (learning to play the piano, juggle a soccer ball, perform a complex dance movement); or problem with another person (a coach, your dorm resident assistant, a job supervisor). To encourage you to think about the past from the perspective of the present, try asking yourself the question, "How do I see the experience differently now from the way I saw it then?" Imagine that you are doing a debriefing of your participation in the experience. Working on your own for ten minutes, freewrite reflectively about your performance. What did you do well? What wasn't working for you? What could you have done better?

Then in groups or as a whole class, share what you have learned through your reflective freewrites. How did the process of looking back give you a new perspective on your experience? How might reflective writing help you bring about changes and improvements in future performances?

Why Is Reflective Writing Important?

According to learning theorists, reflective writing can substantially enhance both your learning and your performance.* Reflective writing helps you gain the insights needed to transfer current knowledge to new situations. For example, one of our students recently reported that the most important thing she had learned in her first-year writing course was that research could be used in the service of her own argument. In high school, she had thought of research as merely assembling and reporting information she had found in various sources. Now she realized that writers must make their own arguments, and she saw how research could help her

*Learning theorists who have made this general claim include J. H. Flavel, "Metacognitive Aspects of Problem-Solving," in L. B. Resnick (ed.), *The Nature of Intelligence* (Hillsdale, NJ: Erlbaum, 1976); Donald Schon, *Educating the Reflective Practitioner* (San Francisco: Jossey-Bass, 1987); and Stephen Brookfield, *Becoming a Critically Reflective Teacher* (San Francisco: Jossey-Bass, 1995). Throughout this chapter we are indebted to Kathleen Blake Yancey, *Reflection in the Writing Classroom* (Logan, UT: Utah State UP, 1998), who has translated and extended this work on reflection for writing instructors. We are also indebted to Donna Qualley, *Turns of Thought: Teaching Composition as Reflexive Inquiry* (Portsmouth, NH: Boynton/Cook, Heinemann, 1997), who draws on feminist and other critical theorists to argue for the value of reflexive approaches to writing instruction.

do so. Clearly, this new understanding of the relationship between argument and research will help this student do the kind of research writing expected in upper-level college courses.

Learning theorists call this kind of thinking "metacognition": the ability to monitor consciously one's intellectual processes or, in other words, to be aware of how one "does" intellectual work. Reflection enables you to control more consciously the thinking processes that go into your writing, and it enables you to gain the critical distance you need to evaluate and revise your writing successfully.

Reflective Writing Assignments

In this section we describe the kinds of reflective writing that your instructors across the disciplines may ask of you.

Single Reflection Assignments

Single reflection assignments are usually informal, exploratory pieces, similar to other kinds of informal writing you have done. Like the exploratory writing described in Chapter 2, Concept 5, single reflections are conversational in tone, open in form, and written mainly for yourself and, perhaps, a friendly, nonjudgmental audience. However, single reflections differ from most other kinds of exploratory writing in timing, focus, and purpose.

Whereas exploratory writing helps you generate ideas early in the writing process, single reflection writing is usually assigned between drafts or after you have completed an essay. Its focus is your writing itself, both the draft and the processes that produced it. Its aim is critical understanding, usually for the purpose of revision. In it, you think about what's working or not working in the draft, what thinking and writing processes went into producing it, and what possibilities you see for revising it. An example of a single reflection is Jaime Finger's essay in the Readings section at the end of this chapter (see p. 687).

Instructors use a variety of assignments to prompt single reflections. Some examples of assignments are the following:

- ***Process log:*** Your instructor asks you to keep a process log in which you describe the writing processes and decisions made for each essay you write throughout the term. In particular, you should offer a detailed and specific account of the problems you encountered (your "wallowing in complexity") and the rhetorical and subject-related alternatives considered and choices made.
- ***Writer's memo:*** Your instructor asks you to write a memorandum to turn in with your draft. In it, you answer a series of questions: How did you go about composing this draft? What problems did you encounter? What do you see as this draft's greatest strengths? What are its greatest weaknesses? What questions about your draft would you like the instructor to address?
- ***Companion piece:*** Less structured than a formal memorandum, a companion piece asks you to reflect briefly on one or two questions. A typical assignment might be this: "Please turn in (1) your draft and (2) an additional piece telling me what you would do with this draft if you had more time."

- ***Talk-to:*** In this type of companion piece, your instructor asks you to do four things: (1) believe this is the best paper you've ever written and explain why; (2) doubt that this paper is any good at all and explain why; (3) predict your instructor's response to this paper; and (4) agree or disagree with what you expect your instructor's response to be.
- ***Talk-back:*** In another type of companion piece, the instructor asks you to respond to his or her comments after you get the paper back: (1) What did I value in this text as a reader? (2) Do you agree with my reading? and (3) What else would you like for me to know?*

Guidelines for Writing a Single Reflection

If you are inexperienced with reflective writing, your tendency at first may be to generalize about your writing. That is, you may be tempted to narrate your writing process in generic, blow-by-blow procedural terms ("First I took some notes. Then I wrote a first draft and showed it to my roommate, who gave me some suggestions. Then I revised") or to describe your rhetorical choices in general, prescriptive terms ("I started with a catchy introduction because it's important to grab your reader's attention").

To write an effective single reflection, select only a few ideas to focus on, look at specific aspects of a specific paper, explore dialectically your past thinking versus your present thinking, and support your analysis with adequate details. We suggest the following questions as a guide to producing such reflections. But don't answer them all. Rather, pick out the two or three questions that best apply to your performance and text. (Try to select your questions from at least two different categories.) Your goal should be depth, not a broad survey. The key criteria are these: Be *selective*, be *specific*, show *dialectic thinking*, and include *adequate details*.

Process questions: What specific writing strategies did I use to complete this work?

- Which strategies were the most or least productive?
- Did this writing project require new strategies, or did I rely on past strategies?
- What was the biggest problem I faced in writing this piece, and how successful was I in solving that problem?
- What has been my major content-level revision so far?
- What were my favorite sentence- or word-level revisions?
- What did I learn about myself as a writer or about writing in general by writing this paper?

Subject-related questions: How did the subject of my writing cause me to "wallow in complexity"?

- What tensions did I encounter between my ideas/experiences and those of others? Between the competing ideas about the subject in my own mind?
- Did I change my mind or come to see something differently as a result of writing this work?

*We are indebted to Kathleen Blake Yancey and Donna Qualley for a number of the definitions, specific assignments, and suggestions for single and comprehensive reflection tasks that are discussed in the rest of this chapter. Yancey explains the "Talk-To" and "Talk-Back" assignments in her book *Reflection in the Writing Classroom* (Logan, UT: Utah State UP, 1998).

- What passages show my independent thinking about the subject? My unresolved problems or mixed feelings about it?
- What were the major content problems I had, and how successful was I in resolving them?
- What did writing about this subject teach me?

Rhetoric-related questions: How did the audience I imagined influence me in writing this paper?

- How did my awareness of genre influence my choices about subject matter and rhetorical features?
- What do I want readers to take away from reading my work?
- What rhetorical strategies please me most (my use of evidence, my examples, my delayed thesis, etc.)? What effect do I hope these strategies have on my audience?
- How would I describe my voice in this work? Is this voice appropriate? Similar to my everyday voice or to the voices I have used in other kinds of writing?
- Did I take any risks in writing this?
- What do readers expect from this genre of writing, and did I fulfill those expectations?

Self-assessment questions: What are the most significant strengths and weaknesses in this writing?

- Do I think others will also see these as important strengths or weaknesses? Why or why not?
- What specific ideas and plans do I have for revision?

Comprehensive Reflection Assignments

You may also be asked to write a final, comprehensive reflection on your development as a writer over a whole term. Although end-of-the-term reflective essays differ in scope and audience from single reflections, similar qualities are valued in both: selectivity, specificity, dialectical thinking, and adequate detail.

In some cases, the comprehensive reflective essay will introduce the contents of a final portfolio; in other cases, this will be a stand-alone assignment. Either way, your goal is to help your readers understand more knowledgeably how you developed as a writer. Most important, in explaining what you have learned from this review of your work, you also make new self-discoveries.

Guidelines for Writing a Comprehensive Reflection

Instructors look for four kinds of knowledge in comprehensive reflections: self-knowledge, content knowledge, rhetorical knowledge, and critical knowledge or judgment. Here we suggest questions that you can use to generate ideas for your comprehensive reflective letter or essay. Choose only a few of the questions to respond to, questions that allow you to explain and demonstrate your most important learning in the course. Also, choose experiences to narrate and passages to cite that illustrate more than one kind of knowledge.

Self-Knowledge

By *self-knowledge*, we mean your understanding of how you are developing as a writer. Think about the writer you were, are, or hope to be. You can also contemplate how the subjects you have chosen to write about (or the way you have approached your subjects) relate to you personally beyond the scope of your papers. Self-knowledge questions you might ask are the following:

- What knowledge of myself as a writer have I gained from the writing I did in this course?
- What changes, if any, have occurred in my writing practices or my sense of myself as a writer?
- What patterns or discontinuities can I identify between the way I approached one writing project versus the way I approached another?
- How can I best illustrate and explain through reference to specific writing projects the self-knowledge I have gained?

Content Knowledge

Content knowledge refers to what you have learned by writing about various subjects. It also includes the intellectual work that has gone into the writing and the insights you gained from considering multiple points of view and grappling with your own conflicting ideas. Perhaps you have grasped ideas about your subjects that you have not shown in your papers. These questions about content knowledge can prod your thinking:

- What kinds of content complexities did I grapple with this term?
- What *earned insights** did I arrive at through confronting clashing ideas?
- What new perspectives did I gain about particular subjects from my considerations of multiple or alternate viewpoints?
- What new ideas or perspectives did I gain that may not be evident in the writings themselves?
- What passages from various papers best illustrate the critical thinking I did in my writing projects for this course?

Rhetorical Knowledge

Our third category, *rhetorical knowledge*, focuses on your awareness of your rhetorical decisions—how your contemplation of purpose, audience, and genre affected your choices about content, structure, style, and document design. The following questions about rhetorical choices can help you assess this area of your knowledge:

- What important rhetorical choices did I make in various works to accomplish my purpose or to appeal to my audience? What parts of my various works best illustrate these choices? Which of these choices are particularly effective and why? About which choices am I uncertain and why?
- What have I learned about the rhetorical demands of audience, purpose, and genre, and how has that knowledge affected my writing and reading practices?
- How do I expect to use this learning in the future?

*Thomas Newkirk, in *Critical Thinking and Writing: Reclaiming the Essay* (Urbana, IL: NCTE, 1989), coined the phrase "earned insights," a phrase that Donna Qualley also refers to in *Turns of Thought: Teaching Composition as Reflexive Inquiry* (Portsmouth, NH: Boynton/Cook, Heinemann, 1997), pp. 35–37.

Critical Knowledge or Judgment

A fourth area of knowledge, *critical knowledge* or *judgment*, concerns your awareness of significant strengths and weaknesses in your writing. This area also encompasses your ability to identify what you like or value in various pieces of writing and to explain why. You could ask yourself these questions about your critical knowledge:

- Of the works in my portfolio, which is the best and why? Which is the weakest and why?
- How has my ability to identify strengths and weaknesses changed during this course?
- What role has peer, instructor, or other reader feedback had on my assessments of my work?
- What improvements would I make in these works if I had more time?
- How has my writing changed over the term? What new abilities will I take away from this course?
- What are the most important things I still have to work on as a writer?
- What is the most important thing I have learned in this course?
- How do I expect to use what I've learned from this course in the future?

Guidelines for Writing a Comprehensive Reflective Letter

Because the letter (sometimes an essay) that you write to introduce your portfolio shows your insights not only about your writing abilities but also about your abilities as a reflective learner, it may be one of the most important pieces of writing you do for a writing course. Here we offer some additional suggestions geared specifically toward introducing your writing portfolio:

- Review the single reflections you have written about specific writing projects during the term. As you reread these process log entries, writer's memos, companion pieces, and so on, what do you discover about yourself as a writer?
- Consider key rhetorical concepts that you have learned in this course. Use the detailed table of contents of Chapters 1 through 4 to refresh your memory about these concepts (see pp. vii–ix). How can you show that you understand these concepts and have applied them in your writing?
- Take notes on your own writing as you review your work and reconstruct your writing processes for particular writing projects. What patterns do you see? What surprises you? How can you show the process behind the product? How can you show your growth as a writer through specific examples?
- Be honest. Identifying weaknesses is as important as identifying strengths. How can you use this opportunity to discover more about yourself as a writer or learner?

Our first reading is a single reflection by student Jaime Finger. She writes about what she sees as the strengths and weaknesses of an exploratory essay in which she was asked to pose a question raised but not clearly answered in a collection of essays on issues of race and class. (She posed the question, "What motivates people to behave as they do?") She was then asked to investigate various perspectives on the question that were offered by the readings, to consider other perspectives drawn from her own knowledge and experience, and to assess the strengths and weaknesses of differing points of view.

Jaime Finger (student)

A Single Reflection on an Exploratory Essay

1 Although this paper was harder than the first one, I believe I have a good opening question. I like how I divided her [the author of the essays] ideas about motivation into two parts—individual and social. I also like how I used examples from many different essays (this proves I really read the whole book!). Another thing I like about this essay is how I include some examples of my own, like the Michael Jordan example of how he did not make the basketball team in his freshman year and that motivated him to practice every day for a year before making the team his sophomore year. I wonder if he ever would have been as good as he is if he had made the team his freshman year? I wish I could or would have added more of my own examples like this one.

2 What I'm not sure about is if I later ask too many other questions, like when I ask, "If someone is doing something because of society's pressures, is he responsible for that behavior?" and "How much are we responsible to other people like the homeless?" I felt that I piled up questions, and also felt I drifted from my original questions. The paper was confusing for me to write, and I feel that it jumps around. Maybe it doesn't, but I don't know.

3 Since *Alchemy* [the title of the essay collection] was such a hard book, I'm kind of happy with my paper (although after hearing some of the others in my peer group, I don't know if it's up to par!!).

THINKING CRITICALLY
about "A Single Reflection on an Exploratory Essay"

1. To what extent does this reflection show that Jaime has deepened her thinking about the question, "What motivates people to behave as they do?"
2. Where does Jaime show an awareness of audience and purpose in her self-reflection on her essay?
3. To what extent does Jaime show us that she can identify strengths and weaknesses of her essay?
4. What are Jaime's most important insights about her essay?

5. How would you characterize Jaime's voice in this reflection? Does this voice seem appropriate for this kind of reflective writing? Why or why not?
6. What are the greatest strengths and weaknesses in Jaime's single reflection?

Our second reading is the draft of a comprehensive reflective letter written by a student, Bruce Urbanik, for a second-semester composition course that involved a large-scale portfolio assessment. Bruce's portfolio as a whole will be read and scored (Pass or Fail) by two outside readers (and a third if the first two disagree). The contents of Bruce's portfolio include two essays written outside of class and revised extensively and one essay written in class under test conditions. As his letter suggests, his two out-of-class essays were classical arguments (see Chapter 14) written in response to the nonfiction texts that his class read during the semester. The assignment he was given for this comprehensive reflection is similar to the one on pages 684–686.

Bruce Urbanik (student)

A Comprehensive Reflective Letter

Dear Portfolio Reader:

1 This is my first college course in five years. I left school for financial reasons and a career opportunity that I couldn't pass up. I thought of contesting the requirement of this course because I had completed its equivalent back in 1993. But, as I reflected on the past few years, I realized that the only books I have read have been manuals for production machinery. My writing has consisted of shorthand, abbreviated notes that summarize a shift's events. Someday, after I finish my degree and move up in my company, I'm going to have to write a presentation to the directors on why we should spend millions of dollars on new machinery to improve productivity. I need this course if I expect to make a persuasive case.

2 I was very intimidated after I read the first book in the course, *No Contest: The Case Against Competition*, by Alfie Kohn. The author used what seemed to me a million outside sources to hammer home his thesis that competition is unhealthy in our society and that cooperation is the correct route. I felt very frustrated with Kohn and found myself disagreeing with him although I wasn't always sure why. I actually liked many of his ideas, but he seemed so detached from his argument. Kohn's sources did all the arguing for him. I tried to take a fresh perspective by writing about my own personal experience. I also used evidence from an interview I conducted with a school psychologist to back up my argument about the validity of my own experiences with cooperative education. The weakness of this paper is my lack of opposing opinions.

3 For my second essay, on Terry Tempest Williams's *Refuge: An Unnatural History of Family and Place*, I certainly could not use any personal experience. Williams, a Mormon woman, writes about the deaths of her mother, grandmother, and other female relatives from breast cancer, believed to be caused by the atomic testing in Utah. I argued that the author, Williams, unfairly blamed men and the role women play in the Mormon religion

for the tragic death of her mother and other relatives. She thinks that if the Mormon Church had not discouraged women from questioning authority, maybe some of them would have protested the nuclear testing. But I think this reasoning ignores the military and government pressures at the time and the fact that women in general didn't have much power back in the '50s. Since I didn't know anything about the subject, I asked a Mormon woman that I know to comment on these ideas. Also, my critique group in class was comprised of myself and three women. I received quite a bit of verbal feedback from them on this essay. I deal with men at work all day. This change, both for this essay and the entire semester, was welcome.

4 In-class, timed essay writing was my biggest downfall. I have not been trained to develop an idea and present support for it on the fly. Thoughts would race through my head as I tried to put them on paper. I thought I was getting better, but the in-class essay in this portfolio is just awful. I really wish I could have had more practice in this area. I'm just not comfortable with my writing unless I've had lots of time to reflect on it.

5 A few weeks ago, I found a disk that had some of my old papers from years ago stored on it. After reading some of them, I feel that the content of my writing has improved since then. I know my writing has leaped huge steps since my first draft back in September. As a student not far from graduation, I know I will value the skills practiced in this course.

THINKING CRITICALLY
about "A Comprehensive Reflective Letter"

1. What kinds of self-knowledge does Bruce display in his reflective letter?
2. Does Bruce demonstrate dialectical thinking about himself as a writer? If so, where? What multiple writing selves does Bruce identify in his letter?
3. What has Bruce learned from writing about *No Contest* and *Refuge?* What specific examples does he give of "earned insights" or dialectical thinking regarding his subjects?
4. Does Bruce demonstrate his ability to make judgments about his essays' strengths and weaknesses?
5. What learning from this course do you think Bruce is likely to use in the future?
6. Which of the four kinds of writer's knowledge would you like Bruce to address more closely in revising this reflective letter? What kinds of questions does he overlook? Which points could he build up more? Where could his comments be more text-specific and adequately detailed?

For additional writing, reading, and research resources, go to **www.MyCompLab.com** and choose **Ramage/Bean/Johnson's *The Allyn & Bacon Guide to Writing,* Fifth Edition.**

APPENDIX
ACKNOWLEDGMENTS
INDEX

This energy poster is part of a series produced by Energy Conservation Awareness Products (www.energyconservationposters.com). These posters are intended to make people conscious of how they use and waste energy and of alternative energy sources that can lessen the use of fossil fuels. Consider how the poster's words, the features of this image, and the use of color all work together to attract viewers and make them think about their energy habits. This poster relates to various readings on energy and various For Writing and Discussion exercises throughout Parts 1 and 2 of this text.

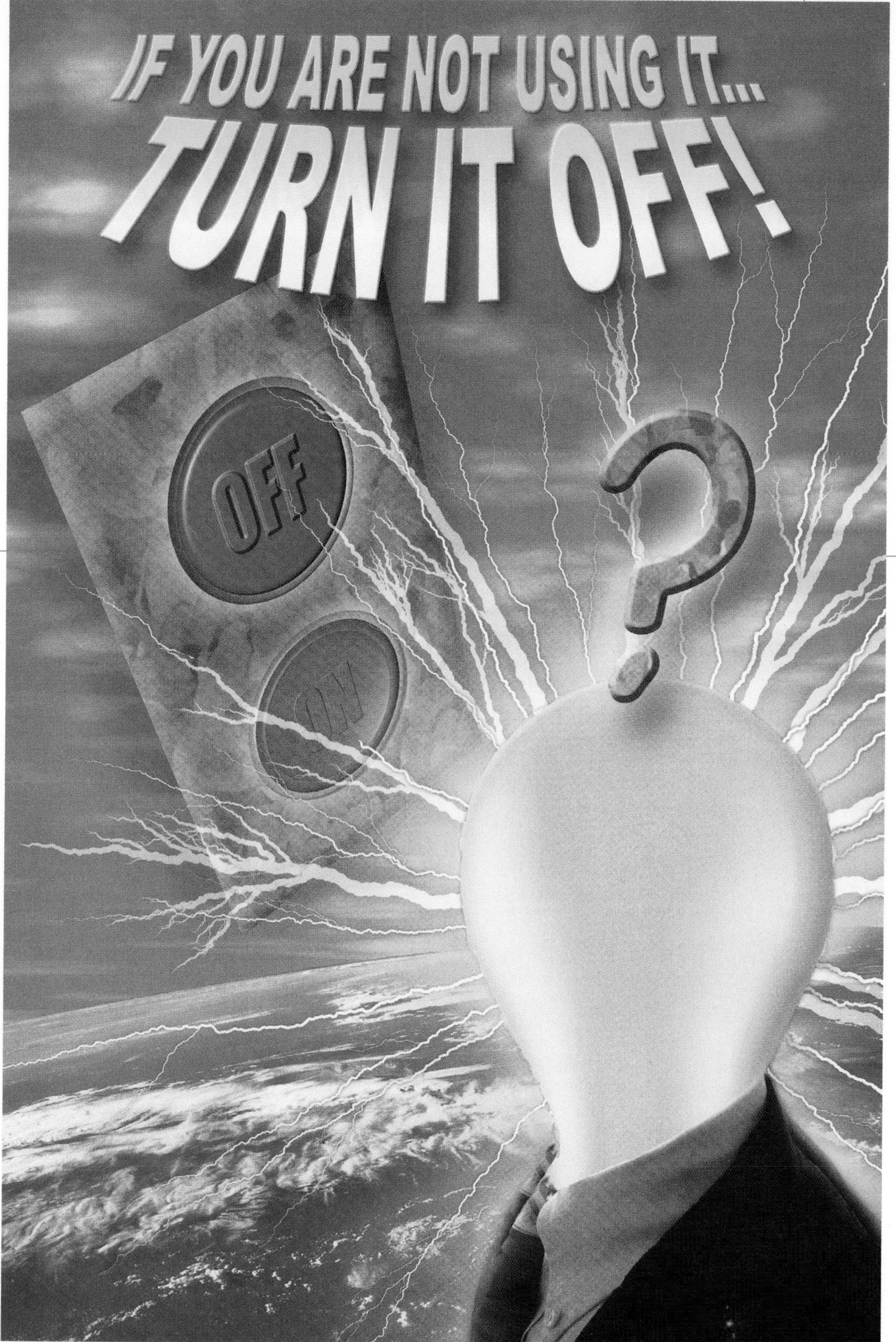
IF YOU ARE NOT USING IT...
TURN IT OFF!
OFF
ON

APPENDIX
A Guide to Avoiding Plagiarism

Plagiarism is using someone else's work—words, ideas, or illustrations, published or unpublished—without giving the creator of that work sufficient credit. A serious breach of scholarly ethics, plagiarism can have severe consequences. Students risk a failing grade or disciplinary action ranging from suspension to expulsion. A record of such action can adversely affect professional opportunities in the future as well as graduate school admission.

Documentation: The Key to Avoiding Unintentional Plagiarism

It can be difficult to tell when you have unintentionally plagiarized something. The legal doctrine of **fair use** allows writers to use a limited amount of another's work in their own papers and books. However, to make sure that they are not plagiarizing that work, writers need to take care to credit the source accurately and clearly for *every* use. **Documentation** is the method writers employ to give credit to the creators of material they use. It involves providing essential information about the source of the material, which enables readers to find the material for themselves. It requires two elements: (1) a list of sources used in the paper and (2) citations in the text to items in that list. To use documentation and avoid unintentionally plagiarizing from a source, you need to know how to

- Identify sources and information that need to be documented.
- Document sources in a Works Cited list.
- Use material gathered from sources: in summary, paraphrase, and quotation.
- Create in-text references.
- Use correct grammar and punctuation to blend quotations into a paper.

Identifying Sources and Information That Need to Be Documented

Whenever you use information from **outside sources**, you need to identify the source of that material. Major outside sources include books, newspapers, magazines, government sources, radio and television programs, material from electronic databases, correspondence, films, plays, interviews, speeches, and information from Web sites. Virtually all the information you find in outside sources requires documentation. The one major exception to this guideline is that you do not have to document common knowledge. **Common knowledge** is widely known information about current events, famous people, geographical facts, or familiar history. However, when in doubt, the safest strategy is to provide documentation.

Documenting Sources in a Works Cited List

You need to choose the documentation style that is dominant in your field or required by your instructor. Take care to use only one documentation style in any one paper and to follow its documentation formats consistently. The most widely used style manuals are ***MLA Handbook for Writers of Research Papers***, published by the **Modern Language Association (MLA)**, which is popular in the fields of English language and literature; the ***Publication Manual of the American Psychological Association*** (APA), which is favored in the social sciences; and ***The Chicago Manual of Style***, published by the **University of Chicago Press (CMS)**, which is preferred in other humanities and sometimes business. Other, more specialized style manuals are used in various fields. Certain information is included in citation formats in all styles:

This text covers MLA and APA style in Chapter 23, Skills 32 and 33. For CMS style, visit www.chicagomanualofstyle.org

- Author or other creative individual or entity
- Source of the work
- Relevant identifying numbers or letters
- Title of the work
- Publisher or distributor
- Relevant dates

Constructing a Works Cited List in MLA Style

As an accompaniment to your English text, this guide explores MLA style. MLA lists are alphabetized by authors' last names. When no author is given, an item can be alphabetized by title, by editor, or by the name of the sponsoring organization. MLA style spells out names in full, inverts only the first author's name, and separates elements with a period. In the MLA citation examples below, note the use of punctuation such as commas, colons, and angle brackets to separate and introduce material within elements.

For more examples of MLA citations, see Chapter 23, Skill 32. For examples of APA citations, see Chapter 23, Skill 33.

Books

Chernow, Ron. Alexander Hamilton. New York: Penguin, 2004.

Claiborne, Robert. Our Marvelous Native Tongue: The Life and Times of the English Language. New York: New York Times, 1983.

Maupassant, Guy de. "The Necklace." Trans. Marjorie Laurie. An Introduction to Fiction. Ed. X. J. Kennedy and Dana Gioia. 7th ed. New York: Longman, 1999. 160–66.

Periodicals

"Living on Borrowed Time." Economist 25 Feb.–3 Mar. 2006: 34–37.

"Restoring the Right to Vote." Editorial. New York Times 10 Jan. 2006, late ed., sec. A: 24.

Ulrich, Lars. "It's Our Property." Newsweek 5 June 2000: 54.

Williams, N. R., M. Davey, and K. Klock-Powell. "Rising from the Ashes: Stories of Recovery, Adaptation, and Resiliency in Burn Survivors." Social Work Health Care 36.4 (2003): 53–77.

Zobenica, Jon. "You Might As Well Live." Rev. of A Long Way Down by Nick Hornby. Atlantic July–Aug. 2005: 148.

Electronic Sources

Glanz, William. "Colleges Offer Students Music Downloads." Washington Times 25 Aug. 2004. 17 Oct. 2004 <http://washingtontimes.com/business/20040824-103654-1570r.htm>.

McNichol, Elizabeth C., and Iris J. Lav. "State Revenues and Services Remain below Pre-Recession Levels." Center on Budget Policy Priorities. 6 Dec. 2005. 10 Mar. 2006 <http://www.cbpp.org/12-6-05sfp2.html>.

Reporters Without Borders. "Worldwide Press Freedom Index 2005." Reporters Without Borders. 2005. 28 Feb. 2006 <http://www.rsf.org/article.php3?id_article=15331>.

Using Material Gathered from Sources: Summary, Paraphrase, Quotation

You can integrate material into your paper in three ways—by summarizing, paraphrasing, and quoting. A quotation, paraphrase, or summary must be used in a manner that accurately conveys the meaning of the source.

For more on using summary, paraphrase, and quotation, see Chapter 22, Skill 28.

A **summary** is a brief restatement in your own words of the source's main ideas. Summary is used to convey the general meaning of the ideas in a source, without giving specific details or examples that may appear in the original. A summary is always much shorter than the work it treats. Take care to give the essential information as clearly and succinctly as possible in your own language.

Summary: Rules to Remember

1. Write the summary using your own words.
2. Indicate clearly where the summary begins and ends.
3. Use attribution and parenthetical reference to tell the reader where the material came from.
4. Make sure your summary is an accurate restatement of the source's main ideas.
5. Check that the summary is clearly separated from your own contribution.

A **paraphrase** is a restatement, in your own words and using your own sentence structure, of specific ideas or information from a source. The chief purpose of a paraphrase is *to maintain your own writing style* throughout your paper. A paraphrase can be about as long as the original passage.

Paraphrase: Rules to Remember

1. Use your own words and sentence structure. Do not duplicate the source's words or phrases.
2. Use quotation marks within your paraphrase to indicate words and phrases you do quote.

3. Make sure your readers know where the paraphrase begins and ends.
4. Check that your paraphrase is an accurate and objective restatement of the source's specific ideas.
5. Immediately follow your paraphrase with a parenthetical reference indicating the source.

A **quotation** reproduces an actual part of a source, word for word, to support a statement or idea, to provide an example, to advance an argument, or to add interest or color to a discussion. The length of a quotation can range from a word or a phrase to several paragraphs. In general, quote the least amount possible that gets your point across to the reader.

Quotation: Rules to Remember

1. Copy the words from your source to your paper exactly as they appear in the original. Do not alter the spelling, capitalization, or punctuation of the original. If a quotation contains an obvious error, you may insert "[sic]," which is Latin for "so" or "thus," to show that the error is in the original.
2. Enclose short quotations (four or fewer lines of text) in quotation marks, and set off longer quotations as block quotations.
3. Immediately follow each quotation with a parenthetical reference that gives the specific source information required.

Creating In-Text References

For more on attribution, see Chapter 22, Skill 28. For more on parenthetical citations in MLA style, see Chapter 23, Skill 31.

In-text references need to supply enough information to enable a reader to find the correct source listing in the Works Cited list. To cite a source properly in the text of your report, you generally need to provide some or all of the following information for each use of the source:

- Name of the person or organization that authored the source.
- Title of the source (if there is more than one source by the same author or if no author is given).
- Page, paragraph, or line number, if the source has one.

For parenthetical references in APA style, see Chapter 23, Skill 33.

These items can appear as an attribution in the text ("According to Smith . . .") or in a parenthetical reference placed directly after the summary, paraphrase, or quotation. The examples that follow are in MLA style.

Using an Introductory Attribution and a Parenthetical Reference

The author, the publication, or a generalized reference can introduce source material. Remaining identifiers (title, page number) can go in the parenthetical reference at the end, as in the first sentence of the example below. If a source, such as a Web site, does not have page numbers, it may be possible to put all the necessary information into the in-text attribution, as in the second sentence of the example below.

The Economist noted that since 2004, "state tax revenues have come roaring back across the country" ("Living" 34). However, McNichol and Lav, writing for the Center on Budget and Policy Priorities, claim that recent gains are not sufficient to make up for the losses suffered.

Identifying Material by an Author of More Than One Work Used in Your Paper

The attribution and the parenthetical reference combined must provide the title of the work, the author, and the page number of the citation.

Describing the testing of the first atom bomb, Jennet Conant says, "The test had originally been scheduled for 4:00 A.M. on July 16, when most of the surrounding population would be sound asleep and there would be the least number of witnesses" (109 East Palace 304–05).

Identifying Material That the Source Is Quoting

To use material that has been quoted in your cited source, add "*qtd. in,*" for "quoted in."

The weather was worrisome, but procrastination was even more problematic. General Groves was concerned that "every hour of delay would increase the possibility of someone's attempting to sabotage the tests" (qtd. in Conant, 109 East Palace 305).

Using Correct Grammar and Punctuation to Blend Quotations into a Paper

Quotations must blend seamlessly into the writer's original sentence, with the proper punctuation, so that the resulting sentence is neither ungrammatical nor awkward.

For more details on how to quote source material, see Chapter 22, Skill 29.

Using a Full-Sentence Quotation of Fewer Than Four Lines

A quotation of one or more complete sentences can be enclosed in double quotation marks and introduced with a verb, usually in the present tense and followed by a comma. Omit a period at the close of a quoted sentence, but keep any question mark or exclamation mark. Insert the parenthetical reference, then a period.

One commentator asks, "What accounts for the government's ineptitude in safeguarding our privacy rights?" (Spinello 9).

"The test had originally been scheduled for 4:00 A.M. on July 16," Jennet Conant writes, "when most of the surrounding population would be sound asleep" (109 East Palace 304–05).

Introducing a Quotation with a Full Sentence

Use a colon after a full sentence that introduces a quotation.

Spinello asks an important question: "What accounts for the government's ineptitude in safeguarding our privacy rights?" (9).

Introducing a Quotation with "That"

A single complete sentence can be introduced with a *that* construction.

> Chernow suggests that "the creation of New York's first bank was a formative moment in the city's rise as a world financial center" (199–200).

Quoting Part of a Sentence

Make sure that quoted material blends grammatically into the new sentence.

> McNichol and Lav assert that during that period, state governments were helped by "an array of fiscal gimmicks."

Using a Quotation That Contains Another Quotation

Replace the internal double quotation marks with single quotation marks.

> Lowell was "famous as a 'confessional' writer, but he scorned the term," according to Bidart (vii).

Adding Information to a Quotation

Any addition for clarity or any change for grammatical reasons should be placed in square brackets.

> Describing how the weather would affect the testing of the first atom bomb, Jennet Conant says, "The test had originally been scheduled for 4:00 A.M. on July 16, [1945,] when most of the surrounding population would be sound asleep" (<u>109 East Palace</u> 304–05).

Omitting Information from Source Sentences

Indicate an omission with ellipsis marks (three dots).

> Describing how the weather would affect the testing of the first atom bomb, Jennet Conant says, "The test had originally been scheduled for 4:00 A.M. on July 16, when . . . there would be the least number of witnesses" (<u>109 East Palace</u> 304–05).

Using a Quotation of More Than Four Lines

Begin a long quotation on a new line and set off the quotation by indenting it one inch from the left margin and double spacing it throughout. Do not enclose it in quotation marks. Put the parenthetical reference *after* the period at the end of the quotation.

> Human Rights Watch recently documented the repression of women's rights in Libya:
>
> > The government of Libya is arbitrarily detaining women and girls in "social rehabilitation" facilities, . . . locking them up indefinitely without due process. Portrayed as "protective" homes for wayward women and girls, . . . these facilities

are de facto prisons . . . [where] the government routinely violates women's and girls' human rights, including those to due process, liberty, freedom of movement, personal dignity, and privacy. (Human)

Is It Plagiarism? Test Yourself on In-Text References

Read the Original Source excerpt. Can you spot the plagiarism in the examples that follow it?

For more examples, see Chapter 22, Skill 30.

Original Source

To begin with, language is a system of communication. I make this rather obvious point because to some people nowadays it isn't obvious: they see language as above all a means of "self-expression." Of course, language is one way that we express our personal feelings and thoughts—but so, if it comes to that, are dancing, cooking and making music. Language does much more: it enables us to convey to others what we think, feel and want. Language-as-communication is the prime means of organizing the cooperative activities that enable us to accomplish as groups things we could not possibly do as individuals. Some other species also engage in cooperative activities, but these are either quite simple (as among baboons and wolves) or exceedingly stereotyped (as among bees, ants and termites). Not surprisingly, the communicative systems used by these animals are also simple or stereotypes. Language, our uniquely flexible and intricate system of communication, makes possible our equally flexible and intricate ways of coping with the world around us: in a very real sense, it is what makes us human. (Claiborne 8)

Works Cited entry:

Claiborne, Robert. Our Marvelous Native Tongue: The Life and Times of the English Language. New York: New York Times, 1983.

Plagiarism Example 1

One commentator makes a distinction between language used as **a means of self-expression** and **language-as-communication**. It is the latter that distinguishes human interaction from that of other species and allows humans to work cooperatively on complex tasks (8).

What's Wrong?
The source's name is not given, and there are no quotation marks around words taken directly from the source (in **boldface** in the example).

Plagiarism Example 2

Other animals also **engage in cooperative activities**. However, these actions are not very complex. Rather they are either the very **simple** activities of, for example, **baboons and wolves** or the **stereotyped** activities of animals such as **bees, ants and termites** (Claiborne 8).

What's Wrong?

A paraphrase should capture a specific idea from a source but must not duplicate the writer's phrases and words (in **boldface** in the example). In the example, the wording and sentence structure follow the source too closely.

Evaluating Sources

For more on evaluating sources, see Chapter 21, Skills 24–26.

It's very important to evaluate critically every source you consult, especially sources on the Internet, where it can be difficult to separate reliable sources from questionable ones. Ask these questions to help evaluate your sources:

- Is the material relevant to your topic?
- Is the source well respected?
- Is the material accurate?
- Is the information current?
- Is the material from a primary source or a secondary source?

Avoiding Plagiarism: Note-Taking Tips

For detailed suggestions on effective note taking, see Chapter 21, Skill 24.

The most effective way to avoid unintentional plagiarism is to follow a systematic method of note taking and writing.

- **Keep copies of your documentation information.** For all sources that you use, keep photocopies of the title and copyright pages and the pages with quotations you need. Highlight the relevant citation information in color. Keep these materials until you've completed your paper.
- **Quotation or paraphrase?** Assume that all the material in your notes is direct quotation unless you indicated otherwise. Double-check any paraphrase for quoted phrases, and insert the necessary quotation marks.
- **Create the Works Cited or References list *first*.** Before you start writing your paper, your list is a **working bibliography**, a list of possible sources to which you add source entries as you discover them. As you finalize your list, you can delete the items you decided not to use in your paper.

LINDA STERN, PUBLISHING SCHOOL OF CONTINUING AND PROFESSIONAL STUDIES, NEW YORK UNIVERSITY

ACKNOWLEDGMENTS

Page 5. Rodney Kilcup, "A Modest Proposal for Reluctant Writers," *Newsletter of the Pacific Northwest Writing Consortium 2,* no. 3 (September 1982): 5.

Page 6. Andrea Lunsford and Lisa Ede, *Singular Texts/Plural Authors: Perspective on Collaborative Writing* (Carbondale and Edwardsville, IL: Southern Illinois University Press, 1992): 21, 45–48.

Page 7. David M. Rockwood, letter to editor, *The Oregonian* (January 1, 1993): E4. Copyright © 1993 David Rockwood. Used with permission.

Page 8. Thomas Merton, "A Festival of Rain," from *Raids on the Unspeakable* by Thomas Merton. Copyright © 1966 by The Abbey of Gethsemani, Inc. Reprinted by permission of New Directions Publishing Corp.

Page 12. Excerpt from a workshop for new faculty members, Jeffrey R. Stephens (Department of Chemistry, Seattle University).

Page 13. Paulo Freire, *Pedagogy of the Oppressed* (New York: Continuum, 1989).

Page 14. Brittany Tinker, "Can the World Sustain an American Standard of Living?" student writing. Reprinted with the permission of the author.

Page 18. Dylan Loeb McClain, "Growing More Oil Dependent, One Vehicle at a Time," *The New York Times* (June 20, 2004). Copyright © 2004 New York Times Co., Inc. Used with permission.

Page 28. A. Kimbrough Sherman, in *Thinking and Writing in College: A Naturalistic Study of Students in Four Disciplines* by Barbara E. Walvoord and Lucille P. McCarthy (Urbana, IL: NCTE, 1990): 51.

Page 29. Stephen D. Brookfield, *Developing Critical Thinkers: Challenging Adults to Explore Alternative Ways of Thinking and Acting* (San Francisco: Jossey-Bass, 1987):5.

Page 29. William G. Perry, *Forms of Intellectual and Ethical Development in the College Years* (Troy, MO: Holt, Rinehart & Winston, 1970).

Page 33. James Gardiner, student writing. Copyright © James Gardiner. Used with permission.

Page 36. Peter Elbow, *Writing Without Teachers* (New York: Oxford University Press, 1973): 14–15.

Page 36. Paul Theroux, *Sunrise with Seamonsters* (Boston: Houghton Mifflin, 1985).

Page 39. E. E. Cummings, "next to of course god america i," from *Complete Poems: 1904–1962* by E. E. Cummings, edited by George J. Firmage. Copyright 1926, 1954, © 1991 by the Trustees for the E. E. Cummings Trust. Copyright © 1985 by George James Firmage. Used by permission of Liveright Publishing Corporation.

Page 41. Peter Elbow, *Writing Without Teachers* (New York: Oxford University Press, 1973): 147–190.

Page 49. Kenneth Burke, *Permanence and Change,* 3rd rev. ed. (Berkeley: University of California Press, 1984): 49.

Page 49. Nayan Chanda, quoted in Thomas Friedman, "Think Global, Act Local," *The New York Times* (June 6, 2004): WK13.

Page 60. Kenneth Burke, *A Rhetoric of Motives* (New York: Prentice Hall, 1950): 43.

Page 64. Marianne Means, "Bush, Cheney Will Face Wall of Opposition if They Try to Resurrect Nuclear Power," (April 12, 2001). © 2001 Hearst Newspapers. Used with permission.

Page 68. Michael A. Chaney, from "Representations of Race and Place in *Static Shock, King of the Hill,* and *South Park,*" *Journal of Popular Film and Television,* Vol. 31, No. 4 (Winter 2004). Copyright Heldref Publications.

Page 69. Kevin Michael Grace, from "*South Park* Is a Snort of Defiance against a World Gone to Hell," *Alberta Report/Newsmagazine,* Vol. 25, No. 35 (August 17, 1998). Copyright © 1998 Kevin Michael Grace. Used with permission.

Page 80. Dale Kunkel, Kristie M. Cope, and Erica Biely, from "Sexual Messages on Television," *The Journal of Sex Research,* Vol. 36, No. 3 (August 1999): 230. Copyright © 1999 by The Society for the Study of Sexuality. Used with permission.

Page 81. Deborah A. Lott, from "The New Flirting Game," *Psychology Today* (January/February 1999): 42. Copyright © 1999 Sussex Publishers. Reprinted with permission.

Page 83. Penny Parker, "For Teeth, Say Cheese," from *New Scientist* (April 6, 1991). Copyright © 1991 New Scientist. Used with permission.

Page 83. Carlo Patrono, "Aspirin as an Antiplatelet Drug," *The New England Journal of Medicine* 330, (May 5, 1994): 1287–1294. Copyright © 1994 Massachusetts Medical Society. Used with permission.

Page 90. From "ANWR Information Brief," from www.anwr.org/tech-facts.pdf, accessed September 24, 2001. Reprinted by permission of Arctic Power.

Page 90. Jimmy Carter, "Make This National Treasure a National Monument." *The New York Times* (Dec. 28, 2000), p. A23. Copyright © 2000, The New York Times. Reprinted by permission of the New York Times Company.

Page 95. Lorna Marshal, *The !Kung of Nyae Nyae* (Cambridge: Harvard University Press, 1976): 177–178.

Page 95. P. Draper, "!Kung Women: Contrasts in Sexual Egalitarianism in Foraging and Sedentary Contexts," in *Toward an Anthropology of Women,* ed. R. Reiter (New York: Monthly Review Press, 1975): 82–83.

Page 105. Henry Morton Stanley, "Henry Morton Stanley's Account" and "Mojimba's Account" from Donald

C. Holsinger, "A Classroom Laboratory for Writing History" from *Social Studies Review* 31, no. 1 (1991): 59–64. Copyright © 1991 Social Studies Review. Used with permission.

Page 106. Tamlyn Rogers, "Two Descriptions of the Same Classroom and a Self-Reflection," student essay. Reprinted with the permission of the author.

Pages 110 and 137. Andrés Martin, M.D., "On Teenagers and Tattoos," *Journal of the American Academy of Child and Adolescent Psychiatry* 36, no. 6 (June 1997): 860–861. Copyright © 1997. Used with permission.

Page 115. Robert B. Cullen with Sullivan, "Dangers of Disarming," *Newsweek* (October 27, 1986). Copyright © 1986. All rights reserved. Reprinted by permission.

Page 116. Carl Rogers, *On Becoming a Person: A Therapist's View of Psychotherapy,* 3rd ed. (Boston: Houghton Mifflin, 1961).

Page 127. Sean Barry, "Why Do Teenagers Get Tattoos? A Response to Andrés Martin," student essay. Reprinted with the permission of the author.

Page 142. Thomas L. Friedman, "30 Little Turtles," *The New York Times* (Feb. 29, 2004). Copyright © 2004 New York Times Company Inc. Used with permission.

Page 143. Stephanie Malinowski, "Questioning Thomas L. Friedman's Optimism in '30 Little Turtles,'" student essay. Reprinted with the permission of the author.

Page 148. Froma Harrop, "New Threat to Skilled U.S. Workers." *Seattle Times* (April 17, 2007). Copyright © 2007 Froma Harrop. Reprinted with permission.

Page 154. Richard Wright, excerpt from *Black Boy* by Richard Wright, pp. 216–217. Copyright © 1937, 1942, 1944, 1945 by Richard Wright; renewed © 1973 by Ellen Wright. Reprinted by permission of HarperCollins Publishers.

Page 161. Megan Lacy, "Excerpt from Literacy Narrative," student writing. Copyright © 2007, Megan Lacy. Used with permission.

Page 161. Jeffrey Cain, "Excerpt from Literacy Narrative," student writing. Copyright © 2007, Jeffrey Cain. Used with permission.

Page 165. Kris Saknussemm, "Phantom Limb Pain." Reprinted by permission of Kris Saknussemm.

Page 167. Patrick José, "No Cats in America?", student essay. Reprinted with the permission of the author.

Page 169. Sheila Madden, "Letting Go of Bart," *Santa Clara Magazine* (Summer 1994). Copyright © 1994. Reprinted by permission.

Page 171. Jennifer Ching, "Once Upon a Time," student essay. Copyright © Jennifer Ching. Used with permission.

Page 176. Anonymous, "Essay A/Essay B" from "Inventing the University," in *When A Writer Can't Write* by David Bartholomae. Reprinted with the permission of The Guilford Press.

Page 191. James Gardiner, "How Do On-Line Social Networks Affect Communication?" student essay. Copyright © James Gardiner. Used with permission.

Page 196. James Gardiner, "The Effect of Online Social Networks on Communication Skills: An Annotated Bibliography," student writing. Copyright © James Gardiner. Used with permission.

Page 199. Jane Tompkins, "'Indians': Textualism, Morality and the Problem of History." *Critical Inquiry* (October 1, 1986). Copyright © 1986 The University of Chicago Press. Used with permission.

Page 209. EnchantedLearning.com, "Tarantulas." www.enchantedlearning.com/subjects/arachnids/spider. © Copyright EnchantedLearning.com. Used by permission.

Page 210. Rod Crawford, "Myths About 'Dangerous' Spiders" from the Burke Museum Web site. www.washington.edu/burkemuseum/spidermyth/index.html. Copyright © Burke Museum. Reprinted by permission of Burke Museum, Seattle, WA.

Page 212. "About the Scanning Mode," DVD Video Player XV-N40BK/XV-N44SL Instructions, JVC, 2003, p. 4.

Page 213, Figure 9.1. From *The Best Recipe* by editors of Cook's Illustrated Magazine. Copyright © 1999 Boston Common Press. Used with permission.

Page 216. Article abstract of "Reefer Madness" by Eric Schlosser (August 1994). Abstract reprinted with the permission of *The Atlantic Monthly.*

Page 226. Kerry Norton, "Winery Yeast Preparation Instructions." Copyright © 2007. Reprinted by permission.

Page 228. "Muslim Americans: Middle Class and Mostly Mainstream" (May 22, 2007). Copyright © 2007 Pew Research Center. Used with permission.

Page 231. Kerri Ann Matsumoto, "How Much Does It Cost to Go Organic?" student essay. Reprinted with the permission of the author.

Page 232. Cheryl Carp, "Behind Stone Walls," student essay. Reprinted with the permission of the author.

Page 234. Shannon King, "Will the Hydrogen Economy Solve the Energy Crisis and Protect Our Environment?" student essay. Reprinted with the permission of the author.

Page 236. Eugene Robinson, "You Have the Right to Remain a Target of Racial Profiling," *Washington Post* (May 1, 2007). Original title, "Pulling Over for Prejudice." © 2007, The Washington Post Writers Group. Reprinted with permission.

Page 257. Robert H. Aseltine, Jr., and Ronald C. Kessler, "Marital Disruption and Depression in a Community Sample," *Journal of Health and Social Behavior* 34 (Sept. 1993): 237–251; adapted from Russell K. Schutt, *Investigating the Social World: The Process and Practice of Research,* 2nd ed. (Thousand Oaks, CA: Pine Forge Press, 1999): 470.

Page 266. J. Adam Luckenbach, John Godwin, and Russell Borski, "Southern Flounder Exhibit Temperature-Dependent Sex Determination." Copyright © 2006. Used by permission. "Ecology Meets Endocrinology: Environmental Sex Determination in Fishes," by John Godwin, J.

Adam Luckenbach, and Russell J. Borski. Contact John Godwin, Department of Zoology, North Carolina State University, Raleigh, NC 27695-7617, USA; e-mail John_Godwin@ncsu.edu. "Gonadal Differentiation and Effects of Temperature on Sex Determination in Southern Flounder (Paralichthys Lethostigma)," by J. Adam Luckenbach, John Godwin, Harry V. Daniels, and Russell J. Borski. Contact Russell J. Borski, Department of Zoology, North Carolina State University, Box 7617, Raleigh, NC 27695, USA.

Page 269. Gina Escamilla, Angie L. Cradock, and Ichiro Kawachi, "Women and Smoking in Hollywood Movies: A Content Analysis," *American Journal of Public Health,* Vol. 90, Issue 3 (March 2000): 412ff. Copyright © 2000 by APHA. Used with permission.

Page 275. Lauren Campbell, Charlie Bourain, and Tyler Nishida, "A Comparison of Gender Stereotypes in *SpongeBob SquarePants* and a 1930s Mickey Mouse Cartoon," student essay. Reprinted with the permission of the authors.

Page 284. Lauren Campbell, Charlie Bourain, and Tyler Nishida, "SpongeBob SquarePants Has Fewer Gender Stereotypes," student poster. Reprinted with the permission of the authors.

Page 285. John Berger, *About Looking* (New York: Vintage Books, 1980), p. 52.

Page 303. Erving Goffman, *Gender Advertisements* (New York: Harper & Row, 1979).

Page 311. Paul Messaris, from *Visual Persuasion: The Role of Images in Advertising* by Paul Messaris (Thousand Oaks, CA: Sage, 1997). Copyright © 1997 Sage Publications. Used with permission.

Page 316. Stephen Bean, "How Cigarette Advertisers Address the Stigma Against Smoking: A Tale of Two Ads," student essay. Reprinted with the permission of the author.

Page 321. Evelyn Dahl Reed, "Medicine Man," from *Coyote Tales from the Indian Pueblos* by Evelyn Dahl Reed. Copyright © 1988 by Evelyn Dahl Reed. Reprinted with the permission of Sunstone Press, P.O. Box 2321, Sante Fe, NM 87504-2321.

Page 333. Alice Walker, "Everyday Use," from *In Love & Trouble: Stories of Black Women* by Alice Walker. Copyright © 1973 by Alice Walker. Reprinted by permission of Harcourt, Inc.

Page 339. Sherman Alexie, "The Lone Ranger and Tonto Fistfight in Heaven," from *The Lone Ranger and Tonto Fistfight in Heaven.* Copyright © 1993, 2005 by Sherman Alexie. Used by permission of Grove/Atlantic, Inc.

Page 343. Elizabeth M. Weiler, "Who Do You Want to Be?", student essay. Reprinted with the permission of the author.

Page 347. Nikki Swartz, "Mobile Phone Tracking Scrutinized," *Information Management Journal* (March/April 2006). Copyright © 2006. Used with permission.

Page 348. Terry J. Allen, "Reach Out and Track Someone," *In These Times* (May 2006). Copyright © 2006 Terry J. Allen. Used with permission.

Pages 353, 358, 361, 363. Kate MacAulay, student writings. Reprinted with the permission of the author.

Pages 358, 359, 361, 362, 364. Kara Watterson, student writings. Reprinted with the permission of the author.

Page 370. Dee, "Comprehensive Immigration Reform: PROs and ANTIs, at http://immigrationmexicanamerican.blogspot.com. Used with permission.

Page 371. Byron Williams, "Immigration Frenzy Points Out Need for Policy Debate." Copyright © 2006 Byron Williams. Used with permission.

Page 372. Victor Davis Hanson, "The Global Immigration Problem." Tribune Media Services, June 6, 2007. Copyright © 2007.

Page 374. Mike Crapo, excerpt from "Immigration Policy Must Help Economy While Preserving Ideals," July 7, 2007. Blog.thehill.com.

Page 375. Jake McIntrye, excerpt from "The Progressive Case Against the Immigration Bill," by Trapper John, posted on www.dailykos.com. Copyright © 2007. Used with permission.

Page 384. Stephen Toulmin, *The Uses of Argument* (Cambridge: Cambridge University Press, 1958).

Page 387. Michael Levin, "The Case for Torture," *Newsweek* (June 7, 1982).

Page 393. Walter Wink, "Biting the Bullet: The Case for Legalizing Drugs," *The Christian Century* (August 8–15, 1990).

Page 404. Ross Taylor, "Paintball: Promoter of Violence or Healthy Fun?" student essay. Reprinted with the permission of the author.

Page 407. William Sweet, "Better Planet: Dirty Coal Plants Are Killers ..." Copyright © 2007 William Sweet. Used with permission.

Page 412. "No to Nukes," *Los Angeles Times,* July 23, 2007. Copyright © 2007. Used with permission.

Page 415. Leonard A. Pitts, Jr., "Spare the Rod, Spoil the Parenting," *The Seattle Times* (September 6, 2001). Copyright © 2001 by the Miami Herald. Reprinted by permission.

Page 417. A. J. Chavez, "The Case for (Gay) Marriage," student essay. Reprinted with the permission of the author.

Page 423. Walvoord, Barbara E. and Lucille P. McCarthy. *Thinking and Writing in College: A Naturalistic Study of Students in Four Disciplines*. Urbana: NCTE, 1990: 7–8.

Page 424, Figure 15.1. Data from Presley, Cheryl, Yuqui Cheng, and Edgardo Pimentel, "Alcohol and Drugs on American College Campuses: A Report to College Presidents," Core Institute, Southern Illinois University, 2000: 11.

Page 426, Figure 15.3. Data from Wechsler, Henry, "Harvard School of Public Health College Alcohol Study," Cambridge: Harvard School of Public Health, 2000: 9.

Page 435. Katie Tiehen, from "Some may challenge ...," student essay. Reprinted with the permission of the author.

Page 440. Jackie Wyngaard, "EMP: Music History or Music Trivia?" student essay. Reprinted with the permission of the author.

Page 442. Diane Helman and Phyllis Bookspan, "*Sesame Street*: Brought to You by the Letters M-A-L-E," *The Seattle Times* (July 28, 1992). Reprinted with permission.

Page 444. Teresa Filice, "Parents: The Anti-Drug: A Useful Site." Copyright © Teresa Filice. Reprinted with the permission of the author.

Page 469. Jane Kester, "A Proposal to Reduce High-Risk Drinking Through Student Awareness Workshops," student writing. Reprinted with the permission of the author.

Page 472. Rebekah Taylor, "A Proposal to Provide Cruelty-Free Products on Campus," student essay. Reprinted with the permission of the author.

Page 477. Jennifer Allen, "The Athlete on the Sidelines," *New York Times* (February 20, 2004). Copyright © 2004 The New York Times. Reprinted by permission.

Page 479. Dylan Fujitani, "The Hardest of the Hardcore: Let's Outlaw Hired Guns in Contemporary American Warfare," student essay. Reprinted with the permission of the author.

Page 489. Jonathan Swift, "A Modest Proposal," in *The Prose Works of Jonathan Swift* (London: Bell, 1914).

Page 490. Peter Elbow, *Writing Without Teachers* (New York: Oxford University Press, 1973): 14–15.

Page 506. Kenneth Burke, *The Grammar of Motives* (Berkeley: University of California Press, 1969).

Page 506. James Jones, quoted in Jon Winokur (Ed.), *Writers on Writing* (Philadelphia: Running Press, 1986).

Pages 507–508. Adapted from J. D. Bransford and M. K. Johnson, "Conceptual Prerequisites for Understanding," *Journal of Learning Behavior* 11 (1972): 717–726.

Page 513. Lynnea Clark, excerpt and outline from "Women Police Officers: Should Size and Strength Be Criteria for Patrol Duty?", student essay. Reprinted with the permission of the author.

Pages 515–520, 526. James Gardiner, student writing. Copyright © James Gardiner. Used with permission.

Pages 528, 529, 539, 540. Dao Do, "Choose Life," student writing. Reprinted with the permission of the author.

Page 529. Tiffany Linder, excerpt from "Salvaging Our Old-Growth Forests," student essay. Reprinted with the permission of the author.

Pages 535, 536. David Popenoe, "Where's Papa?" from *Life Without Father: Compelling New Evidence that Fatherhood and Marriage Are Indispensable for the Good of Children and Society*. As published in "The Decline of Fatherhood," *Wilson Quarterly* (September/October 1996).

Page 547. Patrick Klein, "Berkeley Blues," in *University of Arizona First Year Composition Guide*. Copyright © 1995 by University of Arizona First Year Composition Program. Reprinted with permission.

Page 551. Val Plumwood, excerpt from "Being Prey," *Utne Reader* (July/August 2000): 56–57. Originally published in *The Ultimate Journey* by Val Plumwood. Copyright © 2000 Val Plumwood. Used by permission of the author.

Page 552. Richard Brautigan, excerpt from "Leaves" from *The Tokyo-Montana Express* by Richard Brautigan. Copyright © 1979 by Richard Brautigan. Used with permission.

Page 553. Jon Krakauer, excerpt from *Into Thin Air*. Copyright © 1997 by Jon Krakauer. Published by Anchor Books.

Page 553. Hitomaro, "A Strange Old Man," by Hitomaro, translated by Kenneth Rexroth, from *One Hundred Poems from the Japanese*. Copyright © New Directions Publishing Corp. Used with permission.

Page 555. *College Composition and Communication,* Viponid Interview with John McPhee (May 1991): 203–204.

Page 556. Tom Wolfe, "New Journalism," introduction to *New Journalism,* ed. Tom Wolfe and E. W. Johnson (New York: Harper & Row, 1973): 32. Nicholas Tomalin, in *New Journalism,* ed. Wolfe and Johnson: 201.

Page 560. Isak Dinesen, "The Iguana," *Out of Africa* (New York: Modern Library, 1952).

Page 561. Victoria Register-Freeman, from "My Turn: Hunks and Handmaidens," *Newsweek* (November 4, 1996): 16.

Page 563. John Kaufeld, *Paradox 5 for Windows for Dummies* (San Mateo, CA: IDG Books Worldwide, Inc., 1994).

Pages 564–565. Michael F. Graves and Wayne H. Slater, "Could Textbooks Be Better Written and Would It Make a Difference?" *American Educator* (Spring 1986): 36–42.

Page 566. Annie Dillard, "Living Like Weasels," in *Teaching a Stone to Talk: Expeditions and Encounters:* 11–16. Copyright © 1982 by Annie Dillard. Reprinted by permission of HarperCollins Publishers, Inc.

Page 571. Women Against Gun Control home page, © 2007 Women Against Gun Control. www.wagc.org.

Page 577. James Gardiner, excerpt from exploratory essay, student writing. Copyright © James Gardiner. Used with permission.

Page 587, Figure 20.2. EbscoHost search screen. © EBSCO Publishing, 2007. Used with permission.

Page 589, Figure 20.3. Google search results. © Google, Inc., 2007.

Page 606, Figure 21.1. Excerpts from Million Mom March home page. © 2007 Million Mom March Chapters of the Brady Campaign to Prevent Gun Violence. Used with permission. www.millionmommarch.org.

Page 611. Roger D. McGrath, "The Myth of Violence in the Old West," from *Gunfighters, Highwaymen, and Vigilantes: Violence on the Frontier.* Copyright © 1984 by The Regents of the University of California. Used with permission.

Page 634, Figure 23.1. EbscoHost results screen. Copyright © 2007 EBSCO. M. Kyle Matsuba et al. "Searching for Self and Relationships Online." *Cyber Psychology & Behavior* 9.3 (June 1, 2006): 275–284. Copyright © 2006 Mary Ann Liebert, Inc. Used with permission.

Page 637, Figure 23.2. John Barrett, excerpt from "MySpace Is a Natural Monopoly." *ECommerce Times*. (Jan. 17, 2007). ECT News Network, http://www.ecommercetimes.com/story/55185.html. Reproduced with permission of TechNewWorld.com and ECT News Network. Copyright © 2007 ECT News Network, Inc. All rights reserved.

Page 640, Figure 23.3. Jeremy Wright, "MySpace Is the New Blogosphere." Blog posting (Feb. 21, 2006). Ensight.org, http://www.ensight.org. © Jeremy Wright, 2007. Used with permission.

Pages 643–651. James Gardiner, "Why Facebook Might Not Be Good for You: Some Dangers of Online Social Networks," student essay. Copyright © James Gardiner. Reprinted by permission.

Page 657, Figure 23.4. EbscoHost results screen. Copyright © 2007 EBSCO. Daniel E. Scharrer et al., "Working hard or hardly working?" *Mass Communication and Society, 9*(2), 215–238. Copyright © 2006. Reprinted by permission of Taylor & Francis.

Page 663. Anonymous undergraduate students at the University of Oklahoma, paraphrased from responses written when asked to comment on their experiences with essay examinations. Randall Popken, "Essay Exams and Papers: A Contextual Comparison," *Journal of Teaching Writing* 8 (1989): 51–65.

Page 680. Susan Meyers, excerpt from an e-mail message, student writing. Reprinted with the permission of the author.

Page 687. Jaime Finger, "A Single Reflection," student essay. Reprinted with the permission of the author.

Page 688. Bruce Urbanik, "A Comprehensive Reflective Letter," student essay. Reprinted with the permission of the author.

Illustrations

Page 3. Bob Jacobson/Corbis

Page 59. Allan H. Shoemake/Taxi/Getty

Page 62. Jeff Greenberg/The Image Works

Page 62. Frank Micelotta/Getty

Page 63. Bill Bachmann/The Image Works

Page 63. Leland Bobbe/Taxi/Getty

Page 91. Top: AP; Bottom: Alaska Stock

Page 146. David Horsey/2003/Seattle Post Intelligencer

Page 147. Mike Lane/PoliticalCartoons.com

Page 158. Left: Ken Bube; Right: Masakazu Watanabe / Aflo / Jupiter Images

Page 159. Left: Photos Alyson/Getty; Right: Ken Bube

Page 284. SpongeBob SquarePants: Paramount/Everett Collection; Mickey Mouse: Walt Disney Co./Everett Collection

Page 287. Top left: Karen Kasmauski/Corbis; Top right: GUILLERMO ARIAS/AP; Bottom left: J. Emilio Flores/Corbis; Bottom right: Carlos Barria/Corbis

Page 288. Top left: Mark E. Gibson/Fotosearch; Top right: Isaac Brekken/AP; Bottom left: Lindsay Hebberd/Corbis; Bottom right: Mel Evans/AP

Page 294. Photography copyright The Art Institute of Chicago

Page 302. Courtesy of Hoover Company

Pages 305 and 306. Advertising Archive

Page 314. Top: Photograph by Katrine Naleid, Pinesol is a registered trademark of the Clorox Company. Used with permission. Copyright 2001 The Clorox Company, reprinted with permission.

Page 315. Top and bottom: Advertising Archives

Page 425. Cartoon Research Library

Page 426. Courtesy of the University of Massachusetts

Page 433. Courtesy of Experience Music Project

Page 441. Stan Eales/Cartoon Stock

Page 487. Rhetoricians at a Window—Jan Steen, The Philadelphia Museum of Art / Art Resource, NY

Page 661. Courtesy of American Indian College Fund. All rights reserved.

INDEX

Abstraction scale
  explanation of, 69–71
  writing low on, 554–556
Abstracts, 117, 262. *See also* Summary writing
Academic disciplines
  essay examinations for, 663–675 (*See also* Essay examinations)
  as field of inquiry and argument, 30–31
  scholarly questions for assorted, 31–32
Academic writing. *See also* Scholarly publications
  APA style for, 652–659
  document design for, 76–79
  examples of, 24
  layout for, 78
  MLA style for, 628–651
  transition words in, 530–532
Active voice, use of, 538
Ad hominem, 396
Advertisements
  advocacy, 455, 459–461
  analysis of, 295–296, 298–300
  cultural perspectives on, 301–305
  examples of, 299, 301, 302, 304–306, 314, 315
  goal of, 295
  MLA style for citing, 641
  targeting of audiences for, 296–297
Advice-centered workshops, 504–505
Advocacy, degree of, 600
Advocacy advertisements, 455, 459–461
Alexie, Sherman, 339–343
all about writing, 512–514
Allen, Jennifer, 477–479
Allen, Terry J., 348–350
American Psychological Association (APA). *See* APA style
Amis, Martin, 66
Analogy, 452
Analysis. *See also* Idea analysis and synthesis; Image analysis; Literary analysis
  of advertisements, 295–296, 298–300
  of angle of vision, 54
  of essay exam questions, 666–671
  explanation of, 285, 346
  of research reports, 256–259
and then writing. *See* Chronological order
Anecdotal conclusions, 545
Angle of vision
  analysis of, 54
  in description, 103–104
  examples of, 51, 52
  of images, 289, 291
  perception and, 93–95
  persuasion through, 57, 59
  recognition of, 50–51
  of research sources, 598–600
  strategies for constructing, 54–55
  thought exercise on, 50
Annotated bibliography
  examples of entries for, 188–189
  explanation of, 175, 187
  features of, 187–188
  peer reviews for, 190
  shaping, drafting, and revising, 189–190
  writing critical preface for, 189
Anthologies
  APA style for citing, 655
  MLA style for citing, 631–632
Anxiety, 468, 673
APA style
  for articles in magazines and newspapers accessed in print, 655–656
  for articles in scholarly journals accessed in print, 655
  for books, 627–628, 653–655
  for books downloaded from database, 656–657
  for edited anthologies, 655
  features of, 652
  for films, 659
  for government publications, 659
  for indirect sources, 653
  in-text citations in, 652–653
  for podcasts, 659
  for print articles downloaded from database, 656–657
  "Reference" list in, 595, 628, 653
  for sound recordings, 659
  student example of research paper in, 275–282
  for television programs, 658
  for unpublished papers presented at meetings, 659
  use of, 76, 188, 652
  for Web and Internet sources, 657–658
Appeals
  bandwagon, 397
  to *ethos,* 55–56, 58, 122, 393–394, 455
  to false authority, 397
  to *logos,* 55, 58, 122, 394, 447, 455
  to *pathos,* 56, 58, 122, 393–395, 447, 455
Argument. *See also* Classical argument; Evaluative writing; Proposal writing
  addressing objections and counterarguments in, 389–391
  articulating reasons in, 382–383
  articulating unstated assumptions in, 383–384
  components of, 377
  from consequence, 452, 453
  creating frame for, 380–382
  evaluating evidence for, 387–388
  generating and exploring ideas for, 399–401
  keeping focus on, 613–615
  misleading views of, 377–378
  from precedent or analogy, 452, 453
  from principle, 452, 453
  readings in, 404–421
  rebuttal to, 392
  responding to objects, counterarguments, and alternative views in, 392–393
  shaping and drafting, 401–402
  stages of development of, 279–280
  structure of, 384*n,* 398–399
  using evidence for, 385–387
Aristotle, 55
Articles
  APA style for citing downloaded, 656–657
  APA style for citing print, 655
  MLA style for citing downloaded, 629
  MLA style for citing print, 632–633
Assumptions, 383–384
"The Athlete on the Sidelines" (Allen), 477–479

Attributive tags
to create context and shape reader response, 619
explanation of, 118, 119, 617
methods for using, 620
to separate writer's ideas from source's ideas, 617–618
using parenthetical citations without, 618
with and without quotations, 620, 621
Audience
for advertisements, 296–297
for arguments, 401–402
assessment of, 22–24
attempts to change views of, 41–42
desire for direction and clarity, 557–559
expectations of, 507–511
point of view of, 21–22
writing for purpose to, 19–22
Authority, creating air of, 76
Autobiographical narratives
character in, 154
elements of, 150–152
generating and exploring ideas for, 151–153, 157–158
opposition of contraries in, 152
peer reviews for, 164
plot in, 153, 157–158
revision of, 159
setting in, 155
shaping and drafting, 158–159
theme in, 156

Back-and-forth pattern, 542, 543
Background knowledge, 114
Bandwagon appeals, 397
Banking method, 13–14
Bar graphs, 254, 255
Barry, Sean, 127–129
Bean, Stephen, 316–318
"Behind Stone Walls" (Carp), 232–233
Beliefs, 94
Believing and doubting game, 36, 37, 48
Berger, John, 285–286
"Berkeley Blues" (Klein), 547–549, 556, 558
Bibliographic citations, 187–188
Bibliography, 76, 187. *See also* Annotated bibliography
"The Bird and the Machine" (Eisley), 558
Black Boy (Wright), 154
Block quotations, 624
Blogs
angle of vision of, 599
APA style for citing, 658
examples of, 369–376
explanation of, 369
MLA style for citing, 639, 640
Bloom, Benjamin, 346
Books
APA style for citing, 627–628, 653–655
e-books, 635–636
MLA style for books downloaded from database, 634–636
MLA style for citing, 630–631
as research sources, 579–581
searching library's online catalog for, 583–584
Bookspan, Phyllis, 442–443
Boolean search commands, 586
Bourain, Charlie, 275–282
Brackets, 622
Brautigan, Richard, 552
Broadcast transcripts, 635, 639, 656, 658
Brookfield, Stephen, 681*n*
Bullets, 542
Burke, Kenneth, 49, 60, 506, 557
Bush, George W., 51, 57

Campbell, Lauren, 275–282
"Can the World Sustain an American Standard of Living?", 14–15
Carp, Cheryl, 224, 232–233
Cartoons, 641
"The Case for (Gay) Marriage" (Chavez), 417–421
Category questions, 250
Causality, 257–258
Chanda, Nayan, 49
Chaney, Michael A., 68
Characters
asking questions about, 324
in autobiographical narratives, 154
Chavez, A. J., 417–421, 448
Ching, Jennifer, 171–174
Chronological order
closed-end prose and, 511–512
open-form prose and, 547–552
Circular reasoning, 397
Citations. *See* Research source citations
Clarity, reader's desire for, 557–559
"Clash on the Congo: Two Eyewitness Accounts" (Stanley & Mojimba), 105–106
Classical argument. *See also* Argument; Evaluative writing
addressing objections and counterarguments in, 389–391
appeals to *ethos* and *pathos* in, 393–395
articulating reasons in, 382–383
articulating unstated assumptions in, 383–384
creating frame for, 380–381
evaluating evidence for, 387–388
exploration prior to drafting, 400–401
function of, 378–379
generating and exploring ideas for, 399–401
informal fallacies in, 395–397
peer reviews for, 403
readings in, 404–421
responding to objects, counterarguments, and alternative views in, 392–393
revision of, 403
shaping and drafting, 401–402
stages of development in, 379–380
structure of, 384*n,* 398–399
using evidence for, 385–387
Closed-form prose
appropriate use of, 25, 28
binding sentences together in, 533–538
choice of, 10–11
conclusions in, 543–545
example of, 7
for exploratory writing, 184
humor in, 563
introductions in, 522–526
language use in, 70
for literary analysis, 326
open vs., 9–11, 22, 546–547, 557, 559
organizing and developing ideas in, 539–543
planning and visualizing structure in, 514–520
purpose statements in, 22
reader expectations for, 507–511
thesis in, 45–47
thesis/support structures in, 511–514

titles for, 521–522
topic sentences for paragraphs in, 527–530
transitions and signposts in, 530–532
using open-form elements to create voice in, 562–565
Clothing, 60–61
Coherence, 507–509
COIK (Clear Only If Known), 212
Colomb, Gregory, 507*n*
Color, 78–79
Commentators, 599
Companion pieces, 682
Comparison/contrast strategy, 542–543
"A Comparison of Gender Stereotypes in *SpongeBob SquarePants* and a 1930s Mickey Mouse Cartoon" (Campbell, Bourain, and Nishide), 275–282
Comparison questions, 244, 245
Composition process, 180–186
"A Comprehensive Reflective Letter" (Urbanik), 688
"Comprehensive Immigration Reform: PROs and ANTIs" (Dee), 369
Comprehensive reflection, 677, 684–686
Conclusions
delayed-thesis, 545
to essay examination responses, 675
hook and return, 545
larger significance, 544
proposal, 544
scenic or anecdotal, 545
simple summary, 544
strategies for writing, 543–545
Concrete words, 554–556
Conference presentations, 641
Conjunctions, coordinating, 73
Connectedness, 552
Consequence
argument from, 452, 453
evaluation of, 451
prediction of, 451
Consumer items, rhetoric of, 60–61
Consumers, 296–297
Content knowledge, 685
Coordinating conjunctions, to join independent sentences, 73
Coordination, 73–74
Correlation questions, 244, 245
Cost, in determining criteria, 431
Council of Writing Program Administrators outcomes
composition and revision, 488
rhetorical guide to research, 572
rhetoric for college writers, 4
writing for assessment, 662
writing projects, 88
Counterarguments
concession to, 392–393
methods of addressing, 389–391
Cradock, Angie L., 269–274
Crapo, Mike, 374
Crawford, Rod, 210–211, 215–216
Credibility, of research sources, 597
Criteria, for evaluation arguments, 427–431
Criteria-match process, 427–428, 439
Critical knowledge, 686
Critical thinking
Council of Writing Program Administrators outcomes for, 4, 88, 572, 662
exploratory strategies for, 32–36
function of, 29
skills for, 30
writing as, 5
Critiques
ideas, 124–125
rhetorical, 122–123
Cultural differences
advertising and, 301–306
perception and, 94
Cyberspace. *See* Internet; Web sites; World Wide Web

Databases
APA style for citing material downloaded from, 656–657
licensed, 584–588, 634–635, 656
methods for searching, 586–588
MLA style for citing material downloaded from, 627–629, 634–636
Data collection
interviews for, 247–249
observation for, 245–247
questionnaires for, 249–251
Deadlines, 497–498
Debate, 377–378
Declaration of Independence, 450
Delayed-thesis conclusions, 545
Descriptive writing
generating details for, 100–101
rationales for writing opposing, 100
revision of, 103–104
shaping and drafting, 101
show and *tell* words in, 102–103
Design. *See* Document design
Details, generation of, 100–101
Dewey Decimal System, 584
Dialectic thinking
explanation of, 35–36
for exploratory essays, 178
Dillard, Annie, 559, 566–568
Dinesen, Isak, 560
Division-into-parallel-parts strategy, 541–542
Doctorow, E. L., 546
Documentation. *See* Research source documentation
Document design
for advocacy advertisements, 459, 460
color and, 78–79
for empirical research reports, 261
examples of, 79–81
explanation of, 76
goal of, 66
graphics and images and, 79
rhetorical messages sent by, 76–77
space and layout and, 78
technology use and, 76
type and, 77
Does statement, 132
Domain-specific skills, 30–31
Double-entry research notes, 181–183
Doubting, 36–38
Douglass, Frederick, 160
Drafts. *See also* Revision
for advocacy advertisements, 460
for annotated bibliographies, 189–190
for autobiographical narratives, 158–159
for classical argument, 401–402
for evaluative writing, 438
example of, 491
for exploratory essays, 183–186
function of multiple, 490–492
for image analysis, 309
for informative writing, 218, 220, 223–225
for literacy narratives, 163–164
for literary analysis, 331
methods used to produce, 490, 496, 497
peer review of, 498–505
for proposal writing, 457
for research reports, 261–262
of summaries, 133–134
for synthesis writing, 365

Eales, Stan, 411
E-books, 635–636, 658
EBSCOhost, 585, 587, 589
Ede, Lisa, 6
Edited anthologies
  APA style for citing, 655
  MLA style for citing, 631–632
Editorials, 412–414
Eisley, Loren, 558
Either/or reasoning, 396
E-journals, 639
Elbow, Peter, 36, 41, 490
Electronic bulletin boards, 658
Electronic databases. *See* Databases
Electronic newsgroups, 658
Ellipses, 622
E-mail
  APA style for citing, 658
  MLA style for citing, 639
"EMP: Music History or Music Trivia?" (Wyngaard), 440–441
Emphasis, sentence structure to control, 73–74
Empirical data, 430–431
Empirical research, 239–242. *See also* Field research; Field research data; Research; Research reports
EnchantedLearning.com, 209–210, 215
Encyclopedic structure, 512–513
Engfish writing, 514
ERIC (Educational Resources Information Center), 635, 656
Escamilla, Gina, 269–274
Essay examinations
  analysis of questions on, 666–671
  essays vs., 664
  function of, 663–664
  guidelines for successful responses on, 675
  preparation for, 664–666
  strategies for handling test situation during, 673–675
Essays. *See also specific forms of writing*
  essay exams vs., 664
  thesis statement for, 41–44
Ethical guidelines
  of National Institutes of Health, 260
  for research, 259–260
Ethos
  appeals to, 55–56, 58, 122, 393–394, 455
  explanation of, 55
Evaluative annotations, 187–188
Evaluative writing
  establishing criteria for, 427–431
  examples of, 432–435, 440–446
  exploration of, 424–426
  generating and exploring ideas for, 437, 438
  making choices for, 436–437
  overview of, 423–424
  peer reviews for, 439
  revision of, 439
  shaping and drafting, 438, 439
  using planning schema to develop, 431–432
"Everyday Use (For Your Grandmama)" (Walker), 333–338
Evidence
  in essay examination responses, 675
  evaluation of, 387–388
  particulars as, 47
  types of, 385–387
Examinations. *See* Essay examinations
Examples, as evidence, 385
"Excerpt from 'Immigration Policy Must Help Economy While Preserving Ideals'" (Crapo), 374
"Excerpt from 'The Progressive Case Against the Immigration Bill'" (Trapper John), 375–376
Exigency, 21
Existence questions, 244, 245
Experimental questions, 244, 245
Exploratory writing
  to discover and clarify ideas, 496
  double-entry research notes for, 181–183
  exploring, 176–177
  function of, 175, 176
  generating and exploring ideas for, 180–181
  peer reviews for, 186
  readings in, 191–207
  revision of, 186
  shaping and drafting, 183–186
  strategies for, 184
  structure of, 185
  understanding, 178–179

Facebook.com, 33, 577
Facts, 385
Fallacies, 395–397
False analogy, 396
Feminism and the Mastery of Nature (Plumwood), 551–552
"A Festival of Rain" (Merton), 8
Field research. *See also* Research reports
  analyzing results from, 256–259
  ethical standards for, 259–260
  methods for reporting results from, 252–256
  scientific posters and, 265–267
Field research data. *See also* Research reports
  analysis of, 239–240
  empirical research report structure and, 240–242
  interviews to gather, 247–249
  observation to gather, 245–247
  posing research questions and, 243, 244
  questionnaires to gather, 249–251
  reading research reports and, 242–243
Field research reports
  designing and drafting introduction and method sections of, 261–262
  examples of, 268–281
  generating ideas for, 261
  methods for reading, 242–243
  peer reviews for, 262–263
  research and writing guidelines for, 262
  revision of, 262
  team writing for, 264
Figurative language, 559–560
Figures, 254
Filice, Teresa, 444–446
Films
  APA style for citing, 659
  MLA style for citing, 640–641
Finger, Jaime, 687
FirstSearch Databases, 585
Fixed-choice questions, 250
Flavel, J. H., 681*n*
Flowcharts, 519, 520
"Flying Elsewhere" (Markham), 562
Focused freewriting, 34
Fonts, 77
Forecasts
  in closed-form prose, 510–511, 546
  in introductions, 525–526
for example, 539–540
Framework charts, 185, 241, 309, 367, 398, 439, 457
Freewriting
  example of, 33–34
  explanation of, 32–33
  focused, 34

Freire, Paulo, 13, 14
Friedman, Thomas L., 142–143
Fujitani, Dylan, 447, 479–483
Fulfillment, 510–511
Fulkerson, Richard, 387
"Funnel" introductions, 522

Gardiner, James, 33, 181, 182, 191–199, 515, 516, 518, 519, 586, 593, 643–651
Gender Advertising (Goffman), 303
Gender roles, 302–305
Genre
  in college-level reading, 114
  examples of, 24
  how writers think about, 24–25
  overlap in, 126–127
"The Global Immigration Problem" (Hanson), 372–374
Goffman, Erving, 303
Google, 589, 590
Gopen, George, 507*n*
Goswamie, Dixie, 507*n*
Government publications
  APA style for citing, 659
  MLA style for citing, 641–642
Grace, Kevin Michael, 69
Graphics. *See also* Images; Photographs; Visual aids
  guidelines for using, 79
  in research reports, 254–255
  revision of, 256
Graphs, 253–255
Groups, 223

Hanson, Victor Davis, 372–374
"'The Hardest of the Hardcore': Let's Outlaw Hired Guns in Contemporary American Warfare" (Fujitani), 479–483
Harrop, Froma, 148–149
Hasty generalizations, 396
Headings, to signal transitions, 533
Hegel, George Wilhelm Friedrich, 346
Helman, Diane, 442–443
Hitomaro, 553
Home pages, 590
Hook and return conclusions, 545
Hopper, Edward, 294–295
Horsey, David, 146
"How Cigarette Advertisers Address the Stigma Against Smoking: A Tale of Two Ads" (Bean), 316–318
"How Clean and Green Are Hydrogen Fuel-Cell Cars? (King), 234–236
"How Do Online Social Networks Affect Communication?" (Gardiner), 191–195
however, 540
"How Much Does It Cost to Go Organic?" (Matsumoto), 231
Humor, 563

Idea analysis and synthesis. *See also* Synthesis writing
  elements of, 350–352
  exploring main themes and similarities and differences for, 360–361
  formulating your synthesis views and, 363–364
  generating and exploring your own ideas for, 362–363
  learning logs and, 357
  organization for, 367–368
  overview of, 346
  peer reviews for, 368
  readings in, 353–355, 369–376
  revision of, 368
  rhetorical strategies and, 359–360
  shaping and drafting, 365–366
  summary/strong response writing and, 352, 357–358
  synthesis questions and, 350–351, 356–357
  writing thesis for, 366–367
Idea generation
  for advocacy advertisements, 459–460
  for autobiographical writing, 151–153, 157–158
  for classical argument, 399–401
  for empirical research reports, 261
  for evaluative writing, 437, 438
  for exploratory essays, 180–181
  for image analysis, 308–309
  for informative writing, 218, 220, 222–223
  for literacy narratives, 162–163
  for literary analysis, 329–331
  for proposal writing, 456–457
  reading for structure and content for, 131–133
  for self-reflection, 104
  in small groups, 223
  for synthesis writing, 362–363
  using elements of literary narrative for, 162–163
Idea mapping, 34, 35
Ideas critique, 124–125
Ideology, 378
"The Iguana" (Dinesen), 560
Ill-structured problems, 13*n*
Image analysis
  for advertisements, 295–306 (*See also* Advertisements)
  exploration of, 286–289
  generating and exploring ideas about, 308–309
  overview of, 285–286
  peer reviews of, 310
  readings about, 311–319
  revising essays on, 309–310
  shaping and drafting, 309
Images. *See also* Photographs; Visual aids
  compositional features of, 291–295
  cultural importance of, 285–286
  persuasion through, 57–59
  rhetorical effect of, 289–291
  use of, 79
"Immigration Frenzy Points Out Need for Policy Debate" (Williams), 371–372
"'Indians': Textualism, Morality, and the Problem of History" (Tompkins), 199–207
Indirect quotations, 629
Inflated voice, 74–75
Information
  converted to meaning, 45–46
  data collection methods to gather, 245–251
  introduction of suprising, 216–217
  presenting old before new, 509–510
Informative reports, 214–215
Informative writing
  categories of, 208–209
  examples of, 226–238
  exploration of, 209–210
  function of, 208, 214–215
  generating and exploring ideas for, 218, 220, 222–223
  instructions as, 217–218
  in magazines, 215–217, 221–222
  need-to-know, 212–213
  peer reviews for, 219, 221, 225
  reports as, 214–215
  research sources incorporated into, 614–615
  revision of, 219, 221, 225

Informative writing (*continued*)
shaping and drafting of, 218, 220, 223–225
thesis-based, 208
workplace, 219–220
In medias res, 153
Inner-directed consumers, 297
Institutional Review Boards, 260
Instructions, 212–213
Internet. *See also* Web sites; World Wide Web
blogging on, 369–376
MLA style for citing sources from, 636–640
print sources vs. sources from, 582
search engines for, 588–591
Interviews
APA style for citing, 658
ethical guidelines for, 260
methods for conducting, 247–248
MLA style for citing, 641
preparing for, 248–249
In-text citations
APA style for, 652–653
MLA style for, 628–629
"Into Thin Air" (Krakauer), 558
Introductions
for closed-form prose, 522–525
elements of, 524–525
for forecasting the whole, 525–526
strategies for, 522–523
Issue questions, 381

Jensen, William, 677
Jones, James, 506
José, Patrick, 156, 167–168
Journals
APA style for citing articles in, 655
MLA style for citing articles in, 632
JSTOR, 585
Judson, Olivia, 385
Justification
in proposals, 449–450, 458
three-approach strategy for, 451–452
Juxtapositions, 558

Kawachi, Ichiro, 269–274
Keller, Helen, 160
Kester, Jane, 448, 465, 469–471
Key terms, 668
Keyword searches
library catalog, 583–584
methods for, 586
Kilbourne, Jean, 303
Kilcup, Rodney, 5, 13
King, Shannon, 216, 234–236
Klein, Patrick, 547–549, 556, 558
Knowledge
applied on essay exams, 665–666
background, 114
content, 685
critical, 686
rhetorical, 685
Knowledge of conventions, Council of Writing Program Administrators outcomes for, 4, 488, 572
Krakauer, Jon, 552

"Labor Day Blues" (Lane), 147
Lane, Mike, 147
Language
aesthetic use of, 547
concrete, 554–556
figurative, 559–560
revelatory, 556
vivid, 394
Larger significance conclusions, 544
Learning logs, 357
Lectures, 641
"A Letter to the Editor" (Rockwood), 7
Letters, comprehensive reflective, 686
Lexis-Nexis Academic Universe, 585
Libraries
home page for, 583
searching licensed databases in, 584–588
searching online catalogs of, 583–584
strategies for searching, 582–583
Library of Congress classification system, 584
Library of Congress Subject Headings, 584
Licensed databases. *See also* Databases
citing sources from, 634–635, 656
explanation of, 584–585
searches using, 586–588
Line graphs, 253, 254
Listserv, 658
Literacy, visual, 285
Literacy narratives
explanation of, 160
features of, 161
generating and exploring ideas for, 162–163
revision of, 164
shaping and drafting, 163–164
Literary analysis
generating and exploring ideas for, 329–330
guidelines for understanding, 322–326
guidelines for writing, 326–327
literal vs. literary readings and, 320–321
overview of, 320
peer reviews for, 332
reading logs and, 327
readings for, 321–322, 332–345
revision of, 331
shaping and drafting, 331
tasks for, 327–329
Literary nonfiction. *See* Open-form prose
"Living Like Weasels" (Dillard), 559, 566–568
Logos
appeals to, 55, 58, 122, 394, 447, 455
explanation of, 55
"The Lone Ranger and Tonto Fistfight in Heaven" (Alexie), 339–343
Los Angeles Times, 412–414
Lunsford, Andrea, 6

MacAulay, Kate, 352–355
Magazines
angle of vision of, 599
APA style for citing, 655–656
informative articles in, 215–217, 221–222
MLA style for citing, 632–633
popular, 564–565
Malinowski, Stephanie, 139, 140
Manuscripts, 76
Markham, Beryl, 562
Marshal, Lorna, 95
Martin, Andrés, 110–113, 118–119, 129, 132, 137, 139
"Masks," 169–171
Matsumoto, Kerri Ann, 223, 231
McCarthy, Lucille, 423
McGrath, Roger D., 611–613
McPhee, John, 555
Meaning, converting information to, 45–46
Measurement questions, 244, 245
"The Medicine Man" (Reed), 321–322
Memorizers, 13
Memory-soaked words, 556
Mencken, H. L., 154
Merton, Thomas, 7, 9

Messages
nonverbal, 57–61
persuasive power of, 55
Messaris, Paul, 311–313
Metaphors, 559–560
MLA Handbook for Writers of Research Papers (Modern Language Association), 626
MLA style
for advertisements, 641
for articles in scholarly journals accessed in print, 632
for books, 627–628, 630–631
for cartoons or advertisements, 641
citation system in, 628–629
for edited anthologies, 631–632
example using, 118–119, 643–649
for film or video recordings, 640–641
formatting in, 627
for government publications, 641–642
for interviews, 641
for journal articles accessed in print, 632
for lectures, speeches, or conference presentations, 641
for magazine and newspaper articles accessed in print, 632–633
for podcasts, 641
for print articles downloaded from database, 634–636
for sound recordings, 641
student example of research papers in, 643–651
for television and radio programs, 640
use of, 76, 188
for Web and Internet sources, 636–640
for "Works Cited" list, 595, 626, 629–630, 650–651
"Mobile Phone Tracking Scrutinized" (Swartz), 347–348
Modern Language Association (MLA) style. *See* MLA style
Mojimba, 105–106
Mood
observing scenes in different, 100
perception and, 94
Multiplists, 29–30
"Muslim Americans: Middle Class and Mostly Mainstream" (Pew Research Center for the People and the Press), 228–230
MySpace.com, 33, 577
"Myths about 'Dangerous' Spiders" (Crawford), 210–211, 215
"The Myth of Violence in the Old West" (McGrath), 611–613
"My Turn: Hunks and Handmaidens" (Register-Freeman), 561

Narrative. *See also* Literacy narratives
autobiographical, 151–159, 164
literacy, 160–164
open-form prose as, 161, 547–551
Narrators
in open-form prose, 546–547
point of view of, 324–325
National Institutes of Health, 260
Needs-driven consumers, 296
Newkirk, Thomas, 685*n*
Newsmagazines, 580
Newspapers
APA style for citing, 656, 658
MLA style for citing, 632–633, 639
as research source, 580, 599
"New Threat to Skilled U. S. Workers" (Harrop), 148–149
Nishide, Tyler, 274–282
"No Cats in America?" (José), 156, 167–168
Non sequitur, 397
NoodleTools.com, 590
Norton, Kerry, 226–227
Notes
avoiding plagiarism and, 624
double-entry, 181–183
research, 595–597
"No to Nukes" (Los Angeles Times), 412–414
NTIS (National Technical Information Service), 635, 656

Objections
methods for addressing, 389–391
responses to, 392–395
Observation, to gather information, 245–247
Observational writing
exploring rationales in, 99–100
using *show* rather than *tell* words in, 102–103
Odell, Lee, 507*n*
Old-before-new principle, 522–523
Old/new contract
active voice vs. passive voice in, 538–539
links to old in, 535–537
repetition and, 537–538
in sentences, 509–510, 533–534
use of *this* and, 537
"Once Upon a Time" (Ching), 171–174
"One Hundred Poems from the Japanese" (Hitomaro), 553
Online social networks (OSNs), 577–578. *See also* Facebook.com; MySpace.com
"On Teenagers and Tattoos" (Martin), 110–113
Open-ended questions, 13, 250
Open-form prose
for academic writing, 25
characteristics of, 546–547
closed vs., 9–11, 22, 546–547, 557, 559
concrete language in, 554–556
connectedness in, 552
to create voice in closed-form prose, 562–565
depicting events through time in, 551–552
disrupting reader's desire for direction and clarity in, 557–559
for exploratory writing, 184
figurative language in, 559–560
as narrative, 161, 547–551
resolution, recognition, or retrospective interpretation in, 553–554
revelatory and memory-soaked language in, 556
tension and conflict in, 552–553
use of styles in, 561–562
Oral presentations
MLA style for citing, 641
outlines for, 462–463
peer reviews of, 468
proposal arguments as, 447–448
revision of, 468
strategies for delivery of, 467–468
with visual aids, 461–468
Organization
of essay examination responses, 675
for synthesis writing, 367–368
Organizational cues, 667–668
Outer-directed consumers, 296
Outlines
for closed-form prose, 515–518
detailed, 515–516
example of, 518
for oral presentations, 462–463
scratch, 515

"Paintball: Promoter of Violence or Healthy Fun?" (Taylor), 404–406
Parallel structure, 103
Paraphrases
 of research source information, 615–617
 with and without attributive tag, 620
Parenthetical citations, 618, 626–628
"Parents: The Anti-Drug: A Useful Site" (Filice), 444–446
Particulars
 supporting thesis with, 45–47
 to support points, 529–530
Passive voice, use of, 538
Pathos
 appeals to, 56, 58, 122, 393–395, 447, 455
 explanation of, 56
Peer review guide, 500–501
Peer reviews
 for advocacy advertisements, 461
 for annotated bibliography, 190
 for autobiographical narrative, 164
 for classical argument, 403
 for evaluative writing, 439
 for exploratory essays, 186
 function of, 498, 581
 for image analysis, 310
 for informative essays, 219, 221, 225
 for literary analysis, 332
 for proposal writing, 458
 for research reports, 262–263
 responses from, 505
 for scientific posters, 268
 for seeing rhetorically, 104
 for speeches, 468
 strategies for, 498–501
 for synthesis writing, 368
Peer review workshops, 503–505
Perception, elements of, 93–94
Periodicals. *See also specific types of periodicals*
 explanation of, 580
 as research sources, 579–582
Perry, William, 29
Persona, 74–75
Personal correspondence, 658
Personification, 559
Persuasion. *See also* Argument; Classical argument; Evaluative writing
 explanation of, 377, 378
 power and, 55
 research sources incorporated into, 614
 rhetoric as, 55–56
 strategies for, 97, 394
"Phantom Limb Pain" (Saknussemm), 165–166
Photographs. *See also* Graphics; Image analysis; Visual aids
 analysis of, 288–289
 angle of vision of, 289–291
 purposes of, 285–286
Phrases, transition, 531–532
Pie charts, 253, 254
Pitts, Leonard, Jr., 415–417
Plagiarism, 624–625
Planning schema
 to anticipate argument objections, 390–391
 to develop evaluation arguments, 431–432
Plot
 asking questions about, 323–324
 for autobiographical narratives, 153, 157–158
 explanation of, 153
Plumwood, Val, 551–552, 554–555
Podcasts, 641, 659
Point of view
 asking questions about, 324–325
 desire to change reader's, 21–22
Points
 adding particulars to support, 529–530
 supporting thesis with, 45–47
Policy proposals, 447
Political stance, 598, 599
Popular magazines
 fonts used in, 77
 as research sources, 580
 techniques used in, 564–565
Portable document format (.pdf) files, 580
Portfolios
 collecting work for, 678–679
 overview of, 677–678
 reflective writing to introduce work in, 677
 selecting work for, 679
Posters. *See* Scientific posters
Post hoc, ergo propter hoc argument, 395–396
PowerPoint (Microsoft), 447–448, 455, 463
Practical proposals, 447
Precedent, 452
Prediction, disruption of, 558
Prefaces, 189
Presentations. *See* Oral presentations
Presentation software, 447–448, 463–464
Primary sources, 604
Principle, argument from, 452, 453
Print sources. *See also specific sources*
 books as, 579–581
 categories of, 578–579
 cyberspace vs., 582
 in libraries, 582–588
 periodicals as, 579–582
Problematic questions, 13–17
Problematizers, 13, 14
Problems
 description of, 257
 ill-structured, 13*n*
 for proposal writing, 449
 subject-matter, 12–13
Process logs, 682
Process questions, 683
"A Proposal to Provide Cruelty-Free Products on Campus" (Taylor), 472–476
Proposal conclusions, 544
"A Proposal to Reduce High-Risk Drinking Through Student Awareness Workshops" (Kester), 469–471
Proposal writing
 as advocacy advertisements, 459–461
 developing justification section in, 451–453
 elements of, 449–454
 exploration of, 448–449
 generating and exploring ideas for, 456–457
 overview of, 447–448
 peer reviews for, 458
 readings in, 469–483
 revision of, 458
 shaping and drafting, 457
 with visual aids, 455, 461–469
ProQuest, 585
Prose, closed-form vs. open-form, 9–11, 22, 546–547, 557, 559 (*See also* Closed-form prose; Open-form prose)
Protagonists, 324
Public affairs magazines, 579
Punctuation
 brackets, 622

ellipses, 622
quotation marks, 119, 622, 623
Purpose
as desire to change reader's view, 21–22
as response to motivating occasion, 19, 21
as rhetorical aim, 19
taking notes according to, 596

Qualley, Donna, 681*n,* 683*n,* 685*n*
"Questioning Thomas L. Friedman's Optimism in '30 Little Turtles'" (Malinowski), 143–145
Questionnaires
construction of, 249
ethical guidelines for, 260
example of, 251
types of questions used in, 250
Questions
about audience, 22–23
about characters, 324
about plot, 323–324
about point of view, 324–325
about setting, 324
about short stories, 329–331
about theme, 325–326
elements of good, 14
on essay exams, 666–671
issue, 381
open-ended, 13
problematic, 13–17
process, 683
questionnaire, 250
research, 243–245
rhetoric-related, 684
for scholarly disciplines, 31–32
significant, 14–15, 17
subject-matter, 12–14, 32–36
synthesis, 350–352
thesis, 526
for writing ideas critique, 124–125
for writing reflective response, 126
for writing rhetorical critique, 122–123
Quotation marks, 119, 622, 623
Quotations
block, 624
brackets in, 622
ellipses in, 623
in examination questions, 667
Quotations (*continued*)
from indirect sources, 629
inserted, 621
within quotations, 623
of research source information, 615–617
uses for, 620–621
with and without attributive tag, 620, 621

Radio programs, 640
Random samples, 249
"Reach Out and Track Someone" (Allen), 348–350
Reader energy, 507. *See also* Audience
Readers. *See* Audience
Reading
Council of Writing Program Administrators outcomes for, 4, 88, 572, 662
difficulties of college-level, 114
literally, 320–321
research sources, 592–597
rhetorical, 109–119 (*See also* Rhetorical reading)
strategies for, 115–117, 135, 136
for structure and content, 131–133
Reading logs, 327–329
Reasons, 382–383
Rebuttal, 392
Recognition, 553–554
Red herring, 397
Reed, Evelyn Dahl, 321–322
"Reefer Madness" (Scholosser), 216
Reference books, 579
"References" list, 595, 626, 653
Reflective writing
comprehensive, 677, 684–686
explanation of, 677, 679–681
generating and exploring ideas for, 104
importance of, 681–682
in portfolios, 677
readings in, 680, 687–689
single, 678, 682–684
strong responses as, 125–126
Register-Freeman, Victoria, 561
Relativism, 30
Reliability, of research sources, 597
Repetition, 537–538
Reports
informative, 214–215
workplace, 215
Rereading strategies, 135, 136
Research. *See also* Field research; Field research data
analyzing results from, 256–259
ethical standards for, 259–260
as evidence, 386
methods for reporting results from, 252–256
scientific posters and, 265–267
use of, 239
Research data
analysis of, 239–240
empirical research report structure and, 240–242
interviews to gather, 247–249
observation to gather, 245–247
posing research questions and, 243, 244
questionnaires to gather, 249–251
reading research reports and, 242–243
Researchers, 575–576
Research questions, 574–575
Research reports. *See also* Field research; Field research data; Field research reports
in APA style, 275–282
case study of, 577–578
designing and drafting introduction and method sections of, 261–262
examples of, 268–281
generating ideas for, 261
methods for reading, 242–243
in MLA style, 628–651
overview of, 573–574
peer reviews for, 262–263
research and writing guidelines for, 262
revision of, 262
team writing for, 264
Research source citations
MLA style for, 628–651
parenthetical system of, 626–628
Research source documentation
APA style for, 652–659 (*See also* APA style)
MLA style for, 628–651 (*See also* MLA style)
parenthetical citation, 626–628
Research sources. *See also* Libraries; Web sites; *specific types of research sources*
avoiding plagiarism and, 624–625
differences in, 578–579
evaluation of, 597–610
incorporated into your own prose, 615–619
library, 582–588
note taking from, 595–597
primary and secondary, 604
rhetorically reading, 593–595
taking notes from, 595–597

Resnick, L B., 681*n*
Resolution, 553–554
Response-centered workshops, 504
Response writing. *See also* Essay examinations
  exploring ideas in, 135
  function of, 121
  as ideas critique, 124–125
  as reflection, 125–126
  rereading strategies to stimulate strong, 135, 136
  revision of, 140
  as rhetorical critique, 122–123
  shaping and drafting for, 139–140
  student example of, 143–145
  thesis for strong, 138–139
Retrospective interpretation, 553–554
Revelatory words, 556
Revision. *See also* Drafts
  of advocacy advertisements, 461
  of annotated bibliographies, 189–190
  of autobiographical narratives, 159
  of classical argument, 403
  of descriptive writing, 103–104
  of evaluative writing, 439
  of exploratory essays, 186
  function of, 492–493
  global and local, 493–496
  of image analysis, 309–310
  of informative writing, 219, 221, 225
  of literacy narratives, 164
  of literary analysis, 331
  of proposal writing, 458
  of research reports, 262
  of speeches, 468
  of summaries, 133–134
  of synthesis writing, 368
  for unity, 528–529
  using points and particulars during, 47
Rhetoric
  angle of vision and, 50–52
  of clothing and consumer items, 60–61
  logos, ethos, and *pathos* and, 55–56, 58
  visual, 57–59
Rhetorical analysis
  of observational writing, 96, 97
  of research sources, 578–579, 605–607
  strong response as, 122–123
Rhetorical context
  in college-level reading, 114
  document design choices and, 76–81
  scale of abstraction choices and, 69–70
Rhetorical effects
  of attributive tags, 617–621
  of images, 57–59, 289–291
Rhetorical knowledge
  Council of Writing Program Administrators outcomes for, 4, 88, 488, 572, 662
  to evaluate Web sources, 600–610
  function of, 685–686
Rhetorical reading
  exploration of, 109–110
  strategies for, 115–116, 359–360
  understanding, 114
Rhetorical thinking
  about audience, 19
  about genre, 19
  about purpose, 19–21
  Council of Writing Program Administrators outcomes for, 4, 88, 488, 572, 662
  overview of, 49
  thought exercise on, 50
  for writing, 496
Rhetorical triangle, 56
Rhetoric-related questions, 684
Robinson, Eugene, 236–238
Rockwell, Norman, 57–58
Rockwood, David, 7, 9, 21, 59, 71, 395
Rogers, Carl, 116
Rogers, Tamlyn, 106–108

Saknussemm, Kris, 165–166
Sans serif fonts, 77
Satisfice, 497
Says statement, 132, 133
Scaled-answer questions, 250
Scale of abstraction, 69–71, 554
Scenarios, 385
Scenic conclusions, 545
Schema, planning, 390–391, 431–432
Scholarly publications. *See also* Academic writing
  APA style for citing, 655, 658
  document design in, 77–79
  MLA style for citing, 632, 639
  as research sources, 579, 581, 582
Scholosser, Eric, 216
Scientific posters
  content of, 265
  designing and revising, 266
  example of, 267
  explanation of, 265
  features of, 265–266
  peer reviews for, 268
Scratch outlines, 515
Search engines, 588–591
Secondary sources, 604
Self-knowledge, 684–685
Self-reflection. *See* Reflective writing
Sensory details, 100–101
Sentences
  controlling emphasis in, 73–74
  inserting quoted words and phrases into, 621
  old/new contract in, 509–510, 533–534
  topic, 527–529
Serif fonts, 77
"*Sesame Street*: Brought to You by the Letters M-A-L-E" (Helman & Bookspan), 442–443
Setting
  asking questions about, 324
  in autobiographical narratives, 155
Sherman, A. Kimbrough, 28, 29
Show words, 102–103
Short stories. *See* Literary analysis
Side-by-side pattern, 542, 543
Signaling phrases, 118
Significant questions, 14–15, 17
Similes, 559
Simple summary conclusions, 544
Single reflection assignments, 682–684
"A Single Reflection on an Exploratory Essay" (Finger), 687
Slides, 463–466
Slim Hopes: Advertising and the Obsession with Thinness, 303
Slippery slope, 397
Small groups, idea generation in, 223
Software
  desktop publishing, 76
  presentation, 447–448, 463–464
Sound recordings
  APA style for citing, 659
  MLA style for citing, 641
Source documentation. *See* Research source documentation
Sources. *See* Research sources
"Spare the Rod, Spoil the Parenting" (Pitts), 415–417
Speeches
  MLA style for citing, 641
  outlines for, 462–463
  peer reviews of, 468
  proposal arguments as, 447–448
  revision of, 468

strategies for delivery of, 467–468
with visual aids, 461–468 (*See also* Visual aids)
Standards, 430
Stanley, Henry Morton, 105–106
STAR criteria for evaluating evidence, 387–388, 396
Statistics, 386
Steen, Jan Havickszoon, 294
Stem cell research, 51, 52
Still Killing Us Softly, 303
"The Stolen Watch," 549–550
Strong response writing. *See* Response writing
Structure
chronological, 511–512
for closed-form prose, 520
encyclopedic, 512–513
engfish and, 514
planning and visualizing, 514–520
thesis/support, 511–514
Study plans, 666
Style
choices regarding, 66, 72–73
expanding your repertoire of, 561–562
factors affecting, 67, 68
goal of effective, 66
in popular magazines, 68–69
in scholarly journal, 68
Subarguments, 387
Subject matter
changing reader's view of, 41–42
for essay exams, 664–666
Subject-matter questions
explanation of, 12
exploratory strategies to think critically about, 32–36
posing ones own, 13–14
that unite writers and readers, 12–13
Subject-related questions, 683–684
Subject searches, 583–584
Summary/however strategy, 540
Summary-only annotations, 187, 188
Summary writing
drafting and revising in, 133–134
exploring texts through, 357–358
focus on structure and content for, 131–132
function of, 117–118
guidelines for, 118–119
removing particulars to create, 46–47
of research source information, 615–617
thesis for, 138, 139
Surprise, in thesis, 41–44
Surprising-reversal strategy
explanation of, 42–44, 217
informative writing using, 217
Swan, Judith, 507*n*
Swartz, Nikki, 347–348
Sweet, William, 407–410
Swift, Jonathan, 489
Symbols, rhetorical power of, 60–61
Synthesis. *See also* Idea analysis and synthesis
explanation of, 346
of ideas, 346–368
Synthesis questions
construction of, 350–352
ideas for, 356–357
Synthesis writing. *See also* Idea analysis and synthesis
assignments for, 351
developing your views for, 363–364
elements of, 352
as extension of summary/strong response writing, 352
generating ideas for, 362–363
organization of, 367–368
student example of, 352–355

Tables, 252–254
Talk-Back assignments, 683
Talk-To assignments, 683
"Tarantulas" (EnchantedLearning.com), 209–210, 215
Taylor, Rebekah, 447, 472–476
Taylor, Ross, 404–406
Team writing, for research reports, 264
"Technology's Peril and Potential" (MacAulay), 352–355
Technology use, for document design, 76
Television programs
APA style for citing, 658
MLA style for citing, 640
Tenses. *See* Verb tenses
Tension
autobiographical, 152
in open-form prose, 552–553
in thesis, 42–43
Test anxiety, 673
Testimony, 386–387
Texts
analyzing and critiquing, 130
angle of vision in, 50–52
visual-verbal, 129–130
Theme
asking questions about, 325–326
in autobiographical narratives, 156
process for clarifying, 360–361
Theroux, Paul, 36, 37
Thesis
changing reader's view in, 41–42
creating tension in, 42–43
creating working, 517
in *engfish* writing, 514
for response essays, 138–140
for synthesis writing, 366–367
using points and particulars to support, 45–47
Thesis questions, 526
Thesis statements
in closed-form prose, 522–523
in essay exams, 675
function of strong, 41
in research reports, 257
for response essays, 138–140
suprising readers in, 41–44
Thesis/support structure
chronological, 511–512
encyclopedic, 512–513
engfish and, 514
explanation of, 511
Think tanks, 598, 599
"30 Little Turtles" (Friedman), 142–143
this, 537
"This Is the End of the World" (Tuchman), 562
Time
depicting events through, 551–552
point of view and, 325
Time/Life books, 564–565
Time management
for composition process, 496
during essay exams, 673–674
Tinker, Brittany, 14–15
Titles, for closed-form prose, 521–522
"Today's Economic Indicator" (Horsey), 146
Tomalin, Nicholas, 559
Tompkins, Jane, 199–207
Topic sentences, 527–529
Toulmin, Stephen, 384*n*
Trade books, 579, 581
Trade magazines, 579
Transitions
headings and subheadings to indicate, 533
between parts, 533
signaling relationships with, 531–532

Transition words/phrases
in closed-form prose, 530–532
for concessions, 393
use of, 536
Trapper John, 375–376
Tree diagrams, 517, 519
Truth, of literary events, 322–323
Truth seeking. *See also* Argument
in argument, 377, 378, 382
increasing attention to, 380
Tuchman, Barbara, 562
Tufte, Edward, 66–67
"Two Descriptions of the Same Classroom and a Self-Reflection: (Rogers), 106–108
Type, 77
Typeface, 77

Unity
in closed-form prose, 507–509
in paragraphs, 528–529
Unpublished papers, 659
Unstated assumptions, 383–384
Urbanik, Bruce, 688
URLs (universal resource locators), 590–591, 638

VALS (Values and Lifestyle System), 296, 297
Values, 94, 450
Verbs, in essay questions, 668–671
Verb tenses, literary analysis and, 325
Video recordings, 640–641
Visual aids. *See also* Graphics; Graphs; Images
bar graphs as, 254
line graphs as, 253
pie charts as, 253, 254
for proposal arguments, 455, 461–469
revision of, 256
tables as, 252–253
Visual literacy, 285
Visual Persuasion: The Role of Images in Advertising (Messaris), 311–313
Visual rhetoric, 57–59. *See also* Graphics; Image analysis
Visual-verbal texts
questions for analyzing, 130
summary/strong response of, 129–130, 133

Vocabulary, 114
Voice
active, 538–539
inflated vs. natural speaking, 74–75
open-form elements to create, 562–565
passive, 538–539

Walker, Alice, 333–338
Walvoord, Barbara, 423
Watterson, Kara, 358–360
Web sites. *See also* World Wide Web
analyzing purpose for using, 604–610
APA style for citing, 657–658
evaluation of, 600–610
library, 583
MLA style for citing, 627–628, 636–640
as research sources, 580–581
rhetorical overview of, 602–604
strategies for searching, 588–591
Weiler, Betsy, 343–345
"Welcome to Sellafield" (Eales), 411
"What Is the Effect of Online Social Networks on Communication Skills?" (Gardiner), 196–199
"Who Do You Want to Be?" (Weiler), 343–345
"Why Do Teenagers Get Tattoos? A Response to Andrés Martin" (Barry), 127–129
"Why Uranium Is the New Green" (Sweet), 407–410
Williams, Byron, 371–372
Williams, Joseph, 507*n*
"Winery Yeast Preparation Instructions" (Norton), 226–227
Wolfe, Tom, 556
"Women and Smoking in Hollywood Movies: A Content Analysis" (Escamilla, Cradock, & Kawachi), 269–274
Wordiness, 72–73
Words
abstract vs. concrete, 69–71
concrete, 554–556
memory-soaked, 556
revelatory, 556
show vs. *tell*, 102–103
transition, 531–532
Workplace reports, 215

"Works Cited" list, 595, 626, 629–630, 650–651
WorldCat, 585
World Wide Web. *See also* Web sites
APA style for citing sources from, 657–658
determining your location on, 590–591
methods for searching, 588–591
MLA style for citing sources from, 636–640
print sources vs. sources from, 82
rhetorical environment of, 600–601
search engines for, 588–591
Wright, Richard, 154
Writers, as questioners, 5
Writer's memo, 682
Writing. *See also* Academic writing; Response writing; *specific types of writing*
closed vs. open, 9–10
Council of Writing Program Administrators outcomes for, 4, 88, 488, 572, 662
as critical thinking, 5
motivation for, 21
purpose for, 19–24
reasons to study, 5–6
subject-matter problems in, 12–13
summary, 117–119
variations in, 6–7
Writing process. *See also* Composition process
expert habits to improve, 496–498
as recursive process, 493
role of drafts in, 490–492 (*See also* Drafts)
role of peer reviews in, 498–505 (*See also* Peer reviews)
role of revision in, 492–496 (*See also* Revision)
Writing skills, 6–7
Wyngaard, Jackie, 440–441

Yancey, Kathleen Blake, 677, 681*n*, 683*n*
"You Have the Right to Remain a Target of Racial Profiling" (Robinson), 236–238

Zitkala-Sa (Gertrude Bonnin), 160

READINGS AND VISUAL TEXTS IN *THE ALLYN & BACON GUIDE TO WRITING*

The Allyn & Bacon Guide to Writing contains 61 readings—35 by professional writers and 26 by student writers—from a wide variety of sources, as well as more than 60 visual texts.

PROFESSIONAL READINGS

Scholarly Journal Articles

Kunkel, Cope, and Biely, from "Sexual Messages on Television" (Ch. 4)
Patrono, from "Aspirin as an Antiplatelet Drug" (Ch. 4)
Martin, "On Teenagers and Tattoos" (Ch. 6)
Tompkins, "'Indians': Textualism, Morality, and the Problem of History" (Ch. 8)
Escamilla, Cradock, and Kawachi, "Women and Smoking in Hollywood Movies" (Ch. 10)

Newspaper Editorial

Los Angeles Times, "No to Nukes" (Ch. 14)

Op-Ed Pieces

Friedman, "30 Little Turtles" (Ch. 6)
Harrop, "New Threat to Skilled U.S. Workers" (Ch. 6)
Robinson, "You Have the Right to Remain a Target of Racial Profiling" (Ch. 9)
Pitts, "Spare the Rod, Spoil the Parenting" (Ch. 14)
Helman and Bookspan, "*Sesame Street*: Brought to You by the Letters M-A-L-E" (Ch. 15)
Allen, "The Athlete on the Sidelines" (Ch. 16)

Letter to the Editor

Rockwood, "A Letter to the Editor" (Ch. 1)

Public Affairs Magazine Article

Allen, "Reach Out and Track Someone" (Ch. 13)

Popular Magazine Article

Sweet, "Why Uranium Is the New Green" (Ch. 14)

Trade Journal Article

Swartz, "Mobile Phone Tracking Scrutinized" (Ch. 13)

Article Posted on Web Site

EnchantedLearning.com, "Tarantulas" (Ch. 9)
Crawford, "Myths about 'Dangerous' Spiders" (Ch. 9)

Blogs

Dee, "Comprehensive Immigration Reform" (Ch. 13)
Williams, "Immigration Frenzy Points Out Need for Policy Debate" (Ch. 13)
Crapo, "Immigration Policy Must Help Economy While Preserving Ideals" (Ch. 13)
John, "The Progressive Case Against the Immigration Bill" (Ch. 13)

Workplace Writing

Norton, "Winery Yeast Preparation Instructions" (Ch. 9)
Pew Research Center, "Muslim Americans: Middle Class and Mostly Mainstream" (Ch. 9)

Book Excerpts

Merton, "A Festival of Rain" (Ch. 1)
Saknussemm, "Phantom Limb Pain" (Ch. 7)
Messaris, from *Visual Persuasion: The Role of Images in Advertising* (Ch. 11)
Dillard, "Living Like Weasels" (Ch. 19)
McGrath, "The Myth of Violence in the Old West" (Ch. 22)

Historical Document

"Clash on the Congo: Two Eyewitness Accounts" (Ch. 5)

Short Stories

"The Medicine Man" (Native American legend; Ch. 12)
Walker, "Everyday Use (For Your Grandmama)" (Ch. 12)
Alexie, "The Lone Ranger and Tonto Fistfight in Heaven" (Ch. 12)

Poem

cummings, "next to of course god america" (Ch. 2)

VISUAL TEXTS

Paintings

Rockwell, *Doc Melhorn and the Pearly Gates* (Ch. 3)
Hopper, *Nighthawks* (Ch. 11)
Steen, *Rhetoricians at a Window* (Part 3)

Design and Architecture

Journal of Sex Research, scholarly journal article layout (Ch. 4)
Psychology Today, magazine article layout (Ch. 4)
Gehry, Experience Music Project Museum (Ch. 15)

Editorial Cartoons

Auth, "Stem Cells" (Ch. 3)
Horsey, "Today's Economic Indicator" (Ch. 6)
Lane, "Labor Day Blues" (Ch. 6)
Eales, "Welcome to Sellafield" (Ch. 14)
"Hellgate Exchange" (Ch. 15)

Information Graphics

Graphics on oil supply and petroleum usage (Ch. 1, 2)
Graphs and charts for scientific reports (Ch. 10)
Graphs on binge drinking (Ch. 15)
Graph and data on violent crime (Ch. 21)

Photographs

Wind turbines (Part 1)
High-technology medicine (Ch. 3)
Clothing (Ch. 3)
Arctic National Wildlife Refuge (Ch. 5)
Four settings (Ch. 7)
Eight immigration photographs (Ch. 11)